P9-DXO-678

ROGET'S THESAURUS OF SYNONYMS AND ANTONYMS

BY

PETER MARK ROGET, M.D., F.R.S.

ENLARGED BY

JOHN LEWIS ROGET, M.A.

NEW EDITION REVISED AND ENLARGED BY

SAMUEL ROMILLY ROGET, M.A.

Galahad Books • New York City

Library of Congress Number 73-91324
ISBN Number 0-88365-148-3

Printed in U.S.A.

PLAN OF CLASSIFICATION

Class	Section		Nos.
I. ABSTRACT RELATIONS	I.	Existence	1 to 8
	II.	Relation	9— 24
	III.	Quantity	25— 57
	IV.	Order	58— 83
	V.	Number	84— 105
	VI.	Time	106— 139
	VII.	Change	140— 152
	VIII.	Causation	153— 179
II. SPACE	I.	Generally	180— 191
	II.	Dimensions	192— 239
	III.	Form	240— 263
	IV.	Motion	264— 315
III. MATTER	I.	Generally	316— 320
	II.	Inorganic	321— 356
	III.	Organic	357— 449
	Division		
IV. INTELLECT	(I.)	Formation of Ideas	450— 515
	(II.)	Communication of Ideas	516— 599
V. VOLITION	(I.)	Individual	600— 736
	(II.)	Intersocial	737— 819
	Section		
VI. AFFECTIONS	I.	Generally	820— 826
	II.	Personal	827— 887
	III.	Sympathetic	888— 921
	IV.	Moral	922— 975
	V.	Religious	976—1000

TABULAR SYNOPSIS OF CATEGORIES

Class I. ABSTRACT RELATIONS

I. EXISTENCE		
1°. Abstract...........	1. Existence.	2. Inexistence.
2°. Concrete..........	3. Substantiality.	4. Unsubstantiality.
3°. Formal............	*Internal.*	*External.*
	5. Intrinsicality.	6. Extrinsicality.
4°. Modal.............	*Absolute.*	*Relative.*
	7. State.	8. Circumstance.
II. RELATION		
1°. Absolute..........	9. Relation.	10. Irrelation.
	11. Consanguinity.	
	12. Correlation.	
	13. Identity.	14. Contrariety.
	15. Difference.	
2°. Continuous........	16. Uniformity.	16*a*. Non-uniformity.
3°. Partial...........	17. Similarity.	18. Dissimilarity.
	19. Imitation.	20. Non-imitation.
	20*a*. Variation.	
	21. Copy.	22. Prototype.
4°. General..........	23. Agreement.	24. Disagreement.
III. QUANTITY		
1°. Simple............	*Absolute.*	*Relative.*
	25. Quantity.	26. Degree.
	27. Equality.	28. Inequality.
2°. Comparative.......	29. Mean.	
	30. Compensation.	
	By Comparison with a Standard.	
	31. Greatness.	32. Smallness.
	By Comparison with a similar Object.	
	33. Superiority.	34. Inferiority.
	Changes in Quantity.	
	35. Increase.	36. Decrease.
3°. Conjunctive......	37. Addition.	38. Non-addition. Subduction.
	39. Adjunct.	40. Remainder.
		40*a*. Decrement.
	41. Mixture.	42. Simpleness.
	43. Junction.	44. Disjunction.
	45. Vinculum.	
	46. Coherence.	47. Incoherence.
	48. Combination.	49. Decomposition.

4°. CONCRETE	50. Whole.	51. Part.
	52. Completeness.	53. Incompleteness.
	54. Composition.	55. Exclusion.
	56. Component.	57. Extraneous.

IV. ORDER

1°. GENERAL	58. Order.	59. Disorder.
	60. Arrangement.	61. Derangement.
2°. CONSECUTIVE	62. Precedence.	63. Sequence.
	64. Precursor.	65. Sequel.
	66. Beginning.	67. End.
	68. Middle.	
	69. Continuity.	70. Discontinuity.
	71. Term.	
3°. COLLECTIVE	72. Assemblage.	73. Non-assemblage. Dispersion.
	74. Focus.	
4°. DISTRIBUTIVE	75. Class.	
	76. Inclusion.	77. Exclusion.
	78. Generality.	79. Speciality.
5°. CATEGORICAL	80. Rule.	81. Multiformity.
	82. Conformity.	83. Unconformity.

V. NUMBER

1°. ABSTRACT	84. Number.	
	85. Numeration.	
	86. List.	
2°. DETERMINATE	87. Unity.	88. Accompaniment.
	89. Duality.	
	90. Duplication.	91. Bisection.
	92. Triality.	
	93. Triplication.	96. Trisection.
	94. Quadruplication.	
	95. Quaternity.	97. Quadrisection.
	98. Five, &c.	99. Quinquesection, &c.
3°. INDETERMINATE	100. Plurality.	100*a*. Fraction.
		101. Zero.
	102. Multitude.	103. Fewness.
	104. Repetition.	
	105. Infinity.	

VI. TIME

1°. ABSOLUTE	106. Time.	107. Neverness.
	Definite.	*Indefinite.*
	108. Period.	109. Course.
	108*a*. Contingent Duration.	
	110. Diuturnity.	111. Transientness.
	112. Perpetuity.	113. Instantaneity.
	114. Chronometry.	115. Anachronism.
2°. RELATIVE — 1. *to Succession*	116. Priority.	117. Posteriority.
	118. Present time.	119. Different time.
	120. Synchronism.	
2°. RELATIVE — 2. *to a Period*	121. Futurity.	122. Preterition.
	123. Newness.	124. Oldness.
	125. Morning.	126. Evening.
	127. Youth.	128. Age.
	129. Infant.	130. Veteran.
	131. Adolescence.	
2°. RELATIVE — 3. *to an Effect or purpose*	132. Earliness.	133. Lateness.
	134. Occasion.	135. Intempestivity.
3°. RECURRENT	136. Frequency.	137. Infrequency.
	138. Periodicity.	139. Irregularity.

SYNOPSIS OF CATEGORIES

VII. CHANGE

1°. Simple	140. Change.	141. Permanence.
	142. Cessation.	143. Continuance.
	144. Conversion.	145. Reversion.
	146. Revolution.	
	147. Substitution.	148. Interchange.
2°. Complex	149. Changeableness.	150. Stability.
	Present.	*Future.*
	151. Eventuality.	152. Destiny.

VIII. CAUSATION

1°. Constancy of Sequence	153. *Constant Antecedent.* Cause.	154. *Constant Sequent.* Effect.
	155. *Assignment of Cause.* Attribution.	156. *Absence of Assignment.* Chance.
2°. Connection between Cause and Effect	157. Power.	158. Impotence.
	Degrees of Power.	
	159. Strength.	160. Weakness.
3°. Power in Operation	161. Production.	162. Destruction.
	163. Reproduction.	
	164. Producer.	165. Destroyer.
	166. Paternity.	167. Posterity.
	168. Productiveness.	169. Unproductiveness.
	170. Agency.	
	171. Energy.	172. Inertness.
	173. Violence.	174. Moderation.
4°. Indirect Power	175. Influence.	175*a*. Absence of Influence.
	176. Tendency.	
	177. Liability.	
5°. Combinations of Causes	178. Concurrence.	179. Counteraction.

Class II. SPACE

I. SPACE IN GENERAL

1°. Abstract Space		180*a*. Inextension.
	180. *Indefinite.* Space.	181. *Definite.* Region.
		182. *Limited.* Place.
2°. Relative Space	183. Situation.	
	184. Location.	185. Displacement.
3°. Existence in Space	186. Presence.	187. Absence.
	188. Inhabitant.	189. Abode.
	190. Contents.	191. Receptacle.

II. DIMENSIONS

1°. General	192. Size.	193. Littleness.
	194. Expansion.	195. Contraction.
	196. Distance.	197. Nearness.
	198. Interval.	199. Contiguity.
2°. Linear	200. Length.	201. Shortness.
	202. Breadth. Thickness.	203. Narrowness. Thinness.
	204. Layer.	205. Filament.
	206. Height.	207. Lowness.
	208. Depth.	209. Shallowness.

SYNOPSIS OF CATEGORIES

2°. LINEAR—*continued*		210. Summit.	211. Base.
		212. Verticality.	213. Horizontality.
		214. Pendency.	215. Support.
		216. Parallelism.	217. Obliquity.
		218. Inversion.	
		219. Crossing.	
3°. CENTRICAL	1. *General*	220. Exteriority.	221. Interiority.
		222. Centrality.	
		223. Covering.	224. Lining.
		225. Investment.	226. Divestment.
		227. Circumjacence.	228. Interjacence.
		229. Circumscription.	
		230. Outline.	
		231. Edge.	
		232. Inclosure.	
		233. Limit.	
	2. *Special*	234. Front	235. Rear.
		236. Laterality.	237. Contraposition.
		238. Dextrality.	239. Sinistrality.

III. FORM

1°. GENERAL	240. Form.	241. Amorphism.
	242. Symmetry.	243. Distortion.
2°. SPECIAL	244. Angularity.	
	245. Curvature.	246. Straightness.
	247. Circularity.	248. Convolution.
	249. Rotundity.	
3°. SUPERFICIAL	250. Convexity.	252. Concavity.
	251. Flatness.	
	253. Sharpness.	254. Bluntness.
	255. Smoothness.	256. Roughness.
	257. Notch.	
	258. Fold.	
	259. Furrow.	
	260. Opening.	261. Closure.
	262. Perforator.	263. Stopper.

IV. MOTION

1°. MOTION IN GENERAL	264. Motion.	265. Quiescence.
	266. Journey.	267. Navigation.
	268. Traveler.	269. Mariner.
	270. Transference.	
	271. Carrier.	
	272. Vehicle.	273. Ship.
2°. DEGREES OF MOTION	274. Velocity.	275. Slowness.
3°. CONJOINED WITH FORCE	276. Impulse.	277. Recoil.
4°. WITH REFERENCE TO DIRECTION	278. Direction.	279. Deviation.
	280. Precession.	281. Sequence.
	282. Progression.	283. Regression.
	284. Propulsion.	285. Traction.
	286. Approach.	287. Recession.
	288. Attraction.	289. Repulsion.
	290. Convergence.	291. Divergence.
	292. Arrival.	293. Departure.
	294. Ingress.	295. Egress.
	296. Reception.	297. Ejection.
	298. Food.	299. Excretion.
	300. Insertion.	301. Extraction.
	302. Passage.	
	303. Overstep.	304. Shortcoming.

4°. With Reference to Direction—*cont.*	305. Ascent.	306. Descent.
	307. Elevation.	308. Depression.
	309. Leap.	310. Plunge.
	311. Circuition.	
	312. Rotation.	313. Evolution.
	314. Oscillation.	
	315. Agitation.	

Class III. MATTER

I. MATTER IN GENERAL		316. Materiality.	317. Immateriality.
		318. World.	
		319. Gravity.	320. Levity.
II. INORGANIC MATTER			
1°. Solids		321. Density.	322. Rarity.
		323. Hardness.	324. Softness.
		325. Elasticity.	326. Inelasticity.
		327. Tenacity.	328. Brittleness.
		329. Texture.	
		330. Pulverulence.	
		331. Friction.	332. Lubrication.
2°. Fluids	1. *In General*	333. Fluidity.	334. Gaseity.
		335. Liquefaction.	336. Vaporization.
	2. *Specific*	337. Water.	338. Air.
		339. Moisture.	340. Dryness.
		341. Ocean.	342. Land.
		343. Gulf. Lake.	344. Plain.
		345. Marsh.	346. Island.
	3. *In motion*	347. Stream.	
		348. River.	349. Wind.
		350. Conduit.	351. Air-pipe.
3°. Imperfect Fluids		352. Semiliquidity.	353. Bubble.
		354. Pulpiness.	355. Unctuousness.
			356. Oil.
			356*a*. Resin.
III. ORGANIC MATTER			
1°. Vitality	1. *In General*	357. Organization.	358. Inorganization.
		359. Life.	360. Death.
			361. Killing.
			362. Corpse.
			363. Interment.
	2. *Special*	364. Animality.	365. Vegetability.
		366. Animal.	367. Vegetable.
		368. Zoology.	369. Botany.
		370. Cicuration.	371. Agriculture.
		372. Mankind.	
		373. Man.	374. Woman.

SYNOPSIS OF CATEGORIES

Division (II.). COMMUNICATION OF IDEAS

I. NATURE OF IDEAS COMMUNICATED

516. Meaning. — 517. Unmeaningness.
518. Intelligibility. — 519. Unintelligibility.
520. Equivocalness.
521. Metaphor.
522. Interpretation. — 523. Misinterpretation.
524. Interpreter.

II. MODES OF COMMUNICATION

525. Manifestation. — 526. Latency.
527. Information. — 528. Concealment.
529. Disclosure. — 530. Ambush.
531. Publication.
532. News. — 533. Secret.
534. Messenger.
535. Affirmation. — 536. Negation.
537. Teaching. — 538. Misteaching. 539. Learning.
540. Teacher. — 541. Learner.
542. School.
543. Veracity. — 544. Falsehood. 545. Deception. 546. Untruth.
547. Dupe. — 548. Deceiver. 549. Exaggeration.

III. MEANS OF COMMUNICATION

1°. *Natural Means*

550. Indication.
551. Record. — 552. Obliteration.
553. Recorder.
554. Representation. — 555. Misrepresentation.
556. Painting.
557. Sculpture.
558. Engraving.
559. Artist.

2°. *Conventional Means*

1. *Language generally*

560. Language.
561. Letter.
562. Word. — 563. Neology.
564. Nomenclature. — 565. Misnomer.
566. Phrase.
567. Grammar. — 568. Solecism.
569. Style.

Qualities of Style.

570. Perspicuity. — 571. Obscurity.
572. Conciseness. — 573. Diffuseness.
574. Vigour. — 575. Feebleness.
576. Plainness. — 577. Ornament.
578. Elegance. — 579. Inelegance.

2. *Spoken Language*

580. Voice. — 581. Aphony.
582. Speech. — 583. Stammering.
584. Loquacity. — 585. Taciturnity.
586. Allocution. — 587. Response.
588. Interlocution. — 589. Soliloquy.

3. *Written Language*

590. Writing. — 591. Printing.
592. Correspondence. — 593. Book.
594. Description.
595. Dissertation.
596. Compendium.
597. Poetry. — 598. Prose.
599. The Drama.

Class IV. INTELLECT

Division (I.). Formation of Ideas

I. Operations of Intellect in General	450. Intellect.	450*a*. Absence of Intellect.
	451. Thought.	452. Incogitancy.
	453. Idea.	454. Topic.
II. Precursory Conditions and Operations	455. Curiosity.	456. Incuriosity.
	457. Attention.	458. Inattention.
	459. Care.	460. Neglect.
	461. Inquiry.	462. Answer.
	463. Experiment.	
	464. Comparison.	
	465. Discrimination.	465*a*. Indiscrimination.
	466. Measurement.	
III. Materials for Reasoning	467. Evidence.	468. Counter-evidence.
	469. Qualification.	
	Degrees of Evidence.	
	470. Possibility.	471. Impossibility.
	472. Probability.	473. Improbability.
	474. Certainty.	475. Uncertainty.
IV. Reasoning Processes	476. Reasoning.	477. Intuition. Sophistry.
	478. Demonstration.	479. Confutation.
V. Results of Reasoning	480. Judgement.	481. Misjudgement.
	480*a*. Discovery.	
	482. Over-estimation.	483. Under-estimation.
	484. Belief.	485. Unbelief. Doubt.
	486. Credulity.	487. Incredulity.
	488. Assent.	489. Dissent.
	490. Knowledge.	491. Ignorance.
	492. Scholar.	493. Ignoramus.
	494. Truth.	495. Error.
	496. Maxim.	497. Absurdity.
	Faculties.	
	498. Intelligence. Wisdom.	499. Imbecility. Folly.
	500. Sage.	501. Fool.
	502. Sanity.	503. Insanity.
		504. Madman.
VI. Extension of Thought — 1°. *To the Past*	505. Memory.	506. Oblivion.
VI. Extension of Thought — 2°. *To the Future*	507. Expectation.	508. Inexpectation.
		509. Disappointment.
	510. Foresight.	
	511. Prediction.	
	512. Omen.	
	513. Oracle.	
VII. Creative Thought	514. Supposition.	
	515. Imagination.	

SYNOPSIS OF CATEGORIES

2°. SENSATION

(1) *General*

375. Sensibility.	376. Insensibility
377. Pleasure.	378. Pain.

(2) *Special*

1. *Touch*

379. Touch.	
380. Sensations of Touch	381. Numbness

2. *Heat*

382. Heat.	383. Cold.
384. Calefaction.	385. Refrigeration.
386. Furnace.	387. Refrigeratory.
388. Fuel.	
389. Thermometer.	

3. *Taste*

390. Taste.	391. Insipidity.
392. Pungency.	
393. Condiment.	
394. Savouriness.	395. Unsavouriness.
396. Sweetness	397. Sourness.

4. *Odor*

398. Odor.	399. Inodorousness.
400. Fragrance.	401. Fœtor.

5. *Sound*

(i.) *Sound in General.*

402. Sound.	403. Silence.
404. Loudness.	405. Faintness.

(ii.) *Specific Sounds.*

406. Snap.	407. Roll.
408. Resonance.	408*a*. Non-resonance.
	409. Sibilation.
410. Stridor.	
411. Cry.	412. Ululation.

(iii.) *Musical Sounds.*

413. Melody. Concord.	414. Discord.
415. Music.	
416. Musician.	
417. Musical Instruments.	

(iv.) *Perception of Sound.*

418. Hearing.	419. Deafness.

6. *Light*

(i.) *Light in General.*

420. Light.	421. Darkness.
422. Dimness.	
423. Luminary.	424. Shade.
425. Transparency.	426. Opacity.
427. Semitransparency.	

(ii.) *Specific Light.*

428. Color.	429. Achromatism.
430. Whiteness.	431. Blackness.
432. Gray.	433. Brown.
434. Redness.	435. Greenness.
436. Yellowness.	437. Purple.
438. Blueness.	439. Orange.
440. Variegation.	

(iii.) *Perceptions of Light.*

441. Vision.	442. Blindness.
443. Dimsightedness.	
444. Spectator.	
445. Optical Instruments.	
446. Visibility.	447. Invisibility.
448. Appearance.	449. Disappearance.

SYNOPSIS OF CATEGORIES

CLASS V. VOLITION

Division (I.). INDIVIDUAL VOLITION

I. VOLITION IN GENERAL	1°. *Acts*....	600. Will.	601. Necessity.
		602. Willingness.	603. Unwillingness.
		604. Resolution.	605. Irresolution.
		604*a*. Perseverance. / 606. Obstinacy.	607. Tergiversation.
			608. Caprice.
		609. Choice.	609*a*. Absence of Choice. / 610. Rejection.
		611. Predetermination.	612. Impulse.
		613. Habit.	614. Desuetude.
	2°. *Causes*..	615. Motive.	615*a*. Absence of Motive. / 616. Dissuasion.
		617. Plea.	
	3°. *Objects*..	618. Good.	619. Evil.
II. PROSPECTIVE VOLITION........	1°. *Conceptional*..	620. Intention.	621. Chance.
		622. Pursuit.	623. Avoidance.
			624. Relinquishment.
		625. Business.	
		626. Plan.	
		627. Method.	
		628. Mid-Course.	629. Circuit.
		630. Requirement.	
	2°. *Subservience to Ends*...	1. *Actual Subservience.*	
		631. Instrumentality.	
		632. Means.	
		633. Instrument.	
		634. Substitute.	
		635. Materials.	
		636. Store.	
		637. Provision.	638. Waste.
		639. Sufficiency.	
		641. Redundance.	640. Insufficiency.
		2. *Degree of Subservience.*	
		642. Importance.	643. Unimportance.
		644. Utility.	645. Inutility.
		646. Expedience.	647. Inexpedience.
		648. Goodness.	649. Badness.
		650. Perfection.	651. Imperfection.
		652. Cleanness.	653. Uncleanness.
		654. Health.	655. Disease.
		656. Salubrity.	657. Insalubrity.
		658. Improvement.	659. Deterioration.
		660. Restoration.	661. Relapse.
		662. Remedy.	663. Bane.
		3. *Contingent Subservience.*	
		664. Safety.	665. Danger.
		666. Refuge.	667. Pitfall.
		668. Warning.	
		669. Alarm.	
		670. Preservation.	
		671. Escape.	
		672. Deliverance.	

SYNOPSIS OF CATEGORIES

II. PROSPECTIVE VOLITION—*cont.*	3°. *Precursory Measures*	673. Preparation.	674. Non-preparation.
		675. Essay.	
		676. Undertaking.	
		677. Use.	678. Disuse. 679. Misuse.
III. ACTION	1°. *Simple*...	680. Action.	681. Inaction.
		682. Activity.	683. Inactivity.
		684. Haste.	685. Leisure.
		686. Exertion.	687. Repose.
		688. Fatigue.	689. Refreshment.
		690. Agent.	
		691. Workshop.	
	2°. *Complex* .	692. Conduct.	
		693. Direction.	
		694. Director.	
		695. Advice.	
		696. Council.	
		697. Precept.	
		698. Skill.	699. Unskilfulness.
		700. Proficient.	701. Bungler.
		702. Cunning.	703. Artlessness.
IV. ANTAGONISM	1°. *Conditional*....	704. Difficulty.	705. Facility.
	2°. *Active*....	706. Hindrance.	707. Aid.
		708. Opposition.	709. Co-operation.
		710. Opponent.	711. Auxiliary.
		712. Party.	
		713. Discord.	714. Concord.
		715. Defiance.	
		716. Attack.	717. Defence.
		718. Retaliation.	719. Resistance.
		720. Contention.	721. Peace.
		722. Warfare.	723. Pacification.
		724. Meditation.	
		725. Submission.	
		726. Combatant.	
		727. Arms.	
		728. Arena.	
V. RESULTS OF ACTION.....		729. Completion.	730. Non-completion.
		731. Success.	732. Failure.
		733. Trophy.	
		734. Prosperity.	735. Adversity.
		736. Mediocrity.	

Division (II.). INTERSOCIAL VOLITION

I. GENERAL..............	737. Authority.	738. Laxity.
	739. Severity.	740. Lenity.
	741. Command.	
	742. Disobedience.	743. Obedience.
	744. Compulsion.	
	745. Master.	746. Servant.
	747. Sceptre.	
	748. Freedom.	749. Subjection.
	750. Liberation.	751. Restraint.
		752. Prison.
	753. Keeper.	754. Prisoner.
	755. Commission.	756. Abrogation.
		757. Resignation.
	758. Consignee.	
	759. Deputy.	

II. Special
- 760. Permission. — 761. Prohibition.
- 762. Consent.
- 763. Offer. — 764. Refusal.
- 765. Request. — 766. Depreciation.
- 767. Petitioner.

III. Conditional
- 768. Promise. — 768*a*. Release.
- 769. Compact.
- 770. Conditions.
- 771. Security.
- 772. Observance. — 773. Non-observance.
- 774. Compromise.

IV. Possessive Relations

1°. *Property in General*
- 775. Acquisition. — 776. Loss.
- 777. Possession. — 777*a*. Exemption.
- 778. Participation.
- 779. Possessor.
- 780. Property.
- 781. Retention. — 782. Relinquishment.

2°. *Transfer of Property*
- 783. Transfer.
- 784. Giving. — 785. Receiving.
- 786. Apportionment.
- 787. Lending. — 788. Borrowing.
- 789. Taking. — 790. Restitution.
- 791. Stealing.
- 792. Thief.
- 793. Booty.

3°. *Interchange of Property*
- 794. Barter.
- 795. Purchase. — 796. Sale.
- 797. Merchant.
- 798. Merchandise.
- 799. Mart.

4°. *Monetary Relations*
- 800. Money.
- 801. Treasurer.
- 802. Treasury.
- 803. Wealth. — 804. Poverty.
- 805. Credit. — 806. Debt.
- 807. Payment. — 808. Non-payment.
- 809. Expenditure. — 810. Receipt.
- 811. Accounts.
- 812. Price. — 813. Discount.
- 814. Dearness. — 815. Cheapness.
- 816. Liberality. — 817. Economy.
- 818. Prodigality. — 819. Parsimony.

Class VI. AFFECTIONS

I. AFFECTIONS GENERALLY
- 820. Affections.
- 821. Feeling.
- 822. Sensibility. — 823. Insensibility.
- 824. Excitation.
- 825. Excitability. — 826. Inexcitability.

SYNOPSIS OF CATEGORIES

II. PERSONAL

1°. PASSIVE	827. Pleasure.	828. Pain.
	829. Pleasureableness.	830. Painfulness.
	831. Content.	832. Discontent. 833. Regret.
	834. Relief.	835. Aggravation.
	836. Cheerfulness.	837. Dejection.
	838. Rejoicing.	839. Lamentation.
	840. Amusement.	841. Weariness.
	842. Wit.	843. Dulness.
	844. Humorist.	
2°. DISCRIMINATIVE	845. Beauty.	846. Ugliness.
	847. Ornament.	848. Blemish.
		849. Simplicity.
	850. Taste.	851. Vulgarity.
	852. Fashion.	
		853. Ridiculousness.
		854. Fop.
		855. Affection.
		856. Ridicule.
		857. Laughing-stock.
3°. PROSPECTIVE	858. Hope.	859. Hopelessness. 860. Fear.
	861. Courage.	862. Cowardice.
	863. Rashness.	864. Caution.
	865. Desire.	867. Dislike.
	866. Indifference.	
		868. Fastidiousness.
		869. Satiety.
4°. CONTEMPLATIVE	870. Wonder.	871. Expectance.
	872. Prodigy.	
5°. EXTRINSIC	873. Repute.	874. Disrepute.
	875. Nobility.	876. Commonalty.
	877. Title.	
	878. Pride.	879. Humility.
	880. Vanity.	881. Modesty.
	882. Ostentation.	
	883. Celebration.	
	884. Boasting.	
	885. Insolence.	886. Servility.
	887. Blusterer.	

III. SYMPATHETIC

1°. SOCIAL	888. Friendship.	889. Enmity.
	890. Friend.	891. Enemy.
	892. Sociality.	893. Seclusion.
	894. Courtesy.	895. Discourtesy.
	896. Congratulation.	
	897. Love.	898. Hate.
	899. Favorite.	
		900. Resentment.
		901. Irascibility.
		901*a*. Sullenness.
	902. Endearment.	
	903. Marriage.	904. Celibacy. 905. Divorce.

2°. **Diffusive**	906. Benevolence.	907. Malevolence.
		908. Malediction.
		909. Threat.
	910. Philanthropy.	911. Misanthropy.
	912. Benefactor.	913. Evil doer.
3°. **Special**	914. Pity.	914*a*. Pitilessness.
	915. Condolence.	
4°. **Retrospective**	916. Gratitude.	917. Ingratitude.
	918. Forgiveness.	919. Revenge.
		920. Jealousy.
		921. Envy.

IV. MORAL

1°. **Obligations**	922. Right.	923. Wrong.
	924. Dueness.	925. Undueness.
	926. Duty.	927. Dereliction.
		927*a*. Exemption.
2°. **Sentiments**	928. Respect.	929. Disrespect.
		930. Contempt.
	931. Approbation.	932. Disapprobation.
	933. Flattery.	934. Detraction.
	935. Flatterer.	936. Detractor.
	937. Vindication.	938. Accusation.
3°. **Conditions**	939. Probity.	940. Improbity.
		941. Knave.
	942. Disinterestedness.	943. Selfishness.
	944. Virtue.	945. Vice.
	946. Innocence.	947. Guilt.
	948. Good Man.	949. Bad Man.
	950. Penitence.	951. Impenitence.
	952. Atonement.	
4°. **Practice**	953. Temperance.	954. Intemperance.
		954*a*. Sensualist.
	955. Asceticism.	
	956. Fasting.	957. Gluttony.
	958. Sobriety.	959. Drunkenness.
	960. Purity.	961. Impurity.
		962. Libertine.
5°. **Institutions**	963. Legality.	964. Illegality.
	965. Jurisprudence.	
	966. Tribunal.	
	967. Judge.	
	968. Lawyer.	
	969. Lawsuit.	
	970. Acquittal.	971. Condemnation.
	973. Reward.	972. Punishment.
		974. Penalty.
		975. Scourge.

V. RELIGIOUS

1°. **Superhuman Beings and Regions**	976. Deity.	
	977. Angel.	978. Satan.
	979. Jupiter.	980. Demon.
	981. Heaven.	982. Hell.
2°. **Doctrines**	983. Theology.	
	983*a*. Orthodoxy.	984. Heterodoxy.
	985. Revelation.	986. Pseudo-revelation.
3°. **Sentiments**	987. Piety.	988. Impiety.
		989. Irreligion.

SYNOPSIS OF CATEGORIES

4°. ACTS	990. Worship.	991. Idolatry
		992. Sorcery.
		993. Spell.
		994. Sorcerer.
5°. INSTITUTIONS	995. Churchdom.	
	996. Clergy.	997. Laity.
	998. Rite.	
	999. Canonicals.	
	1000. Temple.	

ABBREVIATIONS, &c.

Adj.	*adj.*	Adjectives, Participles, and Words having the power of Adjectives.
Adv.	*adv.*	Adverbs and Adverbial Expressions.
Int.	*int.*	Interjections.
Phr.	*phr.*	Phrases.
V.	*v.*	Verbs.

The numbers are those of the headings, or Categories.

Words in italics within parentheses are not intended to explain the meanings of the words which precede them, but to indicate the nature of allied group of words under the numbers which follow them.

See also the Editor's Preface.

THESAURUS

OF

ENGLISH WORDS AND PHRASES

1. Existence.—N. existence, being, entity, *ens, esse,* subsistence, quiddity.

reality, realness, actuality; positiveness etc. *adj.*; fact, matter of fact, sober reality; truth etc. 494; actual existence.

presence etc. (*existence in space*) 186; coexistence etc. 120.

stubborn fact; not a -dream etc. 515; no joke.

substance, essence, prime constituent, hypostatis.

[Science of existence], ontology.

V. exist, be; have -being etc. *n.*; subsist, live, breathe, stand, obtain, be the case; occur etc. (*event*) 151; have place, rank, prevail; find oneself, pass the time, vegetate.

consist in, lie in, reside in, inhere in.

come into -existence etc. *n.*; arise etc. (*begin*) 66; come forth etc. (*appear*) 446.

become etc. (*be converted*) 144; bring into existence etc. 161; coexist, preexist, endure etc. 141.

Adj. existing etc. *v.*; existent, subsistent, under the sun; in -existence etc. *n.*; extant; afloat, on foot, current, prevalent, rife, in force, -vogue; undestroyed.

real, actual, positive, absolute; true etc. 494; substan-tial, -tive; self-existing, -ent.

well-founded, -grounded; un-ideal, -imagined; not -potential etc. 2.

Adv. actually etc. *adj.*; in -fact, – point of fact, – reality; indeed; *de –, ipso-facto.*

2. Nonexistence.—N. nonexistence; inexistence, -subsistence; nonentity, *nil*; negativeness etc. *adj.*; nullity; nihil-ity, -ism; *tabula rasa,* blank; abeyance; absence etc. 187; no such thing etc. 4; nothingness, oblivion, *non esse.*

annihilation; extinction etc. (*destruction*) 162.

V. not -exist etc. 1; have no -existence etc. 1; be null and void; cease to -exist etc. 1; pass away, perish; be –, become-extinct etc. *adj.*; die out; disappear etc. 449; melt away, dissolve, leave not a rack behind, leave no trace; go, be no more; die etc. 360.

annihilate, render null, nullify; abrogate etc. 756; destroy etc. 162; take away; remove etc. (*displace*) 185.

Adj. inexistent, non-existent etc. 1; negative, blank, null and void; missing, omitted; absent etc. 187; visionary etc. 515.

unreal, potential, virtual; baseless, *in nubibus*; unsubstantial etc. 4; vain.

un-born, -created, -begotten, -conceived, -produced, -made.

perished, annihilated etc. *v.*; extinct, exhausted, gone, lost, departed; defunct etc. (*dead*) 360; fabulous, ideal etc. (*imaginary*) 515; suppositious etc. 514.

Adv. negatively, virtually, etc. *adj.*

3. Substantiality.—N. substantiality, *hypostasis*; person, thing, object, article; something, a being, an existence; creature, body, substance, flesh and blood, stuff, *substratum*; matter etc. 316; physical nature.

[Totality of existences], world etc. 318; *plenum.*

Adj. substan-tive, -tial, concrete; hypostatic; personal, bodily; tangible etc. (*material*) 316; real, corporeal, evident.

Adv. substantially etc. *adj.*; bodily, essentially.

4. Unsubstantiality.—N. un-, in-substantiality; nothingness, nihility.

nothing, naught, *nil*, nullity, zero, cipher, no one, nobody; never [illegible], ne'er a one, no such thing, none in the world; nothing -whatever, – at all, – on earth; not a -particle etc. (*smallness*) 32; all -talk, – moonshine, – stuff and nonsense, matter of no import.

thing of naught, man of straw, John Doe and Richard Roe; *nominis umbra,* nonentity, figurehead, lay figure; flash in the pan, *vox et praeterea nihil.*

shadow; phantasm, phantom etc. (*fallacy of vision*) 443; dream etc. (*imagination*) 515; *ignis fatuus* etc. (*luminary*) 423; 'such stuff as dreams are made of;' air, thin air; bubble etc. 353; 'baseless fabric of a vision;' mockery.

hollowness, blank; vacuity, void etc. (*absence*) 187.

inanity, fool's paradise, fatuity, stupidity, emptiness of mind.

V. vanish, evaporate, fade, sink, fly –, die –, melt- away, dissolve, disappear etc. 449; become extinct, become invisible.

Adj. unsubstantial; fleeting; base-, ground-less; ungrounded; without –, having no- foundation.

visionary etc. (*imaginary*) 515; immaterial etc. 317; spectral etc. 980; dreamy; shadowy; ethereal, airy, imponderable, tenuous, vague.

vacant, vacuous; empty etc. 187; eviscerated; blank, hollow; nominal; null; inane.

Phr. there's nothing in it.

5. Intrinsicality.—N. intrinsicality, inbeing, inherence, inhesion, immanence; subjectiveness; *ego*; essence; essentialness etc. *adj.*; essential part, essential stuff, substance, quintessence, incarnation, quiddity, gist, pith, core, kernel, marrow, sap, lifeblood, backbone, heart, soul, life, flower; important part etc. (*importance*) 642.

principle, nature, constitution, character, ethos, type, quality, crasis, *diathesis*.

habit; temper, -ament; spirit, humor, grain, disposition, streak, tendency etc. 176.

endowment, capacity; capability etc. (*power*) 157; moods, declensions, features, aspects; peculiarities etc. (*specialty*) 79; idiosyncrasy; idiocrasy; diagnostics.

V. be –, run- in the blood; be born so; be -intrinsic etc. *adj.*

Adj. derived from within, subjective; idiocratic, idiosyncratic, intrin-sic, -sical; fundamental, cardinal, normal, inherent, essential, natural; in-nate, -born, -bred, -dwelling, -grained; -wrought; radical, incarnate, thoroughbred, hereditary, inherited, immanent; congen-ital, -ite; connate, running in the blood; coeval with birth, genetic, ingenerate, -genite; indigenous; in the -grain etc. *n.*; bred in the bone, instinctive; inward, internal etc. 221; to the manner born; virtual.

characteristic etc. (*special*) 79, (*indicative*) 550; invariable, incurable, ineradicable, fixed, settled, constant, unchanging.

Adv. intrinsically etc. *adj.*; at bottom, in the main, in effect, essentially, practically, virtually, substantially, *au fond*; fairly.

6. Extrinsicality.—N. extrinsicality, objectiveness, *non ego;* extraneousness etc. 57; accident; letter of the law.

Adj. derived from without; objective; extrinsic, -sical; extraneous etc. (*foreign*) 57; modal, adventitious, additional, supervenient, fortuitous; a-, ad-scititious; incidental, casual, accidental, unessential, non-essential, accessory.

implanted, ingrafted; instilled, inculcated.

outward etc. (*external*) 220.

Adv. extrinsically etc. *adj.*

7. State.—N. state, condition, category, estate, lot, case, trim, mood, pickle, plight etc. 704; temper; aspect etc. (*appearance*) 448.

constitution, habitude, *diathesis;* frame, fabric etc. 329; stamp, set, fit, mold.

mode, modality, schesis; fettle; form etc. (*shape*) 240.

tone, tenor, turn; trim, guise, fashion, light, complexion, style, character.

V. be in –, possess –, enjoy –, labor under- a -state etc. *n.;* be on a footing, do, fare; come to pass.

Adj. conditional, modal, formal; structural, organic.

Adv. conditionally etc. *adj.;* as -the matter stands, – things are; such being the case etc. 8.

8. Circumstance.—N. circumstance, situation, phase, position, posture, attitude, place, point; terms; *régime;* footing, standing, status.

occasion, juncture, conjuncture; contingency etc. (*event*) 151.

predicament; emergen-ce, -cy; exigency, crisis, pinch, pass, push; turning point; crossroads.

bearings, how the land lies.

Adj. circumstantial; given, conditional, provisional; critical; modal; contingent, incidental; adventitious etc. (*extrinsic*) 6.

Adv. in the circumstances etc. *n.*, under the conditions etc. 7; thus, in such wise.

accordingly; that –, such- being the case; that being so, since, seeing that.

as matters stand; as -things, – times- go.

conditionally, provided, if, in case; if -so, – so be, – it be so; if it so -happen, – turn out; in the event of; in such a -contingency, – case, – event; provisionally, unless, without.

according to -circumstances, – the occasion; as it may -happen, – turn out, – be; as the -case may be, – wind blows; *pro re natâ.*

9. Relation.—N. relation, bearing, reference, connection, apposition, interconnection, concern, cognation; applicability, appositeness; correlation etc. 12; analogy; similarity etc. 17; affinity, intimacy, friendship; homology, alliance, homogeneity, association, rapport; approximation etc. (*nearness*) 197; filiation etc. (*consanguinity*) 11; interest; relevancy etc. 23; relationship, relative position; relativity; interrelation etc. 12.

comparison etc. 464; ratio, proportion.

link, tie, bond, bond of union.

V. be-related etc. *adj.;* have a relation etc. *n.;* relate –, refer- to; bear upon, regard, concern, touch, affect, have to do with; pertain –, belong –, appertain- to; have respect to; answer to; interest.

bring -into relation with, – to bear upon; connect, associate, draw a parallel; link etc. 43.

Adj. relative; correlative etc. 12; cognate; relating to etc. *v.;* relative to, in relation with, referable *or* referrible to; belonging to etc. *v.;* appurtenant to, in common with.

related, connected; implicated, associated, affiliated, akin, allied to; collateral, cognate, congenial, kindred, affinitive, *en rapport*, in touch with.

approxima-tive, -ting; approaching; proportion-al, -ate, -able; allusive, comparable.

in the same -category etc. 75; like etc. 17; relevant etc. (*apt*) 23.

Adv. relatively etc. *adj.;* pertinently etc. 23.

thereof; as -to, – for, – respects, – re-gards; about; concerning etc. *v.;* anent; relating –, as relates- to; with -relation, – reference, – respect, – regard-to; in respect of; while speaking –, *à propos*-of; in connection with; by the -way, – by; whereas; for –, in -as much as; in point of, as far as; on the -part, – score- of; *quoad hoc; pro re natâ;* under the -head etc. (*class*) 75- of; in the matter of, *in re.*

Phr. 'thereby hangs a tale.'

10. Irrelation. [Want, or absence of relation.]—**N.** irrelation, dissociation; inapplicability; inconnection; multifariousness; disconnection etc. (*disjunction*) 44; inconsequence, independence; incommensurability; irreconcilableness etc. (*disagreement*) 24; heterogeneity;

unconformity etc. 83; irrelevancy, impertinence, *nihil ad rem;* intrusion etc. 24.

V. have no -relation etc. 9 to, — bearing upon, — concern etc. 9 with, — business with; not -concern etc. 9; have -nothing to do with, — no business there; intrude, etc. 24.

bring —, drag —, haul —, lug- in head and shoulders.

Adj. irrelative, irrespective, unrelated, irrelated; arbitrary; independent, unallied; un-, dis-connected; adrift, isolated, insular; extraneous, strange, alien, foreign, outlandish, exotic.

not comparable, incommensurable, heterogeneous; unconformable etc. 83.

irrelevant; rambling etc. 279; inapplicable; not -pertinent, — to the purpose; impertinent, inapposite, beside the mark, *à propos de bottes;* away from —, foreign to —, beside- the -purpose, — question, — transaction, — point; misplaced etc. (*intrusive*) 24.

remote, far fetched, out of the way, forced, neither here nor there, quite another thing; detached, segregated, segregate.

multifarious; discordant etc. 24.

incidental, parenthetical, *obiter dictum,* episodic.

Adv. parenthetically etc. *adj.;* by the -way, — by; *en passant,* incidentally; irrespecitively etc. *adj.;* without reference, — regard- to; in the abstract etc. 87; *a se.*

11. Consanguinity. [Relations of kindred.]—**N.** consanguinity, relationship, kindred, blood; parentage etc. (*paternity*) 166; filiation, affiliation; lineage, agnation, connection, cognation, alliance; family -connection, — tie; ties of blood; blood relationship; nepotism.

kins-man, -folk; people; kith and kin; relation, -tive; connection; sib; next of kin; uncle, aunt, nephew, niece; cousin, -german; first —, second- cousin; cousin -once, — twice etc.- removed; near —, distant-relation; brother, sister, one's own flesh and blood.

family, patriarch, matriarch; fraternity; brother-, sister-, cousin-hood.

race, stock, generation; sept etc. 166 ; stirps, side; strain; breed, clan, tribe.

V. be -related etc. *adj.* — to; claim -relationship etc. *n.*- with.

Adj. related, akin, consanguineous, matrilinear, patrilineal, of the blood, family, allied, collateral; cog-, ag-, con-nate; kindred; affiliated, affine; fraternal, avuncular.

intimately —, nearly —, closely —, remotely —, distantly- related, — allied; german.

12. Correlation. [Double or reciprocal relation.]—**N.** reciprocalness etc. *adj.;* recipro-city, -cality, -cation; mutuality, correlation, correspondence, interdependence; interchange etc. 148; exchange, barter; interrelation, interconnection; alternation, see-saw.

V. reciprocate, alternate; interchange etc. 148; exchange; counterchange; interact, correspond, mutualize, give and take.

Adj. reciprocal, mutual, commutual, correlative; alternate; interchangeable; international; correspondent, complementary, analogous.

Adv. *mutatis mutandis; vice versâ;* each other; by turns etc. 148; reciprocally etc. *adj.;* to and fro etc. 314.

13. Identity.—**N.** identity, sameness, oneness, ditto, homogeneity; unity, coincidence, coalescence; convertibility; equality etc. 27; selfness, self, oneself; identification.

monotony, tautology etc. (*repetition*) 104.

synonym.

fac-simile etc. (*copy*) 21; *alter ego* etc. (*similar*) 17; *ipsissima verba* etc. (*exactness*) 494; same; self —, very —, one and the same; very —, actual-thing, no other.

V. be -identical etc. *adj.;* match, coincide, coalesce.

treat as —, render--the same, —identical; identify; recognize the identity of.

Adj. identical; self, ilk; the -same etc. *n.;* self same; synonymous; one and the same.

coincid-, coalesc-ent, -ing; indistinguishable; one; equivalent etc. (*equal*) 27; much -the same, — of a muchness; unaltered.

Adv. identically etc. *adj.;* on all fours, ibid-, -em.

14. Contrariety. [Non-coincidence.]—**N.** contrariety, contrast, foil, antithesis, oppositeness; counterpole; contradiction; antagonism etc. (*opposition*) 708; counteraction etc. 179.

inversion etc. 218; the -opposite, — reverse, — inverse, — converse, — antipodes, — other extreme etc. 237.

antonym.

V. be -contrary etc. *adj.;* contrast with, oppose; differ *toto coelo.*

invert, reverse, turn the tables etc. 218.

contra-dict, -vene; antagonize etc. 708.

Adj. contrar-y, -ious, -iant; opposite, counter, dead against; ad-, con-, reverse; opposed, antithetical, contrasted, antipodean, antagonistic, opposing; conflicting, inconsistent, contradictory, at cross purposes; negative; hostile etc. 708.

differing *toto coelo;* diametrically opposite; as opposite as -black and white, — light and darkness, — fire and water, — the poles, as different as chalk from cheese; 'Hyperion to a satyr;' quite the -contrary, — reverse; no such thing, just the other way, *tout au contraire.*

Adv. contrarily etc. *adj.; contra,* contrariwise, *per contra,* on the contrary, nay rather; topsy-turvy; *vice versâ;* on the other hand etc. (*in compensation*) 30.

15. Difference.—**N.** difference, unlikeness; heterogeneity; vari-ance, -ation, -ety; diversity, dissimilarity etc. 18; disagreement etc. 24; disparity etc. (*inequality*) 28; distinction, contradistinction; distinctness; discrepancy, divergence, contrast etc. 18; nonconformity, incompatibility, antithesis.

discord etc. 713.

modification, moods and tenses.

nice —, fine —, delicate —, subtle- distinction; shade of difference, *nuance;* discrimination etc. 465; *differentia.*

different thing, something else, variant, apple

off another tree, horse of another color, another pair of shoes; this that or the other.

V. be -different etc. *adj.;* differ, vary, ablude, mismatch, contrast; diverge –, depart –, deviate- -from; divaricate; differ -*toto coelo,* — *longo intervallo.*

disagree etc. 713.

vary, modify etc. (*change*) 140.

discriminate etc. 465.

Adj. differing etc. *v.;* different, diverse, divided, heterogeneous; distinguishable; varied, modified; divergent, incongruous, diversified, various; discrepant, dissentient, differential; divers, all manner of; variform etc. 81; discordant etc. 713.

other, another, not the same; unequal etc. 28; unmatched; widely apart.

distinctive, characteristic; discriminative; distinghishing.

Adv. differently etc. *adj.*

Phr. *il y a fagots et fagots; tot nomines tot sententiae;* one man's meat is another man's poison.

16. Uniformity.—N. uniformity; homogeneity, -ousness; continuity, stability, consistency; connatural-ity, -ness; homology; accordance; conformity etc. 82; agreement etc. 23.

regularity, constancy, even tenor, routine; monotony, evenness, sameness, dead level; steadiness, equability, unity.

V. be -uniform etc. *adj.;* accord with etc. 23; run through.

become -uniform etc. *adj.;* conform to etc. 82.

render uniform etc. *adj.;* assimilate, level, smooth, dress.

Adj. uniform; homo-geneous, -logous; of a piece, consistent, steady; connatural; monotonous, changeless, dreary, even, invariable, equable, level, regular, stereotyped, unchanged, unvarying; methodical etc. 60; habitual etc. 613.

Adv. uniformly etc. *adj.;* uniformly with etc. (*conformably*) 82; in harmony with etc. (*agreeing*) 23; in a -rut, – groove.

always, ever etc. 112; invariably, without exception, never otherwise; by clock-work; endlessly etc. 112.

Phr. *ab uno disce omnes.*

16a. Non-uniformity. [Absence or want of uniformity.]–**N.** diversity, irregularity, unevenness; multiformity etc. 81; unconformity etc. 83; roughness etc. 256; heterogeneity, heteromorphism.

Adj. diversified, varied, irregular, uneven, rough etc. 256; multifarious; multiform etc. 81; of various kinds; all -manner, – sorts, – kinds- of.

Adv. in all manner of ways, here there and everywhere.

17. Similarity.—N. similarity, resemblance, likeness, similitude, semblance; affinity, approximation, parallelism; parity; agreement etc. 23; ana-logy, -logicalness; correspondence, equality etc.

connatural-ness, -ity; brotherhood, family likeness.

alliteration, rhyme, pun.

repetition etc. 104; sameness etc. (*identity*) 13; uniformity etc. 16.

analogue; the like; match, *pendant,* fellow, companion, pair, mate, twin, double, counterpart, brother, sister; one's second self, *alter ego,* chip of the old block, *par nobile fratrum, Arcades ambo,* birds of a feather, *et hoc genus omne.*

parallel; simile; type etc. (*metaphor*) 521; image etc. (*representation*) 554; photograph; close –, striking –, speaking –, faithful etc *adj.* – likeness, – resemblance.

V. be -similar etc. *adj.;* look like, resemble, bear resemblance, favor; savor –, smack- of; approximate; parallel, match, rhyme with; take after; imitate etc. 19; run in pairs.

Adj. similar; resembling etc. *v.;* like, alike; twin.

analog-ous, -ical; parallel, of a piece; such as, so.

connatural, congeneric, allied to; corresponding, cognate; akin to etc. (*consanguineous*) 11.

approximate, much the same, near, close, something like, such like; a show of; mock, *pseudo,* simulating, representing.

exact etc. (*true*) 494; lifelike, faithful, realistic; true to -nature, – the life; the -very image – picture- of; for all the world like, *comme deux gouttes d'eau;* as like as -two peas, – it can stare; *instar omnium,* case in the same mold, ridiculously like.

Adv. as if, so to speak; as –, as if- it were; *quasi,* just as, *veluti in speculum.*

18. Dissimilarity.—N. dissimil-arity, -itude; unlikeness, diversity, disparity, dissemblance; divergence, inequality, difference etc. 15; novelty; variation, variety, originality, disguise.

V. be -unlike etc. *adj.;* vary etc. (*differ*) 15; bear no resemblance to, differ *toto coelo.*

render -unlike etc. *adj.;* vary etc. (*diversify*) 140.

Adj. dissimilar, unlike, disparate; of a different kind etc. (*class*) 75; unmatched, unique; new, novel; unprecedented etc. 83; original.

nothing of the kind; no such –, quite another- thing; far from it, other than, cast in a different mold, *tertium quid,* as like a dock as a daisy, 'very like a whale;' as different as -chalk from cheese, – Macedon and Monmouth; *lucus a non lucendo.*

diversified etc. 16*a*.

Adv. otherwise, *alias.*

19. Imitation.—N. imitation; copying etc. *v.;* transcription; repetition, mimeograph, mimeotype, duplication, reduplication; quotation; reproduction.

mockery, mimicry, mime, simulation, personation; representation etc. 554; semblance, pretence; copy etc. 21; assimilation.

paraphrase, parody etc. 21.

plagiarism; forgery etc. (*falsehood*) 544.

imitator; echo, cuckoo, parrot, ape, monkey, mocking-bird, mimic, impersonator, copyist.

V. imitate, copy, mirror, reflect, reproduce, repeat, borrow; do like, echo, re-echo, catch; transcribe; match, parallel.

mock, take off, mimic, ape, simulate, personate, impersonate; forge; act etc. (*drama*) 599; represent etc. 554; counterfeit, duplicate; portray, parody, travesty, caricature, burlesque.

follow —, tread- in the- -steps, — footsteps, — wake- of; pattern after, take pattern by; follow - suit, — the example of; walk in the shoes of, take a leaf out of another's book, strike in with; take —, model -after; emulate.

Adj. imitated etc. *v.;* mock, mimic; counterfeit, false, pseudo; modelled after, molded on, paraphrastic; literal; imitative, apish; second-hand; imitable; sham etc. 545.

Adv. literally, to the letter, strictly, precisely, *verbatim, literatim, sic, totidem verbis,* word for word, *mot à mot.*

Phr. like master like man.

20. Non-Imitation.—N. no imitation, genuineness, originality; creativeness.

Adj. unimitated, uncopied; unmatched, unparalleled; inimitable etc. 33; *unique,* original, primordial, primary, pristine, underived, first-hand, archetypal, prototypal.

20a. Variation.—N. variation; alteration etc. (*change*) 140. modification, moods and tenses; modulation.

divergency etc. 291; deviation etc. 279; aberration; innovation.

V. vary etc. (*change*) 140; deviate etc. 279; diverge etc. 291.

Adj. varied etc. *v.;* modified; dissimilar etc. 18; diversified etc. 16*a.*

21. Copy. [Result of imitation.]—**N.** copy, facsimile, counterpart, *effigies,* effigy, symbol, image, form, likeness, similitude, semblance, resemblance, cast, electrotype, stereotype, tracing, ectype; imitation etc. 19; model, representation, adumbration, study; counterfeit presentment, portrait etc. (*representment*) 554.

duplicate; transcript, -ion; reflex, -ion; shadow, echo; chip of the old block; reprint, reproduction, casting, engraving, replica; transfer; second edition etc. (*repetition*) 104; *réchauffé* apograph, fair copy; revise.

parody, caricature, cartoon, burlesque, travesty, paraphrase.

servile -copy, — imitation; counterfeit etc. (*deception*) 545; *pasticcio.*

Adj. faithful; lifelike etc. (*similar*) 17.

22. Prototype. [Thing copied.]—**N.** prototype, original, model, pattern, founding, precedent, standard, scantling, type, arche-, anti-type; protoplast, copy-book, module, exemplar, example, ensample, specimen; paradigm; guide; templet; lay-figure.

text, copy, manuscript, MS., design: fugleman, keynote.

die, mold; matrix, engraving, last, plasm; pro-, proto-plasm; mint; seal, punch, *intaglio,* negative, stamp.

V. be —, set- an example; set a copy; standardize.

23. Agreement.—N. agreement; ac-cord, -cordance; unison, harmony, concord etc. 714; concordance, concert, understanding, convention, *entente -cordiale, consortium,* consensus of opinion, pact, mutual understanding, unanimity.

conformity etc. 82; conformance; uniformity etc. 16; consonance, consentaneousness, consistency; congruity, -ence; keeping; congeniality; correspondence, concinnity, parallelism, apposition, union.

fitness, aptness etc. *adj.;* relevancy; pertinence, -cy; sortance; case in point; aptitude, propriety, applicability, admissibility, commensurability, compatibility, suitability; cognation etc (*relation*) 9.

adaptation, adjustment, arrangement, graduation, accommodation; reconcil-iation - ement; assimilation; attunement.

consent etc. (*assent*) 448; concurrence etc. 178; co-operation etc. 709.

right man in the right place, very thing; quite —, just- the thing.

V. be -accordant etc. *adj.;* agree, accord, harmonize; correspond, tally, respond; meet, suit, fit, befit, do, adapt itself to; fall in —, chime in —, square —, quadrate —, consort —, comport- with; dovetail, assimilate; fit like a glove; fit to a -tittle, — T; match etc. 17; become one.

consent etc. (*assent*) 488.

render -accordant etc. *adj.;* fit, suit, adapt, accommodate; graduate; adjust etc. (*render equal*) 27; dress, regulate, readjust; accord, harmonize, reconcile; fadge, dovetail, square.

Adj. agreeing, suiting etc. *v.;* in accord, accordant, concordant, consonant, congruous, consentaneous, correspondent, corresponding, homologous, congenial; becoming; harmonious, reconcilable, conformable; in -accordance, — harminy, — keeping, — unison, etc. *n.;*-with; at one with, of one mind, of a piece; consistent, compatible, proportionate, answerable; commensurate; on all fours.

apt, apposite, pertinent, pat; to the -point, — purpose; happy, felicitous, germane, *ad rem,* in point, bearing upon, applicable, relevant, admissible.

fit, adapted, *in loco, à propos,* appropriate, seasonable, sortable, suitable, idoneous, deft; meet etc. (*expedient*) 646.

at home, in one's proper element.

Adv. *à propos of;* pertinently etc. *adj.; pro rata.*

Phr. *rem acu tetigisti,* the cap fits.

24. Disagreement.—N. disagreement, discord, -cordance; disunion, dissonance, dissidence, discrepancy; unconformity etc. 83; incongru-ity, -ence; discongruity, *mésalliance, oxymoron;* jarring etc. *v.;* clash, collision, dissension etc. 713; conflict etc. (*opposition*) 708; controversy etc. 720; falling out, wrangle, argument.

disparity, mismatch, misfit, disproportion; disproportionateness etc. *adj.;* variance, divergence, repugnance.

unfitness etc. *adj.;* inaptitude, impropriety; inapplicability etc. *adj.;* inconsistency, inconcinnity; irrelevancy etc. (*irrelation*) 10.

misjoin-ing, -der; syncretism, intrusion, interference; *concordia discors.*
fish out of water.
V. disagree; clash, quarrel, jar etc. (*discord*) 713; interfere, intrude, come amiss; not concern etc. 10; mismatch; *hymano capiti cervicem jungere equinam.*
Adj. disagreeing etc. *v.;* discordant, discrepant; at -variance, — war; hostile, antagonistic, repugnant, factious, contradictory, dissentious, incompatible, irreconcilable, inconsistent with; unconformable, exceptional etc. 83; intrusive, incongruous; disproportionate, -ed; unharmonious; unconsonant; divergent, repugnant to.
inapt, unapt, inappropriate, inept, infelicitous, improper; unsuit-ed, -able; inapplicable; un-fit, -fitting, -befitting; unbecoming; ill-timed, ill-adapted, unseasonable, *mal â propos,* inadmissible; inapposite etc. (*irrelevant*) 10.
uncongenial; ill-assorted, -sorted, -matched; mis-matched, -mated, -joined, -placed; unaccommodating, irreducible, uncommensurable, unsympathetic.
out of -character, — keeping, — proportion, — joint, — tune, — place, — season, — its element; at -odds, — variance with.
Adv. in -defiance, — contempt, — spite-of; discordantly etc. *adj.; à tort et à travers.*

25. Quantity. [Absolute quantity.]—**N.** quantity, magnitude; size etc. (*dimensions*) 192; amplitude, mass, amount, *quantum,* measure, measurement, substance, strength.
[Science of quantity.] Mathematics, Mathesis.
[Definite or finite quantity] arm-, hand-, mouth-, spoon-, thimble-, capful; stock, batch, lot, dose, ration, quotum, quota, pittance, driblet, part, portion etc. 51.
Adj. quantitative, some, any, more or less.
Adv. to the tune of.

26. Degree. [Relative quantity.]—**N.** degree, grade, extent, measure, proportion, amount, ratio, stint, standard, height, pitch; reach, amplitude, range, scope, size, caliber; gradation, shade; tenor, compass; sphere, station, rank, standing; rate, way, sort.
point, mark, step, stage etc. (*term*) 71; intensity, strength etc. (*greatness*) 31.
V. compare, graduate, calibrate, measure.
Adj. comparative; gradual, shading off, gradational; within the bounds etc. (*limit*), 233.
Adv. by degrees, gradually, inasmuch, *pro tanto*; how-ever, -soever; step by step, bit by bit, little by little, inch by inch, drop by drop, gradatim; by -inches, — slow degrees, — little and little; in some -degree, — measure; to some extent; just a bit.

27. Equality. [Sameness of quantity or degree.]—**N.** equality, parity, co-extension, symmetry, balance, poise; evenness, monotony, level.
equivalence; equi-pollence, -poise, -librium, -ponderance; par, quits; not a pin to choose; distinction without a difference, six of one and half a dozen of the other; identity etc. 13; similarity etc. 17; isotropism; coequality.
equalization, equation, equilibration, coordination, adjustment, readjustment.
drawn -game, -battle, draw, stalemate; neck and neck race; tie, dead heat.
match, peer, compeer, equal, mate, fellow, brother; equivalent.
V. be -equal etc. *adj.;* equal, match, reach, keep pace with, run abreast; come —, amount —, come upto; be —, lie- on a level with; balance; cope with; come to the same thing; level off.
render -equal etc. *adj.;* equalize, level, dress, balance, equate, handicap, give points, trim, adjust, poise; fit, accommodate; adapt etc. *render accordant*) 23; strike a balance; establish -, restore- equality, — equilibrium; readjust; stretch on the bed of Procrustes.
Adj. equal, even, level, monotonous, coequal, symmetrical, coordinate; on a -par, — level, — footing- with; up to the mark; equiparent.
equivalent, tantamount; quits; homologous; synonymous etc. 522; resolvable into, convertible, much at one, as broad as long, neither more nor less; much the same —, the same thing —, as good- as; all -one, — the same; equi-pollent, -ponderant, -ponderous, -balanced; equalized etc. *v.;* drawn; half and half; isochronous; isoperimetrical.
Adv. equally etc. *adj.; pari passu, ad eundem, caeteris paribus; in equilibrio;* to all intents and purposes.
Phr. it -comes, -adds up, — amounts- to the same thing.

28. Inequality. [Difference of quantity or degree.]—**N.** inequality; dis-, im-parity; odds; difference etc. 15; ill-balanced; unevenness; inclination of the balance, partiality; shortcoming; casting —make- weight; superiority etc. 33; inferiority etc. 34.
V. be -unequal etc. *adj.;* countervail; have —, give- the advantage; turn the scale; kick the beam; topple, -over; over-match etc. 33; not come up to etc. 34.
Adj. unequal, uneven, disparate, partial; un-, over-balanced; top-heavy, lop-sided.
Adv. *haud passibus aequis.*

29. Mean.—**N.** mean, medium, intermedium, average, run of the mill, normal, balance; mediocrity, generality, rule, ordinary -run, -ruck; golden mean etc. (*mid-course*) 628; middle etc. 68; compromise etc. 774; neutrality; middle point, middle course.
V. split the difference; take the -average etc. *n.,* reduce to a -mean etc. *n.;* strike a balance, pair off.
Adj. mean, intermediate; medial; middle etc. 68; average, normal, standard, neutral; middling, moderate.
médiocre, middle-class; *bourgeois,* commonplace etc. (*unimportant*) 643.
Adv. on an average, in the long run; taking -one with another, — all things together, — it for all in all; *communibus annis,* in round numbers.

30. Compensation.—**N.** compensation, equation; commutation; indemnification; compromise etc. 774; neutralization, nullification; counteraction etc. 179; reaction; measure for measure; retaliation etc. 718; equalization etc. 27; redemption, recoupment, recompense.

set-off, offset; make- casting-weight; counterpoise, equipoise, ballast; indemnity, reparation etc. 790; equivalent, *quid pro quo;* bribe, hush-money, tribute etc. 784· amends etc. (*atonement*) 952; counterclaim, counterbalance, equiponderance, countervail, cross demand.

V. make -amends, – compensation; compensate, -pense; indemnify; counter-act, -vail, -poise; equiponderate; balance; out-, over-, counterbalance, set off, offset, cancel; hedge, square, give and take; make up -for, – lee way; cover, fill up, neutralize, nullify; equalize etc. 27; make good; redeem etc. (*atone*) 952; recoup, pay etc. 973.

Adj. compensat-ing, -ory; amendatory, reparative, countervailing etc. *v.;* in the opposite scale; equivalent etc. (*equal*) 27.

Adv. in -return, – consideration; but, however, yet, still, notwithstanding; neverthe-, nathless; although, though; al-, how-beit; in spite of, despite; mauger; at -all events, – any rate; be that as it may, for all that, even so, on the other hand, at the same time, *quoad minus, quand même,* however that may be; after all, – is said and done; taking one thing with another etc. (*average*) 29.

31. Greatness.– N. greatness etc. *adj.;* magnitude; size etc. (*dimensions*) 192; multitude etc. (*number*) 102; immensity, enormity, infinity etc. 105; might, strength, intensity, fulness; importance etc. 642; fame etc. 873.

great quantity, quantity, deal, power, sight, pot, volume, world; mass, heap etc. (*assemblage*) 72; stock etc. (*store*) 636; peck, bushel, load, cargo; cart –, wagon –, car –, truck –, ship-load; flood, spring tide; abundance etc. (*sufficiency*) 639.

principal –, chief –, main –, greater –, major –, best –, essential- part; bulk, mass etc. (*whole*) 50.

V. be -great etc. *adj.;* run high, soar, loom up, tower, bulk large, transcend; rise –, carry- to a great height; know no bounds; scale, overtop, ascend.

enlarge etc. (*increase*) 35, (*expand*) 194.

Adj. great; greater etc. 33; large, considerable, fair, above par; big, massive, huge etc. (*large in size*) 192; ample; abundant etc. (*enough*) 639; Herculean etc. 159; full, intense, strong, sound, passing, heavy, plenary, deep, high; signal, at its height, in the zenith.

world-wide, wide-spread, extensive; wholesale; many etc. 102.

goodly, noble, precious, mighty; sad, grave, serious; far gone, arrant, downright; utter, -most; crass, gross, arch, profound, intense, consummate; rank, unmitigated, red-hot, desperate; glaring, flagrant, stark staring; thorough-paced, -going; roaring, thumping, thundering, strapping, whacking; extraordinary; important etc. 642; unsurpassed etc. (*supreme*) 33; complete etc. 52.

vast, immense, enormous, extreme; inordinate, excessive, extravagant, exorbitant, outrageous, preposterous, unconscionable, swinging, monstrous, over-grown; towering, stupendous, prodigious, astonishing, incredible; terrific, frightful; marvelous etc. (*wonder*) 870; grand.

unlimited etc. (*infinite*) 105; unapproachable, unutterable, indescribable, ineffable, unspeakable, inexpressible, beyond expression, fabulous.

un-diminished, -abated, -reduced, -restricted.

absolute, positive, stark, decided, unequivocal, essential, perfect, finished.

remarkable, of mark, marked, pointed, veriest; noticeable, uncommon, noteworthy, eminent etc. 873.

Adv. [in a positive degree] truly etc. (*truth*) 494; decidedly, unequivocally, purely, absolutely, seriously, essentially, fundamentally, radically, downright, in all conscience; for the most part, in the main.

[in a complete degree] entirely etc. (*completely*) 52; abundantly, etc. (*sufficiently*) 639; widely, far and wide.

[in a great or high degree] greatly etc. *adj.;* much, muckle, well, indeed, very, very much, a deal, no end of, most not a little; pretty, – well; enough, in a great measure, passing richly; to a -large, – great, – gigantic- extent; on a large scale; so; never –, ever- so; ever so much; by wholesale; mightily, mighty, powerfully; with a witness, *ultra,* in the extreme, extremely, exceedingly, intensely, exquisitely, acutely, indefinitely, immeasurably; beyond -compare, – comparison, – measure, – all bounds; incalculably, infinitely.

[in a supreme degree] pre-eminently, superlatively etc. (*superiority*) 33.

[in a too great degree] immoderately, unduly, monstrously, grossly, preposterously, inordinately, exorbitantly, excessively, enormously, out of all proportion, with a vengeance.

[in a marked degree] particularly, remarkably, singularly, curiously, uncommonly, unusually, peculiarly, notably, signally, strikingly, pointedly, mainly, chiefly; famously, egregiously, prominently, glaringly, emphatically, strangely, wonderfully, amazingly, surprisingly, astonishingly, incredibly, marvelously, awfully, stupendously.

[in an exceptional degree] peculiarly etc. (*unconformity*) 83.

[in a violent degree] furiously etc. (*violence*) 173; severely, desperately, tremendously, extravagantly, confoundedly, deucedly, devilishly, with a vengeance; *à –, à toute- outrance.*

[in a painful degree] painfully, sadly, grossly, sorely, bitterly, piteously, grievously, miserably, cruelly, woefully, lamentably, shockingly, frightfully, dreadfully, fearfully, terribly, horribly, distressingly, balefully.

32. Smallness.—N. smallness etc. *adj.;* littleness etc. (*small size*) 193; tenuity; paucity; fewness etc. (*small number*) 103; meanness, insignificance etc. (*unimportance*) 643; mediocrity, moderation.

small quantity, *modicum, minimum;* vanishing point; material point, electron, atom, particle, molecule, corpuscle, point, dab, fleck, speck, dot, mote, jot, iota, ace; *minutiae,* details; look, thought, idea, *soupçon,* whit, tittle, shade, shadow; spark, *scintilla,* gleam; touch, cast; grain, scruple, granule, globule, minim, sup, sip, sop, spice, drop, droplet, sprinkling, dash, smack, tinge, tincture; inch, patch, scantling, dole; scrap, shred, tag, splinter, rag, tatter, cantlet, flitter, gobbet, mite, bit, morsel, crumb, seed, fritter, shive; snip, -pet; snick, snack, snatch, slip, scrag; chip, -ping; shiver, sliver, driblet, clipping, paring, shaving, hair.

nutshell; thimble-, spoon-, hand-, cap-, mouthful; fragment; fraction etc. (*part*)51; drop in the ocean, drop in the bucket.

animalcule etc. 193.

trifle etc. (*unimportant thing*) 643; mere –, next to- nothing; hardly anything; just enough to swear by; the shadow of a shade.

finiteness, finite quantity.

V. be -shall etc. *adj.;* lie in a nutshell.

diminish etc. (*decrease*) 36, (*contract*) 195.

Adj. small, little, tiny, weeny; diminutive etc. (*small in size*) 193; minute; minikin, fine, inconsiderable, dribbling, paltry etc. (*unimportant*) 643; faint etc. (*weak*) 160; slender, light, slight, scanty, scant, limited; meager etc. (*insufficient*) 640; sparing; few etc. 103; low, so-so, middling, tolerable, no great shakes; below –, under-par, – the mark; at a low ebb; halfway; moderate, modest; tender, subtle; petty, shallow, skin-deep.

inappreciable, evanescent, infinite-simal, homeopathic, very small, atomic, molecular, ultra-, -microscopic.

petty, shallow etc. 499.

mere, simple, sheer, stark, bare; near run.

Adv. [in a small degree] to a small extent, on a small scale; a -little, – wee, – tiny bit; slightly etc. *adj.;* imperceptibly; miserably, wretchedly; insufficiently etc. 640; imperfectly; faintly etc. '60; passably, pretty well, well enough.

[in a certain or limited degree] partially, in part; in –, to a certain degree; to a certain extent; comparatively; some, rather; in some -degree, -measure; some-thing, -what; simply, only, purely, merely; at –, at the- -least, – most; ever so little, as little as may be, *tant soit peu,* in ever so small a degree; thus far, *pro tanto;* within bounds, in a manner, after a fashion.

almost, nearly, well nigh, short of, not quite, all but; near –, close- upon; *peu s'en faut,* near the mark; within an -ace, – inch- of; on the brink of; scarcely, hardly, barely, only just, no more than.

[in an uncertain degree] about, therabouts, somewhere about, nearly, say; be the same - more, – little more- or less.

[in no degree] no- ways, – wise; not -at all, – in the least, – a bit, – a bit of it, – a whit, – a jot, – a shadow; in no -wise, – respect; by no - means, – manner of means; on no account, at no hand.

33. Superiority.—N. superiority, supremacy, majority; greatness etc. 31; advantage, odds, pull; preponderance, -ation; predominance, vantage ground, coign of vantage, prevalence, partiality; personal superiority; sovereignty etc. 737; nobility etc. (*rank*) 875; Triton among the minnows, *primus inter pares, nulli secundus,* superman; captain etc. 475.

supremacy, pre-eminence; primacy, lead, *maximum;* record; climax, crest, top; culmination etc. (*summit*) 210; transcendence; *ne plus ultra;* lion's share, Benjamin's mess; excess; bisque, surplus etc. (*remainder*) 40, (*redundance*) 641.

V. be -superior etc. *adj.;* exceed, excel, transcend; out-do, -balance, -weigh, -rival, -Herod, outrank, pass, surpass, surmount, get ahead of; over-top, -ride, -pass, -balance, -weigh, -match; top, o'er-top, cap, beat, win out, cut out; beat hollow; outstrip etc. 303; eclipse, throw into the shade, take the shine out of, put one's nose out of joint; have the -upper hand, – whip hand of, – advantage; turn the scale, play first fiddle etc. (*importance*) 642; preponderate, predominate, prevail; precede, take precedence, come first; come to a head, culminate; beat etc. all others, bear the palm; break the record, take the cake.

become –, render- -larger, etc. (*increase*) 35, (*expand*) 194.

Adj. superior, greater, major, higher; exceeding etc. *v.;* great etc. 31; distinguished, *ultra;* vaulting; more than a match for.

supreme, greatest, maximal, maximum, utmost, paramount, pre-eminent, foremost, crowning; first-rate etc. (important) 642, (*excellent*) 648; unrivalled; peer-, match-less; none such, second to none, *sans pareil;* un-paragoned, -paralleled, -equalled, -approached, -surpassed; superlative, inimitable, *facile princeps,* incomparable, sovereign, without parallel, *nulli secundus, ne plus ultra;* beyond -compare, – comparison; culminating etc. (*topmost*) 210; transcendent, -ental; *plus royaliste que le Roi.*

increased etc. (*added to*) 35; enlarged etc. (*expanded*) 194.

Adv. beyond, more, over; over –, above- the mark; above par; upwards –, in advance- of; over and above; at the top of the scale, on the crest, at it height.

[in a superior or supreme degree] eminently, egregiously, pre-eminently, surpassing, prominently, superlatively, supremely, above all, of all things, the most, to crown all, *par excellence,* principally, especially, particularly, peculiarly, *a fortiori,* even, yea, still more.

Phr. 'we shall not look upon his like again.'

34. Inferiority.—N. inferiority, minority, subordinancy; shortcoming, deficiency; handicap; *minimum;* smallness etc. 32; imperfection, shabbiness.

[personal inferiority] commonalty etc. 876; subordinate, substitute, sub.

V. be -inferior etc. *adj.;* fall –, come- short of; not -pass, – come up to; want.

become –, render- smaller etc. (decrease) 36, (*contract*) 195; hide its diminished head, retire into the shade, yield the palm, play second fiddle, take a back seat; bow.

Adj. inferior, smaller; small etc. 32; minor, less, lesser, deficient, minus, lower, subordinate, secondary; second-rate etc. (*imperfect*) 651; sub, subaltern; thrown into the shade; weighed in the balance and found wanting; not fit to hold a candle to.

least, smallest etc. (*see* little, small etc. 193); lowest.

diminished etc. (*decreased*) 36; reduced etc. (*contracted*) 195; unimportant etc. 643.

Adv. less; under –, below- -the mark, – par; at -the bottom of the scale, – a low ebb, – a disadvantage; short of, under.

35. Increase.—N. increase; augmentation, addition, enlargement, extension; dilatation etc. (*expansion*) 194; multiplication; increment, accretion; accession etc. 37; production etc. 161; development, growth; aggrandizement, aggravation, intensification; rise; ascent etc. 305; anabasis; ex-aggeration, -acerbation; spread etc. (*dispersion*) 73; flood-, spring-, -tide; gain, produce, profit etc. 618; booty, plunder etc. 793.

V. increase, augment, add to, enlarge; dilate etc. (*expand*) 194; grow, wax, mount, swell, get ahead, gain strength; advance; run –, shoot- up; rise; ascend etc. 305; sprout etc. 194.

aggrandize; raise; exalt; deepen, heighten; lengthen; thicken; strengthen; intensify, enhance, inflate, magnify, double, redouble; multiply; aggravate, exaggerate; ex-asperate, -acerbate; add fuel to the flame, *oleum addere camino*, superadd etc. (*add*) 37; spread etc. (*disperse*) 73.

Adj. increased etc. *v.;* on the increase, undiminished, additional etc. (*added*) 37; increasing etc. *v.;* growing, crescent, intensive, cumulative.

Adv. *crescendo*, increasingly.

Phr. *vires acquirit eundo.*

36. Non-Increase, Decrease.—N. decrease, diminution, lessening etc. *v.;* subtraction etc. 38; reduction, abatement, declension; shrinkage etc. (*contraction*) 195; coarctation; abridgment etc. (*shortening*) 201; extenuation.

subsidence, catabasis, wane, ebb-, neap-tide, decline; descent etc. 306; decrement, reflux, depreciation; erosion, wear and tear, deterioration etc. 659; anticlimax; mitigation etc. (*moderation*) 174.

V. decrease, diminish, lessen; abridge etc. (*shorten*) 201; shrink etc. (*contract*) 195; drop –, fall –, tail- off; fall away, waste, wear, erode; wane, ebb, decline; descent etc. 306; subside; deliquesce, melt –, die -away; retire into the shade, hide its diminished head, fall to a low ebb, run low, languish, decay, crumble, consume away.

bate, abate, dequantitate; discount; depreciate; extenuate, lower, weaken, attenuate, fritter away; mitigate etc.(*moderate*) 174; belittle, minimize; dwarf, throw into the shade; keep down, reduce etc. 195; shorten etc. 201; subtract etc. 38.

Adj. unincreased etc. (*see* increase etc. 35); decreased etc. *v.;* decreasing etc. *v.;* on the -wane etc. *n.;* deliquescent.

Adv. *diminuendo, decrescendo*, decreasingly.

37. Addition.—N. addition, annexation, adjection; junction etc. 43; super-position, -addition, -junction, -fetation; accession, reinforcement; increase etc. 35; increment, supplement; accompaniment etc. 88; interposition etc. 228; insertion etc. 300; summation etc. 85; adjunct etc. 39.

V. add, annex, adject, affix, attach, superadd, subjoin, superpose; clap –, saddle- on; tack to, postfix, append, tag; ingraft; saddle with; sprinkle; introduce etc. (*interpose*) 228; insert etc. 300.

become added, accrue; ad-, supervene; add up etc. 85.

reinforce, strengthen, swell the ranks of; augment etc. 35.

Adj. added etc. *v.;* additional; supplement, -al, -ary; suppletory, subjunctive; adjec-, adsci-, ascititious; additive, extra, spare, further, fresh, more, new, ulterior, other, auxiliary, supernumerary, accessory.

Adv. in addition, more, plus, extra; and, also, likewise, too, furthermore, further, item; and - also, – eke; else, besides, to boot, *et cetera;* etc.; and so -on, – forth; into the bargain, *cum multis aliis*, over and above, moreover.

with, withal; including, inclusive, as well as, not to mention, let alone; together –, along –, coupled –, in conjunction- with; conjointly; jointly etc. 43.

38. Non-Addition. Subduction.—N. sub-traction, -duction; deduction, retrenchment; removal; ab-, sub-lation; abstraction etc. (*taking*) 789; garbling etc. *v.;* mutilation, detruncation; amputation, severance; abs-, ex-, re-cision; curtailment etc. 201; minuend, subtrahend; decrease etc. 36; abrasion.

V. sub-tract, -duct; rebate, de-duct, – duce; bate, retrench; remove, withdraw; take – from, – away; detract.

garble, mutilate, amputate, sever, detruncate; cut -off, – away, – out; expurgate; abscind, excise; pare, thin, prune, decimate; abrade, scrape, file; geld, castrate, emasculate, unman, spay, caponize; eliminate.

diminish etc. 36; curtail etc. (*shorten*) 201; deprive of etc. (*take*) 789; weaken.

Adj. subtracted etc. *v.;* subtractive.

tailless, acaudal.

Adv. in -deduction etc. *n.;* less; short of; minus, without, except, excepting, with the exception of, barring, bar, save, exclusive of, save and except, with a reservation.

39. Adjunct. [Thing added.]—**N.** adjunct, addit-ion, -ament; *additum*, affix, appendage, annex; augment, -ation; increment, reinforcement, supernumerary, accessory, item; garnish, sauce; accompaniment etc. 88; adjective, *addendum*, accession, complement, supplement; continuation; extension, subscript, tag, appendix, postscript, interlineation, interpolation, insertion.

rider, codicil, off-shoot, episode, side issue, corollary; piece; flap, lapel, label, tab, strip, fold, lappet, apron, skirt, embroidery, trappings, *cortège*; tail, suffix etc. (*sequel*) 65; wing.

Adj. additional etc. 37.

Adv. in addition etc. 37.

40. Remainder. [Thing remaining.]—**N.** remainder, residue; remains, *remanet*, remnant, rest, relic, relict; leavings, heel-tap, odds and ends, cheese-parings, candle ends, orts; *residuum;* dottle, dregs, etc. (*dirt*) 653; refuse etc. (*useless*) 645; stubble, result, educt; fag-end, stub; ruins, wreck, skeleton, stump; *alluvium*.

surplus, overplus, excess; balance, complement; superfluity etc. (*redundance*) 641; surviv-al, -ance; afterglow.

V. remain; be -left etc. *adj.*; exceed, survive; leave.

Adj. remaining, left; left -behind, – over;

residu-al, -ary; over, odd; unconsumed, sedimentary; surviving; net; exceeding, over and above; outlying, -standing; cast off etc. 782; superfluous etc. (*redundant*) 641.

V. remain; be -left; left -behind, – over; redidual, -ary; over, odd; unconsumed, sedimentary; surviving; net; exceeding, over and above; outlying, -standing; cast off etc. 782; superfluous etc. (*redundant*) 641.

40a. Decrement. [Thing deducted.]—**N.** decrement, discount, rebate, defect, loss, deduction, eduction, tare; drawback; waste, wastage; reprise.

41. Mixture. [Forming a whole without coherence.]—**N.** mix-, admix-, commix-ture, -tion, mingling; commixion, immixture, interfusion, intermixture, alloyage, matrimony; junction etc. 43; combination etc. 48; entanglement, interlacing; miscegenation, interbreeding.

impregnation; in-, dif-, suf-, transfusion; infiltration; seasoning, sprinkling, interlarding; interpolation etc. 228; adulteration, sophistication.

[Thing mixed] tinge, tincture, touch, dash, smack, sprinkling, spice, seasoning, infusion, *soupçon*.

[Compound resulting from mixture] alloy, brass, bronze, pewter etc.; amalgam, *magma*, blend, half-and-half, *mélange*, *tertium*, *quid*, miscellany, *ambigu*, medley, mess, hash, hotchpotch, hodgepodge, *pasticcio*, patchwork, odds and ends, all sorts; jumble etc. (*disorder*) 59; salad, sauce, mash, *omnium gatherum*, gallimaufry, ragout, *olla podrida*, *olio*, salmagundi, *potpourri*, Noah's ark; texture, mingled yarn; mosaic etc. (*variegation*) 440.

half-blood, -caste, -breed, Eurasian; mulatto; terc-, quart-, quinteron etc.; quad-, octo-roon; *griffo*, *zambo*; cross, hybrid, mongrel etc. 83.

V. mix; join etc. 43; combine etc. 48; com-, im-, inter-mix; mix up with, mingle; com-, inter-, bemingle; shuffle etc. (*derange*) 61; pound together; hash –, stir- up; knead, brew; impregnate with; interlard etc. (*interpolate*) 228; intertwine, -weave etc. 219; associate with, miscegenate, interbreed.

be mixed etc.; get among, be entangled with.

instil, imbue; in-, suf-, trans-fuse; infiltrate, dash, tinge, tincture, season, sprinkle, besprinkle, attemper, medicate, blend, cross; alloy, amalgamate, compound, adulterate, sophisticate, infect.

Adj. mixed etc. *v.*; implex, composite, half-and-half, linsey-wolsey, hybrid, mongrel, heterogeneous; motley etc. (*variegated*) 440; miscellaneous, promiscuous, indiscriminate; miscible.

Adv. among, amongst, amid, amidst, with; in the midst of, in the crowd.

42. Simpleness [Freedom from mixture.]—**N.** simpleness etc. *adj.*; purity, homogeneity.

elimination; sifting etc. *v.*; purification etc. (*cleanness*) 652.

V. render -simple etc. *adj.*; simplify.

sift, winnow, bolt, eliminate; narrow down; get rid of, exclude etc. 55; clear; purify etc. (*clean*) 652; disentangle etc. (*disjoin*) 44.

Adj. simple, uniform, of a piece, homogeneous, single, pure, clear, sheer, neat; Attic.

un-mixed, -mingled, -blended, -combined, -compounded; elementary, undecomposed; unadulterated, -sophisticated, -alloyed, -tinged, -fortified; pure and simple.

free –, exempt- from; exclusive.

Adv. simply etc. *adj.*; only.

43. Junction.—**N.** junction; joining etc. *v.*; joinder, union; con-nection, -junction, -jugation, compendency, annex-ion, -ation, -ment; coalition; astriction, attachment, compagination, vincture, ligation, alligation; accouplement; marriage etc. (*wedlock*) 903; infibulation, inosculation, symphysis, anastomosis, confluence, communication, concatenation; concurrence, meeting, reunion; assemblage etc. 72.

copulation, coition, intercourse.

joint, joining, juncture, chiasma, pivot, hinge, articulation, commissure, seam, suture, gusset, stitch, splice; link etc. 45; miter, mortise.

closeness, tightness etc. *adj.*; coherence etc. 46; combination etc. 48.

V. join, unite; con-join, -nect; associate; put –, lay –, clap –, hang –, lump –, hold –, piece –, tack –, fix –, bind up- together; embody, re-embody; roll into one.

attach, fix, affix, saddle on, fasten, bind, secure, clinch, twist, make -fast etc. *adj.*; tie, pinion, string, strap, sew, lace, stitch, tack, paste, knit, button, buckle, hitch, lash, truss, bandage, braid, splice, swathe, gird, tether, moor, picket, harness, chain; fetter etc. (*restrain*) 751; lock, latch, belay, brace, hook, grapple, leash, couple, accouple, link, yoke, bracket; marry etc. (*wed*) 903; bridge over, span.

pin, nail, bolt, hasp, clasp, clamp, screw, rivet; impact, solder, braze, cement, set; weld –, fuse-together; wedge, rabbet, mortise, miter, jam, dovetail, enchase; graft, ingraft, inosculate; en-, in-twine; inter-link, -lace, -twine, -twist, -weave; entangle; twine round, belay; tighten; trice –, screw-up.

be -joined etc.; hang –, hold- together; cohere etc. 46.

Adj. joined etc. *v.*; joint; con-joint, -junct; corporate, compact; hand in hand.

firm, fast, close, tight, taut, taught, tense, secure, set, intervolved; in-separable, -dissoluble, -secable, -severable.

Adv. jointly etc. *adj.*; in conjunction with etc. (*in addition to*) 37; fast, firmly etc. *adj.*; intimately.

44. Disjunction.—**N.** dis-junction, -connection, -unity, -union, -association, -engagement, -sociation; discontinuity etc. 70; inconnection; abstraction, -edness; isolation; insul-arity, -ation; oasis; separateness etc. *adj.*; severalty; *disjecta membra*; dispersion etc. 73; apportionment etc. 786.

separation; parting etc. *v.*; detachment, segregation; divorce, sejunction, seposition, diduction, diremption, discerption; elision; *caesura*, division, subdivision, break, fracture, rupture; compartition; dis-memberment, -integration, -location; luxation; sever-, dis-severance; scission; re-, ab-scission; circumcision;

lacer-, dilacer-ation; dis-, ab-ruption; avulsion, divulsion; section, resection, cleavage; fission; separability; separatism.

fissure, breach, rent, split, rift, crack, slit, slot, incision.

dissection, anatomy; decomposition etc. 49; cutting instrument etc. (*sharpness*) 253; saw.

V. be -disjoined etc.; come —, fall- -off, — to pieces; peel off; get loose.

dis-join, -connect, -engage, unite, -sociate, -pair; divorce, part, dispart, detach, uncouple, separate, cut off, rescind, segregate; set —, keep- apart; insulate, isolate; throw out of gear; cut adrift; loose; un-loose, -do, -bind, -tie, -hitch, -chain, -lock etc. (*fix*) 43, -pack, -ravel; disentangle; set free etc. (*liberate*) 750.

sunder, divide, subdivide, sectionalize, sever, dissever, abscind; cut; segment; in-cide, -cise; circumcise; saw, snip, nib, nip, cleave, rive, rend, slit, split, splinter, chip, crack, snap, break, tear, burst; rend etc. -asunder, — in twain; wrench, rupture, shatter, shiver, cranch, crunch, craunch, chop; rip up; hack, hew, slash; whittle; haggle, hackle, discind, lacerate, scamble, mangle, gash, hash, slice.

cut up, carve, quarter, dissect, anatomize; take —, pull —, pick —, tear- to pieces; tear to tatters, — piecemeal; divellicate; skin etc. 226; dis-integrate, -member, -branch, -band; disperse etc. 73; dis-locate, -joint; break up; mince; comminute etc. (*pulverize*) 330; distribute, apportion etc. 786.

part, — company; separate, leave; alienate, estrange.

Adj. disjoined etc. *v.;* discontinuous etc. 70; bipartite, multipartite, abstract; digitate; disjunctive; isolated etc. *v.;* insular, separate, disparate, discrete, apart, asunder, far between, loose, free; unattached, -annexed, -associated, -connected; distinct; adrift; straggling; rift, reft, cleft, split.

[capable of being divided] scissile, partible, divisible, separable, severable, detachable.

Adv. separately etc. *adj.;* one by one, severally, apart; adrift, asunder, in twain; in the abstract, abstractedly.

45. Vinculum. [Connecting medium.]—**N.** vinculum, link, *nexus*; connec-tive, -tion; junction etc. 43; bond of union, copula, intermedium, hyphen; bracket; bridge, stepping-stone, isthmus.

bond, tendon, tendril; fiber; cord, -age; riband, ribbon, rope, guy, cable, line, halser, hawser, painter, moorings, wire, chain; string etc. (*filament*) 205.

fastening, tie; liga-ment, -ture; strap; bowline, halliard, tackle, lanyard, rigging, shrouds; standing —, running- rigging; traces, harness; yoke; band, -age; brace, roller, fillet; inkle; with, withe, withy; thong, braid; girder, tie-beam; girt, cinch, girth, girdle, cestus, garter, braces, suspenders, halter, noose, lasso, lariat, surcingle, knot, hitch, running knot, frog.

pin, corking pin, nail, brad, tack, skewer, staple, cleat, clamp; cramp, screw, button, buckle, clasp, hasp, hinge; hank, catch, latch, bolt, ring, latchet, pawl, tag; tooth; stud; hook, — and eye; morse, lock, holdfast, padlock, rivet; anchor, grappling-iron, drawbar, coupler, drawhead, coupling, treenail, trennel, stake, pale, pile, post, bollard.

cement, glue, gum, paste, size, wafer, solder, lute, putty, bird-lime, mortar, stucco, plaster, grout.

shackle, rein etc. (*means of restraint*) 752; suspender etc. 214; prop etc. (*support*) 215.

V. bridge over, span; connect etc. 43; hang etc. 214.

46. Coherence.—**N.** co-, ad-herence, -hesion, -hesiveness; concretion, accretion; con-, agglutination, -glomeration; aggregation; consolidation, set, cementation; sticking, soldering etc. *v.;* connection.

tenacity, toughness; stickiness etc. 352; insepara-bility, -bleness; bur, remora.

conglomerate, concrete etc. (*density*) 321.

V. cohere, adhere, stick, cling, cleave, hold, take hold of, hold fast, close with, embrace, clasp, hug; grow —, hang-together; twine round etc. (*join*) 43.

stick like -a leech, — wax; stick close; cling like -ivy, — a bur; adhere like -a remora, — Dejanira's shirt.

glue; ag-, con-glutinate; cement, lute, paste, gum; solder, weld; cake, coagulate, consolidate etc. (*solidify*) 321; agglomerate.

Adj. co-, ad-hesive, -hering etc. *v.;* tenacious, tough; sticky etc. 352.

united, unseparated, sessile, inseparable, inextricable, infrangible; compact etc. (*dense*) 321.

47. Incoherence. [Want of adhesion, non-adhesion, immiscibility.]—**N.** non-adhesion; immiscibility; incoherence; looseness etc. *adj.;* laxity; relaxation; loosening etc. *v.*; freedom; disjunction etc. 44; rope of sand.

V. make -loose etc. *adj.;* loosen, slacken, relax; un-glue etc. 46; detach etc. (*disjoin*) 44

Adj. non-adhesive, immiscible; incoherent, detached, loose, slack, baggy, lax, relaxed, flapping, streaming; dishevelled; segregated, like grains of sand; un-consolidated etc. 321; -combined etc. 48; non-cohesive.

48. Combination.—**N.** combination; mixture etc. 41; alloy; junction etc. 43; union, unification, synthesis, incorporation, amalgamation, embodiment, coalescence, crasis, fusion, blend, blending, absorption, centralization, federation.

compound, amalgam, composition, *tertium quid;* resultant, impregnation.

V. combine, unite, incorporate, alloy, intertwine etc. 41; amalgamate, embody, absorb, reembody, blend, merge, fuse, melt into one, consolidate, coalesce, centralize, impregnate; put —, lump- together; federate, associate; fraternize; cement a union, marry, wed, couple, pair, ally.

Adj. combined etc. *v.;* conjunctive, conjugate, conjoint, allied, confederate; impregnated with, ingrained, inoculated.

49. Decomposition.—**N.** decomposition, analysis, diaeresis dissection, resolution, catalysis, electrolysis, hydrolysis, photolysis, dissolution; dispersion etc. 73; disjunction etc. 44;

putrescence, caries, necrosis, corruption etc. (*uncleanness*) 653.

V. decom-pose, -pound; analyze, disembody, dissolve; resolve –, separate- into its elements; electrolyze; dissect, decentralize, break up; disintegrate; disperse etc. 73; unravel etc. (*unroll*) 313; crumble into dust; decay etc. *n.;* deteriorate etc. 659.

Adj. decomposed etc. *v.;* catalytic, analytical.

50. Whole. [Principal part.]—**N.** whole, totality, integrity; totalness etc. *adj.;* entirety, *ensemble,* collectiveness; unity etc. 87; completeness etc. 52; indivisibility, indiscerptibility; integration, embodiment; integer, integral.

all, the whole, total, aggregate, one and all, gross amount, sum, sum-total, *tout ensemble,* length and breadth of, Alpha and Omega, 'be all and end all,' lock, stock and barrel.

bulk, mass, lump, tissue, staple, body, torso, *compages;* truck, bole, hull, hulk, skeleton; greater –, major –, best –, principal –, main-part; essential part etc. (*importance*) 642; lion's share, Benjamin's mess; the long and the short; nearly –, almost- all.

V. form –, constitute- a whole; integrate, embody, amass; aggregate etc. (*assemble*) 72; amount to, come to.

Adj. whole, total, integral, entire; complete etc. 52; one, individual.

un-broken, -cut, -divided, -severed, -clipped, -cropped, -shorn; seamless; undiminished; undemolished, -dissolved, -destroyed, -bruised.

in-divisible, -dissoluble, -dissolvable, -discerptible.

wholesale, sweeping, comprehensive.

Adv. wholly, altogether; totally etc. (*completely*) 52; entirely, all, all in all, considering all things, in a body, collectively, all put together; in the -aggregate, – lump; – mass, – gross, – main, – long run; *en masse,* on the whole, as a whole, bodily, *en bloc, in extenso,* throughout, every inch; substantially.

51. Part.—**N.** part, portion; dose; item, particular; aught, any; division, ward; subdivision, section; chapter, verse; article, clause, count, paragraph, passage; phrase; number, volume, book, fascicule; sector, segment; fraction, fragment; cantle, -t; frustum; detachment, parcel, unit, class etc. 75.

piece, lump, bit; cut, -ting; chip, chunk, collop, slice, scale, shard; lamina etc. 204; moiety; small part; morsel, scrap, crumb; particle etc. (*smallness*) 32; instalment, dividend; share etc. (*allotment*) 786.

débris, odds and ends, oddments, *detritus; excerpta;* member, limb, lobe, lobule, arm, wing, scion, branch, bough, joint, link, offshoot, rami fication, twig, stipule, tendril, bush, spray, sprig; runner; leaf, -let; stump; constituent, ingredient, component part etc. 56.

compartment; department etc. (*class*) 75; county etc. (*region*) 181.

V. part, divide, break etc. (*disjoin*) 44; partition etc. (*apportion*) 786.

Adj. fractional, fragmentary; sectional, aliquot; divided etc. *v.;* in compartments, multifid, incomplete, partial, divided etc. 44.

Adv. partly, in part, partially; piecemeal, part by part; by -instalments, – snatches, – inches, – driblets; bit by bit, inch by inch, foot by foot, drop by drop; in -detail, – lots.

52. Completeness.—**N.** completeness etc. *adj.;* completion etc. 729; integration; integrality.

entirety; universality; totality; perfection etc. 650; solid-ity, -arity; unity; all; *ne plus ultra,* ideal, limit.

complement, supplement, make-weight; filling up etc. *v.*

impletion; satur-ation, -ity; high water; high –, flood –, spring- tide; fill, load, bumper, bellyful; brimmer; sufficiency etc. 639.

V. be -complete etc. *adj.*; come to a head.

render -complete etc. *adj.*; complete etc. (*accomplish*) 729; fill, charge, load, replenish; make-up, – good; piece –, eke- out; supply deficiencies; fill -up, – in, – to the brim, – the measure of; saturate etc. 869.

go the whole -hog, – length, go all lengths.

Adj. complete, entire; whole etc. 50; perfect etc. 650; full, good, absolute, thorough, plenary; solid, undivided; with all its parts.

exhaustive, radical, sweeping, thorough-going; dead.

regular, consummate, unmitigated, sheer, unqualified, unconditional, free; abundant etc. (*sufficient*) 639.

brimming; brim-, top-ful; chock –, choke-full; as full as- an egg is of meat, – a vetch, – a tick; saturated, crammed; replete etc. (*redundant*) 641; fraught, laden; full-laden, -fraught, -charged; heavy laden.

completing etc. *v.;* supplement-al, -ary; ascititious.

Adv. completely etc. *adj.;* altogether, outright, wholly, totally, *in toto,* quite; over head and ears; effectually, for good and all, nicely, fully, through thick and thin, head and shoulders; neck and -heel, – crop; all out; in -all respects, – every respect; at all points, out and out, to all intents and purposes; *toto coelo;* utterly, clean, – as a whistle; to the -full, – utmost, – backbone; hollow, stark; heart and soul, root and branch; down to the ground.

to the top of one's bent, as far as possible. *à outrance.*

throughout; from -first to last, – beginning to end, – end to end, – one end to the other, – Dan to Beersheba, – head to foot, – head to heels, – top to toe, – top to bottom; *de fond en comble; à fond, a capite ad calcem, ab ovo usque ad mala,* fore and aft; every -whit, – inch; *cap-à-pie,* to the end of the chapter; up to the -brim, – ears, – eyes; as ... as can be.

on all accounts; *sous tous les rapports;* with a -vengeance, – witness.

53. Incompleteness.—**N.** incompleteness etc. *adj.;* deficiency, short -measure, – wieght; shortcoming etc. 304; insufficiency etc. 640; imperfection etc. 651; immaturity etc. (*nonpreparation*) 674; half measures.

[part wanting] defect, deficit, shortage, ullage, defalcation, omission, *caret;* interval etc. 198; break etc. (*discontinuity*) 70; non-completion etc. 730; missing link.

V. be -incomplete etc. *adj.;* fall short of etc. 304; lack etc. (*be insufficient*) 640; neglect etc. 460.

Adj. incomplete; imperfect etc. 651; unfinished; uncompleted etc. (*see* complete etc. 729); defective, deficient, wanting; failing; in -default, – arrear; short, – of; hollow, meagre, lame, half-and-half, perfunctory, sketchy; crude etc. (*unprepared*) 674.

mutilated, garbled, mangled, docked, lopped, truncated; bobtailed, cropped, bobbed, shingled.

in -progress, – hand; going on, proceeding.

Adv. incompletely etc. *adj.;* by halves.

Phr. *caetera desunt; caret.*

54. Composition.—N. composition, constitution, crasis, synthesis; make-up; combination etc. 48; inclusion, admission, comprehension, reception; embodiment, formation, conformation, production.

compilation etc. 72. (*musical*) composition etc. 415; painting etc. 556; writing etc. 590; typography etc. 591.

V. be -composed, – made, – formed, – made up- of; consist of, be resolved into.

include etc. (*in a class*) 76; subsume; synthesize; contain, hold, comprehend, take in, admit, embrace, embody; involve; implicate, drag into.

compose, constitute, form, make; make –, fill –, build- up; weave, construct, fabricate; compile; write, draw; set up (*printing*); enter into the composition of etc. (*be a component*) 56.

Adj. containing, constituting etc. *v.*

55. Exclusion.—N exclusion, non-admission, omission, exception, rejection, repudiation; exile etc. (*seclusion*) 893; preclusion, lock out, ostracism, prohibition; disbarment, expulsion, ban.

separation, segregation, seposition, elimination, coffer-dam.

V. be excluded from etc.

exclude, bar, ban; leave –, shut –, thrust –, bar- out; reject, repudiate, spurn, blackball; ostracize, boycott; lay –, put –, set-apart, – aside; relegate, segregate; throw overboard; strike -off, – out; neglect etc. 460; banish etc. (*seclude*) 893; separate etc. (*disjoin*) 44.

pass over, omit; garble; eliminate, weed, winnow.

Adj. excluding etc. *v.;* exclusive.

excluded etc. *v.;* unrecounted, not included in; inadmissible; preventive, interdictive.

Adv. exclusive of, barring, except; with the exception of; save, bating.

56. Component.—N. component; component –, integral –, integrant-part; element, constituent, ingredient, leaven; part and parcel; contents; appurtenance; feature; member etc. (*part*) 51; personnel.

V. enter into, – the composition of; be a - component etc. *n.;* be –, form- part of; merge –, be merged- in; be implicated in; share in etc. (*participate*) 778; belong –, appertain- to.

form, make, constitute, compose.

Adj. forming etc. *v.;* inclusive; inherent etc. 5.

57. Extraneousness.—N. extraneousness etc. *adj.;* extrinsicality etc. 6; exteriority etc. 220; alienism.

foreign -body, – substance, – element; alien, stranger, intruder, interloper, foreigner, tramontane, *novus homo,* new comer, immi-, emi-grant; creole, Afrikander; outsider, outlander, tenderfoot.

Adj. extraneous, foreign, alien, ulterior; exterior, external, outside, outlandish; oversea; tra-, ultra-montane.

excluded etc. 55; inadmissible; exceptional.

Adv. in foreign -parts, – lands; abroad, beyond seas, overseas.

58. Order.—N. order, regularity etc. 80; uniformity, symmetry, *lucidus ordo;* harmony, music of the spheres.

gradation, progression; series etc. (*continuity*) 69.

subordination; course, even tenor, routine; method, disposition, arrangement, array, system, economy, discipline; orderliness etc. *adj.*

rank, place etc. (*term*) 71.

V. be –, become- in order etc. *adj.;* form, fall in, draw up; arrange –, range –, place- itself; adjust; fall into –, take- -one's place, – rank; rally round; arrange etc. 60.

Adj. orderly, regular; in -order, – trim, – apple-pie order, according to Cocker, – its proper place, neat, neat as a pin, tidy, *en règle,* well regulated, correct, methodical, uniform symmetrical, ship-shape, business-like, systematic; habitual; unconfused etc. (*see* confuse etc. 61) arranged etc. 60.

Adv. in order; methodically etc. *adj.;* in -turn, – its turn; step by step; by regular -steps, – gradations, – stages, – intervals; *seriatim,* systematically, by clockwork, *gradatim;* at stated periods etc. (*periodically*) 138.

59. Disorder. [Absence, or want of Order, etc.]—**N.** disorder; derangement etc. 61; irregularity; anomaly etc. (*unconformity*) 83; anar-chy, -chism; want of method; dishevelment, untidiness etc. *adj.;* disunion; discord etc. 24.

confusion; confusedness etc. *adj.;* disarray, jumble, mix-up, huddle, litter, lumber; *cahotage;* farrago; mess, muss, mash, muddle, hash; hotchpotch; *imbroglio,* chaos, *omnium gatherum,* medley; mere -mixture etc. 41; fortuitous concourse of atoms, *disjecta membra, rudis indigestaque moles.*

complexity; complexness etc. *adj.;* com-, implication; intri-cacy, -cation; perplexity; network, maze, labyrinth, wilderness, jungle; involution, ravelling, entanglement; coil etc. (*convolution*) 248; sleave, tangled skein, knot, Gordian know, kink, web; wheels within wheels.

turmoil; ferment, etc. (*agitation*) 315; to do, trouble, pudder, pother, row, disturbance, convulsion, tumult, pandemonium, uproar, riot, rumpus, stour, scramble, *fracas,* embroilment, *mêlée,* spill and pelt, rough and tumble; whirlwind etc. 349; bear garden, Babel, Saturnalia, Donnybrook Fair, confusion worse confounded, most admired disorder, *concordia discors;* Bedlam –, hell- broke loose; bull in a china shop;

all the fat in the fire, *diable à quatre,* Devil to pay; pretty kettle of fish; pretty piece of -work, — business.

slattern, slut, sloven; draggle-tail.

V. be -disorderly etc. *adj.;* ferment, play at cross purposes.

put out of order; derange etc. 61; ravel etc. 219; ruffle, rumple; bungle, botch.

Adj. disorderly, orderless; out of -order; — place, — gear, — whack; irregular, desultory; anomalous etc. (*unconformable*) 83; acephalous, disorganized, straggling; un-, im-methodical; unsymmetric; unsystematic; untidy, slovenly, bedraggled, messy; dislocated; out of sorts; promiscuous, indiscriminate; chaotic, anarchical, lawless; unarranged etc. 60; confused, tumultuous, turbulent, tempestuous; deranged etc. 61; topsy turvy etc. (*inverted*) 218; shapeless etc. 241; disjointed, out of joint.

com-plex, -plexed; intricate, complicated, perplexed, involved, ravelled, entangled, knotted, tangled, inextricable; irreducible.

troublous; riotous etc. (*violent*) 173.

Adv. irregularly etc. *adj.;* by fits and -snatches, — starts; pell-mell; higgledy-piggledy; helter-skelter, harum-scarum; in a ferment; at -sixes and sevens, — cross purposes; upside down etc. 218.

Phr. the cart before the horse, chaos is come again.

60. Arrangement. [Reduction to Order.]—**N.** arrangement; plan etc. 626; preparation etc 673 dispos-al, -ition; col-, al-location; disbribution; sorting etc. *v.;* assortment, allotment; grouping; apportionment, *taxis,* taxonomy, *syn-taxis,* graduation, organization, grading; re-organization, rationalization.

analysis, classification, division, digestion; systematism.

[Result of arrangement] order, orderliness, form, array; digest, synopsis etc. (compendi -um) 596; *syntagma,* table, atlas; register etc. (*record*) 551; score etc. 415; cosmos, organism, architecture.

[Instrument for sorting] sieve etc. 260; file, card index.

V. reduce to —, bring into- order; introduce order into; rally.

arrange, dispose, place, form; put —, set —, place- in order; straighten up, tidy up; set out, collocate, allocate, pack, marshal, range, size, rank, array, group, parcel out, allot, space, distribute, deal; cast —, assign- the parts; dispose of, assign places to; assort, sort; sift, riddle; put —, set- -to rights, — into shape, — in trim, — in array.

class, -ify; divide; file, string together, thread; register etc. (*record*) 551; list, catalogue, tabulate, index, alphabeticize, graduate, digest, grade, codify; orchestrate, score.

methodize, regulate, systematize, standardize, co-ordinate, organize, settle, fix.

unravel, disentangle, ravel, card; disembroil.

Adj. arranged etc. *v.;* embattled, in battle array; cut and dried; methodical, orderly, regular, systematic, tabular.

61. Derangement. [Subversion of Order; bringing into disorder.]—**N.** derangement etc. *v.;* disorder etc. 59; evection, discomposure, disturbance; dis-, de-organization; involvement; dislocation; perturbation, interruption; shuffling etc. *v.;* inversion etc. 218; corrugation etc. (*fold*) 258; insanity etc. 503.

V. derange; dis-, mis-arrange; dis-, mis-place; mislay, discompose, disorder, de-, dis-organize; embroil, unsettle, disturb, confuse, trouble, perturb, jumble, tumble; huddle, shuffle, muddle, toss, hustle, fumble, riot; bring —, put —, throw- into -disorder etc. 59; break the ranks, disconcert, convulse; break in upon.

unhinge, dislocate, put out of joint, throw out of gear.

turn topsy-turvy etc. (*invert*) 218; bedevil; complicate, involve, perplex, confound; im-, embrangle; tangle, en-tangle, ravel, tousle, dishevel, ruffle, rumple etc. (*fold*) 258; dement.

litter, scatter; mix etc. 41.

Adj. deranged etc. *v.;* syncre-tic, -tistic.

62. Precedence.—N. precedence; coming before etc. *v.;* the lead, *le pas;* superiority etc. 33; importance etc. 642; anteced-ence, -ency; anteriority etc. (*front*) 234; precursor etc. 64; priority etc. 116; precession etc. 280; anteposition, preference.

V. precede; come -before, — first; forerun, head, lead, take the lead; lead the -way, — dance; introduce, usher in; have the *pas;* set the fashion etc. (*influence*) 175; lead off, kick off, open the ball; take —, have- precedence; outrank; have the start etc. (*get before*) 280.

place before; prefix; premise, prelude, preface.

Adj. preceding etc. *v.;* pre-, antecedent; anterior, prior etc. 116; before; former, foregoing; before-, above-mentioned; aforesaid, said; precurs-ory, -ive; prevenient, preliminary, prefatory, introductory; prelus-ive, -ory; proemial, preparatory.

Adv. before; in advance etc. (*precession*) 280.

Phr. *seniores priores.*

63. Sequence.—N. sequence, coming after; going after etc. (*following*) 281; consecution, succession; posteriority etc. 117.

continuation; prolongation, order of succussion; successiveness; Elijah's mantle.

secondariness; subordinancy etc. (*inferiority*) 34.

V. succeed; come -after, — on, — next; follow, ensue, step into the shoes of; alternate.

place after, suffix, append.

Adj. succeeding etc. *v.;* sequent; sub-, consequent; sequacious, proximate, next; consecutive etc. (*continuity*) 69; alternate, amoebaean.

latter; posterior etc. 117.

Adv. after, subsequently; behind etc. (*rear*) 235.

64. Precursor.—N. precursor, antecedent, precedent, predecessor; forerunner, van-courier, *avant-coureur,* pioneer, prodrome, *prodromos,* outrider; leader, bell-wether; herald, harbinger; dawn.

prelude, preamble, preface, prologue, foreword, *avant-propos, protasis,* prolusion, proem, *prolepsis, prolegomena,* prefix, introduction;

lead, heading, frontispiece, groundwork; preparation etc. 673; overture, voluntary, *exordium*, symphony, *ritornello;* premises.

prefigurement etc. 511; omen etc. 512.

Adj. precursory; prelu-sive, -sory, -dious; proemial, introductory, prefatory, prodromous, inaugural, preliminary; precedent etc. (*prior*) 116.

65. Sequel.—N. sequel, suffix, successor; tail, *queue*, train, wake, trail, rear; retinue, suite; appendix, postscript, subscript; epilogue; conclusion; peroration; codicil; continuation, *sequela;* appendage etc. 39; tail —, heel-piece; tag, more last words; *colophon.*

follower, after-glow, -growth, -crop, -taste, -math.

after-part, -piece, -course, -thought, -game; *arrière pensée*, second thoughts.

66. Beginning.—N. beginning, commencement, opening, outset, incipience, inception, inchoation; introduction etc. (*precursor*) 64; *alpha;* initial; foundation; inauguration, *début, le premier pas*, embarcation, rising of the curtain; zero hour; exordium, curtain raiser; maiden speech; prelude; outbreak, onset, brunt; initiative, move, first move; gambit, narrow —, thin- end of the wedge; fresh start, new departure; forefront.

origin etc. (*cause*) 153; source, rise; bud, germ etc. 153; egg, rudiment; genesis, birth, nativity, cradle, infancy, incunabula; start, starting-point etc. 293; dawn etc. (*morning*) 125.

title-page; head, -ing, caption; van etc. (*front*) 234.

en-trance, -try; inlet, orifice, mouth, chops, lips, porch, portal, portico, *propylon*, door; gate, -way; postern, wicket, threshold, vestibule; skirts, border etc. (*edge*) 231; tee.

first -stage, — blush, — glance, — impression, — sight.

rudiments, elements, outlines, *principia*, grammar, *protasis;* alphabet, ABC.

V. begin, commence, inchoate. rise, arise, originate, institute, conceive, initiate, open, dawn, set in, take its rise, enter upon, start; enter; set out etc. (*depart*) 293; embark in.

usher in; lead -off, — the way; take the -lead, — initiative; inaugurate, head; stand -at the head, — first, — for; lay the foundations etc. (*prepare*) 673; found etc. (*cause*) 153; set -up, — on foot, — agoing, — abroach, — the ball in motion; apply the match to a train; launch, broach; open -up, — the door to; set -about, — to work; make a -beginning, — start; handsel; take the first step, lay the first stone, cut the first turf; break -ground, — the ice, — cover; pass —, cross- the Rubicon; open -fire, — the ball; ventilate, air; undertake etc. 676.

come into -existence, — the world; make one's *début*, take birth; burst forth, break out; spring —, crop- up.

begin -at the beginning, — *ab ovo*, — again, — *de novo;* start afresh, make a fresh start, shuffle the cards, resume, recommence.

Adj. beginning etc. *v.;* initi-al, -atory, -ative; inceptive, introductory, incipient; proemial, inaugural; incho-ate, -ative; embryonic, rudimental; primogenial; primeval etc. (*old*) 124; rudimentary, aboriginal; natal, nascent.

first, foremost, front, leading, head; maiden. begun etc. *v.;* just -begun etc. *v.*

Adv. at —, in- the beginning etc. *n.;* first, in the first place, *imprimis*, first and foremost; *in limine;* in -the bud, — embryo, — its infancy; from -the beginning, — its birth; *ab -initio*, — *ovo*, — *incunabilis*, primarily, originally.

67. End.—N. end, close, termination; desinence, conclusion, *finis*, *finale*, period, term, *terminus*, last, *omega;* extreme, -tremity; gable —, butt —, fagend; tip, nib, point; tail etc. (*rear*) 235; verge etc. (*edge*) 231; tag, epilogue, peroration; *bonne bouche*, bitter end, tail end; terminal; *apodosis;* appendix.

consummation, *dénouement;* finish etc. (*completion*) 729; fate; doom, -sday; crack of doom, day of Judgment, fall of the curtain, wind-up; goal, destination; limit, stoppage, end all, determination; expiration, expiry; death etc. 360; end of all things; finality; eschatology.

break up, *commencement de la fin*, last stage, turning point; *coup de grâce*, death-blow; knock-out.

V. end, close, finish, terminate, conclude, be all over; expire; die etc. 360; come —, draw- to a -close etc. *n.;* have run its course; run out, pass away.

bring to an -end etc. *n.;* put an end to, make an end of; determine; get through; achieve etc. (*complete*) 729; stop etc. (*make to cease*) 142; shut up shop.

Adj. ending etc. *v.;* final, terminal, definitive, conclusive; crowning etc. (*completing*) 729; last, ultimate; hindermost; rear etc. 235; caudal.

contermin-ate, -ous, -able.

ended etc. *v.;* at an end; settled, decided, over, played out, set at rest.

penultimate; last but -one, — two, etc.

unbegun, uncommenced; fresh.

Adv. finally etc. *adj.;* in fine; at the last; once for all.

68. Middle.—N. middle, midst, mediety; mean etc. 29; medium, middle term; center etc. 222; mid-course etc. 628; *mezzo termine; juste milieu* etc. 628; half-way house, nave, navel, omphalos; nucle-us, -olus.

equidistance, bisection, half-distance; equator, diaphragm, midriff; interjacence etc. 228.

Adj. middle, medial, mesial, mean, mid; middle-, mid-most; middling; mediate; intermediate etc. (*interjacent*) 228; equidistant; central etc. 222; mediterranean, equatorial.

Adv. in the middle; in the thick; mid-, half-way; midships, *in medias res.*

69. Continuity. [Uninterrupted sequence.]—**N.** continuity; consecu-tion,, -tiveness etc. *adj.;* succession, round, suite, progression, series, train, chain; cat-, concatenation; catena; scale; gradation, course, constant flow, perpetuity.

procession, column; retinue, *cortège*, cavalcade, rank and file, line of battle, array.

pedigree, genealogy, lineage, race etc. 166.

rank, file, line, row, range, tier, string, thread, team; suit; colonnade.

V. follow in —, form- a series etc. *n.;* fall in.

arrange in a -series etc. *n.;* string together, catenate, file, thread, graduate, tabulate.

Adj. continu-ous. -ed; consecutive; progressive, gradual; serial, successive; immediate, unbroken, entire; linear; in a -line, — row etc. *n.;* uninter-rupted, -mitting; unremitting; perennial, evergreen; constant.

Adv. continuously etc. *adj.; seriatim;* in a -line etc. *n.*; in -succession, — turn; running, gradually, step by step, *gradatim,* at a stretch; in -file, — column, — single file, — Indian file.

70. Discontinuity. [Interrupted sequence.]—**N.** discontinuity; disjunction etc. 44; anacoluthon; interruption, break, fracture, flaw, fault, split, crack, cut; gap etc. (*interval*) 198; solution of continuity, *caesura*; broken thread; parenthesis, episode; rhapsody, patchwork; intermission; alternation etc. (*periodicity*) 138; dropping fire.

V. be -discontinuous etc. *adj.;* alternate, intermit.

discontinue, pause, interrupt; intervene; break, — in upon; interpose etc. 228; break —, snap- the thread; disconnect etc. (*disjoin*) 44.

Adj. discontinuous, unsuccessive, broken, interrupted, *décousu;* dis-, un-connected, discrete, disjunctive; fitful etc. (*irregular*) 139; spasmodic, desultory, intermit-ting etc. *v.;* -tent; alternate; recurrent etc. (*periodic*) 138; few and far between.

Adv. at intervals; by -snatches, — jerks, — skips, — catches, — fits and starts; skippingly, *per saltum; longo intervallo.*

71. Term.—**N.** term, rank, station, stage, step; degree etc. 26; scale, remove, grade, link, peg, round —, rung- of the ladder, *status,* position, place, point, mark, *pas,* period, pitch; stand, -ing; footing, range.

V. hold —, occupy —, fall into- a place etc. *n.*

72. Assemblage.—**N.** assemblage; col-lection, location, -ligation; compilation, levy, gathering, ingathering, mobilization, meet, foregathering, muster, *attroupement*; con-course, -flux, -gregation, -tesseration, -vergence etc. 290; meeting, *levée, réunion,* drawing room, at home; conversazione etc. (*social gathering*) 892; assembly, congress, eisteddfod; conven-tion, -ticle; gemote; conclave, etc. (*council*) 696; posse, *posse comitatus;* Noah's ark.

miscellany, *collectanea,* symposium; museum, menagerie, etc. (*store*) 636.

crowd, throng, multitude; flood, rush, deluge; rout, rabble, mob, press, crush, *cohue,* jam, horde, body, tribe; crew, gang, knot, squad, band, party; swarm, shoal, school, covey, flock, herd, drove, kennel; array, bevy, galaxy; *corps,* company, troop, *troupe;* army, force, regiment, etc. (*combatants*) 726; host etc. (*multitude*) 102; populousness.

clan, brotherhood, association etc. (*party*) 712.

volley, shower, storm, cloud.

group, cluster, Pleiades, clump, pencil; set, batch, lot, pack; budget, *dossier,* assortment, bunch; parcel; pack-et, -age; bundle, *fasciculus,* fascine, bale; ser-on, oon; faggot, wisp, truss, tuft; shock, rick, fardel, stack, sheaf, swath, gavel, haycock, stook.

accumulation etc. (*store*) 636; congeries, heap, lump, pile, *rouleau,* tissue, mass, pyramid; drift; snow-ball, -drift; acervation, cumulation; amassment, glom-, agglom-eration; conglobation; conglomeration, -ate; coacervation, coagmentation, aggregation, concentration, congestion, *omnium gatherum, spicilegium,* black hole of Calcutta; quantity etc. (*greatness*) 31.

collector, gatherer; whip, -per in.

V. [be or come together] assemble, collect, muster; meet, unite, join, rejoin; cluster, flock, swarm, surge, stream, herd, crowd, throng, associate; con-gregate, -glomerate, -centrate; center round, *rendezvous,* resort; come —, flock —, get —, pig- together; forgather; huddle; reassemble.

[get or bring together] assemble, muster, mobilize; bring —, get —, put —, draw —, scrape —, lump- together; col-lect, -locate, -ligate; get —, whip- in; gather; hold a meeting; con-vene, -voke, -vocate; rake up, dredge; heap, mass, pile; pack, put up, truss, cram; acervate; ag-glomerate, -gregate; compile; group, aggroup, concentrate, unite; collect —, bring- into a focus; amass, accumulate etc. (*store*) 636; collect in a drag-net; heap Ossa upon Pelion.

Adj. assembled etc. *v.;* closely packed, dense, serried, crowded to suffocation, teeming, swarming, populous; as thick as hops; all of a heap, fasciculated; cumulative.

Phr. the plot thickens.

73. Non-assemblage. Dispersion.—**N.** dispersion; disjunction etc. 44; divergence etc. 291; scattering etc. *v.*; dissemination, broadcasting, diffusion, dissipation, distribution; apportionment etc. 786; spread, respersion, circumfusion, interspersion, spargefaction.

waifs and estrays, flotsam and jetsam, *disjecta membra.*

V. disperse, scatter, sow, disseminate, radiate, diffuse, shed, spread, ted, bestrew, overspread, dispense, disband, disembody, demobilize, dismember, distribute; apportion etc. 786; blow off, let out, dispel, cast forth, draught off; strew, straw, strow; spirtle, cast, sprinkle, shatter; issue, deal out, retail, utter; re-, inter-sperse; set abroach, circumfuse.

turn —, cast- adrift; scatter to the winds; sow broadcast.

spread like wildfire, disperse themselves.

Adj. unassembled etc. (*see* assemble etc. 72); dispersed etc. *v.*; sparse, dispread, broadcast, sporadic, widespread; far-flung; epidemic etc. (*general*) 78; adrift, stray; dishevelled, streaming.

Adv. *sparsim,* here and there, *passim.*

74. Focus. [Place of meeting.]—**N.** focus; point of- convergence etc. 290; corradiation; center etc. 222; gathering-place, resort; haunt; retreat; *venue, rendezvous;* rallying point, head-quarters, home, club; *dépôt* etc. (*store*) 636; tryst, trysting-place; place of -meeting, — resort, — assignation; *point de —, lieu de- réunion;* issue.

V. bring to- a point, — a focus, — an issue; focus.

75. Class.—**N.** class, category, *categorema,* head, order, section; division, subdivision; department, province, domain, sphere.

kind, sort, genus, species, variety, branch, family, race, tribe, caste, sept, clan, breed; *clique, coterie;* type, kit, sect, set; assortment; feather, kidney; suit; range; gender, sex, kin.

manner, description, denomination, persuasion, connection, designation, character, stamp; predicament; conviction etc. 484.

similarity etc. 17.

76. Inclusion. [Comprehension under, or reference to a class.]—**N.** inclusion, admission, incorporation, comprehension, reception.

composition etc. (*inclusion in a compound*) 54.

V. be -included in etc.; come –, fall –, range- under; belong –, pertain- to; range with; merge in.

include, compromise, comprehend, contain, admit, embrace, receive; enclose etc. (*circumscribe*) 229; incorporate, cover, embody, encircle.

reckon –, enumerate –, number- among; refer to; place –, arrange-under, – with; take into account.

Adj. includ-ed; -ing etc. *v.;* inclusive; comprehensive, all-embracing; congen-er, -erous; of the same -class etc. 75.

Phr. *et hoc genus omne,* etc.; *et caetera.*

77. Exclusion.*—**N.** exclusion etc. 55.

* The same set of words is used to express *Exclusion from a class* and *Exclusion from a compound.* Reference is therefore made to the former at 55. This identity does not occur with regard to *Inclusion,* which therefore constitutes a separate category

78. Generality.—**N.** general-ity, -ization; universality; catholic-ity, -ism; miscel-lany, -laneousness; drag-net.

every-one, -body; all hands, all the world and his wife; any body, N or M, all sorts; *tout le monde.*

prevalence, run.

V. be -general etc. *adj.;* prevail, obtain, be going about, stalk abroad.

render -general etc. *adj.;* generalize; spread, broadcast.

Adj. general, usual, current, generic, collective; broad, comprehensive, sweeping; encyclopedical, panoramic, widespread etc. (*dispersed*) 73.

universal; catho-lic, -lical; common, worldwide; e-cumenical; transcendental; prevalent, prevailing, rife, epidemic, besetting; all over, covered with.

every, all; indeterminate, indefinite, unspecified, impersonal.

customary etc. (*habitual*) 613.

Adv. what-ever, -soever; to a man, one and all, without exception.

generally etc. *adj.;* always, for better for worse; in general, generally speaking; speaking generally; for the most part; in the long run etc. (*on an average*) 29.

79. Speciality.—**N.** speciality, *spécialité;* individ-uality, -uity; particularity, peculairity; idiocrasy etc. (*tendency*) 176; personality, characteristic, mannerism, idiosyncrasy, attribute specificness etc. *adj.;* singularity etc. (*unconformity*) 83; reading, version, lection; state; *trait;* distinctive feature; technicality; *differentia.*

particulars, details, minutiae, items, counts.

I, self, I myself, *ego;* my-, him-, her-, it-self.

V. specify, particularize, individualize, realize, specialize, designate, differentiate, determine, define, denote, indicate, itemize, detail.

descend to particulars, enter into detail, come to the point.

Adj. special, particular, individual, specific, proper, personal, intimate, original, private, respective, definite, concrete, determinate, especial, certain, esoteric, endemic, partial, party, peculiar, marked, appropriate, several, characteristic, diagnistic, exact, exclusive; singular etc. (*exceptional*) 83; idiomatic; typical, representative, distinctive.

this, that; yon, -der.

Adv. specially etc. *adj.;* in particular, *in propriâ personâ; ad hominem;* for my part.

each, apiece, one by one; severally, respectively, each to each; *seriatim,* in detail, bit by bit; *pro hac vice,* – *re natâ.*

namely, that is to say, *videlicet,* viz., to wit.

80. Rule.—**N.** regularity, uniformity etc. 16; clock-work precision; punctuality etc. (*exactness*) 494; routine etc. (*custom*) 613; formula; system; rut; canon, convention, maxim; rule etc. (*form, regulation*) 697; key-note, standard, model; precedent etc. (*prototype*) 22; conformity etc. 82.

nature, principle; law; order of things; normal –, natural –, ordinary –, model- -state, – condition; standing -dish, – order; normality; Procrustean law; law of the Medes and Persians; hard and fast rule.

Adj. regular, uniform, symmetrical, constant, steady; according to rule etc. (*conformable*) 82; customary etc. 613; orderly etc. 58.

81. Multiformity.—**N.** multi-, omniformity; variety, diversity; multifariousness etc. *adj.*

Adj. multi-form, -fold, -farious, -generous; multiplex, variform, manifold, many-sided, multiplicate; omni-form, -genous, -farious; polymorphic; protean; heterogeneous, motley, mosaic; epicene, indiscriminate, desultory, irregular, diversified, different, divers; all manner of; of -every description, – all sorts and kinds; *et hoc genus omne;* and what not? *de omnibus rebus et quibusdam aliis.*

82. Conformity.—**N.** conform-ity, -ance; observance.

naturalization; conventionality etc. (*custom*) 613; agreement etc. 23.

example, instance, specimen, sample, quotation; exemplification, illustration, case in point; object lesson.

conventionalist, formalist, Philistine.

pattern etc. (*prototype*) 22.

V. conform to, – rule; accommodate –, adapt- oneself to; rub off corners.

be -regular etc. *adj.;* move in a groove; follow –, observe –, go by –, bend to –, obey- -rules, – precedents; comply –, tally –, chime in –, fall in-with; be -guided, – regulated- by; fall into a -custom, – usage; follow the -fashion, – multitude; pass muster, do as others do, *hurler aves les loups;* do at Rome as the Romans do; go –, swim- with the -stream, – current, – tide; tread the beaten track etc. (*habit*) 613; rubber-stamp; keep one in countenance.

exemplify, illustrate, cite, quote, put a case; produce an- instance etc. *n.*

Adj. conformable to rule, adaptable, compliant, consistent, agreeable; regular etc. 80; according to -regulation, – rule, – Cocker; *en règle, selon les règles,* well regulated, orderly; symmetric etc. 242.

conventional commonplace etc. (*customary*) 613; of -daily, – every day- occurrence; in the natural order of things; ordinary, common, – or garden, prosaic, habitual, usual.

in the order of the day; naturalized.

typical, normal, formal; canonical, orthodox, sound, strict, rigid, positive, uncompromising, Procrustean; point device.

secundum artem, ship-shape, technical.

exemplary, illustrative, in point.

Adv. conformably etc. *adj.;* by rule; agreeably to; in -conformity, – accordance, – keeping-with; according to; consistently with; as usual, *ad instar, instar omnium; more -solito, – majorum.*

for the sake of conformity; of –, as a matter of- course; *pro formâ,* for form's sake, by the card; according to plan.

invariably etc. (*uniformly*) 16.

for -example, – instance; *exempli gratiâ; e.g.; inter alia.*

Phr. *cela va sans dire, ex pede Herculem, noscitur a sociis.*

83. Unconformity.—N. non-conformity etc. 82; un-, dis-conformity; unconventionality, informality, abnormity, anomaly; anomalousness etc. *adj.;* exception, peculiarity, etc. 79; infraction –, breach –, violation –, infringement- of -law, – custom, – usage; eccentricity, *bizarrerie,* oddity, *je ne sais quoi,* monstrosity, rarity; freak of Nature.

individuality, idiosyncrasy, singularity, oritinality, mannerism.

aberration; irregularity; variety; singularity; exemption; salvo etc. (*qualification*) 469.

nonconformist; nondescript, character, original, nonsuch, monster, prodigy, wonder, miracle, curiosity, missing link, flying fish, black swan, *lusus naturae, rara avis,* queer fish; mongrel; half-caste, -blood, -breed; *métis,* cross breed, hybrid, mule, mulatto, sacatra, marabou; *tertium quid,* hermaphrodite, gynander, androgyn.

phoenix, chimera, hydra, sphinx, minotaur; griff-in, -on; centaur; hippogriff, -centaur; sagittary; kraken; cockatrice, wyvern, roc, liver, dragon, sea-serpent; mermaid; unicorn; Cyclops, 'men whose heads do grown beneath their shoulders:, Teratolgy.

fish out of water; neither -one thing nor another, – fish flesh nor fowl nor good red herring; one in a -way, – thousand; out-cast, -law; Ishmael, pariah; oasis.

V. be -unconformable etc. *adj.;* leave the beaten -track, – path; infringe –, break –, violate- a -law, – habit, – usage, – custom; drive a coach and six through; stretch a point; have no business there; baffle –, beggar- all description.

Adj. unconformable, exceptional; abnorm-al, -ous; anomal-ous, -istic; out of -order, – place, – keeping, – tune, – one's element; irregular, arbitrary; lawless, informal, aberrant, stray, wandering, wanton; peculiar, exclusive, unnatural, eccentric, crotchety, egregious; out of the -beaten track, – common, – common run, – pale of; misplaced; funny.

un-usual, -accustomed, -customary, -wonted, -common; rare, singular, *unique,* curious, odd, extraordinary, strange, monstrous; wonderful etc. 870; unexpected, unaccountable; *outré,* out of the way, remarkable, noteworthy; queer, quaint, nondescript, none such, *sui generis;* original, unconventional, Bohemian, unfashionable; un-described, -precedented, -paralleled, -exampled, -heard of, -familiar; fantastic, newfangled, grotesque, *bizarre;* outlandish, exotic, *tombé de nues,* preternatural; denaturalized.

heterogeneious, heteroclite, amorphous, mongrel, amphibious, epicene, half-blood, hybrid; androgyn-ous, -al; unsymmetric etc. 243.

qualified etc. 469.

Adv. unconformably etc. *adj.;* except, unless, save, barring, beside, without, save and except, let alone.

however, yet, but.

Int. what -on earth! – in the world!

Phr. never was -seen, – heard, – known- the like.

84. Number.—N. number, symbol, numeral, figure, cipher, digit, integer; counter; round number; formula; function; series.

sum, total, aggregate, difference, complement, subtrahend; product; multipli-cand, -er, -cator; coefficient, multiple; dividend, divisor, factor, quotient, sub-multiple, fraction; mixed number; numerator, denominator; decimal, circulating decimal, repetend; common measure, aliquot part; reciprocal; prime number; totitive, totient.

permutation, combination, variation; election.

ratio, proportion; progression; arithmetical –, geometrical –, harmonical- progression; percentage.

figurate –, pyramidal –, polygonal- numbers.

power, root, exponent, index, logarithm, antilogarithm; modulus.

differential, integral, fluxion, fluent.

Adj. numeral, complementary, divisible, aliquot, reciprocal, prime, fractional, decimal, figurate, incommensurable.

proportional, exponential, logarithmic, logometric, differential, fluxional, integral.

positive, negative; rational, irrational; surd, radical, real, imaginary, impossible.

85. Numeration.—N. numeration, numbering etc. *v.;* pagination; tale, tally, recension, enumer-

ation, summation, reckoning, computation, supputation; calcu-lation, -lus; algorithm, rhabdology, dactylonomy; measurement etc. 466; statistics.
arithmetic, analysis, algebra, fluxions; differential —, integral —, infinitesimal-calculus; calculus of differences.
[Statistics] dead reckoning, muster, poll, census, capitation, roll-call, recapitulation; account etc. (*list*) 86.
[Operations] notation, addition, subtraction, multiplication, division, proportion, rule of three, practice, equations, extraction of roots, reduction, involution, evolution, approximation, interpolation, differentiation, integration.
[Instruments] abacus, swan-pan, logometer, sliding —, slide- rule, tallies, Napier's bones, calculating —, adding- machine, difference engine; cash register.
arithmetician, calculator, abacist; mathematician, actuary, statistician, surveyor, geodesist.
V. number, count, tell; call —, run- over, take an account of, enumerate, call the roll, muster, poll, recite, recapitulate; sum; sum —, cast- up; tell off, score, cipher, compute, calculate, set a price, reckon, — up, estimate; suppute, add, subtract, multiply, divide, extract roots.
check, prove, demonstrate, balance, audit, overhaul, take stock; affix numbers to, page, foliate, paginate.
amount —, come- to.
Adj. numer-al, -ical; arithmetical, analytic, algebraic, statistical, numerable, computable, calculable; commensur-able, -ate; incommensur-able, -ate.

86. List.—N. list, catalogue, enumeration, inventory, schedule; register etc. (*record*) 551; account; bill, — of costs, syllabus; terrier, tally, file; almanac, calendar, index, table, atlas, contents, card index; rota, ticket; book, ledger; synopsis, *catalogue raisonné, tableau,* scroll, manifest, invoice, bill of lading; prospectus, *programme;* bill of fare, *menu, carte;* score, census, statistics, returns; Red —, Blue —, Domesday- book; *cadaster;* directory, gazetteer, dictionary, glossary, lexicon, thesaurus, gradus.
roll; check —, chequer —, bead- roll, — of honor; muster -roll, — book; roster, panel; cartulary, diptych.
V. list, enrol, schedule, register etc. *n.;* indent, post, docket; matriculate.
Adj. cadastral, listed etc. *v.*

87. Unity.—N. unity; oneness etc. *adj.;* individuality; solitude etc. (*seclusion*) 893; isolation etc. (*disjunction*) 44; unification etc. 48.
one, unit, ace; item; individual; solo, none else, no other, naught beside.
V. be -one, — alone etc. *adj.;* dine with Duke Humphrey.
isolate etc. (*disjoin*) 44.
render one; unite etc. (*join*) 43, (*combine*) 48.
Adj. one, sole, single, solitary, only- begotten; individual, apart, alone; kithless.
un-accompanied, -attended; *solus,* single-handed; singular, odd, unique, unrepeated, azygous, first and last; isolated etc. (*disjoined*) 44; insular; unitary.
lone; lone-ly, -some; desolate, dreary.
in-secable, -severable, -discerptible; compact, irresolvable.
Adv. singly etc. *adj.;* alone, by itself, *per se,* only, apart, in the singular number, in the abstract; one -by one, — at a time; simply; one and a half, *sesqui-.*
Phr. *natura il fece, e poi roppe la stampa.*

88. Accompaniment.—N. accompaniment; appurtenance, adjunct etc. 39; context.
coexistence, concomitance, company, association, companionship; part-, copart-nership; coefficiency.
concomitant, accessory, coefficient; companion, attendant, fellow, associate, consort, spouse, colleague, *fidus Achates;* part-, co-partner; satellite, hanger on, shadow; excort, *entourage,* suite, *cortège;* convoy, follower etc. 65; attribute.
V. accompany, coexist, attend, convoy, chaperon; hang —, wait- on; go hand in hand with; synchronize etc. 120; bear —, keep- company; row in the same boat; bring in its train, associate —, couple- with.
Adj. accompanying etc. *v.;* concomitant, fellow, twin, joint; associated —, coupled- with; accessory, attendant, *obbligato.*
Adv. with, withal; together —, along —, in company- with; hand in hand, side by side; cheek by -jowl, — jole; arm in arm; there-, here-with; and etc. (*addition*) 37.
together, in a body, collectively.

89. Duality.—N. dual-ity, -ism; duplicity; biplicity, -formity; span, polarity.
two, deuce, couple, couplet, doublet, brace, pair, cheeks, twins, Castor and Pollus, *gemini,* Siamese twins; fellows; yoke, conjugation, dyad, distich.
V. [unite in pairs] pair, couple, bracket, yoke; conduplicate, mate.
Adj. two, twain; dual, -istic; binary, binomial; twin, biparous; dyadic; conduplicate; duplex etc. 90; *tête-à-tête;* paired; dihedral.
coupled etc. *v.;* conjugate.
both, — the one and the other.

90. Duplication.—N. duplication, doubling etc. *v.;* gemi-, ingemi-nation; reduplication; iteration etc. (*repetition*) 104; renewal.
V. double; re-double, -duplicate; geminate; repeat etc. 104; renew etc. 660; duplicate, copy etc. 21.
Adj. double; doubled etc. *v.;* bicameral, bicapital, bi-fold, -form, -lateral, -farious, -facial; two-fold, -sided, -headed, -edged etc.; duplex; double-faced; twin, duplicate, ingeminate; second; dual etc. 29.
Adv. twice, once more; over again etc. (*repeatedly*) 104; as much again; twofold.
secondly, in the second place, again.

91. Bisection. [Division into two parts.]—**N.** bi-section, -partition; di-, subdi-chotomy; halving etc. *v.;* dimidiation; *hendiadis.*
bifurcation, forking, branching, furcation, ramification, divarication; fork, prong; fold,

half, moiety.

V. bisect, halve, divide, split, cut in two, cleave, dimidiate, dichotomize, divaricate.

go halves, divide with.

separate, fork, bifurcate; branch -off, – out; ramify.

Adj. bisected etc. *v.;* cloven, cleft; bipartite, biconjugate, bicuspid, bifid; bifur-cous, -cate, -cated; semi-, demi- hemi-.

92. Triality.—N. triality, trinity,* triplicity.

three, triad, triplet, trey, trio, ternion, trinomial, leash; tierce; triennium; trefoil, triangle, trident, tripod, triumvirate, *troika.*

third power, cube.

Adj. three; tri-form, -nal, -nomial; tertiary; triune.

**Trinity* is hardly ever used except in a theological sense; *see* Deity 976.

93. Triplication.—N. tripli-cation, -city; trebleness, trine, trilogy.

V. treble, triple, triplicate, cube.

Adj. treble, triple; tern, -ary; triplex, triplicate, threefold, trilogistic; third; trinal; trihedral.

Adv. three -times, – fold; thrice, in the third place, thirdly; trebly etc. *adj.*

94. Trisection. [Division into three parts.]**—N.** tri-section, -partition, -chotomy; third, – part.

V. trisect, divide into three parts, trifurcate.

Adj. trifid; trisected etc. *v.;* tripartite, -chotomous, -sulcate.

95. Quaternity.—N. quaternity, four, tetrad, quartet, quaternion, square, quadrature, quarter, quadruplet; quadrilateral, quadrangle, quatrefoil; *quadriga.*

V. reduce to a square, square.

Adj. four; quat-ernary, -ernal; quadratic; quartile, quartic, tetractic, tetrad, tetrahedral; quadrennial; quadrivalent.

96. Quadruplication.—N. quadruplication.

V. multiply by four, quadruplicate, biquadrate.

Adj. fourfold; quad-ruple, -ruplicate, -rible; quadruplex; fourth.

Adv. four times; in the fourth place, fourthly.

97. Quadrisection. [Division into four parts.]—N. quadri-section, -partition; quartering etc. *v.;* fourth; quart, -er, -ern; farthing (*i.e.* fourthing); quarto.

V. quarter, divide into four parts, quadrisect.

Adj. quartered etc. *v.;* quadri-fid, -partite.

98. Five, etc.—N. five, cinque, quint, quincunx, quintuplet, quintet, pentagon, pentameter, Pentateuch; six, half-a-dozen; sextet, hexagon, hexameter; seven, Heptarchy; eight, octet, octagon, octave; nine, three times three; ten, decade; eleven; twelve, dozen; thirteen; long –, baker's-dozen.

twenty, score; twenty-four, four and twenty, two dozen; twenty-five, five and twenty, quarter of a hundred; forty, two score; fifty, half a hundred; sixty, three score, sexagenarian; seventy, three score and ten, septuagenarian; eighty, four score, octogenarian; ninety, four score and ten, nonagenarian.

hundred, centenary, hecatomb, century; hundredweight, cwt.; one hundred and forty-four, gross; bicentenary, tercentenary etc.

thousand, chiliad; myriad, millennium, ten thousand; lac, lakh, one hundred thousand, plum; million; thousand million, *milliard.*

billion, trillion etc.

V. centuriate.

Adj. five, quinary, quintuple; fifth; senary, sextuple; sixth; seventh; octuple; eighth; nine-fold, ninth; tenfold, decimal, denary, decuple, tenth; eleventh; duo-denary, -denal; twelfth; in one's 'teens, thirteenth.

vices-, viges-imal; twentieth; twenty-fourth etc. *n.*

cent-uple, -uplicate, -ennial, -enary, -urial; secular, hundredth; thousandth; millenary etc.

99. Quinquesection, etc.—N. division by -five etc. 98; quinquesection etc.; fifth etc.; decimation.

V. decimate, quinquesect.

Adj. quinque-fid, -partite; quinquarticular; octifid; decimal, tenth, tithe, teind; duodecimal, twelfth; sexagesimal, -genary; hundredth, centesimal; millesimal etc.

100. Plurality. [More than one.]**—N.** plurality; a -number, – certain number; one or two, two or three etc.; a few, several; multitude etc. 102.

Adj. plural, more than one, upwards of, some, certain; not -alone etc. 87.

Adv. *et cetera, etc.,* etc.

Phr. *non deficit alter.*

100a. Fraction [Less than one.]**—N.** fraction, fractional part, fragment; part etc. 51.

Adj. fractional, fragmentary, partial.

101. Zero.—N. zero, nothing, naught, nought, duck's egg, goose egg; cipher, none, nobody; not a soul; *âme qui vive*; absence etc. 187; unsubstantiality etc. 4.

Adj. not -one, – any.

102. Multitude.—N. multitude; numerousness etc. *adj.*; numer-osity, -ality; multiplicity; profusion etc. (*plenty*) 639; legion, host; great –, large –, round –, enormous- number; a quantity, numbers, array, sight, army, sea, galaxy; scores, peck, bushel, school, shoal, swarm, draft, bevy, cloud, flock, herd, drove, flight, covey, hive, brood, litter, farrow, fry, nest; mob, crowd etc. (*assemblage*) 72; lots, loads, heaps; all the world and his wife.

[Increase of number] greater number, majority; multiplication, multiple.

V. be -numerous etc. *adj.*; swarm –, teem –, crawl –, creep -with; crowd, swarm, come thick upon; outnumber, multiply; people; swarm like -locusts, – bees.

Adj. many, several, sundry, divers, various,

not a few; a -hundred, — thousand, — myriad, — million, — thousand and one; some -ten or a dozen, — forty or fifty etc.; half a -dozen, — hundred etc.; very —, full —, ever so- many; numer-ous, -ose; profuse, in profusion; manifold, multiplied, multitudinous, multiferous, multiple, multinomial, teeming, crawling, populous, peopled, crowded, thick, studded; galore.

thick coming, many more, more than one can tell, a world of; no end -of, — to; *cum multis aliis*; thick as -hops, — hail; plenty as blackberries; numerous as the -stars in the firmament, — sands on the sea-shore, — hairs on the head; and -what not, — heaven knows what; endless etc. (*infinite*) 105.

Phr. their name is 'Legion.'

103. Fewness.—N. fewness etc. *adj.*; paucity, small number; small quantity etc. 32; scarcity, sparsity; rarity; infrequency etc. 137; handfull; maniple; minority, exiguity.

[Diminution of number] reduction; weeding etc. *v.*; elimination, sarculation, decimation.

V. be -few etc. *adj.*

render -few etc. *adj.*; reduce, diminish the number, weed; eliminate, thin, decimate.

Adj. few; scarce; scant, -y; thin, rare, thinly scattered, few and far between; exiguous; infrequent etc. 137; *rari nantes*; hardly —, scarcely- any; to be counted on one's fingers; reduced etc. *v.*; unrepeated.

Adv. here and there.

104. Repetition.—N. repetition, iteration, reiteration, duplication, ding-dong, alliteration; *epistrophe;* harping, recurrence, succession, run; batto-, tauto-logy; monotony, tautophony; rhythm etc. 138; pleonasm, redundancy, diffuseness.

chimes, repetend, echo, *ritornello*, burden of a song, *refrain;* rehearsal; encore; *réchauffé, rifacimento,* recapitulation.

cuckoo etc. (*imitation*) 19; reverberation etc. 408; drumming etc. (*roll*) 407; renewal etc. (*restoration*) 660.

twice-told tale; old -story, — song, chestnut; second —, new- edition; reprint, new impression; return game, return match, reappearance, reproduction; periodicity etc. 138.

V. repeat, iterate, reiterate, reproduce, parrot, echo, re-echo, drum, harp upon, battologize, hammer, redouble.

recur, revert, return, reappear; renew etc. (*restore*) 660.

rehearse; do —, say- over again; ring the changes on; harp on the same string; din —, drum- in the ear; conjugate in all its moods, tenses and inflexions, begin again, go over the same ground, go the same round, never hear the last of; resume, return to, recapitulate, reword.

Adj. repeated etc. *v.*; repetition-al, -ary; recurrent, -ring; ever recurring, thick coming; frequent, incessant, redundant, pleonastic, tautological.

monotonous, harping, iterative; mocking, chiming; retold; aforesaid, -named; above-mentioned, said; habitual etc. 613; another.

Adv. repeatedly, often, again, afresh, anew, over again, once more; ditto, *encore, de novo, bis, da capo.*

again and again; over and over, — again; many times over; time- and again, — after time; year after year; day by day etc.; many —, several —, a number of- times; many —, full many- a time; times out of number, year in and year out, morning, noon and night; frequently etc. 136.

Phr. *ecce iterum Crispinus, toujours perdrix,* cut and come again; 'tomorrow and tomorrow.'

105. Infinity.—N. infini-ty, -tude, -teness etc. *adj.;* perpetuity etc. 112.

V. be -infinite etc. *adj.;* know —, have- no -limits, — bounds; go on for ever.

Adj. infinite, immense; number-, count-, sum-, measure-less; innumer-, immeasur-, incalcul-, illimit-, intermin-, unfathom-, unapproach-able; exhaustless, inexhaustible, indefinite; without -number, — measure, — limit, — end; incomprehensible; limit-, end-, bound-, termless; un-told, -numbered, -measured, -bounded, -limited; illimited; perpetual etc. 112.

Adv. infinitely etc. *adj.; ad infinitum.*

106. Time.—N. time, duration; period, term, stage, space, span, spell, season; the whole -time, — period; course etc. 109.

intermediate, time, while, *interim,* interval, bit, pendency; inter-vention, -mission, -mittence, -regnum, -lude; respite.

era, epoch, eon, cycle; time of life, age, year, date; decade etc. (*period*) 108; moment, etc. (*instant*) 113; reign etc. 737.

glass —, ravages —, whirligig —, noiseless foot- of time; scythe.

V. continue, last, endure, go on, hold out, remain, stay, persist, abide, run; intervene; elapse etc. 109.

take —, take up —, fill —, occupy- time.

pass —, pass away —, spend —, while away —, consume —, talk against —, kill- time; tide over; use —, employ- time; tarry etc. 110; seize an opportunity etc. 134; waste time etc. (*be inactive*) 683.

Adj. continuing etc. *v.;* on foot; permanent etc. (*durable*) 110.

Adv. while, whilst, during, pending; during the -time, — interval; in the course of; for the time being, day by day; in the time of, when; meantime, -while; in the -meantime, — *interim; ad interim, pendente lite; de die in diem;* from -day to day, — hour to hour etc.; hourly, always; for a -time, — season; till, until, up to, yet; the whole —, all the- time; all along; throughout etc. (*completely*) 52; for good etc. (*diuturnity*) 110.

here-, there-, where-upon; then; *anno,* — *Domini;* A.D.; *ante Christum;* A.C.; before Christ; B.C.; *anno urbis conditae;* A.U.C.; *anno regni,* A.R.; once upon a time, one fine morning.

Phr. time -runs, — runs against; *tempus fugit.*

107. Neverness.—N. 'neverness;' absence of time, no time; *dies non;* Tib's eve; Greek Kalends.

Adv. never; at no -time, — period; on no occasion, never in all one's born days, nevermore, *sine die.*

108. Period. [Definite duration, or portion of time.]—**N.** period; second, minute, hour, day, week, sennight, octave, month, moon, quarter, semester, year, *lustrum, quinquennium,* decade, *decennium,* indiction, lifetime, generation, epoch, era, cycle.

century, age, *millennium; annus magnus.*

Adj. horary; hourly, annual etc. (*periodical*) 138.

108a. Contingent Duration.—Adv. during - pleasure, – good behavior; *quamdiu se bene gesserit.*

109. Course. [Indefinite duration.]—**N.** course –, progress –, process –, succession –, lapse –, flow –, flux –, effluxion, stream –, tract –, current –, sweep –, tide –, march –, step –, flight- of time; duration etc. 106.

[Indefinite time] aorist.

V. elapse, lapse, flow, run, proceed, advance, pass; roll –, wear –, press –, drag- on; flit, fly, slip, slide, glide, crawl; run -its course.

out; expire; go –, pass- by; be -past etc. 122.

Adj. elapsing etc. *v.;* aoristic; progressive, transient etc. 111.

Adv. in due -time, – season; in -course, – process, – the fulness- of time; in time.

Phr. *labitur et labetur; truditur dies die; fugaces labuntur anni;* 'tomorrow and tomorrow and tomorrow creeps in this petty pace from day to day.'

110. Diuturnity. [Long duration.]—**N.** diuturnity; a -long –, length of -time; an age, a century, an eternity, aeons; slowness etc. 275; perpetuity etc. 112; blue moon.

dura-bleness, -bility; persistence, lastingness etc. *adj.;* continuance, assiduity, endurance, standing; permanence etc. (*stability*) 150; survi-val, -vance; longevity etc. (*age*) 128; distance of time.

protraction –, prolongation –, extension- of time; delay etc. (*lateness*) 133.

V. last, endure, stand, remain, abide, continue, brave a thousand years.

tarry etc. (*be late*) 133; drag -on, – its slow length along, – a lengthening chain; protract, prolong; spin –, eke –, draw –, lengthen- out; temporize; gain –, make –, talk against- time.

out-last, -live; survive; live to fight again.

Adj. durable; perdurable; lasting etc. *v.;* of long -duration, – standing; permanent, chronic, long-standing; intransi-ent, -tive; intransmutable, persistent; life-, live-long; longeval, long-lived, macrobiotic, diuturnal, sempervirent, evergreen, perennial; unin-, ter-, unremitting; perpetual etc. 112.

lingering, protracted, prolonged, spun out etc. *v.;* long-pending, -winded; slow etc. 275.

Adv. long; for -a long time, – an age, – ages, – ever so long, – many a long day; long ago etc. (*in a past time*) 122; *longo intervallo.*

all the -day long, – year round; the livelong day, as the day is long, morning, noon and night; hour after hour, day after day, etc.; for good; permanently etc. *adj.*

111. Transientness. [Short duration.]—**N.** transientness etc. *adj.;* evanescence, impermanence, fugacity, transitoriness, volatility, caducity, mortality, span; flash in the pan, nine days' wonder, bubble, May-fly; spurt; temporary arrangement, interregnum.

velocity etc. 274; suddenness etc. 113; changeableness etc. 149.

V. be -transient etc. *adj.;* flit, pass away, fly, gallop, vanish, fade, fleet, melt away, evaporate; pass away like a -cloud, – summer cloud, – shadow, – dream.

Adj. transi-ent, -tory, -tive; passing, evanescent, fleeting; flying etc. *v.;* fug-acious, -itive; shifting, slippery; spasmodic.

tempor-al, -ary; provis-ional, -ory; cursory, short-lived, ephemeral, deciduous; perishable, mortal, precarious; impermanent.

brief, quick, brisk; cometary, meteoric, extemporaneous, summary; pressed for time etc. (*haste*) 684; sudden, momentary etc. (*instantaneous*) 113.

Adv. temporarily etc. *adj.; pro tempore;* for - the moment, – a time; awhile, *en passant, in transitu;* in a short time; soon etc. (*early*) 132; briefly etc. *adj.;* at short notice; on the -point, – eve -of; *in articulo;* between cup and lip.

Phr. one's days are numbered; the time is up; her to-day and gone tomorrow; *non semper erit aestas; eheu! fugaces labuntur anni; sic transit gloria mundi.*

112. Perpetuity. [Endless duration.]—**N.** perpetuity, eternity, timelessness; everness, aye, sempiternity, immortality, athanasia; everlastingness etc. *adj.;* perpetuation; infinite duration.

V. last –, endure –, go on- for ever; have no end.

eternize, eternify, perpetuate, immortalize.

Adj. perpetual, eternal, eterne; everlasting, - living, -flowing; continual, constant, sempiternal; co-eternal; endless, unending; ceaseless, incessant, uninterrupted, indesinent, unceasing; interminable, having no end; unfading, evergreen, amaranthine; neverending, -dying, -fading; deathless, immortal, undying, imperishable.

Adv. perpetually etc. *adj.;* always, ever, evermore, aye; for -ever, – aye, – evermore, – ever and a day, –, ever and ever; in all ages, from age to age; without end; world –, time- without end; *in saecula saeculorum;* to the -end of time, – crack of doom, – 'last syllable of recorded time;' till doomsday; constantly etc. (*very frequently*) 136.

Phr. *esto perpetuum; labitur et labetur in omne volubilis aevum.*

113. Instantaneity. [Point of time.]—**N.** instantane-ity, -ousness; sudden-, abrupt-ness.

moment, instant, second, minute; twinkling, trice, flash, breath, crack, jiffy, *coup,* burst, flash of lightning, stroke of time.

epoch, time; time of -day, – night; hour, minute; very -minute etc., – time, – hours; present –, right –, true –, exact –, correct- time.

V. be -instantaneous etc. *adj.;* twinkle, flash.

Adj. instantaneous, momentary, extempore, sudden, instant, abrupt; subitaneous, hasty; quick as- thought,* – lightning, – a flash; rapid as electricity.

Adv. instantaneously etc. *adj.*; in – in less than- no time; *presto, subito, instanter*, suddenly, at a stroke, like- a shot, – greased lightning; in a trice, in a moment etc. *n.*; eftsoons, in the twinkling of - an eye, – a bed post; at one jump, in the same breath, *per saltum, uno saltu*; at –, all at- once; in one's tracks; plump, slap; 'at one fell swoop;' at the same -instant etc. *n.*; immediately etc. (*early*) 132; *ex tempore*, on the -spot, – spur of the moment, – dot; just then; slap- dash etc. (*haste*) 684; before you could -turn round, – say -knife, – Jack Robinson.

Phr. touch and go; no sooner said than done.
*See note on 264.

114. Chronometry. [Estimation, measurement, and record of time.]—**N.** chrono-, horo-metry, -logy; date, epoch; style, era.

almanac, calendar, ephemeris; register, -try; chronicle, annals, journal, diary, chronogram.

[Instruments for the measurement of time] clock, watch; chrono-meter, -scope, -graph; repeater, alarum; time-keeper, -piece; dial, sundial, *gnomon, pendule*, horologe, pendulum, hourglass, water clock, clepsydra.

mean –, Greenwich –, solar –, sidereal –, local –, summer- time; daylight saving.

chrono-grapher, -loger, -logist; annalist.

V. fix –, mark- the time; date, register, chronicle; measure –, beat –, mark- time; bear date.

Adj. chrono-logical, -metrical, -grammatical; isochronal.

Adv. o'clock; *a.m., p.m.*

115. Anachronism. [False estimate of time.]—**N.** ana-, meta-, para-, prochronism; *prolepsis*, misdate; anticipation, antichronism.

disregard –, neglect –, oblivion- of time.

intempestivity etc. 135.

V. mis-, ante-, post-, over-date; anticipate; take no note of time.

Adj. misdated etc. *v.*; undated; overdue; out of date; anachronous etc. *n.*

116. Priority.—**N.** priority, antecedence, anteriority, pre-existence, precedence etc. 62; precession etc. 280; precursor etc. 64; the past etc. 122; premises.

V. precede, come before; forerun; antecede, go before etc. (*lead*) 280; pre-exist; dawn; premise, presage etc. 511.

be -beforehand etc. (*be early*) 132; steal a march upon, anticipate, forestall; have –, gain- the start.

Adj. prior, previous; preced-ing, -ent; anterior, antecedent; pre-existing, -existent; foresighted; former, foregoing; afore –, before-, above-mentioned; aforesaid, said; introductory etc. (*precursory*) 64; pre-war.

Adv. before, prior to; earlier; previously etc. *adj.*; afore, ere, theretofore, erewhile, ere –, before- -then, – now; erewhile, already, yet, beforehand; aforetime; on the eve of, in anticipation.

117. Posteriority.—**N.** posteriority; succession, sequence; following etc. 281; subsequence, supervention; futurity etc. 121; successor; sequel etc. 65; remainder, reversion.

V. follow etc. 281 –, come –, go- after; ensue, result; succeed, supervene; step into the shoes of.

Adj. subsequent, posterior, following, after, later, succeeding, postliminious, postnate; successive etc. 63; postdiluvial, -an; *puisné*; posthumous; post-war, future etc. 121.

Adv. subsequently, after, afterwards, since, later; at a -subsequent, – later- period; next, in the sequel, close upon, thereafter. thereupon, upon which, eftsoons; from that -time, – moment; after a -while, – time; in process of time.

postcenal, postcibal, postprandial, after-dinner.

118. The Present Time.—**N.** the present -time, – day, – moment, – juncture, – occasion; the times, existing time, time being; twentieth century; nonce, crisis, epoch, day, hour.

age, time of life.

Adj. present, actual, instant, current, latest, existing, that is.

Adv. at this -time, – moment etc. 113; at the - present time etc. *n.*; now, at present.

at this time of day, to-day, now-adays; already; even –, but –, just-now; on the present occasion; for the -time being, – nonce; *pro hâc vice*; on the -nail, – spot; on the spur of the -moment, – occasion.

until now; to -this, – the present day.

119. Different Time. [Time different from the present.]—**N.** different –, other- time.

[Indefinite time] aorist.

Adj. aoristic.

Adv. at that –, at which- -time, – moment, – instant; then, on that occasion, upon.

when; when-ever, -soever; upon which, on which occasion; at -another, – a different, – some other, – any - time; at various times; some –, one- -of these days, – fine morning, – day; sooner or later; some time or other; once upon a time, once.

120. Synchronism.—**N.** synchronism; coexistence, coincidence; simultaneousness etc. *adj.*; concurrence, concomitance, unity of time, interim.

[Having equal times] isochronism, syntony.

contemporary, coetanian.

V. coexist, concur, accompany, go hand in hand, keep pace with; synchronize, isochronize.

Adj. synchron-ous, -al, -ical, -istical; simultaneous, coexisting, coincident, concomitant, concurrent; coev-al, -ous; contempora-ry, -neous; coetaneous; coterminous, coeternal; isochronous.

Adv. at the same time; simultaneously etc. *adj.*; together, in concert, during the same time; in the same breath; *pari passu*; in the interim.

at the -very moment etc. 113; just as, as soon as; meanwhile etc. (*while*) 106.

121. Futurity. [Prospective time.]—**N.** futurity, -ition; future, hereafter, time to come; approaching –, coming –, after- -time, – age, – days, – hours, – years, – ages, – life;

morrow, to-morrow, by and by; millennium, doomsday, day of judgment, crack of doom, remote future.

approach of time, advent, time drawing on, womb of time; destiny etc. 152; eventuality.

heritage, heirs, posterity, descendants.

prospect etc. (*expectation*) 507; foresight etc. 510.

V. look forwards; anticipate etc. (*expect*) 507, (*foresee*) 510; forestall etc. (*be early*) 132.

come –, draw- on; draw near; approach, await, threaten; impend etc. (*be destined*) 152.

Adj. future, to come; coming etc. (*impending*) 152; next, near; near –, close- at hand; eventual, ulterior; expectant, prospective, in prospect etc. (*expectation*) 507.

Adv. prospectively, hereafter, on the knees of the gods, in future; to-morrow, the day after to-morrow; in -course, – process, – the fulness- of time; eventually, ultimately, sooner or later; *proximo; paulo post futurum;* in after time; one of these days; after a -time, – while.

from this time; hence-forth, -forwards; thence; thence-forth, -forward; whereupon, upon which.

soon etc. (*early*) 132; on the -eve, – point, – brink- of; about to; close upon.

122. Preterition. [Retrospective time.]—**N.** preterition, priority etc. 116; the past, past time; days –, times- -of yore, – of old, – past, – gone by; bygone days, good old days; old –, ancient –, former -times; fore time; yesterdays; the olden –, good old- time; auld lang syne; eld.

antiquity, antiqueness, *status quo;* time immemorial; distance of time; remote -age, – time; ancient history; remote past; rust of antiquity; ancientness.

pale-ontology, -ography, -ology; palaetiology,* archaeology; archaism, antiquarianism, mediaevalism, pre- Raphaelitism; retrospection, looking back, memory etc. 505.

laudator temporis acti; mediaevalist, pre-Raphaelite; antiqu-ary, -arian; archaeologist etc.; Oldbuck, Dryasdust.

ancestry etc. (*paternity*) 166.

V. be -past etc. *adj.;*have -expired etc. *adj.;* – run its course, – had its day; pass; pass –, go- -by, – away, – off; lapse, blow over.

look –, trace –, cast the eyes- back; exhume.

Adj. past, gone, gone by, over, passed away, bygone, foregone; elapsed, lapsed, preterlapsed, expired, no more, run out, blown over, that has been, whilom, extinct, never to return, exploded, forgotten, irrecoverable; obsolete etc. (*old*) 124; extinct as the dodo.

former, pristine, *quondam, ci-devant,* late; ancestral.

foregoing; last, latter; recent, overnight; past, preterite, preter-perfect, -pluperfect, past perfect.

looking back etc. *v.;* retro-spective, -active; archaelogical etc. *n.*

Adv. formerly; of -old, –yore; erst, whilom, erewhile, time was, ago, over; in -the olden time etc. *n.;* anciently, long -ago, – since; a long -while, – time- ago; years –, ages-ago; some time -ago, – since, – back.

yesterday, the day before yesterday; last -year, – season, – month etc.; *ultimo,* lately etc. (*newly*) 123.

retrospectively; ere –, before –, till- now; hitherto, heretofore; no longer; once, – upon a time; from time immemorial; in the memory of man; time out of mind; already, yet, up to this time; *ex post facto.*

Phr. time was; the time -has, – hath- been. *Whewell.

123. Newness.—**N.** newness etc. *adj.;* neologism, neoterism; novelty, recency; immaturity; youth etc. 127; gloss of novelty.

innovation; renovation etc. (*restoration*) 660.

modernist, neologist, neoteric.

modernism, modernity; mushroom; latest fashion, *dernier cri.*

upstart, *parvenu, nouveau riche.*

V. renew etc. (*restore*) 660; modernize.

Adj. new, novel, recent, fresh, green; young etc. 127; evergreen; raw, immature; virgin; untried, -handseled, -used, -trodden, -beaten; fledgling.

late, modern, neoteric; new-born, -fashioned, -fangled, -fledged; of yesterday; just out, brand –, span-new, up to date, topical; vernal, renovated; innovatory.

fresh as -a rose, – a daisy, – paint; spick and span.

Adv. newly etc. *adj.;* afresh, anew, lately, just now, only yesterday, the other day; latterly, of late.

not long –, a short time- ago.

124. Oldness.—**N.** oldness etc. *adj.*; age, antiquity; cobwebs of antiquity.

maturity, ripeness; decline, decay; senility etc. 128.

seniority, eldership, primogeniture.

archaism etc. (*the past*) 122; thing –, relic- of the past; megatherium.

tradition, prescription, custom, folklore, immemorial usage, common law.

V. be -old etc. *adj.;* have -had, – seen- its day; become -old etc. *adj.;* age, fade.

Adj. old, olden, ancient, antique; of long standing, time-honored, venerable; eld-er, -est; first-born.

prime; prim-itive, -eval, -igenous; primordi-al, -nate; aboriginal etc. (*beginning*) 66; diluvian, antediluvian; pre-historic; patriarchal, preadamite; paleocrystic; fossil, paleozoic, preglacial, ante-mundane; archaic, classic, mediaeval, pre-Raphaelite, ancestral, black-letter.

immemorial, traditional, prescriptive, customary, whereof the memory of man runneth not to the contrary; inveterate, rooted.

antiquated, of other times, rococo, of the old school, after-age, obsolete; fusty, moth-eaten; out of -date, – fashion; stale, old-fashioned, behind the -age, – times; exploded; gone out, – by; *passé,* outworn, run out; disused; senile etc. 128; time-worn; crumbling etc. (*deteriorated*) 659; second-hand.

old as -the hills, – Methuselah, – Adam, – history.

Adv. since the -world was made, – year one, – days of Methuselah.

125. Morning. [Noon.]—**N.** morning, morn, matins, forenoon, *a.m.*, prime, dawn, daybreak, daylight, sun-up, peep –, break- of day; aurora,

Eos; first blush —, prime- of the morning; twilight, crepuscule, sunrise, cockcrow.

spring; vernal equinox.

noon; mid-, noon-day; noontide, meridian, prime.

summer, midsummer; summer solstice.

Adj. matin, matutinal; vernal, aestival.

Adv. at -sunrise etc. *n.*; with the lark, when the morning dawns.

126. Evening. [Midnight.]—**N.** evening, eve; decline —, fall —, close- of day; eventide, evensong, vespers; candlelight; nightfall, curfew, dusk, twilight, blind man's holiday; eleventh hour; sun-set, -down; going down of the sun, cock-shut, dewy eve, gloaming, bed-time.

afternoon, *post meridiem, p.m.*

autumn; fall, — of the leaf; autumnal equinox, Indian summer, harvest-time.

midnight; dead —, witching time- of night; winter, — solstice.

Adj. vespertine, autumnal, nocturnal, wintry, brumal, hiemal.

127. Youth.—N. youth; juven- -ility, -escence; juniority; infancy; baby-, child-, boy-, girl-, youth-hood; *incunabula;* minority, immaturity, nonage, teens, tender age, bloom.

cradle, nursery, leading-strings, pupilage, puberty, *pucelage.*

prime —, flower —, spring-tide —, seedtime —, golden season - of life; heyday of youth, school days; rising generation, younger generation.

Adj. young, youthful, juvenile, green, callow, budding, sappy, *puisné,* beardless, unfledged, unripe, under age, in one's teens; *in statu pupillari;* younger, junior.

128. Age.—N. age; oldness etc. *adj.;* old —, advanced- age, sen-ility, -escence, years, anility, grey hairs, climacteric, grand climacteric, declining years, decrepitude, hoary age, caducity, superannuation; second childhood, -ishness; dotage; vale of years, decline of life, 'sear and yellow leaf;' three-score years and ten; green old age, ripe old age; longevity; time of life.

seniority, eldership; elders etc. (*veteran*) 130; firstling; *doyen,* dean, father; primogeniture; nostology.

V. be -aged etc. *adj.;* grow —, get- old etc. *adj.;* age; decline, wane.

Adj. aged; old etc. 124; elderly, senile; matronly, anile; in years; ripe, mellow, run to seed, declining, waning, past one's prime; grey, -headed; hoar, -y; venerable, time-worn, antiquated, *passé,* effete, doddering, decrepit, superannuated; advanced in -life, — years; stricken in years; wrinkled, marked with the crow's foot; having one foot in the grave; doting etc. (*imbecile*) 499.

old-, eld-er, -est; senior; first-born.

turned of, years old; of a certain age, no chicken, old as Methuselah; gerontic; ancestral; patriarchal etc. (*ancient*) 124.

129. Infant.—N. infant, babe, baby; nurse-, suck-, year-, wean-ling; *papoose, bambino.*

child, bairn, little- one, — tot, — mite, chick, brat, chit, pickaninny, kid, urchin; bant-, brat-ling; elf.

youth, boy, lad, slip, sprig, stripling, youngster, cub, unlicked cub, younker, callant, whipster, whipper-snapper, schoolboy, hobbledehoy, hopeful, cadet, minor, master.

scion; sap-, seed-ling; tendril, olive branch, nestling, chicken, duckling; larva, caterpillar, chrysalis, cocoon; tadpole, whelp, cub, pullet, fry, callow; codlin, -g; *foetus,* calf, colt, pup, foal, kitten; lamb, -kin.

girl; lass, -ie; wench, miss, damsel, *demoiselle,* damozel; maid, -en; virgin; nymph; colleen; minx, baggage, school-girl; tomboy, flapper, hoyden.

Adj. infant-ine, -ile; puerile; boy-, girl-, child-, baby-, kitten-ish; baby; new-born, unfledged, new-fledged, callow.

in -the cradle, — swaddling clothes, — long clothes, — arms, — leading strings; at the breast; in one's teens; young etc. 127.

130. Veteran.—N. veteran, old man, seer, patriarch, greybeard, dugout, grand-father, -sire; grandam, beldam; gaffer, gammer; hag, crone; pantaloon; sexage-, octoge-, nonage-, cente-narian; old stager; dotard etc. 501.

preadamite, Methuselah, Nestor, Rip van Winkle, old Parr; elders; forefathers etc. (*paternity*) 166.

131. Adolescence.—N. adolescence, pubescence, majority; adultness etc. *adj.;* manhood, virility, maturity; flower of age; prime —, meridian- of life.

man etc. 373; woman etc. 374; adult, no chicken.

V. come -of age, — to man's estate, — to years of discretion; attain majority, assume the *toga virilis;* have -cut one's eye-teeth, — sown one's wild oats, settle down.

Adj. adolescent, pubescent, of age; of -full, — ripe- age; out of one's teens, grown up, mature, full- blown, — grown, in one's prime, in full bloom, manly, virile, adult; womanly, matronly; marriageable, nubile.

132. Earliness.—N. earliness etc. *adj.;* morning etc. 125.

punctuality; promptitude etc. (*activity*) 682; haste etc. (*velocity*) 274; suddenness etc. (*instantaneity*) 113.

prematurity, precocity, precipitation, anticipation; prevenience, a stitch in time.

V. be -early etc. *adj.;* — beforehand etc. *adv.;* keep time, take time by the forelock, anticipate, forestall; have —, gain- the start; steal a march upon; gain time, draw on futurity; bespeak, secure, engage, pre-engage.

accelerate; expedite etc. (*quicken*) 274; make haste etc. (*hurry*) 684.

Adj. early, prime, timely, in time, punctual, forward; prompt etc. (*active*) 682; summary.

premature, precipitate, precocious; prevenient, anticipatory; rathe.

sudden etc. (*instantaneous*) 113; unexpected etc. 508; impending, imminent; near, — at hand; immediate.

Adv. early, soon, anon, betimes, rathe; eft, -soons; ere —, before- long; punctually etc. *adj.;* to the minute; in time; in -good, — military, — pudding, — due- time; time enough.

beforehand; prematurely etc. *adj.;* precipitately etc. (*hastily*) 684; too soon; before -its, — one's- time; in anticipation; unexpectedly etc. 508.

suddenly etc. (*instantaneously*) 113; before one can say 'Jack Robinson,' at short notice, extempore; on the spur of the -moment, — occasion; at once; on the -spot, — instant; at sight; off —, out of- hand; *à vue d'oeil;* straight, -way, -forth; forthwith, incontinently, summarily, instanter, immediately, briefly, shortly, quickly, speedily, apace, before the ink is dry, almost immediately, presently, at the first opportunity, in no long time, by and by, in a while, directly.

Phr. touch and go, no sooner said than done.

133. Lateness.—N. lateness etc. *adj.;* tardiness etc. (*slowness*) 275.

de-lay, -lation; cunctation, procrastination; detention; deferring etc. *v.;* filibuster, postponement, adjournment, prorogation, retardation, respite, reprieve, stay; protraction, prolongation, moratorium; contango; demurrage; remand; Fabian policy, *médecine expectante,* chancery suit; leeway; high time.

V. be -late etc. *adj.;* tarry, wait, stay, bide, take time; dawdle etc. (*be inactive*) 683; linger, loiter, saunter, lag behind; bide —, take- one's time; hang -about, — around, — back, — in the balance; gain time; hang fire; stand —, lie-over.

put off, defer, delay, lay over, suspend; shift —, stave- off; waive, retard, remand, postpone, adjourn; procrastinate; dally; prolong, protract; spin —, draw —, lengthen- out; prorogue; keep back; tide over; push —, drive- to the last; let the matter stand over; reserve etc. (*store*) 636; temporize; consult one's pillow, sleep upon it.

shelve, table, lay on the table.

lose an opportunity etc. 135; be kept waiting, dance attendance; kick —, cool- one's heels; *faire antichambre;* wait impatiently; await etc. (*expect*) 507; sit up, — at night.

Adj. late, tardy, slow, behindhand, belated, postliminious, posthumous, backward, unpunctual; dilatory etc. (*slow*), overdue 275; delayed etc. *v.;* in abeyance.

Adv. late; late-, back-ward; late in the day; at -sunset, — the eleventh hour, — length, — last, — long; ultimately; after —, behind- time; too late; too late for etc. 135.

slowly, leisurely, deliberately, at one's leisure; *ex post facto; sine die.*

Phr. *nonum prematur in annum.*

134. Occasion.—N. occasion, opportunity, opening, room, scope, field; suitable —, proper- -time, — season; high time; opportuneness etc. *adj.;* tempestivity.

crisis, turn, juncture, emergency, conjuncture; turning point; given time.

nick of time; golden —, well-timed —, fine —, favorable- opportunity; clear stage, fair field; *mollia tempora; fata Morgana;* spare time etc. (*leisure*) 685.

V. seize etc. (*take*) 789 —, use etc. 677 —, give etc. 784- an -opportunity, — occasion; improve the occasion.

suit the occasion etc. (*be expedient*) 646.

strike the iron while it is hot, *battre le fer sur l'enclume,* make hay while the sun shines, take time by the forelock, *prendre la balle au bond.*

Adj. opportune, timely, well-timed, timeous, timeful, seasonable.

providential, lucky, fortunate, happy, favorable, propitious, auspicious, critical; suitable etc. 23; *obiter dicta.*

Adv. opportunely etc. *adj.* ; in -proper, — due- -time, — course, — season; for the nonce; in the -nick, — fulness- of time; all in good time; just in time, at the eleventh hour, now or never.

by the -way, — by; *en passant, à propos; pro re natâ, — hac vice; par parenthèse,* parenthetically, by way of parenthesis; while -speaking of, — on this subject; *ex tempore;* on the spur of the -moment, — occasion; on the spot etc. (*early*) 132.

Phr. *carpe diem; occasionem cognosce;* one's hour is come, the time is up; that reminds me.

135. Intempestivity.—N. intempestivity; unseasonableness; unsuitable —, improper-time; unreasonableness etc. *adj.;* evil hour; *contretemps;* intrusion; anachronism etc. 115.

V. be -ill timed etc. *adj.;* mistime, intrude, come amiss, break in upon; have other fish to fry; be -busy, — engaged, — tied up, — occupied.

lose —, throw away —, waste —, neglect etc. 460- an opportunity; allow —, suffer- the -opportunity, — occasion- to -pass, — slip, — go by, — escape, — lapse; waste time etc. (*be inactive*) 683; let slip through the fingers, lock the stable door when the steed is stolen.

Adj. ill-, mis-timed; untimely, intrusive, unseasonable; out of -date, — season; inopportune, timeless, untoward, *mal à propos,* unlucky, inauspicious, unpropitious, unfortunate, unfavorable; unsuited etc. 24; inexpedient etc. 647.

unpunctual etc. (*late*) 133; too late for; premature etc. (*early*) 132; too soon for; wise after the event.

Adv. inopportunely etc. *adj.;* as ill luck would have it, in an evil hour, the time having gone by, a day after the fair.

Phr. after meat mustard, after death the doctor.

136. Frequency.—N. frequency, oftness; repetition, etc. 104.

V. recur etc. 104; do nothing but; keep, — on.

Adj. frequent, many times, not rare, thickcoming, incessant, perpetual, continual, constant, recurrent, repeated etc. 104; habitual etc. 613; hourly, etc. 138.

Adv. often, often to be met with, oft; oft-, often-times; frequently; repeatedly etc. 104; unseldom, not unfrequently; in -quick, — rapid-succession; many a time and oft; daily, hourly etc.; every -day, — hour, — moment etc.

perpetually, continually, constantly, incessantly, without ceasing, at all times, daily and hourly, night and day, day and night, day after day, morning, noon and night, ever and anon.

most often; commonly etc. (*habitually*) 613.

sometimes, occasionally, at times, now and then, from time to time, there being times when, *toties quoties*, often enough, again and again etc. 104.

137. Infrequency.—N. infrequency, infrequence, rareness, rarity; fewness etc. 103; seldomness, uncommonness.

V. be -rare etc. *adj.*

Adj. un-, in-frequent; uncommon, sporadic, rare, — as a blue diamond; few etc. 103; scarce; almost unheard of, unprecedented, which has not occurred within the memory of the oldest inhabitant, not within one's previous experience.

Adv. seldom, rarely, scarcely, hardly; not often, unfrequently, infrequently, unoften; scarcely —, hardly- ever; once in a blue moon.

once; once -for all, — in a way; *pro hac vice;* like angels' visits, few and far between.

138. Regularity of recurrence. **Periodicity.—N.** periodicity, intermittence; beat; oscillation etc. 314; pulse, pulsation; rhythm; alternation, -nateness, -nativeness, -nity.

bout, round, revolution, rotation, turn.

anniversary, birthday, jubilee, centenary, bi-, ter-centenary.

[Regularity of return] rota, cycle, period, stated time, routine; days of the week; Sunday, Monday etc.; months of the year; January etc.; feast, fast, saint's day etc.; Christmas, Easter, New Year's Day etc. 998; quarter-, Lady-, Midsummer-, Michaelmas-day; May Day, the King's Birthday; leap year, seasons.

punctuality, regularity, steadiness.

V. recur in regular -order, — succession; return, revolve, rotate; come -again, — in its turn; come round, — again; beat, pulsate; alternate; intermit.

Adj. periodic, -al; serial, recurrent, cyclic-, -al, rhythmic-, -al, even, recurring etc. *v.;* inter-, remittent; alternate, every other.

hourly; diurnal, daily; quotidian, tertian, weekly; hebdomad-al, -ary; bi-weekly, fortnightly; monthly, menstrual, catamenial; yearly, annual; biennial, triennial, etc.; bissextile; centennial, secular; paschal, lenten, etc.

regular, steady, punctual, constant, methodical, regular as clockwork.

Adv. periodically etc. *adj.;* at -regular intervals, — stated times; at -fixed, — established-periods; punctually etc. *adj.; de die in diem;* from day to day, day by day.

by turns, in -turn, — rotation; alternately, every other day, off and on, ride and tie, round and round.

139. Irregularity of recurrence.**—N.** irregularity, uncertainty, unpunctuality; fitfulness etc. *adj.*

Adj. irregular, uneven, uncertain, unpunctual, capricious, erratic, desultory, fitful, flickering; rambling, rhapsodical; spasmodic, unsystematic, unequal, variable, halting.

Adv. irregularly etc. *adj.;* by fits and starts etc. (*discontinuously*) 70.

140. Change. [Difference at different times.]**—N.** change, alteration, mutation, permutation, variation, modification, modulation, inflexion, mood, qualification, innovation, *metastasis,* deviation, shift, turn; diversion; break.

transformation, transfiguration; metamorphosis; metabolism; transmutation; transsubstantiation; metagenesis, transanimation, transmigration, metempsychosis; version, metathesis, transmogrification; catalysis; *avatar;* alterative.

conversion etc. (*gradual change*) 144; revolution etc. (*sudden or radical change*) 146; inversion etc. (*reversal*) 218; displacement etc. 185; transference etc. 270.

changeableness etc. 149; tergiversation etc. (*change of mind*) 607.

V. change, alter, vary, wax and wane; modulate, diversify, qualify, tamper with; turn, shift, veer, jibe, tack, chop, shuffle, swerve, dodge, warp, deviate, turn aside, evert, intervert; pass to, take a turn, turn the corner, resume.

work a change, modify, vamp, revamp, superinduce; trans-form, —mute, -ume, -figure etc. *n.;* metamorphose, ring the changes; convert, resolve; revolutionize; chop and change; patch, re-shape.

innovate, introduce new blood, shuffle the cards, spin the wheel; give a -turn, — color- to; influence, turn the scale; shift the scene, turn over a new leaf.

recast etc. 146; reverse etc. 218; disturb etc. 61; convert into etc. 144.

Adj. changed etc. *v.;* new-fangled; changeable etc. 149; transitional; modifiable; alterative.

Adv. *mutatis mutandis.*

Int. *quantum mutatus!*

Phr. 'a change came o'er the spirit of my dream;' *nous avons changé tout cela; tempora mutantur et nos mutamur in illis; non sum qualis eram.*

141. Permanence. [Absence of change.]**—N.** stability etc. 150; quiescence etc. 265; obstinacy etc. 606.

permanence, -cy, persistence, fixity, fixity of purpose, endurance, durability; standing, *status quo;* maintenance, preservation, conservation; conservatism; *laissez-faire;* law of the Medes and Persians; standing dish.

V. let -alone, — be; persist, remain, stay, tarry, rest; hold, — on; last, endure, bide, abide, aby, dwell, maintain, keep; stand, — still, — fast; subsist, live, outlive, survive; hold —, keep- one's ground, — footing; hold good.

Adj. stable etc. 150; persisting etc. *v.;* permanent; established, fixed; durable; unchanged etc. (change etc. 140); unrenewed; intact, inviolate; persistent; monotonous, uncheckered; unfailing.

un-destroyed, -repealed, -suppressed; conservative, *qualis ab incepto;* prescriptive etc. (*old*) 124; stationary etc. 265.

Adv. *in statu quo;* for good, finally; at a stand, -still; *uti possidetis;* without a shadow of turning.

Phr. as you were!; *j'y suis j'y reste; esto perpetua; nolumus leges Angliae mutari;* let sleeping dogs lie.

142. Cessation. [Change from action to

rest.]—**N.** cessation, discontinuance, desistance, desinence.

inter-, re-mission; sus-pense, -pension, interruption, hitch; hartal; stop; stopping etc. *v.;* closure, stoppage, halt; arrival etc. 292.

pause, rest, lull, respite, truce, armistice, drop; interregnum, abeyance.

closure etc. 261.

dead -stop, – stand, – lock; checkmate; comma, colon, semicolon, period, full stop; end etc. 67; death etc. 360; *caesura.*

V. cease, discontinue, desist, stay; break –, leave- off; hold, stop, pull up, stall, stop short, check; stick, deadlock, hand fire; halt; pause, rest.

have done with, give over, surcease, shut up shop; give up etc. (*relinquish*) 624.

hold –, stay- one's hand; rest on one's oars, repose on one's laurels.

come to a -stand, – standstill, – dead lock, – full stop; arrive etc. 292; go out, die away, peter out; wear -away, – off; pass away etc. (*be past*) 122; be at an end.

intromit, interrupt, suspend, interpel; inter-, re-mit; put -an end, – a stop, – a period- to; bring to a stand, -still; stop, cut out, cut short, arrest, avast; stem the -tide, – torrent; pull the check string; switch off.

Int. halt! hold! stop! enough! avast! have done! a truce to! soft! leave off! shut up! give over! chuck it!

143. Continuance in action.—**N.** continu-ance, -ation; run; extension, prolongation; maintenance, perpetuation; persistence etc. (*perseverance*) 604a; repetition etc. 104.

V. continue, persist; go –, jog –, keep –, carry –, run – hold- on; abide, keep, pursue, stick to; endure; take –, maintain- its course; keep up.

sustain, uphold, hold up, keep on foot; follow up, perpetuate, prolong; maintain; preserve etc. 604*a*; harp upon etc. (*repeat*) 104.

keep -going, – alive, – at it, – the pot boiling, – the ball rolling, – up the ball; plod-, plug-along; slog on; die in harness; hold on –, pursue- the even tenor of one's way.

let be; *stare super antiquas vias; quieta non movere;* let things take their course.

Adj. continuing etc. *v.;* uninterrupted, unintermitting, unremitting, unvarying, unshifting; unreversed, unstopped, unrevoked, unvaried; sustained; undying etc. (*perpetual*) 112; inconvertible.

follow-up.

Int. carry on! right away!

Phr. *vestigia nulla retrorsum, labitur et labetur.*

144. Conversion. [Gradual change to something different.]—**N.** conversion, reduction, transmutation, transformation, development, resolution, assimilation; assumption; naturalization.

chemistry, alchemy; progress, growth, lapse, flux.

passage; transit, -ion; transmigration, shifting etc. *v.;* conjugation; convertibility.

crucible, alembic, caldron, retort, test tube etc convert, neophyte, proselyte, pervert, renegade, deserter, apostate, turncoat.

V. be converted into; become, get, wax; come –, turn- -to, – into; turn out, lapse, shift; run –, fall –, pass –, slide –, glide –, grow –, ripen –, open –, resolve itself –, settle –, merge- into; melt, grow, come round to, mature, mellow; assume the -form, – shape, – state, – nature, – character- of; illapse; assume a new phase, undergo a change.

convert –, resolve- into; make, render; mold, form etc. 240; remodel, new model, refound, reform, reorganize; assimilate –, bring –, reduce- to; transform.

Adj. converted into etc. *v.;* convertible, resolvable into; transitional; naturalized.

Adv. gradually etc. (*slowly*) 275; *in transitu* etc. (*transference*) 270.

145. Reversion.—N. reversion, return; revulsion; reaction.

turning point, turn of the tide; *status quo ante bellum;* calm before a storm.

alternation etc. (*periodicity*) 138; inversion etc. 219; recoil etc. 277; regression etc. 283; restoration etc. 660; relapse etc. 661; vicinism, atavism, throwback.

V. revert, turn back, return; relapse etc. 661; recoil etc. 277; retreat etc. 283; restore etc. 660; undo, unmake; turn the -tide, – scale; escheat.

Adj. reverting etc. *v.;* revulsive, reactionary.

Adv. *à rebours,* wrong side out.

146. Revolution. [Sudden or violent change.]—**N.** revolution, *bouleversement,* subversion, break up; destruction etc. 162; sudden –, radical –, sweeping –, organic- change; clean sweep, *coup d'état,* overthrow, *débâcle*; counter-revolution, rebellion etc. 742.

transilience, jump, leap, plunge, jerk, start; explosion; spasm, convulsion, throe, revulsion; storm, earthquake, eruption, upheaval, cataclysm.

legerdemain etc. (*trick*) 545.

V. revolutionize; new model, remodel, recast; strike out something new, break with the past; change the face of, unsex; revert etc. 742.

Adj. unrecognizable.

Revolutionary, Bolshevik etc. 742.

147. Substitution. [Change of one thing for another.]—**N.** substitution, subrogation, commutation; supplanting etc. *v.;* supersession, metonymy etc. (*figure of speech*) 521.

[Thing substituted.] substitute, *succedaneum,* make-shift, temporary expedient, shift, *pis aller,* stop-gap, jury-mast, *locum tenens,* warming-pan, dummy, goat, scape-goat; double; changeling; *quid pro quo,* alternative; remount; representative etc. (*deputy*) 759; palimpsest.

price, purchase-money, consideration, equivalent.

V. substitute, put in the place of, change for; make way for, give place to; supply –, take- the place of; supplant, supersede, replace, cut out, serve as a substitute; step into –, stand in- the shoes of; make a shift –, put up- with; borrow of Peter to pay Paul; commute, redeem, compound for.

Adj. substituted etc. *v.;* vicarious, subditit-ious; substitutional.

Adv. instead; in -place, – lieu, – the stead, – the room- of; *faute de mieux.*

148. Interchange. [Double or mutual change.]—**N.** inter-, ex-change; com-, per-, inter-mutation; reciprocation, transposal, transposi-tion, shuffling; reciprocity, castling [at chess]; hocus-pocus.

interchange-ableness, -ability.

barter etc. 794; tit for tat etc. (*retaliation*) 718; cross fire, battledore and shuttlecock; *quid pro quo.*

V. inter-, ex-, counter-change; bandy, trans-pose, shuffle, change hands, swap, trade, per-mute, reciprocate, commute; give and take, return the compliment; play at -puss in the corner, – battledore and shuttlecock; retaliate etc. 718; barter etc. 794.

Adj. interchanged etc. *v.;* reciprocal, mutual, commutative, interchanged etc. *v.;* interchange-able, intercurrent.

Adv. in exchange, *vice versâ, mutatis mu-tandis,* backwards and forwards, by turns, turn and turn about, turn about; each –, every one- in his turn.

149. Changeableness.—**N.** changeableness etc. *adj.*; mutability, inconstancy; versatility, mo-bility; instability, unstable equilibrium; vacilla-tion etc. (*irresolution*) 605; fluctuation, vicissi-tude; alternation etc. (*oscillation*) 314.

restlessness etc. *adj.;* fidgets, disquiet; dis-, in-quietude; unrest; agitation etc. 315.

moon, Proteus, chameleon, kaleidoscope, quicksilver, shifting sands, weathercock, har-lequin, Cynthia of the minute, April showers; wheel of Fortune; transientness etc. 111.

V. fluctuate, vary, waver, flounder, flicker, flitter, flit, flutter, shift, shuffle, shake, totter, tremble, vacillate, wamble, turn and turn about, ring the changes; sway –, shift- to and fro; change and change about; oscillate etc. 314; vibrate –, oscillate- between two extremes; alter-nate; have as many phases as the moon.

Adj. change-able, -ful; changing etc. 140; mutable, variable, checkered, ever changing, kaleidoscopic, prote-an, -iform; versatile.

unstaid, inconstant; un-steady, -stable, -fixed, -settled; fluctuating etc. *v.;* restless; mercurial; agitated etc. 315; erratic, fickle; irresolute etc. 605; capricious etc. 608; touch-and-go; incon-sonant, fitful, spasmodic; vibratory; afloat; alternating; alterable, plastic, mobile; fleeting, transient etc. 111.

Adv. see-saw etc. (*oscillation*) 314; off and on.

150. Stability.—**N.** stability; immutability etc. *adj.;* unchangeableness etc. *adj.;* constancy; stable equilibrium, immobility, soundness, vitality, stabiliment, stabilization, stiffness, ankylosis, solidity, *aplomb.*

establishment, fixture; rock, pillar, tower, foundation, leopard's spots, Ethiopian's skin, law of the Medes and Persians.

stabilimeter, stabilizator.

permanence etc. 141; obstinacy etc. 606.

V. be -firm etc. *adj.;* stick fast; stand –, keep –, remain- firm; weather the storm.

settle, establish, stablish, ascertain, fix, set, stabilitate, stabilize; retain, stet, keep hold; make -good, – sure; fasten etc. (*join*) 43; set on its legs, float; perpetuate.

settle down; strike –, take- root; take up one's abode etc. 184; build one's house on a rock.

Adj. unchangeable, immutable; unalter-ed, -able; not to be changed, constant; permanent etc. 141; invariable, undeviating; stable, durable; per-ennial etc. (*diuturnal*) 110.

fixed, steadfast, firm, fast, steady, balanced; confirmed, valid, fiducial, immovable, irremov-able, riveted, rooted; settled, established etc. *v.;* vested; incontrovertible, stereotyped, indeclin-able.

tethered, anchored, moored, at anchor, on a rock, firm as a rock; firmly -seated, – establish-ed etc. *v.;* deep-rooted, ineradicable; inveterate; obstinate etc. 606.

transfixed, stuck fast, aground, high and dry, stranded.

indefeasible, irretrievable, intransmutable, incommutable, irresoluble, irrevocable, irrevers-ible, reverseless, inextinguishable, irreducible; indissol-uble, -vable; indestructible, undying, im-perishable, indelible, indeciduous; insusceptible, – of change.

Int. *stet.*

151. Eventuality.—**N.** eventuality, event, oc-currence, incident, affair, transaction, proceed-ing, fact; matter of –, naked- fact; phenomenon; advent.

business, concern; circumstance, particular, casualty, happening, accident, adventure, passage, crisis, pass, emergency, contingency, consequence etc. 154.

the world, life, things, doings, affairs, mat-ters; things –, affairs- in general, the times, state of affairs, order of the day; course –, tide –, stream –, current –, run –, march- of -things, – events; ups and downs of life; chapter of accidents etc. (*chance*) 156; situation etc. (*cir-cumstances*) 8.

V. happen, occur; take -place, – effect; come, become of; come -off, – about, – round, – into existence, – forth, – to pass, – on; pass, pre-sent itself; fall; fall –, turn- out; run, be on foot, fall in; be-fall, -tide, -chance; prove, eventuate, draw on; turn –, crop –, spring –, cast- up; super-, sur-vene; issue, emanate, arrive, ensue, arise, start, hold, take its course; pass off etc. (*be past*) 122.

meet with; experience; fall to the lot of; be one's -chance, – fortune, – lot; find; encounter, undergo; pass –, go- through; endure etc. (*feel*) 821.

Adj. happening etc. *v.;* going on, doing, cur-rent; in the wind, afloat; on -foot, – the *tapis;* at issue, in question; incidental.

eventful, momentous, signal; stirring, bustling, full of incident.

Adv. eventually, ultimately, in -the event of, – case; in the course of things; in the -natural, – ordinary- course of things; as -things, – times-go; as the world -goes, – wags; as the -tree falls, – cat jumps; as it may -turn out, – happen.

Phr. the plot thickens

152. Destiny.—**N.** destiny etc. (*necessity*) 601; hereafter, future —, post- existence; future state, next world, world to come, after life; futurity etc. 121; everlasting -life, — death; prospect etc. (*expectation*) 507.

V. impend; hang —, lie —, hover- over; threaten, loom, await, come on, approach, stare one in the face; fore-, pre-ordain; predestine, doom, foredoom, foreshadow, have in store for.

Adj. impending etc. *v.*; destined; about to -be, — happen; coming, in store, to come, going to happen, instant, at hand, near; near —, close- at hand; overhanging, hanging over one's head, imminent; brewing, preparing, forthcoming; in the wind, on the cards, in reserve; that -will, — is to-be; in prospect etc. (*expected*) 507; looming in the -distance, — horizon, — future; unborn, in embryo; in the womb of -time; — futurity; on the knees of the gods; pregnant etc. (*producing*) 161.

Adv. in -time, — the long run; all in good time; eventually etc. 151; whatever may happen etc. (*certainly*) 474; as -chance etc. 156- would have it.

153. Cause. [Constant antecedent.]—**N.** cause, origin, source, principle, element; occasioner, prime mover, engine, turbine, motor, *primum mobile; vera causa*; author etc. (*producer*) 164; main-spring, agent; dynamo, generator, battery (electric); leaven; groundwork, foundation etc. (*support*) 215.

spring, fountain, well, font; fountain —, spring- head; *fons et origo*, genesis; descent etc. (*paternity*) 166; remote cause; influence.

pivot, hinge, turning-point, lever; key; kernel, core; proximate cause, *causa causans;* last straw that breaks the camel's back.

ground; reason, — why; why and wherefore, rationale, occasion, derivation; final cause etc. (*intention*) 620; *le dessous des cartes;* undercurrents.

rudiment, egg, germ, embryo, fetus, bud, root, *radix*, radical, etymon, nucleus, seed, stem, stalk, stock, *stirps*, trunk, tap-root; latent organism.

nest, cradle, nursery, womb, *nidus*, birth-, breeding-place, hot-bed.

caus-ality, -ation; origination; production etc. 161.

V. be the -cause etc. *n.*- of; originate; give -origin, — rise, — occasion- to; cause, occasion, sow the seeds of, kindle, suscitate; bring -on, — to pass, — about; produce; create etc. 161; set -up, — afloat, — on foot; found, broach, institute, lay the foundation of, inaugurate; lie at the root of.

procure, induce, draw down, open the door to, superinduce, evoke, entail, operate; elicit, provoke.

conduce to etc. (*tend to*) 176; contribute; promote; have a -hand in, — finger in- the pie; determine, decide, turn the scale, give the casting vote; have a common origin; derive its origin etc. (*effect*) 154.

Adj. caused etc. *v.*; causal, original; prim-ary, -itive, -ordial; aboriginal; radical; inceptive, embry-onic, -otic; *in -embryo, — ovo;* seminal, germinal; formative, productive etc. 168; at the bottom of; connate, having a common origin.

Adv. because etc. 155; behind the scenes.

154. Effect. [Constant sequent.]—**N.** effect, consequence, sequela; derivative, -tion; result; result-ant, -ance; upshot, issue, *dénouement;* outcome; termination, end etc. 67; development, outgrowth, fruit, crop, harvest, product, bud, blossom, florescence, ear.

production, produce, product, finished product, work, handiwork, fabric, performance; creature, creation; offspring, -shoot; first-fruits, -lings; *prémices*.

V. be the -effect etc. *n.*- of; be -due, — owing-to; originate -in, — from; rise —, arise —, take its rise —, spring —, proceed —, emanate —, come —, grow —, bud —, sprout —, germinate —, issue —, flow —, result —, follow —, derive its origin —, accrue- from; come -to, — of, — out of; depend —, hand —, hinge —, turn- upon.

take the consequences, sow the wind and reap the whirlwind.

Adj. owing to; resulting from etc. *v.*; resultant; derivable from; due to; caused etc. by, 153; dependent upon; derived —, evolved- from; derivative; hereditary.

Adv. of course, it follows that, naturally, consequently; as a —, in- consequence; through all, all along of, necessarily, eventually.

Phr. *cela va sans dire*, thereby hangs a tale.

155. Attribution. [Assignment of cause.]—**N.** attribution, theory, etiology, ascription, reference to, rationale; accounting for etc. *v.*; imputation, derivation from.

fil-, affil-iation; pedigree etc. (*paternity*) 166.

explanation etc. (*interpretation*) 522; reason why etc. (*cause*) 153.

V. attribute —, ascribe —, impute —, refer —, lay —, point —, trace —, bring home- to; put —, set- down- to; charge —, ground- on; invest with, assign as cause, charge with, blame, lay at the door of, father upon; saddle with; affiliate; account for, derive from, point out the -reason etc. 153; theorize; tell how it comes; put the saddle on the right horse.

Adj. attributed etc. *v.*; attributable etc. *v.*; refer-able, -rible; due to, derivable from; owing to etc. (*effect*) 154; putative.

Adv. hence, thence, therefore, for, since, on account of, because, owing to; on that account; from -this, — that- cause; thanks to, forasmuch as; whence, *propter hoc*.

why? wherefore? whence? how -comes, — is, — happens- it? how does it happen?

in -some, — some such- way; somehow, — or other.

Phr. that is why; *hinc illae lachrymae; cherchez la femme*.

156. Chance.† [Absence of assignable cause.]—**N.** chance, indetermination, accident, fortune, hazard, hap, haphazard, chance-medley, random, luck, *raccroc*, casualty, fortuity, contingence, coincidence, adventure, hit; fate etc. (*necessity*) 601; equal chance; lottery, raffle, tombola, sweepstake; toss up etc. 621; turn of the -table, — cards; hazard of the die, chapter of accidents; cast —, throw- of the dice; heads or tails, wheel of Fortune, whirligig of chance; *sortes; — Virgilianae*.

probability, possibility, contingency, odds, long odds, run of luck; main- chance.

theory of -probabilities, – chances; bookmaking; assurance; speculation, gamble, gaming etc. 621.

V. chance, hap, turn up; fall to one's lot; be one's -fate etc. 601; stumble on, light –, blunder –, hit- upon; take one's chance etc. 621.

Adj. casual, fortuitous, accidental, haphazard, random, stray, adventitious, adventive, causeless, incidental. contingent, uncaused, undetermined, indeterminate; possible etc. 470; unintentional etc. 621.

Adv. by -chance, – accident; casually; perchance etc. (*possibly*) 470; for aught one knows; as -good, – bad, – ill-luck etc. *n.*- would have it; as it may -be, – chance, – turn up, – happen; as the case may be.

†The word *Chance* has two distinct meanings: the first, the absence of assignable *cause*, as above; and the second, the absence of *design*—for the latter see 621.

157. Power.—N. power; poten-cy, -tiality; puissance, might, force; energy etc. 171; dint; right -hand, – arm; ascendency, sway, control; pre-potency, -pollence; almightiness, omnipotence; authority etc. 737; strength etc. 159.

ability; ableness etc. *adj.*; competency; efficiency, -cacy; validity, cogency; enablement; vantage ground; influence etc. 175; horse power; dynamometer.

pressure; elasticity; gravity; attraction, repulsion; *vis -inertiae, – mortua, – viva;* friction, suction.

electricity, magnetism, galvanism, voltaic electricity, voltaism, electro-magnetism, electrostatics, electrification; electric – current, – power; potential –, dynamic –, kinetic –, electrical –, chemical –, atomic- energe; electric field, circuit, charge, discharge, shock, polarity, pole; amperage, voltage, wattage, resistance, conduction, induction, electrification, electrolysis.

electronics, radionics, electron physics, electrophysics, avionics, radiometry, photoelectronics; electron, negatron, positron, photoelectron, thermion, barytron; electronic effect; electron emission; electron –, cathode –, anode –, positive – ray; electron – current, – flow – stream, – beam, – volt; electronic circuit; conductance; electron tube, tube vacuum tube, photoelectric tube, call; transistor.

capability, capacity; *quid valeant humeri quid ferre recusent;* faculty, quality, attribute, endowment, virtue, gift, property, qualification, susceptibility.

V. be -powerful etc. *adj.*; gain -power etc. *n.*

belong –, pertain- to; lie –, be- in one's power; can.

electrify, generate, magnetize.

give –, confer –, exercise- power etc. *n.*; empower, enable, invest; in-, en-due; endow, arm; strengthen etc. 159; compel etc. 744.

Adj. powerful, puissant; potent, -ial; capable, able; equal –, up- to; cogent, valid; effect-ive, -ual; efficient, efficacious, adequate, competent; multi-, pleni-, omni-, armi- potent; mighty, ascendent; almighty.

electric, electrical, electronic etc.

forcible etc. *adj.* (*energetic*) 171; influential etc. 175; productive etc. 168.

Adv. powerfully etc. *adj.*; by -virtue, – dint-of.

158. Impotence.—N. impotence; in-, dis-ability; disablement, impuissance, imbecility, caducity; incapa-city, -bility; inapt-, inept-itude; indocility; invalidity, inefficiency, incompetence, disqualification.

telum imbelle, brutum fulmen, blank cartridge, flash in the pan, *vox et praeterea nihil,* dead le ter, bit of waste paper, dummy; scrap of paper.

inefficacy etc. (*inutility*) 645; failure etc. 732.

helplessness etc. *adj.*; prostration, paralysis, palsy, ataxia, apoplexy, syncope, sideration, *deliquium*, collapse, exhaustion, softening of the brain, e nasculation, inanition, senility etc. 128; castrato, eunuch.

cripple, old woman, muff, molly-coddle, milksop.

V. be -impotent etc. *adj.*; not have a leg to stand on.

vouloir -rompre l'anguille au genou, – prendre la lune avec les dents.

collapse, faint, swoon, fall into a swoon, drop; go by the board; end in smoke etc. (*fail*) 732.

render -powerless etc. *adj.*; deprive of power; decontrol; dis-able, -enable; disarm, incapacitate, disqualify, unfit, invalidate, undermine, deaden, cramp, tie the hands; double up, prostrate, paralyze, muzzle, cripple, becripple, maim, lame, hamstring, draw the teeth of; throttle, strangle, *garrotte;* ratten, silence, sprain, clip the wings of, render *hors de combat,* spike the guns; take the wind out of one's sails, scotch the snake, put a spoke in one's wheel; break the -neck, – back; un-hinge, -fit; put out of gear.

unman, unnerve, devitalize, attenuate, enervate; emasculate, spay, caponize, castrate, geld; effeminize.

shatter, exhaust; weaken etc. 160.

Adj. powerless, impotent, unable, incapable, incompetent; ineff-icient, -ective; inept; un-fit, -fitted; un-, dis-qualified; unendowed; in-, un-apt; crippled, decrepit; disabled etc. *v.*; armless.

harmless, unarmed, weaponless, defenceless, *sine ictu*, unfortified, indefensible, vincible, pregnable, untenable.

para-lytic, -lyzed; palsied, imbecile; nerve-, sinew-, marrow-, pith-, lust-less; emasculate, disjointed, out of -joint, – gear; un-nerved, -hinged; water-logged, on one's beam ends, rudderless; laid on one's back; done up, dead beat, exhausted, shattered, demoralized; gravelled etc. (*in difficulty*) 704; helpless, unfriended, fatherless; without a leg to stand on, *hors de combat,* laid on the shelf.

null and void, nugatory, imoperative, good for nothing; dud; invertebrate; ineffectual etc. (*failing*) 732; inadequate etc. 640; inefficacious etc. (*useless*) 645.

159. Strength. [Degree of power.]—**N.** strength; power etc. 157; energy etc. 171; vigor, force; main –, physical –, brute- force; spring, elasticity, tone, tension, tonicity.

stoutness etc. *adj.*; lustihood, stamina, nerve,

muscle, sinew, thews and sinews, *physique;* pith, -iness; virility, vitality.

athlet-ics, -icism; gymnastics, feats of strength.

adamant, steel, iron, oak, heart of oak; iron grip; grit, bone.

athlete, gymnast, tumbler, acrobat; Atlas, Hercules, Antaeus, Samson, Cyclops, Goliath, Titan; tower of strength; giant refreshed.

strengthening etc. *v.;* invigoration, refreshment, refocillation.

[Science of forces] dynamics, statics.

V. be -strong etc. *adj.*, — stronger; overmatch.

render -strong etc. *adj.;* give -strength etc. *n.;* strengthen, invigorate, brace, nerve, fortify, buttress, sustain, harden, case-harden, steel; gird; screw —, wind —, set- up; gird —, brace- up one's loins; recruit, set on one's legs; vivify; refresh etc. 689; refect; reinforce etc. (*restore*) 660.

Adj. strong, mighty, vigorous, forcible, hard, adamantine, stout, robust, sturdy, hardy, powerful, potent, puissant, valid.

resistless, irresistible, invincible, proof against, impregnable, unconquerable, indomitable, inextinguishable, unquenchable; incontestable; more than a match for; over-powering, -whelming; all-powerful; sovereign.

able-bodied; athletic, gymnastic; Herculean, Cyclopean, Atlantean; muscular, husky, brawny, wiry, well-knit, broad-shouldered, sinewy, strapping, stalwart, gigantic.

man-ly, -like, -ful; masculine, male, virile, in the prime of manhood.

un-weakened, -allayed, -withered, -shaken, -worn, -exhausted; in full -force, — swing; in the plenitude of power.

stubborn, thick-ribbed, made of iron, deep-rooted; strong as -a lion, — a horse, — brandy; sound as a roach; in -fine, — high- feather; in fine fettle; like a giant refreshed.

Adv. strongly etc. *adj.*; by -force etc. *n.*; by main force etc. (*by compulsion*) 744.

Phr. 'our withers are unwrung.'

160. Weakness.—N. weakness etc. *adj.;* debility, atony, relaxation, languor, enervation; impotence etc. 158; infirmity; effeminancy, feminality; fragility, flaccidity; inactivity etc. 683.

declension —, loss —, failure- of strength; delicacy, invalidation, decrepitude, asthenia, adynamy, cachexy, *cachexia*, anemia, bloodlessness, sprain, strain.

reed, thread, rope of sand, broken reed, house -of cards, — built on sand.

soft-, weak-ling; infant etc. 129; youth etc. 127.

V. be -weak etc. *adj.;* drop, crumble, give way, totter, tremble, shake, halt, limp, fade, languish, decline, flag, fail, have one foot in the grave.

render -weak etc. *adj.;* weaken, enfeeble, debilitate, shake, deprive of strength, relax, enervate; un-brace, -nerve; cripple, unman, etc. (*render powerless*) 158; cramp, reduce, sprain, strain, blunt the edge of; dilute, impoverish; decimate; extenuate; reduce -in strength, — the strength of; invalidate; *mettre de l'eau dans son vin.*

Adj. weak, feeble, debile; impotent etc. 158; relaxed, unnerved etc. *v.*; sap-, strength-, powerless; weakly, unstrung, flaccid, adynamic, asthenic; nervous.

soft, effeminate, feminate, womanish.

frail, fragile, shattery, frangible, brittle etc. 328; flimsy, unsubstantial, gimcrack, gingerbread; rickety, cranky; creachy; drooping, tottering etc. *v.;* broken, lame, halt, game, withered, shattered, shaken, crazy, shaky, tumble-down; palsied etc. 158; decrepit; C3.

lanquid, poor, poorly, infirm; faint, -ish; sickly etc. (*disease*) 655; dull, slack, evanid, spent, short-winded, effete; weatherbeaten; decayed, rotten, worn, seedy, languishing, wasted, washy, wishy-washy, laid low, pulled down, the worse for wear.

un-strengthened etc. 159, -supported, -aided, -assisted; aidless, defenceless etc. 158.

on its last legs; weak as a -child, — baby, — chicken, — cat, — rat; weak as -water, — water gruel, — gingerbread, — milk and water; colorless etc. 429.

Phr. *non sum qualis eram.*

161. Production.—N. production, creation, construction, formation, fabrication, manufacture; building, architecture, erection, edification; coinage; organization; *nisus formativus;* putting togeher etc. *v.;* establishment; workmanship, performance; achievement etc. (*completion*) 729; effect etc. 154.

flowering, fructification fruition.

bringing forth etc. *v.;* parturition, birth, birth-throe, child-birth, delivery, confinement, *accouchement*, travail, labour, midwifery, obstetrics; geniture; gestation etc. (*maturation*) 673; evolution, development, growth; genesis, fertilization, breeding, conception, germination, generation, *epigenesis*, pro-creation, -generation, -pagation; fecundation, impregnation; spontaneous generation; *arche-genesis, -biosis; bio-, abio-, homo-, xeno-genesis.*

authorship, publication; works, *oeuvre, opus.*

edifice, building, structure, fabric, erection, pile, tower, flower, fruit.

V. produce, perform, operate, do, make, gar, form, construct, fabricate, frame, contrive, manufacture; weave, forge, coin, carve, chisel; build, raise, edify, rear, erect, put together; set —, run- up; establish, constitute, compose, organize, institute, get up; achieve, accomplish etc. (*complete*) 729.

flower, sprout, blossom, burgeon, bear fruit, fructify, spawn, teem, ean, yean, farrow, drop, calf, pup, whelp, kitten, kindle; bear, lay, bring forth, give birth to, lie in, be brought to bed of, evolve, pullulate, usher into the world.

make productive etc. 168; create; beget, conceive, get, generate, fecundate, impregnate; procreate, -generate, -pagate; engender; bring —, call- into -being, — existence; breed, hatch, develop, bring up.

induce, superinduce; suscitate; cause etc. 153; acquire etc. 775.

Adj. produc-ed, -ing etc. *v.;* productive of; prolific etc. 168; creative; formative; gen-etic, -ial, -ital; fertile, pregnant; *enceinte*, big —, fraught-with; with child, in the family way, teeming, parturient, in the straw, brought to bed of; puerper-al, -ous.

architectonic; constructive.

162. Destruction. [Non-production.]—**N.** destruction; waste, dissolution, breaking up; di-, dis-ruption; consumption; disorganization.

fall, downfall, ruin, perdition, crash, smash, havoc, *délabrement, débâcle;* break -down, – up; prostration; desolation, *bouleversement*, wreck, crack-up, crash, wrack, shipwreck, cataclysm; Caudine Forks, Sedan.

extinction, annihilation; destruction of life etc. 361; knock-out, knock-down blow; doom, crack of doom.

destroying etc. *v.*; demo-lition, -lishment; biblioclasm; overthrow, subversion, suppression; abolition etc. (*abrogation*) 756; sacrifice; ravage, devastation, *sabotage, razzia*; incendiarism; revolution etc. 146; extirpation etc. (*extraction*) 301; *commencement de la fin*, road to ruin; dilapidation etc. (*deterioration*) 659.

V. be -destroyed etc.; perish; fall, – to the ground; tumble, topple; go –, fall- to pieces; break up; crumble, – to dust; go to -the dogs, – the wall, – smash, – shivers, – wreck, – pot, – wrack and ruin; go -by the board, – all to smash, – to pieces, – under; be all -over, – up- with; totter to its fall.

destroy; do –, make- away with; nullify; annul etc. 756; sacrifice, demolish; tear up; over-turn, -throw, -whelm; upset, subvert, put an end to; seal the doom of, do for, dish, undo; break -, cut- up; break –, cut –, pull –, mow –, blow –, beat- down; suppress, quash, put down; cut short, take off, blot out; dispel, dissipate, dissolve; consume.

smash, – to smithereens, quell, squash, squelch, crumple up, shatter, shiver; batter; tear –, crush –, cut –, shake –, pull –, pick- to pieces; nip; tear to -rags, – tatters; crush –, knock- to atoms; pulverize; ruin; strike out; throw –, knock- -down, – over; lay by the heels; fell, sink, swamp, scuttle, wreck, crash, shipwreck, engulf, submerge; lay in -ashes, – ruins; sweep away, erase, expunge, strike out, delete, efface, raze; level, – with the -ground, – dust.

deal destruction, lay waste, ravage, gut; disorganize; dismantle etc. (*render useless*) 645; devour, swallow up, desolate, devastate, sap, mine, blast, confound; exterminate, extinguish, quench, annihilate; snuff –, put –, stamp –, trample- out; lay –, trample- in the dust; prostrate; tread –, crush –, trample- under foot; lay the axe to the root of; make -short work, – a clean sweep, – mincemeat- of; cut up root and branch; fling –, scatter- to the winds; throw overboard; strike at the root of, sap the foundations of, spring a mine, blow up; ravage with fire and sword; cast to the dogs; eradicate etc. 301.

Adj. destroyed etc. *v.;* perishing etc. *v.;* trembling –, nodding –, tottering- to its fall; in course of destruction etc. *n.;* extinct.

destructive, subversive, ruinous, incendiary, deletory; destroying etc. *v.*; suicidal; deadly etc. (*killing*) 361.

Adv. with -crushing effect, – a sledge-hammer.

Phr. *delenda est Carthago.*

163. Reproduction.—**N.** reproduction, renovation; restoration etc. 660; renewal; new edition, reprint etc. 21; revival, regeneration, palingenesia, revivification; apotheosis; resuscitation, reanimation, resurrection, resurgence, reappearance, atavism; Phoenix; reincarnation.

generation etc. (*production*) 161; multiplication.

V. reproduce; restore etc. 660; revive, renovate, renew, regenerate, revivify, resuscitate, reanimate, refashion, stir the embers, put into the crucible; multiply, repeat, resurge.

crop up, spring up like mushrooms.

Adj. reproduced etc. *v.;* renascent, reappearing; reproductive; resurgent; progenitive; Hydra-headed.

164. Producer.—**N.** producer, creator, deviser, designer, originator, inventor, author, founder, generator, mover, architect; grower, constructor, maker etc. (*agent*) 690.

165. Destroyer.—**N.** destroyer etc. (destroy etc. 162); cankerworm etc. (*bane*) 663; iconoclast; assassin etc. (*killer*) 361; executioner etc. (*punish*) 975; Hun, Vandal, nihilist, anarchist.

166. Paternity.—**N.** paternity; parentage; fatherhood; consanguinity etc. 11.

parent, father, sire, dad, daddy, papa, governor, *pater, paterfamilias, abba;* genitor, progenitor, procreator, begetter; ancestor; grandsire, -father; great-grandfather.

house, stem, truck, tree, stock, *stirps*, pedigree, lineage, line, family, tribe, sept, race, clan; genealogy, descent, extraction, birth, ancestry; forefathers, forbears, patriarchs.

motherhood, maternity; mother, dam, mamma, *materfamilias;* grand-mother; matriarch.

Adj. paternal, parental; maternal; family, ancestral, linear, matrilinear, patrilineal, patriarchal.

167. Posterity.—**N.** posterity, progeny, breed, issue, offspring, brood, litter, seed, farrow, spawn, spat; family, children, grandchildren, heirs; great-grandchild.

child, son, daughter; kid; infant etc. 129; bantling, scion; shoot, sprout, olive branch, sprit, branch; off-shoot, -set; ramification; descendant; heir, -ess; heir -apparent, – presumptive; chip of the old block; heredity; rising generation.

straight descent, sonship, line, lineage, filiation, promogeniture.

Adj. filial.

168. Productiveness.—**N.** productiveness etc. *adj.;* fecundity, fertility, luxuriance, uberty.

pregnancy, pullulation, fructification, multiplication, propagation, procreation; superfetation.

milch cow, rabbit, hydra, warren, seed-plot, land flowing with milk and honey; second crop, after-crop, -growth, -math; fertilization.

V. make -productive etc. *adj.;* fructify; procreate, generate, fertilize, spermatize, impregnate; fecund-ate, -ify; teem, pullulate, multiply; produce etc. 161; conceive.

Adj. productive, prolific; teem-ing, -ful; fertile, fruitful, frugiferous, fruit-bearing; fructiferous; fecund, luxuriant; pregnant, uberous.

procre-ant, -ative; generative, life-giving, spermatic; originative; multiparous; omnific; propagable.

parturient etc. (*producing*) 161; profitable etc. (*useful*) 644.

169. Unproductiveness.—N. unproductiveness etc. *adj.;* infertility, steril; ity, infecundity; impotence etc. 158- unprofitableness etc. (*inutility*) 645.

waste, desert, Sahara, wild, wilderness, howling wilderness.

V. be -unproductive etc. *adj.;* hang fire, flash in the pan, come to nothing.

Adj. unproductive, inoperative, barren, addle, unfertile, unprolific, arid, sterile, unfruitful, acarpous, infecund; *sine prole;* fallow; teem-, issue-, fruitless; unprofitable etc. (*useless*) 645; null and void, of no effect.

170. Agency.—N. agency, operation, force, working, strain, function, office, maintenance, exercise, work, swing, play; inter-working, -action, procuration, procurement.

causation etc. 153; instrumentality etc. 631; influence etc. 175; action etc. (*voluntary*) 680; *modus operandi* etc. 627.

quickening —, maintaining- power; home stroke.

V. be -in action etc. *adj.;* operate, work; act, — upon; perform, play, support, sustain, strain, maintain, take effect, quicken, strike.

come —, bring- into -operation, — play; have - play, — free play; bring to bear upon.

Adj. operative, efficient, efficacious, practical, effectual.

at work, on foot; acting etc. (*doing*) 680; in - operation, — force, — action, — play, — exercise; acted —, wrought- upon.

Adv. by the -agency etc. *n.*- of; through etc. (*instrumentality*) 631; by means of etc. 632.

171. Physical Energy.—N. energy, physical energy, force; keenness etc. *adj.;* intensity, vigor, strength, elasticity; go; pep, live wire, high pressure; backbone, mettle, fire, vim.

acri-mony, -tude, -dity; causticity, virulence, poignancy; harshness etc. *adj.;* severity, edge, point; pungency etc. 392.

cantharides; Spanish fly; seasoning etc. (*condiment*) 393, stimulant, excitant.

activity, agitation, effervescence; ferment, -ation; ebullition, splutter, perturbation, stir, bustle; voluntary energy etc. 682; quicksilver.

resolution etc. (*mental energy*) 604; exertion etc. (*effort*) 686; excitation etc. (*mental*) 824.

V. give -energy etc. *n.;* energize, stimulate, kindle, excite, activate, exert; sharpen, pep up, intensify; inflame etc. (*render violent*) 173; wind up etc. (*strengthen*) 159.

strike, — into, — hard, — home; make an impression.

Adj. strong, energetic, forcible, active; strenuous, forceful, mettlesome, enterprising, go ahead; intense, deep-dyed, severe, keen, vivid, sharp, acute, incisive, trenchant, brisk, vigorous, live.

rousing, irritating; poignant; virulent, caustic, corrosive, mordant, harsh, stringent; double-edged, — shotted, — distilled; drastic, escharotic; racy etc. (*pungent*) 392; sarcastic etc. 932.

potent etc. (*powerful*) 157; radio-active.

Adv. strongly etc. *adj.; fortiter in re;* with telling effect.

Phr. the steam is up; *vires acquirit eundo.*

172. Physical Inertness.—N. inertness, dulness etc. *adj.;* inertia, *vis inertiae,* inertion, inactivity, torpor, languor; dormancy, quiescence etc. 265; latency, inaction, passivity.

mental inertness; sloth etc. (*inactivity*) 683; inexcitability etc. 826; irresolution etc. 605; obstinacy etc. 606; permanence etc. 141.

V. be -inert etc. *adj.;* hang fire, smoulder.

Adj. inert, inactive, passive, pacific; torpid etc. 683; sluggish, stagnant, dull, heavy, flat, slack, tame, slow, blunt; lifeless, dead, uninfluential.

latent, dormant, smouldering, unexerted.

Adv. inactively etc. *adj.;* in -suspense, -abeyance.

173. Violence.—N. violence, inclemency, vehemence, might, impetuosity; boisterousness etc.; *adj.;* effervescence, ebullition; turbulence, bluster; uproar, riot, row, rumpus, *le diable à quatre,* devil to pay, all the fat in the fire.

severity etc. 739; ferocity, rage, berserk, fury; exacerbation, exasperation, malignity; fit, paroxysm, orgasm; force, brute force; outrage; *coup de main;* strain, shock, shog; spasm, convulsion, throe; hysterics, passion etc. (*state of excitability*) 825.

out-break, -burst; burst, bounce, dissilience, discharge, volley, explosion, blow up, blast, detonation, rush, eruption, displosion, torrent.

turmoil etc. (*disorder*) 59; ferment etc. (*agitation*) 315; storm, tempest, rough weather; squall etc. (*wind*) 349; earthquake, volcano, thunderstorm.

fury, dragon, demon, tiger, beldame, Tisiphone, Megaera, Alecto, madcap, wild beast; fire-eater etc. (*blusterer*) 887.

V. be -violent etc. *adj.*; run high; ferment, effervesce; romp, rampage; run -wild, — riot; break the peace; rush, tear; rush head-long, -foremost; run amuck, raise a storm, make a riot; make —, kick up- a row, — a fuss; bluster, rage, roar, riot, storm; boil, — over; fume, foam, come in like a lion, wreak, bear down, ride roughshod, out-Herod Herod; spread like wildfire.

break —, fly —, burst- out; bounce, shock, strain; break-, pry-, force-, prize- open.

render -violent etc. *adj.;* sharpen, stir up, quicken, excite, incite, urge, lash, stimulate; irritate, inflame, exacerbate, kindle, suscitate, foment; accelerate, aggravate, exasperate, convulse, infuriate, madden, lash into fury; fan —, add fuel to- the flame; *oleum addere camino.*

explode, go off, displode, fly, detonate, thunder, blow up, flash, flare, erupt, burst; let -off, — fly; discharge, detonize, fulminate.

Adj. violent, vehement, forcible; warm; acute, sharp; rough, rude, ungentle, bluff, boisterous, wild, vicious; brusque, abrupt, waspish; impetuous; rampant.

turbulent; disorderly; blustering, raging etc. *v.*; troublous, riotous; tumultu-ary, -ous; obstreperous, uproarious; extravagant; unmitigated; ravening, tameless; frenzied etc. (*insane*) 503; desperate etc. (*rash*) 863; infuriate, towering, furious, outrageous, frantic, hysteric, in hysterics.

fiery, flaming, scorching, hot, red-hot, ebullient.

savage, fierce, ferocious, fierce as a tiger.

excited etc. *v.*; un-quelled, -quenched, -extinguished, -repressed, -bridled, -ruly; headstrong; un-governable, -appeasable, -mitigable; un-, in-controllable; insup-, irre-pressible.

spasmodic, convulsive, explosive; detonating etc. *v.*; volcanic, meteoric; stormy etc. (*wind*) 349.

Adv. violently etc. *adj.*; amain; by -storm, — force, — main force; with might and main; tooth and nail, *vi et armis*, at the point of the -sword, — bayonet: at one fell swoop; with a high hand, through thick and thin; in desperation, with a vengeance; *à —*, *à touteoutrance*; head-long, -foremost, -first; like a bull at a gate.

174. Moderation.—N. moderation; lenity etc. 740; temperance, temperateness, gentleness etc. *adj.*; sobriety; quiet; mental calmness etc. (*inexcitability*) 826.

moderating etc. *v.*; relaxation, remission, mitigation etc. 834; tranquilization, alleviation, assuagement, appeasement, contemporation, pacification.

measure, *juste milieu*, golden mean etc. 29.

moderator; lullaby, sedative, lenitive, demulcent, rose-water, balm, soothing syrup, poppy, opiate, anodyne, milk, opium, laudanum, 'poppy or mandragora;' wet blanket; palliative, calmative.

V. be -moderate etc. *adj.*; keep within -bounds, — compass; sober —, settle- down; keep the pease, remit, relent; take in sail.

moderate, soften, mitigate, temper, accoy; at-, con-temper; mollify, lenify, dull, take off the edge, blunt, obtund, sheathe, subdue, chasten; sober —, tone —, smooth- down; censor, blue-pencil, weaken etc. 160; lessen etc. (*decrease*) 36; check; palliate.

tranquilize, assuage, appease, dulcify, swage, lull, soothe, compose, still, calm, cool, quiet, hush, quell, sober, pacify, tame, damp, lay, allay, rebate, slacken, smooth, alleviate, rock to sleep, deaden, smother; throw -cold water on, — a wet blanket over; slake; curb etc. (*restrain*) 751; tame etc. (*subjugate*) 749; smooth over; pour oil on the -waves, — troubled waters; pour balm into, *mettre de l'eau dans son vin*.

go out like a lamb, 'roar you as gently as any sucking dove.'

Adj. moderate; lenient etc. 740; gentle, mild; cool, sober, temperate, reasonable, measured; tempered etc. *v.*; calm, unruffled, quiet, tranquil, still; slow, smooth, untroubled; tame; peaceful, -able; pacific, halcyon.

un-exciting, -irritating; soft, bland, oily, demulcent, lenitive, anodyne; hypnotic etc. 683; sedative; assuaging.

mild as mother's milk; milk and water; gentle as a lamb.

Adv. moderately etc. *adj.*; gingerly; *piano*; under easy sail, at half speed; within -bounds, — compass; in reason.

Phr. *est modus in rebus*.

175. Influence.—N. influence; importance etc. 642; weight, pressure, preponderance, prevalence, sway, pull; predomi-nance, -nancy; ascendency; control, dominance, reign; authority etc. 737; capability etc. (*power*) 157; interest; spell, magic, magnetism.

footing; purchase etc. (*support*) 215; play, leverage, vantage ground.

tower of strength, host in himself; protection, patronage, auspices.

V. have -influence etc. *n.*; be -influential etc. *adj.*; carry weight, actuate, sway, bias, weigh, tell; have a hold upon, magnetize, bear upon, gain a footing, work upon; take -root, — hold; strike root in.

run through, pervade, prevail, dominate, predominate, subject; out-, over-weigh; over-ride, -bear, — come; gain head; rage; be -rife etc. *adj.*; spread like wildfire; have —, get —, gain- -the upper hand, — full play.

be -recognized, — listened to; make one's voice heard, gain a hearing; play a -part, — leading part- in; lead, control, rule, master; get the mastery over; make one's influence felt, cut ice with; take the lead, pull the strings; turn —, throw one's weight into- the scale; set the fashion, lead the dance.

Adj. influential; important etc. 642; weighty; prevailing etc. *v.*; prevalent, rife, rampant; dominant, regnant, predominant, in the ascendant, hegemonical; authoritative, recognized, telling, with authority.

Adv. with telling effect.

175a. Absence of Influence.—N. impotence etc. 158; inertness etc. 172; irrelevancy etc. 10.

V. have no -influence etc. 175.

Adj. uninfluential; unconduc-ing, -ive, -ting to; powerless etc. 158; irrelevant etc. 10.

176. Tendency.—N. tendency; apt-ness, -itude; proneness, proclivity, bent, turn, tone, bias, set, warp, leaning to, predisposition, inclination, conatus, propensity, susceptibility; liability etc. 177; quality, nature, temperament; characteristic, idio-crasy, -syncrasy; cast, vein, grain; humor, mood; drift etc. (*direction*) 278; conduciveness, -ducement; applicability etc. (*utility*) 644; subservience etc. (*instrumentality*) 631.

V. tend, contribute, conduce, lead, dispose, incline, verge, bend to, warp, turn, trend, affect, carry, redound to, bid fair to, gravitate towards; promote etc. (*aid*) 707.

Adj. tending etc. *v.*; conducive, working towards, in a fair way to, calculated to; liable etc. 177; subservient etc. (*instrumental*) 631; useful etc. 644; subsidiary etc. (*helping*) 707.

Adv. for, whither.

177. Liability.—N. lia-bility, -bleness; possibility, contingency; suscepti-vity, -bility.

V. be -liable etc. *adj.;* incur, lay oneself open to; run the —, stand a- chance; lie under, expose oneself to, open a door to.

Adj. liable, subject; in danger etc. 665; open —, exposed —, obnoxious- to; answerable, responsible, accountable, amenable; unexempt from; apt to; dependent on; incident to.

contingent, incidental, possible, on the cards, within range of, at the mercy of.

178. Concurrence.—N. concurrence, co-operation, coagency; coincidence, consilience; union; agreement etc. 23; consent etc. (*assent*) 488; alliance; concert etc. 709; partnership etc. 712; collaboration, conformity.

V. con-cur, -duce, -spire, -tribute; agree, unite, harmonize; hang —, pull- together etc. (*co-operate*) 709; help to etc. (*aid*) 707.

keep pace with, run parallel to; go —, go along —, go hand in hand- with.

Adj. concurring etc. *v.;* concurrent, conformable, joint, co-operative, concordant, coincident, concomitant, harmonious; in alliance with, banded together, of one mind, at one with; parallel.

Adv. with one consent.

179. Counteraction.—N. counteraction, opposition; contrariety etc. 14; antagonism, polarity; clashing etc. *v.;* collision, interference, resistance, renitency, friction; reaction; retroaction; repercussion etc. (*recoil*) 277; counterblast; neutralization etc. (*compensation*) 30; *vis inertiae;* check etc. (*hindrance*) 706.

voluntary -opposition etc. 708. — resistance etc. 719; repression etc. (*restraint*) 751.

V. counteract; run counter, clash, cross; interfere —, conflict- with; jostle; go —, run —, beat —, militate- against; stultify; antagonize, frustrate, oppose etc. 708; withstand etc. (*resist*) 719; hinder etc. 706; repress etc. (*restrain*) 751; react etc. (*recoil*) 277.

undo, neutralize, cancel; counterpoise etc. (*compensate*) 30; overpoise.

Adj. counteracting etc. *v.;* antagonistic, conflicting, retroactive, renitent, reactionary; contrary etc. 14.

Adv. although etc. 30; in spite of etc. 708; *malgré;* against.

180. Space. [Indefinite space.]—**N.** space, extension, extent, superficial extent, expanse, stretch; capacity, volume, room, accommodation, scope, range, latitude, field, way, expansion, compass, sweep, play, swing, spread.

dimension, fourth dimension; relativity, geometry.

spare —, elbow —, house- room; stowage, roomage, margin; opening, sphere, arena; lee-, sea-, head-way.

open —, free- space; wide open spaces, void etc. (*absence*) 187; waste; wild-, wilder-ness; up-, bottom-, moor -land; *campagna, veldt,* prairie, steppe.

abyss etc. (*interval*) 198; unlimited space; infinity etc. 105; world, wide world; ubiquity etc. (*presence*) 186; length and breadth of the land.

proportions, acreage; acres, — roods and perches; square -inches, — yards etc.

V. reach, extend, stretch, sweep, spread, range, cover, thrust out, reach forth.

Adj. spacious, roomy, extensive, expansive, capacious, ample; wide-spread, vast, world-wide, uncircumscribed; boundless etc. (*infinite*) 105; shore-, track-, path-less; large etc. 192.

spatial, dimensional, proportional; two-, three-, four-dimensional; stereoscopic.

Adv. extensively etc. *adj.;* wherever; everywhere; far and -near, — wide; right and left, all over, all the world over; throughout the -world, — length and breadth of the land; under the sun, in every quarter; in all -quarters, — lands; here, there and everywhere; from -pole to pole, — China to Peru, — Indus to the pole, — Dan to Beersheba, — end to end; on the face of the earth, in the wide world, from all points of the compass; to the -four winds, — uttermost parts of the earth.

180a. Inextension.—N. in-, non-extension; point; atom etc. (*smallness*) 32; pinprick; limitation etc. 229.

181. Region. [Definite space.]—**N.** region, sphere, sphere of influence, corridor, ground, soil, area, realm, hemisphere, quarter district, beat, orb, orbit, zone, belt, circuit, circle; pale etc. (*limit*) 233; com-, department; domain, tract, territory, terrain, country, canton, county, shire, province, *arrondissement,* diocese, parish, township, borough, constituency, *commune,* ward, wapentake, hundred, riding, lathe, garth, soke, tithing, bailiwick; empire, kingdom, principality, duchy, grand —, arch- duchy, palatinate, republic, commonwealth, dominion, colony, state, island.

arena, precincts, *enceinte,* walk, march; patch, plot, enclosure, etc. 232; close, *enclave,* field, court; street etc. (*abode*) 189.

clime, climate, zone, meridian, latitude.

Adj. territorial, local, parochial, provincial, insular.

182. Place. [Limited space.]—**N.** place, lieu, spot, point, dot; niche, nook, etc. (*corner*) 244; hole; pigeonhole etc. (*receptacle*) 191; compartment; premises, precinct, station, confine; area, court, yard, quadrangle, square, compound; abode etc. 189; locality etc. (*situation*) 183.

ins and outs; every hole and corner.

Adv. somewhere, in some place, wherever it may be, here and there, in various places, *passim.*

183. Situation.—N. situation, position, locality, *locale, status*, latitude and longitude; footing, standing, standpoint, post; stage, aspect, attitude, posture, *pose*.

place, site, base, station, seat, *venue*, whereabouts, environment, neighborhood; bearings etc. (*direction*) 278; spot etc. (*limited space*) 182.

top-, ge-, chor-ography; map etc. 554.

V. be -situated, — situate; lie; have its seat in.

Adj. situ-ate, -ated; local, topical, topographical etc. *n*.

Adv. *in -situ, — loco;* here and there, *passim;* here-, there-, whereabouts; in place, here, there.

in —, amidst- such and such- -surroundings, — *environs, — entourage.*

184. Location.—N. loca-tion, -lization; lodgement; de-, re-position; stow-, pack-age; collocation; packing, lading; establishment, settlement, installation; fixation; insertion etc. 300.

anchorage, roadstead, mooring, mooring mast, encampment, camp, bivouac.

plantation, colony, settlement, cantonment, encampment, reservation; colonization, domestication, situation; habitation etc. (*abode*) 189; cohabitation; 'a local habitation and a name;' indenization, naturalization.

V. place, situate, locate, localize, make a place for, put, lay, set, seat, station, lodge, quarter, post, install; storehouse, stow; extablish, fix, pin, root; graft; plant etc. (*insert*) 300; shelve, pitch, camp, lay down, deposit, reposit; cradle; moor, tether, picket; pack, tuck in; embed; vest, invest in.

billet on, quarter upon, saddle with; load, lade, freight; pocket, put up, bag.

inhabit etc. (*be present*) 186; domesticate, colonize, populate, people; take —, strike-root; anchor; cast —, come to an- anchor; sit —, settle- down; settle; take up one's -abode, — quarters; plant —, establish —, locate- oneself; squat, perch, hive, *se nicher*, bivouac, burrow, get a footing; encamp, pitch one's tent; put up -at, — one's horses at; keep house.

indenizen, naturalize, adopt.

put back, replace etc. (*restore*) 660.

Adj. placed etc. *v.;* situate, posited, ensconced, embedded, embosomed, rooted; domesticated; vested in unremoved; settled, stationed, established.

moored etc. *v.;* at anchor.

185. Displacement.—N. displacement, elocation, transposition.

ejectment etc. 297; exile etc. (*banishment*) 893; removal etc. (*transference*) 270; unshipment.

misplacement, dislocation etc. 61; fish out of water.

V. dis-place, -plant, -lodge, -nest, -establish; misplace, unseat, disturb; exile etc. (*seclude*) 893; ablegate, set aside, remove; take —, cart- away; take —, draft- off; lade etc. 184, unship.

unload, empty etc. (*eject*) 297; transfer etc. 270; dispel.

vacate; depart etc. 293.

Adj. displaced etc. *v.;* un-placed, -housed, -harbored, -established, -settled; house-, homeless; out of -place, — a situation.

misplaced, out of its element.

186. Presence.—N. presence; occupancy, -ation; attendance; whereness.

permeation, pervasion; diffusion etc. (*dispersion*) 73.

ubi-ety, -quity, -quitariness; omnipresence.

bystander etc. (*spectator*) 444.

V. exist in space, be -present etc. *adj.;* assist at; make one -of, — at; look on, attend, remain; find —, present- oneself; show one's face; fill in the way of, occur in a place; lie, stand; occupy.

people; inhabit, dwell, reside, stay, sojourn, live, room, abide, bunk, lodge, nestle, roost, perch; take up one's abode etc. (*be located*) 184; tenant, occupy.

resort to, frequent, haunt; revisit.

fill, pervade, permeate; be -diffused, — disseminated- through; over-spread, -run; run through; meet one at every turn.

Adj. present; occupying, inhabiting etc. *v.;* moored etc. 184; residential, resi-ant, -dent, -dentiary; domiciled.

ubiquit-ous, -ary; omnipresent.

peopled, populous, full of people, inhabited.

Adv. here; there, where, everywhere, aboard, on board, at home, afield; on the spot; here, there and everywhere etc. (*space*) 180; in presence of, before; under the -eyes, —nose- of; in the face of; *in propriâ personâ.*

187. Absence. [Nullibiety.]**—N.** absence; inexistence etc. 2; non-residence, absenteeism; non-attendance, *alibi*.

emptiness etc. *adj.;* void, *vacuum;* vac-uity, -ancy; *tabula rasa;* exemption; *hiatus* etc. (*interval*) 198; no man's land.

truant, absentee.

nobody; nobody -present, — on earth; no one; not a soul; *âme qui vive.*

V. be -absent etc. *adj.;* keep -away, — out of the way; play truant, absent oneself, stay away.

withdraw, make oneself scarce, vacate; go away, slip out, slip away, retreat etc. 293.

Adj. absent, not present, away, nonresident, gone, from home; missing; lost; wanted, wanting; omitted; nowhere to be found; inexistent etc. 2.

empty, void; blank, vac-ant, -uous; untenanted, -occupied, -inhabited; tenantless; desert, -ed; devoid; un-, uninhabitable.

exempt from, not having.

Adv. without, *minus*, nowhere; elsewhere; neither here nor there; in default of; *sans;* behind one's back.

Phr. the bird has flown, *non est inventus.*

188. Inhabitant.—N. inhabitant; habitant, resident, -iary; dweller, in-dweller; occup-ier, -ant, farmer, planter; householder, lodger, boarder, paying guest; inmate, tenant, renter, incumbent, sojourner, *locum tenens*, commorant; settler, squatter, backwoodsman, colonist; islander; denizen, citizen; burgher, oppidan, cockney, cit, townsman, burgess; villager; cottager, -tier, -ter; compatriot.

native, indigene, aboriginal, aborigines, autochthones; Briton, Englishman, John Bull; new comer etc. (*stranger*) 57.

garrison, crew; population; people etc. (*mankind*) 372; colony, settlement; household.

V. inhabit etc. (*be present*) 186; indenizen etc. (*locate oneself*) 184.

Adj. indigenous; enchorial; national, nat-ive, -al; autochthonous; British, English; colonial; domestic, domiciliated, -ed; naturalized, vernacular, domesticated; domiciliary.

in the occupation of; garrisoned –, occupied-by.

189. Abode. [Place of habitation, or resort.]—**N.** abode, dwelling, lodging, -s; diggings, domicile, residence, address, habitation, where one's lot is cast, local habitation, berth, seat, lap, sojourn, housing, quarters, headquarters, resiance, tabernacle, throne, ark.

home, fatherland, mother country, country etc. 181; home-stead, -stall; fireside, chimney corner; hearth, – stone; household gods, *lares et penates*, roof, household, housing, *dulce domum*, paternal domicile; native -soil, – land, blighty.

nest, *nidus*, snuggery; arbor, bower etc. 191; lair, den, cave, hole, hidingplace, cell, *sanctum sanctorum*, aerie, eyry, rookery, hive; *habitat*, haunt, covert, resort, retreat, perch, roost; nidification.

bivouac, camp, encampment, cantonment, castrametation; barrack, casemate, casern.

tent etc. (*covering*) 223; building etc. (*construction*) 161; chamber etc. (*receptacle*) 191.

tenement, messuage, farm, farmhouse, grange, *hacienda*.

cot, cabin, log cabin, shack, hut, *châlet*, croft, shed, booth, stall, hovel, bothy, shanty, igloo, tepee, wigwam; pen etc. (*inclosure*) 232; barn, bawn; kennel, sty, dog-hole, cote, coop, hutch, byre; cowhouse, -shed; stable, dove-cote, shippen.

house, mansion, place, villa, cottage, box, lodge, hermitage, *rus in urbe*, folly, rotunda, tower, *château*, castle, pavilion, hotel, court, manor-house, capital messuage, hall, palace, alcazar; country seat; kiosk, bungalow; temple etc. 1000; home of rest, alms-, poor-, work-house, asylum; boarding-, lodging-house; flat, maisonette, duplex, penthouse, suite of rooms, apartments, rooms, room building etc. 161; Mansion House, town hall, Capitol.

assembly-room, auditorium, coliseum, meeting-house, pump-room, spa, health resort, watering-place; club; theatre etc. 840; drill hall, gymnasium, church etc. 1000; Houses of Parliament etc. 696; school etc. 542; inn; hostel, -ry; hotel, tavern, caravansary, khan, hospice; public-, ale-, pot-, mug-house; gin-palace, gin mill; coffee-, eating-house; canteen, *restaurant*, *rotisserie*, cafeteria, grill-room, *buffet*, *café*, *estaminet*, *posada*, *bodega*; bar; saloon, speakeasy, shebeen.

hamlet, village, thorp, dorp, ham, kraal; borough, burgh, town, county-seat, – town, city, capital, metropolis; suburb, quarter, parish etc. 181; ghetto; province, country.

street, place, terrace, parade, esplanade, promenade, pier, embankment, road, villas, row, walk, lane, alley, court, quadrangle, quad, wynd, close, yard, passage, rents, mansions, buildings, mews.

square, polygon, circus, crescent, mall, *piazza*, arcade, colonnade, peristyle, cloister; gardens, grove, residences; block of buildings, market-place, *place*.

anchorage, roadstead, roads; dock, basin, wharf, quay, port, harbor; dry-, graving-, floating-dock.

garden, park, pleasure-ground, pleasance, demesne.

V. take up one's abode etc. (*locate oneself*) 184; inhabit etc. (*be present*) 186.

Adj. urban, oppidan, metropolitan; suburban; provincial, rural, rustic; countrified; regional, parochial, domestic; cosmopolitan; palatial.

190. Contents. [Things contained.]—**N.** contents; cargo, lading, freight, shipment, load, bale, burden; cart-, ship-load; cup –, basket –, etc. (*receptacle*) 191 - of; inside etc. 221; stuffing, ullage.

V. load, lade, ship, charge, fill, stuff.

191. Receptacle.—N. receptacle, container; inclosure etc. 232; recipient, receiver, reservatory.

compartment; cell, -ule; follicle; hole, corner, niche, recess, nook; crypt, stall, pigeon-hole, cove oriel; cave etc. (*concavity*) 252.

capsule, vesicle, cyst, pod, calyx, *cancelli*, utricle, bladder, udder.

stomach, paunch, *venter*, abdomen, ventricle, crop, craw, ingluvies, maw, gizzard, bread-basket, belly, little Mary; mouth.

pocket, pouch, fob, sheath, scabbard, socket, bag, vanity bag, compact, sac, sack, saccule, despatch –, attaché-, tachy- case, wallet, scrip, card-, note-, case, billfold, poke, knit, knap-, haver-, ruck-sack, sachel, satchel, reticule, budget, net; ditty-, -box, -bag, kitbag; portfolio; saddlebags, holster; quiver etc. (*magazine*) 636.

chest, box, coffer, caddy, case, casket, pyx, pix, *caisson*, desk, *bureau*, reliquary, shrine; trunk, portmanteau, band-box, *valise*, suitcase, hand-, traveling-, overnight-, Gladstone-, carpet-bag, brief case; boot, imperial; *vache*; cage, manger, rack.

vessel, vase, bushel, barrel; canister, jar; pottle, basket, punnet, pannier, buck-basket, hopper, maund, creel, cran, crate, cradle, bassinet, wisket, whisket, *jardinière*, *corbeille*, hamper, wastepaper basket, dosser, dorser, tray, hod, scuttle, utensil, spittoon, cuspidor.

[For liquids] cistern etc. (*store*) 636; vat, caldron, barrel, cask, puncheon, keg, rundlet, tun, butt, firkin, hogshead, kilderkin, carboy, amphora, ampulla, bottle, jar, leather bottle, decanter, ewer, cruse, carafe, crock, kit, canteen, flagon; demijohn; flask, -et; stoup, noggin, vial, phial, ampoulé, cruet, caster; gourd; urn, *épergne*, salver, *patella*, *tazza*, *patera*; pig-, big-gin; tea-, coffee-pot, percolator, *samovar*; tyg, nipperkin, pocket-pistol; tub, bucket, pail, skeel, pot, tankard, jug, pitcher, toby, mug, pipkin; gal-, gall-ipot, pannikin; matrass, receiver, retort, alembic, bolthead, can, kettle; bowl, basin, jorum, punch-bowl, cup, goblet, chalice, tumbler, glass, wineglass, rummer, beaker, tass, horn, saucepan, skillet, posnet, tureen, terrine, *casserole*, sauce-, gravy-boat.

plate, platter, paten, dish, vegetable –, *entrée*-dish, trencher, calabash, porringer, potager, saucer, pan, crucible.

shovel, trowel, spoon; table-, dessert-, tea-, egg-,

salt-spoon; spatula, ladle; dipper; baler; watch-glass, thimble.

closet, commode, cupboard, cellaret, *chiffonnière*, locker, bin, bunker, *buffet*, press, safe, sideboard, drawer, chest of drawers, till, *scrutoire*, *secrétaire*, *escritoire*, davenport, book-case, cabinet, canterbury; corner cupboard, wardrobe.

chamber, apartment, room, cabin; office, court, hall, atrium; suite of rooms, flat, story; saloon, *salon*, parlor; presence-chamber; sitting-, drawing-, reception-, state-, living-, work-room; gallery, cabinet, closet, cubicle; pew, box; *boudoir*; *adytum, sanctum*; bed-room, dormitory, dressing-room; refectory, dining-room, *salle-à-manger*; nursery, schoolroom; library, study; *studio*; billiard-, bath-, smoking-room; den, canteen, mess, officers' mess; gun-, ward-, mess-room.

attic, loft, garret, cockloft, clerestory; cellar, vault, hold, cockpit; *entre-sol*; mezzanine floor; ground-floor, *rez-de-chaussée*; basement, kitchen, cook-house, galley, pantry, scullery, offices; store-room etc. (*depository*) 636; lumber-room; dust-hole, -bin; dairy, laundry, coachhouse; *garage*; *hangar*; out-, pent-house; lean-to.

portico, porch, piazza, verandah, lobby, court, hall, vestibule, corridor, passage; ante-room, -chamber; lounge; *foyer, loggia*.

conservatory, green-house, glass-house, vinery, bower, arbor, summer-house, alcove, grotto, hermitage, pergola.

lodging etc. (*abode*) 189; bed etc. (*support*) 215; carriage etc. (*vehicle*) 272.

Adj. capsular; saccu-lar, -lated; recipient; ventricular, cystic, vascular, vesicular, cellular, camerated, locular, multilocular, poly-gastric; marsupial; siliqu-ose, -ous.

192. Size.—N. size, magnitude, dimension, bulk, volume; largeness etc. *adj.*; greatness etc. (*of quantity*) 31; expanse etc. (*space*) 180; amplitude, mass; proportions.

capacity; ton-, tun-nage; caliber, scantling.

turgidity etc. (*expansion*) 194; corpulence, obesity; plumpness, etc. *adj.*; *embonpoint*, corporation, flesh and blood, lustihood.

hugeness etc. *adj.*; enormity, immensity, monstrosity.

giant, Brobdingnagian, Antaeus, Goliath, Gog and Magog, Gargantua, monster, mammoth, Cyclops; whale, porpoise, behemoth, leviathan, elephant, hippopotamus; colossus; tun, lump, bulk, block, loaf, mass, clod, nugget, bushel, thumper, whopper, spanker, strapper; Triton among the minnows.

mountain, mound; heap etc. (*assemblage*) 72.

largest portion etc. 50; full-, life-size.

V. ve- large etc. *adj.*; become -large etc. (*expand*) 194.

Adj. large, big; great etc. (*in quantity*) 31; considerable, bulky, voluminous, ample, massive, massy; capacious, comprehensive; spacious etc. 180; mighty, towering, fine, magnificent.

corpulent, stout, fat, plump, squab, full, lusty, strapping, bouncing; portly, burly, well-fed, full-grown; stalwart, brawny, fleshy; goodly; in good -case, – condition; in condition; chopping, jolly; chub-, chubby-faced.

lubberly, hulky, unwieldy, lumpish, gaunt, spanking, whacking, whopping, thumping, thundering, hulking; overgrown; puffy etc. (*swollen*) 194.

huge, immense, enormous, mighty; vast, -y; amplitudinous, stupendous; monst-er, -rous; gigantic, elephantine; giant, -like; colossal, Cyclopean, Brobdingnagian, Garguantuan, Titanic; infinite etc. 105.

large as life; plump as a dumpling, – partridge; fat as -a pig, – a quail, – butter, – brawn, – bacon.

193. Littleness.—N. littleness etc. *adj.*; smallness etc. (*of quantity*) 32; exiguity, inextension; parvi-tude, -ty; duodecimo; Elzevir edition, epitome, microcosm; rudiment; vanishing point; thinness etc. 203.

dwarf, pigmy, atomy, Liliputian, midget, chit, pigwidgeon, urchin, elf; doll, puppet; Tom Thumb, Hop-o'-my thumb, Humpty-dumpty; man-, mannikin; *homunculus*, dapperling, fingerling, dandiprat, cock-sparrow, scalawag.

animalcule, monad, mite, insect, emmet, fly, midge, gnat, shrimp, minnow, worm, maggot, entozoon; *bacillus*, microbe, micro-organism, *bacteria*; *infusoria*; microbe; grub; tit, tomtit, runt, mouse, small fry; millet-, mustard-seed; barleycorn; pebble, grain of sand; mole-hill, button, bubble.

point; atom etc. (*small quantity*) 32; fragment etc. (*small part*) 51; powder etc. 330; point of a pin, mathematical point; *minutiae* etc. (*unimportance*) 643.

micro-graphy, -meter, -scope; vernier; scale.

V. be -little etc. *adj.*; lie in a nutshell; become small etc. (*decrease*) 36, (*contract*) 195.

Adj. little; small etc. (*in quantity*) 32; minute, diminutive, microscopic; inconsiderable etc. (*unimportant*) 643; exiguous, puny, tiny, wee, petty, minikin, miniature, pigmy, elfin; under sized; dwarf, -ed, -ish; spare, stunted, limited; cramp, -ed; pollard, Liliputian, dapper, pocket; port-ative, -able; duodecimo; dumpy, squat; compact, handy; short etc. 201.

impalpable, intangible, evanescent, imperceptible, invisible, inappreciable, infinitesimal, homeopathic; atomic, corpuscular, molecular; rudiment-ary, -al; embryonic.

weazen, scant, scraggy, scrubby; thin etc. (*narrow*) 203; granular etc. (*powdery*) 330; shrunk etc. 195.

Adv. in a -small compass, – nutshell; on a small scale.

194. Expansion.—N. expansion; increase etc. 35 -of size; enlargement, extension, augmentation; ampli-fication, -ation; aggrandizement, spread, increment, growth, development, pullulation, swell, dilation, dilatation, rarefaction; turg-escence, -idness, -idity; obesity etc. (*size*) 192; dropsy, tumefaction, intumescence, swelling, tumor, *diastole*, distension; puff-ing, -iness; inflation; pandiculation.

dilatability, expansibility.

germination, growth, upgrowth; accretion etc. 35.

over-growth, -distension; hypertrophy, tympany.

bulb etc. (*convexity*) 250; plumper; superiority of size.

V. become -larger etc. (large etc. 192); expand, widen, enlarge, extend, grow, increase, incrassate, swell, gather; fill out; deploy, take open order, dilate, stretch, spread; mantle, was; grow –, spring- up; bud, bourgeon, shoot, sprout, germinate, put forth, vegetate, pullulate, open, burst forth, flower, blow etc. 734; gain –, gather- flesh; outgrow; spread like wildfire, overrun.

be larger than; surpass etc. (*be superior*) 33.

render -larger etc. (large etc. 192); expand, spread, extend, aggrandize, distend, develop, amplify, spread out, widen, magnify, rarefy, inflate, puff, puff out, blow up, stuff pad, cram; exaggerate; fatten.

Adj. expanded etc. *v.*; larger etc. (large etc. 192); swollen; expansive; wide-open, -spread; fan-shaped; flabelliform; overgrown, exaggerated, bloated, fat, turgid, tumid, hypertrophied, dropsical; pot-, swag-bellied; edematous, obese, puffy, pursy, blowzy, distended; patulous; bulbous etc. (*convex*) 250; full-blown, -grown, -formed; big etc. 192.

195. Contraction.—N. contraction, reduction, diminution; decrease etc. 36- of size; defalcation, decrement; lessening, shrinkage; collapse, emaciation, attenuation, tabefaction, consumption, marasmus, atrophy; systole, neck, hourglass.

condensation, compression, constraint, compactness; compendium etc. 596; squeezing etc. *v.*; strangulation; corrugation; astringency, constringency; astringents, sclerotics; contractility, compressibility; coarctation.

inferiority in size.

V. become -small, – smaller; lessen, decrease etc. 36; grow less, dwindle, shrink, contract, narrow, shrivel, collapse, wither, lose flesh, wizen, fall away, waste, wane, ebb; decat etc. (*deteriorate*) 659.

be smaller than, fall short of; not come up to etc. (*be inferior*) 34.

render smaller, lessen, diminish, contract, draw in, shrink, shrivel, narrow, coarctate; constrict, constringe; condense, compress, boil down, deflate, exhaust, empty; squeeze, corrugate, crush, crumple up, warp, purse up, pack, stow; pinch, tighten, strangle; cramp; dwarf, bedwarf; shorten etc. 201; circumscribe etc. 229; restrain etc. 751; fold etc. 258.

pare, reduce, attenuate, rub down, scrape, file, grind, chip, shave, shear.

Adj. contracting etc. *v.*; astringent; shrunk, contracted etc. *v.*; strangulated, tabid, wizened, stunted, tabescent; marasmic; waning etc. *v.*; neap; compact; shriveled, preshrunk.

unexpanded etc. (expand etc. 194); inswept; contractile; compressible; smaller etc. small etc. 193).

196. Distance.—N. distance; space etc. 180; remoteness, farness; far- cry to; longinquity, elongation; offing, background; removedness; parallax; reach, span, stride; drift.

out-post, -skirt; horizon, sky-line; aphelion; foreign parts, *ultima Thule*, *ne plus ultra*, antipodes; long range, giant's stride.

dispersion etc. 73.

V. be -distant etc. *adj.*; extend –, stretch –, reach –, spread –, go –, get –, stretch away- to; range, outrange, outreach.

remain at a distance; keep –, stand- -away, – off, – aloof, – clear of.

Adj. distant; far -off, away; remote, telescopic, distal, wide of; stretching to etc. *v.*; yon, -der; ulterior; trans-marine, -pontine, -atlantic, -pacific, -continental, -polar, -equatorial, -alpine; tramontane; ultra-montane, -mundane; hyperborean, antihodean; inaccessible, out of the way; unapproached, -able; incontiguous.

Adv. far -off, – away; afar, -off; off; away; a -long, – great, – good- way off; wide away, aloof; wide –, clear- of; out of -the way, – reach; abroad, yonder, farther, further, beyond; *outre mer*, over the border, far and wide, over the hills and far away; from pole to pole etc. (*over great space*) 180; to the -uttermost parts, – ends- of the earth; out of -hearing, – range, nobody knows where, *à perte de vue*, out of the sphere of, wide of the mark; a far cry to.

apart, asunder; wide -apart, – asunder; *longo intervallo*; at arm's length.

197. Nearness.—N. nearness etc. *adj.*; proximity, propinquity; vicinity, -age; neighborhood, adjacency; contiguity etc. 199.

short -distance, – step, – cut; earshot, close quarters, brief span; stone's throw; bow –, gun –, pistol- shot; hair's breadth, span; close-up.

purlieus, neighborhood, vicinage, *environs*, *alentours*, suburbs, confines, *banlieue*, borderland; whereabouts.

bystander; neighbor, borderer.

approach etc. 286; convergence etc. 290; perihelion.

V. be -near etc. *adj.*; adjoin, hang about, trench on; border-, verge upon; stand by, approximate, tread on the heels of, cling to, clasp, hug; cuddle, huddle; hang about the skirts of, hover over; burn; abut.

bring –, draw- -near etc. 286; converge etc. 290; crowd etc. 72; place -side by side etc. *adv.*

Adj. near, nigh; close-, near- at hand; close, neighboring, propinquent, bordering upon; adjacent, adjoining, limitrophe; proxim-ate, -al; at hand, handy; near the mark, near run; home, intimate.

Adv. near, nigh; hard –, fast- by; close -to, upon, – up; at the point of; next door to; within -reach, – call, – hearing, – earshot, – range; within an ace of; but a step, not far from, at no great distance; on the -verge, – brink, – skirts- of; in the -environs etc. *n.*; at one's -door, – feet, – elbow, – finger's end, – side; on the tip of one's tongue; under one's nose; within a -stone's throw etc. *n.*; in -sight, – presence- of; at close quarters; cheek by -jole, – jowl; beside, alongside, side by side, *tête-à-tête*; in juxtaposition etc. (*touching*) 199; yard-arm to yard-arm; at the heels of; on the confines of, at the threshold, bordering upon, verging to; in the way.

about; here-, there-abouts; rougly, in round

numbers; approxim- -ately, – atively; as good as, well nigh.

198. Interval.—N. interval, interspace; separation etc. 44; break gap, opening; hole etc. 260; chasm, *hiatus,* caesura; inter-ruption,-regnum; interstice, *lacuna,* cleft, mesh, crevice, chink, rime, creek, cranny, crack, chap, slit, slot, fissure, scissure, rift, flaw, breach, fracture, rent, gash, cut, leak, dike, ha-ha.

gorge, defile, ravine, canon, *crevasse,* abyss, abysm; gulf; inlet, frith, strait, gully, gulch, nullah; pass; notch; furrow etc. 259; yawning gulf; *hiatus - maxime, – valde- deflendus*; parenthesis etc. (*interjacence*) 228; void etc. (*absence*) 187; incompleteness etc. 530.

V. gape etc. (*open*) 260; part, remove.

Adj. with an interval, far between; separated, spaced, split.

Adv. at intervals etc. (*discontinuously*) 70; *longo intervallo.*

199. Contiguity.—N. contiguity, contact, proximity, apposition, juxtaposition, touching etc. *v.*; abutment, osculation; meeting, appulse, appulsion, *rencontre,* rencounter, syzygy, coincidence, conjunction, coexistence; adhesion etc. 46.

border-land; frontier etc. (*limit*) 233; tangent.

V. be -contiguous etc. *adj.*; join, adjoin, abut on, march with, border; tick, graze, touch, meet, osculate, kiss, come in contact; coincide; coexist; adhere etc. 46.

Adj. contiguous; touching etc. *v.*; in -contact etc. *n.*, conterminous, end to end, osculatory; pertingent; tangential.

hand to hand; close to etc. (*near*) 197; with no - interval etc. 198.

200. Length.—N. length, longitude, span, extent, mileage.

line, bar, rule, stripe, streak, spoke, radius.

lengthening etc. *v.*; pro-longation, -duction, - traction; ten-sion, -sure; extension.

[Measures of length] line, nail, inch, hand, palm, foot, cubit, yard, ell, fathom, rod, pole, perch, furlong, mile, league; chain, meter, kilo-, centi-, milli- etc meter.

pedometer, perambulator, odometer, odograph, speedometer, cyclometer, log, telemeter, range finder; scale etc. (*measurement*) 466.

V. be -long etc. *adj.*; stretch out, sprawl; extend –, reach –, stretch -to; make a long arm, 'drag its slow length along.'

render -long etc. *adj.*; lengthen, extend, elongate; stretch; pro-long, -duce, -tract; let –, pay –, draw –, spin- out; drawl.

enfilade, look along, view in perspective.

Adj. long, -some; lengthy, lank, wiredrawn, outstretched; stretched, drawn out, lengthened etc. *v.*; sesquipedalian etc. (*words*) 577; interminable, no end of.

line-ar, -al; longitudinal, oblong.

as long as -my arm, –to-day and to-morrow; unshortened etc. (shorten etc. 201).

Adv. lengthwise, at length, longitudinally, endlong, along; *tandem*; in a line etc. (*continuously*) 69; in perspective.

from -end to end; –stem to stern, –head to foot, –the crown of the head to the sole of the foot, – top to toe, –head to heels; fore and aft.

201. Shortness.—N. shortness etc. *adj.*; brevity; littleness etc. 193; a span.

shortening etc. *v.*; abbrevia-tion, -ture; abridgment, concision, retrenchment, curtailment, decurtation; reduction etc. (*contraction*) 195; epitome etc. (*compendium*) 596.

abridger, abstractor, epitomiser.

elision, ellipsis; conciseness etc. (*in style*) 572.

V. be -short etc. *adj.*; render -short etc. *adj.*; shorten, curtail, abridge, abbreviate, take in, reduce; compress etc. (*contract*) 195; epitomize etc. 596.

retrench, cut short, obtruncate; scrimp, cut, chop up, hack, hew; cut –, pare- down; clip, snip, dock, lop, prune; shear, shave, mow, reap, crop; snub; truncate, pollard, stunt, nip, nip in the bud, check the growth of; [in drawing] foreshorten.

Adj. short, brief, curt; compendious, compact; stubby, scrimp; shorn, stubbed; stumpy, thickset, podgy, stocky, pug; squab, -by; squat, dumpy; little etc. 193; curtailed of its fair proportions; short by; oblate; concise etc. 572; summary.

Adv. shortly etc. *adj.*; in short etc. (*concisely*) *572.*

202. Breadth. Thickness.—N. breadth, width, latitude, amplitude; diameter, bore, calibre, radius; superficial extent etc. (*space*) 180.

thickness, crassitude; corpulence etc. (*size*) 192; dilatation etc. (*expansion*) 194.

V. be -broad etc. *adj.*; become –, render- - broad etc. *adj.*; expand etc. 194; thicken, widen.

Adj. broad, wide, ample, extended; discous; fanlike; out-spread, -stretched; wide as a church-door.

thick, dumpy, squab, squat, thickset, tubby; thick as a rope, stubby etc. 201.

203. Narrowness. Thinness.—N. narrowness etc. *adj.*; closeness, exility; exiguity etc. (*little*) 193.

line; hair's –, finger's -breadth; strip, streak, vein.

thinness etc. *adj.*; tenuity; emaciation, slenderness, macilency, *marcor.*

shaving, slip etc. (*filament*) 205; threadpaper, skeleton, shadow, scrag, anatomy, spindle-shanks, barebones, lantern jaws, mere skin and bone.

middle construction, stricture, neck, waist, isthmus, wasp, hour-glass; ridge, *ghaut*, pass; ravine etc. 198.

narrowing, coarctation, angustation, tapering; contraction etc. 195.

V. be-narrow etc. *adj.*; narrow, taper, diminish, contract etc. 195; render -narrow etc. *adj.*

Adj. narrow, close; slender, thin, fine; *svelte;* thread-like etc. (*filament*) 205; finespun, taper, slim, gracile, slight, slight-made; scant, -y; spare, delicate, incapacious; contracted etc. 195; unexpanded etc. (expand etc. 194); slender as a thread, capillary.

emaciated, lean, meager, gaunt, macilent; lank, -y; weedy, skinny, scrawny, scraggy; starv-ed, -eling; attenuated, shrivelled; wizened, pinched, peaky, skeletal, spindling, spindle- -legged, -shanked; extenuated, tabid, marcid, bare-bone, raw-boned; herring-gutted; worn to a shadow, lean as a rake; thin as a -lath,—whipping post,—wafer; hatchet-faced; lantern-jawed.

204. Layer.—N. layer, stratum, course, bed, zone, *substratum*, floor, flag, stage, story, tier, slab, escarpment, table, tablet, panel, plaque; board, plank; trencher, platter.

plate; lam-ina, -ella; sheet, flake, foil, wafer, scale, coat, peel, pellicle, ply, thickness, membrane, film, leaf, slice, shive, cut, rasher, shaving, integument etc. (*covering*) 223.

V. slice, shave, pare, peel; plate, coat, veneer; cover etc. 223.

Adj. lamell-ar, -ated, -iform; laminated, -iferous; micaceous; schist-ose, -ous; scaly; filmy, membranous, flaky, squamous; folia-ted, -ceous; stratified, -form; tabular, discoid, spathic.

205. Filament.—N. filament, line; fiber, fibril; funicle, vein, hair, capillament, *cilium*, tendril, gossamer; hair-stroke; harl.

wire, string, thread, packthread, cotton, sewing-silk, twine, twist, whip-cord, cord, rope, cable, yarn, hemp, oakum, jute, wool, worsted.

strip, shred, slip, spill, list, band, fillet, *fascia*, ribbon, riband, tape, roll, lath, slat, strake, splinter, shiver, shaving.

beard etc. (*roughness*) 256; ramification; strand.

Adj. fil-amentous, -aceous, -iform; fibr-ous, -illous; thread-like, wiry, stringy, ropy; capill-ary, -iform; funicular, wire-drawn; anguilliform; flagelliform; hairy etc. (*rough*) 256; ligulate.

206. Height.—N. height, altitude, elevation, ceiling; eminence, pitch; loftiness etc. *adj.*; sublimity.

tallness etc. *adj.*; stature, procerity; prominence etc. 250.

colossus etc. (*size*) 192; giant, grenadier, giraffe.

mount, -ain; hill, butte, monticle, fell, knap; cape; head-, fore-land; promontory; ridge, hog's back, dune; rising —, vantage- ground; down; moor, -land; Alp; up-, table-, high-lands; heights etc. (*summit*) 210; knoll, hummock, hillock, barrow, mound, mole, *kopje*; steeps, bluff, cliff, craig, tor, peak, pike, clough; escarpment, edge, ledge, brae; dizzy height.

tower, pillar, column, pylon, obelisk, monument, steeple, spire, minaret, *campanile*, belfry, turret, roof, dome, cupola, pagoda, pyramid; sky scraper; Eiffel tower.

pole, pikestaff, maypole, flagstaff; mast, top—, topgallant- mast.

ceiling etc. (*covering*) 223.

high water; high—, flood—, spring-tide.

altimetry etc. (*angle*) 244; altimeter, height-finder, hypsometer, barograph.

V. be -high etc. *adj.*; tower, soar, command; hover; cap, culminate; overhang, hang over, impend, beetle; bestride, ride, mount; perch, surmount; cover etc. 233; overtop etc. (*be superior*) 33; stand on tiptoe.

become -high etc. *adj.*; grow, — higher, — taller; upgrow; rise etc. (*ascend*) 305.

render -high etc. *adj.*; heighten etc. (*elevate*) 307.

Adj. high, elevated, eminent, exalted, lofty, supernal; tall; gigantic etc. (*big*) 192; Patagonian; towering, beetling, soaring, hanging [gardens]; elevated etc. 307; upper; highest etc. (*topmost*) 210; monticulous, perching, hill-dwelling.

up-, moor-land; hilly, mountainous, alpine, subalpine, heaven-kissing; cloud-topt, -capt, -touching; aerial.

overhanging etc. *v.*; incumbent, overlying; super-incumbent, -natant, -imposed; prominent etc. 250.

tall as a -maypole, —poplar,—steeple; lanky etc. (*thin*) 203.

Adv. on high, high up, aloft, up, above, aloof, overhead; up—, above- stairs; in the clouds; on -tiptoe, —stilts,—the shoulders of; over head and ears; breast high.

over, upwards; from top to bottom etc. (*completely*) 52.

207. Lowness.—N. lowness etc. *adj.*; debasement, depression; prostration etc. (*horizontal*) 213; depression etc. (*concave*) 252.

molehill; lowlands; bottomlands; basement-ground-floor; *rez de chaussée* etc. 211; hold; feet, heels.

low water; low—, ebb—, neap—, spring- tide.

V. be -low etc. *adj.*; lie -low, —flat; underlie; crouch, slouch, wallow, grovel; lower etc. (*depress*) 308.

Adj. low, neap, debased; nether, -most; flat, level with the ground; lying low etc. *v.*; crouched, subjacent, squat, prostrate etc. (*horizontal*) 213.

Adv. under; be-, under-neath; below; down, -wards; adown, at the foot of; under-foot, -ground; down—, below-stairs; at a low ebb; below par.

208. Depth.—N. depth; deepness etc. *adj.*; profundity, depression etc. (*concavity*) 252.

hollow, pit, shaft, well, crater, abyss; gulf etc. 198; bowels of the earth, bottomless pit, hell.

soundings, sonar, depth of water, water, draught, submersion; plummet, sound, probe; sounding -rod, — line, — machine; lead; submarine, diving bell, bathysphere; diver.

V. be -deep etc. *adj.*; render -deep etc. *adj.*; deepen.

plunge etc. 310; sound, heave the lead, take soundings; dig etc. (*excavate*) 252.

Adj. deep, -seated; profound, sunk, buried; submerged etc. 310; sub-aqueous, -marine, -terranean, -terrene; underground.

bottom-, sound-, fathom-less; unfathom-ed, -able; abysmal; deep as a well, deep-sea.

knee-, ankle-deep.

Adv. beyond—, out of- one's depth; over head and ears, over one's head.

209. Shallowness.—N. shallowness etc. *adj.*; shoals; mere scratch; veneer, gloss, pinprick.

Adj. shallow, superficial; skin—, ankle—, knee-deep; just enough to wet one's feet; shoal, -y.

V. shallow, shoal, skim— over, —the surface, touch on.

210. Summit.—N. summit, -y; top, vertex, apex, zenith, pinnacle, acme, acropolis, culmination, meridian, utmost height, *ne plus ultra,* height, pitch, maximum, climax, apogee; culminating —, crowning —, turning- point; turn of the tide, fountain head; water-shed, -parting; sky, pole.

tip, -top; crest, crow's nest, cap, truck, peak, nib; end etc. 67; crown, brow; head, nob, noddle, pate, skull, cranium.

high places, heights.

top-, top-gallant mast, sky scraper; quarter —, hurricane- deck.

architrave, frieze, cornice, coping, coping-stone, zoophorus, capital, headpiece, capstone, epistyle, sconce, pediment, entablature; tympanum; ceiling etc. (*covering*) 223.

attic, loft, garret, house-top, upper story, roof.

topping, icing, frosting.

V. culminate, cap, crown, top; overtop etc. (*be superior to*) 33.

Adj. highest etc. (high etc. 206); top; top-, up-per-most; tip-top; culminating etc. *v.*; meridi-an, -onal; capital, head, polar, supreme, supernal, top-gallant.

Adv. a-top, at the top of — the tree, — the heap.

211. Base.—N. base, -ment; plinth, dado, wainscot, baseboard; foundation etc. (*support*) 215; substructure, *sub · stratum,* sump, ground, earth, pavement, floor, paving, flag, carpet, ground-floor, deck; footing, groundwork, basis; hold, bilge, orlop deck

bottom, nadir, foot, sole, toe, hoof, keel, kelson, root.

Adj. bottom; under-, nether-most; fundamental; founded —, based —, grounded —, built- on.

212. Verticality.—N. verticality; erectness etc. *adj.*; perpendicularity; right angle, normal; azimuth circle.

wall, palisade, precipice, cliff, steep, bluff.

elevation, erection; square, plumb-line, plummet.

V. be -vertical etc. *adj.*; stand -up, — on end, — erect, — upright; stick —, cock-up.

render -vertical etc. *adj.*; set —, stick —, raise —, cock- up; erect, rear, raise, pitch, raise on its legs.

Adj. vertical, upright, erect, perpendicular, normal, plumb, straight, bolt upright; rampant; straight —, standing- up etc. *v.*; rectangular, orthogonal.

Adv. vertically etc. *adj.*; up, on end; up —, right- on end; *à plomb*, endwise; on one's legs; at right angles.

213. Horizontality.—N. horizontality; flatness; level, plane; stratum etc. 204; dead -level, — flat; level plane.

recumbency; lying down etc. *v.*; reclination, decumbence; de-, discumbency; proneness etc. *adj.*; accubation, supination, resupination, prostration; azimuth.

plain, floor, platform, bowling-green; cricket-ground; court; gridiron; base-ball diamond; hockey rink; tennis-, croquet-ground, — lawn; billiard table; terrace, estrade, esplanade, *parterre,* table-land, *plateau,* ledge.

spirit-, level; T-square.

V. be -horizontal etc. *adj.*; lie, recline, couch; lie -down, — flat, — prostrate; sprawl, loll; sit down.

render -horizontal etc. *adj.*; lay, — down, — out; level, flatten, even, raze, equalize, smooth, align; prostrate, knock down, floor, fell, ground.

Adj. horizontal, level, even, plane; flat etc. 251; flat as a -billiard table, — bowling green; alluvial; calm, — as a mill-pond; smooth, —as glass.

re-, de-, pro-, ac-cumbent; lying etc. *v.*; prone, supine, couchant, jacent, prostrate.

Adv. horizontally etc. *adj.*; on -one's back, —all fours, — its beam ends.

214. Pendency.—N. pend-, dependency; suspension, hanging etc. *v.*

pendant, drop, tippet, tassel, lobe, tail, train, flap, lappet, skirt, pig-tail, queue, pendulum, hanger, suspender, supporter.

peg, knob, button, hook, nail, stud, ring, staple, tenterhook; davit; fastening etc. 45; spar, horse.

chande-, gase-, electro-lier.

V. be -pendent etc. *adj.*; hang, depend, swing, dangle, droop, sag; swag; daggle, flap, trail, flow.

suspend, hang, sling, hook up, hitch, fasten to, append.

Adj. pend-ent, -ulous; pensile; hanging etc. *v.*; dependent; suspended etc. *v.*; lowering, overhanging, beetling, decumbent; loose, flowing.

having a -peduncle etc. *n.*; pedunculate, tailed, caudate.

215. Support.—N. support, backing, ground, foundation, base, basis; *terra firma*; bearing, fulcrum, *point d'appui*, caudex, purchase, footing, hold, *-locus standi*; landing, — stage, — place; stage, platform; block; rest, resting-place; ground-work, *substratum*, sustentation, subvention; floor etc. (*basement*) 211.

supporter; aid etc. 707; prop, stand, anvil, fulciment; hod, stay, shore, skid, rib, sprag, truss, bandage; sleeper; stirrup, stilts, shoe, sole, heel, splint, lap; bar, rod, boom, sprit, outrigger.

staff, stick, crutch, alpenstock, bourdon; *bâton*, maulstick, colstaff, cowlstaff, staddle; stalk, pedicel, -icle, — uncle.

post, pillar, shaft, column, pilaster; pediment, pedestal; plinth, shank, leg, socle, zocle; buttress, jamb, mullion, abutment; pile, baluster, banister, stanchion, king post; balustrade.

frame, -work, body, *chassis*, *fuselage*; scaffold, skeleton, beam, rafter, girder, lintel, joist, cantilever, travis, trave, corner-stone, summer, transom; rung, round, step, sill.

columella, back-bone; key-stone; axle, -tree; axis; arch, ogive, mainstay

trunnion, pivot, rowlock; peg etc. (*pendency*)

214; tie-beam etc. (*fastening*) 45; thole pin.

board, ledge, shelf, hob, bracket, trevet, trivet, arbor, rack, hatrack; mantel, -piece, -shelf; slab, console; counter, dresser; flange, corbel; table, trestle, teapoy; shoulder; perch; horse; easel, desk; retable, predella.

seat, throne, dais; divan, musnud; chair, bench, form, stool, camp-stool, sofa, settee, davenport, stall, miserere, arm —, easy —, elbow —, rocking-chair; couch, day bed, *fauteuil*, woolsack, ottoman, settle, squab, bench, box, dicky; saddle, pannel, pillion; side —, pack- saddle; pommel.

bed, berth, pallet, tester, crib, cot, bassinet, hammock, shakedown, camp bed, bunk, truckle-bed, cradle, litter, stretcher, bedstead; four-poster, French bed; bedding, mattress, *paillasse;* pillow, bolster; mat, rug, cushion.

stool, footstool, hassock, faldstool, *prie-dieu*; tabouret; tripod.

Atlas, Persides, Atlantes, Caryatides, Hercules.

V. be -supported etc.; lie —, sit —, recline —, lean —, loll —, rest —, stand —, step —, repose —, abut —, beat —, be based etc.- on; have at one's back; be-stride, -straddle.

support, bear, carry, hold, sustain, shoulder; hold —, back —, bolster —, shore- up; up-hold, -bear; prop; under-prop,-pin, -set; bandage, etc. 43; brace, truss; cradle, pillow.

give —, furnish —, afford —, supply —, lend- -support, — foundations; bottom, found, base, ground, embed.

maintain, keep on foot; aid etc. 707.

Adj. support-ing, -ed, etc.*v.*; atlantean, columellar; sustentative, fundamental, basal.

Adv. astride on, astraddle; pick-a-back.

216. Parallelism.—N. parallelism; coextension, concentricity, collimation.

V. be —, lie- parallel to; collimate; equate, match.

Adj. parallel; coextensive, collateral, concentric, concurrent, abreast, aligned.

Adv. alongside, abreast etc. (*laterally*) 236.

217. Obliquity.—N. obliquity, inclination, skew, slope, slant; crookedness etc. *adj.*; slopeness; leaning etc. *v.*; bevel, bezel, ramp, tilt; bias, list, twist, warp, swag, cant, lurch; distortion etc. 243; bend etc. (*curve*) 245; tower of Pisa.

acclivity, rise, ascent, grade, gradient, *glacis*, rising ground, hill, bank, declivity, downhill, dip, fall, devexity; gentle —, rapid- slope; easy -ascent, —descent; shelving beach; *talus; montagne Russe; facilis descensus Averni.*

steepness etc. *adj.*; cliff, precipice etc. (*vertical*) 212; escarpment, scarp.

[Measure of inclination]clinometer, theodolite, level, sextant, quadrant, protractor; angle, sine, cosine, tangent etc. hypothenuse.

diagonal; zigzag, chevron.

V. be -oblique etc. *adj.*; slope, slant, lean, incline, shelve, stoop, decline, descent, bend, heel, careen, sag, swag, seel, slouch, cant, sidle.

render -oblique etc. *adj.*; sway, bias; slope, slant; incline, bend, crook; cant, tilt; distort etc. 243.

Adj. oblique, inclined; sloping etc. *v.*; tilted etc. *v.*; recumbent, clinal, skew, askew, slant, aslant, bias, plagiedral, indirect, wry, awry, ajee, crooked; knock-kneed etc. (*distorted*) 243; bevel, out of the perpendicular.

uphill, rising, ascending, acclivous; downhill, falling, descending; declining, declivous, devex, anticlinal; steep, abrupt, precipitous, breakneck.

diagonal; trans-verse, -versal; athwart, antiparallel; curved etc. 245.

Adv. obliquely etc. *adj.*; on —, all on- one side; askew, askant, askance, aslope, asquint, edgewise, at an angle; side-long, -ways; slope-, slant-wise; by a side wind.

218. Inversion.—N. in-, e-, sub-, re-, retro-, intro-version; contraposition etc. 237; contrariety etc. 14; reversal; turn of the tide.

overturn; upset, capsize; somer-sault, -set; summerset; *culbute*; revulsion; *pirouette.*

transposition, transposal, anastrophy, *metastasis, hyperbaton, anastrophe, hysteron--proteron,* hypallage, *synchysis, tmesis,* parenthesis; *metathesis*; palindrome; Spoonerism.

pronation and supination.

V. be -inverted etc.; turn —, go —, wheel- -round, — about, — to the right about; turn —, go —, tilt —, topple-over; capsize, turn turtle.

in-, sub-, retro-, intro-vert; reverse; up-, overturn, -set; turn -topsy turvy etc. *adj.*; *culbuter*; transpose, put the cart before the horse, turn the tables.

Adj. inverted etc. *v.*; wrong side -out, — up; inside out, upside down; bottom —, keel- upwards; supine, on one's head, topsy turvy, *sens dessus sens dessous.*

inverse; reverse etc. (*contrary*) 14; opposite etc. 237.

topheavy, unstable.

Adv. inversely etc.*adj.*; hirdie-girdie; heels over head, head over heels.

219. Crossing.—N. crossing etc. *v.*; intersection, — lacement, — twinement, -digitation; decussation, transversion; convolution etc. 248.

reticulation, meshwork, network; inosculation, anastomosis, inter-texture, mortise.

net, *plexux*, web, mesh, twill, skein, sleeve, felt, lace; wicker; mat, -ting; plait, trellis, wattle, lattice, grating, *grille*, gridiron, tracery, fretwork, filigree, reticle; tissue, netting, mokes.

cross, crucifix, rood, crisscross, crux; chain, wreath, braid, cat's cradle,knot; entanglement etc. (*disorder*) 59.

[woven fabrics] cloth, linen, muslin, cambric, drill, homespun, tweed, broadcloth etc.

V. cross, decussate; inter-sect, -lace, -twine, -twist, -weave, -digitate, -link.

twine, entwine, weave, inweave, twist, wreathe; anastomose, inosculate, dovetail, splice, link.

mat, plait, plat, braid, felt, twill; tangle, entangle, ravel; net, knot; dishevel, raddle.

Adj. crossing etc.*v.*; crossed, matted etc. *v.*; transverse.

cross, cruciform, crucial; reti-form, -cular, -culated; areolar, cancellated, mullioned, latticed, grated, barred, streaked; textile, secant, plexal; interfretted.

Adv. across, thwart, athwart, transversely, crosswise.

220. Exteriority.—N. exteriority; outside, exterior; surface, superficies; skin etc. (*covering*) 223; *superstratum*; disk, disc; face, facet, external, the open.

excentricity; circumjacence etc. 227.

V. be -exterior etc. *adj.*; lie around etc. 227.

place -exteriorly, — outwardly, — outside; put —, turn- out.

Adj. exter-ior, -nal; extraneous, outer, -most; out-ward, -lying, -side, -door; round about etc. 227; extramural.

superficial, skin-deep; frontal, discoid.

extraregarding; eccentric; outstanding; extrinsic etc. 6.

Adv. externally etc. *adj.*; out, without, over, outwards, *ab extra*, out of doors; *extra muros*.

in the open air; *sub -Jovè, — dio; à la belle étoile, al fresco.*

221. Interiority.—N. interiority; inside, -land, interior, endocrine; interspace, subsoil, *substratum*.

contents etc. 190; substance, pith, marrow; backbone etc. (*center*) 222; heart, bosom, breast, abdomen; vitals, viscera, entrails, bowels, belly, intestines, guts, chitterlings, womb, lap; gland, cell; internal organs, *penetralia*, recesses, innermost recesses; cave etc. (*concavity*) 252.

inhabitant etc. 188.

V. be -inside etc. *adj.*, — within etc. *adv.*

place —, keep- within; enclose etc. (*circumscribe*) 229; intern; embed etc. (*insert*) 300.

Adj. inter-ior, -nal; inner, inside, intimate, inward, intraregarding; in-, inner-most; deep-seated; visceral, intestine, -tinal; inland; subcutaneous; interstitial etc. (*interjacent*) 228; inwrought etc. (*intrinsic*) 5; enclosed etc. *v.*

home, domestic, indoor, intramural, vernacular; endemic.

Adv. internally etc. *adj.*; inwards, within, in, inly; here-, there-, where-in; *ab intra*, withinside; in —, within- doors; at home, in the bosom of one's family.

222. Centrality.—N. centrality, centricalness, center; middle etc. 68; focus etc. 74.

core, kernel; nucleus, nucleolus; heart, pole, axis, pivot, fulcrum, bull's eye; hub, nave, navel; *umbilicus*, spine, backbone, marrow, pith; hot-bed; concentration etc. (*convergence*) 290; centralization; symmetry.

center of -gravity, — pressure, — percussion, — oscillation, — buoyancy etc. metacenter.

V. be -central etc. *adj.*; converge etc. 290.

render central, centralize, concentrate; bring to a focus.

Adj. centr-al, -ical; middle etc. 68; axial, pivotal, focal, umbilical, concentric; middlemost, nuclear, centric, centraidal; spinal, vertebral.

Adv. middle; midst; centrally etc. *adj.*

223. Covering.—N. covering, cover; canopy, tilt, awning, baldachin, tent, marquee, *tente d'abri*, umbrella, parasol, sunshade; veil (*shade*) 424; shield etc. (*defense*) 717; hall.

roof, dome, cupola, mansard roof; ceiling; thatch, tile; pan-, pen-tile; tiling, shingles, slates, slating, leads; shed etc. (*abode*) 189.

top, lid, coverele, door, *operculum*, eyelid, blind, curtain.

bandage, plaster, lint, wrapping, dossil, finger stall.

coverlet, counterpane, sheet, quilt, comforter, eiderdown; tarpaulin, blanket, rug, drugget, linoleum, oilcloth; housing.

in-, tegument; skin, pellicle, fleece, fell, fur, ermine, miniver, sable, sealskin etc.; fabrikoid; leather, morocco, calf, pigskin, elk, kid, cowhide etc.; shagreen, hide; pelt, -ry; cuticle, *dermis*, scarf-skin, *epidermis*.

clothing etc. 225; mask etc. (*concealment*) 530.

peel, crust, bark, rind, *cortex*, husk, shell, coat.

capsule; ferrule; sheath, -ing; pod, cod; casing, case, theca; *elytron; involucrum;* wrapp-ing, -er, cellophane; envelope, vesicle; dermatology, conchology.

armor, -plate, armoring; veneer, facing; pavement; scale etc. (*layer*) 204; coating, paint, stain; varnish etc. (*resin*) 356*a*; anointing etc. *v.*; inunction; incrustation, superposition, obduction, ground, enamel, whitewash, plaster, stucco, rough cast, pebble dash, compo; rendering; cerement; ointment etc. (*grease*) 356.

V. cover; super-pose, -impose; over-lay, -spread; wrap etc. 225; incase; face, case, veneer, pave, paper; tip, cap, bind, revet.

coat, paint, varnish, pay, incrust, stucco, cement, dab, plaster, tar; wash; be-, smear; be-, daub; anoint, do over; gild, plate, electroplate, japan, laquer, lacker, enamel, whitewash; lay it on thick.

over-lie, -arch; conceal etc. 528.

Adj. covering etc. *v.*; cutaneous, dermal, cortical, cuticular, tegumentary, skinny, scaly, squamous; covered etc. *v.*; imbricated, loricated, armor-plated, iron-clad; under cover, hooded, cloaked, cowled.

224. Lining.—N. lining, inner coating; coating etc. (*covering*) 223; stalactite, -agmite.

filling, stuffing, wadding, padding, bushing.

wainscot, *parietes*, wall brattice.

V. line, stuff, incrust, wad, pad, fill.

Adj. lined etc. *v.*

225. Investment.—N. investment; covering etc. 223; dress, clothing, raiment, drapery, costume, attire, guise, toilet, *toilette*, trim; habiliment; vesture, -ment; garment, garb, palliament, apparel, wardrobe, wearing apparel, clothes, things.

array; tailoring, millinery; best bib and tucker; finery etc. (*ornament*) 847; full dress etc. (*show*) 882; garniture; theatrical properties.

outfit, equipment, *trousseau*; uniform, khaki, regimentals; academicals, canonicals etc. 999; livery, gear, harness, turn out, accoutrement, caparison, suit, rigging, trappings, traps, slops, togs, toggery; masquerade.

dishabille, morning dress, lounge suit, tea-gown, *kimono*, *négligé*, dressing-gown, *peignoir*, wrapper, undress; shooting-coat; smoking jacket, mufti; rags, tatters, old clothes; mourning, weeds; duds; slippers.

robe, tunic, dolman, *paletot*, habit, gown, coat, coatee, frock, blouse, *pelisse*, middy, sagum, *toga*, smock-frock; frock-, dress-, morning-, tail- coat; dress-suit, — clothes, swallow-tail coat, dinner-, Eton-jacket.

cloak, pall; mantle, mantlet, mantua, shawl, *pelisse*, veil, yashmak; cape, tippet, kirtle, plaid, muffler, comforter, Balaclava helmet, haik, huke, chlamys, mantilla, tabard, housing, horse-cloth, burnous, *roquelaure*, *houppelande*; sur-, top-, over-, great-coat; *surtout*, spencer, cardigan, sweater, blazer; mackintosh, waterproof, slicker, raincoat, oilskin, trench coat, ulster, monkey-, pea-, pilot-jacket, redingote; wraprascal, poncho, cardinal, pelerine, talma.

jacket, jumper, vest, jerkin, waistcoat, doublet, *camisole*, gabardine; stays, *corsage*, corset, corselet, bodice; stomacher; skirt, petticoat, slip, farthingale, kilt, jupe, crinoline, bustle, hobble skirt, *panier*, apron, pinafore; loin cloth.

trousers; breeches, trews, pantaloons, unmentionables, inexpressibles, overalls, pajamas, smalls, small-clothes; tights, pants, shorts, drawers; knickerbockers, knickers, plus fours, bloomers, divided skirt; phil-, fill-ibeg.

head-dress, -gear; cap, *béret*, tam o' shanter, glengarry, topee, sombrero; hat; cocked —, high —, tall —, top —, silk —, opera —, crush - hat, *gibus*, beaver, castor, bonnet, tile, wideawake, billy-cock; bowler; soft felt —, straw —, leghorn- hat, panama; toque; wimple; night-, mob-, skull-cap, biretta; hood, cowl, coif; capote, calach; scull-cap; kerchief, snood; head, *coiffure*; crown etc. (*circle*) 247; *chignon*, pelt, wig, front, peruke, periwig; caftan, turban, fez, *tarboosh*, taj, shako, csako, busby; *képi*, forage cap, bearskin; helmet etc. 717; mask, domino.

body clothes, linen; shirt, sark, smock, shift, *chemise*, *lingerie*; night-gown, -shirt; bed-gown, *sac de nuit*; jersey, guernsey; underclothing, -waistcoat.

neck-erchief, -cloth; tie, ruff, collar, cravat, stock, handkerchief, bandana, scarf; bib, tucker; dicky; boa; girdle etc. (*circle*) 247; cummerbund.

shoe, pump, brogue, boot, slipper, sandal, galoche, galoshes, arctics, rubber boots, overshoes, patten, clog, sabot; high-low; Blucher —, Wellington —, Hessian —, jack —, top- boot; Balmoral; legging, puttee, buskin, greave, galligaskin, moccasin, *gamache*, gambado, gaiter, spatter-dash, spat, antigropeles; stocking, hose, gaskins, trunk-hose, sock, hosiery.

glove, gauntlet, mitten, cuff, muffettee, wristband, sleeve.

swaddling cloth, baby-linen, *layette*; pocket-handkerchief.

shroud, etc. 363.

clothier, tailor, milliner, *costumier*, sempstress, seamstress, snip; dress-, habit-, breeches-, shoemaker; cordwainer, cobbler, Crispin, hosier, hatter; draper, linendraper, haberdasher, mercer.

V. invest; cover etc. 223; envelop, lap, involve; in-, en-wrap; wrap; fold —, wrap —, lap —, muffle-up; overlap; sheathe, swathe, swaddle, roll up in, shroud, circumvest.

vest, clothe, array, dress, dight, drape, robe, enrobe, attire, tire, garb, habilitate, apparel, accouter, rig, fit out; bedizen, deck etc. (*ornament*) 847; perk; equip, harness, caparison; dress up, wear; don; put —, huddle —, slip- on; mantle.

Adj. invested etc. *v.*; habited; dight, -ed; clad, *costumé*, shod, *chaussé*; *en grande tenue* etc. (*show*) 882.

sartorial.

226. Divestment.—N. divestment; taking off, stripping, removal etc. *v.*

nudity; bareness etc. *adj.*; undress; dishabille etc. 225, altogether; nu-, denu-dation; decortication, depilation, excoriation, desquamation; molting; exfoliation.

baldness, alopecia, acomia.

V. divest; uncover etc. (*cover* etc. 223); denude, bare, strip; undress, unclothe, disrobe etc. (dress, enrobe, etc. 225); uncoif; dismantle; uncase; put —, take —, cast- off; shed, doff; husk, peel, pare, decorticate, desquamate, excoriate, skin, scalp, flay, bark, expose, lay open; exfoliate, molt, mew; cast the skin.

Adj. divested etc. *v.*; bare, naked, nude; undressed, -draped, -clad, -clothed, -appareled; exposed; in dishabille; *décolleté*; bald, threadbare, ragged, callow, roofless.

in -a state of nature, — nature's garb, — buff, — native buff, — birthday suit; *in puris naturalibus*; with nothing on, stark naked; bald as a coot, bare as the back of one's hand; out at elbows; barefoot; bareback; leaf-, nap-, hairless, shaved, clean shaven, tonsured, beardless, bald-headed, acomous.

227. Circumjacence.—N. circumjacence, -ambience; environment, encompassment; atmosphere, medium; surroundings, *entourage*.

outpost; border etc. (*edge*) 231; girdle etc. (*circumference*) 230; outskirts, *boulevards*, suburbs, purlieus, precincts, *faubourgs*, *environs*, *banlieue*, neighborhood, vicinity.

V. lie -around etc. *adv.*; surround, beset, compass, encompass, environ, inclose, enclose, encircle, circle, embrace, circumvent, lap, gird; begird, girdle, engird; skirt, twine round; hem in etc. (*circumscribe*) 229; besiege, invest, blockade.

Adj. circum-jacent, -ambient, -fluent; ambient; surrounding etc. *v.*; circumferential, suburban.

Adv. around, about; without; on -every side, — all sides; right and left, all round, round about; in the neighborhood.

228. Interjacence.—N. inter-jacence, currence, -venience, -location, -digitation, penetration; permeation.

inter-jection, -polation, -lineation, -spersion, calation; embolism.

inter-vention, -ference, -position; in-, ob-trusion; insinuation; insertion etc. 300; dovetailing; infiltration; intromission.

intermedi-um, -ary; go-between, agent, middleman, medium, bodkin, intruder, interloper; parenthesis, episode; fly-leaf.

partition, *septum*, diaphragm, mid-riff; party-wall, panel, vail, bulkhead, brattice, *cloison*; half way house.

V. lie —, come —, get- between; intervene, slide in, interpenetrate, permeate.

put between, introduce, intromit, import; throw –, wedge –, edge –, jam –, worm –, foist –, run –, plough –, work- in; interpose, -ject, -calate, -polate, -line, -leave, -sperse, -weave, -lard, -digitate; let in, dovetail, splice, mortise; insinuate, smuggle; infiltrate, ingrain.

interfere, put in an oar, thrust one's nose in; intrude, obtrude; have a finger in the pie; introduce the thin end of the wedge; thrust in etc. (*insert*) 300.

Adj. inter-jacent, -current, -venient, -vening etc. *v.*, -mediate, -mediary, -calary, -sitital, -costal, -mural, -planetary, -stellar; embolismal.

parenthetical, episodic; mediterranean; intrusive; embosomed; merged, mean, middle, medium, median.

Adv. between, betwixt; 'twixt; among, -st; amid, st; 'mid, -st; in the thick of; betwixt and between; sandwich-wise; parenthetically, *obiter dictum.*

229. Circumscription.—N. circumscription, limitation, inclosure; confinement etc. (*restraint*) 751; circumvallation, encincture; envelope etc. 232.

V. circumscribe, limit, bound, confine, restrict, enclose; surround etc. 227; compass about; imprision etc. (*restrain*) 751; hedge –, wall –, rail-in; fence –, hedge- round; embar; picket, corral.

enfold, bury, incase, pack up, enshrine, inclasp; wrap up etc. (*invest*) 225; embosom.

Adj. circumscribed etc. *v.*; begirt, lapt; circumambient; buried –, immersed- in; embosomed, in the bosom of, imbedded, encysted, mewed up; imprisoned etc. 751; land-locked, in a ring fence.

230. Outline.—N. outline, circumference; perimeter, -phery; ambit, circuit, lines, *tournure, contour*, profile, *silhouette*, lineaments; bounds, coastline.

zone, belt, girth, band, baldric, zodiac, girdle, tire, cingle, clasp, girt; *cordon* etc. (*inclosure*) 232; circlet etc. 247.

V. outline, delineate, *silhouette*, circumscribe etc. 229; profile, block out.

Adj. outlined etc. *v.*; circumferential, perimetric, peripheral.

231. Edge.—N. edge, verge, brink, brow, brim, margin, border, confines, skirt, rim, felloe, felly, flange, side, mouth; jaws, chops, chaps, *fauces*; lip, muzzle.

threshold, door, porch; portal etc. (*opening*) 260; coast, shore, strand, beach, bank, wharf, quay, dock.

frame, fringe, flounce, frill, list, trimming, edging, skirting, hem, selvedge, welt; furbelow, valance, exergue.

Adj. border, marginal, skirting; labial; labiated, marginated.

232. Inclosure.—N. inclosure, enclosure, envelope; package, box, crate, case etc. (*receptacle*) 191; wrapper; girdle etc. 230.

pen, fold, croft, sty; pen-, in-, sheep--fold; paddock, pound, corral, kraal; yard, compound; net, seine net.

wall; hedge, -row; *espalier*; fence etc. (*defence*) 717; pale, paling, balustrade, rail, railing, gunwale; quickset hedge, park paling, circumvallation, *enciente*, ring fence.

barrier, barricade; gate; -way; door, hatch, *cordon*; prison etc. 752.

dike, dyke, ditch, fosse, moat, trench.

V. inclose; circumscribe etc. 229.

233. Limit.—N. limit, boundary, bounds, confine, *enclave*, term, bourn, verge, kerb-stone, curbstone, but, pale; termin-ation, -us; stint, frontier, precinct, marches.

boundary line, landmark; line of -demarcation, – circumvallation; pillars of Hercules; Rubicon, turning-point; *ne plus ultra*; sluice, flood-gate.

V.limit, bound, confine, define, circumscribe, demarcate, delimit, encompass.

Adj.definite; contermin-ate, -able, terminable, limitable; terminal, frontier, border, bordering, boundary.

Adv.thus far, – and no further.

234. Front.—N.front; fore, – part; foreground; forefront, face, disk, disc, frontage, *façade, proscenium*, facia, frontispiece; priority, anteriority; obverse [of a medal].

fore –, front- rank, first line; van, -guard; advanced guard; outpost, scout.

brow, forehead, visage, physiognomy, phiz, features, countenance, map, mug; rostrum, beak, bow, stem, prow, prore, jib, bowsprit; forecastle.

pioneer etc (*precursor*) 64; metoposcopy.

V. be –, stand- in front etc. *adj.*; front, face, confront, breast, brave; bend forwards; come to the -front, – fore.

Adj. fore, forward, anterior, front, frontal, head-on, leading, first, primary.

Adv. before; in -front, – the van, – advance; ahead, right ahead; fore-, head-most, in the foreground; before one's -face, – eyes; face to face, *vis-à-vis*.

235. Rear.—N. rear, back, posterior-ity; rear -rank, – guard; background, *hinterland*.

occiput, nape, scruff, chine; heels; tail, rump, croup, buttock, posteriors, bottom, seat, backside, scut, breech, *dorsum*, loin, dorsal –, lumbar-region; hind quarters.

stern poop, after-part, counter, postern, heel-, tail-piece, crupper.

wake; train etc. (*sequence*) 281.

reverse; other side of the shield.

V. be -behind etc. *adv.*, fall astern; bend backwards; bring up the rear; follow etc. 622; tail, shadow.

Adj. back, rear; hind, -er, -most, -ermost; postern, -erior; dorsal, after; caudal, lumbar; mizzen.

Adv. behind; in the -rear, – ruck, – background; behind one's back; at the -heels, – tail, – back- of; back to back.

after, -most, aft, abaft, astern, stern- most, aback, rear-, hind-, back-ward.

236. Laterality.—N. laterality; side, flank, beam, quarter, lee; hand; cheek, jowl, jole, wing; profile; temple, *parietes*, loin, haunch, hip.

gable, -end; broadside; lee side.

points of the compass; East, Orient, Levant; West, occident; orientation.

V. be -on one side etc. *adv.*; flank, outflank; sidle; skirt, border.

Adj. lateral, sidelong; collateral; parietal, flanking, skirting; flanked; sideling.

many-sided; multi-, bi-, tri-, quadri- lateral.

East-ern, -ward, -erly; orient, -al, auroral, Levantine; West-ern, -ward, -erly; occidental, Hesperian; equatorial.

Adv. side-ways, -long; broadside on; on one side, abreast, abeam, alongside, beside, aside; by, – the side of; side by side; cheek by jowl etc. (*near*) 197; to -windward, – leeward; laterally etc. *adj.*; right and left; on her beam ends.

237. Contraposition.—N. contraposition, opposition; polarity; inversion etc. 218; opposite side, antithesis; reverse, inverse; counterpart; antipodes; opposite poles, North and South.

V. be -opposite etc. *adj.*; subtend.

Adj. opposite; reverse, inverse; antipodal, subcontrary; fronting, facing, diametrically opposite.

Northern, Septentrional, Boreal, arctic; Southern, Austral, antarctic, polar.

Adv. over, – the way, – against; against; face to face, vis-à-vis; as poles asunder.

238. Dextrality.—N. dextrality; right, – hand; dexter, offside, starboard.

Adj. dextral, right-handed; ambidextral; dexterous, dextrorsal etc.

239. Sinistrality.—N. sinistrality; left, – hand; *sinister*, nearside, larboard, port.

Adj. sinistral, sinister, sinistrorsal etc., left-handed, sinistromanual, sinistrous.

240. Form.—N. form, figure, shape, physique; con-formation, -figuration; make, formation, frame, construction, design, cut, set, build, trim, cut of one's jib; stamp, type, cast, mold; fashion; contour etc. (*outline*) 230, structure etc. 329.

feature, lineament, outline, turn, phase etc. (*aspect*) 448; posture, attitude, *pose*.

[Science of form] morphology.

[Similarity of form] isomorphism.

forming etc. *v.*; form-, figur-, efform- ation, sculpture.

V. form, shape, figure, fashion, efform, carve, cut, chisel, hew, cast; rough-hew, -cast; sketch, block –, hammer- out; trim, lick –, put- into shape; model, knead, work up into, set, mold, sculpture; cast, stamp; built etc. (*construct*) 161.

Adj. formed etc. *v.*

[Receiving form] plastic, fictile, full- fashioned etc.

[Giving form] plasmic, etc.

[Similar in form] isomorphous etc.

241. Amorphism. [Absence of form.]—**N.** amorphism, informity, uncouthness; unlicked cub, rough diamond; *rudis indigestaque moles*; disorder etc. 59; deformity etc. 243.

disfigure-, deface-ment, deformation; mutilation.

V. [Destroy form] deface, disfigure, deform, mutilate, truncate; derange etc. 61.

Adj. shapeless, amorphous, malformed, formless; un-formed, -hewn, -fashioned, -shapen; rough, rude, Gothic, barbarous, rugged, in the rough; misshapen etc. 243.

242. Symmetry. [Regularity of form.]—**N.** symmetry, shapeliness, finish; beauty etc. 845; proportion, eurythmy, eurythmic, uniformity, parallelism; bi-, tri-, multi-lateral symmetry; centrality etc. 222.

arborescence, branching, ramification.

Adj. symmetrical, shapely, well set, finished; beautiful etc. 845; classic, chaste, severe.

regular, uniform, balanced; equal etc. 27; parallel, coextensive.

arbor-escent, -iform; dendr-iform, -oid; branching; ramous, ramose.

243. Distortion. [Irregularity of form.]—**N.** dis-, de-, con-tortion; knot, mop, warp, buckle, screw, twist; crookedness etc. (*obliquity*) 217; grimmace; deformity; mal-, malcon-formation; monstrosity, misproportion, want of symmetry, *anamorphosis*; ugliness etc. 846; teratology.

V. distort, contort, twist, warp etc. *n.*; wrest, writhe, make faces, deform, misshape.

Adj. distorted etc. *v.*; out of shape, irregular, unsymmetric, awry, wry, askew, crooked, sinuous; anamorphous; not -true, – straight; on one side, crump, deformed; mis-shapen, -begotten; mis-, ill-proportioned; ill-made; grotesque, crooked as a ram's horn; hump-, hunch-, bunch-, crook-backed; bandy; bandy-, bow-legged; bow-, knock-kneed; splay-, club-footed; taliped; round-shouldered; snub-nosed; curtailed of one's fair proportions; scalene, stumpy etc. (*short*) 201; gaunt etc. (*thin*) 203; bloated etc. 194.

Adv. all manner of ways.

244. Angularity.—N. angular-ity, -ness; aduncity; angle, cusp, bend; fold etc. 258; notch etc. 257; fork, bifurcation.

elbow, knee, knuckle, ankle, groin, crotch, crane, fluke, scythe, sickle, zigzag, kimbo.

corner, nook, recess, niche, oriel.

right angle etc. (*perpendicular*) 212; obliquity etc. 217; angle of 45 degrees, miter; acute –, obtuse –, salient –, re-entrant –, spherical –, solid –, dihedral- angle.

angular -measurement, – elevation, – distance, – velocity; trigon-, goni-ometry; altimetry; clin-, graph-, goni-ometer; theodolite; transit circle; sextant, quadrant; dichotomy.

triangle, trigon, wedge; rectangle, square, lozenge, diamond; rhomb, -us; quadr-angle, -ilateral; parallelogram; quadrature; poly-, penta-, hexa-, hepta-, octa-, deca-gon.

Platonic bodies; cube, rhomboid; tetra-, penta-, hexa-, octa-, dodeca-, icosa-hedron; prism, pyramid; parallelopiped.

V. bend, fork, bifurcate, crinkle, divaricate, branch, ramify.

Adj. angular, bent, crooked, aduncous, uncinated, aquiline, jagged, serrated; falc-iform, -ated; furcular, furcated, forked, bifurcate, crotched; zigzag; dovetailed; knock-kneed, crinkled, akimbo, kimbo, geniculated; oblique etc. 217.

fusiform, wedge-shaped, cuneiform; tri-angular, -gonal, -lateral; quadr-angular, -ilateral; rectangular, square, foursquare, multilateral; polygonal etc. *n.*; cubical, rhomboidal, pyramidal.

245. Curvature.—N. curv-ature, -ity, -ation; incurv-ity, -ation; bend; flex- ure, -ion; conflexure; crook, hook, bought, bending; de-, inflexion; arcuation, devexity, turn; deviation, *détour*, sweep; curl, -ing; bough; recurv-ity, -ation; sinuosity etc. 248; aduncity.

curve, arc, arch, arcade, vault, dome, bow, crescent, *meniscus*, half-moon, lunule, horse-shoe, loop, crane-neck; para-, hyper-bola; catenary, festoon; conch-, cardi-oid; caustic, instep; tracery.

V. be -curved etc. *adj.*; sweep, swag, sag; deviate etc. 279; turn; re-enter.

render -curved etc. *adj.*; bend, curve, incurvate; de-, in-flect; crook; turn, round, arch, arcuate, arch over, loop the loop, concamerate; bow, coil, curl, recurve, frizzle.

Adj. curved etc. *v.*; curvi-form, -lineal, -linear, devex, devious; recurv-ed, -ous; *retroussé*; crump; bowed etc. *v.*; vaulted; hooked; falc-iform, -ated; semicircular, crescentic; lun-iform, -ular; semilunar, meniscal; conchoidal; cord-iform, -ated; cardioid; heart-, bell-, pear-, fig-shaped; reniform; lenti-form, -cular; bow-legged etc. (*distorted*) 243; oblique etc. 217; circular etc. 247.

246. Straightness.—N. straightness, rectilinearity, directness; inflexibility etc. (*stiffness*) 323; straight –, right –, direct-, bee- line; short cut.

V. be -straight etc. *adj*; have no turning; not -incline, – bend, – turn, – deviate- to either side; go straight; steer for etc. (*direction*) 278.

render straight, straighten, rectify; set –, put- straight; un-bend, -fold, -curl etc. 248, -ravel etc. 219, -wrap.

Adj. straight; rectiline-ar, -al; direct, even, right, true, in a line; unbent etc. *v.*; un-deviating, -turned, -distorted, -swerving; straight as an arrow etc. (*direct*) 278; inflexible etc. 323.

247. Circularity. [Simple circularity.]**—N.** circularity, roundness; rotundity etc. 249.

circle, circlet, ring, washer, areola, hoop, roundlet, *annulus*, annulet, bracelet, armlet, armilla; ringlet; eye, loop, wheel; cycle, orb, orbit, rundle, zone, belt, *cordon*, band; sash, girdle, cestus, cincture, baldric, fillet, *fascia*, wreath, garland; crown, corona, coronet, chaplet, snood, necklace, collar; noose, lasso, lariat.

ellipse, oval, ovule; ellipsoid, cycloid; epicycloid, -cycle; semi-circle; quadrant, sextant, sector.

V. make -round etc. *adj.*; round.

go round; encircle etc. 227; describe -a circle etc. 311.

Adj. round, rounded, circular, annular, orbicular; oval, ovate; elliptic, -al; ovoid, egg-shaped; pear-shaped etc. 245; cycloidal etc. *n.*; spherical etc. 249.

248. Convolution. [Complex circularity.]**—N.** winding etc. *v.*; con-, in-, circum-volution; wave, undulation, tortuosity, anfractuosity; sinu-osity, -ation, sinuousness; meandering, circuit, circumbendibus, twist, twirl, windings and turnings, *ambages*; torsion; inosculation; reticulation etc. (*crossing*) 219.

coil, roll, curl, buckle, spire, spiral, helix, corkscrew, worm, volute, whorl, rundle; tendril; scollop, scallop, escalop; kink.

serpent, snake, eel, maze, labyrinth.

V. be -convoluted etc. *adj.*; wind, twine, turn and twist, twirl; wave, undulate, meander; inosculate; entwine, intwine; twist, coil, roll; wrinkle, curl, crisp, twill; frizz, -le; crimp, crape, indent, scollop, scallop; wring, intort; contort; wreathe etc. (*cross*) 219.

Adj. convoluted; winding, twisted etc. *v.*; tortile, tortive; wavy; und-ated, -ulatory; circling, snaky, snake-like, serpentine; serpent-, anguill-, vermiform; vermicular; mazy, tortuous, anfractuous, sinuous, flexuous, wavy, sigmoidal.

involved, intricate, complicated, perplexed; labyrinth-ic, -ian, -ine; circuitous; peristaltic; daedalian, curly.

wreathy, frizzly, *crêpé*, buckled; ravelled etc. (*in disorder*) 59.

spiral, coiled, helical, turbinated.

Adv. in and out, round and round.

249. Rotundity.—N. rotundity; roundness etc. *adj.*; cyclindricity; spher-icity, -oidity; globosity.

cylin-der, -droid; barrel, drum; roll, -er; *rouleau*, column, rolling-pin, rundle; chimney-pot, drain-pipe.

cone, conoid; pear-, egg-, bell-shape.

sphere, globe, orb, orbit, ball, boulder, bowlder; spher-, ellips-, ge-, glob-oid, oblong –, oblate-spheroid; drop, spherule, globule, vesicle, bulb, bullet, pellet, *pelote*, clew, pill, marble, pea, knob, pommel, knot.

V. render -spherical etc. *adj.*; form into a sphere, sphere, roll into a ball; give -rotundity etc. *n.*; round.

Adj. rotund; round etc. (*circular*) 247; cylindric, -ical, -oid; columnar, lumbriciform; conic, -al; spher-ical, -oidal; glob-ular, -ated, -ous, -ose; egg-, bell-, pear-shaped; ov-oid, -iform; gibbous; campaniform, -ulate, -iliform; fungiform, bead-like, moniliform, pyriform, bulbous; *teres atque rotundus*; round as -an orange, — an apple, — a ball, — a billiard ball, — a cannon ball.

250. Convexity.—N. convexity, prominence, projection, swelling, gibbosity, bilge, bulge, protuberance, protrusion; excrescency, camber.

intumescence; tumor; tubercle, -osity; excrescence; hump, hunch, bunch, gnarl.

tooth, knob, elbow, process, *apophysis*, condyle, bulb, node, nodule, nodosity, tongue, *dorsum*, boss, embossment, bump, clump; sugar-loaf etc. (*sharpness*) 253; bow; mamelon.

pimple, wen, wheal, *papula*, postule, pock, proud flesh, growth, goiter, *sarcoma*, caruncle, corn, bunion, wart, furuncle, polypus, adenoid, fungus, fungosity, *exostosis*, bleb, blister, blain; boil etc. (*disease*) 655; bubble, blob.

papilla, nipple, teat, pap, breast, dug, mammilla; proboscis, ,ose, neb, beak, snout, nozzle, snozzle; Adam's apple; belly, paunch, corporation; withers, back, shoulder, lip, flange.

peg, button, stud, ridge, rib, jutty, trunnion, snag.

cupola, dome, bee-hive; arch, balcony, eaves; pilaster.

relief, relievo, *cameo*; *basso-*, *mezzo-*, *alto-rilievo*; low-, bas-, high-relief.

hill etc. (*height*) 206; cape, promontory, mull; fore-, head-land; point of land, naze, ness, mole, jetty, hummock, ledge, spur.

V. be -prominent etc. *adj.*; project, bulge, protrude, bag, belly, pout, bouge, bunch; jut —, stand —, stick —, poke- out; stick —, bristle —, start —, cock —, shoot- up; swell —, hang —, bend-over; beetle.

render -prominent etc. *adj.*; raise 307; emboss, chase.

Adj. convex, prominent, protuberant, underhung, undershot; projecting etc. *v.*; bossed, bossy, nodular, bunchy; clav-ate, -ated; hummocky, *moutonné*, mammiform; papul-ous, -ose; hemispheric, bulbous; bowed, arched; bold; bellied; tuber-ous, -culous; tumorous; cornute, knobby, odontoid; lenti-form, -cular; gibbous.

salient, in relief, raised, *repoussé*; bloated etc. (*expanded*) 194.

251. Flatness.—N. flatness etc. *adj.*; smoothness etc. 255.

plane; level etc. 213; plate, platter, table, tablet, slab.

V. render flat, flatten, squash; level etc. 213.

Adj. flat, plane, even, flush, scutiform, discoid; level etc. (*horizontal*) 213; smooth; flat as -a pancake, — a fluke, — a flounder, — a board, — my hand.

252. Concavity.—N. concavity, depression, dip; hollow, -ness; indentation, *intaglio*, cavity, antrum, dent, dint, dimple, follicle, pit, *sinus*, *alveolus*, *lacuna*; excavation, trench, shaft, sap, mine, tunnel, burrow; trough etc. (*furrow*) 259; honeycomb.

cup, basin, crater, punch-bowl; cell etc. (*receptacle*) 191; socket, faucet.

valley, vale, dale, dell, gap, dingle, combe, bottom, slade, strath, glade, grove, glen, cave, cavern, cove; grot, -to; alcove, *cul-de-sac*, blind alley; gully etc. 198; arch etc. (*curve*) 245; bay etc. (*of the sea*) 343.

excavator, sapper, miner.

V. be -concave etc. *adj.*; retire, cave in.

render -concave etc. *adj.*; depress, hollow; scoop, — out; gouge, dig, delve, excavate, dent, dint, mine, sap, undermine, burrow, tunnel, stave in.

Adj. depressed etc. *v.*; concave, hollow, stove in; dished; spoon-like; retiring; retreating; cavernous; porous etc. (*with holes*) 260; cellular, spongy, spongious; honeycombed, alveolar; infundibul-ar, -iform; funnel-, bell-shaped; campaniform, capsular; vaulted, arched.

253. Sharpness.—N. sharpness etc. *adj.*; acuity, acumination; spinosity.

point, spike, spine, *spiculum*, tine; needle, pin; tack, nail; prick, -le; spur, rowel, barb; spit, cusp; horn, antler; snag; tag; thorn, bristle.

nib, tooth, incisor, tusk; spoke, cog, ratchet.

crag, crest *arête*, cone, peak, sugar-loaf, pike, *aiguille*; spire, pyramid, steeple.

beard, *chevaux de frise*, porcupine, hedgehog, brier, bramble, thistle; comb, awn, bur.

wedge; knife-, cutting- edge; blade, edge-tool, cutlery, knife, penknife, whittle, razor; scalpel, bistoury, lancet; chisel; ploughshare, coulter; hatchet, axe, pick-axe, mattock, pick, adze, bill; bill-hook, cleaver, cutter; skiver; scythe, sickle, scissors, shears; sword etc. (*arms*) 727; bodkin etc. (*perforator*) 262.

sharpener, hone, strop; grind-, whet-stone; steel, emery.

V. be -sharp etc. *adj.*; taper to a point; bristle with.

render -sharp etc. *adj.*; sharpen, point, aculeate, acuminate, whet, barb, spiculate, set, strop, grind.

cut etc. (*sunder*) 44.

Adj. sharp, keen; acute; aci-cular, -form; aculeated, -minated; pointed; tapering; conical, pyramidal; mucron-ate, -ated; spindle-, needle-shaped; spiked, spiky, ensiform, peaked, salient, cusp-ed; -idate, -idated; corn-ute, -uted, -iculate; prickly; spiny, spinous; thorny, bristling, muricated, pectinated, studded, thistly, briery; craggy etc. (*rough*) 256; snaggy; digitated, two-edged, fusiform; denti-form, -culated; toothed; odontoid; star-like; stell-ated, -iform; arrow-headed; arrowy, barbed, spurred, sagittal; spear-shaped, hastate; horned; conical.

cutting; sharp-, knife-edged; sharp —, keen- as a razor; sharp as a needle; sharpened etc. *v.*; set.

254. Bluntness.—N. bluntness etc. *adj.*; abruptness, dullness.

V. be —, render- blunt etc. *adj.*; obtund, dull; take off the -point, — edge; turn.

Adj. blunt, obtuse, dull, bluff.

255. Smoothness.—N. smoothness etc. *adj.*; polish, gloss; lubric-ity, -ation.

down, velvet, silk, satin; slide; bowling green etc. (*level*) 213; glass, ice; asphalt, pavement, flags.

roller, steam-roller; iron, flat-iron, tailor's goose; sand-, emery-paper; burnisher, turpentine and bees-wax.

V. smooth, -en; plane; file; mow, shave; level, roll; macadamize; polish, burnish, planish, levigate, calender, glaze; iron, hot-press, mangle; lubricate etc. (*oil*) 332.

Adj. smooth; polished etc. *v.*; even; level etc. 213; plane etc. (*flat*) 251; sleek, glossy; silken, silky; lanate, downy, velvety; glabrous, slippery, glassy, lubricous, oily, soft; unwrinkled; smooth as -glass, — ice, — velvet, — oil; slippery as an eel; wooly etc. (*feathery*) 256.

256. Roughness.—N. roughness etc. *adj.*; tooth, grain, texture, ripple; asperity, rugosity, salebrosity, corrugation, nodosity; arborescence etc. 242.

brush, hair, beard, shag, mane, whisker, mutton-chops, *moustache*, *mustachio*, imperial, Van Dyke, tress, lock, curl, ringlet, *fimbriae*, *cilia*, *villi*; eye-lashes, eye-brows, love-lock.

plum-age, -osity; plume, *panache*, crest; feather, tuft, tussock, fringe, toupee.

wool, velvet, plush, nap, pile, floss, fluff, fur, down; byssus, moss, bur.

V. be -rough etc. *adj.*; go against the grain.

render -rough etc. *adj.*; roughen, rough cast, knurl; ruffle, crisp, crumple, crinkle, corrugate, engrail; set on edge, stroke —, rub- the wrong way, rumple.

Adj. rough, uneven; scabrous, knotted; nodular; rug-ged, -ose, -ous; asperous, crisp, salebrous, gnarled, unpolished, unsmooth, rough-hewn; knurled, cross-grained, crag-gy, -ged; crankling, scraggy, jagged, unkempt, prickly etc. (*sharp*) 253; arborescent etc. 242; leafy, well-wooded; feathery; plum-ose, -igerous; tufted, fimbriated, hairy, bristly, ciliated, filamentous, hirsute, crin-ose, -ite; bushy, hispid, villous, pappous, bearded, pilous, shaggy, shagged; fringed, befringed; set-ous, -ose, -aceous; 'like quills upon the fretful porcupine;' rough as a -nutmeg grater, — bear.

downy, velvety, flocculent, wolly; lan-ate, -ated; lanugin-ous, ose; tomentous.

Adv. against the grain, in the rough, on edge.

257. Notch.—N. notch, dent, nick, cut; indent, -ation; serration; dimple.

embrasure, battlement, machicolation; saw, tooth, crenelle, scallop, scollop, vandyke.

V. notch, nick, cut, pink, mill, score, dent, indent, jag, scarify, scotch, crimp, scollop, crenulate, vandyke.

Adj. notched etc. *v.*; crenate, -d; dentate, -d; denticulate, -d; toothed, palmated, serrated.

258. Fold.—N. fold, plicature, pleat, plait, ply, crease; tuck, gather; flexion, flexure, joint, elbow, doubling, duplicature, wrinkle, rimple, crinkle, crankle, crumple, rumple, rivel, ruck, ruffle, dog's ear, corrugation, frounce, flounce, lapel; pucker, crow's feet.

V. fold, double, plicate, pleat, plait, crease, wrinkle, crinkle, crankle, curl, smock, cockle up, crocker, rimple, rumple, frizzle, frounce, rivel, twill, corrugate, ruffle, crimple, crumple, pucker; turn —, double- -down, — under; tuck, ruck, hem, gather.

Adj. folded etc. *v.*

259. Furrow.—N. furrow, groove, rut, *sulcus*, scratch, streak, *striae*, crack, score, incision, slit; chamfer, fluting.

channel, gutter, trench, ditch, dike, dyke, moat, fosse, trough, kennel; ravine etc. (*interval*) 198.

V. furrow etc. *n.*; flute, groove, carve, corrugate, plough; incise, chase, enchase, grave, engrave, etch, bite in, cross-hatch.

Adj. furrowed etc. *v.*; ribbed, straited, sulcated, fluted, canaliculated; bisculc-ous, -ate; trisulcate; corduroy.

260. Opening.—N. hole, foramen; puncture, blow-out, perforation; pin-, key-, loop-, port-, peep-, mouse-, pigeon-hole; eye, — of a needle; eyelet; slot.

opening; apert-ure, -ness; hiation, yawning, oscitancy, dehiscence, patefaction, pandiculation; gap, chasm etc. (*interval*) 198.

embrasure, window, casement, light; sky-, fan-light; lattice; bay-, bow-window; oriel; dormer, lantern.

out-, in-let; vent, vomitory; *embouchure*; orifice, mouth, sucker, muzzle, throat, gullet, placket, weasand, wizen, nozzle, *esophagus*.

portal, porch, gate, ostiary, postern, wicket, trap-door, hatch, door; arcade; gate-, door-, hatch-, gang-way; lych-gate.

way, path etc. 627; thoroughfare; channel, passage, tube, pipe, water-pipe etc. 350; air-pipe etc. 351; vessel, tubule, canal, gut, fistula; adjutage, ajutage; chimney, smoke stack, flue, tap, funnel, gully, tunnel, main; mine, pit, adit, shaft; gallery.

alley, aisle, glade, lane, vista.

bore, caliber; pore; blind orifice.

por-ousness, -osity; sieve, cullender, colander; grater, shredder; cribble, riddle, screen; honeycomb.

apertion, perforation; piercing etc. *v.*; terebration, empalement, pertusion, puncture, acupuncture, penetration.

opener, corkscrew, can opener, key, master-key, *passe-partout*.

V. open, ope, gape, dehisce, yawn, bilge; fly open.

perforate, pierce, empierce, tap, bore, drill; mine etc. (*scoop out*) 252; tunnel; trans-pierce, -fix; enfilade, impale, spike, spear, gore, spit, stab, pink, puncture, lance, trepan, trephine, stick, prick, riddle, punch; stave in.

cut a passage through; make -way, — room- for.

un-cover, -close, -rip; lay —, cut —, rip —, throw- open.

Adj. open; perforated etc. *v.*; perforate; wide open, agape, ajar; un-closed, -stopped; oscitant, gaping, yawning; patent.

tubular, cannular, fistulous; per-vious, -meable; foraminous; vesi-, vas-cular; porous, follicular, cribriform, honeycombed, infundibular, riddled; tubul-ous, -ated, piped.

opening etc. *v.*; aperient.

Int. *open sesame!*

261. Closure.—N. closure, occlusion, blockade; shutting up etc. *v.*; obstruction etc. (*hindrance*) 706; gag; embolism; contraction etc. 195; infarction; con-, ob-stipation; blind -alley, – corner; *cul-de-sac*, *caecum*; imperforation, -viousness etc. *adj.*; -meability; stopper etc. 263; *operculum*.

V. close, occlude, plug; block –, stop –, fill –, bung –, cork –, button –, stuff –, shut –, dam-up, obturate; blockade; obstruct etc. (*hinder*) 706; bar, bolt, stop, seal, plumb; choke, throttle; ram down, tamp, dam, cram; trap, clinch; put to –, shut- the door; batten down the hatches.

Adj. closed etc. *v.;* shut, opeculated; unopened.

unpierced, imporous, caecal; imperforate, -vious, -meable; impenetrable; un-, im-passable; invious; path-, way-less; untrodden.

unventilated; air-, water-tight; hermetically sealed; tight, snug.

262. Perforator.—N. perforator, piercer, borer, auger, gimlet, stylet, drill, wimble, awl, bradawl, scoop, terrier, corkscrew, dibble, trocar, trepan, trephine, probe, bodkin, needle, stiletto, broach, reamer, rimer, warder, lancet; punch, -eon; spikebit, gouge; spear etc. (*weapon*) 727.

263. Stopper.—N. stopper, stopple; plug, cork, bung, spike, spill, stop-cock, tap; rammer; ram, -rod; piston; stopgap; wadding, stuffing, padding, stopping, dossil, pledget, tompion, tourniquet, obturator; wad.

cover etc. 223; valve, slide valve; vent-peg, spigot.

janitor, door –, gate- keeper, porter, commissionaire, *concierge*, warder, beadle, Cerberus, usher, guard, sentry, sentinel; ostiary.

264. Motion. [Successive change of place.*]—**N.** motion, movement, move; motivity, motility, going etc. *v.*; unrest.

stream, current, flow, flux, run, course, stir; conduction, evolution; kinematics.

step, rate, pace, tread, stride, gait, clip, port, footfall, cadence, carriage, velocity, angular velocity; progress, locomotion; journey etc. 266; voyage etc. 267; transit etc. 270.

restlessness etc. (*changeableness*) 149; mobility; movableness, motive power; laws of motion; mobilization.

V. be -in motion etc. *adj.*; move, go, hie, gang, budge, stir, pass, flit; hover -round, – about; shift, slide, slither, glide; roll, – on; flow, stream, run, drift, sweep along; wander etc. (*deviate*) 279; walk etc. 266; change –, shift- one's -place, – quarters; dodge; keep -going, – moving.

put –, set- in motion; move; impel etc. 276; propel etc. 284; render movable, mobilize.

Adj. moving etc. *v.*; in motion; motile, transitional; motory, motive; shifting, movable, mobile, mercurial, unquiet; restless etc. (*changeable*) 149; nomadic etc. 266; erratic etc. 279.

Adv. under way; on the -move, – wing, – tramp, – march.

*A thing cannot be said to *move* from one place to another, unless it passes in succession through every intermediate place; hence motion is only such a change of place as is *successive*. 'Rapid, swift, etc., as thought' are therefore incorrect expressions.

265. Quiescence.—N. rest; stillness etc. *adj.*; quiescence; stag-nation, -nancy; fixity, immobility, catalepsy; indisturbance; quietism.

quiet, tranquillity, calm; repose etc. 687; peace; dead calm, anticyclone; statue-like repose; silence etc. 403; not a -breath of air, – mouse stirring; sleep etc. (*inactivity*) 683.

pause, lull etc. (*cessation*) 142; stand, – still; standing still etc. *v.*; lock; dead -lock, – stop, – stand; full stop; fix; embargo.

resting-place; bivouac; home etc. (*abode*) 189; pillow etc. (*support*) 215; haven etc. (*refuge*) 666; goal etc. (*arrival*) 292.

V. be -quiescent etc. *adj.*; stand –, lie- still; keep quiet, repose, hold the breath.

remain, stay; stand, lie to, ride at anchor, remain *in situ*, mark time, tarry; bring –, heave –, lay- to; pull –, draw- up; hold, halt; stop, – short; rest, pause, anchor; cast –, come to an- anchor; rest on one's oars; repose on one's laurels, take breath; stop etc. (*discontinue*) 142.

stagnate, vegetate; *quieta non movere*; let -alone, – well alone; abide, rest and be thankful; keep within doors, stay at home, go to bed.

dwell etc. (*be present*) 186; settle etc. (*be located*) 184; alight etc. (*arrive*) 292.

stick, – fast; stand, – like a post; not stir a -peg, – step; be at a -stand etc. *n.*

quell, becalm, hush, stay, lull to sleep, lay an embargo on; put the brake on.

Adj. quiescent, still; motion-, move-less; fixed; stationary; at -rest, – a stand, – a stand-still, – anchor; stock-still; immotile; standing still etc. *v.*; sedentary, untravelled, stay-at-home; becalmed, stagnant, quiet; un-moved, -disturbed, -ruffled; calm, restful; cataleptic; immovable etc. (*stable*) 150; sleeping etc. (*inactive*) 683; silent etc. 403; still as -a statue; – a post, – a mouse, – death.

Adv. at a stand etc. *adj.*; *tout court*; at the halt.

Int. stop! stay! avast! halt! hold, – hard! whoa!

Phr. *requiescat in pace*.

266. Journey. [Locomotion by land.]—**N.** travel; traveling etc. *v.*; wayfaring, campaigning.

journey, excursion, expedition, tour, trip, grand tour, circuit, peregrination, discursion, ramble, pilgrimage, *trek*, course, ambulation, march, walk, hike, promenade, constitutional, stroll, saunter, tramp, jog-trot, turn, stalk, perambulation; noctambulation; somnambulism, sleep walking; outing, ride, drive, airing, jaunt.

equitation, horsemanship, riding, *manège*, ride and tie.

roving, vagrancy, pererration; marching and countermarching; nomadism; vagabond-ism, -age; gadding; flit, -ting; migration; e-, im-, de-, inter- migration.

plan, itinerary, guide; hand-, road- book; Baedeker, Murray, Bradshaw, time table.

procession, parade, cavalcade, caravan, file, *cortège*, column.

[Organs and instruments of locomotion] vehicle etc. 272; locomotive etc. 271; legs, feet, pegs, pins, trotters.

traveler etc. 268.

V. travel, journey, course; tour; take —, go- a journey, take —, go out for- -a walk etc. *n.*; have a run; take the air.

flit, take wing; migrate, emigrate, *trek*; rove, prowl, roam, range, patrol, pace up and down, traverse; scour —, traverse- the country; peragrate; per-, circum-ambulate; nomadize, wander, ramble, stroll, saunter, hover, go one's rounds, straggle; gad; — about; expatiate.

walk, march, step, tread, pace, plod, wend; promenade; trudge, tramp; stalk, stride, straddle, strut, foot it, stump, bundle, bowl along, toddle; paddle; tread —, follow —, pursue- a path.

take horse, ride, drive, trot, amble, canter, prance, fisk, frisk, *caracoler*; gallop etc. (*move quickly*) 274; motor, cycle, taxi; go by -car, — train, — tram, — bus, — plane.

peg —, jog —, wag —, shuffle- on; stir one's stumps; bend one's -steps, — course; make —, find —, wend —, pick —, thread —, plough- one's way; coast, slide, glide, skim, skate, ski; march in procession, file off, defile.

go —, repair —, resort —, hie —, betake oneself- to.

Adj. traveling etc. *v.*; ambulatory, itinerant, peripatetic, perambulatory, roving, rambling, gadding, discursive, vagrant, migratory, nomadic; circumforane-an, -ous; somnambular, nocti-, mundivagant; locomotive, automotive, self-moving.

way-faring, worn; travel-stained.

Adv. on -foot, — horseback, — Shanks's mare; by the Marrowbone stage; *in transitu* etc. 270; *en route* etc. 282.

Int. come along!

267. Navigation. [Locomotion by water, or air.]—**N.** navigation; aquatics; boating, cruising, yachting; ship etc. 273; oar, scull, sweep, punt pole, paddle, — wheel, screw, propeller, stern wheel, sail, canvas.

natation, swimming; fin, flipper, fish's tail.

aeronautics, aviation, flying, winging, cruising, gliding, ballooning; blind —, instrument — flying; avigation, take-off.

flight, trip, run; solo —, nolo (pilotless) —, supersonic —, test — flight; air -lift, -drop; shuttle, reconnaisence, mission, dry run (coll.), search mission, combat flight, sortie, air raid, bombing mission; air — support, — cover, — umbrella; formation flying, maneuvers, aerobatics, stunt flying (coll.), diving, rolling, barrel roll, spin, tail spin, loop, buzzing.

landing, instrument —, crash — landing

angle, center, axis, stability, load, pressure, torsion, torque, thrust, propulsion, jet propulsion, pitch, lift, dray, yaw, resistance, drift, flow, wash.

course, heading, altitude; air -route, -lane.

voyage, sail, cruise, passage, circumnavigation, *periplus*; head-, stern-, lee-way.

astro-, cosmo- nautics; space —, interplanetary — travel; space — exploration, — flight.

mariner, aeronaut etc. 269.

V. sail; put to sea etc. (*depart*) 293; take ship, get under way; spread -sail, — canvas; gather way, have way on; make —, carry- sail; plough the - waves, — deep, — main, — ocean; walk the waters.

navigate, warp, luff, scud, boom, kedge; drift, course, cruise, coast; hug the -shore, — land; circumnavigate.

ply the oar, row, paddle, pull, scull, punt, steam.

swim, float; buffet the waves, ride the storm, skim, *effleurer*, dive, wade.

fly, pilot, copilot, astronavigate, solo, take off, taxi, ascend, climb, stunt, spin, loop, roll, dive, buzz, land, descend, level off, bail out, parachute.

Adj. sailing etc. *v.*; seafaring, nautical, maritime, naval; sea-going, coasting; afloat; navigable, aquatic, natatory.

volitant, volant, aerostatic, aerial, aeronautic; alar, alate, pennate.

Adv. under -way, — sail, — canvas, — steam; on the wing.

268. Traveler.—N. traveler, wayfarer, voyager, itinerant, passenger.

tourist, excursionist, globe-trotter; explorer, adventurer, mountaineer, Alpine Club; peregrinator, wanderer, rover, straggler, rambler; bird of passage; gad-about, -ling; vagrant, scatterling, landloper, waifs and estrays, wastrel, stray; loafer; tramp, -er, hobo, beachcomber, vagabond, nomad, Bohemian, gipsy, Arab, Wandering Jew, Hadji, pilgrim, palmer; peripatetic; somnambulist; sleep walker, noctambulist; emigrant, fugitive, refugee, *émigré*.

runner, courier, King's messenger; Mercury, Iris, Ariel, comet.

pedestrian, walker, foot-passenger; cyclist; wheelman.

rider, horseman, equestrian, cavalier, jockey, rough rider, trainer, breaker, huntsman.

driver, coachman, whip, Jehu, charioteer, postilion, post-boy, carter, wagoner, drayman, truckman; cab-man, -driver; *voiturier*, *vetturino*, *condottiere*; engine-driver; stoker, fireman, guard, brakeman, conductor; chauffeur, automobilist, motorist, motor —, truck —, taxi- driver.

269. Mariner.—N. sailor, mariner, navigator, argonaut; sea-man, -farer, -faring man; yachtsman; tar, jack tar, salt, gob, sea-dog, shellback, able seaman, A.B.; man-of-war's man, bluejacket, marine, jolly; midshipman, middy, reefer; captain, commander, master mariner, skipper, mate; ship-, boat-, ferry-, water-, lighter-, barge-, longshoreman, hoveller; bargee, gondolier; oar-, -sman; rower; boat-, cock-swain; coxswain; steersman, helmsman, pilot; crew; lascar.

aerial navigator, navigator; aero-, astro-, cosmonaut; balloonist, Icarus, aviator, pilot, flyer, copilot, spaceman; fighter —, bomber — pilot; bombardier, gunner; meteorologist; stewardess, aviatrix, aviatress; ground crew, aeromechanic, aeronautical engineer, parachutist, paratrooper.

270. Transference.—N. transfer, -ence; trans-, e-location; displacement; *meta-stasis, -thesis*; removal; re-, a-motion; relegation; de-, as-portation; extradition, conveyance, draft; carrying, carriage; convection, -duction, -tagion, infection; transfusion; transfer etc. (*of property*) 783.

transit, transition; passage, ferry, gestation; portage, porterage, carting, cartage; shoveling etc. *v.*; vect-ion, -ure, -itation; shipment, freight, wafture; trans-mission, -port, -portation, -umption, -plantation, -lation; shift-, dodg ing; dispersion etc. 73; transposition etc. (*interchange*) 148; traction etc. 285.

[Thing transferred] drift, alluvium, detritus, *moraine*; gift, legacy, bequest, lease; freight, mails, cargo, luggage, baggage, goods.

V. trans-fer, -mit, -port, -place, -plant; convey, assign, carry, bear, fetch and carry; carry —, ferry-over; hand, pass, forward; shift; conduct, convoy, bring, fetch, reach.

send, delegate, consign, mail post, relegate, turn over to, pass the buck, deliver; ship, embark; waft; switch, shunt; transpose etc. (*interchange*) 148; displace etc. 185; throw etc. 284; drag etc. 285.

shovel, lade, dip, ladle, bale, decant, draft off, transfuse.

Adj. transferred etc. *v.*; drifted; movable, portable, -ative; conductive; contagious, infectious.

transferable, assignable, conveyable, devisable, negotiable, transmissible.

Adv. from -hand to hand, — pillar to post.

on —, by- the way; on the -road, — wing; as one goes; *in transitu, en route, chemin faisant, en passant*, in mid-progress.

271. Carrier.—N. carrier, porter, red cap, bearer, messenger, postman, tranter, conveyer; stevedore; coolie; conductor, locomotive, tractor, caterpillar tractor, motor.

beast of burden, cattle, horse steed, nag, palfrey, Arab, blood horse, thorough-bred, galloway, charger, courser, racer, hunter, jument, pony, filly, colt, foal, barb, roan, jade, hack, *bidet*, pad, cob, tit, punch, roadster, goer; race-, pack-, draft-, cart-, dray-, post-horse, mount; Shetland pony, sheltie; garran; jennet, genet, bayard, mare, stallion, gelding; stud.

Pegasus, Bucephalus, Rozinante.

ass, donkey, jackass, mule, hinny; sumpter - horse, — mule; reindeer; camel, dromedary, mehari, llama, elephant; carrier pigeon.

carriage etc. (*vehicle*) 272; ship etc. 273.

Adj. equine, asinine.

272. Vehicle.—N. vehicle, conveyance, carriage, car, caravan, van, furniture van, pantechnicon; wagon, wain, dray, cart, lorry.

carriole; sledge, sled, sleigh, bob-sleigh, toboggan, *luge*, truck, tram; limber, tumbrel, pontoon; barrow; wheel-, hand- -barrow, — cart, trolley; perambulator; Bath —, wheel —, sedan-chair, jinriksha, rickshaw; ekka; chaise; palankeen, -quin; litter, horse-litter, brancard, crate, hurdle, stretcher, ambulance; velocipede, hobby-horse, coaster, scooter, go-cart; cycle; bi-, tri-, quadri-cycle; tandem, safety; skate, roller —, ice — skate; sled, sleigh; ski, snow-shoe.

equipage, turn-out; coach, chariot; *quadriga*, chaise, phaëton, break, brake, mail-phaëton, wagonette, drag, curricle, tilbury, whisky, landau, *barouche*, victoria, brougham, clarence, calash, *calèche*, britzska, *araba*, kibitka; berlin; sulky, *désobligeant*, sociable, *vis-à-vis*, *dormeuse*; jaunting —, outside- car; *tarantass*; runabout; shay.

post-chaise; diligence, stage; stage —, mail —, hackney —, glass- coach; stage-wagon; car, omnibus, bus, fly, *cabriolet*, cab, hansom, shofle, fourwheeler, growler, *droshki*, drosky.

dog-cart, trap, gig, whitechapel, buggy, four-in-hand, unicorn, random, tandem; shandredhan, *char-à-banc*.

automobile, motor-, auto-, touring-, racing-, cycle-, side-, steam-, electric- car; motor — cycle, — bike; motorized vehicle; bus, mini-bus; buggy, crate, tub, flivver, jalopy, wreck, clunker, dog, heap (all slang); coupe, coup, sedan, convertible, hard-top; camper, trailer, mobile home; limosine, landaulette, cabriolet, *coupé*, *voiturette*, runabout, electromobile, taxi, -cab.

train; passenger —, express —, freight —, subway —, special —, corridor —, parliamentary —, luggage —, goods- train, *train de luxe*; 1st-, 2nd-, 3rd- class- -train, — carriage, — compartment; Pullman —, sleeping-, club-, observation-, dining-, restaurant-car; mail-, luggage-, brake-van, coach, car, carriage; rolling stock; horse-box, cattle- truck.

273. Ship.—N. ship, vessel, sail; craft, bottom.

navy, marine, fleet, flotilla, squadron; shipping.

man of war etc. (*combatant*) 726; transport, tender, store-ship; merchant ship, merchantman; packet, liner; whaler, slaver, collier, coaster, tanker, freighter, freight steamer, cargo boat, lighter; fishing-, pilot- boat; trawler, drifter; cable ship; hulk; yacht; floating palace, ocean greyhound.

ship, bark, barque, brig, snow, hermaphrodite brig; brigantine, barquentine; schooner; topsail —, fore and aft —, three masted- schooner; *chasse-marée*; sloop, cutter, corvette, clipper, foist, yawl, dandy, ketch, smack, lugger, barge, hoy, cat-, -boat, buss; sail-er, -ing vessel, wind jammer; steamer, -boat, -ship; mail—, paddle —, screw —, stern-wheel- steamer; tug; train-ferry; line of steamers etc.

boat, pinnace, launch, motor-boat, picket-boat; hydroplane; life-, long-, jolly-, bum-, fly-, cock-, ferry-, canal- boat, dory, dugout, galliot; shallop, gig, funny, skiff, dingy, scow, cockleshell, wherry, coble, punt, cog, lerret; eight-, four-, pair- oar; randan; out- rigger; float, raft, pontoon; prame, ice-yacht.

state barge, bucentaur.

catamaran, coracle, gondola, carvel, caravel; felucca, caique, canoe; trireme; galley, — foist; bilander, dogger, hooker, howker; argosy, carack; galliass, galleon; galliot, polacca, polacre, corsair, tartane, junk, lorcha, praam, proa, prahu, saick, sampan, xebec, dhow; dahabeah; nuggar, cayak, piroque; trireme.

submarine, submersible.

aircraft (*combatant*) etc. 726; flying machine, air mail, aero-, air-, mono-, bi-, tri-, hydro aeroplane, plane, cabin —, transport —, propeller — plane; *avion*, flying boat, glider; helicopter, rotor —, gyro-plane, whirlybird, autogyro, gyrodine; sea-, hydro-plane; amphibian; jet, — plane; turbo-, ram-, pulse-, subsonic —, supersonic —, strato-jet; rocket — plane, — ship.; space ship; war-, combat — plane; kamikaze, fleet, armada; trainer, flight simulator; aerostat, dirigible, blimp (coll.), zeppelin; parachute, chute (coll.); kite.

rocket, flying —, ballistic —, guided — missile; projectile; rocket —, robot —, buzz-bomb; multistage —, step —, test — rocket; booster; satellite; flying saucer, unidentified flying object, (UFO).

nacelle, car, gondola, aileron; hangar, airport, landing field, airdrome; catwalk, controls, rudder, tail.

Adj. marine, maritime, naval, nautical, seafaring, sea-, ocean-going, sea-worthy.

aerial, aeronautical, air-worthy, flying etc. *n.*

Adv. afloat, aboard; on -board, — ship board, — board ship.

274. Velocity.—N. velocity, speed, celerity; swiftness etc. *adj.*; rapidity, eagle speed; expedition etc. (*activity*) 682; pernicity; acceleration; haste etc. 684.

spurt, rush, dash, race, steeplechase; smart —, lively —, swift etc. *adj.* —, rattling —, spanking —, strapping- -rate, — pace; round pace; flying, flight.

gallop, canter, trot, round trot, run, scamper; hand —, full- gallop; swoop.

lightning, light, electricity, wind; cannon-ball, rocket, arrow, dart, quicksilver; telegraph, express train; torrent; swallow flight.

eagle, antelope, courser, race-horse, gazelle, greyhound, hare, doe, squirrel.

Mercury, Ariel, Camilla, Harlequin.

[Measurement of velocity.] speedometer, log, -line, tachometer.

air speed, speed of sound, sonic —, subsonic —, supersonic —, ultrasonic —, hypersonic —, transonic — speed.

V. move quickly, trip, fisk; speed, hie, hasten, sprint, spurt, post, spank, scuttle; scud, -dle, scurry; scour, — the plain; scamper, sprint, dash, run, — like mad; fly, race, run a race, cut away, cut and run, shoot, tear, whisk, whiz, sweep, skim, brush; cut —, bowl- along; rush etc. (*be violent*) 173; dash -on, — off, — forward; bolt; trot, gallop, bound, flit, spring, dart, boom; march in -quick, — double-time; ride hard; et over the ground, scorch.

hurry etc. (*hasten*) 684; accelerate, put on; quicken; quicken —, mend- one's pace; clap spurs to one's horse; make-haste, — rapid strides, — forced marches, — the best of one's way; put one's best leg foremost, stir one's stumps, wing one's way, set off at a score; carry —, crowd- sail; go off like a shot, go ahead, gain ground; outstrip the wind, fly on the wings of the wind.

keep -up, — pace- with; outstrip etc. 303.

Adj. fast, speedy, swift, rapid, quick, fleet; nimble, agile, expeditious; express; active etc. 682; flying, galloping etc. *v.*; light- nimble-footed; winged; eagle-winged, mercurial, electric telegraphic; light-legged; light of heel; swift as -an arrow etc. *n.*; quick as -lightning etc. *n.*, — thought.*

Adv. swiftly etc. *adj.*; with -speed etc. *n.*; apace; at -a great rate, — full speed, — railway speed; full - drive, — gallop; post-haste, in full sail, tantivy; trippingly; instantaneously etc. 113; like a shot.

under press of -sale, — canvas, — sail and steam; *velis et remis*, on eagle's wing, in double quick time; with -rapid, — giant- strides; *à pas de géant*; in seven league boots; whip and spur; *ventre à terre*; as fast as one's -legs, — heels- will carry one, as fast on one can lay feet to the ground, at the top of one's speed; by leaps and bounds; with haste etc. 684; in- high — gear, — speed.

Phr. *vires acquirit eundo.*

*See note on *274.*

275. Slowness.—N. slowness etc. *adj.*; languor etc. (*inactivity*) 683; drawl; creeping etc. *v.*, lentor.

retardation; slackening etc. *v.*; delay etc. (*lateness*) 133; claudication.

jog-, dog-trot, walk; mincing steps; slow -march, — time.

slow -goer, — coach, — back; lingerer, loiterer, sluggard, tortoise, snail; dawdle etc. (*inactive*) 683.

V. move -slowly, etc. *adv.*; creep, crawl, lag, slug, walk, drawl, linger, loiter, saunter; plod, trudge, stump along, lumber; trail; drag; dawdle etc. (*be inactive*) 683; grovel, worm one's way, steal along; jog —, rub —, bundle- on; toddle, waddle, wabble, slug; traipse, slouch, shuffle, halt, hobble, limp, claudicate, shamble; flag, falter totter, stagger; mince, step short; march in -slow time, — funeral procession; take one's time; hang fire etc. (*be late*) 133.

retard, relax; slacken, check, moderate, rein in, curb; reef; strike —, shorten —, take in- sail; put on the drag, apply the brake; clip the wings; reduce the speed, decelerate; slacken -speed, — one's pace, lose ground; back -water, — pedal, put the engines astern, throttle down.

Adj. slow, slack; tardy; dilatory etc. (*inactive*) 683; gentle, easy; leisurely; deliberate, gradual; insensible, imperceptible; languid, sluggish, apathetic, phlegmatic, slow-paced, tardigrade, snail-like; creeping etc. *v.*

Adv. slowly etc. *adj.*; leisurely; *piano*, *adagio*; *largo*, *larghetto*; at half speed, under easy sail; at a -foot's, — snail's, — funeral- pace; slower than molasses in January; in slow time; with -mincing steps, — clipped wings; *haud passibus aequis*; in- low —, gear, — speed.

gradually etc. *adj.*; *gradatim*; by -degrees, — slow degrees, — inches, — little and little; step by step; inch by inch, bit by bit, little by little, *seriatim*; consecutively.

276. Impulse.—N. impulse, impulsion, impetus; momentum; push, pulsion, thrust, shove, jog, jolt, brunt, booming, boost, throw; explosion etc. (*violence*) 173; propulsion etc. 284, jet propulsion; firing, launching, projection, trajection.

percussion, concussion, collision, occursion, clash, encounter, cannon, *carambole*, appulse, shock, crash, bump; impact; *élan*; charge etc. (*attack*) 716; beating etc. (*punishment*) 972.

blow, dint, stroke, knock, tap, rap, slap, smack, pat, dab; fillip, slam, bang; hit, whack, thwack, clout; cuff etc. 972; squash, dowse, whap, swap, punch, thump, swipe, jab, pelt, kick, punce, calcitration; *ruade*; arietation; cut, thrust, lunge, yerk.

hammer, sledge-hammer, mall, maul, mallet, flail; ram, -mer; battering-ram, monkey, pile-driver, punch, bat, tamper, tamping iron; cudgel etc. (*weapon*) 727; axe etc. (*sharp*) 253.

[Science of mechanical forces] mechanics, dynamics etc.

V. give an -impetus etc. *n.*; impel, push; start, give a start to, set going; drive, urge, boom; thrust, prod, foin; cant; elbow, shoulder, jostle, justle, hustle, hurtle, shove, jog, jolt, bean, encounter; run –, bump –, butt- against; knock –, run- one's head against; impinge.

fire, launch, project, traject, propel, 284.

strike, knock, hit, bash, tap, rap, bat, slap, flap, dab, pat, thump, beat, bang, slam, dash; punch, thwack, whack; hit –, strike- hard; swap, batter, dowse, baste; pelt, patter, skelter, buffet, belabor, tamp; fetch one a blow, swat; poke at, pink, lunge, yerk; kick, calcitrate; butt; strike at etc. (*attack*) 716; whip etc. (*punish*) 972; propel etc. 284.

come –, enter- into collision; collide; foul; fall –, run- foul of.

throw etc.

Adj. impelling etc. *v.*; im-pulsive, -pellent; booming; dynamic, -al; impelled etc. *v.*

277. Recoil.—N. recoil; re-, retro-action; revulsion; rebound, *ricochet*; re-percussion, -calcitration; kick, *contre-coup*; springing back etc. *v.*; elasticity etc. 325; reflexion, reflex, reflux; reverberation etc. (*resonance*) 408; rebuff, repulse; return.

ducks and drakes; boomerang; spring; reactionist, reactionary.

V. recoil, resile, react; spring –, fly –, bound-back; rebound, reverberate, repercuss, recalcitrate, echo, *ricochet*.

Adj. recoiling etc. *v.*; re-fluent, -percussive, -calcitrant, -actionary; retroactive.

Adv. on the -recoil etc. *n.*

278. Direction.—N. direction, bearing, course, set, drift, tenor; tendency etc. 176; incidence; bending, trending etc *v.*; dip, tack, aim, collimation; steer-ing, -age.

point of the compass, cardinal –, half –, quarter- points; North, East, South, West; N by E, ENE, NE by N, NE etc; rhumb, azimuth, line of collimation.

line, path, road, range, quarter, line of march; alignment; straight shot, bee-line.

course, bearing, heading, altitude, air -route, -lane, angle, center, axis, torsion, torque, pitch, lift, drift, flow, wash.

V. tend –, bend –, point- towards; conduct –, go- to; point -to, – at; bend, trend, verge, incline, dip, determine.

steer –, make- -for, – towards; aim –, level-at; take aim; keep –, hold- a course; be bound for; bend one's steps towards; direct –, steer –, bend –, shape- one's course; align –, align- one's march; go straight, – to the point; march -on, – on a point.

ascertain one's -direction etc. *n.*; *s'orienter*, see which way the wind blows; box the compass.

Adj. directed etc. *v.*, – towards; pointing towards etc. *v.*; bound for; aligned –, with; direct, straight; un-deviating, -swerving; straightforward; North, -ern, -erly, etc. *n.*

directable etc. *v.*

Adv. towards; on the -road, – high road- to; versus, to; hither, thither, whither; directly; straight, – forwards, – as an arrow; point blank; in a -direct, – straight- line -to, – for, – with; in a line with; full tilt at, as the crow flies.

before –, near –, close to –, against- the wind; windwards, in the wind's eye.

through, *via*, by way of; in all -directions, – manner of ways; *quaqua-versum*, from the four winds.

279. Deviation.—N. deviation; swerving etc. *v.*; obliquation, warp, refraction; flection, flexion; sweep; de-flection, -flexure; declination.

diversion, digression, departure from, aberration, drift, sheer; divergence etc. 291; zigzag; *détour* etc. (*circuit*) 629.

[Desultory motion] wandering etc. *v.*; vagrancy, evagation; by-paths and crooked ways.

[Motion sideways, oblique motion] sidling etc. *v.*; *échelon*, leeway; knight's move (at chess).

V. alter one's course, deviate, depart from, turn, trend; bend, curve, etc. 245; swerve, heel, bear off.

intervert; deflect; divert, – from its course; put on a new scent, shift, shunt, switch, wear, draw aside, crook, warp, short circuit.

stray, straggle; sidle, edge; diverge etc. 291; tralineate, digress, divagate, wander; wind, twist, meander, meander around Robin Hood's barn; veer, tack, sheer; turn -aside, – a corner, – away from; wheel, steer clear of; ramble, rove, drift; go -astray, – adrift; yaw, dodge; step aside, ease off, make way for, shy.

fly off at a tangent; glance off; turn, wheel –, face- about; turn –, face- to the right about; wabble etc. (*oscillate*) 314; go out of one's way etc. (*perform a circuit*) 629; lose one's way.

Adj. deviating etc. *v.*; aberrant, errant; ex-, dis-cursive; devious, desultory, loose; rambling; stray, erratic, vagrant, undirected; circuitous, indirect, zigzag; crab-like.

Adv. astray from, round about, wide of the mark; to the right about; all manner of ways; circuitously etc. 629.

obliquely, sideling, like the move of the knight on a chessboard.

280. Precession. [Going before.]**—N.** precession, leading, heading; precedence etc. 62; priority etc. 116; the lead, *le pas*; van etc. (*front*) 234; precursor etc. 64.

V. go -before, – ahead, – in the van, – in advance; precede, forerun; usher in, introduce, herald, head, take the lead; lead, – the way, – the dance; get –, have- the start; steal a march; get -before, – ahead, – in front of; outstrip etc. 303; take precedence etc. (*first in order*) 62.

Adj. foremost, first, leading etc. *v.*

Adv. in advance, before, ahead, in the van; fore-head-most; in front.

Phr. *seniores priores.*

281. Sequence. [Going after.]—**N.** sequence, run; coming after etc. (*order*) 63; (*time*) 117; following; pursuit etc. 622.

follower, attendant, satellite, shadow, dangler, train.

V. follow; pursue etc. 622; go –, fly- after.

attend, beset, dance attendance on, dog, be-dog; tread -in the steps of, – close upon; be –, go –, follow- in the -wake, – trail, – rear- of; trail, follow as a shadow, hang on the skirts of; tread –, follow- on the heels of, tag after.

lag, get behind.

Adj. following etc. *v.*

Adv. behind; in the -rear etc. 235, – train of, wake of; after etc. (*order*) 63, (*time*) 117.

282. Progression. [Motion forwards; progressive motion.]—**N.** progress, -ion, -iveness; advancing etc. *v.*; advance, -ment; ongoing; flood-tide, headway; march etc. 266; rise; improvement etc. 658.

V. advance; proceed, progress; get -on, – along, – over the ground; gain ground; jog –, rub –, wag- on; go with the stream; keep –, hold on- one's course; go –, move –, come –, get –, pass –, push –, press- -on, – forward, – forwards, – ahead; press onwards, step forward; make –, work –, carve –, push –, force –, edge –, elbow- one's way; make -progress, – head, – way, – headway, – advances, – strides, – rapid strides etc. (*velocity*) 274; go –, shoot- ahead; distance; make up leeway.

Adj. advancing etc. *v.*; pro-gressive, -fluent; advanced.

Adv. forward, onward; forth, on ahead, under way, *en route* for, on -one's way, – the way, – the road, – the high road- to; in -progress, – mid progress; *in transitu* etc. 270.

Phr. *vestigia nulla retrorsum.*

283. Regression. [Motion backwards.]—**N.** regress, -ion; retro-cession, -gression, -gradation, -action; *reculade*; retreat, withdrawal, retirement, remigration; recession etc. (*motion from*) 287; recess; crab-like motion.

re-fluence, -flux; backwater, regurgitation, ebb, return; resilience; reflexion (*recoil*) 277; *volte-face*.

counter -motion, – movement, – march; veering, tergiversation, recidivation, backsliding, fall, relapse; deterioration etc. 659.

turning point etc. (*reversion*) 145.

V. re-cede, -grade, -turn, -vert, -treat, -tire; retro-grade, -cede; back, – down, – out, crawl; withdraw; rebound etc. 277; go –, come –, turn –, hark –, draw –, fall –, get –, put –, run- back; lose ground; fall –, drop- astern; back water, put about; veer, – round; double, wheel, counter-march; ebb, regurgigate; *jib*, shrink, shy.

turn -tail, – round, – upon one's heel, – one's back upon; retrace one's steps, dance the back step; sound –, beat- a retreat; go home.

Adj. receding etc. *v.*; retro-grade, -gressive; re-gressive, -fluent, -flex, -cidivous, -silient; crab-like; reactionary etc. 277; counter-clockwise.

Adv. back, -wards; reflexively, to the right about; *à reculons*, *à rebours*.

Phr. *revenons à nos moutons*, as you were.

284. Propulsion. [Motion given to an object situated in front.]—**N.** pro-pulsion, -jection; *vis a tergo*; push etc. (*impulse*) 276; e-, jaculation; ejection etc. 297; throw, fling, toss, shot, discharge, shy.

[Science of propulsion] steam –, gas –, diesel –, jet –, rocket – propulsion, gunnery, ballistics, archery.

missile, projectile, ball, *discus*, javelin, hammer, quoit, brickbat, shot, bullet; arrow, shaft, gun etc. (*arms*) 727.

shooter, shot; gunner, gun-layer; archer, toxophilite; bow-, rifle-, marks- man; good –, crack- shot; sharpshooter etc. (*combatant*) 726.

V. propel, project, throw, fling, cast, pitch, chuck, toss, jerk, heave, shy, hurl; flirt, fillip.

dart, lance, tilt; e-, jaculate; fulminate, bolt, drive, sling, pitchfork.

send; send –, let –, fire- off; discharge, shoot; launch, send forth, let fly; dash.

put –, set- in motion; set agoing, start; give -a start, – an impulse- to; push, impel etc. 276; trundle etc. (*set in rotation*) 312; expel etc. 297.

carry one off one's legs; put to flight.

Adj. propelled etc. *v.*; propelling etc. *v.*; propulsive, -jectile.

285. Traction. [Motion given to an object situated behind.]—**N.** traction; drawing etc. *v.*; draft, pull, tug, haul; rake; 'a long pull, a strong pull and a pull all together;' towage, haulage.

V. draw, pull, haul, lug, rake, drag, draggle, tug, tow, trail, trawl, train; take in tow.

wrench, jerk, twitch.

Adj. drawing etc. *v.*; tractive, tractile; ductile, pulling, hauling, tugging, towing.

286. Approach. Motion towards.]—**N.** approach, approximation, appropinquation; access; appulse; afflux, -ion; advent etc. (*approach of time*) 121; pursuit etc. 622; convergence etc. 290.

V. approach, approximate; near; get –, go –, draw- near; come, – near, – to close quarters; move –, set in- towards; drift; make up to; gain upon; pursue etc. 622; tread on the heels of; bear up; make the land; hug the -shore, – land.

Adj. approaching etc. *v.*; approximative; convergent; affluent; impending, imminent etc. (*destined*) 152.

Adv. on the road.

Int. come hither! approach! here! come! come near!

287. Recession. [Motion from.]—**N.** recession, retirement, withdrawal; retreat; retrocession etc. 283; departure etc. 293; recoil etc. 277; flight etc. (*avoidance*) 623.

V. recede, go, move from, retire, ebb, withdraw, shrink; come –, move –, go –, get –, drift- away; depart etc. 293; retreat etc. 283; move –, stand –, sheer- off; swerve from; fall back, stand aside; run away etc. (*avoid*) 623.

remove, shunt, side track, switch off.

Adj. receding etc. *v.*

288. Attraction. [Motion towards, actively.]—**N.** attract-ion, -iveness; pull; drawing to, pulling towards, adduction, magnetism, gravity, attraction of gravitation; lure, bait, decoy.

lode-stone, -star; magnet, siderite, magnetite.

V. attract; draw –, pull –, drag- towards; adduce.

lure, bait, decoy.

Adj. attracting etc. *v.*; attrahent, attractive, adducent, adductive, alluring.

289. Repulsion. [Motion from, actively.]—**N.** repulsion; driving from etc. *v.*; repulse; abduction.

V. repel; push –, drive – etc. 276; from; chase, dispel; retrude; abduce, abduct; send away, repulse, dismiss.

keep at arm's length, turn one's back upon, give the cold shoulder; send packing; send -off, – away- with a flea in one's ear, – about one's business.

Adj. repelling etc. *v.*; repellant, repulsive; abducent, abductive.

290. Convergence. [Motion nearer to.]—**N.** con-vergence, -fluence, -course, -flux, -gress, -currence, -centration; appulse, meeting; corradiation.

assemblage etc. 72; resort etc. (*focus*) 74; asymptote.

V. converge, concur; come together, unite, meet, fall in with; close -with, – in upon; center -round, – in; enter in; pour in.

gather together, unite, concentrate, bring into a focus.

Adj. converging etc. *v.*; con-vergent, -fluent, -current; centripetal; asymptotical.

291. Divergence. [Motion further off.]—**N.** diverg-ence, -ency; divarication, ramification, radiation; separation etc. (*disjunction*) 44; dispersion etc. 73; deviation etc. 279; aberration, declination.

V. diverge, divaricate, radiate; ramify; branch –, glance –, file- off; fly off, – at a tangent; spread, scatter, disperse etc. 73; deviate etc. 279; part etc. (*separate*) 44; splay apart.

Adj. diverging etc. *v.*; divergent, radiant, centrifugal; aberrant.

292. Arrival. [Terminal motion at.]—**N.** arrival, advent; landing; de-, disem-barkation; reception, welcome, *vin d'honneur.*

home, goal, bourn; landing-place, -stage; resting –, stopping -place; destination, harbor, haven, port; terminal, terminus, railway station, depot, airport; halt, halting -place, – ground; anchorage etc. (*refuge*) 666.

return, recursion, remigration; meeting; ren-, encounter.

completion etc. 729.

V. arrive; get to, come to; come; reach, attain; come up, – with, – to; overtake; make, fetch; complete etc. 729; join, rejoin.

light, alight, dismount; land, go ashore; debark, disembark; put -in, – into; visit, cast anchor, pitch one's tent; sit down etc. (*be located*) 184; get to one's journey's end; make the land; be in at the death; come –, get- -back, – home; return; come in etc. (*ingress*) 294; make one's appearance etc. (*appear*) 446; drop in; detrain; outspan.

come to hand; come -at, – across; hit; come –, light –, pop –, bounce –, plump –, burst –, pitch- upon; meet; en- ren-counter; come in contact.

Adj. arriving etc. *v.*; homewardbound; terminal.

Adv. here, hither.

Int. welcome! hail! all hail! good- day, – morrow; greetings! hullo! well!

293. Departure. [Initial motion from.]—**N.** departure, decession, decampment; embarkation; take-off; outset, start; removal; exit etc. (*egress*) 295; exodus, Hejira, flight.

leave-taking, *congé*, valediction, valedictory, adieu, farewell, good-bye, stirrup-cup.

starting -point, – post; point –, place- of -departure, – embarkation; port of embarkation.

V. depart; go, – away; take one's departure, set out; set –, march –, put –, start –, be –, move –, get –, whip –, pack –, go –, take oneself- off; start, issue, march out, debouch; go –, sally- forth; sally, set forward; be gone.

leave a place, quit, vacate, evacuate, abandon; go off the stage, make ones' exit; retire, withdraw, remove; go -one's way, – along, – from home; take -flight, – wing; spring, fly, flit, wing one's flight; fly –, whip- away; take off, hop off; embark; go -on board, – aboard; set sail; put –, go- to sea; sail, take ship; hoist blue Peter; get under way, weigh anchor; strike tents, break camp, decamp; walk one's chalks, make tracks, cut one's stick; cut and run; take leave; say –, bid- -good-bye etc. *n.*; disappear etc. 449; abscond etc. (*avoid*) 623; entrain, embus, emplane; saddle –, harness –, hitch- up; inspan.

Adj. departing etc. *v.*; valedictory; outward bound.

Adv. whence, hence, thence; with a foot in the stirrup; on the -wing, – move.

Int. begone! etc. (*ejection*) 297; to horse! all aboard! farewell! adieu! good-bye, – day! *au revoir! auf wiedersehen!* fare you well! so long! God -bless you, – speed! *bon vayage!*

294. Ingress. [Motion into.]—**N.** ingress; entrance, entry; introgression; influx; intrusion, inroad, incursion, invasion, irruption; pene-, interpene- tration; illapse, import, importation, infiltration; immigration; admission etc. (*reception*) 296; insinuation etc. (*interjacence*) 228; insertion etc. 300.

inlet; way in; mouth, door etc. (*opening*) 260; path etc. (*way*) 627; conduit etc. 350; immigrant, visitor, incomer, newcomer, colonist.

V. have the *entrée*; enter; go –, come –, pour –, flow –, creep –, slip –, pop –, break –, burst- -into, – in; set foot on; burst –, break-in upon; invade, intrude, butt in, horn in, crash; insinuate itself; inter-, penetrate; infiltrate; find one's way –, wriggle –, worm oneself- into.

give entrance to etc. (*receive*) 296; insert etc. 300.

Adj. incoming, ingressive etc. *n.*; inward bound.
Adv. inward.

295. Egress. [Motion out of.]—**N.** egress, exit, issue; emer-sion, -gence; disemboguement; outbreak, -burst; e-, pro-ruption; emanation; evacuation; ex, trans-udation; extravasation, perspiration, sweating, leakage, percolation, distillation, oozing; gush etc. (*water in motion*) 348; outpour, -ing; effluence, effusion; efflux, -ion; drain; dribbling etc. *v.*; defluxion; drainage; outcome, -put; discharge etc. (*excretion*) 299.

export; expatriation; e-, re-migration; *débouche*; exodus etc. (*departure*) 293; emigrant, migrant, *émigré*, colonist.

outlet, vent, spout, tap, sluice, floodgate; pore; vomitory, out-gate, sally-port; way out; mouth, door etc. (*opening*) 260; path etc. (*way*) 627; conduit etc. 350; air-pipe etc. 351.

V. emerge, emanate, issue; go –, come –, move –, pass –, pour –, flow- out of; pass off, evacuate; migrate.

ex-, trans-ude; leak; run, – out, – through; per-, trans-colate; seep; strain, distil; perspire, sweat, drain, ooze; filter, filtrate; dribble, gush, spout, flow out; well, – out; pour, trickle etc. (*water in motion*) 348; effuse, extravasate, disembogue, discharge itself, debouch; come –, break-forth; burst- out, – through; find vent, escape etc. 671.

Adj. effused etc. *v.*; outgoing, outward bound.
Adv. outward.

296. Reception. [Motion into, actively.]—**N.** reception; admission, admittance, *entrée*, importation; initiation; intro-duction, -mission, -ception; immission, ingestion, imbibition, absorption, ingurgitation, inhalation; suction, sucking; eating, drinking etc. (*food*) 298; insertion etc. 300; interjection etc. 228.

V. give -entrance to, – admittance to, – the *entrée*; intro-duce, -mit; usher, admit, receive, import, initiate, bring in, open the door to, throw open, ingest, absorb, imbibe, inhale, infiltrate; let –, take –, suck- in; re-admit, -sorb, -absorb; snuff up; swallow, ingurgitate; enfulf, engorge; gulp; eat, drink etc. (*food*) 298.

Adj. admit-ting etc. *v.*, -ted etc. *v.*; admissible; absorbent; introductory, introceptive, intromittent, initiatory.

297. Ejection. [Motion out of, actively.]—**N.** ejection, emission, effusion, rejection, expulsion, eviction, extrusion, trajection; discharge.

egestion, evacuation, vomition, disgorgement, voidance, eruption, eruptiveness; ruc-, eruc-tation, blood-letting, venesection, phlebotomy, paracentesis; tapping, drainage; clear-ance, -age, voidance; vomiting, excretion etc. 299.

deportation; banishment etc. (*punishment*) 972; rogue's march; relegation, extradition; dislodgment.

V. give -exit, – vent- to; let –, give –, pour –, send- out; des-, dis-patch; exhale, excern, excrete, disembogue, secrete, secern; extravasate, shed, void, evacuate, egest, emit; open the -sluices, – floodgates; turn on the tap; extrude, detrude; effuse, spend, expend; pour forth; squirt, spirt, spill, slop; perspire etc. (*exude*) 295; breathe, blow etc. (*wind*) 349.

tap, draw off; bale –, lade- out; let blood, broach.

eject, reject; expel, discard; cut, send to Coventry, boycott, ostracize; *chasser*; banish etc. (*punish*) 972; throw etc. 284 -out, – up, – off, – away, – aside; push etc. 276 -out, – off, – away, – aside; shovel –, sweep- -out, – away; brush –, whisk –, turn –, send- -off, – away; discharge; send –, turn –, cast- adrift; turn –, bundle- out; throw overboard; give the sack to; send -packing, – about one's business, – to the right about; strike off the roll etc. (*abrogate*) 756; turn out- neck and heels, – head and shoulders, – neck and crop; pack off; send away with a flea in the ear; send to Jericho; bow out, show the door to, dismiss, fire, sack.

turn out of -doors, – house and home; evict, oust; exorcise, un-house, -kennel; dislodge; un-, dis-people; depopulate; relegate, deport.

empty; drain, – to the dregs; sweep off; clear, – off, – out, – away; such, draw off, extract; clean out, make a clean sweep of, clear decks, purge.

em-, dis-, disem-bowel; eviscerate, gut; unearth, root -out, – up; averruncate; weed –, get out; eliminate, get rid of, do away with, shake off; exenterate.

vomit, spew, puke, keck, retch; belch, – out, eruct, eructate; cast –, bring- up; disgorge; expectorate, salivate, clear the throat, hawk, spit, sputter, splutter, slobber, drool, drivel, slaver, slabber.

unpack, unlade, unload, unship; break bulk.

be let out; ooze etc. (*emerge*) 295.

Adj. emitt-ing, -ed etc. *v.*

begone! get you gone! get –, go- away, along, – along with you! go your way! away, – with! off with you! go, – about your business! be off! avaunt! aroynt! get out!

298. Food. [Eating.]—**N.** eating etc. *v.*; deglutition, gulp, epulation, mastication, manducation, rumination, gastronomy, gastrology; panto-, hippo-, ichthyo-phagy etc.; gluttony etc. 957; carnivorousness, vegetarianism.

mouth, jaws, mandible, mazard, chops.

drinking etc. *v.*; potation, draught, libation; carousal etc. (*amusement*) 840; drunkenness etc. 959.

food, *pabulum*; aliment, nourishment, nutriment; susten-ance, -tation; nurture, subsistence, provender, feed, fodder, provision, ration, keep, commons, board; commissariat etc. (*provision*) 637; prey, forage, pasture, pasturage; fare, cheer; diet, -ary; regimen; belly timber, staff of life; bread, -and cheese; proteins, carbohydrates, vitamines.

comestibles, eatables, victuals, edibles, *ingesta*; grub, prog, tack, hard tack, meat; bread, -stuffs; cereals; viands, cates, delicacy, dainty, creature comforts, contents of the larder, flesh-pots; festal board; ambrosia; good -cheer, – living.

hors-d'oeuvre; soup, pottage, *potage*, broth,

bouillon, *consommé*, *purée*, *borsch*, stock, skilly, gumbo; fish, – cakes, – pie; joint, *rôti*, *pièce de résistance*, *relevé*, hash, *réchauffé*, stew, *ragoût*, fricassee, mince, *salim*, *goulash*, *bouillabaisse*, *remove*, *entrée*, *croquette*, *rissole*, sausage, curry, bubble and squeak; haggis, collops, giblets; poultry, game etc.; biscuit, bun, scone, rusk, pancake, pie, pastry, pasty, patty, *patisseria*, tart, turnover, *vol-au-vent*, *soufflé*, dumpling, pudding, duff, *compote*, fritters, cake, napoleon, *blancmange*, custard, jelly, jam, sweets etc. 396; *entremet*; oatmeal, porridge, hasty pudding, gruel; eggs, omelet, cheese, matzoon, savory; vegetable, salad, *mayonnaise*, fruit; sauce, condiment etc. 393; kickshaws.

table, *cuisine*, bill of fare, *menu*, *table d'hôte*, ordinary, *à la carte*; cover.

meal, repast, feed, spread; mess; dish, plate, course, side dish; regale; regale-, refresh-, entertain-ment; refection, collation, picnic, feast, banquet, junket; breakfast; lunch, -eon, *déjeuner*, bever, tiffin, tea, dinner, supper, snack, whet, bait, dessert; pot-luck, *table d'hôte*, *déjeuner à la fourchette*; hearty –, square –, substantial –, full- - meal; blow out; light refreshment; pemmican.

mouthful, bolus, gobbet, tit-bit, morsel, sop, sippet.

drink, beverage, liquor, broth, soup; potion, dram, draft, drench, swill; nip, peg, sip, sup, gulp.

wine, champagne, spirits, *liqueur* beer, porter, stout, ale, malt liquor, julep, Sir John Barleycorn, stingo, heavy wet, bitter, lager- beer, cider; grog, toddy, flip, purl, punch, negus, cup, bishop, posset, wassail; bitters, *apéritif*, high-ball, cocktail; whisky, rum, absinthe; gin etc. (*intoxicating liquor*) 959; coffee, chocolate, cocoa, tea, *maté*, the cup that cheers but not inebriates.

eating-house etc. 189.

V. eat, feed, fare, devour, swallow, take; gulp, bolt, snap; fall to; despatch, dispatch; discuss; take –, get –, gulp-down; lay –, tuck- in; lick, pick, peck; gormandize etc. 957; bite, champ, munch, cranch, craunch, crunch, chew, masticate, nibble, gnaw, mumble.

live on; feed –, batten –, fatten –, feast- upon; browse, graze, crop, regale; carouse etc. (*make merry*) 840; eat heartily, do justice to, play a good knife and fork, banquet.

break -bread, – one's fast; breakfast; lunch, dine, take tea, sup.

drink, – in, – up, – one's fill; quaff, sip, sup; suck, – up; lap; swig; swill, tipple etc. (*be drunken*) 959; empty one's glass, drain the cup; toss -off, – one's glass; wash down, crack a bottle, wet one's whistle.

cater, purvey etc. 637.

Adj. eatable, edible, esculent, comestible, alimentary; cereal, cibarious; dietetic; culinary; nutri-tive, -tious; succulent; drinkable, pot-able, -ulent; bibulous.

omn-, carn-, herb-, frug-, gran-, gramin-, phytivorous; ichthyophagous.

prandial.

299. Excretion.—N. excretion, discharge, emanation; ejection etc. 297; exhalation, exudation, extrusion, secretion, effusion, extravasation, *ecchymosis*, evacuation, cacation, defecation, dysentery, dejection, *feces*, excrement; perspiration, sweat; sub-, exud-ation; *diaphoresis*; sewage.

saliva, spittle, rheum; ptyalism, salivation, catarrh, distemper; diarrhea; *ejecta*, *egesta*, *sputum*, *sputa*; *excreta*; lava; *exuviae* etc. (*uncleanness*) 653.

hemorrhage, bleeding; catamenia, menses; outpouring etc. (*egress*) 295; leucorrhea.

V. excrete etc. (*eject*) 297; emanate etc. (*come out*) 295.

Adj. excretory, fecal, secretory; ejective, eliminant.

300. Insertion. [Forcible ingress.]—**N.** insertion, implantation, intercalation, embolism, introduction; interpolation, insinuation etc. (*intervention*) 228; planting etc. *v.*; injection, inoculation, importation, infusion; forcible -ingress etc. 294; immersion; submersion, -gence; dip, plunge; bath etc. (*water*) 337; interment etc. 363.

V. insert; intro-duce, -mit; put –, run- into; import; inject; interject etc. 228; infuse, instil, inoculate, impregnate, imbue, imbrue.

graft, ingraft, bud, plant, implant; dovetail.

obtrude; thrust –, stick –, ram –, stuff –, tuck –, press –, drive –, pop –, whip –, drop –, put- in; impact; empierce etc. (*make a hole*) 260.

embed; immerse, immerge, merge; bathe, soak etc. (*water*) 337; dip, plunge etc. 310.

bury etc. (*inter*) 363.

insert etc. -itself; plunge *in medias res*.

Adj. inserted etc. *v.*

301. Extraction. [Forcible egress.]—**N.** extraction; extracting etc. *v.*; removal, elimination, extrication, eradication, evolution.

evulsion, avulsion; wrench; expression, squeezing; extirpation, extermination; ejection etc. 297; export etc. (*egress*) 295; distillation.

extractor, corkscrew, forceps, pliers.

V. extract, draw, pit; take –, draw –, pull –, tear –, pluck –, pick –, get- out; wring from, wrench; extort; root –, weed –, grub –, rake-up, – out; eradicate; pull –, pluck- up by the roots; averruncate; unroot; uproot, pull up, extirpate, dredge.

remove; educe, elicit; evolve, extricate; eliminate etc. (*eject*) 297; eviscerate etc. 297.

express, squeeze –, press- out; distil.

Adj. extracted etc. *v.*

302. Passage. [Motion through.]—**N.** passage, transmission; permeation; pene-, interpene-tration; transudation, infiltration; *osmosis*, osmose, endos-, exos-mose; intercurrence; ingress etc. 294; egress etc. 295; path etc. 627; conduit etc. 350; opening etc. 260; journey etc. 266; voyage etc. 267.

V. pass, – through; perforate etc. (*hole*) 260; penetrate, permeate, thread, thrid, enfilade; go -through, – across; go –, pass- over; cut across; ford, cross; pass and repass, work; make –, thread –, worm –, force- one's way; make –, force- a passage; cut one's way through; find its -way, –

vent; transmit, make way, clear the course; traverse, go over the ground.

Adj. passing etc. *v.*; intercurrent; osmotic etc. *n.*

Adv. *en passant* etc. (*transit*) 270.

303. Overstep. [Motion beyond.]—**N.** transcursion, -ilience, -gression; infraction, intrusion; trespass; encroach-, infringe-ment; extravagation, transcendence; redundance etc. 641; ingress etc. 294.

V. transgress, surpass, pass; go- beyond, – by; show in –, come to the- front; shoot ahead of; steal a march –, gain- upon.

over-step, -pass, -reach, -go, -ride- -leap, -jump, -skip, -lap, -shoot the mark; out-strip, -leap, -jump, -go, -step, -run, -ride, -rival, -do; beat, – hollow; distance; leave in the -lurch, – rear; go one better, throw into the shade; exceed, transcend, surmount; soar etc. (*rise*) 305.

encroach, intrude, trespass, infringe, invade, trench upon, intrench on; strain; stretch –, strain- a point; pass the Rubicon.

Adj. surpassing etc. *v.*

Adv. beyond the mark, ahead.

304. Shortcoming. [Motion short of.]—**N.** shortcoming, failure; delinquency; falling short etc. *v.*; de-fault, -falcation; leeway; labor in vain, no go.

incompleteness etc. 53; imperfection etc. 651; insufficiency etc. 640; noncompletion etc. 730; failure etc. 732.

V. come –, fall –, stop- -short, – short of; not reach; want; keep within -bounds, – the mark, – compass.

break down, stick in the mud, collapse, come to nothing; fall -through, – to the ground, – down; cave in, end in smoke, fizzle out, miss the mark, fail; lose ground; miss stays, slump

Adj. unreached; deficient; short, – of; *minus*; out of depth; perfunctory etc. (*neglect*) 460.

Adv. within -the mark, – compass, – bounds; behindhand; *re infectâ*; to no purpose; far from it.

Phr. the bubble burst.

305. Ascent. [Motion upwards.]—**N.** ascent, ascension; rising etc. *v.*; rise, upgrowth; leap etc. 309; acclivity, hill etc. 217; stair, stairs, stair-case, -way, flight of -steps, – stairs; ladder, companion, – way; lift, elevator etc. 307.

rocket, lark; sky-rocket, -lark; Alpine Club.

V. ascend, rise, mount, arise, uprise; go –, get –, work one's way –, start –, spring –, shoot- up; zoom; aspire.

climb, clamber, ramp, scramble, swarm, *escalade*, surmount; scale, – the heights.

tower, soar, hover, spire, plane, swim, float, surge; leap etc. 309.

Adj. rising etc. *v.*; scandent, buoyant; supernatant, -fluitant; excelsior.

Adv. uphill.

306. Descent. [Motion downwards.]—**N.** descent, descension, declension, declination; fall; falling etc. *v.*; drop, cadence; subsidence, lapse; come-down, downfall, tumble, slip, tilt, trip, lurch; cropper, *culbute*; titubation, stumble; fate of Icarus; dive, nose-dive, *volpané*.

avalanche, *débâcle*, landslip, slide.

V. descend; go –, drop –, come-down; fall, gravitate, drop, slip, slide, glissade, dive, plunge, settle; decline, slump, set, sink, droop, come down a peg.

dismount, alight, light, get down; swoop; stoop etc. 308; fall prostrate, precipitate oneself; let fall etc. 308.

tumble, trip, stumble, titubate, lurch, pitch, swag, topple; topple –, tumble- -down, – over; tilt, sprawl, plump down, come a cropper.

Adj. descending etc. *v.*; descendent, declivitous; downcast; decur-rent, sive; labent, deciduous; nodding to its fall.

Adv. down, -hill, -wards.

307. Elevation.—**N.** elevation; raising etc. *v.*; erection, lift; sublevation, upheaval; sublimation, exaltation; prominence etc. (*convexity*) 250.

lever etc. 633; crane, derrick, windlass, capstan, winch, dredger, lift, elevator, escalator, dumb waiter.

V. heighten, elevate, raise, lift, erect; set –, stick –, perch –, perk –, tilt- up; rear, hoist, heave; up-lift, -raise, -rear, -bear, -cast, -hoist, -heave; buoy, weigh, mount, give a lift; exalt, sublimate; place –, set- on a pedestal.

take –, drag –, fish- up; dredge.

stand –, rise –, get –, jump- up, spring to one's feet; hold -oneself, – one's head- up; draw oneself up to his full height.

Adj. elevated etc. *v.*; standing up; stilted, attollent, rampant.

Adv. on -stilts, – the shoulders of, – one's legs, – one's hind legs.

308. Depression.—**N.** lowering etc. *v.*; depression; dip etc. (*concavity*) 252; abasement; detrusion; reduction.

over-throw, -set, -turn; upset; prostration, subversion, precipitation.

bow; courtesy, curtsy; genuflexion, *kowtow*, obeisance, *salaam*.

V. depress, lower; let –, take- -down, – down a peg; cast; let -drop, – fall; sink, debase, bring low, abase, slash, reduce, detrude, pitch, precipitate.

over-throw, -turn, -set; upset, subvert, prostrate, level, fell; cast –, take –, throw –, fling –, dash –, pull –, cut –, knock –, hew- down; raze, – to the ground; humiliate, trample in the dust, pull about one's ears.

sit, – down; couch, squat, crouch, stoop, bend, bow, courtsey, curtsy; bob, duck, dip, genuflect, kneel; *kowtow*, *salaam*, make obeisance, prostrate oneself; bend, bow- the -head, – knee; incline the head; bow down; cower; recline etc. (*be horizontal*) 213.

Adj. depressed etc. *v.*; at a low ebb; prostrate etc. (*horizontal*) 213; detrusive.

309. Leap.—**N.** leap, jump, hop, spring, bound, vault, saltation.

dance, caper, gambol; curvet, caracole; *gambade*, *-bado*; capriole, demivolt; buck, – jump; hop, skip and jump.

kangaroo, jerboa, chamois, goat, frog, grasshopper, flea.

V. leap; jump -up, – over the moon; hop, spring, bound, vault, ramp, cut capers, gambol, trip, skip, dance, caper, curvet, *caracole*; foot it, bob, bounce, flounce, start, frisk etc. (*amusement*) 840; jump about etc. (*agitation*) 315; trip it on the light fantastic toe, dance oneself off one's legs.

Adj. leaping etc. *v.*; saltatory, frisky.

Adv. on the light fantastic toe.

310. Plunge.—N. plunge, dip, dive, header; ducking etc. *v.*; submergence, immersion, diver.

V. plunge, dip, souse, duck; dive, plump; take a -plunge, – header, make a plunge; bathe etc. (*water*) 337

sub-merge, -merse; immerse, douse, sink, engulf, send to -the bottom, – Davy Jones' locker.

get out of one's depth; go -to the bottom, – down like a stone; founder, welter, wallow

311. Circuition. [Curvilinear motion.]—**N.** circuition, circulation; turn, curvet; excursion; circum-vention, -navigation, -ambulation; north-west passage; ambit, gyre, lap, circuit etc. 629.

turning etc. *v.*; wrench; evolution; coil, helix, spiral; corkscrew.

V. turn, bend, wheel; go –, put- about; heel; go –, turn -round, – to the right about; turn on one's heel; make –, describe- a -circle, – complete circle; encircle; go –, pass- through -180°, – 360°.

circum-navigate, -aviate, -ambulate, -vent; put a girdle round the earth, go the round, make the round of.

turn –, round- a corner; double a point.

wind, circulate, meander; whisk, twirl; twist etc. (*convolution*) 248; make a *détour* etc. (*circuit*) 629.

Adj. turning etc. *v.*; circuitous; circumforaneous, -fluent; devious, roundabout, circumambient, -flex, -navigable.

Adv. round about.

312. Rotation. [Motion in a continued circle.]—**N.** rotation, revolution, gyration, circulation, roll; circum-rotation, -volution, -gyration; volutation, circination, turbination, *pirouette*, convolution.

verticity; whir, whirl, swirl, eddy, vortex, whirlpool, gurge; cyclone, tornado; surge; *vertigo*, dizzy round; Maelstrom, Charybdis; Ixion; wheel of Fortune.

wheel, screw, propeller, whirligig, rolling stone, windmill; top, teetotum, merry-go-round; roller; cog-, fly-wheel, spit; jack; caster.

axis, axle, spindle, spool, pivot, pin, hinge, pole, swivel, gimbals, arbor, bobbin, mandrel, shaft.

[Science of rotatory motion] trochilics, gyrostatics.

V. rotate; roll, – along; revolve, spin; turn, – round; circumvolve; circulate; gyre, gyrate, wheel, whirl, swirl, twirl, trundle, troll, bowl; slew round.

roll up, furl; wallow, welter; box the compass; spin like a -top, – teetotum.

Adj. rotating etc. *v.*; rota-tory, -ry; circumrotatory, trochilic, vertiginous, gyratory; vortic-al, -ose.

Adv. head over heels, round and round, like a horse in a mill.

313. Evolution. [Motion in a reverse circle.]—**N.** evolution, unfolding, development; eversion etc. (*inversion*) 218.

V. evolve; un-fold, -roll, -wind, -coil, -twist, -furl, -twine, -ravel; disentangle; develop.

Adj. evolving etc. *v.*; evolved etc. *v.*

314. Oscillation. [Reciprocating motion, motion to and fro.]—**N.** oscillation; vibration, libration; motion of a pendulum; nutation; undulation; pulsation; pulse; throb; seismic disturbance.

alternation; coming and going etc. *v.*; ebb and flow, flux and reflux, ups and downs; wave, vibratiuncle, swing, beat, shake, wag, see-saw, dance, lurch, dodge; fluctuation; vacillation etc. (*irresolution*) 605.

seismometer, vibroscope, seismograph.

V. oscillate; vi-, li-brate; alternate, undulate, wave; sway, rock, swing; pulsate, beat; wag, -gle; nod, bob, courtesy, curtsy; tick; play; chatter, wamble, wabble; teeter, dangle, swag.

fluctuate, dance, curvet, reel, quake; quiver, quaver, shake, flicker; wriggle; roll, toss, pitch; flounder, stagger, totter, waddle; move –, bob- up and down etc. *adv.*; pass and repass, ebb and flow, come and go, shuttle; vacillate etc. 605.

brandish, shake, flourish.

Adj. oscillating etc. *v.*; oscill-, undul-, puls-, libr-atory; vibrat-ory, -ile; pendulous, shutterwise, seismic.

Adv. to and fro, up and down, backwards and forwards, see-saw, zigzag, wibble-wabble, in and out, from side to side, like buckets in a well.

315. Agitation. [Irregular motion.]—**N.** agitation, stir, tremor, shake, ripple, jog, jolt, jerk, shock, succession, trepidation, quiver, quaver, dance; jactit-ation, -ance; shuffling etc. *v.*; twitter, flicker, flutter.

disquiet, perturbation, commotion, turmoil, turbulence; tumult, -uation; hubbub, rout, bustle, fuss, racket, *subsultus*, staggers, megrims, epilepsy, fits, twitching, vellication, St. Vitus' dance.

spasm, throe, throb, palpitation, convulsion, paroxysm; tetanus.

disturbance etc. (*disorder*) 59; restlessness etc. (*changeableness*) 149.

ferment, -ation; ebullition, effervescence, hurly burly, *cahotage*; tempest, storm, ground swell, heavy sea, whirlpool, vortex etc. 312; whirlwhind etc. (*wind*) 349.

V. be -agitated etc.; shake; tremble, – like an aspen leaf; quiver, quaver, quake, shiver, twitter, twire, dither, dodder; twitch, writhe, toss, shuffle, tumble, stagger, bob, reel, sway; wag, -gle, wiggle; wriggle, – like an eel; squirm; dance, stumble, shamble, flounder, totter, flounce, flop, curvet, prance.

throb, pulsate, beat, palpitate, go pit-a-pat; flutter, flitter, flicker, bicker; bustle.

ferment, effervesce, foam; boil, – over; bubble, – up; simmer.

toss –, jump- about; jump like a parched pea; shake like an aspen leaf; shake to its -center, – foundations; be the sport of the winds and waves; reel to and fro like a drunken man; move –, drive- from post to pillar and from pillar to post; keep between hawk and buzzard.

agitate, shake, convulse, toss, tumble, bandy, wield, brandish, flap, flourish, whisk, jerk, hitch, jolt; jog, -gle; hostle, buffet, hustle, disturb, stir, shake up, churn, jounce, wallop, whip, vellicate.

Adj. shaking etc. *v.*; agitated, tremulous; de-, sub-sultory; shambling; giddy-paced, saltatory, convulsive, jerky, unquiet, restless, all of a twitter.

Adv. by fits and starts; subsultorily etc. *adj.*: *per saltum*; hop, skip and jump; in -convulsions, – fits, pit-a-pat.

316. Materiality.—N. material-ity, -ness; materialization; corpor-eity, -ality; substantiality, material existence, incarnation, flesh and blood, *plenum*; physical condition.

matter, body, substance, brute matter, stuff, element, principle, protoplasm, plasma, *parenchyma*, material, *substratum*, hyle, *corpus*, *pabulum*; frame.

object, article, thing, something; still life; stocks and stones; materials etc. 635.

[Science of matter] physics; somatology, -ics; natural –, experimental- philosophy; physical science, *philosophie positive*, materialism, hylism; applied –, micro-, molecular –, nuclear – physics.

atomics, atomic science, nucleonics, quantum mechanics, radiology.

atom, radical, tracer, isotope, pleiad; atomic – nucleus, – cluster; nuclear particle, neutron, protron, shell, valence electron.

materialist, physicist, atomic scientist, radiologist.

V. materialize, incorporate, incarnate, substantiate, embody.

atomize, split –, smash – the atom; radio-activate.

Adj. material, bodily; corpor-eal, -al; physical; somat-ic, -oscopic; sensible, tangible, ponderable, palpable, substantial; fleshly, incarnate.

physical, bio-, electro-, geo-physical; atomic, nuclear, thermonuclear, radio-active.

objective, impersonal, neuter, unspiritual, materialistic.

317. Immateriality.—N. immaterial-ity, -ness; incorporeity, dematerialization, unsubstantiality, spirituality; inextension; astral plane.

personality; I, myself, me; *ego*, spirit etc. (*soul*) 450; astral body; immaterialism; spiritual-ism, -ist; subliminal –, subconscious- self.

V. disembody, spiritualize, dematerialize.

Adj. immateri-al, -ate; incorpor-eal, -al; asomatous, unextended; un-, dis-embodied; extramundane, supersensible, unearthly; pneumatoscopic; spiritual etc. (*psychical*) 450; aery.

personal, subjective.

318. World.—N. world, creation, nature, universe; earth, globe, wide world; *cosmos*; terraqueous globe, sphere; macro-, mega-cosm; music of the spheres; strato-, tropo-sphere.

heavens, sky, welkin, empyrean; starry -heaven, – host; firmament; vault –, canopy- of heaven; celestial spaces.

heavenly bodies, stars, luminaries, nebulae; galaxy, milky way, galactic circle, *via lactea*.

sun, orb of day, Apollo, Phoebus; photo-, chromo-sphere; solar system; planet, -oid, asteroid; comet; satellite; moon, orb of night, Diana, Luna; aerolite, meteor; falling –, shooting-star; meteorite.

constellation, zodiac, signs of the zodiac, Charles's wain, Great Bear, Southern Cross, Orion's belt, Cassiopeia's chair, Pleiades etc.

colures, equator, ecliptic, orbit.

[Science of heavenly bodies] astronomy; urano-graphy, -logy; cosmo-logy, -graphy, -gony; *eidouranion*, orrery; geography; geodesy etc. (*measurement*) 466; star-gazing, -gazer; astronomer; cosmogonist, geodesist, geographer; observatory.

Adj. cosmic, cosmical, mundane; terr-estrial, -estrious, -aqueous, -ene, -eous; telluric, earthly, geotic, geodetic, cosmogonal, under the sun; sublunary, -astral.

solar, heliacal; lunar; celestial, heavenly, empyreal, sphery; starry, stellar; sider-eal, -al; astral; nebular.

Adv. in all creation, on the face of the globe, here below, under the sun.

319. Gravity.—N. gravi-ty, -tation, weight; heaviness etc. *adj.*; specific gravity; ponderosity, pressure, load; bur-den, -then; ballast, counterpoise; lump –, mass –, weight- of.

lead, millstone, mountain, Ossa on Pelion.

weighing, ponderation, trutination; weights; avoirdupois –, troy –, apothecaries'- weight; grain, scruple, drachm, ounce, pound, lb., load, stone, hundredweight, cwt., ton, quintal, carat, pennyweight, tod, gram, kilogram etc.

[Weighing instrument] balance, scales, steelyard, beam, weighbridge, spring balance, weighing machine.

[Science of gravity] statics.

V. be -heavy etc. *adj.*; gravitate, weigh, press, cumber, load.

[Measure the weight of] weigh, poise.

Adj. weighty; weighing etc. *v.*; heavy, – as lead; ponder-ous, -able; lump-ish, -y; cumber-, burden-some; cumbrous, unwieldy, massive.

in-, superin-cumbent.

320. Levity.—N. levity; lightness etc. *adj.*; imponderability, imponderables, buoyancy, volatility.

feather, dust, mote, down, thistledown, flue, cobweb, gossamer, straw, cork, bubble; float, bouy; ether, air.

leaven, ferment, barm, yeast, enzyme.
V. be -light etc. *adj.*; float, swim, be buoyed up.
render -light etc. *adj.*; lighten, levitate; leaven.
Adj. light, subtile, subtle, airy; imponder-ous, -able; astatic, weightless, ethereal, sublimated; uncompressed, volatile; buoyant, floating etc. *v.*; barmy, frothy; portable.
light as -a feather, – thistle down, – air.
fermenting etc. *n.*

321. Density.—N. density, solidity; solidness etc. *adj.*; impenetra-, impermea-bility; incompressibility; imporosity; cohesion etc. 46; constipation, consistence, spissitude.
specific gravity; hydro-, areo-meter.
condensation; solid-ation, -ification; consolidation; concretion, caseation, coagulation; petrifaction etc. (*hardening*) 323; crystallization, precipitation; deposit, precipitate, silt; inspissation; thickening etc. *v.*
indivisibility, indiscerptibility, indissolvableness.
solid body, mass, block, knot, lump; con-cretion, -crete, -glomerate; cake, clot, stone, curd, coagulum, grume; bone, gristle, cartilage.
V. be -dense etc. *adj.*; become –, render- solid etc. *adj.*; solid-ify, -ate; concrete, set, take a set, consolidate, congeal, coagulate; curd, -le; fix, clot, cake, candy, precipitate, deposit, cohere, crystallize; petrify etc. (*harden*) 323.
condense, thicken, inspissate, incrassate; compress, squeeze, ram down, constipate.
Adj. dense, solid, solidified etc. *v.*; cohe-rent, -sive etc. 46; compact, close, serried, thickset; substantial, massive, lumpish; impenetrable, impermeable, imporous; incompressible; constipated; concrete etc. (*hard*) 323; knot-ted, -ty; gnarled; crystal-line, -lizable; thick, grumous, stuffy.
un-dissolved, -melted, -liquified, -thawed.
in-divisible, -discerptible, -frangible, dissolvable, -dissoluble, -soluble, -fusible.

322. Rarity.—N. rarity; tenuity; absence of -solidity etc. 321; subtility; sponginess, compressibility.
rarefaction, expansion, dilatation, inflation, subtilization.
ether etc. (*gas*) 334.
V. rarefy, expand, dilate, subtilize, attenuate, thin.
Adj. rare, subtile, thin, fine, tenuous, compressible, flimsy, slight; light etc. 320; cavernous, spongy etc. (*hollow*) 252.
rarefied etc. *v.*; unsubstantial; uncom-pact, -pressed.

323. Hardness.—N. hardness etc. *adj.*; rigidity, renitence, inflexibility, temper, callosity, durity.
induration, petrifaction; lapid-ification, -escence; vitri-, ossi-, corni-fication; crystallization.
stone, pebble, flint, marble, rock, fossil, crag, crystal, quartz, granite, adamant; bone, cartilage; heart of oak, block, board, deal board; iron, steel; cast –, wrought- iron; nail; brick, concrete; cement.
V. render -hard etc. *adj.*; harden, stiffen, indurate, petrify, temper, ossify, vitrify.
Adj. hard, rigid, stubborn, stiff, firm; starch, -ed; stark, unbending, unlimber, unyielding; inflexible, tense; indurate, -d; gritty, proof.
adamant-ine, -ean; concrete, stony, rocky, lithic, granitic, vitreous; crystalline; horny, corneous; bony; oss-eous, -ific; cartilaginous; hard as a -stone etc. *n.*; stiff as -buckram, – a poker.

324. Softness.—N. softness, pliableness etc. *adj.*; flexibility; pli-ancy, -ability; sequacity, malleability; flabbiness; duct-, tract-ility; extend-, extensibility; plasticity; inelasticity; flaccidity, laxity.
clay, wax, butter, dough, pudding; cushion, pillow, feather-bed, pad, down, padding, wadding.
mollification; softening etc. *v.*
V. render -soft etc. *adj.*; soften, mollify, mellow, relax, temper; mash, knead, squash, *massage*.
bend, yield, relent, relax, give.
Adj. soft, tender, supple; pli-ant, -able; flex-ible, -ile; lithe, -some; lissom, limber, plastic; ductile; tract-ile, -able; malleable, extensile, sequacious, inelastic, mollient.
yielding etc. *v.*; flabby, limp, flimsy.
flaccid, flocculent, downy; spongy, edematous, medullary, doughy, argillaceous, mellow.
soft as -butter, – down, – silk; yielding as wax; tender as a chicken.

325. Elasticity.—N. elasticity, springiness, spring, resilience, renitency, buoyancy.
india-rubber, caoutchouc, gutta-percha, whalebone, gum elastic.
V. be -elastic etc. *adj.*; spring back etc. (*recoil*) 227.
Adj. elastic, tensile, springy, ductile, resilient, renitent, buoyant.

326. Inelasticity.—N. want of –, absence of-elasticity etc. 325; inelasticity etc. (*softness*) 324.
Adj. inelastic etc. (*soft*) 324.

327. Tenacity.—N. tenacity, toughness, strength; cohesion etc. 46; sequacity; stubbornness etc. (*obstinacy*) 606; viscidity etc. 352.
leather; gristle, cartilage.
V. be -tenacious etc. *adj.*; resist fracture.
Adj. tenacious, tough, cohesive, adhesive, strong, resisting, sequacious, stringy, gristly, cartilaginous, leathery, coriaceous, tough as whit-leather; stubborn etc. (*obstinate*) 606.

328. Brittleness.—N. brittleness etc. *adj.*; frag-, friab-, frangib-, fiss-ility; frailty; house of -cards, – glass.
V. be -brittle etc. *adj.*; live in a glass house.
break, crack, snap, split, shiver, splinter, crumble, break short, burst, fly, give way; fall to pieces; crumble -to, – into- dust.

Adj. breakable, brittle, frangible, fragile, frail, friable, delicate, gimcrack, shivery, fissile; splitting etc. *v.*; lacerable, splintery, crisp, crimp, short, brittle as glass.

329. Texture. [Structure.]—**N.** structure, organization, anatomy, frame, mold, fabric, construction; frame-work, carcass, architecture; stratification, cleavage.

substance, stuff, *compages*, *parenchyma*; constitution, staple, organism.

[Science of structures] organ-, oste-, my- splanchn-, neur-, angi-, aden-ology; angi-, aden-ography.

texture; inter-, con-texture; tissue, grain, web, surface; warp and -woof, – weft; tooth, nap etc. (*roughness*) 256; fineness –, coarseness- of grain.

[Science of textures] histology.

Adj. structural, organic; anatomic, -al.

text-ural, -ile; fine-, coarse-grained; fine, delicate, subtile, gossamery, filmy; coarse; homespun; linsey-woolsey.

330. Pulverulence. [State of powder.]—**N.** pulverulence; sandiness etc. *adj.*; efflorescence; friability.

powder, dust, sand, shingle; sawdust; grit; attrition; meal, bran, flour, *farina*, spore, sporule; crumb, seed, grain; particle etc. (*smallness*) 32; thermion; limature, filings, *débris*, *detritus*, scobs, magistery, fine powder; *flocculi*.

smoke; cloud of -dust, – sand, – smoke; puff –, volume -of smoke; sand –, dust- storm.

[Reduction to powder] pulverization, comminution, attenuation, granulation, disintegration, subaction, contusion, trituration, levigation, abrasion, detrition, multure; limation; filing etc. *v.*

[Instruments for pulverization] mill, millstone, grater, rasp, file, pestle and mortar, nutmeg grater, teeth, molar, grinder, chopper, grindstone, kern, quern, muller.

V. come to dust; be -disintegrated, – reduced to powder etc.

reduce –, grind- to powder; pulverize, comminute, granulate, triturate, levigate; scrape, file, abrade, rub down, grind, grate, rasp, pound, bray, bruise; con-tuse, -tund; beat, crush, cranch, craunch, crunch, muller, scranch, crumble, disintegrate; attenuate etc. 195.

Adj. powdery, pulverulent, granular, mealy, floury, farinaceous, branny, furfuraceous, flocculent, dusty, sandy, sabulous; aren-ose, -arious, -aceous; gritty; efflorescent, impalpable.

pulverizable; friable, crumbly, shivery; pulverized etc. *v.*; attrite; in pieces.

331. Friction.—**N.** friction, attrition; rubbing etc. *v.*; erasure; con-frication, -trition; affriction, abrasion, arrosion, limature, frication, rub; elbow-grease; rosin; *massage*.

V. rub, scratch, abrade, scrape, scrub, fray, rasp, graze, curry, scour, polish, rub out, erase, gnaw; file, grind etc. (*reduce to powder*) 330; *massage*.

set one's teeth on edge; rosin.

Adj. anatriptic, abrasive.

332. Lubrication. [Absence of friction. Prevention of friction.]—**N.** smoothness etc. 255; unctuousness etc. 355.

lubri-cation, -fication; anointment; oiling etc. *v.*

synovia; lubricant, graphite, glycerine, oil etc. 356; saliva; lather.

V. lubri-cate, -citate; oil, grease, lather, soap; wax.

Adj. lubricated etc. *v.*

333. Fluidity.—**N.** fluidity, liquidity; liquidness etc. *adj.*; gaseity etc. 334; liquefaction etc. 334.

fluid, inelastic fluid; liquid, liquor; lymph, humor, juice, sap, serum, blood, serosity, gravy, rheum, ichor, sanies.

solu-bility, -bleness.

[Science of liquids] hydro-logy, -statics, -dynamics, hydraulics. etc.

V. be -fluid etc. *adj.*; flow etc. (*water in motion*) 348; liquefy etc. 335.

Adj. liquid, fluid, serous, juicy, succulent, sappy; fluent etc. (*flowing*) 348.

liquefied etc. 335; uncongealed; soluble, hydrostatic etc. *n.*

334. Gaseity.—**N.** gaseity, gaseousness, vapourousness etc. *adj.*; flatulence, -lency; volatility, aeration, gasification.

elastic fluid, gas, air, vapor, ether, steam, fume, reek, *effluvium*, *flatus*; cloud etc. 353.

[Science of elastic fluids] pneumat-ics, -ostatics; aero-statics, -dynamics etc.

gas-, gaso-meter.

V. gassify, aerate, aerify; emit vapor etc. 336.

Adj. gaseous, aeriform, ethereal, aerial, airy, vaporous, volatile, evaporable; flatulent; aerostatic etc. *n.*

335. Liquefaction.—**N.** liquefaction; liquescen-ce, -cy, deliquescence; melting etc. (*heat*) 384; colliqu-ation, -efaction; thaw; de-, liquation; lixiviation, dissolution.

solution, apozem, lixivium, infusion, decoction, flux.

solvent, diluent, menstruum, alkahest, *aqua fortis*.

V. render -liquid etc 333; liquefy, run, deliquesce; melt etc. (*heat*) 384; solve; dissolve, resolve; liquate; hold in solution; leach, lixiviate.

Adj. lique-fied etc. *v.*, -scent, -fiable; deliquescent, soluble, colliquative; solvent.

336. Vaporization.—**N.** vapor-, volatilization; gasification; e-, vaporation; distillation, cohobation, sublimation, exhalation; volatility.

vaporizer, still, retort, spray, atomizer; fumigation, steaming.

V. render -gaseous etc. 334; vaporize, volatilize; distil, sublime; evaporate, exhale, smoke, transpire, emit vapor, fume, reek, steam, fumigate.

Adj. volatilized etc. *v.*; reeking etc. *v.*; volatile; evaporable, vaporizable.

337. Water.—N. water; serum, serosity; lymph; rheum; diluent.

dilution, maceration, lotion; washing etc. *v.*; im-, mersion; humectation, infiltration, spargefaction, affusion, irrigation, *douche*, balneation, bath.

deluge etc. (*water in motion*) 348; high water, flood-, spring-tide.

V. be -watery etc. *adj.*; reek.

add water, water, wet; moisten etc. 339; dilute, dip, immerse; merge; im-, sub-merge; plunge, souse, duck, drown; soak, steep, macerate, pickle, wash, sprinkle, sparge, lave, bathe, affuse, splash, swash, douse, slosh, drench; dabble, slop, slobber, irrigate, inundate, deluge; syringe, inject, gargle; infiltrate, percolate.

Adj. watery, aqueous, aquatic, lymphatic; balneal, diluent; drenching etc. *v.*; diluted etc. *v.*; weak; wet etc. (*moist*) 339.

Phr. the waters are out.

338. Air.—N. air etc. (*gas*) 334; common –, atmospheric- air; atmosphere, stratosphere, isothermal layer, troposphere, Heaviside layer.

open, – air; sky, welkin; blue, – sky; cloud etc. 353.

weather, climate, rise and fall of the barometer, isobar.

[Science of air] pneumatics, aero-logy, -scopy, -graphy; meteorology, climatology; eudio-, baro-, aero-meter; aneroid, baro-graph, -scope; weather-gauge, -glass, -cock.

exposure to the -air, – weather; ventilation; aero-station; -nautics; -naut etc. 265 and 269.

V. air, ventilate; fan etc. (*wind*) 349.

Adj. containing air, flatulent, effervescent; windy etc. 349.

atmospheric, airy; aeri-al, -form; pneumatic; meteorological; weather-wise.

Adv. in the open air, out of doors, *à la belle étoile, al fresco*; *sub -Jove, – dio.*

339. Moisture.—N. moisture; moistness etc. *adj.*; hum-idity, -ectation; madefaction, dew; *serein*; marsh etc. 345; Hygromet-ry, -er.

V. moisten, wet; humect, -ate; sponge, damp, dampen, bedew; imbue, imbrue, infiltrate, saturate; seethe, sop; soak, drench etc. (*water*) 337.

be -moist etc. *adj.*; not have a dry thread; perspire etc. (*exude*) 295.

Adj. moist, damp; watery etc. 337; undried, humid, wet, dank, muggy, dewy; roric; roscid; juicy.

wringing wet; wet -through, – to the skin; saturated etc. *v.*

swashy, soggy, dabbled; reeking, seething, dripping, soaking, soft, sodden, sloppy, muddy; swampy etc. (*marshy*) 345; irriguous.

340. Dryness.—N. dryness etc. *adj.*; siccity, aridity, drought, ebb-, neap-tide, low water.

drying, ex-, de-siccation; evaporation; dehydration; arefaction, dephlegmation, drainage.

drier, desiccator.

V. be -dry etc. *adj.*; render -dry etc. *adj.*; dry; dry –, soak- up; sponge, swab, wipe; ex-, desiccate, dehydrate, anhydrate; drain, parch.

be fine, hold up.

Adj. dry, anhydrous, arid, waterless; dried etc. *v.*; undamped; juice-, sap- less; sear; husky; rainless, without rain, fine; dry as -a bone, – dust, – a stick, – a mummy, – a biscuit; disiccated; dehydrated; water-proof, -tight.

341. Ocean.—N. sea, ocean, main, deep, brine, salt water, waters, waves, billows, high seas, offing, great waters, watery waste, 'vasty deep,' briny ocean, herring pond, steamer track, the seven seas; wave, tide etc. (*water in motion*) 348.

hydrograph-y, -er, oceanography; Neptune, Thetis, Triton, Naiad, Nereid; sea-nymph, Siren, mer-maid, -man; trident, dolphin.

Adj. oceanic; mar-ine, -itime; pleagic, -ian; sea-going, -worthy; hydrographic.

Adv. at –, on- sea; afloat, on the high seas.

342. Land.—N. land, earth, ground, dry land, *terra firma*.

continent, mainland, peninsula, delta; tongue –, neck- of land; isthmus; oasis; promontory etc. (*projection*) 250; highland etc. (*height*) 206.

coast, shore, scar, strand, beach; bank, lea; seaboard, -side, -shore, -bank, -coast, -beach; rock-, iron- bound coast; loom of the land; derelict; innings; *alluvium*, alluvion.

soil, glebe, clay, loam, marl, clodge, chalk, gravel, mold, subsoil, clod, clot; rock, crag, cliff.

acres; real estate etc. (*property*) 780; landsman, land-lubber, farmer.

geography etc. 318; agriculture etc. 371.

V. land, come to land; set foot on -the soil, – dry land; come –, go- ashore.

Adj. earthy; continental, midland; littoral, riparian, ripuarian; alluvial; terrene etc. (*world*) 318; landed, predial, territorial.

Adv. ashore; on -shore, – land.

343. Gulf. Lake.—N. land covered with water, gulf, gulph, bay, inlet, bight, estuary, arm of the sea, fiord, armlet; frith, firth, ostiary, mouth; lagune, lagoon; indraught; cove, creek; natural harbor; roads; strait, narrows; Euripus; sound, belt, gut, kyles.

lake, loch, lough, mere, tarn, plash, broad, pond, pool, lin, puddle, well, artesian well, tank, sump; standing –, dead –, sheet of- water; fish –, mill-pond; race; ditch, dike, dyke, dam; reservoir etc. (*store*) 636.

Adj. lacustrine; land locked.

344. Plain.—N. plain, table land, mesa, face of the country; open –, champaign-country; basin, downs, waste, weary waste, desert, tundra, wild, steppe, pampas, savanna, prairie, champaign, heath, common, wold, veld; moor, -land, uplands, fell; bush; *plateau* etc. (*level*) 213; *campagna*.

meadow, mead, haugh, pasturage, park, field,

lawn, green, plat, plot, grass-plat, greensward, sward, grass, turf, sod, heather; lea, ley, lay; grounds.

Adj. campestrian, champaign, alluvial.

345. Marsh.—N. marsh, swamp, morass, marish, moss, fen, bog, quagmire, slough, sump, wash; mud, squash, slush.

Adj. marsh, -y; swampy, boggy, plashy, poachy, quaggy, soft; muddy, sloppy, squashy, spongy; paludal; moor-ish, -y; fenny.

346. Island.—N. island, isle, islet, eyot, ait, holm, reef, atoll, breaker; archipelago; islander.

Adj. insular, sea-girt.

347. Stream. [Fluid in motion.]**—N.** stream etc. (*of water*) 348, (*of air*) 349.

V. flow etc. 348; blow etc. 349.

348. River. [Water in motion.]**—N.** running water.

jet, spirt, squirt, spout, splash, swash, rush, gush, *jet d'eau*; sluice, chute.

water-spout, -fall; fall, cascade, force, foss; lin, -n, ghyll, Niagara; cata-ract, -dupe, -clysm; *débâcle*, inundation, deluge.

rain, -fall; *serein*; shower, scud; downpour, cloud burst; driving –, pouring –, drenching-rain; hyeto-logy, -graphy; rainy season, monsoon; predominance of Aquarius, reigh of St. Swithin; mizzle, drizzle, *stilliciduim*, plash; dropping etc. *v.*

stream, course, flux, flow, profluence; effluence etc. (*egress*) 295; defluxion; flowing etc. *v.*; current, tide, race.

spring; fount, -ain; rill, rivulet, gill, gullet, rillet; stream-, brook-let; runnel, sike, burn, beck, brook, stream, river; reach; tributary.

body of water, torrent, rapids, flush, flood, swash, spate; spring –, high –, full-tide; bore; eagre, *hugre*; fresh, -et; undertow, indraught, reflux, undercurrent, eddy, vortex, gurge, whirlpool, Maelstrom, regurgitation, overflow; confluence, corrivation.

wave, billow, surge, swell, ripple; roller, ground swell, surf, breaker, white horses; comber, beach-comber; rough –, heavy –, cross –, long –, short –, chopping –, choppy- sea, choppiness; tidal wave.

[Science of fluids in motion] Hydrodynamics; Hydraul-ics etc.; raingauge etc.

water-bearer, – carrier, Aquarius.

irrigation etc. (*water*) 337; pump; watering-pot, – cart; hydrant, standpipe, hose, sprinkler, drencher; fire engine, squirt, syringe.

V. flow, run; meander; gush, pour, spout, roll, jet, well, issue; drop, drip, dribble, plash, squirt, spurt, spirtle, trill, trickle, distil, percolate; stream, overflow, inundate, deluge, flow over, splash, swash; guggle, murmur, babble, bubble, purl, gurgle, sputter, regurgitate; ooze, flow out etc. (*egress*) 295.

rain, – hard, – in torrents, – cats and dogs, – pitchforks; come down in sheets; pour with rain, drizzle, mizzle, spit, sprinkle, set in.

flow –, fall –, open –, drain- into; discharge itself, desembogue.

[Cause a flow] pour; pour out etc. (*discharge*) 297; shower down; irrigate, drench etc. (*wet*) 337; spill, splash.

[Stop a flow] stanch; dam, -up etc. (*close*) 261; obstruct etc. 706.

Adj. fluent; dif-, pro-, af-fluent; tidal; flowing etc. *v.*; meand-ering, -ry, -rous; fluvi-al, -atile, streamy, showery, rainy, drizzly, drizzling, pluvial, pluviose, stillicidous.

349. Wind. [Air in motion.]**—N.** wind, draught, *flatus*, *afflatus*, air; breath, – of air; puff, whiff, zephyr; blow, drift; *aura*; stream, current; under-current.

gust, blast, breeze, squall, gale, half a gale, storm, tempest, hurricane, whirlwind, tornado, samiel, cyclone, typhoon; simoon; harmattan, monsoon, trade wind, sirocco, *mistral*, *bise*, *föhn*, tramontane, levanter; capful of wind; fresh –, stiff- breeze; keen blast; blizzard.

windiness etc. *adj.*; ventosity; rough –, dirty –, ugly –, stress of- weather; dirty-, windy-, mackerel- sky; mare's tail; thick –, black –, white- squall.

anemography, aerodynamics; windgauge, anemometer, weather-cock, vane.

suf-, insuf-, per-, in-, af-flation; blowing, fanning etc. *v.*; ventilation.

sneezing etc. *v.*; sternutation; hic-cup, -cough; catching of the breath; breathing etc.

Eolus, Eurus, Boreas, Zephyr, cave of Eolus.

air-pump, lungs, bellows, blow-pipe, fan, blower; pulmotor, ventilator, punkah, aspirator, exhauster, ejector.

V. blow, waft; blow -hard, – great guns, – a hurricane etc. *n.*; whistle, roar, howl, ring in the shrouds; stream, issue.

respire, breathe, in-, ex-hale, puff; whif, -fle; gasp, wheeze; snuff, -le; sniff, -le; sneeze, cough, belch.

fan, ventilate; in-, per-flate; blow –, pump- up.

Adj. blowing etc. *v.*; windy, airy, aeolian, flatulent; breezy, gusty, squally; stormy, tempestuous, blustering; boisterous etc. (*violent*) 173.

pulmon-ic, -ary.

350. Conduit. [Channel for the passage of water.]**—N.** conduit, channel, duct, watercourse, race; head –, tail- race; adit, aqueduct, canal, trough, flume, gutter, pantile; dike, canyon, ravine, gorge, hollow, main, gully, moat, ditch, drain, sewer, culvert, *cloaca*, sough, kennel, siphon, *piscina*; pipe etc. (*tube*) 260; funnel; tunnel etc. (*passage*) 627; water –, waste- pipe; emunctory, gully-hole, artery, aorta, vein, blood vessel; lymphatic; throat, alimentary canal, intestine; pore, spout, scupper; ad-, a-jutage; hose; gar-, gurgoyle; penstock, weir; flood-, water-gate; sluice, lock, valve; rose; waterworks.

Adj. vascular etc. (*with holes*) 260.

351. Air-pipe. [Channel for the passage of air.]**—N.** air-pipe, – shaft, – way, – passage, –

tube; shaft, flue, chimney, funnel, vent, blow-hole, nostril, nozzle, throat, weasand, *trachea*; *bronchus*, *-ia*; larynx, tonsils, wind-pipe, spiracle; ventiduct, -lator; louvre, Venetian blinds; blow-pipe etc. (*wind*) 349; pipe etc. (*tube*) 260.

352. Semiliquidity.—N. semiliquidity; stickiness etc. *adj.*; visc-idity, -osity; gumm-, glutin-, muc-osity; spiss-, crass-itude; lentor; adhesiveness etc. (*cohesion*) 46.

inspiss-, incrass-ation; thickening, coagulation.

jelly, aspic, mucilage, gelatin, isinglass; colloid, mucus, phlegm; pituite, lava; glair, starch, gluten, albumen, milk, cream, protein; syrup, treacle; gum, size, glue, paste; wax, bee's-wax; emulsoid, emulsion, soup; squash, mud, slush, slime, ooze; moisture etc. 339; marsh etc. 345.

V. inspiss-, incrass-ate; coagulate, gelatinize, gelatinify, gel, jell, emulsify, thicken; mash, squash, churn, beat up.

Adj. semi-fluid, -liquid; half-melted, -frozen; milky, muddy etc. *n.*; lact-eal, -ean, -eous, -escent, -iferous; emulsive, curdled, thick, succulent, uliginous.

gelat-, album-, mucilag-, glut-inous; gelatine, mastic, amylaceous, ropy, clammy, clotted; vis-cid, -cous; sticky, tacky; slab, -by; lentous, pituitous; mu-cid, -culent, -cous.

353. Bubble. [Mixture of air and water.] [Cloud.]—**N.** bubble; foam, froth, head, fume, spume, lather, suds, spray, surf, yeast, barm, spindrift.

cloud, vapor, fog, mist, haze, steam; scud, rack, *nimbus*; *cumulus*, woolpack, *cirrus*, *stratus*; *cirro-*, *cumulo-stratus*; *cirro-cumulus*; mackerel sky, mare's tail, dirty sky.

[Science of clouds] nephelognosy, nephology.

effervescence, fermentation; bubbling etc. *v.*

nebula; cloudiness etc. (*opacity*) 426; nebulosity etc. (*dimness*) 422.

V. bubble, boil, foam, froth, spume, mantle, sparkle, guggle, gurgle; effervesce, ferment, fizzle; aerate; cloud, overcast, befog.

Adj. bubbling etc. *v.*; frothy, nappy, effervescent, sparkling, *mousseux*, up, fizzy, with a head on.

cloudy etc. *n.*; vaporous, nebulous, overcast; nubiferous, nephological; foggy, brumous.

354. Pulpiness.—N. pulpiness etc. *adj.*; pulp, paste, dough, sponge, curd, pap, rob, jam, pudding, mush, fool, poultice, grume.

Adj. pulpy etc. *n.*; pultaceous, grumous.

V. pulp, pulpify, mash.

355. Unctuousness.—N. unctuousness etc. *adj.*; unctuosity, lubricity; ointment etc. (*oil*) 356; anointment; lubrication etc. 332.

V. oil etc. (*lubricate*) 332.

Adj. unctuous, oily, oleaginous, adipose, sebaceous; fat, -ty; greasy; waxy, butyraceous, soapy, saponaceous, pinguid, lardaceous; slippery.

356. Oil.—N. oil, fat, butter, cream, grease, tallow, suet, lard, dripping, margarine, oleomargarine, exunge, blubber; glycerine, stearine, elaine, oleagine; soap; soft soap, wax, cerement; paraffin, spermaceti, adipocere; petroleum, mineral –, rock –, crystal- oil, kerosene, vegetable –, colza –, olive –, linseed –, cotton seed –, rape –, nut –, fusel- oil; animal –, neat's foot –, signal –, train- oil; ointment, unguent, liniment, salve, pomade, pomatum, brilliantine, spike –, nard.

356a. Resin.—N. resin, rosin, colophony; gum; lac, shellac, sealing-wax; amber, -gris; bitumen, pitch, tar, asphalt, -e, -um; varnish, copal, mastic, magilp, lacquer, japan.

V. varnish etc. (*overlay*) 223.

Adj. resinous, bituminous, pitchy, tarry.

357. Organization.—N. organized -world, – nature; living –, animated- nature; living beings; organic remains, organism; fossils; animal and vegetable kingdom, *fauna* and *flora*, biota.

prot-oplasm, -ein; albumen; structure etc. 329; organ-ization, -ism.

[Science of living beings] biology; natural history,* organic –, bio-chemistry, anatomy, physiology, embryology, morphology, evolution, Darwinism, Lamarkism, zoology etc. 368; botany etc. 369; naturalist, biologist etc.

Adj. organ-ic, -ized.

*The term *Natural History* is also used as relating to all the objects in Nature whether organic or inorganic, and including therefore *Mineralogy*, *Geology*, *Meteorology*, etc.

358. Inorganization.—N. mineral -world, – kingdom; unorganized –, inorganic –, brute –, inanimate- matter.

[Science of the mineral kingdom] mineralogy; geo-logy, -gnosy, -scopy; metall-urgy, -ography; lithology; orycto-logy, -graphy.

V. turn to dust, pulverize.

Adj. in-organic, -animate; unorganized; azoic; mineral.

359. Life.—N. life; vi-tality, -ability; animation; vital -spark, – flame, – force.

respiration, wind; breath -of life, – of one's nostrils; life-blood; Archeus; existence etc. 1.

vivification, vitalization; revivification etc. 163; Prometheus; life to come etc. (*destiny*) 152.

[Science of life] physiology, etiology, embryology, biology; animal economy.

nourishment, staff of life etc. (*food*) 298.

V. be -alive etc. *adj.*; live, breathe, respire; subsist etc. (*exist*) 1; walk the earth; strut and fret one's hour upon a stage; be spared.

see the light, be born, come into the world; fetch –, draw- -breath, – the breath of life; quicken; revive; come to, – life.

give birth to etc. (*produce*) 161; bring to life, put into life, vitalize; vivi-fy, -ficate; reanimate etc. (*restore*) 660; keep -alive, – body and soul together, – the wolf from the door; support life.

have nine lives like a cat.

Adj. living, alive; in -life, – the flesh, – the land of the living; on this side of the grave, above ground, breathing, quick, animated, viable; lively etc. (*active*) 682; alive and kicking; tenacious of life.

vital; vivi-fying; -fied etc. *v.*; Promethean.

Adv. *vivendi causâ.*

360. Death.—N. death, dying etc. *v.*; de-cease, -mise; dissolution, departure, *obit*, release, rest, *quietus*, fall; loss, bereavement.

end etc. 67 –, cessation etc. 142 –, loss –, extinction –, ebb- of -life etc. 359.

death-warrant, -watch, -rattle, -bed; stroke –, agonies –, shades –, valley of the shadow –, jaws –, hand- of death; last -breath, – gasp, – agonies; dying -day, – breath, – agonies; swan song, *chant du cygne*; *rigor mortis*; Stygian shore; crossing the bar, the great adventure.

King -of terrors, – Death, Death, Angel of Death; mortality; doom etc. (*necessity*) 601.

euthanasia; happy release; break up of the system; natural -death, – decay; sudden –, violent- death; untimely end, watery grave; suffocation, *asphyxia*; heart failure; fatal disease etc. (*disease*) 655; death-blow etc. (*killing*) 361.

necrology, bills of mortality, obituary; death-song etc. (*lamentation*) 839.

V. die, expire, perish; meet one's -death, – end; pass away, be taken; yield –, resign- one's breath; resign one's -being, – life; end one's -days, – life, – earthly career; breathe one's last; cease to -live, – breathe; depart this life; be -no more etc. *adj.*; go –, drop –, pop -off; lose –, lay down –, relinquish –, surrender- one's life; drop –, sink- into the grave; close one's eyes; fall –, drop- dead, – down dead; break one's neck; give –, yield- up the ghost; be all over with one.

pay the debt to nature, shuffle off this mortal coil, take one's last sleep; go the way of all flesh; join the -greater number, – majority, – choir invisible, to life immortal awake; come –, turn- to dust; cross the Stygian ferry; go to -one's long account, – one's last home, – Davy Jones's locker, – the wall; receive one's death warrant, make one's will, die a natural death, go out like the snuff of a candle; come to an untimely end; catch one's death; go off the hooks, kick the bucket, pet out; go West; hop the twig, turn up one's toes; die a violent death etc. (*be killed*) 361; make the supreme sacrifice.

Adj. dead, lifeless; deceased, demised, departed, defunct; late, gone, no more; ex-, in-animate; out of the world, taken off, released; departed this life etc. *v.*; dead and gone; bereft of life, stone dead, dead as -a door nail, – a door post, – mutton, – a herring, – nits; launched into eternity, gathered to one's fathers, numbered with the dead, gone to a better land, behind the veil, beyond the grave, – mortal ken.

dying etc. *v.*; mori-bund, -ent, Acherontic; hippocratic; *in -articulo, – extremis*; in the -jaws, – agony- of death; going, – off; *aux abois*; on one's -last legs, – death bed; at -the point of death, – death's door, – the last gasp; near one's end, given over, booked, fey; with one foot in –, tottering on the brink of- the grave.

still-born; mortuary; deadly etc. (*killing*) 361.

Adv. *post -obit, – mortem.*

Phr. life -ebbs, – fails, – hangs by a thread; one's -days are numbered, – hour is come, – race is run, – doom is sealed; Death -knocks at the door, – stares one in the face; the breath is out of the body; the grave closes over one; *sic itur ad astra.*

361. Killing. [Destruction of life; violent death.]—**N.** killing etc. *v.*; homicide, manslaughter, murder, assassination, trucidation, occision; lynching, effusion of blood; blood, -shed; gore, slaughter, carnage, butchery; *battue*, gladiatorial combat.

massacre; *fussillade*, *noyade*, *pogrom*; thuggism; racketeering.

death blow, finishing stroke, *coup de grâce*, *quietus*; execution etc. (*capital punishment*) 972; judicial murder; martyrdom.

butcher, slayer, murderer, Cain, assassin, cutthroat, garrotter, *bravo*, thug, racketeer, gunman, mobster, gangster, Moloch, *matador*, *sabreur*; *guet-à-pens*; gallows, executioner etc. (*punishment*) 975; man-eater.

regicide, parricide, fratricide, infanticide, aborticide etc.

suicide, *felo de se*, *suttee*, *hara kiri*, Juggernaut; immolation, holocaust.

suffocation, strangulation, *garrotte*; hanging etc. *v.*

deadly weapon etc. (*arms*) 727; Aceldama; the potter's field, the field of blood.

fatal accident, violent death, casualty.

[Destruction of animals] slaughtering; phthiozoics;' sport, -ting; the chase, venery; hunting, coursing, shooting, fishing; pig-sticking; sports-, hunts-, fisher-man; hunter, Nimrod; slaughterer, knacker, slaughter-house, shambles, *abattoir*.

V. kill, put to death, slay, shed blood; murder, assassinate, butcher, slaughter; victimize, immolate; massacre; take away –, deprive of- life; make away with, put an end to; despatch, dispatch; burke settle, do, – to death, – for.

strangle, garrotte, hang, lynch, throttle, choke, stifle, suffocate, stop the breath, smother, asphyxiate, drown.

saber; cut -down, – to pieces, – the throat; jugulate; stab, run through the body, bayonet; put to the -sword, – edge of the sword.

shoot, – dead; blow one's brains out; brain, knock on the head; stone, lapidate; give –, deal- a death blow; give a *-quietus*, – *coup de grâce.*

behead, bowstring etc. (*execute*) 972.

hunt, shoot etc. *n.*

cut off, nip in the bud, launch into eternity, send to one's last account, bump off, rub out, sign one's death warrant, strike the death knell of.

give no quarter, pour out blood like water; decimate; run amuck, wade knee-deep –, imbrue one's hands- in blood.

die a violent death, welter in one's blood; dash –, blow- out one's brains; commit suicide; kill –, -make away with –, put an end to- oneself.

Adj. killing etc. *v.*; murd-, slaught-erous; sanguin-ary, -olent; blood-stained, -thirsty;

homicidal, red-handed; bloody, -minded; ensanguined, gory, sanguineous.

mortal fatal, lethal; dead-, death-ly; mort-, lethiferous; unhealthy etc. 657; internecine; suicidal.

sporting; piscator-ial, -y.

Adv. in at the death.

*Bentham, 'Chrestomathia.'

362. Corpse.—N. corpse, corse, carcass, bones, skeleton, dry-bones; defunct, relics, *relinquiae*, remains, mortal remains, dust, ashes, earth, clay; mummy; carrion; food for- worms, – fishes; tenement of clay, this mortal coil.

shade, ghost, *manes*, apparition etc. 980.

organic remains, fossils.

Adj. cadaverous, corpse-like; unburied etc. 363.

363. Interment.—N. interment, burial, inhumation, sepulture, entombment; in-, humation; obs-, ex-equies; funeral, wake, pyre, funeral pile; cremation.

funeral -rite, – solemnity; knell, passing bell, tolling; dirge etc. (*lamentation*) 839; cypress; *obit*, dead march, muffled drum; coroner, mortician, undertaker, mute, mourner, professional mourner, pallbearer; elegy; funeral -oration, – sermon; epitaph.

grave clothes, shroud; winding-sheet, cere-cloth; cerement.

coffin, shell, sarcophagus, urn, pall, bier, hearse, catafalque, cinerary urn.

grave, pit, sepulcher, tomb, vault, crypt, catacomb, mausoleum, *Golgotha*, house of death, narrow house, long home; cemetery, necropolis, boneyard; burial-place, -ground; grave-, churchyard; God's acre; mortuary, tope, cromlech, dolmen, menhir, barrow, tumulus, cairn; ossuary; bone-, charnel-, dead-house; *Morgue*; lich-gate; crematorium.

sexton, grave-digger.

monument, memorial, cenotaph, shrine; grave-, head-, tomb-stone; *memento mori*; hatchment, stone, cross.

exhumation, disinterment; necropsy, autopsy, *post mortem* examination.

V. inter, bury, lay in –, consign to- the -grave, – tomb; en-, in-tomb; inhume; lay out, prepare for burial, embalm, mummify; conduct a funeral, hold services; toll the knell; put to bed with a shovel.

exhume, disinter, unearth.

Adj. buried etc. *v.*; burial; fune-real, -brial; mortuary, sepulchral, cinerary; elegiac; necroscopic.

Adv. *in memoriam*; *post-obit*, *-mortem*; beneath –, under- the sod.

Phr. *hic jacet, ci-git, requiescat in pace.*

364. Animality.—N. animal life; anima-tion, -lity, -lization; breath.

flesh, – and blood; corporeal nature; *physique*; strength etc. 159.

V. animalize, incorporate.

Adj. fleshly, incarnate, carnal, corporeal, human.

365. Vegetability.—N. vegetable life; vegetation, -bility; herbage.

V. vegetate, germinate, sprout, shoot; cultivate.

Adj. vegetable etc. 367; rank, lush.

366. Animal.*—N. animal, – kingdom; *fauna*; brute creation.

beast, brute, creature, created being; creeping –, living- thing; dumb -animal, – creature.

flocks and herds, live stock; domestic –, wild- animals; game, *ferae naturae*; beasts of the fields, fowls of the air, denizens of the day.

vertebrate, bi-, quadru-ped, mammal, marsupial, bird, reptile, batrachian, amphibian, fish, crustacean, shell fish, articulate, mollusc, worm, insect, zoophyte; protozoon, animalcule etc. 193.

horse etc. (*beast of burden*) 271; cattle, kine, ox; bull, -ock; steer, stot; cow, milch-cow, calf, heifer, shorthorn; sheep; lamb, -kin; ewe –, pet-lamb; ewe, ram, tup; pig, swine, boar, hog, shoat, sow tag, teg, wether.

dog, bitch, hound; pup, -py; whelp, cur, mutt, mongrel; house-, watch-, sheep-, shepherd's, sporting-, fancy-, lap-, toy-, bull-, badger-dog; mastiff; blood-, grey-, stag-, deer-, fox-, otter-, hound; harrier, beagle, spaniel, pointer, setter, retriever; Newfoundland; water -dog, – spaniel; pug, poodle; dachshund; Pinscher; turnspit; terrier; fox –, Skye- terrier; Dandie Dinmont; colley.

cat; puss,-y; kitten; grimalkin; gib-, tom-cat; mouser; fox, Reynard, vixen, stag, deer, hart, buck, doe, roe, antelope.

bird; poultry, fowl, cock, hen, chicken, chanticleer, partlet, rooster, dunghill cock, barn-door fowl; feathered -tribes, – songster; singing –, dicky- bird; canary; finch; auk, dodo, moa, roc, phoenix.

snake, serpent, viper, adder; newt, eft; asp, vermin.

Adj. animal, zoological.

equine, bovine, vaccine, canine, feline; fishy; piscator-y, -ial; molluscous, vermicular.

*Extended lists of names of specific varieties of animals, vegetables, etc., are beyond the scope of this work.

367. Vegetable.*—N. vegetable, – kingdom; *flora*, verdure.

plant; tree, shrub, bush; creeper; vine; herb, -age; grass.

annual; per-, bi-, tri-ennial; exotic.

timber; primeval –, virgin- forest; wood, -lands; hurst; frith, holt, weald, park, chase, greenwood, brake, grove, copse, coppice, *bocage*, *tope*, clump of trees, thicket, spinet, spinney; under-, brushwood; boscage, scrub; the oak and the ash and the bonny ivy tree.

bush, jungle, prairie; heath, -er; fern, bracken, furze, gorse, whin, broom; grass, turf, grassland, greensward, green, lawn, meadow; pas-ture, -turage; turbary; sedge, rush, weed; fungus, mushroom, toadstool; lichen, moss, conferva, mold; seaweed etc.; growth, crop.

foliage, leafage, branch, bough, ramage; spray etc. 51; leaf, frond, flag, petal, shoot, tendril.

flower, blossom, bud, bloom, bine; flowering plant; tree, sapling, pollard; timber-, fruit-tree; palm-, gum-tree; pulse, legume.

Adj. veget-able, -ous; herb-aceous, -al; botanic; sylvan, silvan; arbor- ary, -eous, -escent, -ical; dendritic, dendriform; woody, grassy; ver-dant, -durous; floral, mossy; lign-ous, -eous; wooden, leguminous; end-, ex-ogenous.

*Extended lists of names of specific varieties of animals, vegetables, etc., are beyond the scope of this work.

368. Zoology. [The science of animals.]—**N.** zoo-logy, -nomy, -graphy, -tomy; anatomy; comparative anatomy; animal –, comparative-physiology; morphology.

anthrop-, ornith-, ichthy-, herpet-, ophi-, malac-, helminth-, entom-, oryct-, paleont-ology; ichthy- etc. -otomy; taxidermy.

zo- etc. -ologist.

Adj. zoological etc. *n.*

369. Botany. [The science of plants.]—**N.** botany; phyto-graphy, -logy, -tomy; vegetable physiology, herborization, dendr-, myc-, fung-, algology; flora, pomona; botanist etc.; botanic garden etc. (*garden*) 371; *hortus siccus*, *herbarium*, herbal.

herb-ist, -arist, -alist, -orist, -arian etc.

V. botanize, herborize.

Adj. botanical etc. *n.*

370. Cicuration. [The economy or management of animals.]—**N.** taming etc. *v.*; cicuration, zoohygiantics; domestication, -ity; *manège*; veterinary art; breeding, pisciculture, apiculture etc.

menagery, vivarium, zoological garden, zoo; bear-pit; aviary, apiary, hive; aquarium, fishery, fish hatchery; duck-, fish-pond; stud-farm; stock farm, dairy.

[Destruction of animals] phthisozoics etc. (*killing*) 361.

neat-, cow-, shep-herd, shepherdess; grazier; drover, cowboy, cowkeeper; trainer, breeder, groom, ostler etc. 746; veterinary surgeon, vet, horse doctor; farrier; keeper; game keeper.

cage etc. (*prison*) 752; hen-coop, bird-cage, cauf; sheep-fold etc. (*inclosure*) 232.

V. tame, domesticate, acclimatize, breed, tend, break in, train, corral, round up; cage, bridle etc. (*restrain*) 751; ride etc. 266.

drive, yoke, harness, hitch; groom, curry-comb; milk; shear; hatch; incubate.

Adj. pastoral, bucolic; tame, domestic, domesticated, broken in, gentle, docile.

371. Agriculture. [The economy or management of plants.]—**N.** agriculture, cultivation, husbandry, farming; georgics, geoponics; tillage, tilth, agronomy, gardening, spade husbandry, vintage; hort-, arbor-, silv-, citr-, vit-, flor-iculture; intensive culture; landscape gardening; forestry, afforestation.

husbandman, horticulturist, citriculturist, gardener, florist; agricult-or, -urist; yeoman, farmer, cultivator, tiller of the soil, ploughman, sower, reaper; woodcutter, backwoodsman, forester; vine grower, vintager; Boer; Triptolemus.

field, meadow, garden; botanic –, winter –, ornamental –, flower –, kitchen –, truck –, market –, hop- garden; nursery; green-, hot-, glass-house; conservatory, cucumber frame, *cloche*, bed, border, seed-plot; grass-plat, lawn; park etc. (*pleasure ground*) 840; *partere*, shrubbery, plantation, avenue, *arboretum*, pinery, *pinetum*, orchard, vineyard, vinery; orangery; farm etc. (*abode*) 189.

V. cultivate; till, – the soil; farm, garden; sow, plant; reap, mow, cut; manure, dress the ground, dig, delve, dibble, hoe, plough, plow, harrow, rake, weed, lop and top, force, transplant, thin out, bed out, prune, graft.

Adj. agr-icultural, -airan, -estic.

arable; predial, rural, rustic, country, bucolic, Boeotian; horticultural.

372. Mankind.—**N.** man, -kind; human -race, – species, – nature; humanity, mortality, flesh, generation.

[Science of man] anthropo-logy, -graphy, -sophy; ethno-logy, -graphy; humanitarianism.

human being; person, -age; individual, creature, fellow creature, mortal, body, somebody, one; such a –, someone; soul, living soul; earthling; party, head, hand; *dramatis personae*.

people, persons, folk, public, society, world; community, – at large; general public; nation, -ality; state, realm; common-weal, -wealth; republic, body politic; million etc. (*commonalty*) 876; population etc. (*inhabitant*) 188.

cosmopolite; lords of the creation; ourselves.

Adj. human, mortal, personal, individual, national, civic, public, cosmopolitan; anthropoid.

373. Man.—**N.** man, male, he; manhood etc. (*adolescence*) 131; gentleman, sir, master; yeoman, wight, swain, fellow, guy, blade, *beau*, chap, gaffer, good man, husband etc. (*married man*) 903; Mr., mister, *monsieur*, *sahib*, *Herr*, *señor*, *signor*; boy etc. (*youth*) 129; Adonis.

[Male animal] cock, drake, gander, dog, boar, stag, hart, buck, horse, entire horse, stallion; gib-, tom-cat; he-, Billy-goat; ram, tup; bull, -ock; capon, ox, gelding; steer, stot.

Adj. male, he, masculine; manly, virile; unwomanly, -feminine.

374. Woman.—**N.** woman, she, female, petticoat, skirt, moll, broad.

feminality, feminity, muliebrity; womanhood etc. (*adolescence*) 131; feminism; gynecology, gyniatrics, gynics.

womankind; the -sex, – fair; fair –, softer- sex; weaker vessel; the distaff side.

dame, madam, *madame*, mistress, Mrs., lady, *mem-sahib*, *Frau*, *señora*, *signora*, *donna*, *belle*, matron, dowager, goody, gammer; good -woman, – wife; squaw; wife etc. (*marriage*) 903; matronage, -hood.

Venus, nymph, wench, *grisette*; little bit of fluff; girl etc. (*youth*) 129.

inamorata (love) etc. 897; courtesan etc. 962.

spinster, old maid, virgin, bachelor girl, new woman, amazon.

[Female animal] hen, slut, bitch, sow, doe, roe, mare; she-, Nanny-goat; ewe, cow; lioness, tigress; vixen.

gynecaeum, harem, *seraglio*, *zenana*, *purdah*.

Adj. female, she; feminine, womanly, ladylike, matronly, maidenly; womanish, effeminate, unmanly, gynecic.

375. Physical Sensibility.—N. sensibility; sensitiveness etc. *adj.*; physical sensibility, feeling, perceptivity, anaphylaxis, susceptibility, esthetics; moral sensibility etc. 882.

sensation, impression, effect; consciousness etc. (*knowledge*) 490.

external senses.

V. be -sensible etc. *adj.* -of; feel, perceive.

render, -sensible etc. *adj.*; excite, stir, sharpen, cultivate, tutor.

cause sensation, impress; excite –, produce- an impression.

Adj. sens-ible, -itive, -uous; esthetic, perceptive, sentient; conscious etc. (*aware*) 490; impressionable, responsive, alive to.

acute, sharp, keen, vivid, lively, impressive, thin-skinned.

Adv. to the quick.

376. Physical Insensibility.—N. insensibility, physical insensibility; obtuseness etc. *adj.*; palsy, paralysis, *anesthesia*, *analgesia*, *narcosis*, *hypnosis*, twilight sleep, stupor, coma, trance, catalepsy; sleep etc. (*inactivity*) 683; moral insensibility etc. 823; numbness etc. 381.

anesthetic agent, general –, local- anesthetic, opium, ether, chloroform, cocaine, novocaine, chloral; nitrous oxide, laughing gas; refrigeration.

V. be -insensible etc. *adj.*; have a -thick skin, – rhinoceros hide.

render -insensible etc. *adj.*; blunt, pall, obtund, benumb, deaden, paralyze; anesthetize, drug, dope; put under the influence of -chloroform etc. *n.*; hypnotize; stupefy, stun, narcotize.

Adj. insensible, unfeeling, senseless, comatose, dazed, impercipient, callous, thick-skinned, pachydermatous; hard, -ened; case-hardened; proof; obtuse, dull; anesthetic; paralytic, palsied, numb, dead.

377. Physical Pleasure.—N. pleasure; physical –, sensual –, sensuous- pleasure; bodily enjoyment, animal gratification, sensuality; hedonism, luxuriousness etc. *adj.*; dissipation, round of pleasure; titillation, *gusto*, creature comforts, comfort, ease; pillow etc. (*support*) 215; luxury, lap of luxury; purple and fine linen; bed of -down, – roses; velvet, clover; cup of Circe etc. (*intemperance*) 954.

treat; diversion, divertisement, entertainment; refreshment, regale; feast; *délice*; dainty etc. 394; *bonne bouche*.

source of pleasure etc. 829; happiness etc. (*mental enjoyment*) 827.

V. feel –, experience –, receive- pleasure; enjoy, relish; luxuriate –, revel –, riot –, bask –, swim –, wallow- in; feast on; gloat -over, – on; smack the lips.

live -on the fat of the land, – in comfort etc. *adv.*; bask in the sunshine, *faire ses choux gras*.

give pleasure etc. 829.

Adj. enjoying etc. *v.*; luxurious, voluptuous, sensual, hedonistic, comfortable, cosy, snug, in comfort, at ease.

agreeable etc. 829; grateful, refreshing, comforting, cordial, genial; sensuous; palatable etc. 394; sweet etc. (*sugar*) 396; fragrant etc. 400; melodious etc. 413; lovely etc. (*beautiful*) 845.

Adv. in -comfort etc. *n.*; on -a bed of roses etc. *n.*; at one's ease.

378. Physical Pain.—N. pain; suffering, -ance; bodily – physical -pain, – suffering; mental suffering etc. 828; dolor, ache; aching etc. *v.*; smart; shoot, -ing; twinge, twitch, gripe, head-, ear-, toothache; *migraine*, neuralgia, neuritis, lumbago, gout, sciatica; hurt, cut; sore, -ness; discomfort, *malaise*; *tic douloureux*.

spasm, cramp; nightmare, *ephialtes*; crick, stitch, kink; thrill, convulsion, throe; throb etc. (*agitation*) 315; pang.

sharp –, piercing –, throbbing –, shooting –, gnawing –, burning- pain; anguish, agony.

torment, torture; rack; cruci-ation, -fixion; martyrdom; martyr, toad under a harrow, vivisection.

V. feel –, experience –, suffer –, undergo- pain etc. *n.*; suffer, ache, smart, bleed; tingle, shoot; twinge, twitch, lancinate; writhe, wince, make a wry face; sit on -thorns, – pins and needles.

give –, inflict- pain; pain, hurt, chafe, sting, bite, gnaw, gripe, stab, grind; pinch, tweak; grate, gall, fret, prick, pierce, wring, convulse; torment, torture; rack, agonize; crucify; excruciate; break on the wheel, put to the rack; flag etc. (*punish*) 972; grate on the ear etc. (*harsh sound*) 410.

Adj. in -pain etc. *n.*; – a state of pain; pained etc. *v.*

painful; aching etc. *v.*; biting, poignant; sore, raw, tender, with exposed nerve.

379. Touch. [Sensation of pressure.] **—N.** touch; tact, -ion, -ility; feeling; palp-ation, -ability; manipulation; brush, tick, graze, contact etc. 199.

[Organ of touch] hand, finger, fore-finger, thumb, paw, feeler, *antenna*.

V. touch, feel, handle, finger, thumb, paw, fumble, grope, grabble; twiddle, tweedle; pass –, run- the fingers over, massage, rub, knead; palpate, stroke, manipulate, wield; throw out a feeler.

Adj. tact-ual, -ile; tangible, palpable; lambent.

380. Sensations of Touch.—N. itching etc. *v.*; titillation, formication, *aura*.

V. itch, tingle, creep, thrill, sting; prick, -le; tickle, titillate.

Adj. itching etc. *v.*

381. Numbness. [Insensibility to touch.] **—N.**

numbness etc. (*physical insensibility*) 376; pins and needles.

local anesthetic, cocaine novocaine etc.; morphia.

V. benumb etc. 376; freeze, dull, deaden.

Adj. numb; benumbed etc. *v.*; intangible, impalpable.

382. Heat.—N. heat, caloric; temperature, warmth, fervor, calidity; incal-, incand-, recal-, decal-escence; glow, flush, blush; fever, hectic.

phlogiston; fire, spark, scintillation, flash, flame, blaze; arc; bonfire; firework, pyrotechny; wild-fire; sheet of fire, lambent flame; devouring element; conflagration.

summer, dog-days, canicule; baking etc. 384 –, white –, tropical –, Afric –, Bengal –, summer –, blood- heat; heat wave, sirocco, simoon; broiling sun; isolation; warming etc. 384.

sun etc. (*luminary*) 423; fire worshipper etc. 991; furnace etc. 386.

geyser, hot spring, volcano.

: Science of heat. pyrology; thermology, -otics; thermometer etc. 389.

V. be -hot etc. *adj.*; glow, incandesce, flush, sweat, swelter, bask, smoke, reek, stew, simmer, seethe, boil, burn, singe, scorch, scald, grill, broil, blaze, flame; smoulder; parch, fume, pant.

heat etc. (*make hot*) 384; thaw, fuse, melt, give.

Adj. hot, heated, warm, mild, genial, tepid, lukewarm, unfrozen; therm-al, -ic; calorific; fervent, -id; ardent; aglow.

sunny, torrid, tropical, estival, canicular; close, sultry, stifling, stuffy, suffocating, oppressive; reeking etc. *v.*; baking etc. 384.

red –, white –, smoking –, bruning etc. *v.* –, piping- hot; like -a furnace, – an oven; hot as -fire, – pepper; hot enough to roast an ox.

fiery; incand-, incal-escent; candent, ebullient, glowing, smoking; on fire; blazing etc. *v.*; in -flames, – a blaze; alight, afire, ablaze; un quenched, -extinguished; smouldering; in a -heat, – glow, – fever, – perspiration, – sweat; sudorific; swelter-ing, -ed; blood-hot, -warm; warm as -a toast, – wool; recalescent, thermogenic, pyrotechnic, feverish, febrile, inflamed.

volcanic, plutonic, igneous; isother-mal, -mic, -al.

Phr. Not a breath of air.

383. Cold.—N. cold, -ness etc. *adj.*; frigidity, gelidity, algidity, inclemency, *fresco*..

winter; depth of –, hard- winter; Siberia, Nova Zembla; Ant-, arctic, North –, South- Pole.

ice; snow, – flake, – crystal – drift; sleet; hail, -stone; rime, frost; hoar –, white –, hard –, sharp- frost; icicle, thick-ribbed ice; fall of snow, snow storm, heavy fall, *avalanche*; ice-berg, -floe; floe, berg; *glacier*; *nevée*, *serac*.

[Sensation of cold] chilliness etc. *adj.*; chill shivering etc. *v.*; goose- skin, -flesh; *rigor*, horripilation, chattering of teeth; frostbite, chilblain.

V. be -cold etc. *adj.*; shiver, starve, quake, shake, tremble, shudder, didder, quiver; perish with cold; chill etc. (*render cold*) 385.

Adj. cold, cool; chill, -y; gelid, frigid, algid; fresh, keen, bleak, raw, inclement, bitter, biting, niveous, cutting, nipping, piercing, pinching; clay-cold; starved etc. (*made cold*) 385; shivering etc. *v.*; aguish, *transi de froid*; frost- bitten, -bound, -nipped.

cold as -a stone, – marble, – lead, – iron, – a frog, – charity, – Christmas; cool as -a cucumber, – custard.

icy, glacial, frosty, freezing, wintry, brumal, hibernal, boreal, arctic, antarctic, polar, Siberian, hyemal; hyperbore-an, -al; ice-bound; frozen out.

un-warmed, -thawed, -heated; isocheimal, -chimenal.

Adv. coldly, bitterly etc. *adj.*; *à pierre fendre*.

384. Calefaction.—N. increase of temperature; heating etc. *v.*; cale-, tepe-, torre-faction; melting, fusion; liquefaction etc. 335; burning etc. *v.*; kindling, combustion; in-, ac-cension; con-, cremation; scorification; cauter-y, -ization; ustulation, calcination; in-, cineration; cupellation; carbonization.

ignition, inflammation, adustion, flagration; de-, con-flagration; empyrosis, incendiarism; arson; *auto da fé*; suttee.

boiling etc. *v.*; coction, ebullition, estuation, elixation, decoction.

furnace etc. 386; blanket, flannel, fur, muffler, wrap; wadding etc. (*lining*) 224; clothing etc. 225.

match etc. (*fuel*) 388; incendiary, pryomaniac; *pétroleur, pétroleuse*; cauterant, caustic, lunar caustic, apozem, moxa.

sunstroke, *coup de soliel*; insolation, sunburn.

pottery, ceramics, crockery, porcelain, china; earthen-, stone-ware; pot, mug, *terra-cotta*, brick, clinker; cinder, ash, *scoriae*; embers, dress, slag, products of combustion, coke, carbon, charcoal.

inflamma-, combusti-bility.

[Transmission of heat] diathermancy, transcalency, diathermy.

V. heat, warm, chafe, stive, foment; make -hot etc. 382; sun oneself, bask in the sun.

fire; set -fire to, – on fire; kindle, enkindle, light, ignite, strike a light; apply the -match, – torch- to; re-kindle, -lume; fan –, add fuel to- the flame; poke –, stir –, blow- the fire; make a bonfire of; burn at the stake.

melt, thaw, fuse; liquefy etc. 335.

burn, inflame, roast, toast, fry, grill, singe, parch, bake, torrefy, scorch; brand, cauterize, sear, burn in; corrode, char, carbonize, calcine, incinerate; smelt, cupel, scorify; reduce to ashes; burn to a cinder; commit –, consign- to the flames.

boil, digest, stew, cook, seethe, scald, parboil, simmer; do to rags.

take –, catch- fire; blaze etc. (*flame*) 382.

Adj. heated etc. *v.*; molten, sodden; réchauffe; heating etc. *v.*

inflammable, burnable, inflammatory, combustible; diatherm-al, -anous; burnt etc. *v.*; volcanic.

386. Refrigeration.—N. refrigeration, infrigidation, reduction of temperature; cooling etc. *v.*; con-gelation, -glaciation; ice etc. 383; solidification etc. (*density*) 321; refrigerator etc. 387.

extincteur; fire, – engine, – extinguisher, – annihilator, – brigade, – man; sprinkler, hose, hydrant, standpipe.

incombusti-bility, -bleness etc. *adj.*

V. cool, fan, refrigerate, refresh, ice; congeal, freeze, glaciate; benumb, starve, pinch, chill, petrify, chill to the marrow, nip, cut, pierce, bite, make one's teeth chatter; damp, slack; quench; put –, stamp- out; extinguish.

go –, burn- out.

Adj. cooled etc. *v.*; frozen out; cooling etc. *v.*; frigorific.

incombustible; un-, unin-flammable; fire-proof.

386. Furnace.—N. furnace, blast furnace, fire-box, stove, incinerator, destructor, crematorium, crematory, kiln, oven, oast-house; hot-, bake-, wash-house; laundry; conservatory; hearth, focus; athanor, hypocaust, reverberatory; volcano; forge, fiery furnace; *tuyère*, brasier, salamander, heater, warming-pan, foot-warmer, hot-water bottle; radiator; boiler, geyser, caldron, seething caldron, pot; urn, kettle; chafing-dish; retort, crucible, alembic, still; saggar.

fire-place, -dog, -irons; hearth, ingle, grate, range, kitchener; kitchen range; oil-, gas-, electric, -cooker, -stove; fireless cooker; fire; galley; ca-, cam-boose; poker, tongs, shovel, hob, trivet; and-, grid-iron; frying-, stew-pan etc.

hot –, Turkish –, Russian –, vapor –, shower –, warm- bath; *calidarium*, *tepidarium*, *sudatorium*, sudatory; *hammam*.

387. Refrigerator.—N. refrigerator, -y; *frigidarium*; cold storage; refrigerating-plant, – machine; ice-house, -pail, -bag, -chest, -pack; cooler, damper; wine-cooler, freezing mixture.

388. Fuel.—N. fuel, firing, combustible, coal, wallsend, anthracite, bituminous coal, slack, culm, cannel coal, lignite, briquette, coke, carbon, charcoal; turf, peat, fire-wood, bobbing, faggot, log, yule log, ember, cinder etc. (*products of combustion*) 384; kindling wood, tinder, touch-wood; fumigator, sulphur, brimstone; incense; port-fire; fire-barrel, -ball, -brand.

fuel oil, gas, gasoline, electricity.

brand, torch, fuse; wick; spill, match, safety match, light, lucifer, congreve, vesuvian, vesta, fusee, locofoco; linstock; illuminant.

candle etc. (*luminary*) 423; oil etc. (*grease*) 356; petrol, gasoline, methylated –, spirit; gas, acetylene.

Adj. carbonaceous; combustible, inflammable.

V. stoke, fire, feed, add fuel to the flames.

389. Thermometer.—N. thermo-meter, -scope, -stat, -pile, differential thermometer; pyro-, calorimeter; radio micrometer etc.

390. Taste.—N. taste, flavor, gust, *gusto*, relish, savor; sapor, sapidity; twang, smack, smatch; after-taste, tang.

tasting; de-, gustation.

palate, tongue, tooth, stomach.

V. taste, savor, smatch, smack, flavor, twang; tickle the palate etc. (*savory*) 394; smack the lips.

Adj. sapid, saporific; gusta-ble, -tory; strong; flavored, spiced, savory; palatable etc. 394.

391. Insipidity.—N. insipidity; tastlessness etc. *adj.*

V. be -tasteless etc. *adj.*

Adj. void of -taste etc. 390; insipid; jejune; taste-, gust-, savor-less; ingustible, mawkish, milk and water, weak, stale, flat, vapid, *fade*, wishy-washy, mild; untasted.

392. Pungency.—N. pungency, piquancy, poignancy, *haut-goût*, strong taste, twang, race, tang.

sharpness etc. *adj.*; acrimony, acridity; roughness etc. (*sour*) 397; unsavoriness etc. 395.

niter, saltpeter; mustard, cayenne, caviar; seasoning etc. (*condiment*) 393; brine.

dram, cordial, nip, pick-me-up, bracer, potion.

nicotine, tobacco, snuff, quid; segar; cigar, -ette, gasper, fag; cheroot; weed; fragrant –, Indian-weed; pipe, clay pipe, churchwarden, brier, meerschaum, hookah, hubble-bubble.

V. be -pungent etc. *adj.*; bite the tongue.

render -pungent etc. *adj.*; season, spice, salt, pepper, pickle, brine, devil, curry.

smoke, chew, take snuff.

Adj. pungent, strong; high-, full-flavored; high-tasted, -seasoned; gamy; sharp, stinging, rough, *piquant*, racy; biting, mordant; spicy; seasoned etc. *v.*; hot; – as pepper; peppery, vellicating, escharotic, meracious; acrid, acrimonious, bitter; rough etc. (*sour*) 397; unsavory etc. 395.

salt, saline, brackish, briny; salt as -brine, – a herring, – Lot's wife.

393. Condiment.—N. condiment, flavoring, salt, mustard, pepper, cayenne, curry, seasoning, sauce, spice, cinnamon, chillies, relish, *sauce piquante*, caviare, pot-herbs, onion, garlic, pickle, chutney, nutmeg etc.

V. season etc. (*render pungent*) 392.

394. Savoriness.—N. savoriness etc. *adj.*; relish, zest.

tit-bit, dainty, delicacy, ambrosia, nectar, *bonne bouche*; game, turtle, venison.

V. taste good, be -savory etc. *adj.*; tickle the -palate, – appetite; flatter the palate.

render -palatable etc. *adj.*

relish, like, smack the lips.

Adj. savory, well-tasted, to one's taste, tasty, good, palatable, nice, dainty, delectable; tooth-ful, -some; gustful, appetizing, lickerish, delicate, delicious, exquisite, rich, luscious, ambrosial.

Adv. *per amusare la bocca.*

Phr. *cela se laisse manger.*

395. Unsavoriness.—N. unsavoriness etc. *adj.*; amaritude; acri-mony, -tude; roughness etc. (*sour*) 397; acerbity, austerity; gall and worm-wood, rue, quassia, aloes; sickener.

V. be -unpalatable etc. *adj.*; sicken, disgust, nauseate, pall, turn the stomach.

Adj. un-savory, -palatable, -sweet; ill-flavored, un-appetizing, -eatable, inedible; bitter, – as gall; acrid, acrimonious; rough.

offensive, repulsive, nasty; sickening etc. *v.*; nauseous; loath-, ful-some; unpleasant etc. 830.

396. Sweetness.—N. sweetness, dulcitude, saccharinity.

sugar, cane-, beet-sugar; saccharine, glucose, syrup, treacle, molasses, honey, manna; confection, -ary; sweets, grocery, conserve, preserve, *confiture*, jam, marmalade, julep; sugar-candy, -plum; licorice, liquorice, plum, lollipop, *bon bon*, *jujube*, comfit, sweetmeat, caramel, toffee, butterscotch.

nectar; hydromel, mead, metheglin, honeysuckle, *liqueur*, sweet wine.

pastry, pie, tart, puff, pudding, cake.

dulc-ification, -oration.

V. be sweet etc. *adj.*

render -sweet etc. *adj.*; sugar, saccharize, sweeten; edulcorate; dulc-orate, -ify; candy; mull.

Adj. sweet, sugary; sacchar-ine, -iferous; dulcet, honied, candied, luscious, nectarious, melliferous; sweetened etc. *v.*

sweet as -a nut, – sugar, – honey.

397. Sourness.—N. sourness etc. *adj.*; acid, -ity; acetous fermentation; acerbity.

vinegar, verjuice, crab, alum.

V. be –, turn- -sour etc. *adj.*; set the teeth on edge.

render -sour etc. *adj.*; acid-ify, -ulate.

Adj. sour; acid, -ulous, -ulated; acerb; tart, crabbed; acet-ous, -ose; sour as vinegar, sourish, acescent, sub-acid; styptic, hard, rough; unripe, green.

398. Odor.—N. odor, smell, odorament, scent, effluvium; eman-, exhal-ation; fume, essence, trail, nidor, redolence.

sense of smell; scent; act of -smelling etc. *v.*

V. have an -odor etc. *n.*; smell, – of, – strong of; exhale; give out a -smell etc. *n.*; scent.

smell, scent; snuff, – up; sniff, nose, inhale.

Adj. odor-ous, -iferous; smelling, strong-scented; redolent, graveolent, nidorous, pungent.

[Relating to the sense of smell] olfactory, quick-scented.,

399. Inodorousness.—N. inodorousness; absence –, want- of smell.

V. be -inodorous etc. *adj.*; not smell, deodorize.

Adj. inodor-ous, -ate; scentless; without –, wanting- smell etc. 398.

deodoriz-ed, -ing.

400. Fragrance.—N. fragrance, aroma, redolence, perfume, *bouquet*; sweet smell, aromatic perfume.

perfumery; incense; musk, frankincense; pastil, -le; myrrh, perfumes of Arabia, chypre; otto, ottar, attar; bergamot, balm, civet, *pot-pourri*, pulvil; nosegay, *boutonnière*; scent, -bag; *sachet*, scent-bottle, smelling bottle, *vinaigrette*; toilet water, *eau de Cologne*; thurible, censer, thurification.

perfumer; incense bearer.

V. be -fragrant etc. *adj.*; have a -perfume etc. *n.*; smell sweet, scent, perfume, thurify, embalm.

Adj. fragrant, aromatic, redolent, spicy, balmy, scented; sweet-smelling, -scented; perfum-ed, -atory; thuriferous; fragrant as a rose, muscadine, ambrosial.

401. Fetor.—N. fetor, fetidness; bad etc. *adj.*; -smell, – odor; stench, stink; mephitis, foul –, mal- odor; *empyreuma*; mustiness etc. *adj.*; rancidity; foulness etc. (*uncleanness*) 653.

stoat, polecat, skunk; asafetida; fungus, garlic; stink-pot, -bomb.

V. have a -bad smell etc. *n.*; smell; stink, – in the nostrils, – like a polecat; smell -strong etc. *adj.*; – offensively.

Adj. fetid; strong-smelling; high, bad, strong, fulsome, offensive, noisome, rank, rancid, reasty, tainted, musty, fusty, frouzy; olid, -ous; nidorous; smelling, stinking; putrid etc. 653; suffocating, mephitic; empyreumatic.

402. Sound.—N. sound, noise, strain; accent, twang, intonation, tone, tune; cadence; sonority, sonorousness etc. *adj.*; audibility; resonance etc. 408; voice etc. 580.

[Science of sound] acou-, acu-stics; catacoustics; cataphonics; phon-ics, -etics, -ology, -ography; diacoustics, -phonics.

telephone, phonograph etc. 418.

V. produce sound; sound, make a noise; give out –, emit- sound; phonetize, phonate; resound etc. 408.

Adj. sounding; soniferous; sonorific; resonant, audible, acoustic, auditory, distinct; stertorous; phonic, sonant; phonetic.

403. Silence.—N. silence; stillness etc. (*quiet*) 265; peace, hush, lull, rest; muteness etc. 581; solemn –, awful –, dead –, deathlike- silence.

V. be -silent etc. *adj.*; hold one's tongue etc. (*not speak*) 585.

render -silent etc. *adj.*; silence, still, hush; stifle, muffle, gag, stop; muzzle, put to silence etc. (*render mute*) 581.

Adj. silent; still, -y; calm, quiet; noise-, sound-, speech-less; hushed etc. *v.*; mute etc. 581; aphonic.

soft, solemn, awful, deathlike, silent as the grave; inaudible etc. (*faint*) 405.

Adv. silently etc. *adj.*; *sub silentio*; in perfect silence.

Int. hush! 'sh! silence! soft! whist! tush! chut! tut! *pax!* mum's the word! hold your tongue! shut up! be silent! be quiet! stop that noise! hold your row! dry up! peace, be still!

Phr. one might hear a -feather, – pin- drop.

404. Loudness.—N. loudness, power; loud noise, din; clang, -or; clatter, noise, bombilation, roar, uproar, racket, static, grinders, hubbub, *fracas, charivari*, trumpet blast, blare, flourish of trumpets, fanfare, *tintamarre*, peal, swell, blast, alarum, boom; resonance etc. 408.

vociferation; pandemonium, hullaballoo etc. 411; lungs; Stentor; megaphone; siren.

artillery, cannon, gunfire, shellburst, bomb; thunder.

V. be -loud etc. *adj.*; peal, swell, clang, boom, thunder, fulminate, roar; resound etc. 408; speak up, shout etc. (*vociferate*) 411; bellow etc. (*cry as an animal*) 412; give tongue.

rend the -air, – skies; fill the air; din –, ring –, thunder- in the ear; pierce –, split –, rend-the-ears, – head; deafen, stun; *faire le diable a quatre*; make one's windows shake; awaken –, startle- the echoes; make the welkin ring.

Adj. loud, sonorous; high-, big- sounding; blatant; deep, full, powerful, noisy, clangorous, multisonous, *fortisimo*; thundering, deafening etc. *v.*; trumpet-tongued; ear-splitting, -rending, -deafening; piercing; obstreporous, rackety, uproarious; enough to wake the -dead, – seven sleepers.

shrill etc. 410; clamorous etc. (*vociferous*) 411; stentor-ian, -ophonic.

Adv. loudly etc. *adj.*; aloud; at the top of one's voice, lustily, in full cry.

Phr. the air rings with.

405. Faintness.—N. faintness etc. *adj.*; faint sound, whisper, breath; under-tone, -breath; murmur, hum, rustle, buzz, purr; plash; sough, moan, sigh, susurration; tinkle; 'still small voice.'

hoarseness etc. *adj.*; raucity.

silencer, soft pedal, damper, mute, *sourdine*.

V. whisper, breathe, murmur, purl, hum, gurgle, ripple, babble, flow; tinkle; mutter etc. (*speak imperfectly*) 583.

steal on the ear; melt in –, float on- the air.

muffle, mute, deaden, damp, stifle.

Adj. inaudible; scarcely –, just- audible; low, dull; stifled, muffled; hoarse, husky; gentle, soft, faint; floating; purling, flowing etc. *v.*; whispered etc. *v.*; liquid; soothing; dulcet etc. (*melodious*) 413.

Adv. in a whisper, with bated breath, *sotto voce*, between the teeth, aside; *pian-o, -issimo*; *à la sourdine*; *con sourdine*; out of earshot, inaudibly etc. *adj.*

406. Snap. [Sudden and violent sounds.]—**N.** snap etc. *v.*; rapping etc. *v.*; de-, crepitation; smack, clap, report; thud; burst, explosion, discharge, detonation, blow-out, back-fire, firing, salvo, volley, pistol-shot.

squib, cracker, gun, rifle, pop-gun.

V. rap, snap, tap, knock; click; clash; crack, -le; crash; pop; slam, bang, clap, thump, plump; toot; back-fire, explode, burst on the ear.

Adj. rapping etc. *v.*

Int. crash! bang!

407. Roll. [Repeated and protracted sounds.]—**N.** roll etc. *v.*; drumming etc. *v.*; tattoo; ding-dong; tantara; rataplan; whirr; rat-a-tat; rub-a-dub; pit-a-pat; quaver, clutter, *charivari*, racket; cuckoo; repetition etc. 104; peal of bells, devil's tattoo; reverberation etc. 408.

drumfire, barrage.

machine gun.

V. roll, drum, rumble, rattle, clatter, rustle, roar, drone, patter, clack.

hum, trill, shake; chime, peal, toll; tick, beat.

drum –, din- in the ear.

Adj. rolling etc. *v.*; monotonous etc. (*repeated*), 104; like a bee in a bottle.

408. Resonance.—N. resonance; ring etc. *v.*; ringing etc. *v.*; tintinnabulation; reflection, reverberation, clangor.

low –, base –, bass –, flat –, grave –, deep –, pedal- note; bass; *basso*, – *profondo*; bari-, bary-tone; *contralto*.

V. re-sound, -verberate, -echo; ring, ding, sing, jingle, gingle, chink, clink; tink, -le; chime; gurgle etc. 405; plash, guggle, echo, ring in the ear.

Adj. resounding etc. *v.*; resonant, tinnient; tintinnabulary; deep-toned, -sounding, -mouthed; hollow, sepulchral; gruff etc. (*harsh*) 410.

408a. Non-resonance.—N. thud, thump, dead sound; non-resonance; muffled drums, cracked bell; silencer, damper; mute, *sourdine*.

V. sound dead; stop –, damp- the -sound, – reverberations; deaden, muffle.

Adj. non-resonant, dead, muted, muffled.

409. Sibilation. [Hissing sounds.]—**N.** sibilation; hiss etc. *v.*; sternutation; high note etc. 410.

goose, serpent, snake.

V. hiss, buzz, whiz, rustle; fizz, -le, sizzle, swish; wheeze, whistle, snuffle; squash; sneeze.

Adj. sibilant; hissing etc. *v.*; wheezy.

410. Stridor. [Harsh sounds.]—**N.** creak etc. *v.*; creaking etc. *v.*; discord etc. 414; stridor; harshness, roughness, sharpness etc. *adj.*; cacophony.

acute –, high- note; *soprano*, treble, tenor, *alto*, falsetto, *voce di testa*; shriek, cry etc. 411.

piccolo, fife, penny -whistle, – trumpet.

V. creak, grate, jar, burr, pipe, twang, jangle, clank, clink; scream etc. (*cry*) 411; yelp etc. (*animal sound*) 412; buzz etc. (*hiss*) 409.

set the teeth on edge, écorcher les orielles; pierce –, split- the -ears, – head; offend –, grate upon –, jar upon- the ear.

Adj. creaking etc. *v.*; strident, stridulous, harsh,

coarse, hoarse, horrisonous, raucous, metallic, rough, gruff, grum, sepulchral.

sharp, high, acute, shrill, high-pitched; trumpet-toned; piercing, ear-piercing; cracked; discordant etc. 414; cacophonous.

411. Cry.—N. cry etc. *v.*; voice etc. (*human*) 580; bark etc. (*animal*) 412.

vociferation, outcry, hullaballoo, chorus, clamor, hue and cry, plaint; lungs; stentor.

V. cry, roar, shout, bawl, brawl, halloo, halloa, hail, hoop, whoop, yell, bellow, howl, scream, screech, screak, shriek, shrill, squeak, squeal, squall, whine, whinny, pule, pipe, yaup.

cheer, hurrah; hoot; grumble, maon, groan.

snore, snort; grunt etc. (*animal sounds*) 412.

vociferate; raise –, lift up- the voice; call –, sing –, cry- out; exclaim; rend the air; thunder –, shout- at the -top of one's voice, – pitch of one's breath; *s'égosiller*; strain the -throat, – voice, – lungs; give a -cry etc.

Adj. crying etc. *v.*; clam-ant, -orous; vociferous; stentorian etc. (*loud*) 404; open-mouthed.

412. Ululation. [Animal sounds.]**—N.** cry etc. *v.*; crying etc. *v.*; ululation, latration, belling; reboation; call, note; bark, howl, yelp; twittering, woodnote; insect cry, fritinancy, drone; screech; cuckoo.

V. cry, ululate, howl, roar, bellow, blare, rebellow, bark, yelp; bay, – the moon; yap, growl, yarr, yawl, snarl, howl; grunt, -le; snort, squeak; neigh, bray; mew, mewl; purr, caterwaul, pule; bleat, low, moo; troat, croak, crow, screech, caw, coo, gobble, quack, cackle, gaggle, guggle; chuck, -le; cluck; clack; cheep, chirp, chirrup, twitter, sing, cuckoo; pout, wail, hum, buzz; hiss, blatter; hoot.

Adj. crying etc. *v.*; blatant, latrant; re-, mugient; deep-, full-mouthed.

Adv. in full cry.

413. Melody. Concord.—N. melody, rhythym, measure; rhyme etc. (*poetry*) 597.

pitch, *timbre*, intonation, tone, overtone.

scale, gamut; diapason; diatonic –, chromatic –, enharmonic- scale; key, clef, chords.

modulation, temperament, syncope, syncopation, preparation, suspension, resolution.

staff, stave, line, space, brace; bar, rest; *appogiato*, *-tura*; *acciaccatura*, shake, *arpeggio*.

note, musical note, notes of a sclae; sharp, flat, natural; high note etc. (*shrillness*) 410; low note etc. 408; interval; semitone; second, third, fourth etc.; diatessaron.

breve, semibreve, minim, crotchet, quaver; semi-, demisemi- quaver; sustained note, drone, burden.

tonic; key-, leading-, fundamental-, note; supertonic, mediant, dominant; sub-mediant, -dominant, organ-, pedal-point; octave, tetrachord; major –, minor- -mode, – scale, – key; Doric mode, passage, phrase.

concord, harmony; unison, -ance; chime, homophony; euphon-y, -ism; tonality; consonance; concent; part.

orchestration; harmonization, – phrasing.

[Science of harmony] harmon-y, -ics; thorough-, fundamental- bass; counterpoint; faburden.

piece of music etc. 415; composer, harmonist, contrapuntist.

V. be -harmonious etc. *adj.*; harmonize, chime, symphonize, transpose; put in tune, tune, accord, string; score, arrange, orchestrate.

Adj. harmoni-ous, -cal; in -concord etc. *n.*, – tune, – concert; unisonant, concentual, symphonizing, isotonic, homophonous, assonant, consonant.

measured, rhythmical, diatonic, chromatic, enharmonic.

melodious, musical; tuneful, tunable; sweet, dulcet, canorous; mell-ow, -ifluous; soft; clear, – as a bell; silvery; euphon-ious, -ic, -ical; symphonious; enchanting etc. (*pleasure-giving*) 829; fine-, full-, silver-toned.

Adv. harmoniously etc. *adj.*

414. Discord.—N. discord, -ance; dissonance, cacaphony, caterwauling; harshness etc. 410; consecutive fifths.

[Confused sounds] Babel, pandemonium; Dutch –, cat's- concert; marrow-bones and cleavers.

V. be -discordant etc. *adj.* : jar etc. (*sound harshly*) 410.

Adj. discordant; dis-, ab-sonant; out of tune, tuneless; un-musical, -tunable; un-, im-melodious; un-, in-harmonious; sing-song; cacophonous; jarring, harsh etc. 410.

415. Music.—N. music, classical –, modern –, descriptive- music; concert, recital; strain, tune, air, *motif*; melody etc. 413; *aria*, *arietta*; piece of music, *sonata*; *rond-o*, *-eau*; *pastorale*, *cavatina*, roulade, *fantasia*, *toccata*, *concerto*, overture, symphony, symphonic poem, tone poem, prelude, voluntary, *intermezzo*, variations, *cadenza*; cadence; fugue, canon, serenade, *nocturne*, *notturno*, rhapsody, romance, *aubade*, dithyramb; opera, operetta; oratorio; composition, movement, stave.

instrumental music; full-, orchestral- score; minstrelsy, tweedledum and tweedledee, band, orchestra etc. 416; concerted piece, *potpourri*, medley, *capriccio*, incidental music; improvisation; peal.

vocal music, vocalism; chaunt, chant; psalm, -ody; hymn; song etc. (*poem*) 597; canticle, canzonet, *cantata*, *bravura*, *coloratura*; lay, ballad, ditty, carol, barcarolle, pastoral, recitative, *recitativo*, *solfeggio*, tonic sol-fa.

Lydian measures; slow -music, – movement; *adagio* etc. *adv.*; minuet; siren strains, soft music, lullaby; *berceuse*, cradle song, dump; dirge etc. (*lament*) 839; pibroch; martial music, march, funeral-, dead- march; dance music; waltz etc. (*dance*) 840; rag-time, syncopation, jazz.

solo, duet, *duo*, *trio*; quartet; quintet, sextet, septet; part song, descant, glee, madrigal, catch, round, chorus, *chorale*; antiphon, -y; accompaniment, second –, alto –, tenor –, bass-part; score, thorough bass; counterpoint.

composer etc. 413; musician etc. 416.
V. compose, perform etc. 416; attune.
Adj. musical; instrumental, orchestral, vocal, choral, lyric, operatic; harmonious etc. 413.
Adv. *adagio*; *largo*, *larghetto*, *andan-te*, *-tino*; *alla capella*; *maestoso*, *moderato*; *allegr-o*, *-etto*; *spiritoso*, *vivace*, *veloce*; *prest-o*, *-issimo*; *pian-o*, *-issimo*, *fort-e*, *-issimo*, *sforzando*; *con brio*; *capriccioso*; *scherz-o*, *-ando*; *legato*, *sostenuto*, *staccato*, *crescendo*, diminuendo, *rallentando*, *affettuoso*, *arioso*; *parlante*, *cantabile*; *obbligato*; *pizzacato*, *tremolo*, *vibrato*.

416. Musician. [Performance of Music.]—**N.** musician, *artiste*, *virtuoso*, performer, player, minstrel; bard etc. (*poet*) 597; instrumental-, organ-, accompan-, pian-, violin-, flaut-, harp-ist; harper, fiddler, fifer, trumpeter, piper, drummer; catgut scraper.
band, orchestra, waits.
vocal-, melod-ist; singer, warbler; songst-, chaunt-er, -ress; *diva*, *cantatrice*, coloratura, soprano, mezzo-soprano, alto, contralto, tenor, baritone, bass, *basso*, *-profundo*.
choir, quire, chorister; chorus, – singer; choral society, festival, *eisteddfod*.
nightingale, philomel, thrush; siren; Orpheus, Apollo, the Muses, Erato, Euterpe, Terpsichore; tuneful -nine, – quire.
composer etc. 413.
performance, virtuosity, execution, touch, expression, solmization.
V. play, pipe, strike –, tune-up, sweep the chords, tickle –, paw- the ivories, vamp, tweedle, fiddle; strike the lyre, beat the drum; blow –, sound –, wind- the horn; grind the organ; touch the -guitar etc. (*instruments*) 417; thrum, strum, twang, drum, beat –, keep- time, conduct.
execute, perform; accompany; sing –, play- a second; compose, write music, set to music, arrange, harmonize, orchestrate.
sing, chaunt, chant, hum, warble, carol, chirp, chirrup, lilt, purl, quaver, trill, shake, twitter, whistle; sol-fa; intone.
have -an ear for music, – a musical ear, – a correct ear, – absolute pitch.
Adj. playing etc. *v.*; musical, lyric.
Adv. *adagio*, *andante* etc. (*music*) 415.

417. Musical Instruments.—N. musical instruments; band; string-, brass-, drum and fife-, military-, bugle-, German-, dance-, jazz-band; orchestra, string quartet; orchestration, orchestrelle.
[Stringed instruments] mono-, poly-chord; harp, lyre, lute, archlute, thearbo; mandol-a, -in, -ine; guitar; *ukulele*; psaltery, zither; bandore, cither, -n; gittern, rebeck, *bandurria*, banjo, zither banjo, *balalaika*, *samisen*; plectrum.
viol, -in, Cremona, Stradivarius; fiddle; kit; *vielle*, *viola*, – *d'amore*, – *di gamba*; tenor, *violoncello*, cello; bass, bass-, bass-viol; double-bass, *contrabasso*, *violone*, hurdy-gurdy; strings, catgut; bow, fiddlestick.
piano, -forte; grand –, concert grand –, baby –, upright –, cottage- piano; pianino, pianette; harpsi-, clavi-, clari-, mani-chord; *clavier*, spinet, virginals; dulcimer, *cymbalo*; Eolian harp; piano-organ, -player, electric piano, player-piano, pianola.
[Wind instruments] organ, church –, pipe –, American- organ; harmoni-um, -phon; accordion, seraphina, concertina; melodeon; barrel- organ; humming top.
flute, fife, piccolo, flageolet, penny-whistle, reed instrument; clari-net, -onet; bass clarionet; saxophone; basset horn, *corno di bassetto*; musette, shawm, oboe, hautboy, *cor Anglais*, *corno Inglese*, bassoon, double bassoon, *contrafagotto*; bag-, union-pipes; ocarina, Pandean pipes; calliope; sirene, pipe, pitch-pipe; sourdet; whistle, catcall.
horn, bugle, key bugle, cornet, *cornet-à-pistons*, cornopean, clarion, trumpet, trombone, ophicleide, serpent; English-, French-, bugle-, sax-, flugel-, alt-, helicon-, post-horn; sackbut, euphonium, bombardon, tuba, bass tuba.
[Vibrating surfaces] cymbal, bell, gong, peal of bells, *carillon*; tambour, -ine; drum, tom-tom, tabor, -ret, -ourine, -orin; *sistrum*, *grand caisse*, bass-, big-, side-, kettle-drum; *tympani*; war drums; tymbal, timbrel, castanet, bones; musical-glasses, -stones; harmonica, sounding– board, rattle; gramophone, phonograph.
[Vibrating bars] reed, tuning-fork, triangle, Jew's harp, musical box, harmonicon, xylophone, marimba, *celeste*.
sord-ine, -et; *sourd-ine*, *-et;* mute.

418. Hearing. [Sense of sound.]—**N.** hearing etc. *v.*; audition, auscultation; eavesdropping; audibility; acoustics etc. 402.
acute –, nice –, delicate –, quick –, sharp –, correct –, musical -ear; ear for music.
ear, auricle, lug, acoustic organs, auditory apparatus, ear-drum, tympanum; ear-, speaking-trumpet, megaphone; telephone, radiophone, stethoscope, phonograph, gramophone, microphone.
hearer, auditor, listener, eavesdropper; audi-tory, -ence.
V. hear, overhear; hark, -en; list, -en; give –, lend –, bend- an ear; give attention; catch a sound, prick up one's ears; give -a hearing, – audience -to.
hang upon the lips of, be all ear, listen with both ears, monitor.
become audible; meet –, fall upon –, catch –, reach- the ear; be heard; ring in the ear etc. (*resound*) 408.
Adj. hearing etc. *v.*; auditory, auricular, aural, auditive, acoustic.
Adv. *arrectis auribis.*
Int. hark, – ye! hear! list, -en! *Oyez!* attention! lend me your ears!

419. Deafness.—N. deafness, hardness of hearing, surdity; inaudibility.
V. be -deaf etc. *adj.*; have no ear; shut –, stop –, close- one's ears; turn a deaf ear to.
render deaf, stun, deafen.
Adj. deaf, earless, surd; hard –, dull- of hearing; deaf-mute, stunned, deafened; stone deaf; deaf as -a post, – an adder, – a beetle, – a trunk-maker.
inaudible etc. 405; out of hearing.

420. Light.—N. light, ray, beam, stream, gleam, streak, pencil; sun-, moon-beam; dawn, aurora.

day; sunshine; light of -day, – heaven; sun etc. (*luminary*) 432, day-, broad day-, noontide- light; noon-tide, -day; glare.

glow etc. *v.*; afterglow, sunset; glimmering etc. *v.*; glint; play –, flood- of light; phosphorescence,

flush, halo, glory, nimbus, aureole, *aureola*.

spark, *scintilla*; *facula*; sparkling etc. *v.*; emication, scintillation, flash, blaze, coruscation, fulguration; flame etc. (*fire*) 382; lightning, *ignis fatuus*, etc. (*luminary*) 423, radio-activity.

luster, sheen, shimmer, reflection; gloss, tinsel, spangle, brightness, brilliancy, splendor; ef-, refulgence; ful-gor, -gidity; dazzlement, resplendence, transplendency; luminousness etc. *adj.*; luminosity; lucidity; renitency; radi-ance, -ation; irradiation, illumination, phosphorescence, luminescence.

radiation, radiant heat, infra-red rays, visible radiation, ultra-violet –, actinic- rays, actinism; X –, Roentgen- rays; phot-, heli-ography; optical instruments etc. 445.

[Science of light] optics; photo-logy, -metry; di-, cat-optrics.

[Distribution of light] *chiaroscuro*, *clair-obscur*, clear obscure, breadth, light and shade, black and white, tonality, half-tone, mezzotint.

reflection, refraction, dispersion, double refraction, polarization, diffraction, interference.

illuminant etc. 423.

V. shine, glow, glitter, phosphoresce; glis-ter, -ten; twinkle, gleam; flare, – up; glare, beam, shimmer, glimmer, flicker, sparkle, scintillate, coruscate, flash, fulgurate, blaze; be -bright etc. *adj.*; reflect light, daze, dazzle, bedazzle, raidate, shoot out beams.

clear up, brighten.

lighten, enlighten; light, – up; irradiate, shine upon; give –, hang out- a light; cast –, throw –, shed- -luster, – light- upon; illum-e, -ine, -inate; relume, strike a light; kindle etc. (*set fire to*) 384.

Adj. shining etc. *v.*; lumin-ous, -iferous; luc-id, -ent, -ulent, -ific, -iferous; illuminating, light, -some; bright, vivid, splendent, nitid, lustrous, shiny, brilliant, beamy, scintillant, radiant, lambent; sheen, -y; glossy, burnished, glassy, sunny, orient, meridian; noon-day, -tide; cloudless, clear; unclouded, -obscured.

garish; re-, tran-splendent; re-, effulgent; ful-gid, -gent; relucent, splendid, blazing, in a blaze, ablaze, rutilant, meteoric, phosphorescent; aglow.

bright as silver; light –, bright- as -day, – noonday, – the sun at noonday.

optical, actinic; photo-genic, -graphic; heliographic, radioactive.

421. Darkness.—N. darkness etc. *adj.*; blackness etc. (*dark color*) 431; obscurity, gloom, murk; dusk etc. (*dimness*) 422;, tenebrosity, umbrageousness.

Cimmerian –, Stygian –, Egyptian- darkness; night; midnight; dead of –, witching time of- night; blind man's holiday; darkness -visible; – that can be felt; palpable, obscure; Erebus.

shade, shadow, umbra, penumbra; sciagraphy; *silhouette*; radiograph, skiagraph.

obscuration; ad-, ob-umbration; obtenebration, offuscation, caligation; extinction; eclipse, total eclipse; gathering of the clouds.

shading; distribution of shade; *chiaroscuro* etc. (*light*) 420.

noctivagation, noctograph, noctuary.

obscurantist.

V. be -dark etc. *adj.*

darken, obscure, shade; dim; tone down, lower; over-cast, -shadow; cloud, eclipse; ob-, of-fuscate; ob-, ad-umbrate, cast into the shade; be-cloud, -dim, -darken; cast –, throw –, spread- a -shade, – shadow, – gloom.

extinguish; put –, blow –, snuff- out; doubt.

Adj. dark, -some, -ling; obscure, tenebrous, tenebrious, sombrous, pitch dark, pitchy, caliginous; black etc. (*in color*) 431.

sunless, lightless etc. (*see* sun, light etc. 423); somber, dusky; unilluminated etc. (*see* illuminate etc. 420); nocturnal; dingy, lurid, gloomy; murk-y, -some; shady, umbrageous; overcast etc. (*dim*) 422; cloudy etc. (*opaque*) 426; darkened etc. *v.*

dark as -pitch, – a pit, – Erebus.

benighted; noctivag-ant, -ous.

Adv. in the -dark, – shade; at night.

422. Dimness.—N. dimness etc. *adj.*; darkness etc. 421; paleness etc. (*light color*) 429.

half-light, *demi-jour*; partial -shadow, – eclipse; shadow of a shade; glimmer, -ing; nebulosity; cloud etc. 353; eclipse.

aurora, dusk, twilight, gloaming, blind man's holiday, shades of evening, crepuscule, cockshut time; break of day, daybreak, dawn.

moon-light, -beam, -shine; star- owl's-, candle-, rush-, fire-light; farthing candle.

V. be –, grow- -dim etc. *adj.*; flicker, twinkle, glimmer; loom, lower; fade; darken; pale, – its ineffectual fire.

render -dim etc. *adj.*; dim, bedim, obscure.

Adj. dim, dull, lack-luster, dingy, darkish, shorn of its beams; dark 421.

faint, shadowed forth; glassy; bleary; cloudy; misty etc. (*opaque*) 426; muggy, fuliginous; nebulous, -ar; obnubilated, overcast, crepuscular, twilight, muddy, lurid, leaden, dun, dirty; looming etc. *v.*

pale etc. (*colorless*) 429; confused etc. (*invisible*) 447.

423. Luminary. [Source of light.]—**N.** luminary; light etc. 420; flame etc. (*fire*) 382.

spark, *scintilla*; phosphorescence.

sun, orb of day, day star, Phoebus, Apollo, Helios, Phaethon, Hyperion, Ra, Aurora; star, orb, meteor; falling –, shooting- star; blazing –, dog-star; Sirius, canicula, Aldebaran; morning star, Lucifer, Phosphor, evening star; Hesperus, Venus, planet, moon etc. 318; constellation, galaxy; northern light, *aurora -borealis*, – *australis*, zodiacal light; mock sun, parhelion.

lightning; fork –, sheet –, summer- lightning, St. Elmo's fire; phosphorus; *ignis fatuus*; Jack o' – Friar's- lantern; Will o' the wisp, fire-drake, *Fata Morgana*.

glow-worm, fire-fly.

radium, luminous paint.

[Artificial light] gas; gas –, lime –, electric –, head –, search –, spot –, flash –, flood –, foot-light; lamp, oil –, gas –, arc –, incandescent-lamp; flare; lant-ern, -horn; dark lantern, bull's eye, projector; candle, *bougie*, tallow –, wax-candle; dip, farthing dip; taper, rush-light; oil etc. (*grease*) 356; wick, burner; Argand, moderator, duplex; torch, *flambeau*, link, brand; cresset; gase-, chande-, electro-lier; candelabrum, *girandole*, sconce, luster, candle-stick.

firework, fizgig; pyrotechnics; Roman candle, Very light, star shell, parachute light; rocket, lighthouse etc. (*signal*) 550.

V. illuminate etc. (*light*) 420.

Adj. self-luminous, incandescent; phosphor-ic, -escent; luminescent, fluorescent, radiant etc. (*light*) 420.

424. Shade.—N. shade; awning etc. (*cover*) 223; parasol, sunshade, umbrella; screen, curtain, shutter, blind, gauze, veil, mantle, mask; cloud, mist, gathering of clouds; smoke screen; smoked glasses, colored spectacles; blinkers, blinders.

umbrage, glade; shadow etc. 421.

V. draw a curtain; put up –, close- a shutter; veil etc. *v.*; cast a shadow etc. (*darken*) 421; screen, obstruct the view.

Adj. shady, umbrageous, bowery.

425. Transparency.—N. transparen-ce, -cy; translucen-ce, -cy; diaphaneity; luc-, pelluc-, limp-idity.

transparent medium, glass, crystal, mica; lymph, water.

v. be -transparent etc. *adj.*; transmit light.

Adj. transparent, pellucid, lucid, diaphanous; trans-, tra-lucent; limpid, clear, serene, crystalline, clear as crystal, vitreous, transpicuous, glassy, hyaline.

426. Opacity.—N. opacity; opaqueness etc. *adj.*

film; cloud etc. 353.

V. be -opaque etc. *adj.*; obstruct the passage of light; ob-, of-fuscate.

Adj. opaque, impervious to light.

dim etc. 422; turbid, thick, muddy, opacous, obfuscated, fuliginous, cloudy, hazy, foggy, vaporous, nubiferous, muggy.

smoky, fumid, murky, dirty.

427. Semitransparency.—N. semitransparency, opalescence, milkiness, pearliness; gauze, muslin; film; mist etc. (*cloud*) 353; frosted glass.

Adj. semi-transparent, -pellucid, -diaphanous, -opacous, -opaque; opal-escent, -ine; pearly, milky, frosted, mat; misty.

428. Color.—N. color, hue, tint, tinge, dye, complexion, shade, tincture, cast, livery, coloration, chromatism, glow, flush; tone, key.

pure –, positive –, primary –, primitive –, complementary- color; three primaries; spectrum, chromatic dispersion; broken –, secondary –, tertiary- color.

local color, coloring, keeping, tone, value, aerial perspective.

[Science of color] chromatics, spectrum analysis; prism, spectroscope.

pigment, coloring matter, paint, dye, wash, distemper, stain; medium; mordant; oil-paint etc. (*painting*) 556.

V. color, dye, tinge, stain, tint, tinct, tone, paint, wash, ingrain, grain, illuminate, emblazon, imbue; paint etc. (*fine art*) 556; daub.

Adj. colored etc. *v.*; colorific, tingent, tinctorial; chormatic, prismatic; full-, high-, deep-colored; doubly-dyed; polychromatic.

bright, vivid, intense, deep; fresh, unfaded; rich, gorgeous; highly colored; gay; variegated etc. 440.

gaudy, florid; garish; showy, flaunting, flashy; raw, crude; glaring, flaring; discordant, inharmonious.

mellow, harmonious, pearly, sweet, delicate, tender, refined.

429. Achromatism. [Absence of color.]**—N.** achromatism; de-, dis-coloration; pall-or, -idity; paleness etc. *adj.*; etoilation; neutral tint, monochrome, black-and-white.

V. lose -color etc. 428; fade, fly, go; become -colorless etc. *adj.*; turn pale, pale, whiten.

deprive of color, decolorize, bleach, tarnish, achromatize, blanch, etiolate, wash out, tone down.

Adj. uncolored etc. (*see* color etc. 428); colorless, achromatic, hueless, pale, pallid; pale-, tallow-faced; faint, dull, cold, muddy, leaden, dun, wan, sallow, dead, dingy, ashy, ashen, ghastly, cadaverous, glassy, lack-luster; discolored etc. *v.*

light-colored, fair, *blond*; white etc. 430.

pale as -death, – ashes, – a witch, – a ghost, – a corpse.

430. Whiteness.—N. whiteness etc. *adj.*; argent.

albification, albescence, albinism, etiolation.

snow, paper, chalk, milk, lily, ivory, silver, alabaster; white lead, chinese –, flake –, ivory –, zinc- white, white-wash, -ning, whiting.

V. be -white etc. *adj.*

render -white etc. *adj.*; whiten- bleach, blanch, etiolate, whitewash, silver, frost.

Adj. white; milky, milk-, snow-white; snowy, niveous, candid, chalky; hoar, -y; frosted, silvery; argent, -ine; canescent.

whitish, creamy, pearly, ivory, fair, *blond*, ash-blond, platinum blond; blanched etc. *v.*; high in tone, light.

white as -a sheet, – driven snow, – a lily, – silver; like -ivory etc. *n.*

431. Blackness.—N. blackness etc. *adj.*; darkness etc. (*want of light*) 421; swarthness, lividity, dark color, tone, color; *chiaroscuro* etc. 420.

nigrification, infuscation, denigration.
jet, ink, ebony, coal, pitch, soot, smudge, charcoal, sloe, raven, crow; black.
[Pigments] lamp –, ivory –, blue-black; writing –, printing –, printer's –, Indian- ink.
V. be -black etc. *adj.*
render -black etc. *adj.*; blacken, infuscate, denigrate; blot, -ch; smutch; smirch; darken etc. 421.
Adj. black, sable, swarthy, somber, dark, inky, ebon, atramentous, jetty; coal-, jet-black; fuliginous, pitchy, sooty, swart, dusky, dingy, murky, low-toned, low in tone; of the deepest dye.
black as -jet etc. *n.*, – my hat, – a shoe, – a tinker's pot, – November, – thunder, – midnight; nocturnal etc. (*dark*) 421; nigrescent; gray etc. 432; obscure etc. 421.
Adv. in mourning.

432. Gray.—N. gray etc. *adj.*; neutral tint, silver, pepper and salt, *chiaroscuro*, *grisaille*, grayness.
[Pigments] Payne's gray; black etc. 431.
Adj. gray, grey; steel –, iron- gray, dun, drab, dingy, leaden, livid, somber, sad, pearly; silver, -y, -ed; ash-en, -y; ciner-eous, -itious; grizzl-y, -ed; dove-, slate-, stone-, mouse-, ash-colored; mole; cool.

433. Brown.—N. brown etc. *adj.*
[Pigments] bister, ocher, sepia, Vandyke brown.
Adj. brown, adust, bay, dapple, auburn, chestnut, nutbrown, cinnamon, hazel, fawn, puce, *écru*, russet, tawny, fuscous, chocolate, maroon, foxy, tan, brunette, whitey-brown; snuff-, liver-colored; brown as -a berry, – mahogany; reddish brown; copper-, rust-, colored; henna, bronze, khaki russet, roan, sorrel.
sub-burnt; tanned etc. *v.*
V. render -brown etc. *adj.*; tan, embrown, bronze.

434. Redness.—N. red, scarlet, vermilion, cardinal, Post Office, red, carmine, crimson, pink, lake, *cerise*, cherry red, maroon, carnation, *couleur de rose*, *rose du Barry*; magenta, damask; flesh -color, – tint; color; fresh –, high- color; warmth; gules.
ruby, garnet, carbuncle; rose; rust, iron-mold.
[Dyes and pigments] cinnabar, cochineal; fuchsine; ruddle, madder, redlead; light –, Venetian- red; red ink, annotto.
redness etc. *adj.*; rub-escence, -icundity, -ification; erubescence, blush.
V. be –, become- -red etc. *adj.*; blush, flush, color up, mantle, redden.
render- red etc. *adj.*; redden, rouge; rub-ify, -ricate; incarnadine; ruddle.
Adj. red etc. *n.*; -dish; rufous, ruddy, florid, incarnadine, sanguine, bloody, gory; ros-y, -eate; blowz-y, -ed; brunt; rubi-cund, -form; lurid, stammel, blood-red; russet, murrey, carroty, sorrel, lateritious.
rose-, ruby-, cherry-, claret-, wine-, plum-, flame-, flesh-, peach-, salmon-, brick-, brickdust-colored, reddish brown etc. 433.
red as -fire, – blood, – scarlet, – a turkeycock, – a lobster; warm, hot; foxy.

435. Greenness.—N. green etc. *adj.*; blue and yellow; vert.
emerald, verd antique, verdigris, malachite, beryl, aquamarine, reseda.
[Pigments] *terre verte*, verditer, bice, chlorophyl.
greenness, verdure, verdancy; viridity, -escence.
Adj. green, verdant; glaucous, olive; porraceous; green as grass.
emerald –, pea –, grass –, apple –, sea –, olive –, bottle –, leaf- green.
greenish; vir-ent, -escent.

436. Yellowness.—N. yellow etc. *adj.*; or.
[Pigments] gamboge; cadmium –, chrome –, Indian –, lemon- yellow; orpiment, yellow ocher, Claude tint, aureolin.
crocus, saffron, topaz, gold.
jaundice; London fog; yellowness etc. *adj.*
Adj. yellow, aureate, gold, golden, gilt, gilded, flavous, citrine, fallow; fulv-ous, -id; sallow, luteous, fawny, creamy, sandy; xanth-ic, -ous; jaundiced.
gold-, citron-, saffron-, lemon-, sulphur-, amber-, straw-, primrose-, cream-colored; flazen, yellowish, buff.
yellow as a -quince, – guinea, – crow's foot.

437. Purple.—N. purple etc. *adj.*; blue and red, bishop's purple; aniline dyes, gridelin, amethyst; purpure.
livid-ness, -ity.
V. empurple.
Adj. purple, violet, plum-colored, lavender, lilac, puce, *mauve*; livid.

438. Blueness.—N. blue etc. *adj.*; garter-blue; watchet.
[Pigments] ultramarine, smalt, cobalt, cyanogen; Prussian –, syenite- blue; bice, indigo, woad.
lapis lazuli, sapphire, turquoise.
blue-, bluish-ness; bloom
Adj. blue, azure, cerulean; sky-blue, -colored, -dyed; navy-blue, aquamarine, electric blue, royal blue, cyanic; bluish; atmospheric, retiring; cold.

439. Orange.—N. orange, red and yellow; gold; or; flame etc. color, *adj.*
[Pigments] ochre, Mars orange, cadmium.
V. gild, warm.
Adj. orange; ocherous; orange-, gold-, flame-, copper-, brass-, apricot-colored; warm, hot, glowing.

440. Variegation.—N. variegation; di-, tri-chromism; iridescence, irisation, play of colors, polychrome, maculation, spottiness, striae.

spectrum, rainbow, iris, tulip, peacock, chameleon, butterfly, tortoiseshell; mackerel. – sky; zebra, leopard, mother-of-pearl, nacre, opal, marble, batik.

check, plaid, tartan, patchwork; mar-, parquetry; mosiac, *tesserae*, tesselation, chess-board, checkers, chequers; harlequin; Joseph's coat; tricolor; patches, bands, stripes, spots etc of color.

V. be -variegated etc. *adj.*; variegate, stripe, streak, checker, chequer; be-, speckle, fleck; be-, sprinkle; stipple, maculate, dot, bespot; tattoo, inlay, tesselate, damascene; embroider, braid, quilt.

Adj. variegated etc. *v.*; many-colored, -hued; divers-, parti-colored; di-, poly-chromatic; bi-, tri-, versi-color; of all -the colors of the rainbow, – manner of colors; kaleidoscopic.

iridescent; opal-ine, -escent; prismatic, nacreous, pearly, shot, *gorge de pigeon*, *chatoyant*, irisated.

pied, piebald, skewbald; motley; mottled, marbled; pepper and salt, paned, dappled, clouded, cymophanous.

mosiac, tesselated, chequered, plaid; tortoiseshell etc. *n.*

spott-ed, -y; punctuated, powdered; speckled etc. *v.*; freckled, fleabitten, studded; fleck-ed, -ered; striated, barred, veined; brind-ed, -led; tabby; watered; grizzled; listed; embroidered etc. *v.*; daedal.

441. Vision.—N. vision, sight, optics, eye-sight.

view, look, espial, glance, ken, *coup d'oeil*; glimpse, peep, glint; gaze, stare, leer; perlustration, contemplation; conspect-ion, -uity; regard, survey; in-, intro-spection; *reconnaissance*, speculation, watch, espionage, *espionnage*, autopsy; ocular - inspection, – demonstration; sight-seeing.

macrography, micrography.

point of view; view-, stand- point; gazebo, loophole, *belvedere*, watchtower.

field of view; theater, amphitheater, arena, vista, horizon; commanding –, bird's eye –, panoramic- view; periscope.

visual organ, organ of vision; eye; naked –, unassisted- eye; eye-ball, retina, pupil, iris, cornea, white; optics, orbs; saucer –, goggle –, gooseberry-eyes.

short sight etc. 443; clear –, sharp –, quick –, eagle –, piercing-, –, penetrating- -sight, – glance, – eye; perspicacity, discernment; catopsis.

eagle, hawk; cat, lynx; Argus.

evil eye; basilisk, cockatrice.

spectacles, telescope etc. 445.

V. see, behold, discern, perceive, have in sight, descry, sight, make out, discover, distinguish, recognize, spy, espy, ken; get –, have –, catch- a - sight, – glimpse- of; command of view of; witness, contemplate, speculate; cast –, set- the eyes on; be a -spectator etc. 444- of; look on etc. (*be present*) 186; see sights etc. (*curiosity*) 445; see at a glance etc. (*intelligence*) 498.

look, view, eye; lift up the eyes, open one's eye; look -at, – on, – upon, – over, – about one, – round; survey, scan, inspect; run the eye -over, – through; reconnoiter, glance -round, – on, – over; turn –, bend- one's looks upon; direct the eyes to, turn the eyes on, cast a glance, make eyes at.

observe etc. (*attend to*) 457; watch etc. (*care*) 459; see with one's own eyes; watch for etc. (*expect*) 507; peek, peep, peer, pry, take a peep; play at bo-peep.

look -full in the face, – hard at, – intently; strain one's eyes; fix –, rivet- the eyes upon; stare, gaze; pore over, gloat -over, – on; leer, ogle, glare; goggle; cock the eye, squint, gloat, look askance; give the glad eye.

Adj. seeing etc. *v.*; visual, ocular, -al; ophthalmic.

far-, clear-sighted etc. *n.*; eagle-, hawk-, lynx-, keen-, Argus-eyed.

visible etc. 446.

Adv. visibly etc. 446; in sight of, with one's eyes open.

at -sight, – first sight, – a glance, – the first blush; *primâ facie*.

Int. look! etc. (*attention*) 457.

Phr. the scales falling from one's eyes.

442. Blindness.—N. blindness, anopsia, cecity, excecation, *amaurosis*, cataract, ablepsy, prestriction; dim-sightedness etc. 443.

V. be -blind etc. *adj.*; not see; lose sight of; have the eyes bandaged; grope in the dark.

not look; close –, shut –, turn away –, avert- the eyes; look another way; wink etc. (*limited vision*) 443; shut the eyes –, be blind- to; wink –, blink- at.

render -blind etc. *adj.*; blind, -fold; hoodwink, dazzle; put one's eyes out; throw dust into one's eyes; *jeter de la poudre aux yeux*; screen from sight etc. (*hide*) 528.

Adj. blind; eye-, sight-, vision-less; dark; stone-, sand-, stark-blind; undiscerning; dim-sighted etc. 443.

blind as -a bat, – a buzzard, – a beetle, – a mole, – an owl; wall-eyed.

blinded etc. *v.*

Adv. blind-ly, -fold; darkly.

443. Dim-sightedness. [Imperfect vision.] [Fallacies of vision.]—**N.** dim –, dull –, half –, short –, near –, long –, double –, astigmatic –, failing- sight; dim etc -sightedness; snow blindness; purblindness, lippitude; my-, presby-opia; confusion of vision; astigmatism; nystagmus; color-blindness, dichromism, chromato-pseudo-blepsis, Daltonism; nyctalopy; *strabismus*, strabism, squint, cast in the eye, swivel eye, goggle eyes; obliquity of vision.

winking etc. *v.*; nictitation; blinkard, albino.

dizziness, swimming, scotomy; cataract; ophthalmia.

[Limitation of vision] eye shade, blinker, blinder; screen etc. (*hider*) 530.

[Fallacies of vision] *deceptio visûs*; refraction, distortion, illustion, false light, *anamorphosis*, virtual image, *spectrum*, *mirage*, looming, phasma; phant-asm, -asma, -om; vision; specter, apparition, ghost; *ignis fatuus* etc. (*luminary*) 423; specter of the Brocken; magic mirror; magic lantern etc. (*show*) 448; mirror, lens etc. (*instrument*) 445.

V. be -dim-sighted etc. *n.*; see double; have a -mote in the eye, – mist before the eyes, – film over the eyes; see through a -prism, – glass darkly; wink, blink, nictitate; squint; look ask-ant, -ance; screw up the eyes, glare, glower.

dazzle, glare, blur, swim, loom.

Adj. dim-sighted etc. *n.*; my-, presby-opic; astigmatic; moon-, mope-, blear-, goggle-, gooseberry-, one-eyed; blind of one eye, monoculous; half-, pur-, color-blind; dichromatic.

blind as a bat etc. (*blind*) 442; winking etc. *v.*

444. Spectator.—N. spectator, beholder, observer, inspector, viewer, looker-on, onlooker, witness, eye-witness, bystander, passer by; sight-seer.

spy, scout; sentinel etc. (*warning*) 668.

v. witness, behold etc. (*see*) 441; look on etc. (*be present*) 186.

445. Optical Instruments.—N. optical instruments; lens, meniscus, magnifier, reading –, burning- glass; micro-, mega-, teino-scope; spectacles, glasses, barnacles, goggles, giglamps, eyeglass, *pince-nez*, monocle; periscopic lens; telescope, glass, lorgnette, binocular; spy-, opera-, field-glass, periscope, range finder.

mirror, reflector, speculum; looking-, pier-, cheval-, hand-glass.

prism; camera, *camera-lucida*, *-obscura*; projector, stereopticon, magic lantern etc. (*show*) 448; chro-, thau-matrope; stereo-, pseudo-, poly-, kaleido-scope.

photo-, opto-, erio-, actino-, luci-, radio-, spectro-meter; polari-, polemo-, spectro-scope, diffraction grating.

optics, optician, optometry, optometrist; microscop-y, -ist; photometry, photography; photographer.

446. Visibility.—N. visibility, perceptibility; conspicuousness, distinctness etc. *adj.*; conspicuity; appearance etc. 448; exposure; manifestation etc. 525; ocular -proof, – evidence, – demonstration; field of view etc. (*vision*) 441.

V. be –, become- -visible etc. *adj.*; appear, emerge, open to the view; meet –, catch- the eye; present –, show –, manifest –, produce –, discover –, reveal –, expose –, betray- itself; stand -forth, – out; show; arise; peep –, peer –, crop- out; start –, spring –, show –, turn –, crop- up; glimmer, glitter, glow, loom; glare; burst forth, scintillate; burst upon the -view, – sight; heave in sight; come -in sight, – into view, – out, – forth, – forward; see the light of day; break through the clouds; make its appearance, show its face, materialize, appear to one's eyes, come upon the stage, enter; float before the eyes, speak for itself. etc. (*manifest*) 525; attract the attention etc. 457; reappear; live in a glass house.

expose to view etc. 525.

Adj. visible, perceptible, perceivable, discernible, apparent; in -view, – full view, – sight; exposed to view, *en évidence*; unclouded.

obvious etc. (*manifest*) 525; plain, clear, distinct, definite; well-defined, -marked; in focus; recognizable, palpable, autoptical; glaring, staring, conspicuous; stereoscopic; in -bold, – strong, – high- relief.

periscopic, panoramic.

before –, under- one's eyes; before one, *à vue d'oeil*, in one's eye, *oculis subjecta fidelibus.*

Adv. visibly etc. *adj.*; in sight of; before one's eyes etc. *adj.*; *veluti in speculum.*

447. Invisibility.—N. invisibility, nonappearance, imperceptibility; indistinctness etc. *adj.*; mystery, delitescence.

concealment etc. 528; latency etc. 526.

V. be -invisible etc. *adj.*; be hidden etc. (*hide*) 528; lurk etc. (*lie hidden*) 526; escape notice.

render -invisible etc. *adj.*; conceal etc. 528; put out of sight.

not see etc. (*be blind*) 442; lose sight of.

Adj. invisible, imperceptible; un-, in-discernible; un-, non-apparent; out of –, not in- sight; *à perte de vue*; behind the -scenes, – curtain; view-, sightless; in-, un-conspicuous; unseen etc. (*see* see etc. 441); covert etc. (*latent*) 526; eclipsed, under an eclipse.

dim etc. (*faint*) 422; mysterious, dark, obscure, confused; indistin-ct, -guishable; shadowy, indefinite, undefined; ill-defined, -marked; blurred, fuzzy, out of focus; misty etc. (*opaque*) 426; veiled etc. (*concealed*) 528; delitescent.

448. Appearance.—N. appearance, phenomenon, sight, spectacle, show, premonstration, scene, species, view, *coup d'oeil*; look-out, out-look, prospect, vista, perspective, bird's-eye view, scenery, landscape, picture, *tableau*; display, exposure, *mise en scène*; scenery, *décor*; rising of the curtain.

phant-asm, -om etc. (*fallacy of vision*) 443.

pageant, *spectacle*; peep-, raree-, gallanty-show; *ombres chinoises*; projector, optical –, magic-lantern, phantasmagoria, dissolving views; cinema, -tograph; bio-scope, -graph; moving pictures, movies, film, screen etc.; pan-, di-, cosm-, georama; *coup* –, *jeu- de théâtre*; pageantry etc. (*ostentation*) 882; insignia etc. (*indication*) 550.

aspect, phase, *phasis*, seeming; shape etc. (*form*) 240; guise, look, complexion, color, image, mien, air, cast, carriage, port, demeanor; presence, expression, first blush, face of the thing; point of view, light.

lineament, feature, trait, lines; out-line, -side; contour, *silhouette*, face, countenance, physiognomy, visage, phiz, mug, cast of countenance, profile, *tournure*, cut of one's jib, metoposcopy; outside etc. 220.

V. appear; be –, become- visible etc. 446; seem, look, show; present –, wear –, carry –, have –, bear –, exhibit –, take –, take on –, assume- the -appearance, – semblance- of; look like; cut a figure, figure; present to the view; show etc. (*make manifest*) 525.

Adj. apparent, seeming, ostensible; on view.

Adv. apparently; to all -seeming, – appearance; ostensibly, seemingly, as it seems, on the face of it, *primâ facie*; at the first blush, at first sight; in the eyes of; to the eye.

449. Disappearance.—N. disappearance, evanescence, eclipse, occultation.

departure etc. 293; exit, vanishing point; dissolving views.

V. disappear, vanish, dissolve, fade, melt away, pass, go, avaunt; be -gone etc. *adj.*; leave -no trace, – 'not a rack behind;' go off the stage etc. (*depart*) 293; suffer –, undergo- an eclipse; be lost to –, retire from- -sight, – view.

lose sight of.

efface etc. 552.

Adj. disappearing etc. *v.*; evanescent; missing, lost; lost to -sight, – view; gone; *spurlos versenki.*

Int. vanish! disappear! avaunt! etc. (*ejection*) 297.

450. Intellect.—N. intellect, mind, understanding, reason, thinking principle; rationality; cogitative –, cognitive –, intellectual- faculties; faculties, senses, consciousness, observation, percipience, apperception, mentality, intelligence, intellection, intuition, association of ideas, instinct, flair, conception, judgment, wits, parts, capacity, intellectuality, reasoning power, brains, genius; wit etc. 498; ability etc. (*skill*) 698; wisdom etc. 498.

soul, spirit, ghost, inner man, heart, breast, bosom, *penetralia mentis, divina particula aurae*, heart's core; ego, psyche, pneuma, subconsciousness, subconscious, subliminal self; dual personality.

organ –, seat- of thought; *sensorium*, sensory, brain, gray matter; head, -piece; pate, noddle, skull, scull, *pericranium*, *cerebrum*, *cranium*, brain-pan, -box; sconce, upper story.

[Science of mind] metaphysics; psychics, psycho-logy, -metry, -genesis, -analysis, -physics, psychi-atry, -cal research, thought reading etc. 992; ideology; mental –, moral- philosophy; philosophy of the mind; pneumat-, phren-ology; no –, craniology, -scopy.

ideal-ity, -ism; transcendental-, spiritual-ism; immateriality etc. 317.

metaphysician, psychologist etc.

V. note, notice, mark; take -notice, – cognizance- of; be -aware, – conscious- of; realize; appreciate; ruminate etc. (*think*) 451; fancy etc. (*imagine*) 515; conceive, reason, understand.

Adj. [Relating to intellect] intellectual, mental, rational, subjective, metaphysical, nooscopic, spiritual; ghostly; psych-ical, -ological; cerebral.

immaterial etc. 317; endowed with reason.

Adv. *in petto.*

450a. Absence or want **of Intellect.—N.** absence –, want- of -intellect etc. 450; imbecility etc. 499; brutality; brute -instinct, – force.

Adj. unendowed with reason.

451. Thought.—N. thought; exercitation –, exercise- of the intellect; reflection, cogitation, consideration, meditation, study, lucubration, speculation, deliberation, pondering; head-, brainwork; cerebration; mentation, deep reflection; close study, application etc. (*attention*) 457.

abstract thought, abstraction, contemplation, musing; brown study etc. (*inattention*) 458; reverie, Platonism; depth of thought, workings of the mind, thoughts, inmost thoughts; self-counsel, communing, -consultation.

association –, succession –, flow –, train –, current- of -thought, – ideas.

after –, mature- thought; reconsideration, second thoughts; retrospection etc. (*memory*) 505; excogitation; examination etc. (*inquiry*) 461; invention etc. (*imagination*) 515.

thoughtfulness etc. *adj.*

V. think, reflect, reason, cogitate, excogitate, consider, deliberate; bestow -thought, – consideration- upon; speculate, contemplate, meditate, ponder, muse, dream, ruminate; brood –, conover; animadvert, study; bend–, apply- the mind etc. (*attend*) 457; digest, discuss, hammer at, weigh, perpend; realize, appreciate; fancy etc. (*imagine*) 515; trow.

take into consideration; take counsel etc. (*be advised*) 695; commune with –, bethink- oneself; collect one's thoughts; revolve –, turn over –, run over- in the mind; chew the cud –, sleep- upon; take counsel of –, advise with- one's pillow.

rack –, ransack –, crack –, beat –, cudgel- one's brains; set one's -brain, – wits- to work.

harbor –, entertain –, cherish –, nurture- an idea etc. 453; take into one's head; bear in mind; reconsider.

occur; present –, suggest- itself; come –, get- into one's head; strike one, flit across the view, come uppermost, run in one's head; enter –, pass in –, cross –, flash on –, flash across –, float in –, fasten itself on –, be uppermost in –, occupy- the mind; have in one's mind.

make an impression; sink –, penetrate- into the mind; engross the thoughts.

Adj. thinking etc. *v.*; thoughtful, pensive, meditative, reflective, cogitative, museful, wistful, contemplative, speculative, deliberative, studious, sedate, introspective, Platonic, philosophical.

lost –, engrossed –, rapt –, absorbed- in thought etc. (*inattentive*) 458; deep musing etc. (*intent*) 457.

in the mind, under consideration, in contemplation.

Adv. all things considered; taking everything into account.

Phr. the mind being on the stretch; the -mind, – head- -turning, – running- upon.

452. Incogitancy. [Absence or want of thought.]—**N.** incogitancy, vacancy, inunderstanding; inanity, fatuity etc. 499; thoughtlessness etc. (*inattention*) 458.

V. not -think etc. 451; not think of; dismiss from the -mind, – thoughts etc. 451.

indulge in reverie etc. (*be inattentive*) 458.

put away thought; unbend –, relax –, divert- the mind.

Adj. vacant, unintellectual, unideal, unoccupied, unthinking, inconsiderate, thoughtless; absent etc. (*inattentive*) 458; diverted; irrational etc. 499; narrow-minded etc. 481.

un-thought of, -dreamt of, -considered; off one's mind; incogitable, not to be thought of, inconceivable.

453. Idea. [Object of thought.]—**N.** idea, notion, conception, thought, apprehension, impression, perception, image, sentiment, reflection, observation, consideration; abstract idea, principle; archetype.

view etc. (*opinion*) 484; theory etc. 514; conceit, fancy; phantasy etc. (*imagination*) 515.

point of view etc. (*aspect*) 448; field of view.

454. Topic. [Subject of thought.]—**N.** subject of –, material for- thought; food for the mind, mental *pabulum*.

subject, -matter; matter, theme, topic, what it is about, *thesis*, text, business, affair, matter in hand, argument; motion, resolution; head, chapter; case, point; proposition, theorem; field of inquiry; moot point, problem, etc. (*question*) 461.

V. float –, pass- in the mind etc. 451.

Adj. thought of; uppermost in the mind; *in petto*.

Adv. under -discussion, – consideration, – advisement; in -question, – the mind; on -foot, – the carpet, – the *tapis*; before the house, relative to etc. 9.

455. Curiosity. [The desire of knowledge.]—**N.** interest, thirst for knowledge; curi-osity, -ousness; inquiring mind; inquisitiveness.

sight-seer, quidnunc, newsmonger, Paul Pry, peeping Tom, eavesdropper; gossip etc. (*news*) 532; questioner, *enfant terrible*.

V. be -curious etc. *adj.*; take an interest in, stare, gape; prick up the ears, see sights, lionize; pry, speer; dig up.

Adj. curious, inquisitive, burning with curiosity, overcurious, nosey; inquiring etc. 461; prying; inquisitorial; agape etc. (*expectant*) 507; attentive etc. 457.

Phr. what's the matter? what next?

456. Incuriosity. [Absence of curiosity.]—**N.** incuriosity; incuriousness etc. *adj.*; *insouciance* etc. 866; indifference, apathy.

V. be -incurious etc. *adj.*; have no -curiosity etc. 455; take no interest in etc. 823; mind one's own business.

Adj. incurious, uninquisitive, uninterested, indifferent, bored; impassive etc. 823.

457. Attention.—**N.** attention; mindfulness etc. *adj.*; intent-ness, -iveness; thought etc. 451; adverten-ce, -cy; observ-ance, -ation; consideration, reflection, perpension; heed; particularity; notice, regard etc. *v.*; circumspection etc. (*care*) 459; study, scrutiny, once-over; in-, intro-spection; revision, -al.

active –, diligent –, exclusive –, minute –, close –, intense –, deep –, profound –, abstract –, labored –, deliberate- -thought, – attention, – application, – study.

minuteness, attention to detail etc. 459.

absorption of mind etc. (*abstraction*) 458.

indication, calling attention to etc. *v.*

V. be -attentive etc. *adj.*; attend, advert to, observe, look, see, view, remark, notice, regard, take notice, mark; give –, pay- -attention, – heedto; listen in, incline –, lend- an ear to; trouble one's head about; give a thought –, animadvert to; occupy oneself with; contemplate etc (*think of*) 451; look -at, – to, – after, – into, – over; see to; turn –, bend –, apply –, direct –, give- the - mind, – eye, – attention- to; have -an eye to, – in one's eye; bear in mind; take into -account, – consideration; keep in -sight, – view; have regard to, heed, mind, take cognizance of, be engaged in, entertain, recognize; make –, take- note of; note.

examine cursorily; glance -at, – upon, – over; cast –, pass- the eyes over; run over, turn over the leaves, dip into, perstringe; skim etc. (*neglect*) 460; take a cursory view of.

examine, – closely, – intently; scan, scrutinize, consider; give –, bend- one's mind to; overhaul, revise, pore over; inspect, review, pass under review; take stock of; fix –, rivet –, focus –, devote- the - eye, – mind, – thoughts, – attention- on *or* to; hear –, think- out; mind one's business.

revert –, hark back- to; watch etc. (*expect*) 507, (*take care of*) 459; hearken –, listen- to; prick up the ears; have –, keep- the eyes open; come to the point.

meet with attention; fall under one's -notice, – observation; be -under consideration etc. (*topic*) 454.

catch –, strike- the eye; attract notice; catch –, awaken –, wake –, invite –, solicit –, attract –, claim –, excite –, engage –, occupy –, strike –, arrest –, fix –, engross –, absorb –, rivet-the- attention, – mind, – thoughts; be -present to, – uppermost in- the mind.

bring under one's notice; point -out, – to, – at, – the finger at, lay the finger on, indigitate, indicate; direct –, call- attention to; show; put a - mark etc. (*sign*) 550- upon; call soldiers to 'attention;' bring forward etc. (*make manifest*) 525.

Adj. attentive, mindful, heedful, observant, regardful; alive –, awake- to, alert; observing etc. *v.*; taken up –, occupied- with; engaged –, engrossed –, interested –, wrapped- in; absorbed, rapt; breathless; pre-occupied etc. (*inattentive*) 458; watchful etc. (*careful*) 459; intent on, open-eyed, breathless, undistracted, upon the stretch; on the watch etc. (*expectant*) 507.

steadfast.

Int. see! look, – here, – out, – alive, – you, – to it! mark! lo! behold! soho! hark, – ye! mind ! halloo! observe! lo and hehold! attention! *nota bene*; N.B.; *, †; I'd have you to know; notice! take notice! O yes! *Oyez!*

Phr. this is –, these are- to give notice.

458. Inattention.—**N.** in-attention, - consideration; inconsiderateness etc. *adj.*; oversight; inadverten-ce, -cy; non-observance, disregard.

supineness etc. (*inactivity*) 683; *étourderie*; want of thought; heedlessness etc. (*neglect*) 460; *insouciance* etc. (*indifference*) 866.

abstraction; absence —, absorption- of mind; preoccupation, distraction, reverie, brown study, deep musing, fit of abstraction, woolgathering.

V. be -inattentive etc. *adj.*; overlook, disregard; pass by etc. (*neglect*) 460; not -observe etc. 457; think little of.

close —, shut- one's eyes to; wink at; pay no attention to; dismiss —, discard —, discharge- from one's -thoughts, — mind; drop the subject, think no more of; set —, turn —, put- aside; turn -away from, — one's attention from, — a deaf ear to, — one's back upon.

abstract oneself, dream, indulge in reverie.

escape -notice, — attention; come in at one ear and go out at the other; forget etc. (*have no remembrance*) 506.

call off —, draw off —, call away —, divert —, distract- the -attention, — thoughts, — mind; put out of one's head; dis-concert, -compose; put out, confuse, perplex, bewilder, fluster, muddle, dazzle; throw a sop to Cerberus.

Adj. inattentive; un-observant, -mindful, heeding, -discerning; inadvertent; mind-, regard-, respect-less; listless etc. (*indifferent*) 866; blind, deaf; flighty, hand over head; cur-, percur-sory; giddy-, scatter-, hare-brained; unreflecting, *écervelé*, inconsiderate, off-hand, thoughtless, dizzy, muzzy, brainsick; giddy, — as a goose; wild, harum-scarum, ranipole, high-flying; heed-, careless etc. (*neglectful*) 460.

absent, absent-minded, abstracted, *distrait*; lost; lost —, wrapped- in thought, woolgathering; rapt, in the clouds, bemused; dreaming —, musing- on other things; pre-occupied; engrossed etc. (*attentive*) 457; in a -reverie etc. *n.*; off one's guard etc. (*inexpectant*) 508; napping; dreamy.

disconcerted, put out etc. *v.*; rattled.

Adv. inattentively, inadvertently etc. *adj.*; *per incuriam, sub silentio.*

Int. stand -at ease, — easy!

Phr. the attention wanders; one's wits gone a -woolgathering, — bird's nesting; it never entered into one's head; the mind running on other things; one's thoughts being elsewhere; had it been a bear it would have bitten you.

459. Care. [Vigilance.]—**N.** care, solicitude, heed; heedfulness etc. *adj.*; scruple etc. (*conscientiousness*) 939.

watchfulness etc. *adj.*; vigilance, *surveillance*, eyes of Argus, watch, vigil, look out, watch and ward, *l'oeil du maître*.

alertness etc. (*activity*) 682; attention etc. 457; prudence etc., circumspection etc. (*caution*) 864; forethought etc. 510; precaution etc. (*preparation*) 673; tidiness etc. (*order*) 58, (*cleanliness*) 652; accuracy etc. (*exactness*) 494; minuteness, attention to detail; meticulousness, nicety, circumstantiality.

V. be -careful etc. *adj.*; reck; take care etc. (*be cautious*) 864; pay attention to etc. 457; take care of; look —, see- -to, — after; keep -an eye, — a sharp eye- upon; keep -watch, — watch and ward; mount guard, set watch, watch; keep in -sight, — view; chaperon, play gooseberry; mind, — one's business.

look -sharp, — about one; look with one's own eyes; keep a -good, — sharp- look-out; have all one's -wits, — eyes- about one; watch for etc. (*expect*) 507; stand to; keep one's eyes —, have the eyes —, sleep with one eye- open.

take precautions etc. 673; protect etc. (*render safe*) 664.

do one's best etc. 682; mind one's Ps and Qs, speak by the card, pick one's steps.

Adj. care-, regard-, heed-ful; taking care etc. *v.*; particular; prudent etc. (*cautious*) 864; considerate; thoughtful etc. (*deliberative*) 451; provident etc. (*prepared*) 673; alert etc. (*active*) 682; sure-footed.

guarded, on one's guard; on the -*qui vive*, — alert, — watch, — look-out; awake, broad awake, vigilant; watch-, wake-, wist-ful; Argus-, lynx-eyed; wide awake etc. (*intelligent*) 498; on the watch for etc. (*expectant*) 507.

tidy etc. (*orderly*) 58, (*clean*) 652; accurate etc. (*exact*) 494; scrupulous etc. (*conscientious*) 939; *cavendo tutus* etc. (*safe*) 664.

Adv. carefully etc. *adj.*; with care, gingerly.

Phr. *quis custodiet ipsos custodes?*

460. Neglect.—**N.** neglect; carelessness etc. *adj.*; trifling etc. *v.*; negligence; omission, laches, default; remissness, slackness, procrastination; supineness etc. (*inactivity*) 683; inattention etc. 458; *nonchalance* etc. (*insensibility*) 823; imprudence, recklessness etc. 863; slovenliness etc. (*disorder*) 59; (*dirt*) 653; improvidence etc. 674; non-completion etc. 730; inexactness etc. (*error*) 495.

paraleipsis [in rhetoric].

trifler, slacker, waster, waiter on Providence; Micawber.

V. be -negligent etc. *adj.*; take no care of etc. (take care of etc. 459); neglect; let -slip, — go; lay —, set —, cast —, put- aside; keep —, leave- out of sight; lose sight of.

overlook, disregard; pass -over, — by; let pass; blink; wink —, connive- at; gloss over; take no -note, — notice, — thought, — account- of; pay no regard to; *laisser aller*; allow to lie on the table.

scamp; trifle, fribble; do by halves; skimp; cut; slight etc. (*despise*) 930; play —, trifle- with; slur; skim, — the surface; *effleurer*; take a cursory view of etc. 457.

slur —, slip —, skip —, jump- over; pretermit, miss, skip, jump, omit, give the go-by to, push aside, throw into the background, shelve, sink; ignore, shut one's eyes to, refuse to hear, turn a deaf ear to; leave out of one's calculation; not -attend to etc. 457, — mind; not trouble -oneself, — one's head- -with, — about; forget etc. 506; be caught napping etc. (*not expect*) 508; leave a loose thread; let the grass grow under one's feet.

render -neglectful etc. *adj.*; put —, throw- off one's guard.

Adj. neglecting etc. *v.*; unmindful, negligent, neglectful; heedless, careless, thoughtless; perfunctory, remiss, slack.

inconsiderate; un-, in-circumspect; off one's guard; un-wary, -watchful, -guarded; offhand.

supine etc. (*inactive*) 683; inattentive etc 458; *insouciant* etc. (*indifferent*) 823; imprudent, reckless etc. 863; slovenly etc. (*disorderly*) 59, (*dirty*) 653; inexact etc. (*erroneous*) 495; improvident etc. 674.

neglected etc. *v.*; un-heeded, -cared for, -

perceived, -seen, -observed, -noticed, -noted, -marked, -attended to, -thought of, -regarded, -remarked, -missed; shunted, shelved.

un-examined, -studied, -searched, -scanned, -weighed, -sifted, -explored.

Adv. negligently etc. *adj.*; hand over head, anyhow; in an unguarded moment etc. (*unexpectedly*) 508; *per incuriam*.

Int. never mind, no matter, let it pass; it will be all the same a hundred years hence.

461. Inquiry. [Subject of Inquiry. Question.]—**N.** inquiry; request etc. 765; search, research, quest; pursuit etc. 622.

examination, review, scrutiny, investigation, indagation; per-quisition, -scrutation, -vestigation; inqu-est, -isition; exploration; *exploitation*, ventilation.

sifting; calculation, analysis, dissection, resolution, induction; Baconian method.

strict —, close —, searching —, exhaustive- inquiry; narrow —, strict- search; study etc. (*consideration*) 451.

scire facias, *ad referendum*; trial.

questioning etc. *v.*; interroga-tion, -tory; third degree; interpellation; challenge, examination, cross-examination, catechism; feeler, Socratic method, zetetic philosophy; leading question; discussion etc. (*reasoning*) 476; questionnaire, questionary.

reconnoitering, *reconnaissance*; prying etc. *v.*; espionage, *espionnage*; domiciliary visit, peep behind the curtain; lantern of Diogenes.

question, query, problem, *desideratum*, point to be solved, porism; subject —, field- of -inquiry, — controversy; point —, matter- in dispute; moot-point; issue, question at issue; bone of contention etc. (*discord*) 713; plain —, fair —, open- question; enigma etc. (*secret*) 533; knotty point etc. (*difficulty*) *704*; *quod-libet*; threshold of an inquiry.

inquirer, investigator, experimenter, inquisitor, inspector, querist, examiner, catechist; scrut-ator, -ineer; analyst; quidnunc etc. (*curiosity*) 455.

V. make -inquiry etc. *n.*; inquire, seek, search, frisk, speer, look -for, — about for, — out for; scan, reconnoiter, explore, sound, rummage, ransack, pry, peer, look round; look —, go- -over, — through; spy, over-haul.

scratch the head, slap the forehead.

look —, peer —, pry- into every hole and corner; look behind the scenes; trace up; hunt —, fish —, dig —, ferret- out; unearth; leave no stone unturned.

seek a -clue, — clew; hunt, track, trail, shadow, mouse, dodge, trace; follow the -trail, — scent; pursue etc. 622; beat up one's quarters; fish for; feel for etc. (*experiment*) 463.

investigate; take up —, institute —, pursue —, follow up —, conduct —, carry on —, prosecute- -an inquiry etc. *n.*; look -at, — into; pre-examine; discuss, canvass, agitate.

examine, study, consider, calculate; dip —, dive —, delve —, go deep- into; make sure of, probe, sound, fathom; probe to the -bottom, — quick; scrutinize, analyze, anatomize, dissect, parse, resolve, sift, winnow; view —, try- in all its phases; thresh out.

bring in question, subject to examination; put to the proof etc. (*experiment*) 463; audit, tax, pass in review; take into consideration etc. (*think over*) 451; take counsel etc. 695.

ask, question, demand; put —, pop —, propose —, propound —, moot —, start —, raise —, stir —, suggsst —, put forth —, ventilate —, grapple with —, go into- a question.

put to the question, interrogate, catechize, pump, grill; cross-question, -examine; dodge; require an answer; pick —, suck- the brains of; feel the pulse.

be -in question etc. *adj.*; undergo examination.

Adj. inquiry etc. *v.*; inquisitive etc. (*curious*) 455; requisit-ive, -ory; catechetical, inquisitorial, analytic; in -search, — quest- of; on the look-out for, interrogative, zetetic; all-searching.

un-determined, -tried, -decided; in -question, — dispute, — issue, — course of inquiry; under -discussion, — consideration, — investigation etc. *n.*, *sub judice*, moot, proposed; doubtful etc. (*uncertain*) 475.

Adv. what? why? wherefore? whence? whither? where? *quaere?* how -comes, — happens, — is- it? what is the reason? what's -the matter, — up, in the wind? what on earth? when? who?

462. Answer.—**N.** answer, response, reply, replication, *riposte*, rejoinder, surrejoinder, rebutter, surrebutter, counter-evidence etc. 468, counter-charge, defence, plea; retort, repartee; contradiction etc. 536; rescript, -ion; antiphon, -y; acknowledgment; password; echo.

discovery etc. 480*a*; solution etc. (*explanation*) 522; rationale etc. (*cause*) 153; clue etc. (*indication*) 550.

Oedipus; oracle, etc. 513; return etc. (*record*) 551.

V. answer, respond, reply, rebut, retort, rejoin; give —, return for- answer; acknowledge, echo.

explain etc. (*interpret*) 522; solve etc. (*unriddle*) 522; discover etc. 480*a*; fathom, hunt out etc. (*inquire*) 461; satisfy, set at rest, determine.

Adj. answering etc. *v.*; respon-sive, -dent; oracular; antiphonal; conclusive.

Adv. because etc. (*cause*) 153; on the -scent, — right scent.

Int. *eureka!*

463. Experiment.—**N.** experiment; essay etc. (*attempt*) 675; research etc. (*investigation*) 461; trial, tentative method, *tâtonnement*.

verification, probation, *experimentum crucis*, proof, criterion, diagnostic test, tryout, crucial test, acid test.

crucible, reagent, check, touchstone, pix; assay, ordeal; ring.

empiricism, rule of thumb.

feeler; pilot —, messenger- balloon, *ballon d'essai*; pilot engine; scout; straw to show the wind.

speculation, random shot, leap in the dark.

analy-zer, -st; adventurer, explorer, sourdough, prospector; experiment-er, -ist, -alist; assayer.

V. experiment; essay etc. (*endeavor*) 675; try, assay, sample; make -an experiment, — trial of; give a trial to; put upon —, subject to- trial; experiment upon; rehearse; put —, bring —, submit-to the -test, — proof; prove, verify, test, touch, practise upon, try one's strength.

grope; feel —, grope- -for, — one's way; fumble; *tâttonner, aller à tâtons*; put —, throw- out a feeler; send up a pilot balloon; see how the -land lies, — wind blows; consult the barometer; feel the pulse; fish —, bob- for; cast —, beat- about for; angle, trawl, cast one's net, beat the bushes.

venture, try one's fortune etc. (*adventure*) 675; explore etc. (*inquire*) 461.

Adj. experimental; probat-ive, ory, -ionary; analytic, docimastic; tentative; empirical; speculative, tentive.

under probation, on one's trial, on trial, on approval.

464. Comparison.—N. comparison, collation, contrast; identification.

sim-ile, -ilitude; allegory etc. (*metaphor*) 521.

V. compare -to, — with; collate, confront; place side by side etc. (*near*) 197; set —, pit- against one another; contrast balance.

identify, draw a parallel, parallel.

compare notes; institute a comparison; *parva componere magnis*.

Adj. comparative, relative; metaphorical etc. 521.

compared with etc. *v.*; comparable.

Adv. relatively etc. (*relation*) 9; as compared with etc. *v.*

465. Discrimination.—N. discrimination, distinction, differentiation, diagnosis, diorism; nice perception; perception —, appreciation- of difference; acuteness; estimation etc. 466; nicety, refinement; taste etc. 850; *critique*, judgement, tact; insight, discernment etc. (*intelligence*) 498; *nuances*.

V. discriminate, distinguish, differentiate, severalize; separate; draw the line, sift; separate —, winnow- the chaff from the wheat; split hairs.

estimate etc. (*measure*) 466; know -which is which, — one's stuff, — one's way about, — what is what, — 'a hawk from a handsaw.'

take into -account, — consideration; give —, allow- due weight to; weigh carefully.

Adj. discriminating etc. *v.*; dioristic, discriminative, critical, distinctive; nice.

Phr. *il y a fagots et fagots*; *rem acu tetigisti*.

465a. Indiscrimination.—N. indiscrimination; promiscuity; indistinctness, -ion; uncertainty etc. (*doubt*) 475; obtuseness.

V. not -indiscriminate etc. 465; overlook etc. (*neglect*) 460- a distinction; con-found, -fuse, jumble; swallow whole.

Adj. indiscriminate, undiscriminating, promiscuous; undistinguish-ed, -able, -ing; unmeasured.

466. Measurement.—N. measurement, admeasurement, mensuration, survey, valuation, appraisment, assessment, assize; estim-ate, -ation; dead reckoning; reckoning etc. (*numeration*) 85; gauging etc. *v.*

metrology, weights and measures, compound arithmetic.

measure, yard measure, standard, rule, foot-rule, chain, tape, staff, compass, callipers; dividers; gage, gauge, planimeter; meter, line, rod, check.

volt, kilowatt, ampere, candle power; horse power; axle load; foot pound.

flood —, high water- mark; Plimsoll mark; index etc. 550.

scale; gradu-ation, -ated scale; nonius; vernier etc. (*minuteness*) 193; pedo (*length*)- 200, sounding line etc. (*depth*) 208, thermo (*heat* etc. 398)-, baro (*air* etc. 338)-, dynamo (*power*)- 276, anemo (*wind* 349)-, gonio (*angle* 244)- meter; landmark etc. (*limit*) 233; balance etc. (*weight*) 310; optical instruments etc. 445.

co-ordinates, ordinate and abscissa, polar co-ordinates, latitude and longitude, declination and right ascension, altitude and azimuth.

geo-, stereo-, hypso-metry; metage; surveying, land surveying; geo-desy, -detics, -desia; ortho-, alti-metry; *cadastre*.

astrolabe, armillary sphere.

land, -surveyor; geometer, topographer, cartographer, hydrographer.

V. measure, meter, mete; value, assess, rate, appraise, estimate, form as estimate, set a value on; appreciate; standardize.

span, pace, step; apply the -compass etc. *n.*; gauge, plumb, probe, calliper, sound, fathom etc. 208; heave the -log, — lead; weigh etc. 319; survey.

take an average etc. 29; graduate.

Adj. measuring etc. *v.*; metric, -al; measurable; geodetical, cadastral, topographical.

467. Evidence. [on one side]**—N.** evidence; facts, premises, *data*, *praecognita*, grounds.

indication etc. 550; criterion etc. (*test*) 463.

testi-mony, -fication; attestation; deposition etc. (*affirmation*) 535; examination.

admission etc. (*assent*) 488; authority, warrant, credential, diploma, voucher, certificate, docket; record etc. 551; document, muniments; *pièce justificative*; deed, warranty etc. (*security*) 771; signature, seal etc. (*identification*) 550; exhibit, citation, reference.

witness, indicator; eye-, ear-witness; deponent; sponsor.

oral —, documentary —, hearsay —, external —, extrinsic —, internal —, intrinsic —, circumstantial —, cumulative —, *ex parte* —, presumptive —, collateral —, constructive- evidence; proof etc. (*demonstration*) 478; evidence in chief; finger prints, dactylogram.

secondary evidence; confirmation, corroboration, adminicle, support; ratification etc. (*assent*) 488; authentication, verification; compurgation, wager of law, comprobation.

citation, reference.

V. be -evidence etc. *n.*; evince, show, betoken, tell of; indicate etc. (*denote*) 550; imply, involve, argue, bespeak, breathe.

have —, carry- weight; tell, speak volumes; speak for itself etc. (*manifest*) 525.

rest –, depend- upon; repose on.

bear -witness etc. *n.*; give -evidence etc. *n.*; testify, depose, witness, vouch for; sign, seal, undersign, set one's hand and seal, sign and seal, deliver as one's act and deed, certify, attest; acknowledge etc. (*assent*) 488.

make absolute, confirm, ratify, corroborate, endorse, countersign, support, bear out, vindicate, uphold, warrant.

adduce, attest, cite, quote; refer –, appeal- to; call, – to witness; bring -forward, – into court; allege, plead; produce –, confront- witnesses; collect –, bring together –, rake up- evidence.

have –, make out- a case; establish, circumstantiate, authenticate, substantiate, verify, make good, quote chapter and verse; bring -home to, – to book.

Adj. showing etc. *v.*; evidential, indica-tive, -tory; deducible etc. 478; grounded –, founded –, based- on; first hand, authentic, verifiable; corroborative, confirmatory; significant, conclusive.

Adv. by inference; according to, witness, *a fortiori*; still -more, – less; *raison de plus*; in corroboration etc. *n.* of; *valeat quantum*; under -seal, – one's hand and seal.

468. Counter-evidence. [Evidence on the other side, on the other hand.]—**N.** counter-evidence; evidence on the other -side, – hand; disproof; refutation etc. 479; negation etc. 536; conflicting evidence.

plea etc. 617; vindication etc. 937; counter-protest; *tu quoque* argument; other side –, reverse- of the shield.

V. countervail, oppose; run counter; rebut etc. (*refute*) 479; subvert etc. (*destroy*) 162; check, weaken; contravene; contradict etc. (*deny*) 536; tell another story, turn the -tables, – scale; alter the case; cut both ways; prove a negative, *audire alteram partem*.

Adj. countervailing etc. *v.*; contradictory, in rebuttal.

un-attested, -authenticated, -supported by evidence; supposititious, trumped up.

Adv. *per contra*, conversely, on the other hand.

469. Qualification.—N. qualification, limitation, modification, coloring.

allowance, grains of allowance, consideration, extenuating circumstances.

condition, proviso, exception; exemption; salvo, saving clause; discount etc. 813.

V. qualify, limit, modify, affect, temper, leaven, give a color to, introduce new conditions.

allow –, make allowance- for; admit exceptions, take into account.

take exception, object.

Adj. qualifying etc. *v.*; conditional; extenuatory; exceptional etc. (*unconformable*) 83.

hypothetical etc. (*supposed*) 514; contingent etc. (*uncertain*) 475.

Adv. provided, – always; if, unless, but, yet; according as; conditionally, admitting, supposing; on the supposition of etc. (*theoretically*) 514; with the understanding, even, although, though, for all that, after all, at all events.

with grains of allowance, *cum grano salis*; *exceptis excipiendis*; wind and weather permitting; if possible etc. 470.

subject to; with this -proviso etc. *n.*

470. Possibility.—N. possibility, potentiality; what -may be, – is possible etc. *adj.*; compatibility etc. (*agreement*) 23.

practicability, feasibility; practicableness etc. *adj.*

contingency, chance etc. 156.

V. be -possible etc. *adj.*; stand a chance, have a leg to stand on; admit of, bear.

render -possible etc. *adj.*; put in the way of.

Adj. possible; on the -cards, – dice; *in posse*, within the bounds of possibility, conceivable, credible, imaginable; compatible etc. 23.

practicable, feasible, workable, performable, achievable; within -reach, – measurable distance; accessible, superable, surmountable; at-, obtainable; contingent etc. (*doubtful*) 475.

Adv. possibly, by possibility; perhaps, -chance, -adventure; may be, haply, mayhap.

if possible, wind and weather permitting, God willing, *Deo volente*, D.V.

471. Impossibility.—N. impossibility etc. *adj.*; what -cannot, – can never- be; sour grapes; infeasibility, impracticability; hopelessness etc. 859.

V. be -impossible etc. *adj.*; have no chance whatever.

attempt impossibilities; square the circle; discover the -philosopher's stone – elixir of life, – secret of perpetual motion; wash a blackamoor white; skin a flint; make -a silk purse out of a sow's ear, – bricks without straw; have nothing to go upon; weave a rope of sand, build castles in the air, *prendre la lune avec les dents*, extract sunbeams from cucumbers, set the Thames on fire, milk a he-goat into a sieve, catch a weasel asleep, *rompre l'anguille au genou*, be in two places at once.

Adj. impossible; not -possible etc. 470; absurd, contrary to reason; unlikely, at variance with facts; unreasonable etc. 477; incredible etc. 485; beyond the bounds of -reason, – possibility; from which reason recoils; visionary; inconceivable etc. (*improbable*) 473; prodigious etc. (*wonderful*) 870; un-, in-imaginable, unthinkable, not a Chinaman's chance.

impracticable, unachievable; un-, in-feasible; insuperable; un-, in-surmountable; unat-, unobtainable; out of -reach, – the question; not to be -had, – thought of; beyond control; desperate etc. (*hopeless*) 859; incompatible etc. 24; inaccessible, uncomeatable, impassable, impervious, innavigable, inextricable.

out of –, beyond- one's -power, – depth, – reach, – grasp; too much for; *ultra crepidam*.

Phr. the grapes are sour; *non possumus*; *non nostrum tantas componere lites*.

472. Probability.—N. probability, likelihood; likeliness etc. *adj.*

vraisemblance, verisimilitude, plausibility;

color, semblance, show of; presumption; presumptive —, circumstantial- evidence; credibility.

reasonable —, fair —, good —, favorable- -chance, — prospect; prospect, well-grounded hope; chance etc. 156.

V. be -probable etc. *adj.*; give —, lend- color to; point to; imply etc. (*evidence*) 467; bid fair etc. (*promise*) 511; stand fair for; stand —, run- a good chance.

presume, infer, suppose, take for granted.

think likely, dare say, flatter oneself; expect etc. 507; count upon etc. (*believe*) 484.

Adj. probable, likely, hopeful, to be expected, in a fair way.

plausible, specious, ostensible, colorable, *ben trovato*, well-founded, reasonable, credible, easy of belief, presumable, presumptive, apparent.

Adv. probably etc. *adj.*; belike; in all -probability, — likelihood; very —, most- likely; as likely as not; like enough; ten etc. to one; apparently, seemingly, according to every reasonable expectation; *primâ facie*; to all appearance etc. (*to the eye*) 448.

Phr. the -chances, — odds- are; appearances —, chances- are in favor of; there is reason to -believe, — think, — expect; I dare say; all Lombard Street to a China orange.

473. Improbability.—N. improbability, unlikelihood; unfavorable —, bad —, little —, small —, poor —, scarcely any —, no —, not a ghost of a- chance; bare possibility; long odds; incredibility etc. 485.

V. be -improbable etc. *adj.*; have a -small chance etc. *n.*

Adj. improbable, unlikely, contrary to all reasonable expectation, implausible.

rare etc. (*infrequent*) 137; unheard of, inconceivable; un-, in-imaginable; incredible etc. 485; more than doubtful.

Int. not likely! no fear!

Phr. the chances are against.

474. Certainty.—N. certainty; necessity etc. 601; certitude, certainness, surety, assurance, sureness; dead —, moral- certainty; infallibleness etc. *adj.*; infallibility, reliability.

gospel, scripture, church, pope, court of final appeal; *res judicata, ultimatum.*

positiveness; dogmat-ism, -ist, -izer; *doctrinaire*, know-all, bigot, -ry; opinionist, Sir Oracle; *ipse dixit*; zealot.

fact; positive —, matter of- fact; *fait accompli.*

V. be -certain etc. *adj.*; stand to reason.

render -certain etc. *adj.*; in-, en-, as-sure; clinch, make sure; determine, decide, set at rest, 'make assurance double sure;' know etc. (*believe*) 484; dismiss all doubt.

dogmatize, lay down the law.

Adj. certain, sure; assured etc. *v.*; solid, well-founded.

unqualified, absolute, positive, determinate, definite, clear, unequivocal, categorical, unmistakable, decisive, decided, ascertained.

inevitable, unavoidable, ineluctable, avoidless.

unerring, infallible; unchangeable etc. 150; to be depended on, trustworthy, reliable, bound.

un-impeachable, -deniable, -questionable; in-disputable, -contestable, -controvertible, -defeasible, -dubitable; irrefutable etc. (*proven*) 478; conclusive, without power of appeal, final.

indubious; without —, beyond a —, without a shade or shadow or- -doubt — question; past dispute; beyond all -question, — dispute; un-doubted, -contested, -questioned, -disputed; question-, dount-less.

bigoted, fanatical, dogmatic, opinionat-ed, -ive, *doctrinaire.*

authoritative, authentic, official.

sure as -fate, — death and taxes, — a gun.

evident, self-evident, axiomatic; clear, — as day, — as the sun at noonday; obvious.

Adv. certainly etc. *adj.*; for certain, certes, sure, no doubt, doubtless, and no mistake, *flagrante delicto*, sure enough, to be sure, of course, as a matter of course, *à coup sur*, to a certainty, undoubtedly; in truth etc. (*truly*) 494; at -any rate, — all events; without fail; *coûte que coûte*; whatever may happen, if the worst come to the worst; come —, happen- what -may, — will; sink or swim; rain or shine.

Phr. *cela va sans dire*; there is -no question, — not a shadow of doubt; the die is cast etc. (*necessity*) 601.

475. Uncertainty.—N. uncertainty, incertitude, doubt; doubtfulness etc. *adj.*; dubi-ety, -tation, -tancy, -ousness.

hesitation, suspense; perplexity, embarrassment, dilemma, quandary, Morton's fork, bewilderment; timidity etc. (*fear*) 860; indecision, vacillation etc. 605; *diaporesis*, indetermination.

vagueness etc. *adj.*; haze, fog; obscurity etc. (*darkness*) 421; ambiguity etc. (*double meaning*) 520; contingency, double contingency, possibility upon a possibility; conjecture; open question etc. (*question*) 461; *onus probandi*; blind bargain, pig in a poke, leap in the dark, something or other; needle in a bottle of hay; roving commission.

fallibility, unreliability, untrustworthiness, precariousness.

V. be -uncertain etc. *adj.*; wonder whether.

lose the -clue, — clew, — scent; miss one's way.

not know -what to make of etc. (*unintelligibility*) 519, — which way to turn, — whether one stands on one's head or one's heels; float in a sea of doubt, hesitate, flounder; lose -oneself, — one's head, — one's way, wander aimlessly; muddle one's brains.

render -uncertain etc. *adj.*; put out, pose, puzzle, perplex, embarrass; confuse, -found; bewilder, mystify, bother, nonplus, addle the wits, throw off the scent; *ambiguas in vulgus spargere voces*; keep in suspense.

doubt etc. (*disbelieve*) 485; hang —, tremble- in the balance; depend.

Adj. uncertain; casual; random etc. (*aimless*) 621; changeable etc. 149.

doubtful, dubious; indecisive; unsettled, -decided, -determined; in suspense, open to discussion; controvertible; in question etc. (*inquiry*) 461; insecure, unstable.

vague; in-determinate, -definite; ambiguous, equivocal; undefin-ed, -able; confused etc. (*indistinct*) 447; mystic, mysterious, veiled, obscure, cryptic, oracular.

perplexing etc. *v.*; enigmatic, paradoxical; apocryphal, problematical, hypothetical; experimental etc. 463.

fallible, questionable, precarious, slippery, ticklish, debatable, disputable; un-reliable, -trustworthy.

contingent, — on, dependent on; subject to; dependent on circumstances; occasional; provisional.

unauth-entic, -enticated, -oritative; unascertained, -confirmed; undemonstrated; un-told, -counted.

in a -state of uncertainty, — cloud, — maze; ignorant etc. 491; on the horns of a dilemma; afraid to say; out of one's reckoning, astray, adrift; as -sea, — fault, — a loss, — one's wit's end, — a *nonplus*; puzzled etc. *v.*; lost abroad, *désorienté*; dis-tracted, -traught.

Adv. *pendente lite*; *sub spe rati*.

Phr. Heaven knows; who can tell? who shall decide when doctors disagree?

476. Reasoning.—N. reasoning; ratio-cination, -nalism; dialectics, induction, generalization.

discussion, comment; ventilation; inquiry etc. 461.

argumentation, controversy, debate; polemics, wrangling; contention etc. 720; logomachy; disputation, -ceptation; paper war.

art of reasoning, logic.

process —, train —, chain- of reasoning; de-, induction; systhesis, analysis.

argument; case, plea, *plaidoyer*, opening; *lemma*, proposition, terms, premises, postulate, *data*, starting point, principle; inference etc. (*judgment*) 480.

pro-, syllogism; enthymeme, sorites, dilemma, *perilepsis*, *a priori* reasoning, *reductio ad absurdum*, horns of a dilemma, *argumentum ad hominem*, comprehensive argument.

reasoner, logician, dialectician; disputant; controver-sialist, -tist; wrangler, arguer, debater, polemic, casuist, rationalist; scientist.

logical sequence; good case; correct —, just —, sound —, valid —, cogent —, logical —, forcible —, persuasive —, persuasory —, consectary —, conclusive etc. 478 —, subtle- reasoning; force of argument; strong -point, — argument.

arguments, reasons, pros and cons.

V. reason, argue, discuss, debate, dispute, wrangle; bandy -words, — arguments; chop logic; hold —, carry on- an argument; controvert etc. (*deny*) 536; canvass; comment —, moralize-upon; consider etc. (*examine*) 461.

open a -discussion, — case; join —, be at- issue; moot; come to the point; stir —, agitate —, ventilate —, torture- a question; try conclusions; take up a -side, — case.

contend, take one's stand upon, insist, lay stress on; infer etc. 480.

follow from etc. (*demonstration*) 478.

Adj. rational; reasoning etc. *v.*; rationalistic; argumentative, controversial, dialectic, polemical; discurs-ory, -ive; disputations.

debatable, controvertible.

logical; in-, de-ductive; synthetic, analytic; relevant etc. 23.

Adv. for, because, hence, whence, seeing that, since, sith, then, thence, so; for -that, — this, — which- reason; for-, inasmuch as; whereas, *ex concesso*, considering, in consideration of; there-, where-fore; consequently, *ergo*, thus, accordingly; *a fortiori*.

in -conclusion, — fine; finally, after all, *au bout du compte*, on the whole, taking one thing with another.

rationally etc. *adj*.

477. Sophistry. [The absence of reasoning.] **Intuition.** [False or vicious reasoning; show of reason.]—**N.** intuition, instinct, association; presentiment; rule of thumb.

sophistry, paralogy, perversion, casuistry, jesuitry, equivocation, evasion, mental reservation; chicane, -ry; quiddit, quiddity; mystification; special pleading; speciousness etc. *adj.*; nonsense etc. 497; word-, tongue-fence.

false —, vicious- reasoning; *petitio principii*, *ignoratio elenchi*; *post hoc ergo propter hoc*; *non sequitur*, *ignotum per ignotius*.

misjudgment etc. 481; false teaching etc. 538.

sophism, solecism, paralogism; quibble, quirk, *elenchus*, elench, fallacy, *quodlibet*, subterfuge, subtlety, quillet; inconsistency, antilogy; 'a mockery, a delusion and a snare;' claptrap, mere words; 'lame and impotent conclusion.'

meshes —, cobwebs- of sophistry; flaw in an argument; weak point, bad case.

over-refinement; hair-splitting etc. *v.*

sophist, casuist, paralogist.

V. judge -intuitively, — by intuition; hazard a proposition, talk at random.

reason -ill, falsely etc. *adj.*; paralogize; misjudge etc. 481.

pervert, quibble; equivocate, mystify, evade, elude; gloss over, varnish; misteach etc. 538; mislead etc. (*error*) 495; cavil, refine, subtilize, split hairs; misrepresent etc. (*lie*) 544.

beg the question, reason in a circle, cut blocks with a razor, beat about the bush, play fast and loose, blow hot and cold, prove that black is white and white black, travel out of the record, *parler à tort et à travers*, put oneself out of court, not have a leg to stand on.

Adj. intuitive, instinctive, impulsive; independent of —, anterior to- reason; gratuitous; hazarded; unconnected.

unreasonable, illogical, false, unsound, invalid; unwarranted, not following; inconsequent, -ial; inconsistent, incongruous; abson-ous, -ant; unscientific; untenable, inconclusive, incorrect; fall-acious; -ible; groundless, unproved.

deceptive, sophistical, sophisticated, casuistical, jesuitical; illus-ive, -ory; specious, hollow, plausible, *ad captandum*, evasive; irrelevant etc. 10.

weak, feeble, poor, flimsy, loose, vague, irrational; nonsensical etc. (*absurd*) 497; foolish etc. (*imbecile*) 499; frivolous, pettifogging, quibbling; finespun, over-refined.

at the end of one's tether, *au bout de son latin*.

Adv. intuitively etc. *adj.*; by intuition; illogically etc. *adj.*

Phr. *non constat*; that goes for nothing.

478. Demonstration.—N. demonstration, proof; conclusiveness etc. *adj.*; *apodixis*, probation, comprobation.

logic of facts etc. (*evidence*) 467; *experimentum curcis* etc. (*test*) 463; argument etc. 476; irrefragability.

V. demonstrate, prove, establish, make good; show; evince etc. (*be evidence of*) 467; verify etc. 467; settle the question, reduce to demonstration, set the question at rest.

make out, — a case; prove one's point, have the best of the argument; draw a conclusion etc. (*judge*) 480.

follow, — of course; stand to reason; hold -good, — water.

Adj. demonstra-ting etc. *v.*, -tive, -ble; probative, unanswerable, conclusive; apodictic, -al; irre-sistible, -futable, -fragable, undeniable.

categorical, decisive, crucial.

demonstrated etc. *v.*; proven; unconfuted, -answered, -refuted; evident etc. 474.

deducible, consequential, consectary, inferential, following.

Adv. of course, in consequence, consequently, as a matter of course.

Phr. *probatum est*; there is nothing more to be said, Q.E.D., it must follow.

479. Confutation.—N. con-, re-futation; answer, complete answer; disproof, conviction, redargution, invalidation; expos-ure, -ition; clincher; retort; ***reductio ad absurdum***; knock down —, *tu quoque*- argument.

V. con-, re-fute; parry, negative, disprove, redargue, expose, show the fallacy of, rebut, defeat; demolish etc. (*destroy*) 162; over-throw, -turn; scatter to the winds, explode, invalidate; silence; put —, reduce- to silence; clinch -an argument, — a question; give one a set down, stop the mouth, shut up; have, — on the hip; get the better of; confound, convince.

not leave a leg to stand on, cut the ground from under one's feet.

be confuted etc.; fail; expose —, show- one's weak point.

Adj. confut-ing, -ed etc. *v.*; capable of refutation; re-, con-futable.

condemned -on one's own showing, — out of one's own mouth.

Phr. the argument falls to the ground, *cadit quaestio*, it does not hold water, '*suo sibi gladio hunc jugulo.*'

480. Judgment. [Conclusion.]**—N.** result, conclusion, upshot; deduction, inference, ergotism, illation; corollary, porism; moral.

estimation, valuation, appreciation, judication; di-, ad-judication; arbitr- ament, -ement, -ation; assessment, ponderation.

award, estimate; review, criticism, ***critique***, notice, report.

decision, determination, judgment, finding, verdict, sentence, decree, — nisi, — absolute, — interlocutory; dictum; *res judicata.*

plébiscite, referendum, voice, casting vote; vote etc. (*choice*) 609; opinion etc. (*belief*) 484; good judgment etc. (*wisdom*) 498.

judge, jurist, umpire; arbi-ter, -trator; assessor, referee; censor, reviewer, critic; *connoisseur*; commentator etc. 524; inspector, inspecting officer.

V. judge, conclude; come to —, draw —, arrive at- a conclusion; ascertain, determine, make up one's mind.

deduce, derive, gather, collect, draw an inference, make a deduction, weet, ween.

form an estimate, estimate, size up, appreciate, value, count, assess, rate, rank, account; regard, consider, think of; look upon etc. (*believe*) 484.

settle; pass —, give- an opinion; decide, try, pronounce, rule; pass -judgment, — sentence; sentence, doom; find; give —, deliver- judgment; adjud-ge, -icate; arbitrate, award, report; bring in a verdict; make absolute, set a question ar rest; confirm etc. (*assent*) 488.

comment, criticize; review, pass under review etc (*examine*) 457; investigate etc. (*inquire*) 461.

hold the scales, sit in judgment; try —, hear- a cause.

Adj. judging etc. *v.*; judicious etc. (*wise*) 498; determinate, conclusive, censorious, critical etc. 932.

Adv. on the whole, all things considered.

480a. Discovery. [Result of search or inquiry.]**—N.** discovery, invention, detection, disenchantment, disclosure, find, ascertainment, revelation.

trover etc. 775.

V. discover, find, determine, evolve; fix upon; find —, trace —, make —, hunt —, fish —, worm —, ferret —, root-out; fathom; bring —, draw-out; educe, elicit, bring to light, invent; dig —, grub —, fish- up; unearth, disinter.

solve, resolve; un-riddle, -ravel, -lock; pick —, open- the lock; find a -clue, — clew- to; interpret etc. 522; disclose etc. 529.

trace, get at; hit it, have it; lay one's -finger, — hands- upon; spot; get —, arrive- at the -turth etc. 494; put the saddle on the right horse, hit the right nail on the head.

be near the truth, burn; smoke, scent, sniff, smell a rat.

open the eyes to; see -through, — daylight, — in its true colors, — the cloven foot; detect; catch, — tripping.

pitch —, fall —, light —, hit —, stumble —, pop- upon; come across; meet —, fall in- with.

recognize, realize, verify, make certain of, identify.

Int. *eureka!*

481. Misjudgment.—N. misjudgment, obliquity of —, warped- judgment; mis-calculation, -computation, -conception etc. (*error*) 495; hasty conclusion.

prejud-gment, -ication, -ice; foregone conclusion; pre-notion, -vention, -conception, -dilection, -possession, -apprehension, -sumption, -sentiment; fixed —, preconceived- idea; *idée fixe*; *mentis gratissimus error*; fool's paradise.

esprit de corps, party spirit, race —, class-prejudice, partisanship, clannishness, *prestige*.

bias, warp, twist; hobby, fad, whim, craze, quirk, crotchet, partiality, infatuation, blind side, mote in the eye.

one-sided —, partial —, narrow —, confined —, superficial- -views, — ideas,— conceptions, — notions; narrow mind; bigotry etc. (*obstinacy*) 606; *odium theologicum*; pedantry; hypercriticism.

doctrinaire etc. (*positive*) 474.

V. mis-judge, -estimate, -think, -conjecture, -conceive etc. (*error*) 495; fly in the face of facts; mis-calculate, -reckon, -compute.

overestimate etc. 482; underestimate etc. 483.

pre-, fore-judge; pre-suppose, -sume, -judicate; dogmatize; have a -bias etc. *n.*; have only one idea; *jurare in verba magistri*, run away with the notion; jump —, rush- to a conclusion; look only at one side of the shield; view -with jaundiced eye, — through distorting spectacles; not see beyond one's nose; *dare pondus fumo*; get the wrong sow by the ear etc. (*blunder*) 699.

give a -bias, — twist; bias, warp, twist; prejudice, -possess.

Adj. misjudging etc. *v.*; ill-judging, wrong-headed; prejudiced, prejudicial, etc. *v.*; jaundiced; short-sighted, pur-blind; partial, one-sided, superficial.

narrow-minded; confined, insular, provincial, parochial, illiberal, intolerant, narrow, besotted, infatuated, fanatical, cracked, warped, *entêté*, positive, dogmatic, dictatorial; conceited; opin-, opini-ative; opinion-ed, -ate, -ative, -ated; self-opinioned, wedded to an opinion, *opiniâtre*; bigoted etc. (*obstinate*) 606; crotchety, fussy, impracticable; unreason-able, -ing; stupid etc. 499, credulous etc. 486.

misjudged etc. *v.*

Adv. *ex parte*.

Phr. nothing like leather; the wish the father to the thought.

482. Overestimation.—N. overestimation etc. *v.*; exaggeration etc. 549; vanity etc. 880; optim-, pessim-ism, -ist; megalomania.

much -cry and little wool, — ado about nothing; storm in a teacup; fine talking, rodomontade, gush, hot air, gas, bombast.

egotism etc. 880; boasting etc. 884.

V. over-estimate, -rate, -value, -prize, -weigh, -reckon, -strain, -praise; estimate too highly, attach too much importance to, make mountains of molehills, catch at straws; strain, magnify; exaggerate etc. 549; set too high a value upon; think —, make- -much, — too much- of; outreckon.

extol, — to the skies; make the -most, — best, — worst- of, eulogize, panegyrize, gush, puff, boost; make two bites of a cherry.

have too high an opinion of oneself etc. (*vanity*) 880.

Adj. overestimated etc. *v.*; oversensitive etc. (*sensibility*) 822; inflated, puffed up, exaggerated etc. 549.

Phr. all his geese are swans; *parturiunt montes*.

483. Underestimation.—N. underestimation; depreciation etc. (*detraction*) 934; pessim-ism, -ist; undervaluing etc. *v.*; modesty etc. 881.

V. under-rate, -estimate, -value, -reckon; depreciate; disparage etc. (*detract*) 934; not do justice to; mis-, dis-prize; ridicule etc. 856; slight etc. (*despise*) 930; neglect etc. 460; slur over, under-state.

make -light, — little, — nothing, — no account- of; minimize, belittle, run down, think nothing of; set -no store by, — at naught; shake off as dewdrops from the lion's mane.

Adj. depreciat-ing, -ed, -ive, -ory, etc. *v.*; unappreciated, -valued, -prized; pejorative.

484. Belief.—N. belief; credence; credit; assurance; faith, trust, troth, confidence, presumption, sanguine expectation etc. (*hope*) 858; dependence on, reliance on.

persuasion, conviction, convincement, plerophory, self-conviction; certainty etc. 474; opinion, mind, view; conception, thinking; impression etc. (*idea*) 453; surmise etc. 514; conclusion etc. (*judgment*) 480.

tenet, dogma, principle, way of thinking; popular belief etc. (*assent*) 488.

firm —, implicit —, settled —, fixed —, rooted —, deep-rooted —, staunch —, unshaken —, steadfast —, inveterate —, calm —, sober —, dispassionate —, impartial —, well-founded- -belief, — opinion etc.; *uberrima fides*.

system of opinions, school, doctrine, articles, canons; declaration —, profession- of faith; tenets, *credenda*, creed, thirty-nine articles etc. (*orthodoxy*) 983*a*; catechism; assent etc. 488; *propaganda* etc. (*teaching*) 537.

credibility etc. (*probability*) 472.

V. believe, credit; give -faith, — credit, — credence- to; see, realize; assume, receive; set down —, take- for; have —, take- it; consider, esteem, presume.

count —, depend —, calculate —, pin one's faith —, reckon —, lean —, build —, rely —, rest- upon; lay one's account for; make sure of.

make oneself easy -about, — on that score; take on -trust, — credit; take for -granted, — gospel; allow —, attach- some weight to.

know, — for certain; have —, make- no doubt; doubt not; be — rest- -assured etc. *adj.*; persuade —, assure —, satisfy- oneself; make up one's mind.

give one credit for; confide —, believe —, put one's trust- in; place —, repose- implicit confidence in; take -one's word for, — at one's word; place reliance on, rely upon, swear by, regard to.

think, hold; take, — it; opine, be of opinion, conceive, trow, ween, fancy, apprehend: have —, hold —, possess —, entertain —, adopt —, imbibe —, embrace —, get hold of —, hazard —, foster —, nurture —, cherish- -a belief, — an opinion etc. *n.*

view —, consider —, take —, hold —, conceive —, regard —, esteem —, deem —, look upon —, account —, set down- as; surmise etc. 514.

get –, take- it into one's head; come round to an opinion; swallow etc. (*credulity*) 486.

cause to -be believed etc. *v.*; satisfy, persuade, have the ear of, gain the confidence of, assure; convince, -vict, -vert; put across, sell; wean, bring round; bring –, put –, win- over; indoctrinate etc. (*teach*) 537; cram down the throat; produce –, carry- conviction; bring –, drive- home to.

go down, find credence, pass current; be -received etc. *v.*, – current etc. *adj.*; possess –, take hold of –, take possession of- the mind.

Adj. believing etc. *v.*; certain, sure, assured, positive, cocksure, satisfied, confident, unhesitating, convinced, secure.

under the impression; impressed –, imbued –, penetrated- with.

confiding, trustful, suspectless; unsusp-ecting, -icious; void of suspicion; credulous etc. 486; wedded to.

believed etc. *v.*; accredited, putative; unsuspected.

worthy of –, deserving of –, commanding- -belief, – confidence; credible, reliable, trusted, trustworthy, to be depended on, undoubted; satisfactory; probable etc. 472; fiduci-al, -ary; persuasive, impressive.

relating to belief, doctrinal.

Adv. in the -opinion, – eyes- of; *me judice*; me-seems, -thinks; to the best of one's belief; I -dare say, – doubt not, – have no doubt, – am sure; in my opinion; sure enough etc. (*certainty*) 474; depend –, rely- upon it; be –, rest- assured; I'll warrant you etc. (*affirmation*) 535.

485. Unbelief. Doubt.—N. un-, dis-, mis-belief; discredit, miscreance; infidelity etc. (*irreligion*) 989; dissent etc. 489; change of -opinion etc. 484; retraction etc. 607.

doubt etc. (*uncertainty*) 475; skepticism, misgiving, demur; dis-, mis-trust; misdoubt, suspicion, jealousy, scruple, qualm; *onus probandi.*

incredib-ility, -leness; incredulity; unbeliever etc. 487.

V. dis-believe, -credit; not -believe etc. 484; misbelieve; refuse to admit etc. (*dissent*) 489; refuse to believe etc. (*incredulity*) 487.

doubt; be -doubtful etc. (*uncertain*) 475; doubt the truth of; be -skeptical as to etc. *adj.*; diffide; dis-, mis-trust; suspect, smoke, scent, smell a rat; have –, harbor –, entertain- -doubts, – suspicions; have one's doubts.

demur, stick at, pause, hesitate, scruple, waver, stop and consider.

hang in -suspense, – doubt.

throw doubt upon, raise a question; bring –, call- in question; question, challenge, query; dispute; deny etc. 536; cavil; cause –, raise –, start –, suggest –, awake- a -doubt, – suspicion; ergotize.

startle, stagger; shake –, stagger- one's faith, – belief.

Adj. unbelieving; incredulous –, skeptical- as to; distrustful –, shy –, suspicious- of; doubting etc. *v.*

doubtful etc. (*uncertain*) 475; disputable; unworthy –, undeserving- of -belief etc. 484; questionable; sus-pect, -picious; open to -suspicion, – doubt; staggering, hard to believe, incredible, not to be believed, inconceivable.

fallible etc. (*uncertain*) 475; undemonstrable; controvertible etc. (*untrue*) 495.

Adv. *cum grano salis.*

Phr. *fronti nulla fides*; *nimium ne crede colori*; '*timeo Danaos et dona ferentes*;' *credat Judaeus Apella*; let those believe who may.

486. Credulity.—N. credul-ity, -ousness etc. *adj.*; gull-, cull-ibility; gross credulity, infatuation; self-delusion, -deception; blind reasoning; superstition; one's blind side; bigotry etc. (*obstinacy*) 606; hyper-orthodoxy etc. 984; misjudgment etc. 481.

credulous person etc. (*dupe*) 547.

V. be -credulous etc. *adj.*; *jurare in verba magistri*; follow implicitly; swallow, – whole, gulp down; take on trust; take for -granted, – gospel; run away with -a notion, – an idea; jump –, rush- to a conclusion; think the moon is made of green cheese; take –, grasp- the shadow for the substance; catch at straws.

impose upon etc. (*deceive*) 545.

Adj. credulous, gullible; easily -deceived etc. 545; simple, green, soft, childish, silly, stupid; over-credulous, -confident; infatuated, superstitious; confiding etc. (*believing*) 484.

Phr. the wish the father to the thought; *credo quia impossibile.*

487. Incredulity.—N. incredul-ous-ness, -ity; skepticism, pyrrhonism; want of faith etc. (*irreligion*) 989.

suspiciousness etc. *adj.*; scrupulosity; suspicion etc. (*unbelief*) 485; dissent etc. 489.

unbeliever, skeptic, aporetic; atheist, agnostic, infidel, disbeliever, misbeliever, pyrrhonist etc. 989; heretic etc. (*heterodox*) 984.

v. be -incredulous etc. *adj.*; distrust etc. (*disbelieve*) 485; refuse to believe; shut one's -eyes, – ears- to; turn a deaf ear to; hold aloof; ignore; *nullis jurare in verba magistri.*

Adj. incredulous, skeptical, unbelieving, inconvincible; hard –, shy- of belief; suspicious, scrupulous, distrustful, heterodox etc. 984.

488. Assent.—N. assent, -ment; acquiescence, admission; nod; ac-, con-cord, -cordance; agreement etc. 23; affirm-ance, -ation; recognition, acknowledgment, avowal; confession, – of faith.

unanimity, common consent, *consensus*, acclamation, chorus, *vox populi*; popular –, current- -belief, – opinion; public opinion; concurrence etc. (*of causes*) 178; co-operation etc. (*voluntary*) 709.

ratification, confirmation, corroboration, approval, acceptance, *visa*; indorsement etc. (*record*) 551.

consent etc. (*compliance*) 762.

affirmant, consenter, covenantor, subscriber, endorser, upholder.

V. assent; give –, yield –, nod- assent; acquiesce; agree etc. 23; receive, accept, accede, accord, concur, lend oneself to, consent, coincide, reciprocate, go with; be -at one with etc. *adj.*; go along –, chime in –, strike in –, close- with; echo, enter into one's views, agree in opinion; vote –, give one's voice- for; recognize; subscribe –, conform –, defer- to; say -yes, – ditto, – amen, – aye- to.

acknowledge, own, admit, allow, avow, confess; concede etc. (*yield*) 762; come round to; abide by; permit etc. 760.

come to –, arrive at- -an understanding, – terms, – an agreement.

con-, af-firm; ratify, approve, endorse, countersign; visa; corroborate etc. 467.

go –, swim- with the stream, float with the current; be in the fashion, join in the chorus; be in every mouth.

Adj. assenting etc. *v.*; of one -accord, – mind; of the same mind, at one with, agreed, acquiescent, content; willing etc. 602.

un-contradicted, -challenged, -questioned, -controverted.

carried –, agreed- *-nem. con.* etc. *adv.*; unanimous; agreed on all hands, carried by acclamation.

affirmative etc. 535.

Adv. yes, yea, ay, aye, true; good; well; very -well, – true; well and good; granted; *placet*; even –, just- so; to be sure, surely, 'thou hast said;' truly, exactly, precisely, that's just it, indeed, certainly, certes, *ex concesso*; of course, unquestionably, assuredly, no doubt, doubtless, undoubtedly.

be it so; so -be it, – let it be, so mote it be; amen; with all my heart; willingly etc. 602.

with one -consent, – voice, – accord; unanimously, *unâ voce*, by common consent, in chorus, to a man, *nem. con.*; *nemine -contradicente*, – *dissentiente*; without a dissentient voice; as one man, one and all, on all hands.

489. Dissent.—N. dissent; discordance etc. (*disagreement*) 24; difference –, diversity- of opinion.

non-conformity etc. (*heterodoxy*) 984; protestantism, recusancy, schism; disaffection; secession etc. 624; recantation etc. 607.

dissension etc. (*discord*) 713; discontent etc. 832; cavilling.

protest; contradiction etc. (*denial*) 536; non-compliance etc. (*rejection*) 764; disapprobation etc. 932; hartal.

dissent-ient, -er; non-juror, -content; recusant, sectary, schismatic, protestant, non-conformist, separatist, non-co-operator, conscientious objector, passive resister.

V. dissent, demur; call in question etc. (*doubt*) 485; differ in opinion, disagree; say -no etc. 536; refuse -assent, – to admit; cavil, protest, raise one's voice against, make bold to differ; repudiate; contradict etc. (*deny*) 536; agree to differ.

have no notion of, differ *toto caelo*; revolt -at, – from the idea.

shake the head, shrug the shoulders; look -askance, – askant.

secede; recant etc. 607.

Adj. dissenting etc. *v.*; negative etc. 536; dissident, -entient; unconsenting etc. (*refusing*) 764; non-content, -juring; protestant, recusant; unconvinced, -verted.

unavowed, unacknowledged; out of the question.

discontented etc. 832; unwilling etc. 603; extorted.

sectarian, denominational, schismatic, heterodox, intolerant.

Adv. no etc. 536; at -variance, – issue- with; under protest; *non placet*.

Int. God forbid! not for the world; not on your life; I beg to differ; I'll be hanged if; never tell me; your humble servant, pardon me; tell that to the marines.

Phr. many men many minds; *quot homines tot sententiae*; *tant s'en faut*; *il s'en faut bien.*

490. Knowledge.—N. knowledge; cogn-izance, -ition, -oscence; acquaintance, experience, ken, privity, insight, familiarity; com-, ap-prehension; recognition; appreciation etc. (*judgment*) 480; intuition; consci-ence, -ousness; preception, precognition; acroamatics.

light, enlightenment; glimpse, inkling; side light; glimmer, -ing; dawn; scent, suspicion; impression etc. (*idea*) 453; discovery etc. 480*a*.

system –, body- of knowledge; science, philosophy, pansophy; theory, Etiology; circle of the sciences; pandect, doctrine, body of doctrine; cy-, ency-clopedia; school etc. (*system of opinions*) 484.

tree of knowledge; republic of letters etc. (*language*) 560.

erudition, learning, lore, scholarship, reading, letters; literature; booklearning, bookishness; biblio-mania, -latry; information, general information; store of -knowledge etc.; education etc. (*teaching*) 537; culture, attainments; acquirements, -sitions; accomplishments, proficiency; practical knowledge etc. (*skill*) 698; higher education, liberal education; dilettantism; rudiments etc. (*beginning*) 66.

deep –, profound –, solid –, accurate –, acroatic –, acroamatic –, vast –, extensive –, encyclopedical- -knowledge, – learning; omniscience, pantology.

march of intellect; progress –, advance- of -science, – learning; schoolmaster abroad.

V. know, ken, scan, wot; wot –, be aware etc. *adj.*- of; ween, weet, trow, have, possess.

conceive; ap-, com-prehend; take, realize, understand, appreciate; fathom, make out; recognize, discern, perceive, see, get a sight of, experience.

know full well; have –, possess- some knowledge of; be *-au courant* etc. *adj.*; have -in one's head, – at one's fingers' ends; know by -heart, – rote; be master of; *connaître le dessous des cartes*, know what's what etc. 698.

see one's way; learn, discover etc. 480*a*.

come to one's knowledge etc. (*information*) 527.

Adj. knowing etc. *v.*; cognitive; acroamatic.

aware –, cognizant –, conscious- of; acquainted –, made acquainted- with; privy –, no stranger- to; *au -fait*, – *courant*; in the secret; up –, alive- to; sensible of; behind the -scenes, – curtain; let into; apprized –, informed- of; undeceived.

proficient –, versed –, read –, forward –,

strong –, at home- in; conversant –, familiar- with.

erudite, instructed, learned, lettered, educated; high-brow; well-conned, -informed, -read, - grounded, -educated; enlightened, shrewd, insightful, *savant*, blue, bookish, scholastic, solid, profound, deep-read, book-learned; accomplished etc. (*skilful*) 698; omniscient; self-taught, - educated.

known etc. *v.*; ascertained, well-known, recognized, received, notorious, noted; proverbial; familiar, – as household words, to every schoolboy; hackneyed, trite, commonplace.

knowable, cogn-oscible, -izable.

Adv. to –, to the best of- one's knowledge.

Phr. one's eyes being opened etc. (*disclosure*) 529.

491. Ignorance.—N. ignorance, nescience, *tabula rasa*, crass ignorance, *ignorance crasse*; unacquaintance; unconsciousness etc. *adj.*; dark-, blind-ness; incomprehension, inexperience, simplicity.

unknown quantities, *x*, *y*, *z*.

sealed book, *terra incognita*, virgin soil, unexplored ground; dark ages.

[Imperfect knowledge] smattering, superficiality, half-learning, sciolism, glimmering; bewilderment etc. (*uncertainty*) 475; incapacity.

[Affectation of knowledge] pedantry; charlatanry, -ism.

V. be -ignorant etc. *adj.*; not -know etc. 490; know -not, – not what, – nothing of; have no - idea, – notion, – conception; not have the remotest idea; not know chalk from cheese.

ignore, be blind to; keep in ignorance etc. (*conceal*) 528.

see through a glass darkly; have a -film over the eyes, – glimmering etc. *n.*; wonder whether; not know what to make of etc. (*unintelligibility*) 519; not pretend –, not take upon oneself- to say.

Adj. ignorant, nescient; un-knowing, -aware, - acquainted, -apprized, -witting, -weeting, - conscious; wit-, weet-less; a stranger to; unconversant.

un-informed, -cultivated, -versed, -instructed, - taught, -initiated, -tutored, -schooled, -guided, - enlightened; Philistine; behind the age.

shallow, superficial, green, rude, empty, half-learned, illiterate; un-read, -informed, -educated, - learned, -lettered, -bookish; empty-headed; lowbrow; pedantic.

in the dark; be-nighted, -lated; blind-ed, -fold; hoodwinked; misinformed; *au bout de son latin*, at the end of his tether; at fault; at sea etc. (*uncertain*) 475; caught tripping.

un-known, -apprehended, -explained, - ascertained, -investigated, -explored, -heard of, - perceived; concealed etc. 528; novel.

Adv. ignorantly etc. *adj.*; unawares; for - anything, – aught- one knows; not that one knows.

Int. God –, Heaven –, the Lord –, nobody- knows.

Phr. a little learning is a dangerous thing.

492. Scholar.—N. scholar, *connoissuer*, *savant*, pundit, schoolman, professor, graduate, wrangler, moonshee; academ-ician, -ist; fellow, don, post graduate, advanced student; master –, bachelor- of arts; doctor, licentiate, gownsman; philo-sopher, -math; scientist, clerk; soph, -ist, - ister; linguist, classicist; glosso-, etymo-, philologist; philologer; lexico-, glosso-grapher; scholiast, commentator. annotator, grammarian; *littérateur*, *literati*, *dilettanti*, *illuminati*; Mezzofanti, admirable Crichton, Maecenas.

book-worm, ***helluo librorum***, biblio-phile, - maniac; blue-stocking, ***bas-bleu***; big-wig, learned Theban.

learned –, literary- man; ***homo multarum literarum***; man of -learning, – letters, – education; high-brow, intelligentsia.

antiquar-ian, -y; archeologist; sage etc. (*wise man*) 500.

pendant, *doctrinaire*; pedagogue, Dr. Pangloss; pantologist.

teacher etc. 540; schoolboy etc. (*learner*) 541.

Adj. learned etc. 490; brought up at the feet of Gamaliel.

493. Ignoramus.—N. ignoramus, illiterate, moron, dunce, numskull; wooden spoon; no scholar.

sciolist, smatterer, dabbler, half-scholar; *charlatan*; wiseacre.

novice, griffin; greenhorn etc. (*dupe*) 547; tyro etc. (*learner*) 541.

lubber etc. (*bungler) 701; fool etc. 501; pedant etc. 492.*

Adj. bookless, shallow, simple, dense, dumb, thick, dull, ignorant etc. 491.

494. Truth. [Object of knowledge]**—N.** fact, reality etc. (*existence*) 1; plain matter of fact; nature etc. (*principle*) 5; truth, verity; gospel; orthodoxy etc. 983*a*; authenticity; veracity etc. 543.

accuracy, exactitude; exact-, precise-ness etc. *adj.*; precision, delicacy; rigor, mathematical precision, punctuality; clockwork precision etc. (*regularity*) 80.

orthology; *ipsissima verba*; letter of the law, realism.

plain –, honest –, sober –, naked –, unalloyed –, unqualified –, stern –, exact –, intrinsic- truth; *nuda veritas*; the very thing; not an - illusion etc. 495; real Simon Pure; unvarnished tale; the truth, the whole truth and nothing but the truth; just the thing.

V. be -true etc. *adj.*, – the case; stand the test; have the true ring; hold -good, – true, – water; conform to rule.

render –, prove- -true etc. *adj.*; substantiate etc. (*evidence*) 467.

get at the truth etc. (*discover*) 480*a*.

Adj. real, actual etc. (*existing*) 1; veritable, true; certain etc. 474; substantially –, categorically- true etc; true -to the letter; – to life, – to scale, – the facts, – as gospel; unimpeachable; veracious etc. 543; unre-, uncon-futed; un-ideal -imagined; realistic.

exact, accurate, definite, precise, well defined, just, right, correct, strict, severe; close etc. (*similar*) 17; literal; rigid, rigorous; scrupulous etc. (*con-

scientious) 939; religiously exact, punctual, mathematical, scientific; faithful, constant, unerring; curious, particular, punctilious, meticulous, nice, delicate, fine.

genuine, authentic, legitimate, pukka; orthodox etc. 983*a*; official, *ex officio*.

pure, natural, sound, sterling; un-sophisticated, -adulterated, -varnished, -colored; in its true colors.

well-grounded, -founded; solid, substantial, tangible, valid; undis-torted, -guised; un-affected, -exaggerated, -romantic, -flattering.

Adv. truly etc.*adj.*; verily, indeed, in reality; as a matter of fact; beyond -doubt, – question; with truth etc. (*veracity*) 543; certainly etc. (*certain*) 474; actually etc. (*existence*) 1; in effect etc. (*intrinsically*) 5.

exactly etc. *adj.* ; *ad amussim*; *verbatim*, – *et literatim*; word for word, literally, *literatim*, *totidem verbis*, *sic*, to the letter, chapter and verse, *ipsissimis verbis*; *ad unguem*; to an inch; to a -nicety, – hair, – tittle, – turn, – T; *au pied de la lettre*; neither more nor less; in -every respect, – all respects; *sous tous les rapports*; at -any rate, – all events; strictly speaking.

Phr. the -truth, – fact- is; *rem acu tetigisti*.

495. Error.—N. error, fallacy; misconception, -apprehension, -understanding; inexactness etc. *adj.*; laxity; misconstruction etc. (*misinterpretation*) 523; miscomputation etc. (*misjudgment*) 481; *non-sequitur* etc. 477; misstatement, -report; anachronism; malapropism.

mistake; miss, fault, blunder, boner, bloomer, howler, *quid pro quo*, cross purposes, oversight, misprint, *erratum*, *corrigendum*, slip, blot, flaw, loose thread; trip, stumble etc. (*failure*) 732; botchery etc. (*want of skill*) 699; slip of the -tongue, – pen; *lapsus -linguae*, – *calami*, clerical error; bull etc. (*absurdity*) 497.

il-, de-lusion; false -impression, – idea; bubble, self-deceit, -deception; warped notion; mists of error; superstition, exploded notion.

heresy etc. (*heterodoxy*) 984; hallucination etc. (*insanity*) 503; false light etc. (*fallacy of vision*) 443; dream etc. (*fancy*) 515; fable etc. (*untruth*) 546; bias etc. (*misjudgment*) 481; misleading etc. *v.*

V. be -erroneous etc. *adj.*

cause error; mis-lead, -guide; lead -astray, – into error; beguile, misinform etc. (*misteach*) 538; delude; give a false -impression, – idea; falsify, garble, misstate; deceive etc. 545; lie etc. 544.

err; be -in error etc. *adj.*; – mistaken etc. *v.*; be deceived etc. (*duped*) 547; mistake, receive a false impression, deceive oneself; fall into –, lie under –, labor under- -an error etc. *n.*; be in the wrong, blunder; mis-apprehend, -conceive, -understand, -reckon, -count, -calculate etc. (*misjudge*) 481.

play –, be- at cross purposes etc. (*misinterpret*) 523.

trip, stumble; lose oneself etc. (*uncertainty*) 475; go astray; fail etc. 732; take the wrong sow by the ear etc. (*mismanage*) 699; put the saddle on the wrong horse; reckon without one's host; take the shadow for the substance etc. (*credulity*) 486; dream etc. (*imagine*) 515.

Adj. erroneous, untrue, false, devoid of truth, fallacious, faulty, apocryphal, unreal, ungrounded, groundless; unsubstantial etc. 4; heretical etc. (*heterodox*) 984; unsound; illogical etc. 477; wrong.

in-, un-exact; in-accurate, -correct; indefinite etc. (*uncertain*) 475.

illus-ive, -ory; delusive; mock; ideal etc. (*imaginary*) 515; spurious etc. 545; deceitful etc. 544; perverted.

controvertible, unsustain-able, -ed; unauthenticated, untrustworthy.

exploded, refuted, discarded.

in –, under an- error etc. *n.*; mistaken etc. *v.*; tripping etc. *v.*; out, – in one's reckoning; aberrant; beside –, wide of the- -mark, – truth; astray etc. (*at fault*) 475; on -a false, – the wrong-scent; in the wrong box; at cross purposes, all in the wrong, all abroad, at sea.

Adv. more or less.

496. Maxim.—N. maxim, aphorism; apo-, apoph-thegm; *dictum*, saying, gnome, adage, saw, proverb, epigram; sentence, *mot*, motto, word, by-word, precept, moral, phylactery, *protasis*, brocard.

axiom, postulate, theorem, *scholium*, truism.

reflection etc. (*idea*) 453; conclusion etc. (*judgment*) 480; golden rule etc. (*precept*) 697; principle, *principia*; profession of faith etc. (*belief*) 484; formula.

wise –, sage –, received –, admitted –, recognized- maxim etc.; true –, common –, hackneyed –, trite –, commonplace- saying etc.

Adj. aphoristic, proverbial, phylacteric; axiomatic, gnomic.

Adv. as -the saying is, – they say.

497. Absurdity.—N. absurd-ity, -ness etc. *adj.*; imbecility etc. 499; alogy, nonsense, paradox, inconsistency; stultiloquy, once, futility.

blunder, muddle, bull; Irish-, Hibernic-ism; slip-slop; anti climax; bathos; sophism etc. 477.

farce, burlesque, *galimatias*, *amphigouri*, rhapsody; farrago etc. (*disorder*) 59; extravagance, romance; sciomachy.

joke, catch, sell, pun, verbal quibble, macaronic.

jargon, fustian, twaddle etc. (*no meaning*) 517; exaggeration etc. 549; moonshine, stuff; mare's nest.

vagary, tomfoolery, mummery, monkey trick, practical joke, *boutade*, *escapade*.

V. play the fool etc. 499; stultify, blunder, muddle; joke; talk nonsense, *parler à tort et à travers*; *battre la campagne*; be -absurd etc. *adj.*

Adj. absurd, nonsensical, preposterous, egregious, senseless, farcical, inconsistent, ridiculous, extravagant, quibbling, futile; macaronic, punning, paradoxical.

foolish etc. 499; sophistical etc. 477; unmeaning etc. 517; without rhyme or reason; fantastic.

Int. fiddle-de-dee! pish! pish and tush! pho! stuff and nonsense! rubbish! !rot! bosh! in the name of the Prophet—figs!

Phr. *credat Judaeus Apella*; tell it to the marines.

498. Intelligence. Wisdom.—N. intelligence, capacity, comprehension, understanding, intellect etc. 450; nous, parts, sagacity, mother wit, wit, *esprit*, gumption, quick parts, grasp of intellect; acuteness etc. *adj.*; acumen, subtlety, penetration; perspica-cy, -city; discernment; long-headedness, due sense of, good judgment; discrimination etc. 465; craftiness, cunning etc. 702; refinement etc. (*taste*) 850.

head, brains, gray matter, headpiece, upper story, long head; eagle -eye, – glance; eye of a -lynx, – hawk.

wisdom, sapience, sense; good –, common –, plain –, horse- sense; clear thinking; rationality, reason; reasonableness etc. *adj.*; judgment; solidity, depth, profundity, caliber; enlarged views; reach –, compass- of thought; enlargement of mind.

genius, inspiration, *geist*, fire of genius, heaven-born genius, soul; talent etc. (*aptitude*) 698.

[Wisdom in action] prudence etc. 864; vigilance etc. 459; tact etc. 698; foresight etc. 510; sobriety, self-possession, *aplomb*, ballast, mental -poise, – balance.

a bright thought, inspiration, brainwave, not a bad idea.

V. be -intelligent etc. *adj.*; have all one's wits about one; understand etc. (*intelligible*) 518; catch –, take in- an idea; take a -joke, – hint.

see -through, – at a glance, – with half an eye, – far into, – through a millstone; penetrate; discern etc. (*descry*) 441; foresee etc. 510.

discriminate etc. 465; know what's what etc. 698; listen to reason.

Adj. [Applied to persons] intelligent, quick of apprehension, keen, acute, alive, brainy, awake, bright, quick, sharp; quick-, keen-, clear-, sharp- -eyed, -sighted, -witted; wide awake; canny, shrewd, astute; clear-headed; far-sighted etc. 510; discerning, perspicacious, penetrating, piercing; argute nimble-, needle-witted; sharp as a needle; alive to etc. (*cognizant*) 490; clever etc. (*apt*) 698; arch etc. (*cunning*) 702; *pas si bête*; acute etc. 682.

wise, sage, sapient, sagacious, reasonable, rational, sound, in one's right mind, sensible, *abnormis sapiens*, judicious, strong-minded.

un-prejudiced, -biassed, -bigoted, -prepossessed; un-dazzled, -perplexed; of unwarped judgment, impartial, equitable, fair, broad-minded.

cool; cool-, long-, hard-, strong-headed; long-sighted, calculating, thoughtful, reflecting; solid, deep, profound.

oracular; heaven-directed, -born.

prudent etc. (*cautious*) 864; sober, staid, solid; considerate, politic, wise in one's generation; watchful etc. 459; provident etc. (*prepared*) 673; in advance of one's age; wise as -a serpent, – Solomon, – Solon.

[Applied to actions] wise, sensible, reasonable, judicious; well-judged, -advised; prudent, politic; expedient etc. 646.

499. Imbecility. Folly.—N. want of -intelligence etc. 498, – intellect etc. 450; shallow-, silli-, foolish-ness etc. *adj.*; imbecility, incapacity, vacancy of mind, poverty of intellect, clouded perception, poor head, apartments to let; stup-, stolidity; hebetude, dull understanding, meanest capacity; short-sightedness; incompetence etc. (*unskilfulness*) 699.

one's weak side; bias etc. 481; infatuation etc. (*insanity*) 503.

simplicity, puerility, babyhood; dotage, anility, second childishness, senile dementia, fatuity; idiocy, -tism; driveling.

folly, frivolity, desipience, irrationality, trifling, ineptitude, nugacity, inconsistency, lip-wisdom, conceit; sophistry etc. 477; giddiness etc. (*inattention*) 458; eccentricity etc. 503; extravagance etc. (*absurdity*) 497; rashness etc. 863.

act of folly etc. 699.

V. be -imbecile etc. *adj.*; have no -brains, – sense etc. 498.

trifle, drivel, *radoter*, dote; ramble etc. (*madness*) 503; play the -fool, – monkey, – goat, take leave of one's senses; not see an inch beyond one's nose; stultify oneself etc. 699; talk nonsense etc. 497.

Adj. [Applied to persons] un-intelligent, -intellectual, -reasoning; mind-, wit-, reason-, brainless; having no -head etc. 498; not -bright etc. 498; inapprehensible.

weak-, addle-, puzzle-, blunder-, muddle-, muddy-, pig-, beetle-, maggotty-, gross-headed; beef-, fat- -witted, -headed.

weak, feeble-minded; dull-, shallow-, rattle-, lack-brained; half-, nit-, short-, dull-, blunt-witted; shallow-, clod-, addle-pated; dim-, short-sighted; thick-skulled; weak in the upper story.

shallow, *borné*, weak, wanting, soft, nutty, sappy, spoony; dull, – as a beetle; stupid, heavy, insulse, obtuse, blunt, stolid, doltish, asinine; inapt etc. 699; prosaic etc. 843.

child-ish, -like; infant-ine, -ile; baby-, bab-ish; puerile; anile; simple etc. (*credulous*) 486.

fatuous, idiotic, imbecile, moronic, driveling; blatant, babbling; vacant; sottish; bewildered etc. 475.

blockish, unteachable; Boeot-ian, -ic; bovine; un-gifted, -discerning, -enlightened, -wise, philosophical; apish.

foolish, silly, senseless, irrational, insensate, nonsensical, inept; maudlin.

narrow-minded etc. 481; bigoted etc. (*obstinate*) 606; giddy etc. (*thoughtless*) 458; rash etc. 863; eccentric etc. (*crazed*) 503.

[Applied to actions] foolish, unwise, indiscreet, injudicious, improper, unreasonable, without reason, ridiculous, silly, stupid, asinine; ill-imagined, -advised, -judged, -devised; inconsistent, irrational, unphilosophical; extravagant etc. (*nonsensical*) 497; sleeveless, idle; useless etc. 645; inexpedient etc. 647; frivolous etc. (*trivial*) 643; absurd etc. 497.

Phr. *Davis sum non Oedipus.*

500. Sage.—N. sage, wise man; pundit; master -mind, – spirit of the age; longhead, thinker, philosopher.

authority, oracle, mentor, luminary, shining light, *esprit fort*, *magnus Apollo*, Solon, Solomon, Nestor, Magi, 'second Daniel.'

man of learning etc. 492; expert etc. 700; wizard etc. 994.

[Ironically] wiseacre, bigwig.

Adj. wise, learned; authoritative, oracular; erudite etc. 490; venerable, reverenced, revered, *emeritus*.

501. Fool.—N. fool, idiot, tomfool, wiseacre, simpleton, Simple Simon, nit-wit, witling, dizzard, donkey, ass; ninny, -hammer; moron, dolt, booby, Tom Noddy, looby, hoddy-doddy, noddy, nonny, noodle, nizy, owl; goose, -cap; *imbécile*; gaby, *radoteur*, nincompoop, *badaud*, zany; trifler, babbler; pretty fellow; natural, *niais*.

child, baby, infant, innocent, milksop, sop.

oaf, lout, loon, lown, dullard, doodle, calf, colt, buzzard, block, put, stick, stock, numps, tony.

bull-, dunder-, addle-, block-, dull-, logger-, jolt-, jolter-, beetle-, gross-, thick-, giddy-head; num-, thick- skull; lack-, shallow-brain; half-, lack-wit; dunder-pate; fat-head, poor stick.

sawney, gowk; clod, -hopper; clod-, clot-poll, -pate; bull-calf; men of Boeotia, wise men of Gotham.

un sot à triple étage, sot; jobbernowl, changeling, mooncalf, *gobemouche*.

dotard, driveller; old -fogey, – woman; crone, grandmother.

greenhorn etc. (*dupe*) 547· dunce etc. (*ignoramus*) 493; lubber etc. (*bungler*) 701; madman etc. 504.

one who -will not set the Thames on fire, – did not invent gunpowder; *qui n'a pas inventé la poudre*; no conjuror.

502. Sanity.—N. sanity; soundness etc. *adj.*; rationality, normality, sobriety, lucidity, lucid interval; senses, sober senses, sound mind, *mens sana*.

V. be -sane etc. *adj.*; retain one's senses, – reason.

become -sane etc. *adj.*; come to one's senses, sober down.

render -sane etc. *adj.*; bring to one's senses, sober.

Adj. sane, rational, reasonable, *compos mentis*, of sound mind; sound, -minded.

self-possessed; sober, -minded.

in one's -sober senses, – right mind; in possession of one's faculties.

Adv. sanely etc. *adj.*

503. Insanity.—N. disordered -reason, – intellect; diseased –, unsound –, abnormal- mind; derangement, unsoundness.

insanity, lunacy; madness etc. *adj.*; mania, *rabies*, *furor*, mental aliénation, paranoia, aberration; *amentia*, dementation, -tia, -cy; *dementia praecox*; *morosis*, idiocy, phrenitis, frenzy, raving, incoherence, wandering, delirium, calenture of the brain, delusion, hallucination; lycanthropy, brain storm, *delirium tremens*, D.T.'s.

vertigo, dizziness, swimming; sunstroke, *coup de soleil*, siriasis.

fanatisism, infatuation, craze; oddity, eccentricity, twist, monomania; klepto-, dipso-mania; hypochondriasis etc. (*low spirits*) 837; *melancholia*, hysteria.

screw –, tile –, slate- loose; bee in one's bonnet, rats in the upper story.

dotage etc. (*imbecility*) 499.

V. be –, become- -insane etc. *adj.*; lose one's senses, – reason, – faculties, – wits; go –, run-mad, run amuck; rave, dote, ramble, wander; drivel etc. (*be imbecile*) 499; have a -screw loose etc. *n.*, – devil; *avoir le diable au corps*; lose one's head etc. (*be uncertain*) 475.

derange, render –, drive- -mad etc. *adj.*; madden, dementate, addle the wits, derange the head, infatuate, befool; turn -the brain, – one's head.

Adj. insane, mad, lunatic; crazy, crazed, *aliéné*, *non compos mentis*; not right, cracked, touched; bereft of reason; unhinged, deranged, unsettled in one's mind; insensate, reasonless, beside oneself, demented, daft; phren-, fren-zied, -etic; possessed, – with a devil; far gone, maddened, moonstruck; shatterpated; barmy; mad-, scatter-, shatter-, crack-brained, off one's head; bug-house, *loco*.

maniacal; manic, manic-depressive; delirious, light-headed, incoherent, rambling, doting, wandering; frantic, raving, stark staring mad, amok, amuck.

corybantic, dithyrambic; rabid, giddy, vertiginous, dizzy, wild, haggard, mazed; flighty; distracted, -aught; bewildered etc. (*uncertain*) 475.

mad as a -March hare, – hatter; of -unsound mind etc. *n.* touched –, wrong –, not right- in one's -head, – mind, – wits, – upper story; out of one's -mind, – senses, – wits; not in one's right mind.

fanatical, infatuated, odd, eccentric; hypp-ed, -ish.

imbecile, silly etc. 499.

Adv. like one possessed.

Phr. the mind having lost its balance; the reason under a cloud; *tête -exaltée, -montée*.

504. Madman—N. madman, lunatic, maniac, bedlamite, candidate for Bedlam, raver, madcap; energumen; paranoiac; auto-, mono-, pyro-, megalo-, dipso-, klepto-maniac; hypochondriac etc. (low spirit) 837.

dreamer etc. 515; rhapsodist, seer, high-flier, enthusiast, crank, eccentric, nut, fanatic, *fanatico*; *exalté*; knight errant, Don Quixote.

idiot etc. 501.

505. Memory.—N. memory, remembrance; reten-tion, -tiveness; tenacity; *veteris vestigia flammae*; tablets of the memory; readiness.

reminiscence, recognition, recurrence, recollection, rememoration; retrospect, -ion; after-thought.

suggestion etc. (*information*) 527; prompting etc. *v.*; hint, reminder, token of remembrance, *memento*, *souvenir*, keepsake, relic, *memorandum*; remembrancer, flapper; memorial etc. (*record*) 551; commemoration etc. (*celebration*) 883.

things to be remembered, *memorabilia*.

art of –, artificial- memory; *memoria technica*; mnemo-nics, -technics; phrenotypics; Mnemosyne; memorandum-, note-, engagement-, prompt-book.

retentive –, tenacious –, green –, trustworthy –, capacious –, faithful –, correct –, exact –, ready –, prompt- memory.

V. remember, mind; retain the -memory, – remembrance- of; keep in view.

have –, hold –, bear –, carry –, keep –, retain- in *or* in the -thoughts, – mind, – memory, – remembrance; be in –, live in –, remain in –, dwell in –, haunt –, impress- one's -memory, – thoughts, – mind.

sink in the mind; run in the head; not be able to get it out of one's head; be deeply impressed with; rankle etc. (*revenge*) 919.

recur to the mind; flash -on the mind, – across the memory.

recognize, recollect, bethink oneself, recall, call up, conjure up, retrace; look –, trace- -back, – backwards; think –, look back- upon; review; call –, recall –, bring- to mind; remembrance; carry one's thoughts back; rake up the past.

suggest etc. (*inform*) 527; prompt; put –, keep- in mind; remind; fan the embers; call –, summon –, rip- up; renew; *infandum renovare dolorem*; task –, tax –, jog –, flap –, refresh –, rub up –, awaken- the memory; pull by the sleeve; bring back the memory, put in remembrance, memorialize.

get –, have –, learn –, know –, say –, repeat- by -heart, – rote; drive –, get- into -one's head; say one's lesson; repeat, – as a parrot; have at one's finger's ends.

commit to memory; memorize; con, – over; fix –, rivet –, imprint –, impress –, stamp –, grave –, engrave –, store –, treasure up –, bottle up –, embalm –, enshrine- in the memory; load –, store –, stuff –, burden- the memory with.

redeem from oblivion; keep the memory -alive, – green; *tangere ulcus*; keep up the memory of; commemorate etc. (*celebrate*) 883.

make a note of etc. (*record*) 551.

Adj. remember-ing, -ed etc. *v.*; mindful, reminiscential; retained in the memory etc. *v.*; pent up in one's memory; fresh; green, – in remembrance, still vivid; unforgotten, present to the mind; within one's -memory etc. *n.*; indelible; not to be forgotten, unforgettable, enduring; uppermost in one's thoughts; memorable etc. (*important*) 642.

Adv. by -heart, – rote; without book, *memoriter*.

in memory of; *in memoriam*; suggestive.

Phr. *manet altâ mente repostum*; *forsan et haec olim meminisse juvabit.*

506. Oblivion.—N. oblivion; forgetfulness etc. *adj.*; obliteration etc. 552, of –, insensibility etc. 823 to- the past.

short –, treacherous –, loose –, slippery –, failing- memory; decay –, failure –, lapse- of memory; memory like a sieve; waters of -Lethe, – oblivion, *amnesia*.

pardon, acquittal, amnesty, oblivion; absolution.

V. forget; be -forgetful etc. *adj.*; fall –, sink- into oblivion; have -a short memory etc. *n.* – no head.

forget one's own name, have on the tip of one's tongue, come in at one ear and go out at the other.

slip –, escape –, fade from –, die away from- the memory; lose, – sight of.

unlearn; efface etc. 552 –, discharge- from the memory; consign to -oblivion, – the tomb of the Capulets; think no more of etc. (*turn the attention from*) 458; cast behind one's back, wean one's thoughts from; let bygones be bygones etc. (*forgive*) 918.

Adj. forgotten etc. *v.*; unremembered, past recollection, bygone, out of mind; buried –, sunk- in oblivion; clean forgotten; gone out of one's -head, – recollection.

forgetful, oblivious, mindless, heedless, Lethean; insensible etc. 823- to the past.

Phr. *non mi ricordo*; the memory -failing, – deserting one, – being at (*or* in) fault.

507. Expectation.—N. expect-ation, -ance, -ancy; anticipation, reckoning, calculation; contingency; foresight etc. 510.

contemplation, prospection, look out; prospect, perspective, horizon, vista; destiny etc. 152.

suspense, waiting, abeyance; curiosity etc. 455; anxious –, ardent –, eager –, breathless –, sanguine- expectation; torment of Tantalus.

presumption, hope etc. 858; trust etc. (*belief*) 484; prognostication, auspices etc. (*prediction*) 511.

V. expect; look -for, – out for, – forward to; hope for, anticipate; have in -prospect, – contemplation; keep in view; contemplate, promise oneself; not -wonder etc. 870 -at, – if.

wait –, tarry –, lie in wait –, watch –, bargain- for; keep a -good, – sharp- look-out for; await; stand at 'attention,' abide, bide one's –, mark- time, watch.

foresee etc. 510; prepare for etc. 673; forestall etc. (*be early*) 132; count upon etc. (*believe in*) 484; think likely etc. (*probability*) 472; make one's mouth water.

lead one to expect etc. (*predict*) 511; have in store for etc. (*destiny*) 152.

prick up one's ears, hold one's breath.

Adj. expectant; expecting etc. *v.*; in -expectation etc. *n.*; on the watch etc. (*vigilant*) 459; open -eyed, -mouthed; agape, gaping, all agog; on -tenterhooks, – tiptoe, – the tiptoe of expectation; *aux aguets*; ready; curious etc. 455; looking forward to; prepared for; on the rack.

expected etc. *v.*; long expected, foreseen; in prospect etc. *n.*; prospective; in -one's eye, – view, – the horizon; impending etc. (*destiny*) 152.

Adv. expectantly; in the event of; on the watch etc. *adj.*; with -breathless expectation etc. *n.*; – bated breath, – eyes, – ears strained; *arrectis auribus*; on edge.

Phr. we shall see; *nous verrons.*

508. Inexpectation.—N. in-, non-expectation; false expectation etc. (*disappointment*) 509; miscalculation etc. 481; unforeseen contingency, the unforeseen, the unexpected.

surprise, sudden burst, thunderclap, blow, shock; bolt out of the blue; eye-opener; wonder etc. 870.

V. not -expect etc. 507; be taken by surprise; start; miscalculate etc. 481; not bargain for; come –, fall- upon.

be -unexpected etc. *adj.*; come -unawares etc. *adv.*; turn up, pop, drop from the clouds; come –, burst –, flash –, bounce –, steal –, creep- upon one; come –, burst- like a thunder-clap; -bolt; take –, catch- -by surprise, – unawares, – napping.

pounce –, spring a mine- upon.

surprise, startle, take aback, electrify, stun, stagger, take away one's breath, throw off one's guard; astonish etc. (*strike with wonder*) 870.

Adj. non-expectant; surprised etc. *v.*; unwarned, -aware; off one's guard; inattentive etc. 458.

un-expected, -anticipated, -prepared for, -looked for, -foreseen, -hoped for; dropped from the clouds; beyond –, contrary to –, against- expectation; out of one's reckoning; unheard of etc. (*exceptional*) 83; startling; sudden etc. (*instantaneous*) 113.

Adv. abruptly, unexpectedly, plump, pop, *à l'improviste*, unawares; without -notice, – warning, – saying 'by your leave;' like a -thief in the night, – thunderbolt; in an unguarded moment; suddenly etc. (*instantaneously*) 113.

Int. heyday! etc. (*wonder*) 870.

Phr. little did one -think, – expect; nobody would ever -suppose, – think, – expect; who would have thought?'

509. Disappointment. [Failure of expectation.]—**N.** disappointment, disillusionment; blighted hope, balk; blow; slip 'twixt cup and lip; non-fulfilment of one's hopes; sad –, bitter- disappointment; trick of fortune; afterclap; false –, vain- expectation; miscalculation etc 481; fool's paradise; much cry and little wool.

V. be disappointed; look -blank, – blue; look –, stand- -aghast etc. (*wonder*) 870; find to one's cost; laugh on the wrong side of one's mouth; find one a false prophet.

disappoint; crush –, dash –, balk –, disappoint –, blight –, falsify –, defeat –, not realize- one's -hope, – expectation; balk, jilt, bilk; play one -false, – a trick; dash the cup from the lips; tantalize; dumb-found, -founder; disillusion, -ize; dissatisfy, disgruntle.

Adj. disappointed etc. *v.*; disconcerted, aghast; out of one's reckoning; disgruntled.

Phr. the mountain brought forth a mouse; *nascitur ridiculus mus*; *parturiunt montes*; *diis aliter visum*, the bubble burst; one's countenance falling.

510. Foresight.—N. foresight, prospicience, prevision, longsightedness; anticipation; providence etc. (*preparation*) 673.

fore-thought, -cast; pre-deliberation, -surmise; foregone conclusion etc. (*prejudgment*) 481; prudence etc. (*caution*) 864.

foreknowledge; *prognosis*; pre-cognition, -science, -notion, -sentiment; second sight; sagacity etc. (*intelligence*) 498.

prospect etc. (*expectation*) 507; foretaste; prospectus etc. (*plan*) 626.

V. foresee; look -forwards to, – ahead, – beyond; scent from afar; feel in one's bones; look –, pry –, peep into the future.

see one's way; see how the -land lies, – wind blows, – cat jumps.

anticipate; expect etc. 507; be beforehand etc. (*early*) 132; predict etc. 511; fore-know, -judge, -cast; surmise; have an eye to the -future, – main chance; *respicere finem*; keep a sharp look-out etc. (*vigilance*) 459; forewarn etc. 668.

Adj. foreseeing etc. *v.*; prescient; anticipatory; far-seeing, -sighted; sagacious etc. (*intelligent*) 498; weather-wise; provident etc. (*prepared*) 673; prospective etc. 507.

Adv. against the time when.

511. Prediction.—N. prediction, announcement; program, programme etc. (*plan*) 626; premonition etc. (*warning*) 668; *prognosis*, prophecy, vaticination, Mantology, prognostication, premonstration, augur-y, -ation; a-, ha-riolation; fore-, a-boding; bode-, abode-ment; omin-ation, -ousness; auspices, forecast; sign, presage, prognostic; omen etc. 512; horoscope, nativity; sooth, -saying; fortune-telling; divination; crystal gazing, necromancy etc. 992; prophet etc. 512.

[Divination by the stars] astrology, horoscopy, astromancy, judicial astrology.*

[Place of prediction] *adytum*.

prefigur-ation, -ement; prototype, type.

V. predict, prognosticate, prophesy, vaticinate, divine, foretell, soothsay, augurate, tell fortunes; cast a -horoscope, – nativity; advise; forewarn etc. 668.

presage, augur, bode; a-, fore-bode, -cast; fore-, be-token; pre-figure, -show; portend; fore-show, -shadow, shadow forth, typify, ominate, signify, point to, precurse.

usher in, herald, premise, announce; lower.

hold out –, raise –, excite- -expectation, – hope; bid fair, promise, lead one to expect; be the -precursor etc. 64.

Adj. predicting etc. *v.*; predictive, prophetic, fatidical, vaticinal, oracular, Sibylline, haruspical, weatherwise.

ominous, presageful, portentous; augur-ous, -al, -ial; auspici-al, -ous; prescious, monitory, extispicious, premonitory, precusory, significant of, pregnant with, big with the fate of.

Phr. 'coming events cast their shadows before.'

*The following terms, expressive of different forms of divination, have been collected from various sources, and are here given as a curious illustration of bygone superstitions:

Divination *by oracles*, Theomancy; *by the Bible*, Bibliomancy, *by ghosts*, Psychomancy; *by spirits seen in a magic lens*, Cristallomantia; *by shadows or manes*, Sciomancy; *by appearances in the air*, Aeromancy, Chaomancy, *by the stars at birth*, Genethliacs; *by meteors*, Meteoromancy; *by winds*, Austromancy; *by sacrificial appearances*, Aruspicy (*or* Haruspicy), Hieromancy, Hieroscopy; *by the entrails of animals sacrificed*, Hieromancy; *by the entrails of a human sacrifice*, Anthropomancy; *by the entrails of fishes*, Ichthyomancy; *by sacrificial fire*, Pyromancy; *by red-hot iron*, Sideromancy; *by smoke from the alter*, Capnomancy; *by mice*, Myomancy; *by birds*, Orniscopy, Ornithomancy; *by a cock picking up grains*, Alectryomancy (*or* Alectoromancy); *by fishes*, Ophiomancy; *by herbs*, Botanomancy; *by water*, Hydromancy; *by fountains*, Pegomancy; *by a wand*, Rhabdomancy; *by dough of cakes*, Crithomancy; *by meal*, Aleuromancy, Alphitomancy; *by salt*, Halomancy; *by dice*, Cleromancy; *by arrows*, Belomancy; *by a balanced hatchet*, Axinomancy; *by a balanced sieve*, Coscinomancy; *by a suspended ring*, Dactyliomancy; *by dots made at random on paper*, Geomancy; *by precious stones*, Lithomancy; *by pebbles*, Pessomancy; *by pebbles drawn from a heap*, Psephomancy; *by mirrors*, Catoptromancy; *by writings in ashes*, Tephramancy; *by dreams*, Oneiromancy; *by the hand*, Palmistry, Chiromancy; *by nails reflecting the sun's rays*, Onychomancy; *by finger rings*, Dactylomancy; *by numbers*, Arithmancy; *by drawing lots*, Sortilege; *by passages in books*, Stichomancy; *by the letters forming the name of the person*, Onomancy, Nomancy; *by the features*. Anthroposcopy: *by the mode of laughing*. Geloscopy: *by ventriloquism*. Gastromancy: *by walking in a circle*. Gyromancy: *by dropping melted wax into water*. Ceromancy: *by currents*. Bletonism.

512. Omen.—N. omen, portent, presage, prognostic, augury, auspice; sigh etc. (*indication*) 550; herald, forerunner, harbinger etc. (*precursor*) 64.

bird of ill omen, signs of the times; gathering clouds; warning etc. 668.

prefigurement etc. 511.

513. Oracle.—N. oracle; prophet, -ess; seer, soothsayer, augur, fortune-teller, palmist, medium, clairvoyant, crystal gazer, witch, geomancer, *aruspex*; a-, ha-ruspice; Sibyl; Python, -ess; Pythia; Pythian –, Delphian- oracle; Monitor, Sphinx, Tiresias, Cassandra, Sibylline leaves; Zadkiel, Old Moore; sorcerer etc. 994; interpreter etc. 524.

514. Supposition.—N. supposition, assumption, postulation, condition, pre-supposition, hypothesis, postulate, *postulatum*, theory, *data*; pro-, position; *thesis*, theorem; proposal etc. (*plan*) 626.

bare –, vague –, loose- -supposition, – suggestion; conceit; conjecture; guess, – work; rough guess, shot; conjecturality; surmise, suspicion, inkling, suggestion, suggestiveness, association of ideas, hint; presumption etc. (*belief*) 484; divination, speculation.

theorist, speculator, doctrinarian, hypothesist.

V. suppose, conjecture, surmise, suspect, guess, divine; theorize; pre-sume, -surmise, -suppose; assume, fancy, wis, take it; give a guess, speculate, believe, dare say, take it into one's head, take for granted.

put forth; pro-pound, -pose; moot; hypothesize; start, put a case, submit, move, make a motion; hazard –, throw out –, put forward- a - suggestion, – conjecture.

allude to, suggest, hint, put it into one's head.

suggest itself etc. (*thought*) 451; run in the head etc. (*memory*) 505; marvel –, wonder- -if, – whether.

Adj. supposing etc. *v.*; given, mooted, postulatory; assumed etc. *v.*; supposit-ive, -itious; gratuitous, speculative, conjectural, hypothetical, suppositional, theoretical, academic, supposable, presumptive, putative.

suggestive, allusive, stimulating.

Adv. if, – so be; an; on the -supposition etc. *n.*; *ex hypothesi*; in -case, – the event of; *quasi*, as if, provided; perhaps etc. (*by possibility*) 470; for aught one knows.

515. Imagination.—N. imagination; originality; invention; fancy; inspiration; *verve*; empathy.

warm –, heated –, excited –, sanguine –, ardent –, fiery –, boiling –, wild –, bold –, daring –, playful –, lively –, fertile- - imagination, – fancy.

'mind's eye;' 'such stuff as dreams are made of.'

ideal-ity, -ism; romanticism, utopianism, castle-building; dreaming; frenzy; ecs-, ex-tasy; calenture etc. (*delirium*) 503; reverie, brown study, trance; somnambulism.

conception, *vorstellung*, ercogitation, 'a fine frenzy,' poetic frenzy, divine afflatus; cloud-, dream-land; flight –, fumes- of fancy; 'thick-coming fancies;' creation –, coinage- of the brain; imagery, word painting.

conceit, maggot, figment, myth, dream, vision, shadow, chimera; phan-tasm, -tasy; fantasy, fancy; whim, -sey; vagary, rhapsody, romance, *extravaganza*; air-drawn dagger, bugbear, nightmare; flying Dutchman, great sea-serpent, man in the moon, castle in the air, *château en Espagne*; Utopia, Atlantis, happy valley, millennium, fairy land; land of Prester John, kingdom of Micomicon; work of fiction etc. (*novel*) 594; poetry etc. 597; drama etc. 599; Arabian nights; *le pot au lait*; dream of Alnaschar etc. (*hope*) 858; day –, golden- dream

illusion etc. (*error*) 495; phantom etc. (*fallacy of vision*) 443; *Fata Morgana* etc. (*ignis fatuus*) 423; vapor etc. (*cloud*) 353; stretch of the imagination etc. (*exaggeration*) 549.

idealist, romanticist, visionary; mopus; romancer, dreamer; somnambulist; rhapsodist etc. (*fanatic*) 504.

V. imagine, fancy, conceive; ideal-, real-ize; dream, – of; 'give to airy nothing a local habitation and a name.'

create, originate, devise, invent, coin, fabricate; improvise, strike out something new.

set one's wits to work; strain –, crack- one's invention; rack –, ransack –, cudgel- one's brains; excogitate.

give -play, – the reins, – a loose- to the - imagination, – fancy; empathize; indulge in reverie.

conjure up a vision; fancy –, represent –, picture –, figure- to oneself; envisage.

float in the mind; suggest itself etc. (*thought*) 451.

Adj. imagined etc. *v.*; *ben trovato*; air-drawn, -built.

imagin-ing etc. *v.*, -ative; original, inventive, creative, fertile, productive; ingenious.

romantic, high-flown, flighty, extravagant, fanatic, enthusiastic, Utopian, Quixotic; preposterous, rhapsodical.

ideal, unreal; in the clouds, *in nubibus*; unsubstantial etc. 4; illusory etc. (*fallacious*) 495; fictitious, theoretical, hypothetical.

fabulous, legendary; myth-ic, -ological; chimerical; imagin-, vision-ary; notional; fan-cy, -ciful, -tastic, -tastical; whimsical; fairy, -like.

dreamy, entranced, vaporous.

516. Meaning. [Idea to be conveyed.] [Thing signified.]—**N.** meaning; signific-ation, -ance; sense, expression; im-, pur-port; drift, tenor, implication, connotation, essence, force, spirit bearing, coloring; scope.

matter; subject, -matter; argument, text, sum and substance; gist etc. 5.

general –, broad –, substantial – colloquial –, literal –, plain –, simple –, accepted –, natural –, unstrained –, true etc. (*exact*) 494 –, honest etc. 543 –, *primâ facie* etc. (*manifest*) 525- meaning.

literality; literal interpretation; after acceptation; allusion etc. (*latency*) 526; suggestion etc. (*information*) 527; synonym; figure of speech etc. 521; acceptation etc. (*interpretation*) 522.

V. mean, signify, express, connote, denote; im-, pur-port; convey, imply, breathe, indicate, bespeak, bear a sense; tell –, speak- of; touch on; point –, allude- to; drive at; involve etc. (*latency*) 526; delcare etc. (*affirm*) 535.

understand by etc. (*interpret*) 522.

Adj. meaning etc. *v.*; expressive, suggestive, meaningful, allusive; signific-ant, -ative, -atory; pithy; full of –, pregnant with- meaning.

declaratory etc. 535; intelligible etc. 518; literal, metaphrastic; synonymous; tantamount etc. (*equivalent*) 27; implied etc. (*latent*) 526; explicit etc. 525; literal etc. 562.

Adv. to that effect; that is to say etc. (*being interpreted*) 522.

literally; evidently, from the context.

517. Unmeaningness. [Absence of meaning.]—**N.** unmeaningness etc. *adj.*; scrabble, scribble, scrawl, daub, (*painting*), strumming (*music*).

empty sound, dead letter, *vox et praeterea nihil*; 'a tale told by an idiot, full of sound and fury, signifying nothing;' 'sounding brass and a tinkling cymbal.'

nonsense, jargon, gibberish, jabber, mere words, hocus-pocus, fustian, rant, bombast, balderdash, palaver, patter, flummery, *verbiage*, babble, *bavardage*, *baragouin*, platitude, *niaiserie*; inanity; rigmarole, rodomontade; truism; *nugae canorae*; twaddle, twattle, fudge, trash; stuff, – and nonsense; bosh, rubbish, rot, drivel, moonshine, wish wash, fiddle-faddle, flapdoodle; absurdity etc. 497; vagueness etc. (*unintelligibility*) 519.

V. mean nothing; be -unmeaning etc. *adj.*; twaddle, quibble, rant, gabble, scrabble etc. *n.*

Adj. unmeaning; meaning-, sense-less; nonsensical; void of -sense etc. 516.

in-, un-expressive; vacant, fatuous; not significant; insignificant,.

trashy, washy, inane, vague, trumpery, trivial, fiddle-faddle, twaddling, quibbling.

unmeant, not expressed; tacit etc. (*latent*) 526.

inexpressible, undefinable, incommunicable.

Int. rubbish! etc. 497.

518. Intelligibility.—**N.** intelligibility, clearness, clarity, explicitness etc. *adj.*; lucidity, perspicuity; legibility, plain speaking etc. (*manifestation*) 525; precision etc. 494; a word to the wise.

V. be -intelligible etc. *adj.*; speak -for itself, – volumes; tell its own tale, lie on the surface.

render -intelligible etc. *adj.*; popularize, simplify, clear up; elucidate etc. (*explain*) 522.

understand, comprehend; take, – in; catch, grasp, recognize, follow, collect, master, make out; see -with half an eye, – daylight, – one's way; enter into the ideas of; come to an understanding.

Adj. intelligible; clear, – as -day, – crystal, – noonday; lucid; per-, tran-spicuous; luminous, transparent; comprehensible.

easily understood, easy to understand, for the million, intelligible to the meanest capacity, popularized.

plain, distinct, explicit, clear-cut; positive; definite etc. (*precise*) 494.

graphic, vivid, telling; expressive etc. (*meaning*) 516; illustrative etc. (*explanatory*) 522.

un-ambiguous, -equivocal, -mistakable etc. (*manifest*) 525, -confused; legible, recognizable; obvious etc. 525.

Adv. in plain -terms, – words, – English.

Phr. he that runs may read etc. (*manifest*) 525.

519. Unintelligibility.—**N.** unintelligibility, incomprehensibility, imperspicuity; inconceivableness, vagueness etc. *adj.*; obscurity; ambiguity etc. 520; doubtful meaning; uncertainty etc. 475; perplexity etc. (*confusion*) 59; spinosity; *obscurum per obscurius*; mystification etc. (*concealment*) 528; latency etc. 526; transcendentalism.

paradox; enigma, riddle etc. (*secret*) 533; *dignus vindice nodus*; sealed book; steganography, freemasonry.

pons asinorum, asses' bridge; double –, high-Dutch, Greek, Hebrew; jargon etc. (*unmeaning*). 517.

obscurantist.

V. be -unintelligible etc. *adj.*; require - explanation etc. 522; have a doubtful meaning, pass comprehension.

render -unintelligible etc. *adj.*; conceal etc. 528; darken etc. 421; confuse etc. (*derange*) 61; perplex etc. (*bewilder*) 475.

not -understand etc. 518; lose, – the clue; miss; not know what to make of, be able to make nothing of, give it up; not be able to -account for, – make either head or tail of; be at sea etc. (*uncertain*) 475; wonder etc. 870; see through a glass darkly etc. (*ignorance*) 491.

not understand one another; play at cross purposes etc. (*misinterpret*) 523.

Adj. un-intelligible, -accountable, -decipherable, -discoverable, -knowable, -fathomable; incognizable, -explicable, -scrutable; inap-, incomprehensible; insol-vable, -uble; impenetrable.

illegible, indecipherable, as Greek to one, unexplained, paradoxical; enigmatic, -al; puzzling, baffling.

obscure, dark, muddy, clear as mud, seen through a mist, dim, nebulous, shrouded in mystery; undiscernible etc. (*invisible*) 447; misty etc. (*opaque*) 426; hidden etc. 528; latent etc. 526.

indefinite etc. (*indistinct*) 447; perplexed etc. (*confused*) 59; undetermined, vague, loose, ambiguous; mysterious; mystic, -al; transcendental; occult, recondite, esoteric, abstruse, crabbed.

incon-ceivable, -ceptible; searchless; above –, beyond –, past- comprehension; beyond one's depth; unconceived.

inexpressible, undefinable, incommunicable, unutterable, ineffable, unpronounceable.

520. Equivocalness. [Having a double sense.]—**N.** equivocalness etc. *adj.*; double - meaning etc. 516; ambiguity, *double entendre*, pun, paragram, *calembour*, quibble, *équivoque*, anagram; conundrum etc. (*riddle*) 533; word-play etc. (*wit*) 842; homonym, -y; amphibo-ly, -logy; ambiloquy.

Sphinx, Delphic oracle.

equivocation etc. (*duplicity*) 544; white lie, mental reservation etc. (*concealment*) 528.

V. be -equivocal etc. *adj.*; have two -meanings etc. 516; equivocate etc. (*palter*) 544.

Adj. equivocal, ambiguous, amphibolous, homonymous; double-tongued etc. (*lying*) 544.

521. Metaphor.—N. figure of speech; *facon de parler*, way of speaking, colloquialism.

phrase etc. 566; figure, trope, metaphor, tralatition, metonymy, enallage, *catachresis*, *synecdoche*, *autonomasia*; irony, satire, figurativeness etc. *adj.*; image, -ry; *metalepsis*, type, anagoge, simile, personification, *prosopopaeia*, allegory, apologue, parable, fable; allusion, adumbration; application; euphemism; euphuism.

V. employ -metaphor etc. *n.*; personify, allegorize, adumbrate, shadow forth, apply, allude -, refer- to.

Adj. metaphorical etc. *n.*; figurative, catachrestical, typical, tralatitious, parabolic, allegorical, allusive, anagogical; ironical; colloquial.

Adv. so to -speak, - say, - express oneself; as it were.

Phr. *mutato nomine de te fabula nattatur.*

522. Interpretation.—N. interpretation, definition; explan-, explic-ation; solution, answer; rationale; plain -, simple -, strict- interpretation; meaning etc. 516.

translation; rend-ering, -ition; reddition; literal -, free- translation; key, crib; secret; clew etc. (*indication*) 550; Rosetta stone.

exegesis; ex-pounding, -position; Hermeneutics; comment, -ary; inference etc. (*deduction*) 480; illustration, exemplification; gloss, annotation, *scholium*, note; e-, di-lucidation, enucleation; *éclaircissement*, *mot de l'énigme*.

symptomat-, semei-ology; metoposcopy, physiognomy; diagnosis, prognosis; paleography etc. (*philology*) 560.

accept-ion, -ation, -ance; light, reading, lection, construction, version.

equivalent, - meaning etc. 516; synonym; para- meta-phrase; convertible terms, apposition; dictionary etc. 562; polyglot.

V. interpret, explain, define, construe, translate, render; do -, turn- into; transfuse the sense of.

find out etc. 480*a*- -the meaning etc. 516- of; read; spell -, figure -, make- out; decipher, decode, unravel, disentangle, puzzle out; find the key of, enucleate, resolve, solve; read between the lines.

account for; find -, tell- the cause etc. 153- of; throw -, shed- -light, - new light, - a fresh light- upon; clear up, elucidate.

illustrate, exemplify; unfold, expound, comment upon, annotate; popularize etc. (*render intelligible*) 518.

take -, understand -, receive -, accept- in a particular sense; understand by, put a construction on, be given to understand.

Adj. explanatory, expository; explica-tive, -tory; exegetical; hermeneutic, interpretive, illustrative, elucidative, annotative, scholiastic.

polyglot; literal; para-, meta-phrastic; cosignificative, synonymous; equivalent etc. 27.

Adv. in -explanation etc. *n.*; that is to say, *id est*, *videlicet*, to wit, namely, in other words.

literally, strictly speaking; in -plain, - plainer- - terms, - words, - English; more simply.

523. Misinterpretation.—N. misinterpretation, -apprehension, -understanding, - acceptation, -construction, -application; *catachresis*; cross -reading, - purposes; mistake etc. 495.

misrepresentation, perversion, exaggeration etc. 549; false -coloring, - construction; abuse of terms; parody, travesty; falsification etc. (*lying*) 544.

V. mis-interpret, -apprehend, -understand, - conceive, -judge, -doubt, -spell, -translate, - construe, -apply; mistake etc. 495.

misrepresent, pervert; garble etc. (*falsify*) 544; distort; detort; travesty, play upon words; stretch -, strain -, wrest- the -sense, - meaning; explain away; put a -bad, - false- construction on; give a false coloring, look through -rose colored -, - dark - spectacles.

be -, play- at cross purposes.

Adj. misinterpreted etc. *v.*; untranslat-ed, -able.

Adv. at cross purposes.

524. Interpreter.—N. interpreter, translator, ex-positor, -pounder, -ponent, -plainer; demonstrator.

scholiast, commentator, annotator; meta-, paraphrast.

spokesman, speaker, mouthpiece, prolocutor; diplomat etc. 758.

guide, courier, dragoman, *valet de place*, *cicerone*, showman; oneirocritic; Oedipus; oracle etc. 513.

525. Manifestation.—N. manifestation; unfolding; plainness etc. *adj.*; plain speaking; expression; showing etc. *v.*; exposition, demonstration, *séance*; exhibition, production; display, showing off etc. 882; premonstration. [Thing shown] exhibit, show.

indication etc. (*calling attention to*) 457; publicity etc. 531; disclosure etc. 529; openness etc. (*honesty*) 543, (*artlessness*) 703; *épachement*, prominence.

V. make -, render- -manifest etc. *adj.*; bring - forth, - forward, - to the front, - into view; give notice, express; represent, set forth, exhibit; show,

— up; expose; produce; hold up —, expose- to view; set —, place —, lay- before -one, — one's eyes; tell to one's face; trot out, put through one's paces, unfold, show off, show forth, unveil, bring to light, display, demonstrate, unroll; lay open; draw —, bring- out; bring out in strong relief; call —, bring- into notice; hold up the mirror; wear one's heart upon his sleeve; show one's -face, — colors; manifest oneself; speak out; make no -mystery, — secret- of; unfurl the flag; proclaim etc. (*publish*) 531.

indicate etc. (*direct attention to*) 457; disclose etc. 529; elicit etc. 480*a*; interpret etc. 522.

be -manifest etc. *adj.*; appear etc. (*be visible*) 446; transpire etc. (*be disclosed*) 529; speak for itself, stand to reason; stare one in the face; loom large, appear on the horizon, rear its head; give -token, — sign, — indication of; tell its own tale etc. (*intelligible*) 518; go without saying.

Adj. manifest, apparent; salient, striking, demonstrative, prominent, in the foreground, notable, pronounced.

flagrant; notorious etc. (*public*) 531; arrant; stark staring; unshaded, glaring.

defin-ed, -ite; distinct, conspicuous etc. (*visible*) 446; obvious, evident, incontestable, unmistakable, not to be mistaken, plain, clear, palpable, self-evident, autoptical; intelligible etc. 518; clear as -day, — daylight, — noonday; plain as -a pikestaff, — the sun at noonday, — the nose on one's face, — the way to the parish church.

ostensible; open, — as day; overt, patent, express, explicit; naked, bare, literal, downright, undisguised, exoteric.

unreserved; frank, plain spoken etc. (*artless*) 703; barefaced, brazen, bold, shameless, daring, flaunting, loud.

manifested etc. *v.*; disclosed etc. 529; expressible, capable of being shown, producible; in-, un-concealable.

Adv. manifestly, openly etc. *adj.*; before one's eyes, under one's nose, to one's face, face to face, above board, *cartes sur table*, on the stage, in plain sight, in open court, in the open, — streets; at the cross roads; in market overt; in the face of -day, — heaven; in -broad —, open- daylight; without reserve; at first blush, *primâ facie*, on the face of; in set terms.

Phr. *cela saute aux yeux*; he that runs may read; you can see it with half an eye; it needs no ghost to tell us; the meaning lies on the surface; *cela va sans dire*; *res ipsa loquitur*.

526. Latency.—N. latency, inexpression; hidden —, occult- meaning; occultness, occultism, mysticism, mystery, cabala, symbolism, anagoge; silence etc. (*taciturnity*) 585; concealment etc. 528; more than meets the -eye, — ear; Delphic oracle; *les dessous des cartes*, undercurrent.

allusion, insinuation, implication; innuendo etc. 527; adumbration; 'something rotten in the state of Denmark.'

snake in the grass etc. (*pitfall*) 667; secret etc. 533.

darkness, invisibility, impreceptibility.

latent influence, power behind the throne; friend at court, wire puller.

V. be -latent etc. *adj.*; lurk, smoulder, underlie, make no sign; escape -observation, — detection, — recognition; lie hid etc. 528.

laugh in one's sleeve; keep back etc. (*conceal*) 528.

involve, imply, implicate, connote, import, understand, allude to, infer, leave an inference; symbolize; whisper etc. (*conceal*) 528.

Adj. latent; lurking etc. *v.*; secret etc. 528; occult, symbolic, mystic; implied etc. *v.*; dormant.

un-apparent, -known, -seen etc. 441; in the background; invisible etc. 447; indiscoverable, dark; impenetrable etc. (*unintelligible*) 519; spied, -suspected.

un-said, -written, -published, -breathed, -talked of, -told etc. 527, -sung, -exposed, -proclaimed, -disclosed etc. 529, -pronounced, -mentioned, -expressed; not expressed, tacit.

un-developed, -solved, -explained, -traced, -discovered etc. 480*a*, -tracked, -explored, -invented.

indirect, crooked, inferential; by -inference, — implication; implicit; constructive; allusive, covert, muffled; steganographic; under-stood, -hand, -ground; concealed etc. 528; delitescent.

Adv. by a side wind; *sub silentio*; in the background; behind -the scenes, — one's back, — the veil; below the surface; on the tip of one's tongue; secretly etc. 528; between the lines; by a mutual understanding.

Phr. 'thereby hangs a tale.' 'that is another story.'

527. Information.—N. information, enlightenment, acquaintance, knowledge etc. 490; publicity etc. 531.

communication, intimation; not-ice, -ification; e-, an-nunciation; announcement; representation, round robin, presentment

case, estimate, specification, report, advice, monition; news etc. 532; return etc. (*record*) 551; account etc. (*description*) 594; statement etc. (*affirmation*) 535.

mention; acquainting etc. *v.*; instruction etc. (*teaching*) 537; outpouring; intercommunication, communicativeness.

informant, authority, teller, announcer, annunciator, harbinger, herald, intelligencer, commentator, columnist, reporter, exponent, mouthpiece; informer, keek, eavesdropper, delator, detective, sleuth; *mouchard*, spy, stool pigeon, newsmonger; messenger etc. 534; *amicus curiae*.

valet de place, *cicerone*, pilot, guide; guide-, hand-book; *vade mecum*; manual; map, plan, chart, gazetteer; itinerary etc. (*journey*) 266.

hint, suggestion, wrinkle, innuendo, inkling, whisper, passing word, word in the ear, subaudition, cue, by-play; gesture etc. (*indication*) 550; gentle — broad- hint; *verbum sapienti*; word to the wise; insinuation etc. (*latency*) 526.

V. tell; inform, — of; acquaint, — with; impart, — to; make acquainted with, bring to the ears of, apprise, advise, enlighten, awaken.

let fall, mention, express, intimate, represent, communicate, make known; publish etc 531; notify, signify, specify, convey the knowledge of.

let one —, have one to- know; serve notice, give one to understand; give notice; set —, lay —, put-before; point out, put into one's head; put one in possession of; instruct etc. (*teach*) 537; direct the attention to etc. 457.

an-nounce, -nunciate; report, – progress; bring –, send –, leave –, write- word; tele-graph, -phone; ring –, call- up; wire; retail, render an account; give an account etc. (*describe*) 594; state etc. (*affirm*) 535.

disclose etc. 529; show cause; explain etc. (*interpret*) 522.

hint; give an inkling of; give –, drop –, throw out- a hint; insinuate; allude –, make allusion- to; glance at; tip off, tip the wink etc. (*indicate*) 550; suggest, prompt, give the cue, breathe; whisper, – in the ear.

give a bit of one's mind; tell one plainly, – once for all; speak volumes.

un-deceive, -beguile; set right, correct, open the eyes of, disabuse.

be -informed of etc.; know etc. 490; learn etc. 539; get scent of, gather from; awaken –, open one's eyes- to; become -alive, – awake- to; keep posted; hear, overhear, understand.

come to one's -ears, – knowledge; reach one's ears.

Adj. informed etc. *v.*; *communiqué*; reported etc. *v.*; published etc. 531; advisory.

expressive etc. 516; explicit etc. (*open*) 525, (*clear*) 518; plain-spoken etc. (*artless*) 703.

declara-, nuncupa-, exposi-tory; declarative, enunciative, communicat-ive, -ory; oral.

Adv. from information received; according to -rumor, – report; in the air; from what one can gather.

Phr. a little bird told me.

528. Concealment.—N. concealment; hiding etc. *v.*; occultation, mystification.

seal of secrecy; screen etc. 530; disguise etc. 530; masquerade; masked battery; hiding place etc. 530; cipher, code, crypt-, stegan-ography; invisible –, sympathetic- ink; palimpsest; freemasonry.

stealth, -iness; obreption; slyness etc. (*cunning*) 702.

latit-ancy, -ation; seclusion etc. 893; privacy, secrecy, secretness; *incognita.*

reticence; reserve; mental –, reservation, aside; *arrière pensée*, suppression, evasion, white lie, misprision; silence etc. (*taciturnity*) 585; suppression of truth etc. 544; underhand dealing; close-, secretive-ness etc. *adj.*; mystery.

latency etc. 526; snake in the grass; secret etc. 533.

V. conceal, hide, secrete, stow away, put out of sight; lock –, seal –, bottle- up.

cover, screen, cloak, veil, shroud; screen from -sight, – observation; draw the veil; draw –, close- the curtain; curtain, shade, eclipse, throw a veil over; be-cloud, -fog, -mask; mask, disguise; ensconce, muffle, smother; whisper.

keep -from, – back, – to oneself; keep -snug, – close, – secret, – dark; bury; sink, suppress; keep -from, – out of- -view, – sight; keep in –, throw into- the -shade, – background; cover up one's tracks; stifle, hush up, withhold, reserve; fence with a question; ignore etc. 460.

code, codify, use a cipher.

keep -a secret, – one's own counsel; hold one's tongue etc. (*silence*) 585; make no sign, not let it go further; not breathe a -word, – syllable- about; not let the right hand know what the left is doing; hide one's light under a bushel, bury one's talent in a napkin.

keep –, leave- in -the dark, – ignorance; blind, – the eyes; blindfold, hoodwink, mystify; puzzle etc. (*render uncertain*) 475; bamboozle etc. (*deceive*) 545.

be -concealed etc. *v.*; suffer an eclipse; retire from sight, couch; hide oneself; lie -hid, – in ambush, – low, – *perdu*, – snug, – close; seclude oneself etc. 893; lurk, sneak, skulk, slink, pussyfoot, prowl; steal -into, – out of, – by, – along; play at -bopeep, – hind and seek; hide in holes and corners.

Adj. concealed etc. *v.*; hidden; veiled, secret, recondite, mystic, cabalistic, occult, dark; cryptic, -al, private, privy, *in petto*, auricular, clandestine, close, inviolate.

behind a -screen etc. 530; under -cover, – an eclipse; in -ambush, – hiding, – disguise; in a -cloud, – fog, – mist, – haze, – dark corner; in the -shade, – dark; clouded, wrapt in clouds; invisible etc. 447; buried, underground, *perdu*; incommunicado; secluded etc. 893.

un-disclosed etc. 529; -told etc. 527; covert etc. (*latent*) 526; mysterious etc. (*unintelligible*) 519.

irrevealable, inviolable; confidential; esoteric; not ot be spoken of.

obreptitious, furtive, stealthy, feline; skulking etc. *v.*; surreptitious, underhand, hole and corner; sly etc. (*cunning*) 702; secretive, evasive, noncommittal, reserved, reticent, uncommunicative, buttoned up; close, – as wax; taciturn etc. 585.

Adv. secretly etc. *adj.*; in -secret, – private, – one's sleeve, – holes and corners; in the dark etc. *adj.*

janius clausis, with closed doors, *à huis clos*; hugger-mugger, *à la dérobée*; under the -cloak of, – rose, – table; *sub rosâ*, *en tapinois*, in the background, aside, on the sly, with bated breath, *sotto voce*, in a whisper, without beat of drum, *à la sourdine*.

in –, strict- confidence; confidentially etc. *adj.*; between -ourselves, – you and me; *entre nous*, *inter nos*, under the seal of secrecy; in -code, – cipher.

underhand, by stealth, like a thief in the night; stealthily etc. *adj.*; behind -the scenes, – the curtain, – one's back, – a screen etc. 530; *incognito*; *in camerâ*.

Phr. it -must, – will- go no further; 'tell it not in Gath,' nobody the wiser.

529. Disclosure.—N. disclosure; retection; unveiling etc. *v.*; deterration, revealment, revelation; divulgence, expos-ition, -ure; *exposé*; whole truth; tell-tale etc. (*news*) 532.

acknowledgment, avowal; confession, -al; shrift.

bursting of a bubble; *dénouement*.

V. dis-close, -cover, -mask; draw –, draw aside –, lift –, raise –, lift up –, remove –, tear- the -veil, – curtain; un-mask, -veil, -fold, -cover, -seal, -kennel; take off –, break- the seal; lay -open, – bare; expose; open, – up; bare, bring to light; evidence; make -clear, – evident, – manifest; evince.

divulge, reveal, break; let into the secret; reveal the secrets of the prison-house; tell etc. (*inform*) 527; breathe, utter, blab, peach; let -out, – fall, – drop, – the cat out of the bag; betray; tell tales, – out of school; come out with; give -vent, – utterance- to; open the lips, blurt out, vent, whisper about; speak out etc. (*make manifest*) 525; make public etc. 531; unriddle etc. (*find out*) 480*a*; split; blow the gaff; break the news.

acknowledge, allow, concede, grant, admit, own, confess, avow, throw off all disguise, turn inside out, make a clean breast; show one's -hand, – cards; unburden –, disburden- one's -mind, – conscience, – heart; open –, lay bare –, tell a piece of- one's mind; unbosom oneself, own to the soft impeachment; say –, speak- the truth; turn -King's, – Queen's, – States's- evidence.

raise –, drop –, lift –, remove –, throw off- the mask; expose; debunk; lay open; un-deceive, -beguile; disabuse, set right, correct, open the eyes of; *désillusionner.*

be -disclosed etc.; transpire, come to light; come in sight etc. (*be visible*) 446; become known, escape the lips; come –, ooze –, creep –, leak –, peep –, crop- out; show its -face, – colors; discover etc. itself; break through the clouds, flash on the mind.

Adj. disclosed etc. *v.*

Int. out with it!

Phr. the murder is out; a light breaks in upon one; the scales fall from one's eyes; the eyes are opened.

530. Ambush. [Means of concealment.]—**N.** hiding-place; secret -place, – drawer; recess, hole, funk hole, holes and corners; closet, crypt, *adytum*, abditory, *oubliette*, safe, – deposit.

am-bush, -buscade; stalking horse; lurking-hole, -place; secret path, backstairs; retreat etc. (*refuge*) 666.

screen, cover, shade, blinder; veil, curtain, blind, *purdah*, cloak, cloud.

mask, vizor, visor, disguise, masquerade dress, domino; *camouflage*.

pitfall etc. (*source of danger*) 667; trap etc. (*snare*) 545.

v. ambush, ambuscade, lie in ambush etc. (*hide oneself*) 528; lie in wait for; set a trap for etc. (*deceive*) 545.

Adv. *aux aguets.*

531. Publication.—N. publication; public -announcement etc. 527; promulgation, propagation, proclamation, pronouncement, encylical, *pronunciamento*; circulation, indiction, edition, imprint, impression, printing; hue and cry..

publicity, notoriety, currency, flagrancy, cry, *bruit*; *vox populi*; report etc. (*news*) 532.

the Press, fourth estate, public press, newspaper, periodical, journal, gazette; house organ, trade publication, tabloid, daily, weekly, monthly, quarterly, annual, magazine, monograph, book; review; news sheet, special edition, supplement, feature, rotogravure, comic strips; leaflet, pamphlet; telegraphy; publisher etc. *v.*

circular, – letter; manifesto, advertisement, puff, placard, bill, *affiche*, broadside, poster; notice etc. 527; program.

V. publish; make -public, – known etc. (*information*) 527; speak –, talk- of; broach, utter; put forward; circulate, propagate, promulgate; spread –, abroad; rumor, diffuse, disseminate, evulgate; put –, give –, send- forth; emit, edit, get out; issue; cover, report; bring –, lay –, drag before the public; give -out, – to the world; put –, bandy –, hawk –, buzz –, whisper –, bruit –, blaze- about; drag into the -open day, – limelight; voice.

proclaim, herald, blazon; blaze –, noise-abroad; sound a trumpet; trumpet –, thunder-forth; give tongue; announce with -beat of drum, – flourish of trumpets; proclaim -from the housetops, – at Charing Cross, at the cross roads; declare, declaim.

advertise, placard; post, – up; *afficher*, publish in the Gazette, send round the crier.

raise a -cry, – hue and cry, – report; set news afloat.

telegraph, cable, wireless, broadcast.

be -published etc; be –, become- public etc. *adj.*; come out; go –, fly –, buzz –, blow- about; get -about, – abroad, – afloat, – wind; find vent; see the light; go forth, take air, acquire currency, pass current; go -the rounds, – the round of the newspapers, – through the length and breadth of the land; *virum volitare per ora*; pass from mouth to mouth; spread; run –, spread- like wildfire.

Adj. published etc. *v.*; current etc. (*news*) 532; in circulation, public; notorious; flagrant, arrant; open etc. 525; trumpet-tongued; encyclical, promulgatory; exoteric.

Adv. publicly etc. *adj.*; in open court, with open doors; in the limelight.

Int. *Oyez!* O yes! notice!

Phr. notice is hereby given; this is –, these are- to give notice.

532. News.—N. news; information etc. 527; piece –, budget- of -news, – information; report, story, yarn, copy, filler, intelligence, tidings; stop press news.

word, advice, *aviso*, message; dis-, des-patch; telegram, cable, wireless telegram, radio-gram, marconi-gram, communication, errand, embassy; *bulletin.*

microphone; public address system, P.A.; walkie talkie, radio -telephone, -phone.

radio, wireless (Eng.), high fidelity, hi fi, radio set, transistor, receiver; speaker, loudspeaker, amplifier, tweeter, woofer; transmitter, broadcaster; AM –, FM –, short wave – transmitter; radio station, studio, control room, network, hookup, circuit; frequency, kilocycles, megacycles; band, channel, modulation, amplification; broadcast, program, newscast, network show, commerical announcement, serial, sound effects; signature, station – identification, – break, radio listener, audiophile.

television, TV, video, color television; television –, live – broadcast, telecast, TV show; televising, telecasting, transmission, television channel, video, audio, beam, reception, image, test pattern; rain, snow, ghost; television –, TV – station, mobile unit, TVmobile, transmitter, televisor, boost, camera; set, monitor, tube, screen.

rumor, hearsay, *on dit*, flying rumor, news stirring, cry, buzz, *bruit*, fame; talk, *oui-dire*, scandal, eavesdropping; town –, table- talk; tittle-tattle; *canard*, topic of the day, idea afloat.

fresh –, stirring –, old – stale- news; glad tidings; old –, stale- story.

narrator etc. (*describe*) 594; news-, scandal-monger; tale-bearer; tell-tale, gossip, tattler, busybody, chatterer; informer.

broad-, news-, sports-caster; commentator, announcer, master of ceremonies, M.C., programmer, sound man, radioman, ham, radioperator.

television technician, TV man, cameraman, soundman.

V. transpire etc. (*be disclosed*) 529; rumor etc. (*publish*) 531.

broadcast, radio, transmit, send, release, beam; sign – on, – off; go on –, go off – the air, monitor; listen –, tune – in.

tele-vise, -cast; color cast.

Adj. many-tongued; rumored; publicly –, currently- -rumored, – reported; rife, current, floating, afloat, going about, in circulation, in everyone's mouth, all over the town.

Adv. as the story -goes, – runs; as they say, it is said.

533. Secret.—N. secret; dead –, profound-secret; *arcanum*, mystery; latency etc. 526; Asian mystery; sealed book, secrets of the prison-house; *le dessous des cartes*.

enigma, riddle, puzzle, nut to crack, conundrum, charade, rebus, logogriph; mono-, ana-gram; acrostic, cross-word puzzle; Sphinx; *crux criticorum*.

maze, labyrinth, Hyrcynian wood.

problem etc. (*question*) 461; paradox etc. (*difficulty*) 704; unintelligibility etc. 519; *terra incognita* etc. (*ignorance*) 491.

Adj. secret etc. (*concealed*) 528.

534. Messenger.—N. messenger, envoy, emissary, legate; nuncio, internuncio; intermediary; ambassador etc. (*diplomatist*) 758.

marshal, flag-bearer, herald, crier, trumpeter, bellman, pursuivant, *parlementaire*, *apparitor*.

courier, runner, dawk, *estafette*; Hermes, Mercury, Iris, Ariel.

postman, letter carrier, telegraph boy, messenger boy, district messenger; despatch rider, commissionaire, erand-boy.

mail; post, -office; letter-bag; mail -boat, – train, – coach, – van, aerial mail; tele-graph, -phone; cable, wire; carrier-pigeon; wireless telegraph, -phone; radiotele-graph, -phone.

journalist, newspaperman, reporter; gentleman –, representative- of the press; sob sister; penny-a-liner; special –, war –, own- correspondent; spy, scout; informer etc. 527.

535. Affirmation.—N. affirm-ance, -ation; statement, allegation, assertion, predication, declaration, word, averment.

asseveration, adjuration, swearing, oath, affidavit; deposition etc. (*record*) 551; avouchment, assurance; protest, -ation; profession; acknowledgment etc. (*assent*) 488; pledge.

vote, voice, suffrage, ballot.

remark, observation; position etc. (*proposition*) 514; saying, *dictum*, sentence, *ipse dixit*.

emphasis, positiveness, peremptoriness; dogmatism etc. (*certainty*) 474; dogmatist etc. 887.

V. assert; make -an assertion etc. *n.*; have one's say; say, affirm, predicate, declare, state, represent; protest, profess.

put -forth, – forward; advance, allege, propose, propound, enunciate, enounce, broach, set forth, hold out, maintain, contend, pronounce, pretend.

depose, depone, aver, avow, avouch, asseverate, swear; make –, take one's- oath; make –, swear –, put in- an affidavit; take one's Bible oath, kiss the book, vow, *vitam impendere vero*; swear till - one is black in the face, – all's blue; be sworn, call Heaven to witness; vouch, warrant, certify, assure, swear by bell, book and candle.

swear by etc. (*believe*) 484; insist –, take one's stand- upon; emphasize, lay stress on; assert - roundly, – positively; lay down, – the law; raise one's voice, dogmatize, have the last word; rap out; repeat; re-assert, -affirm.

announce etc. (*information*) 527; acknowledge etc. (*assent*) 488; attest etc. (*evidence*) 467; adjure etc. (*put to one's oath*) 768.

Adj. asserting etc. *v.*; declaratory, predicatory, pronunciative, affirmative, *soi-disant*; positive; certain etc. 474; express, explicit etc. (*patent*) 525; absolute, emphatic, flat, broad, round, pointed, marked, distinct, decided, confident, assertive, insistent, trenchant, dogmatic, definitive, formal, solemn, categorical, peremptory; unretracted; predicable, affirmable.

Adv. affirmatively etc. *adj.*; in the affirmative.

with emphasis, *ex cathedrâ*, without fear of contradiction.

I must say, indeed, i' faith, let me tell you, why, give me leave to say, marry, you may be sure, I'd have you to know; upon my -word, – honor; by my troth, egad, I assure you; by -jingo, – Jove, – George, – etc.; troth, seriously, sadly; in –, in sober- -sadness, – truth, – earnest; of a truth, truly, pardi, perdy; in all conscience, upon oath; be assured etc. (*belief*) 484; yes etc. (*assent*) 488; I'll - warrant, – warrant you, – engage, – answer for it, – be bound, – venture to say, – take my oath; in fact, as a matter of fact, forsooth, joking apart; so help me God; not to mince the matter.

Phr. quoth he; *dixi*.

536. Negation.—N. ne-, abne-gation; denial; dis-avowal, -claimer; abjuration; contra-diction, -vention; recusation, protest; rebuttal; recusancy etc. (*dissent*) 489; flat –, emphatic- -contradiction, – denial; *démenti*.

qualification etc. 469; repudiation etc. 610; retraction etc. 607; confutation etc. 479; refusal etc. 764; prohibition etc. 761.

V. deny; contra-dict, -vene; controvert, give denial to, gainsay, negative, shake the head.

dis-own, -affirm, -claim, -avow; recant etc. 607; revoke etc. (*abrogate*) 756.

dispute, impugn, traverse, rebut, join issue upon; bring –, call- in question etc. (*doubt*) 485.

deny -flatly, – peremptorily, – emphatically, – absolutely, – wholly, – entirely; give the lie to, belie.

repudiate etc. 610; set aside, ignore etc. 460; rebut etc. (*confute*) 479; qualify etc. 469; refuse etc. 764.

Adj. denying etc. *v.*, denied etc. *v.*; contradictory; negat-ive, -ory; revocatory; recusant etc. (*dissenting*) 489; at issue upon.

Adv. no, nay, not, nowise; not a -bit, – whit, – jot; not -at all, – in the least, – so; no such thing; nothing of the -kind, – sort; quite the contrary, *tout au contraire*, far from it; *tant s'en faut*; on no account, in no respect; by -no, – no manner of- means; negatively.

phr. there never was a greater mistake; I know better; *non haec in foedera.*

537. Teaching.—N. teaching etc. *v.*; instruction; edification· education; pedagogy; tuition; tutor-, tutel-age; direction, guidance.

qualification, preparation; train-, school-ing etc. *v.*; discipline; exer-cise, -citation; drill, practice.

persuasion, proselytism, propagandism, *propaganda*; in-doctrination, -culcation, oculation.

explanation etc. (*interpretation*) 522; lesson, lecture, sermon, homily; apologue, parable; discourse, prelection, preachment, disquisition.

exercise, task; *curriculum*; course, – of study; grammar, three R's, initiation, A.B.C. etc. (*beginning*) 66.

elementary –, primary –, secondary –, grammar school –, high school –, college –, university –, technical –, liberal –, classical –, religious –, denominational –, moral –, secular- education, technical –, vocational- training; university extension lectures; propaedeutics, moral tuition; evening classes, correspondence course.

physical education, gymnastics, calisthenics, eurythmics; *sloyd*.

V. teach, instruct, edify, school, tutor; cram, prime, coach; enlighten etc. (*inform*) 527.

in-culcate, -doctrinate, -oculate, -fuse, -stil, -fix, -graft, -filtrate; im-bue, -pregnate, -plant; graft, sow the seeds of, disseminate, propagandize.

give an idea of; put -up to, – in the way of; set right.

sharpen the wits, enlarge the mind; give new ideas, open the eyes, bring forward, 'teach the young idea how to shoot;' improve etc. 658.

expound etc. (*interpret*) 522; lecture; prelect; read –, give- a -lesson, – lecture, – sermon, – discourse; hold forth, preach; sermon-, moral-ize; point a moral.

train, discipline; bring up, – to; educate, form, ground, prepare, qualify, drill, exercise, practice, habituate, familiarize with, nurture, dry-nurse, breed, rear, take in hand; break, – in; tame; pre-instruct; initiate; inure etc. (*habituate*) 613.

put to nurse, send to school.

direct, guide; direct attention to etc. (*attention*) 457; impress upon the -mind, – memory; beat into, – the head; convince etc. (*belief*) 484.

Adj. teaching etc. *v.*; taught etc. *v.*; educational; scholastic, academic, doctrinal; disciplinal; instructive, didactic, hortative, pedagogic, tutorial.

Phr. the schoolmaster abroad.

538. Misteaching—N. mis-teaching, -information, -intelligence, -guidance, -direction, -persuasion, -instruction, -leading etc. *v.*; perversion, false teaching; sophistry etc. 477; college of Laputa; the blind leading the blind.

V. mis-inform, -teach, -direct, -guide, -instruct, -correct; pervert; put on a false –, throw off the- scent; deceive etc. 545; mislead etc. (*error*) 495; misrepresent; lie etc. 544; *ambiguas in vulgum spargere voces*, preach to the wise, teach one's grandmother to suck eggs.

render unintelligible etc. 519; bewilder etc. (*uncertainty*) 475; mystify etc. (*conceal*) 528; unteach.

Adj. misteaching etc. *v.*; unedifying.

Phr. *piscem natare doces.*

539. Learning.—N. learning; acquisition of -knowledge etc. 490, – skill etc. 698; acquirement, attainment; edification, scholarship, erudition; lore; information; self-instruction; study, reading, perusal; inquiry etc. 461.

ap-, prenticeship; pupil-age, -arity; tutelage, novitiate, matriculation.

docility etc. (*willingness*) 602; aptitude etc. 698.

V. learn; acquire –, gain –, receive –, take in –, drink in –, imbibe –, pick up –, gather –, get –, obtain –, collect –, glean- -knowledge, – information, – learning.

acquaint oneself with, master; make oneself -master of, – acquainted with; grind, cram; get –, coach- up; learn by -heart, – rote.

read, spell, peruse; con –, pore –, thumb- over; wade through; dip into; run the eye -over, – through; turn over the leaves.

study; be -studious etc. *adj.*; consume the midnight oil, mind one's book.

go to -school, – college, – the university; serve -an (*or* one's) apprenticeship, – one's time; learn one's trade; be -informed etc. 527; be -taught etc. 537.

Adj. studious; schol-astic, -arly; teachable; docile etc. (*willing*) 602; apt etc. 698; industrious etc. 682; learned erudite.

Adv. at one's books; *in statu pupillari* etc. (*learner*) 541.

540. Teacher.—N. teacher, trainer, instructor, institutor, master, tutor, don, director, Corypheus, dry nurse, coach, grinder, crammer; governor, bear-leader; governess, duenna; disciplinarian.

professor, lecturer, reader, prelector, prolocutor, preacher; Boanerges; pastor etc. (*clergy*) 996; schoolmaster, dominie, usher, pedagogue, abecedarian; schoolmistress, dame, monitor, proctor, pupil-teacher.

expositor etc. 524; preceptor, guide; mentor etc. (*adviser*) 695; pioneer, apostle, missionary, propagandist, moonshee; example etc. (*model for imitation*) 22.

professorship etc. (*school*) 542.

tutelage etc. (*teaching*) 537.

Adj. professorial, tutorial etc. 537.

541. Learner.—N. learner, scholar, student, *alumnus*, *élève*, pupil; ap-, prentice; articled clerk; school-boy, -girl, beginner, tyro, abecedarian, alphabetarian.

recruit, novice, neophyte, tenderfoot, inceptor, *débutant*, catechumen, probationer; undergraduate; freshman, frosh; sophomore, junior, senior; junior –, senior- soph; sophister, questionist, fellow-, commoner, pensioner, exhibitioner, sizar, scholar, fellow, advanced –, post graduate –, research- student.

class, form, grade, standard, remove; pupilage etc. (*learning*) 539.

disciple, follower, apostle, proselyte; fellow student, school-mate, -fellow, class mate, condisciple.

Adj. *in statu pupillari*, in leading strings, sophomoric.

542. School.—N. school, academy, university, *alma mater*, college, seminary, Lyceum; instit-ute, -ution, *conservatoire*; *palaestra*, *gymnasium*.

day –, boarding –, public –, preparatory –, elementary –, primary –, nursery –, dame's –, grammar –, Board –, County –, Council –, parochial –, denominational –, Sunday –, religious –, collegiate –, secondary –, continuation –, night –, correspondence –, secretarial –, military –, law –, medical –, business –, technical- school; technical –, training- college; Polytechnic; training ship; *Kindergarten*, nursery, *crèche*, reformatory.

pulpit, desk, reading desk, ambo, class-, lecture-room, theater, amphitheater, forum, stage, rostrum, platform, hustings, tribune.

school –, horn –, text-book; grammar, primer, abecedary, rudiments, manual, *vade mecum*, Lindley, Murray, Cocker.

professor-, lecture-, reader-ship; chair; schoolmaster etc. 540.

School Board, Council of Education; *propaganda*.

Adj. scholastic, academic, collegiate; educational.

Adv. *ex cathedrâ*.

543. Veracity.—N. veracity; truthfulness, frankness etc. *adj.*; truth, sooth, sincerity, candor, honesty, fidelity; plain dealing, *bona fides*; love of truth; probity etc. 939; ingenuousness etc. (*artlessness*) 703.

the truth the whole truth and nothing but the truth; honest –, sober- truth etc. (*fact*) 494; unvarnished tale; light of truth.

V. speak –, tell- the truth; speak by the card; paint in its –, show oneself in ones -true colors; make a clean breast etc. (*disclose*) 529; speak one's mind etc. (*be blunt*) 703; not -lie etc. 544, – deceive etc. 545.

Adj. truthful, true; ver-acious, -edical; scrupulous etc. (*honorable*) 939; sincere, candid, frank, open, straightforward, unreserved; open-, true-, simple- hearted; honest, trustworthy; undissembling etc. (dissemble etc. 544); guileless, pure; unperjured, ture blue, as good as one's word; unaffected, unfeigned, *bonâ fide*; outspoken, ingenuous etc. (*artless*) 703; undisguised etc. (*real*) 494.

Adv. truly etc. (*really*) 494; on oath; in plain words etc. 703; in –, with –, of a –, in good –, very- truth; as the -dial to the sun, – needle to the pole; honor bright; troth; in good -sooth, – earnest; unfeignedly, with no nonsense, in sooth, sooth to say, *bonâ fide*, *in foro conscientiae*; without equivocation; *cartes sur table*, from the bottom of one's heart; by my troth etc. (*affirmation*) 535.

544. Falsehood.—N. false-hood, -ness; fals-ity, -ification; misrepresentation; deception etc. 545; untruth etc. 546; guile; bad faith; lying etc. *v.*; misrepresentation; mendacity, perjury, false swearing; forgery, invention, fabrication; subreption; covin.

perversion –, suppression- of truth; *suppressio veri*; perversion, distortion, false coloring; exaggeration etc. 549; prevarication, equivocation, shuffling, fencing, evasion, fraud; *suggestio falsi* etc. (*lie*) 546; mystification etc. (*concealment*) 528; simulation etc. (*imitation*) 19; dis-simulation, -sembling; deceit.

sham; pretence, pretending, malingering.

lip-homage, – service; mouth honor; hollowness; mere -show, – outside, eye-wash, window dressing; duplicity, double dealing, insincerity, hypocrisy, cant, humbug, casuistry; jesuit-ism, -ry; pharisaism; Machiavelism, 'organized hypocrisy;' crocodile tears, mealy-mouthedness, quackery; charlatan-ism, -ry; gammon; bun-kum, -come; flam, ban, flim-flam, cajolery, flattery; Judas kiss; perfidy etc. (*bad faith*) 940; *il volto sciolto i pensieri stretti.*

unfairness etc. (*dishonesty*) 940; artfulness etc. (*cunning*) 702; misstatement etc. (*error*) 495.

V. be -false etc. *adj.*, – a liar etc. 548; speak -falsely etc. *adv.*; tell a -lie etc. 546; lie, fib; lie like a trooper; swear falsely, forswear, perjure oneself, bear false witness.

mis-state, -quote, -cite, -report, -represent; belie, falsify, pervert, distort; put a false construction upon etc. (*misinterpret*) 523.

prevaricate, equivocate. quibble; palter, – to the understanding; *répondre en Normand*; trim, shuffle, fence, mince the truth, beat about the bush, blow hot and cold, play fast and loose.

garble, gloss over, disguise, give a color to; give –, put- a -gloss, – false coloring- upon; color, varnish, cook, dress up, embroider; varnish right and puzzle wrong, exaggerate etc. 549.

invent, fabricate; trump –, get- up; forge, hatch, concoct; romance etc. (*imagine*) 515; cry 'wolf!'

dis-semble, -simulate; feign, assume, put on, pretend, make believe; play -false, – a double game; coquet; act –, play- a part; affect etc. 855; simulate, pass off for; counterfeit, fake, sham, make a show of; malinger; swing the lead; say the grapes are sour.

cant, play the hypocrite, sham Abraham, *faire pattes de velours*, put on the mask, clean the outside of the platter, lie like a conjuror; hang out –, hold out –, sail under- false colors; 'commend the poisoned chalice to the lips;' *ambiguas in vulgus spargere voces*; deceive etc. 545.

Adj. false, deceitful, mendacious, unveracious,

fraudulent, untruthful, dishonest; faith-, truth-, troth-less; un-fair, -candid; evasive; un-, dis-ingenuous; hollow, insincere, *Parthis mendacior*; forsworn.

canting; hypocrit-, jesuit-, pharisa-ical; tartuffish; Machiavelian; double-tongued, -faced, -handed, -minded, -hearted, -dealing; two-faced, bare-faced; Janus-faced; smooth-faced, -spoken, -tongued; plausible; mealy-mouthed; affected etc. 855.

collus-ive, -ory; artful etc. (*cunning*) 702; perfidious etc. 940, spurious etc. (*deceptive*) 545; untrue etc. 546; falsified etc. *v.*; covinous.

Adv. falsely etc. *adj.*; *à la Tartufe*, with a double tongue; out of whole cloth; slily etc. (*cunning*) 702.

545. Deception.—N. deception; falseness etc. 544; untruth etc. 546; impos-ition, -ture; fraud, deceit, guile; fraudulen-ce, -cy; covin; knavery etc. (*cunning*) 702; misrepresentation etc. (*falsehood*) 544.

delusion, gullery, bluff, spoof, *blague*; juggl-ing, -ery; sleight of hand, legerdemain; presti-giation, -digitation; magic etc. 992; conjur-ing, -ation; hocus pocus, jockeyship; trickery, coggery, hanky-panky, chicanery, pettifogging, sharp practice; *supercherie*, cozenage, circumvention, ingannation, collusion; treachery etc. 940; practical joke.

trick, cheat, wile, ruse, blind, feint, plant, bubble fetch, catch, chicane, juggle, reach, hocus, bite; thimble-rig, card-sharping, artful dodge, machination, swindle, hoax; tricks upon travellers; confidence trick; strategem etc. (*artifice*) 702; theft etc. 791.

snare, trap, pitfall, decoy, gin; sprin-ge, -gle; noose, hook; bait, decoy-duck, tub to the whale, baited trap, *guet-à-pens*; cobweb, net, meshes, toils, mouse-trap, bird-lime; ambush etc. 530; trap-door, sliding panel, false bottom; spring-net, -gun; mask, -ed battery; mine; booby trap.

Cornish hug; wolf in sheep's clothing etc. (*deceiver*) 548; disguise, -ment; false colors, masquerade, mummery, borrowed plumes; *pattes de velours*.

mockery etc. (*imitation*) 19; copy etc. 21; counterfeit, sham, brummagem, make-believe, forgery, fraud, fake; lie etc. 546; 'a mockery, a delusion, and a snare,' hollow mockery.

whited –, painted- sepulcher; tinsel, paste, false jewelry, scagliola, ormolu, German silver, Britannia metal, paint; jerry building; man of straw.

illusion etc. (*error*) 495; *ignis fatuus* etc. 423; *mirage* etc. 443.

V. deceive, take in; defraud, cheat, jockey, do, cozen, diddle, nab, gyp, chouse, double cross, play one false, bilk, cully, jilt, bite, pluck, swindle, victimize; abuse; mystify; blind one's eyes; blindfold, hoodwink, spoof, bluff; throw dust into the eyes, 'keep the word of promise to the ear and break it to the hope,' 'draw a herring across the trail.'

impose –, practice –, play –, put –, palm –, foist- upon; snatch a verdict.

circumvent, overreach; out-reach, -wit, -maneuvre; steal a march upon, give the go-by to, leave in the lurch.

set –, lay- a -trap, – snare- for; bait the hook, forlay, spread the toils, lime; decoy, waylay, lure, beguile, delude, inveigle; tra-, tre-pan; kidnap; let-, hook-in; trick; en-, in-trap, -snare, entoil, benet; nick, springe; catch, – in a trap; sniggle, entangle, illaqueate, hocus, practice on one's credulity, dupe, gull, hoax, fool, befool, bamboozle; hum, -bug; gammon, stuff up, dope, sell; play a -trick, – practical joke- upon one; balk, trip up, throw a tub to a whale; fool to the top of one's bent, send on -a wild goose chase, – a fool's errand, make -game, – a tool, – an April fool, – an ass- of; trifle with, cajole, flatter; come over etc. (*influence*) 615; gild the pill, make things pleasant, divert, put a good face upon; dissemble etc. 544.

cog, – the dice, play with marked cards; live by one's wits, play at hide and seek; obtain money under false pretences etc. (*steal*) 791; conjure, juggle, practice chicanery; gerrymander.

play –, palm –, foist –, fob- off.

lie etc. 544; misinform etc. 538; mislead etc. (*error*) 495; betray etc. 940; be -deceived etc. 547.

Adj. deceived etc. *v.*; deceiving etc. *v.*; cunning etc. 702; prestigi-ous, -atory; decept-ive, -ious; deceitful, covinous; delus-ive, -ory; illus-ive, -ory; elusive, insidious, *ad captandum vulgus.*

untrue etc. 546; mock, sham, make-believe, counterfeit, faked, pseudo, spurious, so-called, pretended, feigned, trumped up, bogus, scamped, fraudulent, tricky, factitious, artificial, bastard; surreptitious, illegitimate, contraband, adulterated, sophisticated; unsound, rotten at the core; colorable; disguised; meretricious; tinsel, pinchbeck, plated; catch-penny; Brummagem; simulated etc. 544.

Adv. under -false colors, – the garb of, – cover of; over the left.

Phr. *fronti nulla fides.*

546. Untruth.—N. untruth, falsehood, lie, story, thing that is not, flb, bounce, crammer, taradiddle, whopper.

forgery, fabrication, invention; mis-statement, -representation; perversion, falsification, gloss, *suggestio falsi*; exaggeration etc. 549.

fiction; fable, nursery tale; romance etc. (*imagination*) 515; untrue –, false –, trumped up- -story, – statement; thing devised by the enemy; *canard*; shave, sell, hum, yarn, traveler's tale, Canterbury tale, cock and bull story, fairy tale, clap-trap.

myth, moonshine, bosh, all my eye, -and Betty Martin, mare's nest, farce.

irony; half truth, white lie, pious fraud; mental reservation etc. (*concealment*) 528.

pretence, pretext; false -plea etc. 617; subterfuge, evasion, shift, shuffle, make-believe; sham etc. (*deception*) 545.

profession, empty words; Judas kiss etc. (*hypocrisy*) 544; disguise etc. (*mask*) 530.

V. have a false meaning; not ring true.

pretend, sham, feign, counterfeit, make believe.

Adj. untrue, false, trumped up; void of –, without- foundation; far from the truth, false as dicer's oaths; unfounded, *ben trovato*, invented, fabulous, fabricated, forged; fict-, fact-, supposit-, surrept-itious; e-, il-lusory; ironical; satirical; evasive; *soi-disant* etc. (*misnamed*) 565.

Phr. *se non e vero e ben trovato.*

547. Dupe.—N. dupe, gull, gudgeon, *gobemouche*, cull, cully, victim, sucker, pigeon, April fool; laughing stock etc. 857; Cyclops, simple Simon, flat, mug, greenhorn; fool etc. 501; puppet, cat's paw.

V. be -deceived etc. 545, – the dupe of; fall into a trap; swallow –, nibble at- the bait; bite; catch a Tartar.

Adj. credulous etc. 486; mistaken etc. (*error*) 495.

548. Deceiver.—N. deceiver etc. (deceive etc. 545); dissembler, hypocrite; sophist, Pharisee, Jesuit, Mawworm, Pecksniff, Joseph Surface, Tartufe, Janus; serpent, snake in the grass, cockatrice, Judas, wolf in sheep's clothing; Molly Maguire; jilt; shuffler.

liar etc. (lie etc. 544; story-teller, perjurer, false-witness, *mentuer à triple étage*, Scapin.

imposter, pretender, capper, decoy, fraud, *soi-disant*, humbug; adventurer; Cagliostro, Fernam Mendez Pinto; ass in lion's skin etc. (*bungler*) 701; actor etc. (*stage player*) 599.

quack, *charlatan*, mountebank, saltimbanco, *saltimbanque*, empiric, quacksalver, medicaster.

conjuror, juggler, magician, necromancer, trickster, prestidigitator, medium, jockey; crimp; decoy-duck, stool pigeon; rogue, knave, cheat; swindler etc. (*thief*) 792; jobber.

549. Exaggeration.—N. exaggeration; expansion etc. 194; hyperbole, stretch, strain, coloring; high coloring, caricature, *caricatura*; extravagance etc. (*nonsense*) 497; Baron Munchausen; men in buckram, yarn, fringe, embroidery, traveler's tale; Pelion upon Ossa.

storm in a teacup; much ado about nothing etc. (*over-estimation*) 482; puffery etc. (*boasting*) 884; rant etc. (*turgescence*) 577.

figure of speech, *façon de parler*; stretch of-fancy, – the imagination; flight of fancy etc. (*imagination*) 515.

false coloring etc. (*falsehood*) 544; aggravation etc. 835.

V. exaggerate, magnify, pile up, aggravate; amplify etc. (*expand*) 194; overestimate etc. 482; hyperbolize; over-charge, -state, -draw, -lay, -shoot the mark, -praise; make -much, – the most- of; strain, – a point; stretch, – a point; go great lengths; spin a long yarn; draw –, shoot with- a long-bow; deal in the marvelous.

out -Herod Herod, run riot, talk at random.

heighten, overcolor; color -highly, – too highly; embroider, *broder*; flourish; color etc. (*misrepresent*) 544; puff etc. (*boast*) 884.

Adj. exaggerated etc. *v.*; overwrought; bombastic etc. (*magniloquent*) 577; hyperbolical, on stilts; fabulous, extravagant, preposterous, egregious, *outré*, high-flying.

Adv. hyperbolically etc. *adj.*

550. Indication.—N. indication; symbol-ism, -ization; semeio-logy, -tics; sign of the times.

lineament, feature, *trait*, characteristic, trick, diagnostic; divining-rod; cloven hoof; footfall; means of recognition; earmark.

sign, symbol; ind-ex, -ice, -icator; point, -er; marker; exponent, note, token, symptom.

type, figure, emblem, cipher, device; representation etc. 554; epigraph, motto, posy.

gest-ure, -iculation; pantomime; wink, glance, leer; nod, shrug, beck; touch, nudge; grip; dactylo-logy, -nomy; freemasonry, telegraphy, chirology, by-play, dumb-show; cue; hint etc. 527; clue, clew, key, scent, tract etc. 551.

signal, -post; rocket, blue light; watch-fire, -tower; telegraph, semaphore, flag-staff; cresset, fiery cross; calumet; heliograph, signal-, flash-lamp; radar, radar signal, pulse –, microwave –, radar; tracing, blips, pips.

mark, line, stroke, dash, score, stripe, streak, scratch, tick, dot, point, notch, nick, blaze; asterisk, red letter, Italics, heavy type, inverted commas, quotation marks, sublineation, underlining, jotting; print; impr-int, -ess, ession; note, annotation, mark of exclamation.

[For identification] badge, criterion; counter-check, -mark, -sign, -foil, duplicate, tally; label, tab, ticket, stub, billet, letter, counter, *tessera*, card, bill, check; witness, voucher; stamp; *cachet*; trade –, Hall- mark; broad arrow; signature; address –, visiting- card; *carte de visite*; credentials etc. (*evidence*) 467; passport, identity book; attestation; hand, – writing, sign-manual; cipher; monogram, – mark, seal, sigil, signet; autograph, -y, paraph, brand; superscription; in-, en-dorsement; title, heading, rubric, docket; *mot -de passe*, – *du guet*; *passe-parole*; shibboleth; watch-, catch-, pass-word; open *sesame*.

insignia, banner, -et, -ol; bandrol; flag, colors, streamer, standard, eagle, labarum, oriflamb, *oriflamme*; figure-head; ensign; pen-non, -nant, -dant; burgee, blue Peter, jack, ancient, gonfalon, union-jack; tricolor, stars and stripes; bunting.

hearldry, crest; coat of –, arms; armorial bearings, hatchment; e-, scutcheon; shield, supporters; livery, uniform; cockade, *epaulette*, brassard, chevron; garland, chaplet, love-knot, fillet, favor.

[Of locality] beacon, cairn, post, staff, flagstaff, hand, pointer, vane, cock, weathercock; guide-, hand-, finger-, directing-, sign-post; pillars of Hercules, pharos, signal fire; land-, sea-mark; lighthouse, balize; pole-, load-, lode-star; cynosure, guide; address, direction, name; sign, -board.

[Of the future] warning etc. 668; omen etc. 512; prefigurement etc. 511. [Of the past] trace record etc. 551. [Of danger] warning etc. 668; alarm etc. 669. [Of authority] scepter etc. 747. [Of triumph] trophy etc. 733. [Of quantity] gauge etc. 466. [Of distance] mile-stone, -post. [Of disgrace] brand, fool's cap, stigma, mark of Cain. [For detection] check, tell-tale; test etc. (*experiment*) 463.

notification etc. (*information*) 527; advertisement etc. (*publication*) 531.

word of command, call; bugle-, trumpet-call; reveille, taps; bell, alarum, cry; battle –, rallying-cry.

church, bell, angelus, sacring bell; muezzin.

exposition etc. (*explanation*) 522; proof etc. (*evidence*) 463; pattern etc. (*prototype*) 22.

V. indicate; be the -sign etc. *n.*- of; denote,

betoken; argue, testify etc. (*evidence*) 467; bear the -impress etc. *n.*- of; con-note, -notate.

represent, stand for; typify etc. (*prefigure*) 511; symbolize.

put -an indication, – a mark, – etc. *n.*; note, mark, tick, blaze, stamp, earmark; set one's seal upon; label, ticket, docket; dot, spot, score, dash, trace, chalk; print; im-print, -press, surprint; engrave, stereotype, electrotype.

signal, transmit, send, radiate, beam, deflect, echo, bounce back, return.

make a -sign etc. *n.*; signalize; give –, hang out- a signal; beck, -on; gesture; not; wink, glance, leer, nudge, shrug, tip the wink; gesticulate; raise –, hold up- the-finger, – hand; saw the air, suit the action to the word.

wave –, unfurl –, hoist –, hang out- a banner etc. *n.*; wave -the hand, – a kerchief; give the cue etc. (*inform*) 527; show one's colors; give –, sound- an alarm; beat the drum, sound the trumpets, raise a cry.

sign, seal, attest etc. (*evidence*) 467; underline etc. (*give importance to*) 642; call attention to etc. (*attention*) 457; give notice etc. (*inform*) 527.

Adj. indicat-ing etc. *v.*; -ive, -ory; de-, connotative; diacritical, representative, typical, symbolic, pantomimic, pathognomonic, symptomatic, ominous, characteristic, demonstrative, diagnostic, exponential, emblematic, armorial; individual etc. (*special*) 79.

known –, recognizable- by; indicated etc. *v.*; pointed, marked.

[Capable of being denoted] denotable; indelible.

Adv. in token of; symbolically etc. *adj.*; in dumb show.

Phr. *ecce signum*; *ex ungue leonem, ex pede Herculem.*

551. Record.—N. trace, vestige, relic, remains; scar, *cicatrix*; foot-step, mark, -print; track, mark, wake, trail, spoor, scent, *piste.*

monument, hatchment, escutcheon, slab, tablet, trophy, achievement; obelisk, pillar, column, monolith, cromlech, dolmen; memorial; *memento* etc. (*memory*) 505; testimonial, medal, ribbon, order; commemoration etc. (*celebration*) 883.

record, note, minute; *dossier*; register, -try; census, roll etc. (*list*) 86; cartulary, diptych, Domesday book; entry, memorandum, indorsement, inscription, copy, duplicate, docket; notch etc. (*mark*) 550; muniment, deed etc. (*security*) 771; document; deposition, *procès-verbal*; affidavit; certificate etc. (*evidence*) 467.

note-, memorandum-, pocket-, commonplace-book; portfolio; scoring-board, -sheet; bulletin board; card index, file; pigeon-holes, *excerpta, adversaria*, jottings, dottings.

gazette, -er; newspaper, magazine etc. 531; alman-ac, -ack; calendar, ephemeris, noctuary, diary, log, journal, account-, cash-, day-book, ledger.

archive, scroll, state-paper, Congressional Record, return, blue-book; statistics etc. 86; *compte rendu*; Acts –, Transactions –, Proceedings- of; Hansard's Debates; chronicle, annals; legend; history, biography etc. 594.

registration; en-, in-rolment; tabulation; entry, booking; signature etc. (*identification*) 550; recorder etc. 553; journalism.

drawing, photograph etc. 554; phonograph –, gramophone- record; music roll.

V. record; put –, place- upon record; go on record; chronicle, calendar, hand down to posterity; keep up the memory of etc. (*remember*) 505; commemorate etc. (*celebrate*) 883; report etc. (*inform*) 527, commit to –, reduce to- writing; put –, set down- -in writing, – in black and white; put –, jot –, take –, write –, note –, set-down; note, minute, put on paper; take –, make- a -note, – minute, – memorandum; make a return.

mark etc. (*indicate*) 550; sign etc. (*attest*) 467.

enter, book; post, – up; insert, make an entry of; mark –, tick- off; register, list, docket, enroll, inscroll; file etc. (*store*) 636.

Adv. on record.

552. Obliteration. [Suppression of sign.]—**N.** obliteration; erasure, rasure; effacement; interference; cancel, -lation; cassation; circumduction; deletion, blot; *tabula rasa.*

V. efface, obliterate, erase, rase, expunge, cancel; blot –, take –, rub –, scratch –, strike –, wipe –, wash –, sponge- out; wipe –, rub- off; wipe away; deface, render illegible; draw the pen through, apply the sponge.

interfere, jam, black-, block-out; clutter, screen.

be -effaced etc.; leave no -trace etc. 449; 'leave not a rack behind.'

Adj. obliterated etc. *v.*; out of print; printless; leaving no trace; intestate; un-recorded, -registered, -written.

Int. *dele*; out with it!

553. Recorder.—N. recorder, notary, clerk; regis-trar, -trary, -ter; prothonotary; amanuensis, secretary, scribe, stenographer, remembrancer, book-keeper, *custos rotulorum*, Master of the Rolls.

annalist; histori-an, -ographer; chronicler, journalist, reporter, columnist; biographer etc. (*narrator*) 594; antiquary etc. (*antiquity*) 122; memorialist.

draughtsman etc. 559; engraver 558; photographer, cinematographer, camera man.

Recording instrument, recorder, camera, phonograph, gramophone, dictaphone, telegraphone, telautograph, printing telegraph, tape recorder, ticker, time recorder, cash register, turnstile, speedometer, voting machine, seismograph, radar, oscilloscope, teletypewriter, pari-mutuel, photostat.

554. Representation.—N. represent-ation, -ment; imitation etc. 19; illustration, delineation, depictment, portrayal; imagery, portraiture, iconography; design, -ing; art, fine arts; painting etc. 556; sculpture etc. 557; engraving etc. 558; photography, radiography, skiagraphy.

person-ation, -ification; impersonation; drama etc. 599.

picture, drawing, sketch, draught, draft; tracing; copy etc. 21; photo-, helio-graph; daguerreo-, talbo-, calo-, helio-type; cabinet, *carte-de-visite*, snapshot; X-ray photograph; radio-gram, -graph, skia-graph, -gram.

image, likeness, icon, portrait; striking –, speaking- likeness; very image; effigy, fac-simile.

figure, – head; puppet, doll, *figurine*, aglet, manikin, lay-figure, model, *marionnette*, *fantoccini*, bust; waxwork, statue, -tte, automaton, Robot.

hieroglyphic, anaglyph; dia-, mono-gram, -graph.

map, plan, chart; ground plan, projection, elevation; ichno-, carto-graphy; atlas; outline, scheme; view etc. (*painting*) 556.

artist, draughtsman etc. 559.

V. represent, delineate; depict, -ure; portray; picture; take –, catch- a likeness etc. *n.*; hit off, photograph, daguerreotype; figure; shadow -forth, – out; adumbrate; body forth; describe etc. 594; trace, copy; mold.

dress up; illustrate, symbolize.

paint etc. 556; carve etc. 557; engrave etc. 558.

person-ate, -ify; impersonate; assume a character; pose as; act; play etc. (*drama*) 599; mimic etc. (*imitate*) 19; hold the mirror up to nature.

Adj. represent-ing etc. *v.*, -ative; illustrative; represented etc. *v.*; imitative, figurative.

like etc. 17; graphic etc. (*descriptive*) 594.

555. Misrepresentation.—N. misrepresentation, distortion, exaggeration; daubing etc. *v.*; bad likeness, daub, sign-painting; scratch, caricature; *anamorphosis*.

V. misrepresent, distort, overdraw, travesty, parody, burlesque, exaggerate, caricature, daub.

Adj. misrepresented etc. *v.*

556. Painting.—N. painting; depicting; drawing etc. *v.*; design; perspective, skiagraphy; *chiaroscuro* etc. (*light*) 420; composition; treatment, values, atmosphere, tone, technique.

historical –, portrait –, miniature –, landscape –, marine –, flower –, scene- painting; scenography.

school, style; the grand style, high art, *genre*, portraiture; ornamental art etc. 847.

mono-, poly-chrome; *grisaille*.

pallet, palette; easel; brush, pencil, stump; blacklead, charcoal, crayons, chalk, pastel; paint etc. (*coloring matter*) 428; water-, body-, oil-color; oils, oil-paint; varnish etc. 356*a*; *gouache*, tempera, distemper, fresco, water-glass; enamel; encaustic painting; *graffito*, *gesso;* mosiac; tapestry.

picture, painting, piece, *tableau*, canvas; oil etc.-painting; fresco, cartoon; easel –, cabinet- picture; drawing, draught, draft; pencil etc. –, watercolor-drawing; sketch; outline; study.

portrait etc. (*representation*) 554; whole –, full –, half- length; kitcat, head; miniature; shade, *silhouette*; profile.

landscape, sea-piece, -scape; view, scene, prospect; interior; bird's- eye view; pan-, di-orama; still life.

picture –, art- gallery; *studio*, *atelier*.

V. paint, design, limn, draw, sketch, pencil, scratch, shade, stipple, hatch, dash off, chalk out, square up; color, dead-color, wash, varnish; draw in -pencil etc. *n.*; paint in -oils etc. *n.*; stencil; depict etc. (*represent*) 554.

Adj. painted etc. *v.*; pictorial, graphic, picturesque, decorative; classical, romantic, pre-Raphaelite, modern, cubist, futurist, vorticist.

pencil, oil etc. *n.*

Adv. in -pencil etc. *n.*

Phr. *fecit, delineavit.*

557. Sculpture.—N. sculpture, insculpture; carving etc. *v.*; statuary, ceramics, plastic arts.

high –, low –, bas- relief; relievo; *basso-*, *alto-*, *mezzo-relievo*; *intaglio*, anaglyph; medal, -lion; *cameo*.

marble, bronze, *terra cotta*; ceramic ware, pottery, porcelain, china, earthenware, faïence, enamel, *cloisonné*.

statue etc. (*image*) 554; cast etc. (*copy*) 21; glyptotheca.

V. sculpture, carve, cut, chisel, model, mold; cast.

Adj. sculptured etc. *v.*; in relief, anaglyptic, ceroplastic, ceramic; parian; marble etc. *n.*

558. Engraving.—N. engraving, chalcography; line –, mezzotint –, stipple –, chalk- engraving; dry-point, bur; etching, aquatinta; plate –, copper-plate –, steel –, wood-, process-, photo-engraving; xylo-, ligno-, glypto-, cero-, litho-, chromolitho-, photolitho-, zinco-, glypho- -graphy, -graph.

impression, print, engraving, plate; steel-, copper-plate; etching; mezzo-, aqua-, litho-tint; cut, woodcut, block; stereo-, grapho-, auto-, helio-type; half-tone; *photogravure*, *rotogravure*.

graver, *burin*, etching-point, style; plate, stone, wood-block, negative; die, punch, stamp.

printing; plate –, copper-plate –, intaglio –, anastatic –, lithographic –, color –, three color-printing; type-printing etc. 591.

illustr-, illumin-ation; *vignette*, initial letter, *cul de lampe*, tail-piece.

V. engrave, grave, stipple, scrape, etch; bite, – in; lithograph etc. *n.*; print.

Adj. insculptured; engraved etc. *v.*

Phr. *sculpsit, imprimit.*

559. Artist.—N. artist; painter, limner, drawer, sketcher, delineator; cartoon-, caricatur-ist, designer, engraver; draughtsman; copyist; enameller, -list.

historical –, landscape –, genre –, marine –, flower –, portrait –, miniature –, scene –, sign-painter; engraver; Apelles; sculptor, carver, chaser, modeller, lapidary, *figuriste*, statuary; Phidias, Praxiteles; Royal Academician.

photographer, retoucher.

560. Language.—N. language; phraseology etc. 569; speech etc. 582; tongue, lingo, vernacular, slang; mother –, vulgar –, native- tongue; household words; King's *or* Queen's English; idiom; dialect etc. 563.

volapuk, esperanto, ido, occidental, Ro.

confusion of tongues, Babel, *pasigraphie*; pantomime etc. (*signs*) 550; *onomatopaeia.*

phil-, gloss-, glott-ology; linguistics, chrestomathy; paleo-logy; -graphy; comparative grammar.

literature, letters, polite literature, *belles lettres*, muses, humanities, *literae humaniores*, republic of letters, dead languages, classics; genius of a language; scholarship etc. (*knowledge*) 490.

linguist etc. (*scholar*) 492.

V. speak, say, express by words etc. 566.

Adj. lingu-al, -istic; dialectic; vernacular, current, colloquial, slangy; bilingual, polyglot; literary.

561. Letter.—N. letter; character; hieroglyphic etc. (*writing*) 590; type etc. (*printing*) 591; capitals; majus-, minus-cule; alphabet, ABC, abecedary, christcross row, chrisscross row.

consonant, vowel, diphthong; mute, surd; sonant, liquid, labial, dental, palatal, gutteral.

syllable; mono-, dis-, poly-syllable; affix, prefix, suffix.

spelling, orthography; phon-ography, -etic spelling; ana-, meta-grammatism.

cipher, monogram, anagram; double – acrostic.

V. spell.

Adj. literal; alphabetical, abecedarian; syllabic; uncial etc. (*writing*) 590; phonetic, voiced, mute etc. *n.*

562. Word.—N. word, term, vocable; name etc. 564; phrase etc. 566; root, etymon; derivative; part of speech etc. (*grammar*) 567.

dictionary, vocabulary, word book, lexicon, index, glossary, thesaurus, *gradus, delectus*, concordance.

etymology, lexicology, derivation; phonology, orthoepy; gloss-, termin-, orism-ology; paleology etc. (*philology*) 560; comparative philology.

lexicograph-er, -y; glossographer etc. (*scholar*) 492; etymologist; logolept.

verbosity, verbiage, loquacity etc. 584.

Adj. verbal, literal; titular, nominal. [Similarly derived] conjugate, paraonymous; derivative.

Adv. verbally etc. *adj.*; *verbatim* etc. (*exactly*) 494.

563. Neology.—N. neolo-gy, -gism; newfangled expression; barbarism; caconym; archaism, black letter, monkish Latin; corruption; missaying, antiphrasis.

paronomasia, play upon words; wordplay etc. (*wit*) 842; *double-entente* etc. (*ambiguity*) 520; palindrome, paragram, clinch; abuse of -language, – terms.

dialect, brogue, *patois*, provincialism, broken English, *lingua franca*; Brit-, Gall-, Scott-, Hibernicism; American-ism; Gipsy lingo, Romany, pidgin English.

dog Latin, macaronics, gibberish, confusion of tongues, Babel; jargon.

colloquialism etc. (*figure of speech*) 521; byword; technicality, lingo, slang, cant, *argot*, St. Giles's Greek, thieves' Latin, peddler's French, flash tongue, Billingsgate, Wall Street slang.

pseudonym etc. (*misnomer*) 565; Mr. So-and-so; what d'ye call 'em, what's his name; thingum-my, -bob; *je ne sais quoi.*

neologist, coiner of words.

V. coin words.

Adj. neologic, -al; rare; archaic; obsolete etc. (*old*) 124; colloquial, dialectic, slang, cant.

564. Nomenclature.—N. nomenclature; naming etc. *v.*; nuncupation, nomination, baptism; orismology; *onomatopaeia*; antonomasia.

name; appella-tion, -tive; designation; title; head, -ing, caption; denomination; by-name, epithet.

style, proper name; prae-, ag-, cog-nomen; patronymic, surname; cognomination; compellation, description; empty -title, – name; handle to one's name; namesake, eponym.

synonym, antonym.

term, expression, noun; by-word; convertible terms etc. 522; technical term; cant etc. 563.

V. name, call, term, denominate, designate, style, entitle, intitule, clepe, dub, christen, baptize, nickname, characterize, specify, define, distinguish by the name of; label etc. (*mark*) 550.

be -called etc. *v.*; take –, bear –, go (*or* be known) by –, go (*or* pass) under –, rejoice in- the name of.

Adj. named etc. *v.*; hight, yclept, known as; what one may -well, – fairly, – properly, – fitly- call.

nuncupa-tory, -tive; cognominal, titular, nominal; orismological.

565. Misnomer.—N. misnomer; *lucus a non lucendo*; Mrs. Malaprop; what d'ye call 'em etc. (*neologism*) 563.

nickname, *sobriquet*, by-name, handle, moniker; assumed -name, – title; *alias*; *nom de - guerre*, – *plume*, – *theâtre*; pseudonym, pen name, stage name.

V. mis-name, -call, - term; nickname; assume -a name, – an alias.

Adj. misnamed etc. *v.*; pseudonymous; *soi-disant*; self-called, -styled, -christened; so-called.

nameless, anonymous; without a –, having no- name; innominate, unnamed.

Adv. in no sense.

566. Phrase.—N. phrase, expression, set phrase; sentence, paragraph; figure of speech etc. 521; idi-om, -otism; turn of expression.

paraphrase etc. (*synonym*) 522; periphrase etc. (*circumlocution*) 573; motto etc. (*proverb*) 496. phraseology etc. 569.

V. express, phrase; word, – it; give -words, – expression- to; voice; arrange in –, clothe in –, put into –, express by- words; couch in terms; find words to express; speak by the card.

Adj. expressed etc. *v.*; idiomatic.

Adv. in -round, – set, – good, set- terms; in set phrases.

567. Grammar.—N. grammar, accidence, syntax, *praxis*, analysis, paradigm, punctuation; parts of speech, inflexion, case, declension, conjugation; *jus et norma loquendi*; Lindley Murray etc. (*school-book*) 542; correct style; philology etc. (*language*) 560.

V. parse, analyze; decline, conjugate; punctuate.

Adj. grammatical; syntactic; inflexional.

568. Solecism.—N. solecism; bad –, false –, faulty- grammar; slip, error; slip of the -pen, – tongue; *lapsus calami-, – linguae*; *faux pas*; slipslop; bull.

V. use -bad, – faulty- grammar; solecize, commit a solecism; murder the -King's, – Queen's- English; break Priscian's head.

Adj. ungrammatical; in-correct, -accurate; faulty, improper, incongruous, abnormal.

569. Style.—N. style, diction, phraseology, wording; manner, strain; composition; mode of expression, choice of words, literary power, ready pen, pen of a ready writer; command of language etc. (*eloquence*) 582; authorship; *la morgue littéraire*.

V. express by words etc. 566; write.

570. Perspicuity.—N. perspicuity etc. (*intelligibility*) 518; plain speaking etc. (*manifestation*) 525; defin-iteness, -ition; exactness etc. 494; perspicuousness, logical acuteness.

Adj. lucid etc. (*intelligible*) 518; explicit etc. (*manifest*) 525; exact etc. 494.

571. Obscurity.—N. obscurity etc. (*unintelligibility*) 519; involution; hard words; ambiguity etc. 520; vagueness etc. 475, inexactness etc. 495; what d'ye call 'em etc. (*neologism*) 563; cloudiness, confusion.

Adj. obscure etc. *n.*; crabbed, involved, confused.

572. Conciseness.—N. conciseness etc. *adj.*; brevity, 'the soul of wit,' laconism; Tacitus; ellipsis; syncope; abridgment etc. (*shortening*) 201; compression etc. 195; epitome etc. 596; monostitch; portmanteau word, telescope word, protogram.

V. be -concise etc. *adj.*; condense etc. 195; abridge etc. 201; abstract etc. 596; come to the point.

Adj. concise, brief, short, terse, close; to the point, exact; neat, compact, condensed, pointed; laconic, curt, pithy, trenchant, summary; pregnant; compendious etc. (*compendium*) 596; succinct; elliptical, epigrammatic, crisp, sententious.

Adv. concisely etc. *adj.*; briefly, summarily; in -brief, – short, – a word, – few words, – a nutshell; for shortness sake; to -come to the point, – make a long story short, – cut the matter short, – be brief; it comes to this, the long and short of it is.

573. Diffuseness.—N. diffuseness etc. *adj.*; amplification etc. *v.*; dilating etc. *v.*; verbosity, *verbiage*, wordiness, cloud of words, *copia verborum*; flow of words etc. (*loquacity*) 584.

poly-, tauto-, batto-, perisso-logy; pleonasm, exuberance, redundance; thrice-told tale; prolixity; circumlocution, *ambages*; periphra-se, -sis; roundabout phrases; episode; expletive; penny-a-lining; padding, drivel, twaddle, rigmarole; richness etc. 577.

V. be -diffuse etc. *adj.*; run out on, descant, expatiate, enlarge, dilate, amplify, expand, inflate, pad; launch –, branch- out; rant.

maunder, prose; harp upon etc. (*repeat*) 104; dwell on, insist upon.

digress, ramble, *battre la campagne*, beat about the bush, perorate, spin a long yarn, protract; spin –, swell –, draw- out, drivel.

Adj. dif-, pro-fuse; wordy, verbose, largiloquent, copious, exuberant, effusive, pleonastic, lengthy; long, -some, -winded, -spun, -drawn out; diffusive, spun out, protracted, prolix, prosing, maundering; circumlocutory, periphrastic, ambagious, roundabout; digressive; dis-, ex-cursive; rambling, episodic; flatulent, frothy.

Adv. diffusely etc. *adj.*; at large, ***in extenso***; about it and about it.

574. Vigor.—N. vigor, power, force; boldness, raciness etc. *adj.*; spirit, point, antithesis, piquancy; *verve*, glow, fire, warmth, ardor, enthusiasm; 'thoughts that breathe and words that burn;' strong language; punch; gravity, sententiousness; elevation, loftiness, sublimity.

eloquence; command of -words, – language.

Adj. vigorous, nervous, powerful, forcible, trenchant, mordant, biting, incisive, impressive; sensational.

spirited, lively, glowing, sparkling, racy, bold, slashing; pungent, *piquant*, full of point, pointed, pithy, antithetical; sententious.

lofty, elevated, sublime, grand, weighty, ponderous; eloquent; vehement, petulant, impassioned; poetic.

Adv. in -glowing, – good set, – no measured- terms.

575. Feebleness.—N. feebleness etc. *adj.*;

Adj. feeble, bald, tame, meager, insipid, nerve-les, jejune, vapid, trashy, cold, frigid, poor, dull, dry, languid; pros-ing, -y, -aic; unvaried, monotonous, weak, frail, washy, wishy-washy, sloppy; sketchy, slight; careless, slovenly, loose, lax; slip-shod, -slop; inexact; dis-jointed, -connected; puerile, childish; flatulent; rambling etc. (*diffuse*) 573.

576. Plainness.—N. plainness etc. *adj.*; simplicity, severity; plain -terms, – English; Saxon English; household words.

V. speak plainly; call a spade 'a spade;' plunge *in medias res*; come to the point.

Adj. plain, simple; un-ornamented, -adorned, -varnished; home-ly, -spun; neat; severe, chaste, pure, Saxon; commonplace, matter of fact, natural, prosaic, sober, unimaginative.

dry, unvaried, monotonous etc. 575.

Adv. in plain -terms, – words, – English, – common parlance; point blank.

577. Ornament.—N. ornament; floridness etc. *adj.*; turg-idity, -escence; altiloquence etc. *adj.*; orotundity; declamation, teratology; well-rounded periods; elegance etc. 578.

inversion, antithesis, alliteration, *paronomasia*; figurativeness etc. (*metaphor*) 521.

flourish; flowers of -speech, – rhetoric; euphuism, -emism.

big-, high-sounding words; macrology, *sesquipedalia verba*, sesquipedalianism; Alexandrine; inflation, pretension; rant, bombast, fustian, bunkum, balderdash, prose run mad; fine writing; Minerva press.

phrasemonger; euph-uist, -emist.

V. ornament, overlay with ornament, overcharge; smell of the lamp.

Adj. ornamented etc. *v.*; beautified etc. 847; ornate, florid, rich, flowery; euph-uistic, -emistic; sonorous; high-, big-sounding; inflated, swelling, tumid; turg-id, -escent; pedantic, pompous, stilted; high-flown, -flowing; sententious, rhetorical, declamatory; grandiose; grand-, magn-, altiloquent; sesquipedal, -ian; Johnsonian, mouthy; bombastic; fustian; frothy, flashy, flaming, flamboyant.

antithetical, alliterative; figurative etc. 521; artificial etc. (*inelegant*) 579.

Adv. *ore rotundo*; with rounded phrase.

578. Elegance.—N. elegance, purity, grace, ease, felicity, distinction, gracefulness, refinement, readiness etc. *adj.*; concinnity, euphony, numerosity, balance, rythym, symmetry, proportion; restraint; good taste, propriety.

well rounded –, well turned –, flowing-periods; the right word in the right place; antithesis etc. 577.

purist, stylist.

V. point an antithesis, round a period.

Adj. elegant, polished, classical, Attic, correct, Ciceronian, artistic; chaste, pure, Saxon, academical.

graceful, easy, readable, fluent, flowing, tripping; unaffected, natural, unlabored; mellifluous; euph-onious, -emistic; rhythmical, balanced, symmetrical.

felicitous, happy, neat; well –, neatly- -put, – expressed.

579. Inelegance.—N. inelegance; vulgarity, bad taste; stiffness etc. *adj.*; unlettered Muse; barbarism; slang etc. 563; solecism etc. 568; mannerism etc. (*affectation*) 855; euphuism; fustian etc. 577; cacophony; want of balance; words that -break the teeth, – dislocate the jaw.

V. be -inelegant etc. *adj.*

Adj. inelegant, graceless, ungraceful, unpolished; harsh, abrupt; dry, stiff, cramped, formal, *guindé*; forced, labored, awkward; artificial, mannered, ponderous; turgid etc. 577; affected, euphuistic; barbarous, uncouth, grotesque, rude, crude, halting; vulgar, offensive to ears polite.

580. Voice.—N. voice; vocality; organ, lungs, bellows; good –, fine –, powerful etc. (*loud*) 404 –, musical etc. 413- voice; intonation; tone etc. (*sound*) 402- of voice.

vocalization; cry etc. 411; strain, utterance, prolation; exclam-, ejacul-, vocifer-ation; enunci-, articul-ation; articulate sound; distinctness; clearness, – of articulation; stage whisper; delivery; attack.

accent, -uation; emphasis, stress; broad –, strong –, pure –, native –, foreign- accent; pronunciation.

[Word similarly pronounced] homonym.

orthoepy; euphony etc. (*melody*) 413.

gastri-, ventri-loquism; ventriloquist; polyphonism, -ist.

[Science of voice] phonology etc. (*sound*) 402.

V. sing, speak, utter, breathe, voice; give -utterance, – tongue; cry etc. (*shout*) 411; ejaculate, rap out; vocalize, prolate, articulate, enunciate, enounce, pronounce, accentuate, aspirate, deliver, mouth; emit, murmur, whisper, – in the ear, croon, yodel.

Adj. vocal, phonetic, oral; ejaculatory, articulate, distinct, stertorous; enunciative; accentuated, aspirated; euphonious etc. (*melodious*) 413.

581. Aphony—N. aphony, *aphonia*; dumbness etc. *adj.*; obmutescence; absence –, want- of voice; dysphony; silence etc. (*taciturnity*) 585; raucity; harsh etc. 410 –, unmusical etc. 414- voice; *falsetto*, 'childish treble;' mute, dummy, deaf mute.

V. keep silence etc. 585; speak -low, – softly; whisper etc. (*faintness*) 405.

silence; render -mute, – silent etc. 403; muzzle, muffle, suppress, smother, gag, strike dumb, dumbfound, -founder; drown the voice, put to silence, stop one's mouth, cut one short.

stick in the throat.

Adj. aphon-ous, -ic, dumb, mute; deaf-mute, –

and dumb; mum; tongue-tied; breath-, tongue-, voice-, speech-, word-less; mute as a -fish, – stock-fish, – mackerel; silent etc. (*taciturn*) 585; muzzled; in-articulate, -audible.

croaking, raucous, hoarse, husky, dry, hollow, sepulchral, hoarse as a raven.

Adv. with -bated breath, – the finger on the lips; *sotto voce*; in a -low tone, – cracked voice, – broken voice; in an aside.

Phr. *vox faucibus haesit.*

582. Speech.—N. speech, faculty of speech; locution, talk, parlance, verbal intercourse, prolation, oral communication, word of mouth, *parole*, palaver, prattle; effusion.

oration, recitation, delivery, say, address, speech, lecture, harangue, sermon, *tirade*, screed, formal speech, salutatory, peroration; prelection; speechifying; soliloquy etc. 589; allocution etc. 586; interlocution etc. 588.

oratory; elo-cution, -quence; rhetoric, declamation; grandi-, multi-loquence; burst of eloquence; facundity; talkativeness; flow –, command- of -words, – language; *copia verborum*; power of speech, gift of the gab; *usus loquendi.*

speaker etc. *v.*; spokesman, pro-, inter-locutor; mouthpiece, Hermes; ora-tor, -trix, -tress; Demosthenes, Cicero; rhetorician; stump –, platform- orator, tub-thumper; elocutionist; speech-maker, patterer, *improvisatore*.

V. speak, – of; say, utter, pronounce, deliver, give utterance to; utter –, pour- forth; breathe, let fall, come out with; rap –, blurt- out; have on one's lips; have at the -end, – tip- of one's tongue.

break silence; open one's -lips, – mouth; lift –, raise- one's voice; give –, wag the- tongue; talk, outspeak; put in a word or two.

hold forth; make –, deliver- -a speech etc. *n.*; speechify, harangue, declaim, stump, flourish, spout, rant, recite, lecture, preach, sermonize, discourse, be on one's legs; have –, say- one's say; expatiate etc. (*speak at length*) 573; speak one's mind.

soliloquize etc. 589; tell etc. (*inform*) 527; speak to etc. 586; talk together etc. 588.

be -eloquent etc. *adj.*; have -a tongue in one's head, – the gift of the gab etc. *n.*

pass –, escape- one's lips; fall from the -lips, – mouth.

Adj. speaking etc., spoken etc. *v.*; oral, lingual, phonetic, not written, unwritten, outspoken; eloquent, -cutionary; orat-, rhetorical; declamatory; grandiloquent etc. 577; talkative etc. 584.

Adv. orally etc. *adj.*; by word of mouth, *vivâ voce*, from the lips of.

Phr. quoth –, said- he etc.

583. Stammering. [Imperfect Speech.]—**N.** inarticulateness; stammering etc. *v.*; hesitation etc. *v.*; impediment in one's speech; aphasia, titubancy, traulism; whisper etc. (*faint sound*) 405; lisp, drawl, tardiloquence; nasal -tone, – accent; twang; *falsetto* etc. (*want of voice*) 581; broken -voice, – accents, – sentences.

brogue etc. 563; slip of the tongue, *lapsus linguae*.

V. stammer, stutter, hesitate, falter, hammer; balbu-tiate, -cinate; haw, hum and haw, be unable to put two words together.

mumble, mutter; maund, -er; whisper etc. 405; mince, lisp; jabber, gabble, gibber; sp-, spl-utter; muffle, mump; drawl, mouth; croak; speak -thick, – through the nose; snuffle, clip one's words; murder the -language, – King's (*or* Queen's) English; mis-pronounce, -say.

Adj. stammering etc. *v.*; inarticulate, guttural, nasal; tremulous.

Adv. *sotto voce* etc. (*faintly*) 405.

584. Loquacity.—N. loquac-ity, -iousness; talkativeness etc. *adj.*; garrulity; multiloquence, much speaking, effusion, wordiness.

jaw; gab, -ble; jabber, chatter; prate, prattle, cackle, clack; twaddle, trattle, rattle; *caquet*, *-terie*; blabber, *bavardage*, bibble-babble, gibble-gabble; small talk etc. (*converse*) 588.

fluency, flippancy, volubility, flowing tongue; flow, – of words; *flux de -bouche*, – *mots*, – *paroles*; *copia verborum*, *cacoëthes loquendi*; verbosity etc. (*diffuseness*) 573; gift of the gab etc. (*eloquence*) 582.

talker; chatter-er, -box; babbler etc. *v.*; rattle; ranter; sermonizer, proser, driveller; wind bag; gossip etc. (*converse*) 588; magpie, jay, parrot, poll, Babel; *moulin à paroles.*

V. be -loquacious etc. *adj.*; talk glibly, pour forth, patter; prate, palaver, prose, chatter, prattle, clack, jabber, jaw; rattle, – on; twaddle, twattle; babble, gabble; out-talk; talk oneself -out of breath, – hoarse; maunder, gush, blatter; talk a donkey's hind leg off; expatiate etc. (*speak at length*) 573; gossip etc. (*converse*) 588; din in the ears etc. (*repeat*) 104; talk -at random, – nonsense etc. 497; be hoarse with talking.

Adj. loquacious, talkative, conversational, garrulous, linguacious, multiloquous; chattering etc. *v.*; chatty etc. (*sociable*) 892; declamatory etc. 582; open-mouthed.

fluent, voluble, glib, flippant; long-tongued, winded etc. (*diffuse*) 573.

Adv. trippingly on the tongue; glibly etc. *adj.*

Phr. the tongue running -fast, – loose, – on wheels.

585. Taciturnity.—N. silence, muteness, obmutescence; taciturnity, pauciloquy, costiveness, curtness; reserve, reticence etc. (*concealment*) 528; *aposiopesis*.

man of few words.

V. be -silent etc. *adj.*; keep silence; hold one's -tongue, – peace, – jaw; not speak etc. 582; say nothing; seal –, close –, put a padlock on- the -lips, – mouth; put a bridle on one's tongue; keep one's tongue between one's teeth; make no sign, not let a word escape one; keep a secret etc. 528; not have a word to say; lay –, place- the finger on the lips; render mute etc. 581.

stick in one's throat.

Adj. silent, mute, mum; silent as -a post, – a stone, – the grave etc. (*still*) 403; dumb etc. 581.

taciturn, sparing of words; close, – mouthed, –

tongued; laconic, costive, inconversable, curt; reserved; reticent etc. (*concealing*) 528.

Int. tush! silence! mum! hush! *chut!* hist! tut! etc. 403.

586. Allocution.—N. allocution, alloquy, address; speech etc. 582; apostrophe, interpellation, appeal, invocation, salutation; word in the ear.

[Feigned dialogue] dialogism.

platform etc. 542; audience etc. (*interview*) 588.

V. speak to, address, accost, make up to, apostrophize, appeal to, invoke; hail, salute; call to, halloo.

take -aside, – by the button, button-hole; talk to in private.

lecture etc. (*make a speech*) 582.

Int. soho! halloo! hey! hist! hi!

587. Response etc.; *see* Answer 462.

588. Interlocution.—N. interlocution; collocution, colloquy, converse, conversation, confabulation, talk, discourse, verbal intercourse; communion, oral communication, commerce; dia-, duo-, tria-logue.

causerie, chat, chit-chat; small –, table –, teatable –, town –, village –, idle- talk; tattle, gossip, tittle-tattle; babble, -ment; *tripotage*, cackle, prittle-prattle, *on dit*; talk of the -town, – village.

conference, parley, interview, audience, *pourparler*; *tête-à-tête*; reception, *conversazione*; congress etc. (*council*) 696; pow-wow.

hall of audience, *durbar*, coliseum, assembly hall, auditorium.

palaver, debate, logomachy, war of words, controversy.

talker, gossip, tattler; Paul Pry; tabby; chatterer etc. (*loquacity*) 584; interlocutor etc. (*spokesman*) 582; conversation-ist, -alist; dialogist.

'the feast of reason and the flow of soul;' *mollia tempora fandi.*

V. talk together, converse, confabulate; hold –, carry on –, join in –, engage in- a conversation; put in a word; shine in conversation; bandy words; parley; palaver; chat, gossip, tattle; prate etc. (*loquacity*) 584.

discourse –, confer –, commune –, commerce- with; hold -converse, – conference, – intercourse; talk it over; be closeted with; talk with one -in private, – *tête-à-tête.*

Adj. conversing etc. *v.*; interlocutory; conversational, -able; discursive, -coursive; chatty etc. (*sociable*) 892; colloquial, *tête-à-tête*, confabulatory.

589. Soliloquy.—N. soliloquy, monologue, apostrophe.

solilo-quist, -quizer, monologist.

V. soliloquize; say –, talk- to oneself; say aside, think aloud, apostrophize.

Adj. soliloquizing etc. *v.*

Adv. aside.

590. Writing.—N. writing etc. *v.*; chiro-, stelo-, cero-graphy, graphology; stylography; pen-craft, -script, -manship; quill-driving; typewriting.

writing, manuscript, MS., *literae scriptae*; these presents.

stroke –, dash- of the pen; *coup de plume*; line; pen and ink.

letter etc. 561; uncial writing, cuneiform character, arrow-head, Ogham, Runes, futhorc; hieroglyphic, hieratic, demotic; script; contraction.

short-hand; steno-, brachy-, tachy-graphy; secret writing, writing in cipher; crypt-, stegan-ography; phono-, pasi-, poly-, logo-graphy.

copy; tran-, re-script; draft, rough –, fair- copy; handwriting; signature, sign-manual; auto-, mono-, holo-graph; hand, fist; mark.

calligraphy; good –, running –, flowing –, cursive –, legible –, copperplate –, round –, bold-hand.

cacography, *griffonage*, *barbouillage*; bad –, cramped –, crabbed –, illegible- hand; scribble etc. *v.*; *pattes de mouche*; ill-formed letters; pothooks and hangers.

stationery; pen, quill, goose-quill, reed; stylographic-, fountain-pen; pencil, style, stylus; paper, foolscap, parchment, vellum, papyrus, pad, tablet, block, note book, slate, marble, pillar, table, black board.

ink-bottle, -pot, -stand, -well, -horn; typewriter.

transcription etc. (*copy*) 21; inscription etc. (*record*) 551; superscription etc. (*indication*) 550.

composition, authorship; *cacoethes scribendi.*

writer, scribe, amanuensis, scrivener, secretary, clerk, penman, copyist, transcriber, quill-driver; writer for the press etc. (*author*) 593.

shorthand writer, stenographer; typewriter, typist.

V. write, pen; copy, engross; write out, – fair; transcribe; scribble, scrawl, scrabble, scratch; interline; stain paper; write down etc. (*record*) 551; sign etc. (*attest*) 467; take down, – in shorthand; typewrite, type.

compose, indite, draw up, redact, draft, formulate; dictate; inscribe, throw on paper, dash off; concoct.

take -up the pen, – pen in hand; shed –, spill –, dip one's pen in- ink.

Adj. writing etc. *v.*; written etc. *v.*; in -writing, – black and white; under one's hand.

uncial, Runic, cuneiform, hieroglyphical etc. *n.*

Adv. *currente calamo*; pen in hand.

591. Printing.—N. printing; block –, type-printing, lino-, mono-type; plate printing etc. (*engraving*) 558; the press etc. (*publication*) 531; composition.

print, letterpress, text, matter, standing type; context, note, page, column; over-running; head-, foot-line, title.

typography; stereo-, electro-, apro-type; type,

black letter, heavy type, font, fount; pi, pie; capitals etc. (*letters*) 561; diamond, pearl, nonpareil, minion, brevier, bourgeois, long primer, small pica, pica, english, great primer.

folio etc. (*book*) 593; copy, impression, pull, proof, galley –, author's –, page- proof, revise.

printer, compositor, reader; printer's devil.

V. print; compose; put –, go- to press; pass –, see- through the press; publish etc. 531; bring out; appear in –, rush into- print.

Adj. printed etc. *v.*; in type; typographical etc. *n.*

592. Correspondence.—N. correspondence, letter, epistle, note, *billet*, post-, letter-card, missive, circular, form letter; favor, *billet-doux*; des-, dis-patch; *bulletin*, communication etc. 532; these presents; rescript, -ion; post etc. (*messenger*) 534; letter writer, correspondent.

V. correspond, – with; write –, send a letter- to; keep up a correspondence; drop a line to; despatch; communicate with; circularize.

Adj. epistolary.

593. Book.—N. book, -let; writing, work, volume, tome, opuscule; tract, -ate; *livret*; *brochure, libretto*, handbook, treatise, text-book, codex, manual, pamphlet, monograph, enchiridion, circular, publication; book of poems; novel; chap-book.

part, issue, number, *livraison*; album, portfolio; periodical, serial, magazine, *ephemeris*, annual, journal.

paper, bill, sheet, broadsheet, screed; leaf, -let; fly-leaf, page; quire, ream.

chapter, section, head, article, paragraph, passage, clause, supplement, appendix; *feuilleton*.

folio, quarto, octavo; duo-, sexto-, octo-decimo.

en-, cyclopedia, dictionary, lexicon, thesaurus, concordance, anthology, bibliography; compilation, compendium, catalogue etc. 86; library, bibliotheca; the press etc. (*publication*) 531.

writer, author, *littérateur*, essayist, journalist, publicist; scribe, penman, war –, special –, correspondent; pen, scribbler, the scribbling race; ghost, hack, literary hack, Grub-street writer; writer for –, gentlemen of –, representative of- the press; reporter, penny-a-liner; editor, sub-editor; playwright etc. 599; poet etc. 597.

bookseller, publisher; biblio-pole, -polist, -grapher; librarian; book -collector, – worm.

book -shop, – club, circulating –, lending –, public- library; publishing house.

knowledge of books, bibliography; book-learning etc. (*knowledge*) 490.

594. Description.—N. description, account, statement, report; *exposé* etc. (*disclosure*) 529; specification, particulars, scenario, plot; state –, summary- of facts; brief etc. (*abstract*) 596; return etc. (*record*) 551; *catalogue raisonné* etc. (*list*) 86; guide-book etc. (*information*) 527.

delineation etc. (*representation*) 554; sketch, vignette; monograph; minute –, detailed –, particular –, circumstantial –, graphic- account; narration, recital, rehearsal, relation.

histori-, chron-ography; historic Muse, Clio; history; bi-, autobi-ography; necrology, obituary.

narrative, history; memoir, memorials; annals etc. (*chronicle*) 551; tradition, legend, saga, epic, epos, story, tale, historiette; personal narrative, journal, letters, life, adventures, fortunes, experiences, confessions; anecdote, ana, *trait*.

work of fiction, short story, novelette, novel, romance, penny dreadful, shilling, shocker, Minerva press; fairy –, nursery- tale; fable, allegory, parable, apologue.

relator etc. *v.*; *raconteur*; historian etc. (*recorder*) 553; biographer, fabulist, novelist, story teller, romancer, teller of tales, spinner of yarns, anecdotist.

V. describe; set forth etc. (*state*) 535; draw a picture, picture; portray etc. (*represent*) 554; characterize, particularize; narrate, relate, recite, recount, sum up, run over, recapitulate, rehearse, fight one's battles over again.

unfold etc. (*disclose*) 529- a tale; tell; give –, render- an account of; report, make a report, draw up a statement.

detail; enter into –, descend to- -particulars, – details.

Adj. descriptive, graphic, narrative, epic, suggestive, well-drawn; historic; auto-, biographical, realistic, expository, tradition-al, -ary; legendary; fabulous, mythical; anecdotic, storied; described etc. *v.*

595. Dissertation.—N. dissertation, treatise, essay; *thesis*, theme; tract, -ate, -ation, excursus; discourse, memoir, disquisition, lecture, sermon, homily, pandect.

commentary, review, *critique*, criticism, article; lead-er, -ing article, editorial; argument, running commentary.

investigation etc. (*inquiry*) 461; study etc. (*consideration*) 451; discussion etc. (*reasoning*) 476; exposition etc. (*explanation*) 522.

commentator, critic, essayist, pamphleteer; publicist, reviewer, leader writer, editor, annotator.

V. dissert –, descant –, write –, touch- upon a subject; dissertate; treat of –, take up –, ventilate –, discuss –, deal with –, go into –, canvass –, handle –, do justice to- a subject; comment, criticize, interpret etc. 522.

Adj. dis-cursive, -coursive; disquisitional, disquisitionary; expository, critical.

596. Compendium.—N. compend, -ium; abstract, *précis*, epitome, *multum in parvo*, analysis, pandect, digest, sum and substance, brief, abridgment, summary, *aperçu*, draft, minute, note; synopsis, textbook, *conspectus*, outlines, syllabus, contents, heads, prospectus.

album; scrap –, note –, memorandum –, commonplace- book; extracts, *excerpta*, cuttings; fugitive -pieces, – writings; *spicilegium*, flowers, anthology, miscellany, *collectanea*, *analecta*; compilation.

recapitulation, *résumé*, review.

abbrevia-tion, -ture; contraction; shortening etc. 201; compression etc. 195.

V. abridge, abstract, epitomize, summarize; make –, prepare –, draw –, compile- an abstract etc. *n.*

recapitulate, review, skim, run over, sum up.

abbreviate etc. (*shorten*) 201; condense etc. (*compress*) 195; compile etc. (*collect*) 72; edit, blue pencil.

Adj. compendious, synoptic, analectic, analytical; abridged etc. *v.*

Adv. in -short, – epitome, – substance, – few words.

Phr. it lies in a nutshell.

597. Poetry.—N. poetry, poetics, poesy, Muse, Calliope, tuneful Nine, Parnassus, Helicon, Pierides, Pierian spring, afflatus, inspiration.

versification, rhyming, making verses; prosody, scansion, orthometry.

poem; epic, – poem; epopee, *epopaea*, ode, epode, idyl, lyric, eclogue, pastoral, bucolic, georgic, dithyramb, anacreontic, sonnet, roundelay, *rondel, rondoletto, rondeau, rondo*, triolet; madrigal, canzonet, *cento*, monody, elegy, palinode; rhapsody.

dramatic –, lyric- poetry; opera; posy, anthology.

song, ballad, lay; love –, drinking –, war –, folk –, sea- song; lullaby; music etc. 415; nursery rhymes.

[Bad poetry] doggerel, Hudibrastic verse, prose run mad; macaronics; macaronic –, leonine-verse; runes.

canto, stanza, distich, verse, line, couplet, triplet, quatrain, sestet; *strophe*, *antistrophe*, refrain, chorus, burden.

verse, rhyme, assonance, crambo, meter, measure, foot, numbers, strain, rhythm; accentuation etc. (*voice*) 580; iambus, dactyl, spondee, trochee, anapaest etc.; hex-, pent-ameter; Alexandrine; blank verse, alliteration.

elegiacs etc. *adj.*; elegiac etc. *adj.* -verse, – meter, – poetry.

poet, – laureate; laureate; minor poet, bard, lyrist, scald, troubadour, *trouvère*; mistrel; minne-, meister-singer; *improvisatore*; versifier, sonneteer; ballad monger; rhym-er, -ist, -ester; poetaster.

V. poetize, sing, versify, make verses, rhyme, scan.

Adj. poetic, -al; lyric, -al; tuneful; epic; dithyrambic etc. *n.*; metrical; a-, catalectic; elegiac, iambic, trochaic, spondaic, anapest; Ionic, Sapphic, Alcaic, Pindaric.

598. Prose.—N. prose, – writer, pros-aism, -aist, -er.

V. prose, write prose.

write -prose, – in prose.

Adj. pros-y, -aic; unpoetical.

rhymeless, unrhymed, in prose, not in verse.

599. Drama.—N. drama, the -drama, – stage, – theater, – play; theatricals, dramaturgy, histrionic art, buskin, sock, *cothurnus*, Melpomene and Thalia, Thespis.

play, stage-play, piece, five-act play, tragedy, comedy, opera, comic opera, *vaudeville, comedietta, lever de rideau*, curtain raiser, interlude, afterpiece, exode, farce, *divertissement, extravaganza*, burletta, harlequinade, pantomime, mimodrama, burlesque, *opéra bouffe*, musical comedy, review, revue, intimate revue, variety, cabaret entertainment, *ballet, spectacle*, masque, *drame, comédie drame*; melo-drama, -drame; *comédie larmoyante*, emotional drama, sensation drama, tragi-, farcical-comedy; mono-drame, -logue; duologue; trilogy; charade, *proverbe*; mystery, miracle –, morality- play.

act, scene, *tableau*; in-, intro-duction; pro-, epilogue, curtain; *libretto*, book, script.

performance, representation, show, *mise en scène*, stagery, *jeu de théâtre*, stage-craft; acting; gesture etc. 550; impersonation etc. 554; stage business, gag, patter, buffoonery.

theater; play-, opera-house; house; music hall; *cabaret*; amphitheater, circus, hippodrome; puppet-show, *fantoccini*; *marionnettes*, Punch and Judy.

cinema, -tograph-, picture –, theater, the pictures, the movies, the talkies.

auditory, *auditorium*, front of the house, stalls, boxes, balcony, dress –, upper- -circle, – boxes, amphitheater, pit, gallery; *foyer*; greenroom; dressing rooms, *coulisses*.

flat; drop, – scene; wing, screen, side-scene; transformation scene, curtain, act-drop, safety –, fire- curtain; *proscenium*, forestage.

stage, revolving stage, scene, the boards; star –, grave –, trap, mezzanine floor; flies; gridiron, floats, battens, footlights; lime –, spot –, flood –, bunch-lights; scenery, set, *décor*; orchestra.

theatrical -costume, – properties, props.

part, *rôle*, character, cast, *dramatis personae*; *répertoire*.

actor, player; stage –, strolling- player; old –, stager, performer; mime, -r; *artiste*; com-, tragedian, straight man; *tragédienne*, Thespian, Roscius, star.

pantomimist, clown, harlequin, *buffo*, buffoon, *farceur, grimacier*, pantaloon, columbine; *Pierrot, Pierrette*; punch, -inello; *pulcinell-o, -a*; mute, *figurante*, general utility; super, -numerary, extra.

mummer, guiser, guisard, gysart, masque.

mountebank, Jack Pudding; tumbler, posture-master, acrobat, equilibrist, juggler, contortionist; *danseuse*, *ballerina*, ballet -dancer, – girl, *coryphée*; *bayadère*, *geisha*; chorus -singer, – girl.

company; first tragedian, *prima donna*, lead, leading lady, protagonist; *jeune premier*; juvenile lead, *débutant, -e*; light –, genteel –, low- -comedy, – comedian; *soubrette*, walking gentleman, *amoroso*, heavy, heavy father, *ingénue, jeune veuve*, *commère*, *compère*.

property man, *costumier*, machinist, stage hand, electrician, prompter, call-boy; director, manager; stage –, acting –, business- manager; *entrepreneur*, *impresario*, producer, press agent.

dramatic -author, – writer; play-writer, -wright; dramatist, mimographer; dramatic critic.

V. act, play, perform; stage, produce, put on the stage; personate etc. 554; mimic etc. (*imitate*) 19; enact; play –, act –, go through –, perform- a part; rehearse, spout, gag, rant; 'strut and fret one's hour upon a stage;' tread the -stage, – boards; come out; star.

Adj. dramatic; theatric, -al; scenic, histrionic, anctorial, comic, tragic, buskined, farcical, tragicomic, melodramatic, operatic; stagey spectacular; stagestruck.

Adv. on the -stage, – boards; before -the floats, – an audience; in the limelight, behind the footlights; behind the scenes.

600. Will.—N. will, volition, conation, velleity; will and pleasure, free-will; freedom etc. 748; discretion; choice, inclination, intent, purpose, option etc. (*choice*) 609; voluntariness; spontane-ity, -ousness; originality.

pleasure, wish, desire, mind; frame of mind etc. (*inclination*) 602; intention etc. 620; predetermination etc. 611; self-control etc. determination etc. (*resolution*) 604; will-power.

V. will, list; see –, think- -fit; determine etc. (*resolve*) 604; settle etc. (*choose*) 609; volunteer.

have a will of one's own; do what one chooses etc. (*freedom*) 748; have it all one's own way; have one's -will, – own way.

use –, exercise- one's discretion; take -upon oneself, – one's own course, – the law into one's own hands; do -of one's own accord, – upon one's own -responsibility, – authority; take the bit between one's teeth; take responsibility; originate etc. (*cause*) 153.

Adj. voluntary, volitive, volitional, wilful; free etc. 748; optional; discretion-al, -ary; volitient; dictatorial.

minded etc. (*willing*) 602; prepense etc. (*predetermined*) 611; intended etc. 620; autocratic; unbidden etc. (bid etc. 741); spontaneous; original etc. (*causal*) 153.

Adv. voluntarily etc. *adj.*; at -will, – pleasure; *à -volonté*, – *discrétion*; *al piacere*; *ad -libitum*, – *arbitrium*; as -one thinks proper, – it seems good to.

of one's own -accord, – free will; *proprio* –, *suo* –, *ex mero- motu*; out of one's own head; by choice etc. 609; purposely etc. (*intentionally*) 620; deliberately etc. 611.

Phr. *stet pro ratione voluntas*; *sic volo sic jubeo.*

601. Necessity.—N. involuntariness; instinct, blind –, natural- impulse; inborn –, innate- proclivity; the force of circumstances.

necessi-ty, -tation, necessarianism; obligation; compulsion etc. 744; subjection etc. 749; stern –, hard –, dire –, imperious –, inexorable –, iron –, adverse- -necessity, – fate; what must be.

desti-ny, -nation; fatality, fate, *kismet*, doom, foredoom, election, predestination; pre-, fore-ordination; lot, fortune; fatalism, determinism; inevitableness etc. *adj.*; spell etc. 993.

star, -s; planet, -s; astral influence; sky, Fates, Norns, *Parcae*, Sisters three, Clotho, Lachesis, Atropos; book of fate; God's will, will of Heaven; wheel of Fortune, Ides of March, Hobson's choice.

last -shift, – resort; *dernier ressort*; *pis aller* etc. (*substitute*) 147; necessaries etc. (*requirement*) 630.

necess-arian, -itarian; fatalist, determinist; automaton.

V. lie under a necessity; be -fated, – doomed, – destined etc., – in for, – under the necessity of; have no -choice, – alternative; be- obliged –, forced –, driven –, one's -fate etc. *n.*- to; be - pushed to the wall, – driven into a corner, – unable to help, – drawn irresistibly.

destine, doom, foredoom, devote; pre-destine, - ordain; cast a spell etc. 992; necessitate; compel etc. 744.

Adj. necessary; needful etc. (*requisite*) 630.

fated; destined etc. *v.*; fateful; elect; spell-bound.

compulsory etc. (*compel*) 744; uncontrollable, inevitable, unavoidable, irrestible, irrevocable, inexorable, binding; avoid-, resist-less; written in the book of fate.

involuntary, instinctive, automatic, blind, mechanical; un-conscious, -witting, -thinking; unintentional etc. (*undesigned*) 621; impulsive etc. 612.

Adv. necessarily etc. *adv.*; of -necessity, – course; *ex necessitate rei*; needs must; perforce etc. 744; *nolens volens*; will he nil he, willy nilly, *bon gré mal gré*, willing or unwilling, *coûte que coûte*, forcefully.

faute de mieux; by stress of; if need be.

Phr. it cannot be helped; there is no- help for, – helping- it; it -will, – must, – must needs- be, – be so, – have its way; the die is cast; *jacta est alea*; *che sarà sarà*; 'it is written;' one's- days are numbered, – fate is sealed; *Fata obstant*; *diis aliter visum.*

602. Willingness.—N. willingness, voluntariness etc. *adj.*; willing mind, heart.

disposition, inclination, leaning, *animus*; frame of mind, humor, mood, vein; bent etc. (*turn of mind*) 820; *penchant* etc. (*desire*) 865; aptitude etc. 698.

doc-ility, -ibleness, tractability; persuasi-bleness, -bility; pliability etc. (*softness*) 324.

geniality, cordiality; goodwill; alacrity, readiness, earnestness, forwardness, enthusiasm; zeal, eagerness etc. (*desire*) 865.

assent etc. 488; compliance etc. 762; pleasure etc. (*will*) 600.

labor of love, self-appointed task; volunteer, -ing, gratuitous service; unpaid worker, amateur.

V. be -willing etc. *adj.*; incline, lean to, mind, propend; had as lief; lend –, give –, turn- a willing ear; have -a, – half a, – a great- mind to; hold –, cling- to; desire etc. 865.

see –, think- -good, – fit, – proper; acquiescence etc. (*assent*) 488; comply with etc. 762.

swallow –, nibble at- the bait; gorge the hook; swallow hook, line and sinker; have –, make- no scruple of; make no bones of; jump –, catch- at; meet half way; volunteer, offer oneself etc. 763.

Adj. willing, minded, fain, disposed, inclined, favorable, favorably- minded, -inclined, -disposed; nothing loth; in the -vein, – mood, – humor, – mind.

ready, forward, enthusiastic, earnest, eager; bent upon etc. (*desirous*) 865; predisposed, propense.

docile; persua-dable, -sible; suasible, easily persuaded, facile, easy-going; amenable; tractable etc. (*pliant*) 324; genial, gracious, cordial, hearty; content etc. (*assenting*) 488.

voluntary, gratuitous, spontaneous; unasked etc. (ask etc. 765); unforced etc. (*free*) 748.

Adv. willing etc. *adj.*; fain, freely, as lief, heart and soul; with -pleasure, – all one's heart, – open arms; with -good, – right good- will; *de bonne volonté, ex animo*; *con amore*, heart in hand, nothing loth, without reluctance, of one's own accord, graciously, with a good grace, without demur.

à la bonne heure; by all -means, – manner of means; to one's heart's content; yes etc. (*assent*) 488.

Int. sure, -ly! of course!

603. Unwillingness.—N. unwillingness etc. *adj.*; indispos-ition, -edness; disinclination, aversation, aversion; nolleity, nolition; renitence; reluctance; indifference etc. 866; backwardness etc. *adj.*; slowness etc. 275; want of -alacrity, – readiness; indocility etc. (*obstinacy*) 606.

scrupul-ousness, -osity; qualms of conscience, delicacy, demur, scruple, qualm, shrinking, recoil; hesitation etc. (*irresolution*) 605; fastidiousness etc. 868.

averseness etc. (*dislike*) 867; dissent etc. 489; refusal etc. 764.

slacker, scrimshanker, *embusqué*, unwilling worker, forced labor.

V. be -unwilling etc. *adj.*; nill; dislike etc. 867; grudge, begrudge; not be able to find it in one's heart to, not have the stomach to.

demur, stick at, scruple, stickle; hang fire, run rusty, slack, shirk, scamp, give up, fight shy of, not pull fair; recoil, shrink, swerve; hesitate etc. 605; avoid etc. 623.

oppose etc. 708; dissent etc. 489; refuse etc. 764.

Adj. unwilling; not in the vein, loth, shy of, disinclined, indisposed, averse, reluctant, not content; adverse etc. (*opposed*) 708; laggard, backward, remiss, slack, slow to; renitent; indifferent etc. 866; scrupulous; squeamish etc. (*fastidious*) 868; repugnant etc. (*dislike*) 867; rest-iff, -ive; demurring etc. *v.*; unconsenting etc. (*refusing*) 764; involuntary etc. 601; grudging, irreconcilable.

Adv. unwilling etc. *adj.*; grudgingly, with a heavy heart; with -a bad, – an ill- grace; against –, sore against- -one's wishes, – one's will, – the grain; *invitâ Minervâ*; *à contre coeur*; *malgré soi*; in spite of -one's teeth, – oneself; *nolens volens* etc. (*necessity*) 601; perforce etc. 744; under protest; no etc. 536; not for the world, far be it from me; not if I can help it; if I must I must.

604. Resolution.—N. determination, will; iron –, unconquerable- will; will of one's own, decision, resolution, backbone, grit; strength of -mind, – will; resolve etc. (*intent*) 620; *intransigeance*; firmness etc. (*stability*) 150; energy, manliness, vigor; game, pluck; resoluteness etc. (*courage*) 861; zeal etc. 682; *aplomb*; desperation; devot-ion, -edness.

mastery over self; self-control, -command, -mastery, -possession, -reliance, -government, -restraint, -conquest, -denial; moral -courage, – strength, – fiber; perseverance etc. 604*a*; tenacity; obstinacy etc. 606; bull-dog; British lion.

V. have -determination etc. *n.*; know one's own mind; be -resolved etc. *adj.*; make up one's mind, will resolve, determine; decide etc. (*judgment*) 480; form –, come to- a -determination, – resolution, – resolve; conclude, fix, seal, determine once for all, bring to a crisis, drive matters to an extremity; take a decisive step etc. (*choice*) 609; take upon oneself etc. (*undertake*) 676.

devote oneself –, give oneself up- to; throw away the scabbard, kick down the ladder, nail one's colors to the mast, set one's back against the wall, set one's teeth, put one's foot down, burn one's bridges, take one's stand; stand firm etc. (*stability*) 150; steel oneself; stand no nonsense, not listen to the voice of the charmer.

buckle to; put –, lay –, set- one's shoulder to the wheel; put one's heart into; run the gantlet, make a dash at, take the bull by the horns; beard the lion in his den; rush –, plunge- *in medias res*; go in for; insist upon, make a point of; set one's heart, – mind- upon.

stick at nothing; make short work of etc. (*activity*) 682; not stick at trifles; go -all lengths, – the whole hog; persist etc. (*persevere*) 604*a*; go down with colors flying, die game; go through fire and water, ride in the whirlwind and direct the storm.

Adj. resolved etc. *v.*determined; strong-willed, -minded; resolute etc. (*brave*) 861; self-possessed, plucky, tenacious; decided, definitive, peremptory; un-hesitating, -flinching, -shrinking; firm, cast iron, indomitable, game to the backbone; inexorable, relentless, not to be -shaken, – put down; *tenax propositi*; inflexible etc. (*hard*) 323; obstinate etc. 606; steady etc. (*persevering*) 604*a*; unbending, unyielding, irrevocable; firm as a rock; grim,

earnest, serious; set –, bent –, intent- upon.

steeled –, proof- against; *in utrumque paratus*.

Adv. resolutely etc. *adj.*; in –, in good- earnest; seriously, joking apart, earnestly, heart and soul; on one's metal; manfully, like a man, with a high hand; with a strong hand etc. (*exertion*) 686.

at any -rate, – risk, – hazard, – price, – cost, – sacrifice; at all -hazards, – risks, – events; cost what it may; *coûte que coûte*; *à tort et à travers*; once for all; neck or nothing; rain or shine; with colors nailed to the mast.

Phr. *spes sibi quisque.*

604a. Perseverance. —N. perseverance; continuance etc. (*inaction*) 143; permanence etc. (*absence of change*) 141; firmness etc. (*stability*) 150.

constancy, steadiness; singleness –, tenacity- of purpose; persistence, plodding, patience; sedulity etc. (*industry*) 682; pertina-cy, -city, -ciousness; iteration etc. 104.

bottom, game, pluck, stamina, backbone, grit; indefatiga-bility, -bleness; bulldog courage.

V. persevere, persist; hold -on, – out; die in the last ditch, be in at the death; stick –, cling –, adhere- to ; stick to one's text, keep on; keep to –, maintain- one's -course, – ground; bear –, keep –, hold up; plod; stick to work etc. (*work*) 686;

continue etc. 143; follow up; die -in harness, – at one's post.

Adj. persevering, constant; stead-y, -fast; undeviating, -wavering, -faltering, -swerving, -flinching, -sleeping, -flagging, -drooping; steady as time; uninter-, un-remitting; plodding; industrious etc. 682; strenuous etc. 686; pertinacious; persisting, -ent.

solid, sturdy, staunch, stanch, ture to oneself; unchangeable etc. 150; unconquerable etc. (*strong*) 159; indomitable, game to the last, indefatigable, untiring, unwearied, never tiring.

Adv. through -evil report and good report, – thick and thin, – fire and water; *per fas et nefas*; without fail, sink or swim, at any price, *vogue la galère*; in sickness and in health.

Phr. never say die; *vestigia nulla retrorsum*.

605. Irresolution.—N. irresolution, infirmity of purpose, indecision; in-, un-determination, loss of will power; unsettlement; uncertainty etc. 475; demur, suspense; hesi-tating etc. *v.*, -tation, -tancy; vacillation; ambivalence; changeableness etc. 149; fluctuation; alternation etc. (*oscillation*) 314; caprice etc. 608; lukewarmness.

fickleness, levity, *légèreté*; pliancy etc. (*softness*) 324; weakness; timidity etc. 860; cowardice etc. 862; half measures.

waverer, ass between two bundles of hay; shuttlecock, butterfly; timeserver, opportunist, turn coat.

V. be -irresolute etc. *adj.*; hang –, keep- in suspense; heave *'ad referendum*;' think twice about, pause; dawdle etc. (*inactivity*) 683; remain neuter; dilly dally. hesitate, boggle, hover, wobble, shilly-shally, hum and haw, demur, not know one's own mind; debate, balance; dally –, coquet- with; will and will not, *chasser-balancer*; go half-way, compromise, make a compormise; be thrown off one's balance, stagger like a drunken man; be afraid etc. 860; let 'I dare not' wait upon 'I would;' falter, waver.

vacillate etc. 149; change etc. 140; retract etc. 607; fluctuate; alternate etc. (*oscillate*) 314; keep off and on, play fast and loose; blow hot and cold etc. (*caprice*) 608.

shuffle, palter, blink; trim.

Adj. irresolute, infirm of purpose, double-minded, half-hearted; un-decided, -resolved, -determined; drifting; shilly-shally; fidgety, tremulous; wobbly; hesitating etc. *v.*; off one's balance; at a loss etc. (*uncertain*) 475.

vacillating etc. *v.*; unsteady etc. (*changeable*) 149; unsteadfast, fickle, unreliable, irresponsible, unstable, without ballast; capricious etc. 608; volatile, frothy; light, -some, -minded; giddy; fast and loose.

weak, feeble-minded, frail; timid etc. 860; cowardly etc. 862; facile; pliant etc. (*soft*) 324; unable to say 'no,' easy-going.

revocable, reversible.

Adv. irresolutely etc. *adj.*; irresolvedly; in faltering accents; off and on; from pillar to post; see-saw etc. 314.

Int. 'how happy could I be with either!'

606. Obstinacy.—N. obstinateness etc. *adj.*; obstinacy, tenacity; perseverance etc. 604*a*; immovability; old school; inflexibility etc. (*hardness*) 323; obdur-acy, -ation; dogged resolution; resolution etc. 604; ruling passion; blind side.

self-will, contumacy, perversity; pervica-cy, -city; indocility.

bigotry, intolerance, dogmatism; opinia-try, -tiveness; fixed idea etc.; intractibility, incorrigibility; (*prejudgment*) 481; fanaticism, zealotry, infatuation, monomania, opinionativeness.

mule; opin-ionist, -ionatist, -iator, -ator; stickler, dogmatist, die-hard, bitter-ender; bigot; zealot, enthusiast, fanatic.

V. be -obstinate etc. *adj.*; stickle, take no denial, fly in the face of facts; opinionate, be wedded to an opinion, hug a belief; have one's own way etc. (*will*) 600; persist etc. (*persevere*) 604*a*; have –, insist on having- the last word.

die -hard, – fighting, fight -against destiny, – to the last ditch; not yield an inch, stand out.

Adj. obstinate, tenacious, stubborn, obdurate, case-hardened; inflexible etc. (*hard*) 323; immovable, not to be moved; inert etc. 172; unchangeable etc. 150; inexorable etc. (*determined*) 604; mulish, obstinate as a mule, pig-headed.

dogged; sullen, sulky; un-moved, -influenced, -affected.

wilful, self-willed, perverse; res-ty, -tive, -tiff; pervicacious, wayward, refractory, unruly; head-y, -strong; *entete*; contumacious; cross-grained.

arbitrary, dogmatic, opinionated, positive, bigoted; prejudiced etc. 481; prepossessed, infatuated; stiff-backed, -necked, -hearted; hard-mouthed, hidebound; unyielding; im-pervious, -practicable, -persuasible; unpersuadable; in-, untractable; incorrigible, deaf to advice, impervious to reason; crotchety etc. 608.

Adv. obstinately etc. *adj.*

Phr. *non possumus*; no surrender.

607. Tergiversation.—N. change of -mind, – intention, – purpose; afterthought.

tergiversation, recantation; palinode, -ody; renunciation; abjur-ation, -ement; defection etc. (*relinquishment*) 624; going over etc. *v.*; apostasy; retract-ion, -ation; withdrawal, disavowal etc. (*negation*) 536; revo-cation, -kement; reversal; repentance etc. 950; *redintegratio amoris*.

coquetry, flirtation; vacillation etc. 605; back-sliding, recidivation.

turn-coat, -tippet; rat, apostate, renegade, mugwump; con-, per-vert; proselyte, deserter; backslider, recidivist; black leg.

time-server, -pleaser; timist, Vicar of Bray, trimmer, ambidexter; weathercock etc. (*changeable*) 149; Janus.

V. change one's -mind, – intention, – purpose, – note; abjure, renounce; withdraw from etc. (*relinquish*) 624; wheel –, turn –, veer- round; turn a *pirouette*; go over –, pass –, change –, skip- from one side to another; go to the right about; box the compass, shift one's ground, go upon another tack; back down, crawl, crawfish.

apostatize, change sides, go over, rat; recant, retract; revoke; rescind etc. (*abrogate*) 756; recall, forswear, abjure, unsay; come -over, – round- to an opinion.

draw in one's horns, eat one's words; eat –,

swallow- the leek; swerve, flinch, back out of, retrace one's steps, think better of it; come back –, return- to one's first love; turn over a new leaf etc. (*repent*) 950.

trim, shuffle, play fast and loose, blow hot and cold, coquet, flirt, hold with the hare but run with the hounds; straddle; *nager entre deux eaux*; wait to see how the -cat jumps, – wind blows.

Adj. changeful etc. 149; irresolute etc. 605; ductile, slippery as an eel, trimming, ambidextrous, timeserving; coquetting etc. *v.*

revocatory, reactionary.

Phr. 'a change came o'er the spirit of my dream.'

608. Caprice.—N. caprice, fancy, humor; whim, -sey, -wham; crotchet, *capriccio*, quirk, freak, maggot, fad, vagary, prank, fit, flim-flam, *escapade*, *boutade*, wild-goose chase; capriciousness etc. *adj.*; kink.

V. be -capricious etc. *adj.*; have a maggot in the brain; take it into one's head, strain at a gnat and swallow a camel; blow hot and cold; play -fast and loose, – fantastic tricks.

Adj. capricious; erratic, eccentric, fitful, hysterical; full of -whims etc. *n.*; maggoty; inconsistent, fanciful, fantastic, whimsical, crotchety, particular, humorsome, freakish, skittish, wanton, wayward; contrary; captious; arbitrary; unrestrained, undisciplined; not amenable to reason; uncomfortable etc. 83; penny wise and pound foolish; fickle etc. (*irresolute*) 605; frivolous, sleeveless, giddy, volatile.

Adv. by fits and starts, without rhyme or reason, at one's own sweet will.

Phr. *nil fuit unquam six impar sibi*; the deuce is in him.

609. Choice.—N. choice, option; discretion etc. (*volition*) 600; preoption; alternative; dilemma; *ambarras de choix*; adoption, cooptation; novation; decision etc. (*judgment*) 480.

election, poll, ballot, vote, voice, suffrage, plumper, cumulative vote; *plebiscitum, plébiscite, vox populi*; *referendum*, electioneering; voting etc. *v.*; franchise; ballot box; slate, ticket.

selection, excerption, gleaning, eclecticism; *excerpta*, gleanings, cuttings, scissors and paste; pick etc. (*best*) 650.

preference, prelation; predilection etc. (*desire*) 865.

V. offer for one's choice, set before; hold out –, present –, offer- the alternative; put to the vote.

use –, exercise –, one's- -discretion, – option; adopt, take up, embrace, espouse; choose, elect, coopt; take –, make- one's choice; make choice of, fix upon.

vote, poll, hold up one's hand; divide.

settle; decide etc. (*adjudge*) 480; list etc. (*will*) 600; make up one's mind etc. (*resolve*) 604.

select; pick, – and choose; pick –, single- out, excerpt; cull, glean, winnow; sift –, separate –, winnow- the chaff from the wheat; pick up, pitch upon; pick one's way; indulge one's fancy.

set apart, reserve, mark out for; mark etc. 550.

prefer; have -rather, – as lief; fancy etc. (*desire*) 865; be persuaded etc. 615.

take a -decided, – decisive- step; commit oneself to a course; pass –, cross- the Rubicon; cast in one's lot with; take for better or for worse.

Adj. optional; co-optative; discretional etc. (*voluntary*) 600; on approval.

ecletic; choosing etc. *v.*; preferential, chosen etc. *v.*; choice etc. (*good*) 648.

Adv. optionally etc. *adj.*; at pleasure etc. (*will*) 600; either, – the one or the other; or; at the option of; whether or not; once for all; for one's money.

by -choice, – preference; in preference; rather, before.

609a. Absence of Choice.—N. no –, Hobson's- choice; first come, first served; necessity etc. 601; not a pin to choose etc. (*equality*) 27; any, the first that comes.

neutrality, indifference; indecision etc. (*irresolution*) 605.

V. be -neutral etc. *adj.*; have no choice; waive, not vote; abstain –, refrain- from voting; leave undecided; make a virtue of necessity.

Adj. neu-tral, -ter; indifferent; undecided etc. (*irresolute*) 605.

Adv. either etc. (*choice*) 609.

610. Rejection.—N. rejection, repudiation, exclusion; declination; refusal etc. 764.

V. reject; set –, lay- aside; give up; decline etc. (*refuse*) 764; exclude, except, eliminate; pluck, spin; cast.

repudiate, scout, set at naught; fling –, cast –, thrown –, toss- -to the winds, – to the dogs, – overboard, – away; send to the right about; disclaim etc. (*deny*) 536; discard etc. (*eject*) 297, (*have done with*) 678.

Adj. rejected etc. *v.*; reject-aneous, -itious; not -chosen etc. 609, – to be thought of; out of the question.

Adv. neither, – the one nor the other; no etc. 536.

Phr. *non haec in foedera.*

611. Predetermination.—N. premeditation, -deliberation, -determination, -destination; foreordination; foregone conclusion; *parti pris*; resolve, propendency; intention etc. 620; project etc. 626.

V. pre-determine, -destine, -meditate, -resolve, -concert; foreordain; resolve beforehand.

Adj. pre-pense, -meditated etc. *v.*, -designed; advised, studied, designed, calculated; aforethought; intended etc. 620; foregone.

well-laid, -devised, -weighed; maturely considered; cut and dried; cunning.

Adv. advisedly etc. *adj.*; with premeditation, deliberately, all things considered, with eyes open, in cold blood; intentionally etc. 620.

612. Impulse.—N. impulse, sudden thought; *impromptu*, improvisation; inspiration, hunch, flash, spurt.

improvisatore, *improvisatrice*, improviser, extemporizer; creature of impulse.

V. flash on the mind.

say what comes uppermost; improvise, extemporize; rise to the occasion; spurt.

Adj. extemporaneous, impulsive, indeliberate; improvis-ed, -ate, -atory; un-, unpre-meditated; *improvisé*; unprompted, -guided; natural, unguarded; spontaneous etc. (*voluntary*) 600; instinctive etc. 601.

Adv. extem-pore, -poraneously; offhand, *impromptu, à l'improviste*; improviso; on the spur of the -moment, – occasion.

613. Habit.—N. habit, -ude; assuetude, -faction; wont; run, way.

common –, general –, natural –, ordinary –, habitual- -course, – run, – state- of things; matter of course; beaten -path, – track, – ground.

prescription, custom, use, usage, immemorial usage, practice; tradition; prevalence, observance; conventionalism, -ity; mode, fashion, vogue; *etiquette* etc. (*gentility*) 852; order of the day, cry; conformity etc. 82.

habitué, addict.

one's old way, old school, consuetude, *veteris vestigia flammae*; *laudator temporis acti*.

rule, standing order, precedent, routine; red-tape, -tapism; pipe-clay; rut, groove.

cacoëthes; bad –, confirmed –, inveterate –, intrinsic etc. 5- habit; addiction, trick.

training etc. (*education*) 537; seasoning, hardening, inurement; radication; second nature, acclimatization; knack etc. (*skill*) 698.

V. be -wont etc. *adj.*

fall into a custom etc. (*conform to*) 82; tread –, follow- the beaten -track, – path; *stare super antiquas vias*; move in a rut, run on in a groove, go round like a horse in a mill, go on in the old jobtrot way.

habituate, inure, harden, season, caseharden; accustom, familiarize; naturalize, acclimatize; keep one's hand in; train etc. (*educate*) 537.

get into the -way, – knack- of; learn etc. 539; cling –, adhere- to; repeat etc. 104; acquire –, contract –, fall into- a -habit, – trick; addict oneself –, take- to; accustom oneself to.

be -habitual etc. *adj.*; prevail; come into use, become a habit, take root; gain –, grow- upon one.

Adj. habitual; ac-, customary; prescriptive; accustomed etc. *v.*; traditional; of -daily, – everyday- occurrence; wonted, usual, general, ordinary, common, frequent, every-day, household, jog-trot; well-trodden, -known; familiar, vernacular, trite, commonplace, banal, bromidic, conventional, regular, set, stock, officinal, established, stereotyped; pre-vailing, -valent; current, received, acknowledged, recognized, accredited; of course, admitted, understood.

conformable etc. 82; according to -use, – custom, – routine; in -vogue, – fashion; fashionable etc. (*genteel*) 852.

wont; used – given – addicted –, attuned –, habituated etc. *v.*- to; in the habit of; *habitué*; at home in etc. (*skilful*) 698; seasoned; permeated –, imbued- with; devoted –, wedded- to; never free from.

hackneyed, fixed, rooted, deep-rooted, ingrafted, permanent, inveterate, besetting; naturalized; ingrained etc. (*intrinsic*) 5.

Adv. habitually etc. *adj.*; always etc. (*uniformly*) 16.

as -usual, – is one's wont, – things go, – the world goes, – the sparks fly upwards; *more -suo, – solito*.

as a rule, for the most part; generally etc. *adj.*; most often, – frequently.

Phr. *cela s'entend.*

614. Desuetude.—N. desuetude, disusage; disuse etc. 678; want of -habit, – practice; inusitation; newness to; new brooms.

infraction of usage etc. (*unconformity*) 83; non-prevalence; 'a custom more honored in the breach than the observance.'

V. be -unaccustomed etc. *adj.*; leave off –, cast off –, break off –, wean oneself of –, violate –, break through –, infringe- -a habit, – a custom, – a usage; break one's fetters; disuse etc. 678; wear off.

Adj. un-accustomed, -used, -wonted, -seasoned, -inured, -habituated, -trained; new; green etc. (*unskilled*) 699; fresh, original, unhackneyed.

unusual etc. (*unconformable*) 83; unconventional, non-observant; disused etc. 678.

Adv. just for once.

615. Motive.—N. motive, springs of action.

reason, ground, call, principle; mainspring, *primum mobile*, key-stone; the why and the wherefore; *pro* and *con*, reason why; secret –, ulterior- motive, *arrière-pensée*; intention etc. 620.

inducement, consideration; attraction etc. 288; loadstone; magnet, -ism, -ic force; allect-ation, -ive; temptation, enticement, *agacerie*, allurement, witchery; bewitch-ment, -ery; charm; spell etc. 993; fascination, blandishment, cajolery; seduc-tion, -ement; honeyed words, voice of the tempter, son of the Sirens; forbidden fruit, golden apple.

persuasi-bility, -bleness; attractability; impress-, suscept-ibility; softness; persuas-, attract-iveness; tantalization.

influence, prompting, dictate, instance; impuls-e, -ion; incit-ement, -ation; press, instigation; provocation etc. (*excitation of feeling*) 824; inspiration; per-, suasion; encouragement, advocacy; exhortation, advice etc. 695; solicitation etc. (*request*) 765; lobbying.

incentive, stimulus, spur, fillip, whip, goad, rowel, provocative, whet, dram.

bribe, lure; decoy, – duck; bait, trail of a red herring; bribery and corruption; sop, – for Cerberus.

prompter, tempter; seduc-er, -tor; suggester, coaxer, wheedler; instigator, firebrand, incendiary; Siren, Circe; *agent provocateur*; lobbyist.

V. induce, move; draw, – on; bring in its train, give an -impulse etc. *n.*- to; inspire; put up to, prompt, call up; attract, beckon.

stimulate etc. (*excite*) 824; spirit up, inspirit; a-, rouse; ecphorize; animate, incite, provoke, instigate, set on, actuate; act –, work –, operate-upon; encourage; pat –, clap- on the -back, – shoulder.

influence, weigh with, bias, sway, incline, dispose, predispose, turn the scale, inoculate; lead, – by the nose; have –, exercise- influence- -with, – over, – upon; go –, come- round one; turn the head, magnetize.

persuade; prevail -with, – upon; overcome, carry; bring -round, – to one's senses; draw –, win –, gain –, come –, talk- over; procure, enlist, engage; invite, court.

tempt, seduce, overpersuade, entice, allure, captivate, fascinate, intrigue, bewitch, carry away, charm, conciliate, wheedle, coax, lure, suggest; inveigle; tantalize; cajole etc. (*deceive*) 545.

tamper with, bribe, suborn, grease the palm, bait with a silver hook, gild the pill, make things pleasant, put a sop into the pan, throw a sop to, bait the hook.

enforce, force; impel etc. (*push*) 276; propel etc. 284; whip, lash, goad, spur, prick, urge; egg –, hound –, hurry- on; drag etc. 285; exhort; advise etc. 695; call upon etc.; press etc. (*request*) 765; advocate.

set -an example, – the fashion; keep in countenance; back up.

be -persuaded etc.; yield to temptation, come round; concede etc. (*consent*) 762; obey a call; follow -advice, – the bent, – the dictates of; act on principle.

Adj. impulsive, motive; suas-, persuas-, hortative, -ory; protreptical; inviting, tempting etc. *v.*; seductive, attractive, irresistible; fascinating etc. (*pleasing*) 829; provocative etc. (*exciting*) 824.

induced etc. *v.*; disposed; persuadable etc. (*docile*) 602; spellbound; instinct –, smitten- with; inspired etc. *v.*- by.

Adv. because, therefore etc. (*cause*) 155; from -this, – that- motive; for -this, – that- reason; for; by reason –, for the sake –, on the score –, on account- of; out of, from, as, forasmuch as.

for all the world; on principle.

615a. Absence of Motive.—N. absence of motive; caprice etc. 608; chance etc. (*absence of design*) 621.

V. have no motive; scruple etc. (*be unwilling*) 603.

Adj. without rhyme or reason; aimless etc. (*chance*) 621.

Adv. capriciously; out of mere caprice.

616. Dissuasion.—N. dissuasion, dehortation, expostulation, remonstrance; deprecation etc. 766.

discouragement, damper, wet blanket; warning.

cohibition etc. (*restraint*) 751; curb etc. (*means of restraint*) 752; check etc. (*hindrance*) 706.

reluctance etc. (*unwillingness*) 603; contraindication.

V. dissuade, dehort, cry out against, remonstrate, expostulate, warn, contraindicate.

disincline, indispose, shake, stagger; dispirit; discourage, -hearten, -enchant; deter; hold –, keep-back etc. (*restrain*) 751; render -averse etc. 603; repel; turn aside etc. (*deviation*) 279; wean from; act as a drag etc. (*hinder*) 706; throw cold water on, damp, cool, chill, blunt, calm, quiet, quench; deprecate etc. 766.

Adj. dissuading etc. *v.*; dissuasive; dehortatory, expostulatory; monit-ive, -ory.

dissuaded etc. *v.*; uninduced etc. (induce etc. 615); unpersuadable etc. (*obstinate*) 606; averse etc. (*unwilling*) 603; repugnant etc. (*dislike*) 867.

617. Plea. [Ostensible motive, ground, or reason assigned.]—**N.** plea, pretext; allegation, advocation; ostensible -motive, – ground, – reason; excuse etc. (*vindication*) 937; color; gloss, guise.

loop-, starting-hole; how to creep out of, salvo, come off.

handle, peg to hang on room, *locus standi*; stalking horse, *cheval de bataille*, cue.

pretence etc. (*untruth*) 546; put off, subterfuge, dust thrown in the eyes; blind; moonshine; mere –, shallow- pretext; lame -excuse, – apology, tub to a whale; flase plea, sour grapes; makeshift, shift, white lie; special pleading etc. (*sophistry*) 477: soft sawder etc. (*flattery*) 933.

V. plead, allege; shelter oneself under the plea of; excuse etc. (*vindicate*) 937; gloss over; lend a color to; furnish a -handle etc. *n.*; make a -pretext, – handle- of; use as a plea etc. *n.*; take one's stand upon, make capital out of; pretend etc. (*lie*) 544.

Adj. ostensible etc. (*manifest*) 525; excusing; alleged, apologetic; pretended etc. 545.

Adv. ostensibly; under -color, – the plea, – the pretence- of.

618. Good. N. good, benefit, advantage; improvement etc. 658; interest, service, behoof, behalf; weal; main chance, *summum bonum*, common weal; 'consummation devoutly to be wished;' gain, boot; profit, harvest.

boon etc. (*gift*) 784; good turn; blessing, benison; world of good; piece of good -luck, – fortune; nuts, prize, windfall, godsend, waif, treasure trove.

good fortune etc. (*prosperity*) 734; happiness etc. 827.

[Source of good] goodness etc. 648; utility etc. 644; remedy etc. 662; pleasure-giving etc. 829.

Adj. commendable etc. 931; useful etc. 644; good etc., beneficial etc. 648.

V. benefit, profit, advantage, serve, help, avail; do good to, gain, prosper, flourish.

Adv. well, aright, satisfactorily, favorably, not amiss; all for the best; to one's -advantage etc. *n.*; in one's -favor, – interest etc. *n.*

Phr. so far so good.

619. Evil.—N. evil, ill, harm, hurt, mischief, nuisance; machinations of the devil, Pandora's box, ills that flesh is heir to.

blow, buffet, stroke, scratch, bruise, wound, gash, mutilation; mortal -blow, – wound; *im-*

medicabile vulnus; damage, loss etc. (*deterioration*) 659.

disadvantage, prejudice, drawback.

disaster, accident, casualty; mishap etc. (*misfortune*) 735; bad job, devil to pay; calamity, bale, woe, catastrophe, tragedy; ruin etc. (*destruction*) 162; adversity etc. 735.

mental suffering etc. 828. [Evil spirit] demon etc. 980. [Cause of evil] bane etc. 663. [Production of evil] badness etc. 649; painfulness etc. 830; evil doer etc. 913.

outrage, wrong, injury, foul play; bad –, ill-turn; disservice; spoliation etc. 791; grievance, crying evil.

V. be in trouble etc. (*adversity*) 735; harm, injure, hurt, do disservice to.

Adj. disastrous, bad etc. 649; awry, out of joint; disadvantageous, injurious, harmful.

Adv. amiss, wrong, ill, to one's cost.

620. Intention.—N. intent, -ion, -ionality; purpose; *quo animo*; project etc. 626; undertaking etc. 676; predetermination etc. 611; design, ambition.

contemplation, mind, *animus*, view, purview, proposal; study; look out.

final cause; *raison d'être*; *cui bono*; object, aim, end; 'the be all and the end all;' drift etc. (*meaning*) 516; tendency etc. 176; destination, mark, point, butt, goal, target, bull's-eye, quintain; prey, quarry, game.

decision, determination, resolve; set –, settled-purpose; *ultimatum*; resolution etc. 604; wish etc. 865; *arrière-pensée*; motive etc. 615.

[Study of final causes] teleology.

V. intend, purpose, design, mean; have to; propose to oneself; harbor a design; have in -view, – contemplation, – one's eye, – *petto*; have an eye to.

bid –, labor- for; be –, aspire –, endeavour-after; be –, aim –, drive –, point –, level- at; take aim; set before oneself; study to.

take upon oneself etc. (*undertake*) 676; take into one's head; meditate, contemplate; think –, dream –, talk- of; premeditate etc. 611; compass, calculate; dest-ine, -inate, propose.

project etc. (*plan*) 626; have a mind to etc. (*be willing*) 602; desire etc. 865; pursue etc. 622.

Adj. intended etc. *v.*; intentional, advised, express, determinate; prepense etc. 611; bound for; intending etc. *v.*; minded, disposed, inclined; bent upon etc. (*earnest*) 604; at stake, on the -anvil, – *tapis*; in -view; – prospect, – the breast of; *in petto*; teleological.

Adv. intentionally etc. *adj.*; advisedly, wittingly, knowingly, designedly, purposely, on purpose, by design, studiously, pointedly; with -intent etc. *n.*; deliberately etc. (*with premeditation*) 611; with one's eyes open, in cold blood.

for; with -a view, – an eye- to; in order -to, – that; to the end –, with the intent- that; for the purpose –, with the view –, in contemplation –, on account- of.

in pursuance of, pursuant to; *quo animo*; to all intents and purposes.

621. Chance.† [Absence of purpose in the succession of events.]—**N.** chance etc. 156; lot, fate etc. (*necessity*) 601; luck; good luck etc. (*good*) 618; bad luck etc. 735; wheel of fortune; mascot; swastika.

speculation, venture, stake, flutter, flier, gamble, game of chance; mere –, random- shot; blind bargain, leap in the dark; pig in a poke etc. (*uncertainty*) 475; fluke, pot-luck.

drawing lots; sorti-legy, -tion; *sortes*, – *Virgilianae*; *rouge et noir*, hazard, *roulette*, pitch and toss, chuck-farthing, cup-tossing, heads or tails, cross and pile, wager; bet, -ting; risk, stake, plunge; gambling; the turf.

stock exchange, bourse, board of trade, curb exchange.

gaming-, gambling-, betting-house; hell; betting ring, totalizator; dice, – box; dicer; gam-bler, -ester, plunger, stock operator, manipulator, punter; man of the turf; adventurer, speculator; bookmaker, layer, backer.

V. chance etc. (*hap*) 156; stand a chance etc. (*be possible*) 470.

toss up; cast –, draw- lots; leave –, trust- -to chance, – to the chapter of accidents; tempt fortune; chance it, take one's chance; run –, incur –, encounter- the -risk, – chance; stand the hazard of the die.

speculate, try one's luck, set on a cast, raffle, put into a lottery, buy a pig in a poke, shuffle the cards.

risk, venture, hazard, stake; lay, – a wager; make a bet, wager, bet, gamble, game, play for; play at chuck-farthing.

Adj. fortuitous etc. 156; unintentional, -ded; accidental; not meant; un-designed, -purposed; unpremeditated etc. 612; never thought of.

indiscriminate, promiscuous; undirected, random; aim-, drift-, design-, purpose-, cause-less; without purpose.

possible etc. 470.

Adv. casually etc. 156; unintentionally etc. *adj.*; unwittingly.

en passant, by the way, incidentally; as it may happen; at -random, – a venture, – haphazard; as luck would have it, by -chance, – good fortune; un-, -luckily.

† See note on 156.

622. Pursuit. [Purpose in action.]—**N.** pursuit; pursuing etc. *v.*; prosecution; pursuance; enterprise etc. (*undertaking*) 676; business etc. 625; adventure etc. (*essay*) 675; quest etc. (*search*) 461; scramble, hue and cry, game; hobby.

chase, hunt, *battue*, race, steeplechase, hunting, coursing; ven-ation, -ery; fox-chase; sport, -ing; shooting, angling, fishing, hawking.

pursuer; hunt-er, -sman; sportsman, Nimrod, the field; hound etc. 366.

V. pursue, prosecute, follow; run –, make –, be –, hunt – prowl- after; shadow; carry on etc. (*do*) 680; engage in etc. (*undertake*) 676; set about etc. (*begin*) 66; endeavor etc. 675; court etc. (*request*) 765; seek etc. (*search*) 461; aim at etc. (*intention*) 620; follow the trail etc. (*trace*) 461; fish for etc. (*experiment*) 463; press on etc. (*haste*) 684; run a race etc. (*velocity*) 274.

chase, give chase, course, dog, hunt, hound, stalk; tread –, follow- on the heels of etc. (*sequence*) 281.

rush upon; rush headlong etc. (*violence*) 173;

ride –, run- full tilt at; make a leap –, jump –, snatch- at; run down; start game.

tread a path; take –, hold- a course; shape –, direct –, bend- one's -steps, – course; play a game; fight –, elbow- one's way; follow up; take - to, – up; go in for; ride one's hobby.

Adj. pursuing etc. *v.*; in quest of etc. (*inquiry*) 461; in -pursuit, – full cry, – hot pursuit; on the scent.

Adv. in pursuance of etc. (*intention*) 620; after.

Int. tally-ho! yoicks! so-ho!

623. Avoidance. [Absence of pursuit.]—**N.** abst-ention, -inence; forbearance; refraining etc. *v.*; inaction etc. 681; neutrality.

avoidance, evasion, elusion; seclusion etc. 893.

avolation, flight; escape etc. 671; retreat etc. 287; recoil etc. 277; departure etc. 293; rejection etc. 610.

shirker etc. *v.*; slacker; truant; fugitive, refugee; runa-way, -gate; renegade; deserter.

V. abstain, refrain, spare, not attempt; not do etc. 681; maintain the even tenor of one's way.

eschew, keep from, let alone, have nothing to do with; keep –, stand –, hold- -aloof, – off; take no part in, have no hand in.

avoid, shun; steer –, keep- clear of; fight shy of; keep -one's, – at a respectful- distance; keep –, get- out of the way; evade, elude, turn away from; set one's face against etc. (*oppose*) 708; deny oneself.

shrink; hang –, hold –, draw- back; recoil etc. 277; retire etc. (*recede*) 287; flinch, blink, blench, shy, shirk, dodge, parry, make way for, give place to.

beat a retreat; turn -tail, – one's back; take to one's heels; run, -away, – for one's life; cut and run; be off, – like a shot; fly, flee; fly –, flee –, run away- from; take –, take to- flight; desert, elope; make –, scamper –, sneak –, shuffle –, sheer- off; break –, burst –, tear oneself –, slip –, slink –, steal- -away, – away from; slip cable, part company, turn on one's heel; sneak out of, play truant, give one the go by, give leg bail, take French leave, slope, decamp, flit, bolt, abscond, levant, skedaddle, absquatulate, cut one's stick, walk one's chalks, show a light pair of heels, make oneself scarce; escape etc. 671; go away etc. (*depart*) 293; abandon etc. 624; reject etc. 610.

lead one a -dance, – a merry chase, – pretty dance; throw off the scent, play at hide and seek.

Adj. unsought, unattempted; avoiding etc. *v.*; neutral; shy of etc. (*unwilling*) 603; elusive, evasive, distant; fugitive, runaway; shy, wild.

Adj. lest, in order to avoid.

Int. forebear! keep –, hands- off! *sauve qui peut!* devil take the hindmost.

624. Relinquishment.—**N.** relinquish-, abandon-ment; desertion, defection, secession, withdrawal; cave of Adullam; *nolle prosequi.*

discontinuance etc. (*cessation*) 142; renunciation etc. (*recantation*) 607; abrogation etc. 756; resignation etc. (*retirement*) 757; desuetude etc. 614; cession etc. (*of property*) 782.

V. relinquish, give up, abandon, desert, forsake, leave in the lurch; depart –, secede –, withdraw- from; back – out of, – down from, leave, go back on one's word, quit, take leave of, bid a long farewell; vacate etc. (*resign*) 757.

renounce etc. (*abjure*) 607; forego, have done with, drop; write off; disuse etc. 678; discard etc. 782; wash one's hands of; drop all idea of; *nolle-pros.*; lose interest in.

break –, leave- off; desist; stop etc. (*cease*) 142; hold –, stay- one's hand; quit one's hold; give over, shut up shop.

throw up the -game, – cards; give up the -point, – argument; pass to the order of the day, move the previous question, table the motion.

Adj. unpursued; relinquished etc. *v.*; relinquishing etc. *v.*

Int. avast etc.! (*stop*) 142.

625. Business.—**N.** business, occupation, employment; pursuit etc. 622; what one is doing-, – about; affair, concern, matter, case, undertaking.

matter in hand, irons in the fire; thing to do, *agendum*, task, work, job, chore, errand, transaction, commission, mission, charge, care; duty etc. 926.

part, *rôle*, cue; province, function, look-out, department, capacity, sphere, orb, field, line; walk, – of life; beat, round, routine; race, career.

office, place, post, incumbency, living situation, appointment, billet, berth, employ; service etc. (*servitude*) 749; engagement; undertaking etc. 676.

vocation, calling, profession, *métier*, cloth, faculty; industry, art; industrial arts; craft, mystery, handicraft; trade etc. (*commerce*) 794.

exercise; work etc. (*action*) 680; avocation; press of business etc. (*activity*) 682.

V. pass –, employ –, spend- one's time in; employ oneself -in, – upon; occupy –, concern- oneself with; make it one's -business etc. *n.*; undertake etc. 676; enter a profession; betake oneself to, turn one's hand to; have to do with etc. (*do*) 680.

drive a trade; carry on –, do –, transact- - business, – a trade etc. *n.*; keep a shop; ply one's task, – trade; labor in one's vocation; pursue the even tenor of one's way; attend to -business, – one's work.

officiate, serve, act; act –, play- one's part; do duty; serve –, discharge –, perform- the -office, – duties, – functions- of; hold –, fill- -an office, – a place, – a situation; hold a portfolio.

be -about, – doing, – engaged in, – employed in, – occupied with, – at work on; have one's hands in, have in hand; have on one's -hands, – shoulders; bear the burden; have one's hands full etc. (*activity*) 682.

be -in the hands of, – on the stocks, – on the anvil; pass through one's hands.

Adj. business-like; work-a-day; professional; official, functional; busy etc. (*actively employed*) 682; on –, in- -hand, – one's hands; afoot; on - foot, – the anvil; going on; acting.

Adv. in the course of business, all in a day's work; professionally etc. *adj.*

626. Plan.—**N.** plan, scheme, design, project; propos-al, -ition; suggestion; resolution, motion;

precaution etc. (*provision*) 673; deep-laid etc. (*premeditated*) 611- plan etc.; racket.

system etc. (*order*) 58; organization etc. (*arrangement*) 60; germ etc. (*cause*) 153; Five Year Plan.

sketch, skeleton, outline, draught, draft, *ébauche*, *brouillon*; rough-cast, – draft, – draught, – copy; proof, revise.

forecast, *programme*, prospectus, scenario; *carte du pays*; card; bill, protocol; order of the day, list of agenda, *memorandum*; bill of fare etc. (*food*) 298; base of operations; platform, plank.

rôle; policy etc. (*line of conduct*) 692.

contrivance, invention, expedient, receipt, nostrum, artifice, device, gadget; stratagem etc. (*cunning*) 702; trick etc. (*deception*) 545; alternative, loophole, shift etc. (*substitute*) 147; last shift etc. (*necessity*) 601.

measure, step; stroke, – of policy; master stroke; trump-, court-card; *chaval de bataille*, great gun; *coup*, – *d'état*; clever –, bold –, good- -move, – hit, – stroke; bright -thought, – idea, great idea.

intrigue, cabal, plot, frame-up, conspiracy, complot, machination; under-, counter-plot.

schem-ist, -atist; stragetist, machinator, schemer; projector, author, builder, artist, promoter, designer etc. *v.*; conspirator; *intrigant* etc. (*cunning*) 702.

V. plan, scheme, design, frame, contrive, project, forecast, sketch; conceive, devise, invent etc. (*imagine*) 515; set one's wits to work etc. 515; spring a project; fall –, hit- upon; strike –, chalk –, cut –, lav –, map-out; lay down a plan; shape –, mark- out a course; predetermine etc. 611; concert, preconcert, preestablish; prepare etc. 673; hatch, – a plot; concoct; take -steps, – measures.

cast, recast, systematize, organize; arrange etc. 60; digest, mature.

plot; counter-plot, -mine; dig a mine; lay a train; intrigue etc. (*cunning*) 702.

Adj. planned etc. *v.*; strategic, -al; planning etc. *v.*; in course of preparation etc. 673; under consideration; on the -*tapis*, – carpet, – table.

627. Method. [Path.]—**N.** method, way, manner, wise, gait, form, mole, fashion, tone, guise; *modus operandi*; procedure etc. (*line of conduct*) 692.

path, road, route, course; line of -way, – road; trajectory, orbit, track, beat, tack.

steps; stair, -case; flight of stairs, ladder, stile.

bridge, viaduct, gauntry, pontoon, stepping stone, plank, gangway, catwalk, drawbridge; pass, ford, ferry, tunnel, subway, elevated; pipe etc. 260.

door; gateway etc. (*opening*) 260; channel, passage, avenue, means of access, approach, perron, adit, entrance; artery, lane, alley, aisle, lobby, corridor, cloister; back- door, -stairs; secret passage; covert-way.

road-, path-, stair-way; thoroughfare; highway, pike, turnpike, trail, parkway, *boulevard*; turnpike –, royal –, coach- road; broad –, King's –, Queen's- highway; beaten -track, – path; horse –, bridle- road, – track, – path; pathway; walk, *trottoir*, foot-path, pavement, flags, side-walk; by –, cross- -road, – path, – way; cut; short -cut etc. (*mid-course*) 628; *carrefour*; private –, occupation- road; highways and byways; rail-, tramroad, -way; funicular, ropeway, causeway; defile, cutting; canal etc. (*conduit*) 350; street etc. (*abode*) 189.

Adv. how; in what -way, – manner; by what mode; so, in this way, after this fashion, on these lines.

one way or another, anyhow; somehow or other etc. (*instrumentality*) 631; by way of; *viâ*; *in transitu* etc. 270; on the high road to.

Phr. *hae tibi erunt artes.*

628 Mid-course.—N. middle-, mid-course; moderation, mean etc. 29; middle etc. 68; *juste milieu*, *mezzo termine*, golden mean, *aurea mediocritas*.

straight etc. (*direct*) 278 -course, – path; short – cross- cut; short- circuit; great circle sailing.

neutrality; half –, half and half- measures; compromise.

V. keep in –, steer –, preserve- -a middle, – an even- course; go straight etc. (*direct*) 278.

go half way, compromise, make a compromise.

Adj. neutral, average, even, impartial, moderate, straight etc. (*direct*) 278.

629. Circuit.—N. circuit, round-about way, digression, divagation, *détour*, circum-ambience, -ambulation, bendibus, *ambages*, loop; winding etc. (*circuition*) 311; zigzag etc. (*deviation*) 279.

V. perform –, make- a circuit; go -round about, – out of one's way; make a *détour*; meander etc. (*deviate*) 27; circumambulate.

lead a pretty dance; beat about, – the bush; make two bites of a cherry.

adj. circuitous, indirect, round-about; zig-zag etc. (*deviating*) 279; circum-ambient, -ambulatory.

Adv. by -a side wind, – an indirect course; in a roundabout way; from pillar to post.

630. Requirement.—N. requirement, need, wants, necessities; necessaries, – of life; stress, exigency, pinch, *sine quâ non*, matter of necessity; case of -need, – life or death.

needfulness, essentiality, necessity, indispensability, urgency, prerequisite.

requisition etc. (*request*) 765, (*exaction*) 741; run upon; demand –, call- for.

desideratum etc. (*desire*) 865; want etc. (*deficiency*) 640.

charge, claim, command, injunction, requisition, mandate, order, *ultimatum*.

V. require, need, want, have occasion for, entail; not be able to -do without, – dispense with; prerequire.

render necessary, necessitate, create a necessity for, call for, put in requisition; make a requisition etc. (*ask for*) 765, (*demand*) 741,

stand in need of; lack etc. 640; desiderate; desire etc. 865; be -necessary etc. *adj.*

Adj. required etc. *v.*; requisite, needful,

necessary, imperative, essential, indispensable, prerequisite; called for; in -demand, – request.

urgent, exigent, pressing, instant, crying, absorbing.

in want of; destitute of etc. 640.

Adv. *ex necessitate rei* etc. (*necessarily*) 601; of –, out of stern- necessity; at a pinch.

Phr. there is no time to lose; it cannot be -spared, – dispensed with.

631. Instrumentality.—N. instrumentality; aid etc. 707; subservien-ce, -cy; mediation, intervention, -mediacy, medium, inter-medium, -mediary, vehicle, hand; agency etc. 170.

minister, handmaid, servant, slave, maid, valet; midwife, *accoucheur*, obstetrician; go-between; cat's paw; stepping-stone.

key; master –, pass –, latch- key; 'open sesame;' passport, *passe partout*, safe-conduct; influence.

instrument etc. 633; expedient etc. (*plan*) 626; means etc. 632.

V. subserve, minister, tend, mediate, intervene; come –, go- between, interpose; pull the strings; be -instrumental etc. *adj.*; pander to.

Adj. instrumental; useful etc. 644; ministerial, subservient, mediatorial; inter-mediate, -vening; conducive.

Adv. through, by, *per*; where-, there-, here-by; by the -agency etc. 170- of; by dint of; by –, in- virtue of; through the -medium etc. *n.*- of; along with; on the shoulders of; by means of etc. 632; by –, with- -the aid etc. (*assistance*) 707- of.

per fas et nefas, by fair means or foul; somehow, – or other; by hook or by crook.

632. Means.—N. means, resources, revenue, wherewithal, ways and means, income; capital etc. (*money*) 800; stock in trade etc. 636; provision etc. 637; a shot in the locker; appliances etc. (*machinery*) 633; means and appliances; conveniences; cards to play; expendients etc. (*measures*) 626; two strings to one's bow; sheet anchor etc. (*safety*) 666; aid etc. 707; medium etc. 631.

V. find –, have –, possess- means etc. *n.*; provide the wherewithal.

Adj. instrumental etc. 631; mechanical etc. 633.

Adv. by means of, with; by -what, – all, – any, – some- means; where-, here-, there-with; wherewithal.

how etc. (*in what manner*) 627; through etc. (*by the instrumentality of*) 631; with –, by- the aid etc. (*assistance*) 707- of; by the -agency etc. 170- of.

633. Instrument.—N. machinery, mechanism, engineering.

instrument, organ, tool, implement, utensil, contrivance, machine, motor, engine, lathe, gin, mill, pump.

gear; tack-le, -ling, trice, rigging, gear, apparatus, appliances; plant, *matériel*; harness, trappings, fittings, accouterments; equip-ment, -age; appointments, furniture, upholstery; chattels; paraphernalia etc. (*belongings*) 780; *impedimenta*.

mechanical powers; lever, -age; mechanical advantage; crow, -bar; handspike, gavelock, jemmy, arm, limb, wing; oar, paddle; pulley, sheave; parbuckle; wheel and axle; wheel-, clock-work; wheels within wheels; pinion, gear wheel, spur –, bevel-gearing, chains, belting, crank, winch, capstan, windlass, crane, derrick, hoist, lift etc. 307; cam; pedal; wheel etc. (*rotation*) 312; inclined plane; wedge; screw; jack; spring, mainspring.

handle, hilt, haft, shaft, heft, shank, blade, trigger, tiller, helm, treadle, key; turnscrew, screwdriver, spanner, wrench.

hammer etc. (*impulse*) 276; edge tool etc. (*cut*) 253; borer etc. 262; vice, teeth etc. (*hold*) 781; nail, rope etc. (*join*) 45; peg etc. (*hang*) 214; support etc. 215; spoon etc. (*vehicle*) 272; arms etc. 727; oar etc. (*navigation*) 267.

Adj. instrumental etc. 631; mechanical, machinal, automatic, self-acting; brachial.

634. Substitute.—N. substitute etc. 147; deputy etc. 759; proxy, alternative, understudy.

635. Materials.—N. material, raw material, stuff, stock, staple; building materials, bricks and mortar; metal; stone; clay, brick; crockery etc. 384; compo, -sition; reinforced –, ferro-, concrete; cement; wood, ore, timber; gravel, cobbles, macadam, asphalt, tarmac.

materials; supplies, munition, fuel, grist, household stuff; *pabulum* etc. (*food*) 298; ammunition etc. (*arms*) 727; contingents; relay, reinforcement; baggage etc. (*personal property*) 780; means etc. 632.

Adj. raw etc. (*unprepared*) 674; wooden etc. *n.*

636. Store.—N. stock, fund, mine, vein, lode, quarry; spring; fount, -ain; well, -spring; milch-cow.

stock in trade, supply; heap etc. (*collection*) 72; treasure; reserve, *corps de réserve*, reserve fund, nest-egg, savings, *bonne bouche*.

crop, harvest, mow, vintage; yield, product, gleanings.

store, accumulation, hoard, rick, stack; lumber; relay etc. (*provision*) 637.

store-house, -room, -closet; depository, *dépôt*, *cache*, safe deposit, vault, pantechnicon, repository, -servatory, -pertory; *repertorium*; promptuary, warehouse, *entrepôt*, magazine, dump, buttery, larder, pantry, panary, lanary, still-room, spence; crib, garner, granary, silo, barn; bunker; thesaurus; bank etc. (*treasury*) 802; armoury; arsenal; dock; gallery, museum, library, conservatory, hot-house; manag-ery, -erie, aquarium, zoological gardens.

reservoir, cistern, tank, sump, pond, mill-pond; gasometer.

budget, quiver, bandolier, portfolio; coffer etc. (*receptacle*) 191.

conservation; storing etc. *v.*; storage.

dictionary etc. 562; list etc. 86.

V. store; put –, lay –, set- by; stow away; set –, lay- apart; store –, hoard –, treasure –, lay –, heap –, put –, garner –, save- up; *cache*; accumulate, amass, hoard, fund, garner, save, bank.

conserve, reserve; keep –, hold- back; husband, – one's resources.

deposit; stow, stack, load, dump; harvest; heap, collect etc. 72; lay -in, – down, – by, store etc. *adj.*; keep, file [papers] lay in etc. (*provide*) 637; preserve etc. 670; put by for a rainy day.

Adj. stored etc. *v.*; in -store, – reserve, – ordinary; spare, supernumerary.

637. Provision.—N. provision, supply; grist, – to the mill; subvention etc. (*aid*) 707; resources etc. (*means*) 632.

provising etc. *v.*; purveyance; reinforcement; commissary, commissariat.

rations; iron –, emergency- rations; provender etc. (*food*) 298; *viaticum*; ensilage.

caterer, purveyor, commissary, quartermaster, steward, housekeeper, manciple, feeder, batman, victualler, storekeeper, grocer, provision merchant, green-, grocer, *comprador*, *restaurateur*; sutler etc. (*merchant*) 797; innkeeper, publican, confectioner, baker, butcher, wine merchant, vintner.

V. provide; make -provision, – due provision for; lay in, – a stock, – a store.

sup-ply, -peditate; furnish; find, – one in; arm.

cater, victual, provision, purvey, forage; beat up for; stock, – with; make good, replenish; fill, – up; recruit, feed, ration.

have in -store, – reserve; keep, – by one, – on foot; have to fall back upon; store etc. 636; provide against a rainy day etc. (*economy*) 817.

638. Waste.—N. consumption, expenditure, exhaustion; dispersion etc. 73; ebb; leakage etc. (*exudation*) 295; loss etc. 776; wear and tear; waste; prodigality etc. 818; misuse etc. 679; wasting etc. *v.*; rubbish etc. (*useless*) 645.

mountain in labor.

v. spend, expend, use, consume, swallow up, exhaust, deplete; impoverish; spill, drain, empty; disperse etc. 73.

cast –, throw –, fling –, fritter- away; burn the candle at both ends, waste; squander etc. 818.

'waste its sweetness on the desert air;' cast -one's bread upon the waters, – pearls before swine; employ a steam engine to crack a nut, waste powder and shot, break a butterfly on a wheel; labor in vain etc. (*useless*) 645; cut a whetstone with a razor, pour water into a sieve; tilt at windmills.

leak etc. (*run out*) 295; run to waste; ebb; melt away, run dry, dry up.

Adj. wasted etc. *v.*; at a low ebb.

wasteful etc. (*prodigal*) 818; penny wise and pound foolish.

Phr. *magno conatu magnas nugas; le jeu n'en vaut pas la chandelle.*

639. Sufficiency.—N. sufficiency, adequacy, enough, withal, *quantum sufficit*, satisfaction, competence; no less.

mediocrity etc. (*average*) 29.

fill; fullness etc (*completeness*) 52; plen-itude, -ty; abundance; copiousness etc. *adj.*; amplitude, galore, lots, profusion; full measure; 'good measure pressed down, shaken together and running over.'

luxuriance etc. (*fertility*) 168; affluence etc. (*wealth*) 803; fat of the land; 'a land flowing with milk and honey;' cornucopia; horn of -plenty, – Amalthaea; mine etc. (*stock*) 636.

outpouring; flood etc. (*great quantity*) 31; tide etc. (*river*) 348; repletion etc. (*reduncance*) 641; satiety etc. 869; rich man etc. 803.

V. be -sufficient etc. *adj.*; suffice, do, just do, satisfy, pass muster; have -enough etc. *n.*; eat –, drink –, have- one's fill; roll –, swim- in; wallow in etc. (*superabundance*) 641.

abound, exuberate, teem, flow, stream, rain, shower down; pour, – in; swarm; bristle with.

render -sufficient etc. *adj.*; replenish etc. (*fill*) 52.

Adj. sufficient, enough, adequate, up to the mark, commensurate, competent, satisfactory, valid, tangible.

measured; moderate etc. (*temperate*) 953.

full etc. (*complete*) 52; ample; plen-ty, -tiful, -teous; plenty as blackberries; copious, abundant; abounding etc. *v.*; replete, enough and to spare, flush; choke-full; well-stocked, -provided; liberal; unstint-ed, -ing; stintless; without stint; un-sparing, -measured; lavish etc. 641; wholesale.

rich, luxuriant etc. (*fertile*) 168; affluent etc. (*wealthy*) 803; wantless; big with etc. (*pregnant*) 161.

un-exhausted, -wasted; exhaustless, inexhaustible.

Adv. sufficiently, amply etc. *adj.*; full; in -abundance etc. *n.*; with no sparing hand; to one's heart's content, *ad libitum*, without stint.

Phr. cut and come again.

640. Insufficiency.—N. insufficiency; inadequa-cy, -teness; incompetence etc. (*impotence*) 158; deficiency etc. (*incompleteness*) 53; imperfection etc. 651; shortcoming etc. 304; paucity; stint; scantiness etc. (*smallness*) 32; none to spare; bare subsistence.

scarcity, dearth; want, need, lack, poverty, exigency; inanition, starvation, famine, drought.

dole, pittance, mite; short -allowance, – commons; half-rations; banyan –, fast- day, Lent.

emptiness, poorness etc. *adj.*; depletion, vacancy, flaccidity; ebb-tide; low water; 'a beggarly account of empty boxes;' indigence etc. (*poverty*) 804; insolvency etc. (*non-payment*) 808; poor man etc. 804; bankrupt etc. 808.

V. be -insufficient etc. *adj.*; not -suffice etc. 639; come short of etc. 304; run dry.

want, lack, need, require; *caret*; be in want etc. (*poor*) 804; live from hand to mouth.

render- insufficient etc. *adj.*; drain of resources; impoverish etc. (*waste*) 638; stint etc. (*begrudge*) 819; put on short -commons, – allowance.

do -insufficiently etc. *adv.*; scotch the snake.

Adj. insufficient, inadequate; too -little etc. 32; not -enough etc. 639; unequal to; incompetent etc. (*impotent*) 158; 'weighed in the balance and found wanting;' perfunctory etc. (*neglect*) 460; deficient etc. (*incomplete*) 53; wanting etc. *v.*; imperfect etc. 651; ill-furnished, -provided, -stored, -off.

slack, at a low ebb; empty, vacant, bare; short –, out –, destitute –, devoid –, bereft etc. 789 –, denuded- of; dry, drained.

un -provided, -supplied, -furnished; unreplenished, -fed; un-stored, -treasured; empty-handed.

meager, poor, thin, scrimp, sparing, spare, stinted, stunted; skimpy; starv-ed, -eling; half-starved, emaciated, famine-stricken, famished, underfed, undernourished; jejune.

scant etc. (*small*) 32; scarce; not to be had, – for love or money, – at any price; scurvy; stingy etc. 819; at the end of one's tether; without -resources etc. 632; in want etc. (*poor*) 804; in debt etc. 806.

Adv. insufficiently etc. *adj.*; in default –, for want- of; failing.

641. Redundance.—N. redundance; too -much, – many; superabundance, -fluity, -fluence, -saturation; nimiety, transcendency, exuberance, profuseness; profusion etc. (*plenty*) 639; repletion, enough in all conscience, *satis superque*, lion's share; more than -enough etc. 639; plethora, engorgement, congestion, load, surfeit, sickener; turgescence etc. (*expansion*) 194; over-dose, -measure, -supply, -flow; inundation etc. (*water*) 348; *avalanche*.

accumulation etc. (*store*) 636; heap etc. 72; drug, – in the market; glut; crowd; burden.

excess; sur-, over-plus, epact; margin; remainder etc. 40; duplicate; surplusage; expletive; work of –, supererogation; *bonus*, *bonanza*.

luxury; intemperance etc. 954; extravagance etc. (*prodigality*) 818; exorbitance, lavishment.

pleonasm etc. (*diffuseness*) 573; too many irons in the fire; embarassment of riches; money to burn.

V. super-, over-abound; know no bounds, swarm; meet one at every turn; creep –, bristle-with; overflow; run –, flow –, well –, brim-over; run riot; over-run, -stock, -lay, -charge, -dose, -feed, -burden, -load, -do, -whelm, -shoot the mark etc. (*go beyond*) 303; surcharge, supersaturate, gorge, glut, load, drench, whelm, inundate, deluge, flood; drug, – the market.

choke, cloy, accloy, suffocate; pile up, lay it on, – with a trowel, lay on thick; impregnate with; lavish etc. (*squander*) 818.

send –, carry- coals to Newcastle, – owls to Athens; teach one's grandmother to suck eggs; *pisces natare docere*; kill the slain, 'gild refined gold,' 'paint the lily;' butter one's bread on both sides, put butter upon bacon; employ a steam-engine to crack a nut etc. (*waste*) 638.

exaggerate etc. 549; wallow in; roll in etc. (*plenty*) 639; remain on one's hands, hang heavy on hand, go a begging.

Adj. redundant; too -much, – many; exuberant, inordinate, superabundant, excessive, overmuch, replete, profuse, lavish; prodigal etc. 818; exorbitant; overweening; extravagant; overcharged etc. *v.*; supersaturated, drenched, overflowing; running -over, – to waste, – down.

crammed –, filled- to overflowing; gorged, stuffed, ready to burst; dropsical, turgid, plethoric, full-blooded; obese etc. 194; voluminous.

superfluous, unnecessary, needless, supervacaneous, uncalled for, to spare, in excess; over and above etc. (*remainder*) 40; *de trop*; adscititious etc. (*additional*) 37; supernumerary etc. (*reserve*) 636; on one's hands, spare, duplicate, supererogatory, expletive; *un peu fort*.

Adj. over, too, over and above; over –, too-much; too far; without –, beyond – out of-measure; with ... to spare; over head and ears; up to one's eyes, – ears; *extra*; beyond the mark etc. (*transcursion*) 303; over one's head.

Phr. It never rains but it pours.

642. Importance.—N. importance, consequence, moment, prominence, consideration, mark, materialness.

import, significance, concern; emphasis, interest.

greatness etc. 31; superiority etc. 33; notability etc. (*repute*) 873; weight etc. (*influence*) 175; value etc. (*goodness*) 648; usefulness etc. 644.

gravity, seriousness, solemnity; no -joke, – laughing matter; pressure, urgency, stress; matter of life and death.

memorabilia, *notabilia*, great doings; red-letter day.

great -thing, – point; main chance, 'the be all and end all,' cardinal point, outstanding feature; substance, gist etc. (*essence*) 5; sum and substance, *gravamen*, head and front; important –, principal –, prominent –, essential- part; half the battle; *sine quâ non*; breath of one's nostrils etc. (*life*) 359; cream, salt, core, kernel, heart, nucleus; key, -note, -stone; corner stone; trumpcard etc. (*device*) 626; salient points.

top-sawyer, first fiddle, *prima donna*, chief, bigwig; triton among the minnows.

V. be -important etc. *adj.*, – somebody, – something; import, signify, matter, be an object; carry weight etc. (*influence*) 175; make a figure etc. (*repute*) 873; be in the ascendant, come to the front, lead the way, take the lead, play first fiddle, throw all else into the shade; lie at the root of; deserve –, merit –, be worthy- -of notice, – regard, – consideration.

attach –, ascribe –, give- importance etc. *n.*-to; value, care for; set store -upon, – by; mark etc. 550; mark with a white stone, underline; write –, put –, print- in -italics, – capitals, – large letters, – large type, – letters of gold; accentuate, emphasize, lay stress on.

make -a fuss, – a stir, – a piece of work, – much ado- about; make -of, – much of.

Adj. important; of -importance etc. *n.*; momentous, material; to the point; not to be -overlooked, – despised, – sneezed at; egregious; weighty etc. (*influential*) 175; of note etc. (*repute*) 873; notable, prominent, salient, signal; memorable, remarkable; worthy of -remark, – notice; never to be forgotten; stirring, eventful.

grave, serious, earnest, noble, grand, solemn, impressive, commanding, imposing.

urgent, pressing, critical, instant.

paramount, essential, vital, all-absorbing, radical, cardinal, chief, main, prime, primary, principal, leading, capital, foremost, overruling; of vital etc. importance.

in the front rank, first-rate, A1; superior etc. 33; considerable etc. (*great*) 31; marked etc. *v.*; rare etc. 137.

significant, telling, trenchant, emphatic, pregnant; *tanti*.

Adv. materially etc. *adj.*; in the main; above all, *par excellence*, to crown all.

643. Unimportance.—N. unimportance, insignificance, nothingness, immateriality.

triviality, trivia, fribble, levity, frivolity; paltriness etc. *adj.*; poverty; smallness etc. 32; vanity etc. (*uselessness*) 645; matter of - indifference etc. 866; no object; side issue.

nothing, – to signify, – worth speaking of, – particular, – to boast of, – to speak of; small –, no great –, trifling etc. *adj.*-matter; mere -joke, – nothing; hardly –, scarcely- anything; nonentity, cipher, figurehead; no great shakes, *peu de chose*; child's play; small beer.

toy, plaything, popgun, paper pellet, gimcrack, geegaw, bauble, trinket, *bagatelle*, kickshaw, knicknack, whim-wham, trifle, 'trifles light as air.'

trumpery, trash, rubbish, stuff, *fatras*, frippery; 'leather or prunello;' chaff, drug, froth, bubble, smoke, cobweb; weed; refuse etc. (*inutility*) 645; scum etc. (*dirt*) 653.

joke, jest, snap of the fingers; fudge etc. (*unmeaning*) 517; fiddlestick, – end; pack of nonsense, mere farce.

straw, pin, fig, continental, button, rush; bulrush, feather, halfpenny, farthing, brass farthing, doit, peppercorn, jot, rap, pinch of snuff, old song.

minutiae, details, minor details, small fry; dust in the balance, feather in the scale, drop in the ocean, flea-bite, molehill; fingle-fangle.

nine days' wonder, *ridiculus mus*; flash in the pan etc. (*impotence*) 158; much ado about nothing etc. (*overestimation*) 482; storm in a teacup.

V. be -unimportant etc. *adj.*; not -matter etc. 642; go for –, matter –, signify- -little, – nothing, – little or nothing; not matter a -straw etc. *n.*

make light of etc. (*underestimate*) 483; catch at straws etc. (*overestimate*) 482.

Adj. unimportant; of -little, – small, – no- - account, – importance etc. 642; immaterial; un-, non-essential; not vital; irrelevant, incidental, indifferent.

subordinate etc. (*inferior*) 34; *médiocre* etc. (*average*) 29; passable, fair, respectable, tolerable, commonplace; uneventful, mere, common; ordinary etc. (*habitual*) 613; inconsiderable, so-so, insignificant, inappreciable, nugatory.

trifling, trivial; slight, slender, light, flimsy, frothy, idle; puerile etc. (*foolish*) 499; airy, shallow; weak etc. 160; powerless etc. 158; frivolous, petty, niggling; pid-, ped-dling; fribble, inane, ridiculous, farcical; fini-cal, -kin; fiddle-faddle, namby-pamby, wishy-washy, milk and water.

poor, paltry, pitiful; contemptible etc. (*contempt*) 930; sorry, mean, meager, shabby, miserable, wretched, vile, scrubby, scrannel, weedy, niggardly, scurvy, putid, beggarly, worthless, twopenny-half penny, cheap, trashy, catchpenny, gimcrack, trumpery, one-horse; toy.

not worth -the pains, – while, – mentioning, – speaking of, – a thought, – a curse, – a straw, – rap etc. *n.*; beneath –, unworthy of- -notice, – regard, – consideration, – contempt; *de lanâ caprinâ*; vain etc. (*useless*) 645.

Adv. slightly etc. *adj.*; rather, somewhat, pretty well, fairly well, tolerably.

for aught one cares.

Int. no matter! pish! tush! tut! pshaw! pugh! pooh, -pooh! fudge! bosh! humbug! fiddle-stick, – end! fiddlededee! never mind! *n'importe!* what - signifies, – matter, – boots it, – of that, –'s the odds! a fig for! stuff! nonsense! stuff and nonsense!

Phr. *magno conatu magnas nugas*; *le jeu n'en vaut pas la chandelle*; it -matters not, – does not signify; it is of no -consequence, – importance.

644. Utility.—N. utility; usefulness etc. *adj.*; efficacy, efficiency, adequacy; service, use, stead, avail; help etc. (*aid*) 707; applicability etc. *adj.*; subservience etc. (*instrumentality*) 631; function etc. (*business*) 625; value; worth etc. (*goodness*) 648; money's worth; productiveness etc. 168; *cui bono* etc. (*intention*) 620; utilization etc. (*use*) 677; step in the right direction.

common weal, public good; utilitarianism etc. (*philanthropy*) 910.

V. be -useful etc. *adj.*; avail, serve; subserve etc. (*be instrumental to*) 631; conduce etc. (*tend*) 176; answer –, serve- -one's turn, – a purpose.

act a part etc. (*action*) 680; perform –, discharge- -a function etc. 625; do –, render- -a service, – good service, – yeoman's service; bestead, stand one in good stead; be the making of; help etc. 707.

bear fruit etc. (*produce*) 161; bring grist to the mill; profit, remunerate; benefit etc. (*do good*) 648.

find one's -account, – advantage- in; reap the benefit of etc. (*be better for*) 658.

render useful etc. (*use*) 677.

Adj. useful; of -use etc. *n.*; serviceable, usable, proficuous, good for; subservient etc. (*instrumental*) 631; conducive etc. (*tending*) 176; subsidiary etc. (*helping*) 707.

advantageous etc. (*beneficial*) 648; profitable, gainful, remunerative, worth one's salt; in-, valuable; prolific etc. (*productive*) 168.

adequate; ef-ficient, -ficacious; effect-ive, -ual; practicable, expedient etc. 646.

applicable, available, ready, handy, at hand, tangible; commodious, adaptable; of all work.

Adv. usefully etc. *adj.*; *pro bono publico*.

645. Inutility.—N. inutility; uselessness etc. *adj.*; inefficacy, futility; inep-, inap-titude; un-subservience; inadequacy etc. (*insufficiency*) 640; inefficiency etc. (*incompetence*) 158; unskilfulness etc. 699; disservice; unfruitfulness etc. (*unproductiveness*) 169; labor -in vain, – lost, – of Sisyphus; lost -trouble, – labor; work of Penelope; sleeveless errand, wild goose chase, mere farce.

tautology etc. (*repetition*) 104; supererogation etc. (*redundance*) 641.

vanitas vanitatum, vanity, inanity, worthlessness, nugacity; triviality etc. (*unimportance*) 643.

caput mortuum, waste paper, dead letter; blunt tool.

litter, rubbish, lumber, odds and ends, cast-off clothes; button-top; shoddy; rags, orts, trash, refuse, sweepings, scourings, off-scourings, dross, slag, waste, rubble, dottle, drast, *débris*; stubble, leavings; broken meat; dregs etc. (*dirt*) 653; weeds, tares; rubbish heap, dust hole; *rudera*, deads.

fruges consumere natus etc. (*drone*) 683.

V. be -useless etc. *adj.*; go a begging etc. (*redundant*) 641; fail etc. 732.

seek –, strive- after impossibilities; use vain efforts, labor in vain, roll the stone of Sisyphus, beat the air, lash the waves; *battre l'eau avec un bâton, donner un coup d'épée dans l'eau*, fish in the air, milk the ram, drop a bucket into an empty well, sow the sand; bay the moon; preach –, speak- to the winds; whistle jigs to a milestone; kick against the pricks, *se battre contre des moulins*; lock the stable door when the steed is stolen etc. (*too late*) 135; hold a farthing candle to the sun; cast pearls before swine etc. (*waste*) 638; carry coals to Newcastle etc. (*redundance*) 641; wash a blackamoor white etc. (*impossible*) 471.

render -useless etc. *adj.*; dis-mantle, -mast, -mount, -qualify, -able; unrig; cripple, lame etc. (*injure*) 659; spike guns, clip the wings; put out of gear.

Adj. useless, inutile, inefficacious, futile, unavailing, bootless; inoperative etc. 158; inadequate etc. (*insufficient*) 640; in-, un- subservient; inept, inefficient etc. (*impotent*) 158; of no -avail etc. (*use*) 644; ineffectual etc. (*failure*) 732; incompetent etc. (*unskilful*) 699; 'stale, flat and unprofitable;' superfluous etc. (*redundant*) 641; dispensable; thrown away etc. (*wasted*) 638; abortive etc. (*immature*) 674.

worth-, value-less; unsaleable; not worth a straw etc. (*trifling*) 643; dear at any price.

vain, empty, inane; gain-, profit-, fruit-less; unserviceable, -profitable; ill-spent; unproductive etc. 169; *hors de combat*; barren, sterile, impotent, unproductive; effete, past work etc. (*impaired*) 659; obsolete etc. (*old*) 124; fit for the -dust-hole, – wastepaper basket; good for nothing; of no earthly use; not worth -having, – powder and shot; leading to no end, uncalled for; un-necessary, -needed, superfluous.

Adv. uselessly etc. *adj.*; to -little, – no, – little or no- purpose.

Int. *cui bono?* what's the good!

646. Expedience. [Specific subservience.]—**N.** expedien-ce, -cy; desirableness, -bility etc. *adj.*; fitness etc. (*agreement*) 23; utility etc. 644; propriety; advantage; opportunism, pragmatism.

high time etc. (*occasion*) 134.

V. be -expedient etc. *adj.*; suit etc. (*agree*) 23; befit; suit –, befit- the -time, – season, – occasion.

conform etc. 82.

Adj. expedient; desir-, advis-, accept-able; convenient; worth while, meet; fit, -ting; due, proper, eligible, seemly, becoming; befitting etc. *v.*; opportune etc. (*in season*) 134; *in loco*; suitable etc. (*accordant*) 23; applicable etc. (*useful*) 644; practical, effective, pragmatical; suitable, handy.

Adv. in the right place; conveniently etc. *adj.*; in the nick of time.

Phr. *operae pretium est.*

647. Inexpedience.—**N.** enexpedien-ce, -cy; undesira-bleness, -bility etc. *adj.*; discommodity, impropriety; unfitness etc. (*disagreement*) 24; inutility etc. 645; inconvenience, inadvisability; disadvantage.

V. be -inexpedient etc. *adj.*; come amiss etc. (*disagree*) 24; embarrass etc. (*hinder*) 706; put to inconvenience; pay too dear for one's whistle.

Adj. inexpedient, undesirable; un-, in-advisable; objectionable; troublesome, in-apt, -eligible, -admissable, -convenient; in-, dis-commodious; disadvantageous; inappropriate, unsuitable, unfit etc. (*inconsonant*) 24.

ill-contrived, -advised; unsatsifactory; unprofitable etc., unsubservient etc. (*useless*) 645; inopportune etc. (*unseasonable*) 135; out of –, in the wrong- place; improper, unseemly.

clumsy, awkward; cum-brous, -bersome; lumbering, unwieldy, hulky; unmanageable etc. (*impracticable*) 704; impedient (*in the way*) 706.

unnecessary etc. (*redundant*) 641.

Phr. it will never do.

648. Goodness. [Capability of producing good. Good qualities.]—**N.** goodness etc. *adj.*; excellence, merit; virtue etc. 944; value, worth, price.

super-excellence, -eminence; superiority etc. 33; perfection etc. 650; *coup de maître*; master-piece, *chef d'oeuvre*, prime, flower, cream, *élite*, pick, A1, none such, *nonpareil*, *crême de la crême*, flower of the flock, cock of the roost, salt of the earth; champion.

tid-bit; gem, – of the first water; *bijou*, precious stone, jewel, pearl, diamond, ruby, brilliant, treasure; good thing; *rara avis*, one in a thousand.

beneficence etc. 906; good man etc. 948.

V. be -beneficial etc. *adj.*; produce –, do- -good etc. 618; profit etc. (*be of use*) 644; benefit; confer a -benefit etc. 618.

be the making of, do a world of good, make a man of.

produce a good effect; do a good turn, confer an obligation; improve etc. 658.

do no harm, break no bones.

be -good etc. *adj.*; excel, transcend etc. (*be superior*) 33; bear away the bell.

stand the -proof, – test; pass -muster, – an examination.

challenge comparison, vie, emulate, rival.

Adj. harm-, hurt-less; unobnoxious; in-nocuous, -nocent, -offensive.

beneficial, valuable, of value; serviceable etc. (*useful*) 644; advantageous, profitable, edifying; salutary etc. (*healthful*) 656.

favorable; propitious etc. (*hopegiving*) 858; fair.

good, – as gold; excellent; better; superior etc. 33; above par; nice, fine; genuine etc. (*true*) 494.

best, choice, select, picked, elect, eximious, *recherché*, rare, priceless; unpara-goned, -lleled etc. (*supreme*) 33; superlatively etc. 33- good; super-fine, -excellent; bonzer; of the first water; first-rate, -class; high-wrought; exquisite, very best, crack, prime, tip-top, gilt-edged, capital, cardinal; standard etc. (*perfect*) 650; inimitable.

admirable, estimable; praiseworthy etc. (*approve*) 931; pleasing etc. 829; *couleur de rose*, precious, of great price; costly etc. (*dear*) 814; worth -its weight in gold, – a Jew's eye, – a king's ransom; matchless, peerless, invaluable, inestimable, precious as the apple of the eye.

tolerable etc. (*not very good*) 651; up to the mark, un-exceptionable, -objectionable; satisfactory, tidy.

in -good, – fair- condition; fresh; unspoiled; sound etc. (*perfect*) 650.

Adv. beneficially etc. *adj.*; well etc. 618.

649. Badness. [Capability of producing evil. Bad qualities.]—**N.** hurtfulness etc. *adj.*; virulence.

evil doer etc. 913; bane etc. 663; plague-spot etc. (*insalubrity*) 657; evil star, ill wind; snake in the grass, skeleton in the closet; *amari aliquid*, thorn in the side; Jonah, jinx, hoodoo.

malignity; malevolence etc. 907; tender mercies [ironically].

ill-treatment, annoyance, molestation, abuse, oppression, persecution, outrage; misusage etc. 679; injury etc. (*damage*) 659.

badness etc. *adj.*; peccancy, abomination; painfulness etc. 830; pestilence etc. (*disease*) 655; guilt etc. 947; depravity etc. 945.

V. be -hurtful etc. *adj.*; cause –, produce –, inflict –, work –, do- evil etc. 619; damnify, endamage, hurt, harm, scathe; injure etc. (*damage*) 659; pain etc. 830.

wrong, aggrieve, oppress, persecute; trample –, tread –, bear hard –, put-upon; overburden; weigh -down, – heavy on; victimize; run down; molest etc. 830.

maltreat, abuse; ill-use, -treat; thwart, buffet, bruise, scratch, maul; smite etc. (*scourge*) 972; do -violence, – harm, – a mischief; stab, pierce, outrage.

do –, make- mischief; bring –, get- into trouble.

destroy etc. 162.

Adj. hurt-, harm-, scath-, bane-, bale-ful; injurious, deleterious, detrimental, noxious, pernicious, mischievous, full of mischief, mischief-making, malefie, malignant, nocuous, noisome; prejudicial; dis-serviceable, advantageous; wide-wasting.

unlucky, sinister; obnoxious, untoward, disastrous.

oppressive, burdensome, onerous; malign etc. (*malevolent*) 907.

corrupting etc. (corrupt etc. 659) virulent, venomous, envenomed, corrosive; poisonous etc. (*morbific*) 657; deadly etc. (*killing*) 361; destructive etc. (*destroying*) 162; inauspicious etc. 859.

bad, ill, arrant, as bad bad can be, dreadful; horrid, -rible; dire; rank, peccant, foul, fulsome; rotten, – at the core.

vile, base, villainous; mean etc. (*paltry*) 643; injured etc., deteriorated etc. 659; unsatisfactory, exception, -able, indifferent; below par etc. (*imperfect*) 651; ill-contrived, -conditioned; wretched, sad, grievous, deplorable, lamentable; piti-ful, -able, woeful etc. (*painful*) 830.

evil, wrong; depraved etc. 945; shocking; reprehensible etc. (*disapprove*) 932.

hateful, – as a toad; abominable, detestable, execrable, cursed, accursed, confounded; damn-ed, -able; infernal; diabolic etc. (*malevolent*) 907.

inadvisable etc. (*inexpedient*) 647; unprofitable etc. (*useless*) 645; incompetent etc. (*unskilful*) 699; irremediable etc. (*hopeless*) 859.

Adv. badly etc. *adj.*; wrong, ill; to one's cost; where the shoe pinches.

Phr. bad is the best; the worst come to the worst.

650. Perfection.—N. perfection; perfectness etc. *adj.*; indefectibility; inpecc-ancy, -ability.

pink, *beau idéal*, phoenix, paragon; pink –, acme- of perfection; *ne plus ultra*; summit etc. 210.

cygne noir; philosopher's stone; chrysolite, Koh-i-noor, black tulip.

model, standard, pattern, mirror, admirable Chrichton; trump; very prince of.

master-piece, -stroke, super-excellence etc. (*goodness*) 648; transcendence etc. (*superiority*) 33.

V. be -perfect etc. *adj.*; transcend etc. (*be supreme*) 33.

bring to perfection, perfect, ripen, mature; consummate, complete etc. 729; put in trim etc. (*prepare*) 673; put the finishing touch to.

Adj. perfect, faultless, ideal; indefective, -ficient, -fectible; immaculate, spotless, impeccable; free from -imperfection etc. 651; un-blemished, -injured etc. 659; sound, – as a roach; in perfect condition; scathless, intact, harmless; seaworthy etc. (*safe*) 644; right as a trivet; *in seipso totus teres atque rotundus*; consummate etc. (*complete*) 52; finished etc. 729; complete in itself.

best etc. (*good*) 648; model, standard; inimitable, unparagoned, unparalleled etc. (*supreme*) 33; superhuman, divine; beyond all praise etc. (*approbation*) 931; *sans peur et sans reproche*.

Adj. to perfection, to the limit; perfectly etc. *adj.*; *ad unguem*; clean, – as a whistle.

651. Imperfection.—N. imperfection; imperfectness etc. *adj.*; deficiency; inadequacy etc. (*insufficiency*) 640; peccancy etc. (*badness*) 649; immaturity etc. 674.

fault, defect, weak point; screw loose; rift within the lute; fly in the ointment; flaw etc. (*break*) 70; gap etc. 198; twist etc. 243; taint, attainder; bar sinister, hole in one's coat; blemish etc. 848; weakness etc. 160; half-blood, touch of the tar brush; shortcoming etc. 304; drawback; seamy side.

mediocrity; no great -shakes, – catch; not much to boast of.

V. be -imperfect etc. *adj.*; have a -defect etc. *n.*; lie under a disadvantage; spring a leak.

not –, barely- pass muster; fall short etc. 304.

Adj. imperfect; not -perfect etc. 650; de-ficient, -fective; faulty, unsound, mutilated, tainted; out of -order, – tune; cracked, leaky; sprung; warped etc. (*distort*) 243; lame; injured etc. (*deteriorated*) 659; peccant etc. (*bad*) 649; frail etc. (*weak*) 160; inadequate etc. (*insufficient*) 640; crude etc. (*unprepared*) 674; incomplete etc. 53; found wanting; below par; shorthanded; below –, under- its full -strength, – complement.

indifferent, middling, ordinary, mediocre; average etc. 29; so-so; *così-così*, milk and water; tolerable, fair, passable; pretty -well, – good; rather –, moderately- good; good –, well-enough; decent; not -bad, – amiss; inobjectionable, admissable, bearable, only better than nothing.

secondary, inferior; second-rate, -best, one-horse.

Adv. almost etc.; to a limited extent, rather etc. 32; pretty, moderately; only; considering, all things considered, enough.

Phr. ***surgit amari aliquid.***

652. Cleanness.—N. cleanness etc. *adj.*; purity; cleaning etc. *v.*; purification, defecation etc. *v.*; purgation, lustration; de-, abs-tersion; epuration, mundation, ablution, lavation, colature; disinfection etc. *v.*; drain-, sewerage.

lavatory, bath, -room; swimming pool, natatorium; public baths; hot –, cold –, Turkish –, Swedish –, Russian – vapor- bath; *hammam*, laundry, washhouse; washerwoman, laundress, laundryman; scavenger, cleaner, sweeper, goodie; crossing sweeper, white wings, dustman, sweep.

brush; broom, besom, carpet-sweeper, vacuum-cleaner, mop, squilgee, rake, shovel, sieve, riddle, screen, filter; scraper, strigil.

napkin, *serviette*, cloth, table-, carving-cloth, table-linen, napery, maukin, handkerchief, towel, sudary; doyley, doily, duster, sponge, mop, swab.

cover, drugget, mat, doormat.

soap, wash, lotion, detergent, cathartic, purgative; purifier etc. *v.*; dentifrice, tooth-powder, -paste; mouth wash; disinfectant.

V. be –, render- clean etc. *adj.*

clean, -se; mundify, rinse, wring, flush, full, wipe, mop, sponge, scour, swab, scrub, holystone, brush up.

wash, shampoo, lave, launder, buck; abs-, deterge; clear, purify; de-purate, -spumate, -fecate; purge, expurgate; Bowdlerize; elutriate, lixiviate, edulcorate, clarify, refine, rack; fil-ter, -trate; drain, strain.

disinfect, sterilize, pasteurize, fumigate, ventilate, deodorize; whitewash.

sift, winnow, screen, riddle, pick, weed, comb, rake, brush, sweep.

rout –, clear –, sweep etc.- out; make a clean sweep of.

Adj. clean, -ly; pure; immaculate; spot-, stain-, taint-less; without a stain, un-stained, -spotted, -soiled, -sullied, -tainted, -infected, -adulterated; aseptic; sweet, – as a nut.

neat, spruce, tidy, trim, gimp, clean as a new penny, like a cat in pattens; cleaned etc. *v.*; kempt.

Adv. neatly etc. *adj.*; clean as a whistle.

653. Uncleanness.—N. uncleanness etc. *adj.*; impurity; immundi-ty, -city; impurity etc. [of mind] 961.

defilement, contamination etc. *v.*; defedation; soil-ure, -iness; abomination; leaven; taint, -ure; fetor etc. 401.

decay; putre-scence, -faction; corruption; mold, must, mildew, dry-rot, *mucor*, rubigo, caries.

slovenry; slovenliness etc. *adj.*; squalor.

dowdy, drab, slut, malkin, slattern, sloven, slammerkin, scrub, draggletail, mudlark, dustman, sweep; beast.

dirt, filth, soil, slop; dust, cobweb, flue; smoke, soot, smudge, smut, grime, raff.

sordes, dregs, grounds, lees; sedi-, settle-ment; heel-tap; dross, -iness; mother, precipitate, *scoria*, ashes, cinders, recrement, slag; scum, froth.

hog-wash, swill, ditch-, dish-, bilge-water; rinsings, cheese-parings; sweepings etc. (*useless refuse*) 645; off-, out-scourings; off-scum; *caput mortuum, residuum*, sprue, feculence, clinker, draff; scurf, -iness; *exuviae*, morphew; fur, -fur; dandruff; tartar.

riffraff; vermin, louse, cootie, flea, bug.

mud, mire, quagmire, *alluvium*, silt, sludge, slime, slush, slosh.

spawn, offal, garbage, carrion; *excreta* etc. 299; slough, peccant humor, pus, matter, suppuration, *lienteria*; *feces*, excrement, ordure, dung; sew-, sewer-age; muck, coprolite; guano, manure, compost.

dunghill, *colluvies*, mixen, midden, bog, laystall, sink, w.c., water-, earth-closet, latrine, privy, jakes, John's, cess, -pool; sump, sough, *cloaca*, drain, sewer, common sewer; Cloacina; dust-hole.

sty, pig-sty, lair, den, Augean stable, sink of corruption; slum, rookery.

V. be –, become- unclean etc. *adj.*; rot, putrefy, fester, rankle, reek; stink etc. 401; mold, -er; go - bad etc. *adj.*

render -unclean etc. *adj.*; dirt, -y; soil, smoke, tarnish, slaver, spot, smear, daub, blot, blur, smudge, smutch, smirch; d-, dr-abble, -aggle; spatter, slubber; be-smear etc.; -mire, -slime, -grime, -foul; splash, stain, distain, maculate, sully, pollute, defile, debase, contaminate, taint, leaven; corrupt etc. (*injure*) 659; cover with -dust etc. *n.*; drabble in the mud.

wallow in the mire; slob-, slab-ber.

Adj. unclean, dirty, filthy, grimy; soiled etc. *v.*, not to be handled with kid gloves; dusty, snuffy, smutty, sooty, smoky; thick, turbid, dreggy; slimy.

uncleanly, slovenly, untidy, sluttish, dowdy, slatternly, draggletailed; un-combed, -kempt, -scoured, -swept, -wiped, -washed, -strained, -purified; squalid.

nasty, coarse, foul, impure, offensive, abominable, beastly, reeky, reechy; fetid etc. 401.

moldy, lentiginous, musty, mildewed, rusty, moth-eaten, mucid, rancid, bad, gone bad, touched, fusty, reasty, rotten, corrupt, tainted, high, fly-blown, maggoty; putr-id, -escent, -efied; purulent, carious, peccant, fec-al, -ulent; stercoraceous, excrementitious; scurfy, impetiginous; gory, bloody; rotting etc. *v.*; rotten as -a pear, – cheese.

crapulous etc. (***intemperate***) 954; gross etc. (***impure in mind***) 961.

654. Health.—N. health, sanity; soundness etc. *adj.*; vigor; good –, perfect –, excellent –, rude –, robust- health; bloom, ***mens sana in corpore sano***; Hygeia; incorrupti-on, -bility; good state –, clean bill- of health, eupepsia.

V. be in health etc. *adj.*; bloom, flourish.

keep -body and soul together, – on one's legs; enjoy -good, – a good state of - health; have a clean bill of health.

return to health; recover etc. 660; get better etc. (*improve*) 658; take a -new, – fresh- lease of life; convalesce, be convalescent, recruit; restore to health; cure etc. (*restore*) 660.

Adj. health-y, -ful; in -health etc. *n.*; well, sound, strong, fit, hearty, hale, fresh, blooming, green, whole; florid, flush, hardy, stanch, staunch, brave, robust, vigorous, weather-proof; convalescent.

un-scathed, -injured, -maimed, -marred, -tainted; sound of wind and limb, safe and sound; without a scratch.

on one's legs; sound as a -roach, – bell; fresh as -a daisy, – a rose, – April; picture of health; bursting with health; fit as a fiddle; hearty as a buck; in -fine, – high- feather; in -good case, – full bloom; in fine fettle; pretty bobbish, tolerably well, as well as can be expected.

sanitary etc. (*health-giving*) 656; sanatory etc. (*remedial*) 662.

655. Disease.*—**N.** disease, illness, sickness etc. *adj.*; ailing etc. *v.*; 'the ills that flesh is heir to;' morb-idity, -osity; infirmity, ailment, indisposition; complaint, disorder, malady; distemper, -ature.

visitation, attack, seizure, stroke, fit, epilepsy, apoplexy, shock, shell-shock.

delicacy, loss of health, valetudinarianism, invalidism, cachexy; *cachexia*, atrophy, *marasmus*; indigestion, *dyspepsia*; decay etc. (*deterioration*) 659; malnutrition, decline, consumption, palsy, paralysis, prostration; occupational diseases.

taint, pollution, infection, contagion, septicity, septicaemia, blood poisoning, pyaemia, epi-, endemic; murrain, plague, pestilence, virus, pox.

sore, ulcer, abscess, fester, boil; pimple etc. (*swelling*) 250; carbuncle, gathering, whitlow, imposthume, peccant humor, issue; rot, canker, cancer, *carcinoma*, *caries*, mortification, corruption, gangrene, *sphacelus*, leprosy, eruption, rash, breaking out, venereal disease.

fever, calenture; inflammation.

fatal etc. (*hopeless*) 859- -disease etc.; dangerous illness, galloping consumption, churchyard cough; general breaking up, break up of the system.

[Disease of the mind] neurasthenia; idiocy etc. 499; insanity etc. 503.

martyr to disease; cripple; 'the halt, the lame and the blind;' valetudinar-y, -ian; invalid, patient, case; sick-room, -chamber, hospital etc. 662.

[Science of disease] path-, eti-, nos-ology, therapeutics, diagnosis, prognosis.

V. be -ill etc. *adj.*; ail, suffer, labor under, be affected with, complain of; droop, flag, languish, halt; sicken, peak, pine, waste away, fail, lose strength; gasp.

keep one's bed; feign sickness etc. (*falsehood*) 544; malinger.

lay -by, – up; take –, catch- -a disease etc. *n.*, – an infection; be stricken by; break out.

Adj. diseased; ailing etc. *v.*; ill, – of; taken ill, seized with; indisposed, unwell, sick, squeamish, poorly, seedy; affected –, afflicted- with illness; laid up, confined, bed-ridden, invalided, in hospital, on the sick list; out of -health, – sorts; valetudinary.

un-sound, -healthy; sickly, morbose, healthless, infirm, chlorotic, unbraced, drooping, flagging, lame, halt, crippled, halting.

morbid, tainted, vitiated, peccant, contaminated, poisoned, septic, tabid, mangy, leprous, cankered; rotten, – to, – at- the core; withered, palsied, paralytic, tuberculous; dyspeptic.

touched in the wind, broken-winded, spavined, gasping; *hors de combat* etc. (*useless*) 645.

weak-ly, -ened etc. (*weak*) 160; decrepit; decayed etc. (*deteriorated*) 659; incurable etc. (*hopeless*) 859; in declining health; cranky; in a bad way, in danger, prostrate; moribund etc. (*death*) 360.

morbific, epidemic etc. 657.

*Extended lists of different diseases are beyond the scope of this work.

656. Salubrity.—**N.** salubrity, salubriousness; healthiness etc. *adj.*

fine -air, – climate; eudiometer.

[Preservation of health] *hygiène*; valetudinarian, -ism, preventorium, sanitarian; *sanitarium*, *sanitorium*, immunity.

V. be -salubrious etc. *adj.*; agree with, be good for; assimilate etc. 23.

Adj. salu-brious, -tary, -tiferous, wholesome; health-y, -ful; sanitary, prophylactic, benign, bracing, tonic, invigorating, good for, nutritious, hyg-eian, -ienic.

in-noxious, -nocuous, -nocent; harmless, uninjurious, uninfectious; immune.

sanative etc. (*remedial*) 662; restorative etc. (*reinstate*) 660; useful etc. 644.

657. Insalubrity.—**N.** insalubrity, unhealthiness etc. *adj.*; non-naturals; plague spot; malaria etc. (*poison*) 663; death in the pot, contagion.

Adj. insalubrious; un-healthy, -wholesome; noxious, noisome, foul; morbi-fic, -ferous; mephitic, septic, azotic, deleterious; pesti-lent, -ferous, -lential; virulent, venomous, envenomed, poisonous, toxic, narcotic.

contagious, infectious, catching, taking, communicable, epidemic, zymotic, sporadic, endemic, pandemic, epizoötic.

innutritious, indigestible, ungenial; uncongenial etc. (*disagreeing*) 24.

deadly etc. (*killing*) 361.

658. Improvement.—**N.** improvement; a-, melioration; betterment; mend, amendment, emendation; mending etc. *v.*; advancement; advance etc. (*progress*) 282; ascent etc. 305; promotion, preferment; elevation etc. 307; increase etc. 35.

cultiv-, civiliz-ation; menticulture, culture, march of intellect; eugenics, euthenics, meliorism, telesis.

reform, -ation; revision, radical reform; second thoughts, correction, *limae labor*, refinement, elaboration; purification etc. 652; repair etc. (*restoration*) 660; recovery etc. 660.

revise; revised –, new- edition.

reformer, radical, progressive.

V. improve; be –, become –, get- better; mend, amend.

advance etc. (*progress*) 282; ascend etc. 305; increase etc. 35; fructify, ripen, mature; pick up, come about, rally, take a favorable turn; turn -over a new leaf, – the corner; raise one's head, sow one's wild oats; recover etc. 660.

be -better etc. *adj.*, – improved by; turn to -right, – good, – best- account; profit by, reap the benefit of; make -good use of, – capital out of; place to good account; take advantage of.

render better, improve, emend, make over, better; a-, meliorate; correct.

improve –, refine- upon; rectify; enrich, mellow, elaborate, fatten.

promote, cultivate, advance, forward, enhance; bring -forward, – on; foster etc. 707; invigorate etc. (*strengthen*) 159.

touch –, rub –, brush –, furbish –, bolster –, vamp –, brighten –, warm- up; polish, cook, make the most of, set off to advantage; prune; repair etc. (*restore*) 660; put in order etc. (*arrange*) 60.

review, revise, edit, redact; make -corrections, – improvements etc. *n.*; doctor etc. (*remedy*) 662; purify etc. 652.

relieve, refresh, revive, infuse new blood into, recruit, re-invigorate, renew, revivify, freshen, build -afresh, – anew; uplift, inspire.

re-form, -model, -organize; new model, civilize.

view in a new light, think better of, appeal from Philip drunk to Philip sober.

palliate, mitigate; lessen etc. 36- an evil.

Adj. improving etc. *v.*; progressive, improved etc. *v.*; better, – off, – for; all the better for; better advised.

reform-, emend-atory; reparatory etc. (*restorative*) 660; remedial etc. 662.

corrigible, improvable, curable, accultural.

Adv. on -consideration, – reconsideration, – second thoughts, – better advice; *ad melius inquirendum*; on the -mend, – up grade.

659. Deterioration.—N. deterioration, debasement; want, ebb; recession etc. 287; retrogradation etc. 283; decrease etc. 36.

degenera-cy, -tion, -teness; degradation; depravation, -ement; depravity etc. 945; demoralization, retrogression.

impairment, inquination, injury, damage, loss, detriment, delaceration, outrage, havoc, inroad, ravage, scath; perversion, prostitution, vitiation, discoloration, oxidation, pollution, defedation, poisoning, venenation, leaven, contamination, canker, corruption, adulteration, alloy.

decl-ine, -ension, -ination; decadence, -cy; falling off etc. *v.*; caducity, decreptitude, senility.

decay, dilapidation, ravages of time, wear and tear; cor-, e-rosion; mouldi-, rotten-ness; moth and rust, dry-rot, blight, marasmus, atrophy, collapse; disorganization; *délabrement* etc. (*destruction*) 162.

wreck, mere wreck, honeycomb, *magni nominis umbra.*

V. be –, become- -worse, – deteriorated etc. *adj.*; have seen better days, deteriorate, degenerate, fall off; wane etc. (*decrease*) 36; ebb; retrograde etc. 283; decline, droop; go down etc. (*sink*) 306; go -downhill, – on from bad to worse, – farther and fare worse; jump out of the frying pan into the fire.

run to -seed, – waste; swale, sweal; lapse, be the worse for; break, – down; spring a leak, crack, start; shrivel etc. (*contract*) 195; fade, go off, wither, molder, rot, rankle, decay, go bad; go to – fall into- decay; 'fall into the sear and yellow leaf,' rust, crumble, shake; totter, – to its fall; perish etc. 162; die etc. 360.

[Render less good] deteriorate; weaken etc. 160; put back; taint, infect, contaminate, poison, empoison, envenom, canker, corrupt, exulcerate, pollute, vitiate, inquinate; de-, em-base; denaturalize, leaven; de-flower, -bauch, -file, -prave, -grade; stain etc. (*dirt*) 653; discolor; alloy, adulterate, sophisticate, tamper with, prejudice.

pervert, prostitute, demoralize, brutalize; render vicious etc. 945; compromise.

embitter, ex-, acerbate, aggravate.

injure, impair, labefy, damage, harm, hurt, shend, scathe, spoil, mar, despoil, dilapidate, waste; overrun; ravage; pillage etc. 791.

wound, stab, pierce, maim, lame, surbate, cripple, hough, hamstring, hit between the wind and water, scotch, mangle, mutilate, disfigure, blemish, deface, warp.

blight, rot; cor-, e-rode, eat away; wear -away, – out; gnaw, – at the root of; sap, mine, undermine, shake, sap the foundations of, break up; dis-organize, -mantle, -mast; destroy etc. 162.

damnify etc. (*aggrieve*) 649; do one's worst; knock down; deal a blow to; play -havoc, – sad havoc, – the mischief, – the deuce, – the very devil- -with, – among; decimate.

Adj. unimproved etc. (improve etc. 658); deteriorated etc. *v.*; altered, – for the worse; injured etc. *v.*; sprung; withering, spoiling, etc. *v.*; on the -wane, – decline; tabid; degenerate; worse; the –, all the- worse for; out of -repair, – tune; imperfect etc. 651; the worse for wear; battered; weather-ed, -beaten; stale, *passé*, shaken, dilapidated, frayed, faded, wilted, shabby, second-hand, second-rate, threadbare; worn, – to- -a thread, – a shadow, – the stump, rags; reduced, – to a skeleton, skeletonized; far gone.

decayed etc. *v.*; moth-, worn-eaten; mildewed, rusty, moldy, spotted, seedy, time-worn, moss-grown; discolored; effete, wasted, crumbling, moldering, rotten, cankered, blighted, tainted; depraved etc. (*vicious*) 945; decrep-id, -it; broken down; done, – for, – up; worn out, used up; fit for the -dust-hole, – wastepaper basket; past work etc. (*useless*) 645.

at a low ebb, in a bad way, on one's last legs, washed -up; – out; undermined, deciduous; nodding to its fall etc. (*destruction*) 162; tottering etc. (*dangerous*) 665; past cure etc. (*hopeless*) 859; fatigued etc. 688; backward, retrograde etc. (*retrogressive*) 283; deleterious etc. 649; behind the times.

Adv. on the down grade; beyond hope.

Phr. out of the frying pan into the fire; *aegrescit medendo.*

660. Restoration.—N. restor-ation, -al; re-instatement, -placement, -habilitation, -

establishment, -construction; reporduction etc. 163; re-novation, -newal; reviv-al, -escence; refreshment etc. 689; re-suscitation, -animation, -vivification, -viction; Phoenix; reorganization.

renaissance, renascence, rebirth, second youth, rejuvenation, rejuvenescence, new birth; regeneration, -cy, -teness; palingenesis, reconversion, resurgence, resurrection.

redress, retrieval, reclamation, recovery; convalescence; resumption, *résumption*.

recurrence etc. (*repetition*) 104; *réchauffé, rifacimento*.

cure, recure, sanation; healing etc. *v.*; redintegration; rectification, instauration.

repair, reparation, mending; recruiting etc. *v.*; cicatrization; disinfection; tinkering.

reaction; redemption etc. (*deliverance*) 672; restitution etc. 790; relief etc. 834.

mender, repairer, renewer; tinker, cobbler; doctor etc. 662; *vis medicatrix* etc. (*remedy*) 662.

curableness.

V. return to the original state; recover, rally, revive; come -to, – round, – to oneself; pull through, weather the storm, be oneself again; get -well, – round, – the better of, – over, – about; rise from -one's ashes, – the grave; resurge, resurrect; survive etc. (*outlive*) 110; resume, reappear; come to, – life again; live –, rise- again; relive.

heal, skin over, cicatrize; right itself.

restore, put back, place *in statu quo*; re-instate, -place, -seat, -habilitate, -establish, -estate, -install.

re-construct, -build, -organize, -constitute; reconvert; re-new, -novate; recondition; regenerate; rejuvenate.

re-deem, -claim, -cover, -trieve; rescue etc. (*deliver*) 672.

redress, recure; cure, heal, remedy, doctor, physic, medicate; break of; bring round, set on one's legs.

re-suscitate, -vive, -animate, -vivify, -call to life, reproduce etc. 163; warm up; reinvigorate, refresh etc. 689.

redintegrate, make whole; recoup etc. 790; make -good, – all square; rectify; put –, set- -right, – to rights, – straight; set up, correct; put in order etc. (*arrange*) 60; refit, recruit; fill up, – the ranks; reinforce.

repair, mend; put in -repair, – thorough repair, – complete repair; retouch, botch, vamp, tinker, doctor, cobble; do –, patch –, plaster –, vamp-up; darn, fine-draw, heel-piece; stop a gap, stanch, staunch, caulk, calk, careen, splice, bind up wounds.

Adj. restored etc. *v.*; *redivivus*, convalescent; in a fair way; none the worse; rejuvenated, renascent.

restoring etc. *v.*; restorative, recuperative; sana-, repara-tive, -tory; curative, remedial.

restor-, recover-, san-, remedi-, retriev-, cur-able.

Adv. *in statu qho*; as you were.

Phr. *revenons a nos moutons.*

661. Relapse.—N. relapse, lapse; falling back etc. *v.*; retrogradation etc. (*retrogression*) 283; deterioration etc. 659.

[Return to, or recurrence of a bad state] backsliding, recidivation, recrudescence.

V. relapse, lapse; fall –, slide –, sink- back; have a relapse; return; retrograde etc. 283; recidivate; fall off etc. 659- again.

662. Remedy.—N. remedy, help, redress; antidote, anti-toxin, -biotic; anti-, counter-poison, prophylactic, antiseptic, germicide, bactericide, corrective, restorative, stimulant, pick-me-up, tonic; sedative etc. 174; palliative; febrifuge; alterant, -ative; specific; emetic, carminative; narcotic etc. *adj.*; Nepenthe, Mithridate.

cure; radical –, perfect –, certain- cure; sovereign remedy.

physic, medicine, patent medicine, Galenicals, simples, drug, wonder –, miracle – drugs; potion, draught, dose, pill, bolus, lozenge, tablet, tabloid, capsule; electuary; linct-us, -ure; medicament.

nostrum, receipt, recipe, prescription; catholicon, panacea, elixir, *elixir vitae*, philosopher's stone; balm, balsam, cordial, theriac, ptisan.

salve, ointment, cerate, oil, lenitive, lotion, cosmetic; plaster; epithem, embrocation, liniment, cataplasm, sinapism, arquebusade, traumatic, vulnerary, pepastic, poultice, collyrium, depilatory.

compress, pledget; bandage etc. (*support*) 215.

treatment, medical treatment, regimen; diet-ary, -etics; *vis medicatrix*, – *naturae*; *médicine expectante*; seton, blood-letting, bleeding, venesection, phlebotomy, cupping, leeches; operation, surgical operation; tonsillectomy, appendectomy; injection, electrolysis, massage.

pharma-cy, -cology, -ceutics; acology; materia medica, pharmacopoeia, therapeutics, therapy, posology, pathology etc. 655; home-, hetero-, all-, hydr-opathy; cold water –, open air- cure; dietetics; sur-, chirur-gery, osteopathy; healing art, leechcraft, practice of medicine; ortho-paedy, -praxy; dentistry, midwifery, obstetrics, gynecology.

faith -cure, – healing, Christian science; psychotherapy, -analysis, psychiatry.

hospital, infirmary, clinic; pest-, lazar-house; lazaretto, lazaret; lock hospital; *maison de santé*; *ambulance*; dispensary; *sanatorium*, *sanitarium*, spa, baths, pump-room, well; *hospice*; Red Cross; nursing home; asylum.

doctor, physician, surgeon; medical –, general-practitioner, consultant, specialist; medical attendant; medical student, medico; chemist, apothecary, pharmacopolist, druggist; leech; Aesculapius, Hippocrates, Galen; *accoucheur*, gynecologist, midwife, oculist, aurist, dentist; operator; osteopath, bonesetter; nurse, monthly nurse, sister; dresser; *masseur*, *masseuse*.

V. apply a -remedy etc. *n.*; doctor, dose, physic, nurse, minister to, attend, dress the wounds, plaster, bandage, poultice; heal, cure, work a cure, kill or cure, remedy, stay (disease), snatch from the jaws of death; prevent etc. 706; relieve etc. 834; palliate etc. 658; restore etc. 660; drench with physic; consult, operate, extract, deliver; bleed, cup, let blood, transfuse; electrolyse; psychoanalyse.

Adj. remedial; restorative etc. 660; corrective, palliative, healing; sana-tory, -tive; prophylactic; salutiferous etc. (*salutary*) 656; medic-al, -inal; therapeutic, surgical, chirurgical, orthopedic, epulotic, paregoric, tonic, corroborant, analeptic, balsamic, anodyne, hypnotic, neurotic, narcotic, sedative, lenitive, demulcent, emollient; depuratory; deter-sive, -gent; abstersive, disinfectant, febrifugal, alternative; traumatic, vulnerary.

dietetic, alimentary; nutrit-ious, -ive; peptic; alexi-pharmic, -teric; remedi-, cur-able.

663. Bane.—**N.** bane, curse, thorn in the -side, -flesh, bugbear, *bête noire*; evil etc. 619; hurtfulness etc. (*badness*) 649; painfulness etc. (*cause of pain*) 830; scourge etc. (*punishment*) 975; *damnosa hereditas*; white elephant.

sting, fang, thorn, tang, bramble, briar, nettle.

poison, leaven, virus, venom; intoxicant; arsenic, Prussic acid, antimony, tartar emetic, strychnine, nicotine, cyanide of potassium, corrosive sublimate; curare; hyoscine etc.; poison-, mustard-, tear-gas; carbon di-, mon-oxide; ptomaine poisoning, botulism; miasm, mephitis, malaria, azote, sewer gas; pest, stench etc. 401.

rust, worm, moth, moth and rust, fungus, mildew; dry-rot; canker, -worm; cancer; torpedo; viper etc. (*evil-doer*) 913; demon etc. 980.

hemlock, hellebore, nightshade, *belladonna*, henbane, aconite; Upas tree.

drugs, dope, opium, morphia, morphine, cocaine, heroin, hashish, bhang.

[*Science of poisons*] Toxicology.

Adj. baneful etc. (*bad*) 649; poisonous etc. (*unwholesome*) 657.

664. Safety.—**N.** safety, security, impregnability; invulnera-bility, -bleness etc. *adj.*; danger -past, – over; storm blown over; coast clear; escape etc. 671; means of escape, safety-valve; safeguard, palladium, sheet anchor, rock, tower of strength.

guardian-, ward-, warden-ship; tutelage, custody, safe keeping; preservation etc. 670; protection, auspices.

safe-conduct, escort, convoy; guard, sheild etc. (*defense*) 717; guardian angel, tutelary -god, – deity, – saint; *genius loci.*

protector, guardian; ward-en, -er; preserver, custodian, *duenna chaperon*, third person.

watch-, ban-dog; Cerberus; watch-, patrol-, police-man, constable, peeler, bobby, copper, cop, bull, flat-foot, detective, armed guard; sentinel, sentry, scout etc. (*warning*) 668; garrison; guard-ship.

[Means of safety] refuge etc., anchor etc. 666; precaution etc. (*preparation*) 673; quarantine, *cordon sanitaire.* [Sense of security] confidence etc. 858.

V. be -safe etc. *adj.*; keep one's head above water, tide over, save one's bacon; ride out –, weather- the storm; light upon one's feet; bear a charmed life; escape etc. 671; possess nine lives.

make –, render- -safe etc. *adj.*; protect, watch over; take care of etc. (*care*) 459; preserve etc. 670; cover, screen, shelter, shroud, flank, ward; guard etc. (*defend*) 717; secure etc. (*restrain*) 751; intrench, fence round etc. (*circumscribe*) 229; house, nestle, ensconce; take charge of.

escort, convoy; garrison; watch, mount guard, patrol, scout, spy.

make assurance double sure etc. (*caution*) 864; take up a loose thread; take precautions etc. (*prepare for*) 673; take in a reef; double reef top-sails.

seek safety; take –, find- shelter etc. 666; run into port.

Adj. safe, secure, sure; in -safety, – security; have an anchor to windward; on the safe side; under the -shield of, – shade of, – wing of, – shadow of one's wing; under -cover, – lock and key; out of -danger, – the meshes, – harm's way; in -harbor, – port; on sure ground, at anchor, high and dry, above water, on *terra firma*; unthreatened, -molested; protected etc. *v.*; cavendo tutus; panoplied etc. (*defended*) 717.

snug, sea-, air-worthy; weather-, water-, fire-, bomb-proof.

defensible, tenable, proof against, invulnerable; un-assailable, -attackable; im-pregnable, -perdible; founded on a rock; inexpugnable.

safe and sound etc. (*preserved*) 670; harmless; scathless etc. (*perfect*) 650; unhazarded; not - dangerous etc. 665.

protecting etc. *v.*; guardian, tutelary; perservative etc. 670; trustworthy etc. 939.

Adv. *ex abundanti cautelâ*; with impunity.

Phr. all's well; all clear; *salva res est*; *suave mari magno*; safety first.

665. Danger.—**N.** danger, peril, insecurity, jeopardy, risk, hazard, venture, precariousness, slipperiness; instability etc. 149; defenselessness etc. *adj.*

exposure etc. (*liability*) 177; vulnerability; vulnerable point, heel of Achilles; forlorn hope etc. (*hopelessness*) 859.

[Dangerous course] leap in the dark etc. (*rashness*) 863; road to ruin, *facilis descensus Averni*, hair-breadth escape.

cause for alarm; source of danger etc. 667. [Approach of danger] rock –, breakers- ahead; storm brewing; clouds -in the horizon, – gathering; warning etc. 668; alarm etc. 669. [Sense of danger] apprehension etc. 860.

V. be -in danger etc. *adj.*; be exposed to –, run into –, incur –, encounter- -danger etc. *n.*; run a risk; lay oneself open to etc. (*liability*) 177; lean on –, trust to- a broken reed; feel the ground sliding from under one, have to run for it; have the -chances, – odds- against one.

hang by a thread, totter; tremble on the -verge, – brink; sleep – stand -on a volcano; sit on a barrel of gunpowder, live in a glass house.

bring –, place –, put- in -danger etc. *n.*; endanger, expose to danger, imperil; jeopard, -ize, compromise; sail too near the wind etc. (*rash*) 863; put one's head in the lion's mouth.

adventure, risk, hazard, venture, stake, set at hazard; run the gauntlet etc. (*dare*) 861; engage in a forlorn hope.

threaten etc. 909- danger; run one hard; lay a trap for etc. (*deceive*) 545.

Adj. in -danger etc. *n.*; endangered etc. *v.*; fraught with danger; danger-, hazard-, peril-, parl-, pericul-ous; unsafe, unprotected etc. (safe, protect etc. 664); insecure, untrustworthy, unreliable; built upon sand, on a sandy basis.

defence-, fence-, guard-, harbor-less; unshielded; vulnerable, expugnable, unsheltered, exposed; open to etc. (*liable*) 177.

aux abois, at bay; on -the wrong side of the wall, – a lee shore, – the rocks.

at stake, in question; precarious, aleatory, critical, ticklish; slip-pery, -py; hanging by a thread etc. *v.*; with a halter round one's neck; between -the hammer and the anvil, – Scylla and Charybdis, – two fires; on the -edge, – brink, – verge of a- -precipice, – volcano; in the lion's den, on slippery ground, under fire; not out of the wood.

un-warned, -admonished, -advised; unprepared etc. 674; off one's guard etc. (*inexpectant*) 508.

tottering; un-stable, -steady; shaky, top-heavy, tumble-down, ramshackle, crumbling, waterlogged; help-, guide-less; in a bad way; reduced to –, at- the last extremity; trembling in the balance; nodding to its fall etc. (*destruction*) 162.

threatening etc. 909; ominous, ill-omened; alarming etc. (*fear*) 860; explosive; poisonous etc. 657.

adventurous etc. (*rash*) 863, (*bold*) 861.

Int. stop! look out! beware! take care!

Phr. *incidit in Scyllam qui vult vitare Charybdim; nam tua res agitur paries dum proximus ardet.*

666. Refuge. [Means of safety.]—**N.** refuge, sanctuary, retreat, fastness; stronghold, keep, last resort; ward; prison etc. 752; asylum, ark, home, almshouse, refuge for the destitute; hiding-place etc. (*ambush*) 530; *sanctum sanctorum* etc. (*privacy*) 893.

roadstead, anchorage; breakwater, mole, port, haven; harbor, – of refuge; sea-port; pier, jetty, embankment, quay.

covert, shelter, abri, screen, lee-wall, wing, shield, umbrella; splash-, dash-board, mudguard.

wall etc. (*inclosure*) 232; fort etc. (*defence*) 717.

anchor, kedge; grap-nel, -pling iron; sheet-, mushroom-anchor, main-stay; support etc. 215; check etc. 706; ballast.

jury-mast; vent-peg; safety -valve, – lamp; lightning conductor.

means of escape etc. (*escape*) 671; life-boat, swimming belt, cork jacket; life preserver, breeches buoy; parachute, plank, stepping-stone.

safeguard etc. (*protection*) 664.

V. seek –, take –, find- refuge etc. *n.*; seek –, find- safety etc. 664; throw oneself into the arms of; claim sanctuary; take to the -hills, – woods; make port, reach shelter, bar –, bolt –, lock -the door, – gete; let the portcullis down; raise the drawbridge.

667. Pitfall. [Source of danger.]—**N.** rocks, reefs, coral reef, sunken rocks, snags; sands, quicksands, Goodwin sands, sandy foundation; slippery ground; breakers, shoals, shallows, bank, shelf, flat, lee shore, iron-bound coast; rock – breakers- ahead; derelict.

precipice; abyss, chasm, pit, crevasse; maelstrom, whirlpool, eddy, vortex, rapids, current, bore, tidal wave; storm, squall, hurricane, whirlwind; volcano; ambush etc. 530; pitfall, trap-door; trap etc. (*snare*) 545.

sword of Damocles; wolf at the door, snake in the grass, viper in one's bosom, death in the pot; latency etc. 526.

ugly customer, dangerous person, *le chat qui dort*; firebrand, hornet's nest.

Phr. *latet anguis in herbâ*; *proximus ardet Ucalegon.*

668. Warning.—N. warning, caution, *caveat*; notice etc. (*information*) 527; premoni-tion, -shment; prediction etc. 511; contraindication; symptom; lesson, dehortation; admonition, monition; alarm etc. 669.

handwriting on the wall, *tekel upharsin*, yellow flag; fog-signal, -horn; siren; monitor, warning voice, Cassandra, signs of the times, Mother Carey's chickens, stormy petrel, bird of ill omen, gathering clouds, clouds in the horizon, cloud no bigger than a man's hand, death-watch.

watch-tower, beacon, signal-post; light-house etc. (*indication of locality*) 550.

sent-inel, -ry; watch, -man; watch and ward; watch-, ban-, house-dog; patrol, vedette, picket, bivouac, scout, spy, spial; advanced –, rear-guard, lookout, flagman..

cautiousness etc. 864.

V. warn, caution; fore-, pre-warn; ad-, premonish; give -notice, – warning; menace etc. (*threaten*) 909; put on one's guard; sound the alarm etc. 669; croak.

beware, ware; take -warning, – heed at one's peril; watch out for; keep watch and ward etc. (*care*) 459.

Adj. warning etc. *v.*; premonitory, monitory, cautionary; admonitory, -tive; ominous, threatening, lowering, minatory, symptomatic.

warned etc. *v.*; on one's guard etc. (*careful*) 459; (*cautious*) 864.

Adv. *in terrorem* etc. (*threat*) 909.

Int. beware! ware! take care! mind –, take care-what you are about; mind! look out!

Phr. *ne reveillez pas le chat qui dort*; *foenum habet in cornu.*

669. Alarm. [Indication of danger.]—**N.** alarm; alarum, larum, alarm bell, tocsin, *alerte*, beat of drum, sound of trumpet, note of alarm, hue and cry, signal of distress, S.O.S.; blue-lights; war-cry, -whoop; warning etc. 668; fog-signal, -horn; siren; yellow flag; danger signal; red -light, – flag; fire -bell, – alarm; burglar alarm, police whistle, watchman's rattle.

false alarm, cry of wolf; bug-bear, -aboo.

V. give –, raise –, sound –, beat- the *or* an -alarm etc. *n.*; alarm; warn etc. 668; ring the tocsin; *battre la générale*; cry wolf.

Adj. alarming etc. *v.*

Int. *sauve qui peut! qui vive?* who goes there?

670. Preservation.—N. preservation; safe keeping; conservation etc. (*storage*) 636; maintenance, upkeep, support, sustentation, conservatism; *vis conservatrix*; salvation etc. (*deliverance*) 672; drying etc. *v.*

[Means of preservation] prophylaxis; preserv-er, -ative; canned goods; cold pack; hygi-astics, -antics; cover, durgget; *cordon sanitaire.*

[Superstitious remedies] charm etc. 993.

V. preserve, maintain, keep, sustain, support; keep -up, – alive; not willingly let die; shore –, bank- up; nurse; save, rescue; be –, make- safe etc. 664; take care of etc. (*care*) 459; guard etc. (*defend*) 717.

stare super antiquas vias; hold one's own; hold –, stand- -one's ground etc. (*resist*) 719.

embalm, dry, cure, smoke, salt, pickle, season, kyanize, bottle, pot, tin, can; husband etc. (*store*) 636.

Adj. preserving etc. *v.*; conservative; prophylatic; preserva-tory, -tive; hygienic.

preserved etc. *v.*; un-impaired, -broken, -injured, -hurt, -singed, -marred; safe, – and sound; intact, with a whole skin, without a scratch.

Phr. *nolumus leges Angliae mutari.*

671. Escape.—N. escape, scape; avolation, elopment, flight, get-away; evasion etc. (*avoidance*) 623; retreat; narrow –, hairbreadth- escape; close –, near- shave; come off, impunity.

[Means of escape] loophole etc. (*opening*) 260; path etc. 627; secret -door, – passage; refuge etc. 666; vent, – peg; safety-valve; drawbridge, fire-escape.

reprieve etc. (*deliverance*) 672; liberation etc. 750.

refugee etc. (*fugitive*) 623.

V. escape, scape; make –, effect –, make good- one's escape, make a get-away; get -off, – clear off, – well out of; *échapper belle*, save one's bacon; weather the storm etc. (*safe*) 664; escape scot-free.

elude etc., make off etc. (*avoid*) 623; march off etc. (*go away*) 293; give one the slip; slip through the -hands, – fingers; slip the collar, wriggle out of; break -loose, – from prison; break –, slip –, get- away; find -vent, – a hole to creep out of.

Adj. escap-ing, -ed etc. *v.*; stolen away, fled.

Phr. the bird has flown.

672. Deliverance.—N. deliverance, extrication, rescue; repriev-e, -al; respite; ransom; liberation etc. 750; truce, armistice; redemption, salvation; riddance; gaol delivery; exemption, day of grace; redeemableness.

V. deliver, extricate, rescue, save, redeem, ransom, free, liberate, release, set free, redeem, emancipate; bring -off, – through; *tirer d'affaire*, get the wheel out of the rut; snatch from the jaws of death, come to the rescue; rid; retrieve etc. (*restore*) 660; be –, get- rid of.

Adj. saved etc. *v.*; extric-, redeem-, rescu-able.

Phr. to the rescue!

673. Preparation.—N. preparation; providing etc. *v.*; provi-sion, -dence; anticipation etc. (*foresight*) 510; precaution, -concertation, -disposition; forecast etc. (*plan*) 626; rehearsal, not of preparation.

[Putting in order] arrangement etc. 60; clearance; adjustment etc. 23; tuning; equipment, outfit, accoutrement, armament, array.

ripening etc. *v.*; maturation, evolution; elaboration, concoction, digestion; gestation, hatching, incubation, sitting.

groundwork, datum, first stone, cradle, stepping-stone; foundation, scaffold etc. (*support*) 215; scaffolding, *échafaudage.*

[Preparation -of men] training etc. (*education*) 537; inurement etc. (*habit*) 613; novitiate; [– of food] cook-ing, -ery; brewing, culinary art; [– of the soil] till-, plough-, sow-ing; semination, cultivation.

[State of being prepared] prepared-, readi-, ripe-, mellow-ness; maturity; *un impromptu fait à loisir.*

[Preparer] preparer, teacher, coach, trainer, pioneer; *avant-courrier*, *-coureur*; sappers and miners, paver, navvy; packer, stevedore; warmingpan; precursor etc. 64.

V. prepare; get –, make- ready; make preparations, settle preliminaries, get up, sound the note of preparation; address oneself to.

set –, put- in order etc. (*arrange*) 60; forecast etc. (*plan*) 626; prepare –, plough –, dress- the ground; till –, cultivate- the soil; predispose, sow the seed, lay a train, dig a mine; lay –, fix- the -foundations, – basis, -groundwork; dig the foundations, erect the scaffolding; lay the first stone etc. (*begin*) 66.

rough-hew; cut out work; block –, hammer-out; lick into shape etc. (*form*) 240.

elaborate, mature, ripen, mellow, season, bring to maturity; nurture etc.

(*aid*) 707; hatch, cook, brew; temper; anneal, smelt; dry, cure etc. 670.

equip, arm, man; fit-out, -up; furnish, rig, dress, garnish, betrim, accouter, array, fettle, fledge; dress –, furbish –, brush –, vamp- up; refurbish; sharpen one's tools, trim one's foils, set, prime, attune; whet the -knife, – sword; wind –, screw- up; adjust etc. (*fit*) 27; put in- trim, – train, – gear, – working order, – tune, – a groove for, – harness; pack, stow away, store.

train etc. (*teach*) 537; inure etc. (*habituate*) 613; breed; prepare etc.- for; rehearse; make provision for; take -steps, – measures, – precautions; provide, – against; beat up for recruits; open the door to etc. (*facilitate*) 705.

set one's house in order, make all snug; clear -decks, – for action; close one's ranks; shuffle the cards.

prepare oneself; serve an apprenticeship etc. (*learn*) 539; lay oneself out for, get into harness, gird up one's loins, buckle on one's armor, *reculer pour mieux sauter*, prime and load, shoulder arms, get the steam up, put the horses to.

guard –, make sure- against; forearm, make sure, prepare for the evil day, have a rod in pickle, provide against a rainy day, feather one's nest; lay in provisions etc. 637; make investments; keep on foot.

be -prepared, – ready etc. *adj.*; hold oneself in readiness, watch and pray, keep one's powder dry; lie in wait for etc. (*expect*) 507; anticipate etc. (*foresee*) 510; *principiis obstare*; *veniente occurrere morbo.*

Adj. preparing etc. *v.*; in -preparation, – course

of preparation, – agitation, – embryo, – hand, – train; afoot, afloat; on -foot, – the stocks, – the anvil; under consideration etc. (*plan*) 626; brewing, hatching, forthcoming, brooding; in -store for, – reserve.

precautionary, provident; prepara-tive, -tory; provisional, inchoate, under revision; preliminary etc. (*precedent*) 62.

prepared etc. *v.*; in readiness; ready, – to one's hand, – made, cut and dried; ready for use, reach me down; made to one's hand, handy, on the table, made to order; in gear; in working -order, – gear; snug; in practice.

ripe, mature, mellow; practiced etc. (*skillet*) 698; labored, elaborate, highly-wrought, smelling of the lamp, worked up.

in -full feather, – best bib and tucker; in –, at-harness; in – the saddle, – arms, – battle array, – war paint; up in arms; armed -at all points, – to the teeth, – *cap-à-pie*; sword in hand; booted and spurred.

in utrumque –, *semper- paratus*; on the alert etc. (*vigilant*) 459; at one's post.

Adv. in -preparation, – anticipation of; afoot, astir, abroad; abroach.

674. Non-preparation.—N. non-, absence of –, want of- preparation; unpreparedness; inculture, inconcoction, improvidence.

immaturity, crudity; rawness etc. *adj.*; abortion; disqualification.

[Absence of art] nature, state of nature; virgin soil, unweeded garden; rough diamond, neglect etc. 460.

rough copy etc. (*plan*) 626; germ etc. 153; raw material etc. 635.

improvisation etc. (*impulse*) 612.

V. be -unprepared etc. *adj.*; want –, lack-preparation; lie fallow; *s'embarquer sans biscuits*; live from hand to mouth.

[Render unprepared] dismantle etc. (*render useless*) 645; undress etc. 226.

extemporize, improvise.

surprise, pay a surprise visit, take by surprise, drop in upon, take unawares; take pot-luck.

Adv. un-prepared etc. prepare etc. 673] without -preparation etc. 673; incomplete etc. 53; rudimental, embryonic, abortive; immature, unripe, raw, green, crude; coarse; rough, -cast, -hewn; in the rough; un-hewn, -formed, -fashioned, -wrought, -labored, -blown, -cooked, -boiled, -concocted, -cút, -polished.

callow, un-hatched, -fledged, -nurtured, -licked, -taught, -educated, -cultivated, -trained, -tutored, -drilled, -exercised; precocious, premature; un-, indigested; un-mellowed, -seasoned, -leavened.

fallow; un-sown, -tilled; natural, in a state of nature; undressed; in dishabille, *en déshabille, en négligé.*

un-, dis-qualified; unfitted; ill-digested; unbegun, -ready, -arranged, -organized, -furnished, -provided, -equipped, -trimmed; out of -gear, – order; dismantled etc. *v.*

shiftless, improvident, unthrifty, thoughtless, unguarded; happy-go-lucky; caught napping etc. (*inexpectant*) 508; unpremeditated etc. 612.

Adv. extempore etc. 612.

675. Essay.—N. essay, trial, endeavor, aim, attempt; venture, adventure, speculation, *coup d'essai, début*; probation etc. (*experiment*) 463.

V. try, essay; experiment etc. 463; endeavor, strive; tempt, tackle, take on, attempt, make an attempt; venture, adventure, speculate, take one's chance, tempt fortune; try one's -fortune, – luck, – hand; use one's endeavor; feel –, grope –, pick- one's way.

try hard, push, make a bold push, use one's best endeavor; do one's best etc. (*exertion*) 686.

Adj. essaying etc. *v.*; experimental etc. 463; tentative, empirical, probationary.

Adv. experimentally etc. *adj.*; on trial, at a venture; by rule of thumb.

if one may be so bold.

676. Undertaking.—N. undertaking, compact etc. 769; engagement etc. (*promise*) 768; enter-, em-prise; venture etc. 675; pilgrimage; matter in hand etc. (*business*) 625; move; first move etc. (*beginning*) 66.

V. undertake; engage –, embark- in; launch –, plunge- into; volunteer; apprentice oneself to; engage etc. (*promise*) 768; contract etc. 769; take upon -oneself, – one's shoulders; devote oneself to etc. (*determination*) 604.

take -up, – in hand; tackle; set –, go- about; set fall- -to, – to work; launch forth; set up shop; put in -hand, – execution; set forward; break the neck of a business, be in for; put one's hand to; betake oneself to, turn one's hand to, go to do; begin etc. 66; broach, institute, etc. (*originate*) 153; put –, lay- one's -hand to the plough, – shoulder to the wheel.

have in hand etc. (*business*) 625; have many irons in the fire etc. (*activity*) 682.

Adj. undertaking etc. *v.*; on the anvil etc. 625; adventurous, venturesome.

Int. here goes!

677. Use.—N. use; employ, -ment; exer-cise, -citation; appli-cation, -ance; adhibition, disposal; consumption; agency etc. (*physical*) 170; usufruct; usefulness etc. 644; recourse, resort, avail, pragmatism.

[Conversion to use] utilization, service, wear.

[Way of using] usage.

V. use, make use of, employ, put to use; apply, put in -action, – operation, – practice; set -in motion, – to work.

ply, work, wield, handle, manipulate; play, – off; exert, exercise, practice, avail oneself of, profit by; resort –, have recourse –, recur –, take –, betake oneself- to; take -up with, – advantage of; lay one's hands on, try.

render useful etc. 644; mold; turn to -account, – use; convert to use, utilize, administer; work up; call –, bring- into play; put into requisition; call –, draw- forth; press –, enlist- into the service; bring to bear upon, devote, dedicate, consecrate, apply, adhibit, dispose of; make a -handle, – cat's paw- of.

fall beak upon, make a shift with; make the -most, – best- of.

use –, swallow- up; consume, absorb, expend; tax, task, wear, put to task.

Adj. in use; used etc. *v.*; well-worn, -trodden. useful etc. 644; subservient etc. (*instrumental*) 631; utilitarian; pragmatical.

678. Disuse.—N. forbearance, abstinence; disuse; relinquishment etc. 782; desuetude etc. (*want of habit*) 614.

V. not use; do without, dispense with, let alone, not touch, forbear, abstain, spare, waive, neglect; keep back, reserve.

lay -up, – by, – on the shelf, – up in a napkin; shelve; set –, put –, lay- aside; disuse, leave off, have done with; supersede; discard etc. (*eject*) 297; dismiss, give warning.

throw aside etc. (*relinquish*) 782; make away with etc. (*destroy*) 162; cast –, heave –, throw- overboard; cast to the -dogs, – winds; dismantle etc. (*render useless*) 645.

lie –, remain- unemployed etc. *adj.*

Adj. not used etc. *v.*; un-employed, -applied, -disposed of, -spent, -exercised, -touched, -trodden, -essayed, -gathered, -culled; uncalled for, not required.

disused etc. *v.*; done with; run down, used up, cast off.

679. Misuse.—N. mis-use, -usage, -employment, -application, -appropriation.

abuse, profanation, prostitution, desecration; waste etc. 638.

V. mis-use, -employ, -apply, -appropriate.

desecrate, abuse, profane, prostitute; waste etc. 638; over-task, -tax, -work; squander etc. 818.

cut a whetstone with a razor, employ a steam-engine to crack a nut; catch at a straw.

Adj. misused etc. *v.*

680. Action.—N. action, performance; doing etc. *v.*; perpetration; exercise, -citation; movement, operation, evolution, work; labor etc. (*exertion*) 686; *praxis*, execution; procedure etc. (*conduct*) 692; handicraft; business etc. 625; agency etc. (*power at work*) 170.

deed, act, overt act, stitch, touch, gest; transaction, job, doings, dealings, proceeding, measure, step, maneuver, bout, passage, move, stroke, blow; *coup*, – *de main*, – *d'état*; *tour de force* etc. (*display*) 882; feat, exploit, stunt; achievement etc. (*completion*) 729; handiwork, workmanship, craftsmanship; manufacture; stroke of policy etc. (*plan*) 626.

actor etc. (*doer*) 690.

V. do, perform, execute; achieve etc. (*complete*) 729; transact, enact; commit, perpetrate, inflict; exercise, prosecute, carry on, work, practice, play.

employ oneself, ply one's task; officiate, have in hand etc. (*business*) 625; labor etc. 686; be at work; pursue a course; shape one's course etc. (*conduct*) 692.

act, operate; take -action, – steps; strike a blow, lift a finger, stretch forth one's hand; take in hand etc. (*undertake*) 676; put oneself in motion; put in practice; carry into execution etc. (*complete*) 729; act upon.

be -an actor etc. 690; take –, act –, play –, perform- a part in: participate in; have a -hand in, – finger in the pie; have to do with; be a -party to, – participator in; bear –, lend- a hand; pull an oar, run in a race; mix oneself up with etc. (*meddle*) 682.

be in action; come into operation etc. (*power at work*) 170.

Adj. doing etc. *v.*; acting; in action; in harness; on duty; at work; in operation etc. 170; up to one's ears in work, in the midst of things.

Adv. in the -act, – midst of, – thick of; red-handed, *in flagrante delicto*; while one's hand is in.

681. Inaction.—N. inaction, passiveness, abstinence from action; non-interference; Fabian –, conservative- policy; neglect etc. 460; stagnation, vegetation; loafing.

inactivity etc. 683; rest etc. (*repose*) 687; quiescence etc. 265; want of –, in- occupation; unemployment; idle hours, time hanging on one's hands, *dolce far niente*; sinecure.

V. not -do, – act, – attempt; be -inactive etc. 683; abstain from doing, do nothing, hold, spare; not -stir, – move, – lift- a -finger, – foot, – peg; fold one's -arms, – hands; leave –, let- alone; let -be, – pass, – things take their course, – it have its way, – well alone; *quieta non movere*; *stare super antiquas vias*; rest and be thankful, live and let live; lie –, rest- upon one's oars; *laisser -aller*, – *faire*; stand aloof; refrain etc. (*avoid*) 623; keep oneself from doing; remit –, relax- one's efforts; desist etc. (*relinquish*) 624; stop etc. (*cease*) 142; pause etc. (*be quiet*) 265.

wait, lie in wait, bide one's time, take time, tide it over.

cool –, kick- one's heels; loaf, while away the -time, – tedious hours; pass –, fill –, beguile- the time; talk against time; waste time etc. (*inactive*) 683.

lie -by, – on the shelf, – in ordinary, – idle, – to, – fallow; keep quiet, slug; have nothing to do, whistle for want of thought; twiddle one's thumbs.

undo, do away with; take -down, – to pieces; destroy etc. 162.

Adj. not doing etc. *v.*; not done etc. *v.*; undone; passive; un-occupied, -employed; out of -employ, – work, – a job; fallow; *désoeuvré*.

Adv. *re infectâ*, at a stand, *les bras croisés*, with folded arms; with the hands -in the pockets, – behind one's back; *pour passer le temps*.

Int. so let it be! stop! etc. 142; hands off!

Phr. nothing doing; *cunctando restituit rem*.

682. Activity.—N. activity; briskness, liveliness etc. *adj.*; animation, life, vivacity, spirit, verve, dash, energy, go.

nimbleness, agility; smartness, quickness etc. *adj.*; velocity etc. 274; alacrity, promptitude; des-, dis-patch; expedition; haste etc. 684; punctuality etc. (*early*) 132.

eagerness, zeal, ardor, *perfervidum ingenium*, *empressement*, earnestness, intentness; *abandon*; vigor etc. (*physical energy*) 171; devotion etc. (*resolution*) 604; exertion etc. 686.

industry, assiduity; assiduousness etc. *adj.*; sedulity; laboriousness; drudgery etc. (*labor*) 686; painstaking, diligence; perseverance etc. 604*a*; indefatigation; habits of business.

vigilance etc. 459; wakefulness; sleep-, restlessness; *pervigilium, insomnia*; racketing.

movement, bustle, hustle, stir, fuss, ado, bother, pottering; fidget, -iness; flurry etc. (*haste*) 684.

officiousness; dabbling, meddling; inter-ference, -position, -meddling, butting in, intrusiveness; tampering with, intrigue.

press of business, no sinecure, plenty to do, many irons in the fire, great doings, busy hum of men, battle of life, thick of -things, – the action; the madding corwd.

housewife, busy bee; new brooms; sharp fellow, blade; hustler, devotee, enthusiast, fan, zealot, fanatic; meddler, intermeddler, intriguer, busybody, kibitzer, pickthank.

V. be -active etc. *adj.*; busy oneself in; stir, -about, – one's stumps; bestir –, rouse- oneself; speed, hasten, peg away, lay about one, bustle, fuss; raise –, kick up- a dust; push; make a -push, – fuss, – stir; go ahead, push forward; flight –, elbow- one's way; make progress etc. 282; toil etc. (*labor*) 686; drudge, plod, persist etc. (*persevere*) 604*a*; keep -up the ball, – the pot boiling.

look sharp; have all one's eyes about one etc. (*vigilance*) 459; rise, arouse oneself, get up early, hustle, push; be about, keep moving, steal a march, kill two birds with one stone; seize the opportunity etc. 134; lose no time, not lose a moment, make the most of one's time, not suffer the grass to grow under one's feet, improve the shining hour, make short work of; dash off; make haste etc. 684; do one's best, take pains etc. (*exert oneself*) 686; do –, work- wonders.

have -many irons in the fire, – one's hands full, – much on one's hands; have other -things to do, – fish to fry; be busy; not have a moment -to spare, – that one can call one's own.

have one's fling, run the round of; go all lengths, stick at nothing, run riot.

outdo; over-do, -act, -lay, -shoot the mark; make a toil of a pleasure.

have a hand in etc. (*act in*) 680; take an active part, put in one's oar, have a finger in the pie, mix oneself up with, trouble one's head about, intrigue; agitate.

tamper with, meddle, moil; inter-meddle, -fere, -pose; obtrude; poke –, thrust- one's nose in, butt in.

Adj. active; brisk, – as a lark, – as a bee; lively, animated, vivacious; alive, – and kicking; frisky, spirited, stirring.

nimble, – as a squirrel; agile; light-, nimble-footed; featly, tripping.

quick, prompt, yare, instant, ready, alert, spry, sharp, smart, slick, go-ahead; fast etc. (*swift*) 274; quick as a lamplighter, expeditious; awake, broad awake; wide awake etc. (*intelligent*) 498.

forward, eager, ardent, strenuous, zealous, enterprising, pushing, in earnest; resolute etc. 604.

industrious, assiduous, diligent, sedulous, notable, painstaking; intent etc. (*attention*) 457; indefatigable etc. (*persevering*) 604*a*; unwearied; unsleeping, sleepless, never tired; plodding, hard-working etc. 686; business-like, workaday.

bustling; restless, – as a hyena; fussy, fidgety, pottering; busy, – as a hen with one chicken. working, laboring, at work, on duty, in harness; up in arms; on one's legs, at call; up and -doing, – stirring.

busy, occupied; hard at -work, – it; up to one's ears in, full of business, busy as a bee.

meddling etc. *v.*; meddlesome, pushing, officious, overofficious, *intrigant*.

astir, stirring; a-going, -foot; on foot; in full swing; eventful; on the alert etc. (*vigilant*) 459.

Adv. actively etc. *adj.*; with -life and spirit, – might and main etc. 686, – haste etc. 684, – wings; full tilt, *in mediis rebus*.

Int. be –, look- -alive, – sharp! move –, push-on! keep moving! go ahead! stir your stumps! *age quod agis!*

Phr. *carpe diem* etc. (*opportunity*) 134; *nulla dies sine lineâ*; *nec mora nec requies*; no sooner said than done etc. (*early*) 132; catch a weasel asleep.

683. Inactivity.—N. inactivity; inaction etc. 681; inertness etc. 172; obstinacy etc. 606.

lull etc. (*cessation*) 142; quiescence etc. 265; rust, -iness.

idle-, remiss-ness etc. *adj.*; sloth, indolence, indiligence; otiosity, dawdling etc. *v.*

dullness etc. *adj.*; languor; segni-ty, -tude; lentor; sluggishness etc. (*slowness*) 275; procrastination etc. (*delay*) 133; torp-or, -idity, -escence; stupor etc. (*insensibility*) 823; somnolence; drowsiness etc. *adj.*; nodding etc. *v.*; oscitation, -ancy; pandiculation, hypnotism, lethargy; heaviness, heavy eye-lids, sand in the eyes.

sleep, slumber; sound –, heavy –, balmy-sleep; Morpheus, dreamland; coma, trance, catalepsy, hypnosis, *ecstasis*, dream, hibernation, nap, doze, snooze, *siesta*, wink of sleep, forty winks, snore; Hypnology.

dull work; pottering; relaxation etc. (*loosening*) 47; Castle of Indolence.

[Cause of inactivity] lullaby, *berceuse*; anesthetic, sedative etc. 174; torpedo.

idler, drone, droil, dawdle, mopus; do-little, *fainéant*, dummy, sleeping partner; afternoon farmer; truant etc. (*runaway*) 623; lounger, *lazzarone*, floater, loafer, tramp, beggar, cadger; lubber, -bard; slow-coach etc. (*slow*) 275; opium –, lotus- eater; slug; lag-, slug-gard, lie-abed; slumberer, dormouse, marmot; waiter on Providence, *fruges consumere natus*.

V. be -inactive etc. *adj.*; do nothing etc. 681; move slowly etc. 275; let the grass grow under one's feet; take one's time, dawdle, poke, drawl, droil, lag, hang back, slouch; loll, -op; lounge, loaf, loiter; go to sleep over; sleep at one's post; *ne battre que d'une aile*.

take -it easy, – things as they come; lead an easy life, vegetate, swim with the stream, eat the bread of idleness; loll in the lap of -luxury, – indolence; waste –, consume –, kill –, lose time; burn daylight, waste the precious hours.

idle –, trifle –, fritter –, fool- away time; spend –, take- time in; ped-, pid-dle; potter, putter, dabble, faddle, fribble, fiddle-faddle; dally, dilly-dally.

sleep, slumber, be asleep; hibernate; oversleep; sleep like a -top, – log, – dormouse; sleep -soundly, – heavily; doze, drowze, snooze, nap; take a -nap etc. *n.*; dream; snore; settle –, go –, go off- to sleep; drop off; fall –, drop- asleep; close –, seal up- -the -eyes, – eyelids; weigh down the eyelids; get sleepy, nod, yawn; go to bed, turn in.

languish, expend itself, flag, hang fire; relax.

render -idle etc. *adj.*; sluggardize; mitigate etc. 174.

Adj. inactive; motionless etc. 265; unoccupied etc. (*doing nothing*) 681.

indolent, lazy, slothful, idle, otiose, lusk, remiss, slack, inert, torpid, sluggish, languid, supine, heavy, dull, leaden, lumpish; exanimate, soulless; listless; dron-y, -ish; lazy as Ludlam's dog.

dilatory, laggard; lagging etc. *v.*; slow etc. 275; rusty, flagging; lackadaisical, maudlin, fiddle-faddle; pottering etc. *v.*; shilly-shally etc. (*irresolute*) 605.

sleeping etc. *v.*; alseep; fast –, dead –, sound-alseep; in a sound sleep; sound as a top, dormant, comatose; in the -arms, – lap- of Morpheus.

sleep-y, -ful; dozy, drowsy, somnolent, torpescent; lethargic, -al; heavy, – with sleep; napping; somni-fic, -ferous; sopor-ous, -ific, -iferous; hypnotic; balmy, dreamy; un-, una-wakened.

sedative etc. 174.

Adv. inactively etc. *adj.*; at leisure etc. 685.

Phr. the eyes begin to draw straws.

684. Haste.—N. haste, urgency; des-, dis-patch; acceleration, spurt, spirt, forced march, rush, dash; velocity etc. 274; precipit-ancy, -ation, -ousness etc. *adj.*; impetuosity; *brusquerie*; hurry, scurry, scuttle, drive, scramble, push, hustle, bustle, fuss, fidget, flurry, flutter, splutter.

V. haste, hasten; make -haste, – a dash etc. *n.*; hurry –, dash –, whip –, push –, press- -on, – forward; hurry, skurry, scuttle along, bundle on, dart to and fro, bustle, flutter, scramble; plunge, – headlong; run, race, speed; dash off; rush etc. (*violence*) 173.

bestir oneself etc. (*be active*) 682; lose -no time, – not a moment, – not an instant; make short work of, make the best of one's -time, – way.

be -precipitate etc. *adj.*; jump at; be in -haste, – a hurry etc. *n.*; have -no time, – not a moment- -to lose, – to spare; work -under pressure, – against time.

quicken etc. 274; accelerate, expedite, put on, precipitate, urge, whip, spur, flog, goad.

Adj. hasty, hurried, *brusque*; scrambling, cursory, precipitate, headlong, furious, boisterous, impetuous, hot-headed; feverish, fussy; pushing.

in -haste, – a hurry etc. *n.*; in -hot, – all- haste; breathless, pressed for time, hard pressed, urgent.

Adv. with -haste, – all haste, – breathless speed; in haste etc. *adj.*; apace etc. (*swiftly*) 274; amain; all at once etc. (*instantaneously*) 113; at short notice etc., immediately etc. (*early*) 132; posthaste; by -express, – telegraph, – wire, – wireless, – air mail.

hastily, precipitately etc. *adj.*; helter-skelter, hurry-skurry, holusbolus; slap-dash, -bang; full-tilt, -drive; heels over head, head and shoulders, headlong, *à corps perdu*.

by -fits and starts, – spurts; hop, skip and jump.

Phr. *sauve qui peut*, devil take the hindmost, no time to be lost; no sooner said than done etc. (*early*) 132; a word and a blow.

Int. hurry up! look alive! get a move on! buck up! double march! rush! urgent!

685. Leisure.—N. leisure; spare -time, – hours, – moments; vacant hour; time, – to spare, – on one's hands; holiday etc. (*rest*) 687; *otium cum dignitate*, ease.

V. have -leisure etc. *n.*; take one's -time, – leisure, – ease; repose etc. 687; move slowly etc. 275; while away the time etc. (*inaction*) 681; be -master of one's time, – an idle man; *desipere in loco*.

Adj. leisurely; slow etc. 275; deliberate, quiet, calm, undisturbed; at -leisure, – one's ease, – a loose end.

Phr. time hanging heavy on one's hands.

686. Exertion.—N. exertion, effort, strain, tug, pull, stress, force, pressure, throw, stretch, struggle, spell, spurt, spirt; stroke –, stitch- of work.

'a stong pull, a long pull and a pull all together;' dead lift; heft; gymnastics, sports; exer-cise, -citation; wear and tear; ado; toil and trouble; uphill –, hard –, warm- work; harvest time.

labor, work, toil, travail, manual labor, sweat of one's brow, swink, operoseness, drudgery, slavery, fagging, hammering; *limae labor*.

trouble, pains, duty; resolution etc. 604; energy etc. (*physical*) 171.

V. exert oneself; exert –, tax- one's energies; use exertion.

labor, work, toil, moil, sweat, fag, drudge, slave, drag a lengthened chain, wade through, strive, strain; make –, stretch- a long arm; pull, tug, ply; ply –, tug at- the oar; do the work; take the laboring oar.

bestir oneself (*be active*) 682; take trouble, trouble oneself.

work hard; rough it; put forth -one's strength, – a strong arm; fall to work, bend the bow; buckle to, set one's shoulder to the wheel etc. (*resolution*) 604; work like a -Briton, – horse, – carthorse, – galley-slave, – coalheaver; labor –, work-day and night; redouble one's efforts; do double duty; work double -hours, – tides; sit up, burn the -midnight oil, – candle at both ends; stick to etc. (*persevere*) 604*a*; work –, fight- one's way; lay about one, hammer at.

take pains; do one's -best, – level best, – utmost; do -the best one can, – all one can, – all in one's power, – as much as in one lies, – what lies in one's power; use one's -best, – utmost- endeavor; try one's -best, – utmost; play one's best card; put one's -best, – right- leg foremost; have one's whole soul in one's work, put all one's strength into, strain every nerve; spare no -efforts, – pains; go all lengths; go through fire and water etc. (*resolution*) 604; move heaven and earth, leave no stone unturned.

Adj. laboring etc. *v.*

laborious, operose, elaborate; strained; toil-, trouble-, burden-, weari-some; uphill; herculean, gymnastic, athletic, palestric.

hardworking, painstaking, strenuous, energetic, hard at work, on the stretch.

Adv. laboriously etc. *adj.*; lustily; with -might and main, – all one's might, – a strong hand, – sledge-hammer, – much ado; to the best of one's abilities, *totis viribus*, *vi et armis*, *manibus pedibusque*, tooth and nail, *unguibus et rostro*, hammer and tongs, heart and soul; through thick and thin etc. (*perseverance*) 604*a*.

by the sweat of one's brow, *suo Marte*.

687. Repose.—N. repose, rest, silken repose; sleep etc. 683.

relaxation, breathing time; halt, pause etc. (*cessation*) 142; respite.

day of rest, *dies non*, Sabbath, Lord's day, holiday, red-letter day, vacation, recess.

V. repose; rest, – and be thankful; take -rest, – one's ease.

relax, unbend, slacken; take breath etc. (*refresh*) 689; rest upon one's oars; pause etc. (*cease*) 142; stay one's hand.

lie down; recline, – on a bed of down, – on an easy chair; go to -rest, – bed, – sleep etc. 683.

take a holiday, shut up shop; lie fallow etc. (*inaction*) 681.

Adj. reposing etc. *v.*; unstrained.

Adv. at rest.

688. Fatigue.—N. fatigue; weariness etc. 841; yawning, drowsiness etc. 683; lassitude, tiredness, fatigation, exhaustion; sweat.

anhelation, shortness of breath, panting; faintness; collapse, prostration, swoon, fainting, *deliquium*, syncope, lipothymy.

V. be -fatigued etc. *adj.*; yawn etc. (*get sleepy*) 683; droop, sink, flag; lose -breath, – wind; gasp, pant, puff, blow, drop, swoon, faint, succumb.

fatigue, tire, weary, bore, irk, fag, jade, harass, exhaust, knock up, wear out, prostrate.

tax, task, strain; over-task, -work, -burden, -tax, -strain.

Adj. fatigued etc. *v.*; weary etc. 841; drowsy etc. 683; drooping etc. *v.*; haggard; toil-, way-worn; footsore, surbated, weatherbeaten; faint; done –, used –, knock- up; exhausted, prostrate, spent; over-tired, -spent, -fatigued; forspent; unre-freshed, -stored.

worn, – out; battered, shattered, pulled down, seedy, altered.

breath-, wind-less; short of –, out of -breath, – wind; blown, puffing and blowing; short-breathed; anhelous; broken-, short-winded.

ready to drop, more dead than alive, dog -tired, – weary, walked off one's legs, tired to death, on one's last legs, played out, *hors de combat*.

fatiguing etc. *v.*; tire-, irk-, weari-some; weary; trying.

689. Refreshment.—N. bracing etc. *v.*; recovery of -strength etc. 159; restoration, revival etc. 660; repair, refection, refocillation, refreshment, regalement, bait; relief etc. 834.

V. brace etc. (*strengthen*) 159; reinvigorate; air, freshen up, refresh, recruit; repair etc. (*restore*) 660; fan, revocillate.

breathe, respire; draw –, take –, gather –, take a long –, regain –, recover- breath; get better, raise one's head; recover –, regain –, renew- one's strength etc. 159; perk up.

come to oneself etc. (*revive*) 660; feel like a giant refreshed.

Adj. refreshing etc. *v.*; recuperative etc. 660. refreshed etc. *v.*; un-tired, -wearied.

690. Agent.—N. doer, actor, agent, performer, perpetrator, operator; execu-tor, -trix; practitioner, worker, stager.

bee, ant, working bee, laboring oar, shaft horse, servant –, maid- of all work, general servant, factotum.

workman, artisan; crafts-, handicrafts-man; mechanic, operative; working –, laboring- man; hewers of wood and drawers of water, laborer, navvy; hand, man, day laborer, journeyman, hack; mere -tool etc. 633; porter, docker, stevedore, beast of burden, drudge, fag.

maker, artificer, artist, wright, manufacturer, architect, contractor, builder, mason, bricklayer, smith, forger, Vulcan; black-, tin-smith; carpenter; ganger, platelayer.

machinist, mechanician, engineer, electrician, plumber, gasfitter etc.

semp-, sem-, seam-stress; needle-, char-, work-woman; tailor, cordwainer.

minister etc. (*instrument*) 631; servant etc. 746; representative etc. (*commissioner*) 758; (*deputy*) 759.

co-worker, fellow-worker, party to, participator in, co-operator, colleague, associate, collaborator, *particeps criminis, dramatis personae*; *personnel*.

Phrs. *'quorum pars magna fui.'*

691. Workshop.—N. work-shop, -house; laboratory; manufactory, mill, factory, armory, arsenal, mint, forge, loom; cabinet, *studio*, *bureau*, *atelier*· hive, – of industry; nursery; hot-house, -bed; kitchen, kitchenette; dock, -yard; slip, yard, wharf; found-ry, -ery; furnace; vineyard, orchard, farm, kitchen garden.

melting pot, crucible, alembic, caldron, mortar, *matrix*.

692. Conduct.—N. dealing, transaction etc. (*action*) 680; business etc. 625.

tactics, game, policy, polity; general-, statesman-seaman-ship; strate-gy, -gics; plan etc. 626.

husbandry; house-keeping, -wifery; stewardship; *ménage*; regimen, *régime*; econom-y, -ics; political economy; management; government etc. (*direction*) 693.

execution, manipulation, treatment, campaign, career, life, course, walk, race.

conduct; behavior; de-, com-portment; carriage, *maintien*, demeanor, guise, bearing, manner, mien, air, observance.

course –, line- of -conduct, – action, – proceeding; *rôle*; process, ways, practice, procedure, *modus operandi*; method etc., path etc. 627.

V. transact, execute; des-, dis-patch; proceed with, discharge; carry -on, – through, – out, – into effect; work out; go –, get- through; enact; put into practice; officiate etc. 625.

behave –, comport –, demean –, carry –, bear –, conduct –, acquit- oneself.
run a race, lead a life, play a game; take –, adopt- a course; steer –, shape- one's course; play one's- part, – cards; shift for oneself; paddle one's own canoe.
conduct; manage etc. (*direct*) 693.
deal –, have to do- with; treat, handle a case; take -steps, – measures.
Adj. conducting etc. *v.*; strategical, businesslike, practical, economic, executive.

693. Direction.—N. direction; manage-ment, -ry; government, gubernation, conduct, legislation, regulation, guidance; steer-, pilot-age; reins, – of government; helm, rudder, controls, joy stick, needle, compass, binnacle; guiding –, load –, lode –, pole- star; cynosure.
super-vision, -intendence; *surveillance*, oversight; eye of the master; control, charge, auspices; board of control etc. (*council*) 696; command etc. (*authority*) 737.
premier-, senator-ship; director etc. 694; chair, seat, portfolio.
statesmanship; state-, king-craft.
minis-try, -tration; administration; steward-, proctor-ship; agency.
V. direct, manage, govern, conduct; order, prescribe, cut out work for; head, lead; lead –, show- the way; take the lead, lead on; regulate, guide, steer, pilot; take –, be at- the helm; have –, handle –, hold –, take- the reins, handle the ribbons; drive, tool; tackle.
super-intend, -vise; overlook, control, keep in order, look after, see to, oversee, legislate for; administer, ministrate; patronize; have the -care, – charge- of; have –, take- the direction; pull the -strings, – wires; rule etc. (*command*) 737; have –, hold- -office, – the portfolio; preside, – at the board; take –, occupy –, be in- the chair; pull the stroke oar.
Adj. directing etc. *v.*; executive, supervisory, hegemonic.
Adv. at the -helm, – head of, in charge of; under the auspices of.

694. Director.—N. director, manager, governor, rector, comptroller; super-intendent, -visor; intendant; over-seer, -looker; foreman, boss, straw boss; supercargo, husband, inspector, visitor, ranger, surveyor, aedile, moderator, monitor, taskmaster; master etc. 745; leader, ringleader, demagogue, corypheus, conductor, fugleman, precentor, bellwether, agitator.
guiding star etc. (*guidance*) 693; adviser etc. 695; guide etc. (*information*) 527; pilot; helmsman; steers-man, -mate; man at the wheel; wirepuller.
driver, whip, Jehu, charioteer; coach-, car-, cabman, jarvey; postilion, *vetturino*, muleteer, teamster; whipper in; engineer, engine driver, motorman, *chauffeur*.
head, – man; principal, president, speaker; chair, -man; captain etc. (*master*) 745; superior; dean; mayor etc. (*civil authority*) 745; vice-president, prime minister, premier, vizier, grand vizier; dictator.
officer, functionary, minister, official, red-tapist, bureaucrat; man –, Jack- in office; office-bearer; person in authority etc. 745.
statesman, strategist, legislator, lawgiver, politician, administrator, statist, statemonger; Minos, Draco; arbiter etc. (*judge*) 967; king maker, power behind the throne.
board etc. (*council*) 696.
secretary, – of state; Reis Effendi; vicar etc. (*deputy*) 759; steward, factor; agent etc. 758; bailiff, middleman; ganger, clerk of works; landreeve; factotum, major-domo, seneschal, housekeeper, shepherd, *croupier*; proctor, procurator, curator, librarian.
Adv. *ex officio*.

695. Advice.—N. advice, counsel, adhortation; word to the wise; suggestion, submonition, recommendation, advocacy, consultation.
exhortation etc. (*persuasion*) 615; expostulation etc. (*dissuasion*) 616; admonition etc. (*warning*) 668; guidance etc. (*direction*) 693.
instruction, charge, injunction.
adviser, prompter; counsel, -lor; monitor, mentor, Nestor, *magnus Apollo*, senator; teacher etc. 540.
guide, manual, chart etc. (*information*) 527.
physician, leech, archiater; arbiter etc. (*judge*) 967.
refer-ence, -ment; consultation, conference, parley, *pourparler* etc. 696.
V. advise, counsel; give -advice, – counsel, – a piece of advice; suggest, prompt, submonish, recommend, prescribe, advocate; exhort etc. (*persuade*) 615.
enjoin, enforce, charge, instruct, call; call upon etc. (*request*) 765; dictate.
expostulate etc. (*dissuade*) 616; admonish etc. (*warn*) 668.
advise with; lay heads –, consult- together; compare notes; hold a council, deliberate, be closeted with.
confer, consult, refer to, call in; take –, follow- advice; follow implicitly; be advised by, have at one's elbow, take one's cue from.
Adj. recommendatory; hortative etc. (*persuasive*) 615; dehortatory etc. (*dissuasive*) 616; admonitory etc. (*warning*) 668; consultative.
Int. go to!

696. Council.—N. council, committee, subcommittee, *comitia*, court, chamber, cabinet, board, bench, staff; consultation.
senate, *senatus*, parliament, house, – of Lords, – Peers, – Commons, legislature, legislative assembly, federal council, chamber of deputies, directory, *reichsrath*, *rigsdag*, *cortes*, storthing, witenagemote, *junta*, divan, *musnud*, *sanhedrim*, Amphictyonic council; *duma*, *zemstvo*, *soviet*, *cheka*, *ogpu*; *Dail Eireann*; caput, consistory, chapter, syndicate; court of appeal etc. (*tribunal*) 966; board of -control, – works; vestry; county –, borough –, district –, parish –, town- council, local board.

cabinet –, privy- council, royal commission; cockpit, convocation, synod, congress, congregation, convention, diet, states-general, aulic council.

League of Nations, assembly, *caucus*, conclave, *clique*, conventicle; meeting, sitting, *séance*, conference, session, hearing, palaver, *pourparler*, *durbar*, pow-wow, house; *quorum*.

senator; member, – of parliament; councilor, M.P., representative of the people.

Adj. senatorial, curule, parliamentary.

697. Precept.—N. precept, direction, instruction, charge; prescript, -ion; *recipe*, receipt; golden rule; maxim etc. 496.

commandment, rule, ruling, canon, law, code, *corpus juris*, *lex scripta*, common –, unwritten –, canon- law; the Ten Commandments; act, statute, convention, rubric, stage direction, regulation; form, -ula, -ulary; technicality; nice point.

order etc. (*command*) 741.

698. Skill.—N. skill, skilfulness, address; dexter-ity, -ousness; adroitness, expertness etc. *adj.*; proficiency, competence, craft, callidity, facility, knack, trick, sleight; master-y, -ship; excellence, panurgy; ambidext-erity, -rousness; sleight of hand etc. (*deception*) 545.

sea-, air-, marks-, horse-manship; tight-, rope-dancing.

accomplish-, acquire-, attain-ment; art, science; techn-icality, -ology, -ique; practical –, technical- knowledge; technocracy; finish, technic.

knowledge of the world, world wisdom, *savoir-faire*; tact; mother wit etc. (*sagacity*) 498; discretion etc. (*caution*) 864; *finesse*; craftiness etc. (*cunning*) 702; management etc. (*conduct*) 692; *ars celare artem*; self-help.

cleverness, talent, ability, ingenuity, capacity, parts, talents, faculty, endowment, *forte*, turn, gift, genius, flair, feeling; intelligence etc. 498; sharpness, readiness etc. (*activity*) 682; invention etc. 515; apt-ness, -itude; turn –, capacity –, genius- for; felicity, capability, *curiosa felicitas*, qualification, habilitation.

proficient etc. 700.

masterpiece, *coup de maître*, *chef- d'oeuvre*, *tour de force*; good stroke etc. (*plan*) 626.

V. be -skilful etc. *adj.*; excel in, be master of; have -a turn for etc. *n.*

know -what's what, – a hawk from a handsaw, – what one is about, – on which side one's bread is buttered, – what's o'clock, – a thing or two; have cut one's -eye, – wisdom- teeth.

see -one's way, – where the wind lies, – which way the wind blows; have -all one's wits about one, – one's hand in; *savoir vivre*; *scire quid valeant humeri quid ferre recusent*

look after the main chance; cut one's coat according to one's cloth; live by one's wits; exercise one's discretion, feather the oar, sail near the wind; stoop to conquer etc. (*cunning*) 702; play one's -cards well, – best card; hit the right nail on the head, put the saddle on the right horse.

take advantage of, make the most of; profit by etc. (*use*) 677; make a hit etc. (*succeed*) 731; make a virtue of necessity; make hay while the sun shines etc. (*occasion*) 134.

Adj. skilful, dexterous, adroit, expert, apt, slick, handy, quick, deft, ready, resourceful, gain; smart etc. (*active*) 682; proficient, good at, up to, at home in, master of, a good hand at, *au fait*, thoroughbred, masterly, crack, accomplished; conversant etc. (*knowing*) 490.

experienced, practiced, skilled; up –, well up- in; in -practice, – proper cue; competent, efficient, qualified, capable, fitted, fit for, up to the mark, trained, initiated, prepared, primed, finished.

clever, able, ingenious, felicitous, gifted, talented, endowed, cute, inventive etc. 515; shrewd, sharp etc. (*intelligent*) 498; cunning etc. 702; alive to, up to snuff, not to be caught with chaff; discreet.

neat-handed, fine-fingered, ambidextrous, sure-footed; cut out –, fitted- for.

technical, artistic, scientific, daedalian, shipshape; workman-, business-, statesman-like.

Adv. skilfully etc. *adj.*; well etc. 618; artistically; with -skill, – consummate skill; *secundum artem*, *suo Marte*; to the best of one's abilities etc. (*exertion*) 686; like a machine.

699. Unskillfulness.—N. unskillfulness etc. *adj.*; want of -skill etc. 698; incompeten-ce, -cy; in-ability, -felicity, -dexterity, -experience; clumsiness; disqualification, unproficiency; quackery.

folly, stupidity etc. 499; indiscretion etc. (*rashness*) 863; thoughtlessness etc. (*inattention*) 458, (*neglect*) 460.

mis-management, -conduct; impolicy; maladministration; mis-rule, -government, -application, -direction, -feasance.

absence of rule, rule of thumb; bungling etc. *v.*; failure etc. 732; screw loose; too many cooks.

blunder etc. (*mistake*) 495; *étourderie*, *gaucherie*, act of folly, *balourdise*; botch, -ery; bad job, sad work.

sprat sent out to catch a whale, much ado about nothing, wildgoose chase.

bungler etc. 701; fool etc. 501.

layman, amateur.

V. be -unskillful etc. *adj.*; not see an inch beyond one's nose; blunder, bungle, boggle, fumble, muff, botch, bitch, flounder, loppet, stumble, trip; hobble etc. 275; put one's foot in it; make a -mess, – hash, – sad work- of; overshoot the mark.

play -tricks with, – Puck; mismanage, -conduct, -direct, -apply, -send.

stultify –, make a fool of –, commit- oneself; act foolishly; play the fool; put oneself out of court; lose one's -head, – cunning.

begin at the wrong end; do things by halves etc. (*not complete*) 730; make two bites of a cherry; play at cross purposes; strain at a gnat and swallow a camel etc. (*caprice*) 608; put the cart before the horse; lock the stable door when the horse is stolen etc. (*too late*) 135.

not know -what one is about, – one's own interest, – on which side one's bread is buttered; stand in one's own light, quarrel with one's bread and butter, throw a stone in one's own garden, kill the goose which lays the golden eggs, pay dear for one's whistle, cut one's own throat, burn one's fingers; knock –, run- one's head against a stone wall; fall into a trap, catch a Tartar, bring the house about one's ears; have too many -eggs in one basket (*imprudent*) 863, – irons in the fire.

mistake etc. 495; take the shadow for the substance etc. (*credulity*) 486; be in the wrong box, aim at a pigeon and kill a crow; take –, get- the wrong sow by the ear, – the dirty end of the stick; put -the saddle on the wrong horse, – a square peg into a round hole, – new wine into old bottles.

cut a whetstone with a razor; hold a farthing candle to the sun etc. (*useless*) 645; fight with –, grasp at- a shadow; catch at straws, lean on a broken reed, reckon without one's host, pursue a wildgoose chase; go on a fool's –, sleeveless- errand; go further and fare worse; loose –, miss- one's way; fail etc. 732.

Adj. un-skillful etc. 698; unskilled, inexpert; bungling etc. *v.*; awkward, clumsy, unhandy, lubberly, *gauche*, *maladroit*; left-, heavy-handed; sloverly, slatternly; gawky.

adrift, at fault.

in-, un-apt; inhabile; un-tractable, -teachable; giddy etc. (*inattentive*) 458; inconsiderate etc. (*neglectful*) 460; stupid etc. 499; inactive etc. 683; incompetent; un-, dis-, ill-qualified; unfit; quackish; raw, green, inexperienced, rusty, out of practice.

un-accustomed, -used, -trained etc. 537; -initiated, -conversant etc. (*ignorant*) 491; shiftless; unbusinesslike, unpractical; unstatesmanlike.

un-, ill-, mis-advised; ill-devised, -imagined, -judged, -contrived, -conducted; un-, mis-guided; misconducted, foolish, wild; infelicitous; penny wise and pound foolish etc. (*inconsistent*) 608.

Phr. one's fingers being all thumbs; the right hand forgets its cunning.

il se noyerait dans une goutte d'eau.

incidit in Scyllam qui vult vitare Charybdim; *out of the frying pan into the fire.*

700. Proficient.—N. proficient, expert, adept, dab; *connoisseur* etc. (*scholar*) 492; master, -hand; top-sawyer, *prima donna*, first fiddle, *chef de cuisine*; protagonist; past master; profess-or, -ional, specialist.

picked man; medalist, prizeman.

veteran; old -stager, – campaigner, – soldier, – file, – hand; man of -business, – the world.

nice –, good –, clean- hand; practised –, experienced- -eye, – hand; marksman; good –, dead –, crack- shot; rope-dancer, funambulist, acrobat, contortionist; cunning man; conjuror etc. (*deceiver*) 548; wizard etc. 994.

genius; master-mind, – head, – spirit.

cunning –, sharp -blade, – fellow; jobber; cracksman etc. (*thief*) 792; politician, tactician, diplomat, -ist, strategist.

pantologist, admirable Crichton, Jack of all trades; prodigy of learning; walking encyclopedia; mine of information.

701. Bungler.—N. bungler; blunderer, -head; marplot, fumbler, lubber, lout, oaf, duffer, stick, clown; bad –, poor- -hand, – shot; butter-fingers.

no conjuror, flat, muff, slow coach, looby, lubber, swab; clod, yokel, hick, awkward squad, novice, greenhorn, jaywalker, *blanc-bec*.

land lubber; fresh water –, fair weather- sailor; horse-marine; fish out of water, ass in lion's skin, jackdaw in peacock's feathers; quack etc. (*deceiver*) 548; Lord of Misrule.

sloven, slattern, trapes.

Phr. *il n'a pas inventé la poudre*; he will never set the Thames on fire.

702. Cunning.—N. cunning, craft; cunningness, craftiness etc. *adj.*; subtlety, artificiality; maneuvring etc. *v.*; temporization; circumvention.

chicane, -ry; sharp practice, knavery, jugglery; concealment etc. 528; nigger in the woodpile; guile, duplicity etc. (*falsehood*) 544; foul play.

diplomacy, politics; Machiavellism; jobbery, back-stairs influence, gerrymandering.

art, -ifice; device, machination; plot etc. (*plan*) 626; maneuver, stratagem, dodge, artful dodge, wile; trick, -ery etc. (*deception*) 545; *ruse*, – *de guerre; finesse*, side-blow, thin end of the wedge, shift, go by, subterfuge, evasion; white lie etc. (*untruth*) 546; juggle, *tour de force*; tricks -of the trade, – upon travelers; imposture, deception; *espiè-glerie*, net, trap etc. 545.

Ulysses, Machiavel, sly boots, fox, reynard; Scotch-, Yorkshire-man; Jew, Yankee; intriguer, *intrigant*, schemer, trickster.

V. be -cunning etc. *adj.*; have cut one's eyeteeth; contrive etc. (*plan*) 626; live by one's wits; maneuver; intrigue, gerrymander, *finesse*, double, temporize, stoop to conquer, *reculer pour mieux sauter*, circumvent, steal a march upon; overreach etc. 545; throw off one's guard; surprise etc. 508; outdo, get the better of, snatch from under one's nose; snatch a verdict; waylay, undermine, introduce the thin end of the wedge; play a deep game, – tricks with; have an axe to grind; *ambiguas in vulgum spargere voces*; flatter, make things pleasant.

Adj. cunning, crafty, artful; skilful etc. 698; subtle, feline, vulpine; cunning as a -fox, – serpent; deep, – laid; profound; designing, contriving; intriguing etc. *v.*; strategic, diplomatic, politic, Machiavellian, time-serving; artificial; trick-y, -sy; wily, sly, slim, insidious, stealthy, foxy; underhand etc. (*hidden*) 528; subdolous; deceitful etc. 545; double-tongued, -faced; shifty; crooked; arch, pawky, shrewd, acute; sharp, – as a needle; canny, astute, leery, knowing, up to snuff, too clever by half, not to be caught with chaff.

Adv. cunningly etc. *adj.*; slily, on the sly, by a side wind.

Phr. diamond cut diamond.

703. Artlessness.—N. artlessness etc. *adj.*; nature, simplicity; innocence etc. 946; *bonhomie*, *naiveté*, *abandon*, candor, sincerity; singleness of -purpose, – heart; honesty etc. 939; plain speaking; *épanchement*.

rough diamond, matter of fact man; *le palais de vérité*; *enfant terrible*.

V. be -artless etc. *adj.*; look one in the face; wear one's heart upon his sleeves for daws to peck at; think aloud; speak -out, — one's mind; be free with one, call a spade a spade.

Adj. artless, natural, pure, native, simple, plain, inartificial, untutored, unsophisticated, *ingénu*, unaffected, *naïve*; sincere, frank; open, — as day; candid, ingenuous, guileless, unsuspicious, childlike; honest etc. 939; innocent etc. 946; Arcadian; undesigning, straightforward; unreserved, unvarnished, above-board; simple-, single-minded; frank-, open-, single-, simple-hearted; open and above-board.

free-, plain-, out-spoken; blunt, downright, direct, matter of fact, unpoetical; unflattering.

Adv. in plain -words, — English; without mincing the matter; not to mince the matter etc. (*affirmation*) 535.

Phr. *Davus sum non Oedipus*; *liberavi animam meam.*

704. Difficulty.—N. difficulty; hardness etc. *adj.*; impracticability etc. (*impossibility*) 471; tough —, hard —, uphill- work; hard —, Herculean —, Augean- task; task of Sisyphus, Sisyphean labor, tough job, teaser, rasper, dead lift.

dilemma, embarrassment; perplexity etc. (*uncertainty*) 475; involvement; intricacy; entanglement etc. 59; cross fire; awkwardness, delicacy, ticklish card to play, deadlock, knot, Gordian knot, *dignus vindice nodus*, net, meshes, maze; coil etc. (*convolution*) 248; crooked path.

nice —, delicate —, subtle —, knotty-point; vexed question, *vexata quaestio*, poser; puzzle etc. (*riddle*) 533; paradox; hard —, nut to crack; bone to pick, *crux*, *pons asinorum*, where the shoe pinches.

nonplus, quandary, strait, pass, pinch, pretty pass, stress, brunt; critical situation, crisis; trial, rub, emergency, exigency, scramble.

scrape, hobble, slough, quagmire, hot water, hornet's nest; sea —, peck- of troubles; pretty kettle of fish; pickle, stew, *imbroglio*, mess, muddle, botch, fuss, bustle, ado; false position; set fast, stand; dead -lock, — set; fix, horns of a dilemma, *cul de sac*; hitch; stumbling block etc. (*hindrance*) 706.

V. be -difficult etc. *adj.*; run one hard, go against the grain, try one's patience, put one out; put to one's -shifts, — wit's end; go hard with —, try- one; pose, perplex etc. (*uncertain*) 475; bother, nonplus, gravel, bring to a dead lock; be -impossible etc. 471; be in the way of etc. (*hinder*) 706.

meet with —, labor under —, get into —, plunge into —, struggle with —, contend with —, grapple with- difficulties; labor under a disadvantage; be -in difficulty etc. *adj.*

fish in troubled waters, buffet the waves, swim against the stream, scud under bare poles.

have -much ado with, — a hard time of it; come to the -push, — pinch; bear the brunt.

grope in the dark, lose one's way, weave a tangled web, walk among eggs.

get into a -scrape etc. *n.*; bring a hornet's nest about one's ears; be put to one's shifts; flounder, boggle, struggle; not know which way to turn etc. (*uncertain*) 475; get -tangled up, — wound up; *perdre son latin*; stick - at, — in the mud, — fast; come to a -stand, — dead lock; hold the wolf by the ears.

render -difficult etc. *adj.*; encumber, embarrass, ravel, entangle; put a spoke in the wheel etc. (*hinder*) 706; lead a pretty dance.

Adj. difficult, not easy, hard, tough; trouble-, toil-, irk-some; operose, laborious, onerous, arduous, Herculean, formidable; sooner —, more easily- said than done; difficult —, hard- to deal with; ill-conditioned, crabbed; not -to be handled with kid gloves, — made with rosewater.

awkward, unwieldy, unmanageable; intractable, stubborn etc. (*obstinate*) 606; perverse, refractory, plaguy, trying, thorny, rugged; knot-ted, -ty; invious; path-, track-less; labyrinthine etc. (*convoluted*) 248; intricate, complicated etc. (*tangled*) 59; impracticable etc. (*impossible*) 471; not -feasible etc. 470; desperate etc. (*hopeless*) 859.

embarrassing, perplexing etc. (*uncertain*) 475; delicate, ticklish, critical; beset with —, full of —, surrounded by —, entangled by —, encompassed with- difficulties.

under a difficulty; in -difficulty, — hot water, — the suds, — a cleft stick, — a fix, — the wrong box, — a scrape etc. *n.*; — deep water, — a fine pickle; *in extremis*; between -two stools, — Scylla and Charybdis; surronded by -shoals, — breakers, — quicksands; at cross purposes; not out of the wood.

reduced to straits; hard —, sorely- pressed; run hard; pinched, put to it, straitened; hard -up, — put to it, — set; put to one's shifts; puzzled, at a loss etc. (*uncertain*) 475; at -the end of one's tether, — one's wit's end, — a nonplus, — a standstill; graveled, nonplussed, stranded, aground; stuck —, set- fast; up a tree, at bay, *aux abois*, driven -into a corner, — from post to pillar, — to extremity, — to one's wit's end, — to the wall; *au bout de son latin*; out of one's -depth, — reckoning; put —, thrown -out.

accomplished with difficulty; hard-fought, -earned.

Adv. with -difficulty, — much ado; hardly etc. *adj.*; uphill; against the -stream, — grain; *à rebours*; *invitâ Minervâ*; in the teeth of; at —, upon- a pinch; at long odds.

Phr. ay there's the rub; *hic labor hoc opus*; things are come to a pretty pass.

705. Facility.—N. facility, ease; easiness etc. *adj.*; capability; feasibility etc. (*practicability*) 470; flexibility, pliancy etc. 324; smoothness etc. 255; convenience.

plain —, smooth —, straight- sailing; mere child's play, holiday task.

smooth water, fair wind; smooth — royal- road; clear -coast, — stage; *tabula rasa*; *full play* etc. (*freedom*) 748.

disen-cumbrance, -tanglement; deoppilation; permission etc. 760.

V. be -easy etc. *adj.*; go on —, run- smoothly; have -full play etc. *n.*; go —, run- on all fours; obey the helm, work well.

flow —, swim —, drift —, go- with the- -stream, — tide; see one's way; have -it all one's own way, — the game in one's own hands; walk over the course, win -at a canter, — hands down; make -light of, — nothing of; be at home in etc. (*skilful*) 698.

render -easy etc. *adj.*; facilitate, smooth, ease; popularize; lighten, – the labor; free, clear; disencumber, -embarrass, -entangle, -engage; deobstruct, unclog, extricate, unravel; untie –, cut- the knot; disburden, unload, exonerate, emancipate, free from, deoppilate; humor etc. (*aid*) 707; lubricate etc. 332; relieve etc. 834.

leave -a hole to creep out of, – a loophole, – the matter open; give -the reins to, – full play, – full swing; make way for; open the -door to, – way; prepare –, smooth –, clear- the -ground, – way, – path, – road; pave the way, bridge over; permit etc. 760.

Adj. easy, facile; feasible etc. (*practicable*) 470; easily -managed, – accomplished; within reach, accessible, easy of access, for the million, open to.

manageable, wieldy; towardly, tractable; submissive; yielding, ductile; pliant etc. (*soft*) 324; glib, slippery; smooth etc. 255; on -friction wheels, – velvet; convenient.

un-, dis-burdened, -encumbered, -embarrassed; exonerated; un-loaded, -obstructed, -trammeled, -impeded, -restrained etc. (*free*) 748; at ease, light.

at –, quite at- home; in -one's element, – smooth water.

Adv. easily etc. *adj.*; readily, smoothly, swimmingly, *ad lib.*, on easy terms, single-handed.

Phr. touch and go.

Int. all clear!

706. Hindrance.—N. prevention, preclusion, obstruction, stoppage; prohibition; inter-ruption, -ception, -clusion; hindrance, impedition; retardment, -ation; constriction; embarrassment, oppilation; coarctation, stricture, restriction; anchor etc. 666; restraint etc. 751 & 752; inhibition etc. 761; blockade etc. (*closure*) 261; picketing.

inter-ference, -position; obtrusion; discouragement, -countenance, -approval, -approbation; opposition etc. 708.

impediment, let, obstacle, obstruction, knot, knag; check, hitch, *contretemps, impasse*, screw loose, grit in the oil.

bar, stile, barrier; turn-stile, -pike; gate, portcullis; bulwark, parapet, barricade etc. (*defence*) 717; wall, dead wall, breakwater, groyne; bulkhead, block, buffer; stopper etc. 263; boom, dam, weir, burrock.

drawback, objection; stumbling-block, -stone; lion in the path; snag; snags and sawyers.

en-, in-cumbrance; clog, skid, shoe, spoke; brake, drag, – chain, – weight; stay, stop; preventive, prophylactic; contraception; load, burden, fardel, *onus*, millstone round one's neck, *impedimenta*; dead weight; lumber, pack; nightmare, Ephialtes, incubus, old man of the sea; remora.

difficulty etc. 704; insuperable etc. 471- obstacle; estoppel; ill wind; head wind etc. (*opposition*) 708; trammel, tether etc. (*means of restraint*) 752; hold back, counterpoise; damper, wet blanket, hinderer, marplot, kill-joy, dog in the manger, interloper; trail of a red herring; opponent etc. 710.

V. hinder, impede, impedite, embarrass.

keep –, stave –, ward- off; picket; obviate; a-, ante-vert; turn aside, draw off, prevent, forefend, nip in the bud; retard, slacken, check, let; counteract, -check; preclude, debar, foreclose, estop; inhibit etc. 761; shackle etc. (*restrain*) 751; restrict, restrain, cohibit.

obstruct, filibuster, stop, stay, bar, bolt, lock; block, – up; belay, barricade; block –, stop- the way; dam up etc. (*close*) 261; put on the -brake etc. *n.*; scotch –, lock –, put a spoke in- the wheel; put a stop to etc. 142; traverse, contravene; inter-rupt, -cept; oppose etc. 708; hedge -in, – round; cut off; interclude.

inter-pose, -fere, -meddle etc. 682.

cramp, hamper; clog, – the wheels; cumber; en-, in-cumber; handicap; choke; saddle –, load- with; overload, lay; lumber, trammel, tie one's hands, put to inconvenience; in-, discommode; discompose; hustle, drive into a corner; choke off.

run –, fall- foul of; cross the path of, break in upon.

thwart, frustrate, disconcert, balk, foil, baffle, snub, override, circumvent; defeat etc. 731; spike guns etc. (*render useless*) 645; spoil, mar, clip the wings of; cripple etc. (*injure*) 659; put an extinguisher on; damp; dishearten etc. (*dissuade*) 616; discountenance, throw cold water on, spoil sport; lay –, throw- a wet blanket on; cut the ground from under one, take the wind out of one's sails, undermine; be –, stand- in the way of; act as a drag; hang like a millstone round one's neck.

Adj. hindering etc. *v.*; obstr-uctive, -uent; impedi-tive, -ent; intercipient; prophylactic etc. (*remedial*) 662.

in the way of, unfavorable; onerous, burdensome; cumb-rous, -ersome; obtrusive.

hindered etc. *v.*; wind-bound, water-logged, heavy laden; hard pressed.

unassisted etc. (*see* assist etc. 707); single-handed, alone; deserted etc. 624.

707. Aid. N. aid, -ance; assistance, help, opitulation, succor; support, lift, advance, furtherance, promotion; coadjuvancy etc. (*co-operation*) 709.

patronage, championship, countenance, favor, interest, advocacy, auspices.

sustentation, subvention, subsidy, bounty, alimentation, nutrition, nourishment, maintenance; manna in the wilderness; food etc. 298; means etc. 632.

ministr-y, -ation; subministration; accomodation.

relief, rescue; help at a dead lift; supernatural aid; *deus ex machinâ*.

supplies, reinforcements, succors, contingents, recruits; support etc. (*physical*) 215; adjunct, ally etc. (*helper*) 711.

V. aid, assist, help, succor, lend one's aid; come to the aid etc. *n*- of; contribute, subscribe to; bring –, give –, furnish –, afford –, supply- -aid etc. *n.*; render assistance; give –, stretch –, lend –, bear –, hold out- a -hand, – helping hand; give one a -lift, – cast, – turn; take -by the hand, – in tow; help a lame dog over a stile, lend wings to.

relieve, rescue; set -up, – agoing, – on one's legs; bear –, pull- through; give new life to, be the making of; reinforce, recruit; set –, put –, push- forward; give -a lift, – a shove, – an impulse- to; promote, further, forward, advance; speed, expedite, quicken, hasten.

support, sustain, uphold, prop, hold up, bolster,

cradle, nourish; nurture, nurse, dry nurse, suckle, put out to nurse; manure, cultivate, force; foster; cherish, foment; feed –, fan- the flame.

serve; do service to, tender to, pander to; ad-, sub-, minister to; tend, attend, wait on; take care of etc. 459; entertain; smooth the bed of death.

oblige, accomodate, consult the wishes of; humor, cheer, encourage.

second, stand by; back, – up; pay the piper, abet; work –, make interest –, stick up –, take up the cudgels- for; take up –, espouse –, adopt- the cause of; advocate, beat up for recruits, press into the service; squire, give moral support to, keep in countenance, countenance, patronize; lend - oneself, – one's countenance- to; smile –, shine- upon; favor, befriend, take up, take in hand, enlist under the banners of; side with etc. (*co-operate*) 709.

be of use to; subserve etc. (*instrument*) 631; benefit etc. 648; render a service etc. (*utility*) 644; conduce etc. (*tend*) 176.

Adj. aiding etc. *v.*; auxiliary, adjuvant, helpful; coadjuvant etc. 709; subservient, ministrant, ancillary, accessory, subsidiary.

at one's beck; friendly, amicable, favorable, propitious, well-disposed; neighborly; obliging etc. (*benevolent*) 906.

Adv. with –, by- -the aid etc. *n.*- of; on –, in-behalf of; in -aid, – the service, – the name, – favor, – furtherance- of; on account of; for the sake of, on the part of; *non obstante*.

Int. help! save us! to the rescue! S.O.S.!

708. Opposition.—N. opposition, antagonism, oppug-nancy, -nation; impugnation; contravention; counteraction etc. 179; counterplot.

cross-fire, under-current, head-wind.

clashing, collision, conflict, lack of harmony, contest.

competition, two of a trade, rivalry, emulation, race; war to the knife.

absence of -aid etc. 707; resistance etc. 719; restraint etc. 751; hindrance etc. 706.

V. oppose, conteract, run counter to; withstand etc. (*resist*) 719; control etc. (*restrain*) 751; hinder etc. 706; antagonize, oppugn, fly in the face of, go dead against, kick against, fall foul of; set –, pit- against; face, confront, cope with; make a -stand, – dead set- against; set -oneself, one's face- against; protest –, vote –, raise one's voice- against; disfavor, turn one's back upon; set at naught, slap in the face, slam the door in one's face.

be –, play- at cross purposes; counter-work, - mine; thwart, overthwart.

stem, breast, encounter; stem –, breast- the - tide, – current, – flood; buffet the waves; beat up –, make head- against; grapple with; kick against the pricks etc. (*resist*) 719; contend etc. 720 –, do battle etc. (*warfare*) 722- -with, – against.

contra-dict, -vene; belie; go –, run –, beat –, militate- against; come in conflict with.

emulate etc. (*compete*) 720; rival, spoil one's trade.

Adj. oppos-ing, -ed etc. *v.*; adverse, antagonistic; ambivalent; contrary etc. 14; at variance etc. 24; at issue, at war with; in opposition; 'agin the Government.'

un-favorable, -friendly; hostile, inimical, cross, unpropitious.

in hostile array, front to front, with crossed bayonets, at daggers drawn; up in arms; resistant etc. 791.

competitive, emulous.

Adv. against, *versus*, counter to, in conflict with, at cross purposes.

against the -grain, – current, – stream, – wind, – tide; with a headwind; with the wind - ahead, – in one's teeth.

in spite, in despite, in defiance; in the -way, – teeth, – face- of; across; a-, over-thwart; where the shoe pinches.

though etc. 30; even; *quand même*; *per contra*.

Phr. *nitor in adversum*.

709. Co-operation.—N. co-operation; coadju-vancy, -tancy; coagency, coefficiency; concert, concurrence, complicity, participation; union etc. 43; amalgamation, combination etc. 48; collusion.

association, alliance, colleagueship, jointstock, copartnership, trust, cartel, pool, ring, combine, interlocking directorate; confederation etc. (*party*) 712; federation, coalition, fusion; a long pull, a strong pull and a pull all together; log-rolling, freemasonry.

unanimity etc. (*assent*) 488; *esprit de corps*, party spirit; clan-, partisan-ship; reciprocity, concord etc. 714.

V. co-operate, co-adjute, concur; conduce etc. 178; combine, cartelize, unite one's efforts; keep –, draw –, pull –, club –, hang –, hold –, league –, band –, be banded- together; stand –, put- shoulder to shoulder; act in concert, join forces, fraternize, cling to one another, conspire, concert, lay one's heads together; confederate, be in league with; collude, understand one another, play into the hands of, hunt in couples.

side –, take side –, go along –, go hand in hand –, join hands –, make common cause –, strike in –, unite –, join –, mix oneself up –, take part –, play along –, cast in one's lot- with; join –, enter into- partnership with; rally round, follow the lead of; come to, pass over to, come into the views of; be –, row –, sail- in the same boat; sail on the same tack.

be a party to, lend oneself to; participate; have a -hand in, – finger in the pie; take –, bear- part in; second etc. (*aid*) 707; take the part of, play the game of; espouse a -cause, – quarrel.

Adj. co-operating etc. *v.*; in -co-operation etc. *n.*, – league etc. (*party*) 712; coadju-vant, -tant; hand and glove with.

favorable etc. 707- to; un-opposed etc. 708.

Adj. as one man etc. (*unanimously*) 488; shoulder to shoulder; in co-operation with.

710. Opponent.—N. opponent, antagonist, adversary; adverse party, opposition; enemy etc. 891; assailant.

oppositionist, obstructive; obscurantist; brawler, wrangler, brangler, disputant, extremist, irreconcilable, diehard, bitter-ender.

malcontent; Jacobin, Fenian etc. 742; demagogue, reactionist.

passive resister, conscientious objector.

rival, competitor, contestant.

711. Auxiliary.—N. auxiliary; recruit; assistant; adju-vant, -tant; adjunct; help, er, -mate, -ing hand; midwife; colleague, partner, mate, *confrère*, co-operator; coadju-tor, -trix; collaborator.

ally; friend etc. 890; confidant, *fidus Achates*, pal, chum, buddy, *alter ego*.

confederate; ac-, complice; accessory, – after the fact; *particeps criminis*.

aide-de-camp, secretary, clerk, associate, marshal; right-hand; candle-, bottle-holder; hand-maid; servant etc. 746; puppet, cat's-paw; stooge, dependent, creature, jackal; tool, *âme damnée*; satellite, adherent, parasite.

votary, disciple; secta-rian, -ry; seconder, backer, upholder, supporter, abettor, advocate, partisan, champion, patron, friend at court, mediator.

friend in need, Jack at a pinch, *deus ex machinâ*, guardian angel, fairy godmother; special providence, tutelary genius.

712. Party.—N. party, faction, side, denomination, class, communion, set, crowd, crew, band, horde, posse, phalanx; regiment etc. 726; family, clan etc. 166.

Tories, Conservatives, Unionists, Whigs, Liberals, Radicals, Labour party, Socialists, Communists etc.; Republicans, Democrats, Farmer-Labor; *Fascisti*, Revolutionaries etc. 742.

community, body, fellowship, sodality, solidarity; con-, fraternity; sorority; brother-, sisterhood.

Freemasons, Knights Templars, Odd Fellows, Ku Klux Klan etx.

knot, gang, *clique*, ring, circle; *coterie*, club, *casino*.

corporation, corporate body, guild; establishment, company, copartnership, firm, house, joint concern, joint-stock company, trust, investment trust, combine etc. 709.

society, association; instit-ute, -ution; union; trade-union; league, syndicate, alliance, *Verein*, *Bund*, *Zollverein*, combination; league –, alliance- offensive and defensive; coalition; federation; confedera -tion, -cy; junto, cabal, *camarilla*, *camorra*, *brigue*; freemasonry; party spirit etc. (*co-operation*) 709.

staff; cast, *dramatis personae*.

V. unite, join; club together etc. (*co-operate*) 709; cement –, form- a party etc. *n.*; associate etc. (*assemble*) 72.

Adj. in -league, – partnership, – alliance etc. *n.*

bonded –, banded –, linked etc. (*joined*) 43- together; embattled; confederated, federative, joint, corporate, leagued, fraternal, masonic, cliquish.

Adv. hand in hand, side by side, shoulder to shoulder, *en masse*, in the same boat.

713. Discord.—N. disagreement etc. 24; discord, -accord, -sidence, -sonance; jar, clash, shock; jarring, jostling etc. *v.*; screw loose.

variance, difference, dissension, misunderstanding, cross purposes, odds, *brouillerie*; division, split, rupture, disruption, division in the camp, house divided against itself, rift within the lute; disunion, breach; schism etc. (*dissent*) 489; feud, faction.

quarrel, dispute, rippet, spat, tiff, *tracasserie*, squabble, altercation, words, high words; wrangling etc. *v.*; jangle, brabble cross questions and crooked answers, snip-snap; family jars.

polemics; litigation; strife etc. (*contention*) 720; warfare etc. 722; outbreak, open rupture; breaking off of negotiations, recall of ambassadors; declaration of war.

broil, brawl, row, racket, hubbub, rixation; embroilment, embranglement, *imbroglio*, *fracas*, breach of the peace, piece of work, scrimmage, rumpus; breeze, squall; riot, disturbance etc. (*disorder*) 59; commotion etc. (*agitation*) 315; bear garden, Donnybrook Fair.

subject of dispute, ground of quarrel, battle ground, disputed point; bone -of contention, – to pick; apple of discord, *casus belli*; question at issue etc. (*subject of inquiry*) 461; vexed question, *vexata quaestio*, brand of discord.

troublous times; cat-and-dog life; contentiousness etc. *adj.*; enmity etc. 889; hate etc. 898; Kilkenny cats; disputant etc. 710; strange bedfellows.

V. be -discordant etc. *adj.*; disagree, come amiss etc. 24; clash, jar, jostle, pull different ways, conflict, have no measures with, misunderstand one another; live like cat and dog; differ; dissent etc. 489; have a -bone to pick, – crow to pluck- with.

fall out, quarrel, dispute; litigate; controvert etc. (*deny*) 536; squabble, wrangle, jangle, brangle, bicker, nag; spar etc. (*contend*) 720; have -words etc. *n.* with; fall foul of.

split; break –, break squares –, part company- with; declare war, try conclusions; join –, put in- issue; pick a quarrel, fasten a quarrel on; sow –, stir up- -dissension etc. *n.*; embroil, estrange, entangle, disunite, widen the breach; set -at odds, – together by the ears; set –, pit- against; rub up the wrong way.

get into hot water, fish in troubled waters, brawl; kick up a -row, – dust; turn the house out of window.

Adj. discordant; disagreeing etc. *v.*; out of tune, dissonant, inharmonious, harsh, grating, jangling, ajar, on bad terms; dissentient etc. 489; inconsistent, contradictory, incongruous, discrepant; un- reconciled, -pacified.

quarrelsome, unpacific; gladiatorial, controversial, polemic, disputatious; factious; liti-gious, -gant; pettifogging.

at odds, at loggerheads, at daggers drawn, at variance, at issue, at cross purposes, at sixes and sevens, at feud, at high words; up in arms, together by the ears, in hot water, embroiled.

torn, disunited.

Phr. *quot homines tot sententiae*; no love lost between them, *non nostrum tantas componere lites*.

714. Concord.—N. concord, accord, harmony, symphony, homology; aggreement etc. 23; sympathy etc. (*love*) 897; response; union, unison, unity; bonds of harmony; peace etc. 721; unanimity etc. (*assent*) 488; league etc. 712; happy family.

rapprochement; *réunion*; amity etc. (*friendship*) 888; reciprocity; alliance, *entente cordiale*, good understanding, conciliation, arbitration, peacemaker etc. 724.

V. agree etc. 23; accord, harmonize with; fraternize; be -concordant etc. *adj.*; go hand in hand; blend –, tone in- with; run parallel etc. (*concur*) 178; understand one another; pull together etc. (*co-operate*) 709; put up one's horses together, sing in chorus.

side –, sympathize –, go –, chime in –, fall in- with; come round; be pacified etc. 723; assent etc. 488; enter into the -ideas, – feelings- of; reciprocate.

hurler avec les loups; go –, swim- with the stream.

pour oil on troubled waters, keep in good humor, render accordant, put in tune; come to an understanding, meet half-way; keep the –, remain at- peace.

Adj. concordant, congenial; agreeing etc. *v.*; in-accord etc. *n.*; harmonious, united, cemented; banded together etc. 712; allied; friendly etc. 888; fraternal; conciliatory; at one with; of one mind etc. (*assent*) 488.

at peace, in still water; tranquil etc. (*pacific*) 721.

Adv. with one voice etc. (*assent*) 488; in concert with, hand in hand; on one's side, unanimously.

715. Defiance.—N. defiance; daring etc. *v.*; dare, challenge, *cartel*; threat etc. 909; war-cry, -whoop.

V. defy, dare, beard; brave etc. (*courage*) 861; bid defiance to; set at -defiance, – naught; hurl defiance at; dance the war dance; snap the fingers at, laugh to scorn; disobey etc. 742.

show -fight, – one's teeth, – a bold front; bluster, look big, stand akimbo; double –, shake- the fist; threaten etc 909.

challenge, call out; throw –, fling- down the -gauntlet, – gage, – glove.

Adj. defiant; defying etc. *v.*; with arms akimbo; rebellious, insolent; reckless, greatly daring.

Adv. in -defiance, – the teeth- of; under one's very nose.

Int. do your worst! come if you dare! come on! marry come up! hoity toity!

Phr. *noli me tangere*; *nemo me impune lacessit*.

716. Attack.—N. attack; assault, – and battery; onset, onslaught, charge.

aggression, drive, offence; incursion, inroad; invasion; irruption; outbreak; *estrapade*, *ruade*; *coup de main*, sally, *sortie*, *camisade*, raid, foray; run -at, – against; dead set at.

storm, -ing; boarding, *escalade*; siege, investment, obsession, bombardment, cannonade; air raid.

fire, volley; platoon –, file –, rapid-fire; *fusillade*; sharp-shooting, sniping; broadside; raking –, cross –, machine gun- fire; – volley of grapeshot, *feu d'enfer*; salvo.

cut, thrust, lunge, pass, *passado*, *carte* and *tierce*, home thrust, *coup de pied*; kick, punch, etc. (*impulse*) 276.

battue, *razzia*, *Jacquerie*, *dragonnade*; devastation etc. 162.

assailant, aggressor, invader.

base of operations, point of attack.

V. attack, assault, assail; set –, fall- upon; charge, impugn, break a lance with, enter the lists.

assume –, take- the offensive; be –, become- the aggressor; strike the first blow, fire the first shot, throw the first stone at; lift a hand –, draw the sword- against; take up the cudgels; advance –, march- against; march upon, invade, harry; come on, show fight.

strike at, poke at, thrust at; aim –, deal- a blow at; give –, fetch- one a -blow, – kick; have a -cut, – shot, – fling, – shy- at; be down –, pounce- upon; fall foul of, pitch into, launch out against; bait, slap on the face; make a -thrust, – pass, – set, – dead set- at; dunt; bear down upon.

close with, come to close quarters, bring to bay.

ride full tilt against; let fly at, dash at, run a tilt at, rush at, tilt at, run at, fly at, hawk at, have at, let out at; make a -dash, – rush at; attack tooth and nail; strike home; drive –, press- one hard; be hard upon, run down, strike at the root of.

lay about one, run amuck.

fire -upon, – at, – a shot at; shoot at, pop at, level at, let off a gun at; open fire, pepper, bombard, shell, pour a broadside into; fire -a volley, – red-hot shot; spring a mine.

throw -a stone, – stones- at; stone, lapidate, pelt; hurl -at, – against, – at the head of.

beset, besiege, beleaguer; lay siege to, invest, open the trenches, plant a battery, sap, mine; storm, board, scale the walls.

cut and thrust, bayonet, butt; kick, strike etc. (*impulse*) 276; whip etc. (*punish*) 972.

Adj. attacking etc. *v.*; aggressive, offensive, obsidional.

up in arms; on the warpath; over the top.

Adv. on the offensive.

Int. 'up and at them!'

717. Defense.—N. defense, protection, guard, ward; shielding etc. *v.*; propugnation; preservation etc. 670; guardianship.

self-defense, -preservation; resistance etc. 719.

safeguard etc. (*safety*) 664; screen etc. (*shelter*) 666, (*concealment*) 530; barrage; fortification; muni-tion, -ment; bulwark, fosse, moat, ditch, intrenchment, trench, dugout, gas mask; dike, dyke; parapet, parados, sunk fence, embankment, mound, mole, bank; earth- field-work, gabions; fence, wall, dead wall, contravallation; paling etc. (*inclosure*) 232; palisade, haha, stockade, *stoccado, laager, sangar*; barri-er, -cade; boom; portcullis, *chevaux de frise*; aba-, abat-, abba-tis; *vallum,* circumvallation, battlement, rampart, scarp; e-, counter-scarp; glacis, casemate.

mine, countermine.

buttress, abutment; shore etc. (*support*) 215.

breastwork, *banquette,* curtain, mantlet, bastion, demilune, redan, ravelin; advanced –, horn –, out- work, lunette; barb-acan, -ican; redoubt; fortelage, -alice; lines; coast defense.

loop-hole, machicolation; sally-port, postern gate.

hold, stronghold, fastness; asylum etc. (*refuge*) 666; keep, donjon, fortress, citadel; capitol, castle; tower, – of strength; fort, barracoon, pah, sconce, martello tower, peel-house, block-house, rath; wooden walls; turret, barbette.

buffer, corner-stone, fender, apron, mask, gauntlet, thimble, carapace, armor, shield, buckler; target, targe, aegis, breastplate, cuirass, plastron, habergeon, mail, coat of mail, brigandine, hauberk, lorication, helmet, helm, basinet, sallet, salade, heaume, morion, murrion, armet, cabaset, vizor, casquetel, siege-cap, head-piece, casque, steel helmet, tin hat; *pickelhaube*, csako; shako etc. (*dress*) 225; bearskin; panoply; truncheon etc. (*weapon*) 727.

garrison, picket, piquet; defender, protector; guardian etc. (*safety*) 664; trabant, body guard, champion; knight-errant, Paladin; propugner.

V. defend, forfend, fend; shield, screen, shroud; fence round etc. (*circumscribe*) 229; fence, intrench; guard etc. (*keep safe*) 664; guard against; take care of etc. (*vigilance*) 459; bear harmless; keep –, ward –, beat- off; hinder etc. 706.

parry, repel, propugn, put to flight; give a warm reception to [*ironical*]; hold –, keep- at -bay, – arm's length.

stand –, act- on the defensive; show fight; maintain –, stand- one's ground; stand by; hold one's own; bear –, stand- the brunt; fall back upon, hold, stand in the gap.

Adj. defending etc. *v.*; defensive; mural; armed, – at all points, – *cap-à-pie*, – to the teeth; panoplied; accoutred, harnessed; iron-plated, -clad; loop-holed, castellated, machicolated; casemated; defended etc. *v.*; proof against, bomb-, bullet-proof; protective.

Adv. defensively; on the -defense, – defensive; in defense; at bay, *pro aris et focis*.

Int. no surrender! *il ne passeront pas!*

Phr. defense not defiance.

718. Retaliation.—N. retaliation, reprisal, retort; counter-stroke, -blast, -plot, -project; retribution, *lex talionis*; reciprocation etc. (*reciprocity*) 12.

requital, desert, tit for tat, give and take, blow for blow, *quid pro quo*, a Roland for an Oliver, measure for measure, an eye for an eye, diamond cut diamond, the biter bit, a game at which two can play; boomerang.

recrimination etc. (*accusation*) 938; revenge etc. 919; compensation etc. 30; reaction etc. (*recoil*) 277.

V. retaliate, retort, turn upon; pay -off, – back; pay in -one's own, – the same- coin; cap; reciprocate etc. 148; turn the tables upon, return the compliment; give -a *quid pro quo* etc. *n.*, – as much as one takes; give and take, exchange -blows, – fisticuffs; be -quits, – even- with; pay off old scores.

serve one right, be hoist on one's own petard, throw a stone in one's own garden, cathch a Tartar.

Adj. retaliating etc. *v.*; retalia-tory, -tive; retributive, recriminatory, reciprocal.

Adv.. in retaliation; *en revanche*.

Phr. *mutato nomine de te fabula narratur; par pari refero; tu quoque*; you're another; *suo sibi gladio hunc jugulo*.

719. Resistance.—N. resistance, stand, front, oppugnation; opposition etc. 708; renitence, reluctation, recalcitration, recalcitrance; repugnance; kicking etc. *v.*

repulse, rebuff.

insurrection etc. (*disobedience*) 742; strike; turn –, lock –, barring- out; *levée en masse*, *Jacquerie*; riot etc. (*disorder*) 59.

V. resist; not -submit etc. 725; repugn, reluctate, withstand; stand up –, strive –, bear up –, be proof –, make head- against; stand, – firm, – one's ground, – the brunt of, – out; hold -one's ground, – one's own, – out.

breast the -wave, – current; stem the -tide, – torrent; face, confront, grapple with; show a bold front etc. (*courage*) 861; present a front; make a –, take one's- stand.

kick, – against; recalcitrate, kick against the pricks; oppose etc. 708; fly in the face of; lift the hand against etc. (*attack*) 716; rise up in arms etc. (*war*) 722; strike, turn out; draw up a round robin etc. (*remonstrate*) 932; revolt etc. (*disobey*) 742; make a riot.

prendre le mors aux dents; take the bit between the teeth; sell one's life dearly, die hard, keep at bay; repel, repulse.

Adj. resisting etc. *v.*; resist-ive, -ant; refractory etc. (*disobedient*) 742; recalcitrant, re-nitent, -pulsive, -pellant; up in arms.

proof against; unconquerable etc. (*strong*) 159; stubborn, unconquered; indomitable etc. (*persevering*) 604*a*; unyielding etc. (*obstinate*) 606.

Int. hands off! keep off!

720. Contention.—N. contention, strife; contest, -ation; struggle; belligerency; opposition etc. 708.

controversy, polemics; debate etc. (*discussion*) 476; war of words, logomachy, litigation; paper war, ink slinging; high words etc. (*quarrel*) 713; sparring etc. *v.*

competition, rivalry; corrival-ry, -ship; agonism, *concours*, match, race, horse-racing, heat, steeple chase, point-to-point race, handicap; boat race, regatta; field-day; sham fight, Derby day; turf, sporting, bull-fight, tauromachy, *gymkhana*, rodeo, Olympiad.

wrestling, *ju-jitsu*, pugilism, boxing, fisticuffs, spar, mill, set-to, scrap, round, bout, event; prize-fighting; quarter-staff, single stick; gladiatorship, gymnastics; athletic-s, – sports; games of skill etc. 840.

shindy; *fracas* etc. (*discord*) 713; clash of arms; tussle, scuffle, broil, fray; affray, -ment; velitation; col-, luctation; brabble, *brique*, scramble, *mêlée*, scrimmage, stramash, bush-fighting.

free –, stand up –, hand to hand –, running-fight.

conflict, skirmish; ren-, en-counter; *rencontre*, collision, affair, brush, fight; battle, – royal; combat, action, engagement, joust, tournament; tilt, -ing; tourney, list; pitched battle, guerilla warfare.

death-struggle, struggle for life or death, Armageddon; hard knocks, sharp contest, tug of war.

naval -engagement, – battle; *naumachia*, sea-fight.

duel, -lo; single combat, monomachy, satisfaction, *passage d'armes*, passage of arms, affair of honor; triangular duel; hostile meeting, digladiation; appeal to arms etc. (*warfare*) 722.

deeds –, feats- of arms; pugnacity; combativeness etc. *adj.*; bone of contention etc. 713.

V. contend; contest, strive, struggle, scramble, wrestle; spar, square; exchange -blows, – fisticuffs; scrap, mix with, fib, justle, tussle, tilt, box, stave, fence; skirmish; fight etc. (*war*) 722; wrangle etc. (*quarrel*) 713.

contend etc. –, grapple –, engage –, close –, buckle –, bandy –, try conclusions –, have a brush etc. *n.* –, tilt- with; encounter, fall foul of, pitch into, clapperclaw, run a tilt at; oppose etc. 708; reluct.

join issue, come to blows, be at loggerheads, set-to, come to the scratch, exchange shots, measure swords, meet hand to hand; take up the -cudgels, – glove, – gauntlet; enter the lists; couch one's lance; give satisfaction; appeal to arms etc. (*warfare*) 722.

lay about one; break the peace.

compete –, cope –, vie –, race- with; outvie, emulate, rival; run a race; contend etc. –, stipulate –, stickle- for; insist upon, make a point of.

Adj. contending etc. *v.*; together by the ears, at loggerheads, at war, at issue.

competitive, rival; belligerent; contentious, combative, bellicose, unpeaceful; warlike etc. 722; quarrelsome etc. 901; pugnacious; pugilistic, gladiatorial; palestric, -al.

Phr. *a verbis ad verbera*; a word and a blow.

721. Peace.—N. peace; amity etc. (*friendship*) 888; harmony etc. (*concord*) 714; tranquility etc. (*quiescence*) 265; truce etc. (*pacification*) 723; pacificism; pipe –, calumet- of peace.

piping time of peace, quiet life; neutrality.

V. be at peace; keep the peace etc. (*concord*) 714; make peace etc. 723.

Adj. pacific; peace-able, -ful; calm, tranquil, untroubled, halcyon; bloodless; neutral.

Phr. the storm blown over; the lion lies down with the lamb.

722. Warfare.—N. warfare; fighting etc. *v.*; hostilities; war, arms, the sword; Mars, Bellona, grim visaged war, *horrida bella*, Armageddon.

appeal to -arms, – the sword; ordeal –, wager- of battle; *ultima ratio regum*, arbitrament of the sword.

battle array, campaign, crusade, expedition; mobilization; state of siege; battle-field etc. (*arena*) 728; warpath.

art of war, tactics, strategy, castrametation; general-, soldier-ship; aerial –, submarine –, naval –, chemical-, atomic-, guerilla- warfare; military evolutions, ballistics, gunnery; chivalry; poison gas; gun-powder, shot, – and shell.

battle, tug of war etc. (*contention*) 720; service, campaigning, active service, tented field; fiery cross, trumpet, clarion, bugle, pibroch, slogan; war-cry, -whoop; battle cry, beat of drum, rappel, tom-tom; word of command; pass-, watch-word.

war to the -death, – knife; *guerre à -mort*, – *outrance*; open –, internecine –, civil- war.

V. arm; raise –, mobilize- troops; raise up in arms; take up the cudgels etc. 720; take up –, fly to –, appeal to- -arms, – the sword; draw –, unsheathe- the sword; dig up the hatchet; go to –, declare –, wage –, let slip the dogs of- war; cry havoc; kindle –, light- the torch of war; raise one's banner, send round the fiery cross; hoist the black flag; throw –, fling- away the scabbard; enrol, enlist, join up; take the field; take the law into one's own hands; do –, give –, join –, engage in –, go to- battle; flesh one's sword; set to, fall to, engage, measure swords with, draw the trigger, cross swords; come to -blows, – close quarters; fight; combat; contend etc. 720; battle –, break a lance- with.

serve; see –, be on- -service, – active service; campaign; wield the sword, shoulder a musket, smell powder, be under the fire; spill –, imbrue the hands in- blood; be on the warpath.

carry on -war, – hostilities; keep the field; fight the good fight; go over the top; cut one's way through; fight -it out, – like devils, – one's way, – hand to hand; sell one's life dearly.

Adj. conten-ding, -tious etc. 720; armed, – to the teeth, – cap-à-pie; sword in hand; in –, under –, up in- arms; at war with; bristling with arms; in -battle array, – open arms, – the field; embattled.

unpacific, unpeaceful; belligerent, combative, armigerous, bellicose, martial, warlike; mili-tary, -tant; soldier-like, -ly; chivalrous; strategical, internecine.

Adv. *flagrante bello*, in the -thick of the fray, – cannon's mouth; at the -swords's point, – point of the bayonet.

Int. *vae victis!* to arms! to your tents O Israel!

Phr. the battle rages.

723. Pacification.—N. pacification, conciliation; reconcil-iation, -ement; shaking of hands, accomodation, arrangement, adjustment; terms, compromise; amnesty, deed of release.

peace-offering; olive-branch; overtures; pipe –, calumet –, preliminaries- of peace.

truce, armistice; suspension of -arms, – hostilities; breathing-time; convention; *modus vivendi*; flag of truce, white flag, *parlementaire*, *cartel*.

hollow truce, *pax in bello*; drawn battle.

V. pacify, tranquilize, compose; allay etc. (*moderate*) 174; reconcile, propitiate, placate, conciliate, meet half-way, hold out the olive-branch, heal the breach, make peace, restore harmony, bring to terms.

settle –, arrange –, accommodate- -matters, – differences; set straight; make up a quarrel, *tantas componere lites*; come to -an understanding, – terms; bridge over, hush up; make -it, – matters- up; shake hands.

raise a siege; put up –, sheathe- the sword; bury the hatchet, lay down one's arms, turn swords into ploughshares; smoke the calumet of peace, close the temple of Janus; keep the peace etc. (*concord*) 714; be -pacified etc.; come round.

Adj. conciliatory, pacificatory; composing etc. *v.*; pacified etc. *v.*

Phr. *requiescat in pace*.

724. Mediation.—N. media-tion, -torship, -tization; inter-vention, -position, -ference, -meddling, -cession; parley, negotiation, arbitration; flag of truce etc. 723; good offices, peace -offering; diploma-tics, -cy; compromise etc. 774.

mediator, intercessor, peacemaker, make-peace, negotiator, go-between; diplomatist etc. (*consignee*) 758; moderator, propitiator, umpire, arbitrator.

V. media-te, -tize; inter-cede, -pose, -fere, -vene; step in, negotiate; meet half-way; arbitrate; *magnas componere lites.*

Adj. mediatory, propitiatory, diplomatic.

725. Submission.—N. submission, yielding, acquiescence, compliance; non-resistance; obedience etc. 743; submissiveness, deference.

surrender, cession, capitulation, resignation.

obeisance, homage, kneeling, genuflexion, courtesy, curtsy, *salaam, kowtow,* prostration.

V. succumb, submit, yield, bend, resign, defer to, accede.

lay down –, deliver up- one's arms; hand over one's sword; lower –, haul down –, strike- one's flag, – colors; deliver the keys of the city.

surrender, – at discretion; cede, capitulate, come to terms, retreat, beat a retreat; draw in one's horns etc. (*humility*) 879; give -way, – ground, – in, – up; cave in; suffer judgment by default; bend, – to one's yoke, – before the storm; reel back; bend –, knuckle- -down, – to, – under; knock under.

humble oneself; eat -dirt, – the leek, – humble pie; bite –, lick- the dust; be –, fall- at one's feet; craven; crouch before, throw oneself at the feet of; swallow the -leek, – pill; kiss the rod; turn the other cheek; *avaler des couleuvres,* gulp down.

obey etc. 743; kneel to, bow to, pay homage to, cringe to, truckle to; bend the -neck, – knee; kneel, fall on one's knees, bow submission, courtesy, curtsy, *kowtow*; make obeisance.

pocket the affront; make -the best of, – a virtue of necessity; grin and abide, shrug the shoulders, resign oneself; submit with a good grace etc. (*bear with*) 826.

Adj. surrendering etc. *v.*; submissive, resigned, crouching; down-trodden; down on one's marrow bones; on one's bended knee; weak-kneed, un-, non-resisting; pliant etc. (*soft*) 324; undefended.

untenable, indefensible; humble etc. 879.

Phr. have it your own way; it can't be helped; amen etc. (*assent*) 488.

726. Combatant.—N. combatant; disputant, controversialist, polemic, litigant, belligerent; competitor, rival, corrival; fighter, assailant, aggressor; champion, Paladin; moss-trooper, swashbuckler, fire-eater, duellist, bully, bludgeon-man, rough, fighter, fighting-man, prize-fighter, pugilist, pug, boxer, bruiser, the fancy, gladiator, athlete, wrestler; fighting-, game-cock; swordsman, *sabreur.*

warrior, soldier, Amazon, man-at-arms, armigerent; campaigner, veteran; red-coat, military man, *rajpoot*, brave.

armed force, troops, soldiery, military, forces, sabaoth, the army, standing army, regulars, the line, troops of the line, militia, territorials, yeomanry, volunteers, trainband, fencible; auxiliary –, reserve- forces; reserves, *posse comitatus*, national guard, *gendarme*, beefeater; guards, -man; yeoman of the guard, life guards, household troops.

janissary; myrmidon; Mama-, Mame-luke; spahee, *spahi*, Cossack, Croat, Pandour; irregular, free lance, *franc-tireur, bashi-bazouk, guerilla, condottiere*; mercenary.

levy, draught, commando; *Land-wehr, -sturm*; conscript, recruit, rookie, cadet, raw levies.

private, – soldier; Tommy Atkins, rank and file, peon, trooper, doughboy, sepoy, *askari, legionnaire*, legionary, food for powder, cannon fodder; officer etc. (*commander*) 745; subaltern, ensign, shave-tail, standard bearer, non-com; spear-, pike-man; halberdier, lancer; musketeer, carabineer, rifleman, sharpshooter, yager, skirmisher; grenadier, fusileer; archer, bowman.

horse and foot; horse –, foot- soldier; cavalry, horse, artillery, horse –, field –, heavy –, mountain- artillery, infantry, light horse, *voltigeur, Uhlan*, mounted rifles, dragoon, hussar, trooper; light –, heavy- dragoon; heavy; *cuirassier*; gunner, cannoneer, bombardier, artillery-man, matross; sapper, – and miner; engineer; light infantry, rifles, *chasseur, zouave*; military train, supply and transport, coolie.

army, – corps, *corps d'armée*, host, division, column, wing, detachment, *escadrille*, garrison, flying column, brigade, regiment, *corps*, battalion, squadron, company, platoon, battery, subdivision, section, squad; piquet, picket, guard, rank, file; legion, phalanx, cohort; cloud of skirmishers; impi.

war-horse, charger, *destrier.*

armored -train, – car; tank.

marine, man of war's man etc. (*sailor*) 269; navy, first line of defense, wooden walls; naval forces, fleet, flotilla, armada, squadron.

man-of-war, warship; H M S., U.S.S.; capital ship; line-of-battle ship, battle ship; super-, dreadnought, battle –, armored –, protected – light-cruiser; scout, flotilla leader; destroyer, torpedo boat; submarine, submersible, U-boat; submarine chaser, eagle boat, mystery ship, Q-boat; mine-layer, -sweeper; ship of the line, iron-clad, turret-ship, ram, Monitor, floating battery; first-rate, frigate, sloop of war, corvette, gunboat, bomb-vessel, fire-boat; flag ship, guard ship, cruiser; airplane carrier; privateer; tender; depôt –, parent-ship; store –, troop- ship; transport, catamaran.

aircraft etc. 273; air force, scout, fighter, bomber, troop carrier, aerial patrol, seaplane, flying boat, torpedo plane; airship, Zeppelin; rigid –, semi-rigid –, non-rigid- airship; dirigible –, free –, captive –, kite –, observation- balloon.

anti-aircraft guns, searchlights, sound locators; catapult.

727. Arms.—N. arm, -s; weapon, deadly weapon; arma-ment, -ture; panoply, stand of arms; armor etc. (*defense*) 717; armory etc. (*store*) 636.

ammunition; powder, – and shot; explosive; propellant; gun-powder, -cotton; dynam-, melin-, cord-, lydd-ite; trinitrotoluene, T.N.T., ammonal; cartridge; ball cartridge, *cartouche*, fire-ball; dud, black Marie; 'villainous saltpeter;' poison –, mustard –, lachrymatory –, tear- gas.

sword, saber, broadsword, cutlass, falchion, scimitar, cimeter, brand, whinyard, bilbo, glaive, glave, rapier, skean, Toledo, Ferrara, tuck, claymore, creese, kris, *kukri*, dagger, dirk, hanger, poniard, stiletto, stylet, dudgeon, bayonet; sword-bayonet, -stick; side arms, foil, blade, steel; axe, bill; pole-, battle-axe; gisarm, halberd, partisan, tomahawk, bowie-knife; at-, att-, yat-aghan; yatachan; good –, trusty –, naked- sword; cold –, naked-steel.

club, mace, truncheon, staff, bludgeon, cudgel, life-preserver, shillelagh, sprig; hand-, quarter-staff; bat, cane, stick, knuckle-duster, sand bag.

gun, piece; fire-arms; artillery, ordnance; siege –, battering-train; park, battery; cannon, gun of position, heavy –, siege –, field –, mountain –, anti-aircraft –, breech loading –, quick firing-gun; field piece, mortar, trench mortar; mine –, flame- -thrower, napalm; howitzer, carronade, culverin, basilisk; falconet jingal, swivel, *pederero, bouche à feu*; smooth bore, rifled cannon; Armstrong –, Lancaster –, Paixhan –, Whitworth –, Parrott –, Krupp –, Gatling –, Maxim –, Vickers –, Hotchkiss –, Lewis –, machine- gun; tommy gun, Thompson's submachine gun; *mitrailleu-r, -se*; pompom; blow pipe.

small arms; musket, -ry, firelock, flintlock, fowling-piece, shot gun, rifle, *fusil*, caliver, carbine, blunderbuss, musketoon, Brown Bess, matchlock, harquebuss, *arquebuse*, haguebut; petronel; smallbore; breech-, muzzle-loader; Minié –, Enfield –, Westly Richards –, Snider –, Springfield –, Martini-Henry –, Lee-Metford –, Lee-Enfield –, Mauser –, Männlicher –, magazine –, repeating- rifle; needle-gun, *chassepot*; pis-tol, -et; revolver, automatic pistol, automatic; wind-, air-gun; flame –, gas- projector.

bow, cross-bow, arbalest, balister, catapult, sling; battering-ram etc. (*impulse*) 276; gunnery; ballistics etc. (*propulsion*) 284.

missile, bolt, projectile, shot, pellet, ball; grape; grape –, canister –, bar –, cannon –, langrel –, langrage –, round –, chain- shot; explosive; incendiary –, expanding –, soft-nosed –, dum-dum- bullet; slug, stone, brickbat; hand –, rifle-grenade; high explosive –, incendiary –, stink-, A-, H-, atomic –, hydrogen – bomb; petard, torpedo, carcass, rocket; congreve, – rocket; shrapnel, *mitraille*; thunderbolt; mine, land mine, infernal machine.

pike, lance, spear, spontoon, javelin, assagai, throwing stick, dart, djerrid, arrow, reed, shaft, bolt, boomerang, harpoon, gaff.

728. Arena.—N. arena, field, platform; scene of action, theater; walk, course; hustings; stage, boards etc. (*playhouse*) 599; amphitheater; Coli-, Colos-seum; Flavian amphitheater, hippodrome, circus, race-course, track, *stadium*, *corso*, turf, cockpit, bear-garden, play-ground, playing fields, *gymnasium, palaestra*, ring, lists; tilt-yard, -ing ground; *Campus Martius, Champ de Mars*; aerodrome, airport, air base, flying field.

theater –, seat- of war; battle-field, -ground; field of -battle, – slaughter; no man's land; Aceldama, camp; the enemy's camp; trysting- place etc. (*place of meeting*) 74.

729. Completion.—N. completion; accomplish-, achieve-, fulfil-ment; performance, execution; des-, dis-patch; consummation, culmination, climax; finish, conclusion, effectuation; close etc. (*end*) 67; terminus etc. (*arrival*) 292; winding up; *finale, dénouement*, catastrophe, issue, upshot, result; final –, last –, crowning –, finishing- -touch, – stroke; last finish, *coup de grâce*; crowning of the edifice; coping-, keystone; missing link etc. 53; superstructure, *ne plus ultra*, work done, *fait accompli*.

elaboration; finality; completeness etc. 52.

V. effect, -uate; accomplish, achieve, compass, consummate, hammer out; bring to -maturity, – perfection; perfect, complete; elaborate.

do, execute, make; go –, get- through; work out, enact; bring -about, – to bear, – to pass, – through, – to a head.

des-, dis-patch; knock –, finish –, polish- off; make short work of; dispose of, set at rest; perform, discharge, fulfil, realize; put in -practice, – force; carry -out, – into effect, – into execution; make good; be as good as one's word.

do thoroughly, not do by halves, go the whole hog; drive home; be in at the death etc. (*persevere*) 604*a*; carry through, play out, exhaust, deliver the goods, fill the bill.

finish, bring to a close etc. (*end*) 67; wind up, stamp, clinch, seal, set the seal on, put the seal to; give the -final touch etc. *n.* to; put the -last, – finishing- hand to; crown, – all; cap.

ripen, culminate; come to a -head, – crisis; come to its end; die -a natural death, – of old age; run -its course, – one's race; touch –, reach –, attain- the goal; reach etc. (*arrive*) 292; get in the harvest.

Adj. completing, final; conclu-ding, -sive; crowning etc. *v.*; exhaustive, complete, mature, perfect, consummate.

done, completed etc. *v.*; done for, sped, wrought out; highly wrought etc. (*preparation*) 673; thorough etc. 52; ripe etc. (*ready*) 673.

Adv. completely etc. (*thoroughly*) 52; to crown all, out of hand.

Phr. the race is run; *actum est*; *finis coronat opus*; *consummatum est*; *c'en est fait*; it is all over; the game is played out, the bubble has burst.

730. Non-Completion.—N. non-completion, -fulfilment; shortcoming etc. 304; incompleteness etc. 53; drawn -battle, – game; work of Penelope, task of Sisyphus.

non-performance, inexecution; neglect etc. 460.

V. not -complete etc. 729; leave -unfinished etc. *adj.*, – undone; neglect etc. 460; let -alone, – slip; lose sight of.

fall short of etc. 304; do things by halves; scotch the snake, not kill it; hang fire; be slow to; collapse etc. 304.

Adj. not completed etc. *v.*; incomplete etc. 53; uncompleted, unfinished; unaccomplished; unperformed, unexecuted; sketchy, addle.

in progress, in hand; going on, proceeding; on one's hands; on the fire; on the stocks; in preparation; lacking the finishing touch.

Adv. *re infectâ*.

731. Success.—N. success, -fulness; speed; advance etc. (*progress*) 282.

trump card; hit, stroke; lucky –, fortunate –, good- -hit, – stroke; bold –, master- stroke; *coup de maître*, checkmate; half the battle, prize; profit etc. (*acquisition*) 775; best seller.

continued success; good fortune etc. (*prosperity*) 734; time well spent.

advantage over; edge; upper-, whiphand; ascendancy, mastery; expugnation, conquest, victory, subdual; subjugation etc. (*subjection*) 749.

triumph etc. (*exultation*) 884; proficiency etc. (*skill*) 698; conqueror, victor, winner, champion; master of the -situation, – position.

V. succeed; be -successful etc. *adj.*; gain one's -end, – ends; crown with success.

gain –, attain –, carry –, secure –, win- -a point, – an object; put over; make a go of; manage to, contrive to; accomplish etc. (*effect, complete*) 729; do –, work- wonders.

come off -well, – successfully, – with flying colors; make short work of; take –, carry- by storm; bear away the bell; win -one's spurs, – the battle; win –, carry –, gain- the -day, – prize, – palm; climb on the bandwagon; have -the best of it, – it all one's own way, – the game in one's own hands, – the ball at one's feet, – one on the hip; walk over the course; carry all before one, remain in possession of the field; score a success, win hands down.

speed; make progress etc. (*advance*) 282; win –, make –, work –, find- one's way; strive to some purpose; prosper etc. 734; drive a roaring trade; make profit etc. (*acquire*) 775; reap –, gather- the -fruits, – benefit of, – harvest; make one's fortune, get in the harvest, turn to good account; turn to account etc. (*use*) 677.

triumph, be triumphant; gain –, obtain- -a victory, – an advantage; chain victory to one's car.

surmount –, overcome –, get over- -a difficulty, – an obstacle etc. 706; *se tirer d'affaire*; make head against; stem the torrent, – tide, – current; weather -the storm, – a point; turn a corner, keep one's head above water, tide over; master; get –, have –, gain- the -better of, – best of, – upper hand, – ascendancy, – whip hand, – start of; distance; surpass etc. (*superiority*) 33.

defeat, conquer, vanquish, discomfit; over-come, throw, -power, -master, -match, -set, -ride, -reach; out-wit, -do, -flank, -maneuver, -general, -vote; take the wind out of one's adversary's sails; beat, – hollow; rout, lick, drub, floor, worst; put -down, – to flight, – to the rout, – *hors de combat*; – out of court.

silence, quell, nonsuit, checkmate, upset, confound, nonplus, trump; baffle etc. (*hinder*) 706; circumvent, elude; trip up – the heels of; drive -into a corner, – to the wall; run hard, put one's nose out of joint.*

settle, do for; break the -neck of, – back of; capsize, sink, shipwreck, drown, swamp; subdue; subjugate etc. (*subject*) 749; reduce; make the enemy bite the dust; victimize, roll in the dust, trample under foot, put an extinguisher upon.

answer, – the purpose; avail, prevail, take effect, do, turn out well, work well, take, tell, bear fruit; hit -it, – the mark, – the right nail on the head; nick it; turn up trumps, make a hit; find one's account in.

Adj. succeeding etc. *v.*; successful; prosperous etc. 734; triumphant; flushed –, crowned- with success; victorious; set up; in the ascendant; unbeaten etc. (*see* beat etc. *v.*); well-spent; felicitous, effective, in full swing.

Adv. successfully etc. *adj.*; with flying colors, in triumph, swimmingly; *à merveille*, beyond all hope; to some –, good- purpose; to one's heart's content.

Phr. *veni vidi vici*, the day being one's own, one's star in the ascendant; *omne tulit punctum*.

732. Failure.—N. failure; non-success, -fulfilment; dead failure, successlessness; abortion, miscarriage; *brutum fulmen* etc. 158; labor in vain etc. (*inutility*) 645; no go; inefficacy; inefficaciousness etc. *adj.*; vain –, ineffectual –, abortive- -attempt, – efforts; flash in the pan, 'lame and impotent conclusion;' frustration; slip 'twixt cup and lip etc. (*disappointment*) 509.

blunder etc. (*mistake*) 495; fault, omission, miss, oversight, slip, trip, stumble, claudication, footfall; false –, wrong- step; *faux pas*, titubation, *bévue*, *faute*, lurch; botchery etc. (*want of skill*) 699; scrape, jam, mess, muddle, foozle, *fiasco*, breakdown.

mishap etc. (*misfortune*) 735; split, collapse, smash, blow, explosion.

repulse, rebuff, defeat, rout, overthrow, discomfiture; beating, drubbing; *quietus*, nonsuit, subjugation; check-, fool's-mate.

fall, downfall, ruin, perdition; wreck etc. (*destruction*) 162; death-blow; bankruptcy etc. (*non-payment*) 808.

losing game, *affaire flambée*.

victim, prey; bankrupt.

V. fail; be -unsuccessful etc. *adj.*; not -succeed etc. 731; make -vain efforts etc. *n.*; do –, labor –, toil- in vain; lose one's labor, take nothing by one's motion; bring to naught, make nothing of; wash a blackamoor white etc. (*impossible*) 471; roll the stone of Sisyphus etc. (*useless*) 645; do by halves etc. (*not complete*) 730; lose ground etc. (*recede*) 283; flunk; fall short of etc. 304.

miss, – one's aim, – the mark, – one's footing, – stays; slip, trip, stumble; make a -slip etc. *n.*, – blunder etc. 495, – mess of, – botch of; bitch it, miscarry, abort, go up like a rocket and come down like the stick, reckon without one's host; get the wrong sow by the ear etc. (*blunder, mismanage*) 699.

limp, halt, hobble, titubate; fall, tumble; lose one's balance; fall -to the ground, – between two stools; flounder, falter, stick in the mud, run aground, split upon a rock; run –, knock –, dash-one's head against a stone wall; break one's back; break down, sink, drown, founder, have the ground cut from under one; get into -trouble, – a mess, – a scrape; come to grief etc. (*adversity*) 735; go to -the wall, – the dogs, – pot; lick –, bite- the dust; be -defeated etc. 731; have the worst of it, lose the day, come off second best, lose; fall a prey to; succumb etc. (*submit*) 725; not have a leg to stand on.

come to nothing, end in smoke; fall -to the ground, – through, – dead, – still-born, – flat; slip through one's fingers; hang –, miss- fire; flash in the pan, collapse; topple down etc. (*descent*) 305; go to wrack and ruin etc. (*destruction*) 162.

go amiss, go wrong, go cross, go hard with, go on a wrong tack; go on –, come off –, turn out

–, work- ill; take -a wrong, – an ugly- turn; gang agley.

be all -over with, – up with; explode; dash one's hopes etc. (*disappoint*) 509; defeat the purpose; upset the apple cart; sow the wind and reap the whirlwind, jump out of the frying pan into the fire.

Adj. unsuccessful, successless; failing, tripping etc. *v.*; at fault; unfortunate etc. 735.

abortive, addle, still-born; fruitless, sterile, bootless; ineffect-ual, -ive; inefficient etc. (*impotent*) 158; inefficacious; lame, hobbling, *décousu*; insufficient etc. 640; unavailing etc. (*useless*) 645; of no effect.

aground, grounded, swamped, stranded, cast away, wrecked, foundered, capsized, shipwrecked, non-suited; foiled; defeated etc. 731; struck –, borne –, broken- down; down-trodden; over-borne, -whelmed; all up with; beaten to a frazzle.

lost, undone, ruined, broken; bankrupt etc. (*not paying*) 808; played out; done -up, – for; dead beat, ruined root and branch, *flambé*, knocked on the head; destroyed etc. 162.

frustrated, thwarted, crossed, unhinged, disconcerted, dashed; thrown -off one's balance, – on one's back, – on one's beam ends; unhorsed, in a sorry plight; hard hit.

stultified, befooled, dished, hoist on one's own petard, victimized, sacrificed.

wide of the mark etc. (*error*) 495; out of one's reckoning etc. (*inexpectation*) 508; left in the lurch; thrown away etc. (*wasted*) 638; unattained; uncompleted etc. 730.

Adv. unsuccessfully etc. *adj.*; to little or no purpose, in vain, *re infectâ*.

Phr. the bubble has burst, the game is up, all is lost; the devil to pay; *parturiunt montes* etc. (*disappointment*) 509.

733. Trophy.—N. trophy; medal, prize, palm; ribbon, blue ribbon, *cordon bleu*; citation; cup, laurel, -s; bays, crown, chaplet, wreath, civic crown; Victoria Cross, V.C., *Croix de Guerre*, Iron Cross; Distinguished Service Cross, Medal of Honor, Congressional Medal; insignia etc. 550; feather in one's cap etc. (*honor*) 873; decoration etc. 877; garland, triumphal arch.

triumph etc. (*celebration*) 883; flying colors etc. (*show*) 882.

monumentum aere perennius.

734. Prosperity.—N. prosperity, welfare, well-being; affluence etc. (*wealth*) 803; success etc. 731; thrift, roaring trade; chicken in every pot, the full dinner paid; good –, smiles of- fortune; blessings, godsend.

luck; good –, run of- luck; sunshine; fair -weather, – wind; palmy –, bright –, halcyon-days; piping times, tide, flood, high tide.

Saturnia regna, Saturnian age; golden -time, – age; bed of roses; fat of the land, milk and honey, loaves and fishes, fleshpots of Egypt.

made man, lucky dog, *enfant gâté*, spoiled child of fortune.

upstart, *parvenu, nouveau riche*, profiteer, skip-jack, mushroom.

V. prosper, thrive, flourish; be -prosperous etc. *adj.*; drive a roaring trade; go on -well, – smoothly, – swimmingly; sail before the wind, swim with the tide; run -smooth, – smoothly, – on all fours.

rise –, get on- in the world; work –, make- one's way; look up; lift –, raise- one's head, make one's -fortune, – pile, feather one's nest.

flower, blow, blossom, bloom, fructify, bear fruit, fatten, batten.

keep oneself afloat; keep –, hold- one's head above water; light –, fall- on one's -legs, – feet; drop into a good thing; bear a charmed life; bask in the sunshine; have a -good, – fine- time of it; have a run, – of luck; have the -good fortune etc. *n.* to; take a favorable turn; live -on the fat of the land, – in clover.

Adj. prosperous; thriving etc. *v.*; in a fair way, buoyant; well -off, – to do, – to do in the world; set up, at one's ease; rich etc. 803; in good case; in -full, – high- feather; fortunate, lucky, in luck; born -with a silver spoon in one's mouth, – under a lucky star; on the sunny side of the hedge.

auspicious, propitious, providential.

palmy, halcyon; agreeable etc. 829; *couleur de rose*.

Adv. prosperously etc. *adj.*; swimmingly; as good luck would have it; beyond all -expectation, – hope, – one's wildest dreams.

Phr. one's star in the ascendant, all for the best, one's course runs smooth.

735. Adversity.—N. adversity, evil etc. 619; failure etc. 732; bad –, ill –, evil –, adverse –, hard- -fortune, – hap, – luck, – lot; frowns of fortune; evil -dispensation, – star, – genius; ups and downs of life, broken fortunes; hard -case, – lines, – life; sea –, peck- of troubles; hell upon earth; slough of despond; jinx.

trouble, humiliation, hardship, curse, blight, blast, load, pressure.

pressure of the times, iron age, evil day, time out of joint; hard –, bad –, sad- times; rainy day, cloud, dark cloud, gathering clouds, ill wind; visitation, infliction; affliction etc. (*painfulness*) 830; bitter -pill, – cup; care, trial; the sport of fortune.

mis-hap, -chance, -adventure, -fortune; disaster, calamity, catastrophe; accident, casualty, cross, reverse, check, *contretemps*, rub, pinch, setback.

losing game; falling etc. *v.*; fall, down-fall, come-down; ruin-ation, -ousness; undoing; extremity; ruin etc. (*destruction*) 162.

V. be -ill off etc. *adj.*; go hard with; fall on evil, – days; go on ill; not -prosper etc. 734.

go -downhill, – to rack and ruin etc. (*destruction*) 162, – to the dogs; fall, – from one's high estate; decay, sink, decline, go down in the world; have seen better days; bring down one's grey hairs with sorrow to the grave; come to grief; be all -over, – up- with; bring a -wasp's, – hornet's- nest about one's ears.

Adj. unfortunate, unblest, unhappy, unlucky; im-, un-prosperous; luck-, hap-less; out of luck; in trouble, in a bad way, in an evil plight; under a cloud; clouded; ill –, badly- off; in adverse circumstances; poor etc. 804; behindhand, down in the world, decayed, undone; on the road to ruin, on its last legs, on the wane; in one's utmost need.

planet-struck, devoted; born -under an evil star, – with a wooden ladle in one's mouth; ill-fated, -starred, -omened; inconspicuous, ominous, doomed, unpropitious.

adverse, untoward; disastrous, calamitous, ruinous, dire, deplorable.

Adv. if the worst come to the worst, as ill luck would have it, from bad to worse, out of the frying pan into the fire.

Phr. one's star is on the wane; one's luck -turns, – fails; the game is up, one's doom is sealed, the ground crumbles under one's feet, *sic transit gloria mundi, tant va la cruche à l'eau qu'à la fin elle se casse.*

736. Mediocrity.—N. moderate –, average- circumstances; respectability; middle classes, *bourgeoisie*; mediocrity; golden mean etc. (*mid-course*) 628, (*moderation*) 174.

V. jog on; go –, get on- -fairly, – quietly, – peaceably, – tolerably, – respectably; steer a middle course etc. 628.

Adj. middling, so-so, fair, medium, moderate, mediocre, second-, third- etc. -rate.

737. Authority.—N. authority; influence, patronage, power, preponderance, credit, *prestige*, prerogative, jurisdiction; right etc. (*title*) 924.

divine right, dynastic rights, authoritativeness; absolut-eness, -ism; despotism, tyranny; *jus nocendi.*

command, empire, sway, rule; domin-ion, -ation; sovereignty, supremacy, suzerainty; lord-, head-ship; chiefdom; seignior-y, -ity, hegemony, patriarchate, patriarchy; master-y, -ship, -dom; government etc. (*direction*) 693; dictation, control.

hold, grasp; grip, -e; reach; iron sway etc. (*severity*) 739; fangs, clutches, talons; rod of empire etc. (*scepter*) 747.

reign, regnancy, *régime*, dynasty; director-, dictator-ship; protector-ate, -ship; caliphate, pashalic, electorate; presiden-cy, -tship; administration; pro-, consulship; prefecture; seneschalship; magistra-ture, -cy; raj.

empire; monarchy; king-hood, -ship; royalty, regality, autocracy, monocracy, arist-archy, -ocracy; oligarchy, democracy, demogogy; republic, -anism, federalism; socialism, collectivism; communism, bolshevism, syndicalism; mob law, mobocracy, ochlocracy, ergatocracy; *vox populi, imperium in imperio*; bureaucracy; beadle-, bumble-dom; stratocracy; martial law, military -power, – government; feodality, feudal system, feudalism.

Thearchy, diarchy; du-, tri-, heter-archy; du-, triumvirate; auto-cracy, -nomy; limited monarchy; constitutional -government, – monarchy; home rule, autonomy; self-government, -determination; representative government; Soviet government.

gyn-archy, -ocracy, -aeocracy; petticoat government, matriarchate, matriarchy.

[Vicarious authority] commission etc. 755; deputy etc. 759; permission etc. 760.

country, state, realm, commonwealth, canton, constituency, toparchy, municipality, polity, body politic, *posse comitatus.*

person in authority etc. (*master*) 745; judicature etc. 965; cabinet etc. (*council*) 696; usurper; seat of -government, – authority; head-quarters.

[Acquisition of authority] accession; installation etc. 755; usurpation.

V. authorize etc. (*permit*) 760; warrant etc. (*right*) 924; dictate etc. (*order*) 741; have –, hold –, possess –, exercise –, exert –, wield- -authority etc. *n.*

be -at the head of etc. *adj.*; hold –, be in –, fill an- office; hold –, occupy- a post; be -master etc. 745.

rule, sway, command, control, administer; govern etc. (*direct*) 693; lead, preside over, reign; possess –, be seated on –, occupy- the throne; sway –, wield- the scepter; wear the crown.

have –, get- the -upper, – whip- hand; gain a hold upon, preponderate, dominate, boss, rule the roost; over-ride, -rule, -awe; lord it over, hold in hand, keep under, make a puppet of, lead by the nose, hold in the hollow of one's hand, turn round one's little finger, bend to one's will, hold one's own, wear the breeches; have -the ball at one's feet, – it all one's own way, – the game in one's own hand, – on the hip, – under one's thumb; be master of the situation; take the lead, play first fiddle, set the fashion; give the law to; carry with a high hand; lay down the law; 'ride in the whirlwind and direct the storm;' rule with a rod of iron etc. (*severity*) 739.

ascend –, mount- the throne, take the reins, – into one's hand; assume -authority etc. *n.*, – the reins of government; take –, assume the- command.

be -governed by, – in the power of; be under -the rule of, – the domination of.

Adj. ruling etc. *v.*; regnant, at the head, dominant, paramount, supreme, predominant, preponderant, in the ascendant, influential; gubernatorial; imperious; authoritative, executive, administrative, clothed with authority, official, *ex officio*, ministerial, bureaucratic, departmental, imperative, peremptory, overruling, absolute; hegemonic, -al; arbitrary; compulsory etc. 744; stringent.

regal, sovereign; royal, -ist; monarchical, kingly; imperial, -istic; princely; feudal; aristo-, auto-cratic; oligarchic etc. *n.*; democratic, republican, dynastic.

at one's command; in one's -power, – grasp; under control; authorized etc. (*due*) 924.

Adv. in the name of, by the authority of, *de par le Roi*, in virtue of; under the auspices of, in the hands of.

at one's pleasure; by a -dash, – stroke- of the pen; *ex mero motu*; *ex cathedrâ.*

Phr. the grey mare the better horse; 'every inch a king.'

738. Laxity. [Absence of authority.]—**N.** laxity; lax-, loose-, slack-ness; toleration etc. (*lenity*) 740; freedom etc. 748.

anarchy, interregnum; relaxation; loosening etc. *v.*; remission; dead letter, *brutum fulmen*, misrule; license, licentiousness; insubordination etc. (*disobedience*) 742; lynch law etc. (*illegality*) 964; nihilism.

[Deprivation of power.] dethronement, deposition, usurpation, abdication.

V. be -lax etc. *adj.*; *laisser -faire*, – *aller*; hold a loose rein; give -the reins to, – rope enough, – a loose to; tolerate; relax; misrule.

go beyond the length of one's tether; have one's -swing, – fling; act without -instructions, – authority; act on one's own responsibility, usurp authority.

dethrone, depose; abdicate.

Adj. lax, loose; slack; remiss etc. (*careless*) 460; weak.

relaxed; licensed; reinless, unbridled; anarchical; unauthorized etc. (*unwarranted*) 925.

739. Severity.—N. severity; strictness, formalism, harshness etc. *adj.*; rigor, stringency, austerity; inclemency etc. (*pitilessness*) 914*a*; arrogance etc. 885.

arbitrary power; absolut-, despot-ism; dictatorship, autocracy, tyranny, domineering, oppression; assumption, usurpation; inquisition, reign of terror, martial law; iron -heel, – rule, – hand, – sway; tight grasp; brute -force, – strength; coercion etc. 744; strong –, tight- hand.

hard -lines, – measure; tender mercies [ironical.]; sharp practice; bureaucracy, red tape; pipe-clay, officialism.

tyrant, disciplinarian, martinet, stickler, formalist, bashaw, despot, hard master, Draco, oppressor, inquisitor, extortioner, harpy, vulture, bird of prey.

V. be -severe etc. *adj.*

assume, usurp, arrogate, take liberties; domineer, bully etc. 885; tyrannize, inflict, wreak, stretch a point, put on the screw; be hard upon; bear –, lay- a heavy hand on; be –, come- down upon; ill-treat; deal-hardly with, – hard measure to; rule with a rod of iron, chastise with scorpions; dye with blood; oppress, override; trample –, tread- -down, – upon, – under foot; crush under an iron heel, ride roughshod over; rivet the yoke; hold –, keep- a tight hand; force down the throat; coerce etc. 744; give no quarter etc. (*pitiless*) 914*a*.

Adj. severe; strict, hard, harsh, dour, rigid, stiff, stern, rigorous, uncompromising, exacting, exigent, *exigeant*, inexorable, inflexible, obdurate, austere, relentless, Spartan, Draconian, stringent, strait-laced, puritanical, prudish, searching, unsparing, ironhanded, hard-headed, peremptory, absolute, positive, arbitrary, imperative; coercive etc. 744; tyrannical, despotic, masterful, extortionate, grinding, withering, oppressive, inquisitorial; inclement etc. (*ruthless*) 914*a*; cruel etc. (*malevolent*) 907; haughty, arrogant etc. 885.

Adv. severely etc. *adj.*; with a -high, – strong, – tight, – heavy-hand.

at the point of the -sword, – bayonet.

Phr. *Delirant reges plectuntur Achivi.*

740. Leniency.—N. leni-ency, -ence, -ty; moderation etc. 174; toler-ance, -ation; mildness, gentleness; favor; indulgen-ce, -cy; clemency, mercy, forbearance, quarter; compassion etc. 914.

V. be -lenient etc. *adj.*; tolerate, bear with; *parcere subjectis*, give quarter.

indulge, allow one to have his own way, spoil.

Adj. lenient; mild, – as milk; gentle, soft; tolerant, indulgent, easy-going; clement etc. (*compassionate*) 914; forbearing; complaisant, long-suffering.

741. Command.—N. command, order, ordinance, act, *fiat*, bidding, *dictum*, hest, behest, call, beck, nod.

des-, dis-patch; message, direction, injunction, charge, instructions; appointment, fixture.

demand, exaction, imposition, requisition, claim, reclamation, revendication; *ultimatum* etc. (*terms*) 770; request etc. 765; requirement.

dictation; dict-, mand-ate; *caveat*, decree, decree -nisi, – absolute, *senatus consultum*; precept; pre-, re-script; writ, ordination, bull, edict, decretal, dispensation, prescription, brevet, placet, ukase, *firman*, hatti-sheriff, warrant, passport, *mittimus, mandamus*, summons, subpoena, *nisi prius*, interpellation, citation; word, – of command; *mot d'ordre*; bugle –, trumpet- call; beat of drum, tattoo; order of the day; enactment etc. (*law*) 963; *plébiscite* etc. (*choice*) 609.

V. command, order, decree, enact, ordain, dictate, direct, give orders.

prescribe, set, appoint, mark out; set –, prescribe –, impose- a task; set to work, put in requisition etc. 926.

bid, enjoin, charge, call upon, instruct; require, – at the hands of; exact, impose, tax, task; demand; insist on etc. (*compel*) 744.

claim, lay claim to, revendicate, reclaim.

cite, summon; call –, send- for; subpoena; beckon.

issue a command; make –, issue –, promulgate- -a requisition, – a decree, – an order etc. *n.*; give the -word of command, – word, – signal; call to order; give –, lay down- the law; assume the command etc. (*authority*) 737; remand.

be -ordered etc.; receive an order etc. *n.*

Adj. commanding etc. *v.*; authoritative etc. 737; decret-ory, -ive, -al; imperative, jussive, decisive, final.

Adv. in a commanding tone; by a -stroke, – dash- of the pen; by order, at beat of drum, on the first summons; at the word of command.

Phr. the decree is gone forth; *sic volo sic jubeo*; *le Roi le veut.*

742. Disobedience.—N. disobedience, insubordination, contumacy; infraction, -fringement; violation, non-compliance; non-observance etc. 773.

revolt, rebellion, mutiny, outbreak, rising, uprising, putsch, insurrection, *émeute*; riot, tumult etc. (*disorder*) 59; strike etc. (*resistance*) 719; barring out; defiance etc. 715.

mutinousness etc. *adj.*; mutineering; sedition, treason; high –, petty –, misprison of- treason; *premunire*; *lèse- majesté*; violation of law etc. 964; defection, secession, revolution, *sabotage*, bolshevism, *Sinn Fein.*

insurgent, mutineer, rebel, revolter, rioter, traitor, *carbonaro*, *sansculottes*, red republican, communist, Fenian, chartist, *frondeur*; seceder, runagate, brawler, anarchist, demagogue; suffragette; Spartacus, Masaniello, Wat Tyler, Jack Cade; bolshevist, bolshevik, maximalist, ringleader.

V. disobey, violate, infringe; shirk; set at defiance etc. (*defy*) 715; set authority at naught, run riot, fly in the face of, bolt, take the law into one's own hands; kick over the traces.

turn –, run- restive; champ the bit; strike etc. (*resist*) 719; rise, – in arms; secede; mutiny, rebel.

Adj. disobedient; uncompl-ying, -iant; unsubmissive; unruly, ungovernable; insubordinate, impatient of control; rest-iff, -ive; refractory, contumacious; recusant etc. (refuse) 764; recalcitrant; resisting etc. 719; lawless, mutinous, seditious, insurgent, riotous, revolutionary.

disobeyed, unobeyed; unbidden.

743. Obedience.—N. obedience; observance etc. 772; compliance; submission etc. 725; subjection etc. 749; non-resistance; passiveness, passivity, resignation.

allegiance, loyalty, fealty, homage, deference, devotion, fidelity, constancy.

submiss-ness, -iveness; ductility etc. (*softness*) 324; obsequiousness etc. (*servility*) 886.

V. be -obedient etc. *adj.*; obey, bear obedience to; submit etc. 725; comply, answer the helm, come at one's call; do -one's bidding, – what one is told, – suit and service; attend to orders, serve -devotedly, –, loyally, – faithfully.

follow, – the lead of, – to the world's end; serve etc. 746; play second fiddle.

Adj. obedient; compl-ying, -iant; law-abiding, loyal, faithful, leal, devoted; at one's -call, – command, – orders, – beck and call; under -beck and call, – control.

restrainable, resigned, passive; submissive etc. 725; henpecked; pliant etc. (*soft*) 324.

unresist-ed, -ing.

Adv. obediently etc. *adj.*; in compliance with, in obedience to.

Phr. to hear is to obey; as –, if- you please; at your service.

744. Compulsion.—N. compulsion, coercion, coaction, constraint, eminent domain, duress, enforcement, press, conscription.

force; brute –, main –, physical- force; the sword, *ultima ratio*; club –, mob –, lynch- law; *argumentum baculinum, le droit du plus fort*, martial law.

restraint etc. 751; necessity etc. 601; *force majeure*; Hobson's choice; the spur of necessity.

V. compel, force, make, drive, coerce, constrain, enforce, necessitate, oblige.

force upon, press; cram –, thrust –, force- down the throat; say it must be done, make a point of, insist upon, take no denial; put down, dragoon.

extort, wring from; put –, turn- on the screw; drag into; bind, – over; pin –, tie- down; require, tax, put in force; commandeer; restrain etc. 751.

Adj. compelling etc. *v.*; coercive, coactive; inexorable etc. 739; compuls-ory, -atory; obligatory, stringent, peremptory, binding.

forcible, not to be trifled with; irresistible etc. 601; compelled etc. *v.*; fain to.

Adv. by -force etc. *n.*, – force of arms; on compulsion, perforce; *vi et armis*, under the lash; at the point of the -sword, – bayonet; forcibly; by a strong arm.

under protest, in spite of one's teeth; against one's will etc. 603; *nolens volens* etc. (*of necessity*) 601; by stress of -circumstances, – weather; under press of; *de rigueur*.

745. Master.—N. master, *padrone*; lord, – paramount; command-er, -ant; captain; chief, -tain; *sahib*, sirdar, sachem, sheik, head, senior, governor, *duce*, ruler, dictator; leader etc. (*director*) 694.

lord of the ascendant; cock of the -walk, – roost; grey mare; mistress.

potentate; liege, – lord; suzerain, sovereign, monarch, autocrat, despot, tyrant, oligarch, overlord.

crowned head, emperor, king, anointed king, majesty, *imperator*, protector, president, stadtholder, judge.

caesar, kaiser, czar, sultan, grand Turk, caliph, imaum, shah, padishah, sophi, mogul, great mogul, khan, cham; lama, tycoon, mikado, inca, cazique; domn; vaivode; wai-, way-wode; landamman; seyyid, cacique.

prince, duke etc. (*nobility*) 875; arch-duke, doge, elector; seignior; mar-, land-grave; rajah, emir, nizam, nawab, negus.

empress, queen, sultana, czarina, princess, infanta, duchess, margravine, begum, maharani.

regent, viceroy, exarch, palatine, khedive, hospodar, beglerbeg, three-tailed bashaw, pasha, pashaw, bashaw, bey, beg, dey, scherif, tetrarch, satrap, mandarin, subhadar, nabob, maharajah; burgrave; laird etc. (*proprietor*) 779; High Commissioner.

the -authorities, – powers that be, – government; staff, *état major*, aga, official, man in office, person in authority.

[Naval authorities] admiral, -ty, – of the fleet; rear-, vice-, port-admiral; senior-, naval officer, S.N.O., commodore, captain, commander, lieutenant-commander, lieutenant, sub-lieutenant, midshipman, warrant –, petty- officer, leading seaman; skipper, mate, master.

[Military authorities] marshal, field-marshal, *maréchal*; general, -issimo; commander-in-chief, *seraskier, hetman*; lieutenant-, major-general; commandant; colonel, lieutenant-colonel, major, captain, centurion, skipper, lieutenant, second-lieutenant, officer, staff-officer, *aide de camp*, brigadier, brigade-major, adjutant, *jemidar*, ensign, cornet, cadet, subaltern, warrant officer, quartermaster, noncommissioned officer, N.C.O.; sergeant, -major; top-sergeant, color sergeant; corporal, -major; lance-, acting-corporal; drum major; shavetail.

[Air authorities] air -marshal, – commodore; group captain, squadron leader, wing commander, flight lieutenant, flying –, pilot- officer.

[Civil authorities] judge etc. 967; mayor, -alty; prefect, chancellor, archon, provost, magistrate, syndic; alcalde, alcaid; burgomaster, *corregidor*, seneschal, alderman, warden, constable, portreeve; lord mayor, sheriff; officer etc. (*executive*) 965.

746. Servant.—N. subject, liegeman; servant, retainer, follower, henchman, servitor, domestic, menial, help, lady help, *employé, attaché*; official.

retinue, suite, *cortège*, staff, court.

attendant, squire, usher, page, buttons, donzel, footboy; dog robber; train-, cup-bearer; waiter, busboy, tapster, butler, livery servant, lackey, footman, flunkey, valet, *valet de chambre*; boots; scout, gyp; equerry, groom; jockey, hostler, ostler, tiger, orderly, messenger, cad, gillie, caddie; *wallah*; journeyman, herdsman, swineherd.

bailiff, castellan, seneschal, chamberlain, *major-domo*, groom of the chambers.

secretary; under –, assistant- secretary; clerk; clerical staff, stenographer, subsidiary; agent etc. 758; subaltern; under-ling, -strapper; man.

maid, -servant, waitress; handmaid; *confidente*, lady's maid, abigail, *soubrette*; nurse, *bonne, ayah*; nurse-, nursery-, house-, parlor-, waiting-, chamber-, kitchen-, scullery-, between –, laundry –, dairy-maid; *femme –, fille- de chambre*; *camarista*; *chef de cuisine, cordon bleu*, cook, scullion, Cinderella; maid –, servant- of all work, tweeny, general servant, girl, slavey; laundress, bed-maker, goodie, char-woman etc. (*worker*) 690.

serf, vassal, slave, negro, helot; bondsman, -woman; bondslave; *âme damnée, odalisque*, ryot, *adscriptus glebae*; vill-ain, -ein; bead-, bede-sman; sizar; pension-er, -ary; client; dependant, -ent; hanger on, stooge, satellite; parasite etc. (*servility*) 886; led captain; *protégé*, ward, hireling, mercenary, puppet, creature.

badge of slavery; bonds etc. 752.

V. serve; minister to, wait –, attend –, dance attendance –, pin oneself- upon; squire, tend, hang on the sleeve of, char, do for; fag; valet.

Adj. in the train of; in one's -pay, – employ; at one's call etc. (*obedient*) 743; in bonds.

747. Scepter. [Insignia of authority.]—**N.** scepter, regalia, rod of empire, sword of state, mace, *fasces*, wand; staff, – of office; *bâton*, truncheon; flag etc. (*insignia*) 550; ensign –, emblem –, badge –, insignia- of authority, rank marks, brassard, badge, sash; cocked –, brass- hat.

epaulette, aiguilette, crown, star, eagle, bar, double bar, pip, stripe, chevron, curl, ring, anchor, shoulder-strap, tab.

throne, chair, musnud, divan, dais, woolsack.

toga, pall, mantle, robes of state, ermine, purple.

crown, coronet, diadem, tiara, triple crown, miter, crozier, cardinal's hat etc.; cap of maintenance; decoration; title etc. 877; portfolio.

key, signet, seals, talisman; helm; reins etc. (*means of restraint*) 752.

748. Freedom.—N. freedom, liberty, independence; license etc. (*permission*) 760; facility etc. 705.

scope, range, latitude, play; free –, full- -play, – scope; free stage and no favor; swing, full swing, elbow-room, margin, rope, wide berth; Liberty Hall.

franchise, denization; free –, freed-, liveryman; denizen.

autonomy, self-government, homerule, self-determination, liberalism, free trade; non-interference etc. 706.

immunity, exemption; emancipation etc. (*liberation*) 750; en-, af-franchisement; rights, privileges.

free land, freehold; allodium; frankalmoigne, mortmain.

independent, free-lance, -thinker, -trader.

V. be -free etc. *adj.*; have -scope etc. *n.*, – the run of, – one's own way, – a will of one's own, – one's fling; do what one -likes, – wishes, – pleases, – chooses; go at large, feel at home, paddle one's own canoe; stand on one's -legs, – rights; shift for oneself.

take a liberty; make -free with, – oneself quite at home; use a freedom; take -leave, – French leave.

set free etc. (*liberate*) 750; give the reins to etc. (*permit*) 760; allow –, give- scope etc. *n.* to; give a horse his head.

make free of; give the -freedom of, – franchise; en-, af-franchise.

laisser -faire, – aller; live and let live; leave to oneself; leave –, let- alone; mind one's own business.

Adj. free, – as air; out of harness, independent, at large, loose, scot free; left -alone, – to oneself.

in full swing; uncaught, unconstrained, unbuttoned, unconfined, unrestrained, unchecked, unprevented, unhindered, unobstructed, unbound, uncontrolled, untrammeled.

unsubject, ungoverned, unenslaved, unenthralled, unchained, unshackled, unfettered, unreined, unbridled, uncurbed, unmuzzled, unimpeded.

unrestricted, unlimited, unconditional; absolute; discretionary etc. (*optional*) 600.

unassailed, unforced, uncompelled.

unbiassed, unprejudiced, uninfluenced, spontaneous.

free and easy; at –, at one's- ease; *dégagé*, quite at home; wanton, rampant, irrepressible, unvanquished.

exempt; freed etc. 750; freeborn; autonomous, freehold, allodial; *gratis* etc. 815.

unclaimed, going a begging.

Adv. freely etc. *adj.*; *ad libitum* etc. (*at will*) 600.

749. Subjection.—N. subjection; depend-ence, -ance, -ency; subordination; thrall, thraldom, enthralment, subjugation, bondage, serfdom; feudal- -ism, -ity; vassalage, villenage; slavery, enslavement, involuntary servitude.

service; servi-tude, -torship; tendence, employ, tutelage, clientship; liability etc. 177; constraint etc. 751; oppression etc. (*severity*) 739; yoke etc. (*means of restraint*) submission etc. 725; obedience etc. 743.

V. be -subject etc. *adj.*; be –, lie- at the mercy of; depend –, lean –, hang- upon; fall -a prey to, – under; play second fiddle.

be a -mere machine, – puppet, – football; not dare to say one's soul is his own; drag a chain.

serve etc. 746; obey etc. 743; submit etc. 725.

break in, tame; subject, subjugate; master etc. 731; tread -down, – under foot; weigh down; drag at one's chariot wheels; reduce to -subjection, –

slavery; en-, in-, be-thral; enslave, lead captive; take into custody etc. (*restrain*) 751; rule etc. 737; drive into a corner, hold at the sword's point; keep under; hold in -bondage, – leading strings, – swaddling clothes.

Adj. subject, dependent, subordinate; feud-al, -atory; in subjection to, under control; in -leading strings, – harness; subjected, enslaved etc. *v.*; con-strained etc. 751; subservient, servile, fawning, slavish, obsequious, cringing; down-trodden; over-borne, -whelmed; under the lash, on the hip, led by the nose, henpecked; the -puppet, – sport, – plaything- of; under one's -orders, – command, – thumb; like dirt under one's feet; a slave to; at the mercy of; in the -power, – hands, – clutches- of; at the feet of; at one's beck and call etc. (*obedient*) 743; liable etc. 177; parasitical; stipendiary.

Adv. under.

750. Liberation.—N. liberation, disengagement, release, disenthrallment, enlargement, emancipation; af-, en-franchisement; manumission; discharge, dismissal.

deliverance etc. 672; redemption, extrication, acquittance, absolution; acquittal etc. 970; escape etc. 671.

V. liberate, free; set -free, – clear, – at liberty; render free, emancipate, release; en-, af-franchise; manumit; enlarge; dis-band, -charge, -miss, -enthral; let -go, – loose, – out, – slip; cast –, turn- adrift; deliver etc. 672; absolve etc. (*acquit*) 970; reprieve.

unfetter etc. 751; untie etc. 44; loose etc. (*disjoin*) 44; loosen, relax; un-bolt, -bar, -close, -cork, -clog, -hand, -bind, -latch, -chain, -harness; dis-engage, -entangle; clear, extricate, unloose.

gain –, obtain –, acquire- one's -liberty etc. 748; get -rid, – clear- of; deliver oneself from; shake off the yoke, slip the collar; break -loose, – prison; tear asunder one's bonds, cast off trammels, escape etc. 671.

Adj. at -liberty, – large, free, liberated etc. *v.*; out of harness etc. 748; adrift.

Int. unhand me! let me go!

751. Restraint.—N. restraint; hindrance etc. 706; coercion etc. (*compulsion*) 744; cohibition, constraint, repression; discipline, control, self-restraint etc. 604.

confinement; durance, duress; im-, prisonment; incarceration, coarctation, entombment, mancipation, durance vile, thrall, -dom, limbo, captivity; blockade; quarantine; detention.

arrest, -ation; custody, keep, care, charge, ward, restringency.

curb etc. (*means of restraint*) 752; *lettres de cachet.*

limitation, restriction, protection, monopoly; prohibition etc. 761; economic pressure.

prisoner etc. 754.

V. restrain, check; put –, lay- under restraint; en-, in-, be-thral; restrict; debar etc. (*hinder*) 706; constrain; coerce etc. (*compel*) 744; curb, control; hold –, keep- -back, – from, – in, – in check, – within bounds; hold in -leash, – leading strings; withhold.

keep under; repress, suppress; smother; pull in, rein in; hold, – fast; keep a tight hand on; prohibit etc. 761; in-, co-hibit.

enchain; fasten etc. (*join*) 43; fetter, shackle; en-, trammel; bridle, muzzle, gag, pinion, manacle, handcuff, tie one's hands, hobble, bind hand and foot; swathe, swaddle; pin –, peg- down; tether, picket; tie, – up, – down; secure; forge fetters.

confine; shut –, clap –, lock –, box –, mew –, bottle –, cork –, seal –, button- up; shut –, hem –, bolt –, wall –, rail- in; impound, pen, coop; enclose etc. (*circumscribe*) 229; cage; in-, en-cage; close the door upon, cloister; imprison, immure; incarcerate, entomb; clap –, lay- under hatches; put in -irons, – a strait waistcoat; throw –, cast- into prison; put into bilboes.

arrest; take -up, – charge of, – into custody; take –, make- -prisoner, – captive; captivate; lead -captive, – into captivity; send –, commit- to prison; commit; give in -charge, – custody; subjugate etc. 749.

Adj. re-, con-strained; imprisoned etc. *v.*; pent up; jammed in, wedged in; under -restraint, – lock and key, – hatches; serving –, doing- time; in swaddling clothes; on *parole*; in custody etc. (*prisoner*) 754; cohibitive; coactive etc. (*compulsory*) 744.

stiff, restringent, straitlaced, hide-bound.

ice-, wind-, weather-bound; 'cabined, cribbed, confined;' in Lob's pound, laid by the heels.

Adv. in captivity, under arrest, behind the bars, in -prison, – jail, – durance vile.

752. Prison. [Means of restraint.]—**N.** prison, -house; jail, gaol, cage, coop, den, death house, condemned –, cell; stronghold, fortress, keep, donjon, dungeon, *Bastille, oubliette*, bridewell, house of correction, hulks, tool-booth, panopticon, penitentiary, guard-room, clink, can, stir, tronk, jug, lock up, hold, round –, watch –, station –, sponging-house; station; house of detention, black hole, pen, fold, pound; enclosure etc. 232; penal settlement; chain gang; debtors' prison; reformatory; federal penitentiary, state prison; criminal lunatic asylum; bilboes, stocks, limbo, quod.

Dartmoor, Newgate, Fleet, Marshalsea; King's (*or* Queen's) Bench; Sing Sing, Dannemora.

bond; strap, bandage, splint, tourniquet; irons, pinion, gyve, fetter, shackle, trammel, manacle, handcuff, bracelets, darbies, strait waistcoat, strait-jacket.

yoke, collar, halter, harness; muzzle, gag, bit, brake, curb, snaffle, bridle; rein, -s; ribbons, lines, bearing-rein; martingale, leading string; tether, picket, band, guy, chain; cord etc. (*fastening*) 45.

bolt, bar, lock, padlock, rail, wall; paling, palisade; fence; barrier, barricade.

brake, drag etc. (*hindrance*) 706.

753. Keeper.—N. keeper, custodian, *custos*, ranger, warder, jailer, gaoler, turnkey, castellan, guard; watch, -dog, -man; Charley; sen-try, -tinel; watch and ward; *concierge*, coast-guard, *guarda costa*, gamekeeper.

escort, body guard, convoy.

protector, governor, duenna; guardian; governess etc. (*teacher*) 540; nurse, *bonne, ayah, amah.*

754. Prisoner.—N. prisoner, captive, *détenu*, close prisoner.

jail-bird, ticket-of-leave man.

V. stand committed; be -imprisoned etc. 751.

Adj. imprisoned etc. 751; in -prison, – quod, – durance vile, – limbo, – custody, – charge, – chains; under -lock and key, – hatches; on *parole*; detained at his Majesty's pleasure.

755. Commission. [Vicarious authority.]—**N.** commission, delegation; con-, as-signment; procuration; deputation, legation, mission, embassy; agency, agentship; power of attorney, proxy; clerkship.

errand, charge, *brevet*, diploma, *exequatur*, permit etc. (*permission*) 760.

appointment, nomination, return; charter; ordination; installation, inauguration, investiture; accession, coronation, enthronement.

vicegerency; regency, regentship.

viceroy etc. 745; consignee etc. 758; deputy etc. 759.

V. commission, delegate, depute; consign, assign; charge; in-, en-trust; turn over to; commit, – to the hands of; authorize etc. (*permit*) 760.

put in commission, accredit, engage, hire, bespeak, appoint, name, nominate, return, ordain; install, induct, inaugurate, invest, crown; en-roll, -list.

employ, empower; give power of attorney to; set –, place- over; send out.

be commissioned, be accredited; represent, stand for; stand in the -stead, – place, – shoes- of.

Adj. commissioned etc. *v.*

Adv. *per procuratione.*

756. Abrogation.—N. abrogation, annulment, nullification; cancelling etc. *v.*; cancel; revo-cation, -kement; repeal, rescission, defeasance.

dismissal, *congé*, demission; depos-al, -ition; sack, dethronement; disestablish-, disendow-ment; deconsecration.

aboli-tion, -shment; dissolution.

counter-order, -mand; repudiation, retractation; recantation etc. (*tergiversation*) 607.

V. abrogate, annul, cancel; destroy etc. 162; abolish; revoke, repeal, rescind, reverse, retract, recall; over-rule, -ride; set aside; disannul, dissolve, quash, nullify, declare null and void; dis-establish, -endow; deconsecrate.

disclaim etc. (*deny*) 536; ignore, repudiate; recant etc. 607; divest oneself, break off.

counter-mand, -order; do away with; sweep –, brush- away; throw -overboard, – to the dogs; scatter to the winds, cast behind.

dismiss, discard; cast –, turn- -off, – out, – adrift, – out of doors, – aside, – away; send -off, – away, – about one's business; discharge, get rid of, fire out, fire etc. (*eject*) 297; jilt.

cashier; break; oust; set down, unseat, -saddle; un-, de-, disen-throne; depose, uncrown; unfrock, strike off the roll; dis-bar, -bench.

be -abrogated etc.; receive its quietus.

Adj. abrogated etc. *v.*; *functus officio.*

Int. get along with you! begone! go about your business! away with!

757. Resignation.—N. resignation, retirement, abdication, renunciation, abjuration, disclaimer, abandonment, relinquishment.

V. resign; give –, throw- up; lay down, throw up the cards, wash one's hands of, abjure, renounce, forego, disclaim, abandon, relinquish, retract, demit; deny etc. 536.

abrogate etc. 756; desert etc. (*relinquish*) 624; get rid of etc. 782.

abdicate; vacate, – one's seat; accept the stewardship of the Chiltern Hundreds; retire; tender –, send in –, hand in- one's resignation.

Adj. abdicant, renunciatory etc. *v.*

Phr. 'Othello's occupation's gone.'

758. Consignee.—N. consignee, trustee, nominee, committee.

delegate; commiss-ary, -ioner; emissary, envoy, commissionaire; messenger etc. 534.

diplomatist, diplomat, *corps diplomatique*, embassy; am-, em-bassador; representative, resident, consul, legate, nuncio, internuncio, *chargé d' affaires, attaché.*

vicegerent etc. (*deputy*) 759; plenipotentiary.

functionary, placeman, curator; treasurer etc. 801; agent, factor, bailiff, steward, clerk, secretary, attorney, solicitor, proctor, broker, underwriter, commission agent, auctioneer, one's man of business; factotum etc. (*director*) 694; caretaker.

negotiator, go between; middleman; under agent, *employé*; servant etc. 746.

salesman; commercial, – traveler; bagman, *commis-voyageur*, touter.

newspaper –, own –, war –, special- correspondent; reporter.

759. Deputy.—N. deputy, substitute, vice, proxy, *locum tenens*, delegate, representative, next friend, surrogate, secondary.

regent, vicegerent, vizier, minister, vicar; premier etc. (*director*) 694; chancellor, prefect, provost, warden, lieutenant, archon, consul, proconsul; viceroy etc. (*governor*) 745; commissioner etc. 758; plenipotentiary, *alter ego.*

team, eight, eleven; champion.

V. be -deputy etc. *n.*; stand –, appear –, h ld a brief –, answer- for; represent; stand –, walk- in the shoes of; stand in the stead of.

substitute, ablegate, accredit; commission, empower, delegate etc. 755.

Adj. acting; vice, -regal; accredited to.

Adv. in behalf of, by proxy.

760. Permission.—N. permission, leave; allow-, suffer-ance; toler-ance, -ation; liberty, law, license, concession, grace; indulgence etc. (*lenity*) 740; favor, dispensation, exemption, release; connivance; vouchsafement.

authorization, warranty, accordance, admission.

permit, warrant, *brevet*, precept, sanction, authority, *firman*; pass, -port; furlough, license, *carte blanche*, ticket of leave; grant, charter, patent.

V. permit; give -permission etc. *n.*, – power;

let, allow, admit; suffer, bear with, tolerate, recognize; concede etc. 762; accord, vouchsafe, favor, humor, gratify, indulge, stretch a point; wink at, connive at; shut one's eyes to.

grant, empower, charter, enfranchise, privilege, confer a privilege, license, authorize, warrant; sanction; entrust etc. (*commission*) 755.

give -*carte blanche*, – the reins to, – scope to etc. (*freedom*) 748; leave -alone, – it to one, – the door open; open the -door to, – floodgates; give a loose to.

let off; absolve etc. (*acquit*) 970; release, exonerate, dispense with.

ask –, beg –, request- -leave, – permission.

Adj. permitting etc. *v.*; permissive, indulgent; permitted etc. *v.*; patent, chartered, permissible, allowable, lawful, legitimate, legal; legalized etc. (*law*) 963; licit; unforbid, -den; unconditional.

Adv. permissibly; by –, with –, on- -leave etc. *n.*; *speciali gratiâ*; under favor of; *pace*; *ad libitum* etc. (*freely*) 748, (*at will*) 600; by all means etc. (*willingly*) 602; yes etc. (*assent*) 488.

761. Prohibition.—N. pro-, in-hibition; *veto*, disallowance; interdict, -ion; injunction; embargo, ban, *verboten*, taboo, proscription; *index expurgatorius*; restriction etc. (*restraint*) 751; hindrance etc. 706; forbidden fruit.

V. pro-, in-hibit; forbid, put one's *veto* upon, disallow; bar; debar etc. (*hinder*) 706, forefend.

keep -in, – within bounds; restrain etc. 751; cohibit, withhold, limit, circumscribe, clip the wings of, restrict, narrow; interdict, taboo; put –, place- under -an interdiction, – the ban; proscribe, censor; exclude, shut out; shut –, bolt –, show- the door; warn off; dash the cup from one's lips; forbid the banns.

Adj. prohibit-ive, -ory; interdictive; proscriptive; restrictive, exclusive; forbidding etc. *v.*

prohibited etc. *v.*; not -permitted etc. 760; unlicensed, contraband, under the ban of; illegal etc. 964; unauthorized, not to be thought of.

Adv. on no account etc. (*no*) 536.

Int. forbid it heaven! etc. (*deprecation*) 766.

hands –, keep- off! hold! stop! avast!

Phr. that will never do.

762. Consent.—N. consent; assent etc. 488; acquiescence; approval etc. 931; compliance, agreement, concession; yield-ance, -ingness; accession, acknowledgment, acceptance, agnition.

settlement, ratification, confirmation, adjustment.

permit etc. (*permission*) 760; promise etc. 768.

V. consent; assent etc. 488; yield assent, admit, allow, concede, grant, yield; come -over, – round; give in to, acknowledge, agnize, give consent, comply with, acquiesce, agree to, fall in with, accede, accept, embrace an offer, close with, take at one's word, have no objection.

satisfy, meet one's wishes, settle, come to terms etc. 488; not -refuse etc. 764; turn a willing ear etc. (*willingness*) 602; jump at; deign, vouchsafe; promise etc. 768.

Adj. consenting etc. *v.*; agreeable, compliant; agreed etc. (*assent*) 488; unconditional.

Adv. yes etc. (*assent*) 488; by all means etc. (*willingly*) 602; if –, as- you please; be it so, so be it, well and good, of course.

763. Offer.—N. offer, proffer, presentation, tender, bid, overture; propos-al, -ition; motion, invitation; candidature; offering etc. (*gift*) 784.

V. offer, proffer, present, tender; bid; propose, move; make -a motion, – advances; start; invite, hold out, place- at one's disposal, – in one's way, put forward.

hawk about; offer for sale etc. 796; press etc. (*request*) 765; lay at one's feet.

offer –, present- oneself; volunteer, come forward, be a candidate; stand –, bid- for; seek; be at one's service; go a begging; bribe etc. (*give*) 784.

Adj. offer-ing, -ed etc. *v.*; in the market, for sale, to let, disengaged, on hire.

764. Refusal.—N. refusal, rejection; non-, incompliance; denial; declining etc. *v.*; declension; peremptory –, flat –, point blank- refusal; repulse, rebuff; discountenance.

recusancy, renunciation, abnegation, negation, protest, disclaimer; dissent etc. 489; revocation etc. 756.

V. refuse, reject, deny, decline; nill, negative; refuse –, withhold- one's assent; shake the head; close the -hand, – purse; grudge, begrudge, be slow to, hang fire.

be deaf to; turn -a deaf ear to, – one's back upon; set one's face against, discountenance, not hear of, have nothing to do with, wash one's hands of, stand aloof, forswear, set aside, cast behind one; not yield an inch etc. (*obstinacy*) 606.

resist, cross; not -grant etc. 762; repel, repulse; shut –, slam- the door in one's face; rebuff; send -back, – to the right about, – away with a flea in the ear; deny oneself, not be at home to; discard etc. (*repudiate*) 610; rescind etc. (*revoke*) 756; disclaim, protest; dissent etc. 489.

Adj. refusing etc. *v.*; rest-ive, -iff; recusant; uncomplying, noncompliant, unconsenting, uncomplaisant, protestant; not willing to hear of, deaf to.

refused etc. *v.*; ungranted, out of the question, not to be thought of, impossible.

Adv. no etc. 536; on no account, not for the world; no thank you.

Phr. *non possumus*; [ironically] your humble servant; *bien obligé*.

765. Request.—N. requ-est, -isition; claim etc. (*demand*) 741; petition, suit, prayer; begging letter, round-robin.

motion, overture, application, canvass, address, appeal, apostrophe; imprecation; rogation; proposal, proposition.

orison etc. (*worship*) 990; incantation etc. (*spell*) 993.

mendicancy; asking, panhandling, begging etc. *v.*; postulation, solicitation, invitation, entreaty, importunity, supplication, instance, impetration, imploration, obsecration, obtestation, invocation, interpellation.

V. request, ask; beg, crave, sue, pray, petition, solicit, invite, pop the question, make bold to ask; beg -leave, – a boon; apply to, call to, put to; call -upon, – for; make –, address –, prefer –, put up- a -request, – prayer, – petition; make -application, – a requisition; ask –, trouble- one for; claim etc. (*demand*) 741; offer up prayers etc. (*worship*) 990; whistle for.

beg hard, entreat, beseech, plead, supplicate, implore, apostrophize; conjure, adjure; obtest; cry to, kneel to, appeal to; invoke, evoke; impetrate, imprecate, ply, press, urge, beset, importune, dun, tax, clamor for; cry -aloud, – for help; fall on one's knees; throw oneself at the feet of; come down on one's marrow-bones.

beg from door to door, send the hat round, go a begging; mendicate, mump, cadge, panhandle, beg one's bread.

dance attendance on, besiege, knock at the door.

bespeak, canvass, tout, make interest, court; seek, bid for etc. (*offer*) 763; publish the banns.

Adj. requesting etc. *v.*; precatory; suppli-ant, -cant, -catory; invoc-, imprec-, rog-atory; postulant, mendicant.

importunate, clamorous, urgent; solicitous; cap in hand; on one's -knees, – bended knees, – marrow-bones.

Adv. prithee, do, please, pray; be so good as, be good enough; have the goodness, vouchsafe, will you, I pray thee, if you please.

Int. for -God's, – heaven's, – goodness', – mercy's- sake.

766. Deprecation. [Negative request.]—**N.** deprecation, expostulation; remonstrance; intercession, mediation.

V. deprecate, protest, expostulate, enter a protest, intercede for.

Adj. deprecatory, expostulatory, intercessory, mediatorial.

deprecated, protested.

un-, unbe-sought; unasked etc. (*see* ask etc. 765).

Int. cry you mercy! God forbid! forbid it Heaven! Heaven -forefend, – forbid! far be it from! hands off! etc. (*prohibition*) 761.

767. Petitioner.—N. petitioner, solicitor, applicant; suppli-ant, -cant; suitor, candidate, claimant, postulant, aspirant, competitor, bidder; place –, pot- hunter; prizer.

beggar, mendicant, mumper, sturdy beggar, cadger, panhandler.

canvasser, barker, touter etc. 768.

sycophant, parasite etc. 886.

768. Promise.—N. promise, undertaking, word, troth, plight, pledge, *parole*, word of honor, vow; oath etc. (*affirmation*) 535; profession, assurance, warranty, guarantee, insurance, obligation; contract etc. 769.

engagement, pre-engagement; affiance; betroth, -al, -ment; marriage -compact, – vow.

V. promise; give a -promise etc. *n.*; undertake, engage; make –, form- an engagement; enter -into, – on- an engagement; bind –, tie –, pledge –, commit –, take upon- oneself; vow; swear etc. (*affirm*) 535; give –, pass –, pledge –, plight- one's -word, – honor, – credit, – troth; betroth, plight faith; take the vows.

assure, warrant, guarantee, vouch for, avouch, covenant etc. 769; attest etc. (*bear witness*) 467.

hold out an expectation; contract an obligation; become -bound to, – sponsor for; answer –, be answerable- for; secure; give security etc. 771; underwrite.

adjure, administer an oath, put to one's oath, swear a witness.

Adj. promising etc. *v.*; promissory; votive; under hand and seal; upon -oath, – affirmation.

promised etc. *v.*; affianced, pledged, bound; committed, compromised; in for it.

Adv. as one's head shall answer for; upon my honor.

Phr. in for a penny, in for a pound.

768a. Release from engagement.—**N.** release etc. (*liberation*) 750.

Adj. absolute; unconditional etc. (*free*) 748.

769. Compact.—N. compact, contract, agreement, bargain, deal, transaction; affidation; pact, -ion; bond, covenant, indenture.

stipulation, settlement, convention; compromise, *cartel*.

protocol, treaty, *concordat, Zollverein, Sonderbund*, charter, *Magna Charta*, Pragmatic Sanction.

negotiation etc. (*bargaining*) 794; diplomacy etc. (*mediation*) 724; negotiator etc. (*agent*) 758.

ratification, completion, signature, seal, sigil, signet.

V. contract, covenant, agree for, engage etc. (*promise*) 768.

treat, negotiate, stipulate, make terms; bargain etc. (*barter*) 794.

make –, strike- a bargain; come to -terms, – an understanding; compromise etc. 774; set at rest; close, – with; conclude, complete, settle; confirm, ratify, clench, subscribe, underwrite; en-, in-dorse; put the seal to; sign, seal etc. (*attest*) 467; indent.

take one at one's word, bargain by inch of candle.

Adj. contractual, agreed etc. *v.*; conventional; under hand and seal; signed, sealed and delivered.

Phr. *caveat emptor.*

770. Conditions.—N. conditions, terms; articles, – of agreement.

clauses, provisions; proviso etc. (*qualification*) 469; covenant, stipulation, obligation, *ultimatum, sine quâ non*; *casus foederis*.

V. make –, come to- -terms etc. (*contract*) 769; make it a condition, stipulate, insist upon, make a point of; bind, tie up.

Adj. conditional, provisional, guarded, fenced, hedged in.

Adv. conditionally etc. (*with qualification*) 469; provisionally, *pro re natâ*; on condition; with a reservation.

771. Security.—N. security; guaran-ty, -tee; gage, waranty, bond, tie, pledge, plight, mortgage, debenture, hypothecation, bill of sale, lien, pignus, pawn, pignoration; real security; bottomry; collateral, vadium.

stake, deposit, earnest, handsel, caution.

promissory note; bill, – of exchange; I.O.U.: personal security, covenant, specialty; *parole* etc. (*promise*) 768.

acceptance, indorsement, signature, execution, stamp, seal.

spon-sor, -sion, -sorship; surety, bail; mainpernor, hostage.

recognizance; deed –, covenant- of indemnity.

authentication, verfication, warrant, certificate, voucher, docket, doquet; record etc. 551; probate, attested copy.

receipt; ac-, quittance; discharge, release.

muniment, title-deed, instrument; deed, – poll; assurance, insurance, indenture; charter etc. (*compact*) 769; charter-poll; paper, parchment, settlement, will, testament, last will and testament, codicil.

V. give -security, – bail, – substantial bail; go bail; pawn, impawn, hock, spout, mortgage, hypothecate, impignorate.

guarantee, warrant, assure; accept, indorse, underwrite, insure.

execute, stamp; sign, seal etc. (*evidence*) 467.

let, set; grant –, take –, hold- a lease; hold in pledge; lend on security etc. 787.

Adj. secure, -ed; pledged etc. *v.*; in pawn, on deposit.

772. Observance.—N. observance, performance, compliance; obedience, etc. 743; fulfilment, satisfaction, discharge; acquit-tance, -tal.

adhesion, acknowledgment; fidelity etc. (*probity*) 939; exact etc. 494- observance.

V. observe, comply with, respect, acknowledge, abide by; cling to, adhere to, be faithful to, act up to; meet, fulfil; carry -out, – into execution; execute, perform, keep, satisfy, discharge; do one's office.

perform –, fulfill –, discharge –, acquit oneself of- an obligation; make good; make good –, keep- one's -word, – promise; redeem one's pledge; keep faith with, stand to one's engagement.

Adj. observant, faithful, true, loyal; honorable etc. 939; true as the -dial to the sun, – needle to the pole; punct-ual, -ilious; meticulous; literal etc. (*exact*) 494; as good as one's word.

Adv. faithfully etc. *adj.*

773. Non-observance.—N. non-observance etc. 772; evasion, inobservance, failure, omission, neglect, laches, laxity, informality.

infringement, infraction; violation, transgression, retractation, repudiation, nullification; protest; forfeiture.

lawlessness; disobedience etc. 742; bad faith etc. 940.

V. fail, neglect, omit, elude, evade, give the go by to, cut, set aside, ignore; shut –, close- one's eyes to, avoid.

infringe, transgress, pirate, violate, break, trample under foot, do violence to, drive a coach and six through.

discard, protest, repudiate, fling to the winds, set at naught, nullify, declare null and void; cancel etc. (*wipe off*) 552.

retract, go back from, be off, forfeit, go from one's word, palter; stretch –, strain- a point.

Adj. violating etc. *v.*; lawless, transgressive; elusive, evasive; lax, casual; non-observant.

unfulfilled etc. (*see* fulfil etc. 772).

774. Compromise.—N. com-promise, -mutation, -position; middle term, *mezzo termine*; compensation etc. 30; adjustment, mutual concession.

V. com-promise, -mute, -pound; take the mean; split the difference, meet one half way, give and take; come to terms etc. (*contract*) 769; submit to –, abide by- arbitration; patch up, bridge over, fix up, arrange; adjust, – differences; agree; make -the best of, – a virtue of necessity; take the will for the deed.

775. Acquisition.—N. acquisition; gaining etc. *v.*; obtainment; procur-ation, -ement; purchase, descent, inheritance; gift etc. 784.

recovery, retrieval, revendication, replevin; redemption, salvage, trover; find, *trouvaille*, foundling.

gain, thrift; money-making, -grubbing; lucre, filthy lucre, loaves and fishes, the main chance, pelf; emolument etc. 973; wealth etc. 803.

profit, earnings, winnings, innings, clean-up, pickings, perquisite, net profit; income etc. (*receipt*) 810; pro-ceeds, -duce, -duct; out-come, -put; return, fruit, crop, harvest, tilth; second crop, aftermath; benefit etc. (*good*) 618.

sweepstakes, trick, prize, pool.

[Fraudulent acquisition] subreption; theft, stealing etc. 791.

V. acquire, get, gain, win, earn, obtain, procure, gather, annex; collect etc. 72; pick, – up; glean, take etc. 789.

find; come –, pitch –, light- upon; scrape -up, – together; get in, reap and carry, net, bag, sack, bring home, secure, come across, derive, draw, get in the harvest.

profit; make –, draw- profit; turn to -profit, – account; make -capital out of, – money by; obtain a return, reap the fruits of; reap –, gain- an advantage; turn -a penny, – an honest penny; make the pot boil, bring grist to the mill; make –, coin –, raise- money; raise -funds, – the wind; fill one's pocket etc. (*wealth*) 803.

treasure up etc. (*store*) 636; realize, clear; produce etc. 161; take etc. 789.

get back, recover, regain, retrieve, revendicate, replevy, redeem, come by one's own.

come -by, – in for; receive etc. 785; inherit; step into, – a fortune, – the shoes of; succeed to.

get -hold of, – between one's finger and thumb, – into one's hand, – at; take –, come into –, enter into- possession.

be -profitable etc. *adj.*; pay, answer.

accrue etc. (*be received*) 785.

Adj. acquir-ing, -ed etc. *v.*; acquisitive; productive, profitable, advantageous, gainful, remunerative, paying, lucrative.

776. Loss.—N. loss; de-, perdition; forfeiture, lapse.

privation, bereavement; deprivation etc. (*dispossession*) 789; riddance.

V. lose; incur –, experience –, meet with- a loss; miss; mislay, let slip, allow to slip through the fingers, squander; be without etc. (*exempt*) 777*a*; forfeit.

get rid of etc. 782; waste etc. 638.

be lost, lapse.

Adj. losing etc. *v.*; not having etc. 777*a*.

shorn of, deprived of; denuded, bereaved, bereft, *minus*, cut off; dispossessed etc. 789; rid of, quit of; out of pocket.

lost etc. *v.*; long lost; irretrievable etc. (*hopeless*) 859; irredentist; off one's hands.

Int. farewell to! adieu to! good riddance!

777. Possession.—N. possession, seisin; ownership etc. 780; occupancy; hold, -ing; tenure, tenancy, feodality, dependency; villenage; socage, chivalry, knight service.

exclusive possession, impropriation, monopoly, corner; retention etc. 781; pre-possession, -occupancy; nine points of the law.

future possession, heritage, inheritance, heirship, reversion, fee, seigniority, feud, fief.

bird in hand, *uti possidetis*, *chose* in possession.

V. possess, have, hold, occupy, enjoy; be -possessed of etc. *adj.*; have -in hand etc. *adj.*; own etc. 780; command.

inherit; come -to, – in for.

engross, monopolize, forestall, regrate, impropriate, have all to oneself, corner; have a firm hold of etc. (*retain*) 781; get into one's hand etc. (*acquire*) 775.

belong to, appertain to, pertain to; be -in one's possession etc. *adj.*; vest in.

Adj. possessing etc. *v.*; worth; possessed of, seized of, master of, in possession of; endowed –, blest –, instinct –, fraught –, laden –, charged –, instilled –, with.

possessed etc. *v.*; on hand, by one; in hand, in store, in stock; in one's -hands, – grasp, – possession; at one's -command, – disposal; one's own etc. (*property*) 780.

unsold, unshared.

777a. Exemption.—N. exemption; exception, immunity, privilege, release etc. 927*a*; absence etc. 187.

V. not -have etc. 777; be -without etc. *adj.*

Adj. exempt from, devoid of, without, unpossessed of, unblest with, immune from.

not -having etc. 777; unpossessed; untenanted etc. (*vacant*) 187; without an owner.

unobtained, unacquired.

778. Participation. [Joint possession.]**—N.** participation; co-, joint-tenancy; possession –, tenancy- in common; joint –, common- stock; co-, partnership; communion; community of -possessions, – goods; communalism, communism, socialism, collectivism; co-operation etc. 709; profit sharing.

snacks, co-portion, picnic, hotchpotch; co-heirship, -parceny, -parcenary; gavelkind.

participator, sharer; co-, partner; shareholder; co-, joint-tenant; tenants in common; co-heir, -parcener.

communist, socialist.

V. par-ticipate, -take; share, – in; come in for a share; go -shares, – snacks, – halves; share and share alike.

have –, possess –, be seized- -in common, – as joint tenants etc. *n.*

join in; have a hand in etc. (*co-operate*) 709.

Adj. partaking etc. *v.*; communistic, socialistic, co-operative, profit sharing.

Adv. share and share alike.

779. Possessor.—N. possessor, holder; occupant, -ier; tenant; person –, man- -in possession etc. 777; renter, lodger, lessee, under-lessee; zemindar, ryot; tenant -on sufferance, – at will, – from year to year, – for years, – for life.

owner; propriet-or, -ress, -ary; impropriator, master, mistress, lord.

land-holder, -owner, -lord, -lady; lord -of the manor, – paramount; heritor, laird, vavasor, landed gentry, mesne lord.

cestui-que-trust, beneficiary, mortgagor.

grantee, feoffee, relessee, devisee; legat-ee, -ary.

trustee; holder etc.- of the legal estate; mortgagee.

right –, rightful- owner.

[Future possessor] heir, – apparent; – presumptive; heiress; inherit-or, -ress, -rix; reversioner, remainder-man.

780. Property.—N. property, possession, *suum cuique, meum et tuum.*

owner-, proprietor, lord-ship; seignority; empire etc. (*dominion*) 737.

interest, stake, estate, right, title, claim, demand, holding; tenure etc. (*possession*) 777; vested –, contingent –, beneficial –, equitable- interest; use, trust, benefit; legal –, equitable- estate; seisin.

absolute interest, paramount estate, freehold; fee, – simple, – tail; estate -in fee, – in tail, – tail; estate in tail -male, – female, – general.

limitation, term, lease, settlement, strict settlement, particular estate; estate -for life, – for years, – *pur autre vie*; remainder, reversion, expectancy, possibility.

dower, dowry, *dot*, jointure, marriage portion, appanage, inheritance, heritage, patrimony, alimony; legacy etc. (*gift*) 784.

assets, belongings, means, resources, circumstances; wealth etc. 803; money etc. 800; what one -is worth, – will cut up for; estate and effects.

landed –, real- -estate, – property; realty; land, -s; subdivision; plot, site; tenements; hereditaments; corporeal –, incorporeal- hereditaments; acres; ground etc. (*earth*) 342; acquest; messuage.

territory, state, kingdom, principality, realm, empire, protectorate, margravate, dependancy, colony, sphere of influence, mandate.

manor, honor, domain, demesne; farm, ranch, plantation, *hacienda*; allodium etc. (*free*) 748; fieff, feoff, feud, zemindary, dependency.

free-, copy-, lease-holds; chattels real; fixtures, plant, heirloom easement; folkland; right of - common, – user.

personal -property, – estate, – effects; personalty, chattels, goods, effects, movables; stock, – in trade; things, traps, rattle-traps, paraphernalia; equipage etc. 633.

parcels, appurtenances.

impedimenta; lug-, bag-gage; bag and baggage; pelf; cargo, lading.

rent-roll; income etc. (*receipts*) 810.

patent, copyright; *chose* in action; credit etc. 805; debt etc. 806.

V. possess etc. 777; be the -possessor etc. 779- of own; have for one's own, – very own; come in for, inherit; enfeoff.

savor of the realty.

be one's own -property etc. *n.*; belong to; ap-, pertain to.

Adj. one's own; landed, predial, manorial, allodial, seignorial; free-, copy-, lease-hold; feu-, feo-dal; hereditary, entailed, personal.

Adv. to one's -credit, – account; to the good.

to one and -his heirs for ever, – the heirs of his body, – his heirs and assigns, – his executors, administrators and assigns.

781. Retention.—N. retention; retaining etc. *v.*; keep, detention, custody; tenacity, firm hold, grasp, gripe, grip, iron grip.

fangs, teeth, claws, talons, nail, hook, tentacle, *tenaculum*; bond etc. (*vinculum*) 45.

clutches, tongs, forceps, pincers, nippers, pliers, tweezers, vise.

paw, hand, finger, wrist, fist, neaf, neif.

bird in hand; captive etc. 754.

V. retain, keep; hold, – fast, – tight, – one's own, – one's ground; clinch, clench, clutch, grasp, gripe, hug, have a firm hold of.

secure, withold, detain; hold –, keepback; keep close; husband etc. (*store*) 636; reserve; have –, keep- in stock etc. (*possess*) 777; enfail, tie up, settle.

Adj. retaining etc. *v.*; retentive, tenacious.

unforfeited, undeprived, undisposed, uncommunicated.

incommunicable, inalienable; in mortmain; in strict settlement.

Phr. *uti possidetis.*

782. Relinquishment.—N. relinquishment, abandonment etc. (*of a course*) 624; renunciation, expropriation, dereliction; cession, surrender, dispensation; resignation etc. 757; riddance.

derelict etc. *adj.*; jetsam; waif, foundling, orphan.

v. relinquish, give up, surrender, yield, cede; let -go, – slip; spare, drop, resign, forego, renounce, abjure, abandon, expropriate, give away, dispose of, part with; lay -aside, – apart, – down, – on the shelf etc. (*disuse*) 678; set –, put- aside; make away with, cast behind; discard, cast off, dismiss; maroon.

give -notice to quit, – warning; supersede; be –, get- -rid of, – quit of; eject etc. 297.

rid –, disburden –, divest –, dispossess- oneself of; wash one's hands of; divorce, desert; disinherit, cut off.

cast –, throw –, pitch –, fling- -away, – aside, – overboard, – to the dogs; cast –, throw –, sweep- to the winds; put –, turn –, sweep- away; jettison.

quit one's hold.

Adj. relinquished etc. *v.*; cast off, derelict; unowned, unappropriated, unculled; left etc. (*residuary*) 40; divorced; disinherited.

Int. away with!

783. Transfer.—N. transfer, conveyance, assignment, alienation, abalienation; demise, limitation; conveyancing; transmission etc. (*transference*) 270; enfeoffment, bargain and sale, lease and release; exchange etc. (*interchange*) 148; barter etc. 794; substitution etc. 147.

succession, reversion; shifting -use, – trust; devolution.

V. transfer, convey; alien, -ate; assign; grant etc. (*confer*) 784; consign; make –, hand- over; pass, hand, transmit, negotiate; hand down; exchange etc. (*interchange*) 148.

change -hands, – from one to another; devolve, succeed; come into possession etc. (*acquire*) 775; take over.

abalienate; disinherit; dispossess etc. 789; substitute etc. 147.

Adj. alienable, negotiable, transferable, reversional.

Phr. estate coming into possession.

784. Giving.—N. giving etc. *v.*; bestowal, donation; present-ation, -ment; accordance; con-, cession; delivery, consignment, dispensation, communication, endowment; invest-ment, -iture; award.

almsgiving, charity, liberality, generosity; philanthropy etc. 910.

[Thing given] gift, donation, present, *cadeau*; fairing; free gift, boon, favor, benefaction, grant, offering, oblation, sacrifice, immolation.

grace, act of grace, *bonus, bonanza*.

allowance, contribution, subscription, subsidy, tribute, subvention.

bequest, legacy, devise, will, dotation, appanage; dowry; voluntary -settlement, – conveyance etc. 783; amortization.

alms, largess, bounty, dole, sportule, donative, help, oblation, offertory, Peter's pence, *honorarium*, gratuity, Maundy money, Christmas box, Easter offering, vail, tip, *douceur*, drink money, *pourboire, trinkgeld, backsheesh*; fee etc. (*recompense*) 973; consideration.

bribe, bait, ground-bait; peace-offering, handsel.

giver, grantor etc. *v.*; donor, feoffer, settlor; almoner; testator; investor, subscriber, contributor; fairy godmother; Santa Claus, benefactor etc. 816.

V. deliver, hand, pass, put into the hands of; hand –, make –, deliver –, pass –, turn- over.

present, give away, dispense, dispose of; give –, deal –, dole –, mete –, fork –, shell –, squeeze- out.

pay etc. 807; render, impart, communicate.

concede, cede, yield, part with, shed cast; spend etc. 809.

give, bestow, confer, grant, accord, award, assign.

entrust, consign, vest in.

make a present; allow, contribute, subscribe, donate, furnish its quota.

invest, endow, settle upon; bequesth, leave, devise.

furnish, supply, help; ad-, minister to; afford, spare; accommodate –, indulge –, favor- with; shower down upon; lavish, pour on, thrust upon; tip, bribe; tickle –, grease- the palm; offer etc. 763; sacrifice, immolate.

Adj. giving etc. *v.*; given etc. *v.*; allow-ed, -able; concessional; communicable; charitable, eleemosynary, sportulary, tributary; *gratis* etc. 815.

785. Receiving.—N. receiving etc. *v.*; acquisition etc. 775; reception etc. (*introduction*) 296; suscipiency, acceptance, admission.

re-, ac-cipient; assignee, devisee; lega-tee, -tary; grantee, feoffee, donee, relessee, lessee.

sportulary, stipendiary; beneficiary; pension-er, -ary; almsman.

income etc. (*receipt*) 810.

v. receive; take etc. 789; acquire etc. 775; admit.

take in, catch, touch; pocket; put into one's -pocket, – purse; accept; take off one's hands.

be received; come -in, – to hand; pass –, fall-into one's hand; go into one's pocket; fall to one's -lot, – share; come –, fall- to one; accrue; have -given etc. 784 to one.

Adj. receiving etc. *v.*; re-, suscipient.

received etc. *v.*; given etc. 784; second-hand.

not given, unbestowed etc. (*see* give, bestow etc. 784).

786. Apportionment.—N. apportion-, allot-, consign-, assign-, appoint-ment; appropriation; dispensation, -tribution; allocation, division, deal; repartition; administration.

dividend, portion, contingent, share, allotment, lot, cut, split, measure, dose; dole, meed, pittance;, *quantum*, ration; ratio, proportion, quota, *modicum*, mess, allowance.

V. apportion, divide; cut, split, divvy; distribute, administer, dispense; billet, allot, detail, cast, share, mete; portion –, parcel –, dole- out; deal, carve.

partition, assign, appropriate, appoint.

come in for one's share etc. (*participate*) 778.

Adj. apportioning etc. *v.*; respective.

Adv. respectively, each to each.

787. Lending.—N. lending etc. *v.*; loan, advance, accommodation, feneration; mortgage etc. (*security*) 771; investment.

mont de piété, pawnshop, hock shop, spout, my uncle's.

lender, pawnbroker, money lender, usurer, Jew, Shylock.

V. lend, advance, loan, accommodate with; lend on security; pawn etc. (*security*) 771.

intrust, invest; place –, put- out to interest; sink, risk.

let, demise, lease, set, under-, sub-let.

Adj. lending etc. *v.*; lent etc. *v.*; unborrowed etc. (*see* borrowed etc. 788).

Adv. in advance; on -loan, – security.

788. Borrowing.—N. borrowing, pledging, pawning.

borrowed plumes; plagiarism etc. (*thieving*) 791, replevin.

V. borrow, desume; pawn.

hire, rent, farm; take a -lease, – demise; take –, hire- by the -hour, – mile, – year etc.

raise –, take up- money; float bonds; raise the wind; fly a kite, borrow of Peter to pay Paul; run into debt etc. (*debt*) 806.

make use of, plagiarize, pirate.

replevy.

789. Taking.—N. taking etc. *v.*; reception etc. (*taking in*) 296; deglutition etc. (*taking food*) 298; appropriation, prehension, prensation; capture, caption; ap-, de-prehension; abreption, seizure; abduction, -lation; subtraction etc. (*subduction*) 38; abstraction, ademption.

dispossession; depriv-ation, -ement; bereavement; divestment; disherison; distraint, distress; sequestration, confiscation, attachment, execution; eviction etc. 297.

rapacity, extortion, vampirism, predacity, blood-sucking; theft etc. 791.

resumption; repris-e, -al; recovery etc. 775.

clutch, swoop, wrench; grip etc. (*retention*) 781; haul, take, catch; scramble.

taker, captor, capturer; vampire; extortioner.

V. take, catch, hook, nab, bag, sack, pocket, put into one's pocket, scrounge; receive; accept.

reap, crop, cull, pluck; gather etc. (*get*) 775; draw.

ap-, im-propriate; assume, possess oneself of; take possession of; commandeer; lay –, clap- one's hands on; help oneself to; make free with, dip one's hands into, lay under contribution; intercept; scramble for; deprive of.

take –, carry –, bear- -away, – off; abstract; hurry off –, run away- with; abduct; steal etc. 791; ravish; seize; pounce –, spring- upon; swoop -to, – down upon; take by -storm, – assault; snatch, reave.

snap up, nip up, whip up, catch up; kidnap, crimp, capture, lay violent hands on.

get –, lay –, take –, catch –, lay fast –, take firm- hold of; lay by the heels, take prisoner; fasten upon, grip, grapple, embrace, gripe, clasp, grab, clutch, collar, throttle, take by the throat, claw, clinch, clench, make sure of.

catch at, jump at, make a grab at, snap at, snatch at; reach, make a long arm, stretch forth one's hand.

take -from, – away from; deduct etc. 38; retrench etc. (*curtail*) 201; dispossess, ease one of, snatch from one's grasp; tear –, tear away –, wrench –, wrest –, wring- from; extort; deprive of, bereave; disinherit, cut off with a shilling.

oust etc. (*eject*) 297; divest; levy, distrain, confiscate; sequest-er, -rate, accroach; usurp; despoil, strip, fleece, shear, displume, impoverish, eat out of house and home; drain, – to the dregs; gut, dry, exhaust, swallow up; absorb etc. (*suck in*) 296; draw off; suck, – like a leech, – the blood of.

retake, resume; recover etc. 775.

Adj. taking etc. *v.*; privative, prehensile; predaceous, -al, -atory, -atorial; rap-acious, -torial; ravenous; parasitic; all-devouring, -engulfing.

bereft etc. 776.

Adv. at one fell swoop.

Phr. give an inch and take an ell.

790. Restitution.—N. restitution, return; ren-, red-dition; reinstatement, restoration; reinvestment, recuperation; repatriation; rehabilitation etc. (*reconstruction*) 660; reparation, atonement, indemnity, compensation, recompense.

release, replevin, redemption; recovery etc. (*getting back*) 775; remitter, reversion.

V. return, restore; recondition; give –, carry –, bring- back; render, – up; give up; let go, unclutch; dis-, re-gorge; regurgitate; recoup, reimburse, repay, indemnify, reinvest, remit, rehabilitate; repair etc. (*make good*) 660.

redeem, recover etc. (*get back*) 775; take back again; revest, revert.

Adj. restoring etc. *v.*; recuperative etc. 660; in full restitution, to compensate for.

Phr. *suum cuique.*

791. Stealing.—N. stealing etc. *v.*; theft, thievery, robbery, latrociny, direption; abstraction, appropriation; plagiar-y, -ism; rape, kidnapping, depredation; raid, hold up.

spoliation, plunder, pillage; sack, -age; rapine, *brigandage*, highway robbery, foray, *razzia*; blackmail; piracy, privateering, buccaneering; filibustering, -ism; burglary; house-breaking; cattle-stealing, -rustling, -lifting.

peculation, embezzlement; fraud etc. 545; larceny, petty larceny, pilfering, shop-lifting.

thievishness, rapacity, kleptomania, Alsatia; den of -Cacus, – thieves.

license to plunder, letters of marque.

V. steal, thieve, rob, purloin, pilfer, filch, lift, prig, bag, nim, crib, cabbage, palm; abstract; appropriate, plagiarize.

convey away, carry off, abduct, kidnap, shanghai, impress, crimp; make –, walk –, run- off with; run away with; spirit away; seize etc. (*lay violent hands on*) 789.

plunder, pillage, rifle, sack, loot, ransack, spoil, spoliate, despoil, strip, sweep, gut, forage, levy black-mail, pirate, pickeer, maraud, lift cattle, rustle, poach, smuggle, run.

stick –, hold- up.

swindle, peculate, embezzle; sponge, mulct, rook, bilk, pluck, pigeon, skin, fleece, diddle; defraud etc. 545; obtain under false pretences; live by one's wits.

rob –, borrow of- Peter to Paul; set a thief to catch a thief.

disregard the distinction between *meum* and *tuum*.

Adj. thieving etc. *v.*; thievish, light-fingered; furacious, -tive; piratical; pred-aceous, -al, -atory, -atorial; raptorial etc. (*rapacious*) 789.

stolen etc. *v.*

Phr. *sic vos non vobis.*

792. Thief.—N. thief, robber, *homo trium literarum*, pilferer, rifler, filcher, plagiarist.

spoiler, depredator, pillager, marauder; harpy, shark, land-shark, falcon, moss-trooper, bushranger, Bedouin, brigand, freebooter, bandit, thug, dacoit, pirate, corsair, viking, Paul Jones; buccan-eer, -ier; piqu-, pick-eerer; rover, ranger, privateer, filibuster; rapparee, wrecker, picaroon; smuggler, poacher, plunderer; racketeer.

highwayman, Dick Turpin, Claude Duval, Macheath, knight of the road, footpad, sturdy beggar; abductor, kidnapper.

cut-, pick-purse; pick-pocket, light-fingered gentry; sharper; card-, skittle-sharper; crook; thimble-rigger; rook, Greek, blackleg, leg, welsher, defaulter; Autolycus, Cacus, Barabbas, Jeremy Diddler, Robert Macaire, artful dodger, trickster; swell mob, *chevalier d'industrie*; shop-lifter.

swindler, peculator; forger, coiner, counterfeiter, shoful; fence, receiver of stolen goods, duffer; smasher.

burglar, housebreaker; cracks-, mags-man; Bill Sikes, Jack Sheppard, Jonathan Wild, Raffles, cat burglar.

793. Booty.—N. booty, spoil, plunder, price, loot, graft, swag, pickings, boodle; *spolia opima*, prey; blackmail; stolen goods.

Adj. looting etc. *n.*; manubial, spoliative.

794. Barter.—N. barter, exchange, scorse, truck system; interchange etc. 148.

a Roland for an Oliver; *quid pro quo*; commutation, -position.

trade, commerce, mercature, buying and selling, bargain and sale; traffic, business, nundination, custom, shopping; commercial enterprise, speculation, jobbing, stock-jobbing, *agiotage*, brokery, arbitrage.

dealing, transaction, negotiation, bargain.

free trade.

V. barter, exchange, truck, scorse, swop; interchange etc. 148; commutate etc. (*substitute*) 147; compound for.

trade, traffic, buy and sell, give and take, nundinate; carry on –, ply –, drive- a trade; be in -

business, – the city; keep a shop, deal in, employ one's capital in.

trade –, deal –, have dealings- with; transact –, do- business with; open –, keep- an account with.

bargain; drive –, make- a bargain; negotiate, bid for; dicker, haggle, higgle; chaffer, huckster, cheapen, beat down; stickle, – for; out-, under-bid; ask, charge; strike a bargain etc. (*contract*) 769.

speculate, give a sprat to catch a herring; buy in the cheapest and sell in the dearest market; rig the market.

Adj. commercial, mercantile, trading; interchangeable, marketable, staple, in the market, for sale.

wholesale, retail.

Adv. across the counter; on 'change.

795. Purchase.—N. purchase, emption; buying, purchasing, shopping; pre-emption, refusal.

coemption, bribery; slave trade.

buyer, purchaser, *emptor*, vendee; patron, employer, client, customer, *clientèle*.

V. buy, purchase, invest in, procure; rent etc. (*hire*) 788; repurchase, buy in.

keep in one's pay, bribe, suborn; pay etc. 807; spend etc. 809.

make –, complete- a purchase; buy over the counter; pay cash for.

shop, market, go a shopping.

Adj. purchased etc. *v.*

Phr. *caveat emptor.*

796. Sale.—N. sale, vent, disposal; auction, roup, Dutch auction; custom etc. (*traffic*) 794.

vendi-bility, -bleness.

seller, salesman; peddler, smous; vender, vendor, consignor; merchant etc. 797; auctioneer.

V. sell, vend, dispose of, effect a sale; sell -over the counter, – by auction etc. *n.*; dispense, retail; deal in etc. 794; sell -off, – out; turn into money; realize; bring -to, – under- the hammer; put up to auction; auction, offer –, put up- for sale; hawk, peddle, bring to market; offer etc. 763; undersell; dump, unload.

let; mortgage etc. (*security*) 771.

Adj. under the hammer, in the market, for sale.

saleable, marketable, vendible, in demand, having a ready sale; unsaleable etc., unpurchased, unbought; on one's hands.

797. Merchant.—N. merchant, trader, dealer, monger, chandler, salesman; changer; regrater; shop-keeper, -man; trades-man, -people, -folk.

retailer; chapman, hawker, huckster, higgler; peddler, smous, pedlar, *colporteur*, cadger, Autolycus; sutler, *vivandière*; coster-man, -monger; market woman; cheap jack; caterer etc. 637; tallyman.

money-broker, -changer, -lender; stock-broker, -jobber; cambist, usurer, moneyer, banker.

jobber; broker etc. (*agent*) 758; buyer etc. 795; seller etc. 796.

concern; firm etc. (*partnership*) 712.

798. Merchandise.—N. merchandise, ware, commodity, effects, goods, article, stock, produce, staple commodity; stock in trade etc. (*store*) 636; cargo etc. (*contents*) 190.

799. Mart.—N. mart; market, -place, *forum*; fair, bazaar, staple; stock –, exchange; 'change, *bourse*, Wall Street, Rialto, hall, guildhall; toll-booth, custom-house; Tattersalls.

shop, stall, booth; wharf; office, chambers, counting-house, *bureau*; coun-, comp-ter.

ware-house, -room; *dépôt*, interposit, *entrepôt*, *emporium*, establishment; store etc. 636.

open market, market-overt.

800. Money.—N. money -matters, – market; finance; accounts etc. 811; funds, treasure; capital, stock; assets etc. (*property*) 780; wealth etc. 803; supplies, ways and means, wherewithal, sinews of war, almighty dollar, needful, cash.

sum, amount; balance, -sheet; sum total; proceeds etc. (*receipts*) 810.

currency, circulating medium, specie; coin, – of the realm; piece, hard cash, dollar, sterling coin; pounds, shillings and pence; L s. d., guineas; pocket, breeches pocket, purse; money in hand; the best, ready, – money; filthy lucre, shekels, roll, jack, rhino, blunt, dust, bawbees, brass, dibs, dough, mopus, tin, salt, chink, oof, spondulics, pile, wads.

precious metals, gold, silver, copper, nickel; bullion, bar, ingot, nugget.

petty cash; pocket-, pin-money; small –, change; small coin, loose cash; doit, stiver, rap, mite, farthing, *sou*, penny, shilling, bob, tanner, tester, groat, guinea, ducat; *rouleau*; *wampum*; good –, round –, lump- sum; power –, mint –, tons- of money; plum, lac of rupees, millions, money-bags, miser's hoard, stocking, mine of wealth etc. 803.

[Science of coins] numismatics, chrysology.

paper-money; money –, postal –, Post Office-order; note, – of hand; bank –, treasury- note; Bradbury; promissory note; I.O.U., bond; bill, – of exchange; draft, check, order, warrant, *coupon*, debenture, exchequer bill, *assignat*, greenback, gold –, silver- certificate.

copper, nickel, dime, quarter, two bits, half a dollar, dollar, buck, simoleon, fiver, tenner, a twenty, a sawbuck, a century, a grand; eagle, double eagle.

gold standard, bimetallism, fiat money; rate of –, exchange; in-, de-flation.

remittance etc. (*payment*) 807; credit etc. 805; liability etc. 806; solvency etc. 803.

draw-er, -ee; oblig-or, -ee; moneyer, coiner, counterfeiter, forger.

false –, bad- money; base –, counterfeit- coin, flash note, slip, kite; Bank of Elegance.

argumentum ad crumenam.

V. amount to, come to, mount up to; touch the pocket; draw, – upon; endorse etc. (*security*) 771; issue, utter, circulate; discount etc. 813.

forge, counterfeit, coin, circulate –, pass- bad money.

Adj. monetary, pecuniary, crumenal, fiscal, financial, sumptuary, numismatical; sterling; solvent etc. 803.

801. Treasurer.—N. treasurer; bursar, -y; purser, purse-bearer; cash-keeper, banker; depositary; questor, receiver, steward, trustee, chartered –, accountant; Accountant-General, almoner, liquidator, paymaster, cashier, teller; cambist; money-changer etc. (*merchant*) 797.

financier, Chancellor of the Exchequer, minister of finance; Secretary of the Treasury, Director of the Budget, Controller of Currency.

802. Treasury.—N. treasury, bank, exchequer, almonry, fisc, hanaper, bursary; safe; strong-box, -hold, -room; coffer; chest etc. (*receptacle*) 191; depository etc. 636; till, -er; cash-box, -register, purse, pocketbook, wallet; money-bag, -belt, -box, *porte-monnaie*.

purse-strings; pocket, breeches pocket.

sinking fund; stocks; government –, public –, parliamentary- -stocks, – funds, – securities, bonds; gild-edged securities; Consols, Liberty bonds, government bonds, *crédit mobilier*.

803. Wealth.—N. wealth, riches, fortune, handsome fortune, opulence, affluence; good –, easy- circumstances; independence; competence etc. (*sufficiency*) 639; solvency, soundness, solidity.

provision, livelihood, maintenance; alimony, dowry; means, resources, substance; property etc. 780; command of money.

income etc. 810; capital, money; round sum etc. (*treasure*) 800; mint of money, mine of wealth, *El Dorado*, Pactolus, Golconda, Potosi, *bonanza*; philosopher's stone.

long –, full –, well lined –, heavy- purse; purse of Fortunatus.

pelf, Mammon, lucre, filthy lucre; loaves and fishes; fleshpots of Egypt.

rich –, moneyed –, warm- man; man of substance; capitalist, millionaire, Nabob, Croesus, Midas, Plutus, Dives, Timon of Athens; Timo-, Pluto-cracy; Danaë.

V. be -rich etc. *adj.*; roll –, wallow- in -wealth, – riches; have money to burn.

afford, well afford; command -money, – a sum; make both ends meet, hold one's head above water.

become -rich etc. *adj.*; fill one's -pocket etc. (*treasury*) 802; feather one's nest, clean up –, make- a fortune; make money etc. (*acquire*) 775.

enrich, imburse.

worship -Mammon, – the golden calf.

Adj. wealthy, rich, affluent, opulent, moneyed, monied, worth -a great deal, – much; well -to do, – off; warm; well –, provided for.

made of money; rich as Croesus; rolling in -riches, – wealth.

flush, – of -cash, – money, – tin; in -funds, – cash, – full feather; solvent, solid, sound, pecunious, out of debt, all straight; able to pay 20s in the L.

Phr. one's ship coming in.

804. Poverty.—N. poverty, indigence, penury, pauperism, destitution, want; need, -iness; lack, necessity, privation, distress, difficulties, wolf at the door.

bad –, poor –, needy –, embarrassed –, reduced –, straitened- circumstances; slender –, narrow- means; straits; hand to mouth existence, *res angusta domi*, low water, impecuniosity.

beggary; mendi-cancy, -city; broken –, loss of- fortune; insolvency etc. (*non-payment*) 808.

empty -purse, – pocket; light purse; beggarly account of empty boxes.

poor man, pauper, mendicant, mumper, beggar, starveling; *pauvre diable*.

V. be -poor etc. *adj.*; want, lack, starve, live from hand to mouth, have seen better days, go down in the world, be on one's uppers, come upon the parish; go to -the dogs, – wrack and ruin; not have a -penny etc. (*money*) 800, – shot in one's locker; beg one's bread; *tirer le diable par la queue*; run into debt etc. (*debt*) 806.

render -poor etc. *adj.*; impoverish; reduce, – to poverty; pauperize, fleece, ruin, bring to the parish.

Adj. poor, indigent; poverty-striken; badly –, poorly –, ill- off; poor as -a rat, – a church mouse, – Job's turkey, – Job; fortune-, dower-, money-, penni-less; unportioned, unmoneyed; impecunious; broke, flat; out –, short- of -money, – cash; without –, not worth- a rap etc. (*money*) 800; *qui n'a pas le sou*, out of pocket, hard up; out at -elbows, – heels; seedy, bare-footed; beggar-ly, -ed; destitute; fleeced, strapped, stripped; bereft, bereaved; reduced.

in -want etc. *n.*; needy, necessitous, distressed, pinched, straitened; put to one's -shifts, – last shifts; unable to -keep the wolf from the door, – make both ends meet; embarrassed, under hatches; involved etc. (*in debt*) 806; insolvent etc. (*not paying*) 808.

Adv. *in formâ pauperis*.

Phr. *zonam perdidit*.

805. Credit.—N. credit, trust, tick, score, tally, account.

letter of credit, circular note; duplicate; mortgage, lien, debenture, paper credit, floating capital; draft; securities.

creditor, lender, lessor, mortgagee; dun; usurer.

V. keep –, run up- an account with; entrust, credit, accredit.

place to one's -credit, – account; give –, take- credit; fly a kite.

Adj. credit-ing, -ed; accredited.

Adv. on -credit etc. *n.*; to the -account, – credit- of.

806. Debt.—N. debt, obligation, liability, indebtment, debit, score.

arrears, deferred payment, deficit, default; insolvency etc. (*non-payment*) 808; bad debt.

interest; usance, usury; premium; floating -debt, – capital.

debtor, debitor; mortgagor; defaulter etc. 808; borrower.

V. be -in debt etc. *adj.*; owe; incur –, contract- a debt etc. *n.*; run up -a bill, – a score, – an account; go on tick, put on the cuff; borrow etc. 788; run –, get- into debt; outrun the constable.

answer –, go bail- for; back one's note.

Adj. indebted; liable, chargeable, answerable for.

in -debt, – embarrassed circumstances, – difficulties; incumbered, involved; involved –, plunged –, deep –, over head and ears- in debt; deeply involved; fast tied up; insolvent etc. (*not paying*) 808; *minus*, out of pocket.

unpaid; unrequieted, unrewarded; owing, due, in arrear, outstanding.

807. Payment.—N. pay-, defray-ment; discharge; ac-, quittance; settlement, clearance, liquidation, satisfaction, reckoning, arrangement.

acknowledgment, release; receipt, – in full, – in full of all demands; voucher.

repayment, reimbursement, retribution; pay etc. (*reward*) 973; money paid etc. (*expenditure*) 809.

ready money etc. (*cash*) 800; stake, remittance, instalment.

payer, liquidator etc. 801.

V. pay, defray, make payment; pay -down, – on the nail, – ready money, – at sight, – in advance; cash, honor a bill, acknowledge; redeem; pay in kind.

pay one's -way, – shot, – footing; pay -the piper, – sauce for all, – costs; do the needful; come across; shell –, fork- out; come down with, – the dust; tickle –, grease- the palm; expend etc. 809; put –, lay- down.

discharge, settle, quit, acquit oneself of; account –, reckon –, settle –, be even –, be quits- with; strike a balance; settle –, balance –, square- accounts with; quit scores; foot the bill; wipe –, clear- off old scores; satisfy; pay in full; satisfy –, pay in full of- all demands; clear, liquidate; pay - up, – old debts.

disgorge, make repayment; repay, refund, reimburse, retribute; make compensation etc. 30.

Adj. paying etc., paid etc. *v.*; owing nothing, out of debt, all straight, clear of -debt, – encumbrance; unowed, never indebted.

Adv. to the tune of; on the nail; money –, cash- down; cash on delivery.

808. Non-payment.—N. non-payment; default, defalcation; protest, repudiation; application of the sponge; whitewashing.

insolvency, bankruptcy, failure; overdraft, overdrawn account; insufficiency etc. 640; run upon a bank.

waste paper bonds; dishonored –, protested- bills; bogus cheque.

bankrupt, insolvent debtor, lame duck, man of straw, welsher, stag, defaulter, absconder, levanter.

V. non -pay etc. 807; fail, break, stop payment; become -insolvent, – bankrupt; be gazetted.

protest, dishonor, repudiate, nullify.

pay under protest; button up one's pockets, draw the purse strings; apply the sponge; pay over the left shoulder, get whitewashed; swindle etc. 791; run up bills, fly kites.

Adj. not paying; in debt etc. 806; behindhand, in arrear; beggared etc. (*poor*) 804; unable to make both ends meet; *minus*; worse than nothing.

insolvent, bankrupt, in the gazette, gazetted, ruined.

unpaid etc. (*outstanding*) 806; *gratis* etc. 815; unremunerated.

809. Expenditure.—N. expenditure, money going out; out-goings, -lay; expenses, disbursement; prime cost etc. (*price*) 812; circulation; run upon a bank.

[Money paid] payment etc. 807; pay etc. (*remuneration*) 973; bribe etc. 973; fee, footing, garnish; subsidy; tribute, Peter's pence; contingent, quota; donation etc. 784.

pay in advance, earnest, handsel, deposit, instalment.

investment; purchase etc. 795.

V. expend, spend; run –, get- through; pay, disburse; open –, loose –, untie- the purse strings; lay –, shell –, fork- out; bleed; make up a sum, invest, sink money.

fee etc. (*reward*) 973; pay one's way etc. (*pay*) 807; subscribe etc. (*give*) 784; subsidize, bribe.

Adj. expend-ing, -ed etc. *v.*; sumptuary, liberal etc. 816; openhanded, lavish etc. 818; extensive etc. 814.

810. Receipt—N. receipt, accountable –, conditional –, binding –, return- receipt; value received, money coming in; income, incomings, innings, revenue, return, proceeds; gross receipts, net profit; earnings etc. (*gain*) 775.

rent, – roll; rent-al, -age; rack-rent.

premium, *bonus*; sweepstakes, tontine, prize, drawing.

pension, annuity; jointure etc. (*property*) 780; alimony, pittance; emolument etc. (*remuneration*) 973.

V. receive etc. 785; take money; draw –, derive- from; get, be in receipt of, acquire etc. 775; take etc. 789.

bring in, yield, afford, pay, return; accrue etc. (*be received from*) 785.

Adj. receiv-ing, -ed etc. *v.*; profitable etc. (*gainful*) 775.

811. Accounts.—N. accounts, accompts; commercial –, monetary- arithmetic; statistics etc. (*numeration*) 85; money matters, finance, budget, bill, score, reckoning, account.

books, account book, ledger; day –, cash –, pass- book; journal; debtor and creditor –, cash –, petty cash –, running- account; account-current; balance, – sheet; *compte rendu*, account settled.

book-keeping, audit; double –, single- entry; reckoning etc. 85.

chartered –, certified public –, accountant; auditor, actuary, bookkeeper; financier etc. 801; accounting party.

V. keep accounts, enter, post, book, credit, debit, carry over; take stock; balance –, make up –, square –, settle –, wind up –, cast up –, add up –, tot up- accounts; make accounts square.

bring to book, audit, tax, surcharge and falsify.

falsify –, garble –, cook –, doctor- an account.

Adj. monetary etc. 800; account-able, -ing; statistical.

812. Price.—N. price, amount, cost, expense, prime cost, charge, figure, demand, damage, fare, hire; wages etc. (*remuneration*) 973.

dues, duty, toll, tax impost, cess, sess, tallage, levy, capitation-, poll-, income-, sur-, sales-, super-tax; gabel, *gabelle*; gavel, *octroi*, custom, tariff, excise, assessment, taxation, benevolence, tithe, tenths, exactment, ransom, salvage; broker-, wharf-, lighter-, ton-, freight-age.

worth, rate, value, valuation, appraisement, money's worth, par value; penny etc. -worth; price current, market price, quotation; what it will -fetch etc. *v.*

bill etc. (*account*) 811; shot.

V. bear –, set –, fix- a price; appraise, assess, price, charge, demand, ask, require, exact, run up; distrain; run up a bill etc. (*debt*) 806; have one's price; liquidate.

amount to, come to, mount up to; stand one in. fetch, sell for, cost, bring in, yield, afford.

Adj. priced etc. *v.*; to the tune of, *ad valorem*; mercenary, venal.

Phr. no penny, no paternoster; *point d'argent, point de Suisse*, no longer pipe, no longer dance, no song, no supper.

one may have it for.

813. Discount.—N. discount, abatement, concession, reduction, depreciation, allowance, qualification, set off, drawback, poundage, *agio*, percentage; rebate, -ment; backwardation, contango; salvage; tare and tret.

V. discount, bate; a-, re-bate; deduct, reduce, mark down, take off, allow, give, make allowance; tax, depreciate.

Adj. discounting etc. *v.*

Adv. at a discount, below par.

814. Dearness.—N. dearness etc. *adj.*; high –, famine –, fancy- price; overcharge; extravagance; exorbitance, extortion; heavy pull upon the purse; Pyrrhic victory.

V. be -dear etc. *adj.*; cost -much, – a pretty penny; rise in price, look up.

overcharge, bleed, fleece, skin, extort.

pay -too much, – through the nose, –, too dear for one's whistle.

Adj. dear; high, -priced; of great price, expensive, costly, precious, worth a Jew's eye, dear bought; unreasonable, extravagant, exorbitant, extortionate.

at a premium; not to be had, – for love or money; beyond –, above- price; priceless, of priceless value.

Adv. dear, -ly; at great –, heavy- cost; *à grands frais*.

Phr. prices looking up; *le jeu ne vaut pas la chandelle*.

815. Cheapness.—N. cheapness, low price; depreciation; bargain; good penny etc.- worth, *bon marché*.

[Absence of charge] gratuity; free -quarters, – seats, – admission, – warren; pass, Annie Oakley; run of one's teeth; nominal price, peppercorn rent; labor of love.

drug in the market.

V. be -cheap etc. *adj.*; cost little; come down –, fall- in price.

buy for -a mere nothing, – an old song; have one's money's worth; cheapen, beat down.

Adj. cheap; low, – priced; moderate, reasonable; in-, un-expensive; well –, worth the money; *magnifique et pas cher*; good –, cheap- at the price; dirt –, dog- cheap; cheap, -as dirt, – and nasty; catchpenny.

reduced, marked down, half-price, depreciated, unsaleable.

gratuitous, *gratis*, free, for love, – nothing; cost-, expense-less; without charge, not charged, untaxed; scot –, shot –, rent- free; free of -cost, – expense; honorary, unbought, unpaid, complimentary.

Adv. for a mere song; at -cost price, – prime cost, – a reduction, – a bargain; on the cheap.

816. Liberality.—N. liberality, generosity, munificence; bount-y, -eousness, -ifulness; hospitality; charity etc. (*beneficence*) 906.

benefactor, free giver, Lady Bountiful.

V. be -liberal etc. *adj.*; spend –, bleed- freely; shower down upon; open one's purse strings etc. (*disburse*) 809; spare no expense, give -with both hands, – *carte blanche*.

Adj. liberal, free, generous; charitable etc. (*beneficent*) 906; hospitable; bount-iful, -eous; handsome; unsparing, ungrudging; open-, free-, full-handed; open-, large-, free-hearted; munificent, princely, unstinting.

overpaid.

Adv. liberally, ungrudgingly, with open hand.

817. Economy.—N. economy, frugality; thrift, -iness; prudence, care, husbandry, good housewifery, savingness, retrenchment.

savings; prevention of waste, save-all; cheese parings and candle ends, parsimony etc. 819.

V. be -economical etc. *adj.*; economize, save; retrench; cut- down expenses, – one's coat according to one's cloth, make both ends meet, keep within compass, meet one's expenses, pay one's way; keep one's head above water; husband etc. (*lay by*) 636; save –, invest- money; put out to interest; provide –, save- -for, – against- a rainy day; feather one's nest; look after the main chance.

Adj. economical, frugal, careful, thrifty, saving, chary, spare, sparing; parsimonious etc. 819.

underpaid.

Adv. sparingly etc. *adj.*; *ne quid nimis*.

818. Prodigality.—N. prodi-gality, -gence; unthriftiness, waste, -fulness; profus-ion, -eness; extravagance; squandering etc. *v.*; lavishness; malversation.

prodigal; spend-, waste-thrift; losel, play-boy, spender, squanderer, locust.

V. be -prodigal etc. *adj.*; squander, lavish, sow broadcast; pour forth like water; pay through the nose etc. (*dear*) 814; spill, waste, dissipate, exhaust, drain, eat out of house and home, overdraw, outrun the constable; run -out, – through; misspend; throw -good money after bad, – the helve after the hatchet; burn the candle at both ends; make ducks and drakes of one's money;

squander one's substance, spend money like water; fool –, potter –, muddle –, fritter –, throw-away one's money; pour water into a sieve, kill the goose that lays the golden eggs; *manger son blé en herbe*.

Adj. prodigal, profuse, thriftless, unthrifty, improvident, wasteful, losel, extravagant, lavish, dissipated, over liberal; full-handed etc. (*liberal*) 816.

penny wise and pound foolish.

Adv. with an unsparing hand; money burning one's pocket; recklessly profuse.

Int. hang the expense!

819. Parsimony.—N. parsimony, parcity; parsimoniousness, stinginess etc. *adj.*; stint; illiberality, avarice, tenacity, avidity, rapacity, extortion, venality, cupidity; selfishness etc. 943; *auri sacra fames*.

miser, niggard, churl, screw, tightwad, skinflint, crib, codger, muckworm, money-grubber, pinchfist, scrimp, lickpenny, hunks, curmudgeon, *Harpagon*, Silas Marner, harpy, extortioner, Jew, usurer.

V. be -parsimonious etc. *adj.*; grudge, begrudge, stint, skimp, pinch, gripe, screw, dole out, hold back, withhold, starve, famish, live upon nothing, skin a flint.

drive a -bargain, – hard bargain; cheapen, beat down; stop one hole in a sieve; have an itching palm, grasp, grab.

Adj. parsimonious, penurious, stingy, miserly, mean, shabby, peddling, scrubby, pennywise, near, niggardly, frugal to excess; close; fast-, close-, strait-handed; close-, hard-, tight-fisted; tight, sparing; chary; grudging, griping etc. *v.*; illiberal, ungenerous, churlish, hidebound, sordid, mercenary, venal, covetous, usurious, avaricious, greedy, extortionate, rapacious.

Adv. with a sparing hand.

820. Affections.—N. affections, character, qualities, disposition, nature, spirit, tone; temper, -ament; *diathesis*, idiosyncrasy; cast –, habit –, frame- of -mind, – soul; predilection, turn; natural –, turn of mind; bent, bias, predisposition, proneness, proclivity; propen-sity, -sedness, -sion, -dency; vein, humor, mood, grain, mettle; sympathy etc. (*love*) 897.

soul, heart, breast, bosom, inner man; heart's -core, – strings, – blood; heart of hearts, *penetralia mentis*; secret and inmost recesses of the –, cockles of one's- heart; inmost -heart, – soul; back-bone.

passion, pervading spirit; ruling –, master-passion; *furore*; fulness of the heart, heyday of the blood, flesh and blood, flow of soul, force of character.

V. have –, possess- -affections etc. *n.*; be of a -character etc. *n.*; be -affected etc. *adj.*; breathe.

Adj. affected, characterized, formed, molded, cast; at-, tempered; framed; pre-, disposed; prone, inclined; having a -bias etc. *n.*; tinctured –, imbued –, penetrated –, eaten up- with.

inborn, inbred, ingrained, in the grain, congenital, inherent, bred in the bone; deep-rooted, ineffaceable, inveterate; pathoscopic.

Adv. in one's -heart etc. *n.*; at heart; heart and soul etc. 821; in the -vein, – mood.

821. Feeling.—N. feeling; suffering etc. *v.*; endurance, tolerance, sufferance, supportance, experience, response; sympathy etc. (*love*) 897; impression, inspiration, affection, sensation, emotion, pathos, deep sense.

fire, warmth, glow, unction, *gusto*, vehemence; ferv-or, -ency; heartiness, cordiality; earnestness, eagerness; *empressment*, ardor, zeal, passion, enthusiasm, *verve, furore*, fanaticism; excitation of feeling etc. 824; fulness of the heart etc. (*disposition*) 820; passion etc. (*state of excitability*) 825; ecstasy etc. (*pleasure*) 827.

blush, suffusion, flush; hectic; tingling, thrill, kick, turn, shock; agitation etc. (*irregular motion*) 315; quiver, heaving, flutter, flurry, fluster, twitter, tremor; throb, -bing; pulsation, palpitation, painting; trepid-, perturb-ation; ruffle, hurry of spirits, pother, stew, ferment.

V. feel; receive an -impression etc. *n.*; be -impressed with etc. *adj.*; entertain –, harbor –, cherish- -feeling etc. *n.*

respond; catch the -flame, – infection; enter the spirit of.

bear, suffer, support, sustain, endure, brook, thole, aby; abide etc. (*be composed*) 826; experience etc. (*meet with*) 151; taste, prove; labor –, smart- under; bear the brunt of, brave, stand.

swell, glow, warm, flush, blush, change color, mantle; turn -color, – pale, – red, – black in the face; blench, crimson, whiten, pale, tingle, thrill, heave, pant, throb, palpitate, go pit-a-pat, tremble, quiver, flutter, twitter; stagger, reel; shake etc. 315; be -agitated, – excited etc. 824; look -blue, – black; wince, draw a deep breath.

impress etc. (*excite the feelings*) 824.

Adj. feeling etc. *v.*; sentient; sensuous; sensorial, -y; emo-tive, -tional; of –, with- feeling etc. *n.*

warm, quick, lively, smart, strong, sharp, acute, cutting, piercing, incisive; keen, – as a razor; trenchant, pungent, racy, *piquant*, poignant, caustic.

impressive, deep, profound, indelible; deep-, home-, heart-felt; swelling, soul-stirring, deep-mouthed, heart-expanding, electric, thrilling, rapturous, ecstatic.

earnest, wistful, eager, breathless; fer-vent, -vid; gushing, passionate, warmhearted, hearty, cordial, sincere, zealous, enthusiastic, glowing, ardent, burning, red-hot, fiery, flaming; boiling, – over.

pervading, penetrating, absorbing; rabid, raving feverish, fanatical, hysterical; impetuous etc. (*excitable*) 825; overmastering.

impressed –, moved –, touched –, affected –, penetrated –, seized –, imbued etc. 820- with; devoured by; wrought up etc. (*excited*) 824; struck all of a heap; rapt; in a -quiver etc. *n.*; enraptured etc. 829.

Adv. heart and soul, from the bottom of one's heart, *ab imo pectore*, *de profundis*, at heart, *con amore*, heartily, devoutly, over head and ears.

Phr. the heart -big, – full, – swelling, – beating, – pulsating, – throbbing, – thumping, – beating high, – melting, – overflowing, – bursting, – breaking.

822. Sensibility.—N. sensi-bility, -bleness, -tiveness; moral sensibility; impress-, affect-ibility; suscepti-bleness, -bility, -vity; mobility; viva-city, -ciousness; tender-, soft-ness; sentimental-ity, -ism.

excitability etc. 825; fastidiousness etc. 868; physical sensibility etc. 375.

sore -point, – place; where the shoe pinches.

V. be -sensible etc. *adj.*; have a -tender, – warm, – sensitive- heart.

take to –, treasure up in the- heart; shrink. 'die of a rose in aromatic pain;' touch to the quick.

Adj. sensi-ble, -tive; impressi-ble, -onable; suscepti-ve, -ble; alive to, impassion-able, -ed; gushing; warm-, tender-, soft-hearted; tender –, as a chicken; soft, sentimental, romantic; enthusiastic, highflying, spirited, mettlesome, vivacious, lively, expressive, mobile, tremblingly alive; excitable etc. 825; over-sensitive, without skin, thin-skinned; fastidious etc. 868.

Adv. sensibly etc. *adj.*; to the -quick, – inmost core.

823. Insensibility.—N. insensi-bility, -bleness; moral insensibility; inertness, *inertia, vis inertiae*; impassi-bility, -bleness; inappetency, apathy, phlegm, dulness, hebetude, supineness, lukewarmness, insusceptibility, unimpressibility.

cold -fit, – blood, – heart; cold-, cool-ness; frigidity, *sang-froid*; stoicism, imperturbation etc. (*inexcitability*) 826; *nonchalance*, unconcern, dry eyes; *insouciance* etc. (*indifference*) 866; recklessness etc. 863; callousness; heart of stone, stock and stone, marble, deadness.

torp-or, -idity; obstupefaction, lethargy, coma, trance; sleep etc. 683; suspended animation; stupor, -efaction; paralysis, palsy; numbness etc. (*physical insensibility*) 376.

neutrality; quietism, vegetation.

V. be -insensible etc. *adj.*; have a rhinoceros hide; show -insensibility etc. *n.*; not -mind, – care, – be affected by; have no desire for etc. 866; have –, feel –, take- no interest in; *nil admirari*; not care a -straw etc. (*unimportance*) 643 for; disregard etc. (*neglect*) 460; set at naught etc. (*make light of*) 483; turn a deaf ear to etc. (*inattention*) 458; vegetate.

render -insensible, – callous; blunt, obtund, numb, benumb, paralyze, chloroform, deaden, hebetate, stun, stupefy; brut-ify, -alize.

inure; harden, – the heart; steel, case-harden, sear.

Adj. insensible, unconscious; impassi-ve, -ble; blind to, deaf to, dead to; un-, in-susceptible; unimpress-ionable, -ible; passion-, spirit-, heart-, soulless; unfeeling, unmoral.

apathetic; leuco-, phlegmatic; dull, frigid; cold, -blooded, -hearted; unemotional; cold as charity; flat, obtuse, inert, supine, sluggish, torpid; sleepy etc. (*inactive*) 683; languid, half-hearted, tame; numb, -ed; comatose; anesthetic etc. 376; stupefied, chloroformed, palsy-stricken.

indifferent, lukewarm; Laodicean; careless, mindless, regardless; inattentive etc. 458; neglectful etc. 460; disregarding.

unconcerned, *nonchalant, pococurante, insouciant, sans souci*; unambitious etc. 866.

un-affected, -ruffled, -impressed, -inspired, -excited, -moved, -stirred, -touched, -shocked, -struck; unblushing etc. (*shameless*) 885; unanimated; vegetative.

callous, thick-skinned, pachydermatous, impervious; hard, -ened; inured, case-hardened; steeled –, proof- against; imperturbable etc. (*inexcitable*) 826; unfelt.

Adv. insensibly etc. *adj.*; *aequo animo*; without being -moved, – touched, – impressed; in cold blood; with -dry eyes, – withers unwrung.

Phr. never mind; it is of no consequence etc. (*unimportant*) 643; it cannot be helped; nothing coming amiss; it is all -the same, – one- to.

824. Excitation.—N. excitation of feeling; mental –, excitement; suscitation, galvanism, stimulation, piquancy, provocation inspiration, calling forth, infection; interest, animation, agitation, perturbation; subjugation, fascination, intoxication; en-, ravishment; entrancement, high pressure.

unction, impressiveness etc. *adj.*; emotional appeal; melodrama; psychological moment, crisis; sensationalism.

trail of temper, *casus belli*; irritation etc. (*anger*) 900; passion etc. (*state of excitability*) 825; thrill etc. (*feeling*) 821; repression of feeling etc. 826.

V. excite, affect, touch, move, impress, strike, interest, intrigue, animate, inspire, impassion, smite, infect; stir –, fire –, warm- the blood; set astir; a-, wake; a-, waken; call forth; e-, pro-voke; raise up, summon up, call up, wake up, blow up, get up, light up; raise; get up steam, rouse, arouse, stir, fire, kindle, enkindle, apply the torch, set on fire, inflame, illuminate.

stimulate; ex-, suscitate; inspirit; spirit up, stir up, work up; infuse life into, five new life to; bring –, introduce- new blood; quicken; sharpen, whet; work upon etc. (*incite*) 615; hurry on, give a fillip, put on one's mettle.

fan the -fire, – flame; blow the coals, stir the embers; fan, – into a flame; foster, heat, warm, foment, raise to a fever heat; keep -up, – the pot boiling; revive, rekindle; rake up, rip up.

stir –, play on –, come home to- the feelings; touch -a string, – a chord, – the soul, – the heart; go to one's heart, penetrate, pierce, go through one, touch to the quick, open the wound; possess –, pervade –, penetrate –, imbrue –, absorb –, affect –, disturb- the soul.

absorb, rivet the attention; sink into the -mind, – heart; prey on the mind; intoxicate; over-whelm, -power; *bouleverser*, upset, turn one's head.

fascinate; enrapture etc. (*give pleasure*) 829.

agitate, perturb, ruffle, fluster, flutter, shake, disturb, faze, startle, shock, stagger; give one a -shock, – turn; strike -dumb, – all of a heap; stun, astound, electrify, galvanize, petrify.

irritate, sting; cut, – to the -heart, – quick; try one's temper; fool to the top of one's bent, pique; infuriate, madden, make one's blood boil; lash into fury etc. (*wrath*) 900.

be -excited etc. *adj.*; flash up, flare up; catch the infection; thrill etc. (*feel*) 821; mantle; work oneself up; seethe, boil, simmer, foam, fume, flame, rage, rave; run mad etc. (*passion*) 825.

Adj. excited etc. *v.*; wrought up, on the *qui vive*, astir, sparkling; in a -quiver etc. 821, – fever, – ferment, – blaze, – state of excitement; in hysterics; black in the face, over-wrought; hot, red-hot, flushed, feverish; all -of a twitter, – of a flutter, – of a dither, – in a pucker; with -quivering lips, – tears in one's eyes.

flaming; boiling, – over; ebullient, seething; foaming, – at the mouth; fuming, raging, carried away by passion, wild, raving, frantic, mad, distracted, distraught, beside oneself, out of one's wits, amuck, ready to burst, *bouleversé*, demoniacal.

lost, *eperdu*, tempest-tossed; haggard; ready to sink.

stung to the quick, up, on one's high ropes.

exciting etc. *v.*; impressive, warm, glowing, fervid, swelling, imposing, spirit-stirring, thrilling; high-wrought; soul-stirring, -subduing; heart-swelling, -thrilling; agonizing etc. (*painful*) 830; telling, sensational, melodramatic, hysterical; overpowering, -whelming; more than flesh and blood can bear.

piquant etc. (*pungent*) 392; spicy, appetizing, provocative, *provaquant*, tantalizing.

Adv. till one is black in the face.

Phr. the heart -beating high, – going pit-a-pat, – leaping into one's mouth; the blood -being up, – boiling in one's veins; the eye -glistening, – 'in a fine frenzy rolling;' the head turned.

825. Excitability. [Excess of sensitiveness.]—**N.** excitability, impetuosity, vehemence; boisterousness etc. *adj.*; turbulence; impatience, intolerance, non-endurance; irritability etc. (*irascibility*) 901; itching etc. (*desire*) 865; wincing; disquiet, -ude; restlessness; fidge-ts, -tiness; agitation etc. (*irregular motion*) 315.

trepidation, perturbation, ruffle, hurry, -skurry, fuss, flurry; fluster, flutter; pother, stew, ferment; whirl; thrill etc. (*feeling*) 821; state –, fever- of excitement; transport.

passion, excitement, flush, heat; fever, -heat; fire, flame, fume, blood boiling; tumult; effervescence, ebullition; boiling, – over; whiff, gust, storm, tempest; scene, breaking out, burst, fit, paroxysm, explosion; out-break, -burst; agony.

violence etc. 173; fierceness etc. *adj.*; rage, fury, *furor*, *furore*, desperation, madness, distraction, raving, delirium, brain storm; frenzy, hysterics; intoxication; tearing –, raging- passion, towering rage; anger etc. 900.

fascination, infatuation, fanaticism; Quixot-ism, -ry; *tête montée*.

V. be -impatient etc. *adj.*; not be able to -bear etc. 826; bear ill, wince, chafe, champ the bit; be in a -stew etc. *n.*; be out of all patience, fidget, fuss, not have a wink of sleep; toss, – on one's pillow.

lose one's temper etc. 900; break –, burst –, fly- out; go –, fly- -off, – off the handle, – off at a tangent; explode; flare up, flame up, fire up, burst into a flame, take fire, fire, burn; boil, – over; foam, fume, rage, rave, rant, tear; go –, run- -wild, – mad; go into hysterics; run -riot, – amuck; *battre la campagne, faire le diable à quatre*, play the deuce; raise -Cain, – the devil.

Adj. excitable, easily excited, in an excitable state; high strung; irritable etc. (*irascible*) 901; impatient, intolerant.

feverish, febrile, hysterical; delirious, mad, moody, maggoty-headed.

unquiet, mercurial, electric, galvanic, hasty, hurried, restless, fidgety, fussy; chafing etc. *v.*

startlish, mettlesome, high mettled, skittish.

vehement, demonstrative, violent, wild, furious, fierce, fiery, hot-headed, mad-cap.

over-zealous, enthusiastic, impassioned, fanatical; rabid etc. (*eager*) 865.

rampant, clamorous, uproarious, turbulent, tempestuous, tumultuary, boisterous.

impulsive, impetuous, passionate; uncontroll-ed, -able; ungovernable, irrepressible, stanchless, inextinguishable, burning, simmering, volcanic, ready to burst forth.

excit-ed, -ing etc. 824.

Int. pish! pshaw!

Phr. *noli me tangere*.

826. Inexcitability. [Absence of excitability, or of excitement.]—**N.** inexcit-, imperturb-, inirritability; even temper, tranquil mind, dispassion; tolerance, toleration, patience.

passiveness etc. (*physical inertness*) 172; hebetude, -ation; impassibility etc. (*insensibility*) 823; stupefaction.

coolness, calmness etc. *adj.*; composure, placidity, indisturbance, imperturbation, *sang-froid*, tranquility, serenity; quiet, -ude; peace of mind, mental calmness.

staidness etc. *adj.*; gravity, sobriety, Quakerism; philosophy, equanimity, stoicism, command of temper; self-possession, -control, -command, -restraint; presence of mind.

submission etc. 725; resignation; suffer-, support-, endur-, long-suffer-, forbear-ance; longanimity; fortitude; patience -of Job, – 'on a monument,' – 'sovereign o'er transmuted ill;' moderation; repression –, subjugation- of feeling; restraint etc. 751.

tranquilization etc. (*moderation*) 174.

V. be -composed etc. *adj.*

laisser -faire, – *aller*; take things -easily, – as they come; take it easy, run on, live and let live; take -easily, – cooly, – in good part; *aequam serva e mentem*.

bear, – well, – the brunt; go through, support, endure, brave, disregard.

tolerate, suffer, stand, bide; abide, aby; bear –, put up –, abide- with; acquiesce; submit etc. (*yield*) 725; submit with a good grace; resign –, reconcile- oneself to; brook, digest, eat, swallow, pocket, stomach; make -light of, – the best of, – a virtue of necessity; put a good face on, keep one's countenance; carry -on, – through; check etc. 751- oneself.

compose, appease etc. (*moderate*) 174; propitiate; repress etc. (*restrain*) 751; render insensible etc. 823; overcome –, allay –, repress- one's -excitability etc. 825; master one's feelings.

make -oneself, – one's mind- easy; set one's mind at -ease, – rest.

calm –, cool- down; thaw, grow cool.

be -borne, – endured; go down.

Adj. in-, un-excitable; imperturbable; unsusceptible etc. (*insensible*) 823; un-, dispassionate; cold-blooded, inirritable; enduring etc. *v.*; stoical, Platonic, philosophic, staid, stayed; sober, – minded; grave; sober –, grave- as a judge; sedate, demure, cool-, level-headed; steady.

easy-going, peaceful, placid, calm; quiet, – as a mouse; tranquil, serene; cool, – as -a cucumber, – custard; undemonstrative.

temperate etc. (*moderate*) 174; composed, collected; un-excited, -stirred, -ruffled, -disturbed, -perturbed, -impassioned; unoffended; unresisting.

meek, tolerant; patient, – as Job; submissive etc. 725; tame; content, resigned, chastened, subdued, lamblike; gentle, – as a lamb; *suaviter in modo*; mild, – as mother's milk; soft as peppermint; armed with patience, bearing with, clement, forbearant, long-suffering.

Adv. 'like patience on a monument smiling at grief;' *aequo animo*, in cold blood etc. 823; more in sorrow than in anger.

Int. patience! and shuffle the cards.

827. Pleasure.—N. pleasure, gratification, enjoyment, fruition; ob-, de-lectation; relish, zest; *gusto* etc. (*physical pleasure*) 377; satisfaction etc. (*content*) 831; complacency.

well-being; good etc. 618; snugness, comfort, ease; cushion etc. 215; *sans souci*, mind at ease.

joy, gladness, delight, glee, cheer, sunshine; cheerfulness etc. 836.

treat, refreshment; frolic, fun, lark, gambol, merry-making; amusement etc. 840; luxury etc. 377; hedonism.

mens sana in corpore sano.

happiness, felicity, bliss; beati-tude, -fication; enchantment, transport, rapture, ravishment, ecstasy; *summum bonum*; paradise, elysium etc. (*heaven*) 981; third –, seventh- heaven; unalloyed - happiness etc.

honeymoon; palmy –, halcyon- days; golden - age, – time; *Saturnia regna*, Eden, Arcadia, happy valley, Agapemone; Cockaigne.

V. be pleased etc. 829; feel –, experience- pleasure etc. *n.*; joy; enjoy –, hug- oneself; be in - clover etc. 377, – elysium etc. 981; tread on enchanted ground; fall –, go- into raptures.

feel at home, breathe freely, bask in the sunshine.

be -pleased etc. 829- with; receive –, derive- pleasure etc. *n.*- from; take -pleasure etc. *n.*- in; delight in, rejoice in, indulge in, luxuriate in; gloat over etc. (*physical pleasure*) 377; enjoy, relish, like; love etc. 897; take -to, – a fancy to; have a liking for; enter into the spirit of.

take in good part.

treat oneself to, solace oneself with.

Adj. pleased etc. 829; not sorry; glad, -some; pleased as Punch.

happy, blest, blessed, blissful, beatified; happy as -a king, – the day is long; thrice happy, *ter quaterque beatus*; enjoying etc. *v.*; joyful etc. (*in spirits*) 836; hedonic.

in -a blissful state, – paradise etc. 981; – raptures, – ecstasies, – a transport of delight.

comfortable etc. (*physical pleasure*) 377; at ease; content etc. 831; *sans souci*, in clover.

overjoyed, entranced, enchanted; enraptured; en-, ravished; transported; fascinated, captivated.

with -a joyful face, – sparkling eyes.

pleasing etc. 829; ecstatic, beat-ic, -ific; painless, unalloyed, without alloy, cloudless.

Adv. happily etc. *adj.*; with pleasure etc. (*willingly*) 60; with -glee etc. *n.*

phr. one's heart leaping with joy.

828. Pain.—N. mental suffering, pain, dolor; suffer-ing, -ance; ache, smart etc. (*physical pain*) 378; passion.

displeasure, dissatisfaction, discomfort, discomposure, disquiet; *malaise*; inquietude, uneasiness, vexation of spirit; taking; discontent etc. 832.

dejection etc. 837; weariness etc. 841.

annoyance, irritation, worry, infliction, visitation; plague, bore; bother, -ation; stew, vexation, mortification, chagrin, *esclandre*; *mauvais quart d'heure.*

care, anxiety, solicitude, trouble, trial, ordeal, fiery ordeal, shock, blow, cark, dole, fret, burden, load.

concern, grief, sorrow, distress, affliction, woe, bitterness, gloom, heartache; heavy –, aching –, bleeding –, broken- heart; heavy affliction, gnawing grief; unhappiness, infelicity, misery, tribulation, wretchedness, desolation; despair etc. 859; extremity, prostration, depth of misery.

nightmare, *ephialtes*, incubus.

anguish, agony; throe, tor-ture, -ment; crucifixion, martyrdom; pang, twinge, stab; the rack, the stake; purgatory etc. (*hell*) 982.

hell upon earth; iron age, reign of terror; slough of despond etc. (*adversity*) 735; peck –, sea- of troubles; ills that flesh is heir to etc. (*evil*) 619; miseries of human life; unkindest cut of all.

sufferer, victim, prey, martyr, object of compassion, wretch, shorn lamb.

V. feel –, suffer –, experience –, undergo –, bear –, endure- pain etc. *n.*; smart, ache etc. (*physical pain*) 378; suffer, bleed, ail; be the victim of; bear – take up- the cross.

labor under afflictions; quaff the bitter cup, have a bad time of it; fall on evil days etc. (*adversity*) 735; go hard with, come to grief, fall a sacrifice to, drain the cup of misery to the dregs, sup full of horrors.

sit on thorns, be on pins and needles, wince, fret, chafe, worry oneself, be in a taking, fret and fume, take -on, – to heart.

grieve; mourn etc. (*lament*) 839; yearn, repine, pine, droop, languish, sink; give way; despair etc. 859; break one's heart; weigh upon the heart etc. (*inflict pain*) 830.

Adj. in –, in a state of –, full of- pain etc. *n.*; suffering etc. *v.*; pained, afflicted, worried, displeased etc. 830; aching, griped, sore etc. (*physical pain*) 378; on the rack; in limbo; between hawk and buzzard.

un-comfortable, -easy; ill at ease; in a -taking, – way; disturbed; discontented etc. 832; out of humor etc. 901*a*; weary etc. 841.

heavy laden, stricken, crushed, a prey to, victimized, ill-used.

unfortunate etc. (*hapless*) 735; to be pitied, doomed, devoted, accursed, undone, lost, stranded.

unhappy, infelicitous, poor, wretched, miserable, woe-begone; cheerless etc. (*dejected*) 837; careworn.

concerned, sorry; sorrow-ing, -ful; cut up, chagrined, horrified, horror-stricken; in –, plunged in –, a prey to- grief etc. *n.*; in tears etc. (*lamenting*) 839; steeped to the lips in misery; heart-stricken, -broken, -scalded; broken-hearted; in despair etc. 859.

Phr. 'the iron entered into our soul;' *haeret lateri lethalis arundo*;' one's heart bleeding.

829. Pleasurableness. [Capability of giving pleasure; cause or source of pleasure.]—**N.** pleasurable-, pleasant-, agreeable-ness etc. *adj.*; pleasure giving, jocundity, delectability; amusement etc. 840.

attraction etc. (*motive*) 615; attractiveness, -

ability; invitingness etc. *adj.*; charm, fascination, captivation, enchantment, witchery, seduction, winsomeness, winning ways, amenity, amiability, sweetness.

loveliness etc. (*beauty*) 845; sunny –, bright-side; sweets etc. (*sugar*) 396; goodness etc. 648; manna in the wilderness, land flowing with milk and honey.

treat; regale etc. (*physical pleasure*) 377; dainty; tit-, tid-bit; nuts, *sauce piquante*.

V. cause –, produce –, create –, give –, afford –, procure –, offer –, present –, yield- pleasure etc. 827.

please, charm, delight; gladden etc. (*make cheerful*) 836; take, captivate, fascinate; enchant, entrance, enrapture, transport, bewitch; en-, ravish.

bless, beatify; satisfy; gratify –, desire etc. 865; slake, satiate, quench; indulge, humor, flatter, tickle; tickle the palate etc. (*savory*) 394; regale, refresh; enliven; treat; amuse etc. 840; take –, tickle –, hit- one's fancy; meet one's wishes; win –, gladden –, rejoice –, warm the cockles of- the heart; do one's heart good.

attract, allure etc. (*move*) 615; stimulate etc. (*excite*) 824; interest, intrigue.

make things pleasant, popularize, gild the pill, sweeten.

Adj. causing pleasure etc. *v.*; pleasure-giving; pleas-ing, -ant, -urable; agreeable, cushy; grat-eful, -ifying; leef, lief, acceptable; welcome, – as the roses in May; welcomed; favorite; to one's -taste, – mind, – liking, – heart's content; satisfactory etc. (*good*) 648.

refreshing; comfortable; cordial; genial; glad, -some; sweet, delectable, nice, dainty; delic-ate, -ious; dulcet; luscious etc. 396; palatable etc. 394; luxurious, voluptuous; sensual etc. 377.

attractive etc. 615; inviting, prepossessing, engaging; win-ning, -some; taking, fascinating, captivating, killing; seduc-ing, -tive; alluring, enticing; appetizing etc. (*exciting*) 824; cheering etc. 836; bewitching; interesting, absorbing, enchanting, entrancing, enravishing.

charming; delightful, felicitous, exquisite; lovely etc. (*beautiful*) 845; ravishing, rapturous; heartfelt, thrilling, ecstatic; beat-ic, -ific; seraphic; empyrean; elysian etc. (*heavenly*) 981.

palmy, halcyon, Saturnian.

Phr. *decies repetita placebit.*

830. Painfulness. [Capability of giving pain; cause or source of pain.]—**N.** painfulness etc. *adj.*; trouble, care etc. (*pain*) 828; trial; af-, in-fliction; cross, blow, stroke, burden, load, curse; bitter -pill, – draught, – cup; waters of bitterness.

annoyance, grievance, nuisance, vexation, mortification, sickener; bore, bother, pother, hot water, sea of troubles, hornet's nest, plague, pest.

cancer, ulcer, sting, thorn; canker etc. (*bane*) 663; scorpion etc. (*evil-doer*) 913; dagger etc. (*arms*) 727; scourge etc. (*instrument of punishment*) 975; carking –, canker worm of- care.

mishap, misfortune etc. (*adversity*) 735; *désagrément, esclandre*, rub.

source of -irritation, – annoyance; wound, sore subject, skeleton in the closet; thorn in -the flesh, – one's side; where the shoe pinches, gall and wormwood.

sorry sight, heavy news, provocation; affront etc. 929; head and front of one's offending.

infestation, molestation; malignity etc. (*malevolence*) 907.

V. cause –, occasion –, give –, bring –, induce –, produce –, create –, inflict- pain etc. 828; pain, hurt, wound.

pinch, prick, gripe etc. (*physical pain*) 378; pierce, lancinate, cut.

hurt –, wound –, grate upon –, jar upon- the feelings; wring –, pierce –, lacerate –, break –, rend- the heart; make the heart bleed; tear –, rend- the heart-strings; draw tears from the eyes.

sadden; make -unhappy etc. 828; plunge into sorrow, grieve, fash, afflict, distress; cut -up, – to the heart.

displease, annoy, incommode, discommode, discompose, trouble, disquiet, disturb, thwart, cross, perplex, molest, tease, rag, tire, irk, vex, mortify, wherret, worry, plague, bother, pester, bore, pother, harass, harry, badger, heckle, bait, beset, infest, persecute, importune, be troublesome.

wring, harrow, torment, torture; put to the -rack, – question; break on the wheel, rack, scarify; cruci-ate, -fy; convulse, agonize; barb the dart; plant a -dagger in the breast, – thron in one's side.

irritate, provoke, sting, nettle, try the patience, pique, fret, rile, tweak the nose, chafe, gall; sting –, wound –, cut- to the quick; aggrieve, affront, enchafe, enrage, ruffle, sour the temper; give offence etc. (*resentment*) 900.

maltreat, bite, snap at, assail, bully; smite etc. (*punish*) 972.

sicken, disgust, revolt, nauseate, disenchant, repel, offend, shock, stink in the nostrils; go against –, turn- the stomach; make one sick, set the teeth on edge, go against the grain, grate on the ear; stick in one's -throat, – gizzard; rankle, gnaw, corrode, horrify, appal, freeze the blood; chill the spine; make the -flesh creep, – hair stand on end; make the blood -curdle, – run cold; make one shudder.

haunt, – the memory; weigh –, prey- on the -heart, – mind, – spirits; bring one's grey hairs with sorrow to the grave; add a nail to one's coffin.

Adj. causing pain, hurting etc. *v.*; hurtful etc. (*bad*) 649; painful; dolor-ific, -ous; unpleasant; un-, dis-pleasing; disagreeable, unpalatable, bitter, distasteful; uninviting; unwelcome; undesir-able, -ed; obnoxious; unacceptable, unpopular, thankless.

unsatisfactory, untoward, unlucky, uncomfortable.

distressing; afflict-ing, -ive; joy-, cheer-, comfortless; dismal, disheartening; depress-ing, -ive; dreary, melancholy, grievous, piteous; woeful, rueful, mournful, deplorable, pitiable, lamentable; sad, affecting, touching, pathetic.

irritating, provoking, stinging, annoying, aggravating, mortifying, galling; unaccommodating, invidious, vexatious; trouble-, tire-, irk-, weari-some; plagu-ing, -y; awkward.

importunate; teas-, pester-, bother-, harass-, worry-, torment-, cark-ing.

in-toler-, -suffer-, -support-able; un-bear-, -endur-able; past bearing; not to be -borne, – endured; more than flesh and blood can bear; enough to -drive one mad, – provoke a saint, – make a parson swear, – try the patience of Job.

shocking, terrific, grim, appalling, crushing; dreadful, fearful, frightful; thrilling, tremendous, dire; heart-breaking, -rending, -wounding, corroding, -sickening; harrowing, rending.

odious, hateful, execrable, repulsive, repellent, abhorrent; horri-d, -ble, -fic, -fying; offensive; nause-ous, -ating; disgust-, sicken-, revolt-ing; nasty; loath-some, -ful; fulsome; vile etc. (*bad*) 649; hideous etc. 846.

sharp, acute, sore, severe, grave, hard, harsh, cruel, biting, acrimonious, caustic; cutting, corroding, consuming, racking, excruciating, searching, searing, grinding, grating, agonizing; envenomed.

ruinous, disastrous, calamitous, tragical; desolating, withering; burdensome, onerous, oppressive; cumb-rous, -ersome.

Adv. painfully etc. *adj.*; with -pain etc. 828; deuced.

Int. *hinc illae lachrymae!* woe is me!

Phr. *surgit amari aliquid*; the place being too hot to hold one; the iron entering the soul.

831. Content.—N. content, -ment, -edness; complacency, satisfaction, entire satisfaction, ease, heart's ease, peace of mind; serenity etc. 826; cheerfulness etc. 836; ray of comfort; comfort etc. (*well-being*) 827.

re-, conciliation; resignation etc. (*patience*) 826.

waiter on Providence.

V. be -content etc. *adj.*; rest -satisfied, – and be thankful; take the good the gods provide, let well alone, feel oneself at home, hug oneself, lay the flattering unction to one's soul.

take -up with, – in good part; assent etc. 488; be reconciled to, make one's peace with; get over it; take -heart, – comfort; put up with etc. (*bear*) 826.

render -content etc. *adj.*; set at ease, comfort; set one's -heart, – mind- at -ease, – rest; speak peace; conciliate, reconcile, win over, propitiate, disarm, beguile; content, satisfy; gratify etc. 829.

be -tolerated etc. 826; go down, – with; do.

Adj. content, -ed; satisfied etc. *v.*; at -ease, – one's ease, – home; with the mind at ease, *sans souci, sine curâ*, easy-going, not particular; conciliatory; unrepining, of good comfort; resigned etc. (*patient*) 826; cheerful etc. 836.

un-afflicted, -vexed, -molested, -plagued; serene etc. 826; at rest; snug, comfortable; in one's element.

satisfactory, satisfying, ample, sufficient, adequate, tolerable.

Adv. to one's heart's content; *à la bonne heure*; all for the best.

Int. amen etc. (*assent*) 488; very well, so much the better, well and good; it –, that- will do; it cannot be helped.

Phr. nothing comes amiss.

832. Discontent.—N. discontent, -ment; dissatisfaction; dissent etc. 489; labor unrest.

disappointment, mortification; cold comfort; regret etc. 833; repining, taking on etc. *v.*; inquietude, vexation of spirit, soreness; heart-burning, -grief; querulousness etc. (*lamentation*) 839; hypercriticism.

malcontent, grumbler, growler, croaker, *laudator temporis acti*; censurer, complainer, faultfinder, murmurer, Adullamite, Diehard, Bitterender.

the Opposition, cave of Adullam, indignation meeting, 'winter of our discontent.'

V. be -discontented etc. *adj.*; quarrel with one's bread and butter; repine; regret etc. 833; wish one at the bottom of the Red Sea; take -on, – to heart; shrug the shoulders; make a wry –, pull a long- face; knit one's brows; look -blue, – black, – black as thunder, – blank, – glum.

take -in bad part, – ill; fret, chafe, make a piece of work; grumble, croak, grouse; lament etc. 839.

cause -discontent etc. *n.*; dissatisfy, disappoint, mortify, put out, disconcert; cut up; dishearten.

Adj. discontented; dissatisfied etc. *v.*; unsatisfied, ungratified; dissident; dissentient etc. 489; malcontent, exigent, exacting, hypercritical.

repining etc. *v.*; regretful etc. 833; down in the mouth etc. (*dejected*) 837.

in -high dudgeon, – a fume, – the sulks, – the dumps, – bad humor; glum, sulky; sour, – as a crab; soured, sore; out of -humor, – temper.

disappointing etc. *v.*; unsatisfactory.

Int. so much the worse!

Phr. that –, it- will never do.

833. Regret.—N. regret, repining; home sickness, nostalgia; *mal –, maladie- du pays*; lamentation etc. 839; contrition, compunction, penitence etc. 950.

bitterness, heart-burning.

laudator temporis acti etc. (*discontent*) 832.

V. regret, deplore; bewail etc. (*lament*) 839; repine, cast a longing lingering look behind; rue, – the day; repent etc. 950; *infandum renovare dolorem*.

prey –, weigh –, have a weight- on the mind; leave an aching void.

Adj. regretting etc. *v.*; regretful; home-sick

regretted etc. *v.*; much to be regretted, regrettable; lamentable etc. (*bad*) 649.

Int. what a pity! hang it!

Phr. 'tis -pity, – too true.

834. Relief.—N. relief; deliverance; refreshment etc. 689; easement, softening, alleviation, mitigation, palliation etc. 174; soothing, lullaby; cradle song, *berceuse*.

solace, consolation, comfort, encouragement.

lenitive, restorative etc. (*remedy*) 662; poultice etc. *v.*; cushion etc. 215; crumb of comfort, balm in Gilead; aspirin.

V. relieve, ease, alleviate, mitigate, palliate, soothe, addulce; salve; soften, – down; foment, stupe, poultice; assuage, allay.

cheer, comfort, console; encourage, bear up, pat on the back, give comfort, set at ease; enliven, gladden –, cheer- the heart.

remedy; cure etc. (*restore*) 660; refresh; pour - balm into, – oil on.

smoothe the ruffled brow of care, temper the wind to the shorn lamb, lay the flattering unction to one's soul.

disburden etc. (*free*) 705; take off a load of care.

be relieved; breathe more freely, draw a long breath; take comfort; dry –, wipe- the -tears, – eyes.

Adj. relieving etc. *v.*; consolatory, soothing; assua-ging, -sive; bal-my, -samic; lenitive, palliative; anodyne etc. (*remedial*) 662; curative etc. 660.

835. Aggravation.—N. aggravation, heightening; exacerbation; exasperation; overestimation etc. 482; exaggeration etc. 549.

V. aggravate, render worse, heighten, embitter, sour; ex-, acerbate; exasperate, envenom; tease, provoke, enrage.

add fuel to the -fire, – flame; fan the flame etc. (*excite*) 824; go from bad to worse etc. (*deteriorate*) 659.

Adj. aggravated etc. *v.*; worse, unrelieved; aggravable; aggravating etc. *v.*

Adv. out of the frying pan into the fire, from bad to worse, worse and worse.

Int. so much the worse!

836. Cheerfulness.—N. cheerfulness etc. *adj.*; geniality, gaiety, *l'allegro*, cheer, good humor, spirits; high –, animal –, flow of- spirits; glee, high glee, light heart; sunshine of the -mind, – breast; *gaieté de coeur, bon naturel.*

liveliness etc. *adj.*; life, alacrity, vivacity, animation, *allégresse*; jocundity, joviality, jollity; levity; jocularity etc. (*wit*) 842.

mirth, merriment, hilarity, exhilaration; laughter etc. 838; merry-making etc. (*amusement*) 840; heyday, rejoicing etc. 838; marriage bells.

nepenthe, Euphrosyne.

optimism etc. (*hopefulness*) 858; self-complacency.

V. be -cheerful etc. *adj.*; have the mind at ease, smile, put a good face upon, keep up one's spirits; view -the bright side of the picture, – things *en couleur de rose*; *ridentem dicere verum*, cheer up, brighten up, light up, bear up; chirp, take heart, cast away care, drive dull care away, perk up.

rejoice etc. 838; carol, chirrup, lilt; frisk, rollick, give a loose to mirth.

cheer, enliven, elate, exhilarate, gladden, in-spirit, animate, raise the spirits, inspire; put in good humor; cheer –, rejoice- the heart; delight etc. (*give pleasure*) 829.

Adj. cheerful; happy etc. 827; cheer-y, -ly; of good cheer, smiling; blithe; in –, in good- spirits; in high -spirits, – feather; happy as -the day is long, – a king; gay, – as a lark; *allegro*; light, -some, -hearted; buoyant, *débonnaire*, bright, free and easy, airy; janty, jaunty, canty; spright-ly, -ful; spry; spirit-ed, -ful; lively; animated, breezy, vivacious; brisk, – as a bee; sparkling; sportive; full of -play, – spirit; all alive.

sunny, palmy; hopeful etc. 858.

merry, – as a -cricket, – grig, – marriage bell; joyful, joyous, jocund, jovial; jolly, – as a thrush, – as a sandboy; blithesome; glee-ful, -some; hilarious, rattling.

winsome, bonny, hearty, buxom.

play-ful, -some; *folâtre*, playful as a kitten, tricksy, frisky, frolicsome; gamesome; jocose, jocular, waggish; mirth-, laughter-loving; mirthful, rollicking.

elate, -d; exulting, jubilant, flushed; rejoicing etc. 838; cock-a-hoop.

cheering, inspiriting, exhilarating; cardiac, -al; pleasing etc. 829; flourishing, halcyon.

Adv. cheerfully etc. *adj.*

Int. never say die! come! cheer up! hurrah! etc. 838; 'hence loathed melancholy!' begone dull care! away with melancholy!

837. Dejection.—N. dejection; dejectedness etc. *adj.*; depression, prosternation; lowness –, depression- of spirits; weight –, oppression –, damp- on the spirits; low –, bad –, drooping –, depressed- spirits; heart sinking; heaviness –, failure- of heart.

heaviness etc. *adj.*; infestivity, gloom; weariness etc. 841; *taedium vitae*, disgust of life; *mal du pays* etc. (*regret*) 833.

melancholy; sadness etc. *adj.*; *il penseroso, melancholia*, dismals, mumps, mopes, lachrymals, dumps, blues, blue devils, doldrums, vapors, megrims, spleen, horrors, hypochondriasis, pessimism; despondency, slough of Despond; disconsolateness etc. *adj.*; hope deferred, blank despondency.

prostration, – of soul; broken heart; despair etc. 859; cave of -despair, – Trophonius.

demureness etc. *adj.*; gravity, solemnity; long –, grave- face.

hypochondriac, seek-sorrow, self-tormentor, *heautontimorumenos, malade imaginaire, médecin tant pis*; croaker, pessimist; mope, mopus.

[Cause of dejection] affliction etc. 830; sorry sight; *memento mori*; damper, wet blanket, Job's comforter; death's head, skeleton at the feast.

V. be -dejected etc. *adj.*; grieve; mourn etc. (*lament*) 839; take on, give way, lose heart, despond, droop, sink.

lower, look downcast, frown, pout; hang down the head; pull –, make- a long face; laugh on the wrong side of the mouth; grin a ghastly smile; look -blue, – like a drowned man; lay –, take- to heart.

mope, brood over; fret; sulk; pine, – away; yearn; repine etc. (*regret*) 833; despair etc. 859.

refrain from laughter, keep one's countenance; be –, look- grave etc. *adj.*; repress a smile, keep a straight face.

depress; dis-courage, -hearten; dis-pirit; damp, dull, deject, lower, sink, dash, knock down, un-man, prostrate, break one's heart; frown upon; cast a -gloom, – shade- on; sadden; damp –, dash –, wither- one's hopes; weigh –, lie heavy –, prey-on the -mind, – spirits; damp –, depress- the spirits.

Adj. cheer-, joy-, spirit-less; uncheer-ful, -y; unlively; unhappy etc. 828; melancholy, dismal, somber, dark, gloomy, adust, *triste*, clouded, murky, lowering, frowning, lugubrious, Acheron-tic, funereal, mournful, lamentable, dreadful.

dreary, flat; dull, – as -a beetle, – ditchwater; depressing etc. *v.*

'melancholy as a gib cat;' oppressed with –; a prey to- melancholy; down-cast, -hearted; down -in the mouth, – on one's luck; heavy-hearted; in the -dumps, – suds, – sulks, – doldrums; in doleful dumps, in bad humor; sullen; mumpish, dumpish; mopish, moping; moody, glum; sulky etc. (*discontented*) 832; out of -sorts, – humor, – heart, – spirits; ill at ease, low-spirited, in low spirits, a cup too low; weary etc. 841; dis-couraged, -heartened; desponding; chop-, jaw-, crest-fallen.

sad, pensive, *penseroso*, tristful; dole-some, -ful; woebegone, lachrymose, in tears, melancholic, hypped, hypochondriacal, bilious, jaundiced, atrabilious, saturnine, splenetic; lackadaisical.

serious, sedate, staid, stayed; grave, – as -a judge, – an undertaker, – a mustard pot; sober, solemn, demure; grim; grim-faced, -visaged; rueful, wan, long-faced.

disconsolate; un-, in-consolable; forlorn, comfortless, desolate, *désolé*, sick at heart; soul-, heart-sick; *au désepoir*; in despair etc. 859; lost.

overcome; broken-, borne-, bowed-down; heart-stricken etc. (*mental suffering*) 828; cut up, dashed, sunk; unnerved, unmanned; down-fallen, -trodden; broken-hearted; care-worn.

Adv. with -a long face, – tears in one's eyes; sadly etc. *adj.*

Phr. the countenance falling; the heart -failing, – sinking within- one.

838. Rejoicing. [Expression of pleasure.]—**N.** rejoicing, exultation, triumph, jubilation, heyday, flush, revelling; merry-making etc. (*amusement*) 840; jubilee etc. (*celebration*) 883; *paean*, *Te Deum* etc. (*thanksgiving*) 990; congratulation etc. 896; applause etc. 971.

smile, simper, smirk, grin; broad –, sardonic-grin.

laughter, giggle, titter, crow, cheer, chuckle, snicker, snigger, shout; Homeric laughter, horse –, hearty- laugh; guffaw; burst –, fit –, shout –, roar –, peal- of laughter; cachinnation.

risibility; derision etc. 856.

Momus; Democritus the Abderite; rollicker; Laughter holding both his sides.

V. rejoice; thank –, bless- one's stars; congratulate –, hug- oneself; rub –, clap- one's hands; smack the lips, fling up one's cap; dance, skip, caleer; sing, carol, chirrup, chirp; hurrah; cry for –, leap with- joy; exult etc. (*boast*) 884; triumph; hold jubilee etc. (*celebrate*) 883; make merry etc. (*sport*) 840; sing a paean of joy.

smile, simper, smirk; grin, – like a Cheshire cat; mock, laugh in one's sleeve; laugh, – outright; giggle, titter, snigger, crow, smicker, chuckle, snicker, cackle; burst -out, – into a fit of laughter; shout, split, roar.

shake –, split –, hold both- one's sides; roar –, die- with laughter.

raise laughter etc. (*amuse*) 840.

Adj. rejoicing etc. *v.*; jubilant, exultant, triumphant; flushed, elated; laughing etc. *v.*; risible; ready to -burst, – split, – die with laughter; convulsed with laughter.

laughable etc. (*ludicrous*) 853.

Int. hip, hip, -hurrah! huzza! aha! hail! tolderolloll! tra-la la! Heaven be praised! *io triumphe! tant mieux!* so much the better.

Phr. the heart leaping with joy.

839. Lamentation. [Expression of pain.]—**N.** lament, -ation; wail, complaint, plaint, murmur, mutter, grumble, groan, moan, whine, whimper, sob, sigh, suspiration, heaving, deep sigh.

cry etc. (*vociferation*) 411; scream, howl; outcry, wail of woe, frown, scowl.

tear; weeping etc. *v.*; flood of tears, fit of crying, lachrymation, melting mood, weeping and gnashing of teeth.

plaintiveness etc. *adj.*; languishment; condolence etc. 915.

mourning, weeds, willow, cypress, crêpe, crape, deep mourning; sackcloth and ashes; knell etc. 363; dump, deathsong, dirge, coronach, keen, *nenia*, requiem, elegy, *epicedium*; threne; mon-, thren-ody; jeremiad; ululation.

mourner, professional mourner, keener; grumbler etc. (*discontent*) 832; Niobe; Heraclitus.

V. lament, mourn, deplore, grieve, weep over; be-wail, -moan; keen; condole with etc. 915; fret etc. (*suffer*) 828; wear –, go into –, put on- mourning; wear -the willow, – sackcloth and ashes; *infandum renovare dolorem* etc. (*regret*) 833; give sorrow words.

sigh; give –, heave –, fetch- a sigh; 'waft a sigh from Indus to the pole;' sigh 'like furnace;' wail.

cry, weep, sob, greet, blubber, pipe, snivel, bibber, whimper, pule; pipe one's eye; drop –, shed- -tears, – a tear; melt –, burst- into tears; *fondre en larmes*; cry -oneself blind, – one's eyes out.

scream etc. (*cry out*) 411; mew etc. (*animal sounds*) 412; groan, moan, whine, yammer; roar; roar –, bellow- like a bull; cry out lustily, rend the air, yell.

frown, scowl, make a wry face, grimace, gnash one's teeth, wring one's hands, tear one's hair, beat one's breast, roll on the ground, burst with grief.

complain, murmur, mutter, grumble, growl, clamor, make a fuss about, croak, grunt, maunder; deprecate etc. (*disapprove*) 932.

cry out before one is hurt, complain without cause.

Adj. lamenting etc. *v.*; in mourning, in sackcloth and ashes; crying, sorrowing, -ful etc. (*unhappy*) 828; mourn-, tear-ful; lachrymose; plaint-ive, -ful, querulous, -imonious, in the melting mood.

in tears, with tears in one's eyes; with -moistened, – watery- eyes; bathed –, dissolved- in tears; 'like Niobe all tears.'

elagiac, epicedial, threnetic.

Adv. *de profundis*; *les larmes aux yeux*.

Int. heigh-ho! alas! alack! O dear! ah –, woe is me! lackadaisy! well –, lack –, alack- a day! well-a-way! alas the day! *O tempora! O mores!* what a pity! *miserabile dictu!* O lud lud! too true!

Phr. tears -standing in, – starting from- the eyes; eyes -suffused, – swimming, – brimming –, over- flowing- with tears.

840. Amusement.—N. amuse-, entertain-ment; diver-sion, -tissement; reaction, relaxation, solace; pastime, *passetemps*, sport; labor of love; pleasure etc. 827.

fun, frolic, merriment, whoopee, jollity; jovial-ity, -ness; heyday; laughter etc. 838; jocos-ity, -eness; droll-, buffoon-, tomfool-ery; mummery, masquing, pleasantry; wit etc. 842; quip, quirk.

play; game, – at romps; gambol, romp, prank, antic, rig, lark, spree, skylarking, vagary, trick, monkey trick, *gambade*, *fredaine*, *escapade*, *échappée*, bout, *espièglerie*; practical joke etc. (*ridicule*) 856.

dance; round –, square –, solo –, step –, tap –, clog –, skirt –, sand –, folk –, morris-dance, *pas seul*, step, turn, *chassé*, cut, shuffle, double shuffle; hop, reel, rigadoon, saraband, hornpipe, bolero, fandango, pavan, tarantella, minuet, waltz, polka; galop, -ade; Schottische, *pas de quatre*, Boston, one-, two-step, rumba, tango, maxixe, fox-, turkey-trot, shimmy, ragtime, cakewalk, jazz, blues, Charleston; jig, breakdown, fling, strathspey; *allemande*; gavot, -te; mazurka, morisco; quadrille, lancers, country dance, *cotillon*, polonaise, Sir Roger de Coverley, Swedish dance; *ballet* etc. (*drama*) 599; ball; *bal*, – *masqué*, – *costumé*; masquerade, fancy dress ball; *thé dansant*; Terpsichore, choreography, Russian ballet, classical dancing; eurythmics; nautch dance, *danse du ventre*, cancan.

festivity, merry-making; party etc. (*social gathering*) 892; *fête*, festival, gala, *ridotto*; revel-s, -ry, -ling; carnival, brawl, saturnalia, high jinks; feast, banquet etc. (*food*) 298; regale, *symposium*, wassail; carous-e, -al; jollification, junket, wake, pic-nic, *fête champêtre*, garden party, gymkhana, regatta, track meet, field day, jamboree, treat.

round of pleasures, dissipation, a short life and a merry one, racketing, holiday making, high jinks.

rejoicing etc. 838; jubilee etc. (*celebration*) 883.

bonfire, fireworks, *feu-de-joie*, rocket, catherine wheel, roman candle etc.

holiday; gala –, red letter –, play- day; high days and holidays; high –, Bank- holiday; May –, Derby- day; Saint –, Easter –, Whit- Monday; King's birthday, Empire Day; *mi-carême*; *Bairam*; wayzgoose, bean feast, beano.

place of amusement, theater etc. 599; concert-, ball-, assembly-room; music-hall, cinema, movies, talkies, vaudeville; hippodrome, circus, rodeo; *casino*, *kursaal*; winter garden; park, pleasance, arbor; garden etc. 371; pleasure-, play-, cricket-, football-, polo-, croquet-, archery-, hunting-ground; golf links, race course, stadium, gridiron, bowl, speedway, racing track, ring; gymnasium, swimming pool; shooting gallery; tennis-, racket-court; bowling-green, -alley; croquet-lawn, rink, skating rink; roller-coaster, roundabout, carousel, merry-go-round; swing; *montagne russe*; switchback, scenic railway etc.

game, – of -chance, – skill; athletic sports, gymnastics; fencing; archery, rifle-shooting; tournament, pugilism etc. (*contention*) 720; sporting etc. 622; horse-racing, the turf; aquatics etc. 267; skating, roller skating; ski-running, -joring, -jumping, bobsleighing, luging, tobogganing, winter sports; sliding; cricket, tennis, lawn –, table –, deck-tennis, rackets, fives, squash, ping pong, trap bat and ball, battledore and shuttlecock, badminton, *la grâce*; pall mall, tip-cat, croquet, golf, curling, hockey, basketball, soccer, football, Rugby, Association, *pallone*, polo; tent-pegging, tilting at the ring, quintain, greasy pole; quoits, *discus*; throwing the hammer, putting the -weight, – shot, tossing the caber; knurr and spell; leapfrog; hop, skip and jump; French and English, tug of war; blind man's buff, hunt the slipper, hide-and-seek, kiss in the ring; snapdragon; cross questions and crooked answers; jig-saw puzzle; rounders, base-ball, *la crosse* etc.; angling; swimming, diving, water-polo.

billiards, pool, pyramids, snooker, bagatelle; bowls, skittles, ninepins, kail, American bowls.

cards; bridge, auction, contract, whist, rubber; round game, coon-can, loo, cribbage, *bésique*, pinocle, euchre, drole, *écarté*, skat, picquet, all-fours, quadrille, ombre, reverse, Pope Joan, commit; bo-, boa-ston; *vingt-et-un*; *quinze*, thirty-one, put-and-take, speculation, connections, brag, cassino, lottery, commerce, snip-snap-snorem, lift smoke, blind hookey, Polish bank, poker, banker; faro; Earl of Coventry, Napoleon, nap, patience, pairs; old maid, fright, beggar-my-neighbor; *baccarat*, *chemin de fer*, *monté*, *roulette*.

chess, draughts, backgammon, dominoes, checkers, mah jong, merelles, nine men's morris, go-bang, solitaire; game of –, fox and-goose; lotto; etc.

morra; gambling etc. (*chance*) 621.

toy, plaything, bauble; doll etc. (*puppet*) 554; teetotum; knick-knack etc. (*trifle*) 643; magic lantern etc. (*show*) 448; peep-, puppet-, raree-, gallanty-show; marionettes, Punch and Judy; toy-shop; 'quips and cranks and wanton wiles, nods and becks and wreathed smiles.'

sportsman, gamester, gambler etc. 621; reveler, master of the -ceremonies, – revels; *arbiter elegantiarum*.

V. amuse, entertain, divert, eliven; tickle, – the fancy; titillate, raise a smile, put in good humor; cause –, create –, occasion –, raise –, excite –, produce –, convulse with- laughter; set the table in a roar, be the death of one.

recreate, solace, cheer, rejoice; please etc. 829; interest; treat, regale.

amuse oneself; game; play, – a game, – pranks, – tricks; sport, disport, toy, wanton, revel, junket, feast, carouse, banquet, make merry; drown care; drive dull care away; frolic, gambol, frisk, romp; caper; dance etc. (*leap*) 309; keep up the ball; run a rig, sow one's wild oats, have one's fling, paint the town red, take one's pleasure; see life; *desipere in loco*, play the fool.

make –, keep- holiday; go a Maying.

while away –, beguile- the time; kill time, dally.

Adj. amusing, entertaining, diverting etc. *v.*; recreative, lusory; pleasant etc. (*pleasing*) 829; laughable etc. (*ludicrous*) 853; witty etc. 842; festive, -al; jovial, jolly, jocund, roguish, rompish; sporting; playful – as a kitten; sportive, ludibrious.

amused etc. *v.*; 'pleased with a feather, tickled with a straw.'

Adv. 'on the light fantastic toe,' at play, in sport.

Int. *vive la bagatelle! vogue la galère!*

Phr. *Deus nobis haec otia fecit*; *dum vivimus vivamus.*

841. Weariness.—N. weariness, defatigation, boredom, *ennui*; lassitude etc. (*fatigue*) 688; drowsiness etc. 683.

disgust, nausea, loathing, sickness; satiety etc. 869; *taedium vitae* etc. (*dejection*) 837.

wearisome-, tedious-ness etc. *adj.*; dull work, tedium, monotony, twice told tale.

bore, button-hole, proser, wet blanket; heavy hours, 'the enemy' [time].

V. weary; tire etc. (*fatigue*) 688; bore; bore –, weary –, tire- -to death, – out of one's life, – out of all patience; set –, send- to sleep.

pall, sicken, nauseate, disgust.

harp on the same string; drag its -slow, – weary-length along.

never hear the last of; be -tired etc. *adj.* -of, – with; yawn; died with *ennui*.

Adj. wearying etc. *v.*; wearing; weari-, tire-, irksome; uninteresting, stupid, bald, devoid of interest, dry, monotonous, dull, arid, tedious, humdrum, mortal, flat; pros-y, -ing; slow; soporific, somniferous, dormitive.

disgusting etc. *v.*; unenjoyed.

weary; tired etc. *v.*; drowsy etc. (*sleepy*) 683; uninterested, flagging, used up, worn out, *blasé*, life-weary, weary of life; sick of.

Adv. wearily etc. *adj.*; *usque ad nauseam*.

Phr. time hanging heavily on one's hands; *toujours perdrix*; *crambe repetita*.

842. Wit.—N. wit, -tiness; attic -wit, – salt; atticism; salt, *esprit*, point, fancy, whim, humor, drollery, pleasantry.

farce, buffoonery, fooling, tomfoolery; harlequinade etc. 599; broad -farce, – humor; fun, *espièglerie*; *vis comica*.

jocularity; jocos-ity, -eness; facetiousness; waggery, -ishness; whimsicality; comicality etc. 853.

smartness, ready wit, banter, *badinage*, *persiflage*, retort, repartee, *quid pro quo*; ridicule etc. 856.

facetiae, quips and cranks; jest, joke, capital joke; standing -jest, – joke; conceit, quip, quirk, crank, quiddity, *concetto, plaisanterie*, brilliant idea; merry –, bright –, happy- thought; sally; flash, – of wit, – of merriment; scintillation; *mot*, – pour rire; witticism, smart saying, *bon mot, jeu d'esprit*, epigram; jest book; dry joke, *quodlibet*, cream of the jest.

word-play, *jeu de mots*; play -of, – upon-words; pun, -ning; *double entente* etc. (*ambiguity*) 520; quibble, verbal quibble; conundrum etc. (*riddle*) 533; anagram, acrostic, double acrostic, *nugae canorae*, trifling, idle conceit, *turlupinade*.

old joke, Joe Miller, chestnut, hoary-headed jest.

V. joke, jest, cut jokes; crack a joke; perpetrate a -joke, – pun; make -fun of, – merry with; set the table in a roar etc. (*amuse*) 840; scintillate.

retort, flash back; banter etc. (*ridicule*) *856; ridentem dicere verum*; joke at one's expense.

Adj. witty, attic, salty; quick-, nimble-witted; keen, clever, smart, brilliant, pungent, jocular, jocose, funny, waggish, facetious, whimsical, humorous, gilbertian; playful etc. 840; merry and wise; pleasant, sprightly, *spirituel*, sparkling, epigrammatic, full of point, *ben trovato*; comic etc. 853.

Adv. in joke, in jest, in sport, in play.

843. Dullness.—N. dullness, heaviness, flatness; infestivity etc. 837; stupidity etc. 499; want of originality, dearth of ideas.

prose, matter of fact; heavy book, *conte à dormir debout*; platitude.

V. be -dull etc. *adj.*; prose, platitudinize, take *au sérieux*, be caught napping.

render -dull etc. *adj.*; damp, depress, throw cold water on, lay a wet blanket on; fall flat upon the ear; hang fire.

Adj. dull, – as ditch water; dry, insipid, jejune; unentertaining, uninteresting, unlively, unimaginative; heavisome, heavy-gaited; insulse; dry as dust; pros-y, -ing, -aic; matter of fact, commonplace, banal, pointless; 'weary, flat, stale and unprofitable.'

stupid, slow, flat, sluggish, ponderous, humdrum, monotonous; melancholic etc. 837; stolid etc. 499; plodding.

Phr. *Davus sum non Oedipus*.

844. Humorist.—N. humorist, wag, wit, reparteeist, epigrammatist, gag man, punster; *bel esprit*, life of the party; wit-snapper, -cracker, -worm; joker, jester, jokesmith, Joe Miller, *drôle de corps, gaillard*, spark, *persiffleur*, banterer.

buffoon, *farceur*, merry-andrew, mime, tumbler, acrobat, mountebank, charlatan, posturemaster, harlequin, punch, *pulcinella*, scaramouch, clown; wearer of the -cap and bells, – motley; motley fool; pantaloon, gipsy; jack -pudding, – in the green, – a dandy; zany; mad-cap, pickle-herring, witling, caricaturist, *grimacier*.

845. Beauty.—N. beauty, the beautiful, *le beau ideal*, loveliness.

[Science of the perception of beauty] Callaesthetics.

form, elegance, grace, beauty unadorned; symmetry etc. 242; comeliness, fairness etc. *adj.*; pulchritude, polish, gloss; good -effect, – looks; *belle tournure*; bloom, brilliancy, radiance, splendor, gorgeousness, magnificence; sublimi-ty, -fication.

concinnity, delicacy, refinement; charm, *je ne sais quoi*, style, *chic*, swank.

Venus, – of Milo; Aphrodite, Hebe, the Graces, Peri, Houri, Cupid, Apollo, Hyperion, Adonis, Antinous, Narcissus; Helen of Troy.

peacock, butterfly, flower, flow'ret gay, rose, lily, asphodel; garden; flower of, pink of; *bijou*; jewel etc. (*ornament*) 847; work of art.

pleasurableness etc. 829.

beautifying; landscape gardening; decoration etc. 847; calisthenics.

V. be -beautiful etc. *adj.*; shine, beam, bloom; become one etc. (*accord*) 23; set off, grace, flatter one.

render -beautiful etc. *adj.*; beautify; polish, burnish; gild etc. (*decorate*) 847; set out.

'snatch a grace beyond the reach of art.'

Adj. beaut-iful, -eous; handsome; pretty; lovely, graceful, elegant; delicate, dainty, refined, exquisite; fair, personable, comely, seemly; bonny; good-looking; well-favored, -made, -formed, -proportioned; proper, shapely; symmetrical etc. (*regular*) 242; harmonious etc. (*color*) 428; sightly.

fit to be seen, passable, not amiss.

goodly, dapper, tight, jimp; gimp; janty, jaunty; natty, quaint, trim, tidy, neat, spruce, smart, tricksy.

bright, -eyed; rosy-, cherry-cheeked; rosy, ruddy; blooming, in full bloom.

brilliant, shining; beam-y, -ing; sparkling, swanky, splendid, resplendent, dazzling, glowing; glossy, sleek.

showy, specious; rich, gorgeous, superb, magnificent, grand, fine, sublime, imposing; majestic 873.

artistic, -al; aesthetic; pict-uresque, -orial; *fait à piendre*, paintable; well-composed, -grouped, -varied; curious.

enchanting etc. (*pleasure-giving*) 829; attractive etc. (*inviting*) 615; becoming etc. (*accordant*) 23; ornamental etc. 847.

undeformed, undefaced, unspotted; spotless etc. (*perfect*) 650.

846. Ugliness.—N. ugliness etc. *adj.*; deformity, inelegance; disfigurement etc. (*blemsih*) 848; want of symmetry, inconcinnity; distortion etc. 243; squalor etc. (*uncleanness*) 653.

forbidding countenance, vinegar aspect, hanging look, wry face, *'spretae injuria formae.'*

eyesore, object, figure, sight, fright, specter, scarecrow, hag, harridan, satyr, witch, toad, baboon, monster, Caliban, Aesop, *'monstrum horrendum informe ingens cui lumen ademptum.'*

V. be -ugly etc. *adj.*; look ill, grin horribly a ghastly smile, make faces.

render -ugly etc. *adj.*; deface; dis-, de-figure; deform, spoil, distort etc. 243; blemish etc. (*injure*) 659; soil etc. (*render unclean*) 653.

Adj. ugly, – as -sin, – a toad, – a scarecrow, – a dead monkey; plain, bald etc. 226; homely etc. (*unadorned*) 849; ordinary, unornamental, inartistic; unsightly, unseemly, uncomely, unshapely, unlovely; sightless, seemless; not fit to be seen; unbeaut-eous, -iful; beautiless; shapeless etc. (*amorphous*) 241; course; garish, over-decorated etc. 882.

mis-shapen, -proportioned; monstrous; gaunt etc. (*thin*) 203; dumpy etc. (*short*) 201; curtailed of its fair proportions; ill-made, -shaped, -proportioned; crooked etc. (*distorted*) 243; hard-featured, -visaged; ill-, hard-, evil-favored; ill-looking; unprepossessing.

graceless, inelegant; ungraceful, ungainly, uncouth; stiff; rugged, rough, gross, rude, awkward, clumsy, slouching, rickety; gawky; lump-ing, -ish; lumbering; hulk-y, -ing; unwieldy.

squalid, haggard; grim, -faced, -visaged; grisly, ghastly; ghost-, death-like; cadaverous, gruesome.

frightful, hideous, odious, uncanny, forbidding, repellant, repulsive; horri-d, -ble; shocking etc. (*painful*) 830.

foul etc. (*dirty*) 653; dingy etc. (*colorless*) 429; gaudy etc. (*color*) 428; disfigured etc. *v.*; discolored (*blemished*) etc. 848.

847. Ornament.—N. ornament, -ation, -al art; ornat-ture, -eness; adorn-ment, decoration, embellishment; architecture.

garnish, polish, varnish, French polish, gilding, japanning, lacquer, ormolu, enamel.

cosmetics, rouge, powder, lipstick, lip salve, mascara; manicure, nail polish; permanent –, Marcel –, finger-wave.

pattern, diaper, powdering, panelling, graining, pargeting, inlay, detail; texture etc. 329; richness; tracery, molding, beading, reeding, fillet, listel, strapwork, *coquillage*, flourish, *fleur-de-lis*, arabesque, fret, *anthemion*; egg and -tongue, -dart; *astragal*, zigzag, *acanthus, cartouche*; pilaster etc. (*projection*) 250; cyma, ogee.

em-, broidery, needlework; knitting, crochet, tatting, brocade, *brocatelle*, beads, bugles; galloon, lace, gimp, *guipure*, fringe, trapping, border, edging, insertion, *motif*, trimming; *passementerie*; drapery, hanging, tapestry, arras; millinery, ermine.

wreath, festoon, garland, lei, chaplet, flower, nosegay, *bouquet*, posy, 'daisies pied and violets blue.'

tassle, knot; shoulder-knot, *épaulette*, epaulet, aigulet, *aiguilette*, frog; star, rosette, bow; feather, plume, *panache, aigrette*.

jewel, -ry, -lery; bijoutry; *bijou, -terie*; diadem, tiara; pendant, trinket, locket, necklace, armilla, bracelet, bangle, armlet, anklet, ear-, nose- ring, carcanet, chain, *châtelaine*, albert, brooch, torque.

gem, precious stone; diamond, brilliant, beryl, aquamarine, alexandrite, cat's eye, emerald, calcedony, chrysoprase, cornelian, jasper, bloodstone, agate, heliotrope; girasol, -e; onyx, plasma; sard, -onyx; garnet, lapis-lazuli, opal, peridot, chrysolite, sapphire, ruby; spinel, -le; balais; oriental –, topaz; turquois, -e; zircon, jacinth, hyacinth, carbuncle, amethyst; moonstone; pearl, coral.

finery, frippery, gewgaw, gimcrack, knick-knack, tinsel, spangle, sequin, *clinquant*, pinch-beck, paste; excess of ornament etc. (*vulgarity*) 851; gaud, pride, ostentation; frills and furbelows.

illustration, illumination, *vignette*; *fleuron*; head-, tail-piece; *cul-de-lampe*; flowers of rhetoric etc. 577; work of art, article of vertu, *bric-à-brac*, curio, *bibelot*.

V. ornament, embellish, enrich, decorate, adorn, beautify, adonize.

smarten, furbish, polish, gild, varnish, whitewash, enamel, japan, lacquer, paint, grain.

garnish, trim, dizen, bedizen, prink, prank; trick –, fig- out; deck, bedeck, dight, bedight, array; dress, – up, preen, spruce up, titivate; spangle, bespangle, powder; embroider, work; chase, tool, emboss, fret; emblazon, blazon, illuminate; illustrate.

become etc. (*accord with*) 23.

Adj. ornamented, beautified etc. *v.*; ornate, rich, gilt, begilt, tesselated, enamelled, inlaid; festooned; topiary.

smart, gay, tricksy, flowery, glittering; new-gilt, -spangled; fine, – as -a Mayday queen, – fivepence, – a carrot fresh scraped; pranked out, bedight, well-groomed.

in full dress etc. (*fashion*) 852; *en grande -tenue*, – *toilette*; in best bib and tucker, in Sunday best, *endimanché*; dressed to advantage.

showy, flashy; gaudy etc. (*vulgar*) 851; garish; gorgeous.

ornamental, decorative; becoming etc. (*accordant*) 23.

848. Blemish.—N. blemish, disfigurement, deformity; defect etc. (*imperfection*) 651; flaw; injury etc. (*deterioration*) 659; spots on the sun; eyesore.

stain, blot, slur; spot, -tiness; speck, -le; blur, freckle, mole, *macula*, patch, blotch, birthmark, blain, maculation, tarnish, smudge, smear; dirt etc. 653; bruise, black eye, scar, wem; pustule; excrescence, pimple etc. (*protuberance*) 250.

V. disfigure etc. (*injure*) 659; speckle; render ugly etc. 846.

Adj. pitted, freckled, discolored, bloodshot, bruised, disfigured; stained etc. *n.*; imperfect etc. 651; injured etc. (*deteriorated*) 659.

849. Simplicity.—N. simplicity; plain-, homeli-ness; undress, nudity, nakedness, beauty unadorned, chastity, chasteness.

V. be -simple etc. *adj.*

render -simple etc. *adj.*; simplify, chasten, strip of ornament.

Adj. simple, plain; home-ly, -spun; ordinary, household.

natural, unaffected; free from -affectation, – ornament; *simplex munditiis*; *sans façon, en déshabillé*, nude, naked.

chaste, inornate, severe.

un-adorned, -ornamented, -decked, -garnished, -arranged, -trimmed, -varnished.

bald, flat, dull, blank.

850. Taste. [Good taste.]—**N.** taste; good –, refined –, cultivated- taste; delicacy, refinement, fine feeling, gust, *gusto*, tact, *finesse*; nicety etc. (*discrimination*) 465; polish, elegance, grace.

virtu; dilettanteism, virtuosity; fine art; cul-ture, -ivation.

[Science of taste] esthetics.

man of -taste etc.; *connoisseur*, judge, critic, *conoscente, virtuoso, amateur, dilettante*, Aristarchus, Corinthian, *arbiter elegantarum*, stagirite, euphemist.

'caviar to the general.'

V. appreciate, judge, criticize, discriminate etc. 465.

Adj. in good taste; tasteful, tasty; unaffected, pure, chaste, classical, attic; cultivated, refined; dainty; esthetic, artistic; elegant etc. 578; euphemistic.

to one's taste, – mind; after one's fancy; *comme il faut*; *tiré à quatre épingles*.

Adv. elegantly etc. *adj.*

Phr. *nihil tetigit quod non ornavit*.

851. Vulgarity. [Bad taste.]—**N.** vulgar-ity, -ism; barbar-, Vandal-, Gothic-ism; *mauvais goût*, bad taste; Babbittry; *gaucherie*, awkwardness, want of tact; ill-breeding etc. (*discourtesy*) 895; ungentlemanly behavior.

coarseness etc. *adj.*; indecorum, misbehavior.

low-, homeli-ness; low life, *mauvais ton*, rusticity; boorishness etc. *adj.*; brutality; rowdy-, ruffian-, blackguard-ism; ribaldry; slang etc. (*neology*) 563.

bad joke, *mauvaise plaisanterie*.

[Excell of ornament] gaudi-, tawdri-ness; false ornament; finery, frippery, trickery, tinsel, gewgaw, *clinquant*.

rough diamond, tomboy, hoyden, cub, unlicked cub; clown etc. (*commonalty*) 876; Hun, Goth, Vandal, Boeotian; vulgarian; snob, cad, bounder, gent; *parvenu* etc. 876; frump, dowdy; slattern etc. 653.

V. be -vulgar etc. *adj.*; misbehave; talk –, smell of the- shop.

Adj. in bad taste, vulgar, unrefined, gutter.

coarse, indecorus, ribald, gross; unseemly, unbeseeming, unpresentable; *contra bonos mores*; ungraceful etc. (*ugly*) 846.

dowdy, slovenly etc. (*dirty*) 653; ungenteel, shabby genteel; low etc. (*plebeian*) 876;uncourtly; uncivil etc. (*discourteous*) 895; ill-bred, -mannered; underbred; ungentleman-ly, -like; unladylike, unfeminine; wild, – as an unbacked colt.

unkempt, uncombed, untamed, unlicked, unpolished, uncouth, plebeian; incondite; heavy, rude, awkward; home-ly, -spun, -bred; provincial, hick, countrified, rustic, uncultivated, freshwater; boorish, clownish; savage, brutish, blackguard, rowdy, snobbish; barbar-ous, -ic; Gothic, unclassical, doggerel, heathenish, tramontane, outlandish; Bohemian.

obsolete etc. (*antiquated*) 124; unfashionable, old-fashioned, out of date; new-fangled etc. (*unfamiliar*) 83; fantastic, odd etc. (*ridiculous*) 853.

particular; affected etc. 855; meretricious; extravagant, monstrous, horrid; shocking etc. (*painful*) 830.

gaudy, tawdry, bedizened, tricked out, gingerbread; obtrusive, flaunting, loud, flashy, garish, showy.

852. Fashion.—N. fashion, style, *ton*, *bon ton*, society; good –, polite- society; drawing room, civilized life, civilization, town, *beau monde*, high life, court; world; fashionable –, gay- world; Vanity Fair; show etc. (*ostentation*) 822.

manners, breeding etc. (*politeness*) 894; air, demeanor etc. (*appearance*) 448; *savoir faire*; gentlemanliness, gentility, decorum, propriety, *bienséance*; conventions –, dictates- of society; Mrs. Grundy; convention, -ality; punctilio; form, -ality; etiquette, point of etiquette; custom etc. 613; mode, vogue, style, go; rage etc. (*desire*) 865; prevailing taste, *dernier cri*, dress etc. 225.

man –, woman- of -fashion, – the world; height –, pink –, star –, glass –, leader- of fashion; *arbiter elegantiarum* etc. (*taste*) 850; upper ten thousand etc. (*nobility*) 875; *élite* etc. (*distinction*) 873.

V. be -fashionable etc. *adj.*, – the rage etc. *n.*; have a run, pass current.

follow –, conform to –, fall in with- the fashion etc. *n.*; go with the stream etc. (*conform*) 82; *savoir -vivre*, – *faire*; keep up appearances, behave oneself.

set the –, bring into- fashion; give a tone to –, cut a figure in- society, rub shoulders with nobility, keep one's carriage.

Adj. fashionable; in -fashion etc. *n.*; *à la mode, comme il faut*; admitted –, admissible- in -society etc. *n.*; presentable, decorous, punctilious, conventional etc. (*customary*) 613; genteel; well-bred, -mannered, -behaved, -spoken; gentleman-like, -ly; ladylike; civil, polite etc. (*courteous*) 894.

polished, refined, thoroughbred, courtly; *distingué*, aristocratic, unembarrassed, poised, *dégagé*; ja-, jau-nty; dashing, fast, showy, high toned, toney.

modish, stylish, in the latest style, *recherché*; new-fangled etc. (*unfamiliar*) 83.

in -court, – full, – evening- dress; *en grande tenue* etc. (*ornament*) 847.

Adv. fashionably etc. *adj.*; for fashion's sake.

853. Ridiculousness.—N. ridiculousness etc. *adj.*; comical-, odd-ity etc. *adj.*; extravagance, drollery.

farce, comedy; burlesque etc. (*ridicule*) 856; buffoonery etc. (*fun*) 840; frippery; doggerel verses; Irish bull, Hibernianism, Hibernicism; Spoonerism; absurdity etc. 497; bombast etc. (*unmeaning*) 517; anticlimax, bathos; monstrosity etc. (*unconformity*) 83; laughing stock etc. 857.

V. be -ridiculous etc. *adj.*; pass from the sublime to the ridiculous; make one laugh; play the fool, make a fool of oneself, commit an absurdity.

play a joke on, make a -fool of, – sucker of, – monkey of.

Adj. ridiculous, ludicrous; comic, -al; droll, funny, laughable, *pour rire*, grotesque, farcical, odd; whimsical, – as a dancing bear; fanciful, fantastic, queer, rum, quizzical, waggish, quaint, *bizarre*; eccentric etc. (*unconformable*) 83; strange, outlandish, out of the way, *baroque*, *rocaille*, rococo; awkward etc. (*ugly*) 846.

absurd, extravagant, *outré*, monstrous, preposterous, bombastic, inflated, stilted, burlesque, mock heroic.

drollish; serio-, tragic-comic; gimcrack, contemptible etc. (*unimportant*) 643; doggerel; ironical etc. (*derisive*) 856; risible.

Phr. *'risum teneatis amici?' rideret Heraclitus.*

854. Fop.—N. fop, fine gentleman; swell; dand-y, -iprat; exquisite, coxcomb, toff, beau, macaroni, blade, blood, buck, man about town, fast man; fribble, jemmy, spark, popinjay, puppy, prig, *petit maître*; jacka-napes, -dandy; man milliner; Jemmy Jessamy, carpet-knight, masher, Dundreary, Johnnie, dude.

belle, fine lady, *coquette*, flirt.

855. Affectation.—N. affectation; affectedness etc. *adj.*; acting a part etc. *v.*; pretence etc. (*falsehood*) 544; (*ostentation*) 882; boasting etc. 884.

charlatanism, quakery, shallow profundity, humbug, pretension, airs, pedantry, purism, precisianism, euphuism, prunes and prisms; teratology etc. (*altiloquence*) 577.

mannerism, *simagrée*, grimace.

conceit, foppery, dandyism, man millinery, coxcombry, puppyism.

stiffness, formality, buckram; prudery, demureness, coquetry, mock modesty, *minauderie*, sentimentalism; *mauvaise honte*, false shame.

affector, performer, actor; pedant, pedagogue, *doctrinaire*, purist, euphuist, mannerist; shoneen; *grimacier*; lump of affectation, *précieuse ridicule*, *bas bleu*, blue stocking, poetaster; prig, hypocrite; charlatan etc. (*deceiver*) 548; *petit maître* etc. (*fop*) 854; flatterer etc. 935; *coquette*, prude, puritan; precisian, formalist.

V. affect, act a part, put on; give oneself airs etc. (*arrogance*) 885; boast etc. 884; coquet; simper, mince, attitudinize, strike a pose, pose; flirt a fan; over-act, -play, -do.

Adj. affected, full of affectation, pretentious, pedantic, stilted, stagey, theatrical, big-sounding, *ad captandum*, canting, insincere.

not natural, unnatural; self-conscious; *maniéré*; artificial; over-wrought, -done, -acted; euphuistic etc. 577.

stiff, starch, formal, prim, smug, demure, *tiré à quatre épingles*, quakerish, puritanical, prudish, pragmatical, priggish, conceited, coxcomical, foppish, dandified; fini-cal, -kin, -cky, mincing, simpering, namby-pamby, sentimental, languishing.

856. Ridicule.—N. ridicule, derision; sardonic -smile, – grin; irrision; snigger; scoffing etc. (*disrespect*) 929; mockery, quiz, banter, irony, *persiflage*, raillery, chaff, *badinage*; quizzing etc. *v.*

squib, satire, skit, quip, quib, grin.

parody, burlesque, travesty; farce etc. (*drama*) 599; caricature, take-off.

buffoonery etc. (*fun*) 840; practical joke, horseplay.

V. ridicule, deride; laugh at, grin at, smile at; snigger; laugh in one's sleeve; banter, rally, chaff, joke, twit, quiz, poke fun at, jolly, roast, rag; fleer; play –, play tricks- upon; fool, – to the top of one's bent; show up.

satirize, parody, caricature, burlesque, travesty.

turn into ridicule; make merry with; make -fun, – game, – a fool, – an April fool- of; rally; scoff etc. (*disrespect*) 929.

raise a laugh etc. (*amuse*) 840; play the fool, make a fool of oneself.

be ridiculous etc. 853.

Adj. deris-ory, -ive; mock; sarcastic, ironical, quizzical, burlesque, Hudibrastic; scurrilous etc. (*disrespectful*) 929.

Adv. in -ridicule etc. *n.*

857. Laughing-stock. [Object and cause of ridicule.]**—N.** laughing-, jesting-, gazing-stock; butt, game, fair game; April fool etc. (*dupe*) 547.

original, oddity; queer –, odd- fish; quiz, square toes; old –, fogey *or* fogy.

monkey; buffoon etc. (*jester*) 844; pantomimist etc. (*actor*) 599.

jest etc. (*wit*) 842.

858. Hope.—N. hope, -s; desire etc. 865; fervent hope, sanguine expectation, trust, confidence, reliance; faith etc. (*belief*) 484; affiance, assurance; secur-eness, -ity; reassurance.

good -omen, – auspices; promise; well-grounded hopes; good –, bright- prospect; clear sky.

as-, pre-sumption; anticipation etc. (*expectation*) 507.

hopefulness, buoyancy, optimism, enthusiasm, heart of grace, aspiration; optimist, utop-ian, -ist; Pollyanna.

castles in the air, *châteaux en Espagne*, hope chest, *le pot au lait*, Utopia, millennium; day –, golden- dream; dream of Alnaschar; airy hopes, fool's paradise; *mirage* etc. (*fallacies of vision*) 443; fond hope.

beam –, ray –, gleam –, glimmer –, dawn –, flash –, star- of hope; cheer; bit of blue sky, silver lining of the cloud, bottom of Pandora's box, balm in Gilead.

anchor, sheet-anchor, main-stay; staff etc. (*support*) 215; heaven etc. 981.

V. hope, trust, confide, rely on, put one's trust in, lean upon; pin one's -hope, – faith- upon etc. (*believe*) 484.

feel –, entertain –, harbor –, indulge –, cherish –, feed –, foster –, nourish –, encourage –, cling to –, live in- hope etc. *n.*; see land; feel –, rest- -assured, – confident etc. *adj.*

presume; promise oneself; expect etc. (*look forward to*) 507.

hope for etc. (*desire*) 865; anticipate.

be -hopeful etc. *adj.*; look on the bright side of, view on the sunny side, make the best of it, hope for the best; put -a good, – a bold, – the best- face upon; keep one's spirits up; take heart, – of grace; be of good -heart, – cheer; flatter oneself, lay the flattering unction to one's soul.

catch at a straw, hope against hope, count one's chickens before they are hatched.

give –, inspire –, raise –, hold out- hope etc. *n.*; raise expectations; encourage, hearten, cheer, assure, reassure, buoy up, embolden; promise, bid fair, augur well, be in a fair way, look up, flatter, tell a flattering tale.

Adj. hoping etc. *v.*; in -hopes etc. *n.*; hopeful, confident; secure etc. (*certain*) 484; sanguine, in good heart, buoyed up, buoyant, elated, flushed, exultant, enthusiastic; utopian.

unsus-pecting, -picious; fearless, free –, exempt from- -fear, – suspicion, – distrust, – despair; undespairing, self-reliant.

probable, on the high road to; within sight of -shore, – land; promising, propitious; of –, full of-promise; of good omen; auspicious, *de bon augure*; reassuring; encouraging, cheering, inspiriting, looking up, bright, roseate, *couleur de rose*, rose-colored.

Adv. hopefully etc. *adj.*

Phr. *nil desperandum*; never say die, *dum spiro spero, latet scintillula forsan*; all is for the best, *spero meliora*; the wish being father to the thought; 'hope told a flattering tale;' *rusticus expectat dum defluat amnis.*

859. Hopelessness. [Absence, want, or loss of hope.]—**N.** hopelessness etc. *adj.*; despair, desperation; despondency etc. (*dejection*) 837; pessimism.

hope deferred, dashed hopes; vain expectation etc. (*disappointment*) 509.

airy hopes etc. 858; forlorn hope; bad -job, – business; *enfant perdu*; gloomy –, black spots in the- horizon; slough of Despond, cave of Despair.

Job's comforter; bird of -bad, – ill-omen.

V. despair; lose –, give up –, abandon –, relinquish- -all hope, – the hope of; give -up, – over; yield to despair; falter; despond etc. (*be dejected*) 837; *jeter le manche après la cognée.*

inspire –, drive to- despair etc. *n.*; disconcert; dash –, crush –, shatter –, destroy- one's hopes; hope against hope.

Adj. hopeless, desperate, despairing, in despair, *au désespoir*, forlorn; inconsolable etc. (*dejected*) 837; broken-hearted.

out of the question, not to be thought of; impracticable etc. 471; past -hope, – cure, – mending, – recall; at one's last gasp etc. (*death*) 360; given -up, – over.

incurable, cureless, immedicable, remediless, beyond remedy; incorrigible; irre-parable, -mediable, -coverable, -versible, -trievable, -claimable, -deemable, -vocable; ruined, undone; immitigable.

unpromising, unpropitious; inauspicious, ill-omened, threatening, clouded over, lowering, ominous.

Phr. *'lasciate ogni speranza voi ch' entrate;'* its days are numbered; the worst come to the worst.

860. Fear.—N. fear, timidity, diffidence, want of confidence; apprehensive-, fearful-ness etc. *adj.*; solicitude, anxiety, care, apprehension, misgiving; mistrust etc. (*doubt*) 485; suspicion, qualm; hesitation etc. (*irresolution*) 605.

nervous-, restless-ness etc. *adj.*; in-, dis-quietude; flutter, trepidation, fear and trembling, perturbation, tremor, quivering, shaking, trembling, throbbing heart, palpitation, ague fit, cold sweat; abject fear etc. (*cowardice*) 862; mortal funk, heart-sinking, despondency; despair etc. 859.

fright; affright, -ment; alarm, pavor, dread, awe, terror, horror, dismay, consternation, panic, scare, stampede [of horses].

intimidation, terrorism, reign of terror.

[Object of fear] bug-bear, -aboo; scarecrow; hobgoblin etc. (*demon*) 980; daymare, nightmare, Gorgon, Medusa, mormo, ogre, Hurlothrumbo, raw head and bloody bones, fee faw fum, *bête noire, enfant terrible.*

alarmist etc. (*coward*) 862.

V. fear, stand in awe of; be -afraid etc. *adj.*; have -qualms etc. *n.*; apprehend, sit upon thorns, eye askance; distrust etc. (*disbelieve*) 485.

hesitate etc. (*be irresolute*) 605; falter, funk, cower, crouch; skulk etc. (*cowardice*) 862; let 'I dare not' wait upon 'I would;' take -fright, – alarm; start, wince, flinch, shy, shrink; fly etc. (*avoid*) 623.

tremble, shake; shiver, – in one's shoes; shudder, flutter; shake –, tremble- -like an aspen leaf, – all over; quake, quaver, quiver, quail; get the wind up.

grow –, turn- pale; blench, stand aghast; not dare to say one's soul is one's own.

inspire –, excite- -fear, – awe; raise apprehensions; give –, raise –, sound- an alarm; alarm, startle, scare, cry 'wolf,' disquiet, dismay; fright, -en; affright, terrify; astound; frighten from one's propriety; frighten out of one's -wits, – senses, – seven senses; awe; strike -all of a heap, – an awe into, – terror; harrow up the soul, appal, unman, petrify, horrify.

make one's -flesh creep, – hair stand on end, – blood run cold, – teeth chatter; chill one's spine; take away –, stop- one's breath; make one -tremble etc.

haunt, obsess, beset; prey –, weigh- on the mind.

put in -fear, – bodily fear; terrorize, intimidate, cow, daunt, over-awe, abash, deter, discourage; browbeat, bully; threaten etc. 909.

Adj. fearing etc. *v.*, frightened etc. *v.*; in -fear, – a fright etc. *n.*; haunted with the -fear etc. *n.*- of.

afraid, fearful; tim-id, -orous; nervous, diffident, coy, faint-hearted, tremulous, shaky, afraid of one's shadow, apprehensive, restless, fidgety; more frightened than hurt.

aghast; awe-, horror-, terror-, panic- -struck, -stricken; frightened to death, white as a sheet; pale, – as -death, – ashes, – a ghost; breathless, in hysterics.

inspiring fear etc. *v.*; alarming; formidable, redoubtable; perilous etc. (*danger*) 665; portentous; fear-ful, -some; dread, -ful; fell; dire, -ful; shocking; terri-ble, -fic; tremendous; horri-d, -ble, -fic; ghastly; awful, awe-inspiring, eerie, weird; revolting etc. (*painful*) 830.

Adv. *in terrorem.*

Int. 'angels and ministers of grace defend us!'

Phr. *ante tubam trepidat*; *horresco referens*, one's heart failing one, *obstupui steteruntque comae et vox faucibus haesit.*

861. Courage. [Absence of fear.]—**N.** courage, bravery, valor; resolute-, bold-ness etc. *adj.*; spirit, daring, gallantry, intrepidity; contempt –, defiance- of danger; derring-do; audacity; rashness etc. 863; dash; defiance etc. 715; confidence, self-reliance.

man-liness, -hood; nerve, pluck, mettle, game; heart, – of grace; spunk, gameness, grit, face, virtue, hardihood, fortitude; firmness etc. (*stability*) 150; heart of oak; bottom, backbone etc. (*perseverance*) 604*a*.

resolution etc. (*determination*) 604; tenacity, bull-dog courage.

prowess, heroism, chivalry.

exploit, feat, achievement; heroic -deed, – act; bold stroke.

man, – of mettle; hero, demigod, paladin, heroine, Amazon, Hector, Joan of Arc; lion, tiger, panther, bulldog; game-, fighting-cock; bully, fire-eater etc. 863; dare-devil.

V. be -courageous etc. *adj.*; dare, venture, make bold; face –, front –, affront –, confront –, brave –, defy –, despise –, mock- danger; look in the face; look -full, – boldly, – danger- in the face; face; meet, – in front; brave, beard; defy etc. 715.

take –, muster –, summon up –, pluck up- courage; nerve oneself, take heart; take –, pluck up- heart of grace; hold up one's head, screw one's courage to the sticking place; come -to, – up to- the scratch; stand, – to one's guns, – fire, – against; bear up – against; hold out etc. (*persevere*) 604*a*.

put a bold face upon; show –, present- a bold front, face the music; envisage; show fight.

bell the cat, take the bull by the horns, beard the lion in his den, march up to the cannon's mouth, go through fire and water, run the gauntlet, go over the top.

give –, infuse –, inspire- courage; reassure, encourage, embolden, inspirit, cheer, hearten, nerve, put upon one's mettle, rally, raise a rallying cry; pat on the back, make a man of, keep in countenance.

Adj. courageous, brave; val-iant, -orous; gallant, intrepid; spirit-ed, -ful; high-spirited, -mettled; mettlesome, game, plucky; man-ly, -ful; resolute; stout, -hearted; iron-, lion-hearted; heart of oak; Penthesilean.

bold, – spirited; daring, audacious; fear-, daunt-, dread-, awe-less; un-daunted, -appalled, -dismayed, -awed, -blenched, -abashed, -alarmed, -flinching, -shrinking, -blenching; apprehensive; confident, self-reliant; bold as -a lion, – brass.

enterprising, adventurous; ventur-ous, -esome; dashing, chivalrous; soldierly etc. (*warlike*) 722; heroic.

fierce, savage; pugnacious etc. (*bellicose*) 720.

strong-minded, hardy, doughty; firm etc. (*stable*) 150; determined etc. (*resolved*) 604; dogged, indomitable etc. (*persevering*) 604*a*.

up to, – the scratch; upon one's mettle; reassured etc. *v.*; unfeared, undreaded.

Phr. one's blood being up.

862. Cowardice. [Excess of fear.]—**N.** cowardice, pusillanimity; cowardliness etc. *adj.*; timidity, effeminacy.

poltroonery, baseness; dastard-ness, -y; abject fear, funk; Dutch courage; fear etc. 860; white feather, faint heart.

coward, poltroon, dastard, sneak, recreant; shy –, dunghill- cock; coistril, milksop, white-liver, nidget, cur, craven, one that cannot say 'Boo' to a goose; Bob Acres, Jerry Sneak.

alarm-, terror-, pessim-ist; runagate etc. (*fugitive*) 623; shirker.

V. quail etc. (*fear*) 860; be -cowardly etc. *adj.*, – a coward etc. *n.*; funk; cower, skulk, sneak; flinch, shy, fight shy, slink, turn tail; run away etc. (*avoid*) 623; show the white feather, have cold feet, show a yellow streak.

Adj. coward, -ly; fearful, shy; tim-id, -orous; skittish; poor-spirited, spirit-less, soft, effeminate.

weak-minded; infirm of purpose etc. 605; weak-, faint-, chicken-, lily-, pigeon-hearted; yellow; white-, lily-, milk-livered; milksop, smock-faced; unable to say 'Boo' to a goose.

dastard, -ly; base, craven, sneaking, dunghill, recreant; unwar-, unsoldier-like.

'in face a lion but in heart a deer.'

unmanned; frightened etc. 860.

Int. *sauve qui peut!* devil take the hindmost!

Adv. in fear and trembling, in fear of one's life, in a blue funk.

Phr. *ante tubam trepidat*, one's courage oozing out.

863. Rashness.—**N.** rashness etc. *adj.*; temerity, want of caution, imprudence, indiscretion; over-confidence, presumption, audacity.

precipit-ancy, -ation; impetuosity; levity; foolhardi-hood, -ness; heed-, thought-lessness etc. (*inattention*) 458; carelessness etc. (*neglect*) 460; desperation; Quixotism, knight-errantry; fire-eating.

gam-ing, -bling; blind bargain, leap in the dark, fool's paradise; too many eggs in one basket.

desperado, rashling, mad-cap, dare-devil, Hotspur, fire-eater, bully, *bravo*, Hector, scapegrace, *enfant perdu*; Don Quixote, knight-errant, Icarus; adventurer; gam-bler, -ester; dynamitard.

V. be -rash etc. *adj.*; stick at nothing, play a desperate game; run into danger etc. 665; play with -fire, – edge tools.

carry too much sail, sail too near the wind, ride at single anchor, go out of one's depth.

take a leap in the dark, buy a pig in a poke. *donner tête baissée*; knock one's head against a wall etc. (*be unskilful*) 699; rush on destruction; kick against the pricks, tempt Providence, go on a forlorn hope.

count one's chickens before they are hatched; reckon without one's host; catch at straws; trust to –, lean on- a broken reed.

Adj. rash, incautious, indiscreet, injudicious; imprudent, improvident, temerarious; uncalculating; heedless; careless etc. (*neglectful*) 460; without ballast, heels over head; giddy etc. (*inattentive*) 458; wanton, reckless, wild, madcap; desperate, devil-may-care.

hot-blooded, -headed, -brained; head-long, -strong; break-neck; fool-hardy; harebrained; precipitate, impulsive.

over-confident, -weening; ventur-esome, -ous; adventurous, Quixotic; fire-eating, cavalier; free-and-easy.

off one's guard etc. (*inexpectant*) 508.

Adv. post haste, *à corps perdu*, hand over head, *tête baissée*, head- foremost; happen what may.

Phr. neck or nothing, the devil being in one.

864. Caution.—N. caution; cautiousness etc. *adj.*; discretion, prudence, cautel, heed, circumspection, calculation, deliberation; safety first.

foresight etc. 510; vigilance etc. 459; warning etc. 668.

coolness etc. *adj.*; self-possession, -command; presence of mind, *sang froid*; well-regulated mind; worldly wisdom, Fabian policy.

V. be -cautious etc. *adj.*; take -care, – heed, – good care; have a care; mind, – what one is about; be on one's guard etc. (*keep watch*) 459; make assurance double sure; ca' canny.

bespeak etc. (*be early*) 132.

think twice, look before one leaps, keep one's weather eye open, count the cost, look to the main chance, cut one's coat according to one's cloth; feel one's -ground, – way; see how the land lies etc. (*foresight*) 510; wait to see how the cat jumps; bridle one's tongue; *reculer pour mieux sauter* etc. (*prepare*) 673; let well alone, let sleeping dogs lie, *ne pas réveiller le chat qui dort.*

keep out of -harm's way, – troubled waters; keep at a respectful distance, stand aloof; keep –, be- on the safe side.

husband one's resources etc. 636.

caution etc. (*warn*) 668.

Adj. cautious, wary, guarded; on one's guard etc. (*watchful*) 459; *cavendo tutus*; *in medio tutissimus*.

care-, heed-ful; cautelous, stealthy, chary, shy of, circumspect, prudent, canny, safe, non-committal, discreet, politic; sure-footed etc. (*skilful*) 698.

unenterprising, unadventurous, cool, steady, self-possessed; over-cautious.

suspicious, leery, vigilant.

Adv. cautiously, gingerly etc. *adj.*

Int. have a care! look out! *cave canem!*

Phr. *timeo Danaos*; *festina lente*.

865. Desire.—N. desire, wish, fancy, fantasy; want, need, exigency.

mind, inclination, leaning, bent, *animus*, partiality, *penchant*, predilection; propensity etc. 820; willingness etc. 602; liking, love, fondness, relish.

longing, hankering; solicitude, anxiety; yearning, coveting; aspiration, ambition, vaulting ambition; eagerness, zeal, ardor, *empressement*, breathless impatience, over-anxiety; solicitude, impetuosity etc. 825.

appet-ite, -ition, -ence, -ency; sharp appetite, keenness, hunger, stomach, twist; thirst, -iness; drouth, mouth-watering; itch, -ing; prurience, *cacoëthes*, cupidity, lust, concupiscence.

edge of -appetite, – hunger; torment of Tantalus; sweet –, lickerish- tooth; itching palm; longing –, wistful –, sheep's-eye.

avidity; greed, -iness; covetous-, ravenous-ness etc. *adj.*; grasping, craving, canine appetite, rapacity; voracity etc. (*gluttony*) 957.

passion, rage, *furore*, mania, *manie*; inextinguishable desire; dips-, klept-, mon-omania.

[Person desiring] desirer, lover, *amateur*, votary, devotee, aspirant, solicitant, candidate; cormorant etc. 957; sycophant.

[Object of desire] *desideratum*; want etc. (*requirement*) 630; 'consumation devoutly to be wished;' attraction, magnet, allurement, fancy, temptation, seduction, lure, fascination, *prestige*, height of one's ambition, idol; whim, -sey; maggot; hobby, -horse.

Fortunatus's cap, wishing cap, love potion.

V. desire; wish, – for; be -desirous etc. *adj.*; have a -longing etc. *n.*; hope etc. 858.

care for, affect, like, list; take to, cling to, take a fancy to; fancy; prefer etc. (*choose*) 609.

have -an eye, – a mind- to; find it in one's heart etc. (*be willing*) 602; have a fancy for, set one's eyes upon; cast a sheep's eye –, look sweet- upon; take into one's head, have a heart, be bent upon; set one's -cap at, – heart upon, – mind upon; covet.

want, miss, need, lack, desiderate, feel the want of; would fain -have, – do; would be glad of.

be -hungry etc. *adj.*; have a good appetite, play a good knife and fork; hunger –, thirst –, crave –, lust –, itch –, hanker –, run mad- after; raven –, die- for; burn to.

desiderate; sigh –, cry –, gape –, gasp –, pine –, pant –, languish –, yearn –, long –, be on thorns –, hope- for; aspire after; catch at, grasp at, jump at.

woo, court, solicit; fish –, spell –, whistle –, put up- for; ogle.

cause –, create –, raise –, excite –, provoke- desire; whet the appetite; appetize, titillate, allure, attract, take one's fancy, tempt; hold out -temptation, – allurement; tantalize, make one's mouth water, *faire venir l'eau à la bouche.*

gratify desire etc. (*give pleasure*) 829.

Adj. desirous; desiring etc. *v.*; orectic, appetitive; inclined etc. (*willing*) 602; partial to; fain, wishful, optative; anxious, wistful, curious; at a loss for, sedulous, solicitous.

craving, hungry, sharp-set, peckish, ravening, with an empty stomach, esurient, lickerish, thirsty, athirst, parched with thirst, pinched with hunger, famished, dry, drouthy; hungry as a -hunter, – hawk, – horse, – church mouse.

greedy, – as a hog; over-eager, voracious; ravenous, – as a wolf; open-mouthed, covetous, rapacious, grasping, extortionate, exacting, sordid, *alieni appetens*; insati-able, -ate; unquenchable, quenchless; omnivorous.

unsatisfied, unsated, unslaked.

eager, avid, keen; burning, fervent, ardent; agog; all agog; breathless; impatient etc. (*impetuous*) 825; bent –, intent –, set- -on, – upon; mad after, *enragé*, rabid, dying for, devoured by desire.

aspiring, ambitious, vaulting, sky-aspiring.

desirable; popular; desired etc. *v.*; in demand; pleasing etc. (*giving pleasure*) 829; appeti-zing, -ble; tantalizing.

Adv. wistfully etc. *adj.*; fain.

Int. would -that, – it were! O for! *esto perpetua!* if only!

Phr. the wish being the father to the thought; *sua cuique voluptas*; *hoc erat in votis*, the mouth watering, the fingers itching; *aut Caesar aut nullus*.

866. Indifference.—N. indifference, neutrality; coldness etc. *adj.*; unconcern, *insouciance, nonchalance*; want of -interest, – earnestness; anorexy, inappetency; apathy etc. (*insensibility*) 823; supineness etc. (*inactivity*) 683; disdain etc. 930; recklessness etc. 863; inattention etc. 458.

V. be -indifferent etc. *adj.*; stand neuter; take no interest in etc. (*insensibility*) 823; have no -desire etc. 865, – taste, – relish- for; not care for; care nothing -for, – about; not care a -straw etc. (*unimportance*) 643 -about, – for; not mind.

set at naught etc. (*make light of*) 483; spurn etc. (*disdain*) 930.

Adj. indifferent, cold, frigid, lukewarm; cool, – as a cucumber; unconcerned, *insouciant*, phlegmatic, *pococurante*, easy-going, devil-may-care, careless, listless, lackadaisical, feckless; half-hearted; un-ambitious, -aspiring, -desirous, -solicitous, -attracted.

un-attractive, -alluring, -desired, -desirable, -cared for, -wished, -valued, all one to.

insipid etc. 391; vain.

Adv. for aught one cares.

Int. never mind.

867. Dislike.—N. dis-like, -taste, -relish, -inclination, -placency.

reluctance; backwardness etc. (*unwillingness*) 603.

repugnance, disgust, queasiness, turn, nausea, loathing; avers-eness, -ation, -ion; abomination, antipathy, abhorrence, horror; mortal –, rooted- -antipathy, – horror; hatred, detestation; hate etc. 898; animosity etc. 900; hydrophobia.

sickener; gall and wormwood etc. (*unsavory*) 395; shuddering, cold sweat.

V. dis-, mis-like, -relish; mind, object to; have rather not, not care for; have –, conceive –, entertain –, take- -a dislike, – an aversion- to; have no -taste, – stomach- for.

shun, avoid etc. 623; eschew; withdraw –, shrink –, recoil- from; not be able to -bear, – abide, – endure; shrug the shoulders at, shudder at, turn up the nose at, look askance at; make a -mouth, – wry face, – grimace; make faces.

loathe, nauseate, abominate, detest, abhor; hate etc. 898; take amiss etc. 900; have enough of etc. (*be satiated*) 869.

cause –, excite- dislike; disincline, repel, sicken; make –, render- sick; turn one's stomach, nauseate, wamble, disgust, shock, stink in the nostrils; go against the -grain, – stomach; stick in the throat; make one's blood run cold etc. (*give pain*) 830; pall.

Adj. disliking etc. *v.*; averse to, loth, adverse; shy of, sick of, out of conceit with; disinclined; heart-, dog-sick; queasy.

disliked etc. *v.*; uncared for, unpopular; out of favor; repulsive, repugnant, repellent; abhorrent, insufferable, fulsome, nauseous; loath-some, -ful; offensive; disgusting etc. *v.*; disagreeable etc. (*painful*) 830; unsavory etc. 395.

Adv. *usque ad nauseam*.

Int. faugh! foh! ugh!

868. Fastidiousness.—N. fastidiousness etc. *adj.*; nicety, meticulosity, hypercriticism, difficulty in being pleased, *friandise*, epicurism, *omnia suspendens naso*.

discrimination, discernment, good taste, perspicacity.

epicure, gourmet.

[Excess of delicacy] prudery, prudishness, primness.

V. be -fastidious etc. *adj.*; split hairs, discriminate, have a sweet tooth.

mince the matter; turn up one's nose at etc. (*disdain*) 930; look a gift horse in the mouth, see spots on the sun.

Adj. fastidious, meticulous, exacting, nice, delicate, *délicat*, finical, finicky, difficult, dainty, lickerish, squeamish, thin-skinned; s-, queasy; hard –, difficult- to please; querulous, particular, over-particular, straitlaced, prudish, prim, scrupulous; censorious etc. 932; hypercritical, discriminating, discerning, perspicacious.

Phr. *noli me tangere*.

869. Satiety.—N. satiety, satisfaction, saturation, repletion, glut, surfeit; weariness etc. 841.

spoiled child; *enfant gâté*; too much of a good thing, *toujours perdrix*; *crambe repetita*.

V. sate, satiate, satisfy, saturate; cloy, quench, slake, pall, glut, gorge, surfeit; bore etc. (*weary*) 841; tire etc. (*fatigue*) 688; spoil.

have -enough of, – quite enough of, – one's fill, – too much of; be -satiated etc. *adj.*

Adj. satiated etc. *v.*; overgorged; *blasé*, used up, sick of, heart-sick.

Int. enough! hold! *eheu jam satis!*

870. Wonder.—N. wonder, marvel; astonish-, amaze-, wonder-, bewilder-ment; amazedness etc. *adj.*; admiration, awe; stup-or, -efaction; stound, fascination; sensation; surprise etc. (*inexpectation*) 508; cynosure.

note of admiration; thaumaturgy etc. (*sorcery*) 992.

V. wonder, marvel, admire; be -surprised etc. *adj.*; start; stare; open –, rub –, turn up- one's eyes; gloar; gape, open one's mouth, hold one's breath; look –, stand- -aghast, – agog; look blank etc. (*disappointment*) 509; *tomber des nues*; not believe one's -eyes, – ears, – senses.

not be able to account for etc. (*unintelligible*) 519; not know whether one stands on one's head or one's heels.

surprise, astonish, amaze, astound; dumbfound, -er; startle, dazzle; strike, – with -wonder, – awe; electrify; stun, stupefy, petrify, confound, bewilder, flabbergast; stagger, throw on one's beam ends, fascinate, turn the head, take away one's breath, strike dumb; make one's -hair stand on end, – tongue cleave to the roof of one's mouth; make one stare.

take by surprise etc. (*be unexpected*) 508.

be -wonderful etc. *adj.*; beggar –, baffle- description; stagger belief.

Adj. surprised etc. *v.*; aghast, all agog, breathless, agape; open-mouthed; awe-, thunder-, moon-, planet-struck; spell-bound; lost in -amazement, – wonder, – astonishment; struck all of a heap, unable to believe one's senses, like a duck in thunder.

wonderful, wondrous; surprising etc. *v.*; unexpected etc. 508; unheard of; mysterious etc. (*inexplicable*) 519; miraculous; *foudroyant*.

in-describable, -expressible' -effable; unutterable, -speakable.

monstrous, prodigious, stupendous, marvelous; in-conceivable, -credible; in-, un-imaginable; strange etc. (*uncommon*) 83; passing strange.

striking etc. *v.*; over-whelming; wonder-working.

Adv. wonderfully etc. *adj.*; fearfully; for a –, in the name of- wonder; strange to say; *mirabile -dictu*, – visu; to one's great surprise.

with -wonder etc. *n.*, – gaping mouth, – open eyes, – upturned eyes; eyes starting out of one's head.

Int. lo, – and behold! O! hey-day! halloo! what! indeed! really! surely! humph! hem! good -lack, – heavens, – gracious! – lord! by jove! gad so! well a day! dear me! only think! lack-a-daisy! my stars, – goodness! gracious goodness! goodness gracious! mercy on us! heavens and earth! God bless me! bless -us, – my heart! odzookens! *O gemini!* adzooks! hoity-toity! strong! Heaven save –, bless- the mark! can such things be! zounds! 'sdeath! what -on earth, – in the world! who would have thought it! etc. (*inexpectation*) 508; fancy! did you ever? you don't say so! what do you say to that! how now! where am I? well I'm blowed! etc.

Phr. *vox faucibus haesit*; one's hair standing on end.

871. Expectance. [Absence of wonder.]—**N.** expectan-ce, -cy etc. (*expectation*) 507; calmness, composure, tranquillity, serenity, coolness, imperturbability etc. 826.

nine days' wonder.

V. expect etc. 507; not -be surprised, – wonder etc. 870; *nil admirari*, make nothing of.

Adj. expecting etc. *v.*; unamazed, astonished at nothing; *blasé* etc. (*weary*) 841; unimaginative, calm, serene, imperturbable etc. 826; expected etc. *v.*; foreseen.

common, ordinary etc. (*habitual*) 613.

Int. no wonder; of course; why not?

872. Prodigy.—N. prodigy, phenomenon; wonder, -ment; genius, marvel, miracle; freak, monster etc. (*unconformity*) 83; curiosity, lion, infant prodigy, sight, spectacle; *jeu –*, *coup- de théâtre*; gazing-stock; sign; portent etc. 512.

bursting of a -shell, – bomb; volcanic eruption, peal of thunder; thunder-clap, -bolt.

what no words can paint; wonders of the world; *annus mirabilis*; *dignus vindice nodus*.

873. Repute.—N. distinction, mark, name, figure; repute, reputation, character; good –, high- repute; note, notability, notoriety, *éclat*, 'the bubble reputation,' vogue, celebrity; fame, famousness; renown; populairty, *aura popularis*; esteem, approval, approbation etc. 931; credit, *succès d'estime*, *prestige*, talk of the town; name to conjure with.

glory, honor; luster etc. (*light*) 420; illustriouness etc. *adj.*

account, regard, respect; reputableness etc. *adj.*; respectability etc. (*probity*) 939; good -name, – report; fair name.

dignity; stateliness etc. *adj.*; solemnity, grandeur, splendor, nobility, majesty, sublimity.

rank, standing, brevet rank, precedence, *pas*, station, place, *status*; position, – in society; order, degree, *locus standi*, caste, condition.

greatness etc. *adj.*; eminence; height etc. 206; importance etc. 642; pre-, super-eminence; high mightiness, primacy; top of the -ladder, – tree.

elevation; ascent etc. 305; super-, ex-altation; dignification, aggrandizement.

dedication, consecration, enthronement, canonization, apotheosis, deification, celebration, enshrinement, glorification.

hero, man of mark, great card, celebrity, worthy, lion, *rara avis*, notability, somebody; man of rank etc. (*nobleman*) 875; pillar of the -state, – society, – church.

chief etc. (*master*) 745; first fiddle etc. (*proficient*) 700; scholar etc. 492; cynosure, mirror; flower, pink, pearl; paragon etc. (*perfection*) 650; choice and master spirits of the age; *élite*; star, sun, constellation, galaxy.

ornament, honor, feather in one's cap, halo, aureole, nimbus; halo –, blaze- of glory; blushing honors; laurels etc. (*trophy*) 733.

memory, posthumous fame, niche in the temple of fame; immor-tality, -tal name; *magni nominis umbra*.

V. be conscious of glory; be proud of etc. (*pride*) 878; exult etc. (*boast*) 884; be vain of etc. (*vanity*) 880.

be -distinguished etc. *adj.*; shine etc. (*light*) 420; shine forth, figure; make –, cut- a -figure, – dash, – splash.

rival, surpass; out-shine, -rival, -vie, -jump; emulate, vie with, eclipse; throw –, cast- into the shade; overshadow.

live, flourish, glitter, scintillate, flaunt; gain –, acquire- honor etc. *n.*; play first fiddle etc. (*be of importance*) 642; bear the -palm, – bell; lead the way; take -precedence, – the wall of; gain –, win- -laurels, – spurs, – golden opinions etc. (*approbation*) 931; graduate, take one's degree, pass one's examination, win a -scholarship, – fellowship.

make -a, – some- -noise, – noise in the world; leave one's mark, exalt one's horn, star, have a run, be run after; enjoy popularity, come -into vogue, – to the front; raise one's head.

enthrone, signalize, immortalize, deify, exalt to the skies; hand one's name down to posterity.

consecrate; dedicate to, devote to; enshrine, inscribe, blazon, lionize, blow the trumpet, crown with laurel.

confer –, reflect- honor etc. *n.* on; shed a luster on; redound to one's honor, ennoble.

give –, do –, pay –, render- honor to; honor, accredit, pay regard to, dignify, glorify; sing praises to etc. (*approve*) 931; look up to; exalt, aggrandize, elevate, nobilitate.

Adj. distinguished, *distingué*, noted; of -note etc. *n.*; honored etc. *v.*; popular; fashionable etc. 852.

in good odor; in –, in high- favor; reput-, respect-, credit-able.

remarkable etc. (*important*) 642; notable, notorious; celebrated, renowned, in every one's mouth, talked of; fam-ous, -ed; far-famed; conspicuous, to the front; foremost; in the -front rank, – ascendant.

imperishable, deathless, immortal, never fading, *aere perennius*; time-honored.

illustrious, glorious, splendid, brilliant, radiant; bright etc. 420; full-blown; honorific.

eminent, prominent; high etc. 206; in the zenith; at the -head of, – top of the tree; peerless, of the first water; superior etc. 33; super-, pre-eminent.

great, dignified, proud, noble, honorable, worshipful, lordly, grand, stately, august, princely, imposing, solemn, transcendent, majestic, sacred, sublime, heaven-born, heroic, *sans peur et sans reproche*; sacrosanct.

Int. hail! all hail! *ave! viva! vive!* long life to! glory –, honor- be to!

Phr. one's name -being in every mouth, – living for ever; *sic itur ad astra, fama volat, aut Caesar aut nullus*; not to know him argues oneself unknown; none but himself could be his parallel, *palmam qui meruit ferat.*

874. Disrepute.—N. disrepute, discredit; ill-, bad- -repute, -name, -odor, -favor; disapprobation etc. 932; in-gloriousness, derogation; a-, debasement; abjectness etc. *adj.*; degradation, dedecoration; 'a long farewell to all one's greatness;' odium, obloquy, opprobrium, ignominy.

dishonor, disgrace; shame, humiliation; scandal, baseness, vileness; perfidy, turpitude etc. (*improbity*) 940; infamy.

tarnish, taint, defilement, pollution.

stain, blot, spot, blur, stigma, brand, reproach, imputation, slur.

crying –, burning- shame; *scandalum magnatum*, badge of infamy, blot in one's escutcheon; bend –, bar- sinister; champain, point champain; by- word of reproach; Ichabod.

argumentum ad verecundiam; sense of shame etc. 879.

V. be -inglorious etc. *adj.*; incur -disgrace etc. *n.*; have –, earn- a bad name; put –, wear- a halter round one's neck; disgrace –, expose- oneself.

play second fiddle; lose caste; pale one's ineffectual fire; recede into the shade; fall from one's high estate; keep in the background etc. (*modesty*) 881; be conscious of disgrace etc. (*humility*) 879; look -blue, – foolish, – like a fool; cut a -poor, – sorry- figure; laugh on the wrong side of the mouth; make a sorry face, go away with a flea in one's ear, slink away.

cause -shame etc. *n.*; shame, disgrace, put to shame, dishonor; throw –, cast –, fling –, reflect- dishonor etc. *n.* upon; be a -reproach etc. *n.* to; derogate from.

tarnish, stain, blot, sully, taint; discredit, degrade, debase, defile; beggar; expel etc. (*punish*) 972.

impute shame to, brand, post, stigmatize, vilify, defame, slur, cast a slur upon, hold up to shame, send to Coventry; tread –, trample- under foot; show up, drag through the mire, heap dirt upon; reprehend etc. 932.

bring low, put down, snub; take down a peg, – lower, – or two.

obscure, eclipse, outshine, take the shine out of; throw –, cast- into the shade; overshadow; leave –, put- in the background; push into a corner, put one's nose out of joint; put out, – of countenance.

upset, throw off one's center; discompose, disconcert; put to the blush etc. (*humble*) 879.

Adj. disgraced etc. *v.*; blown upon; shorn of -its beams, – one' glory; overcome, down-trodden; loaded with -shame etc. *n.*; in -bad repute etc. *n.*; out of -repute, – favor, – fashion, – countenance; at a discount; under -a cloud, – an eclipse; unable to show one's face; in the -shade, – background; out at elbows, down in the world, down and out.

inglorious; nameless, renownless, obscure, unknown to fame; un-noticed, -noted, -honored, -glorified.

shameful; dis-graceful, -creditable, -reputable; despicable; questionable; unbecoming, unworthy; derogatory; degrading, humiliating, *infra dignitatem*, dedecorous; scandalous, infamous, too bad, unmentionable; ribald, opprobrious; arrant, shocking, outrageous, notorious, shady.

ignominious, scrubby, dirty, abject, vile, beggarly, pitiful, low, mean, shabby; base etc. (*dishonorable*) 940.

Adv. to one's shame be it spoken.

Int. fie! shame! for shame! *proh pudor! O tempora! O mores!* ough! *sic transit gloria mundi!*

875. Nobility.—N. nobility, rank, condition, distinction, optimacy, blood, *pur sang*, birth, high descent, order; quality, gentility; blue blood of Castile; *ancien régime.*

high life, *haut monde*; upper -classes, – ten thousand; *élite*, aristocracy, great folks; fashionable world etc. (*fashion*) 852; salariat.

peer, -age; house of -lords, – peers; lords, – temporal and spiritual; *noblesse*; baronage, knightage; noble, -man; lord, -ling; grandee, *magnifico, hidalgo*; don, -ship; aristocrat, swell, three-tailed bashaw; gentleman, squire, squireen, patrician, laureate.

gentry, gentlefolk; squirarchy, better sort, *magnates, primates, optimates.*

king etc. (*master*) 745; prince, crown prince, *Dauphin*; duke; marquis, -ate; earl, viscount, baron, thane, banneret; baronet, -cy; knight, -hood; count, armiger, laird; sig-, seig-nior; esquire, boyar, margrave, vavasor, sheik, emir, ameer, scherif, *pasha*, effendi, sahib.

queen etc. 745; princess, begum, duchess, marchioness; countess etc.; lady, dame.

personage –, man- of -distinction, – mark, – rank; nota-bles, -bilities; celebrity, big-wig, magnate, great man, star; *magni nominis umbra*; 'every inch a king;' grand Panjandrum

V. be -noble etc. *adj.*

Adj. noble, exalted; of -rank etc. *n.*; princely, titled, patrician, aristocratic; high-, well-born; of gentle blood; genteel, *comme il faut*, gentlemanlike, courtly etc. (*fashionable*) 852; highly respectable.

Adv. in high quarters.

876. Commonalty.—N. commonalty, democracy; obscruity; low -condition, – life, – society, – company; *bourgeoisie*; mass of -the people, – society; Brown, Jones, and Robinson; Tom, Dick, and Harry; lower –, humbler- -classes, – orders; vulgar –, common- herd; rank and file, *hoc genus omne*; the -many, – general, – crowd, – people, – populace, – multitude, – million, – masses, – mobility, – peasantry; king Mob; proletariat, *fruges consumere nati*, great unwashed; man in the street.

mob; rabble, – rout; chaff, rout, horde, *canaille*; scum –, *residuum* –, dregs- of -the people, – society; swinish multitude, *faex populi*; *profanum* –, *ignobile- vulgus*; vermin, riff-raff, tag-rag and bobtail; small fry.

commoner, one of the people, democrat, plebeian, republican, proletary, *prolétaire*, *roturier*, Mr. Snooks, *bourgeois*, *épicier*, Philistine, cockney; *grisette*, *demi-monde*.

peasant, countryman, boor, carle, churl; vill-ain, -ein; serf, kern, tyke, tike, chuff, ryot, fellah; longshoreman; swain, clown, hind; clod, -hopper; hobnail, yokel, hick, rube, cider squeezer, bog-trotter, bumpkin; ploughman, -boy; rustic, chawbacon, tiller of the soil; hewers of wood and drawers of water, groundling; gaffer, loon, put, cub, Tony Lumpkin, looby, lout, under-ling; *gamin*, guttersnipe, street arab, mudlark; rough, rowdy, ruffian, roughneck; pot-wallopper, slubberdegullion; vulgar –, low- fellow; cad, curmudgeon.

upstart, *parvenu*, *nouveau-riche*, skipjack; nobody, – one knows; *hesterni quirites*, *pessoribus orti*; *bourgeois gentilhomme*, *novus homo*, snob, gent, mushroom, no one knows who, adventurer; man of straw.

beggar, panhandler, gaberlunzie, muckworm, mudlark, *sans-culotte*, raff, tatterdemalion, caitiff, ragamuffin, Pariah, outcast of society, tramp, weary Willie, bum, vagabond, *chiffonaier*, rag-picker, Cinderella, cinderwench, scrub, jade; boots, gossoon.

Goth, Vandal, Hottentot, savage, barbarian, Yahoo; unlicked cub, rough diamond.

barbar-ousness, -ism; Boeotia.

V. be -ignoble etc. *adj.*, – nobody etc. *n.*

Adj. ignoble, common, mean, low, base, vile, sorry, scrubby, beggarly, below par; no great shakes etc. (*unimportant*) 643; home-ly, -spun; vulgar, low-minded; snobbish, *parvenu*.

plebeian, proletarian; of -low, – mean- -parentage, – origin, extraction; low-, base-, earthborn, low bred; mushroom, dunghill, risen from the ranks; unknown to fame, obscure, untitled.

rustic, uncivilized; lout-, boor-, clown-, churl-, brut-, raff-ish; rude, unlicked, unpolished.

barbar-ous, -ian, -ic, -esque; cockney, born within sound of Bow bells.

underling, menial, servile, subaltern.

Adv. below the salt.

877. Title.—N. title, honor; knighthood etc. (*nobility*) 875.

royal –, serene- highness, excellency, grace; lordship, worship, Rt. Hon., rever-ence, -end; esquire, sir; madam, *madame*; master, mistress, Mr., Mrs., *signor*, *señor*, *Mein Herr*, *mynheer*; your –, his- honor; handle to one's name.

decoration, laurel, palm, wreath, garland, bays, medal, ribbon, riband, blue ribbon, *cordon*, cross, crown, coronet, star, garter; feather, – in one's cap; chevron, epaulet, *épaulette*, colors, cockade; livery; order, arms, armorial bearings, shield, scutcheon, crest, reward etc. 973.

878. Pride.—N. dignity, self-respect, *mens sibi conscia recti*.

pride; haughtiness etc. *adj.*; high notions, *hauteur*; vainglory, crest; arrogance etc. (*assumption*) 885; pomposity etc. 882.

proud man, highflier; fine -gentleman, – lady; *grande dame*.

V. be -proud etc. *adj.*; put a good face on; look one in the face; stalk abroad, perk oneself up; presume, swagger, strut; rear –, lift up –, hold up- one's head; hold one's head high, look big, take the wall, 'bear like the Turk no rival near the throne,' carry with a high hand; ride the –, mount on one's- high horse; set one's back up, bridle, toss the head; give oneself airs etc. (*assume*) 885; boast etc. 884.

pride oneself on; glory in, take pride in; pique –, plume –, hug- oneself; stand upon, be proud of; put a good face on; not -hide one's light under a bushel, – put one's talent in a napkin; not think small beer of oneself etc. (*vanity*) 880.

Adj. dignified; stately; proud, -crested; lordly, baronial; lofty-minded; high-souled, -minded, -mettled, -handed, -plumed, -flown, -toned.

haughty, paughty, insolent, lofty, high, mighty, swollen, puffed up, flushed, blown; vain-glorious; purse-proud, fine; proud as -a peacock, Lucifer; bloated with pride.

supercilious, disdainful, bumptious, magisterial, imperious; high-handed, – and mighty; overweening, consequential; arrogant etc. 885; unblushing etc. 880.

stiff, -necked; starch; perked –, stuck- up; in buckram, straitlaced; prim etc. (*affected*) 855.

on one's -high horses, – tight ropes, – high ropes; on stilts; *en grand seigneur*.

Adv. with head erect, with one's nose in the air.

Phr. *odi profanum vulgus et arceo*.

879. Humility.—N. hum-ility, -bleness; meek-, low-ness; lowli-ness, -hood; abasement, self-abasement, -effacement; submission etc. 725; resignation.

condescension; affability etc. (*courtesy*) 894.

modesty etc. 881; verecundity, blush, suffusion, confusion; sense of -shame, – disgrace; humiliation, mortification; let –, set- down.

V. be -humble etc. *adj.*; deign, vouchsafe, condescend; humble –, demean- oneself; stoop, – to conquer; carry coals; submit etc. 725; submit with a good grace etc. (*brook*) 826; yield the palm.

lower one's -tone, – note; sing small, draw in one's horns, sober down; hide one's -face, – diminished head; not dare to show one's face, take shame to oneself, not have a word to say for oneself; feel –, be conscious of- -shame, – disgrace; drink the cup of humiliation to the dregs; eat -humble pie, – one's words, – dirt; be humiliated, receive a snub.

blush -for, – up to the eyes; redden, change color; color up; hang one's head, look foolish, feel small.

render humble; humble, humiliate; let –, set –, take –, tread –, frown- down; snub, abash, abase, make one sing small, strike dumb; teach one -his distance, – his place; take down a peg, – lower; throw –, cast- into the shade etc. 874; stare –, put- out of countenance; put to the blush; confuse, ashame, mortify, disgrace, crush; send away with a flea in one's ear.

get a set down.

Adj. humble, lowly, meek; modest etc. 881; humble-, sober-minded; unoffended; submissive etc. 725; servile etc. 886.

condescending; affable etc. (*courteous*) 894.

humbled etc. *v.*; bowed down, resigned; abashed, ashamed, dashed; out of countenance; down in the mouth; down on one's -knees, – marrow-bones; humbled in the dust, brow-beaten; chap-, crest-fallen; dumbfoundered, flabbergasted, struck all of a heap.

shorn of one's glory etc. (*disrepute*) 874.

Adv. with -downcast eyes, – bated breath, – bended knee; on all fours, on one's feet.

under correction, with due deference.

Phr. I am your -obedient, – very humble- servant; my service to you.

880. Vanity.—N. vanity; conceit, -edness; self-conceit, -complacency, -confidence, -sufficiency, -esteem, -love, -approbation, -praise, -glorification, -laudation, -gratulation, -applause, -admiration; *amour-propre*; selfishness etc. 943.

airs, pretensions, mannerism; egotism; prigg-ism, -ishness; coxcombery, gaudery, vainglory, elation; pride etc. 878; ostentation etc. 882; assurance etc. 885.

vox et praeterea nihil; *cheval de bataille*.

ego-ist, -tist; peacock, coxcomb etc. 854; Sir Oracle etc. 887.

V. be -vain etc. *adj.*, – vain of; pique oneself etc. (*pride*) 878; lay the flattering unction to one's soul.

have -too high, – an overweening- opinion of -oneself, – one's talents; blind oneself as to one's own merit; not think -small beer, – *vin ordinaire*- of oneself; put oneself forward; fish for compliments; give oneself airs etc. (*assume*) 885; boast etc. 884.

render -vain etc. *adj.*; inspire with -vanity etc. *n.*; inflate, puff up, turn up, turn one's head.

Adj. vain, – as a peacock; conceited, assured, overweening, pert, forward, perky; vain-glorious, high-flown; ostentatious etc. 882; puffed up, inflated, flushed.

self-satisfied, -confident, -sufficient, -flattering, -admiring, -applauding, -glorious, -opinionated; *entêté* etc. (*wrong-headed*) 481; wise in one's own conceit, pragmatical, overwise, pretentious, priggish; egotistic, -al; *soi-disant* etc. (*boastful*) 884; arrogant etc. 885.

un-abashed, -blushing; un-constrained, -ceremonious; free and easy.

Adv. vainly etc. *adj.*

Phr. how we apples swim!

881. Modesty.—N. modesty; humility etc. 879; diffidence, timidity; retiring disposition, unobtrusiveness, bashfulness etc. *adj.*; *mauvaise honte*; blush, -ing; verecundity; self-knowledge.

reserve, constraint; demureness etc. *adj.*; blushing honors.

V. be -modest etc. *adj.*; retire, reserve oneself; give way to; draw in one's horns etc. 879; hide one's face.

keep -private, – in the background, – one's distance; pursue the noiseless tenor of one's way, 'do good by stealth and blush to find it fame,' hide one's light under a bushel, cast a sheep's eye.

Adj. modest, diffident; humble etc. 879; timid, timorous, bashful; shy, nervous, skittish, coy, sheepish, shamefaced, blushing, over-modest.

unpreten-ding, -tious; un-obtrusive, -assuming, -ostentatious, -boastful, -aspiring; poor in spirit.

out of countenance etc. (*humbled*) 879.

reserved, constrained, demure.

Adv. humbly etc. *adj.*; quietly, privately; without -ceremony, – beat of the drum; *sans façon*.

882. Ostentation.—N. ostentation, display, show, flourish, parade, *étalage*, pomp, array, state, solemnity; dash, splash, glitter, strut, swank, side, swagger, pomposity; preten-se, -sions; showing off; fuss.

magnificence, splendor; *coup d'oeil*; grand doings.

coup de théâter; stage -effect, – trick; clap-trap; *mise en scène*; *tour de force*; *chic*.

demonstration, flying colors; tomfoolery; flourish of trumpets etc. (*celebration*) 883; pageant, -ry; spectacle, exhibition, procession; turn –, set- out; grand function; *fête*, gala, field-day, review, march past, promenade, insubstantial pageant.

dress; court –, full –, evening –, ball –, fancy- dress; tailoring, millinery, man-millinery, frippery; foppery, equipage.

ceremon-y, -ial; ritual; form, -ality; etiquette; punct-o, -ilio, -ilious-ness; starched-, stateli-ness.

mummery, solemn mockery, mouth honor.

attitudinarian; fop etc. 854.

V. be -ostentatious etc. *adj.*; come –, put oneself- forward; attract attention, star it.

make –, cut- a -figure, – dash, – splash; strut, blow one's own trumpet; figure, – away; make a show, – display; glitter.

show -off, – one's paces; parade, march past;

display, exhibit, put forward, hold up; trot –, hang- out; sport, brandish, blazon forth; dangle, – before the eyes.

cry up etc. (*praise*) 931; *prôner*, flaunt, emblazon, prink, set off, mount, have framed and glazed.

put a good, – smiling- face upon; clean the outside of the platter etc. (*disguise*) 544.

Adj. ostentatious, showy, dashing, pretentious; ja-, jau-nty; grand, pompous, palatial; high sounding; turgid etc. (*big-sounding*) 577; garish, gorgeous; gaudy, – as a -peacock, – butterfly, – tulip; flaunting, flashing, flaming, glittering; gay etc. (*ornate*) 847; colorful.

splendid, magnificent, sumptuous.

theatrical, dramatic, spectacular, scenic, ceremonial, ritual, -istic.

solemn, stately, majestic, formal, stiff, ceremonious, punctilious, starch-ed, -y.

en grande tenue, in best bib and tucker, in Sunday best, *endimanché*.

Adv. with -flourish of trumpet, – beat of drum, – flying colors, – a brass band.

ad captandum vulgus.

883. Celebration.—N. celebration, solemnization, jubilee, diamond jubilee, commemoration, ovation, paean, triumph, jubilation.

triumphal arch, bonfire, salute; salvo, – of artillery; *feu de joie*, flourish of trumpets, *fanfare*, colors flying, illuminations, fireworks.

inauguration, installation, presentation; *début*, coming out, birthday anniversary, bi-, ter-, centenary; silver –, golden –, diamond- wedding, - day; coronation; Lord Mayor's show; harvest home, red letter day, festival; trophy etc. 733; *Te Deum* etc. (*thanksgiving*) 990; fête etc. 882; holiday etc. 840.

V. celebrate, keep, signalize, do honor to, commemorate, solemnize, hallow, mark with a red letter, hold high festival, maffick.

pledge, drink to, toast, hob and nob.

inaugurate, install, instate, induct, chair.

rejoice etc. 838; kill the fatted calf, hold jubilee, roast an ox, fire a salute.

Adj. celebrating etc. *v.*; commemorative, celebrated, immortal.

Adv. in -honor, – commemoration, – celebration of.

Int. hail! all hail! *io -paean, – triumphe!* 'see the conquering hero comes!'

884. Boasting.—N. boasting etc. *v.*; boast, vaunt, crake; preten-ce, -sions; puff, -ery; flourish, *fanfaronnade*; gasconade; bluff, swank, brag, - gardism; bravado, bunkum, Buncombe; highfalutin; jact-itation, -ancy; bounce, rant, bluster; venditation, vaporing, rodomontade, bombast, fine talking, tall talk, magniloquence, teratology, heroics; jingoism, Chauvinism; exaggeration etc. 549; gas, hot air.

vanity etc. 880; *vox et praeterea nihil*; much cry and little wool, *brutum fulmen.*

exultation; glorification; flourish of trumpets; triumph etc. 883.

boaster; bragg-art, -adocio; hot air merchant; Gascon, *fanfaron*, pretender, fourflusher, *soi-disant*; windbag, blowhard, bluffer; chauvinist; blusterer etc. 887; charlatan, jack-pudding, trumpeter; puppy etc. (*fop*) 854.

V. boast, make a boast of, brag, vaunt, puff, show off, flourish, crake, crack, trumpet, strut, swagger, vapor, bluff; draw the long bow.

exult, crow over, neigh, chuckle, triumph; glory, gloat, jubilate; throw up one's cap; talk big, *se faire valoir*, *faire claquer son fouet*, take merit to oneself, make a merit of, sing *Io triumphe*, holloa before one is out of the wood.

Adj. boasting etc. *v.*; magniloquent, flaming, Thrasonic, stilted, gasconading, braggart, boastful, pretentious, *soi-disant*; vain-glorious etc. (*conceited*) 880.

elate, -d; jubilant, triumphant, exultant; in high feather; flushed, – with victory; cock-a-hoop; on stilts.

vaunted etc. *v.*

Adv. vauntingly etc. *adj.*; with a brass band.

Phr. 'let the galled jade wince.'

885. Insolence. [Undue assumption of superiority.]—**N.** insolence; haughtiness etc. *adj.*; arrogance, airs; overbearance, brashness, bumptiousness, contumely, disdain; domineering etc. *v.*; tyranny etc. 739.

impertinence; cheek, nerve, sauce; sauciness etc. *adj.*; flippancy, dicacity, petulance, procacity, bluster; swagger, -ing etc. *v.*; bounce; terrorism; jingoism, chauvinism.

as-, pre-sumption; beggar on horseback; usurpation.

impudence, assurance, audacity, self-assertion, hardihood, front, face, brass; shamelessness etc. *adj.*; effrontery, hardened front, face of brass.

assumption of infallibility.

malapert, saucebox etc. (*blusterer*) 887.

V. be -insolent etc. *adj.*; bluster, vapor, swagger, swell, give oneself airs; snap one's fingers, kick up a dust; swear etc. (*affirm*) 535; rap out oaths; roister.

arrogate; as-, pre-sume; make -bold, – free; take a liberty, give an inch and take an ell.

domineer, bully, dictate, hector; lord it over, bulldoze; *traiter de haut*, *regarder de haut en bas*; exact; snub, huff, beard, fly in the face of; put to the blush; bear –, beat- down; browbeat, intimidate; trample –, tread- -down, – under foot; dragoon, ride roughshod over, terrorize.

out-face, -look, -stare, -brazen, -brave; stare out of countenance; brazen out; lay down the law; teach one's grandmother to suck eggs; assume a lofty bearing; talk –, look- big; put on big looks, act the *grand seigneur*; mount –, ride- the high horse; toss the head, carry with a high hand.

tempt Providence, want snuffing.

Adj. insolent, haughty, arrogant, imperious, magisterial, dictatorial, arbitrary; high-handed, high and mighty; contumelious, supercilious, overbearing, intolerant, domineering; overweening, high-flown.

flippant, pert, cavalier, saucy, forward, impertinent, fresh, malapert.

precocious, assuming, would-be, bumptious.

bluff; brazen-, browed-faced, shameless, aweless, unblushing, unabashed; bold-, bare-faced; dead –, lost- to shame.

impudent, audacious, presumptuous, free and easy, devil-may-care, rollicking; janty, jaunty; roistering, blustering, hectoring, swaggering, vaporing; thrasonic, fire-eating, 'full of sound and fury.'

Adv. insolently, with a high hand; *ex cathedrâ.*

Phr. one's bark being worse than his bite.

886. Servility.—N. servility; slavery etc. (*subjection*) 749; obsequiousness etc. *adj.*; subserviency; abasement; pros-tration, -ternation; genuflexion etc. (*worship*) 990; fawning etc. *v.*; tuft-hunting, time-serving, flunkeyism; sycophancy etc. (*flattery*) 933; humility etc. 879.

sycophant, parasite, yes-man; toad, -y, -eater; tuft-hunter; snob, flunkey, lap-dog, spaniel, lickspittle, smell-feast, *Graeculus esuriens*, hanger on, stooge, *cavaliere servente*, led captain, carpet knight; time-server, fortune-hunter, Vicar of Bray, Sir Pertinax Mac Sycophant, pick-thank; flatterer etc. 935; doer of dirty work; *âme damnée*, tool; reptile; slave etc. (*servant*) 746; courtier; sponge, jackal; truckler.

V. cringe, bow, stoop, kneel, bend the knee; fall on one's knees, prostrate oneself; worship etc. 990.

sneak, crawl, crouch, cower, truckle to, grovel, fawn, toady, lick the feet of, kiss the hem of one's garment.

pay court to; feed –, fatten –, batten- on; dance attendance on, pin oneself upon, hang on the sleeve of, *avaler des couleuvres*, keep time to, fetch and carry, do the dirty work of.

go with the stream, follow the crowd, worship the rising sun, hold with the hare and run with the hounds.

Adj. servile, obsequious; supple, – as a glove; soapy, oily, pliant, cringing, fawning, slavish, groveling, sniveling, mealy-mouthed; beggarly, sycophantic, parasitical; abject, prostrate, down on one's marrow-bones; base, mean, sneaking; crouching etc. *v.*

Adv. hat –, cap- in hand.

887. Blusterer.—N. bluster-, swagger-, vapor-, roister-, brawl-er; brazen-face; *fanfaron*; braggart etc. (*boaster*) 884; bully, terrorist, rough, roughneck; hooligan, hoodlum, larrikin, ruffian; Mohock, -hawk; drawcansir, swashbuckler, Captain Boabdil, Sir Lucius O'Trigger, Thraso, Pistol, Parolles, Bombastes Furioso, Hector, Chrononhotonthologos; jingo; desperado, dare-devil, fire-eater; fury etc. (*violent person*) 173; rowdy.

puppy etc. (*fop*) 854; prig; Sir Oracle, dogmatist, *doctrinaire*, stump orator, jack-in-office; saucebox, malapert, jackanapes, minx; bantam-cock.

888. Friendship.—N. friendship, amity; friendliness etc. *adj.*; brotherhood, fraternity, sodality, confraternity, sorosis, sisterhood; harmony etc. (*concord*) 714; peace etc. 721.

firm –, staunch –, intimate –, familiar –, bosom –, cordial –, tried –, devoted –, lasting –, fast –, sincere –, warm –, ardent- friendship.

cordiality, fraternization, *entente cordiale*, good understanding, *rapprochement*, sympathy, fellow-feeling, response, welcomeness; *camaraderie*.

affection etc. (*love*) 897; favoritism; goodwill etc. (*benovolence*) 906; partiality.

acquaintance, familiarity, intimacy, intercourse, fellowship, knowledge of; introduction.

V. be -friendly etc. *adj.*, – friends etc. 890; – acquainted with etc. *adj.*; know; have the ear of; keep- company with etc. (*sociality*) 892; hold communication –, have dealings –, sympathize- with; have a leaning to; bear good will etc. (*benevolence*) 906; love etc. 897; make much of; befriend etc. (*aid*) 707; introduce to.

set one's horses together; hold out –, extend- the right hand of -friendship, – fellowship; become -friendly etc. *adj.*; make -friends etc. 890 with; break the ice, be introduced to; make –, pick –, scrape- acquaintance with; get into favor, gain the friendship of.

shake hands with, fraternize, embrace; receive with open arms, throw oneself into the arms of; meet half way, take in good part.

Adj. friendly, amic-able, -al; well affected, unhostile, neighborly, brotherly, fraternal, sisterly, sympathetic, harmonious, hearty, cordial, warm-hearted, devoted.

friends –, well –, at home –, hand in hand- with; on -good, – friendly, – amicable, – cordial, – familiar, – intimate- -terms, – footing; on -speaking, – visiting- terms; in one's good -graces, – books.

acquainted, familiar, intimate, thick, hand and glove, hail fellow well met, free and easy; welcome.

Adv. amicably etc. *adj.*; with open arms; *sans cérémonie*; arm in arm.

889. Enmity.—N. enmity, hostility; unfriendliness etc. *adj.*; discord etc. 713.

alienation, estrangement; dislike etc. 867; hate etc. 898; antagonism.

heartburning; animosity etc. 900; malevolence etc. 907.

V. be -inimical etc. *adj.*; keep –, hold- at arm's length; be at loggerheads; bear malice etc. 907; fall out; take umbrage etc. 900; harden the heart, alienate, estrange.

Adj. inimical, unfriendly, hostile; at -enmity, – variance, – swords points, – daggers drawn, – open war with; up in arms against; in bad odor with.

on bad –, not on speaking- terms; cool; cold, -hearted; estranged, alienated, disaffected, irreconcilable.

890. Friend.—N. friend, – of one's bosom, intimate acquaintance, neighbor, well-wisher; *alter ego*; best –, bosom –, fast- friend; *amicus usque ad aras*; *fidus Achates*; *persona grata.*

favorer, *fautor*, patron, backer, Maecenas; tutelary saint, good genius, advocate, partisan, sympathizer; ally; friend in need etc. (*auxiliary*) 711.

associate, compeer, comrade, mate, companion, *confrère, camarade, confidante*, colleague; old –, crony; side-kick; chum, buddy, bunkie, roommate, pal; play-fellow, -mate; classmate, schoolfellow; bed-fellow, -mate; maid of honor.

compatriot; fellow –, countryman, – townsman.

shop-, ship-, mess-mate; fellow –, boon –, pot-companion; co-partner.

Arcades ambo, Pylades and Orestes, Castor and Pollux, Nisus and Euryalus, Damon and Pythias, *par nobile fratrum*.

host, Amphitryon, Boniface; guest, visitor, frequenter, *habitué*; *protégé*.

891. Enemy.—N. enemy; antagonist, foeman; open –, bitter- enemy; opponent etc. 710; back friend.

public enemy, enemy to society, traitor, anarchist etc. 743.

Phr. every hand being against one.

892. Sociality.—N. soci-ality, -ability, -ableness etc. *adj.*; social intercourse; consociation; intercourse, -community; consort-, companion-, fellow-, comrade-ship; clubbism; *esprit de corps*.

conviviality; good -fellowship, – company, *camaraderie*; joviality, jollity, *savoir -vivre*, festivity, festive board, merry-making; loving cup; hospitality, heartiness; cheer.

welcome, -ness; greeting; hearty –, warm –, welcome- reception; urbanity etc. (*courtesy*) 894; intimacy, familiarity.

good –, jolly- fellow, good mixer, Rotarian; *bon enfant*.

social –, family- circle; circle of acquaintance, *coterie*, society, company.

social -gathering, – *réunion*; assembly etc. (*assemblage*) 72; party, entertainment, reception, *levée*, at home, *conversazione*, *soirée*, *matinée*, evening –, morning –, afternoon –, garden –, dinner –, tea –, cocktail- party; symposium, sing-song; kettle-, drum; *partie carrée*, dish of tea, *ridotto*, rout, housewarming; ball, prom, hop, dance, *thé dansant*; festival etc. (*amusement*) 840; wedding breakfast; 'the feast of reason and the flow of soul.'

visit, -ing; round of visits; call, morning call; interview etc. (*interlocution*) 588; assignation; tryst, -ing place; appointment.

club etc. (*association*) 712.

V. be -sociable etc. *adj.*; know; be -acquainted etc. *adj.*; associate –, sort –, keep company –, walk hand in hand -with; eat off the same trencher, club together, consort, bear one company, join; make acquaintance with etc. (*friendship*) 888; make advances, fraternize, embrace; intercommunicate.

be –, feel –, make oneself- at home with; make free with; crack a bottle with; take pot luck with, receive hospitality, live at free quarters.

visit, pay a visit; interchange -visits, – cards; call -at, – upon; leave a card; drop in, look in; look one up, beat up one's quarters.

entertain; give a -party etc. *n.*; be at home, see one's friends, hang out, keep open house, do the honors; receive, – with open arms; welcome; give a warm reception etc. *n.* to; kill the fatted calf.

Adj. sociable, companionable, clubbable, clubby, conversable, cosy, cosey, chatty, conversational; homiletical.

convivial; fest-ive, -al; jovial, jolly, hospitable.

welcome, – as the roses in May; *fêté*, entertained.

free and easy, hail fellow well met, familiar, on visiting terms, acquainted.

social, neighborly; international, cosmopolitan, gregarious.

Adv. *en famille*, in the family circle; *sans - façon*, – *cérémonie*, arm in arm.

893. Seclusion. Exclusion.—N. seclusion, privacy; retirement; concealment; reclusion, recess; snugness etc. *adj.*; delitescence; rustication, *rus in urbe*; solitude; solitariness etc. (*singleness*) 87; isolation; loneliness etc. *adj.*; estrangement from the world, anchoritism, voluntary exile; aloofness.

cell, hermitage; convent etc. 1000; *sanctum sanctorum*; study, library, den; hide-out.

depopulation, desertion, desolation; wilderness etc. (*unproductive*) 169; howling wilderness; rotten borough, Old Sarum.

exclusion, excommunication, banishment, exile, ostracism, proscription; cut, – direct; dead cut.

inhospit-ality, -ableness etc. *adj.*; un-, dis-sociability; domesticity, Darby and Joan.

recluse, hermit, eremite, cenobite; anchor-et, -ite; Simon Stylites; Troglodyte, Timon of Athens, Santon, *solitaire*, ruralist, disciple of Zimmermann, closet cynic, Diogenes; outcast, Pariah, castaway, outsider, pilgarlic; wastrel, foundling, orphan.

V. be –, live- secluded etc. *adj.*; keep –, stand –, hold oneself- -aloof, – in the background; keep snug; shut oneself up; deny –, seclude- oneself; creep into a corner, rusticate, *aller planter ses choux*; retire, – from the world; hermetize, take the veil; abandon etc. 624.

cut, – dead; refuse to -associate with, – acknowledge; look cool –, turn one's back –, shut the door- upon; repel, blackball, excommunicate, exclude, exile, expatriate; banish, outlaw, maroon, ostracize, proscribe, cut off from, send to Coventry, keep at arm's length, draw a cordon round; boycott, blockade, lay an embargo on, isolate.

depopulate; dis-, un-people.

Adj. secluded, sequestered, retired, delitescent, private, bye; out of the -world, -way; in a backwater; 'the world forgetting by the world forgot.'

snug, domestic, stay-at-home.

unsociable; un-, dis-social; inhospitable, cynical, inconversable, unclubbable, *sauvage*, eremetic.

solitary; lone-ly, -some; isolated, single.

excluded, estranged; unfrequented; uninhabitable, -ed; tenantless; un-tenanted, -occupied; abandoned; deserted, – in one's utmost need; unfriended; kith-, friend-, home-less; lorn, forlorn, desolate.

un-visited, -introduced, -invited, -welcome; under a cloud, left to shift for oneself, derelict, outcast, outside the gates.

banished etc. *v.*; under an embargo.

Phr. *noli me tangere*.

894. Courtesy.—N. courtesy; respect etc. 928; good -manners, – behavior, – breeding; manners; politeness etc. *adj.*; *bienséance*, urbanity, comity, gentility; gentle –, breeding; polish, presence, cultivation, culture; civili-ty, -zation; amenity, suavity; good -temper, – humor; amiability, easy temper, complacency, soft tongue, mansuetude; condescension etc. (*humility*) 879; affability, complaisance, *prévenance*, amiability, gallantry, chivalry; pink of -politeness, – courtesy.

compliment; fair –, soft –, sweet- words; honeyed phrases, flattering remarks, ceremonial; salutation, reception, presentation, introduction, *accueil*, greeting, recognition; welcome, *abord*, respects, *devoir*, regards, remembrances; kind -regards, – remembrances; love, best love, duty; deference.

obeisance etc. (*reverence*) 928; bow, courtesy, curtsy, scrape, *salaam*, *kow-tow*, bowing and scraping; kneeling; genuflexion etc. (*worship*) 990; obsequiousness etc. 886; capping, shaking hands etc. *v.*; grip of the hand, embrace, hug, squeeze, *accolade*, loving cup, *vin d'honneur*, pledge; love token etc. (*endearment*) 902; kiss, buss, salute.

mark of recognition, not; 'nods and becks and wreathed smiles;' valediction etc. 293; condolence etc. 915.

V. be -courteous etc. *adj.*; show -courtesy etc. *n.*

mind one's P's and Q's, behave oneself, be all things to all men, conciliate, speak one fair, take in good part; make –, do- the amiable; look as if butter would not melt in one's mouth; mend one's manners.

receive, do the honors, usher, greet, hail, bid welcome; welcome, – with open arms; shake hands; hold out –, press –, squeeze- the hand; bid God speed; speed the parting guest; cheer, serenade.

salute; embrace etc. (*endearment*) 902; kiss, – hands; drink to, pledge, hob and nob; move to, nod to; smile upon.

uncover, cap; touch –, take off- the hat; doff the cap; pull the forelock; present arms; make way for; bow; make one's bow; scrape, curtsy, courtesy; bob a -curtsy, – courtesy; kneel; bow –, bend- the knee; salaam, *kowtow*.

visit, wait upon, present oneself, pay one's respects, pay a visit etc. (*sociability*) 892; dance attendance on etc. (*servility*) 886; pay attentions to; do homage to etc. (*respect*) 928.

prostrate oneself etc. (*worship*) 990.

give –, send- one's duty etc. *n.* to.

render -polite etc. *adj.*; polish, civilize, humanize.

Adj. courteous, polite, civil, mannerly, urbane; well-behaved, -mannered, -bred, -brought up, gently bred, of gentle -breeding, – manners, good-mannered, polished, civilized, cultivated; refined etc. (*taste*) 850; gentlemanlike etc. (*fashion*) 852; gallant, chivalrous, on one's good behavior.

fine –, fair –, soft- spoken; honey-mouthed, -tongued; oily, unctuous, bland, suave; obliging, conciliatory, complaisant, complacent; obsequious etc. 886.

ingratiating, winning; gentle, mild; good-humored, cordial, gracious, amiable, tactful, addressful, affable, genial, friendly, familiar; neighborly.

Adv. courteously etc. *adj.*; with a good grace; with -open, – outstretched- arms; *à bras ouverts*; *suaviter in modo*, in good humor.

Int. hail! welcome! well met! *ave!* all hail! good -day, – morning etc., – morrow! God speed! *pax vobiscum!* may your shadow never be less! *chin-chin!*

895. Discourtesy.—N. discourtesy; ill breeding; ill –, bad –, ungainly- manners; in suavity; grouchiness; un-courteousness etc. *adj.*, tactlessness; rusticity, inurbanity; illiberality, incivility, displacency.

disrespect etc. 929; procacity, impudence; barbar-ism, -ity; misbehavior, brutality, blackguard-ism, conduct unbecoming a gentleman, *grossièreté*, *brusquerie*; vulgarity etc. 851.

churlishness etc. *adj.*; spinosity, perversity; moroseness etc. (*sullenness*) 901*a*.

bad-, ill-temper; sternness etc. *adj.*; austerity; moodishness, captiousness etc. 901; cynicism; tartness etc. *adj.*; acrimony, acerbity, virulence, asperity.

scowl, black looks, frown; short answer, rebuff; hard words, contumely; unparliamentary language, personality.

bear, bruin, brute, grouch, blackguard, beast; unlicked cub; frump, cross-patch; saucebox etc. 887.

V. be -rude etc. *adj.*; insult etc. 929; treat with discourtesy; take a name in vain; make -bold, – free- with; take a liberty; stare out of countenance, ogle, point at, put to the blush.

cut; turn -one's back upon, – on one's heel; give the cold shoulder; keep at -a distance, – arm's length; look -cool, – coldly, – black- upon; show the door to, send away with a flea in the ear.

lose one's temper etc. (*resentment*) 900; sulk etc. 901*a*; frown, scowl, glower, pout; snap, snarl, growl.

render -rude etc. *adj.*; brut-alize, -ify.

Adj. dis-, un-courteous; uncourtly; ill-bred, -mannered, -behaved, -conditioned; unbred; unmanner-ly, -ed; im-, un-polite; un-polished, -civilized, -genteel; ungentleman-like, -ly; unladylike; blackguard; vulgar etc. 851; dedecorous; foul-mouthed, -spoken; abusive.

un-civil, -gracious, -ceremonious; cool; pert, forward, obtrusive, impudent, rude, saucy, precocious; insolent etc. 885.

repulsive; un-complaisant, -accommodating, -neighborly, -gallant; inaffable; un-gentle, -gainly; rough, rugged, bluff, blunt, gruff; churl-, boor-, bear-ish; brutal, *brusque*; stern, harsh, austere; cavalier.

tart, sour, crabbed, sharp, short, trenchant, sarcastic, crusty, biting, caustic, virulent, bitter, acrimonious, venomous, contumelious; snarling etc., *v.*; surly, – as a bear; perverse; grim, sullen etc. 901*a*; peevish etc. (*irascible*) 901.

Adv. discourteously etc. *adj.*; with -discourtesy etc. *n.*, – a bad grace.

896. Congratulations.—N. con-, gratulation; felicitation; salute etc. 894; condolence etc. 915; compliments of the season; good –, best- wishes.

V. con-, gratulate; felicitate, compliment; give –, wish one- joy; tender –, offer- one's congratulations; wish -many happy returns of the day, – a merry Christmas and a happy new year.

congratulate oneself etc. (*rejoice*) 838.

Adj. con-, gratulatory.

897. Love.—N. love; fondness etc. *adj.*; liking; inclination etc. (*desire*) 865; regard, dilection, admiration, fancy.

affection, sympathy, fellow-felling; tenderness etc. *adj.*; heart, brotherly love; benevolence etc. 906; attachment.

yearning, tender passion, *affaire de coeur*, *amour*, gallantry, passion, flame, devotion, fervor, enthusiasm, transport of love, rapture, enchantment, infatuation, adoration, idolatry.

narcissism, Oedipus complex, Electra complex.

Cupid, Venus, Eros; myrtle; true lover's knot; love -token, – suit, – affair, – tale, – story; the old story, plighted love; courtship etc. 902; *amourette*.

maternal love.

attractiveness, charm; popularity; favorite etc. 899.

lover, suitor, follower, admirer, adorer, wooer, amoret, beau, sweetheart, inamorato, swain, young man, flame, love, truelove; leman, Lothario, gallant, paramor, *umoroso*, *cavaliere servente*, captive, *cicisbeo*; *caro sposo*, Don Juan, sheik, ladies' man, squire of dames, Knave of Hearts.

inamorata, lady-love, idol, darling, duck, Dulcinea, angel, goddess, *cara sposa*; mistress.

betrothed, affianced, *fiancée*.

flirt, *coquette*; amorette; pair of turtle doves; abode of love, *agapemone*.

V. love, like, affect, fancy, care for, take an interest in, be partial to, sympathize with; be -in love etc. *adj.*- with; have –, entertain –, harbor –, cherish- a -love etc. *n.* for; regard, revere; take to, bear love to, be wedded to; set one's affections on; make much of, feast one's eyes on; hold dear, prize, treasure; hug, cling to, cherish, pet, caress etc. 902.

burn; adore, idolize, love to distraction, *aimer eperdument*; dote -on, – upon.

take a fancy to, fall for, be stuck on, look sweet upon; become -enamored etc. *adj.*; fall in love with, lose one's heart; desire etc. 865.

excite love; win –, gain –, secure –, engage- the -love, – affections, – heart; take the fancy of; have a place in –, wind round- the heart; attract, attach, endear, charm, fascinate, captivate, bewitch, seduce, enamor, enrapture, turn the head.

get into favor; ingratiate –, insinuate –, worm- oneself; propitiate, curry favor with, pay one's court to, make a date with, *faire l'aimable*, set one's cap at, flirt, coquet.

Adv. loving etc. *v.*; fond of; taken –, struck- with; smitten, bitten; attached to, wedded to; enamored; charmed etc. *v.*; in love; lovesick; over head and ears in love.

affectionate, tender, sweet upon, sympathetic, loving, fond, amorous, amatory; erotic, uxurious, ardent, passionate, rapturous, devoted, motherly.

loved etc. *v.*; beloved; well –, dearly- beloved; dear, precious, darling, pet, little; favorite, popular.

congenial; to –, after- one's -mind, – taste, – fancy, – own heart.

in one's good -graces etc. (*friendly*) 888; dear as the apple of one's eye, nearest to one's heart.

lovable, adorable; lovely, sweet; attractive, seductive, winning; charming, engaging, interesting, enchanting, captivating, fascinating, intriguing, bewitching; amiable, like an angel, angelic, seraphic.

898. Hate.—N. hate, hatred, vials of hate; Hymn of Hate.

dis-affection, -favor; alienation, estrangement, coolness; enmity etc. 889; animosity etc. 900.

umbrage, pique, grudge; dudgeon, spleen; bitterness, – of feeling; ill –, bad- blood; acrimony; malice etc. 907; implacability etc. (*revenge*) 919.

repugnance etc. (*dislike*) 867; odium, unpopularity; loathing, detestation, antipathy; object of -hatred, – execration; abomination, aversion, *bête noire*; enemy etc. 891; bitter pill; source of annoyance etc. 830.

V. hate, detest, abominate, abhor, loathe; recoil –, shudder- at; shrink from, view with horror, hold in abomination, revolt against, execrate; scowl etc. 895; disrelish etc. (*dislike*) 867.

owe a grudge; bear -spleen, – a grudge, – malice etc. (*malevolence*) 907; conceive an aversion to.

excite –, provoke- hatred etc. *n.*; be -hateful etc. *adj.*; stink in the nostrils; estrange, alienate, repel, set against, sow dissension, set by the ears, envenom, incense, irritate, rile, ruffle, vex; horrify etc. 830.

Adj. hating etc. *v.*; abhorrent; averse from etc. (*disliking*) 867; set against.

bitter etc. (*acrimonious*) 895; implacable etc. (*revengeful*) 919.

un-loved, -beloved, -lamented, -deplored, -mourned, -cared for, -endured, -valued; disliked etc. 867.

crossed in love, forsaken, rejected, love-lorn, jilted.

obnoxious, hateful, odious, abominable, repulsive; offensive, shocking; disgusting etc. (*disagreeable*) 830.

invidious, spiteful; malicious etc. 907.

insulting, irritating, provoking.

[Mutual hate] at -daggers drawn, – swords points; not on speaking terms etc. (*enmity*) 889.

Phr. no love lost between.

899. Favorite.—N. favorite, pet, cosset, minion, idol, jewel, spoiled child, *enfant gâté*; led captain; crony; fondling; apple of one's eye, man after one's own heart; *persona grata*.

love, dear, darling, duck, honey, jewel; mopsey, moppet; sweetheart etc. (*love*) 897.

general –, universal- favorite; idol of the people; matinée idol, movie –, radio- star.

900. Resentment.—N. resentment, displeasure, animosity, anger, wrath, indignation; vexation, exasperation, bitter resentment, wrathful indignation.

pique, umbrage, huff, miff, soreness, dudgeon, acerbity, virulence, bitterness, acrimony, asperity, spleen, gall; heart-burning, -swelling; rankling.

ill –, bad- -humor, – temper; irascibility etc. 901; ill blood etc. (*hate*) 898; revenge etc. 919.

excitement, irritation; warmth, bile, choler, ire, fume, pucker, dander, ferment, ebullition; towering -passion, – rage, *acharnement*, angry mood, taking, pet, tiff, passion, fit, tantrums.

burst, explosion, paroxysm, storm, rage, fury, desperation; violence etc. 173; fire and fury; vials of wrath; gnashing of teeth, hot blood, high words.

scowl etc. 895; sulks etc. 901*a*.

[Cause of umbrage] affront, provocation, offence; indignity etc. (*insult*) 929; grudge, crow to pluck, sore subject; red rag to a bull; *casus belli*.

Furies, Erinys, Eumenides, Alecto, Megaera, Tisiphone.

buffet, slap in the face, box on the ear, rap on the knuckles.

V. resent; take -amiss, – ill, – to heart, – offence, – umbrage, – huff, – exception; take in -ill part, – bad part, – dudgeon; *ne pas entendre raillerie*; breathe revenge, cut up rough.

fly –, fall –, get- into a -rage, – passion; bridle –, bristle –, froth –, fire –, flare- up; open –, pour out- the vials of one's wrath.

pout, knit the brow, frown, scowl, lower, snarl, growl, gnarl, gnash, snap; redden, color; look -black, – black as thunder, – daggers; bite one's thumb; show –, grind- one's teeth; champ the bit.

chafe, mantle, fume, kindle, fly out, take fire; boil, – over; boil with -indignation, – rage; rage, storm, foam; vent one's -rage, – spleen; lose one's temper, stand on one's hind legs, stamp the foot, kick up a row, fly off the handle, cut up rough; stamp –, quiver –, swell –, foam- with rage; burst with anger; raise Cain, breathe fire and fury.

have a fling at; bear malice etc. (*revenge*) 919.

cause –, raise- anger; affront, offend; give -offence, – umbrage; anger; hurt the feelings; insult, discompose, fret, ruffle, nettle, heckle, huff, pique; excite etc. 824; irritate, stir the blood, stir up bile; sting, – to the quick; rile, provoke, chafe, wound, incense, inflame, enrage, aggravate, add fuel to the flame, fan into a flame, widen the breach, envenom, embitter, exasperate, infuriate, kindle wrath; stick in one's gizzard; rankle etc. 919.

put out of humor; put one's -monkey, – back-up; set –, get- one's back up; raise one's -gorge, – dander, – choler; work up into a passion; make -one's blood boil, – the ears tingle; throw into a ferment, madden, drive one mad; lash into -fury, – madness; fool to the top of one's bent; set by the ears.

bring a hornet's nest about one's ears.

Adj. angry, wrath, irate; ire-, wrath-ful; cross etc. (*irascible*) 901; sulky etc. 901*a*; bitter, virulent; acrimonious etc. (*discourteous*) etc. 895; violent etc. 173.

warm, burning; boiling, – over; fuming, raging; foaming, – at the mouth; convulsed with rage.

offended etc. *v.*; waxy, *acharné*; wrought, worked up; indignant, hurt, sore, peeved; set against.

fierce, wild, rageful, furious, mad with rage, fiery, infuriate, rabid, savage; relentless etc. 919.

flushed with -anger, – rage; in a -huff, – stew, – fume, – pucker, – passion, – rage, – fury; on one's high ropes, up in arms; in high dudgeon.

Adv. angrily etc. *adj.*; in the height of passion; in the heat of -passion, – the moment.

Phr. one's -blood, – back, – monkey- being up; *fervens difficili bile jecur*; the gorge rising, eyes flashing fire; the blood -rising, – boiling; *haeret lateri lethalis arundo*.

901. Irascibility.—N. irascibility, temper; crossness etc. *adj.*; susceptibility, procacity, petulance, irritability, tartness, acerbity, protervity; pugnacity etc. (*contentiousness*) 720.

excitability etc. 825; bad –, fiery –, crooked –, irritable etc. *adj.*- temper; *genus irritabile*, hot blood.

ill humor etc. (*sullenness*) 901*a*; asperity etc., churlishness etc. (*discourtesy*) 895.

huff etc. (resentment) 900; a word and a blow.

Sir Fretful Plagiary; brabbler, Tartar; shrew, vixen, virago, termagant, dragon, scold, Xanthippe; porcupine; spit-fire; fire-eater etc. (*blusterer*) 887; fury etc. (*violent person*) 173.

V. be -irascible etc. *adj.*; have a -temper etc. *n.*, – devil in one; fire up etc. (*be angry*) 900.

Adj. irascible; bad-, ill-tempered; irritable, susceptible; excitable etc. 825; thin-skinned etc. (*sensitive*) 822; fretful, fidgety; on the fret.

hasty, over-hasty, quick, warm, hot, testy, touchy, techy, tetchy; like -touchwood, – tinder; huffy; pet-tish, -ulant; waspish, snapp-y, -ish, peppery, fiery, passionate, choleric, shrewish, 'sudden and quick in quarrel.'

querulous, captious, mood-y, -ish; quarrelsome, contentious, disputatious; pugnacious etc. (*bellicose*) 720; cantankerous, exceptious; restive etc. (*perverse*) 901*a*; churlish etc. (*discourteous*) 895.

cross, – as -crabs, – two sticks, – a cat, – a dog, – the tongs; like a bear with a sore head; fractious, peevish, *acariâtre*.

in a bad temper; sulky etc. 901*a*; angry etc. 900.

resent-ful, -ive; vindictive etc. 919.

Int. pish!

901a. Sullenness.—N. sullenness etc. *adj.*; morosity, spleen; churlishness etc. (*discourtesy*) 895; irascibility etc. 901.

moodiness etc. *adj.*; perversity; obstinacy etc. 606; torvity, spinosity; crabbedness etc. *adj.*

ill –, bad- -temper, – humor; sulks, dudgeon, mumps, doleful dumps, doldrums, fit of the sulks, *bouderie*, black looks, scowl; huff etc. (*resentment*) 900.

V. be -sullen etc. *adj.*; sulk; frown, scowl, lower, glower, grouse, grouch, crab, gloam, pout, have a hang-dog look, glout.

Adj. sullen, sulky; ill-tempered, -humored, -affected, -disposed; in -an ill, – a bad, – a shocking- -temper, – humor; out of -temper, – humor; knaggy, torvous, crusty, crabbed; sore as a boil; surly etc. (*discourteous*) 895.

moody; spleen-ish, -ly; splenetic, cankered.

cross, -grained; perverse, wayward, humorsome; restive; cantankerous, refractory, intractable, exceptious, sinistrous, deaf to reason, unaccommodating, rusty, crust, froward.

dogged etc. (*stubborn*) 606.

grumpy, glum, grim, grum, morose, frumpish; in the -sulks etc. *n.*; out of sorts; scowl-, glower-, growl-ing.

peevish etc. (*irascible*) 901.

902. Endearment. [Expression of affection or love.]—**N.** endearment, caress; blandish-, blandiment; *épanchement*, fondling, billing and cooing, dalliance.

embrace, salute, kiss, buss, smack, osculation,

deosculation; amorous glances; ogle, side glance, sheep's eyes.

courtship, wooing, suit, addresses, the soft impeachment; love-making; an affair; serenading; caterwauling.

flirting etc. *v.*; flirtation, gallantry; coquetry, spooning.

ture lover's knot, plighted love, engagement, bethrothal; love -tale, – token, – letter; *billet-doux*, valentine.

honeymoon; Strephon and Chloe, 'Arry and 'Arriet.

V. caress, fondle, pet, dandle, nurse; pat, – on the -head, – cheek; chuck under the chin, smile upon, coax, wheedle, cosset, coddle, cocker; make -of, – much of, pamper; cherish, foster, kill with kindness.

clasp, hug, cuddle; fold –, strain- in one's arms; nestle, nuzzle, neck, embrace, kiss, buss, smack, blow a kiss; salute etc. (*courtesy*) 894.

bill and coo, spoon, toy, dally, flirt, coquet; galli-, gala-vant; philander; make love; pay one's -court, – addresses, – attentions- to; serenade; court, woo; set one's cap at; be –, look- sweet upon; ogle, cast sheep's eyes upon; *faire les yeux doux*.

fall in love with, win the affections etc. (*love*) 897; die for.

propose; make –, have- an offer; pop the question; plight one's -troth, – faith; become -engaged, – betrothed.

Adj. caressing etc. *v.*; 'sighing like furnace;' love-sick, spoony.

carressed etc. *v.*

903. Marriage.—N. marriage, matrimony, wedlock, union, intermarriage, *vinculum matrimonii*, nuptial tie, knot.

married state, coverture, bed, cohabitation.

match; betrothment etc. (*promise*) 768; wedding, nuptials, Hymen, bridal; e-, spousals; leading to the altar etc. *v.*; nuptial benediction, *epithalamium*,

torch –, temple- of Hymen; hymeneal altar; honeymoon.

bride, bridegroom; brides-maid; -man.

best –, grooms-man, page, usher.

married -man, – woman, – couple; neogamist, Benedick, partner, spouse, mate, yokemate; husband, man, consort, baron; old –, good- man; wife of one's bosom; help-meet, -mate, rib, better half, grey mare, old woman, good wife; feme, – coverte; squaw, lady; matron, -age, -hood; man and wife; wedded pair, Darby and Joan.

affinity, soul-mate.

mono-, bi-, di-, deutero-, tri-, poly-gamy; mormonism; poly-andry; Turk, Bluebeard.

unlawful –, left-handed –, companionate –, morganatic –, ill-assorted- marriage; *mésalliance*; *mariage de convenance*; an affair.

match-maker, marriage broker, matrimonial agent.

V. marry, wive, take to oneself a wife; be -married, – spliced; go –, pair- off; wed, espouse, lead to the hymeneal altar, take 'for better, for worse,' give one's hand to, bestow one's hand upon; remarry; intermarry.

marry, join, handfast; couple etc. (*unite*) 43; tie the nuptial knot; give -away, – in marriage; affy, affiance; betroth etc. (*promise*) 768; publish –, bid- the banns; be asked in church.

Adj. married etc. *v.*; one, – bone and one flesh.

marriageable, nubile.

engaged, betrothed, affianced.

matrimonial, marital, conjugal, connubial, wedded; nuptial, hymeneal, spousal, bridal.

Phr. the gray mare the better horse.

904. Celibacy.—N. celibacy, singleness, single blessedness; bachelor-hood, -ship; miso-gamy, -gyny.

virginity, *pueelage*; maiden-hood, -head.

unmarried man, bachelor, agamist, old bachelor; miso-gamist, -gynist; celibate.

unmarried woman, spinster; maid, -en; virgin, *feme sole*, old maid; bachelor girl; nun etc.

V. live single; keep bachelor hall.

Adj. un-married, -wedded; wife-, spouse-less; single, virgin, celibate.

905. Divorce.—N. divorce, -ment; separation; judicial separation, separate maintenance; *separatio a -mensâ et thoro, – vinculo matrimonii*.

widowhood, viduage, viduity, weeds.

widow, -er; relict; dowager; *divorcée*; cuckold.

V. live -separately, – apart; separate, divorce, disespouse, put away; wear the horns.

906. Benevolence.—N. benevolence, Christian charity; God's -love, – grace; good-will; philanthropy etc. 910; unselfishness etc. 942.

good -nature, – feeling, – wishes; kind-, kindliness etc. *adj.*; lovingkindness, benignity, brotherly love, charity, humanity, fellow-feeling, sympathy; goodness –, warmth- of heart; *bon-homie*; kind-heartedness; amiability, milk of human kindness, tenderness; love etc. 897; friendship etc. 888.

toleration, consideration, generosity; mercy etc. (*pity*) 914.

charitableness etc. *adj.*; bounty, alms-giving; good works, beneficence, the luxury of doing good.

acts of kindness, a good turn; good –, kind- -offices, – treatment.

good Samaritan, sympathizer, well-wisher, philanthropist, *bon enfant*; altruist.

V. be -benevolent etc. *adj.*; have one's heart in the right place, bear good will; wish -well, – God speed; view –, regard- with an eye of favor; take in good part; take –, feel- an interest in; be –, feel-interested- in; sympathize with, feel for; fraternize etc. (*be friendly*) 888.

enter into the feelings of others, do as you would be done by, meet halfway.

treat well; give comfort, smooth the bed of death; do -good, – a good turn; benefit etc. (*goodness*) 648; render a service, be of use; aid etc. 707.

Adj. benevolent; kind, -ly; wellmeaning; amiable; obliging, accommodating, indulgent, considerate, gracious, complacent, good-humored.

warm-, soft-, kind-, tender-, large-, broad-hearted; merciful etc. 914; philanthropic etc. 910; charitable, beneficent, humane, benign, benignant; bount-eous, -iful etc. 816.

good-, well-natured; spleenless; sympath-izing, -etic; complaisant etc. (*courteous*) 894; kindly, well-meant, -intentioned.

fatherly, motherly, brotherly, sisterly; pat-, mat-, frat-ernal; friendly etc. 888.

Adv. with -a good intention, – the best intentions.

Int. God speed! much good may it do!

907. Malevolence.—N. malevolence; bad intent, -ion; un-, dis-kindness; ill -nature, – will, – blood; bad blood; enmity etc. 889; hate etc. 898; malignity; malice, – aforethought, – prepense; maliciousness etc. *adj.*; spite, despite; resentment etc. 900.

uncharitableness etc. *adj.*; incompassionateness etc. 914*a*; gall, venom, rancor, rankling, virulence, mordacity, acerbity; churlishness etc. (*discourtesy*) 895.

hardness of heart, heart of stone, obduracy; cruelty; cruelness etc. *adj.*; brutality, savagery; ferity, -ocity; barbarity, inhumanity, immanity, truculence, ruffianism; evil eye, cloven -foot, – hoof; Inquisition; torture.

ill –, bad- turn; affront etc. (*disrespect*) 929; outrage, atrocity; ill usage; intolerance, bigotry, persecution; tender mercies [ironical]; 'unkindest cut of all.'

V. be -malevolent etc. *adj.*; bear –, harbor- -spleen, – a grudge, – malice; betray –, show- the cloven foot.

hurt etc. (*physical pain*) 378; annoy etc. 830; injure, harm, wrong; do -harm, – an ill office- to; outrage; disoblige, malign, plant a thorn in the breast.

molest, worry, harass, haunt, harry, bait, tease, throw stones at; play the devil with; hunt down, dragoon, hound; persecute, oppress, grind; maltreat; ill-treat, -use.

wreak one's malice on, do one's worst, break a butterfly on the wheel; dip –, imbrue- one's hands in blood; have no mercy etc. 914*a*.

Adj. male-, unbene-volent; unbenign; ill-disposed, -intentioned, -natured, -conditioned, -contrived; evil-minded, -disposed.

malicious; malign, -ant; rancorous; de-, spiteful; mordacious, caustic, bitter, envenomed, acrimonious, virulent; un-amiable, -charitable; maleficent, venomous, grinding, galling.

harsh, disobliging; un-kind, -friendly, -gracious; treacherous; inofficious; invidious; uncandid; churlish etc. (*uncourteous*) 895; surly, sullen etc. 901*a*.

cold, -blooded, -hearted; hard-, flint-, marble-, stony-hearted; hard of heart, unnatural; ruthless etc. (*unmerciful*) 914*a*; relentless etc. (*revengeful*) 919.

cruel; brut-al, -ish; savage, – as a -bear, – tiger; ferine, feral, ferocious; inhuman; barbarous, fell, untamed, tameless, truculent, incendiary; bloodthirsty etc. (*murderous*) 361; atrocious.

fiend-ish, -like; demoniacal; diabolic, -al; devilish, infernal, hellish, Satanic.

Adv. malevolently etc. *adj.*; with -bad intent etc. *n.*

908. Malediction.—N. malediction, malison, curse, imprecation, denunciation, execration, anathema, ban, proscription, excommunication, commination, thunders of the Vatican, fulmination, *maranatha*, aspersion, vilification, vituperation, scurrility.

abuse; foul –, bad –, strong –, unparliamentary- language, Limehouse; Billingsgate, sauce, evil speaking; cursing etc. *v.*; profane swearing, oath.

threat etc. 909; more bark than bite; invective etc. (*disapprobation*) 932.

V. curse, accurse, imprecate, damn, swear at; slang; curse with bell, book and candle; invoke –, call down- curses on the head of; devote to destruction.

execrate, beshrew, scold; anathematize etc. (*censure*) 932; hold up to execration, denounce, proscribe, excommunicate, fulminate, thunder against; threaten etc. 909; curse up hill and down dale.

curse and swear; swear, – like a trooper; fall a cursing, rap out an oath, damn, cuss.

Adj. curs-ing, -ed etc. *v.*; maledictory.

Int. woe to! beshrew! *ruat coelum!* ill –, woe-betide! confusion seize! damn! confound! blast! curse! devil take! hang! out with! a plague –, out-upon! aroynt! *honi soit!*

Phr. *delenda est Carthago.*

909. Threat.—N. threat, menace; defiance etc. 715; abuse, minacity, intimidation; fulmination; commination etc. (*curse*) 908; gathering clouds etc. (*warning*) 668.

V. threat, -en; menace; snarl, growl, gnarl, mutter, bark, bully.

defy etc. 715; intimidate etc. 860; keep –, hold up –, hold out- *in terrorem*; shake –, double –, clinch- the fist at; thunder, talk big, fulminate, use big words, bluster, look daggers.

Adj. threatening, menacing; mina-tory, -cious; comminatory, abusive; *in terrorem*; ominous etc. (*predicting*) 511; defiant etc. 715; under the ban.

Int. *vae victis!* at your peril! do your worst!

910. Philanthropy.—N. philanthropy; altruism, humanit-y, -arianism; universal benevolence; *deliciae humani generis;* cosmopolitanism, utilitarianism, the greatest happiness of the greatest number, social science, sociology.

common weal, public welfare, socialism, communism.

patriotism, civism, nationality, love of country, *amor patriae*, public spirit.

chivalry, knight errantry; generosity etc. 942.

philanthropist, altruist etc. 906; utilitarian, Benthamite, socialist, communist, cosmopolite, citizen of the world, *amicus humani generis*; knight errant; patriot.

Adj. philanthropic, altruistic, humanitarian, utilitarian, cosmopolitan; public-spirited, patriotic; humane, large-hearted etc. (*benevolent*) 906; chival-ric, -rous, generous etc. 942.

Adv. *pro -bono publico, – aris et focis.*

Phr. '*humani nihil a me alienum puto.*'

911. Misanthropy.—N. misanthropy, incivism; egotism etc. (*selfishness*) 943; moroseness etc. 901*a*; cynicism; defeatism.

misanthrope, misanthropist, egotist, cynic, man-hater, Timon, Diogenes.

woman hater, misogynist.

Adj. misanthropic, antisocial, unpatriotic; egotistical etc. (*selfish*) 943; morose etc. 901*a*.

912. Benefactor.—N. benefactor, savior, good genius, tutelary saint, patron, guardian angel, fairy godmother, good Samaritan; *pater patriae*; salt of the earth etc. (*good man*) 948; auxiliary etc. 711.

913. Evil-doer. [*Maleficent being.*]—**N.** evil--doer, – worker; wrong doer etc. 949; mischief maker, marplot; oppressor, tyrant; firebrand, incendiary, pyromaniac, anarchist, destroyer, Hun, *Boche*, Vandal, iconoclast; communist; terrorist, *apache*, gunman, gangster, racketeer.

savage, brute, ruffian, barbarian, semi-barbarian, caitiff, desperado; Mo-hock, -hawk; bludgeon man, bully, rough, hooligan, larrikin, dangerous classes, ugly customer; thief etc. 792.

cockatrice, scorpion, hornet; viper, adder; snake, – in the grass; serpent, cobra, asp, rattlesnake, anaconda; canker-, wire-worm; locust, Colorado beetle; torpedo; bane etc. 663.

cannibal; Anthropophag-us, -ist; bloodsucker, vampire, ogre, ghoul, gorilla; vulture; gyr- ger-falcon.

wild beast, tiger, hyaena, butcher, hangman; cut-throat etc. (*killer*) 361; blood-, sleuth-, hell-hound.

hag, hellhag, beldam, Jezebel.

monster; fiend etc. (*demon*) 980; homicidal maniac, devil incarnate, demon in human shape; Frankenstein's monster.

harpy, siren, vampire; Furies, Eumenides etc. 900.

Attila, scourge of the human race.

Phr. *foenum habet in cornu.*

914. Pity.—N. pity, compassion, commiseration; bowels, – of compassion; condolence etc. 915; sympathy, fellow-feeling, tenderness, yearning, forbearance, humanity, mercy, clemency, exorability; leniency etc. (*lenity*) 740; charity, ruth, long-suffering.

melting mood; ***argumentum ad misericordiam***; quarter, grace, *locus poenitentiae*.

sympathizer, champion, partisan.

V. pity; have –, show –, take- pity etc. ***n.***; commiserate, compassionate; condole etc. 915; sympathize; feel –, be sorry –, yearn- for; weep, melt, thaw, enter into the feelings of.

forbear, relent, relax, give quarter, wipe the tears, *parcere subjectis*, give a *coup de grâce*, put out of one's misery; be cruel to be kind.

raise –, excite- pity etc. *n.*; touch, soften; melt, – the heart; appeal to one's better feelings; propitiate, disarm.

ask for -mercy etc. *n.*; supplicate etc. (***request***) 765; cry for quarter, beg one's life, kneel; deprecate.

Adj. pitying etc. *v.*; pitiful, compassionate, sympathetic, touched.

merciful, clement, ruthful; humane; humanitarian etc. (*philanthropic*) 910; tender, – hearted, – as a chicken; soft, – hearted; unhardened; lenient etc. 740; exorable, forbearing; melting etc. *v.*; weak.

Int. for pity's sake! mercy! have –, cry you-mercy! God help you! poor -thing, – dear, – fellow! woe betide! ***quis talia fando temperet a lachrymis!***

Phr. one's heart bleeding for; ***haud ignara mali miseris succurrere disco.***

914a. Pitilessness.—N. pitilessness etc. *adj.*; inclemency; inexorability, hardness of heart; inflexibility; severity etc. 739; malevolence etc. 907.

V. have no –, shut the gates of- mercy etc. 914; give no quarter.

Adj. piti-, merci-, ruth-, bowel-less; unpitying, unmerciful, inclement; in-, un-compassionate; inexorable, inflexible; harsh etc. 739; cruel etc. 907; unrelenting etc. 919.

915. Condolence.—N. condolence; lamentation etc. 839; sympathy, consolation.

V. condole with, console, sympathize etc. 914; share one's misery; feel for; express –, testify- pity; afford –, supply- consolation; lament etc. 839-with; send one's condolences.

916. Gratitude.—N. gratitude, thankfulness, gratefulness, feeling of obligation.

acknowledgement, recognition, thanksgiving, giving thanks.

thanks, praise, benediction; paean; ***Te Deum*** etc. (***worship***) 990; grace, – before, – after-meat; thank-offering.

requital.

V. be -grateful etc. *adj.*; thank; give –, render –, return –, offer –, tender- thanks etc. *n.*; acknowledge, requite.

feel –, be –, lie- under an obligation; *savoir gré*; not look a gift horse in the mouth; never forget, overflow with gratitude; thank –, bless-one's stars; fall on one's knees.

Adj. grateful, thankful, obliged, beholden, indebted to, under obligation.

Int. thanks! many thanks! gramercy! much obliged! thank you! thank Heaven! Heaven be praised!

917. Ingratitude.—N. ingratitude, thanklessness, oblivion of benefits; unthankfulness.

'benefits forgot;' thankless -task, – office.

V. be -ungrateful etc. *adj.*; forget benefits; look a gift horse in the mouth.

Adj. un-grateful, -mindful, -thankful; thankless, ingrate, wanting in gratitude, insensible of benefits.

forgotten; un-acknowledged, -thanked, -requited, -rewarded; ill-requited.

Int. thank you for nothing! ***'et tu Brute!'***

918. Forgiveness.—N. forgiveness, pardon, condonation, grace, remission, absolution, amnesty, oblivion; indulgence; reprieve.

conciliation; reconciliation etc. (*pacification*) 723; propitiation.

excuse, exoneration, quittance, release, indemnity; bill –, act –, covenant –, deed- of indemnity; exculpation etc. (*acquittal*) 970.

longanimity, placability, forbearance; *amantium irae*; *locus poenitentiae*.

V. forgive, – and forget; pardon, condone, think no more of, let bygones be bygones, shake hands; forget an injury, bury the hatchet; clean the slate.

excuse, pass over, overlook; wink at etc. (*neglect*) 460; bear with; allow –, make allowances- for; let one down easily, not be too hard upon, pocket the affront; blot out one's transgression.

let off, remit, absolve, give absolution, reprieve; acquit etc. 970.

beg –, ask –, implore- pardon etc. *n.*; conciliate, propitiate, placate; make up a quarrel etc. (*pacify*) 723; let the wound heal.

Adj. forgiving, placable, conciliatory.

forgiven etc. *v.*; un-resented, -avenged, -revenged.

Adv. cry you mercy.

Phr. *veniam petimusque damusque vicissim*; more in sorrow than in anger.

919. Revenge.—N. revenge, -ment; vengeance; avenge-ment, -ance; sweet revenge, *vendetta*, death-feud, eye for an eye, blood for blood, a Roland for an Oliver; retaliation etc. 718; day of reckoning.

rancor, vindictiveness, implacability; malevolence etc. 907; ruthlessness etc. 914*a*.

avenger, vindicator, Nemesis, Eumenides.

V. re-, a-venge; take –, have one's- revenge; breathe -revenge, – vengeance; wreak one's -vengeance, – anger; give no quarter.

have -accounts to settle, – a crow to pluck, – a rod in pickle; pay off old scores.

keep the wound green; harbor -revenge, – vindictive feeling; bear malice; rankle, – in the breast; have at one's mercy.

Adj. revenge-, venge-ful; vindictive, rancorous; pitiless etc. 914*a*; ruthless, rigorous, avenging, retaliative.

unforgiving, unrelenting; inexorable, stony-hearted, implacable; relent-, remorse-less.

aeternum servans sub pectore vulnus; rankling, immitigable.

Phr. *manet -cicatrix,– altâ mente repostum*. revenge is sweet.

920. Jealousy.—N. jealous-y, -ness; jaundiced eye, heartburning; green-eyed monster; yellows; Juno.

V. be -jealous etc. *adj.*; view with -jealousy, – a jealous eye.

Adj. jealous, – as a Barbary pigeon; jaundiced, yellow-eyed, horn-mad.

921. Envy.—N. envy; enviousness etc. *adj.*; rivalry; *jalousie de métier*.

V. envy, covet, lust after, crave, burst with envy, regard with envious eyes.

Adj. envious, invidious, covetous; *alieni appetens*.

922. Right.—N. right; what -ought to, – should- be; fitness etc. *adj.*; *summum jus*.

justice, equity; equitableness etc. *adj.*; propriety; fair play, impartiality, measure for measure, give and take, *lex talionis*, square deal.

Astraea, Nemesis, Themis.

scales of justice, even-handed justice, retributive justice, *suum cuique*; clear stage –, fair field- and no favor; Queensberry rules.

morals etc. (*duty*) 926; law etc. 963; honor etc. (*probity*) 939; virtue etc. 944.

V. be -right etc. *adj.*; stand to reason.

see -justice done, – one righted, – fair play; do justice to; recompense etc. (*reward*) 973; hold the scales even, give and take; serve one right, put the saddle on the right horse; give -every one, – the devil- his due; *audire alteram partem*.

deserve etc. (*be entitled to*) 924.

Adj. right, good; just, reasonable; fit etc. 924; equ-al, -able, -itable; evenhanded, fair, – and square.

legitimate, justifiable, rightful; as it -should, – ought to- be; lawful etc. (*permitted*) 760, (*legal*) 963.

deserved etc. 924.

Adv. rightly etc. *adj.*; in -justice, – equity, – reason.

without -distinction of, – regard to, – respect to- persons; upon even terms.

Int. all right!

923. Wrong.—N. wrong; what -ought not to, – should not- be; *malum in se*; unreasonableness, grievance; shame.

injustice; unfairness etc. *adj.*; iniquity, foul play, partiality, leaning; favor, -itism; nepotism, party spirit, partisanship; undueness etc. 925; unlawfulness etc. 964.

robbing Peter to pay Paul etc. *v.*; the wolf and the lamb; vice etc. 945.

a custom more honored in the breach than the observance.

V. be -wrong etc. *adj.*; cry to heaven for vengeance.

do -wrong etc. *n.*; be -inequitable etc. *adj.*; favor, lean towards; encroach; impose upon; reap where one has not sown; give an inch and take an ell; rob Peter to pay Paul.

Adj. wrong, -ful; bad, too bad; unjust, -fair; in-, un-equitable; unequal, partial, one-sided.

objectionable; un-reasonable, -allowable, -warrantable, -justifiable; not cricket, not playing the game; improper, unfit; unjustified etc. 925; illegal etc. 964; iniquitous, criminal; immoral etc. 945; injurious etc. 649.

in the wrong, – box.

Adv. wrongly etc. *adj.*

Phr. it will not do; this is too bad.

924. Dueness.—N. due, -ness; right, privilege, prerogative, prescription, title, claim, pretension, demand, birthright.

immunity, license, liberty, franchise; vested -interest, – right; licitness.
sanction, authority, warranty, charter; warrant etc. (*permission*) 760; constitution etc. (*law*) 963; tenure; bond etc. (*security*) 771.
deserts, merits, dues.
claimant, appellant; plaintiff etc. 938.
V. be -due etc. *adj.*to, – the due etc. *n.*of; have -right, – title, – claim- to; be entitled to; have a claim upon; belong to etc. (*property*) 780.
deserve, merit, be worthy of, richly deserve.
demand, claim; call upon –, come upon –, appeal to- for; re-vendicate, -claim; exact; insist -on, – upon; challenge; take one's stand, make a point of, require, lay claim to, assert, assume, arrogate, make good; substantiate; vindicate a -claim, – right; make out a case.
give –, confer- a right; sanction, entitle; authorize etc. 760; sanctify, legalize, ordain, prescribe, allot.
give every one his due etc. 922; pay one's dues; have one's -due, – rights; stand upon one's rights.
use a right, assert, enforce, put in force, lay under contribution.
Adj. having a right to etc. *v.*; entitled to; claiming; deserving, meriting, worthy of.
privileged, allowed, sanctioned, warranted, authorized; ordained, prescribed, constitutional, chartered, enfranchised.
prescriptive, presumptive; absolute, indefeasible; un-, in-alienable.
imprescriptible, inviolable, unimpeachable, unchallenged; sacrosanct.
due to, merited, deserved, condign, richly deserved, *emeritus*.
allowable etc. (*permitted*) 760; lawful, licit, legitimate, legal; legalized etc. (*law*) 963.
square, unexceptionable, right; equitable etc. 922; due, *en règle*; fit, -ting; correct, proper, meet, befitting, becoming, seemly; decorous; creditable, up to the mark, right as a trivet, just –, quite- the thing; *selon les règles*.
Adv. duly, *ex officio*, *de jure*; by -right, – divine right; as is -fitting, – proper, – fitting and proper; *jure divino*, *Dei gratiâ*, in the name of.
Phr. *civis Romanus sum*.

925. Undueness. [Absence of right.]—**N.** undueness etc. *adj.*; *malum prohibitum*; impropriety; illegality etc. 964.
falseness etc. *adj.*; emptiness –, invalidity- of title; illegitimacy.
loss of right, disfranchisement, forfeiture.
usurpation, assumption, tort, violation, breach, encroachment, presumption, seizure, stretch, exaction, imposition, lion's share.
usurper, pretender, Carlist; imposter.
V. be -undue etc. *adj.*; not be -due etc. 924.
infringe, encroach, trench on, exact; arrogate, – to oneself; give an inch and take an ell; stretch –, strain- a point; usurp, violate, do violence to; sail under false colors.
dis-franchise, -entitle, -qualify; invalidate.
relax etc. (*be lax*) 738; misbehave etc. (*vice*) 945; misbecome.
Adj. undue; unlawful etc. (*illegal*) 964; unconstitutional, *ultra vires*; illicit; un-authorized, -warranted, -allowed, -sanctioned, -justified; un-, dis-entitled, -qualified; un-privileged, -chartered.
illegitimate, bastard, spurious, false; usurped, tortious.
un-deserved, -merited, -earned; unfulfilled.
forfeited, disfranchised.
improper; un-meet, -fit, -befitting, -seemly; un-, mis-becoming; seemless; *contra bonos mores*; not the thing, out of the question, not to be thought of; preposterous, pretentious, would- be.

926. Duty.—N. duty, what ought to be done, moral obligation, accountableness, liability, *onus*, responsibility; bounden –, imperative- duty; call, – of duty.
allegiance, fealty, tie; engagement etc. (*promise*) 768; part; function, calling etc. (*business*) 625.
morality, morals, decalogue; case of conscience; conscientiousness etc. (*probity*) 939; conscience, inward monitor, still small voice within, sense of duty, tender conscience.
dueness etc. 924; propriety, fitness, seemliness, amenableness, decorum; the -thing, – proper thing; the -right, – proper- thing to do.
[Science of morals] eth-ics, -ology; deon-, aretology; moral –, ethical-philosophy; casuistry, polity.
observance, fulfilment, discharge, performance, acquittal, satisfaction, redemption; good behavior.
V. be -the duty of, – incumbent etc. *adj.*on, – responsible etc. *adj.*; behoove, become, befit, beseem; belong –, pertain- to; fall to one's lot; devolve on; lie -upon, – on one's head, – at one's door; rest -with, – on the shoulders of.
take upon oneself etc. (*promise*) 768.
be –, become- -bound to, – sponsor for; be responsible for; incur a -responsibility etc. *n.*; be –, stand –, lie- under an obligation; have to answer for, owe it to oneself.
impose a -duty etc. *n.*; enjoin, require, exact; bind, – over; saddle with, prescribe, assign, call upon, look to, oblige.
enter upon –, perform –, observe –, fulfil –, discharge –, adhere to –, acquit oneself of –, satisfy- -a duty, – an obligation; act one's part, redeem one's pledge, do justice to, be at one's post; do duty; do one's duty etc. (*be virtuous*) 944.
be on one's good behavior, mind one's P's and Q's.
Adj. obligatory, binding; imperative, peremptory; stringent etc. (*severe*) 739; behooving etc. *v.*; incumbent –, chargeable- on; under obligation; obliged –, bound –, tied- by; saddled with.
due –, beholden –, bound –, indebted- to; tied down; compromised etc. (*promised*) 768; in duty bound.
amenable, liable, accountable, responsible, answerable.
right, meet etc. (*due*) 924; moral, ethical, casuistical, conscientious, ethological.
Adv. with a safe conscience, as in duty bound, on one's own responsibility, at one's own risk, *suo periculo*; *in foro conscientiae*; *quamdiu se bene gesserit*; at one's post, on duty.
Phr. *dura lex sed lex*.

927. Dereliction of Duty.—N. dere; liction of duty; fault etc. (*guilt*) 947- sin etc. (*vice*) 945; non-observance, -performance, -co-operation; neglect, carelessness, laziness, incompetence, eye-service, relaxation, infraction, violation, transgression, failure, evasion, indolence; dead letter.

slacker, loafer, striker, non-co-operator.

V. violate; break, – through; infringe; set - aside, – at naught; trample -on, – under foot; slight, neglect, evade, renounce, forswear, repudiate; wash one's hands of; escape, transgress, fail.

call to account etc. (*disapprobation*) 932.

927a. Exemption.—N. exemption, freedom, irresponsibility, immunity, liberty, license, release, exoneration, excuse, dispensation, absolution, franchise, renunciation, discharge; exculpation etc. 970; *aegrotat*.

V. be -exempt etc. *adj*.

exempt, release, acquit, discharge, quit-claim, remise, remit; free, set at liberty, let off, pass over, spare, excuse, dispense with, give dispensation, license; stretch a point; absolve etc. (*forgive*) 918; exonerate etc. (*exculpate*) 970; save the necessity.

Adj. exempt, free, immune, at liberty, scot free; released etc. *v.*; unbound, unencumbered; irresponsible, unaccountable, not answerable; excusable.

928. Respect.—N. respect, regard, consideration; courtesy etc. 894; attention, deference, reverence, honor, esteem, estimation, veneration, admiration; approbation etc. 931.

homage, fealty, obeisance, genuflexion, kneeling, prostration; obsequiousness etc. 886; salaam, *kowtow*, bow, presenting arms, salute.

respects, regards, duty, *devoirs*, *égards*.

devotion etc. (*piety*) 987.

V. respect, regard; revere, -nce; hold in reverence, honor, venerate, hallow; esteem etc. (*approve of*) 931; think much of; entertain –, bear- respect for; have a high opinion of; look up to, defer to; pay -attention, – respect etc. *n.*- to; do –, render- honor to; do the honors, hail; show courtesy etc. 894; salute, present arms; do –, pay- homage to; pay tribute to; kneel to, bow to, bend the knee to; fall down before, prostrate oneself, kiss the hem of one's garment; worship etc. 990.

keep one's distance, make room, observe due decorum, stand upon ceremony.

command –, inspire- respect; awe, impose, overawe, dazzle.

Adj. respecting etc. *v.*; respectful, deferential, decorous, reverential, obsequious, ceremonious, bare-headed, cap in hand, on one's knees; prostrate etc. (*servile*) 886.

respected etc. *v.*; in high -esteem, – estimation; time-honored, venerable, *emeritus*.

Adv. in deference to; with -all, – due, – the highest- respect; with submission.

saving your -grace, – presence; *salva sit reverentia*; *pace tanti nominis*.

Int. hail! all hail! *esto perpetua!* may your shadow never be less!

929. Disrespect.—N. dis-respect, -esteem, -estimation, -favor, -repute; low estimation; disparagement etc. (*dispraise*) 932; (*detraction*) 934.

irreverence; slight, neglect; *spretae injuria formae*; superciliousness etc. (*contempt*) 930.

vilipendency, contumely, affront, dishonor, insult, indignity, outrage, discourtesy etc. 895; practical joking; scurrility, scoffing, sibilation; ir-, derision; mockery; irony etc. (*ridicule*) 856; sarcasm.

hiss, hoot, gibe, flout, jeer, scoff, gleek, taunt, sneer, quip, fling, wipe, slap in the face.

V. hold in disrespect etc (*despise*) 930; misprize, disregard, slight, undervalue, depreciate, trifle with, set at naught, pass by, push aside, overlook, turn one's back upon, laugh in one's sleeve; be -disrespectful etc. *adj.*, – discourteous etc. 895; treat with -disrespect etc. *n.*; set down, browbeat.

dishonor, desecrate; insult, affront, outrage.

speak slightingly of; disparage etc. (*dispraise*) 932; vilipend, call names; throw –, fling- dirt; drag through the mud, point at, indulge in personalities; make -mouths, – faces; bite the thumb; take –, pluck- by the beard; toss in a blanket, tar and feather.

have –, hold- in derision; deride, scoff, sneer, laugh at, snigger, ridicule, gibe, mock, jeer, taunt, twit, niggle, gleek, gird, flout, fleer; roast, turn into ridicule; guy, burlesque etc. 856; laugh to scorn etc. (*contempt*) 930; smoke; fool; make -game, – a fool, – an April fool- of; play a practical joke; rag; lead one a dance, run the rig upon, have a fling at, scout, hiss, hoot, mob.

Adj. disrespectful; aweless, irreverent; disparaging etc. 934; insulting etc. *v.*; supercilious etc. (*scornful*) 930; rude, derisive, contemptuous, sarcastic; scurri-le, -lous; contumelious.

un-respected, -worshipped, -envied, -saluted; un-dis-regarded.

Adv. disrespectfully etc. *adj*.

930. Contempt.—N. contempt, disdain, scorn, sovereign contempt; despi-sal, -ciency; vilipendency, contumely; slight, sneer, spurn, by-word.

contemptuousness etc. *adj.*; scornful eye; smile of contempt; derision etc. (*disrespect*) 929.

[State of being despised] despisedness.

V. despise, contemn, scorn, disdain, feel contempt for, view with a scornful eye, disregard, slight, not mind; pass by etc. (*neglect*) 460.

look down upon; hold -cheap, – in contempt, – in disrespect; think -nothing, – small beer- of; make light of; underestimate etc. 483; esteem - slightly, – of small or no account; take no account of, care nothing for; set no store by; not care a - straw etc. (*unimportance*) 643; set at naught, laugh in one's sleeve, snap one's fingers at, shrug one's shoulders, turn up one's nose at, pooh-pooh, damn with faint praise; sneeze –, whistle –, sneer- at; curl up one's lip, toss the head, *traiter de haut*; laugh at etc. (*be disrespectful*) 929.

point the finger of –, hold up to –, laugh to-scorn; scout, hoot, flout, hiss, scoff at.

turn -one's back, – a cold shoulder- upon; tread –, trample- -upon, – under foot; spurn, kick; fling to the winds etc. (*repudiate*) 610; send away with a flea in the ear.

Adj. contemptuous; disdain-, scorn-ful; withering, contumelious, supercilious, cynical, haughty, bumptious, cavalier; derisive.

contemptible, despicable; pitiable; pitiful etc. (*unimportant*) 643; despised etc. *v.*; downtrodden; unenvied.

Adv. contemptuously etc. *adj.*

Int. a fig for etc. (*unimportant*) 643; bah! never mind! away with! hang it! fiddle-de-dee!

931. Approbation.—N. approbation; approval, -ement; sanction, advocacy; nod of approbation; esteem, estimation, good opinion, golden opinions, admiration; love etc. 897; appreciation, regard, account, popularity, *kudos*, credit; repute etc. 873.

commendation, praise; laud, -ation; good word; meed –, tribute- of praise; encomium; eulog-y, -ium; *éloge*, panegyric; homage, hero worship; benediction, blessing, benison.

applause, plaudit, clap; clapping, – of hands; accl-aim, -amation; cheer; paean, hosannah; shout –, peal –, chorus –, thunders- of -applause etc. Kentish fire; Prytaneum; blurb.

V. approve; think -good, – much of, – well of, – highly of; esteem, value, prize; set great store -by, – on.

do justice to, appreciate; honor, hold in esteem, look up to, admire; like etc. 897; be in favor of, wish God speed; hail, – with satisfaction.

stand –, stick- up for; uphold, hold up, countenance, sanction; clap –, pat- on the back; keep in countenance, endorse, give credit, recommend; mark with a white -mark, – stone.

commend, praise; be-, laud; compliment, pay a tribute, bepraise; clap, – the hands; applaud, cheer, acclaim, acclamate, encore; panegyrize, eulogize, cry up, *prôner*, puff; extol, – to the skies; magnify, glorify, exalt, boost, swell, make much of; flatter etc. 933; bless, give a blessing to; have –, say- a good word for; speak -well, – highly, – in high terms- of; sing –, sound –, chaunt –, resound- the praises of; sing praises to; cheer –, applaud- to the -echo, – very echo.

redound to the -honor, – praise, – credit- of; do credit to; deserve -praise etc. *n.*; recommend itself; pass muster.

be -praised etc.; receive honorable mention; be in -favor, – high favor- with; ring with the praises of, win golden opinions, gain credit, find favor with, stand well in the opinion of; *laudari a laudato viro*.

Adj. approving etc. *v.*; in favor of; lost in admiration.

commendatory, complimentary, benedictory, laudatory, panegyrical, eulogistic, encomiastic, acclamatory, lavish of praise, uncritical.

approved, praised etc. *v.*; un-censured, -impeached; popular, in good odor; in high esteem etc. (*respected*) 928; in –, in high- favor.

deserving –, worthy of- praise etc. *n.*; praiseworthy, commendable, of estimation; good etc. 648; meritorious, estimable, creditable, plausible, unimpeachable; beyond all praise.

Adv. commendably, with credit, to admiration; well etc. 681; with three times three.

Int. hear, hear! well done! *brav-o! -a! -i! bravissimo! euge! macte virtute!* so far so good, that's right, quite right; *optime!* one cheer more; may your shadow never be less! *esto perpetua!* long life to! *viva! enviva!* God speed! *valete et plaudite! encore! bis!*

Phr. *probatum est.*

932. Disapprobation.—N. disapprobation, -val; improbation; dis-esteem, -valuation, -placency; odium; dislike etc. 867; dissent etc. 489.

dis-praise, -commendation; blame, censure, obloquy; detraction etc. 934; disparagement, depreciation; denunciation; condemnation etc. 971; ostracism; boycott; black-list, -ball, *index -expurgatorius*, – *librorum prohibitorum*.

animadversion, reflection, stricture, objection, exception, criticism; sardonic -grin, – laugh; sarcasm, insinuation, innuendo; bad –, poor –, left-handed- compliment.

satire; sneer etc. (*contempt*) 930; taunt etc. (*disrespect*) 929; cavil, carping, censoriousness; hypercriticism etc. (*fastidiousness*) 868.

reprehension, remonstrance, expostulation, reproof, reprobation, admonition, increpation, reproach; rebuke, reprimand, castigation, jobation, lecture, curtain lecture, blow up, wigging, dressing, – down; rating, scolding, trimming; correction, set down, rap on the knuckles, *coup de bec*, rebuff; slap, – on the face; home thrust; hit; frown, scowl, black look.

diatribe; jeremiad; *tirade*, philippic.

clamor, outcry, hue and cry; hiss, -ing; sibilation, cat-call; execration etc. 908.

chiding, upbraiding etc. *v.*; exprobration, abuse, vituperation, invective, objurgation, contumely, personal remarks; hard –, cutting –, bitter- words.

evil-speaking; bad language etc. 908; personality.

V. disapprove; dislike etc. 867; lament etc. 839; object to, take exception to; be scandalized at, think ill of; view with -disfavor, – dark eyes, – jaundiced eyes; *nil admirari*, disvalue, improbate.

frown upon, look grave; bend –, knit- the brows; shake the head at, shrug the shoulders; turn up the nose etc. (*contempt*) 930; look -askance, – black upon; look with an evil eye; make a wry -face, – mouth- at; set one's face against.

dis-praise, -commend, -parage; deprecate, speak ill of, not speak well of, slate, condemn etc. (*find guilty*) 971.

blame; lay –, cast- blame upon; censure, *fronder*, reproach, pass censure on, reprobate, impugn.

remonstrate, expostulate, recriminate.

reprehend, chide, admonish; bring –, call- -to account, – over the coals, – to order; take to task, reprove, lecture, bring to book; read a -lesson, – lecture- to; rebuke, correct.

reprimand, chastise, castigate, lash, blow up, trounce, trim, *laver la tête*, overhaul; give it one, – finely; gibbet.

accuse etc. 938; impeach, denounce; hold up to -reprobation, – execration; expose, brand, gibbet, stigmatize; show –, pull –, take- up; cry 'shame' upon; be outspoken; raise a hue and cry against.

execrate etc. 908; exprobrate, speak daggers, vituperate; abuse, –, like a pickpocket; scold, rate, objurage, upbraid, fall foul of; jaw; rail, – at, – in good set terms; bark at; anathematize, call names; call by -hard, – ugly- names; a-, re-vile; vili-fy, -pend; bespatter; backbite; clapperclaw; rave –, thunder –, fulminate- against; load with reproaches; lash with the tongue.

exclaim –, protest –, inveigh –, declaim –, cry out –, raise one's voice- against.

decry; cry –, run –, frown- down; clamor, hiss,

hoot, mob, ostracize; draw up –, sing- a round robin; black-ball, -list.

animadvert –, reflect- upon; glance at; cast - reflection, – reproach, – a slur- upon; insinuate, damn with faint praise; 'hint a fault and hesitate dislike;' not to be able to say much for.

scoff at, point at; twit, taunt etc. (*disrespect*) 929; sneer at etc. (*despise*) 230; satirize, lampoon; defame etc. (*detract*) 934; depreciate, find fault with, criticize, cut up; pull –, pick- to pieces; take exception; cavil; peck –, nibble –, carp- at; be - censorious etc. *adj.*; pick -holes, – a hole, – a hole in one's coat; make a fuss about.

take –, set- down; snub, snap one up, give a rap on the knuckles; throw a stone -at, – in one's garden; have a -fling, – snap- at; have words with, pluck a crow with; give one a -wipe, – lick with the rough side of the tongue.

incur blame, excite disapprobation, scandalize, shock, revolt; get a bad name, forfeit one's good opinion, be under a cloud, come under the ferule, bring a hornet's nest about one's ears.

take blame, stand corrected; have to answer for.

Adj. disapproving etc. *v.*; scandalized.

disparaging, condemnatory, damnatory, denunciatory, reproachful, abusive, objurgatory, clamorous, vituperative; defamatory etc. 934.

satirical, sarcastic, sardonic, cynical, dry, sharp, cutting, biting, severe, virulent, withering, trenchant, hard upon; censorious, critical, captious, carping, hypercritical; fastidious etc. 868; sparing of –, grudging- praise.

disapproved, chid etc. *v.*; in bad odor, blown upon, unapproved; unblest; at a discount, exploded; weighed in the balance and found wanting.

blameworthy, reprehensible etc. (*guilt*) 947; to –, worthy of- blame, answerable, uncommendable, exceptionable, not to be thought of, bad etc. 649; vicious etc. 945.

un-lamented, -bewailed, -pitied.

Adv. with a wry face; reproachfully etc. *adj.*

Int. it is too bad! it -won't, – will never- do! marry come up! Oh! come! 'sdeath!

forbid it Heaven! God –, Heaven- forbid! out –, fie- upon it! away with! tut! *O tempora! O mores!* shame! fie, – for shame! out on you!

tell it not in Gath!

933. Flattery.—N. flattery, adulation, gloze; bland-ishment, -iloquence; cajolery; fawning, wheedling etc. *v.*; captation, coquetry, sycophancy, obsequiousness, flunkeyism, toad-eating, tuft-hunting; snobbishness.

incense, honeyed words, flummery; bun-kum, -combe; blarney, *placebo*, butter; soft -soap, – sawder; rose water.

voice of the charmer, mouth honor; lip-homage; euphemism; unctuousness etc. *adj.*

V. flatter, praise to the skies, puff; wheedle, cajole, glaver, coax; fawn, –, upon; humor, gloze, soothe, pet, coquet, slaver, butter; be-spatter, -slubber, -plaster, -slaver; lay it on thick, overpraise; earwig, cog, collogue; truckle –, pander *or* pandar –, pay court- to; court; creep into the good graces of; curry favor with, hang on the sleeve of; fool to the top of one's bent; lick the dust.

lay the flattering unction to one's soul, gild the pill, make things pleasant.

overestimate etc. 482; exaggerate etc. 549.

Adj. flattering etc. *v.*; adulatory; mealy-, honey-mouthed; honeyed; smooth, – tongued; soapy, oily, unctuous, blandiloquent, specious; fine-, fair-spoken; plausible, servile, sycophantic, fulsome; courtier-ly, -like.

Adv. *ad captandum.*

934. Detraction.—N. detraction, disparagement, depreciation, vilification, obloquy, scurrility, scandal, defamation, aspersion, traducement, slander, calumny, obtrectation, evil-speaking, backbiting, *scandalum magnatum.*

personality, libel, squib, lampoon, skit, pasquinade; *chronique scandaleuse.*

sarcasm, cynicism; criticism (*disapprobation*) 932; invective etc. 932; envenomed tongue; *spretae injuria formae.*

detractor etc. 936.

V. detract, derogate, decry, depreciate, disparage; run –, cry- down; minimize, make light of; belittle, sneer at etc. (*contemn*) 930; criticize, pull to pieces, pick a hole in one's coat, asperse, cast aspersions, blow upon, bespatter, blacken; vili-fy, -pend; avile; give a dog a bad name, brand, malign, backbite, libel, lampoon, traduce, slander, defame, calumniate, bear false witness against; speak ill of behind one's back.

'damn with faint praise, assent with civil leer; and without sneering, others teach to sneer.'

fling dirt etc. (*disrespect*) 929; anathematize etc. 932; dip the pen in gall, view in a bad light.

Adj. detracting etc. *v.*; defamatory, detractory, derogatory; disparaging, libellous; scurril-e, -ous; abusive; foul-spoken, -tongued, -mouthed; slanderous; calumni-ous, -atory; sar-castic, -donic; satirical, cynical.

935. Flatterer.—N. flatterer, adulator; eulogist, -phemist; optimist, encomiast, *laudator*, whitewasher, booster.

toad-y, -eater; sycophant, courtier, pickthank, Sir Pertinax MacSycophant; *flâneur*, *prôneur*; puffer, touter, *claqueur*; claw-back, ear-wig, doer of dirty work; parasite, hanger on etc. (*servility*) 886.

936. Detractor.—N. detractor, reprover; cens-or, -urer; cynic, critic, caviller, carper, word-catcher.

defamer, backbiter, slanderer, knocker, Sir Benjamin Backbite, lampooner, satirist, traducer, libeller, calumniator, dearest foe, dawplucker, Thersites; Zoilus; good-natured –, candid- friend [satirically]; reviler, vituperator, castigator; shrew etc. 901.

disapprover, *laudator temporis acti.*

937. Vindication.—N. vindication, justification, warrant; exoneration, exculpation; acquittal etc. 970; whitewashing.

extenuation; pallia-tion, -tive; softening, mitigation.

reply, defense; recrimination etc. 938.

apology, gloss, varnish; plea etc. 617; salvo; excuse, extenuating circumstances; allowance, – to be made; *locus poenitentiae*.

apologist, vindicator, justifier; defendant etc. 938.

justifiable charge, true bill.

V. justify, warrant; be an -excuse etc. *n.*- for; lend a color, furnish a handle; vindicate; ex-, disculpate; acquit etc. 970; clear, set right, exonerate, whitewash.

extenuate, palliate, excuse, soften, apologize, varnish, slur, gloze; put a -gloss, – good face-upon; mince; gloss over, bolster up, help a lame dog over a stile.

advocate, defend, plead one's cause; stand –, stick –, speak- up for; contend –, speak- for; bear out, keep in countenance, support; plead etc. 617; say in defense; plead ignorance; confess and avoid, propugn, put in a good word for.

take the will for the deed, make allowance for, do justice to; give -one, – the Devil- his due.

make good; prove -the truth of, – one's case; be justified by the event.

Adj. vindicat-ed, -ing etc. *v.*; vindicat-ive, -ory; palliative; exculpatory; apologetic.

excusable, defensible, pardonable; veni-al, -able; specious, plausible, justifiable.

Phr. *'honi soit qui mal y pense.'*

938. Accusation.—N. accusation, charge, imputation, slur, inculpation, exprobration, delation; crimination; in-, ac-, re-crimination; *tu quoque* argument; invective etc. 932.

de-nunciation, -nouncement; libel, challenge, citation, arraignment; im-, ap-peachment; indictment, bill of indictment, true bill; lawsuit etc. 969; condemnation etc. 971.

gravamen of a charge, head and front of one's offending, *argumentum ad hominem*; scandal etc. (*detraction*) 934; *scandalum magnatum*.

accuser, prosecutor, plaintiff, complainant, petitioner; relator, informer; appellant.

accused, defendant, prisoner, panel, co-, respondent; litigant.

V. accuse, charge, tax, impute, twit, taunt with, reproach.

brand with reproach; stigmatize, slur; cast a -stone at, – slur on; incriminate; inculpate, implicate; call to account etc. (*censure*) 932; take to-blame, – task; put in the black book.

inform against, indict, denounce, arraign; im-, ap-peach; have up, show up, pull up, challenge, cite, lodge a complaint; prosecute, bring an action against etc. 969.

charge –, saddle- with; lay to one's -door, – charge; lay the blame on, bring home to; cast –, throw- in one's teeth; cast the first stone at.

have –, keep- a rod in pickle for; have a crow to pluck with.

trump up a charge.

Adj. accusing etc. *v.*; accusat-ory, -ive; imputative, denunciatory; re-, criminatory.

accused etc. *v.*; suspected; under -suspicion, – a cloud, – *surveillance*; in -custody, – detention; in the -lock up, – watch house, – house of detention.

accusable, imputable; in-defensible, -excusable; un-pardonable, -justifiable; vicious etc. 945.

Int. look at home; *tu quoque* etc. (*retaliation*) 718.

939. Probity.—N. probity, integrity, rectitude; uprightness etc. *adj.*; honesty, faith; honor; good faith, *bona fides*; purity, clean hands.

fairness etc. *adj.*; fair play, justice, equity, impartiality, principle; grace.

constancy; faithfulness etc. *adj.*; fidelity, loyalty; incorrupt-ion, -ibility.

trustworthiness etc. *adj.*; truth, candor, singleness of heart; veracity etc. 543; tender conscience etc. (*sense of duty*) 926.

punctil-iousness, -io; delicacy, nicety; scrupulosity, -ousness etc. *adj.*; scruple; point, – of honor; punctuality.

dignity etc. (*repute*) 873; respectability, -bleness etc. *adj.*; gentleman; man of -honor, – his word; *fidus Achates*, *preux chevalier*; *galantuomo*; truepenny, trump, brick; true Briton, white man, sportsman.

court of honor, a fair field and no favor; *argumentum ad verecundiam*.

V. be -honorable etc. *adj.*; deal -honorably, – squarely, – impartially, – fairly; speak the truth etc. (*veracity*) 543; tell the truth and shame the devil, *vitam impendere vero*; show a proper spirit, make a point of; do one's duty etc. 944; play the game.

redeem one's pledge etc. 926; keep –, be as good as- one's -promise, – word; keep faith with, not fail.

give and take, *audire alteram partem*, give the devil his due, put the saddle on the right horse.

redound to one's honor.

Adj. upright; honest, – as daylight; veracious etc. 543; virtuous etc. 944; honorable; fair, right, just, equitable, impartial, even-handed, square; fair –, open- and aboveboard.

constant, – as the northern star; faithful, loyal, staunch; true, – blue, – to one's colors, – to the core, – as the needle to the pole; true-hearted, trust-y, -worthy; as good as one's word, to be depended on, incorruptible.

manly, straightforward etc. (*ingenuous*) 703; frank, candid, open-hearted.

conscientious, tender-conscienced, right-minded; high-principled, -minded; scrupulous, religious, strict; nice, punctilious, correct, punctual; respect-, reput-able; gentlemanlike.

inviol-able, -ate; un-violated, -broken, -betrayed; un-bought, -bribed.

innocent etc. 946; pure; stainless; un-stained, -tarnished, -sullied, -tainted, -perjured; uncorrupt, -ed; unde-filed, -praved, -bauched; *integer vitae scelerisque purus*; *justus et tenax propositi*.

chivalrous, jealous of honor, *sans peur et sans reproche*; high-spirited.

supra-mundane, unworldly, overscrupulous.

Adv. honorably etc. *adj.*; *bona fide*; on the square, in good faith, honor bright, *foro conscientiae*, with clean hands; by fair means.

940. Improbity.—N. improbity; dishon-esty, -our; deviation from rectitude; disgrace etc. (*disrepute*) 874; fraud etc. (*deception*) 545; lying etc. 544; bad –, Punic- faith; *mala –, Punica, fides*; infidelity; faithlessness etc. *adj.*; Judas kiss, betrayal; scrap of paper.

breach of -promise, – trust, – faith; prodition, disloyalty, divided allegiance, treason, high treason; apostacy etc. (*tergiversation*) 607; nonobservance etc. 773.

shabbiness etc. *adj.*; villainy; baseness etc. *adj.*; abjection, debasement, turpitude, moral turpitude, laxity, trimming, shuffling.

perfidy; perfidiousness etc. *adj.*; treachery, double-dealing; unfairness etc. *adj.*; knavery, roguery, rascality, foul-play; jobb-ing, -ery; Tammany, graft; venality, nepotism; corruption, job, shuffle, fishy transaction, barratry; sharp practice, heads I win, tails you lose; mouth-honor etc. (*flattery*) 933.

V. be -dishonest etc. *adj.*; play false; break one's -word, – faith, – promise; jilt, betray, forswear; shuffle etc. (*lie*) 544; live by one's wits, sail near the wind; play with marked cards.

disgrace –, dishonor –, demean –, degrade- oneself; derogate, stoop, grovel, sneak, lose caste; sell oneself, go over to the enemy; seal one's infamy.

Adj. dishon-est, -orable; un-conscientious, -scrupulous; fraudulent etc. 545; knavish; disgraceful etc. (*disreputable*) 874; wicked etc. 945.

false-hearted, disingenuous; unfair, one-sided; double, -tongued, -faced; time-serving, crooked, tortuous, insidious, Machiavellian, dark, slippery; questionable; fishy; perfidious, treacherous, perjured.

infamous, arrant, foul, base, vile, low, ignominious, blackguard.

contemptible, abject, mean, shabby, little, paltry, dirty, scurvy, scabby, sneaking, groveling, scrubby, rascally, pettifogging; beneath one; not cricket.

low-minded, -thoughted; base-minded.

undignified, indign; unbe-coming, -seeming, fitting; de-rogatory, -grading; *infra dignitatem*; ungentleman-ly, -like; un-knightly, -chivalric, -manly, -handsome; recreant, inglorious.

corrupt, venal; debased, mongrel.

faithless, of bad faith, false, unfaithful, disloyal; untrustworthy; trust-, troth-less; lost to shame, dead to honor.

Adv. dishonestly etc. *adj.*; *malâ fide*, like a thief in the night, by crooked paths; by foul means.

Int. *O tempora! O mores!*

941. Knave.—N. knave, rogue, villain; Scapin, rascal; Lazarillo de Tormes; bad man etc. 949; blackguard etc. 949.

traitor, betrayer, arch-traitor, conspirator, stool pigeon, Judas, Catiline; reptile, serpent, snake in the grass, wolf in sheep's clothing, sneak, Jerry Sneak, tell-tale, squealer, mischief-maker, trimmer; renegade etc. (*tergiversation*) 607; truant, recreant; sycophant etc. (*servility*) 886.

942. Disinterestedness.—N. disinterestedness etc. *adj.*; generosity; liberal-ity, -ism; altruism; benevolence etc. 906; elevation, loftiness of purpose, exaltation, magnanimity; chival-ry, -rous spirit; heroism, sublimity.

self-denial, -abnegation, -effacement, -sacrifice, -immolation, -control etc. (*resolution*) 604; stoicism, devotion, martyrdom, *suttee*.

labor of love.

V. be -disinterested etc. *adj.*; make a sacrifice, lay one's head on the block; put oneself in the place of others, do as one would be done by, do unto others as we would men should do unto us.

Adj. disinterested; unselfish; self-denying, -sacrificing, -devoted; generous.

handsome, liberal, noble; noble-, high-minded; princely, great, high, elevated, lofty, exalted, spirited, stoical, magnanimous; great-, large-hearted, chivalrous, heroic, sublime.

un-bought, -bribed; uncorrupted etc. (*upright*) 939.

943. Selfishness.—N. selfishness etc. *adj.*; self-love, -indulgence, -worship, -interest; ego-tism, -ism; egocentrism, narcissism; *amour propre* etc. (*vanity*) 880; nepotism.

worldliness etc. *adj.*; world wisdom.

illiberality; meanness etc. *adj.*

time-server; tuft-, fortune-hunter; self-seeker; jobber, worldling; egotist, egoist, monopolist, nepotist, profiteer; temporizer, trimmer; dog in the manger, charity that begins at home.

V. be -selfish etc. *adj.*; please –, indulge –, coddle- oneself; consult one's own -wishes, – pleasure; look after one's own interest; feather one's nest; take care of number one, have an eye to the main chance, know on which side one's bread is buttered; give an inch and take an ell; wangle.

Adj. selfish; self-seeking, -indulgent, -interested; wrapt up –, centered- in self; egotistic, -al; egoistical; egocentric.

illiberal, mean, ungenerous, narrowminded; mercenary, venal; covetous etc. 819.

unspiritual; earthly, -minded; mundane; worldly, -minded, -wise; time-serving.

interested; *alieni appetens sui profusus*.

Adv. ungenerously etc. *adj.*; to gain some private ends; from selfish –, interested- motives.

Phr. *après nous le déluge*.

944. Virtue.—N. virtue; virtuousness etc. *adj.*; morality; moral rectitude; integrity etc. (*probity*) 939; nobleness etc. 873.

morals; ethics etc. (*duty*) 926; cardinal virtues.

merit, worth, desert, excellence, credit; self-control etc. (*resolution*) 604; self-denial etc. (*temperance*) 953.

well-doing; good -actions, – behavior; discharge –, fulfilment –, performance- of duty; well spent life; innocence etc. 946.

V. be -virtuous etc. *adj.*; practice -virtue etc. *n.*; do –, fulfil –, perform –, discharge- one's duty; redeem one's pledge etc. 926; act well, – one's part; fight the good fight; acquit oneself well; command –, master- one's passions; keep -straight, – in the right path.

set -an, – a good- example; be on one's -good, – best- behavior.

Adj. virtuous, good; innocent etc. 946; meritorious, deserving, worthy, desertful, correct; dut-iful, -eous; moral; right, -eous, -minded; well-intentioned, creditable, laudable, commendable, praiseworthy; above –, beyond- all praise; excellent, admirable; sterling, pure, noble.

exemplary; match-, peer-less; saint-ly, -like; heaven-born, angelic, seraphic, godlike.

Adv. virtuously etc. *adj.*; *e merito*.

945. Vice.—N. vice; evil-doing, – courses; wrong doing; wickedness, viciousness etc. *adj.*; iniquity, peccability, demerit; sin, Adam; old – offending- Adam.

immorality, impropriety, indecorum, scandal, laxity, looseness of morals; want of -principle, – ballast; obliquity, backsliding, infamy, demoralization, pravity, depravity, pollution; hardness of heart; brutality etc. (*malevolence*) 907; corruption etc. (*debasement*) 659; knavery etc. (*improbity*) 940; profligacy; lust etc. 961; flagrancy, atrocity; cannibalism.

infirmity; weakness etc. *adj.*; weakness of the flesh, frailty, imperfection; error; weak side; foible; fail-ing, -ure; crying –, besetting- sin; defect, deficiency, shortcoming; cloven foot.

lowest dregs of vice, sink of iniquity, Alsatian den; *gusto picaresco*.

fault, crime; criminality etc. (*guilt*) 947.

sinner etc. 949.

V. be -vicious etc. *adj.*; sin, commit sin, do amiss, err, transgress; misdemean –, forget –, misconduct- oneself; mis-do, -behave; fall, lapse, slip, trip, offend, trespass; deviate from the -line of duty, – path of virtue etc. 944; take a wrong course, go astray; hug a -sin, – fault; sow one's wild oats.

render -vicious etc. *adj.*; demoralize, brutalize; corrupt etc. (*degrade*) 659.

Adj.* vicious; sinful; sinning etc. *v.*; wicked, iniquitous, bad, immoral, unrighteous, wrong, criminal; naughty, incorrect; undut-eous, -iful.

unprincipled, lawless, disorderly, *contra bonos mores*, indecorous, unseemly, improper; dissolute, profligate, scampish; unworthy; worth-, desert-less; disgraceful, recreant; reprehensible, blameworthy, uncommendable; dis-creditable, -reputable.

base, sinister, scurvy, foul, gross, vile, black, grave, facinorous, felonious, nefarious, shameful, scandalous, infamous, villainous, of a deep dye, heinous; flag-rant, -itious; atrocious, incarnate, accursed.

Mephistophelian, satanic, diabolic, hellish, infernal, stygian, fiend-ish, -like, hell-born, demoniacal, devilish.

mis-created, -begotten; demoralized, corrupt, depraved.

evil-minded, -disposed; ill-conditioned; malevolent etc. 907; heart-, grace-, shame-, virtueless; abandoned, lost to virtue; unconscionable; sunk –, lost –, deep –, steeped- in iniquity.

incorrigible, irreclaimable, obdurate, reprobate, past praying for; culpable, reprehensible etc. (*guilty*) 947.

unjustifiable; in-defensible, -excusable; inexpiable, unpardonable, irremissible.

weak, frail, lax, infirm, imperfect, indiscreet; demoralizing, degrading.

Adv. wrong; sinfully etc. *adj.*; without excuse.

Int. *O tempora! O mores!*

*Most of these adjectives are applicable both to the act and to the agent.

946. Innocence.—N. innocence; guiltlessness etc. *adj.*; incorruption, impeccability.

clean hands, clear conscience, *mens sibi conscia recti*.

innocent, new born babe, lamb, dove.

V. be -innocent etc. *adj.*; *nil conscire sibi nullâ pallescere culpâ*.

acquit etc. 970; exculpate etc. (*vindicate*) 937.

Adj. innocent, not guilty, unguilty; guilt-, fault-, sin-, stain-, blood-, spot-less; clear, immaculate; *rectus in curiâ*; un-spotted, -blemished, -erring; undefiled etc. 939; unhardened, Saturnian; Arcadian etc. (*artless*) 703.

in-, un-culpable; unblam-ed, -able; blameless, inerrable, above suspicion; irrepr-oachable, -ovable, -ehensible; un-exceptionable, -objectionable, -impeachable; salvable; venial etc. 937.

harmless; in-offensive, -noxious, -nocuous; dove-, lamb-like; pure, harmless as doves; innocent as -a lamb, – the babe unborn; more sinned against than sinning.

virtuous etc. 944; un-reproved, -impeached, -reproached.

Adv. innocently etc. *adj.*; with clean hands; with a -clear, – safe- conscience.

947. Guilt.—N. guilt, -iness; culpability; crimin-ality, -ousness; deviation from rectitude etc. (*improbity*) 940; sinfulness etc. (*vice*) 945; peccability.

mis-conduct, -behavior, -doing, -deed; malpractice, fault, sin, error, transgression; dereliction, delinquency; indiscretion, lapse, slip, trip, *faux pas*, *peccadillo*; flaw, blot, omission; fail-ing, -ure.

offence, trespass; mis-demeanor, -feasance, -prision, tort; mal-efaction, -feasance, -versation; crime, felony.

enormity, atrocity, outrage; deadly –, mortal –, unpardonable- sin; died without a name.

corpus delicti.

Adj. guilty, to blame, culpable, peccable, in fault, censurable, reprehensible, blameworthy, uncommendable, illaudable; weighed in the balance and found wanting; exceptionable, objectionable.

Adv. *in flagrante delicto*; red-handed, in the very act.

948. Good Man.—N. good man, worthy.

good woman, goddess, *madonna*, virgin.

model, paragon etc. (*perfection*) 650; good example; hero, demigod, seraph, angel; innocent etc. 946; saint etc. (*piety*) 987; benefactor etc. 912; philanthropist etc. 910; Aristides.

brick, trump, rough diamond, ugly duckling.

salt of the earth; one in ten thousand; one of the best.

Phr. *si sic omnes!*

949. Bad Man.—N. bad man, wrongdoer, worker of iniquity; evil-doer etc. 913; sinner; the -wicked etc. 945; bad example.

rascal, scoundrel, villain, miscreant, caitiff; wretch, reptile, viper, serpent, cockatrice, basilisk, urchin; tiger, monster; devil etc. (*demon*) 980; devil incarnate; demon in human shape, Nana Sahib; hell-hound, -cat; rake-hell.

bad woman, jade, Jezebel, adultress, etc. 962.

scamp, scapegrace, rip, runagate, ne'er-do-well, reprobate, *roué*, rake; limb; one who has sold himself to the devil, fallen angel, *âme damnée, vaurien, mauvais sujet*, loose fish, sad, dog; lost –, black-sheep; castaway, recreant, defaulter; prodigal etc. 818; libertine etc. 962.

rough, rowdy, ugly customer, ruffian, hoodlum, bully; Jonathan Wild; hangman; incendiary; thief etc. 792; murderer etc. 361.

culprit, delinquent, criminal, melefactor, misdemeanant; felon; convict, jail-bird, ticket-of-leave man; outlaw.

blackguard, *polisson*, loafer, sneak; raps-, rascallion; cullion, mean wretch, varlet, kern, *âme-de-boue, drôle*; cur, dog, hound, whelp, mongrel; lown, loon, runnion, outcast, vagabond; rogue etc. (*knave*) 941; scum of the earth, riff-raff; *Arcades ambo*.

Int. sirrah!

950. Penitence.—N. penitence, contrition, compunction, repentance, remorse; regret etc. 833.

self-reproach, -reproof, -accusation, -condemnation, -humiliation; stings –, pangs –, qualms –, prickings –, twinge –, twitch –, touch –, voice- of conscience; compunctious visitings of nature.

acknowledgment, confession etc. (*disclosure*) 529; apology etc. 952; recantation etc. 607; penance etc. 952; resipiscence.

awakened conscience, deathbed repentance, *locus poenitentiae*, stool of repentance, cutty stool.

penitent, Magdalen, prodigal son, returned prodigal, a sadder and wiser man.

V. repent, be sorry for; be -penitent etc. *adj.*; rue; regret etc. 833; think better of; recant etc. 607; knock under etc. (*submit*) 725; plead guilty; sing -*miserere*, – *de profundis*; cry *peccavi*; own oneself in the wrong; acknowledge, confess etc. (*disclose*) 529; humble oneself; beg pardon etc. (*apologize*) 952; turn over a new leaf, put on the new man, turn from sin; reclaim; repent in sackcloth and ashes etc. (*do penance*) 952; learn by experience.

Adj. penitent; repenting etc. *v.*; repentant, contrite; conscience-smitten, -stricken; self-accusing, -convicted.

penitenti-al, -ary; chastened, reclaimed; not hardened; un-hardened.

Adv. *meâ culpâ.*

Phr. *peccavi*; *erubuit*; *salva res est*; *vous l'avez voulu, Georges Dandin.*

951. Impenitence.—N. impenitence, irrepentance, recusance.

hardness of heart, seared conscience, induration, obduracy.

V. be -impenitent etc. *adj.*; steel –, harden- the heart; die -game, – and make no sign.

Adj. impenitent uncontrite, obdurate; hard, -ened; seared, recusant; unrepentant; relent-, remorse-, grace-, shrift-less.

lost, incorrigible, irreclaimable.

unre-claimed, -formed; unrepented, unatoned.

952. Atonement.—N. atonement, reparation; compromise, composition; compensation etc. 30; quittance, quits; indemni-ty, -fication; expiation, redemption, reclamation, conciliation, propitiation.

amends, apology, *amende honorable*, satisfaction; peace –, sin –, burnt- offering; scapegoat, sacrifice.

penance, fasting, maceration, sackcloth and ashes, white sheet, shrift, flagellation, lustration; purga-tion, -tory.

V. atone, – for; expiate; propitiate; make -amends, – good; reclaim, redeem, repair, ransom, absolve, purge, shrive, do penance, stand in a white sheet, repent in sackcloth and ashes.

set one's house in order, wipe off old scores, make matters up; pay the -forfeit, – penalty.

apologize, beg pardon, express regret, *faire amende honorable*, give satisfaction; come –, fall- down on one's -knees, – marrow bones.

Adj. propitiatory, expiatory; sacrific, -ial, -atory; piacul-ar, -ous.

953. Temperance.—N. temperance, moderation, sobriety, soberness.

forbearance, abnegation; self-denial, -restraint, -control etc. (*resolution*) 604.

frugality; vegetarianism, teetotalism, total abstinence, prohibition; abst-inence, -emiousness, asceticism etc. 955; system of -Pythagoras, – Cornaro; Pythagorism, Stoicism.

vegetarian; Pythagorean, gymnosophist; teetotaler etc. 958; abstainer.

V. be -temperate etc. *adj.*; abstain, forbear, refrain, deny oneself, spare; know when one has had enough; take the pledge; look not upon the wine when it is red.

Adj. temperate, moderate, sober, frugal, sparing; abst-emious, -inent; within compass; measured etc. (*sufficient*) 639.

Pythagorean; vegetarian; teetotal, pussy-foot.

954. Intemperance.—N. intemperance; sensuality, animalism, carnality; pleasure; effeminacy, silkiness; luxur-y, -iousness; lap of -pleasure, – luxury.

indulgence; high-, free- living, in-abstinence, self-indulgence; voluptuousness etc. *adj.*; epicurism, -eanism; sybaritism.

dissipation; licentiousness etc. *adj.*; debauchery; crapulence.

revel-s, -ry; debauch, carousal, jollification, drinking bout, wassail, Saturnalia, orgies; excess, too much; intoxication etc. 959.

Circean cup; drug habit etc. 663.

V. be -intemperate etc. *adj.*; indulge, exceed; live -well, – high, – on the fat of the land; give a loose to -indulgence etc. *n.*; dine not wisely but too well; wallow in -voluptuousness etc. *n.*; plunge into dissipation.

revel, rake, live hard, run riot, sow one's wild oats; slake one's -appetite, – thirst; swill; pamper.

Adj. intemperate, inabstinent, intoxicated etc. 958; sensual, self-indulgent; voluptuous, luxurious, licentious, wild, dissolute, rakish, fast, debauched.

brutish, crapulous, swinish, piggish, hoggish, bestial.

Paphian, Epicurean, Sybaritical; bred –, nursed- in the lap of luxury; indulged, pampered, full-fed.

954a. Sensualist.—N. Sybarite, voluptuary, Sardanapalus, man of pleasure, carpet knight; epicure, -an; *gourm-et, -and;* gormandizer, gutling, glutton, pig, hog; votary —, swine- of Epicurus; sensualist; Heliogabalus; free —, hard- liver; libertine etc. 962; hedonist.

955. Asceticism.—N. asceticism, puritanism, sabbatarianism; cynicism, austerity; total abstinence.

mortification, maceration, sackcloth and ashes, flagellation; penance etc. 952; fasting etc. 956; martyrdom.

ascetic; anchor-et, -ite; martyr; *Heautontimorumenos*; hermit etc. (*recluse*) 893; puritan, sabbatarian, cynic.

Adj. ascetic, austere, puritanical; cynical; over-religious.

956. Fasting.—N. fasting; exrophagy; famishment, starvation; banting.

fast, *jour maigre*; fast —, banyan-day; Lent, quadragesima; Rama-dan, -zan; spare —, meager- diet; lenten -diet, — entertainment; *soupe maigre*, short -rations, — commons; Barmecide feast; hunger strike.

V. fast, starve, clem, famish, perish with hunger; dine with Duke Humphrey; make two bites of a cherry.

Adj. lenten, quadragesimal; unfed; starved etc. *v.*; half-starved; fasting etc. *v.*; hungry etc. 865.

957. Gluttony.—N. gluttony; greed; greediness etc. *adj.*; voracity.

epicurism; good —, high- living; edacity, gulosity, crapulence; gutt-, guzz-ling; over-indulgence.

good cheer, blow out; feast etc. (*food*) 298; gastronomy.

epicure, *bon vivant*, *gourmand*; glutton, cormorant, hog, belly-god, Apicius, gastronome, gormandizer.

V. gormandize, gorge; over-gorge, -eat- oneself; engorge, eat one's fill, cram, stuff, stodge, glut, satiate; gutt-le, guzz-le; bolt, devour, gobble up; gulp etc. (*swallow food*) 298; raven, eat out of house and home.

have the stomach of an ostrich; play a good knife and fork etc. (*appetite*) 865.

Adj. gluttonous, greedy; gormandizing etc. *v.*; edacious, omnivorous, crapulent, swinish, voracious, devouring.

pampered; over-fed, -gorged.

958. Sobriety.—N. sobriety; teetotalism, temperance etc. 953.

water-drinker; teetotal-er, -ist; abstainer, Good Templar, Rechabite, band of hope; prohibitionist, pussyfoot.

V. take the pledge.

Adj. sober, — as a judge; dry, on the water wagon.

959. Drunkenness.—N. drunkenness etc. *adj.*; intemperance; drinking etc. *v.*; inebri-ety, -ation; ebri-ety, -osity; befuddlement; insobriety; intoxication; temulency, bibacity, wine-bibbing; com-, potation; deep potations, bacchanals, *bacchanalia*, libations.

oino-, dipso-mania; ***delirium tremens***, d.t., alcohol, -ism.

drink; alcoholic drinks, alcohol, booze; gin, blue ruin, grog, brandy, port wine; punch, -bowl; cup, rosy wine, flowing bowl; drop, — too much; dram; beer, wine, spirits etc. (***beverage***) 298; cocktail, nip, peg; stirrup cup.

drunkard, sot, toper, tippler, bibber, wine-bibber; hard —, gin —, dram- drinker; soak, soaker, sponge, tun; love-, toss-pot; thirsty soul, reveller, carouser; Bacchanal, -ian; Bacch-al, -ante; devotee to Bacchus, dipsomaniac.

V. get —, be- drunk etc. *adj.*; see double; take a -drop, — glass- too much; drink, tipple, tope, booze, bouse, guzzle, swill, soak, sot, lush, bib, swig, carouse; sacrifice at the shrine of Bacchus; take to drinking; drink -hard, — deep, — like a fish; have one's swill, drain the cup, splice the main brace, take a hair of the dog that bit you.

liquor, — up; wet one's whistle, take a whet; lift one's elbow; crack a —, pass the- bottle; toss of etc. (*drink up*) 298; go to the -ale, — public house.

make one-drunk etc. *adj.*; inebriate, fuddle, fuzzle, get into one's head.

Adj. drunk, tipsy; intoxicated; inebri-ous, -ate, -ated; in one's cups; in a state of -intoxication etc. *n.*; temulent, -ive; fuddled, mellow, cut, boosy, fou, fresh, merry, elevated, squiffy; plastered, befuddled, sozzled; flush, -ed; flustered, disguised, groggy, beery; topheavy; potvaliant, glorious; potulent; over-come, -taken; whittled, screwed, tight, primed, oiled, corned, raddled, sewed up, lushy, nappy, muddled, muzzy, bosky, obfuscated, maudlin; crapulous, dead —, blind- drunk.

Inter pocula; in —, the worse for- liquor, having had a drop too much, half seas over, three sheets in the wind; under the table, blind to the world, one over the eight.

drunk as -a piper, — a fiddler, — a lord, — Chloe, — an owl, — David's sow, — a wheelbarrow.

drunken, bibacious, bibulous, sottish; given —, addicted- to -drink, — the bottle; toping etc. *v.*; wet.

Phr. *nunc est bibendum.*

960. Purity.—N. purity; decency, decorum, delicacy; continence, chastity, honesty, virtue, modesty, shame; pudicity, *pucelage*, virginity.

vestal, virgin, Joseph, Hippolytus; Lucretia, Diana; prude.

Adj. pure, undefiled, modest, delicate, decent, decorous; *virginibus puerisque*; chaste, continent, virtuous, honest, Platonic.

961. Impurity.—N. impurity; uncleanness etc. (*filth*) 653; immodesty; grossness etc. *adj.*; indelicacy, indecency; impudicity; obscenity, ribaldry, smut, bawdry, *double entendre*, *équivoque*; Aretinism; pornography.

concupiscence, lust, carnality, flesh, salacity; pruriency, lechery, lasciviency, lubricity, lewdness.

incontinence, intrigue, *faux pas*; *amour*, *-ette*; gallantry; dabauchery, libertinism, *libertinage*, fornication; *liaison*; wenching, venery, dissipation.

seduction; defloration, defilement, abuse, violation, rape; incest.

social evil, harlotry, stupration, whoredom, concubinage, cuckoldom, adultery, advoutry, *crim. con.*; free love.

seraglio, harem, zenana; brothel, bagnio, stew, bawdy-house, *lupanar*, house of ill fame, *bordel*, kip.

V. be -impure etc. *adj.*; intrigue; debauch, defile, assault, attack, seduce; prostitute; abuse, violate, deflower; commit -adultery etc. *n.*

Adj. impure; unclean etc. (*dirty*) 653; not to be mentioned to ears polite; immodest, shameless; indecorous, -delicate, -decent; loose, suggestive, *risqué*, coarse, gross, broad, free, equivocal, smutty, fulsome, ribald, obscene, bawdy, pornographic.

concupiscent, prurient, lickerish, rampant, lustful; carnal, -minded; lewd, lascivious, lecherous, libidinous, erotic, ruttish, salacious; Paphian; voluptuous; incestuous.

unchaste, light, wanton, licentious, adulterous, debauched, dissolute; of -loose character, – easy virtue; frail, gay, riggish, incontinent, meretricious, rakish, gallant, dissipated; no better than she should be; on the -town, – streets, – *pavé*, – loose.

adulterous, incestuous, bestial.

962. Libertine.—N. libertine; voluptuary etc. 954*a*; rake, debauchee, loose fish, rip, rake-hell, fast man; *intrigant*, gallant, seducer, fornicator, lecher, satyr, goat, whoremonger, *paillard*, adulterer, gay deceiver, Lothario, Don Juan, Bluebeard.

adulteress, advoutress, courtesan, prostitute, strumpet, tart, hustler, chippy, broad, harlot, whore, punk, *fille de joie*; woman, – of the town; street-walker, Cyprian, miss, piece; frail sisterhood, fallen woman; demirep, wench, trollop, trull, baggage, hussy, drab, bitch, jade, skit, rig, quean, mopsy, slut, minx, harridan; woman -of easy virtue etc. (*unchaste*) 961; wanton, fornicatress; Jezebel, Messalina, Delilah, Thaïs, Phryne, Aspasia, Lais, *lorette*, *cocotte*, *petite dame*, *grisette*; *demimonde*; white slave.

concubine, mistress, fancy woman, kept woman, doxy, *chère amie*, *bona roba*.

pimp; pand-er, -ar; bawd, *conciliatrix*, procuress, mackerel; wittol.

963. Legality.—N. legality; legitima-cy, -teness, legitimization.

legislature; law, code, *corpus juris*, constitution, pandect, charter, act, enactment, statute, rule; canon etc. (*precept*) 697; ordinance, institution, regulation; by-, bye-law, rescript; decree etc. (*order*) 741; *ordonnance*; standing order; *plébiscite* etc. (*choice*) 609.

legal process; form, -ula, -ality; rite; arm of the law; *habeas corpus*.

[Science of law] jurisprudence, nomology; legislation, codification.

equity, common law; *lex* –, *lex nonscripta*, unwritten law; law of nations, international law, *jus gentium*; *jus civile*; civil –, criminal –, canon –, statute –, ecclesiastical- law; *lex mercatoria*.

constitutional-ism, -ity; justice etc. 922.

V. legalize, legitimize; enact, ordain; decree etc. (*order*) 741; pass a law; legislate; codify, formulate; authorize.

Adj. legal, legitimate; according to law; vested, constitutional, chartered, legalized; lawful etc. (*permitted*) 760; statut-able, -ory; legislat-orial, -ive.

Adv. legally etc. *adj.*; in the eye of the law; *de jure*.

964. Illegality. [Absence or violation of law.]—**N.** lawlessness; breach –, violation- of law; disobedience etc. 742; unconformity etc. 83.

arbitrariness etc. *adj.*; antinomy, violence, brute force, despotism, outlawry.

mob –, lynch –, club –, Lydford –, martial –, drumhead- law; *coup d'état*; *le droit du plus fort*; *argumentum baculinum*.

illegality, informality, unlawfulness, illegitimacy, bar sinister.

trover and conversion; smuggling, boot-legging, rum-running, poaching; simony.

speakeasy, speakie, blind pig.

V. offend against –, violate- the law; set the law at defiance, ride rough-shod over, drive a coach and six through a statute; make the law a dead letter, take the law into one's own hands.

smuggle, run, poach.

Adj. illegal; prohibited etc. 761; not allowed, unlawful, illegitimate, illicit, contraband, actionable.

unchartered, unconstitutional; unwarrant-ed, -able; unauthorized; informal, unofficial; in-, extra-judicial.

lawless, arbitrary; despotic, -al; summary, irresponsible; un-answerable, -accountable.

null and void; a dead letter.

Adv. illegally etc. *adj.*; with a high hand, in violation of law.

965. Jurisdiction. [Executive.]—**N.** jurisdiction, judicature, administration of justice, soc; executive, commission of the peace; magistracy etc. (*authority*) 737.

judge etc. 967; tribunal etc. 966; municipality, corporation, bailiwick, shrievalty; lord lieutenant; lord –, mayor, city manager, alderman etc. 745; sheriff, bailie, shrieve, chief –, constable; police, – force; constabulary, bumbledom.

officer; proctor, high –, commissioner; bailiff, tipstaff, bum-bailiff, catchpoll, beadle; police-man, -constable, -sergeant; *sbirro*, *alguazil*, *gendarme*, kavass, *lictor*, macebearer, *huissier*, bedel.

press-gang; exciseman, gauger, custom-house officer, *douanier*.

coroner, edile, aedile, portreeve, paritor; *posse comitatus*.

V. judge, sit in judgment.

Adj. executive, administrative, municipal;

inquisitorial, causidical; judic-atory, -iary, -ial; juridical.

Adv. *coram judice.*

966. Tribunal.—N. tribunal, court, board, bench, judicatory, curia; court of -justice, – law, – arbitration; inquisition; guild.

justice –, judgment –, mercy- seat; woolsack; bar, – of justice; dock; forum, hustings, *bureau*, drum-head; jury-, witness-box.

senate-house, town-hall, theater; House of - Lords, – Commons.

assize, eyre; ward-, burgh-mote; superior courts of Westminister; court of -record, – oyer and terminer, – assize, – appeal – error; High court of -Judicature, – Appeal; Judicial Committee of the Privy Council; Star-Chamber; Court of -Chancery, – King's *or* Queen's Bench, – Exchequer, – Common Pleas, – Probate, – Arches, – Admiralty, – Criminal Appeal; Lords Justices' –, Rolls –, Vice Chancellor's –, Stannary –, Divorce –, Palatine –, ecclesiastical –, county –, police- court; sessions; quarter –, petty-sessions; court -leet, – baron, – of pie poudre, – of common council; board of green cloth.

court-martial; drum-head court-martial; *durbar*, divan; Areopagus; *rota.*

Adj. judicial etc. 965; appellate; curial.

967. Judge.—N. judge; justi-ce, -ciar, -ciary; chancellor; justice –, judge- of assize; recorder, common serjeant; puisne –, assistant –, county court- judge; conservator –, justice- of the peace, J.P.; court etc. (*tribunal*) 966; grand –, petty –, coroner's- jury; panel, juror, juryman; twelve men in a box; magistrate, police magistrate, stipendiary, the great unpaid, beak; his -worship, – honor, – lordship; deemster, moderator.

Lord -Chancellor, – Justice; Master of the Rolls, Vice-Chancellor; Lord Chief -Justice, – Baron; Mr. Justice; Baron, – of the Exchequer.

jurat, assessor; arbi-ter, -trator; umpire; refer-ee, -endary; revising barrister; domesman; censor etc. (*critic*) 480; official –, receiver.

archon, tribune, praetor, *ephor*, syndic, *podestà*, mullah, ulema, mufti, cadi, kadi; Rhadamanthus.

litigant etc. (*accusation*) 938.

V. adjudge etc. (*determine*) 480; try a -case, – prisoner.

Adj. judicial etc. 965.

Phr. 'a Daniel come to judgment.'

968. Lawyer.—N. lawyer, jurist, legist, civilian, pundit, publicist, jurisconsult, legal adviser, advocate; barrister, – at law; counsel, -lor; King's *or* Queen's counsel; K.C.; Q.C.; silk gown, leader; junior, – counsel; stuff gown, serjeant-at-law; bencher, tubman; judge etc. 967.

bar, legal profession, gentleman of the long robe; junior –, outer –, inner- bar; Inns of Court; equity draftsman, conveyancer, pleader, special pleader.

solicitor, attorney, proctor; notary, – public; scrivener, cursitor; writer, – to the signet; S.S.C.; limb of the law; pettifogger.

V. practice -at, – within- the bar; plead; call –, to called- -to, – within- the bar; take silk.

Adj. learned in the law; at the bar; forensic.

969. Lawsuit.—N. lawsuit, suit, action, cause, petition; litigation; dispute etc. 713.

citation, arraignment, prosecution, impeachment; accusation etc. 938; presentment, true bill, indictment.

apprehension, arrest; committal; imprisonment etc. (*restraint*) 751.

writ, summons, subpoena, *latitat*, *nisi prius*; *habeas corpus*.

pleadings; declaration, bill, claim; *procès-verbal*, bill of right, information, *corpus delicti*; affidavit, state of facts; answer, replication, plea, demurrer, rebutter, rejoinder; surre-butter, -joinder.

suitor, party to a suit; litigant etc. 938; libellant.

hearing, trial; verdict etc. (*judgment*) 480; appeal, – motion; writ of error; *certiorari*.

case, decision, precedent, ruling; decided case, reports.

V. go to –, appeal to the- law; bring to -justice, – trial, – the bar; put on trial, pull up; accuse etc. 938; prefer –, file- a claim etc. *n.*; take the law of, inform against.

serve with a writ, cite, apprehend, arraign, sue, prosecute, bring an action against, indict, impeach, attach, distrain, commit; arrest; summon, -s; give in charge etc. (*restrain*) 751.

empanel a jury, implead, join issue; close the pleadings; set down for hearing.

try, hear a cause; sit in judgment; adjudicate etc. 480.

Adj. litigious etc. (*quarrelsome*) 713; *qui tam*; *coram* –, *sub- judice*.

Adv. *pendente lite.*

Phr. *adhuc sub judice lis est.*

970. Acquittal.—N. acquit-tal, -ment; clearance, exculpation, exoneration; discharge etc. (*release*) 750; *quietus*, absolution, compurgation, reprieve, respite; pardon etc. (*forgiveness*) 918.

[Exemption from punishment] impunity, immunity.

V. acquit, exculpate, exonerate, clear; absolve, whitewash, assoil, discharge, release; liberate etc. 750.

reprieve, respite; pardon etc. (*forgive*) 918; let off, – scot free.

Adj. acquitted etc. *v.*; un-condemned, -punished, -chastised; recommended to mercy.

971. Condemnation.—N. condemnation, conviction, proscription, damnation; death warrant; penalty etc. 974.

attain-der, -ture, -tment.

V. condemn, convict, cast, bring home to, find guilty, damn, doom, sign the death warrant, sentence, pass sentence on, attaint, confiscate, proscribe, sequestrate; non-suit.

disapprove etc. 932; accuse etc. 938.

stand condemned.

Adj. condem-, dam-natory; condemned etc. *v.*; non-suited etc. (*failure*) 732; self-convicted.

Phr. *mutato nomine de te fabula narratur.*

972. Punishment.—N. punishment, punition; chast-isement, -ening; correction, castigation.

discipline, infliction, trial; judgment; penalty etc. 974; retribution; thunderbolt, Nemesis; requital etc. (*reward*) 973; penology; retributive justice.

lash, scaffold etc. (*instrument of punishment*) 975; imprisonment etc. (*restraint*) 751; chain gang; transportation, banishment, expulsion, deportation, exile, involuntary exile, ostracism; penal servitude, hard labor; galleys etc. 975; beating etc. *v.*; flagellation, fustigation, gantlet, *strappado*, *estrapade*, *bastinado*, *argumentum baculinum*, stick law, rap on the knuckles, box on the ear; blow etc. (*impulse*) 276; stripe, cuff, kick, buffet, pummel; slap, – in the face; wipe, douse; *coup de grâce*; torture, rack; picket, -ing; *dragonnade*; capital punishment, extreme penalty; execution; hanging etc. *v.*; de-capitation, -collation; *garrot-te*, *-to*; electrocution, lethal chamber; crucifixion, impalement; martyrdom, *auto-da-fé*; *noyade*; *hara-kiri*, happy despatch.

V. punish; chast-ise, -en; castigate, correct, inflict punishment, administer correction, deal retributive justice.

visit upon, pay; pay –, serve- out; settle with, get even with, get one's own back; do for; make short work of, give a lesson to, strafe, serve one right, make an example of; have a rod in pickle for; give it one.

strike etc. 276; deal a blow to, administer the lash, smite; slap, – the face; smack, cuff, box the ears, spank, thwack, thump, beat, lay on, swinge, buffet; thresh, thrash, pummel, drub, leather, trounce, baste, belabor; lace, – one's jacket; dress, give a -dressing, – down; trim, warm, wipe, tund, cob, bang, strap, comb, lash, lick, larrup, whallop, whop, flog, scourge, whip, birch, cane, give the stick, switch, flagellate, horsewhip, *bastinado*, towel, rub down with an oaken towel, rib roast, dust one's jacket, fustigate, pitch into, lay about one, beat black and blue; beat to a -mummy, – jelly; give a black eye; hit on the head; sandbag.

tar and feather; pelt, stone, lapidate; mast-head, keelhaul.

execute; bring to the -block, – gallows; behead; de-capitate, -collate; guillotine; hang, turn off, gibbet, bowstring, hang, draw and quarter; shoot; decimate; burn; electrocute; break on the wheel, crucify; em-, im-pale; flay; lynch; put to death.

torture; put -on, – to- the rack; picket.

banish, exile; trans-, de-port; expel, ostracize; rusticate; drum out; dismiss, -bar, -bench; strike off the roll, unfrock; post.

suffer, – for, – punishment; be -flogged, – hanged etc.; come to the gallows, dance upon nothing, die in one's shoes; be rightly served.

Adj. punishing etc. *v.*; penal; puni-tory, -tive; inflictive, castigatory; punished etc. *v.*

Int. *à la lanterne!*

973. Reward.—N. reward, recompense, remuneration, prize, meed, guerdon, reguerdon; indemni-ty, -fication, price; quittance; compensation; reparation, *ersatz*, assythment, redress; retribution, reckoning, acknowledgment, requital, amends, sop; atonement; consideration, return, *quid pro quo*; salvage, perquisite; vail etc. (*donation)* 784; *douceur*, bribe, bait, baksheesh, tip; hush-, smart-money; black-mail; carcelage; *solatium*.

allowance, salary, stipend, wages; pay, -ment; emolument; tribute; batta, shot, scot; premium, fee, *honorarium*; hire.

crown etc. (*decoration of honor*) 877.

V. re-ward, -compense, -pay, -quite; remunerate; compensate; fee, tip, bribe; pay one's footing etc. (*pay*) 807; make amends, indemnify, atone; satisfy, acknowledge.

get for one's pains, reap the fruits of.

Adj. remunerat-ive, -ory; munerary, compensatory, retributive, reparatory.

974. Penalty.—N. penalty; retribution etc. (*punishment*) 972; pain, pains and penalties; *peine forte et dure*; penance etc. (*atonement*) 952; the devil to pay.

fine, mulct, amercement; forfeit, -ure; escheat, damages, deodand, sequestration, confiscation, *premunire*.

V. penalize, fine, mulct, amerce, sconce, confiscate; sequest-rate, -er; escheat; estreat, forfeit.

975. Scourge. [Instrument of punishment.]**—N.** scourge, rod, cane, stick; ra-, rat-tan; birch, – rod; rod in pickle; switch, ferule, cudgel, truncheon; rubber hose.

whip, lash, strap, thong, cowhide, knout; cat, – o'-nine-tails, *sjambok*, quirt; rope's end.

pillory, stocks, whipping-post; cuck-, duck-ing stool; brank; triangle, wooden horse, maiden, thumbscrew, boot, rack, wheel, iron heel; treadmill, crank, galleys.

scaffold; block, axe, *guillotine*; stake; cross; gallows, gibbet, Tyburn tree; drop, noose, rope, halter, bowstring; electric chair, lethal chamber.

house of correction etc. (*prison*) 752.

gaol-, jail-er; executioner; hang-, heads-man; Jack Ketch; lyncher.

976. Deity.—N. Deity, Divinity; God-head, -ship; Omnipotence, Providence.

[Quality of being divine] divin-eness, -ity.

God, Lord, Jehovah, *Deus*; The -Almighty, – Supreme Being, – First Cause; *Ens Entium*; Author –, Creator- of all things; Author of our being; The -Infinite, – Eternal; The All-powerfull, -wise, -merciful, -holy; The Omni-potent, -scient.

[Attributes and perfections] infinite -power, – wisdom, – goodness, – justice, – truth, – love, – mercy; omni-potence, -science, -presence; unity, immutability, holiness, glory, majesty, sovereignty, infinity, eternity.

The -Trinity, – Holy Trinity, – Trinity in Unity, – Triune God; Three in One and One in Three.

God the Father; The -Maker, – Creator, – Preserver.

[Functions] creation, preservation, divine government; The-ocracy, -archy; providence; ways –, dealings –, dispensations –, visitations- of Providence.

God the Son, Jesus, Christ; The -Messiah, – Anointed, – Savior, – Redeemer, – Mediator,

– Intercessor, – Advocate, – Judge; The Son of - God, – Man, – David; The Only Begotten; The Lamb of God, The Word; Em-, Im-manuel; The - King of Kings and Lord of Lords, – King of Glory, – Prince of Peace, – Good Shepherd, – Way, – Truth, – Life, – Bread of Life, – Light of the World; The -Lord our, – Sun of- Righteousness

The -Incarnation, – Hypostatic Union, – Word made Flesh.

[Functions] salvation, redemption, atonement, propitiation, mediation, intercession, judgment.

God the Holy Ghost, The Holy Spirit, Paraclete; The -Comforter, – Consoler, – Spirit of Truth, – Dove.

[Functions] inspiration, unction, regeneration, sanctification, consolation.

eon, aeon, special providence, *Deus ex machinâ*; *Avatar*.

V. create, uphold, preserve, govern etc.

atone, redeem, save, propitiate, mediate etc.

predestinate, elect, call, ordain, bless, justify, sanctify, glorify etc.

Adj. almighty, holy, hallowed, sacred, divine, heavenly, celestial; messianic; sacrosanct; all-powerful, -wise, -seeing, -knowing; omnipotent, omniscient; supreme.

super-human, -natural; ghostly, spiritual, hyper-physical, unearthly; the-istic, -ocratic, deistic; anointed.

Adv. *jure divino*, by divine right; *Deo volente*, D.V.

977. Angel. [Beneficent spirits.]—**N.** angel, archangel; heavenly host, choir invisible, host of heaven, sons of God; Michael, Gabriel etc.; seraph, -im; cherub, -im; ministering spirit, morning star; saint, *Madonna*; Our Lady, the Blessed Virgin, the Virgin Mary.

Adj. angelic, seraphic, cherubic.

978. Satan. [Maleficent spirits.]—**N.** Satan, the Devil, Lucifer, Ahrimanes, Belial; Sammael, Zamiel, Beelzebub, the Prince of the Devils; Mephistopheles, his satanic majesty.

the tempter; the evil -one, – spirit; the -author of evil, – wicked one, – old Serpent; the Prince of -darkness, – this world, – the power of the air; the -foul, – arch- fiend; the devil incarnate; the - common enemy, – angel of the bottomless pit; Abaddon, Apollyon, Mammon.

fallen agnels, unclean spirits, devils; the -rulers, – powers- of darkness; inhabitants of Pandemonium; demon etc. 980.

diabolism; devil-ism, -ship, -dom, -ry, -worship; *diablerie*; satanism, manicheism; the cloven foot; black magic etc. 992.

Adj. satanic, diabolic, devilish, infernal, hell-born.

979. Jupiter.—**N.** god, -dess; heathen gods and goddesses; Pantheon; Jupiter, Jove, Zeus, Apollo, Mars, Mercury, Neptune, Vulcan, Bacchus, Pluto, Saturn, Cupid, Eros, Pan; Juno, Ceres, Proserpina, Dina, Minerva, Pallas, Athenae, Venus, Aphrodite, Vesta; The Fates etc. 601.

Allah, Brahma, Vishnu, Siva, Shiva, Krishna, Juggernaut, Buddha; Ra, Isis, Osiris; Belus, Bel, Baal, Asteroth etc.; Thor, Odin; Mumbo Jumbo; good –, tutelary- genius; demiurge, familiar, – spirit; Sibyl; fairy, fay; sylph, -id; Ariel, peri, nymph, nereid, dryad, oread, sea-maid, Banshee, Benshie, Ormuzd; Oberon, Titania, Mab, hamadryad, naiad, mermaid, kelpie, Ondine, nix, nixie, sprite; denizens of the air; pixy etc. (*bad spirit*) 980.

mythology; heathen –, fairy- mythology; Lemprière, folklore.

Adj. fairy-, sylph-like; sylphic.

980. Demon.—**N.** demon, -ry, -ism, -ology; evil genius, fiend, familiar, – spirit, devil; bad –, unclean- spirit; cacodemon, incubus, Frankenstein's monster, succubus and succuba, Titan, Shedim, Mephistopheles, Asmodeus, Moloch, Belial, Ahriman, fury, The Furies etc. 900; harpy; Friar Rush.

vampire, ghoul; af-, ef-freet; afrite; ogre, -ss; gnome, gin, djinn, imp, deev, *lamia*; bo-gie, -gle; nis, kobold, flibbertigibbet, fairy, brownie, pixy, elf, dwarf, urchin, Puck, Robin Goodfellow; lepre-, cluri-chaune; troll, dwerger, sprite, oaf, changeling, bad fairy, nixe, pigwidgeon, Will-o'-the-wisp; Erl King.

[Supernatural appearance] ghost, specter, apparition, genie, spirit, shade, shadow, vision, phantom etc. 443; materialization (*spiritualism*) 992; hob-, goblin; wraith, spook, werwolf, boggart, banshee, *loup-garou*, *lemures*; evil eye.

nisse, necks; mer-man, -maid, -folk; siren, Lorelei; satyr, faun.

Adj. supernatural, weird, uncanny, unearthly, spectral; ghost-ly, -like; elf-in, -like; fiend-ish, -like; impish, demoniacal; haunted.

981. Heaven.—**N.** heaven; kingdom of - heaven, – God; heavenly kingdom; throne –, presence- of God; inheritance of the saints in light.

Paradise, Eden, abode of the blessed; Holy City, New Jerusalem; celestial bliss, glory.

[Mythological -heaven] Olympus; [– paradise] Elysium, Elysian fields, Arcadia, bowers of bliss, garden of the Hesperides, Islands of the Blessed; happy hunting-ground; third –, seventh-heaven; Valhalla (Scandinavian); Nirvana (Buddhist).

future state, eternity, eternal life, life after death, eternal home, resurrection, translation; resuscitation etc. 660; apotheosis, deification.

Adj. heavenly, celestial, supernal, unearthly, from on high, paradisiacal, beatific, elysian, Olympian, Arcadian.

982. Hell.—**N.** hell, bottomless pit, place of torment; habitation of fallen angels; Pandemonium, Abaddon, Domdaniel.

hell fire; everlasting -fire, – torment; lake of fire and brimstone; fire that is never quenched, worm that never dies.

purgatory, limbo, gehenna, abyss.

[Mythological hell] Tartarus, Hades, Avernus, Styx, Stygian creek, pit of Acheron, Cocytus,

Phlegethon, Lethe; infernal regions, *inferno*, shades below, realms of Pluto.

Pluto, Rhadamanthus, Erebus, Charon, Cerberus; Tophet.

Adj. hellish, infernal, stygian.

983. Theology. [Religious Knowledge.]—**N.** Theology (natural and revealed); Theo-gony, -sophy; Divinity; Hagio-logy, -graphy; Caucasian mystery; monotheism; religion; religious -persuasion, – sect, – denomination; cult; creed etc. (*belief*) 484; articles –, declaration –, profession –, confession- of faith.

theolog-ue, -ian; divine, schoolman, canonist, monotheist.

Adj. theological, religious; canonical; denominational; sectarian etc. 984.

983a. Orthodoxy.—N. orthodoxy; strictness, soundness, religious truth, true faith; truth etc. 494.

Christian-ity, -ism; Catholic-ism, -ity; 'the faith once delivered to the saints;' hyperorthodoxy etc. 984; iconoclasm.

the Holy –, the Orthodox- Church; Catholic –, Universal –, Apostolic –, Established- Church; temple of the Holy Ghost; Church –, body –, members –, disciples –, followers- of Christ; Christian, – community; true believer; canonist etc. (*theologian*) 983; Christendom, collective body of Christians, the Church Militant.

canons etc. (*belief*) 484; thirty-nine articles; Apostles' –, Nicene –, Athanasian- Creed; Church Catechism; textuary.

Adj. orthodox, sound, literal, strict, faithful, catholic, schismless, Christian, evangelical, scriptural, divine, monotheistic; true etc. 494.

984. Heterodoxy. [Sectarianism.]—**N.** heterodoxy; error etc. 495; false doctrine, heresy, schism; schismantic-ism, -alness; recusancy, backsliding, apostasy; atheism etc. (*irreligion*) 989.

bigotry etc. (*obstinacy*) 606; fanaticism, iconoclasm; hyperorthodoxy, precisianism, bibliolatry, hagiolatry, sabbatarianism, puritanism; idolatry etc. 991; superstition etc. (*credulity*) 486; dissent etc. 489.

sectar-ism, -ianism; nonconformity; secularism; syncretism, religious sects; the clash of creeds.

protestant-, advent-, Arian-, Erastian-, Calvin-, quaker-, method-, anabapt-, Pusey-, tractarian-, ritual-, Origen-, Sabellian-, Socinian-, De-, The-, mon-, material-, positiv-, latitudinairan-ism etc.

High –, Low –, Broad –, Free- Church; ultramontanism; monasticism; pap-ism, -istry; papacy; Anglican-, Catholic-, Roman-ism; popery, Scarlet Lady, Church of Rome, Greek Church; Christian Science, The Church of Christ Scientist.

pagan-, heathen-, ethic-ism; mythology; animism; poly-, di-, tri-, pan-theism; dualism; heathendom.

Juda-, Gentil-, Mahometan-, Islam-, Turc-, Brahmin-, Hindoo-, Buddh-, Lama-, Confucian-, Shinto-, Sabian-, Gnostic-, Soofee-, Hylothe-, Mormon-ism.

Theosophy; Spiritualism, Occultism.

heretic, antichrist; pagan, heathen; pai-, pay-nim; *giaour*; gentile; pan-, poly-theist; idolator; misbeliever, apostate, backslider.

bigot etc. (*obstinacy*) 606; fanatic, dervish, abdal, iconoclast.

latitudinarian, limitarian, Deist, Theist, Unitarian; positivist, materialist; agnostic, sceptic etc. 989.

schismatic; sectar-y, -ian, -ist; seceder, separatist, recusant, dissenter; non-conformist, -juror; Huguenot, Protestant; orthodox dissenter, Congregationalist, Independent; Episcopalian, Presbyterian; Lutheran, Calvinist, Quaker, Methodist, Weslayan; Ana-, Baptist; Dunker; Mormon, Latter-day Saint, Irvingite, Sandemanian, Glassite, Erastian; Sub-, Supra-lapsarian; Gentoo, Antinomian, Swedenborgian, Adventist, Plymouth Brother; Theosophist etc.

Catholic, Roman Catholic, Romanist, papist, ultramontane; Old Catholic, tractarian, Anglican, Puseyite, ritualist; Puritan.

Jew, Hebrew, Rabbist; Mahometan, Mohammedan, Mussulman, Moslem, Islamite, Osmanli; Brahm-in, -an; Parsee, Sofi, Soofee; Buddhist; Zoroastrian, Magi, Gymnosophist, fire-worshipper, Sabian, Gnostic, Sadducee, Rosicrucian etc.

Adj. heterodox, heretical; un-orthodox, -scriptural, -canonical; antiscriptural, apocryphal; un-, anti-christian; schismatic, recusant, iconoclastic; sectarian; dis-senting, -sident; secular etc. (*lay*) 997.

pagan; heathen, -ish; ethnic, -al; gentile, painim; pan-, poly-theistic; agnostic, sceptic.

Judaical, Mohammedan, Moslem, Brahminical, Buddhist etc. *n.*; Romish, Protestant etc. *n.*

bigoted etc. (*prejudiced*) 481; (*obstinate*) 606; superstitious etc. (*credulous*) 486; fanatical; idolatrous etc. 991; visionary etc. (*imaginative*) 515.

985. Revelation.—N. revelation, inspiration, *afflatus*.

Word, – of God; Scripture; the -Scriptures, – Bible, – Book of Books; Holy -Writ, – Scriptures; inspired writings, Gospel.

Old Testament, Septuagint, Vulgate, Pentateuch; Octateuch; the -Law, – Jewish Law, – Prophets; major –, minor- Prophets; Hagio-grapha, -logy; Hierographa; Apocrypha.

New Testament; Gospels, Evangelists, Acts, Epistles, Apocalypse, Revelations.

Talmud; Mishna, Masorah.

prophet etc. (*seer*) 513; evangelist, apostle, disciple, saint; the –, the Apostolical- fathers; Holy Men of old, inspired -writers, – penmen.

Adj. scriptural, biblical, sacred, prophetic; evangel-ical, -istic; apostolic, -al; inspired, theopneustic, apocalyptic, ecclesiastical, canonical, textuary.

986. Pseudo-Revelation.—N. the -Koran, – Alcoran; Ly-king, Shaster, Vedas, Zendavesta, Vedidad, Purana, Edda; Go-, Gau-tama; Book of Mormon.

[False prophets and religious founders] Buddha, Zoroaster, Zerdhusht, Confucius, Mahomet.

[Idols] golden calf etc. 991; Baal, Moloch, Dagon.

987. Piety.—N. piety, religion, theism, faith; religiousness, holiness etc. *adj.*; saintship; religionism; sanctimony etc. (*assumed piety*) 988; reverence etc. (*respect*) 928; humility, veneration, devotion; prostration etc. (*worship*) 990; grace, unction, edification; sancti-ty, -tude; consecration.

spiritual existence, odor of sanctity, beauty of holiness.

theopathy, beatification, adoption, regeneration, conversion, justification, sanctification, salvation, inspiration, bread of life; Body and Blood of Christ.

believer, convert, theist, Christian, devotee, pietist; the -good, – righteous, – just, – believing, – elect; Saint, *Madonna.*

the children of -God, – the kingdom, – light.

V. be -pious etc. *adj.*; have -faith etc. *n.*; believe, receive Christ; revere etc. 928; worship etc. 950; be -converted etc.

convert, edify, sanctify, hallow, keep holy, beatify, regenerate, inspire, consecrate, enshrine.

Adj. pious, religious, devout, devoted, reverent, godly, heavenly minded, humble; pure, – in heart; holy, spiritual, pietistic; saint-ly, -like; seraphic, sacred, solemn.

believing, faithful, Christian, Catholic.

elected, adopted, justified, sanctified, regenerated, inspired, consecrated, converted, unearthly, not of the earth.

988. Impiety.—N. impiety; sin etc. 945; irreverence; profan-eness etc. *adj.*, -ity, -ation; blasphemy, desecration, sacrilege; scoffing etc. *v.*

[Assumed piety] hypocrisy etc. (*falsehood*) 544; pietism, cant, pious fraud; lip-devotion, -service, -reverence; mis-devotion, formalism, austerity; sanctimon-y, -ousness etc. *adj.*; pharisaism, precisianism, sabbat-ism, -arianism, *odium theologicum*, sacerdotalism; bigotry etc. (*obstinacy*) 606, (*prejudice*) 481.

hardening, backsliding, declension, perversion, reprobation apostacy, recusancy.

sinner etc. 949; scoffer, blasphemer; sacrilegist; worldling; hypocrite etc. (*dissembler*) 548; Scribes and Pharisees; Tartufe, Maw-worm.

bigot; saint [ironically]; Pharisee, sabbatarian, formalist, methodist, puritan, pietist, precisian, religionist, devotee, ranter, fanatic, wowser.

the -wicked, – evil, – unjust, – reprobate; son of -men, – Belial, – the wicked one; children of darkness.

V. be -impious etc. *adj.*; profane, desecrate, blaspheme, revile, scoff; swear etc. (*malediction*) 908; commit sacrilege.

snuffle; turn up the whites of the eyes; idolize.

Adj. impious; irreligious etc. 989; desecrating etc. *v.*; profane, irreverent, sacrilegious, blasphemous.

un-hallowed, -sanctified, -regenerate; hardened, perverted, reprobate.

hypocritical etc. (*false*) 544; canting, pietistical, sanctimonious, unctuous, pharisaical, over-righteous, righteous over much.

bigoted, fanatical etc. 481 and 606; priest-ridden.

Adv. under the -mask, – cloak, – pretence, – form, – guise- of religion.

989. Irreligion.—N. irreligion, indevotion; ungodliness etc. *adj.*; laxity, quietism, apathy, indifference, passivity.

scepticism, doubt; un-, dis-belief; incredul-ity, -ousness etc. *adj.*; want of -faith, – belief; pyrrhonism; doubt etc. 485; agnosticism.

atheism, deism; hylotheism; materialism; positivism; nihilism.

infidelity, freethinking, antichristianity, rationalism.

atheist, anti-christian, sceptic, unbeliever, deist, infidel, pyrrhonist; *giaour*, heathen, alien, gentile, Nazarene; *esprit fort*, freethinker, latitudinarian, rationalist; materialist, positivist, nihilist, agnostic.

V. be -irreligious etc. *adj.*; disbelieve, lack faith; doubt, question etc. 485.

dechristianize; serve Mammon, love darkness better than light.

Adj. irreligious; in-, un-devout; devout-, god-, grace-less; un-godly, -holy, -sanctified, -hallowed; atheistic, without God.

sceptical, free-thinking; un-believing, -converted; incredulous, faithless, lacking faith; deistical; un-, anti-christian.

worldly, mundane, earthly, carnal, unspiritual; worldly etc.- minded.

Adv. irreligiously etc. *adj.*

990. Worship.—N. worship, adoration, devotion, aspiration, latria, homage, service, humiliation; kneeling, genuflexion, prostration.

prayer, invocation, supplication, rogation, intercession, orison, holy breathing; petition etc. (*request*) 765; collect, litany, Lord's prayer, paternoster, *Ave Maria*, rosary; bead-roll; latria, dulia, hyperdulia, vigils; revival; cult.

thanksgiving; giving –, returning- thanks; grace, praise, glorification, benediction, doxology, hosanna; h-, allelujah; *Te Deum*, *non nobis Domine*, *nunc dimittis*; pacan.

psalm, -ody; hymn, plainsong, chant, chaunt, response, anthem, motet; antiphon, -y.

oblation, sacrifice, incense, libation; burnt –, votive –, thank-offering; offertory, collection.

discipline; self-discipline, -examination, -denial; fasting.

divine service, office, duty; morning prayer; mass, matins, evensong, vespers, compline; holy day etc. (*rites*) 998.

worshipper, congregation, communicant, celebrant.

V. worship, lift up the heart, aspire; revere etc. 928; adore, do service, pay homage; humble oneself, kneel; bow –, bend- the knee; fall -down, – on one's knees; prostrate oneself, bow down and worship, recite the rosary.

pray, invoke, supplicate; put –, offer- up -prayers, – petitions; beseech etc. (*ask*) 765; say one's prayers, tell one's beads.

return –, give- thanks; say grace, bless, praise, laud, glorify, magnify, sing praises; give benediction, lead the choir, intone, chant, sing.

propitiate, offer sacrifice, fast, deny oneself; vow, offer vows, give alms.

work out one's salvation; go to church; attend -service, – mass; communicate etc. (*rite*) 998.

Adj. worshipping etc. *v.*; devout, devotional, reverent, pure, solemn; fervid etc. (*heartfelt*) 821.

Int. h-, allelujah! hosanna! glory be to God! O Lord! pray God that! God -grant, – bless, – save, – forbid! *sursum corda.*

991. Idolatry.—N. idol-atry, -ism; demon-ism, -olatry; idol –, demon –, devil –, fire- worship; zoolatry, fetishism, Mari-, Bibli-, ecclesi-, heli-olatry.

deification, apotheosis, canonization; hero worship.

sacrifices, hecatomb, holocaust; human sacrifices, immolation, mactation, infanticide, self-immolation, *suttee.*

idol, golden calf, graven image, fetish, *avatar*, Juggernaut, joss, *lares et penates*; Baal etc. 986.

idolator etc. *n.*

V. worship -idols, – pictures, – relics; put on a pedestal, bow down to, prostrate oneself before, make sacrifice to; deify, canonize, idolize.

Adj. idolatrous.

992. Sorcery.—N. sorcery; superstition; occult -art, – sciences; black –, magic; the black art, necromancy, theurgy, thaumaturgy; demon-ology, -omy, -ship; *diablerie*, bedevilment; witch-craft, -ery; glamor; fetis-hism, -ism; ghost dance; hoodoo, voodoo; Shamanism [Esquimaux], vampirism; conjuration; bewitchery, exorcism, enchantment, incantation, obsession, possession, mysticism, second sight, mesmerism, animal magnetism; od –, odylic- force; electro-biology, *clairvoyance*; spiritualism, spirit-rapping, table-turning; thought reading, telepathy, thought transference, automatic writing, *planchette*, ouija board; crystal gazing; spirit manifestation, materialization, astral body, ectoplasm etc.

divination etc. (*prediction*) 511; sortilege, ordeal, *sortes Virgilianœ*; hocus-pocus etc. (*deception*) 545; oracle etc. 513.

V. practice -sorcery etc. *n.*; cast a -horoscope, – nativity; conjure, exorcise, charm, enchant; bewitch, -devil; overlook, look on with the evil eye; entrance, mesmerize, magnetize; fascinate etc. (*influence*) 615; taboo; wave a wand; rub the -ring, – lamp; cast a spell; call up spirits, – from the vasty deep; raise spirits from the dead; raise –, lay-ghosts; command genii.

Adj. magic, -al; mystic, weird, cabalistic, talismanic, phylacteric, incantatory; charmed etc. *v.*

993. Spell.—N. spell, charm, incantation, exorcism, weird, cabala, exsufflation, cantrap, runes, abracadabra, hocus-pocus, open *sesame*, countercharm, Ephesian letters, bell, book and candle, Mumbo-jumbo, evil-eye, fee-faw-fum.

talisman, amulet, periapt, telesm, phylactery, philter, wish-bone, merry-thought, mascot, scarab, swastika; fetish; *agnus Dei.*

wand, caduceus, rod, divining rod, lamp of Aladdin, magic carpet, seven-league boots; magic ring; wishing –, Fortunatus's- cap.

994. Sorcerer.—N. sorcerer, magician; thaumat-, the-urgist; conjuror, necromancer, seer, wizard, witch; fairy etc. 980; *lamia*, hag, warlock, charmer, exorcist, voodoo, mage, diviner, dowser; cunning| –, medicine- man, witch doctor; Shaman, figure-flinger, ecstatica, medium, *clairvoyant*, mesmerist, hypnotist; *deus ex machinâ*; astrologer; soothsayer etc. 513.

Katerfelto, Cagliostro, Merlin, Comus, Mesmer, Rosicrucian; Hecate, Circe, Lilith, siren, weird sisters; witch of Endor.

995. Churchdom.—N. church, -dom; ministry, apostleship, priesthood, prelacy, hierarchy, church government, christendom, pale of the church.

clerical-, sacerdotal-, episcopalian-, ultramontan-ism; Theocracy; ecclesiolog-y, -ist; priestcraft, *odium theologicum.*

monach-ism, -y; monasticism, monkhood.

[Ecclesiastical offices and dignities] pontificate, primacy, archbishopric, archiepiscopacy; prelacy; bishop-ric, -dom; episcop-ate, -acy; see, diocese; deanery, stall; canon-ry, -icate; prebend, -aryship; benefice, incumbency, glebe, advowson, living, cure, – of souls; rectorship; vicar-iate, -ship; pastor-ate, -ship; deacon-ry, -ship; -curacy; chaplain, -cy, -ship; cardinal-ate, -ship; abbacy, presbytery.

holy orders, ordination, institution, consecration, induction, reading in, preferment, translation, presentation.

popedom, papacy; the -Vatican, – apostolic see, – see of Rome; religious sects etc. 984.

council etc. 696; conclave, college of cardinals, convocation, synod, consistory, chapter, vestry, presbytery; sanhedrim, *congé d'élire*; ecclesiastical courts, consistorial court, court of Arches.

V. call, ordain, induct, prefer, translate, consecrate, present, elect, bestow.

take -orders, – the veil, – vows.

Adj. ecclesi-astical, -ological; clerical, sacerdotal, priestly, prelatical, pastoral, ministerial, capitular, theocratic; hierarchical, archiepiscopal; episcopal, -ian; canonical; mon-astic, -achal; monkish; abbati-al, -cal; pontifical, papal, apostolic; untramontane, priest-ridden.

996. Clergy.—N. clergy, clericals, ministry, priesthood, presbytery, the cloth, the pulpit.

clergyman, divine, ecclesiastic, churchman, priest, presbyter, hierophant, pastor, shepherd, minister, clerk in holy orders; father, – in Christ; *padre, abbé, curé*; patriarch; reverend; black coat; confessor; sky pilot.

dignitaries of the church; ecclesi-, hier-arch; eminence, reverence, elder, primate, metropolitan, archimandrite, archbishop, bishop, prelate, diocesan, suffragan, dean, subdean, archdeacon, prebendary, canon, rural dean, rector, parson, vicar, perpetual curate, residentiary, beneficiary, incumbent, chaplain, curate, – in charge; deacon, -ess; preacher; lay reader, lecturer; capitular; missionary, propagandist, Jesuit, revivalist, field preacher.

churchwarden, sidesman; clerk, precentor, choir; almoner, *suisse*, verger, beadle, sexton, sacristan; acol-yth, -othyst, -yte; thurifer; chorister, choir boy.

[Roman Catholic priesthood] Pope, *Papa*, Holy

Father, pontiff, high priest, cardinal; ancient –, flamen; confessor, penitentiary; spiritual director.

cenobite, conventual, abbot, prior, monk, friar, lay brother, beadsman, mendicant, pilgrim, palmer; canon-regular, -secular; Jesuit, Franciscan, Friars minor, Minorites; Observant, Capuchin, Dominican, Carmelite; Augustinian; Gilbertine; Austin-, Black-, White-, Grey-, Crossed-, Crutched- Friars; Bonhomme, Carthusian, Benedictine, Cistercian, Trappist, Cluniac, Premonstratensian, Maturine; Templar, Hospitaller.

abb-, prior-, canon-ess; mother superior; *religieuse*, nun, sister, *beguine*, novice, postulant.

[Under the Jewish dispensation] prophet, priest, high priest, Levite; Rabbi, -n; scribe.

[Mohammedan etc.] mullah, ulema, imauam, sheik; so-fi, -phi; mufti, hadji, muezzin, dervish; fakir, -quir; brahmin, gooroo, druid, bonze, santon, abdal, Lama, talapoin, caloyer etc.

V. take orders etc. 995.

Adj. the –, the very –, the Right- Reverend; ordained, in orders, called to the ministry.

997. Laity.—N. laity, flock, fold, congregation, assembly, brethren, people.

temporality, secularization.

layman, civilian; parishioner, catechumen; secularist.

V. secularize.

Adj. secular, lay, laical, civil, temporal, profane.

998. Rite.—N. rite; ceremon-y, -ial; ordinance, observance, function, duty; form, -ulary; solemnity, sacrament; incantation etc. (*spell*) 993; service, psalmody etc. (*worship*) 990; liturgies

ministration; preach-ing, -ment; predication, sermon, homily, exhortation, lecture, discourse, pastoral.

baptism, christening, chrism; immersion; baptismal regeneration; font; circumcision.

confirmation; imposition –, laying on- of hands; churching, purification, ordination etc. (*churchdom*) 995; excommunication.

Eucharist, Lord's supper, communion; the –, the holy- sacrament; celebration, high celebration; *missa cantata*; offertory; introit; consecration; con-, tran-substantiation; real presence; elements, bread and wine; mass; high –, low –, dry- mass.

matrimony etc. 903; burial etc. 363; visitation of the sick.

seven sacraments, impanation, extreme unction, last rites, *viaticum*, invocation of saints, canonization, transfiguration, auricular confession; fasting; maceration, flagellation, sackcloth and ashes; penance etc. (*atonement*) 952; absolution; telling of beads, reciting the rosary, processional; thurification, incense, holy water, aspersion.

relics, rosary, beads, reliquary, host, cross, rood, crucifix, pax, pix, pyx, *agnus Dei*, censer, thurible, patera, urceole; chalice, patten, Holy Grail, sangrail; seven-branch candle stick, monstrance, sacring bell.

ritual, rubric, canon, ordinal; liturgy, prayer-book, book of common prayer, pietas, euchology, litany, lectionary; missal, breviary, mass-book, bead-roll.

psalter; psalm –, hymn- book; hymn-al, -ology; psalmody.

ritual-, ceremonial-ism; sabbat-ism, -arianism; ritualist, sabbatarian.

holyday, feast, fast; Sabbath, Passover, Pentecost; Advent, Christmas, Noel, Epiphany, Lent, Shrove Tuesday, Ash Wednesday, Maundy Thursday; Passion –, Holy- week; Good Friday, Easter, Ascension Day, Whitsuntide; Trinity Sunday, Corpus Christi; All-Saints' –, – Souls'- Day; Candle-, Lam-, Martin-, Michael-mas; hogmanay; Ramadan, -zan; Bairam etc. etc.

V. perform service, do duty, minister, officiate, baptize, dip, sprinkle; confirm, lay hands on; give –, administer –, take –, receive –, attend –, partake of- the -sacrament, – communion; communicate; celebrate mass; administer –, receive- extreme unction; anele, shrive, absolve, confess; do penance; genuflect; cross oneself, make the sign of the cross.

excommunicate, ban with bell, book and candle.

preach, sermonize, predicate, lecture.

Adj. ritual, -istic; ceremonial, liturgic; baptismal, eucharistical; paschal.

999. Canonicals.—N. canonicals, vestments; robe, gown, Geneva gown, frock, pallium, surplice, cassock, dalmatic, scapulary, cope, scarf, tunicle, chasuble, alb, *alba*, stole; fan-on, -nel; tonsure, cowl, hood; calo-te, -tte; bands; capouch, amice, orarium, ephod; apron, lawn sleeves, pontificals, pall; miter, tiara, triple crown; shovel –, cardinal's- hat; biretta; crosier; pastoral staff; costume etc. 225.

1000. Temple.—N. place of worship; house of -God, – prayer.

temple, cathedral, minister, church, kirk, chapel, meeting-house, bethel, tabernacle, conventicle, *basilica*, fane, holy place, chantry, oratory.

synagogue; mosque; marabout; pantheon; pagoda; joss-house; dagobah, tope; kiosk.

parsonage, rectory, vicarage, manse, deanery, glebe, church house; Vatican; bishop's palace; Lambeth.

altar, shrine, sanctuary, Holy of Holies, *sanctum sanctorum*, sacrarium, -isty; communion –, holy –, Lord's- table; table of the Lord; pyx; baptistery, font; piscina, stoup; aumbry; sedile; reredos; rood-loft, – screen; jube.

chancel, quire, choir, nave, aisle, transept, lady chapel, vestry, crypt, cloisters, porch; triforium, clerestory, churchyard, *golgotha*, calvary, Easter sepulcher; stall, pew, sitting; pulpit, ambo, lectern, reading-desk, confessional, prothesis, credence, baldachin, *baldacchino*; jesse, apse, belfry; chapter-house; presbytery.

monastery, priory, abbey, friary, convent, nunnery, cloister.

Adj. claustral, cloistered; monast-ic, -erial; conventual.

INDEX

The numbers refer to the headings under which the words or phrases occur. When the same word or phrase may be used in various senses, the several headings under which it, or its synonyms, will be found, according to those meanings, are indicated by the words printed in Italics. These words in Italics are not intended to explain the meaning of the word or phrase to which they are annexed, but only to assist in the required reference.

When the word given in the Index is itself the title or heading of a category, the number of reference is printed in blacker type, thus: **abode 189.**

abundanti cautelâ, ex – 664
abuse *deceive* 545
ill-treat 649
misuse 679
malediction 908
threat 909
upbraid 932
violate 961
– of language 563
– of terms 523
abusive 895, 934
abut *near* 197 *touch* 199, 215
abutment 717
aby *remain* 141
endure 821, 826
abysmal *deep* 208
abyss *space* 180
depth 208
interval 198
danger 667
hell 982
A.C. 106
academic
teaching 537, 542
theory 514
academical
style 578
academicals 225 *robes*
academician 492
Royal – 559
academy 542
acanthus 847
a capite ad calcem 52
acariâtre 901
acarpous 169
acatalectic 597
acaudal 38
accede 488, 725, 762
accelerate
early 132
stimulate 173
velocity 274
hasten 684
accension 384
accent *sound* 402
tone of voice 580
rhythm 597
accentuate 642
accentuated 580
accept *assent* 488
consent 762
receive 785
take 789
acceptable 646, 829
acceptance 771
acceptation 522
acception 522
access 286
easy of – 705
means of – 627
accessible 470, 705
accession
adjunct 39
increase 35
addition 37
- to office 737, 755
consent 762
accessory
extrinsic 6
additive 37
adjunct 39
accompanying 88
aid 707
auxiliary 711
acciaccatura 413
accidence 567
accident *event* 151
chance 156
disaster 619
misfortune 735
fatal – 361
accidental
extrinsic 6
fortuitous 156
undesigned 621
accidents,
trust to the chapter of – 621
accipient 785
acclamation
assent 488
approbation 931
acclimatize 370, 613
acclivity 217
accloy 641
accolade 894
accommodate
suit 23
adjust 27
aid 707
reconcile 723
give 784
lend 787
– oneself to 82
accommodation
space 180
accommodating
kind 906
accompaniment
adjunct 39
coexistence 88
musical 415
accompany
add 37
coexist 88
concur 120
music 416
accompli, fait – 729
accomplice 711
accomplish
execute 161
complete 729
succeed 731
accomplishment 490, 698
accompts 811
accord
uniform 16
agree 23
music 413
assent 488
concord 714
grant 760
give 784
of one's own – 602
according
– as *qualification* 469
– to *evidence* 467
– to circumstances 8
– to law 963
– to rule
conformably 82
– rumor 527
accordingly
logically 476
accordion 417
accost 586
accoucheur 631, 662
accouchment 161
account *list* 86
adjudge 480
description 594
credit 805
money - 811
fame 873
approbation 931
call to – 932
find one's – in
useful 644
success 731
make no – of 483, 930
not – for 519
on – of *motive* 615
behalf 707
on no – 536
send to one's – 361
take into – 457, 469
small – 643
to one's – 780
turn to –
improve 658
use 677
success 731
gain 775
– as *deem* 484
– book 551
– for 155, 522
– with 794, 807
accountable
liable 177
debit 811
duty 926
accountant 301, 811
certified public – 811
accounts 811
accouple 43
accoutered
armed 717
accouterment
dress 225
appliance 633
equipment 673
accoy 174
accredit
commission 755, 759
money 805
honor 873
accredited 484, 613
– to 755, 759
accretion 35, 46
accrimination 938
accroach 789
accrue *add* 37
result 154
acquire 775
be received 785, 810
accubation 213
accueil 894
accultural 35
accumbent 213
accumulate
collect 72
store 636
redundance 641
accurate 494
– knowledge 490
accurse 908
accursed
disastrous 649
undone 828
vicious 945
accusation 938
accuse
disapprove 932
charge 938
lawsuit 969
accustom 613
ace *small* 32
unit 87
within an – 197
aceldama *kill* 361
arena 728
acephalous 59
acerbate 659, 835
acerbity
acrimony 395
sourness 397
rudeness 895
spleen 900, 901
malevolence 907
acervate 72
acetous 397
acetylene 388
acharné 900
Achates, fidus – 890, 939
ache *physical* 378
mental 828
Acheron
pit of – 982
Acherontic
moribund 360
gloomy 837
achievable 470
achieve *end* 67
produce 161
do 680
accomplish 729
achievement 551, 861
Achilles, heel of –
vulnerable 665
achromatism 429
acicular 253
acid 397
acid test 463
acknowledge
answer 462
assent 488
disclose 529
avow 535
consent 762
observe 772
pay 807
thank 916
repent 950
reward 973
acknowledged
custom 613
acme 210
– of perfection 650
Acology 662
acolyte 996
acomous 226
aconite 663
acoustic 418
– organs 418
acoustics 402
acquaint
– oneself with 539
– with 527
acquaintance
knowledge 490
information 527
friend 890
make – with 888
acquiesce
assent 488
willing 488
consent 762
tolerate 826
acquire
develop 161
get 775
receive 785
– a habit 613
– learning 539
acquirement
knowledge 490
learning 539
talent 698
receipt 810
acquisition
knowledge 490
gain 775
acquit
liberate 750
exempt 927a
vindicate 937
innocent 946
absolve 970
acquit oneself
behave 692
– of a debt 807
– of a duty 926
– of an obligation 772
acquittal 506, 970
acquittance 771
acres *space* 180
land 342
property 780
Acres, Bob 862
acrid 392, 395
acridity 171
acrimony
physical 171
caustic 830
discourtesy 895
hatred 898
anger 900
malevolence 907
acroamatism 490
acrobat
strength 159
actor 599
proficient 700
mountebank 844
Acropolis 210
across 219, 708
acrostic 533, 561, 842
act *imitate* 19
physical 170
- of a play 599
personate 599
voluntary 680
statute 697
in the – 680, 947
– a part *feign* 544
– one's part 625, 926
– upon
physical 170
mental 615
take steps 680
– up to 772
– well one's part 944
– without authority 738
acting *deputy* 759
actinic 420
actinometer 445
action *physical* 170
voluntary 680
battle 720
law 969
line of – 692

aedile 965
aegis 717
aegrescit medendo 659
aegrotat 927a
aeolian 349
— harp 417
aequam servare mentem 826
aequo animo 823 826
aerate 334, 353
aere perennius 873
aerial 273
elevated 206
flying 267
gas 334
air 338
– navigation 267
– navigator 269
– mail 534
– patrol 726
– perspective 428
– warfare 722
aerie 189
aerify 334
aerodonetics 267
aerodrome 728
aerodynamics 267, 334, 349
aerolite 318
aerology 338
aeromancy 511
aeromechanics 267
aerometer 338
aeronaut 269
aeronautical 273
aeronautics 267, 338
aeroplane 273
aerostat *balloon* 273
aerostatics 267, 334
aerostation 338
aery 317
Aesculapius 662
Aesop 846
aesthetic
sensibility **375**
beauty 845
taste 850
aestival 125
aeternum servans sub pectore vulnus 919
afar 196
affable 879, 894
affair *event* 151
topic 454
business 625
battle 720
love 902, 903
– of honour 720
affaires, charge d' – 758
affaire de coeur 897
affect *relate to* 9
tend to 176
qualify 469
feign 544
touch 824
desire 865
love 897
affectation **855**
affected with
feeling 821
disease 655
affectibility 822
affecting 830
affection 821, 897
affections **820**
affettuoso 415
affiance 768, 858
affianced 897, 903
affiche 531
affidation 769
affidavit
affirmation 535
record 551
lawsuit 969
affiliation
relation 9
kindred 11
attribution 155
affine 11
affinitive 9
affinity 9, **17**
mate 905
affirmation **535**, 488
affix *add* 37
sequel 39
fasten 43
letter 561
afflation 349
afflatus 349, 597, 985
afflict 830
– with illness 655
affliction *pain* 828
infliction 830
adversity 735
affluence
sufficiency 639
prosperity 734
wealth 803
affluent *river* 348
afflux 286
afford *supply* 784
wealth 803
yield 810
sell for 812
– aid &c. 707
afforestation 371
affranchise
make free of 748
liberate 750
affray 720
affreet 980
affriction 331
affright 860
affront *molest* 830
provocation 900
insult 929
– danger 861
affuse 337
afield 186
afire 382
afloat *extant* 1
unstable 149
going on 151
ship 273
navigation 267
ocean 341
news 532
preparing 673
keep oneself – 734
set – *publish* 531
afoot *on hand* 625
preparing 673
astir 682
afore 116
aforementioned 116
aforesaid
preceding 62
repeated 104
prior 116
aforethought 611
aforetime 116
afraid 860
be – *irresolute* 605
– to say *uncertain* 475
afresh 104, 123
Afric heat 382
Afrikander **57**
afrite 980
aft 235
after *in order* 63
in time 117
too late 135
rear 235
pursuit 622
be – *intention* 620
pursuit 622
go – *follow* 281
– all *for all that* 30
qualification 469
on the whole 476
– time 133
after acceptation 516
after-age 124
after-clap 509
after-crop 65, 168
after-dinner 117
after-glow 40, 65, 420
after-growth 65
after-life 152
aftermath
sequel 65
fertile 168
profit 775
aftermost 235
afternoon 126
– farmer 683
after-part 65, 235
after-piece 599
after-taste 65, 390
after-thought
thought 451
memory 505
change of mind 607
after-time 121
afterwards 117
age 745
agacerie 615
again 90, 104
– and again 136
come – *periodic* 138
fall off – 661
live – 660
against
counteraction 179
anteposition 237
provision 673
voluntary opposition 708
chances – 473
declaim – 932
false witness – 934
go – 708
set – *actively* 898
set one's face – 764, 932
stand up – *resist* 719
raise &c. one's voice – 489
– one's will 744
– one's expectation 508
– the grain *difficult* 704
painful 830
dislike 867
– the stream 704
– the time when 510
– one's will 744
– one's wishes 603
agamist 904
agape *open* 260
curious 455
expectant 507
wonder 870
Agapemone 827, 897
agate 847
age *time* 106
period 108
long time 110
era 114
present time 118
oldness 124
advanced life **128**
of – 131
from age to – 112
age quod agis! 682
agency
physical **170**
instrumentality 631
means 632
employment 677
voluntary action 680
direction 693
commission 755
agenda 625, 626
agent *physical* 153
intermediary 228
voluntary **690**
consignee 759
– provocateur 615
agentship 755
ages: for – 110
– ago 122
agglomerate 46, **72**
agglutinate 46
aggrandize
in degree 35
in bulk 194
honor 873
aggravate
increase 35
vehemence 173
exaggerate 549
render worse 659
distress 835
exasperate 900
aggravating 830
aggravation **835**
aggregate 50, 72, 84
aggregation 46
aggression 716
aggressor 726
aggrieve 649, 830
aggroup 72
aghast
disappointed 509
fear 860
wonder 870
agile 274, 682
agio 813
agiotage 794
agitate *move* 315
inquire 461
activity 682
excite the feelings 824
– a question 476
agitation [*see* agitate]
changeableness 149
energy 171
motion **315**
in – *preparing* 673
agitator *leader* 694
aglet 554
agley, gang – 732
aglow 382, 420
agnate 11
agnition 762
agnomen 564
agnostic 487
agnosticism 984, 989
agnus Dei 993, 998
ago 122
not long – 123
agog *expectant* 507
desire 865
wonder 870
agoing 682
set – 707
agonism 720
agonizing 824, 830
agony 378, 828
– of death 360
– of excitement 825
agrarian 371
agree *accord* 23
concur 178
assent 488
concord 714
consent 762
compact 769
compromise 774
– in opinion 488
– with *salubrity* 656
agreeable
comfortable 82
physically 377
mentally 829
agreeably to 82
agreement **23** [*see* agree]
compact 769
agrestic 371
agriculture **371**
agronomy 371
aground *fixed* 150
in difficulty 704
failure 732
ague-fit 860
aguets, aux –
expectation 507
ambush 530
aguish *cold* 383
ah me! 839
aha! *rejoicing* 838
ahead 234, 280
go – *progression* 282
shoot – *transcursion* 303
activity 682
rock – 665, 667
Ahrimanes 987, 980
aid **707**, 906
by the – of 631, 632
aide-de-camp 711, 745

aidless 160
aigrette 847
aiguille 253
aiguillette 747, 847
aigulet 847
ail 655, 828
aileron 267, 273
ailment 655
aim 278, 620, 675
– a blow at 716
aimable 894
faire l' – 897
aimer éperdument 897
aimless *without motive* 615a
chance 621
air *unsubstantial* 4
broach 66
lightness 320
gas 334
atmospheric **338**
wind 349
tune 415
appearance 448
refresh 689
demeanor 692
fashionable 852
beat the – 645
fill the – 404
fine – *salubrity* 656
fish in the – 645
fowls of the – 366
in the – 527
rend the – 404
take – 531
air-balloon 273
air base 728
air-commodore 745
aircraft 273, 726
air-drawn 515
airdrome 273
air-force 726
air-gun 727
airing 266
air-mail 273
airman 269
airmanship 698
air-marshal 745
air-passage 351
air-pipe 351
airport 273, 292, 728
air-pump 349
air-raid 716
airs *affectation* 855
pride 878
vanity 880
arrogance 885
air-shaft 351
air service 267
airship 273, 726
air-tight 261
airways 267
airworthy 273, 664
airy [*see* air]
windy 349
unimportant 643
gay 836
– hopes 858, 859
give to – nothing a local habitation &c. 515
aisle *passage* 200
way 627
in a church 1000
ait 346
ajar *open* 260
discordant 713
ajee 217
ajutage 260, 350
akimbo *angular* 244
stand – 715
akin *related* 9
consanguineous 11
similar 17
al fresco 220
alabaster *white* 430
alack! 839
alacrity *willing* 602
active 682
cheerful 836
Aladdin's lamp 993
alar 267
alarm *warning* 668
notice of danger **669**
fear 860
cause for – 665
give an – *indicate* 550
alarmist 862
alarum 114, 550, 669
alas! 839
alate 267
alb 999
albeit 30
albert
chain 847
albification 430
albinescence 430
albinism 430
albino 443
album 593, 596
albumen
semi-liquid 352
protein 357
Alcaic 597
alcaid 745
alcalde 745
alcazar 189
alchemy 144
alcohol 995
Alcoran 986
alcove 191, 252
Aldebaran 423
alderman 745
ale 298
alea, jacta est – 601
aleatory 665
Alecto 173
alectromancy 511
alehouse 189
go to the – 959
alembic
conversion 144
vessel 191
furnace 386
laboratory 691
alentours 197
alert *watchful* 457, 459
active 682
alerte 669
aleuromancy 511
Alexandrine
ornate style 577
verse 597
alexandrite 848
alexipharmic 662
alexiteric 662
algebra 85
algid 383
algology 369
algorithm 85
alguazil 965
alias
otherwise 18
pseudonym 565
alibi 187
alien *irrelevant* 10
foreign 57
transfer 783
gentile 989
alienable 783
alienate
transfer 783
estrange 44, 889
set against 898
alienation
mental – 503
alieni appetens
grasping 865
envious 921
selfish 943
alienism 54
align 278
alight *stop* 265
arrive 292
descend 306
on fire 382
alike 17
share and share – 778
aliment *food* 298
alimentary 662
– canal 350
alimentation
aid 707
alimony
property 780
provision 803
income 810
aliquot 51, 84
aliter visum, diis – 601
alive
living 359
intelligent 498
active 682
cheerful 836
be – with 102
keep – *continue* 143
keep the memory – 505
look – 684
– to *attention* 457
cognizant 490
informed 527
able 698
sensible 822
alkahest 335
all *whole* 50
complete 52
generality 78
– absorbing 642
in – ages 112
– aboard 495
– agog 865
– in all 50
– along 106
– along of 154
– but 32
– colors 440
– considered 451, 480
– day long 110
– devouring 190
in – directions 278
– engrossing 190
at – events *compensation* 30
qualification 469
true 494
resolve 604
– fours *easy* 705
cards 840
– in good time 152
– hail! *welcome* 292
honor to 873
celebration 883
courtesy 894
– hands *everybody* 78
on – hands 488
– of a dither 824
– of a heap 72
– knowing 976
– manner of *difference* 15
multiform 81
with – one's might 686
– at once 113
– one 27, 866
– out 52
– over *end* 67
universal 78
destruction 162
space 180
at – points 52
– in one's power 686
– powerful
mighty 159
God 976
in – quarters 180
with – respect 928
in – respects 52, 494
– right! 922
– Saints' day 998
– searching 461
– seeing 976
on – sides 227
– sorts *diverse* 16a
mixed 41
multiform 81
– talk 4
– things to all men 894
– the time 106
at – times 136
– together 50
– ways 243, 279
– wise 976
– the world and his wife 78
of – work
useful 644
maid - 746
Allah 979
allay
moderate 174
pacify 723
relieve 834
– excitability 826
allective 615
allege *evidence* 467
assert 535
plea 617
allegiance 743, 926
allegory 464, 521, 594
allegro *music* 415
cheerful 836
allelujah 990
allemande 840
all-embracing 76
alleviate 174, 834
alley *court* 189
passage 26
way 627
alliance *relation* 9
kindred 11
physical co-operation 178
voluntary co-operation 709
party 712
union 714
allied to *like* 17
alligation 43
allign 278
alliteration
similarity 17
style in writing 577
poetry 597
allocation 60, 786
allocution 586
allodium *free* 748
property 780
allopathy 662
alloquy 586
allot *arrange* 60
distribute 786
due 924
allow *assent* 488
admit 529
permit 760
consent 762
give 784
– to have one's own way 740
allowable 760, 924
allowance
qualification 469
gift 784
allotment 786
discount 813
salary 973
with grains of – 485
make – for *forgive* 918
vindicate 937
alloy *mixture* 41
combination 48
debase 659
allude *hint* 514
mean 516
refer to 521
latent 526
inform 527
allure *move* 615
create desire 865
alluring 829
allusive
relative 9
alluvial *level* 213
land 342
plain 344
alluvium
deposit 40
land 342
soil 653
ally *combine* 48
auxiliary 711
friend 891
alma mater 542
almanac
list 86
chronometry 114
record 551
almighty 157
Almighty, the – 976
almoner
treasurer 801

giver 784
church officer 996
almonry 802
almost *nearly* 32
not quite 651
– all 50
– immediately 132
alms *gift* 784
benevolence 906
worship 990
almshouse 189, 666
almsman 785
Alnaschar's dream 515, 858
aloes 395
aloft 206
alogy 497
alone *single* 87
unaided 706
let – *not use* 678
not restrain 748
along 200
get – *progress* 282
go – *depart* 293
go – with *concur* 178
assent 488
co-operate 709
– of *caused by* 154
– with *added* 37
together 88
by means of 631
alongside *near* 197
parallel 216
laterally 236
aloof *distant* 196
high 206
secluded 893
stand – *inaction* 681
refuse 764
cautious 864
alopecia 226
aloud 404
think – 589
naïveté 703
Alp 206
alpenstock 215
Alpha 66
– and Omega 50
alphabet
beginning 66
letters 561
alphabetarian 541
alphabeticize 60
alphitomancy 511
alpine *high* 206
Alpine Club 268, 305
already
antecedently 116
even now 118
past time 122
Alsatia 791, 945
also 37
altar 903, 1000
alter 140
– the case 468
– one's course 279
alter ego *similar* 17
auxiliary 711
deputy 759
friend 890
alterable 149
alteram partem, audire – 468, 922
alterative
substitute 634
remedy 662
altercation 713
altered *worn* 688
– for the worse 659
alternate
reciprocal 12
sequence 63
discontinuous 70
periodic 138
changeable 149
oscillate 314
alternative
substitute 147
choice 609
plan 626
although
compensation 30
counteraction 179
unless 469
altiloquence 577
altimetry
height 206
angle 244
measurement 466
altitude *height* 206
– and azimuth 466
alto 410, 416
– part 415
alto-rilievo 250, 557
altogether 50, 51
nude 226
altruism 910, 942
altruist 906
alum 397
alumnus 541
alveolus 252
always
uniformly 16
generally 78
during 106
perpetually 112
habitually 613
a.m. 114, 125
amability 829, 894
amah 753
amain 173, 684
amalgam, -ate 41, 48
amalgamation 709
Amalthea's horn 639
amantium iræ 918
amanuensis 553, 590
amaranthine 112
amari aliquid
bad 649
imperfect 651
painful 830
amaritude 395
amass *whole* 50
collect 72
store 636
amateur *volunteer* 602
layman 699
taste 850
votary 865
amatory 897
amaurosis 442
amaze 870
amazingly 31
Amazon
woman 374
warrior 726
courage 861
ambages
convolutions 248
circumlocution 573
circuit 629
ambagious 573
ambassador
messenger 534
representative 758
recall of –s 713
amber 356a
– color 436
ambidexter
right and left 238
fickle 607
clever 698
ambient 227
ambigu 41
ambiguas spargere voces
uncertain 475
misteach 538
false 544
cunning 702
ambiguous
uncertain 475
unintelligible 519
equivocal 520
obscure 571
ambiloquy 520
ambit 230
ambition 620, 865
ambivalence 605, 708
amble 266
ambo *school* 542
pulpit 1000
ambo, Arcades –
alike 17
friends 890
bad men 949
ambrosia 298
ambrosial 394, 490
ambulance
vehicle 272
hospital 662
ambulation 266
ambuscade 530
ambush 530, 667
lie in – 528
âme – de boue 949
– damnée
catspaw 711
servant 746
servile 886
bad man 949
– qui vive 101, 187
ameer 875
ameliorate 658
amen *assent* 488
submission 725
content 831
amenable 177, 602, 926
not – to reason 608
amend 658
amendatory 20
amende honorable 952
amends
compensation 50
atonement 952
reward 973
amenity 829, 894
amentia 503
amerce 974
American organ 417
Americanism 563
amethyst
purple 437
jewel 847
amiable
courteous 894
loving 897
kind 906
amicable 707, 888
amice 999
amicus – curiæ 527
– humani generis 910
– usque ad aras 890
amidships 68
amidst 41, 228
amiss 619
come – *disagree* 24
mistime 135
inexpedient 647
do – 945
nothing comes – 823
take – 867, 900
amity *concord* 714
peace 721
friendship 888
ammunition 635, 727
amnesia 506
amnesty 506, 723, 918
amnis, rusticus expectat dum defluat – *hope* 858
amœbæan 63
amok 503
among 41, 228
amor patriæ 910
amore, con – 602, 821
amoroso 599
amorous 897
– glances 902
amorphous 83, 241
amorphism 241
amortization 784
amotion 270
amount
quantity 25
degree 26
sum of money 800
price 812
gross – 50
– to 27, 85
amour 897, 961
– propre 880
ampere 466
amphibian 366
amphibious 83
amphibology 520
Amphictyonic council 696
amphigouri 497
amphitheatre
prospect 441
school 542
theater 599
arena 728
Amphitryon 890
amphora 191
ample *much* 31
spacious 180
large 192
broad 202
copious 639
amplify
expand 194
exaggerate 549
diffuse style 573
amplitude
quantity 25
degree 26
size 192
breadth 202
enough 639
ampoulé 191
ampulla 191
amputate 38
amuck 824
run – 503
amulet 247, 993
amusare la bocca, per – 394
amuse 829, 840
amusement 840
place of – 840
amussim, ad – 494
amylaceous 352
an *if* 514
ana 594
Anabaptist 984
anabasis 35
anachronism
false time 115
inopportune 135
error 495
anacoluthon 70
anaconda 913
anacreontic 597
anaglyph 554, 557
anagoge 521, 526
anagram
double sense 520
secret 533
letter 561
wit 842
analecta 596
analeptic 662
analgesia 376
analogy 9, 17
analogous 12
analysis
decomposition 49
arrangement 60
algebra 85
inquiry 461
experiment 463
reasoning 476
grammar 567
compendium 596
analyst 461, 463
anamorphosis
distortion 243
optical 443
misrepresentation 555
anapest 597
anaphylaxis 375
anarchist
destroyer 165
disobedient 742
evil-doer 913
anarchy 59, 738
anastatic printing 558
anastomosis 43, 219
anastrophe 218
anathema 908
anathematize 908
censure 932
detract 934
anatomize *dissect* 44
investigate 461
anatomy
dissection 44
leanness 203
texture 329
anatomy

science 357
comparative – 368
anatriptic 331
ancestral
bygone 122
old 124
aged 128
ancestry 166
anchor
connection 45
stop 265
safeguard 666
badge 747
hope 858
at – *fixed* 150
stationed 184
safe 664
cast – *settle* 184
arrive 292
have an – to windward 664
sheet – *means* 632
anchorage
location 184
roadstead 189
refuge 866
anchored 150
anchorite 893, 955
ancien régime 875
ancient *old* 124
flag 550
– times 122
ancientness 122
ancillary 707
and 37, 88
andante 415
andiron 386
androgynous 83
anecdote 594
anele 998
anemia 160
anemography 349
ἀνεμώλια βάζειν 497
anemometer
wind 349
measure 466
anent 9
aneroid 338
anesthesia 376, 381, 683
anew *again* 104
newly 123
anfractuosity 248
angel
object of love 897
good person 948
supernatural being 977
fallen –
bad man 949
devil 978
guardian –
safety 664
auxiliary 711
benefactor 912
– of Death 362
– 's visits 137
angelic 944
angels and ministers of grace defend us! 860
angelus 550
anger 900
more in sorrow than in – 826, 918
angiology 329
angle 244
try 463
at an – 217
Anglicanism 984
angling 622, 840
anguille au genou, rompre l' – 158, 471
anguilliform 205, 248
anguis in herbâ 667
anguish
physical 378
moral 828
angular 244
– velocity 264
angularity 244
angusta domi, res – 804
angustation 203
anhelation 688
anhydrate 340
anhydrous 340
aniline dyes 437
anility 128, 499
animadvert
consider 451
attend to 457
reprehend 932
animal 366
female – 374
– cries 412
– economy 359
– gratification 377
– life 364
– physiology 368
– spirits 836
– and vegetable kingdom 357
animalcule 193, 366
animalism
sensuality 954
animality 364
animate
induce 615
excite 824
enliven 836
animation
life 359
animality 364
activity 682
vivacity 836
suspended – 823
animism 984
animo, ex – 602
quo – 620
animosity
dislike 867
enmity 889
hatred 898
anger 900
animus
willingness 602
intention 620
desire 865
ankle 244
– deep 208, 209
anklet 847
ankylosis 150
annalist 114, 553
annals
chronology 114
record 551
account 594
anneal 673
annex
addition 37
adjunct 39
junction 43
acquire 775
Annie Oakley 815
annihilate 2, 162
anniversary 138
anno 106
Anno Domini
era 106
old age 124
annotation 522, 550
annotator 524
scholar 492
interpreter 524
editor 595
annotto 434
announce
predict 511
inform 527
publish 531
assert 535
announcer 527
annoy
molest 649, 907
disquiet 830
annoyance 828
source of – 830
annual *periodic* 138
plant 367
book 593
annuity 810
annul 162, 750
annular 247
annunciate 527
annus magnus 108
anodyne
lenitive 174
remedial 662
relief 834
anoint *coat* 223
lubricate 332
oil 355
anointed
deity 976
king 745
anomaly 59, 83
disorder 59
irregularity 83
anon 132
anonymous 565
anopsia 442
anorexy 866
another
different 15
repetition 104
– story 468, 526
go upon – tack 607
– time 119
answer
to an inquiry 462
confute 479
solution 522
succeed 731
pecuniary profit 775
pleadings 969
require an – 461
– for *deputy* 759
promise 768
go bail 806
I'll – for it 535
– the helm 745
– the purpose 731
– to *correspond* 9
– one's turn 644
answerable
agreement 23
liable 177
bail 806
duty 926
censurable 932
ant 690
Antaeus 159, 192
antagonism
difference 14
physical 179
voluntary 708
enmity 889
antagonist 710, 891
antagonistic 24
antarctic 237
antecedence 62, 116
antecedent 64
antechamber 191
ante Christum 106
antedate 115
antediluvian 124
antelope 274
antemundane 124
antenna 379
anteposition 62
anterior
in order 62
in time 116
in place 234
– to reason 477
anteroom 191
antevert 706
anthem 990
anthemion 847
anthology
book 533
collection 596
poem 597
anthracite 388
anthropoid 372
anthropology
zoology 368
mankind 372
anthropomancy 511
anthropophagi 913
anthroposcopy 511
anthroposophy 372
antic 840
anti-aircraft gun 564, 727
antichambre, faire – 133
antichristian 984, 989
antichronism 115
anticipate
anachronism 115
priority 116
future 121
early 132
expect 507
foresee 510
prepare 673
hope 858
in – 116
anticlimax
decrease 36
bathos 497, 853
anticlinal 217
anticyclone 265
antidote 662
antigropelos 225
antilogarithm 84
antilogy 477
antimony 663
Antinomian 984
antinomy 964
Antinous 845
antiparallel 217
antipathy 867, 898
antiphon *music* 415
answer 462
worship 990
antiphrasis 563
antipodes
difference 14
distance 196
contraposition 237
antipoison 660
antiquary
past times 122
scholar 492
historian 553
antiquas vias, stare super – 613, 670
antiquated 128
antique 124
antiquity 122
antiscriptural 984
antiseptic 652, 662
antisocial 911
antistrophe 597
antithesis
contrast 14
difference 15
opposite 237
style 574, 577
antitoxin 662
antitype 22
antler 253
antonomasia
metaphor 521
nomenclature 564
antonym 14
antrum 252
anvil *support* 215
on the –
intended 620
in hand 625
preparing 673
anxiety *pain* 828
fear 860
desire 865
anxious expectation 507
any *some* 25
part 51
no choice 609a
at – price 604a
at – rate
certain 474
true 494
at all hazards 604
anybody 78
anyhow 460, 627
anything one knows, for – 491
aorist 109, 119
aorta 350
apace *early* 132
swift 274
apache 913
apart 44, 87
set – 636
wide – 196
apartment 191
–s 189
–s to let
imbecile 499
apathetic 275
apathy
indifference 465
insensibility 823
irreligion 989
ape *imitate* 19
Apelles 559
aperçu 596
aperture 260

attract – 882
call to – 457
call – to 550
give – 418
pay –s to 894
pay one's –s to 902
attenuate
decrease 36
weaken 158
reduce 195
rarefy 322
attenuated 203
attest
bear testimony 467
affirm 535
adjure 768
attested copy 771
attic *simple* 42
garret 191
summit 210
style 578
wit 842
taste 850
Attila 913
attire 225
attitude
circumstance 8
situation 183
posture 240
attitudinarian 882
attitudinize 855
attollent 307
attorney
consignee 758
at law 968
power of – 755
attract
bring towards 288
induce 615
allure 865
excite love 897
– the attention 457
visible 446
attraction
[see attract]
natural power 157
bring towards 288
attractive
[see attract]
pleasing 829
beautiful 845
attrahent 288
attribute
speciality 79
accompaniment 88
power 157
–s of the Deity 976
– to 155
attribution 155
attrite 330
attrition 330, 331
attroupement 72
attune *music* 415
prepare 673
attuned to
habit 613
attunement 23
auburn 433
A.U.C. 106
auction 796, 840
auctioneer 758, 796
auctorial 599
audacity
courage 861
rashness 863
insolence 885
audible 402
become – 418
scarcely – 405
audience
hearing 418
conversation 588
before an – 599
audire alteram partem
counter-evidence 468
right 922
justice 939
audit
numeration 85
examination 461
accounts 811
auditive 418
auditor
hearer 418
accountant 811
auditorium 189, 588
auditory
sound 402
hearing 418
theater 599
– apparatus 418
au fait 698
au fond 5
auf wiedersehen 293
Augean
– stable 653
– task 704
auger 262
aught 51
for – one cares
unimportant 643
indifferent 866
for – one knows
ignorance 491
conjecture 514
augment
increase 35
thing added 39
expand 194
augur 513
– well 858
augurate 511
augury 512
august 873
Augustinian 996
auk 366
auld lang syne 122
aulic council 696
aumbry 1000
aunt 11
aura *wind* 349
sensation 380
aurea mediocritas 628
aureate 436
aureola 420
aureole 420, 873
aureolin 436
auribus, arrectis – 418
auricular *hearing* 418
clandestine 528
– confession 998
auri sacra fames 819
aurist 662
aurora
dawn 125
light 420, 423
twilight 422
– australes 423
– borealis 423
Auroral 236
ausculation 418
auspice *omen* 512
auspices
influence 175
prediction 511
protection 664
direction 693
aid 707
under the – of 693, 737
auspicious
opportune 134
prosperous 734
hopeful 858
austerity
harsh taste 395
severe 739
discourteous 895
ascetic 955
pietism 988
austral 237
austromancy 511
authentic 467
certain 474
true 494
authentication
evidence 467
security 771
author 164, 593
projector 626
dramatic – 599
– of our being 976
– of evil 978
–'s proof 591
authoritative 474, 741
authority
testimony 467
sage 500
informant 527
power 737
permission 760
right 924
ensign of – 747
person in – 745
do upon one's own – 600
authorized *due* 924
legalized 963
authorship
production 161
style 569
writing 590
autobiography 594
autocar 272
autochthonous 188
autocracy 737, 739
autocrat 745
autocratic 600, 737
auto-da-fe 384, 972
autograph 550, 590
Autolycus *thief* 792
pedlar 797
automaniac 504
automatic 601, 633
- pistol 727
- writing 992
automaton 554, 601
automobile 272
automobilist 268
automotive 266
autonomasia 521
autonomy 737, 748
autopsy
post-mortem 363
vision 441
autoptical 446, 535
autotype 558
autumn 126
auxiliary 711
additional 34
helpful 707
– forces 726
avail *benefit* 618
useful 644
succeed 731
of no – 645
– oneself of 677
avalanche *fall* 306
snow 383
redundance 641
avaler les couleuvres 725, 886
avant-courier 64, 673
avant-propos 64
avarice 819
avast! *stop* 142, 265
desist 624
forbid 761
avatar *change* 140
deity 976
idol 991
avaunt! 297, 449
ave! *honor* 873
courtesy 894
Ave maria 990
avenge 919
avenue
plantation 371
way 627
aver 535
average *mean* 29, 628
médiocre 651
– circumstances 736
take an – 466
Averni, facilis descensus – 217, 665
Avernus 982
averruncate 297, 301
aversion *unwillingness* 603
dislike 867
hate 898
avert 706
– the eyes 442
aviary 370
aviation 267
aviator 269
avidity *avarice* 819
desire 865
airette 273
avile 932, 934
avion 273
aviso 532
avocation 625
avoidance 623
avoidless 474, 601
avoirdupois 319
avolation 623, 671
avouch 535, 768
avow *assent* 488
disclose 529
assert 535
avulsion 44, 301
avuncular 11
await *future* 121
be kept waiting 133
impend 152
expect 507
awake *attentive* 457
careful 459
intelligent 498
active 682
– to life immortal 360
awaken *inform* 527
excite 824
– the attention 457
– the memory 505
award *adjudge* 480
give 784
aware 490
away 187, 196
break – 623
fly – 293
move – 287
take – from 789
get &c. – 671
throw &c. –
eject 297
reject 610
waste 638
relinquish 782
– from *unrelated* 10
– with! 930, 932
do – with *undo* 681
abrogate 756
awe *fear* 860
wonder 870
respect 928
aweless *fearless* 861
insolent 885
disrespectful 329
awful 31, 860
– silence 403
awhile 111
awkward
inelegant 579
inexpedient 647
unskilful 699
difficult 704
painful 830
ugly 846
vulgar 851
ridiculous 853
– squad 701
awl 262
awn 253
awning 223, 424
awry *oblique* 217
distorted 243
evil 619
axe *edge tool* 253
impulse 276
weapon 727
for beheading 975
have an – to grind 702
Axinomancy 511
axiom 496
axiomatic 474
axis *support* 215
center 222
rotation 312
axle 312
wheel and – 633
axle load 466
axletree 215
ay 488
ayah 746, 753
aye *ever* 112
yes 488
azimuth

by instalments 51
in detail 79
slowly 275
– between the teeth 600, 719
bitch *animal* 366
female 374
clumsy 699
fail 732
impure 962
bite *eat* 298
physical pain 378
cold 385
cheat 545
dupe 547
etch 558
mental pain 830
– the dust 725
– in 259
– the thumb 900, 929
– the tongue 392
biter bit 718
biting *pain* 378
cold 383
pungent 392
painful 830
discourteous 895
censorious 932
bitten 897
bitter *beer* 298
cold 383
taste 392, 395
painful 830
acrimonious 895
hate 898
angry 900
malevolent 907
– end 67
– ender 606, 710, 832
– pill 735
– words 932
bitterly *greatly* 31
bitterness
[*see* bitter]
pain 828
regret 833
bitumen 356*a*
bituminous coal 388
bivouac
encamp 184
camp 189
repose 265
watch 668
bi-weekly 138
bizarre 83, 853
blab 529
blabber 584
black *color* 431
crime 945
look – *feeling* 821
discontent 832
angry 900
– art 992
– and blue
beat 972
– board 590
– book 938
– eye 848, 972
– in the face
swear 535
excitement 821, 824
– flag 722
– hole *crowd* 72
prison 752
– lead 556
– letter *old* 124
barbarism 563
print 591
– list 932
– looks
discourteous 895
sullen 901*a*
disapprove 932
magic 998
– mail *theft* 791
booty 793
bribe 973
– sheep 949
– spots in the horizon 859
– swan 83
– and white
chiaroscuro 420
colorless 429
record 551
writing 590
prove that – is white 477
blackamoor 431
wash a – white 471
blackball 55, 893, 932
blackcoat 996
blacken [*see* black]
defame 934
blackguard
vulgar 851
rude 895
base 940
vagabond 949
blackleg 792
black Maria 727
blackness **431**
blacksmith 690
bladder 191
blade *edge tool* 253
man 373
instrument 633
sharp fellow 682
proficient 700
sword 727
fop 854
blague 545
blain 250, 848
blame 155, 932
lay – on 938
take – 932
blameless 946
blameworthy
disapprove 932
vice 945
guilt 947
blanc-bec 701
blancmange 298
blanch 429, 430
bland 174, 894
blandiloquence 933
blandishment
inducement 615
endearment 902
flattery 933
blank 2, 4
empty 187
simple 849
look –
disappointed 509
discontent 832
wonder 870
point – 576
– cartridge 158
– verse 597
blanket 223, 384
wet – 174
toss in a – 929
blare 404, 412
blarney 933
blasé 841, 869
blasphemy 988
blast
destroy 162
explosion 173
wind 349
sound 404
adversity 735
curse 908
– furnace 386
blatant *loud* 404
cry 412
silly 499
blather 584
blatter 412
blaze *heat* 382
light 420
mark 550
excitement 824
– abroad 531
blazer 225
blazing
luminary 423
blazon *publish* 531
repute 873
ornament 847
ostentation 882
blé: manger son – on herbe 818
bleach 429, 430
bleak 383
blear-eyed 443
bleary 422
bloat 412
blob 250
bleed
physical pain 378
remedy 662
spend money 809
extort money 814
moral pain 828
make the heart – 830
– freely *liberal* 816
bleeding
hemorrhage 299
remedy 662
– heart 828
blemish
imperfection 651
injure 659
ugly 846
defect **848**
blench *avoid* 623
whiten 821
fear 860
blend 41, 48
– with 714
bless
give pleasure 829
approve 931
divine function 976
worship 990
– my heart 870
– one's stars 838, 916
blessed 827
abode of the – 981
blessedness
single – 904
blessing *good* 618
approval 931
blessings 734
blest 827
– with 177
bletonism 511
blight
deteriorate 659
adversity 735
– hope 509
blighty 189
blimp 273
blind 223
shade 424
cecity 442
inattentive 458
ignorant 491
conceal 528
screen 530
deception 545
instinctive 601
pretext 617
insensible 823
drunk 959
– alley 261
– bargain
uncertain 475
purposeless 62
rash 863
– the eyes *hide* 528
deceive 545
– hookey 840
– lead the blind 538
– man's buff 840
– man's holiday
evening 126
dark 421, 422
– to one's own merit 880
– to the world 959
– of one eye 443
– reasoning 486
– side *prejudice* 481
credulity 486
obstinacy 606
blinders 424, 443
blindness **442**
blind pig 964
blink *wink* 443
neglect 460
falter 605
avoid 623
– at *blind to* 442, 458
blinkard 443
blinker 424, 530
bliss 827
celestial 981
blister 250
blithe 836
blizzard 349
bloated
expanded 194
misshapen 243
convex 250
– with pride 878
blob 250
block *mass* 192
support 215
dense 321
hard 323
fool 501
engraving 558
writing 590
hinder 706
execution 975
bring to the – 972
wood – 558
– of buildings 189
– out 230, 240, 973
– printing 591
– up 261, 706
blockade
surround 227
close 261
restrain 751
exclude 893
blockhead 501
blockhouse 717
blockish 499
blond 429, 430
blood
consanguinity **11**
fluid 333
kill 361
fop 854
nobility 875
dye with –
severe 739
hands in – *cruel* 907
in the – **5**
life – 359
new – 658, 824
spill – *war* 722
– for blood 919
– boil *excite* 824, 825
anger 900
– run cold 830, 860
– heat 382
– horse 271
– hound 913
– letting 297, 662
– poisoning 655
– red 434
– stained 361
– sucker 789, 913
– thirsty
murderous 361
cruel 907
– up *excited* 824
angry 900
bloodless 160
peace 721
virtue 946
bloody [*see* blood]
red 434
unclean 653
cruel 907
bloom *youth* 127
flower 367
blue 438
health 654
prosperity 734
bloomer 495
bloomers 225
blooming 654, 845
blossom
flower 154, 161, 367
prosperity 734
blot *blacken* 431
error 495
obliterate 552
dirty 653
blemish 848
disgrace 874
guilt 947
– out *destroy* 162
forgive 918
blotch 848
blouse 225
blow *expand* 194
knock 276
wind 349

unexpected 508
disappointment 509
evil 619
action 680
get wind 688
failure 732
prosper 734
pain 828, 830
come to –s 720, 722
deal a – at 716
deal a – to 972
death – 360, 361
– for blow 718
– one's brains out 361
– the coals 824
– down 162
– the fire 384
– the gaff 529
– hole 351
– the horn 416
– hot and cold
lie 544
irresolute 605
tergiversation 607
caprice 608
– a kiss 902
– off *disperse* 73
– out *food* 298
darken 421
gorge 957
– over *past* 122
– pipe 349, 727
– the trumpet 873
– one's own trumpet 882
– up *destroy* 162
eruption 173
inflate 194
wind 349
excite 824
objurgate 932, 934
blower 349
blowhard 884
blown [*see* blow]
fatigued 688
proud 878
storm – over 664, 721
– upon 874, 932
blow-out 406
blowzy *swollen* 194
red 434
blubber *fat* 356
cry 839
Blucher boot 225
bludgeon 727
– man 726, 913
blue *sky* 338
color 438
learned 490
bit of – hope 858
look –
disappointed 509
feeling 821
discontent 832
disrepute 874
out of the – 508
swear till all's – 535
true – 543, 939
– book 86, 551
– blood 875
– devils 837
– jacket 269
– light 550, 669
– pencil 174, 596
– moon 110
– Peter 293, 550
– and red 437
– ribbon 733, 877
– ruin 959
– stocking
scholar 492
affectation 855
– and yellow 435
Bluebeard
marriage 903
libertine 962
blueness 438
blues 837, 840
bluff *violent* 173
high cliff 206
blunt 254
deceive 545
boasting 884
insolent 885
discourteous 895
blunder *error* 495
absurdity 497
awkward 699
failure 732
– upon 156
blunderbuss 727
blunderhead 701
blunderheaded 499
blunt *weaken* 160
inert 172
moderate v. 174
obtuse 254
benumb 376
damp v. 616
plain-spoken 703
cash 800
deaden 823
discourteous 895
– tool 645
– witted 499
bluntness 254
blur
imperfect vision 443
dirt 653
blemish 848
stigma 874
blurb 931
blurred
invisible 447
blurt out 529, 582
blush *flush* 382
redden 434
feel 821
humbled 879
modest 881
at first – *see* 441
appear 448
manifest 525
put to the –
humble 897
browbeat 885
discourtesy 895
blushing honors 873, 881
bluster *violent* 173
defiant 715
boasting 884
insolent 885
threaten 909
blusterer 887
blustering [*see* bluster]
windy 349
Bo to a goose, not say – 862.
boa 225
boanerges 540
boar 366, 373
board *layer* 204
support 215
food 298
hard 323
council 696
attack 716
tribunal 966
festive – 892
go by the – 158, 162
go on – 293
on – 186, 273
preside at the – 693
– of trade 621
– school 542
boarding-house 189
boarder 188
boards 599, 728
boast 884
not much to – of 651
boasting 884
boaston 840
boat 273
in the same – 88
– race 720
boating 267
boatman 269
boatswain 269
bob *depress* 308
leap 309
oscillate 314
agitate 315
money 800
– a curtsy 894
– for *fish* 463
Bobadil, Captain – 887
bobbed
hair 53
bobbin 312
bobbing *fuel* 388
bobbish 654
bobby *police* 664
bobsleigh 272
bobsleighing 840
bobtailed 53
bocage 367
bocca, per amusare la – 394
Boche 913
boddice 225
bode 511
bodega 189
bodily
substantially 3
wholly 50
material 316
– enjoyment 377
– fear 860
– pain 378
bodkin
go between 228
perforator 262
body *substance* 3
whole 50
assemblage 72
frame 215
matter 316
party 712
in a – *together* 88
– and blood of Christ 987
– clothes 225
– color 556
– of doctrine 490
– forth 554
– guard 717, 753
– of knowledge 490
– politic
mankind 372
authority 737
keep – and soul together 654
– of water 438
Boeotian *rustic* 371
stupid 499
fool 501
vulgar 851
ignoble 876
Boer 371
bog 345, 653
– trotter 876
boggart 980
boggle *hesitate* 605
awkward 699
difficulty 704
bogie 980
truck 272
bogle 980
bogus 545
Bohemian
unconventional 83
nomad 268
ungenteel 851
boil *violence* 173
effervesce 315
bubble 353
heat 382, 384
ulceration 655
excitement 824, 825
anger 900
– down 195
boiler 386
boisterous
violent 173
hasty 684
excitable 825
bold *prominent* 250
unreserved 525
vigorous 574
brave 861
make – with 895
show a – front 715, 861
– faced 885
– push *essay* 675
– relief *visible* 446
– stroke *plan* 626
success 731
bole 50
bolero 840
bollard 45
bolshevik 144, 146
bolshevist 737, 742
bolster *support* 215
repair 658
aid 707
– up *vindicate* 937
bolt *sift* 42
fasten 43
fastening 45
close 261
move rapidly 274
propel 284
run away 623
escape 671
hindrance 706
shaft 727
disobey 742
shackle 752
thunder – 872
– the door 761
– food 298, 957
– in 751
– upright 212
bolthead 191
bolus *mouthful* 298
remedy 662
bomb 404, 727
– proof 664, 717
– vessel 726
bombard 716
bombardier 726
bombardon 417
bombast
unmeaning 517
magniloquence 577
ridiculous 853
boasting 884
exaggeration 549
Bombastes Furioso 887
bomber
aeroplane 726
bombilation 404
bon de – augure 858
– enfant *social* 892
kindly 906
– gré mal gré 601
– marché 815
– mot 842
– naturel 836
– ton 852
– vivant 957
– voyage 293
bona – fides
veracity 543
probity 939
– roba 962
bonanza 641, 784
wealth 803
bonbon 396
bond *relation* 9
tie 45
compact 769
security 771
money 800
right 924
– of union 9, 45
government – 802
Liberty – 802
bondage 749
bonded together 712
bonds [*see* bond]
fetters 752
funds 802
in – *service* 746
tear asunder one's – 750
– of harmony 714
bondsman 746
bone *strength* 159
dense 321
hard 323
bred in the – 5
feel it in one's – 510
– of contention 713, 720
one – and one flesh 903
– to pick *difficulty* 704
discord 713

refresh 689
bracelet *circle* 247
handcuff 752
ornament 847
bracer 392
braces 45
brachial 633
Brachygraphy 590
bracing 656
bracken 367
bracket *tie* 43, 45
couple 89
support 215
brackish 392
brad 45
bradawl 262
Bradbury 800
Bradshaw 266
brae 206
brag *cards* 840
boast 884
braggart 884
Braggadocio 884
Brahma 979
Brahmin 984, 996
braid *tie* 43
ligature 45
net 219
variegate 440
brain *kill* 361
intellect 450
skill 498
blow one's –s out 361
coinage of the – 515
suck one's –s 461
rack one's –s 451, 515
brainless 499
brainpan 450
brainsick 458
brain-storm 503, 825
brainwork 451
brainy 498
brake *carriage* 272
copse 367
hindrance 706
curb 752
apply the – 275
brakeman 268
bramble *thorn* 253
bane 663
bran 330
brancard 272
branch *member* 51
class 75
posterity 167
fork 244
tree 367
– off 91, 291
– out *ramify* 91
diffuse style 573
branching
symmetry 242
brand *burn* 384
fuel 388
torch 423
mark 550
sword 727
disrepute 874
censure 932
stigmatize 934
– of discord 713
– new 123
– with reproach 938
brandish
oscillate 314
flourish 315
display 882
brandy 959
brangle 713
brangler 710
brank 975
bras
les – croisés 681
à – ouverts 894
brashness 885
brass *alloy* 41
money 800
insolence 885
bold as – 861
– band 417, 882
with a – 884
– colored 439
– hat 745
– farthing 643
brassard 550, 747
brat 129
brattice 224, 228
bravado 884
brave *confront* 234
healthy 654
defy 715
warrior 726
bear 821, 826
courage 861
– a thousand years 110
bravo
assassin 361
desperado 863
applause 931
bravura 415
brawl *cry* 411
discord 713
revel 840
brawler
disputant 710
rioter 742
blusterer 887
brawny 159, 192
bray *grind* 330
cry 412
Bray, Vicar of – 607, 886
braze 43
brazen 525, 885
– browed 885
– faced 885
brazier 386
breach *crack* 44
gap 198
quarrel 713
violation 925
custom honored in the – 614
– of faith 940
– of law 83, 964
– of the peace 713
bread 298
beg – 765
selfish 943
quarrel with – and butter 699
– of idleness 683
– of life *Christ* 976
piety 987
– upon the waters 638
– and wine 998
breadbasket 191
breadth 202
chiaroscuro 420
break
fracture 44
discontinuity 70
change 140
gap 198
carriage 272
crumble 328
disclose 529
cashier 756
violate 773, 927
bankrupt 808
– away 623
– bread 298
– bulk 297
– camp 293
– of day *morning* 125
twilight 422
– down *destroy* 162
fall short 304
decay 659
fail 732
dance 840
– one's fetters 614
– forth 295
– ground 66
– a habit 614
– the heart *pain* 828, 830
dejection 837
– the ice 888
– in *ingress* 294
domesticate 370
teach 537
tame 749
– in upon *derange* 61
inopportune 135
hinder 706
– a lance 716, 722
– a law 83
– loose 671, 750
– one's neck
powerless 158
die 360
– the neck of
task 676
success 731
– the news 529
– no bones 648
– of 660
– off *cease* 142
relinquish 624
abrogate 756
– out *begin* 66
violent 173
disease 655
excited 825
– the peace 173, 720
– Priscian's head 568
– prison 750
– the ranks 61
– short 328
– silence 582
– the teeth 579
– the thread 70
– through the clouds *visible* 446
disclose 529
– through a custom 614
– up *disjoin* 44
decompose 49
end 67
revolution 146
destroy 162
– up of the system, 360, 665
– on the wheel
physical pain 378
mental pain 830
punishment 972
– with 713
– with the past 146
– word *deceive* 525
improbity 940
breaker
of horses 268
reef 346
wave 348
breakers 348, 667
surrounded by – 704
– ahead 665
breakfast 298
breakneck
precipice 217
rash 863
breakwater
refuge 666
obstruction 706
breast *interior* 221
confront 234
convex 250
mind 450
oppose 708
soul 820
at the – 129
in the – of 620
– the current 719
– high 206
breastplate 717
breastwork 717
breath *instant* 113
breeze 349
life 359
animality 364
faint sound 405
with bated – 581
hold – *quiet* 265
expect 507
wonder 870
not a – of air 265, 382
out of – 688
in the same – 120
shortness of – 688
take – 265, 689
take away one's –
unexpected 508
fear 860
wonder 870
breathe *exist* 1
blow 349
live 359
faint sound 405
evince 467
mean 516
inform 527
disclose 529
utter 580
speak 582
refresh 689
– freely 827, 834
– one's last 360
not – a word 528
breathing time 687, 723
breathless
voiceless 581
out of breath 688
feeling 821
fear 860
eager 865
wonder 870
– attention 457
– expectation 507
– impatience 865
– speed 684
bred in the bone 820
breech 235
– loader 727
breeches 225
wear the – 737
– buoy 666
– maker 225
– pocket
money 800, 802
breed *kind* 75
multiply 161
progeny 167
animals 370
rear 537
breeding 161, 852, 894
breeze *wind* 349
discord 713
breezy 836
brethren 997
breve 413
brevet
warrant 741
commission 755
permit 760
– rank 873
breviary 998
brevier 591
brevity 201, 572
brew 41, 673
brewing
impending 152
storm – 665
bribe *equivalent* 30
tempt 615
offer 763
gift 784
buy 795
expenditure 809
reward 973
bric-à-brac 847
brick *hard* 323
pottery 384
material 635
trump 939, 948
make -s without straw 471
– color 434
brickbat 727
bricklayer 690
bride 903
bridewell 752
bridge 45, 627
– over *join* 43
facilitate 705
make peace 723
compromise 774
cards 840
bridle *restrain* 751
rein 752
– road 627
– one's tongue 585, 864
– up 900
brief *time* 111
space 201
concise 572
compendium 596

hold a – for 759
– case 191
briefly anon 132
brier
sharp 253
pipe 390
bane 663
brig 273
brigade 726
brigadier 745
brigand 792
brigandage 791
brigandine 717
brigantine 273
bright shine 420
color 428
intelligent 498
cheery 836
beauty 845
glory 873
– days 734
– eyed 845
– prospect 858
– side 829
look at the – side 836, 858
– thought
sharp 498
good stroke 626
wit 842
brighten up
furbish 658
brigue 712, 720
brilliant
shining 420
good 648
wit 842
beautiful 845
gem 847
glorious 873
– idea 842
brilliantine 356
brim 231
– over 641
brimful 52
brimstone 388
brindled 440
brine 341, 392
bring 270
– about 153, 729
– back 790
– back to the memory 505
– to bear upon
relation 9
action 170
– into being 161
– to a crisis 604
– forth 161
– forward
evidence 467
manifest 525
teach 537
improve 658
– grey hairs to the grave 735, 830
– grist to the mill 644
– home 775
– home to 155
– in receive 296
income 810
price 812
– to life 359
– to light 480a
– low 874
– to maturity 673, 729
– to mind 505
– under one's notice 457
– off 672
– out
discover 480a
manifest 525
publish 591
– over
persuade 484
– to perfection 677
– into play 677
– to a point 74
– in question 461
– up the rear 235
– round
persuade 615
restore 660
– to terms 723
– to convert 144
halt 265
– together 72
– in its train 88
– to trial 969
– up develop 161
vomit 297
educate 537
– in a verdict 480
– word 527
brink 231
on the –
almost 32
coming 121
near 197
– of the grave 360
briny 392
– ocean 341
brio music 415
active 682
brisk prompt 111
energetic 171
active 682
cheery 836
bristle 253
– up stick up 250
angry 900
– with 639, 641
– with arms 722
bristly 256
Britannia metal 545
Briticism 563
British 188
– lion 604
Briton, true – 939
work like a – 686
brittleness 328
britzska 272
broach begin 66
found 153
reamer 262
tap 297
publish 531
assert 535
broad general 78
space 202
lake 343
emphatic 535
indelicate 961, 962
– accent 580
– awake 459, 682
– daylight 420, 525
– farce 842
– grin 838
– highway 627
– hint 527
– meaning 516
– minded 498
broadcast
disperse 73
spread 78
publish 531
sow – 818
broadcloth 219
broadhearted 906
broadsheet 593
broad-shouldered 159
broadside 236
publication 531
cannonade 716
broadsword 727
Brobdingnagian 192
brocade 847
brochure 593
Brocken, specter of the 443
broder 549
brogue boot 225
dialect 563
broidery 847
broil heat 382
fry 384
fray 713, 720
broke poor 804
broken
discontinuous 70
weak 160
– color 428
– down
decrepit 659
failing 732
dejected 837
– English 563
– fortune 735, 804
– heart 828, 837
hopeless 859
– reed 160, 665
– meat 645
– voice 581, 583
– winded
disease 655
fatigue 688
broker 758, 797
brokerage pay 812
brokery 794
bromidic 613
bronchia 351
bronze alloy 41
brown 433
sculpture 557
brooch 847
brood 102, 167
– over 451, 847
brooding
preparing 673
brook stream 348
bear 821, 826
broom 652
broth 298
brothel 961
brother kin 11
similar 17
equal 27
brotherhood 712
brotherly
friendship 888
love 897
benevolence 906
brougham 272
brought to bed 161
brouillerie 713
brouillon 626
brow top 210
edge 231
front 234
browbeat
intimidate 860
swagger 885
disrespect 929
–en humbled 879
brown 433
– Bess 727
– study 451, 458
Brown, Jones and Robinson 876
brownie 980
browse 298
bruin 895
bruise powder 330
hurt 619
injure 649
blemish 848
bruiser 726
bruit
report 531, 532
brumal 126, 383
brumous 353
Brummagem 545
brunette 433
brunt beginning 66
impulse 276
bear the –
difficulty 704
defence 717
endure 821, 826
brush rough 256
rapid motion 274
graze 379
clean 652
fight 720
paint – 556
– away reject 297
abrogate 756
– up clean 652
furbish 658
prepare 673
brushwood 367
brusque violent 173
haste 684
discourtesy 895
brutal vulgar 851
rude 895
savage 907
brutalize
[see brutal]
corrupt 659
deaden 823
vice 945
brute animal 366
rude 895
maleficent 913
– force
strength 159
violence 173
animal 450a
severe 739
compulsion 744
lawless 964
– matter 316, 358
Brute, et tu 917
brutish [see brute]
vulgar 851
ignoble 876
intemperate 954
brutum fulmen
impotent 158
failure 732
lax 738
boast 884
bubble
unsubstantial 4
transient 111
little 193
convexity 250
light 320
water 348
air 353
error 495
deceit 545
trifle 643
– burst
fall short 304
disappoint 509
fail 732
– reputation 873
– and squeak 298
– up agitation 315
buccaneer 791, 792
bucentaur 273
Bucephalus 271
buck stag 366
male 373
wash 652
money 800
fop 854
– basket 191
– jump 309
– up 684
bucket 191
kick the – 360
drop – in empty well 645
like –s in well 314
buckle tie 43
fastening 45
distort 243
curl 248
– on one's armor 673
– to 604, 686
– with grapple 720
buckler 717
buckram 855, 878
men in – 549
bucolic
pastoral 370
poem 597
bud 367
beginning 66
germ 153
expand 194
graft 300
– from 154
Buddha 979, 986
Buddhism 984
budding young 127
buddy 711, 890
budge 264
budget heap 72
bag 191
store 636
finance 811
– of news 532
buff 436
blind man's – 840
native – 226
buffer
hindrance 706
defence 717
buffet 191
strike 276
agitate 315
evil 619
bad 649
affront 900
smite 972
– the waves 704,

708
bar 189
buffo 599
buffoon *actor* 599
humorist 844
butt 857
buffoonery 840, 842
bug 653
bugaboo 669, 860
bugbear
imaginary 155
bane 663
alarm 669
fear 860
buggy 272
bugle
instrument 417
war-cry 722
ornament 847
– call 550, 741
build *construct* 161
form 240
– anew 658
– upon a rock 150
– up *compose* 54
– upon *belief* 484
builder 626, 690
building material 635
buildings 189
built on *basis* 211
bulb 249, 250
bulge 250
bulk 50, 192
– large 31
bulkhead 228, 706
bull *animal* 366
male 373
error 495
absurdity 497
solecism 568
police 664
ordinance 741
– in a china shop 59
like a – at a gate 173
take the – by the horns 604, 861
Bull, John – 188
bullcalf 501
bulldog *animal* 366
pluck 604, 604*a*
courage 861
bulldoze 885
bullet *ball* 249
arms 727
missile 284
bulletin 532, 592
– board 551
bullfight 720
bullhead 501
bullion 800
bullseye *centre* 222
lantern 423
aim 620
bully *fighter* 726
maltreat 830
frighten 860
courage 861
rashness 863
bluster 885
blusterer 887
threaten 909
evil doer 913
bad man 949
bulrush
worthless 643
bulwark 706, 717
bum 876
bumbailiff 965
bumbledom 737, 965
bumboat 273
bump 250, 276
– off 361
bumper 52
bumpkin 876
bumptious
proud 878
insolent 885
contemptuous 930
bun 298
bunch *collection* 72
protuberance 250
– light 599
bunchbacked 243
Buncombe
[*see* bunkum]
Bund 712
bundle *packet* 72
go 266
– on 275, 684
– out 297
bung 263
– up 261
bungalow 189
bungle 59, 699
bungler 701
bunion 259
bunk 186, 215
bunker 181
bunkie 890
bunkum *lie* 544
style 577
boast 884
flattery 933
bunting 550
buoy *raise* 307
float 320
hope 858
buoyant
floating 305
light 320
elastic 325
prosperous 734
cheerful 836
hopeful 858
bur *clinging* 46
sharp 253
rough 256
in engraving 558
burden *lading* 190
weight 319
melody 413
poetry 597
too much 641
clog 706
oppress 828
care 830
– the memory 505
– of a song
repetition 104
burdensome
[*see* burden]
hurtful 649
laboring 686
bureau *chest* 191
office 691
shop 799
tribunal 960
bureaucracy 737
bureaucrat 694
burgee 550
burgeon
[*see* bourgeon]
burgess 188
burgh 189
burgher 188
burghmote 966
burglar 792
– alarm 669
burglary 791
burgomaster 745
burgrave 745
burial 363
buried *deep* 208
imbedded 229
hidden 528
– in a napkin 460
– in oblivion 506
burin 558
burke 361
burlesque
imitation 19
travesty 21
absurdity 497
misrepresent 555
drama 599
comic 853
ridicule 856
burletta 599
burly 192
burn *near* 197
rivulet 348
hot 382
consume 384
near the truth 480*a*
excited 825
love 897
punish 972
– the candle at both ends
waste 638
exertion 686
prodigal 818
– daylight 683
– one's bridges 604
– one's fingers 699
– in 384
– out 385
– to 865
burner 423
burning [*see* burn]
passion 821
angry 900
– glass 445
– with curiosity 455
– pain 378
– shame 874
burnish *polish* 255
shine 420
beautify 845
burnous 225
burnt [*see* burn]
red 434
– offering 952, 990
burr 410
burrock 706
burrow *lodge* 184
excavate 252
bursar 801
bursary 802
burst *disjoin* 44
instantaneous 113
explosion 173
brittle 328
sound 406
paroxysm 825
bubble –
disclosure 529
all over 729
ready to –
replete 641
excited 824
– of anger 900
– away 623
– of eloquence 582
– of envy 921
– into a flame 825
– forth *begin* 66
expand 194
be seen 446
–ing with health 654
– with grief 839
– in 294
– of laughter 838
– out 295
– upon *arrive* 292
unexpected 508
– into tears 839
burthen
[*see* burden]
bury *enclose* 229
inter 363
conceal 528
– the hatchet 918
– one's talent 528
busboy 746
busby 225
bush *branch* 51
jungle 344
shrub 367
beat about the – 629
bushel *much* 31
multitude 102
receptacle 191
size 192
hid under a – 460
not hide light under a – 878
bush-fighting 720
bushing 224
bushranger 792
bushy 256
business *event* 151
topic 454
occupation 625
commerce 794
full of – 682
man of –
proficient 700
consignee 758
mind one's –
incurious 456
attentive 457
careful 459
let alone 748
send about one's – 297
stage – 599
business-like
orderly 58
business 625
active 682
practical 692
skilful 698
buskin *dress* 225
drama 599
buss *boat* 273
courtesy 894
endearment 902
bust 554
bustle *energy* 171
dress 225
agitation 315
activity 682
haste 684
difficulty 704
bustling
[*see* bustle]
eventful 151
busy 682
busybody 532, 682
but
on the other hand 30
except 83
limit 233
qualifying 469
– now 118
butcher *kill* 361
provisions 637
evil-doer 913
butler 746
butt *cask* 191
push 276
aim 620
attack 716
laughing-stock 857
– in 294, 682
– end 67
butte 206
butter 357
flattery 933
– bread on both sides 641
– not melt in mouth 894
buttered *side*
know – *skill* 698
selfish 943
not know – 699
butter-fingers 701
butterfly
variegated 440
fickle 605
beauty 845
gaudy 882
break – on wheel
waste 638
spite 907
butter-scotch 396
buttery 636
buttock 235
button *fasten* 43
fastening 45
little 193
hanging 214
knob 250
trifle 643
take by the – 586
– hole 586
– up *close* 261
restrain 751
– up one's pockets 808
buttoned-up
reserved 528
buttonholder 841
buttons *page* 746
button-top
useless 645
buttress
strengthen 159
support 215
defence 717
butyraceous 355
buxom 836
buy 795
– a pig in a poke 621
– and sell 794
buzz *hiss* 409
insect cry 412

publish 531
news 532
buzzard *fool* 501
blind as a – 442
between hawk and –
agitation 315
worry 315
by *alongside* 236
instrumental 631
go – *pass* 303
– air mail 684
– and by 121, 132
– the card 82
– the hour &c. *hire* 788
– itself 87
– means of 632
– no means 32
have – one 637, 777
– my troth &c. 535
– the way
à propos 9
beside the purpose 10
parenthetical 134
– wire 684
– wireless 684
bye *departure* 293
sequestered 893
bygone 122, 506
let –s be bygones 918
by-law 963
by-name 565
by-path 279
by-play 527, 550
byre 189
byssus 256
bystander 197, 444
byway 627
by word
maxim 496
cant term 563, 564
reproach 574
contempt 930

C

C 3 160
cab 272
cabal *plan* 626
confederacy 712
cabala 526, 993
cabalistic 528, 992
cabaret 599
cabasset 717
cabbage 791
caber, tossing the – 840
cabin 189, 191
cabined, cribbed, confined 751
cabinet
photograph 554
receptacle 191
workshop 691
council 696
– picture 556
cabin plane 273
cable 45, 205
news 531, 532
slip – 623
telegraphic – 534
cabman 268, 694
caboose 386
cabriolet 272
cacation 299
cache 636
cachet 530
lettre de – 751
cachexy 160, 655
cachinnation 838
cacique 745
cackle *of geese* 412
chatter 584
talk 588
laugh 838
cacodemon 980
cacoëthes 613, 865
– loquendi 584
– scribendi 590
cacography 590
caconym 563
cacophony
stridor 410
discord 414
style 579
Cacus 792
den of – 791
cad *servant* 746
vulgar 851
plebeian 876
cadastre 86, 466
cadaverous
corpse 362
pale 429
hideous 846
caddie 746
caddy 191
cadeau 784
cadence *pace* 264
fall 306
sound 402
music 415
cadenza 415
cadet *junior* 129
soldier 726
officer 745
cadge 765
cadger *idler* 683
beggar 767
huckster 797
cadi 967
cadit quaestio 479
cadmium 439
cadre 726
caduceus 993
caducity
fugacity 111
age 128
impotence 158
decay 659
Caesar 745
aut – aut nullus
ambition 865
fame 873
caesura
disjunction 44
discontinuity 70
cessation 142
interval 198
caetera desunt 53
caeteris paribus 27
café 189
cafeteria 189
caftan 225
cage *receptacle* 191
restrain 751
prison 752
Cagliostro 548, 994
cahotage 59, 315
Cain 361
mark of – 550
raise – 825
caique 273
cairn 363, 550
caisse
grand – 417
caisson 191
caitiff *churl* 876
ruffian 913
villain 949
cajolery
imposition 544, 545
persuasion 615
flattery 933
cake *stick* 46
food 298
consolidate 321
sweet 396
– walk 840
calabash 191
calamity *evil* 619
adversity 735
suffering 830
calamo, currente – 590
calash *cap* 225
vehicle 272
calcedony 847
calcine 384
calcitrate 276
calculate
reckon 85
investigate 461
expect 507
intend 620
– upon 484
calculated
tending 176
premeditated 611
calculation
[*see* calculate]
caution 864
calculating [*ditto*]
prudent 498
– machine 85
calculus 85
caldron
convert 144
vessel 191
heat 386
laboratory 691
calèche 272
caleer 838
calefaction 384
calembour 520
calendar *list* 86
chronicle 114
record 551
calender 255
calenture 503, 655
calf *young* 129
give birth 161
leather 223
animals 366
fool 501
golden – 986, 991
Caliban 846
caliber *degree* 26
size 192
breadth 202
opening 260
intellectual capacity 498
calibrate 26
calidarium 356
calidity 382
caliginous 421
caliph 745
caliphate 737
calisthenics
training 537
beauty 845
caliver 727
calk 660
call *cry* 412
signal 550
name 504
motive 615
visit 892
sanctify 976
ordain 995
at one's – 682, 743
within – 197
– to account 932
– attention to 457
– to the bar 968
– into being 161
– of duty 926
– for *require* 630
order 741
ask 765
– forth
resort to 677
excite 824
– in *advice* 695
– to mind 505
– to the ministry 996
– names 929, 932
– into notice 525
– off the attention 458
– to order 741
– out *cry* 411
challenge 715
– over *number* 85
– into play 677
– in question 485
– the roll 85
– up 527
– up spirits 992
– to 586
– up *recollect* 505
motive 615
excite 824
– upon
demand 741
request 765
visit 892
duty 924, 926
– to witness 467
callæsthetics 845
callant 129
call-boy
theatre 599
called, so – 545
callidity 698
calligraphy 590
calling
business 625
Calliope 417, 597
callipers 466
callosity 323
callous 376, 823
callow *young* 127
infant 129
bare 226
unprepared 674
calm *physical* 174
quiet 265
dissuade 616
leisure 685
peace 721
moral 826
unamazed 871
– belief &c. 484
– before a storm 145
calmative 174
caloric 382
calorimeter 389
calote 999
calotype 556
caloyer 996
calumet *token* 550
– of peace 721, 723
calumniator 936
calumny 934
calvary 1000
Calvinism 984
calyx 191
cam 633
camarade 890
camaraderie 888, 892
camarilla 712
camarista 746
camber 250
cambist 797, 801
camboose 386
camel 271
swallow a – 608, 694
cameo *convex* 250
sculpture 557
camera 445, 553
in – 528
– lucida 445
– obscura 445
camerated 191
camilla 274
camisade 716
camisole 225
camorra 712
camouflage 530
camp *locate* 184
abode 189
military 728
– bed 215
– stool 215
campagna 180, 344
campaign 692, 722
campaigner 726
campaigning 266
campaniform 249, 252
campanile 206
campestrian 344
Campus Martius 728
can *power* 157
mug 191
preserve 670
jail 752
best one – 686
– it be! 870
canaille 876
canal *opening* 260
conduit 350
way 627
– boat 273
canard 532, 546
canary 366
cancan
dance 840
cancel
compensate 30
neutralize 179
obliterate 552
abrogate 756
repudiate 773
cancellated 219
cancelli 191
cancer *disease* 655

accuse 938
– comparison 648
cham 745
chamber *room* 191
council 696
mart 799
sick – 655
chamberlain 746
chambermaid 746
chameleon 149, 440
chamfer 259
chamois 309
champ 298
– the bit *disobedient* 742
chafe 825
angry 900
champagne 298
champaign 344
champain 874
Champ de Mars 728
champêtre, fête – 840
champion
best 648
auxiliary 711
defence 717
combatant 726
representative 759
sympathizer 914
championship 707
chance 156, 621
be one's – 151
game of – 840
great – 472
small – 473
stand a – 177, 470
take one's – 675
–s against one 665
whirligig of – 156
as – would have it 152
chancel 1000
chancellor
president 745
deputy 759
judge 967
– of the exchequer 801
chancery
court of – 966
– suit *delay* 133
chandelier 214, 423
chandelle, le jeu n'en vaut pas la – 638, 643
dear 814
chandler 797
change
alteration 140
mart 799
small coin 800
inter– 148
radical – 146
sudden – 146
– about 149
– color 821
– for 147
– hands 783
– of mind 607
– of opinion 485
– of place 264
changeableness 149, 605
changeful
fickle 607
changeling
substitute 147
fool 501
changeless 16
changer 797
channel
furrow 259
opening 260
conduit 350
way 627
chant *song* 415
sing 416
worship 990
chant du cygne 360
chanter 416
chanticleer 366
chantry 1000
chaomancy 511
chaos 59
chap *crack* 198
jaw 231
fellow 373
– book 593
chapel 1000
chaperon
accompany 88
watch 459
protect 664
chapfallen 878
chaplain 995, 996
chaplet *circle* 247
garland 550
trophy 733
ornament 847
chapman 797
chapter *part* 51
topic 454
book 593
council 696
church 995
– of accidents 156, 621
– house 1000
– and verse 467, 494
char *burn* 384
serve 746
char-à-banc 272
character
nature 5
state 7
class 75
oddity 83
letter 561
drama 599
disposition 820
reputation 873
characteristic
intrinsic 5
special 79
tendency 176
mark 550
characterize 564, 594
characterized 820
charade 533, 599
charcoal *fuel* 384, 388
black 431
drawing 556
charge *fill* 52
contents 190
business 625
requisition 630
direction 693
advice 695
precept 697
attack 716
order 741
custody 751
commission 755
bargain for 794
price 812
accusation 938
in – prisoner 754
justifiable – 937
take – of 664
take in – 751
– on *attribute* 155
– with 155, 777
chargé d'affaires 758
chargeable *debt* 806
– on *duty* 926
charger
carrier 271
fighter 726
Charing Cross, proclaim at – 531
chariot 272
drag at one's – wheels 749
charioteer 268, 694
charity *give* 784
liberal 816
beneficent 906
pity 914
Christian – 906
cold as – 823
– that begins at home 943
charivari 404, 407
charlatan
ignoramus 493
imposter 548
mountebank 844
boaster 884
charlatanism
ignorance 491
falsehood 544
affectation 855
Charles's wain 318
Charleston 840
Charley 753
charm *motive* 615
please 829
beauty 845
love 897
conjure 992
spell 993
bear a –ed life 644, 734
charmer 994
voice of the – 933
not listen to voice of – 604
charnel-house 363
Charon 982
chart 527, 554
charter
commission 755
permit 760
compact 769
security 771
privilege 924
chartered
legal 963
– accountant 801, 811
– libertine 962
Chartist 742
charwoman 690, 746
chary
economical 817
stingy 819
cautious 864
Charybdis 312, 665
chase *emboss* 250
furrow 259
drive away 289
killing 361
forest 367
pursue 622
ornament 847
wild goose – 645
chaser 559
chasm *interval* 198
opening 260
chassé 840
chassemarée 273
chassepot 727
chasser 297
– balancer 605
chasseur 726
chassis 215
chaste
shapely 242
language 576, 578
simple 849
good taste 850
pure 960
chasten
moderate 174
punish 972
chastened
subdued spirit 826
penitent 950
chastise 932, 972
– with scorpions 739
chasuble 999
chat 588
chat qui dort 667, 668
château 189
– en Espagne 858
chatelaine 847
chatoyant 440
chattels 633, 780
chatter 314, 584
chatterbox 584
chattering of teeth
cold 383
chatty 584, 892
chauffeur 268
chaunt
song 415
sing 416
worship 990
chaussé 225
Chauvinism 884, 885
chawbacon 876
cheap 643, 815
hold – 930
– jack 797
cheapen *haggle* 794
begrudge 819
cheapness 815
cheat 545, 548
check
numerical 85
stop 142
moderate 174
counteract 179
slacken 275
plaid 440
experiment 463
measure 466
evidence 468
ticket 550
dissuade 616
hinder 706
misfortune 735
restrain 751
money order 800
– the growth 201
– oneself 826
checkered 149
checkers 440, 840
checkmate
stop 142
success 731
failure 732
check-roll 86
check-string
pull the – 142
cheek *side* 236
impertinence 885
– by jowl *with* 88
near 197
cheeks *dual* 89
cheep 412
cheer *repast* 298
cry 411
aid 707
pleasure 827
relief 834
mirth 836
rejoicing 838
amusement 840
courage 861
sociality 892
welcome 894
applaud 931
good – *hope* 858
high living 957
cheerfulness 836
cheerless 830, 837
cheeseparings
remains 40
dirt 653
economy 817
chef de cuisine
proficient 700
servant 746
chef-d'oeuvre 648, 698
cheka 696
chemin
– de fer
game 840
– faisant 270
chemise 225
chemist 662
Chemistry 144
organic – 357
cheque 800
chequer 440
– roll 86
cherchez la femme 155
chère amie 962
cherish *aid* 707
love 897
endearment 902
– a belief 484
– feelings &c. 821
– an idea &c. 451
cherry
– red 434
two bites of a –
overrate 482
roundabout 629
clumsy 699
cherry-cheeked 845
cherry-colored 434
cheroot 392
cherub 977
Cheshire cat 838

chess 840
chessboard 440
chest 191, 802
chestnut-color 433
cheval-de-bataille
plea 617
plan 626
vanity 880
cheval-glass 445
chevalier 875
– d'industrie 792
chevaux de frise
253, 717
chevron
angle 217
indication 550
badge 747
decoration 877
chew 298
– the cud 451
– tobacco 392
chiaroscuro
light 420
grey 432
painting 556
chiasma 43
chic 845, 882
chicane
sophistry 477
deceit 545
cunning 702
chicken 129, 366
– in every pot 733
count –s before
hatched 858,
863
tender **as a** – *soft*
324
sensitive 822
compassionate
914
chickenhearted 862
chide 932
chief *principal* 642
master 745
evidence in – 467
– constable 765
– part 31
Chief Justice 967
chiefdom 737
chieftain 745
chiffonnier 876
chiffonnière 191
chignon 225
chilblain 383
child
infant 129
offspring 167
fool 501
– of God 987
–'s play 643, 705
with – 161
childbirth 161
childhood 127
childish
credulous 486
foolish 499
feeble 575
– treble 581
childlike 703
chiliad 98
chill *cold* 383
render cold 385
indispose 616
– the spine 830,
860
chillies 393
Chiltern Hundreds
757
chime
repetition 104
roll 407
resonance 408
melody 413
– in with *agree* 23
conform 82
assent 488
concord 714
chimera 83, 515
chimney 260, 351
– corner 189
– pot 249
china 384, 557
China to Peru 180
chine 235
chinese white 430
chink *gap* 198
sound 408
money 800
chip *small* 32
detach 44
bit 51
reduce 195
– of the old block
similar 17
copy 21
offspring 167
chippy 962
Chirography 590
Chirology 550
Chiromancy 511
chirp
bird-note 412
sing 416
cheerful 836
rejoice 838
chirrup [*see* chirp]
chirurgery 662
chisel
fabricate 161
form 240
sharp 253
sculpture 557
chit 129, 193
chit-chat 588
chitterlings 221
chivalry *war* 722
tenure 777
courage 861
courtesy 894
philanthropy 910
honor 939
generosity 942
chlamys 225
chloroform 376, 823
chlorophyl 435
chlorotic 655
chock full 52
chocolate
food 298
color 433
choice *will* 600
election 609
excellent 648
absence of – **609a**
by – 600
– spirits 873
– of words 569
choir *sing* 416
church music 996
church 1000
– boy 996
– invisible 360,
977
choke *close* 261
stifle 361
redundant 641
hinder 706
–full *complete* 52
replete 639
–off 706
choler 900
choleric 901
choose 609
do what one –s 748
chop *disjoin* 44
change 140
– logic 476
– up 201
chopfallen 837
chopper 330
chopping
large 192
– sea 348
chops *mouth* 66
jaws 231
food 298
choral 415
chord 413
chore 625
choreography 840
chorister 416, 996
chorography 183
chorus
shout 411
song 415
singers 416
unanimity 488
poetry 597
opera 599
concord 714
– girl 599
chose
– in action 780
– in possession
777
chouse 545
choux gras, faire
ses – 377
chrestomathy 560
chrism 998
Christ 976
Church of – 893*a*
receive – 987
Christ-cross-row
561
christen 564, 998
Christendom 983*a*,
995
Christian 983*a*, 987
– charity 906
– science 662, 984
Christmas 138, 998
Christmas-box 784
chromatic
color 428
– scale *music* 413
chromato-pseudo-
blepsis 443
chromatrope 445
chrome 436
chromolithograph
558
chromosphere 318
chronic 110
chronicle
measure time 114
annals 551
chronicler 553
chronography
measure time 114
description 594
chronology 114
chronometry 114
Chrononhotontho-
logos 887
chrysalis 129
chrysoprase 847
chrysolite 847
perfection 650
chrysology 800
chubby 192
chuck *throw* 284
animal cry 412
– it 142
– under chin 902
chuck-farthing 621
chuckle
animal cry 412
laugh 838
exult 884
chuff 876
chum 711, 890
chunk 51
Church
infallible 474
orthodox 983*a*
Christendom 995
temple 1000
dignitaries of –
996
go to – 990
High –, Low – &c.
984
– of Christ 983*a*
– bell 550
– house 1000
churchdom **995**
churching 998
churchman 996
churchwarden 996
pipe 392
churchyard 363,
1000
– cough 655
churl *boor* 876
churlish
niggard 819
rude 895
sulky 901*a*
malevolent 907
churn 315, 352
chut! *silent* 403
taciturn 585
chute 348
chutney 393
chypre 400
cibarious 298
cicatrix 551
manet – 919
cicatrize 660
Cicero 582
cicerone 524, 527
ciceronian 578
cicisbeo 897
cicuration **370**
cider 298
cider squeezer 876
ci-devant 122
cigar 392
ci-git 363
cilia 205, 256
cimeter 727
Cimmerian 421
cinch 45
cincture 247
cinder
combustion 384
dirt 653
Cinderella
servant 746
commonalty 876
cinema 448, 599,
840
cinematograph 448
cinematographer
553
cinerary 363
cineration 384
cinereous 432
cingle 230
cinnabar 434
cinnamon 393, 433
cinque 98
cipher
unsubstantial 4
number 84
compute 85
zero 101
concealment 528
mark 550
letter 561
unimportant 643
writing in – 590
Circe 615, 994
–an cup 377, 954
circination 312
circle *region* 181
embrace 227
form 247
party 712
describe a – 311
great – sailing 628
– of acquaintance
892
– of the sciences
490
circlet 247
circling 248
circuit *region* 181
outline 230
winding 248
tour 266
indirect path 311
indirect course
629
circuition **311**
circuitous 279, 311
– method 629
circular *round* 247
publication 531
letter 592
pamphlet 593
– note 805
circularity **247**
circularize 592
circulate
circuit 311
rotate 312
publish 531
circulating medium
800
circulation
[*see* circulate]
in – *news* 532
– of money 809
circumambient 227,
229, 311, 629
circumambulate
travel 266
go round 311, 629
circumaviate 311
circumbendibus
248, 629
circumcision 44,
998
circumduction 552
circumference 230
circumferential 227
circumflex 311

circumfluent
lie round 227
move round 311
circumforaneous
traveling 266
circuition 311
circumfuse 73
circumgyration 312
circumjacence 227
circumlocution 573
circumnavigate
navigation 267
circuition 311
circumrotation 312
circumscribe
surround 229
limit 233, 761
circumscription 229
circumspection
attention 457
care 459
caution 459
circumstance
phase 8
event 151
circumstances
property 780
bad – 804
depend on – 475
good – 803
under the – 8
circumstantial 8
– account 594
– evidence 467
probability 472
circumstantiality 459
circumstantiate 467
circumvallation
enclosure 229, 232
defence 717
line of – 233
circumvent
environ 227
move round 311
cheat 545
cunning 702
hinder 706
defeat 731
circumvest 225
circumvolution
winding 248
rotation 312
circus
buildings 189
drama 599
arena 728
amusement 840
cirrus 353
cistern
receptacle 191
store 636
Cistercian 996
cit 188
citadel 717
citation 467, 733
cite
quote as example 82
as evidence 467
summon 741
accuse 938
arraign 969
cithern 417
citizen 188
– of the world 910
citriculture 371
citrine 436
city 189
in the – 794
city manager 965
civet 400
civic 372
civil *courteous* 894
laity 997
– authorities 745
– crown 733
– law 963
– war 722
civilian *lawyer* 968
layman 997
civilization
improvement 658
fashion 852
courtesy 894
civilized life 852
civism 910
clack *clatter* 407
animal cry 412
talkative 584
clad 225
claim *requisition* 630
demand 741
property 780
right 924
lawsuit 969
– the attention 457
claimant
petitioner 767
right 924
clair-obscur 420
clairvoyance 992
clairvoyant 513, 994
clamant 411
clamber 305
clammy 352
clamor *cry* 411
wail 839
– against 932
– for 765
clamorous
[see clamor]
loud 404
excitable 825
clamp *fasten* 43
fastening 45
clan *race* 11
class 75
family 166
party 712
clandestine 528
clangor 404
clank 410
clannishness 481
clanship 709
clap *explosion* 406
applaud 931
thunder –
prodigy 872
– the hands
rejoice 838
– on 31
– on the shoulder 615
– together 43
– up *imprison* 751
clapperclaw
contention 720
censure 932
claptrap
pretence 546
display 882
claquer 935
faire – son fouet 884
clarence 272
claret color 434
clarify 652
clarinet 417
clarion *music* 417
war 722
clarity 518
clash *disagree* 24
cross 179
concussion 276
sound 406
oppose 708
discord 713
– of arms 720
clasp *fasten* 43
fastening 45
stick 46
come close 197
belt 230
embrace 902
class *arrange* 60
category 75
learners 541
party 712
– prejudice 481
– room 542
classic *old* 124
symmetry 242
classical
elegant writing 578
taste 850
– art 556
– dancing 840
– education 537
– music 415
classicist 492
classics 560
classify 60
classmate 890
clatter 404, 407
claudication
slowness 275
failure 732
clause *part* 51
passage 593
condition 770
clausis, janius – 528
claustral 110
clavate 250
clavichord 417
clavier 417
claw *hook* 781
grasp 789
– back 935
clay *soft* 324
earth 342
corpse 362
material 635
– pipe 392
clay-cold 383
claymore 727
clean
entirely 52
perfect 650
unstained 652
– bill of health 654
– breast
disclose 529
– forgotten 506
– hand
proficient 700
with – hands
honesty 939
innocence 946
– out *empty* 297
– shaven 226
– sweep
revolution 146
destruction 162
clean-up 775
clear *simple* 42
sound 413
light 420
transparent 425
visible 446
certain 474
intelligible 518
manifest 525
easy 705
liberate 750
profit 775
vindicate 937
innocent 946
acquit 975
all – 664, 705
coast – 664
get – off 671
keep – of 623
make – 529
– for action
prepare 673
– articulation 580
– conscience 946
– the course 302
– cut 518
– the ground
facilitate 705
– of *distant* 196
– off *pay* 807
– out *empty* 297
clean 652
– sighted
vision 441
shrewd 498
– sky *hope* 858
– stage
occasion 134
easy 705
right 922
– thinking 498
– the throat 297
– up *light* 420
intelligible 518
interpret 522
clearheaded 498
clear-obscure 420
cleat 45
cleavage
cutting 44
structure 329
cleave *sunder* 44
adhere 46
bisect 91
cleaver 253
cledge 342
clef 413
cleft *divided* 44
bisected 91
chink 198
in a – stick
difficulty 704
clem 956
clement
lenient 740
long-suffering 826
compassionate 914
clench *compact* 769
retain 781
take 789
clepe 564
clepsydra 114
clerestory 191, 1000
clergy 996
clerical 995, 996
– error 495
– staff 746
clerk *scholar* 492
recorder 553
writer 590
helper 711
servant 746
agent 758
clergy 996
articled – 541
– in holy orders 995
– of works 694
clerkship
commission 755
cleromancy 511
clever
intelligent 498
skilful 698
smart 842
too – by half 702
clew *ball* 249
interpretation 522
indication 550
seek a – 461
click 406
client
dependant 746
customer 795
clientship
subjection 749
cliff *height* 206
vertical 212
steep 217
land 342
climacteric 128
climate *region* 181
weather 338
fine – 656
climatology 338
climax
supremacy 33
summit 210
culmination 729
climb 305
– on the band-wagon 731
clime 181
clinal 217
clinch *fasten* 43
close 261
certify 474
pun 563
complete 729
clutch 781
snatch 789
– an argument 47
– the fist at 909
clincher 479
cling *adhere* 46
– to *near* 197
willing 602
persevere 604a
habit 613
observe 772
desire 865
love 897
– to hope 858
– to one another 709
clinic 662
clink
resonance 408
stridor 410

prison 752
clinker *brick* 384
dirt 653
clinometer
oblique 217
angle 244
clinquant
ornament 847
vulgar 851
Clio 594
clip *shorten* 201
– the wings
powerless 158
speed 264
slow 275
useless 645
hinder 706
prohibit 761
– one's words 583
clipper 273
clipping
small piece 51
clique *conclave* 696
party 712
cloaca *conduit* 350
foul 653
Cloacina 653
cloak *dress* 225
conceal 528
disguise 530
cloaked 223
cloche 371
clock 114
clockwork 633
by – *uniform* 16
order 58
regular 80
clod *lump* 192
earth 342
fool 501
bungler 701
clodhopper 876
clodpated
stupid 499
clog *shoe* 225
hinder 706
– dance 840
cloison 228
cloisonné 557
cloister *arcade* 189
way 627
restraint 751
convent 1000
close *similar* 17
tight 43
end 67
field 181
court 189
near 197
narrow 203
shut 261
dense 321
warm 382
hidden 528
concise 572
taciturn 585
complete 729
stingy 819
examine –ly 457
keep – *hide* 528
retain 781
tread – upon 281
– the door upon
restrain 751
– the ears 419
– the eyes
die 360
not see 442
– one's eyes to
not attend 458
set at naught 773
– at hand
to-morrow 121
imminent 152
near 197
– the hand
refuse 764
– in upon 290
– inquiry 461
–ly packed 72
– prisoner 754
– quarters 197
approach 286
attack 716
battle 722
– one's ranks 673
– study
thought 451
attention 457
– up 197, 290
– with *cohere* 46
assent 488
attack 716
contend 720
consent 762
compact 769
close-mouthed 585
closet
receptacle 191
ambush 530
closeted with
conference 588
advice 695
close-up 197
closure 142, 261
clot *solidify* 321
earth 342
cloth *vocation* 625
napkin 652
clergy 996
clothes 225
grave – 363
– basket 191
clothier 225
Clotho 601
clotpoll 501
clotted 352
cloud
assemblage 72
multitude 102
mist 353
shade 424
screen 520
break through the –s 446
drop from the –s 508
in a – 475, 528
in the –s
lofty 206
inattentive 458
dreaming 515
under a –
insane 503
adversity 735
disrepute 874
secluded 893
censured 932
accused 938
– burst 348
–capt 206
– of dust 330, 353
–s gathering
dark 421
danger 665
warning 668
– no bigger than a man's hand 668
– of skirmishers 726
– of smoke 353
– of words 573
clouded
variegated 440
dejected 837
hopeless 859
– perception 499
cloudiness 571
cloudland 515
cloudless
light 420
happy 827
cloudy *dim* 422, 426
clough 206
clout 276
cloven 91
cloven foot
mark 550
malevolence 907
vice 945
Satan 978
see the – 480*a*
show the – 907
clover
luxury 377
prosperity 734
comfort 827
clown
pantomime 599
bungler 702
buffoon 844
vulgar 851
rustic 876
cloy 641, 869
club
place of meeting 74
house 189
association 712
weapon 727
sociality 892
– law
compulsion 744
lawless 964
– together
co-operate 709
clubby 892
club car 272
clubfooted 243
cluck 412
clue 550
seek a – 461
clump
assemblage 72
projecting mass 250
– of trees 367
clumsy
unfit 647
awkward 699
ugly 846
Cluniac 996
clurichaune 980
cluster 72
clutch *retain* 781
seize 789
clutches 737
in the – of 749
clutter 407
coacervation 72
coach
carriage 272
teach 537
tutor 540, 673
– painter 540
– road 627
drive a – and six through 964
– up 539
coachhouse 191
coachman 268, 694
coaction 744
coadjutant 709
coadjutor 711
coadjuvancy 709
coagency 178, 709
coagmentation 72
coagulate
cohere 46
density 321
semi-liquid 352
coal 388
call over the –s 932
carry –s 879
– black 431
carry –s to Newcastle 641
coalesce
identity 13
combine 48
coalheaver
work like a – 686
coalition 43, 709, 712
coaming 232
coaptation 23
coarctation
decrease 36
contraction 195
narrow 203
impede 706
restraint 751
coarse *harsh* 410
dirty 653
unpolished 674
garish 846
vulgar 851
impure 961
– grain 329
coast *border* 231
slide 266
navigate 267
land 342
– defence 717
– line 230
coaster 273
coastguard 753
coat *layer* 204
paint 223
habit 225
cut – according to cloth 698
– of arms 550
– of mail 717
coating, inner – 224
coax *persuade* 615
endearment 902
flatter 933
cob *horse* 271
punish 972
cobalt 438
cobble *mend* 660
cobbler 225
cobbles 635
coble 273
cobra 913
cobweb *light* 320
fiction 545
flimsy 643
dirt 653
–s of antiquity 124
–s of sophistry 477
cocaine 376, 381, 663
cochineal 434
cock *bird* 366
male 373
game – 861
– boat 273
– and bull story 546
– the eye 441
– of the roost
best 648
master 745
– up *vertical* 212
convex 250
cockade *badge* 550
title 877
cock-a-hoop
gay 836
exulting 884
Cockaigne 827
cockatrice
monster 83
piercing eye 548
evil-doer 913
miscreant 949
cockcrow 125
cocked hat 225, 745
cocker *fold* 258
caress 902
Cocker
school book 542
according to – 82
cockle *fold* 258
– of one's heart 820
cockleshell 273
cockloft 191
cockney
Londoner 188
plebeian 876
cockpit *hold* 191
council 696
arena 728
cockshut
morning 125
evening 126
dusk 422
cock-sparrow 193
cocksure 484
cockswain 269
cocktail 298, 959
– party 892
cocoa 298
cocotte 962
coction 384
Cocytus 982
cod *shell* 223
coddle 902
– oneself 943
code *conceal* 528
precept 697
law 963
codex 593
codger 819
codicil *sequel* 65
testament 771
codify 60, 963
codlin 129
coefficient
factor 84
accompany 88

– to *insensible* 823
deafen *loud* 404
deafness 419
deal *much* 31
arrange 60
bargain 768
allot 786
– a blow
injure 659
attack 716
punish 972
– board 323
– in 794
– out *scatter* 73
give 784
– with
treat of 595
handle 692
barter 794
dealer 797
dealings *action* 680
have – with
trade 794
friendly 888
dean 128, 694, 996
deanery *office* 995
house 1000
dear
high-priced 814
loved 897
favorite 899
O – ! *lament* 839
– at any price 646
– me *wonder* 870
pay – for whistle 647
dearest foe 936
dearness 814
dearth 640
– of ideas 843
death 360
house of – 363
in at the
arrive 292
kill 361
persevere 604a
pale as –
colorless 429
fear 860
put to – 361, 972
still as – 265
violent – 361
be the – of one
amuse 480
–'s head 837
– in the pot
unhealthy 657
hidden danger 667
deathbed repentance 950
death-blow
end 67
killing 361
failure 732
death-house 752
deathless
perpetual 112
fame 873
deathlike
silent 403
hideous 846
death-song 839
death-struggle 720
death-warrant 971
death-watch 668
débâcle 145
destruction 162
downfall 306
torrent 348
debar *hinder* 706
restrain 751
prohibit 761
debark 292
debase *depress* 308
foul 653
deteriorate 659
degrade 874
debased
lowered 207
dishonored 940
debate *reason* 476
talk 588
hesitate 605
dispute 720
debatable 475
debauch
spoil 659
intemperance 954
impurity 961
debauchee 962
debenture
security 771
money 800
credit 805
debility 160
debit *debt* 806
accounts 811
debitor 806
débonnaire 836
debouch 293, 295
débris
fragments 51
crumbled 330
useless 645
debt 806
out of – 803
get out of – 807
– of nature 360
debtor 806
– and creditor 811
debunk 529
début *beginning* 66
essay 675
celebration 883
débutant
learner 541
drama 599
decade *ten* 98
period 108
decadence 659
decagon 244
decalescence 382
decalogue 926
decamp
go away 293
run away 623
decant 270
decanter 191
decapitate *kill* 361
punish 972
decay *decrease* 36
decompose 49
shrivel 195
unclean 653
disease 655
spoil 659
adversity 735
natural – 360
– of memory 506
decayed
[*see* decay]
old 124
rotten 160
decease 360
deceit
falsehood 544
deception 545
cunning 702
deceived
in error 495
duped 547
deceiver 548
gay – 962
decelerate 275
decennium 108
decent
mediocre 651
pure 960
decentralize 49
deceptio visûs 443
deception 545
deceptive reasoning 477
decession 293
dechristianize 989
decide
turn the scale 153
judge 480
choose 609
decided *great* 31
ended 67
certain 474
resolved 604
take a – step 609
deciduous
transitory 111
falling 306
spoiled 659
decies repetita placebit 829
decimal 84, 98, 99
decimate
subtract 38
tenth 99
few 103
weaken 160
kill 361
play havoc 659
punish 972
decipher 522
decision
judgment 480
resolution 604
intention 620
law case 969
decisive
certain 474
proof 478
commanding 741
take a – step 609
deck *floor* 211
beautify 847
declaim 531, 582
– against 932
declamatory
style 577
speech 582
declaration
affirmation 535
law pleadings 969
– of faith
belief 484
theology 983
– of war 713
declaratory
meaning 516
inform 527
declare
publish 531
declension
[*see* decline]
grammar 567
backsliding 988
declensions 5
declination
[*see* decline]
deviation 279
measurement 466
rejection 610
decline *decrease* 36
old 124
weaken 160
descent 306
grammar 567
be unwilling 603
reject 610
disease 655
become worse 659
adversity 735
refuse 764
– of day 126
– of life 128
declivity *slope* 217
descent 306
decoction 335, 384
decode 522
decollate 972
décolleté 226
decoloration 429
decomposition 49
deconsecrate 756
decontrol 158
décor 448, 599
decoration
insignia 747
ornament 847
title 877
decorative 556
decorous
[*see* decorum]
fashionable 862
proper 924
respectful 928
decorticate 226
decorum
fashion 852
duty 926
purity 960
décousu
discontinuous 70
failure 732
decoy *attract* 288
deceive 545
deceiver 548
entice 615
decrease 36, 195
decree
judgment 480
order 741
law 963, 969
decrement
decrease 36
thing deducted 40a
contraction 195
decrepit *old* 128
weak 158, 160
disease 655
decayed 659
decrepitate 406
decrescendo 36
decretal 741
decry *underrate* 483
censure 932
detract 934
decumbent 213
decuple 98
decursive 306
decurtation 201
decussation 219
dedecorous
disreputable 874
discourteous 895
dedicate *use* 677
inscribe 873
deduce *deduct* 38
infer 480
deducible
evidence 467
proof 478
deduct *retrench* 38
deprive 789
subtract 813
deduction
[*see* deduce]
decrement 40a
reasoning 476
deed *evidence* 467
record 551
act 680
security 771
–s of arms 720
– without a name 947
deem 484
deemster 967
deep *great* 31
profound 208
sea 341
sonorous 404
cunning 702
plough the – 267
– color 428
– in debt 806
– game 702
– knowledge 490
– mourning 839
– note 408
– potations 959
– reflection 451
– sense 821
– sigh 839
– study 457
in – water 704
deepen 35
deep-dyed
intense 171
black 431
vicious 945
deep-felt 821
deep-laid *plan* 626
deep-mouthed
resonant 408
bark 412
thrilling 821
deep-musing 458
deep-read 490
deep-rooted
stable 150
strong 159
belief 484
habit 613
affections 820
deep-sea 208
deep-seated 208, 221
deer 366
in heart a – 862
deev 980
deface
destroy form 241
obliterate 552
injure 659
render ugly 846
defalcation
incomplete 53
contraction 195
shortcoming 304
non-payment 808
defame *shame* 874

dolt 501
doltish 499
domain
  class 75
  region 181
  property 780
Domdaniel 982
dome *high* 206
  roof 223
  curvature 245
  convex 250
Domesday book
  list 86
  record 551
domesman 967
domestic
  inhabitant 188
  home 189
  interior 221
  servant 746
  secluded 893
  – animals 366
domesticate
  locate 184
  acclimatize 613
  – animals 370
domicile 189
domiciled 186
domiciliary 188
  – visit 461
dominant 175
  note in music 413
domination 737
dominical 998
domineer
  tyrannize 739
  insolence 885
Domini, anno – 106
Dominican 996
Dominie 540
dominion 181, 737
domino *dress* 225
  mask 530
  game 840
domn 745
don *put on* 225
  scholar 492
  teacher 540
  noble 875
Don Juan 897
donation 784
done *finished* 729
  work – 729
  – for *spoilt* 659
  failure 732
  – up
  impotent 158
  tired 688
  have – with
  cease 142
  relinquish 624
  disuse 678
donee 785
donjon 717, 752
donkey *ass* 271
  fool 501
  talk a –'s hind leg off 584
donna 374
Donnybrook Fair
  disorder 59
  discord 713
donor 784
donzel 746
doodle 501
doom *end* 67
  fate 152
  destruction 162
  death 360
  judgment 480
  necessity 601
  sentence 971
  – sealed
  death 360
  adversity 735
doomed 735, 828
doomsday
  end 67
  future 121
  till – 112
door *entrance* 66
  cover 223
  brink 231
  barrier 232
  opening 260
  passage 627
  at one's – 197
  beg from door to – 765
  bolt the – 666
  close the – upon 751
  death's – 360
  keep within –s 265
  lie at one's – 926
  lock the – 666
  open a – to *liable* 177
  open the – to
  receive 296
  facilitate 705
  permit 760
  show the – to
  eject 297
  discourtesy 895
  – mat 652
doorkeeper 263
doorway 260
dope 376, 545, 663
doquet
  security 771
Dorado, El – 803
Doric mode 413
dormant
  inert 172
  latent 526
  asleep 683
dormer 260
dormeuse 272
dormir debout, conte à – 843
dormitive 841
dormitory 191
dormouse 683
dorp 189
dorsal 235
dorser 191
dorsum 235, 250
dory 273
dose *quantity* 25
  part 51
  medicine 662
  apportion 786
dosser 191
dossier *bundle* 72
  record 551
dossil 223, 263
dot *small* 32
  place 182
  little 193
  variegate 440
  mark 550
  dowry 780
  on the – 113
dotage 128, 499
dotard 130, 501
dotation 784
dottle 40, 645
dote *drivel* 499, 503
  – upon 897
douanier 965
double
  similar 17
  increase 35
  duplex 90
  substitute 147
  fold 258
  turn 283
  finesse 702
  march at the – 274
  see –
  dim sight 443
  drunk 959
  –'acrostic
  letters 561
  wit 842
  – dutch 518
  - entry 811
  – the fist 909
  – march 684
  – meaning 520
  – a point 311
  in – quick time 274
  – reef topsails 664
  – sure 474
  work – tides 686
  – up
  render powerless 158
double bar 747
double-bass 417
doublecross 545
double-dealing
  lie 544
  cunning 940
double-distilled 171
double-dyed 428
double-eagle 800
double-edged 90, 171
double entendre
  ambiguity 520
  impure 961
double-faced
  lie 544
  cunning 702, 940
double-headed 90
double-minded 605
double-shotted 171
doublet 225
double-tongued
  lie 544
  cunning 702, 940
doubt
  uncertain 475
  disbelieve 485
  sceptic 989
doubtful 475
  more than – 473
  – meaning
  unintelligible 519
doubtless
  certain 474
  belief 484
  assent 488
douceur 784, 973
douche 337
dough 324, 354, 800
doughty 861
dour 739
douse
  immerse 310
  splash 337
  blow 972
Dove
  Holy Ghost 976
dove
  innocent 946
  roar like sucking – 174
dovecote 189
dovetail
  agree 23
  join 43
  intersect 219
  intervene 228
  angle 244
  insert 300
dowager 374, 905
dowdy 653, 851
dower 780, 803, 810
dowerless 804
down
  below 207
  light 320
  bear – upon 716
  bed of –
  pleasure 377
  repose 687
  come – 306
  get – 306
  go –
  sink 306
  calm 826
  keep – 36
  money – 807
  take –
  lower 308
  rebuff 874
  humble 879
  – on one's marrow-bones 886
  – in the mouth 837
  – and out 874
  – in price 815
  go – like a stone 310
  be – upon
  attack 716
  severe 739
downcast 306, 837
  – eyes 879
downfall
  destruction 162
  fall 306
  failure 732
  misfortune 735
downhill 217, 306
  go –
  adversity 735
downpour 348
downright
  absolute 31
  manifest 525
  sincere 703
downs 206, 344
down-trodden
  submission 725
  vanquished 732
  subject 749
  dejected 837
  disrepute 874
  contempt 930
downwards 306
downy
  smooth 255
  plumose 256
  soft 324
dowry 780, 784
dowse 276
dowser 994
doxology 990
doxy 897
doyer 128
doyley 652
doze 683
dozen 98
drab *color* 432
  slut 653
  hussy 962
drabble 653
drachm 319
Draco 694, 739
draff 653
draft [*see also* draught]
  multitude 102
  drawing 554, 556
  write 590
  abstract 596
  plan 626
  cheque 800
  credit 805
  – off *displace* 185
  transfer 270
draft-horse 271
drag *carriage* 272
  crawl 275
  traction 285
  impediment 706
  put on the – 275
  – a chain
  tedious 109, 110
  exertion 686
  subjection 749
  – into
  implicate 54
  compel 744
  – through mire
  disrepute 874
  disrespect 929
  – on *tedious* 110
  – into open day 531
  towards
  attract 288
  – slow length
  long 200
  weary 841
draggle 285, 653
  – tail 59
drag-net
  all sorts 78
dragoman 524
dragon *monster* 83
  violent 173
  animal 366
  irascible 901
dragonnade
  attack 716
  punish 972
dragoon
  soldier 726
  compel 744
  insolent 885
  worry 907
drain
  flow out 295
  empty 297
  dry 340
  conduit 350
  waste 638
  clean 652
  unclean 653
  exhaust 789
  dissipate 818
  – the cup
  drink 298
  drunken 959

– the cup of misery 828
– into 348
– pipe 249
– of resources 640
drake *male* 373
fire – 423
dram *drink* 298
pungent 392
stimulus 615
– drinking 959
drama 599
dramatic 599
ostentation 882
– author 599
– critic 599
– poetry 597
dramatis personæ
mankind 372
play 599
agents 690
party 712
drapery 225, 847
drast 645
drastic 171
draught
[*see also* draft]
depth 208
traction 285
drink 298
stream of air 349
delineation 554, 556
plan 626
physic 662
troops 726
– off 73
draughts
game 840
draughtsman
artist 559
draw *equality* 27
compose 54
pull 285
delineate 554, 556
– aside 279
– off the attention 458
– back
deduction 40*a*
regret 283
avoid 623
– breath
refresh 689
feeling 821
relief 834
– a cheque 800
– a curtain 424
– down 153
– forth 677
– from 810
– on futurity 132
– in one's horns
tergiversation 607
humility 879
– in 195
– an inference 480
– the line 465
– lots 621
– near *time* 121
approach 286
– off *eject* 297
hinder 706
take 789
– on *time* 121
event 151
induce 615
– out
protract 110
late 133
prolong 200
extract 301
discover 480*a*
exhibit 525
diffuse style 573
– over *induce* 615
– a parallel 9
– the pen through 552
– a picture 594
– profit 775
– and quarter 972
– the sword
attack 716
war 722
– the teeth of 158
– together
assemble 72
co-operate 709
– towards 288
– up *order* 58
stop 265
write 590
– up a statement 594
– upon *money* 800
– the veil 528
drawback *evil* 619
imperfection 651
hindrance 706
discount 813
drawbar 45
drawbridge
way 627
escape 671
raise the – 666
drawcansir 887
drawee 800
drawer
receptacle 191
artist 559
– of water 690
drawers
dress 225
drawhead 45
drawing
delineation 554, 556
prize 810
drawing-room
assembly 72
room 191
fashion 852
drawl *prolong* 200
creep 275
in speech 583
sluggish 683
drawn *equated* 27
– battle
– irresistibly 601
pacification 723
incomplete 730
dray 272
– horse 271
drayman 268
dread 860
dreadful *great* 31
bad 649
dire 830
depressing 837
fearful 860
dreadless 861
dreadnought
warship 726
dream
unsubstantial 4
error 495
fancy 515
sleep 683
golden – 858
– of *think* 451
intend 620
– on other things 458
dreamer
madman 504
imaginative 515
dreamy
unsubstantial 4
inattentive 458
sleepy 683
dreary
monotonous 16
solitary 87
melancholy 830, 837
dredge *collect* 72
extract 301
raise 307
dregs
remainder 40
refuse 645
dirt 653
– of the people 876
– of vice 945
drench *drink* 298
water 337
redundance 641
– with physic 662
drencher 248
drenching rain 348
dress
uniformity 16
agree 23
equalize 27
clothes 225
prepare 673
ornament 847
ostentation 882
full – 852
– circle 599
– the ground 371
– up *falsehood* 541
represent 554
– wounds 662
– to advantage 847
dress-coat 225
dresser
sideboard 215
surgeon 662
dressing 932, 972
– room 191, 599
dressing-gown 225
dressmaker 225
dribble 295, 348
driblet 25, 32
drift
accumulate 72
distance 196
motion 264
flying 267
float 267
transfer 270
direction 278
deviation 279
approach 286
wind 349
meaning 516
intention 620
snow – 383
drifter 273
drifting 605
driftless 621
drill *fabric* 219
bore 260
auger 262
teach 537
prepare 673
– hall 191
drink
swallow 296
liquor 298
tipple 959
– one's fill
enough 639
– in *imbibe* 296, 298
– in learning 539
– to *celebrate* 883
courtesy 894
drinking-bout 954
drink-money 784
drip 295, 348
dripping *wet* 330
fat 356
drive *airing* 266
impel 276
propel 284
break in 370
urge 615
haste 684
direct 693
attack 716
compel 744
– at *mean* 516
intend 620
– a bargain
barter 794
parsimony 819
– care away 836
– a coach and six through 83
– into a corner
difficult 704
hinder 706
defeat 731
subjection 749
– to despair 859
– matters to an extremity 604
– from *repel* 289
– one hard 716
– home 729
– in 300
– to the last 133
– out 297
– trade
business 625
barter 794
drivel *slobber* 297
imbecile 499
mad 503
rubbish 517
driveler 501, 584
driver 268
director 694
driving rain 348
drizzle 348
droil 683
droit du plus fort 744
drôle *cards* 840
drole 949
– de corps 844
drollery
amusement 840
wit 842
ridiculous 853
dromedary 271
drone *slow* 275
sound 407, 412, 413
inactive 683
drool 297
droop
weak 160
hang 214
sink 306
disease 655
decline 659
flag 688
sorrow 828
dejection 837
drop *small quantity* 32
discontinue 142
powerless 158
bring forth 161
spherule 249
emerge 295
fall 306
trickle 348
relinquish 624
discard 782
gallows 975
let – 308
ready to –
fatigue 688
– asleep 683
– astern 283
– from the couds 508
– dead 360
– by drop
by degrees 26
in parts 51
– in the bucket 32
– in upon 674
– into a good thing 734
– into the grave 360
– a hint 527
– all idea of 624
– in *arrive* 292
immerse 300
sociality 892
– the mask 529
– off *decrease* 36
die 360
sleep 683
– in the ocean
trifling 643
– the subject 458
– too much 959
dropping fire 70
drop-scene 599
dropsical 194, 641
droshki 272
dross
remainder 40
slag 384
trash 643, 645
dirt 653
drought
dryness 340
insufficiency 640
drouth *desire* 865
drove
assemblage 72
multitude 102
drover 370
drown
affusion 337
kill 361
ruin 731, 732
– care 840
– the voice 581
drowsy *slow* 275

sleepy 683
weary 841
drub
defeat 731, 732
punish 972
drudge *labour* 686
worker 682, 690
drug
render insensible 376
superfluity 641
trash 643
remedy 662
bane 663
– in the market 815
drugget
cover 223
clean 652
preserve 670
druggist 662
druid 996
drum
repeat 104
cylinder 249
sound 407
music 417
party 892
beat of –
signal 550
alarm 669
war 722
command **741**
parade 882
ear – 418
muffled –
funeral 363
non-resonance 408*a*
– and fife band 417
– fire 407
– out 972
drum-head 964, 966
drum-major 745
drummer 416
drunken 959
reel like a – man 315
drunkenness **959**
dry *arid* 340
style 575, 576, 579
hoarse 581
scanty 640
preserve 670
exhaust 789
tedious 841
dull 842
thirsty 865
cynical 932
teetotal 958
run – 640
with – eyes 823
– dock 189
– joke 842
– land 342
– the tears 834
– up 340, 638
dryad 979
dry-as-dust
antiquarian 122
dull 843
dryness **340**
dry-nurse
teach 537
teacher 540
aid 707
dry-point 558
dry-rot
dirt 653
decay 659
bane 663
dualism 984
duality **89**
duarchy 737
dub 564
dubious 475
ducat 800
duce 745
duchess 745, 875
duchy 181
duck *stoop* 308
plunge 310
water 337
darling 897, 899
play –s and drakes
recoil 277
prodigality 818
–'s egg
zero 101
– in thunder 870
ducking-stool 975
duckling 127
duck-pond 370
duct 350
ductile
elastic 323
flexible 324
trimming 607
easy 705
docile 743
dud 158, 727
dude 854
duds 225
dudgeon
dagger 727
discontent 832
churlishness 895
hate 898
anger 900
sullenness 901*a*
due
expedient 646
owing 806
proper 924, 926
give his – to
right 922
vindication 937
fair 939
in – course 109
occasion 134
– respect 928
– sense of 498
– time
soon 132
– to
cause and effect 154, 155
give – weight 465
duel 720
duelist 726
dueness **924**
duenna
teacher 540
guardian 664
keeper 753
dues 812
duet 415
duff 298
duffer
bungler 701
smuggler 792
dug 250
dug-out
old man 130
boat 273
defence 717
duke *ruler* 745
noble 875
dulce domum 189
dulcet
sweet 396
sound 405
melodious 413
agreeable 829
dulcify 174, 396
dulcimer 417
Dulcinea 897
dulcorate 396
dulia 990
dull *weak* 160
inert 172
moderate 174
blunt 254
insensible 376, 381
sound 405
dim 422
colorless 429
ignorant 493
stolid 499
style 575
inactive 683
unapt 699
callous 823
dejected 837
weary 841
prosing 843
simple 849
– of hearing 419
– sight 443
dullard 501
dullness **843**
duly 924
duma 696
dumb 581
– animal 366
– show 550
– waiter 307
strike –
ignorant 493
astonish 870
humble 879
dumbfounder
disappoint 509
silence 581
astonish 870
humble 879
dummy
substitute 147
impotent 158
speechless 581
inactive 683
dump *music* 415
store 636
lament 839
undersell 796
dumpling 298
dumps
discontent 832
dejection 837
sulk 901*a*
dumpy *little* 193
short 201
thick 202
dun *dim* 422
colorless 429
grey 432
importune 765
creditor 805
dunce
ignoramus 493
fool 501
dunderhead 501
dune 206
dung 653
dungeon 752
dunghill
dirt 653
cowardly 862
baseborn 876
– cock 366
Dunker 984
dunt 716
duo 415
duodecimal 99
duodecimo
little 193
book 593
duodenary 98
duologue
interlocution 588
drama 599
dupe
credulous 486
deceive 545
deceived **547**
duplex 90, 189
duplicate
imitate 19
copy 21
double 90
tally 550
record 551
redundant 641
pawn 805
duplication
imitation 19
doubling **90**
repetition 104
duplicature
fold 258
duplicity
duality 89
falsehood 544
dura lex sed lex 926
durable
long time 110
stable 150
durance 141, 751
in – 754
duration 106
contingent – **108a**
infinite – 112
durbar
conference 588
council 696
tribunal 966
duress
compulsion 744
restraint 751
during 106
– pleasure &c. 108*a*
durity 323
dusk
evening 126
half-light 422
dusky
dark 421
black 431
dust *levity* 320
powder 330
corpse 362
trash 643
dirt 653
money **800**
come to –
die 360
come down with the – 807
humbled in the – 879
kick up a – 885
level with the – 162
lick the –
submit **725**
fail 732
make to bite the – 731
turn to –
deorganized 358
die 360
– in the balance 643
throw – in the eyes
blind 442
deceive 545
plead 617
– one's jacket **972**
duster 652
dust-bin, dust-hole 191, 645
fit for the –
useless 645
dirty 653
spoilt 659
dustman
cleaner 652
dust-storm 330
dusty
powder 330
dirt 653
Dutch
double – 519
high – 519
– auction 796
– courage 862
Dutchman, flying 515
dutiful 944
duty
business 625
work 686
tax 812
courtesy 894
obligation **926**
respect 928
worship 990
rite 998
do one's –
virtue 944
on – 680, 682
duumvirate 737
Duval, Claude – 792
D.V. 470, 976
dwarf
lessen 36
small 193
elf 980
dwell
reside 186
abide 265
– upon
descant 573
dweller 188
dwelling 184, 189
dwindle *lessen* 36
shrink 195
dyad 89
dye 428
dying 360
dyke [*see* dike]
dynamic energy 157
dynamics 276

dynamitard 863
dynamite 727
dynamo 153
dynasty 737
dysentery 299
dyspepsia 655
dysphony 581

E

each 79
– to each 786
– other 12
– in his turn 148
eager
willing 602
active 682
ardent 821
desirous 865
– expectation 507
eagle
standard 550
money 800
– boat 726
– eye *sight* 441
intelligence 498
– winged *swift* 274
insignia 747
eagre 348
ean 161
ear 418
corn 154
come to one's –s 527
din in the –
loud 404
drum 407
all – 418
have the – of
belief 484
friendship 888
lend an –
hear 418
attend 457
meet the – 418
nice – 418
no – 419
offend the – 410
pick up the –s
attention 457
expectation 507
put about one's –s 308
quick – 418
reach one's –s 527
ring in the – 408
set by the –s
discord 713
hate 898
resentment 900
split the –s 404
together by the –s
discord 713
contention 720
up to one's –s
redundance 641
active 680, 682
willing – 602
word in the – 586
– for music 416, 418
in at one – out at the other
inattention 458
forget 506
not for –s polite 961
make the –s tingle
anger 900
– ache 378
ear-drum 418
earl 875
earless 419
earliness **132**
early 132
get up – 682
earmark 550
earn 775
earnest *willing* 602
determined 604
emphatic 642
pledge 771
pay in advance 809
eager 821
in –
affirmation 535
veracious 543
strenuous 682
ear-piercing 410
ear-ring 847
ear-shot 197
out of – 405
ear-splitting 404
earth *ground* 211
world 318
land 342
corpse 362
what on –
inquiry 461
wonder 870
– closet 653
earthenware
baked 384
sculpture 557
earthling 372
earthly 318
end of one's – career 360
of no – use 645
earthly-minded 943, 989
earthquake 146, 173
earthwork 717
earwig *flatter* 933, 935
ear-witness 467
ease *bodily* 377
style 578
leisure 685
facility 705
mental 827
content 831
at one's –
prosperous 734
mind at –
cheerful 836
set at – *relief* 834
take one's – 687
– off *deviate* 297
– one of *take* 789
easel *support* 215
painting 556
– picture 556
easement
property 780
relief 834
easily
[*see* easy]
let one down – 918
– accomplished 705
– deceived 486
– persuaded 602
East 236, 278
Easter *period* 138
rite 998
– Monday
holiday 840
– offering
gift 784
– sepulcher 1000
easy *gentle* 275
style 578
facile 705
make oneself – about 484
take it –
inactive 683
inexcitable 826
– ascent 217
– of belief 472
– chair
support 215
repose 687
– circumstances 803
– going
willing 602
irresolute 605
lenient 740
inexcitable 826
contented 831
indifferent 866
– sail
moderate 174
slow 275
– temper 894
– terms 705
– to understand 518
– virtue 961
eat *food* 298
tolerate 826
– dirt 725, 879
– one's fill
enough 639
gorge 957
– heartily 298
– one's words 879
– out of house and home *take* 789
prodigal 818
gluttony 957
– of the same trencher 892
– one's words 607
eatables 298
eaten up with 820
eau, battre l' – 645
faire venir l' – à la bouche 865
mettre de l' – dans son vin 174
eaves 250
eavesdropper 455, 527
eavesdropping 418, 532
ébauche 626
ebb *decrease* 36
contract 195
regress 283
recede 287
waste 638
spoil 659
low – 36
low 207
depression 308
insufficient 640
– and flow 314
– of life 360
ebb-tide *low* 207
dry 340
ebony 431
ebriety 959
ebullient
violent 173
hot 382
excited 824
ebullition
energy 171
violence 173
agitation 315
heating 384
excitation 825
anger 900
écarté 840
ecce
– iterum Crispinus 104
– signum 550
eccentric 220
irregular 83
foolish 499
crazed 503, 504
capricious 608
ecchymosis 299
ecclesiastic
church 995
clergy 996
ecclesiastical
canonical 985
– court 966
– law 963
ecclesiolatry 991
écervelé 458
échafaudage 673
échappée 840
échapper belle 671
échelon 279
echo *imitate* 19
copy 21
repeat 104
reflection 277
resonance 408
answer 462
assent 488
applaud to the – 931
awake –es 404
éclaircissement 522
éclat 873
eclectic 609
eclipse *surpass* 33
disappearance 449
hide 528
outshine 873, 874
partial – *dim* 422
total – *dark* 421
under an –
invisible 447
out of repute 874
ecliptic 318
eclogue 597
economic pressure 751
economy
order 58
conduct 692
frugality **817**
animal – 359
écorcher les oreilles 410
ecphorize 615
écru 433
ecstasis 683
ecstasy
frenzy 515
transport 821
rapture 827
ecstatic 829
ecstatica 994
ectoplasm 992
ectype 21
ecumenical 78
edacity 957
Edda 986
eddy
whirlpool 348
current 312
danger 667
edematous 194, 324
Eden 827
edge *energy* 171
height 206
brink **231**
sidle 279
advantage 731
cutting – 253
on – 256, 507
take the – off 174
– of hunger 865
– in 228
– one's way 282
edge-tools 253
play with – 863
edgewise 217
edging
obliquity 217
border 231
ornament 847
edible 298
edict 741
edification
building 161
teaching 537
learning 539
piety 987
edifice 161
edifying *good* 648
edile 965
edit
publication 531
condense 596
revise 658
edition, new – 658
editor 593
educate 537
educated 490
self – 490
education
teaching 537
knowledge 490
man of – 492
higher – 490
educational 537, 542
educe *extract* 301
discover 480a
educt 40
eduction 40*a*
edulcorate 396, 652
eel 248
wriggle like an – 315
eerie 860
efface
delete 162
disappear 449
obliterate 552
– from the memory 506
effect
consequence **154**
product 161
impression 375

complete 729
carry into – 692
with crushing – 162
in – 5
take – 731
to that – 516
effective
capable 157
useful 644
effectuation 729
expedient 646
effects 780, 798
effectual 731
effectually 52
effectuate 729
effeminate
weak 160
womenlike 374
timorous 862
sensual 954
effeminize 158
effendi 875
effervesce
energy 171
violence 173
agitate 315
bubble 353
excited 825
effervescent 338
effete *old* 128
weak 160
useless 645
spoiled 659
efficacious
[see efficient]
efficient
power 157
agency 170
utility 644
skill 698
effigy 21, 554
effleurer *skim* 207, 460
efflorescence 330
effluxion of time 109
effluence *egress* 295
flow 348
effluvium 334, 398
efflux 295
efformation 240
effort 686
effreet 980
effrontery 885
effulgence 420
effuse
pour out 295, 297
excrete 299
speech 582
loquacity 584
effusion of blood 361
effusive 573
eft 366
eftsoons 117
egad 535
égards 928
egesta 299
egestion 297
egg *beginning* 66
cause 153
food 298
walk among –s 704
too many –s in one basket
unskilful 699
(*imprudent* 863)
– and dart
ornament 847
– on 615
egg-shaped 247, 249
ego *intrinsic* 5
speciality 79
immaterial 317
non – 6
egocentrism 943
egotism
vanity 880
cynicism 911
selfishness 943
egregious
exceptional 83
absurd 497
exaggerated 549
important 642
egregiously 31, 33
egress 295
Egyptian darkness 421
eheu! fugaces labuntur anni 111
eiderdown 223
eidouranion 318
Eiffel tower 206
eight *number* 98
boat 273
representative 759
eisteddfod 72, 416
eighty 98
either *choice* 609
happy with – 605
ejaculate
propel 284
utter 580
ejection 185, 297
ejecta 299
ejector 349
eke *also* 37
– out *complete* 52
spin out 110
ekka 272
El Dorado 803
elaborate
improve 658
prepare 673
laborious 686
work out 729
elaine 356
élan 276
elapse 109, 122
elastic fluid 334
elasticity
power 157
strength 159
energy 171
spring 325
elate *cheer* 836
rejoice 838
hope 858
vain 880
boast 884
elbow *angle* 244
projection 250
push 276
at one's –
near 197
advice 695
lift one's –
drink 959
out at –s
undress 226
poor 804
disrepute 874
– one's way
progress 282
pursuit 622
active 682
elbow-chair 215
elbow-grease 331
elbow-room 180, 748
elder *older* 124
aged 128
veteran 130
clergy 996
elect *choose* 609
good 648
predestinate 976
pious 987
clergy 996
election
numerical 84
necessity 601
electioneering 609
elector 745
electorate 737
Electra complex 897
electric
swift 274
sensation 821
excitable 825
car 272
– blue 438
– chair 974
– light 423
– piano 417
electrician 599, 690
electricity 157, 388
electrify
unexpected 508
excite 824
astonish 870
electro-biology 992
electrocution 972
electrolier 214, 423
electrolyze 49
electro-magnetism 157
electromobile 272
electron 32
electronics 157
electroplate 223
electrotype 21, 591
electuary 662
eleemosynary 784
elegance
in style 578
beauty 845
taste 859
Bank of – 800
elegy *interment* 363
poetry 597
lament 839
element
component 56
beginning 66
cause 153
matter 316
in one's –
facility 705
content 831
devouring – 382
out of its – 195
elementary 42
– education 537
– school 542
elements
Eucharist 998
elench 477
elephant
large 192
carrier 271
white – *bane* 663
elevated
tipsy 959
elevation
height 206
vertical 212
raising 307
plan 554
– of style 574
improvement 658
glory 873
– of mind 942
angular – 244
élève 541
eleven 98
representative 759
eleventh hour
evening 126
late 133
opportune 134
elf *infant* 129
little 193
imp 980
elicit *cause* 153
draw out 301
discover 480a
manifest 525
eligible 646
Elijah's mantle 63
eliminant 299
eliminate
subduct 38
simplify 42
exclude 55
weed 103
extract 301
reject 610
elision 44, 201
élite *best* 648
distinguished 873
aristocratic 875
elixation 384
elixir 662
– of life 471
elk 223
ell 200
take an –
take 789
insolence 885
wrong 923
undue 925
selfish 943
ellipse 247
ellipsis *shorten* 201
style 572
ellipsoid 247, 249
elocation 185, 270
elocution 582
éloge 931
elongation 196, 200
elopement 623, 671
eloquence 572, 582
else 37
elsewhere 187
elucidate 522
elude
sophistry 477
avoid 623
escape 671
succeed 731
palter 773
elusive 545
elusory 546
elutriate 652
elysian 829, 981
Elysium 827, 981
elytron 223
Elzevir edition 193
emaciation 195, 203, 640
emanate 151
go out of 295
excrete 299
– from 544
emanation 398
emancipate
facilitate 705
free 748, 750
emasculate
impotent 158
embalm
interment 363
perfume 400
preserve 670
– in the memory 505
embankment
esplanade 189
refuge 666
fence 717
embar 229
embargo
stoppage 265
prohibition 761
exclusion 893
embark
transfer 270
depart 293
– in *begin* 66
engage in 676
embarquer sans biscuits, s' – 674
embarras de – choix 609
embarrass 641, 704, 706
embarrassed 804, 806
embarrassing 475
embase 659
embassy
errand 532
commission 755
consignee 758
embattled
arranged 60
leagued 712
war array 722
embed
locate 184
base 215
enclose 221
insert 300
embellish 847
embers 384
embezzle 791
embitter
deteriorate 659
aggravate 835
acerbate 900
emblazon
color 428
ornament 847
display 882
emblem 550, 747
embody
join 43
combine 48
form a whole 50
compose 54
embolden
hope 858
encourage 861

embolism 228, 261, 300
embonpoint 192
embosomed
lodged 184
interjacent 228
circumscribed 229
emboss *convex* 250
ornament 847
embouchure 260
embowel 297
embrace
cohere 46
compose 54
include 76
enclose 227
choose 609
take 789
friendship 888
sociality 892
courtesy 894
endearment 902
– an offer 760
embrangle 61
embranglement 713
embrasure 257, 260
embrocation 662
embroider
variegate 440
lie 544
ornament 847
embroidery
adjunct 39
exaggeration 549
embroil *derange* 61
discord 713
embroilment 59
embrown 433
embryo
beginning 66
cause 153
in – *destined* 152
preparing 673
embryology 357
embryonic 193, 674
embus 293
embusqué 603
emendation 658
emerald *green* 435
jewel 847
emerge 295, 446
emergency
circumstance 8
event 151
difficulty 704
emeritus 500, 928
emersion 295, 446
emery
sharpener 253
– paper
smooth 255
emetic *remedy* 662
émeute 742
emication 420
emigrant 57, 268
emigrate 266, 295
emigré 268, 295
eminence
height 206
fame 873
church dignitary 996
eminent domain 744
eminently 33
emir 745, 875
emissary
messenger 534
consignee 758
emission 297
emit *eject* 297
publish 531
voice 580
– vapour 336
Emmanuel 976
emmet 193
emollient 662
emolument
acquisition 775
receipt 810
remuneration 973
emotion 821
–al appeal 824
–al drama 599
empale 260, 972
empanel 86, 969
empathy 515
emperor 745
emphasis 580
emphatic 535, 642
emphatically 31
empierce
perforate 260
insert 300
empire 737, 789
– day 840
empiric 548
empirical 463, 675
empiricism 463
emplane 293
employ
business 625
use 677
servitude 749
commission 755
in one's – 746
– one's capital in 794
– oneself 680
– one's time in 625
employé
servant 746
agent 758
employer 795
empoison 659
emporium 799
empower
power 157
commission 755
accredit 759
permit 760
empress 745
empressement
activity 682
emotion 821
desire 865
emprise 676
emption 795
emptor 795
caveat – 769
empty *clear* 185
vacant 187
deflate 195
drain 297
ignorant 491
waste 638
deficient 640
useless 645
beggarly account of – boxes
poverty 804
– one's glass 298
– purse 804
– sound 517
– stomach 865
– title *name* 564
undue 925
– words 546
empty-handed 640
empty-headed 4, 491
empurple 437
empyrean *sky* 318
blissful 829
empyreuma 41
empyrosis 384
emulate *imitate* 19
goodness 648
rival 708
compete 720
glory 873
emulsion 352
emunctory 350
en – bloc 50
– masse 50
– passant
parenthetical 10
transient 111
à propos 134
– rapport 9
– règle *order* 58
conformity 82
– route
journey 266
progress 282
enable 157
enact *drama* 599
action 680
conduct 692
complete 729
order 741
law 963
enallage 521
enamel *coating* 223
painting 556
ornament 847
enameller 559
enamor 897
encage 751
encamp 184, 189
encampment 184
encaustic 556
enceinte
with child 161
region 181
inclosure 232
enchafe 830
enchain 751
enchant *please* 829
enchanted 827
enchanting 845, 897
enchantment
sorcery 992
enchase 43, 259
enchiridion 593
enchorial 188
encincture 229
encircle 76, 227, 311
enclave *close* 181
boundary 233
enclose 227, 229
enclosure
region 181
envelope 232
fence 752
encomiast 935
encomium 931
encompass 227, 233
–ed with difficulties 704
encore 104, 931
encounter
undergo 151
clash 276
meet 292
withstand 708
contest 720
– danger 665
– risk 621
encourage
animate 615
aid 707
comfort 834
hope 858
embolden 861
encroach
transcursion 303
do wrong 923
infringe 925
encumber 704, 706
encumbrance
clear of – 807
encyclical 531
encyclopedia 490, 593
walking – 700
encyclopedical
general 78
– knowledge 490
encysted 229
end
termination **67**
effect 154
object 620
at an – 142
come to its – 729
one's journey's – 292
on – 212
put an – to
destroy 162
kill 361
begin at the wrong – 699
– one's days 360
–s of the earth 196
– to end *space* 180
touching 199
length 200
– of life 360
– in smoke 732
– of one's tether
sophistry 477
ignorant 491
insufficient 640
difficult 704
endamage 649
endanger 665
endear 897
endearment **902**
endeavor
pursue 622
attempt 675
use one's best – 686
– after 620
endemic
special 79
interior 221
disease 657
endimanché 847, 882
endless
multitudinous 102
infinite 105
perpetual 112
endlessly 16
endlong 200
endocrine 221
endogenous 367
endorse
evidence 467
assent 488
compact 769
– *a bill* 800
approve 931
endorsement 550
endosmose 302
endow
confer power 157
endowed with
possessed of 777
endowment
intrinsic 5
power 157
talent 698
gift 784
endrogynous 83
endue 157
endure *time* 106
last 110
persist 143
continue 141
undergo 151
feel 821
submit to 826
unable to – 867
– for ever 112
– pain 828
enduring
indelible 505
endwise 212
enemy *time* 841
foe 891
the common – 978
thing devised by the – 546
– to society 891
energumen 504
energy *power* 157
strength 159
physical **171**
resolution 604
activity 682
enervate 158, 160
enfant, bon – 906
– gâté
prosperity 734
satiety 869
favorite 899
– perdu
hopeless 859
reckless 863
– terrible
curiosity 455
artless 703
object of fear 860
enfeeble 160
enfeoff 780, 783
Enfield rifle 727
enfilade
lengthwise 200
pierce 260
pass through 302
enfold 229
enforce *urge* 615
advise 695
compel 744
require 924
enfranchise
free 748
liberate 750
permit 760
enfranchised 924
engage
bespeak 132

induce 615
undertake 676
do battle 722
commission 755
promise 768
compact 769
I'll –
affirmation 535
– the attention 457
– with 720
engaged
marriage 903
be – 135
– in *attention* 457
engagement
business 625
battle 720
betrothal 902
engaging
pleasing 829
amiable 897
engender 161
engine 153, 633
engine-driver 268
engineer 690, 694, 726
engineering 633
engird 227
English 188
broken – 563
king's – 560
murder the king's – 568
plain –
intelligible 518
interpreted 522
style 576
– horn 417
engorge
swallow 296
gluttony 957
engorgement
too much 641
engrail 256
engrave
furrow 259
mark 550
– in the memory 505
engraver 559
engraving 21, 22, 558
engross *write* 590
possess 777
– the thoughts
thought 451
attention 457
engrossed in thought 451
engulf
destroy 162
plunge 310
swallow up 296
enhance
increase 35
improve 658
enharmonic 413
enigma
question 461
secret 533
enigmatic
uncertain 475
unintelligible 517
obscure 519
enigme, mot d' – 522
enjoin *advise* 695
command 741
prescribe 926
enjoy
physically 377
possess 777
morally 827
– health 654
– popularity 873
– a state 7
enkindle *heat* 384
excite 824
enlarge
increase 35
swell 194
in writing 573
liberate 750
– the mind 537
enlarged views 498
enlighten
illumine 420
inform 527
teach 537
enlightened
knowledge 490
enlist *engage* 615
war 722
commission 755
under the banners of 707
– into the service 677
enliven
delight 829
cheer 836
amuse 840
enmity 889
ennoble 873
ennui 841
enormity
crime 947
enormous *great* 31
big 192
number 102
enough *much* 31
no more! 142
sufficient 639
moderately 651
satiety 869
know when one has had – 953
– in all conscience 641
– to drive one mad 830
– and to spare 639
enounce 535, 580
enrage 830, 900
enragé 865
enrapture
excite 824
beatify 829
love 897
enraptured 827
enravish 829
enravished 827
enravishment 824
enrich
improve 658
wealth 803
ornament 847
enrobe 225
enroll *list* 86
record 551
– troops 722
commission 755
ens *essence* 1
Ens Entium 976
ensample 22
ensanguined 361
ensconce
conceal 528
safety 664
ensconced
located 184
ensemble 50
enshrine
circumscribe 229
repute 873
sanctify 987
– in the memory 505
ensiform 253
ensign
standard 550
officer 726
master 745
– of authority 747
ensilage 637
enslave 749
ensnare 545
ensue *follow* 63, 117
happen 151
ensure 474
entablature 210
entail *cause* 153
tie up property 781
entangle
interlink 43
derange 61
ravel 219
entrap 545
embroil 713
entangled
disorder 59
– by difficulties 704
entend, cela s' – 613
entente
agreement 23
alliance 714
friendship 888
enter *go in* 294
appear 446
note 551
accounts 811
– into the composition of 56
– into details
special 79
describe 594
– into an engagement 768
– into the feelings of 914
– into the ideas of
understand 518
concord 714
– in *converge* 290
– the lists
attack 716
contention 720
– the mind 451
– a profession 625
– into the spirit of
feel 821
delight 827
– upon 66
– into one's views 488
enterprise
pursuit 622
undertaking 676
commercial – 794
enterprising
active 171, 682
courageous 861
entertain
bear in mind 457
support 707
amuse 840
sociality 892
– doubts 485
– feeling 821
– an idea 451
– an opinion 484
entertainment 840
pleasure 377
repast 298
entêté 481, 606
enthral
subjection 749
restraint 751
enthrone 873
enthronement 755
enthusiasm
language 574
willingness 602
feeling 821
hope 858
love 897
enthusiast
madman 504
obstinate 606
active 682
enthusiastic
imaginative 515
sensitive 822
excitable 825
sanguine 858
enthymeme 476
entice 615
enticing 829
entire *whole* 50
complete 52
continuous 69
– horse 373
entirely *much* 31
entitle *name* 564
give a right 924
entity 1
entoil 545
entomb *inter* 363
imprison 751
Entomology 368
entourage 88, 183, 227
entozoon 193
entrails 221
entrammel 751
entrance
beginning 66
ingress 294
way 627
enrapture 827, 829
magic 992
give – to 296
entranced 515
entrancement 824
entrap 545
entrain 293
entre nous 528
entreat 765
entrée
reception 296
dish 298
give the – 296
have the – 294
– dish 191
entremet 298
entrepôt 636, 799
entrepreneur 599
entre-sol 191
entrust
commission 755
give 784
credit 805
entry *beginning* 66
ingress 294
record 551
entwine *join* 43
intersect 219
convolve 248
enucleate 522
enumerate 85
– among 76
enumeration 86
enunciate
inform 527
affirm 535
voice 580
envelop 225
envelope 223, 232
envenom
deprave 659
exasperate 835
hate 898
anger 900
envenomed
bad 649
insalubrious 657
painful 830
malevolent 907
– tongue 934
environ 227
environment 183
environs 197
in such and such – 183
envisage 515, 861
envoy
messenger 534
consignee 758
envy 921
enwrap 225
enzyme 320
Eolian harp 417
Eolus 349
eon 976
épanchement
manifest 525
artless 703
endearment 902
epact 641
épaulette
badge 550, 747
ornament 847
decoration 877
éperdu 824
épergne 191
ephemeral 111
ephemeris
calendar 114
record 551
book 593
Ephesian letters 993
ephialtes
physical pain 378
hindrance 706
mental pain 828
ephod 999
ephor 967
epic 594, 597
epicedium 839
epicene 81, 83
épicier 876
epicure
fastidious 868
sybarite 954a
glutton 957

etiology *causes* 155, 359
knowledge 490
disease 655
etiquette
custom 613
fashion 832
ceremony 882
étoile, à la belle –
out of doors 220
in the air 338
Eton jacket 225
étourderie
inattention 458
unskilfulness 699
etymological 560
etymology 562
etymon *origin* 153
verbal 562
Eucharist 998
euchology 998
euchre 840
eudiometer
air 338
salubrity 656
euge! 931
eugenics 658
eulogist 935
eulogize 482
eulogy 931
Eumenides *fury* 900
evil-doers 913
revenge 919
eunuch 158
eupepsia 654
euphemism
metaphor 521
style 577, 578
flattery 933
euphemist
man of taste 850
flatterer 935
euphony 413, 578
Euphrosyne 836
euphuism
metaphor 521
elegant style 577
affected style 579
affectation 855
Eurasian 41
eureka! 462, 480*a*
Euripus 343
Eurus 349
eurythmics 537, 840
eurythmy 242
Euterpe 416
euthanasia 360
euthenics 658
evacuate
quit 293
excrete 295
emit 297
evacuation 299
evade *sophistry* 477
avoid 623
not observe 773
exempt 927
evagation 279
evanescent
small 32
transient 111
little 193
disappearing 449
evangelical 983*a*, 985
Evangelists 985
evanid 160
evaporable 334
evaporate
unsubstantial 4
transient 111
vaporize 336
evaporation 340
evasion
sophistry 477
concealment 528
falsehood 544
untruth 546
avoidance 623
escape 671
cunning 702
non-observance 773
dereliction 927
eve 126
on the – of
transient 111
prior 116
future 121
evection 61
even
uniform 16
equal 27
still more 33
regular 138
level 213
straight 246
flat 251
smooth 255
although 469
in spite of 708
– course 628
– now 118
– so
for all that 30
yes 488
– temper 826
– terms 922
– tenor
uniform 16
order 58
continuity 58
pursue the – tenor
continue 143
avoid 623
business 625
be – with
retaliate 718
pay 807
get – with 972
even-handed 922, 939
evening 126
shades of – 422
– classes 537
– star 423
evenness 16
evensong 126, 990
event 151
bout 720
in the – of
circumstance 8
expectation 507
supposition 514
justified by the – 937
eventful 151
remarkable 642
stirring 682
eventide 126
eventual 121
eventuality 151
eventually
effect 154
ever 16, 112
did you – ? 870
– and anon 136
– changing 149
– recurring 104
ever so 31
– little 32
– long 110
– many 102
evergreen
continuous 69
lasting 110
always 112
fresh 123
everlasting 112
– life 152
– fire 982
evermore 112
eversion 218
evert 140
every 78
– hand against one 891
– day
conformity 82
frequent 136
habit 613
– description 81
– inch 50
in – mouth
assent 488
news 532
repute 873
– other 138
in – quarter 180
in – respect 494
on – side 227
at – turn 186
– whit 52
everybody 78
everyone 78
– his due 922
– in his turn 148
everywhere 180, 186
evict 297
evidence 467
disclose 529
ocular – 446
évidence, en – 446
evident
concrete 3
visible 446
certain 474
manifest 525
evidently 516
evil *harm* 619
badness 649
impious 988
– day
prepare for – 673
adversity 735
– eye *vision* 441
malevolence 907
disapprobation 932
demon 980
sorcery 992
spell 993
– favored 846
– fortune 735
– genius 980
– hour 135
– one 978
– plight 735
through – report &c. 604*a*
– star 649
evil-doer 913
evil-doing 945
evil-minded 907, 945
evil-speaking
malediction 908
censure 932
detraction 934
evince *show* 467
prove 478
disclose 529
eviscerate 297, 301
eviscerated 4
evoke *cause* 153
call upon 765
excite 824
evolution
numerical 85
production 161
motion 264
extraction 301
circuition 311
turning out 313
organization 357
training 673
action 680
military –s 722
evolve
discover 480*a*
evolved from 154
[*and see* evolution]
evulgate 531
evulsion 301
evivva! 931
ewe 366, 374
– lamb 366
ewer 191
ex
– animo 602
– cathedra 542
– officio 494, 924
– parte 467
– pede Herculem 82
– post facto 122, 133
– tempore
instant 113
occasion 134
exacerbate
increase 35
exasperate 173
aggravate 659, 835
exact *similar* 17
special 79
true 494
style 572
require 741
tax 812
insolence 885
claim 924, 926
– meaning 516
– memory 505
– observance 772
– truth 494
exacting
severe 739
discontented 832
grasping 865
fastidious 868
exaction
[*see* exact]
undue 925
exactly
just so 488
exaggeration
increase 35
expand 194
overestimate 482
magnify 549
misrepresent 555
exalt
increase 35
elevate 307
extol 931
– one's horn 873
exalté 504
tête –e 503
exalted *high* 206
repute 873
noble 875
magnanimous 942
examination
[*see* examine]
evidence 467
undergo – 461
examine 457, 461
example
pattern 22
instance 82
bad – 949
good – 948
make an – of 974
set a good – 944
exanimate
dead 360
supine 360
exarch 745
exasperate
exacerbate 173
aggravate 835
enrage 900
excavate 252
excecation 442
exceed *surpass* 33
remain 40
transgress 303
intemperance 954
excel *surpass* 33
– in *skilful* 698
excellence 648, 944
excellence, par – 642
excellency 877
excelsior 305
except *subduct* 38
exclude 55
reject 610
exception
unconformity 83
qualification 469
exemption 777*a*
disapproval 932
take –
qualify 469
resent 900
exceptionable
bad 649
guilty 947
exceptional
original 20
extraneous 57
unconformable 83
in an – degree 31
exceptious 901, 901*a*
exceptis excipiendis 469
excern 297
excerpt 609
excerpta *parts* 51
compendium 596

expose]
appearance 448
– to weather 338
expound
interpret 522
teach 537
expounder 524
express
rapid 274
squeeze out 301
mean 516
declare 525
inform 527
journal 531
intentional 620
by – *haste* 684
– train 272
– by words 566
expressed, well –
578
expressible 525
expression [*see*
express]
musical 416
aspect 448
nomenclature 564
phrase 566
mode of – 569
new fangled – 563
expressive
meaning 516
sensibility 822
exprobation 932,
938
expropriation 782
expugnable 665
expugnation 731
expulsion 55 [*see*
expel]
expunge 162, 552
expurgate 38, 652
expurgatorious,
index 761
exquisite
savory 394
excellent 648
pleasurable 829
beautiful 845
fop 854
exquisitely 31
exsiccate 340
exsudation 299
exsufflation 993
exsuscitate 824
extant 1
extasy [*see* ecstasy]
extemporaneous
[*see* extempore]
transient 111
extempore
instant 113
early 132
occasion 134
off-hand 612
unprepared 674
extend
expand 194
prolong 200
– to 196
extended 202
extensibility 324
extensile 324
extension [*see*
extend] 35, 142,
180
– of time 110
extensive 31, 180
– knowledge 490
extenso, in –
whole 50
diffuse 573
extent 26, 180
extenuate
decrease 36
weaken 160
excuse 937
extenuated 203
extenuating cir-
cumstances
469, 937
extenuatory 469
exteriority 220
exterminate 162
extermination 301
external 57, 220
– evidence 467
– senses 375
extinct
inexistent 2
past 122
destroyed 162
darkness 421
become – 4
extincteur 385
extinction of life
360
extinguish
destroy 162
blow out 385
darken 421
extinguisher 165
put an – upon
hinder 706
defeat 731
extirpate 301
extispicious 511
extol
over-estimate 482
praise 931
extort *extract* 301
compel 744
despoil 789
extorted
dissent 489
extortion 814, 819
extortionate 739,
865
extra 37, 599, 641
ab – 220
extract
draw off 297
take out 301
quotation 596
remedy 662
extraction 301
paternity 166
– of roots 85
extractor 301
extradition 270, 297
extrajudicial 964
extramundane 317
extramural 220
extraneous
extrinsic 6
not related 10
foreign 57
outside 220
extraneousness 57
extraordinary
great 31
exceptional 83
extraregarding 220
extravagant
inordinate 31
violent 173
absurd 497
foolish 499
fanciful 515
exaggerated 549
excessive 641
high-priced 814
prodigal 818
vulgar 851
ridiculous 853
extravagation 303
extravaganza
fanciful 515
drama 599
extravasate 295,
297
extreme
inordinate 31
end 67
– unction 998
extremis, in –
dying 360
difficulty 704
extremist 710
extremity *end* 67
adversity 735
tribulation 828
drive matters to
an – 604
at the last – 665
extricate
take out 301
deliver 672
facilitate 705
liberate 750
extrinsicality 6
extrinsic evidence
467
extrusion 297, 299
exuberant
- *style* 573
redundant 639
exudation 295, 299
exulcerate 659
exult 838, 884
exultant 858
exulting 836
exunge 356
exuviae 653
eye *circle* 247
opening 260
organ of sight 441
all my – and
Betty Martin
546
appear to one's
– 446
before one's –s
front 234
visible 446
manifest 525
cast the –s on
see 441
cast the –s over
attend to 457
catch the – 457
close the –s
blind 442
death 360
sleep 683
dry –s 823
fix the –s on 457
have an – to
attention 457
intention 620
desire 865
in one's –
visible 446
expectant 507
in the –s of
appearance 448
belief 484
keep an – upon
459
look with one's
own –s 459
make –'s at 441
mind's – 515
with moistened –s
839
open the –s to
480*a*
with open –s 870
set one's –s upon
865
shut one's –s to
inattention 458
permit 760
to the –s 448
under the –s of
186
up to one's –s
641
have one's –s
about one 459
– askance 860
–s draw straws 683
an – for an – 718,
919
– glistening 824
in the – of the law
963
– of the master
693
– of a needle 260
–s open
attention 457
care 459
intention 620
–s opened
disclosure 529
–s out 442
eye-ball 441
eyebrows 256
eyeglass 445
eyelashes 256
eyeless 442
eyelet 260
eyelid 223
eye-shade 443
eye-sight 441
eyesore 846, 848
eye-teeth
have cut one's –
adolescence 131
skill 698
cunning 702
eye-wash 544
eye-witness
spectator 444
evidence 467
eyot 346
eyre 966
eyry 189

F

Fabian policy
delay 133
inaction 681
caution 864
fable *error* 495
metaphor 521
fiction 546
description 590
fabric *state* 7
effect 154
texture 329
fabricate
composition 54
make 161
invent 515
falsify 544
fabrication *lie* 546
fabula narratur, de
te – *retaliate* 718
condemn 971
fabulist 594
fabulous
enormous 31
imaginary 515
untrue 546
exaggerated 549
faburden 413
façade 234
face *exterior* 220
covering 223
front 234
aspect 448
oppose 708
resist 719
brave 861
impudence 885
change the – of
146
fly in the – of
disobey 742
put a good – upon
sham 545
calm 826
cheerful 836
hope 858
pride 878
display 882
vindicate 93
in the – of
presence 186
opposite 708
look in the –
see 441
proud 878
make –s
distort 243
ugly 846
disrespect 929
on the – of
manifest 525
show –
present 186
visible 446
not show –
disreputable 874
bashful 879
to one's – 525
wry – 378
– about 279
set one's – against
708
– of the country
344
on the – of the
earth
space 180
world 318
– to face *front* 234
contraposition
237
manifest 525
– of the thing
appearance 448
facet 220
facetiae 842
facetious 842
facia 234
facile *willing* 602

irresolute 605
easy 705
facile princeps 33
facilis descensus Averni
sloping 217
danger 665
facilitate 705
facility *skill* 698
easy 705
facing *covering* 223
facinorous 945
façon de parler 521, 549
fac-simile 21, 554
fact *existence* 1
event 151
certainty 474
truth 494
in – 535
faction 712, 713
factious 24
factitious 545, 546
factor
numerical 84
director 694
consignee 758
factory 691
factotum
agent 690
manager 694
employé 758
facts *evidence* 467
summary of – 594
at variance with – 471
facula 420
faculties 450
in possession of one's – 502
faculty
power 157
profession 625
skill 698
facundity 582
fad 481, 608
faddle 683
fade *vanish* 4
transient 111
become old 124
droop 160
grow dim 422
lose color 429
disappear 449
spoil 659
– from the memory 506
fade 391
fadge 23
faex populi 876
fag *cigarette* 392
labor 686
fatigue 688
drudge 690, 746
– end
remainder 40
end 67
faggot 72, 388
fagots et fagots 15, 465
faïence 557
fail *droop* 160
shortcoming 304
be confuted 479
illness 655
not succeed 732
not observe 773
not pay 808
dereliction 927
failing [*see* fail]
incomplete 53
insufficient 640
vice 945
guilt 947
– heart 837
– luck 735
– memory 506
– sight 443
– strength 160
failure 732
heart – 360
fain *willing* 602
compulsive 744
wish 865
fainéant 683
faint
small in degree 32
impotent 158
weak 160
sound 405
dim 422
color 429
swoon 688
– heart *fear* 860
cowardice 862
damn with – praise 930, 932, 934
faintness 405
fair *in degree* 31
pale 429
white 430
wise 498
important 643
good 648
moderate 651
mart 799
beautiful 845
just 922
honorable 939
– chance 472
– copy *copy* 21
writing 590
– field
occasion 134
– game 857
by – means 631, 940
– name 873
– play 922, 923
– question 461
– sex 374
in a – way
tending 176
probable 472
convalescent 658
prosperous 734
hopeful 858
– weather 734
– weather sailor 701
– wind 705
– words 894
fairing 784
fairly
intrinsically 5
get on – 736
– well 643
fair-spoken
courtesy 894
flattery 933
fairy *fanciful* 515
fay 979
imp 980
– godmother 711, 784, 912
– tale 545, 594
fairy-land 515
fait: au –
knowledge 490
skilful 698
– accompli
certain 474
complete 729
faith *belief* 484
hope 858
honor 939
piety 987
declaration of – 983
bad – 544
i' – 535
keep – with
observe 772
plight –
promise 768
love 902
true –
orthodox 983a
want of –
incredulity 487
irreligious 989
– healing 662
faithful [*see* faith]
like 17
copy 21
exact 494
obedient 743
– memory 505
– to 772
faithless *false* 544
dishonorable 940
sceptical 989
fake 544, 545
fakir 996
falcate 244, 245
falchion 727
falciform
[*see* falcate]
falcon 792
falconet 727
faldstool 215
fall *autumn* 126
happen 151
perish 162
slope 217
regression 283
descend 306
die 360
fail 732
adversity 73
vice 945
let – *lower* 308
inform 527
water– 348
– asleep 683
– astern 235, 283
– away 105
– back *return* 283
recede 287
relapse 661
– back upon 677, 717
have to – back upon 637
– a cursing 908
– of the curtain 67
– into a custom 82
– of day 125
– dead 360
– into decay 659
– down 990
– down before 928
– upon the ear 418
– flat on the ear 843
– at one's feet 725
– foul of *blow* 276
hinder 706
oppose 708
discord 713
attack 716
contention 720
censure 932
– for 897
– to the ground
be confuted 479
fail 732
– into a habit 613
– from one's high estate
adversity 735
disrepute 874
– in *order* 58
continuity 69
event 151
– into
conversion 144
river 348
– in with *agree* 23
conform 82
converge 2
discover 480a
concord 714
consent 762
– on one's knees
submit 725
servile 886
gratitude 916
worship 990
– of the leaf 126
– from the lips 582
– in love with 897
– to one's lot
event 151
chance 156
receive 785
duty 926
– under one's notice 457
– into oblivion 506
– off *decrease* 36
deteriorate 659
– off again 661
– out *happen* 151
quarrel 713
enmity 889
– into a passion 900
– to pieces
disjunction 44
destruction 162
brittle 328
– a prey to 732, 749
– in price 815
– into raptures 827
– short *inferior* 32
contract 195
shortcoming 304
– of snow 383
– through *fail* 734
– to *eat* 298
take in hand 676
do battle 722
– into a trap 547
– under
inclusion 76
subjection 749
– upon
discover 480a
unexpected 508
devise 626
attack 716
– in the way of 186
– to work 686
fallacy *sophistry* 477
error 495
show the – of 497
fallen angel 949, 978
fallible 475, 477
falling-out 24
falling star 318, 423
fallow
unproductive 169
yellow 436
unready 674
inactive 681
false *imitation* 10
sophistry 477
error 495
untrue 544, 546
spurious 925
dishonorable 940
– alarm 669
– coloring
misinterpretation 523
falsehood 544
– construction 523, 544
– doctrine 984
– expectation 509
– hearted 940
– impression 495
– light *vision* 443
– money 800
– ornament 851
– plea *untruth* 546
plea 617
– position 704
– pretences 791
– prophet
disappoint 509
pseudo-revelation 986
– reasoning 477
– scent 495, 538
– shame 855
– statement 546
– step 732
– teaching 538
– witness
deceiver 548
detraction 934
falsehood 544, 546
falsetto *squeak* 410
want of voice 581
falsify *error* 495
falsehood 544, 546
– accounts 811
– one's hope 509
falter *slow* 275
stammer 583
hesitate 605
slip 732
hopeless 859
fear 860
faltering accents 605

unimportant 643
contempt 930
fiddlefaddle
unmeaning 517
trifle 643
dawdle 683
fiddler 416
fiddlestick 417
– end 643
fidelity
veracity 543
obedience 743
observance 772
honor 939
fidget *changes* 149
activity 682
hurry 684
excitability 825
fidgety
irresolute 605
fearful 860
irascible 901
fiducial 156
fiduciary 484
fidus Achates
auxiliary 711
associate 743
friend 890
fie *disreputable* 874
– upon it
censure 932
fief 777
field *opportunity* 134
scope 180
region 181
plain 344
agriculture 371
business 625
arena 728
property 780
the – *hunting* 622
beasts of the – 366
playing –s 728
the potter's – 361
take the – 722
– artillery 726
the – of blood 361
– of inquiry
topic 454
inquiry 461
– of view
vista 441
idea 453
field-day
contention 720
amusement 840
display 882
field-glass 445
field-marshal 745
field-piece 727
field-preacher 996
field-work 717
fiend 913, 980
fiend-like
malevolent 907
wicked 945
fiend 980
fierce *violent* 173
passion 825
daring 861
angry 900
fiery *violent* 173
hot 382
strong feeling 821
excitable 825
angry 900
irascible 901
– cross 550, 722
– furnace 386
– imagination 515
– ordeal 828
fife 417
fifer 416
fifth 98, 99
fifty 98
fig
unimportance 643
in the name of the prophet –s! 497
– out 847
fight
contention 720
warfare 722
show –
defence 717
courage 861
– one's battles again 594
– against destiny 606
– the good fight 944
– it out 722
– shy *avoid* 603, 623
coward 862
– one's way
pursue 622
active 682
exertion 686
fighter 726
fighting-cock 726, 861
fighting-man 726
figment 515
figurante 599
figurate number 84
figuration 240
figurative
metaphorical 521
representing 554
– *style* 577
figure
number 84
form 240
appearance 448
metaphor 521
indicate 550
represent 554
price 812
ugly 846
cut a –
repute 873
display 882
poor – 874
– to oneself 515
– of speech 521
– out 522
exaggeration 549
figure-flinger 994
figure-head 4, 550, 554, 643
figurine 554
figuriste 559
filaceous 205
filament 205
filamentous 256
filch 791
filcher 762
file *subduct* 38
arrange 60
row 69
assemblage 72
list 86
reduce 195
smooth 255
pulverize 330
record 551
store 636
soldiers 726
– a claim &c. 969
– off *march* 266
diverge 291
file-fire 716
filial 167
filiation
consanguinity 11
attribution 155
posterity 167
filibuster 133, 706, 792
filibustering 791
filiform 205
filigree 219
filings 330
fill *complete* 52
occupy 186
contents 190
stuff 224
provision 637
eat one's – 957
have one's –
enough 639
satiety 869
– the bill 229
– an office
business 625
government 737
– out
expand 194
–ed to overflowing 641
– one's pocket 803
– time 106
– up *compensate* 30
compose 54
close 261
restore 660
– up the time
inaction 681
fille
– de chambre 746
– de joie 962
filled
– to overflowing 641
filler 532
fillet *band* 45
filament 205
circle 247
insignia 550
ornament 847
fillibeg 225
filling 224
fillip
impulse 276
propulsion 284
stimulus 615
excite 824
filly 271
film *layer* 204
opaque 426
semitransparent 427
– over the eyes
dim sight 443
cinema 448
ignorant 491
filmy *texture* 329
filter *percolate* 295
clean 652
filth 653
–y lucre 800
filtrate 652
fimbriated 256
fin 267
final *ending* 67
conclusive 474
completing 729
court of – appeal 474
– cause 620
– stroke 729
– touch 729
finale *end* 67
completion 729
finality 67, 729
finally
for good 141
on the whole 476
finance 800, 811
minister of – 801
financier 801
finch 366
find
eventuality 151
adjudge 480
discover 480a
acquire 775
– one's account in 644
– the cause of 522
– a clue to 480a
– to one's cost 509
– credence 484
– it in one's heart 602
– in *provide* 637
– the key of 522
– the meaning 522
– means 632
– oneself *be* 1
present 186
– out 480a
– vent 671
– one's way 731
– one's way into 294
finding
judgment 480
fine *small* 32
large 192
thin 203
rare 322
not raining 340
exact 494
good 648
beautiful 845
adorned 847
proud 878
mulct 974
in – *end* 67
after all 476
– air 656
– arts 554
– feather 159, 654
– feeling 850
– frenzy 515
– gentleman
fop 854
proud 878
– grain 329
– lady 854, 878
one – morning 106
some – morning 119
– powder 330
– talking
overrate 482
boast 884
– writing 577
– time of it 734
– voice 580
fine-draw 660
fine-fingered 698
fine-spoken 894, 933
fine-spun *thin* 203
sophistry 477
fine-toned 413
finem, respicere – 510
finery 847, 851
finesse *tact* 698
artifice 702
taste 850
finger *touch* 379
hold 781
lay the – on
point out 457
discover 480a
lift a – 680
not lift a – 681
point the – at 457
turn round one's little – 737
–'s breadth 203
at one's –s' end
near 197
know 490
remember 505
– on the lips
aphony 581
taciturnity 585
– in the pie
cause 153
interfere 228
act 680
active 682
co-operate 709
fingerling 193
finger-post 550
finger-print 467
finger-stall 223
fingle-fangle 643
finical
trifling 643
affected 855
fastidious 868
finicky 855, 868
finikin 643
finis 67
– coronat opus 729
finish *end* 67
symmetry 242
complete 729
skill 698
finished
absolute 31
perfect 650
skilled 698
finishing
– stroke 361
– touch 729
finite 32
fiord 343
fire *energy* 171
heat 382
make hot 384
stoke 388
vigor 574
discharge 756
enthusiasm 821
excite 824, 825
catch – 384

foozle 732
fop 854
foppery 882
foppish 855
for *cause* 155
tendency 176
reason 476
motive 615
intention 620
preparation 673
have –
price 812
– all that
notwithstanding
30
qualification 469
– all the world
like 17
– aught one
knows 156
– better for worse
78
– ever 112
– example 82
– form's sake 82
– good
complete 52
diuturnity 110
permanence 141
– the most part
great 31
general 78
special 79
– the nonce 118
– nothing 815
– a season 106
– a time 111
– the time being
106
forage
food 298
provision 637
steal 791
forage-cap 225
foramen 260
foraminous 260
forasmuch as
relating to 9
cause 155
reason 476
motive 615
foray *attack* 716
robbery 791
forbear
avoid 623
spare 678
lenity 740
sufferance 826
pity 914
abstain 953
forbearance 918
forbid 761
God –
dissent 489
deprecation 766
censure 932
prayer 990
forbidden fruit
seduction 615
prohibition 761
forbidding
ugly 846
force *corps* 72
power 157
strength 159
agency 170
energy 171
violence 173
cultivate 371, 707
cascade 348
- *of style* 574
urge 615
exertion 686
compulsion 744
armed – 726
brute – 964
put in – 924
– of argument 476
– of arms 744
– of character 820
– down the throat
severe 739
compel 744
– majeure 744
– open 173
– one's way
progression 282
passage 302
forced *irrelative* 10
- *style* 579
be – to 601
– labor 603
– march 744
forcefully 601
forceps
extraction 301
grip 781
forces 726
forcible [*see* force]
ford 302, 627
fore 234
fore and aft
complete 52
lengthwise 200
– schooner 273
fore part 234
forearm 673
forebears 166
forebode 511
forecast
foresight 510
prediction 511
plan 626
foreclose 706
foredoom 152, 601
forefathers 166
forefend
prohibit 761
forefinger 379
forego
relinquish 624
renounce 757
surrender 782
foregoing 62, 116
foregone
past 122
– conclusion
prejudged 481
predetermined
611
foreground 234
in the –
manifest 525
forehead 234
foreign
alien 10
extraneous 57
– accent 580
– parts 196
foreigner 57
forejudge
prejudge 481
foresight 510
foreknow 510
foreland 206, 254
forelay 545
fore ock
pull the – 894
take time by the –
early 132
occasion 134
foreman 694
foremost
superior 33
beginning 66
front 234
in advance 280
important 642
reputed 873
forenoon 125
forensic 968
foreordain 152
foreordination 601,
611
forerun 62, 116, 280
forerunner 64, 512
foresee 507, 510
foreseen 871
foreshadow 152,
511
foreshorten 201
foreshow 511
foresight 116, 510
caution 864
forest 367
forestage 599
forestry 371
forestall
prior 116
early 132
possession 777
foretaste 510
foretell 511
forethought 459,
510
foretoken 511
forewarn 511, 668
foreword 64
forfeit *fail* 773
lose 776
penalty 974
– one's good
opinion 932
forfeiture
disfranchisement
925
forfend 706, 717
forgather 72
forge *imitate* 19
produce 161
furnace 386
trump up 544
workshop 691
– fetters 751
forged
false 546
forger
maker 690
thief 792
forgery
deception 545
forget 506
hand – cunning
699
– benefits 917
– injury 918
– oneself 945
forgive 918
forgo
relinquish 624
renounce 757
surrender 782
forgotten
past 122
ingratitude 917
not to be – 505
– by the world
893
fork *bifid* 91
pointed 244
– lightning 423
– out
give 784
pay 807
expenditure 809
forlorn
dejected 837
hopeless 859
deserted 893
– hope
danger 665
rashness 863
form *state* 7
likeness 21
make up 54
order 58
arrange 60
convert 144
produce 161
bench 215
shape 240
educate 537
pupils 541
manner 627
beauty 845
fashion 852
etiquette 882
law 963
rite 998
– letter 592
– part of 56
– a party 712
– a resolution 604
formal [*see* form]
regular 82
definitive 535
- *style* 579
affected 855
stately 882
– speech 582
formalism 739, 988
formalist 82
formality [*see*
formal]
ceremony 852
affectation 855
law 963
formation
composition 54
production 161
shape 240
formative 153
formed [*see* form]
attempered 820
former
in order 62
prior in time 116
past 122
formication 380
formidable 704, 860
formless 241
formula *rule* 80
arithmetic 84
maxim 496
precept 697
law 963
formulary 998
formulate 590
fornication 961
fornicator 962
foro conscientiæ
veracity 543
duty 926
probity 939
forsake 624
forsaken 898
forsooth 535
forspent 688
forswear *lie* 544
tergiversation 607
refuse 764
transgress 927
improbity 940
fort 666, 717
fort
le droit du plus –
compulsion 744
illegality 964
un peu – 641
fortalice 717
forte 415, 698
fortelage 717
forth 282
come –
egress 295
visible 446
go – *depart* 293
the decree has
gone – 741
forthcoming 152,
673
forthwith 132
fortification 717
fortify 159
fortiori, a – 467, 476
fortissimo 404
fortiter in re 171
fortitude 826, 861
fortnightly 138
fortress 717, 752
fortuitous
extrinsic 6
chance 156
undersigned 621
– concourse of
atoms 59
fortunate
opportune 134
successful 731
prosperous 734
Fortunatus's – cap
wish 865
spell 993
– purse 803
fortune *chance* 156
fate 601
wealth 803
be one's – 151
clean up a – 803
evil – 621, 735
good – 734
make one's –
succeed 731
wealth 803
tempt –
hazard 621
essay 675
trick of – 509
try one's – 675
wheel of – 601, 621
fortune-hunter 886,
943
fortuneless 804
fortune-teller 513
fortune-telling 511

candid – 936
next – 759
friendless 893
friendly 714, 894
friends, be – 888
see one's – 892
friendship 9, 888
frieze 210
frigate 726
fright
cards 840
alarm 860
frightful 31, 830, 846
frightfully 31
frightfulness 860
frigid
cold 383
- *style* 575
callous 823
indifferent 866
frigidarium 387
frigorific 385
frill 231, 248
frills and furbelows 847
fringe
border 231
lace 256
exaggeration 549
ornament 847
frippery
trifle 643
ornament 847
finery 851
ridiculous 853
ostentation 882
frisk *prance* 266
leap 309
search 461
gay 836
amusement 840
frisky 682, 836
frith *chasm* 198
strait 343
forest 367
fritinancy 412
fritter *small* 32
– away *lessen* 36
waste 638
– away time 683
fritters 298
frivolous
unreasonable 477
foolish 499
capricious 608
trivial 643
frizz *curve* 245, 248
fold 258
frock *dress* 225
canonicals 999
– coat 225
frog *fastening* 45
leaper 309
ornament 847
frolic 827, 840
frolicsome 836
from *motive* 615
– this cause 155
– day to day 106, 138
– end to end 52
– that time 117
– time immemorial 122
– time to time 136
frond 367
fronder
censure 932
frondeur
disobey 742
front *foremost* 66
wig 225
fore part 234
resist 719
insolence 885
bring to the –
manifest 525
come to the –
surpass 303
important 642
repute 873
in – 280
present a – 719
– danger 861
– to front 708
– of the house 599
– rank 234
in the – rank
important 642
repute 873
frontage 234
frontal 220
fronti nulla fides
doubt 485
deception 545
frontier 199, 233
fronting 237
frontispiece 64
frosh 541
frost 283
frosted 430
– glass 427
frostbite 383
froth
bubble 353
trifle 643
dirt 653
– up *angry* 900
frothy 320, 353
- *style* 573, 577
irresolute 605
frounce 258
frouzy 401
froward 901a
frown *lower* 837
scowl 839
discourteous 895
angry 900
sulky 901a
disapprove 932
– down
abash 879
–s of fortune 735
frozen 383, 385
fructify
produce 161
be productive 168
improve 658
prosper 734
frugal 817, 953
– to excess 819
fruges consumere natus *drone* 683
peasant 876
frugivorus 298
fruit *result* 154
produce 161
food 298
profit 775
forbidden – 615
reap the –s
succeed 731
reward 973
– tree 367
fruitful 168
fruition 161, 827
fruitless
unproductive 169
useless 645
failure 732
frump 851, 895
frumpish 901a
frustrate 179, 706
frustrated 732
frustum 51
fry *shoal* 102
child 129
heat 384
small –
unimportant 643
commonalty 876
frying-pan 386
out of – into fire
worse 659
clumsy 699
failure 732
misfortune 735
aggravation 835
fuddled 959
fudge 517, 643
fuel 388, 638
add – to the flame 835
– oil 388
increase 35
heat 384
aggravate 835
anger 900
fugaces labuntur anni 111
fugacious 111
fugitive
transient 111
emigrant 268
avoiding 623
– writings 596
fugleman
pattern 22
director 694
fugue 415
fulciment 215
fulcrum 215
fulfil
complete 729
– a duty 926
– an obligation 772
fulgent 420
fuliginous
dim 422
opaque 426
black 431
full *much* 31
complete 52
large 192
loud 404
abundant 639
cleanse 652
hands –
active 682
receipt in – 807
– blooded 641
– bloom 131
health 654
beauty 845
– blown 131
expanded 194
glorious 873
– of business 682
– colored 428
– cry *loud* 404
bark 412
pursuit 622
– dinner pail 734
dress 225
ornament 847
fashion 852
show 882
– drive 274
– feather
prepared 673
– force 159
– gallop 274
– heart 820
– of incident 151
– many 102
– of meaning 516
– measure 639
– of people 186
– play
facility 705
freedom 748
– of point 842
– scope 748
– score 415
– size 912
– of sound and fury &c.
unmeaning 517
– speech 274
– stop
cease 142
rest 265
– swing
strong 159
active 682
successful 731
free 748
– as a tick 52
– tide 348
– tilt *active* 682
haste 684
– view 446
– of whims 608
full-fashioned 240
full-fed 954
full-flavored 392
full-grown 131, 192
full-handed 816, 818
full-length 556
full-mouthed 412
full-toned 413
fully 31
fulminate
violent 173
propel 284
loud 404
malediction 908
threat 909
– against
accuse 932
fulness
[see full]
in the – of time 109
fulsome
nauseous 395
fetid 401
bad 649
abhorrent 867
adulatory 933
impure 961
fulvid 436
fulvous 436
fumble
derange 61
handle 379
grope 463
awkward 699
fumbler 701
fume
violent 173
exhalation 334, 336
froth 353
heat 382
odor 398
excitement 824, 825
anger 900
in a –
discontented 832
–s of fancy 515
fumid 426
fumigate
vaporize 336
cleanse 652
fumigator 388
fumo, dare pondus – 481
fun 827, 840, 842
make – of 856
funambulist 700
function
algebra 84
office 170
business 625
utility 644
pomp 882
rite 998
duty 926
functionary
director 694
consignee 758
functus officio 756
fund *store* 636
sinking – 802
fundamental
intrinsic 5
base 211
support 215
– bass 413
– note 413
fundamentally 31
funds 800
in – 803
public – 802
funebrial 363
funeral 363
– pace 275
– march 415
funereal
interment 363
dismal 837
fungiform 249
fungology 369
fungosity 250
fungus
projection 250
vegetable 367
foetor 401
bane 663
funicle 205
funicular 627
funk 860, 862
– hole 530
funnel *opening* 260
conduit 350
air-pipe 351
funnel-shaped 252
funny *odd* 83
boat 273
humorous 842

– ready 673
– rid of 672
– a sight of 441, 490
– through
end 67
transact 692
complete 729
expend 809
– to
extend to 196
arrive 292
– together 72
– into trouble 732
– the wind up 860
– up *produce* 161
ascend 305
raise 307
learn 539
fabricate 544
prepare 673
rise early 682
foment 824
– into the way of 613
get-away 671
gewgaw
trifle 643
ornament 847
vulgar 851
geyser 382, 386
ghastly
pale 429
hideous 846
frightful 860
ghaut 203
ghetto 189
ghost *shade* 362
fallacy of vision 443
soul 450
writer 593
apparition 980
give up the – 360
needs no – to tell us 525
pale as a –
colorless 429
fear 860
– dance 992
ghost-like
ugly 846
ghostly
intellectual 450
supernatural 976, 980
Ghost, Holy – 976
ghoul 913, 980
ghyll 348
giant
large 192
tall 206
– refreshed
strong 159
refreshed 689
–'s strides
distance 196
swift 294
giaour 984, 989
gibber 583
gibberish 517, 563
gibbet
brand 932
execute 972
gallows 975
gibble-gabble 584
gibbous 249, 250
gib-cat *male* 373
gibe 929
giblets 298
gibus 225
giddy
inattentive 458
vertiginous 503
irresolute 605
capricious 608
bungling 699
giddy-head 501
giddy-paced 315
gift *power* 157
talent 698
given 784
– of the gab 582
look a – horse in the mouth
fastidious 868
ungrateful 917
gifted 698
gig 272, 273
gigantic
strong 159
large 192
tall 206
giggle 838
giglamps 445
Gilbertian 842
Gilbertine 996
gild *coat* 223
color 439
ornament 847
– refined gold 641
– the pill
deceive 545
tempt 615
please 829
flatter 933
Gilead, balm in – 834, 858
Giles's Greek, St. – 563
gill 348
gillie 746
gilt 436, 847
– edged 648
gimbals 312
gimcrack
weak 160
brittle 328
trifling 643
ornament 847
ridiculous 853
gimlet 262
gimp
clean 652
pretty 845
decoration 847
gin *trap* 545
instrument 633
intoxicating 959
demon 980
gin mill 189
gin palace 189
gingerbread
weak 160
vulgar 851
gingerly 174, 459, 864
gingle 408
gipsy
wanderer 268
wag 844
– lingo 563
giraffe 206
girandole 423
girasol 847
gird *bind* 43
strengthen 159
surround 227
jeer 929
– up one's loins
brace 159
prepare 673
girder 45, 215
girdle *bond* 45
encircle 227
circumference 230
circle 247
put a – round the earth 311
girl 129, 374
girlhood 127
girt 45
girth
bond 45
circumference 230
gisarm 727
gist *essence* 5
meaning 516
important 642
gît, ci – 363
gittern 417
give *yield* 324
melt 382
bestow 784
discount 813
– away 782, 784
in marriage 903
– back 790
– birth to 161
– with both hands 816
– in charge
restrain 751
– chase 622
– consent 762
– one credit for 484
– in custody 751
– expression to 566
– forth 531
– the go by 623
– a horse his head 748
– in *submit* 725
– into *consent* 762
– light 420
– the mind to 457
– notice
inform 527
warn 668
– it one
censure 932
punish 972
– out *emit* 297
publish 531
bestow 784
– over *cease* 142
relinquish 624
lose hope 859
– place to
substitute 147
avoid 623
– play to the imagination 515
– points to 27
– quarter 740
– rise to 153
– one the slip 671
– security 771
– and take
reciprocate 12
compensation 30
interchange 148
retaliation 718
compromise 774
barter 794
equity 922
honour 939
– tongue 531
– a turn to 140
– one to understand 527
– up
not understand 519
unwilling 603
reject 610
relinquish 624
submit 725
resign 757
surrender 782
restore 790
hopeless 859
– up the ghost 360
– way *weak* 160
brittle 328
submit 725
pine 828
despond 837
modest 881
given [*see* give]
circumstances 8
supposition 514
received 785
– over *dying* 360
– time 134
– to 613
giving 784
gizzard 191
stick in one's – 900
glabrous 225
glacial 383
glaciate 385
glacier 383
glacis 217, 717
glad 827, 829
give the – eye 441
would be – of 865
– tidings 532
gladden 834, 836
glade *hollow* 252
opening 260
shade 424
gladiator 726
gladiatorial 361, 713, 720
gladsome 827, 829
Gladstone bag 191
glair 352
glaive 727
glamor 992
glance *look* 441
sign 550
see at a – 498
– at
take notice of 457
allude to 527
censure 932
– off *deviate* 279
diverge 291
gland 221
glare *light* 420
stare 441
imperfect vision 443
visible 446
glaring
[*see* glare]
great 31
color 428
visible 446
manifest 525
glass *vessel* 191
smooth 255
brittle 328
transparent 425
lens 445
musical –es 47
see through a – darkly 491
– of fashion 852
live in a – house
brittle 328
visible 446
danger 665
– too much 959
glass-coach 272
glasshouse 191, 371
Glassite 984
glassy [*see* glass]
shining 420
colorless 429
glaucous 435
glave 727
glaver 933
glaze 255
gleam *small* 32
light 420
glean 609, 775
gleanings 636
glebe *land* 342
ecclesiastical 995
church 1000
glee *music* 415
satisfaction 827
merriment 836
gleek 929
glen 252
glengarry 225
glib *voluble* 584
facile 705
glide *lapse* 109
move 264
travel 266
fly 267
– into
conversion 144
glider 273
glimmer
light 420
dim 422
visible 446
slight knowledge 490, 491
glimpse 441, 490
glint 420
glissade 306
glisten 420
glitter
shine 420
appear 446
illustrious 882
glittering
ornament 847
display 882
gloam 901*a*
gloaming 126, 422
gloar *look* 441
wonder 970
gloat 884
– on *look* 441
– over 441
pleasure 377

for –
diuturnal 110
permanent 141
make –
evidence 467
provide 637
restore 660
complete 729
substantiate 924
vindicate 937
atone for 952
so far so – 931
think – 931
to the – 780
turn to – account
731
what's the – 645
– actions 944
– at 698
– auspices 858
– behavior
contingent 108*a*
duty 926
virtue 944
in one's – books
888
– bye 293
in – case 192
– chance 472
– cheer *food* 298
cheerful 826
– circumstances
803
– condition 192
– day
arrival 292
departure 293
courtesy 894
– effect
goodness 648
beauty 845
– enough
not perfect 651
be – enough 765
put a – face upon
cheerful 836
proud 878
– fellow 892
– fight *war* 722
virtue 944
– for
useful 644
salubrious 656
– fortune 734
– Friday 998
– genius
friend 890
benefactor 912
god 979
in one's – **graces**
888
– hand 700
– humor
concord 714
cheerfulness 836
amuse 840
courtesy 894
kindly 906
– intention 906
– judgment 498
– lack! 870
– living
food 298
gluttony 957
– look-out 459
– looks 845
– luck 734
– man *man* 373
husband 903
worthy **948**
– manners 894
much – may it do
906
– morrow 292
– name 873
– nature 906
– night 293
– for nothing
impotence 158
useless 645
in – odor
repute 873
approbation 931
– offices
mediation 724
kind 906
– old time 122
– omen 858
– opinion 931
take in – part
pleased 827
courteous 894
kind 906
– pennyworth 815
– at the price 815
to – purpose 731
– repute 873
– sense 498
– society 852
– taste 578, 850
– temper 894
– thing 648
– time *early* 132
opportune 134
prosperous 734
– turn
kindness 906
– understanding
714
– wife
woman 374
spouse 903
– will
willingness 602
benevolence 906
– word
approval 931
vindication 937
– as one's word
veracity 543
observance 772
probity 939
– works 906
goodie 652, 746
goodly
great 31
large 192
handsome 845
good mixer 892
goodness
[*see* good] **648**
virtue 944
have the –
request 765
– gracious! 870
– of heart 906
goods *effects* 270,
780
merchandise 798
good taste 868
Goodwin sands 667
goody 374
gooroo 996
goose *hiss* 409
game of – 840
giddy as a – 458
tailor's – 255
kill the – with
golden eggs
699, 818
a wild – chase 545
gooseberry
old – 978
play – 459
– eyes 411, 443
goosecap 501
goose egg 101
gooseflesh 383
goosequill 590
goose-skin 383
Gordian knot 59,
704
gore *stab* 260
blood 361
gorge *ravine* 198
conduit 350
fill 641
satiety 869
gluttony 957
raise one's – 900
– the hook 602
gorge de pigeon 440
gorgeous
colour 428
beauty 845
ornament 847
ostentation 882
Gorgon 860
gorilla 913
gormandize 298,
954*a*, 957
gorse 367
gory *red* 434
murderous 361
unclean 653
gospel
certainty 474
truth 494
take for – 484
Gospels 985
gossamer
filament 205
light 320
texture 329
gossip *news* 532
babbler 584
conversation 588
gossoon 876
Gotama 986
Goth 851, 876
Gotham, wise men
of – 501
gothic
amorphous 241
gouache 556
gouge *concave* 252
perforator 262
goulash 298
gourd 191
gourmand 954*a*,
957
gourmet 868, 954*a*
gout 378
goût, haut – 392
goutte d'eau, il se
noyerait dans
une – 699
govern 693, 737
governess 540
[*see* govern]
ruling power 745
divine – 976
petticoat – 699
governor
tutor 540
director 694
ruler 745
keeper 753
gowk 501
gown *dress* 225
canonicals 999
gownsman 492
grab *take* 789
miser 819
grabble 379
grace *style* 578
permission 760
concession 784
elegance 845
polish 850
title 877
pity 914
forgiveness 918
honor 939
piety 987
worship 990
act of – 784
God's – 906
with a bad – 603
with a good –
willing 602
courteous 894
in one's good –s
888
heart of – 861
say – 990
submit with a
good – 826
– before meat 916
grâce: coup de –
914
la – 840
graceless
inelegant 579
ugly 846
vicious 945
impenitent 951
irreligious 989
Graces 845
gracile 203
gracious
willing 602
courteous 894
kind 906
good – 870
grade *degree* 26
arrange 60
term 71
ascent 217
on the down – 658
on the up – 659
gradatim
gradually 26
in order 58
continuous 69
slow 275
gradation
degree 26
order 58
continuity 69
gradient 217
gradual *degree* 26
continuous 69
slow 275
graduate
adjust 23
calibrate 26
arrange 60
series 69
measure 466
scholar 492, 873
graduated scale 466
gradus 86, 562
Graeculus esuriens
886
graft *join* 43
locate 184
insert 300
trees 371
teach 537
booty 794
corruption 940
Grail
holy – 998
grain *essence* **5**
small 32
tendency 176
little 193
rough 256
weight 319
texture 329
powder 330
paint 428
temper 820
ornament 847
against the –
rough 256
unwilling 603
opposing 708
in the – 820
–s of allowance
qualification 469
doubt 485
like –s of sand
incoherent 47
gram 319
gramercy 916
graminivorous 298
grammar
beginning 66
teaching 537
school 542
language **567**
bad – 568
comparative – 560
grammarian 492
gramophone 417,
418, 553
granary 636
grand
great 31
style 574
important 642
money 800
handsome 845
glorious 873
ostentatious 882
– climacteric 128
– doings 882
– duchy 181
– jury 967
en – seigneur
proud 878
insolent 885
en –e tenue
ornament 847
show 882
– piano 417
– style 556
– tour 266
– Turk 745
– vizier 694
grandam 130
grandchildren 167
grandee 875
grande dame 878
grandeur 873

grandfather 130, 166
grandiloquent 577
grandiose 577
grandmother 166
simple 501
teach – 538
grandsire 130, 166
grange 189
granite 323
granivorous 298
grano salis, cum 469, 485
grant *admit* 529
permit 760
consent 762
confer 784
God – 990
– a lease 771
granted 488
take for –
believe 484
suppose 514
grantee
possessor 779
receiver 785
granular 330
granulate 330
granule 32
grapes, sour –
unattainable 471
falsehood 544
excuse 617
grape-shot
attack 716
arms 727
graph 554
graphic
intelligible 518
painting 556
descriptive 594
graphite 332
graphite 556
graphology 590
graphometer 244
graphotype 558
grapnel 666
grapple
fasten 43
clutch 789
– with
- *a question* 461
- *difficulties* 704
oppose 708
resist 719
contention 720
grappling-iron
fastening 45
safety 666
grasp
comprehend 518
power 737
retain 781
seize 789
in one's – 737
possess 777
tight – *severe* 739
– at 865
– of intellect 498
grasping
miserly 819
covetous 865
grass 344, 367
let the – grow under one's feet
neglect 460
inactive 683
not let the – &c.
active 682
grasshopper 309
grass-plat 371
grate *rub* 330
physical pain 378
stove 386
– on the ear
harsh sound 410
– on the feelings 830
grated
barred 219
grateful
physically pleasant 377
agreeable 829
thankful 916
grater 260, 330
gratification
animal – 377
moral – 827
gratify 829
permit 760
please 829
grating [*see* grate]
lattice 219
harsh 713
gratis 815
gratitude **916**
gratuitous
inconsequent 477
supposititious 514
voluntary 602
payless 815
gratuity
gift 784
gratis 815
gratulate 896
gravaman 642
– of a charge 938
grave *great* 31
engrave 259, 558
tomb 363
important 642
composed 826
distressing 830
sad 837
heinous 945
beyond the – 360
look –
disapprove 932
rise from the – 660
silent as the – 403
sink into the – 360
on this side of the – 359
– in the memory 505
– note 408
– trap 599
gravel
earth 342
material 635
puzzle 704
graveolent 398
graven image 991
graver 558
graving dock 189
gravitate
descend 306
weigh 319
– towards 176
gravity *force* 157
weight **319**
vigor 574
importance 642
sedateness 826
seriousness 827
center of – 222
specific –
weight 319
density 321
gravy 333
– boat 191
gray **432** [and *see* grey]
graze *touch* 199
browse 298
rub 331
brush 379
grazier 370
gré, savoir – 916
grease
lubricate 332
oil 356
– the palm
tempt 615
give 784
pay 807
greasy 355
great *much* **31**
big 192
glorious 873
magnanimous 942
(*important* 642)
– bear 318
– circle sailing 628
– coat 225
– doings
importance 642
bustle 682
– folks 875
– gun 626
– hearted 942
– Mogul 745
– number 102
– primer 591
– quantity 31
greater **33**
– number 102
– part 31
nearly all **50**
greatest 33
greatness **31**
greave 225
greed
desire 865
gluttony 957
greedy
avaricious 819
green
new 123
young 127
lawn 344
grass 367
unripe 397
color 435
credulous 486
novice 491
unused 614
healthy 654
immature 674
unskilled 699
board of – cloth 966
– memory 505
– old age 128
greenback 800
green-eyed monster 920
greenhorn
novice 493
dupe 547
bungler 701
greenhouse
receptacle 191
horticulture 371
greenness **435**
green-room 599
greensward 344
Greenwich time 114
greenwood 367
Greek
unintelligible 519
sharper 792
St. Giles's – 563
– Church 984
– Kalends 107
greet *weep* 839
hail 894
greeting
sociality 892
–'s! 292
gregarious 892
grenade 727
grenadier
tall 206
soldier 726
grey 432
– beard 130
– friar 996
– hairs 128
bring – hairs to the grave
adversity 735
harass 830
– mare
ruler 737
master 745
wife 903
– matter
brain 498
hound
swift 274
animal 366
ocean –hound 273
gridelin 437
gridiron
flatness 213
crossing 219
stove 386
stage 599
stadium 840
grief 828
come to – 735
grievance
evil 619
painful 830
wrong 923
grieve *mourn* 828
pain 830
dejected 837
complain 839
grievous 649, 830
grievously 31
griffin 83, 366, 493
griffo 41
griffonage 590
grig *merry* 836
grill 382, 384, 461
– room 189
grille 219
grim
resolved 604
painful 830
doleful 837
ugly 846
discourteous 895
sullen 901*a*
–visaged war 722
grimace 243, 839, 855
grimacier
actor 599
humorist 844
affected 855
grimalkin 366
grimy 652
grin *laugh* 838
ridicule 856
– and abide 725
– a ghastly smile
dejected 837
ugly 846
grind
reduce 195
sharpen 253
pulverize 330
pain 378
learn 539
oppress 907
– the organ 416
– one's teeth 900
grinder
teacher 330
noise 404
grinding 739, 830
grindstone 253, 330
grip
indication 550
power 737
retention 781
clutch 789
– of the hand 894
gripe [*see* grip]
pain 378
parsimony 819
grisaille
grey 432
painting 556
grisette
woman 374
commonalty 876
libertine 962
grisly 846
grist
materials 635
provision 637
– to the mill
useful 644
acquire 775
gristle 321, 327
grit
strength 159
powder 330
stamina 604*a*
courage 861
– in the oil
hindrance 706
gritty 323
grizzled
grey 432
variegated 440
groan 411, 839
groat 800
grocer 637
grocery 396
grog 298, 959
groin 244
groom 370, 746
– well
– of the chambers 746
–'s man 903

in action 680
active 682
subjection 749
– up 293
harp
repeat 104
musical instrument 417
weary 841
Harpagon 819
harper 416
harpist 416
harpoon 727
harpsichord 417
harpy
relentless 739
thief 792
miser 819
evil-doer 913
demon 980
harquebuss 727
harridan 846, 962
harrier 366
harrow
agriculture 371
– up the soul 860
harrowing 830
harry *pain* 830
attack 716
persecute 907
Harry, old – 978
harsh
acrid 171
sound 410
style 579
discordant 713
severe 739
disagreeable 830
morose 895
malevolent 907
– voice 581
hart 366, 373
hartal 142, 489
harum-scarum 59, 458
haruspice 513
Haruspicy 511
harvest
effect 154
profit 618
store 636
acquisition 775
get in the –
complete 729
succeed 731
– home
celebration 883
– time
autumn 126
exertion 686
has been 122
hash *mix* 41
cut 44
confusion 59
food 298
make a – 699
hashish 863
hasp 43, 45
hassock 215
hastate 253
haste
velocity 274
activity 682
hurry 684
hasten
promote 707
hasty
transient 113
hurried 684
impatient 825
irritable 901
– pudding 298
hat 225
cardinal's – 999
send round the – 765
shovel – 999
– in hand 886
hatch
produce 161
gate 232
opening 260
chickens 370
fabricate 544
shading 556
plan 626
prepare 673
– a plot 626
hatches, under –
restraint 751
prisoner 754
poor 804
hatchet
cutting 253
bury the – 918
dig up the – 722
throw the helve after the – 818
hatchet-faced 203
hatchment
funeral 363
arms 550
record 551
hatchway 260
hate 867, 898
hateful 649, 830
hath been, the time – 122
hatrack 215
hatter 225
mad as a – 503
hatti-sheriff 741
hatred [*see* hate]
object of – 898
hauberk 717
haud passibus æquis 28, 275
haugh 344
haughty
proud 878
insolent 885
contemptuous 930
haul *drag* 285
catch of fish &c. 789
– down one's flag 725
– in 10
haunch 236
haunt *focus* 74
presence 186
abode 189
alarm 860
persecute 907
– the memory
remember 505
trouble 830
haunted 980
haut
traiter de –
insolence 885
contempt 930
hautboy 417
haut-goût 392
haut-monde 875
hauteur 878
have *confute* 479
ken 49
possess 777
– the advantage 28, 33
– at 716
– no choice 609*a*
– done! 142
– to do with 9
– no end 112
– other fish to fry 135
– it
discover 480*a*
believe 484
– one to know 527
– some knowledge of 490
– nothing to do with 10
– for one's own 780
– rather 609
– one's rights 924
– the start 116
– in store 152, 637
– to 620
– up 638
– it your own way
submission 725
haven 292, 666
haversack 191
havoc
destruction 162
cry – *war* 722
play – *spoil* 659
haw 583
hawk *spit* 297
stammer 583
eye of a – 498
– about
publish 531
offer 763
sell 796
– at 716
between – and buzzard 315, 828
know a – from a handsaw 465, 698
hawker 796
hawk-eyed 441
hawking *chase* 622
hawser 45
hay while the sun shines, make – 134
haycock 72
hazard
chance 156, 621
danger 665
at all –s 604
– a conjecture 514
– a proposition 477
haze *mist* 353
uncertainty 475
in a –
hidden 528
hazel 433
hazy *opaque* 426
he 373
head *precedence* 62
beginning 66
class 75
summit 210
coiffure 225
lead 280
froth 353
person 372
intellect 450
topic 454
wisdom 498
picture 556
nomenclature 564
chapter 593
direct 693
director 694
master 745
at the – of
direction 693
authority 737
repute 873
bow the – 308
bring to a – 729
come into one's – 451
come to a – 729
drive into one's – 505
gain – 175
get into one's –
thought 451
learn 505
belief 484
intoxicate 959
give a horse his – 748
hang one's – 879
have in one's – 490
from – to heels 52, 200
hit on the – 912
knock on the – 361
knock one's – against
impulse 276
unskilful 699
fail 732
lie on one's – 926
lift up one's – 878
make – against
oppose 708
resistance 719
success 731
never entered into one's – 458
have no – 506
on one's – 218
off one's – 503
can't get out of one's – 505
over – and ears
deep 641
debt 806
love 897
put into one's –
supposition 514
information 527
put out of one's – 458
run in the – 505
not know whether one stands on – or heels
uncertain 475
wonder 870
take into one's –
thought 451
caprice 608
intention 620
turn the – 824
trouble one's – about 457
as one's – shall answer for 768
with – erect 878
from – to foot 200
– and front
important 642
– and front of one's offending
provocation 830
charge 938
– over heels
inversion 218
rotation 312
– light 423
– line 591
– and shoulders
irrelevant 10
complete 52
haste 684
make neither – nor tail of 519
hold one's – up 307
– above water
safe 664
prosperous 743
wealth 803
with a – on 353
headache 378
head-dress 225
header 310
head-foremost
violent 173
rash 863
head-gear 225
heading *prefix* 64
beginning 66
indication 550
title 564
headland
height 206
projection 250
headlong
hurry 684
rush 863
rush –
violence 173
headman 694
headmost
front 234
precession 280
head-piece
summit 210
intellect 450
helmet 717
ornament 847
head-quarters
focus 74
abode 189
authority 737
head-race 350
head-stone 363
heads
compendium 596
– or tails 156, 621
lay – together
advice 695
co-operate 709
– I win tails you lose
unfair 940
headship 737
headsman 975

helicopter 273
Heliogabalus 954*a*
heliograph
signal 550
picture 556
heliography 550
light 420
painting 556
Helios 423
heliotrope 847
heliotype 558
helix 248
hell *abyss* 208
gaming-house 62
gehenna 982
– upon earth
misfortune 735
pain 828
– broke loose 59
hell-born 945, 978
hellebore 663
hell-hound 913, 949
hellish
malevolent 907
vicious 945
hell 982
helluo librorum 492
helm *handle* 633
scepter 747
(*authority* 737)
answer the – 743
at the – 693
obey the – 705
take the – 693
helmet 225, 717
helminthology 368
helmsman 269, 694
helot 746
help *benefit* 618
utility 644
remedy 662
aid 707
servant 746
give 784
it can't be –ed
submission 725
never mind 823
content 831
God – you 914
so – me God 535
– oneself to 789
helper 711
helpless 158, 665
helpmate
auxiliary 711
wife 903
helter-skelter 59, 684
helve
throw the – after the hatchet 818
hem *edge* 231
fold 258
indeed! 870
kiss the – of one's garment 886
– in *enclose* 220
restrain 751
hemi- 91
hemisphere 181
hemispheric 250
hemlock 663
hemorrhage 299
hemp 205
hen 366, 374
female 374
– with one chicken
busy 682
henbane 663
hence
arising from 155
departure 293
deduction 476
– loathed melancholy 836
henceforth 121
henchman 746
hencoop 370
hendiadis 91
henna 433
henpecked 743, 749
heptagon 244
heptarchy 98
Heraclitus 839
rideret – 853
herald
precursor 64
precession 280
predict 511
forerunner 512
proclaim 531
messenger 534
heraldry 550
herb 367
herbage 365
herbal 369
herbivorous 298
herborize 369
herculean
strong 159
exertion 686
difficult 704
Herculem, ex pede – 550
Hercules 159, 215
pillars of – 233, 550
herd 72, 102
herdsman 746
here
situation 183
presence 186
arrival 292
come –! 286
– below 318
– goes 676
– and there
dispersed 73
few 103
place 182, 183
– there and everywhere
diversity 16*a*
space 180
omnipresence 186
– to-day and gone to-morrow 111
hereabouts 183, 197
hereafter 121, 152
hereby 631
hereditament 780
hereditary
intrinsic 5
derivative 154, 167
heredity 167
herein 221
heresy 495, 984
heretic 984
heretofore 122
hereupon 106
herewith 88, 632
heritage
futurity 121
possession 777
property 780
heritor 779
hermaphrodite 83
– brig 273
hermeneutics 522
Hermes 534, 582
hermetically 261
hermit 893, 955
hermitage
house 189
cell 191
seclusion 893
hero *brave* 861
glory 873
good man 948
– worship 931, 991
Herod, out-Herod – 549
heroic [*see* hero]
magnanimous 942
mock – 853
heroics 884
heroin 663
heroine 861
herpetology 368
Herr 373
herring
pungent 392
– pond 341
draw a – across the trail 545
trail of a red – 615, 706
herring-gutted 203
hesitate
uncertain 475
sceptical 485
stammer 583
reluctant 603
irresolute 605
fearful 860
Hesperian 236
Hesperides, garden of the – 981
Hesperus 423
Hessian boot 225
hest 741
hesterni quirites 876
heterarchy 737
heteroclite 83
heterodoxy 489, 984
heterogeneous
unrelated 10
different 15
mixed 41
multiform 81
exceptional 83
heterogeneity 15, 16*a*
heteromorphism 16*a*
hetman 745
hew *cut* 44
shorten 201
fashion 240
– down 308
hewers of wood
workers 690
commonalty 876
hexagon 98, 244
hexahedron 244
hexameter 98, 597
hey! 586
heyday
exultation 838
festivity 840
wonder 870
– of the blood 820
– of youth 127
hiation 260
hiatus 198
hibernal 383
hibernate 683
Hibernicism 497, 563
hic:
– jacet 363
– labor hoc opus 704
hick 701, 851, 876
hiccup 349
hid under a bushel 460
hidalgo 875
hidden 528
– meaning 526
hide *skin* 223
conceal 528
– diminished head
inferior 34
decrease 36
humility 879
– one's face
modesty 881
– and seek
deception 545
avoid 623
game 840
hide-bound 751, 819
hideous 846
hide-out 893
hiding-place
abode 189
ambush 530
refuge 666
hie 264, 274
– to 266
hiemal 126
hierarch 996
hierarchy 995
hieratic 590
hieroglyphic
representation 554
letter 561
writing 590
hierographa 985
hieromancy 511
hierophant 996
hieroscopy 511
higgle 794
higgledy piggledy 59
higgler 797
high *much* 31
lofty 206
fetid 401
treble 410
foul 653
noted 873
proud 878
from on – 981
on – 206
think –ly of 931
– art 556
– celebration 998
– color
color 428
red 434
exaggerate 549
– commissioner 745
– days and holidays 840
in a – degree 31
– descent 875
– and dry
stable 150
safe 664
in – esteem 928
in – feather
strong 159
health 654
cheerful 836
boasting 884
– glee 836
– hand
violent 173
resolved 604
authority 737
severe 739
pride 878
insolence 885
lawless 964
– jinks 840
ride the – horse 878
– hat 225
– life *fashion* 852
rank 875
– living
intemperance 954
gluttony 957
– mass 998
– mightiness 873
– and mighty
pride 878
insolence 885
– note 410
– notions 878
– places 210
– pressure
energy 171
excitation of feeling 824
– price 814
– priest 996
in – quarters 875
– relief 448
– repute 873
–ly respectable 875
on the – road to
way 627
hope 858
on one's – ropes
excitation 824
pride 878
anger 900
– seas 341
in – spirits 836
– tide *wave* 348
prosperity 734
– time *late* 133
occasion 134
– in tone
white 430
– treason
disobedience 742
dishonor 940
– words
quarrel 713
anger 900
high-ball 298
high-born 875

high-brow 492
higher 33
highest 210
highfalutin 884
high-flavored 392
high-flier
madman 504
proud 878
high-flown
imaginative 515
style 577
proud 878
vain 880
insolent 885
high-flying
inattentive 458
exaggerated 549
ostentatious 822
highlands 206
high-low 225
high-mettled
excitable 825
brave 861
high-minded
honorable 939
magnanimous 942
highness *title* 877
high-pitched 410
high-seasoned 392
high-souled 878
high-sounding
loud 404
words 577
display 882
high-spirited 861, 939
hight 564
high-toned 852
high-water
completeness 52
height 206
crater 337
– mark
measure 466
highway 627
–s and byways 627
– robbery 791
highwayman 792
high-wrought
good 648
prepared 673
excited 824
hike 266
hilarity 836
hill *height* 206
convexity 250
ascent 305
descent 306
take to the –s 666
–dwelling 206
hillock 206
hilt 633
hinc illæ lachrymæ 155
hind *back* 235
clown 876
on one's – legs
elevation 307
anger 900
– quarters 235
hinder 706
hindermost 67, 235
Hindooism 984
hindrance 706
hinge *fasten* 43
fastening 45
cause 153
depend upon 154
rotate 312
hinny 271
hint *reminder* 505
suppose 514
inform 527
take a – 498
– a fault &c. 932
hinterland 235
hip 236
have on the –
confute 479
success 731
authority 737
subjection 749
– hip, hurrah! 838
hipped [*see* hypped]
hippocentaur 80
Hippocrates 662
hippocratic 360
hippodrome
drama 599
arena 728
amusement 840
hippogriff 83
Hippolytus 960
hippophagy 298
hippopotamus 192
hirdie-girdie 218
hire
commission 755
borrowing 788
price 812
reward 973
on – 763
hireling 746
hirsute 256
hispid 256
hiss *sound* 409
animal cry 412
disrespect 929
contempt 930
disapprobation 932
hist! 585, 586
histology 329
historian 553
historic 594
historiette 594
historical:
– painter 559
– painting 556
historiographer 553
historiography 594
history *past* 122
record 551
narrative 594
History, Natural – 357
histrionic 599
hit *chance* 156
strike 276
reach 292
succeed 731
censure 932
(*punish* 972)
good – 626
make a – 731
– one's fancy 829
– the mark 731
– off 545
– upon
discover 480a
plan 626
hitch
fasten 43
knot 45
stoppage 142
hang 214
jerk 315
harness 370
difficulty 704
hindrance 706
– up 293
hither 278, 292
come – 286
hitherto 122
hive
multitude 102
location 184
abode 189
bees 870
workshop 691
H.M.S. 726
hoar *aged* 128
white 430
– frost 383
hoard 636
hoarse
husky 405
harsh 410
voiceless 581
talk oneself – 584
hoary [*see* hoar]
hoax 545
hob *support* 215
stove 386
– and nob
celebration 883
courtesy 894
hobble
limp 275
awkward 699
difficulty 704
fail 732
shackle 751
– skirt 225
hobbledehoy 129
hobby
crotchet 481
pursuit 622
desire 865
hobby-horse 272
hobgoblin
fearful 860
demon 980
hobo 268
hobnail 876
Hobson's choice
necessity 601
no choice 609a
compulsion 744
hoc genus omne 876
hock 771
hock shop 787
hockey 840
hockey rink 213
hocus 545
hocus-pocus
interchange 148
unmeaning 517
cheat 545
conjuration 992
spell 993
hod
receptacle 191
support 215
vehicle 272
hoddy-doddy 501
hodge-podge 41, 59
hoe 272, 371
hog *animal* 366
sensualist 954a
glutton 957
(greedy as a – 865
go the whole – 604
hog's back 206
hogmanay 998
hogshead 191
hog-wash 653
hoist 307
– the black flag 722
– a flag 550
– on one's own petard
retaliation 718
failure 732
hoity-toity! 815, 870
hold *cohere* 46
contain 54
remain 141
cease 142
go on 143
happen 151
receptacle 191
cellar 207
base 211
support 215
halt 265
believe 484
be passive 681
defend 717
power 737
restrain 751
prison 752
prohibit 761
possess 777
retain 781
enough! 869
have a firm – 781
have a – upon 175
gain a – upon 737
get – of 789
quit one's – 782
take – 175
– aloof
stay away 187
distrust 487
avoid 623
– an argument 476
– authority 737
– back *avoid* 623
store 636
hinder 706
restrain 751
retain 781
miserly 819
– one's breath
wonder 870
– converse 588
– a council 695
– fast 751, 781
– forth *teach* 537
speak 582
– good 478, 494
– one's ground 141
– in hand 737
– one's hand
cease 142
relinquish 624
– hard 265
– up one's head 861
– a lease 771
– a meeting 72
– off 623
– office 693
– on
continue 141, 143
persevere 604a
– out [*see below*]
– one's own
preserve 670
defend 717
resist 719
– oneself in readiness 673
– in remembrance 505
– both one's sides 838
– a situation 625
– in solution 335
– to 602
– together 43, 709
– one's tongue 403, 585
– up [*see below*]
– oneself up 307
hold out
endure 106
affirm 535
persevere 604a
resist 719
offer 763
brave 861
– expectation
predict 511
promise 768
– temptation 865
hold up
continue 143
support 215
not rain 340
aid 707
rob 791
display 882
extol 931
– one's hand
sign 550
threat 609
– to execration
cures 908
censure 932
– the mirror 525
– to scorn 930
– to shame 874
– to view 525
holder 779
holdfast 45
holding
tenancy 777
property 780
hole *place* 182
hovel 189
receptacle 191
opening 260
ambush 530
– in one's coat 651
– and corner
place 182
peer into – 461
hiding 528, 530
– to creep out of
plea 617
escape 671
facility 705
holiday *leisure* 685
repose 687
amusement 840
– task *easy* 705

hunt *inquiry* 461
pursuit 622
– after 622
– in couples 709
– down 907
– out *inquiry* 461
discover 480a
– slipper 840
hunter *horse* 271
killer 361
pursuer 622
place &c. – 767
hunting 361, 622
hunting-ground 840
happy – 981
hurdle 272
hurdy-gurdy 417
hurl 284
– against 716
– defiance 715
hurler avec les loups 82, 714
Hurlothrumbo 860
hurly-burly 315
hurrah 411, 836, 838
hurricane 349, 667
– deck 210
hurry *haste* 684
excite 825
– forward 684
– off with 789
– on 615
– of spirits 821
– up 684
hurst 367
hurt
physical pain 378
evil 619
maltreat 649
injure 659
more frightened than 860
– the feelings
pain 830
anger 900
hurtful 649
hurtle 276
hurtless 648
husband
store 636
director 694
spouse 903
husbandman 371
husbandry
agriculture 371
conduct 692
economy 817
hush *moderate* 174
stop 265
silence 403
taciturn 585
– up
conceal 528
pacify 723
hush-money 30, 973
husk 223, 226
husky *strong* 159
dry 340
faint sound 405
hoarse 581
hussar 726
hussy 962
hustings
school 542
arena 728
tribunal 966
hustle
perturb 61
push 276
agitate 315
activity 682
hinder 706
hustler 682, 962
hut 189
hutch 189
huzza 838
hyacinth
jewel 847
hyaline 425
hybrid
mixture 41
exception 83
hydra
monster 83, 366
productive 168
– headed 163
hydrant 348, 385
hydraulics 333, 348
hydro-aeroplane 273
hydrodynamics 333, 348
hydrography 341
hydrology 333
hydrolysis 49
hydromancy 511
hydromel 396
hydropathy 662
hydrophobia 867
hydroplane 273
hydrostatics 333
hyemal 383
hyena 913 ×
hyetology 348
hygeian 656
hygiantics 670
hygienic 656, 670
hygre 348
hygrometry 339
hyle 316
hylism 316
hylotheism 984, 989
Hymen 903
hymeneal 903
hymn *song* 415
worship 990
– of hate 898
hymn-book 998
hyoscine 663
hypallage 218
hyperbation 218
hyperbola 245
hyperbole 549
hyperborean
far 196
cold 383
hypercriticism
misjudgment 481
discontent 832
fastidiousness 868
censure 932
hyperdulia 990
Hyperion 423, 845
– to a satyr 14
hyperorthodoxy 984
hyperphysical 976
hypertrophy 194
hyphen 45
hypnology 683
hypnotic
remedy 662
sleep 683
hypnotize 376
hypocaust 386
hypochondriac
madman 504
low spirits 837
hypochondriasis 837
hypocrisy
falsehood 544
religious – 988
hypocrite 548, 855
play the – 544
hypostasis 1, 3
Hypostatic union 976
hypothecate 771
hypothenuse 217
hypothesis 514
hypothesize 514
hypothetical 475, 514
hypped *insane* 503
dejected 837
hypsometer 206
Hyrcynian wood 533
hysteria
insanity 503
hysteric *violent* 173
hysterical
spasmodic 608
emotional 821
excitable 825
hysterics 173
in – *excited* 824
frightened 860
hysteron proteron 218

I

I 79
iambic 597
ibidem 13
Icarus
navigator 269
rash 863
fate of – 306
ice *cold* 383
refrigerate 385
iceberg 383
ice-bound 383
restraint 751
ice-chest 385
ice-house 387
ice-yacht 273
Ichabod 874
ichnography 554
ichor 333
ichthyology 368
ichthyomancy 511
ichthyophagous 298
icicle 383
icon 554
iconoclasm 983a, 984
iconoclast 165, 913
iconography 554
icosahedron 244
id est 522
idea
small quantity 32
notion 453
give an – of 537
ideal *unreal* 2
completeness 52
erroneous 495
imaginary 515
perfect 650
ideality 450, 515
idée fixe 481
identification
identity 13
comparison 464
discovery 480a
identity 13
– book 206
Ideology 450
Ides of March 601
idiocrasy
essence 5
tendency 176
idiocy 499
idiom 560, 566
idiomatic 79
idiosyncrasy
essence 5
speciality 79
unconformity 83
tendency 176
temperament 820
idiot 501
tale told by an – 517
idiotic
foolish 499
idiotism
folly 499
phrase 566
idle *foolish* 499
trivial 643
slothful 683
lie – *inaction* 681
– conceit 842
– hours 681
be an – man
leisure 685
– talk 588
– time away 683
idler 683
Ido 560
idol *desire* 865
favorite 899
fetich 991
– of the people 899
idolater 984
idolatry 897, 991
idolize *love* 897
impiety 988
idoneous 23
idyl 597
if *circumstance* 8
qualification 469
supposition 514
– you please 765
– possible 470
igloo 189
igneous 382
ignis fatuus
luminary 423
phantom 443
ignite 384
ignoble 876
ignominy 874, 940
ignoramus 493
ignorance 491
keep in – 528
plead – 937
ignoratio elenchi 477
ignore
neglect 460
incredulity 487
not known 491
repudiate 756, 773
ignotum per ignotius 477
ilk 13
ill *evil* 619
badness 649
sick 655
go on – *fail* 732
adversity 735
look – 846
take –
discontent 832
anger 900
– betide 908
– blood *hate* 898
malevolence 907
– at ease *pain* 828
dejection 837
house of – fame 961
–s that flesh is heir to *evil* 619
disease 655
– humor
anger 900
sullenness 901a
– luck 735
as – luck would have it 135
– off
insufficient 640
adversity 735
poor 804
do an – office to 907
bird of – omen 668
– repute 874
– turn *evil* 610
spiteful 907
– usage 907
– will 907
wind *bad* 649
hindrance 706
adversity 735
ill-adapted 24
ill-advised
foolish 499
inexpedient 647
unskilful 699
ill-affected 901a
illapse
conversion 144
ingress 294
illaqueate 545
ill-assorted 24
illation 480
illaudable 947
ill-balanced 28
ill-bred 851, 895
ill-conditioned
bad 649
difficult 704
discourteous 895
malevolent 907
vicious 945
ill-conducted 699
ill-contrived
inexpedient 647
bad 649
unskilful 699
malevolent 907

insert 300
mean 516
imply 526
be of consequence 642
importance 642
greatness 30
attach – to 642
attach too much – to 482
of no – 643
importune 765, 830
impose *order* **741**
awe 928
– upon
credulity 486
deceive 545
be unjust 923
imposing
important 642
exciting 824
glorious 873
imposition [*see* impose]
undue 925
– of hands 998
impossibile, credo quia – 486
impossibilities, seek after – 645
impossibility 471
impossible 471
refusal 764
– quantity
algebra 84
impost 812
imposthume 655
impostor 548, 925
imposture 545
impotence 158
impotent conclusion 732
impound 701
impoverish
weaken 160
waste 638
despoil 789
render poor 804
impracticable
impossible 471
misjudging 481
obstinate 606
difficult 704
imprecation
prayer 765
curse 908
impregnable 159, 664
impregnate *mix* 41
combine 48
fecundate 161, 168
insert 300
teach 537
– with 641
impresario 599
imprescriptible 924
impress *cause*
sensation 375
mark 550
compel 791
excite feeling 824
– upon the mind
memory 505
teach 537
impressed with
belief 484
feeling 821
impressible
motive 615
sensibility 822
impression
sensation 375
idea 453
belief 484
printing 531
mark 550
engraving 558
print 591
emotion 821
make an –
act 171
thought 451
impressionable 375, 822
impressive
language **574**
important 642
feeling 821, 824
imprimis 66
imprimit 558
imprint
publisher 531
indication 550
– in the memory 505
imprison
circumscribe 229
restrain 751
punish 972
improbability 473
improbate 932
improbity 940
impromptu 612
– fait à loisir 673
improper
incongruous 24
foolish 499
solecism 568
inexpedient 647
wrong 923
unmeet 925
vicious 945
– time 135
impropriate 777, 789
impropriator 779
improve 658
– the occasion 134
– the shining hour 682
– upon 658
improvement 658
improvident
careless 460
not preparing 674
prodigal 818
rash 863
improvisation
music 415
improvisatore
speech 582
poetry 597
impulse 612
improvise
imagination 515
impulse 612
unprepared 674
improviste, à l'– 508, 612
improvisatrice 612
imprudent 460, 863
impudent 885, 895
impudicity 961
impugn *deny* 536
attack 716
blame 932
impugnation 708
impuissance 158
impulse *push* **276**
sudden thought **612**
motive 615
blind – 601
creature of – 612
give an – to
propel 284
aid 707
impulsive [*see* impulse]
intuitive 477
excitable 825
rash 863
impunity *escape* 671
acquittal 970
with – *safely* 664
impurity 653, 961
imputation
ascribe 155
slur 874
accuse 938
in 221
go – 294
– as much **as**
relation 9
degree 26
– the circumstances 8
– doors 221
– durancevile **751**
– for
– force 1
undertake **676**
promise 768
– re 9
– and out 314
–s and outs 182
in: – articulo 111
– extenso *whole* 50
diffuse 573
– jail 751
– limine 66
– loco 23
– medias res 68
– prison 751
– propriâ personâ 79
– toto 52
– transitu
transient 111
transfer 270
– statu pupillari 127
– statu quo 141
– vogue 1
inability 158, 699
inabstinent 954
inaccessible 196, 471
inaccurate 495, 568
inaction 172, 683
inactivity 683, 172
inadequate
powerless 158
insufficient 640
useless 645
imperfect 651
inadmissible
incongruous 24
excluded 55
extraneous 57
inexpedient 647
inadvertence 458
inadvisable 647
inaffable 895
inalienable
retention 781
right 924
inamorata 897
inane *void* 4
unmeaning 517
unthinking 452
insufficient 640
trivial 643
useless 645
inanimate 360
– matter 358
inanition 158
inanity [*see* inane]
inappetency 823, 866
inapplicable 10, 24
inapposite 10, 24
inappreciable 33, 193
unimportant 643
inapprehensible
stolid 499
unintelligible 519
inappropriate 24, 647
inapt
incongruous 24
impotent 158
useless 645
inexpedient 647
unskilful 699
inarticulate 581, 583
inartificial 703
inartistic 846
inasmuch *whereas* 9
however 26
because 476
inattention 458
inaudible
silence 403
faint sound 405
deaf 419
voiceless 581
inaugural
precursor 64
inaugurate
begin 66
cause 153
install 755
celebrate 883
inauspicious
untimely 135
untoward 649
hopeless 859
inbeing 5
inborn, inbred
intrinsic 5
affections 820
– proclivity 601
inca 745
incage 751
incalculable 31, 105
incalescence 382
incandescence 382
incandescent 423
incantation
invocation 765
sorcery 992
spell 993
incantatory 992
incapable 158
incapacious 203
incapacitate 158
incapacity
impotence 158
ignorance 491
stupidity 499
incarcerate 751
incarnadine 434
incarnate
intrinsic 5
bodily 316
fleshly 364
vicious 945
devil –
bad man 949
Satan 978
Incarnation 976
incase 223, 229
incautious 863
incendiary
destroy 162
burn 384
influence 615
malevolent 907
evil-doer 913
bad man 949
incense *fuel* 388
fragrant 400
hate 898
anger 900
flatter 933
worship 990
rite 998
incension
burning 384
incentive 615
inception 66
inceptive 153
inceptor 541
incertitude 475
incessant
repeated 104
ceaseless 112
frequent 136
incest 961
inch *small* 32
length 200
by –es 275
to an – 494
not yield an – 606
give an – and take an ell 789
– by inch
by degrees 26
in parts 51
slowly 275
not see an – beyond one's nose 699
inchoation 66, 673
incide 44
incidence 278
incident 151
incidental
extrinsic 6
circumstance 8
irrelative 10
occurring 151
casual 156
liable 177
chance 621
trivial 643
– music 415
incinerate 384
incipience 66
incircumspect 460

465a
indispensable 630
indispose
dissuade 616
indisposed
unwilling 603
sick 655
indisputable 474
indissoluble, indissolvable
joined 43
whole 50
stable 150
dense 321
indistinct 447
indistinction 465a
indistinguishable
identical 13
invisible 447
indisturbance 265, 826
indite 590
individual
whole 50
special 79
unity 87
person 372
indivisible *whole* 50
dense 321
indocility 158, 606
indoctrinate 537
indolence 683, 927
indomitable
strong 159
determined 604
persevering 604a
resisting 719
courage 861
indoor 221
indorse 769, 771
indorsement 550, 551
indraught 343, 348
indubitable 474
induce *cause* 153
power 157
produce 161
motive 615
induct 883
induction
inquiry 461
reasoning 476
drama 599
appointment 755
- *of a priest* 995
indulge *lenity* 740
allow 760
please 829
intemperance 954
gluttony 959
– one's fancy 609
– in 827
– oneself 943
– in reverie
inattention 458
fancy 515
– with *give* 784
indulgence
[*see* indulge]
absolution 918
indulgent *kind* 906
induration
hardening 323
impenitence 951
Indus to the pole, from – 180
industry 625, 682
hive of – 691
indweller 188
indwelling 5
inebriety 959
inedible 395
ineffable *great* 31
inexpressible 521
wonderful 870
ineffaceable 820
ineffectual
incapable 158
useless 645
failing 732
– attempt 732
pale its – fire 422
inefficacious
incapable 158
useless 645
failing 732
inefficient 158
inelastic *soft* 324
– fluid 333
inelasticity 326
inelegance 579, 846
ineluctable 474
inept 24, 158, 645
inequality 28
inequitable 923
ineradicable
intrinsic 5
stable 150
inerrable 946
inertia 172
inertness
physical 172
inactive 683
moral 823
inestimable 648
inevitable 474, 601
inexact
erroneous 495
feeble 575
inexcitability 826
inexcusable
accusable 938
vicious 45
inexecution 730
inexhaustible 105, 639
inexistence 2
inexorable
unavoidable 601
resolved 604
stern 739
compelling 744
pitiless 914a
revengeful 919
inexpectation 508
inexpedience 647
inexpensive 815
inexperience 491, 699
inexpert 699
inexpiable 945
inexplicable 519
inexpressible
great 31
unmeaning 517
unintelligible 519
wonderful 870
inexpressibles 225
inexpression
latency 526
inexpensive 517
inexpugnable 664
inextension 180a
littleness 193
immateriality 317
inextinguishable
stable 150
strong 159
excitable 825
– desire 865
inextricable
coherent 46
disorder 59
impossible 471
infallibility 474
assumption of – 885
infamy *shame* 874
dishonor 940
vice 945
infancy 66, 127
infandum renovare dolorem 505, 833
infant 129
fool 501
– prodigy 872
Infanta 745
infanticide 361, 991
infantine 129
foolish 499
infantry 726
infarction 261
infatuation
misjudgment 481
credulity 486
folly 499
insanity 503
obstinacy 606
passion 825
love 897
infeasible 471
infect *mix with* 41
contaminate 659
excite 824
infectâ, re –
shortcoming 304
non-completion 730
failure 732
infection
transference 270
disease 655
infectious 270, 657
infecund 169
infelicity
inexpertness 699
misery 828
infelicitous 24
infer 472
inference 476, 480
by – 467
inferential
demonstrative 478
latent 526
inferiority
in degree 34
in size 195
imperfection 651
personal – 34
infernal *bad* 649
malevolent 907
wicked 945
satanic 978
– machine 727
– regions 982
infertility 169
infest 830
infestivity 837, 843
infibulation 43
infidel 487, 989
infidelity
dishonor 940
irreligion 989
infiltrate *mix* 41
intervene 228
interpenetrate 294
moisten 337, 339
teach 537
infiltration
passage 302
Infinite, the – 976
infinite 105
– goodness 976
infinitely *great* 31
infinitesimal
small 32
little 193
– calculus 85
infinity 105
infirm *weak* 160
disease 655
vicious 945
– of purpose 605
infirmary 662
infirmity
[*see* infirm]
infix 537
inflame
render violent 173
burn 384
excite 824
anger 900
inflamed 382
inflammable 384, 388
inflammation
heating 384
disease 655
inflate *increase* 35
expand 194
blow 349
inflated
overestimation 482
style 573, 577
ridiculous 853
vain 880
inflation
[*see* inflate]
rarefaction 322
currency 800
inflect 245
inflexible *hard* 323
resolved 604
obstinate 606
stern 739
inexorable 914a
inflexion
change 140
curvature 245
grammar 567
inflict *act upon* 680
severity 739
– evil 649
– pain
bodily pain 378
mental pain 830
– punishment 972
infliction
adversity 735
mental pain 828, 830
punishment 972
influence 153
change 140
physical – 175
inducement 615
instrumentality 631
authority 737
absence of – 175a
sphere of – 780
make one's – felt 631
influx 294
infold 232
inform 527
– against
accuse 938
go to law 969
informal 83, 964
informality 773
informant 527
information
knowledge 490
communication 527
learning 539
lawsuit 969
pick up – 539
informer 532
informity 241
infra dignitatem 874, 940
infraction
trespass 303
disobedience 742
non-observance 773
exemption 927
– of usage &c.
unconformity 83
desuetude 614
infrangible
combined 46
dense 321
infra-red rays 420
infrequency 137
infrigidation 385
infringe
transgress 303
disobey 742
not observe 773
undueness 925
dereliction 927
– a law &c. 83
infundibular 252, 269
infuriate
violent 173
excite 824
anger 900
infuscate 431
infuse *mix* 41
insert 300
teach 537
– courage 861
– life into 824
– new blood 658
infusible 321
infusion [*see* infuse]
liquefaction 335
infusoria 193
ingannation 545
ingathering 72
ingemination 90
ingenerate 5
ingenious 515, 698
ingenite 5
ingenium, perfervidum – 682
ingénu *artless* 703
ingénue *actress* 599
ingenuity 698

ingenuous 703
ingesta 298
ingestion 296
ingle 388
inglorious 874, 940
ingluvies 191
ingot 800
ingraft *add* **37**
join 43
insert 300
teach 537
ingrafted
extrinsic 6
habit 613
ingrain
insinuate 228
color 428
ingrained
intrinsic **5**
combined 48
habit 613
character 820
ingrate 917
ingratiate 897
ingratiating 894
ingratitude **917**
ingredient 51, 56
ingress **294**
forcible – 300
ingurgitate 296
ingustible 391
inhabile 699
inhabit 186
inhabitant **188**
inhale *receive* 296
breathe 349
smell 398
inharmonious
discord 713
– color 428
– sound **414**
inhere **1**
inherent 5, 820
inherit 775, 777
inheritance 780
– of the saints 981
inherited
intrinsic **5**
inheritor 779
inhesion 5
inhibit *hinder* 706
restrain 751
prohibit 761
inhospitable 893
inhuman 907
inhume 363
inimaginable
impossible 471
improbable 473
wonderful 870
inimical 708, 889
inimitable
non-imitation 20
supreme 33
very good 648
perfect 650
iniquity 923, 945
worker of – 949
inirritability 826
initial 66
– letter 558
initiate *begin* 66
admit 296
teach 537
initiated *skilful* 698
initiative 66
inject 300, 337
injection 662
injudicial 964
injudicious 499, 863
injunction
acquirement 630
advice 695
command 741
prohibition 761
injure *evil* 619
damage 659
spite 907
injuria formae, spretae – 846, 930
injury *evil* 619
badness 649
damage 659
injustice 923
ink 431
pen and – 590
before the – is dry 132
– slinging **720**
inkle 45
inkling
knowledge 490
supposition 514
information 527
inkstand 590
inland 221
inlay 440, 847
inlet *beginning* 66
interval 198
opening 260
ingress 294
– *of the sea* 343
inly 221
inmate 188
inmost 221
to the – core 822
– soul 820
– thoughts 451
inn 189
– s of Court 968
innate 5, 601
innavigable 471
inner 221
– coating 224
– man *intellect* 450
affections 820
innermost recesses 221
innings *land* 342
acquisition 775
receipt 810
innkeeper 601
innocence **946**
innocent *fool* 501
good 648
healthy 656
artless 703
guiltless 946
innocuous *good* 648
healthy 656
innocent 946
innominate 565
innovation
variation 20*a*
new 123
change 140
innoxious
salubrious 656
innocent 946
innuendo *hint* 527
censure 932
innumerable 105
innutritious 657
inobservance 773
inoccupation 681
inoculate
insert 300
teach 537
influence 615
inodorous **399**
inoffensive 648, 946
inofficious 907
inoperative
powerless 158
unproductive 169
useless 645
inopportune
untimely 135
inexpedient 647
inordinate 31, 641
inorganization **358**
inornate 849
inosculate *join* 43
intersect 219
convoluted 248
inquest 461
inquietude
changeable 149
uneasy 828
discontent 832
apprehension 860
inquinate 659
inquire 461
– into 595
inquirer 461
inquiring mind 455
inquiry **461**
inquisition
inquiry 461
severity 739
torture 907
tribunal 966
inquisitive 455
inquisitorial
prying 455
inquiry 461
severe 739
jurisdiction 965
inroad *ingress* 294
devastation 659
invasion 716
inrolment 551
insalubrity **657**
insanity **503**
insatiable 865
inscribe 590, 873
inscription 551
inscroll 551
inscrutable 519
insculpture 557
insculptured 558
insecable 43, 87
insect *minute* 193
animal 366
– cry 412
insecure
uncertain **475**
danger 665
insensate
foolish 499
insane 503
insensibility
slow 275
physical **376**
moral **823**
– of benefits 917
– to the past 506
inseparable 43, 46
insert *locate* 184
interpose 228
enter 294
put in 300
record 551
– itself 300
insertion **300**
adjunct 39
ornament 847
inservient 645
inseverable 43, 87
inside 221
– out 218
turn – out 529
insidious
deceitful 545
cunning 702
dishonourable 940
insight 465, 490
insignia 550
– of authority **747**
insignificant
unmeaning 517
unimportant 643
insincere 544, 855
insinuate
intervene 228
ingress 294
insert 300
latency 526
hint 527
ingratiate **897**
blame 932
insipid
style **575**
dull 840
insipidity
tasteless **391**
indifferent 866
insist *argue* 476
command 741
– upon *affirm* 535
dwell on 573
be determined 604
contend 720
compel 744
conditions **770**
due 924
insnare 545
insobriety 959
insolation 382, 384
insolence 878, 885
insoluble *dense* 321
unintelligible 519
insolvable 519
insolvent
poverty 804
debt 806
non-payment 808
insomnia 682
insouciance
thoughtlessness 458
supineness 823
indifference 866
inspan 293
inspect 441, 457
inspector 444
inquisitor 461
judge 480
director 694
inspiration
wisdom 498
imagination **515**
poetry 577
impulse 612
motive 615
feeling 821
Deity 976
revelation 985
religious - 987
inspire *improve* 658
prompt 615
animate 824
cheer 836
– courage 861
– hope 858
– respect 928
inspirit *incite* 615
animate 824
encourage 861
inspiriting
hopeful 858
inspissate 321, 352
instability 149
install *locate* 184
commission **755**
celebrate 883
instalment
portion 51
payment 807, 809
instance
example 82
motive 615
solicitation 765
instant *moment* 113
present 118
destiny 152
required 630
importance 642
active 682
lose not an – 684
on the – 132
instantaneity **113**
instanter 113, 132
instar omnium **17**, 82
instate 883
instauration 660
instead 147
instep 245
instigate 615
instil *extrinsic* 6
mix 41
insert 300
teach 537
instinct
intellect 450
intuition 477
impulse 601
– with *motive* 615
possession 777
brute – 450*a*
instinctive
inborn 5
institute *begin* 66
cause 153
produce 161
academy 542
society 712
– an inquiry 461
institution
academy 542
society 712
political - 963
church 995
institutor 540
instruct *teach* 537
advise 695
precept 697
order 741
instructed 490
instructor 540
instrument
implement **633**

security 771
musical – 417
optical – 445
recording – 553
instrumental 631
– music 415
instrumentalist 410
instrumentality 631
insuavity 895
insubordinate 742
insubstantial 4
– pageant 882
insufferable
painful 830
dislike 867
insufficiency 640
insufflation 349
insular unrelated 10
detached 44
single 87
local 181
island 346
prejudice 481
insulate 44
insulse 499, 843
insult rudeness 895
offence 900
disrespect 929
insulting 898
insuperable 471
– obstacle 706
insupportable 830
insuppressible 173
insurance 768, 771
insure
make sure 474
obtain security 771
insurgent 742
insurmountable 471
insurrection 719, 742
insusceptible 823
– of change 150
inswept 195
intact
permanent 141
perfect 650
preserved 670
intaglio mold 22
concave 252
sculpture 557
engraving 558
intangible little 193
numb 381
integer 50, 84
integer vitæ scelerisque purus 939
integral 50
– calculus 85
– part 56
integrate 50
integrity whole 50
probity 939
virtue 944
integument 223
intellect 450
absence of – 450a
exercise of the – 451
intellectual 450
intelligence
mind 450
capacity 498
news 532
intelligencer 527
intelligentsia 492
intelligibility 518
intemperance 954
drunkenness 959
intempestivity 135
intend 620
intendant 694
intended will 600
predetermined 611
intense great 31
energetic 171
– color 428
– thought 457
intensification 35
intensify
increase 35
stimulate 171
intensity degree 26
greatness 31
energy 171
intensive culture 371
intent attention 457
will 600
design 620
active 682
– upon desire 865
resolved 604
intention 620
bad – 607
good – 906
intently, look – 441
intents and purposes, to all – 27, 52
inter 363
interact 12
inter: – alia 82
– nos 528
interaction 170
interbreeding 41
intercalate 228
intercalation 300
intercede
mediate 724
deprecate 766
intercept
hinder 706
take 789
intercession
[see intercede]
worship 990
Intercessor 976
interchange 148
barter 794
– visits &c. 892
interchangeable 12
intercipient 706
interclude 706
intercommunication 527
intercommunity 892
interconnection 9
intercourse
copulation 43
friendship 888
sociality 892
verbal – 582, 588
intercurrence
interchange 148
interjacence 228
passage 302
interdependence 12
interdict 761
interdictive 55
interdigitate 219, 228
interest concern 9
influence 175
curiosity 455
advantage 618
importance 642
property 780
debt 806
excite 824
please 829
amuse 840
devoid of – 841
feel an – in 906
not know one's own – 699
make – for 707
place out at –
lend 787
economy 817
take an – in
curiosity 455
love 897
take no – in
insensibility 823
indifference 866
want of – 866
interested
selfish 943
– in 457
interesting
lovable 897
interfere disagree 24
counteract 179
intervene 228
activity 682
thwart 706
mediate 724
interference
light 420
interfretted 219
interfusion 41
interim 106, 120
interior 221
painting 556
interjacence 68, 228
interject 228, 300
interlace join 43
twine 219
interlacing 41
interlard 41, 228
interleave 228
interline
interpolate 288
write 590
interlineation 39
interlink 43, 219
interlocation 228
interlocking directorate 709
interlocution 588
interlocutor 582
interloper
extraneous 57
intervene 228
obstruct 706
interlude
time 106
dramatic 599
intermarriage 903
intermeddle 682, 706
intermeddling 724
intermediary 534
intermediate
mean 29
middle 68
intervening 228
ministerial 631
– time 106
intermedium
mean 29
link 45
intervention 228
instrument 631
interment 363
insertion 300
intermezzo 415
intermigration 266
interminable
infinite 105
eternal 112
long 200
intermingle 41
intermission 106, 142
intermit
interrupt 70
recur 138
discontinue 142
intermittence
time 106
intermix 41, 48
intermutation 148
intermural 278
intern 221
internal 5, 221
– evidence 467
international
reciprocal 12
sociality 892
– law 963
internecine 361
– war 722
internuncio 534, 758
interpel 142
interpellation
inquiry 461
address 586
summons 741
appeal 765
interpenetration
interjacence 228
ingress 294
passage 302
interpolation
adjunct 39
analytical 85
interpose 228
insertion 300
interpose
intervene 228
act 682
hinder 706
mediate 724
interposit 799
interplane ary 228
interpretation 522
interpreter 524
interrelation 9, 12
interregnum
intermission 106
transient 111
discontinuance 142
interval 198
laxity 738
interrogate 461
interrupt
discontinuity 70
cessation 142
hinder 706
interruption
derangement 61
interval 198
intersect 219
interspace 198, 221
intersperse 73, 228
interstellar 228
interstice 198
interstitial 221, 228
intertexture
intersection 219
tissue 329
inter-twine, -twist
unite 43
cross 219
interval
– of time 106
– of space 198
– in music 413
at –s
discontinuously 70
at regular –s 138
intervene
– in order 70
– in time 106
– in space 228
be instrumental 631
mediate 724
intervert 140, 279
interview 588, 892
intervolved 43
interweave join 43
cross 219
interjacence 228
interworking 170
intestate 552
intestine 221
inthral 749, 751
intimacy 9
intimate
personal 79
close 197
inside 221
tell 527
friendly 888, 892
intimately
joined 43
intimidate
frighten 860
insolence 885
threat 909
intitule 564
into: go – 294
put – 300
run – 300
intolerable 830
intolerance
prejudice 481
dissent 489
obstinacy 606
impatience 825
insolence 885
malevolence 907
intomb 363
intonation
sound 402
musical 313
voice 580
intone 416, 992
intort 248
intoxicant 663
intoxication
excitement 824, 825

inebriation 959
intra, ab – 221
intractable
obstinate 606
difficult 704
sullen 901*a*
intramural 221
intransient 110
intransigeance 604
intransitive 110
intransmutable 110, 150
intrap 545
intraregarding 221
intrench 717
– on 303
intrepid 861
intricate
confused 59
convoluted 248
difficult 704
intrigant
meddlesome 682
cunning 702
libertine 962
intrigue *fascinate* 615, 897
plot 626
activity 682
cunning 702
excite 824
interest 829
licentiousness 961
intrinsic 5
– evidence 467
– habit 613
– truth 494
intrinsicality 5
introception 296
introduce *lead* 62
interpose 228
precede 280
insert 300
– new blood 140
– new conditions 469
– to 888
introduction
[*see* introduce]
preface 64
reception 296
drama 599
friendship 888
courtesy 894
introductory
precursor 64
beginning 66
priority 116
introgression 294
introit 998
intromission 228
intromit
discontinue 142
receive 296
introspection 441, 457
introspective 451
introvert 218
intrude
interfere 24
inopportune 135
intervene 228
enter 294
encroach 303
intruder 57
intrusiveness 682
intrust 755, 787
intuition *mind* 450
unreasoning **477**
knowledge 490
intumescence 194, 250
intwine 43, 243
inunction 223
inundate
effusion 337
flow 348
redundance 641
inunderstanding 452
inurbanity 895
inure 613, 673
inured
insensible 823
inusitation 614
inutility **645**
invade *ingress* 294
encroach 303
attack 716
invalid
powerless 158
illogical 477
diseased 655
undue 925
invalidate
disable 158
weaken 160
confute 479
invaluable 648
invariable
intrinsic 5
uniform 16
conformable 82
stable 150
invasion
ingress 294
attack 716
invective 932
inveigh 932
inveigle 545, 615
invent
discover 480*a*
imagine 515
lie 544
devise 626
invented
untrue 546
invention 480*a*
inventive
skilful 698
inventor 164
inventory 86
inverse 14, 218
inversion
derangement 61
change 140
of position **218**
contraposition 237
reversion 145
language 577
invertebrate 158
invest
empower **157**
clothe 225
besiege 227, 716
commission 755
give 784
lend 787
expend 809
– in *locate* 184
purchase 795
– money 817
– with *ascribe* 155
investigate 461
investment **225**
– trust 712
make –s 673
inveterate *old* 124
established 150
inborn 820
– belief 484
– habit 613
invidious
painful 830
hatred 898
spite 907
envy 921
invigorate
strengthen 159
invigorating
healthy 656
invincible 159
inviolable
secret 528
right 924
honor 939
inviolate
permanent 141
secret 528
honorable 939
invious *closed* 261
pathless 704
invisibility **447**
invisible *small* 193
not to be seen 447
concealed 526
– ink 528
become – 4
invitâ Minervâ 603, 704
invite *induce* 615
offer 763
ask 765
– the attention 457
inviting
[*see* invite]
pleasing 829
invoice 86
invoke *address* 586
implore 765
pray 990
– curses 908
– saints 998
involucrum 223
involuntary
necessary 601
unwilling 603
– servitude 749
involution [*see* involve]
algebra 85
involve *include* **54**
derange 61
wrap 225
evince 467
mean 516
latency 526
involved
disorder 59
convoluted 248
obscure style 571
in debt 806
involvement 704
invulnerable 664
inward *intrinsic* 5
inside 221
– bound 294
– monitor 926
inweave 219
inwrap 225
inwrought 5
io triumphe! 838, 883
Ionic 597
iota 32
I. O. U. 771, 800
ipse dixit 474, 535
ipsissima verba 494
ipso facto 1
irae
amantium — 918
tantaene animis coelestibus — 900
irascibility **901**
irate 900
ire 900
iridescent 440
Iris 268, 534
iris 440, 441
Irish Bull 353
Irishism 497
irk 688, 830
irksome
tiresome 688
difficult 704
painful 830
weary 841
iron *strength* 159
smooth 255
hard 323
resolution 604
rule with a rod of – 739
– age *adversity* 735
pain 828
– cross 733
– gray 432
– grip 159
– gripe 781
– heel 739
– necessity 601
– rule 739
– entering into the soul 828, 830
– sway 739
– will 604
iron-bound coast
land 342
danger 667
iron-clad
covering 223
defence 717
man of war 726
iron-handed 739
iron-hearted 861
iron-mold 434
irons 752
fire – 386
put in – 751
– in the fire
business 625
redundance 641
active 682
unskilful 699
irony
figure of speech 521
untruth 546
ridicule 856
irradiate 420
irrational
number 84
illogical 477
silly 499
irreclaimable
hopeless 859
vicious 945
impenitent 951
irreconcilable
unrelated 10
discordant 24
unwilling 603
opponent 710
enmity 889
irrecoverable
past 122
hopeless 859
irredeemable 859
irredentist 776
irreducible
discordant 24
out of order 59
unchangeable 150
irrefragable 478
irrefutable 474, 478
irregular
diverse 16*a*
out of order 59
multiform 81
against rule 83
- *in recurrence* 139
distorted 243
combatant 726
irregularity **139**
irrelation 10
irrelevant
unrelated 10
unaccordant 24
sophistical 477
unimportant 643
irreligion **989**
irremediable
bad 649
hopeless 859
(*spoiled* 659)
irremissible 945
irremovable 150
irreparable
hopeless 859
irrepentance 951
irreprehensible 946
irrepressible
violent 173
free 748
excitable 825
irreproachable 946
irreprovable 946
irresistible
strong 159
demonstration 478
necessary 601
irresoluble 150
irresolution **605**
irresolvable 87
irresolvedly 605
irrespective 10
irresponsible
irresolute 605
exempt 927*a*
arbitrary 964
irretrievable
stable 150
lost 776
hopeless 859
irrevealable 528
irreverence 929, 988
irreversible
stable 150
hopeless 859
irrevocable

John Doe and Richard Roe 4
Johnny 894
John's 653
Johnsonian 577
joie, feu de – 883
join *connect* 43
assemble 72
contiguous 199
arrive 292
party 712
sociality 892
marry 903
– battle 722
– in the chorus 488
– forces, hands, 709
– in 778
– issue *discuss* 476
deny 536
quarrel 713
contend 720
lawsuit 969
– the majority 360
– up
enlist 723
– with 709
joint *junction* 43
part 51
accompanying 88
concurrent 178
meat 298
– concern 721
joint-stock 709, 778
joint-tenancy 778
jointure 780
joist 215
joke *absurdity* 497
trifle 643
wit 842
ridicule 856
in – 842
mere – 643
no – *existing* 1
important 642
practical –
deception 545
ridicule 856
disrespect 929
take a – 498
joker 844
jokesmith 844
joking apart 535, 604
jole 236
jollification
amusement 840
intemperance 954
jollity 840, 892
jolly *plump* 192
marine 269
gay 836
ridicule 856
– boat 273
– fellow 892
jolt 276, 315
jolthead 501
Jonah 649
Jones
Davy –' locker 360
Paul – 792
jorum 191
Joseph 960
–'s coat 440
joss 991
– house 1000
jostle *rush* 276
jog 315
clash 713
jot 32, 643
jotting 550, 551
jounce 315
journal *annals* 114
newspaper 531
record 551
magazine 593
narrative 594
accounts 811
journalist
messenger 534
recorder 553
author 593
journey **266**
journeyman
artisan 690
servant 746
joust 720
Jove 979
by – 870
sub –
out of doors 220
air 338
jovial *gay* 836
amusement 840
social 892
jowl 236
joy 827
give one – 896
joyful 836
joyless *painful* 830
sad 837
joy stick 693
J.P. 967
Juan, Don – 962
jube 1000
jubeo, sic volo sic – 741
jubilant *gay* 836
rejoicing 838
boastful 884
jubilee 138, 883
jubilitate 884
Judaeus Apella, credat –
disbelief 485
absurdity 497
Judaism 984
Judas *deceiver* 548
knave 941
– kiss
hypocrisy 544
base 940
judge *decide* 480
master 745
taste 850
magistrate **967**
Judge *deity* 976
Judgment
Day of – 67
judgment
intellect 450
discrimination 465
decision **480**
wisdom 498
sentence 972
judgment-seat 966
judicata, res –
certain 574
judgment 480
judication 480
judicatory 965, 966
judicature 965
Judicature, High Court of – 966
judice: coram –
jurisdiction 965
lawsuit 969
me – 481
sub – *inquiry* 461
lawsuit 969
judicial 965
– Astrology 511
– murder 361
– separation 905
judicious 498
jug 191, 752
juggernaut
kill 361
god 979
idolatry 991
juggle *deceive* 545
cunning 702
juggler 548, 599
jugulate 361
juice 333
juiceless 340
juicy 339
jujitsu 718
jujube 396
julep 396
jumble *mixture* 41
confusion 59
derange 61
indiscriminate 465a
jument 271
jump
sudden change 146
leap 309
neglect 460
at one – 113
– about 315
– at *willing* 602
pursue 622
hasten 684
consent 762
seize 789
desire 865
– to a conclusion
misjudge 481
credulous 486
– over 460
– up 307, 309
jumper 225
junction **43**
juncture
circumstance **8**
junction 43
period 134
jungle *disorder* 59
vegetation 367
junior 127, 541
– counsel 968
junk 273
junket *dish* 298
merry-making 840
Juno 920, 979
junta 696
junto 712
jupe 225
Jupiter **979**
jurare in verba magistri 481, 486
jurat 967
jure: de – *due* 924
legal 963
– divino *due* 924
God 976
juridical 965
jurisconsult 968
jurisdiction **965**
authority 737
Jurisprudence 963
jurist 480, 968
jury 967
empanel a – 969
– box 966
– mast
substitute **147**
refuge 666
jus: summum – 922
– civile
– gentium 963
– nocendi 737
– et norma loquendi 567
jussive 741
just *accurate* 494
right 922
equitable 939
pious 987
– as *similar* 17
same time 120
– do 639
– now 118
– out 123
– reasoning 476
– so 488
– then 113
– the thing
agreement 23
exact 494
– in time 134
juste milieu
middle 68
moderation 174
mid-course 628
justice
right 922
honor 939
magistrate 967
administration of – 965
bring to – 969
court of – 966
do – to *eat* 298
duty 926
praise 931
vindicate 937
not do – to 483
retributive – 922, 972
– seat 966
justifiable 922, 937
justification
vindication 937
religious 987
justle *push* 276
contend 720
jut out 250
jute 205
jutty 250
juvenile 127
– lead 599
juxtaposition 199
j'y suis j'y reste 141

K

kadi 967
kail 840
kaiser 745
kaleidoscope 149, 445
καλόν, τὸ – 845
kangaroo 309
κατ' ἐξοχήν
greatness 31
superiority 33
importance 642
Katerfelto 994
kavass 965
K.C. 968
keck 297
kedge *navigate* 267
anchor 666
keek 527
keel 211
– upwards 21
keelhaul 972
keen *energetic* 171
sharp 253
sensible 375
cold 383
intelligent 498
poignant 821
lament 839
witty 842
eager 865
– blast 349
keener 839
keen-eyed 441
keep *do often* 136
persist 141
continue 143
food 298
store 636
provision 637
refuge 666
preserve 670
citadel 717
custody 751
prison 752
observe 772
retain 781
celebrate 883
– alive 359, 670
– aloof 196, 623
– accounts 811
– an account with 805
– apart 44
– at it 143
– away 187
– back *late* 133
conceal 528
dissuade 616
not use 678
restrain 751
retain 781
– the ball rolling 143
– one's bed 655
– body and soul together *life* 359
health 654
– within bounds 304
– close 781
– company 88
– one in countenance
conformity 82
induce 615
aid 707
encourage 861
– one's countenance
unexcitable 826

sad 837
– one's course 282
– an eye upon 459
– the field 722
– firm 150
– on foot
continuance 143
support 215
preparation 673
– from *conceal* 528
refrain 623
not do 681
restrain 751
– going
continue 143
move 264
– one's ground 141
– one's hand in 613
– one's head above water 731, 817
– hold 150
– holy 987
– house 184
– in ignorance 528
– in *restrain* 751
prohibit 761
– on one's legs 654
– a good look out for 507
– in mind 505
– moving 682
– off *avoid* 623
hinder 706
defend 717
resist 719
prohibition 761
– on *do often* 136
continue 143
persevere 604a
– to oneself 528
– in order 693
– out
- *of the way* 187
- *of harm's way* 864
– pace with 27, 120
– the peace 714
– posted 527
– the pot boiling 143
– one's promise 772
– quiet 265
– a secret 528
– a shop 625
– in sight 459
– silence 585
– straight 944
– in suspense
uncertainty 475
irresolution 605
– in the thoughts 505
– time
punctual 132
music 416
– to 604a
– together 709
– under
authority 737
subjection 749
restraint 751
– up [*see below*]
– in view
attend to 457
remember 505
expect 507
– waiting 133
– watch 459
– one's word 939
keep up
continue 143
preserve 670
stimulate 824
– appearances 852
– the ball 682, 840
– a correspondence 592
– the memory of 505
– one's spirits 836
– with 274
keeper 370, **753**
keeping
congruity 23
in – 82
safe – *safety* 664
preservation 670
keepsake 505
keg 191
kelpie 979
kelson 211
kempt 652
ken 441, 490
beyond mortal – 360
kennel
assemblage 72
hovel 189
ditch 259
conduit 350
Kentish fire 931
képi 225
kérb-stone 233
kerchief 225
wave a – 550
kern *quern* 330
low fellow 876
varlet 949
kernel *heart* 5
cause 153
central 222
important 642
kerosene 356
ketch
ship 273
Ketch, Jack – 975
kettle *vessel* 191
caldron 386
– drum *music* 417
tea-party 892
– of fish
disorder 59
difficulty 704
key *cause* 153
opener 260
music 413
color 428
interpretation 522
indication 550
instrument 631, 633
emblem of authority 747
deliver the –s of the city 725
key-hole 260
key-note *model* 22
rule 80
music 413
key-stone
support 215
motive 615
importance 642
completion 729
khaki 225, 433
khan *inn* 189
governor 745
khedive 745
kibitka 272
kibitzer 682
kick *impulse* 276
recoil 277
assault 716
thrill 821
spurn 930
punish 972
– against
oppose 708
resist 719
– against the pricks
useless 645
rash 863
unequal 28
superior 33
– up a dust
active 682
discord 713
insolent 885
– a row 900
– one's heels
kept waiting 133
nothing to do 681
– off 62
– up a row
violent 173
discord 713
– over the traces 742
kicking, alive and – 359
kickshaw *food* 298
trifle 643
kid *child* 129
progeny 167
leather 223
not to be handled with – gloves
dirty 653
difficult 704
kidnap
deceive 545
take 789
steal 791
kidney *class* 75
kilderkin 191
Kilkenny cats 713
kill 361
– or cure 662
– the fatted calf 883
– the goose with golden eggs 699
– with kindness 902
– the slain 641
– time 106
inactivity 683
amusement 840
– two birds with one stone 682
killing 361
delightful 829
kill-joy 706
kiln 386
kilowatt 466
kilt 225
kimbo 244
kimono 225
kin 75
kind *class* 75
benevolent 906
– regards 894
kinder-garten 542
kindle *cause* 153
produce 161
quicken 171
inflame 173
set fire to 384
excite 824
incense 900
kindling wood 388
kindred 9, 11
kine 366
kinematics 264
kinetic energy 157
king 745
every inch a –
authority 737
rank 875
–maker 694
King –'s Bench 752, 966
–'s birthday 268
–'s counsel 968
– Death 360
–'s English 560
–'s evidence 529
–'s highway 627
–'s ransom 648
– of Kings 976
kingcraft 693
kingdom
region 181
property 780
– of heaven 981
kingly 737
king-post 215
kink 248, 378, 608
kiosk 189, 1000
kip 961
kirk 1000
kirtle 225
kismet 601
kiss *touch* 199
courtesy 894
endearment 902
– the book 535
– the hem of one's garment 928
– in the ring 840
– the rod 725
kit *class* 75
equipment 191
fiddle 417
–bag 191
kitcat 556
kitchen 191, 691
– maid 746
– range 386
kitchener 386
kitchenette 691
kite *fly* 273
bill 800
fly a – *credit* 805
insolvency 808
– balloon 273, 726
kith 11
kithless 87
kitten *animal* 366
young 129
bring forth 161
playful as a – 836, 840
kleptomania
insanity 502
stealing 791
desire 865
kleptomaniac 504
knack 698
get into the – 613
knacker 361
knag 706
knaggy 901a
knap 206
knapsack 191
knave 548, **941**
– of hearts 897
knavery
deception 545
cunning 702
improbity 940
vice 945
knead *mix* 41
mold 240
soften 324
stroke 379
knee *angle* 244
bend the –
stoop 30
submission 725
down on one's –s
humble 879
on one's –s
beg 765
respect 928
atone 952
on the –s of the gods 121, 152
knee-deep 208, 209
kneel *stoop* 308
submit 725
beg 765
servility 886
courtesy 894
ask mercy 914
respect 928
worship 990
knell 363
strike the death – 361
knickerbockers 225
knicknack 643, 847
knife 253
play a good – and fork *eat* 298
appetite 865
war to the – 708
knight 875
– errant
madman 504
defender 717
rash 863
philanthropist 910
–'s move 279
– service 777
– of the road 792
– Templar 71
knit 43
well – 159
– the brow
discontent 832
anger 900
disapprobation 932
knitting 847
knob *pendency* 214
ball 249
protuberance 250
knock *blow* 276
sound 406
hard –s 720

484
– apart
exclude 55
relinquish 782
– aside
neglect 460
reject 610
disuse 678
give up 782
– on the table 133
– the axe at the root of tree 162
– bare 529
– before 527
– brother 996
– by *store* 636
sickness 655
disuse 678
– to one's charge 938
– claim to 924
– in the dust 162
– eggs 161
– at the door of 155
– down [*see* below]
– at one's feet 763
– figure *nonentity* 4
model 22
representation 554
– one's finger upon 480*a*
– the first stone 66
– the flattering unction to one's soul 831, 834
– the foundations 153, 673
– ghosts 992
– hands on
use 677
take 789
rite 998
– under hatches 751
– one's head on the block 942
– heads together 695, 709
– in *eat* 298
store 636
provide 637
– on 972
open *divest* 226
opening 260
show 525
disclose 529
– oneself open to 177
– out
horizontal 213
corpse 363
plan 626
expend 809
– oneself out for 673
– over 133
– reader 996
– under restraint 751
– in ruins 162
– siege to 716
– stress on 642
– to *attribute* 155
rest 265
– it on thick
cover 223
too much 641
flatter 933
– together 43
– train 626
– up *store* 636
sickness 655
disuse 678
– waste 162
lay down *locate* 184
horizontal 213
assert 535
renounce 757
relinquish 782
pay 807
– one's arms
pacification 723
submission 725
– the law
certain 474
assert 535
command 741
insolence 885
– one's life 360
– a plan 626
layer 204
layette 225
layman 699, 997
laystall 653
lazaret 662
lazar-house 662
lazy 683, 927
lazzarone 683
lb. 319
lea *land* 342
plain 344
leach 335
lead *superiority* 33
in order 62
pioneer 64
influence 175
tend 176
soundings 208
- in motion 280
heavy 319
rôle 599
induce 615
direct 693
authority 737
heave the – 466
red – 434
take the –
influence 175
importance 642
authority 737
white – 420
– to the altar 903
– astray 495
– captive
subject 749
restraint 751
– a merry chase 623
– the choir 990
– a dance
run away 623
circuit 629
difficulty 704
disrespect 929
– the dance 280
– one to expect 511
– a life 692
– on 693
– to no end 645
– by the nose 737
– off 62
– the way
precedence 62
begin 66
precession 280
importance 642
direction 693
repute 873
leaden *dim* 422
colorless 429
grey 432
inactive 683
leader
precursor 64
dissertation 595
director 694
counsel 968
– writer 593
leading
beginning 66
important 642
– article 595
– lady 599
– note *music* 413
– part 175
– question 461
– seaman 745
– strings
childhood 127
child 129
pupil 541
subject 749
restraint 751, 752
leads 223
leaf *part* 51
layer 204
plant 367
- of a book 593
turn over a new – 658
– green 435
leafless 226
leaflet 531
leafy 256
league *length* 200
co-operation 709
party 712
– of Nations 696
leak *crack* 198
dribble 295
waste 638
spring a –
injury 659
– out
disclosure 529
leaky *imperfect* 651
leal 743
lean *thin* 203
oblique 217
– on 215
– to *shed* 191
willing 602
– towards 923
– upon *belief* 484
subjection 749
hope 858
leaning
tendency 176
willingness 602
desire 865
friendship 888
favoritism 923
leap
sudden change 146
ascent 305
jump 309
–s and bounds 274
make a – at 622
– in the dark
experiment 463
uncertain 475
chance 621
rash 863
– with joy 838
– year 138
leap-frog 840
learn 490, 539
– by experience 950
– by heart 505
learned 490
learner 541
learning 490, 539
lease *property* 780
lending 787
grant a – 771
take a new – of life 654
– and release 783
leasehold 780
leash *lie* 43
three 92
hold in – 751
least
– *in quantity* 34
– *in size* 193
at the – 32
leather *skin* 223
tough 327
beat 972
nothing like – 481
– bottle 191
– or prunello 643
leave *remainder* 40
part company 44
relinquish 624
permission 760
bequeathe 784
French – 623
take – *depart* 293
freedom 748
– alone
inaction 681
freedom 748
permit 760
– the beaten track 83
– to chance 621
– an inference 526
– a loophole 705
– in the lurch
pass 303
decisive 545
– no trace
be no more 2
disappear 449
obliterate 552
– it to one 76
– to oneself 748
– off *cease* 142
desuetude 614
relinquish 624
disuse 678
– out 55
– out of one's calculation 460
– a place 293
– ad referendum 605
give me – to say 535
– undecided 609*a*
– undone 730
– a void *regret* 833
– word 527
leaven
component 56
cause 153
lighten 320
qualify 469
unclean 653
deterioration 659
bane 663
leavings
remainder 40
useless 645
lecher 962
lechery 961
lectern 1000
lection *special* 79
interpretation 522
lectionary 998
lecture *teach* 537
speak 582
dissertation 595
censure 932
sermon 998
– room 542
lecturer
teacher 540
preacher 996
lectureship 542
led – captain
follower 746
servile 886
favorite 899
– by the nose 749
ledge *height* 206
horizontal 213
shelf 215
projection 250
ledger *list* 86
record 551
accounts 811
lee 236
leech 662, 695
leef 829
leek eat the –
recant 607
submit 725
Lee-Metford
rifle 727
leer *stare* 441
dumb-show 550
leery 702, 864
lees 653
lee-shore 665, 667
leet, court – 936
lee-wall 666
leeward 236
lee-way *space* 180
tardy 133
navigation 267
deviation 279
progression 282
shortcoming 304
left *residuary* 40
sinistral 239
over the – 545
– alone 748
– in the lurch 732
– to shift for oneself 893
pay over the – shoulder 808
left-handed
clumsy 699
– compliment 932
– marriage 903
leg *support* 215
walker 266

debauched 961
lichgate 363
lichen 367
licit 760, 924
lick *lap* 298
conquer 731
punish 972
– the dust 933
– into shape 240
lickerish
savory 394
desirous 865
fastidious 868
licentious 961
lickpenny 819
lickspittle 886
lictor 965
lid 223
lie *situation* 183
presence 186
recline 213
falsehood 544
untruth 546
give the – to 536
white – 617
– abed 683
– in ambush 528
– by 681
– at one's door 926
– down *flat* 213
rest 687
– fallow 674
– hid 528
– in *be* 1
give birth 161
– low 528
– under a necessity 601
– in a nutshell 32
– on 215
– over *defer* 133
destiny 152
– in one's power 157
– at the root of 153
– still 265
– to
quiescence 265
inaction 681
– under 177
– in wait for
expect 507
inaction 681
lief *pleasant* 829
as – *willing* 602
choice 609
liege 745
liegeman 746
lien 771, 805
lienteria 653
lieu 182
in – of 147
lieutenant 745, 759
lord – 965
life *essence* 5
events 151
vitality 359
biography 594
activity 682
conduct 692
cheerful 836
animal – 364
battle of – 682
come to – 660
infuse into
excite 824
put – into 359
recall to – 660
see – 840
support – 359
take away – 361
tenant for – 779
– to come 152
– after death 981
– or death
need 630
important 642
contention 720
– and spirit 682
Life, the 976
life-blood 5, 359
life-boat 273, 666
life-giving 168
lifeguards 726
lifeless 172, 360
lifelike 17
lifelong 110
life-preserver 666, 727
life-size 192
lifetime 108
life-weary 841
lift *raise* 307
aid 707
steal 791
– cattle 791
– up the eyes 441
– a finger 680
– hand against 716
– one's head 734
– up the heart 990
– the mask 529
– the voice
shout 411
speak 582
lift-smoke 840
ligament 45
ligation 43
ligature 45
light *state* 7
small 32
window 260
velocity 274
arrive 292
descend 306
levity 320
kindle 384
watch 388
luminosity 420
luminary 423
- *in colour* 429
white 430
aspect 448
knowledge 490
interpretation 522
unimportant 643
easy 705
gay 836
loose 961
blue – *signal* 550
bring to –
discover 480a
manifest 525
disclose 529
children of – 987
come to – 529
false – 443
foot –s 599
half – 422
make – of
underrate 483
easy 705
inexcitable 826
despise 930
in one's own – 699
obstruct the – 426
side – 490
see the – *life* 359
publication 531
transmit – 425
throw – upon 522
a – breaks in upon one 529
– under a bushel
hide 528
not hide 878
modesty 881
– comedy 599
– cruiser 726
– fantastic toe 309
– upon one's feet 664
– heart 836
– of heel 274
– horse 726
– infantry 726
– purse 804
– and shade 420
– of truth 543
– up *illumine* 420
excite 824
cheer 836
– upon *chance* 156
arrive at 292
discover 480a
acquire 775
Light of the World 976
lighten
make light 320
illume 420
facilitate 705
lighter *boat* 273
lighterage 812
lighterman 269
light-fingered 791, 792
light-footed 274, 682
light-headed 503
lighthouse 550
lightless 421
light-minded 605
lightning
velocity 274
flash 420
spark 423
like greased – 113
lightsome
luminous 420
irresolute 605
cheerful 836
ligneous 367
lignite 388
lignography 558
ligulate 205
like *similar* 17
relish 394
enjoy 377, 827
wish 865
love 897
do what one –s 748
look – 448
we shall not look upon his – again 33
– master like man 19
– a pin in paper 58
likely 472
think – 507
likeness 21, 554
bad – 555
likewise 37
liking 865, 897
have a – for 827
to one's – 829
lilac *color* 437
Liliputian 193
Lillith 994
lilt 416, 836
lily *white* 430
beauty 845
paint the – 641
lily-livered 862
limæ labor
improve 658
toil 686
limature 330, 331
limb *member* 51
instrument 633
scamp 949
– of the law 968
limber 272, 324
limbo *prison* 751, 752
pain 828
purgatory 982
lime *entrap* 545
– light 423, 531, 599
Limehouse 908
limine, in – 66
limit *complete* 52
end 67
circumscribe 229
boundary 233
qualify 469
restrain 751
prohibit 761
limitarian 984
limitation [*see* limit]
estate 780, 783
limited
- *in quantity* 32
- *in size* 393
to a – extent
imperfect 651
limitless 105
limitrophe 197
limn 556
limner 559
limousine 272
limp *weak* 160
slow 275
supple 324
fail 732
limpid 425
lin 343, 348
lincture 662
line *fastening* 45
continuous 69
ancestors 166
descendants 167
length 200
no breadth 203
string 205
lining 224
outline 230
straight 246
of steamers 273
direction 278
music 413
appearance 448
measure 466
mark 550
writing 590
verse 597
vocation 625
army and navy 726
boundary – 233
draw the – 465
drop a – to 526
in a –
continuous 69
straight 246
in a – with 278
read between the –s 522
sounding – 208
straight – 246
troops of the – 726
– of action 692
– of battle 69
– of battle ship 726
– engraving 558
– of march 278
– of road 627
lineage *kindred* 11
series 69
ancestry 166
posterity 167
lineament
outline 230
feature 240
appearance 448
mark 550
linear
continuity 69
pedigree 166
length 200
linen 225
liner 273
lines
fortification 717
hard –
adversity 735
severity 739
reins 752
linger *protract* 110
delay 133
loiter 275
lingerie 225
lingo 560, 563
lingua franca 563
linguacious 584
lingual 560, 582
linguist 492
linguistics 560
liniment 356, 662
lining 224
link *relation* 9
connect 43
connecting - 45
part 51
term 71
crossing 219
torch 423
golf –s 840
missing – 53, 729
linked together
party 712
linoleum 223
linotype 591
linseed oil 356
linsey-wolsey 41
linstock 388
lint 223
lintel 215

serve – 989
mammoth 192
man *adult* 131
mankind 372
male 373
prepare 673
workman 690
servant 746
courage 861
husband 903
make a – of 648, 861
Son of – 976
straight – 599
to a – 488
–at-arms 726
one's – of business 758
–'s estate 131
– in office 745
– in the street 876
–of-war 273, 726
–of-war's man 269
– at the wheel 694
– and wife 903
manacle 751, 752
manage 693
– to *succeed* 731
manageable 705
management
conduct 692
skill 698
manager
stage - 599
director 694
managery 693
manche après la cognée, jeter le – 859
mancible 637
mancipation 751
mandamus 741
mandarin 745
mandate 630, 741
mandible 298
mandolin 417
mandragora 174
mandrel 312
manducation 298
mane 256
man-eater 361
manége 266, 370
manes 362
manet: – altâmente repostum 505
– cicatrix 919
maneuver 680, 702
manful *strong* 159
resolute 604
brave 861
manger 191
manger:
cela se laisse – 394
– son blé en herbe 818
mangle
separate 44
smooth 255
injure 659
mangled 53
mangy 655
man-hater 911
manhood 131, 861
mania *insanity* 503
desire 865
maniac 504
manibus pedibus-que 686
manic 503
manic-depressive 503
manicure 847
manicheism 978
manichord 417
manie 865
maniéré 855
manifest
list 86
visible 446
obvious 525
disclose 529
manifestation 525
manifesto 531
manifold 81, 102
manikin *dwarf* 193
image 554
maniple 103
manipulate
handle 379
use 677
conduct 692
manipulator 621
mankind 372
manly
adolescent 131
strong 159
male 373
brave 861
honest 939
manna *food* 396
– in the wilderness
aid 707
pleasing 829
manner *kind* 75
style 569
way 627
conduct 692
in a – 32
by all – of means 536
by no – of means 602
to the – born 5
mannered 579
mannerism
special 79
unconformity 83
affectation 855
vanity 880
mannerly 894
manners 852, 894
manor 780
lord of the – 779
– house 189
manorial 780
Mansard roof 223
manse 1000
mansion 189
manslaughter 361
mansuetude 894
mantelpiece 215
mantilla 225
mantle *spread* 194
dress 225
foam 353
shade 424
redden 434
robes 747
flush 821, 824
anger 900
mantlet *cloak* 225
defence 717
Mantology 511
manual *guide* 527
schoolbook 542
book 593
advice 695
– labor 686
manubial 793
manufactory 691
manufacture 161, 680
manufacturer 690
manumission 750
manure
agriculture 371
dirt 653
aid 707
manuscript 22, 590
many 102
the – 876
for – a day 110
– irons in the fire 682
– men many minds 489
– times
repeated 104
frequent 136
many-colored 440
many-sided 81, 236
many-tôngued 532
map 234, 527, 554
– out 626
mar 659, 706
marabou 83
marabout 1000
maranatha 908
marasmus
shrinking 195
atrophy 655
deterioration 659
maraud 791
marauder 792
marble *ball* 249
hard 323
sculpture 557
tablet 590
insensible 823
marble 440
marble-hearted 907
march *region* 181
journey 266
progression 282
music 415
dead – 363
forced – 684
on the – 264
steal a –
advance 280
go beyond 303
deceive 545
active 682
cunning 702
– against 716
– of events 151
– of intellect
knowledge 490
improvement 658
– off 293
– on a point 278
– past 882
– of time 109
– with 199
March, Ides of – 601
marches 233
marchioness 875
marcid 203
marconigram 523
marcor 203
mare *horse* 271
female 374
–'s nest 497, 546
–'s tail *wind* 349
cloud 353
marechal 745
margarine 356
margin *space* 180
edge 231
redundance 641
latitude 748
margravate 780
margrave 745, 875
marimba 417
marine *fleet* 273
sailor 269
oceanic 341
soldier 726
tell it to the –s 489, 497
– painter 559
– painting 556
mariner 269
Mariolatry 991
marionnette
representation 554
drama 599
amusement 840
marish 345
marital 903
maritime 267, 341
mark *degree* 26
term 71
take cognizance of 450
attend to 457
indication 550
record 551
writing 590
object 620
importance 642
repute 873
beyond the – 303
leave one's – 873
man of – 873, 875
near the – 197
overshoot the – 699
put a – upon 457
save the – 870
up to the –
enough 639
good 648
skill 698
due 924
wide of the – 196, 495
within the – 304
– down 813
– off 551
– out *choose* 609
plan 626
command 741
– of recognition 894
– with a red letter 883
– time
chronometry 114
halt 265
wait 507
– with a white stone 931
marked [*see* mark]
great 31
affirmed 535
well- 446
in a – degree 31
play with – cards 545
– down 815
marker 550
market *buy* 795
mart 799
bring to – 796
buy in the cheapest &c. – 794
in the –
offered 763
barter 794
sale 796
rig the – 794
– garden 371
– overt
manifest 525
mart 799
– place *street* 189
mart 799
– price 812
– woman 797
marketable 794, 796
marksman 700
marksmanship 698
marl 342
marmalade 396
marmot 683
maroon
color 433, 434
abandon 782, 893
marplot
bungler 701
obstacle 706
malicious 913
marque, letters of – 791
marquee 223
marquetry 440
marquis 875
marriage 903
companionate – 903
ill-assorted – 904
– bells 836
– portion 780
marriageable 131, 903
marrow *essence* 5
interior 221
central 222
chill to the – 385
marrow-bones, on one's –
submit 725
beg 765
humble 879
servile 886
atonement 952
marrowless 158
marry *combine* 48
assertion 535
wed 903
– come up
defiance 715
anger 900
censure 932
Mars 722, 979
– orange 439
marsh 345
marshal
arrange 60
messenger 534
auxiliary 711
officer 745

merged 228
meridian
region 181
room 125
summit 210
light 420
– of life **131**
merit
goodness 648
due 924
virtue 944
make a – of 884
– notice 642
merito, e – 944
meritorious 931
Merlin 994
mermaid 341
monster 83
mythology 979, 980
merman 341
mero motu, ex – 600
merriment
cheerful 836
amusement 840
merry *cheerful* 836
drunk 959
make – *sport* 840
make – with
wit 842
ridicule 856
wish a – Christmas &c. 896
– and wise 842
merry-andrew 844
merry-go-round 312, 840
merry-making 827, 840, 892
merry-thought 842
mersion 337
meruit ferat, palmam qui – 873
merveille, à – 731
mesa 344
mésalliance 24, 903
meseems 484
mesh 198, 219
meshes *trap* 545
difficulty 704
– of sophistry **477**
meshwork 219
mesial
middle 68
mesmerism 992
mesmerist 994
mesne lord 779
mess *mixture* 41
disorder 59
barracks 191
meal 298
difficulty 704
portion 786
make a –
unskilful 699
fail 732
message
intelligence 532
command 741
Messalina 962
messenger 271
envoy **534**
servant 746
– balloon 463
Messiah 976
messianic 976
messmate 890
messuage 189
messy 59
metabolism 140
metacenter 222
metachronism 115
metage 466
metagenesis 140
metagrammatism 561
metal 635
Brittania – **545**
metallic *sound* 410
metalepsis 521
metallurgy 358
metamorphosis 140
metaphor
comparison 464
figure **521**
(*analogy* 17)
metaphrase 522
metaphrast 524
metaphrastic 516
metaphysics 450
metastasis, metathesis
change 140
inversion 218
displacement 270
mete *measure* 466
distribute 786
– out *give* 784
metempsychosis 140
meteor 318, 423
meteoric 173, 420
meteorology 338
meteoromancy 466
meter 466
meter
length 200
poetry 597
metheglin 396
methylated spirit 388
methinks 484
method *order* 58
way **627**
want of – 59
methodical 60
Methodist 984
methodist
journalist 988
methodize 60
Methuselah 130
old as – 12
since the days of – 124
meticulous 772
métier 625
métis 83
metonymy 521
metoposcopy
front 234
appearance 44
interpret 522
metrical
measured 466
verse 597
metrology 466
moderation 174
mid-course 628
metropolis 189
metropolitan
archbishop 996
mettle *spirit* 820
courage 861
man of – 861
on one's –
resolved 604
put on one's –
excite 824
encourage 861
mettlesome
energetic **171**
sensitive 822
excitable 825
brave 861
mettre de l'eau dans son vin 160
meum et tuum 780
disregard distinction between – 791
mew *moult* 226
cry 412
– up 751
mewed up 229
mewl 412
mews 189
mezzanine floor 191, 599
mezzo rilievo
convex 250
sculpture 557
mezzo termine
middle 68
mid-course 628
compromise 774
Mezzofanti 492
mezzosoprano 416
mezzotint 420, 558
miasm 663
mica 425
micacious 204
mi-carême 840
Micawber 460
Michael 977
Michaelmas 998
Micomicon 515
microbe 163, 193
microcosm 193
micrography 193, 441
micrometer 193
micro-organism 193
microphone 418
microscope 193, 445
microscopic 32, 193
mid 68
Midas 803
mid-course **628**
mid-day 125
midden 653
middle - *in degree* 29
- *in order* **68**
- *in space* 222, 228
– classes 736
– constriction 203
– course 29, 628
– man *director* 694
agent 758
– point 29
– term 68
compromise 774
middlemost 222
middling 29, 32, 68, 651
middy 225, 269
midge 193
midget 193
midland 342
midnight *night* 126
dark 421
– oil 539, 689
mid-progress 282
midriff 68, 228
midshipman 269, 745
midships 68
midst - *in order* 68
central 222
interjacent 228
in the – of
mixed with 41
doing 680
midsummer **125**
– day 138
midway 68
midwife
instrument 631
remedy 662
auxiliary 711
midwifery 161, 662
mien 448, 692
miff 900
might *power* **157**
violence 173
energy 686
mightily 31
mighty *much* 31
strong 159
large 192
haughty 878
migraine 378
migrate 266, 295
mikado 745
milch cow
productive 168
animal 366
store 636
mild *moderate* 174
warm 382
insipid 391
lenient 740
calm 826
courteous 894
mildew 653, 663
mildewed
spoiled 659
mile 200
milestone 550
whistle jigs to a – 645
milieu, juste – 174, 628
militant 722
church – 983*a*
military
warfare 722
soldiers 726
– authorities 745
– band 417
– power 737
– time 132
– train 726
militate against 708
militia 726
milk *moderate* 174
semiliquid 352
cows &c. 370
white 430
mild 740
– a he-goat into a sieve 471
flow with – and honey *plenty* 639
prosperity 734
pleasant 829
– of human kindness 906
– the ram **645**
– and water
weak 160
insipid 391
unimportant 643
imperfect 651
milk-livered 862
milksop
incapable **158**
fool 501
coward 862
milky [*see* milk]
semitransparent 427
whiteness **430**
– way 318
mill 330
notch 257
machine **633**
workshop 691
fight 720
like a horse in a – 312
millennium
number 98
period 108
futurity 121
utopia 515
hope 858
millesimal 99
millet seed 193
milliard 98
milliner 225
man – 854
millinery *dress* 225
ornament 847
display 882
man – 855
million 98
multitude 102
people 372
populace 876
for the –
intelligible **518**
easy 705
–s *money* 800
millionaire 803
mill-pond *level* 213
pond 343
store 636
mime 19, 599, 844
mimeograph 19
mimeotype 19
mimic 19
mimodrama 599
minacity 909
minaret 206
minatory 668
minauderie 855
mince *cut up* 44
slow 275
food 298
stammer 583
affected 855
extenuate 937
– the matter 868
not – the matter
affirm 525
artless 703
– the truth **544**
mincemeat of
make – 162
mincing 855

greater – 536
misteaching 538
mister 373
misterm 565
misthink 481
mistime 135
mistral 349
mistranslate 523
mistress *lady* **374**
master 745
possessor **779**
title 877
love 897
concubine 962
mistrust 485
misty [*see* mist]
semi-transparent 427
misunderstand
misinterpret 523
misunderstanding 495, 713
misuse 679
mite *bit* 32
small 193
insufficiency 649
money 800
little – 129
miter *junction* 43
angle 244
crown 747, 999
Mithridate 662
mitigate *abate* 174
improve 658
relieve 834
mitigation
[*see* mitigate]
extenuation 937
mitraille 727
mitrailleur 727
mitten 225
mittimus 741
mix 41
– oneself up with
meddle 682
co-operate 709
– with 720
mixen 653
mixture 41
mere – 59
mix-up 59
mizzen 235
mizzle 348
mnemonics 505
Mnemosyne 505
moa 366
moan 405
cry 411
lament 839
moat *enclosure* 232
ditch 259
canal 350
defence 717
mob *crowd* 72
multitude 102
vulgar 876
hustle 929
scold 932
king – 876
– cap 225
– law
authority 737
illegality 964
mobile
inconstant 149
movable 264
sensitive 822
mobility, the – 876
mobilize
assemblage 72
render movable 264
– troops 722
mobocracy 737
mobster 361
moccasin 225
mock *imitate* **17**, 19
repeat 104
erroneous 495
deceptive 545
chuckle 838
ridicule 856
disrespect 929
– danger 861
– modesty **855**
– sun 423
mockery
[*see* mock]
unsubstantial **4**
solemn – 882
– delusion and snare
sophistry **477**
deception 545
mocking-bird 19
modal 6, 7, 8
mode *state* **7**
music 413
habit 613
method 627
fashion 852
– of expression 569
mode, à la – 852
model *copy* 21
prototype **22**
rule 80
form 240
representation 554
sculpture 557
perfection 650
good man 948
new – 658
– after 19
– condition 80
modeller 559
moderate
average 29
small 32
allay **174**
slow 275
sufficient 639
cheap 815
temperate 953
– circumstances
mediocrity 736
moderately
imperfect 651
moderation [*see* moderate] **174**
mid-course 628
inexcitability 826
moderato *music* 415
moderator 174
lamp 423
director 694
mediator 724
judge 967
modern 123
music 415
art 556
modest *small* 32
modesty
humility **881**
purity 960
mock – 855
modicum *little* 32
allotment 786
modification
difference 15
variation 20*a*
change 140
qualification 469
modish 852
modulation
variation 20*a*
change 140
music 413
module 22
modulus 84
modus: – operandi
method 627
conduct 692
– in rebus 174
– vivendi 723
mogul 745
Mohammedan 984
Mohawk
swaggerer 887
evil-doer 913
moiety 51, 91
moil *active* 682, 686
exertion 686
moisture *wet* 337
humid **339**
mokes 219
molar 330
molasses 396
mole *mound* 206
mold *condition* **7**
matrix 22
convert **144**
form 240
structure 329
earth 342
vegetation 367
model 554
carve 557
decay 653
turn to account 677
molded 820
– on 19
molder 653, 659
molding 847
moldy 653, 659
prominence 250
color 432
refuge 666
defence 717
spot 848
molecular 32
molecule 193
molehill *little* 193
low 207
trifling 643
molest *trouble* 830
molestation
damage 649
malevolence 907
mollia tempora 134
– fandi 588
mollify *allay* **174**
soften 324
mollusk 366
mollycoddle 158
Molly Maguire 548
Moloch
slaughter 361
demon 980
heathen deity 986
molten 384
moment
– *of time* **113**
importance 642
for the – 111
lose not a – 684
not have a – 682
on the spur of the – 612
momentous 152
momentum 276
Momus 838
monachism 995
monad 193
monarch 745
monarchy 737
monastery 1000
monastic 995
monasticism 984
monetary 800
– arithmetic 11
money 800
wealth 803
bad – 800
command of – 803
for one's – 609
made of – 803
make – 775
raise – 788
save – 817
throw away one's – 818
– to burn 641, 803
– burning one's pocket 818
– coming in 810
– down 807
– going out 809
– market 800
– matters 811
– paid 809
–'s worth
useful 644
price 812
cheap 815
money-bag 800, 802
money-belt 800
money-broker 797
money-changer 797, 801
moneyed 803
moneyer 797
money-grubbing 775
moneyless 804
monger 797
mongrel
mixture 41
anomalous 83
dog 366
base 949
moniker 565
moniliform 249
monism 984
monition 527, 668
information 527
warning 668
monitor *hear* 418
oracle 513
pupil-teacher 540
director 694
adviser 695
war-ship 726
inward – 926
monitory
prediction 511
dissuasion 616
warning 668
monk 996
monkey
imitative 19
support 215
catapult 276
ridiculous 857
play the – 499
–jacket 225
– trick
absurdity 497
sport 840
– up 900
monkhood 995
monkish Latin 563
monochord 417
monochrome 429, 556
monocracy 737
monoculous 443
monode 445
monodrame 599
monody 597, 839
monogamist 904
monogamy 903
monogram
sign 550
cipher 533
diagram 554
letter 561
monograph
publication 531
writing 590
book 593
description **594**
monolith 551
monolithic 983*a*
monologue
soliloquy 589
drama 599
monomachy 720
monomania 503
obstinacy 606
fanaticism 825
monomaniac 504
monomark 550
monoplane 273
monopolist 943
monopoly
restraint 751
possession **777**
monostich 572
monosyllable 561
monotheism 983
monotonous
uniform 16
equal 27
repetition 104
permanent 141
- *style* 575
weary 841
dull 843
monotype 591
monsoon 349
monsieur 370
monster
exception 83
large 192
ugly 846
prodigy 872
evil-doer 913
ruffian 949
monstrance 998
monstrosity
[*see* monster]

mutable 149
mutation 140
mutatis mutandis
correlation 12
change 140
interchange 148
mutato nomine de te &c.
parable 521
retaliation 718
mute *funeral* 363
silent 403
sordine 405, 408*a*, 417
letter 561
speechless 581
taciturn 585
dramatis persona 599
deaf – 419
render – 581
mutilate
retrench 38
deform 241
injure 659
mutilated 53
mutilation 619
mutineer 742
mutiny 742
mutt 366
mutter
faint sound 405
mumble 583
grumble 839
threaten 909
mutton-chop
whiskers 256
mutual 12, 148
mutualize 12
mutual understanding 23
muzzle
powerless 158
edge 231
opening 260
silence 403
render speechless 581
restrain 751
gag 752
muzzle-loader 727
muzzy 458
in liquor 959
my: all – eye 546
– stars! 870
mycology 369
mynheer 877
myology 329
myomancy 511
myopia 443
myriad 98, 102
myrmidon 726
myrrh 400
myrtle 897
myself *I* 79
immateriality 317
mysterious
invisible 447
uncertain 475
obscure 519
concealed 528
mystery
[*see* mysterious]
latency 526
secret 533
play 599
craft 625
– ship 726
mystic
uncertain 475
obscure 519
latent 526
concealed 528
sorcery 992
puzzle 475
mystify *falsify* 477
hide 528
misteach 538
deceive 545
myth 515, 546
mythology 979, 984

N

nab *deceive* 545
seize 789
Nabob 745, 803
nacelle 273
nacre 440
nadir 211
nag *horse* 271
quarrel 713
nager entre deux eaux 607
Naiad 341, 979
nail *fasten* 43
fastening 45
measure of length 200
peg 214
sharp 253
hard 323
retain 781
on the –
present 118
pay 807
hit the right – on the head
discover 480*a*
skill 698
– polish 847
naïveté 703
naked *denuded* 226
manifest 525
simplicity 849
– eye 441
– fact 151
– steel 727
– sword 727
– truth 494
namby-pamby 643, 855
name
indication 550
appellation 564
appoint 755
celebrity 873
assume a – 565
call –s
disrespect 929
disapprobation 932
fair – 873
good – 873
in the – of
aid 707
authority 737
due 924
– to conjure with 873
nameless 565, 874
namely 79, 522
namesake 564
Nana Sahib 949
Nanny-goat 374
nap *down* 256
texture 329
sleep 683
cards 840
nape *back* 235
napery 652
Napier's bones 85
napkin 652
buried in a – 460
lay up in a – 678
napless 226
Napoleon *food* 298
cards 840
napping
inattentive 458
inexpectant 508
dull 843
nappy *frothy* 353
tipsy 959
narcissism 897, 943
Narcissus 845
narcosis 376
narcotic 657, 662
nard 356
narration 594
narrow
contract 195
thin 203
intolerant 481
restrict 761
– down 42
– end of the wedge 66
– escape 671
– house 363
– means 804
– search 461
narrow-minded 481, 943
narrowness 203
narrows 343
nasal accent 583
nascent 66
nascitur: – ridiculus mus 509
– a sociis 82
naso, omnia suspendens – 868
nasty
unsavory 395
foul 653
offensive 830
cheap and – 815
natâ, pro re – 770
natal *birth* 66
indigenous 188
natation 267
natatorium 652
nathless 30
nation 372
national 188, 372
– guard 726
nationality 372, 910
nations, law of 963
native
inhabitant 188
artless 703
– accent 580
– land 189
– soil 189
– tongue 560
nativity *birth* 66
cast a –
predict 511
sorcery 992
natty 845
natura il fece e poi roppe la stampa 87
naturae, vis medicatrix – 662
natural *intrinsic* 5
musical note 413
true 494
fool 501
- *style* 576, 578
spontaneous 621
not prepared 674
artless 703
simple 849
– course of things 613
– death *death* 360
completion 729
– impulse 601
– meaning 516
– order of things 82
– state 90
– turn 820
Natural – History 357
– Philosophy 316
– Theology 983
naturalist 357
naturalization
conformity 82
conversion 144
location 184
naturalize
habit 613
naturalized
inhabitant 188
naturally 154
nature *essence* 5
rule 80
tendency 176
world 318
reality 494
artlessness 703
affections 820
animated – 357
organized – 357
second – 613
state of –
naked 226
raw 674
in –'s garb 226
naught *nothing* 4
zero 101
bring to – 732
set at –
make light of 483
opposition 708
disobey 742
not observe 773
disrespect 929
contempt 930
naughty 945
naumachia 720
nausea 841, 867
nauseate 395, 830
nauseous
unsavory 395
unpleasant 830
disgusting 867
nautch dancer 840
nautical 267
naval 267
– authorities 745
– engagement 720
– forces 726
nave *middle* 68
centre 222
church 1000
navel 68, 222
navigation 267
navigator 269
navvy 673, 690
navy 273, 726
– blue 438
nay 536
– rather 14
Nazarene 989
naze 250
N.C.O. 745
ne plus ultra
supreme 33
complete 52
distance 196
summit 210
limit 233
perfection 650
completion 729
neaf 781
neap 195, 207
– tide 36, 340
near *like* 17
- *in space* 197
- *in time* 121
soon 132
impending 152
approach 286
stingy 819
bring – 17
draw – 197
come – 286
– one's end 360
– at hand 132
– the mark 32
– run 32
– side 239
– sight 443
– the truth 480*a*
– upon 3
sail – the wind
skilful 698
rash 863
nearly 32
nearness 197
neat *simple* 42
order 58
in writing 572, 576, 578
clean 652
spruce 845
–'s foot oil 356
– as a pin 58
neat-handed 698
neatherd 370
neb 250
nebula *stars* 318
mist 353
nebular *dim* 422
nebulous *misty* 353
obscure 519
necessarian 601
necessaries 630
necessarily 154
necessitate 630
necessity *fate* 601
requirement 630
compulsion 744
indigence 804
make a virtue of – 698
neck
contraction 195
narrow 203

make love 902
break one's – 360
– and crop
completely 52
turn out - 297
– of land 342
– and neck 27
– or nothing
resolute 604
rash 863
neckcloth 225
necklace 247, 847
necks 980
necrology 360, 594
necromancer 548, 994
necromancy 992
necropsy 363
necroscopic 363
necrosis 49
nectar 394, 396
need *necessity* 601
requirement 637
insufficiency 640
indigence 804
desire 865
friend in – 711
in one's utmost – 735
needful
necessary 601
requisite 630
money 800
do the – *pay* 807
needle *sharp* 253
perforator 262
compass 693
as the – to the pole
veracity 543
observance 772
honour 939
– in a bottle of hay 475
needle-gun 727
needle-shaped 253
needless 641
needle-witted 498
needlewoman 690
needlework 847
ne'er-do-well 949
nefarious 945
negation **536,** 764
negative
inexisting 2
contrary 14
prototype 22
quantity 84
confute 479
deny 536
photograph 558
refuse 764
prove a – 468
neglect **460**
disuse 678
leave undone 730
omit 773
evade 927
disrespect 929
– of time 115
négligé 225, 674
negligence 460
negotiable 270
negotiate
mediate 724
bargain 769
transfer 783
traffic 794
negotiations
breaking off – 713
negotiator 724, 758
negro 431, 746
negus
drink 298
king 745
neif 781
neigh *cry* 412
boast 884
neighbor 197, 890
neighborhood 183, 197, 227
neighborly
aid 707
friendly 888
social 892
courteous 894
neither 610
– here nor there
irrelevant 10
absent 187
– more nor less
equal 27
true 494
– one thing nor another 83
nem. con. 488
Nemesis
vengeance 919
justice 922
punishment 972
nemine contra-dicente 488
nemo me impune lacessit 715
nenia 839
neogamist 903
neologism 123
neology **563**
neophyte 144, 541
neoteric 123
nepenthe 662, 836
nephelogy 353
nephew 11
nepotism
nephew 11
wrong 923
dishonest 940
selfish 943
Neptune 341
Nereid 341, 979
nerve 159, 861, 885
exposed – 378
nerveless 158
nervous *weak* 160
style 574
timid 860
modest 881
nescience 491
nest
multitude 102
cradle 153
lodging 189
– of boxes 204
nest-egg 636
nestle *lodge* 186
safety 664
endearment 902
nestling 129
Nestor *veteran* 130
sage 500
advice 695
net *remainder* 40
receptacle 191
intersection 219
inclosure 232
snare 545
difficulty 704
gain 775
– profit *gain* 775
receipt 810
nether 207
nethermost 211
netting 219
nettle *bane* 663
sting 830
incense 900
network
disorder 59
crossing 219
neuralgia 378
neurasthenia 655
neuritis 378
neurology 329
neurotic 662
neuter *matter* 316
no choice 609*a*
remain –
irresolute 605
stand –
indifferent 866
neutral *mean* 29
no choice 609*a*
avoidance 623
– tint
colorless 429
grey 432
peace 721
neutrality
mid-course 628
peace 721
insensibility 823
indifference 866
neutralize
compensate 30
counteract 179
névé 383
never 107
– say die
persevere 604*a*
cheerful 836
hope 858
it will – do
inexpedient 647
prohibit 761
discontent 832
disapprobation 932
–dying 112
–ending 112
–fading
perpetual 112
glory 873
– forget 916
– to be forgotten 642
– indebted 807
– hear the last of 841
– mind
neglect 460
unimportant 643
insensible 823
indifferent 866
contempt 930
– more 107
– a one 4
– otherwise 16
– to return 122
– was seen the like 83
– so 31
– tell me 489
– thought of 621
– tired *active* 682
– tiring
persevering 604*a*
neverness **107**
nevertheless 30
new *different* 18
additional 37
novel 123
unaccustomed 614
– birth 660
– blood *change* 140
improve 658
excite 824
– brooms 614, 682
– comer 57
– conditions 469
– departure 66
– edition
repetition 104
reproduction 163
improvement 658
– ideas 537
turn over a – leaf
change 140
repeat 950
give – life to 707, 824
view in a – light 658
put on the – man 950
New Year's Day 138
newaub **745**
new-born 123, 129
Newcastle, carry coals to – 641
new-fangled
unfamiliar 83
change 140
neology 563
new-fashioned 123
new-fledged 129
Newfoundland dog 366
Newgate 752
new-gilt 847
new-model
convert 144
revolutionize 146
improve 658
newness **123**
news **532**
– sheet 531
newsmonger
curious 455
informant 527
news 532
newspaper 531, 551
– correspondent 758
newspaperman 534
newt 366
next
following 63
later 117
future 121
near 197
– friend 759
– of kin 11
– to nothing 32
– world 152
nexus 45
Niagara 348
niais 501
niaiserie 517
nib *cut* 44
end 67
summit 210
point 253
nibble *eat* 298
– at *censure* 932
– at the bait
dupe 547
willing 602
nice
savory 394
discriminative 465
exact 494
good 648
pleasing 829
fastidious 868
honorable 939
– ear 418
– hand 700
– perception 465
– point 704
nicely
completely 52
Nicene Creed 983*a*
nicety 466
niche *recess* 182
receptacle 191
angle 244
– in the temple of fame 873
nicher, se – 184
nick *notch* 257
deceive 545
mark 550
– it 731
– of time 124
Nick, Old – 978
nickel
money 800
nicknack 643
nickname 565
nicotine 392, 663
nictitate 443
nidget 862
nidification 189
nidor 398
nidorous 401
nidus 153, 189
niece 11
niggard 819
nigger 431
– in the woodpile 702
niggle *mock* 929
niggling 643
nigh 197
night 421
labor day and – 686
orb of – 318
– and day 136
– school 542
night-cap 225
nightfall 126
nightingale 416
night-gown 225
nightmare
bodily pain 378
dream 515
incubus 706
mental pain 828
alarm 860
nightshade 663
nigrescent 431
nigrification 431

non-uniformity 16*a*
noodle 501
nook *place* 182
receptacle 191
corner 244
noology 450
noon *mid-day* 125
noon-day *light* 420
clear as –
intelligible 518
manifest 525
nooscopic 450
noose *ligature* 45
loop 247
snare 545
gallows 975
norma loquendi 567
normal
intrinsic 5
mean 29
regular 82
perpendicular 212
– condition
rule 80
normality 80, 502
Normand, répondre en – 544
Norns 601
North 278
- and South 237
Northern 237
– light 423
– star
constant 939
North-west passage 311
nose *prominence* 250
smell 398
with one's – in the air 878
lead by the – 615, 737
led by the – 749
not see beyond one's –
misjudge 481
folly 499
unskilful 699
speak through the – 583
thrust one's – in
interjacence 228
busy 682
under one's –
present 186
near 197
manifest 525
defy 715
put one's – out of joint *defeat* 731
disrepute 874
– ring 847
nose-dive 306
nosegay 400, 847
nosey 455
Nosology 655
nostalgia 833
nostril 351
breath of one's –s 359
stink in the –s 401
nostrum 626, 662
not *negation* 536
what is – 546
what ought – 923
– at all 32
– allowed 964
– amiss 618, 651, 845
– any 101
– bad 651
– bargain for 508
– a bit 536
– to be borne 830
– a Chinaman's chance 471
– come up to 34
– cricket 923
– to be despised 642
it will – do 923
– of the earth 987
– expect 508
– fail 939
– far from 197
– a few 102
– fit to be seen 846
– following 477
– grant 764
– guilty 946
– to be had 471, 640
– having 187, 777*a*
– hardened 950
– hear of 764
– included 55
– know what to make of 519
– a leg to stand on 158
– likely 473
– a little 31
– matter 643
– to mention 37
– mind 823, 930
– often 137
– on your life 489
– one 101
– a particle 4
– particular 831
– pay 808
– a pin to choose 27
– playing the game 923
– within previous experience 137
– to be put down 604
– quite 32
– reach 304
– right 503
– sorry 827
– a soul 101
– on speaking terms 889
– the thing 925
– to be thought of
incogitancy 452
impossible 471
refusal 764
hopeless 859
undue 925
disapprobation 932
– trouble oneself about 460
– understand 519
– vote 609*a*
– wonder 871
– for the world 603, 764
– worth
trifling 643
useless 645
nota bene 457
notabilia 642
notabilities 875
notable
manifest 525
important 642
active 682
distinguished 873
notables 875
notably 31
notary 553, 968
notation 85
notch 198, **257**, 550
note *cry* 412
music 413
take cognizance 450
remark 457
explanation 522
sign 550
record 551
printing 591
epistle 592
minute 596
money 800
fame 873
change one's – 607
make a – of 551
of – 873
take – of 457
– of admiration 870
– of alarm 669
– of preparation 673
note-book
memorandum 505
record 551
compendium 569
writing 590
noted 490, 873
noteworthy
great 31
exceptional 83
important 642
nothing *nihility* 4
zero 101
trifle 643
come to – 304, 732
do – 681
for – 815
go for – 643
good for – 646
make – of
under-estimate 483
fail 732
take – by 732
think of – 930
worse than – 808
– comes amiss 831
– to do 681
– to do with 764
– doing 681
– to go upon 471
– in it 4
– of the kind 18, 536
– loth 602
– on 226
– more to be said 478
– to signify 643
nothingness 2
notice *intellect* 450
observe 457
review 480
information 527
warning 668
bring into – 525
deserve – 642
give –
manifest 525
inform 527
indicate 550
short – 111
take – of 450
this is to give – 457
worthy of – 642
– is hereby given
publication 531
– to quit 782
noticeable 31
notification 527
notion *idea* 453
notional 515
notoriety 531, 873
notorious
known 490
public 531
famous 873
infamous 874
notturno 415
notwithstanding 30
nought
[*see* naught]
noun 564
nourish 707
nourishment
food 298
nous 498
nous avons changé tout cela 140
nouveau riche 123, 734, 876
Nova Zembla 383
novation 609
novel
dissimilar 18
new 123
unknown 491
tale 594
novelette 594
novelist 594
novice
ignoramus 493
learner 541
bungler 701
religious 996
novitiate 539, 673
novocaine 376, 381
novus homo 57, 876
now 118
– and then 136
– or never 134
noways 32
nowhere 187
nowise 32, 536
noxious 649, 657
noyade 361, 972
noyerait dans une goutte d'eau, il se – 699
nozzle
projection 250
opening 260
air-pipe 351
nuance 15, 465
nubibus, in – 2, 515
nubiferous 353, 426
nubile 131, 903
nucleus *middle* 68
cause 153
centre 222
kernel 642
nuda veritas 494
nude 226, 849
nudge 550
nudity 226
nugacity 499, 645
nugae canorae 517, 842
nugas, magno conatu magnas – 643
nugatory 158
unimportant 643
nuggar 273
nugget *mass* 192
money 800
nuisance 619, 830
null 4
– and void
inexistence 2
powerless 158
unproductive 169
illegal 964
declare – and void
abrogation 756
non-observance 773
nulla dies sine lineâ 682
nullah 198
nullâ pallescere culpâ, nil conscire sibi – 946
nulli secundus 33
nullibiety 187
nullify *inexistence* 2
compensate 30
destroy 162
abrogate 756
not observe 773
not pay 808
nullity 2, 4
nullius jurare in verba magistri 487
numb
physically insensible 376, 381
morally insensible 823
-skull 493
number
part 51
abstract - **84**
count 85
plural 100
- *of a magazine* &c. 593
– among 76
take care of – one 943
– of times 104
numbered: days –
kill 361
necessity 601
hopeless 859
– with the dead 360
numberless 105
numbers *many* 102
verse 597
numbness 375, **381**
numerable 85

ocean 341
plough the – 267
oceanography 341
ocher 433, 439
yellow – 436
ochlocracy 737
o'clock 114
know what's – 698
octagon 244
octahedron 244
Octateuch 895
octave
eight 98
music 413
period 108
octavo 593
octet 98
octifid 99
octodecimo 593
octogenarian 98, 130
octoroon 41
octroi 812
octuple 98
ocular 441
– demonstration
see 441
visible 446
– inspection 441
oculis subjecta fidelibus 446
oculist 662
od force 992
odalisque 746
odd *remaining* 40
exception 83
single 87
insane 503
vulgar 851
ridiculous 853
– fellows 712
– fish 857
oddity 857
oddments 51
odds *inequality* 28
superiority 33
chance 156
discord 713
at – 24, 713
long – 704
what's the – 643
– against one 665
the – are 472
– and ends
remainder 40
mixture 41
part 51
useless 645
ode 597
odi profanum vulgus 878
Odin 979
odious
disagreeable 830
ugly 846
hateful 898
odium *disgrace* 874
hatred 898
blame 932
odium theologicum 481, 988
church 995
odograph 200
odometer 200
odontoid 250, 253
odor 398
in bad – 932
– of sanctity 897
odylic force 992
odzookens 870
Oedipus 462, 524
– complex 897
Davus sum non – 703
oeil de maitre 459
o'er [*see* over]
oeuvre 161
of: – all things 33
– course 82, 154
– late 123
– one mind 23
– no effect 169
– old 122
– a piece
uniform 16
similar 17
agreeing 23
off 196
be – 623
keep – 623
make – with 791
move – 287
sheer – 287
stand – 287
start – 293
– one's balance 605
throw – one's center 874
– one's guard 260, 508
– one's hands 776
take – one's hands 785
– one's head 503
– one's legs 284, 309
– one's mind 452
– and on
periodical 138
changeable 149
irresolute 605
throw – the scent
uncertain 475
avoid 623
– side 238
– with you 297
offal 653
offence *attack* 716
anger 900
guilt 947
offend 830, 945
– against the law 964
offensive
unsavory 395
fetid 401
foul 653
aggressive 716
displeasing 830
distasteful 867
obnoxious 898
– and defensive alliance 712
– to ears polite 579
offer *proposal* **763**
– the alternative 609
– a choice 609
– of marriage 902
– oneself 763
– up prayers 990
– sacrifice 990
– for sale 796
offering *gift* 784
burnt – 990
sin – 952
offertory *gift* 784
worship 990
rite 998
off-hand *soon* 132
inattentive 458
careless 460
spontaneous 612
office *doing* 170
room 191
business 625
mart 799
worship 900
do one's – 772
good –s 724, 906
hold – 693
kind –s 906
do an ill – 907
man in – 694
officer *director* 694
commander 745
constable 965
offices
kitchen &c. 191
official *certain* 474
true 494
business 625
man in office 694
authoritative 737
master 745
servant 746
officialism 739
officiate
business 625
act 680
conduct 692
religious 998
officio ex –
officer 694
authority 737
duly 924
officinal 613
officious 682
offing 196, 341
offscourings 645, 653
offset
compensation 30
offspring 167
offshoot *adjunct* 39
part 51
effect 154
offspring 167
offspring *effect* 154
posterity 167
offuscate 121, 426
often *repeated* 104
frequent 136
most – 613
– to be met with 136
ogee 847
Ogham 590
ogive 215
ogle *look* 441
desire 865
rude 895
endearment 902
ogpu 696
ogre *bugbear* 860
evil-doer 913
demon 980
oil *lubricate* 332
grease 355, **356**
pour – on
relieve 834
– on the troubled waters 174, 714
– lamp 423
– stove 386
oiled *drunk* 959
oilcloth 223
oilskin 386
oil-painting 556
oily *smooth* 255
greasy 355
servile 886
courteous 894
flattery 933
oinomania 959
ointment
grease 356
remedy 662
O.K. 58
old 124
of – 122
– age 128
die of – age 729
– bachelor 904
– clothes 225
– fashioned 851
– fogey 501, 857
– joke 842
– maid *cards* 840
spinster 904
– man *veteran* 130
husband 903
– man of the sea 706
– Nick 978
– school 124
obstinate 606
habit 613
pay off – scores 718
– song
repetition 104
trifle 643
cheap 815
– stager
veteran 130
actor 599
proficient 700
– story
repetition 104
stale news 532
love 897
– times 122
one's – way 613
– woman *fool* 501
wife 903
Oldbuck 122
olden 124
older 128
oldest inhabitant
not in memory of – 137
old-fashioned 124, 851
oldness 124
oleagine 356
oleaginous 355
oleomargarine 356
oleum addere camino 35, 173
olfactory 398
olid 401
oligarch 745
oligarchy 737
olio 41
olive-branch
infant 129
offspring 167
pacification 723
olive-green 435
olla podrida 41
Olympiad 720
Olympus 981
omber 840
ombres chinoises 448
omega *end* 67
omelet 298
omen 512
ominate 511
ominous
predicting 511
indicating 550
danger 665
hopeless 859
omission
incomplete 53
exclusion 55
neglect 460
failure 732
non-observance 773
guilt 947
omitted 2, 187
omne tulit punctum 731
omnibus 272
omnifarious 81
omnific 168
omniform 81
omnigenous 81
omnipotence 157, 976
omnipresence 186, 976
omniscience 490, 976
omnium gatherum
mixture 41
confusion 59
assemblage 72
omnivorous
eating 298
desire 865
gluttony 957
omphalos 68
on *forwards* 282
– account of 155
– all accounts 52
– that account 155
– approval 463
– an average 29
– the brink of 32
– the cards 152
– foot *duration* 106
event 151
doing 170
– the fire 730
– all fours 13, 23
– the other hand 30
– one's head 218
– the increase 35
– a large scale 31
– these lines 627
– the move 264
– the nail 118
– no account 32
– no occasion 107
– a par 27
– the part of 9
– the point of 111
– the present oc-

full – 175
full of – 836
in – 842
– along with 709
– one's best card 686, 698
– of colors 440
– at cross purposes 59, 523
– a deep game 702
– the deuce 825
– the devil 907
– one false
disappoint 509
falsehood 544
deception 545
– fast and loose
falsehood 544
irresolute 605
tergiversation 607
caprice 608
– on the feelings 824
– first fiddle 642, 873
– the fool
folly 499
clumsy 699
amusement 840
ridiculous 853
ridicule 856
– for *chance* 621
– a game
pursue 622
conduct 692
pastime 840
– the game 939
– into the hands of 709
– havoc 659
– hide and seek 528, 623
– a joke 853
give – to the imagination 515
– of light 420
– the monkey 499
– off 545
– a part
false 544
drama 599
action 680
– one's part 625, 692
– second fiddle 34, 749
– one a trick 509, 545
– tricks with 699, 702
– truant 623
– upon 545, 856
– with 460
– upon words
misinterpret 523
neology 563
wit 842
play-boy 818
play-day 840
played out
end 67
fatigue 688
completion 729
failure 732
player
musician 416
actor 599
– piano 417
playfellow 890
playful 836
– imagination 515
playground 728, 840
play-house 599
playmate 890
playsome 836
plaything
trifle 643
toy 840
make a – of 749
playwright 599
plea
defence 462
argument 476
excuse 617
vindication 937
lawsuit 969
plead *argue* 467
plea 617
beg 765
– one's cause 937
– guilty 950
pleader *lawyer* 968
pleading, special – 477
pleadings 969
pleasance 189, 840
pleasant
agreeable 829
amusing 840
witty 842
make things –
deceive 545
induce 615
please 829
flatter 933
pleasantry 840, 842
please 829
as you – 743
do what one –s 748
if you –
obedience 743
consent 762
request 765
– oneself 943
pleasurableness 829
pleasure
physical - 377
will 600
moral - 827
dissipation 954
at – 600
at one's – 737
during – 108*a*
give – 829
man of – 954*a*
make a toil of – 682
take one's – 840
will and – 600
with –
willingly 602
pleasure-giving 829
pleasure-ground
demesne 189
amusement 840
pleat 258
plebeian 851, 876
plébiscite 480, 609
plectrum 417
plectuntur Achivi 739
pledge *affirmation* 535
promise 768
security 771
borrow 788
drink to 883, 894
hold in – 771
take the – 771, 958
– oneself 768
– one's word 768
pledget 263, 662
Pleiades 72, 318
plenary 31, 52
plenipotent 157
plenipotentiary
consignee 758
deputy 759
plentitude 639
in the – of power 159
plenty
multitude 102
sufficient 639
– to do 682
plenum *substance* 3
matter 316
pleonasm
repetition 104
diffuseness 573
redundance 641
plerophory 484
plethora 64
plexal 219
plexus 219
pliable 324
pliant *soft* 324
irresolute 605
facile 705
servile 886
plicature 258
pliers 301, 781
plight *state* 7
promise 768
security 771
evil – 735
– one's faith 902
– one's troth 768, 902
plighted love 897, 902
Plimsoll mark 466
plinth 211, 215
plod *journey* 266
slow 275
persevere 604*a*
work 682
– along 143
plodding 604*a*, 682
dull 843
plot - *of ground* 181
plain 344
story 594
plan 626
realty 780
the – thickens
assemblage 72
plough *furrow* 259
agriculture 371
– the ground 673
– in 228
– the waves 267
– one's way 266
ploughboy
commonalty 876
ploughman 371
ploughshare 253
pluck *cheat* 545
resolution 604
persevere 604*a*
reject 610
take 789
steal 791
courage 861
– up courage 861
– a crow with 932
– out 301
plug 261, 263
– along 143
plum *number* 98
sweet 396
money 800
plumage 256
plumb *vertical* 212
close 261
measure 466
plumber 690
plumb-line 212
plum-colored 437
plume *feather* 256
ornament 847
borrowed –s 788
– oneself 878
plume
coup de – 590
nom de – 565
plumigerous 256
plummet 208, 212
plumose 256
plump
instantaneous 113
fat 192
plunge 310
unexpected 508
– down 306
– upon 292
plumper
expansion 194
vote 609
plunder 791, 793
plunderer 792
plunge
revolution 146
insert 300
dive 306, 310
immerse 337
hurry 684
– into difficulties 704
– into dissipation 954
– headlong 684
– into 676
– in medias res 576, 604
– into sorrow 830
plunged
– in debt 806
– in grief 828
plunger 621
plurality 100
plus 37
plus fours 225
plush 256
Pluto 979, 982
realms of – 982
Plutocracy 803
plutonic 382
Plutus 803
pluvial 348
ply *layer* 204
fold 258
use 677
exert 686
request 765
– one's task 680
– one's trade 625
– a trade 794
Plymouth Brother 984
p.m. 114, 126
pneumatics 334, 338
pneumatology 450
pneumatoscopic 317
poach 791, 964
poacher 792
poachy 345
pock 250
pocket *place* 184
pouch 191
diminutive 193
receive 785
take 789
money 800
treasury 802
brook 826
button up one's – 808
out of – 776, 806
touch the – 800
– the affront 725, 918
pocket-book 551
pocket-handkerchief 225
pocket-money 800
pocket-pistol
bottle 191
pococurante 823, 866
pocula, inter – 959
pod 191, 223
podestà 967
podgy 201
poem 597
book of –s 593
poenitentiae, locus-
pity 914
forgive 918
vindicate 937
repent 950
poesy 597
poet 597
poetaster 597, 855
poetic *style* 574
poetic frenzy 515
poetry 597
poignancy
physical energy 171
pain 378
pungency 392
feeling 821
pogrom 361
point *condition* 8
degree 26
small 32
end 67
term 71
poignancy 171
no magnitude 180*a*
place 182
speck 193
sharp 253
topic 454
mark 550
vigor 574
intention 620
wit 842

– an inquiry 461
– the tenor of one's way 625, 881
pursuer 622
pursuit 622
pursuivant 534
pursy 194
purulent 653
purvey 637
purview 620
pus 653
Puseyite 984
push *exigency* 8
impel 276
progress 282
propel 284
essay 675
activity 682
haste 684
come to the – 704
– aside 460, 929
– forward 682, 707
– from 289
– to the last 133
– on *haste* 684
– out *eject* 297
pushing 282, 284, 682
pusillanimity 862
puss 366
play – in the corner 148
pussy-foot 528, 958
pustule 250, 848
put *place* 184
fool 501
cards 840
clown 876
neatly – 576
– across 484
– about
turn back 283
go round 311
publish 531
– aside
exclude 55
inattention 458
neglect 460
disuse 678
– away
- *thought* 452
relinquish 782
divorce 905
– back
turn back 283
deteriorate 659
restore 660
– before 527
– by 636
– a case 82, 514
– in commission 755
– a construction on 522
– on the cuff 806
– down
destroy 162
record 551
conquer 731
compel 744
pay 807
humiliate 874
– an end to
end 67
stop 142
destroy 162
- *oneself* 361
– in force
complete 729
compel 744
– forth
expand 194
suggest 514
publish 531
assert 535
- *a question* 461
- *strength* 686
– forward
suggest 514
publish 531
ostentation 882
– one's hand to 676
– the horses to 673
– in [*see below*]
– to inconvenience 647
– a mark upon 457
– one's nose out of joint 33
– off *late* 133
divest 226
depart 293
plea 617
– on *clothe* 225
deceive 544
hasten 684
affect 855
– out [*see below*]
– on paper 551
– over 484, 731
– a question 461
– right 660
– the saddle on the right horse 155
– the seal to 729, 769
– to [*see below*]
– together *join* 43
combine 48
assemble 161
– one's trust in 484
– up [*see below*]
– upon 545, 649
put in *arrive* 292
insert 300
– an affidavit 535
– hand 676
– one's head 514
– mind 505
– motion 264
– order 60
– the place of 147
– one's pocket 785
– practice 692
– remembrance 505
– shape 60
– trim 60, 673
– the way of 470
– a word 582, 588
put out
destroy 162
outside 220
extinguish 385
darken 421
distract the attention 458
uncertain 475
difficult 704
discontent 832
– of countenance 874
oneself – of court
sophistry 477
bungling 699
– of gear 158
– of one's head 458
– of joint 61
– of one's misery 914
– to nurse 707
– of order 59
put to *attribute* 155
request 765
– the blush 879
– death 361
– the door 261
– it 704
– one's oath 768
– press 591
– the proof 463
– the question 830
– the rack 830
– rights 60
– sea 293
– shame 874
– silence 581
– the sword 361
– task 677
– use 677
– the vote 609
put up *assemble* 72
locate 184
store 636
– to auction 796
– for 865
– a petition } 765
– a prayer } 990
– for sale 796
– a shutter 424
– the sword 723
– to 615
– with 147, 826
putative
attributed 155
believed 484
supposed 514
putid 643
putrefy 653
putrescence 49
putrid 653
putsch 742
puttee 225
putter 683
putting the weight 840
putty 45
puzzle *uncertain* 475
conceal 528
enigma 533
– out 522
puzzled 475, 533
puzzle-headed 499
puzzling 519
pyæmia 655
pyjamas 225
Pylades and Orestes 890
pylon 206
pyramid *heap* 72
height 206
point 253
pyramids
billiards 840
pyre 363
pyriform 249
pyrology 282
pyromaniac 384, 504, 913
pyromancy 511
pyrometer 389
pyrotechnics 423
pyrotechny 382
Pyrrhic victory 814
pyrrhonism 487, 989
Pythagorean 953
Pythia *oracle* 513
Python, -ess 513
pyx *vessel* 191, 998
temple 1000

Q

Q-boat 726
Q.C. 968
Q.E.D. 478
quack *cry* 412
imposter 548
quackery
falsehood 544
want of skill 699
affectation 855
quacksalver 548
quad 189
quadragesima 956
quadrangle
four-sided 95
precinct 182
house 189
angular 244
quadrant 244, 247
quadrate with 23
quadratic 95
quadrature
four 95
angle 244
quadrennial 95
quadrible 96
quadrifid 97
quadriga 95, 272
quadrilateral
sides 236
angles 244
quadrille 840
quadripartition 97
quadrisection 97
quadrivalent 95
quadroon 41
quadruped 366
quadruplet 96
quadruplex 96
quadruplication 96
quaere 461
quaff 298
– the bitter cup 828
quaggy 345
quagmire
marsh 345
dirty 653
difficult 704
quail 860, 862
quaint *odd* 83
pretty 845
ridiculous 853
quake *oscillate* 314
shake 315
cold 383
fear 860
quakerish 826, 855
Quakerism 984
qualification
[*see* qualify]
power 157
modification **469**
skill 698
discount 813
qualify *change* **140**
modify 469
deny 536
teach 537
qualis ab incepto 141
qualities
character 820
quality *nature* **5**
power 157
tendency 176
nobility 875
qualm *disbelieve* 485
unwilling 603
fear 860
qualms of conscience 950
quamdiu se bene gesserit 108*a*
quand même
compensating 30
opposed 708
quandary 475, 704
quantity **25**, 31, 102
quantum *amount* 25
allotment 786
– mutatus 140
– sufficit 639
quaquaversum 278
quarantine 664, 751
quarrel 24, 713
– with one's bread and butter
bungling 699
discontent 832
quarrelsome 901
quarry *object* 620
mine 636
quart 97
quarter *cut up* **44**
fourth 95
quadrisection **97**
period 108
region 181
locate 184
abode 189
side 236
direction 278
forbearance 740
money 800
mercy 914
give – 914
give no –
kill 361
severe 739
pitiless 914*a*
revenge 919
– of a hundred 98
– upon 184
quarter-day 138
quarter-deck 210
quarterly
periodical 531
quartermaster 637
quartern 95
quarteron 41
quarters *abode* 189
take up one's – 184

R

radically 31
radication 613
radio 532
radio-active 171
316
radio-activity 420
radio-graph 421,
554
radiogram
wireless 532
X-ray 554
radiometer 420, 445
radiomicrometer
389
radiophone 418
radio star 899
radiotelegraph 534
radiotelephone 534
radium 423
radius 200, 202
radix 153
radoter 499
radoteur 501
raff 653, 876
raffle 156
Raffles
thief 792
raft 273
rafter 215
rag 32
tease 830, 856,
929
ragamuffin 876
rage *violence* 173
influence 175
excitement 824,
825
fashion 852
desire 865
wrath 900
the battle –s 722
ragged 226
ragoût 41, 298
rag-picker 876
rags *clothes* 225
useless 645
do to – 384
tear to – 162
worn to – 659
ragtime 415, 473
raid 716, 791
rail *inclosure* 232
prison 752
– at 932
– in
circumscribe 229
restrain 751
railing 232
raillerie, ne pas en-
tendre – 900
raillery 856
railway 627
– speed 274
– station 292
raiment 225
rain *stream* 348
sufficient 639
– or shine 474,
604
rainbow 440
raincoat 225
rainless 340
rains but it pours,
never – 641
rainy day 735
provide against
a – 673, 817
rainy season 348
raise *increase* 35
produce 161
erect 212
elevate 307
excite 824
– alarm 860
– anger 900
– one's banner
722
– a cry 531
– a dust 682
– expectations 858
– the finger 550
– funds 775
– one's head
improve 658
refresh 689
prosperity 734
repute 873
– ghosts 992
– hope 511
– a hue and cry
against 932
– a laugh 840
– the mask 529
– money 788
– a question 461,
485
– a report 531
– a siege 723
– the spirits 836
– spirits from the
dead 992
– a storm 173
– troops 722
– up 212, 824
– the voice 441
– one's voice 535,
932
– the wind 775,
778
raised *convex* 250
raison:
– d'être 620
– de plus 467
raj 737
rajah 745
rajpoot 726
rake *drag* 285
gardening 371
clean 652
profligate 949
intemperance 954
libertine 962
– out 301
– up *collect* 72
extract 301
recall 505
excite 824
– up evidence 467
rake-hell 949, 962
raking-fire 716
rakish
intemperate 954
licentious 961
rallentando 415
rally *arrange* 60
improve 658
restore 660
ridicule 856
encourage 861
– round *order* 58
co-operate 709
rallying: – cry 550,
861
– point 74
ram *impulse* 276
sheep 366
male 373
man-of-war 726
milk the – 645
– down 261, 321
– in 300
Ramadan 956, 993
ramage 367
ramble *stroll* 266
wander 279
folly 499
delirium 503
digress 573
rambler 269
rambling 139
ramification *part* 51
bisection 91
posterity 167
filament 205
symmetry 242
divergence 291
rammer 263, 276
ramose 242
ramp *slope* 217
climb 305
leap 309
rampage 173
rampant
violent 173
prevalent 175
vertical 212
raised 307
free 748
vehement 825
licentious 961
rampart 717
ramrod 263
ramshackle 665
ranch 780
rancid 401, 653
rancor 907, 919
randan 273
random *casual* 156
carriage 272
uncertain 475
aimless 621
talk at –
sophistry 477
exaggerate 549
loquacity 584
- *experiment* 463
chance 621
range *extent* 26
collocate 60
series 69
term 71
class 75
space 180
distance 196
roam 266
direction 278
stove 386
freedom 748
out– 196
long – 196
within – 197
–finder 200
– itself 58
– under, – with 76
ranger
director 694
keeper 753
thief 792
rank *have place* 1
degree 26
thorough 31
collocate 60
row 69
term 71
vegetation 365
fetid 401
estimate 480
bad 649
soldiers 726
glory 873
nobility 875
man of – 875
– and file
continuity 69
soldiers 726
commonalty 876
– marks 745
rankle *unclean* 653
corrupt 659
painful 830
animosity 900
malevolence 907
revenge 919
ranks
fill up the – 660
risen from the –
876
ransack *seek* 461
deliver 672
plunder 791
price 812
atonement 952
– one's brains
451, 515
ransom 672
rant
unmeaning 517
exaggeration 549
diffuse style 573
turgescence 577
speech 582
acting 599
excitement 825
boasting 884
ranter *talker* 584
false piety 988
rantipole 458
rap *blow* 276
sound 406
trifle 643
money 800
not worth a – 804
– on the knuckles
angry 900
censure 932
punish 972
– out *affirm* 535
voice 580
speak 582
– out oaths 885,
908
rapacity
taking 789
stealing 791
avarice 819
greed 865
rape 791, 961
– oil 356
rapid 274
– slope 217
– strides
progress 282
velocity 274
– succession 136
rapids 348
rapier 727
rapine 791
rapparee 792
rappel 722
rapping, spirit –
992
rapport 9
rapports, sous tous
les – 494
rapprochement
714, 888
rapscallion 949
rapt *attention* 457
inattention 458
emotion 821
– in thought 451
raptorial 789, 791
rapture 827, 897
rapturous 827
rara avis
exceptional 83
good 648
famous 873
rare *exceptional* 83
few 103
infrequent 137
light 322
excellent 648
raree show 448, 840
rarefaction 194, 322
rari nantes 103
rarity 322
rasa, tabula – 552
rascal 941, 949
rascality 940
rase *obliterate* 552
rash
skin disease 655
reckless 863
rasher 204
rashness 863
rasp 330, 331
rasper *difficult* 704
rasure 552
rat *recant* 607
smell a –
discover 480*a*
doubt 485
rataplan 407
rat-a-tat 407
ratchet 253
rate *degree* 26
motion 264
measure 466
estimation 480
price, tax 812
abuse 932
at a great – 274
rath *early* 132
fort 717
rather 32, 643
have – 609
– good 651
have – not 867
ratification
confirm 467
affirm 488
consent 762
compact 769
ratio *relation* 9
degree 26
proportion 84
apportionment
786
ratiocination 476
ration *quantity* 25
food 298
provisions 637
allotment 786
short –s 956

refluence *recoil* 277
regress 283
reflux *decrease* 36
recoil 277
regress 283
current 348
refocillate
strengthen 159
refresh 689
reform *convert* 144
improve 658
reformatory 542, 752
reformer 658
refound 144
refraction
deviation 279
light 420
fallacy of vision 443
refractory
obstinate 606
difficult 704
mutinous 742
ill-tempered 901a
refrain *poetry* 597
avoid 623
do nothing 681
temperate 953
– from laughter 837
– from voting 609a
refrain 104
refresh
strengthen 159
cool 385
refit 658
restore 660
recruit 689
relieve 834
– the memory 505
refreshing 377, 829
refreshment
food 298
recruiting **689**
delight 827
refrigeration
anesthetic 376
making cold **385**
refrigerator **387**
reft 44
refuge **666**
refugee 268, 623
refulgence 420
refund 807
refurbish 673
refusal **764**
pre-emption 795
refuse *remains* 40
useless 645
not consent 764
– assent 489
– to associate with 893
– to believe 487
– to hear 460
refute 479
refuted 495
regain 775
– breath 689
regal 737
regale *feast* 298
physical pleasure 377
refresh 689
pleasing 829
amusement 840
regalia 747
regality 737
regard
relation 9
view 441
attention **457**
judge 480
credit 873
love 897
respect 928
approbation 931
have – to 457
merit – 642
pay – to
believe 484
honor 873
– as 484
regardful 457, 459
regardless 458, 823
regards 894, 928
regatta 720, 840
regency 755
regenerate
reproduce 163
restore 660
piety 987
regeneration
divine function 976
baptismal – 998
regent 745, 759
regicide 361
régime
circumstances **8**
conduct 692
authority 737
ancien – 875
regimen *diet* 298
remedy 662
conduct 692
regiment 72, 726
regimentals 225
region **181**
register
arrange 60
list 86
chronicle 114
record 551, 553
registrar 553
registration 551
registry 114
règle: en – 924
regnant 175, 737
regni, anno – 106
regorge 790
regrade 283
regrate 777
regrater 797
regression **283**
regret **833**, 950
express – 952
regretted, to be – 833
reguerdon 973
regular
uniform 16
complete 52
order 58
arrangement 60
rule 80
conformity 82
periodic 138
symmetric 242
habitual 613
by – intervals 58
– return 138
regulars 726
regulate
adjust 23
arrange 60
direct 693
regulated by
conformity 82
regulation 697, 963
regurgitate
return 283
flow 348
restore 790
rehabilitate 660, 790
rehearse
repeat 104
try 463
describe 594
drama 599
prepare 673
Reichsrath 696
reign 175, 737
– of terror 739, 860
reimburse 790, 807
rein 752
– in 275, 751
reincarnation 163
reindeer 271
re infectâ 304, 681
reinforce
strengthen 159
restore 660
aid 707
reinforced concrete 635
reinforcement
addition 37
adjunct 39
materials 635
provision 637
aid 707
reinless 738
reins [*see* rein]
direction 693
give the – to
facilitate 705
lax 738
permit 760
hold the – 693
take the – 737
give – to the imagination 515
reinstall 660
reinstate 660, 790
reinvest 790
reinvigorate 658, 689
Reis Effendi 694
reiterate 104
reject
exclude 55
eject 297
refuse 764
rejected
hateful 898
rejection **610**
rejoice *exult* 838
amuse 840
– the heart
gratify 829
cheer 836
– in 827
– in the name of 564
rejoicing **838**
rejoin *assemble* 72
arrive 292
rejoinder
answer 462
law pleadings 969
rejuvenescence 660
rekindle
ignite 384
excite 824
relapse
turn back 145, 283
fall back **661**
relate *narrate* 594
– to *refer* 9
related *kin* 11
relation **9**
kin 11
narrative 594
relationship 9
relative 11, 464
– position
relativity 9
relator
accuser 938
relax *loose* 47
weaken 160
moderate 174
slacken speed 275
soften 324
inactive 683
repose 687
misrule 738
liberate 750
relent 914
– one's efforts 681
– the mind 452
relaxation
[*see* relax]
amusement 840
dereliction 927
relaxed *weak* 160
relay 635, 637
release *death* 360
deliverance 672
liberate 750
exempt 760
from engagement **768a**
security 771
restore 790
repay 807
forgive 918
exempt 927a
discharge 970
deed of – 923
relegate *banish* 55
transfer 270
remove 297
relent *moderate* 174
soften 324
pity 914
relentless
resolute 604
severe 739
wrathful 900
malevolent 907
revenge 919
impenitent 951
relessee
possessor 779
receiver 785
relevancy 9, 23
relevé 298
reliable 474
reliance
confidence 484
hope 858
relic *remainder* 40
reminiscence 505
token 551
relics *corpse* 362
sacred 998
relict 40, 905
relief
prominence 250
aid 707
comfort **834**
bas – 250, 557
in strong – 446, 525
relieve *improve* 658
aid 707
comfort 834
relievo 250, 557
religieuse 996
religion 983, 987
under the mask of – 988
religionist 988
religious
honorable 939
theological 983
pious 987
over- 955
– education 537
– persuasion 983
– sects 984
religiously exact 494
relinquish 757
– hope 859
– life 360
– property 782
– a purpose 624
recant 607
relinquishment 624, 782
reliquary 191, 998
reliquiæ 362
relish *pleasure* 377
savor 390
condiment 393
savory 394
delight 827
desire 865
relive 660
relucent 420
reluct 720
reluctance
dissuasion 616
unwilling 603
dislike 867
reluctation 719
relume 384, 420
rely 484, 858
rem acu tetigisti 23
remain *be left* 40
endure 106
long time 110
continue 141
be present 186
stand 265
– firm 150
– on one's hands 641
– in one's mind 505
– neuter 605
– in possession of the field 731
remainder **40**
estate 780
in – *posterior* 117
remainder-man 779
remains

riggish 961
right *dextral* 238
straight 246
true 494
property 780
just **922**
privilege 924
duty 926
honor 939
virtuous 944
bill of – 969
by – 924
have a – to 924
set – *inform* 527
disclose 529
that's – 931
– about [*see below*]
– ahead 234
– angle 212
– ascension 466
– away 133
step in the – direction 644
– hand [*see below*]
– itself 660
– and left 180, 227, 236
– line 246
– man in the right place 23
in one's – mind 498, 502
hit the – nail on the head 480*a*, 698
– owner 779
keep the – path 944
in the – place 646
– thing to do 926
– as a trivet 650
– word in the right place 578
right about: to the – 283
go to the – 311, 607
send to the –
eject 297
reject 610
refuse 764
turn to the – 218, 279
right hand
power 157
dextrality 238
help 711
not let the – know what the left is doing 528
– of friendship 888
righteous 944
the – 987
– overmuch 988
Righteousness:
Lord our – 976
Sun of – 976
rightful 922
– owner 779
rightly served, be – 972
right-minded 939, 944
rights 748
put to – 660
set to – 60
stand on one's – 748
rigid *regular* 82
hard 323
exact 494
severe 739
rigmarole 517, 573
rigor 383
– mortis 360
rigorous *exact* 494
severe 739
revengeful 919
rigor 494, 739
Rigsdag 696
rigueur
de – 744
rile *annoy* 830
hate 898
anger 900
rilievo *convex* 250
sculpture 557
rill 348
rim 231
rime *chink* 198
frost 283
rimer 262
rimple 258
rind 223
ring
fastening 45
pendency 214
circle 247
loud 404
resonance 408
test 463
combination 709
clique 712
arena 728, 840
badge 747
rub the – 992
have the true – 494
– the changes
repeat 104
change 140
changeable 149
– in the ear 408
in a – fence 229, 232
– with the praises of 931
– the tocsin 669
– up 527
ringleader
director 694
mutineer 742
ringlet 247, 256
rink 840
rinse 652
rinsings 653
riot *confusion* 59
derangement 61
violence 173
discord 713
resist 719
mutiny 742
run – *activity* 682
excitement 825
intemperance 954
– in *pleasure* 742
rioter 742
riotous 173
rip 949, 962
– open 260
– up *tear* 44
recall the past 505
excite 824
Rip van Winkle 130
riparian 342
ripe 673
– age *old* 128
ripen *perfect* 650
improve 658
prepare 673
complete 729
– into 144
rippet 713
riposte 462
ripple *ruffle* 256
shake 315
water 348
murmur 405
ripuarian 342
rire, pour – 853
rise *grow* 35
begin 66
slope 217
progress 282
ascend 305
stir 682
revolt 742
– again 660
– in arms 722
– from 154
– to the occasion 612
– in price 814
– up *elevation* 307
– in the world 734
risible 838, 853
rising [*see* rise]
– of the curtain 66, 448
– generation 127, 167
– ground
height 206
slope 217
worship the – sun 886
risk *chance* 621
danger 665
invest 787
at any – 604
risqué 961
rissole 298
risum teneatis amici? 853
rite 963, **998**
funeral – 363
ritornello 64, 104
ritual
ostentation 882
rite 998
ritualism 984
rival
emulate 648
oppose 708
opponent 710
compete 720
combatant 726
outshine 873
rivalry *envy* 921
rive 44
rivel 258
river 348
rivet 43, 45
– the attention 457, 824
– the eyes upon 441
– in the memory 505
– the yoke 739
riveted *firm* 150
rivulet 348
rixation 713
Ro 560
road *street* 189
direction 278
way 627
on the –
transference 270
progression 282
approach 286
on the high – to 278
– to ruin
destruction 162
danger 665
adversity 735
road-book 266
roads *lake* 343
roadstead 154
abode 189
refuge 666
roadster 271
roadway 627
roam 266
roan *horse* 271
color 433
roar *violence* 173
wind 349
sound 404, 407
bellow 411, 412
laugh 838
weep 839
roaring *great* 31
– trade 731, 734
roast *heat* 384
ridicule 856
rib – 972
– and boiled 298
– an ox 883
rob 354, 791
robber 792
robbery 791
robe 225, 999
robes – of state 747
Robin Goodfellow 980
Robinson
say Jack – 132
Robot 554
robust *strong* 159, 654
roc 83
rocaille 853
rock *firm* 150
oscillate 314
hard 323
land 342
safety 664
danger 667
build on a – 150
founded on a – 664
split upon a – 732
– ahead 665
–bound coast 342
– oil 356
rocket *rapid* 274
rise 305
light 423
ship 273
signal 550
arms 727
fireworks 840
go up like a – and come down like the stick 732
rocking-chair 215
rococo 124, 853
rod *support* 215
measure 466
scourge 975
divining 993
kiss the – 725
sounding – 208
– of empire 747
– in pickle
prepared 673
accusation 938
punishment 972
scourge 975
rodeo 720, 840
rodomontade
exaggeration 482
unmeaning 517
boast 884
roe 366, 374
Roentgen rays 420
rogation
request 765
worship 990
rogue *cheat* 548
knave 941
scamp 949
–'s march 297
roguery 940
roguish
playful 840
Roi le veut, le – 741
roister 885
roisterer 887
Roland for an Oliver
retaliation 716
revenge 719
barter 794
rôle *drama* 599
business 625
plan 626
conduct 692
roll *list* 86
fillet 205
convolution 248
rotundity 249
make smooth 255
move 264
fly 267
rotate 312
rock 314
flow 384
sound **407**
record 551
money 800
strike off the – 756, 972
– along 312
– in the dust 731
– on the ground 839
– of honour 86
– in 639, 641
– on 109
– into one 43
– in riches 803
– up 312
– up in 225
– in wealth 803
roll-call 85
roller *fillet* 45
round 249
clothing 255
rotate 312

impose 741
lease 771, 787
make a dead – at 716
– about 66, 676
– abroach 73
– one's affections on 897
– afloat 153, 531
– against
oppose 708
quarrel 713
hate 898
angry 900
– against one another 464
– agoing
impulse 276
propulsion 284
aid 717
– apart
separate 44
exclude 55
select 609
– aside
displace 185
disregard 458
neglect 460
negative 536
reject 610
disuse 678
annul 756
refuse 764
not observe 773
relinquish 782
dereliction 927
– one's back up 878
– before
inform 527
choice 609
– before oneself 620
– by 636
– one's cap at 897, 902
– on a cast 621
– down [*see below*]
– by the ears 898
– at ease 831
– an example
model 22
motive 615
– the eyes on 441
– one's face against
oppose 708
refuse 764
disapprove 932
– the fashion
influence 175
authority 737
fashion 852
– fast 704
– on fire
ignite 384
excite 824
– on foot 66
– foot on 294
– forth *show* 525
assert 535
describe 594
– forward 293
– free 750
– going [*see* – agoing]
– one's hand to 467
– one's heart upon 604, 865
– at hazard 665
– in *begin* 66
rain 348
– on its legs 150
– on one's legs 159, 669
– in motion 264, 677
– to music 416
– at naught
make light of 483
reject 610
oppose 708
defy 715
disobey 742
not observe 773
dereliction 927
– no store by 483, 930
– off
compensation 30
depart 293
improve 658
discount 813
adorn 845
display 882
– on 615
– in order 60
– out *arrange* 60
begin 66
depart 293
decorate 845
display 882
– over 755
– phrase 566
– a price 85, 812
– purpose 620
– at rest *end* 67
answer 462
adjudge 480
complete 729
compact 760
– right
inform 527
disclose 529
teach 537
reinstate 660
vindicate 937
– to rights 60
– sail 293
– the seal on 729
– one's seal to 467
– store by 642
– straight 246, 723
– the table in a roar 840
– one's teeth 604
– terms
manifest 525
phrase 566
style 574
– a trap for 545
– to 720, 722
– in towards 286
– up
printing 54
originate 153
strengthen 159
produce 161
upright 212
raise 307
successful 731
prosperous 734
– up shop 676
– upon
resolved 604
attack 716
desirous 865
– too high a value upon 482
– watch 459
– one's wits to work *think* 451
imagine 515
plan 626
– to work
undertake 676
impose 741
set-back 735
set down
record 551
unseat 756
humiliate 879
slight 929
censure 932
give one a –
confute 479
– as 484
– for 484
– a cause for hearing 969
– to 155
– in writing 551
setaceous 256
seton 662
setose 256
settee 215
setter 366
settle *regulate* 60
establish 150
be located 184
bench 215
come to rest 265
subside 306
kill 361
decide 480
choose 609
vanquish 731
consent 762
compact 769
pay 807
– accounts 807, 811
– down 133
stability 150
moderate 174
locate oneself 184
– into 144
– matters 723
– preliminaries 673
– property 781
– the question 478
– to sleep 683
– upon *give* 784
– with 807, 992
settled [*see* settle]
characteristic 5
ended 67
account – 811
– opinion 484
– purpose 620
settlement [*see* settle]
location 184
colony 188
dregs 653
compact 769
deed 771
property 780
strict – 781
settler 188
settlor 784
seven 98
-league boots 274, 992
wake the – sleepers 404
seventy 98
sever 38, 44
several *special* 79
plural 100
many 102
– times 104
severalize 465
severally 44, 79
severalty 44
severance 38
severe
energetic 171
symmetry 242
exact 494
- *style* 576
harsh 739
painful 830
simple 849
critical 932
severely *very* 31
severity 739
sew 43
sewage 299, 653
sewed up
drunk 959
sewer 350, 653
sewerage 652, 653
sewer-gas 663
sewing-silk 205
sex *kind* 75
women 374
fair – 374
sexagenarian 98, 130
sexagenary 99
sextant 217, 244, 247
sextet 98
sextodecimo 593
sexton 363, 996
sextuple 98
seyyid 745
sforzando 415
shabbiness 34
shabby *trifling* 643
deteriorated 659
stingy 819
mean 874
disgraceful 940
shabby-genteel 851
shack 189
shackle
fastening 45
hinder 706
restrain 751
fetter 752
shade *degree* 26
small quantity 32
manes 362
darkness 421
shadow 424
color 428
conceal 528
screen 530
paint 556
ghost 980
eye – 443
in the – 528, 874
shadow of a – 32, 422
throw into the –
surpass 303
conceal 528
glory 873
throw all else into the – 642
thrown into the – 34, 874
under the – of 664
without a – of doubt 474
shades:
– below 982
– of death 360
– of difference 15
– of evening 422
shading 421
– off 26
shadow
unsubstantial 4
copy 21
small 32
accompaniment 88
thin 203
be behind 235
sequence 281
dark 421
shade 424
pursue 461, 622
dream 515
demon 980
fight with a – 699
follow as a – 281
partial – 422
without a – of turning 141
worn to a –
thin 203
worse for wear 659
– of coming events 511
– forth *dim* 422
predict 511
metaphor 521
represent 554
may your – never be less
courtesy 894
respect 928
approbation 931
take the – for the substance
credulous 486
mistake 495
unskilful 699
under the – of one's wing 664
shadowy 4, 447
shady 874
shaft *deep* 208
frame 215
pit 260
missile 284
axis 312
air-pipe 351
handle 633
weapon 727
shaggy 256
shagreen 223
shah 745
shake *totter* 149
weak 160
vibrate 314
agitation 315
shiver 383

smooth *uniform* 16
calm 174
flattery 213, 251
not rough 255
easy 705
– the bed of death 707, 906
– down 174
– over 174
– the ruffled brow of care 834
– sailing 705
– water *easy* 705
– the way 705
smooth-bore 727
smoothly, go on – *prosperous* 734
smoothness 255
smooth-tongued 544, 933
smother
repress 174
kill 361
stifle sound 581
restrain 751
smoulder *inert* 172
burn 382
latent 526
smous 796, 797
smudge 431, 653, 848
smug *affected* 855
smuggle
introduce 228
steal 791
illegal 964
smuggler 792
smut
dirt 653
impurity 961
smutch 431
snack
small quantity 32
food 298
snacks, go – 778
snaffle 752
snag *projection* 250
sharp 253
danger 667
hindrance 706
snail *slow* 275
snake *undulation* 248
serpent 366
hissing 406
miscreant 913
scotch the – 640
– in the grass
hidden 528
deceiver 548
bad 649
source of danger 667
evil-doer 913
knave 941
snake-like
convoluted 248
snap *break* 44
eat 298
brittle 328
noise 406
rude 895
– at *seize* 789
bite 830
censure 932
– of the fingers
trifle 643
– one's fingers at
defy 715
insolence 885
despise 930
– the thread 70
– up *seize* 789
– one up
censure 932
–shot 554
snap-dragon 840
snappish 901
snare *deception* 545
snarl *growl* 412
rude 895
angry 900
threaten 909
snatch
small quantity 32
seize 789
– at *pursue* 622
seize 789
– a grace beyond the reach of art 845
– from one's grasp 789
– from the jaws of death 662, 672
– from under one's nose 702
– a verdict 545, 702
snatches, by – 70
sneak *hide* 528
coward 862
servile 886
base 940
knave 941
bad man 949
– off, – out of 623
sneer *disparage* 929
contempt 930
blame 932
sneeze *blow* 349
snuffle 409
– at *despise* 930
sneezed at, not to be – 642
snick 32, 51
snicker 838
sniff *blow* 349
odor 398
discovery 480a
sniffle 349
snigger *laugh* 838
ridicule 856
disrespect 929
sniggle 545
snip
small quantity 32
cut 44
short 201
tailor 225
sniping 716
snippet 32
snip-snap 713
snip-snap-snorem 840
snivel *weep* 839
sniveling
servile 886
snob *vulgar* 851
plebeian 876
servile 886
snobbishness
flattery 933
snood
headdress 225
circle 247
snooker 840
Snooks, Mr. – 876
snooze 683
snozzle 250
snore 411, 683
snort 411, 412
snout 250
snow *ship* 273
ice 383
white 430
snow-ball 72
snow-blindness 443
snow-drift 72
snow-shoe 272
snow-storm 383
snub *short* 201
hinder 706
cast a slur 874
humiliate 879
bluster 885
censure 932
snub-nosed 243
snuff *blow* 349
pungent 392
odor 398
up to – 698, 702
go out like the – of a candle 360
– out 162, 421
– up 296, 398
snuff-color 433
snuffing, want – *pert* 885
snuffle *blow* 349
hiss 409
stammer 583
hypocrisy 988
snuffy 653
snug *closed* 261
comfortable 377
safe 664
prepared 673
content 831
secluded 893
keep – 528, 893
make all – 673
snuggery 189
snugness 827
so *similar* 17
very 31
therefore 476
method 627
– be it 488, 762
– far so good 618
– let it be 681
– much the better 831, 838
– much the worse 832, 835
– to speak 17, 521
soak *immerse* 300
water 337
moist 339
drunkenness 959
– up 340
So-and-so, Mr. – *neology* 563
soap *lubricate* 332
oil 356
cleanser 652
soapy *unctuous* 355
servile 886
flattery 933
soar *great* 31
height 206
fly 267
rise 305
sob 839
sober *moderate* 174
wise 498
sane 502
style 576
grave 837
temperate 953
abstinent 958
– down 174, 502
humility 879
in – sadness
affirmation 535
– senses 502
– truth *fact* 494
sober-minded 502
calm 826
humble 879
sobriety 958
sobriquet 565
sob sister 534
so-called 545, 565
soc *jurisdiction* 965
socage 777
soccer 840
sociable
carriage 272
sociality 892
social *mankind* 372
sociable 892
– circle 892
– evil 961
– gathering 892
– science 910
socialism
government 737
participation 778
philanthropy 910
socialist 712
sociality 892
society
mankind 372
party 712
fashion 852
sociality 892
position in – 873
Socinianism 984
sociology 712
sock *hosiery* 225
drama 599
socket 191, 252
socle 215
Socratic method 461
sod 344
beneath the – 363
sodality 712, 888
sodden 339, 384
sofa 215
Sofi 984, 996
soft *stop!* 142
weak 160
moderate 174
smooth 255
not hard 324
moist 339
marsh 345
silence! 403
- *sound* 405
dulcet 413
credulous 486
silly 499
lenient 740
tender 822
timid 862
own to the – impeachment 529
– music 415
– pedal 405
– sawder 617, 933
– soap 356, 933
– tongue, – words 894
soften [*see* soft]
moderate 174
relieve 834
pity 914
palliate 937
softening of the brain 158
softer sex 374
soft-hearted 914
softling 160
softness 324
persuasibility 615
soft-spoken 894
soggy 339
soho
attention 457
parley 586
hunting 622
soi-disant
asserting 535
pretender 548
misnomer 565
vain 880
boastful 884
soil *region* 18
land 342
dirt 653
deface 846
till the – 371, 673
soirée 892
sojourn 186, 189
sojourner 188
soke 181
solace *relief* 834
recreation 840
– oneself with
pleasure 827
solar 318
– system 318
– time 114
solatium 973
sold to the devil 949
soldan [*see* sultan]
solder *join* 43
cement 45
cohere 46
soldier 726
soldier-like 722, 861
sole *alone* 87
base 211
support 215
feme – 904
solecism 568
soleil, coup de –
hot 384
mad 503
solemn
affirmation 535
important 642
grave 837
glorious 873
ostentatious 882
religious 987
worship 990
– mockery 882
– silence 403
solemnity *rite* 998
solemnization 883
sol-fa 416

solfeggio 415
solicit *induce* 615
request 765
desire 865
– the attention 457
solicitor *agent* 758
petitioner 767
lawyer 968
solicitous 865
solicitude *care* 459
pain 828
anxiety 860
desire 865
solid *complete* 52
dense 321
certain 474
learned 490
exact 494
wise 498
persevering 604a
solvent 803
– angle 244
solidarity
party 712
solidify 321
soliloquy **589**
solitaire *game* 840
hermit 893
solitary } *alone*
solitude } 87
secluded 893
solmization 416
solo 87, 415
– dance 840
Solomon } *wise*
Solon } 498
sage 500
solstice 125, 126
soluble *fluid* 333
liquefy 335
solus 87
solution
liquefaction 335
answer 462
explanation 522
– of continuity 70
solve *liquefy* 335
discover 480a
unriddle 522
solvent
liquefier 335
monied 803
somatics 316
somber *dark* 421
black 431
grey 432
sad 837
sombrero 225
some *indefinite quantity* 25
small quantity 32
more than one 100
–body *person* 372
important or distinguished 642
in – degree
degree 26
small 32
at – other time 119
in – place 182
– ten or a dozen 102
– time ago 122
– time or other 119
somehow or other
cause 155
instrument 631
somersault 218
something *thing* 3
small degree 32
matter 316
– else 15
– like 17
– or other 475
sometimes 136
somewhat
a little 32
a trifle 643
somewhere 182
– about 32
somnambulism
walking 266
trance 515
somnambulist
walker 268
dreamer 515
somniferous
sleepy 683
weary 841
somnolence 683
son 167
Son, God the – **976**
sonant 402
letter 561
sonata 415
Sonderbund 769
song *music* 415
poem 597
death – 360, 839
love– 597
for a mere – 815
no – no supper 812
old – 643
songster 416
soniferous 402
sonnet 597
sonneteer 597
sonorous *sound* 402
loud 404
language 577
sons of:
– Belial 988
– God 977
Soofeeism 984
soon *transient* 111
future 121
early 132
too – for 135
sooner: – or later
another time 119
future 121
– said than done 704
soot 431, 653
sooth 511
in good – **543**
soothe
allay 174
relieve 834
flatter 933
soothing
faint sound 405
– syrup 174
soothsay 511
soothsayer 513, 994
soothsaying 511
sop
small quantity 32
food 298
fool 501
inducement 615
reward 973
– to Cerberus 458
– in the pan 615
soph 492, 541
Sophi 745, 996
sophism 477, 497
sophist *scholar* 492
dissembler 548
sophister 492
student 541
sophistical 477
sophisticate *mix* 41
debase 659
sophisticated
spurious 545
sophistry **477**
sophomore 541
soporific 683, 841
soporous 683
soprano 410, 416
sorbet 298
sorcerer **994**
sorcery **992**
sordes 653
sordet 417
sordid *stingy* 819
covetous 865
sordine 417
sore
bodily pain 378
disease 655
mental suffering 828, 830
discontent 832
anger 900
– as a boil 901a
– place 822
– subject 830, 900
sorely *very* 31
s'orienter 278
sorites 476
sorority 712
sorrel 433, 434
sorrow 828
give – words 839
sorry *trifling* 643
grieved 828
mean 876
make a – face 874
cut a – figure 874
be – for 750, 914
in a – plight 732
– sight 830, 837
sort *degree* 26
arrange 60
kind 75
– with
sociality 892
sortable }
sortance }
agreement 23
sortes
chance 156, 621
– Virgilianae
sorcery 992
sortie 716
sortilege
prediction 511
sorcery 992
sortilegy 621
sortition 621
sorts, out of –
ill-health 655
sulky 901a
S.O.S. 669, 707
so-so *small* 32
trifling 643
imperfect 651
sostenuto 415
sot *fool* 501
drunkard 959
sot à triple étage 501
sotto voce
faint sound 405
conceal 528
voiceless 581
sou *money* 800
qui n'a pas le – 804
soubrette 599, 746
sough *conduit* 350
noise 405
cloaca 653
soul *essence* 5
person 372
intellect 450
genius 498
affections 820
cure of –s 995
flow of – 588
not a – 187
not dare to say one's – is his own *subjection* 749
fear 860
– of wit 572
have one's whole – in his work 686
soulless 683, 823
soul-mate 905
soul-sick 837
soul-stirring 821, 824
sound *great* 31
conformable 82
stable 150
strong 159
fathom 208
bay 343
noise **402**
investigate 461
measure 466
true 494
wise 498
sane 502
good 648
perfect 650
healthy 654
solvent 803
orthodox 983a
catch a – 418
safe and – 654, 670
– the alarm
indication 550
warning 668
alarm 669
fear 860
– asleep 683
full of – and fury
unmeaning 517
insolent 885
– the horn 416
– of limb 654
– locator 726
– mind 502
– the praises of 931
– the note of preparation 673
– reasoning 476
– a retreat 283
– sleep 683
– a trumpet
publish 531
alarm 669
– of wind 654
sounding: big – 577
– brass 517
sounding-board **417**
soundings 208
soundless
unfathomable 208
silent 403
soup 298, 352
soupçon 32, 41
souplé 298
sour *acid* 397
discontented 832
embitter 835
uncivil 895
sulky 901
– grapes
impossible 471
excuse 617
– the temper 830
source *beginning* 66
cause 153
sourdet 417
sourdine 417
à la – *noiseless* 405
concealed 528
sourdough 463
soured 832
sourness **397**
sous tous les rapports 52
souse 310, 337
South *direction* 278
North and –
opposite 237
Southern
antipodes 237
– Cross 318
souvenir 505
sovereign
superior 33
all-powerful 159
authorities 737
ruler 745
– contempt 930
– remedy 662
Soviet 696, 737
sow *scatter* 73
pig 366
agriculture 371
female 374
get the wrong – by the ear
misjudgment 481
error 495
mismanage 699
fail 732
– broadcast 818
– dissension 713, 898
– the sand 645
– the seed
prepare 673
– the seeds of
cause 153
teach 537
– one's wild oats
improve 658
amusement 840
vice 945
intemperance 954

cess 653
sumpter-horse 271
sumptuary 800, 809
sumptuous 882
sum-total 50
sun 318
luminary 423
glory 873
bask in the – 377
going down of the – 126
farthing candle to the – 645
under the – 180, 318
as the – at noonday *bright* 420
certain 474
plain 525
– oneself 384
Sun:
– of Righteousness 976
sunbeam 420
–s from cucumbers 471
sunburn *heat* 384
sunburnt *brown* 433
Sunday:
– Monday &c. 138
–'s best 847, 882
– school 542
sunder 44
sundial 114
sundown 126
sundry 102
sunk [*see* sink]
deep 208
– fence 717
– in iniquity 945
– in oblivion 508
sunken rocks 667
sunless 421
sunlight 420
sunny *warm* 382
luminous 420
cheerful 836
sunny side 829
view the – 858
– of the hedge 734
sun-painting 556
sunrise 125
sunset 126
at – 133
sunshade 223, 424
sunshine *light* 420
prosperity 734
happy 827
cheerful 836
sunstroke 384, 503
sun-up 125
suo: – periculo 926
– sibi gladio hunc jugulo
absurdity 479
retaliation 718
sup *small quantity* 32
feed 298
– full of horrors 828
super *theatrical* 599
superable 470
superabound 641
superadd 37
superannuated 128
superb 845
supercargo 694
supercherie 545
supercilious
proud 878
insolent 885
disrespectful 929
scornful 930
superdreadnought 726
supereminence 648, 873
supererogation 641, 645
superexaltation 873
superexcellence 648
superfetation 37, 168
superficial
shallow 209
outside 220
misjudging 481
ignorant 491
– extent 180
superficies 220
superfine 648
superfluitant 305
superfluity 40, 641
superfluous 645
superhuman 650, 976
superimpose 233
superimposed 206
superincumbent 206, 319
superinduce
change 140
cause 153
produce 161
superintend 693
superintendent 694
superior *greater* 33
– *in size* 194
important 642
good 648
director 694
superiority 33
superjunction 37
superlative 33
superlatively good 648
superman 33
supernal 206, 210, 981
supernatant 206, 305
supernatural 976, 980
– aid 707
supernumerary
adjunct 39
theatrical 599
reserve 636
redundant 641
superpose 37, 223
supersaturate 641
superscription 550, 590
supersede
substitute 147
disuse 678
relinquish 782
supersensible 317
superstition
credulity 486
error 495
religion 984
superstratum 220
superstructure 729
supertax 812
supertonic 413
supervacaneous 641
supervene
extrinsic 6
be added 37
succeed 117
happen 151
supervise 693
supervisor 694
supination 213
supine
horizontal 213
inverted 218
sluggish 683
mentally torpid 823
suppeditate 637
supper 298
supplant 147
supple *soft* 324
servile 886
supplement
addition 37
adjunct 39
completion 52
publication 531
book 593
suppletory 37
suppliant 765, 767
supplicate *beg* 765
pity 914
worship 990
supplies
materials 635
aid 707
money 800
supply *store* 636
provide 637
give 784
– aid 707
– deficiencies 52
– the place of 147
– and transport 726
support *perform* 170
sustain 215
evidence 467
preserve 670
aid 707
feel 821
endure 826
vindicate 937
– life 359
supporter 711
–s *heraldic* 550
suppose 514
supposing 469
supposition 514
supposititious 546
suppress
destroy 162
conceal 528
silent 581
restrain 751
suppression of truth 544
suppuration 653
suppute 85
supralapsarian 984
supramundane 939
supremacy 33, 737
supreme 33
summit 210
authority 737
in a – degree 31
Supreme Being 976
surbate 659
surbated 688
surcease 142
surcharge 641
– and falsify 811
surcingle 45
surcoat 225
surd *number* 84
deaf 419
silent letter 561
sure *certain* 474
belief 484
safe 664
make – against 673
make – of
inquire 461
take 789
you may be – 535
to be – *assent* 488
on – ground 664
security 771
sure-footed
careful 459
skilful 698
cautious 864
surely 489, 602, 870
sureness 474
surety 474, 664
surf 348, 353
surface *outside* 220
texture 329
below the – 526
lie on the – 518, 525
skim the – 460
Surface, Joseph – 548
surfeit 641, 869
surge *swarm* 72
swell 305
rotation 312
wave 348
surgeon 662
surgery 662
surgit amari aliquid 651
surly *gruff* 895
sullen 901a
unkind 907
surmise 514
surmount *be superior* 33
tower 206
transcursion 303
ascent 305
– a difficulty
overcome 731
surmountable 470
surname 564
surpass
be superior 33
grow 194
go beyond 303
outshine 873
surplice 999
surplus 40, 641
surplusage 641
surprint 550
surprise
non-expectation 508
unprepared 674
wonder 870
surprisingly 31
surrebutter &c.
answer 462
pleadings 969
surrender 725, 782
– one's life 360
surreptitious
furtive 528
deceptive 545
untrue 540
surrogate 759
surround 227, 229
surroundings
amidst such and such – 183
sursum corda 990
surtax 812
surtout *coat* 225
surveillance
care 459
direction 693
under – 938
survene 151
survey 441, 466
surveyor 85, 694
survive *remain* 40
long time 110
permanent 141
susceptibility
power 157
tendency 176
liability 177
sensibility 375
motive 615
impressibility 822
irascibility 901
suscipient 785
suscitate *cause* 153
produce 161
stir up 173
excite 824
suspect *doubt* 485
suppose 514
suspected 938
suspectless 484
suspend *defer* 133
discontinue 142
hang 214
suspended animation 823
suspender 45, 214
suspense
cessation 142
uncertainty 475
expectation 507
irresolution 605
in – *inert* 172
suspension
cessation 142
hanging 214
music 413
– of arms 723
suspicion *doubt* 485
incredulity 487
knowledge 490
supposition 514
fear 860
under – 938
suspiration 839
sustain
continue 143
strength 159
perform 170
support 215
preserve 670
aid 707
endure 821

T

insolent 885
threat 909
- glibly 584
- nonsense 497
- of *signify* 516
publish 531
intend 620
- to oneself 589
- oneself out of breath 584
- over
confer 588
persuade 615
- to in private 586
- at random
illogical 477
loquacity 584
together 588
- against time
time 106
protract 110
inaction 681
- of the town
gossip 588
fame 873
talkative 582, 584
talked of 873
talkies 599, 840
talking, fine –
over-estimation 482
tall 206
- hat 225
- talk 884
tallage 812
tallies 85
tallow 356
- candle 423
tallow-faced 429
tally *agree* 23
list 85, 86
sign 550
credit 805
- with *conform* 82
tally-ho 622
tally-man 797
talma 225
Talmud 985
talons
authority 737
claws 781
talus 217
tam-o'-shanter 225
tambourine 417
tame *inert* 172
moderate 174
domesticate 370
teach 537
feeble 575
subjugate 749
insensible 823
calm 826
tameless
violent 173
malevolent 907
Tammany 940
tamp 261, 276
tamper with
alter 140
seduce 615
injure 659
meddle 682
tan *color* 433
tandem
at length 200
vehicle 272
tang *taste* 390
bane 663
tangent 199
angle 217
fly off at a –
deviate 279
diverge 291
excitable 825
tangere ulcus 505
tangible
material 316
touch 379
exact 494
sufficient 639
useful 644
tangle 61, 219
tangled 59, 704
weave a – web 704
tango 840
tank *pool* 343
reservoir 636
armored vehicle 726
tankard 191
tanker 273
tant: – mieux 838
- s'en faut 489
- soit peu 32
tantaene animis coelestibus irae 900
tantalize *balk* 509
induce 615
desire 865
tantalizing
exciting 824
Tantalus: torment of 507, 865
tantamount 27, 516
tantara 407
tantas componere lites 723
tanti 642
tantivy *speed* 274
tantrums 900
tap *open* 260
plug 263
hit 276
let out 295, 297
sound 406
turn on the – 297
tap-dance 840
tape *string* 205
measure 466
- machine 553
taper *contract* 195
narrow 203
candle 423
- to a point 253
tapestry 556, 847
tapinois, en – 528
tapis: on the –
event 151
topic 454
intention 620
plan 626
tap-root 153
taps 550
tapster 746
tar *cover* 223
sailor 269
pitch 356a
- and feather 929, 972
taradiddle 546
tarantass 272
tarantella 840
tarboosh 225
tardiloquence 583
tardy 133, 275
tare 40*a*
- and tret 813
tares 645
targe 717
target 620
shield 717
tariff 812
tarmac 635
tarn 343
tarnish
discoloration 429
soil 653
deface 848
disgrace 874
tarpaulin 223
tarry *remain* 110, 265
later 133
continue 141
- for *expect* 507
tart *pastry* 298, 396
acid 397
rude 895
irascible 901
harlot 962
tartan 440
tartane 273
Tartar *choleric* 901
catch a – *dupe* 547
unskilful 699
retaliation 718
tartar *dirt* 653
- emetic 663
Tartarus 982
Tartufe
hypocrisy 544
deceiver 548
impiety 988
task *lesson* 537
business 625
put to use 677
fatigue 688
command 741
hard – 704
set a – 741
take to – 932
- the memory 505
taskmaster 694
tass 191
tassel 847
taste *sapidity* **390**
experience 821
good taste **850**
man of – 850
to one's – *savory* 394
pleasant 829
love 897
tasteful 850
tasteless *insipid* 391
tasty 394, 850
tâtonner 463
tatter
small quantity 32
tatterdemalion 876
Tattersalls 799
tatters *garments* 225
tear to – 162
tatting 847
tattle 588
tattler 532, 588
tattoo
drumming 407
mottled 440
summons 741
taught [*see* teach]
fastened 43
taunt 929, 938
tauromachy 720
taut 43
tautology 104, 573
tavern 189
tawdry 851
tawny 433, 436
tax *inquire* 461
employ 677
fatigue 688
command 741
compel 744
request 765
accounts 811
impost 812
discount 813
accuse 938
- one's energies 686
- the memory 505
taxi 266
taxi-cab 272
taxi-driver 268
taxidermy 368
taxis 60
taxonomy 60
tazza 191
Te Deum 990
te fabula narratur, de – *retaliate* 718
condemn 971
tea 298
teach 537
- one's grandmother 641, 885
- one his place 879
teachable 539
teacher **540**, 673
teaching **537**
false – 538
teacup, storm in a –
overrate 482, 549
exaggerate 549
teagown 225
team *assemblage* 69, 72
teamster 694
tea-party 892
tea-pot 191
tear *separate* 44
violence 173
move rapidly 274
excite 825
weeping 839
- away from 789
- oneself away 623
- asunder one's bonds 750
- one's hair 839
- out 301
- to pieces
separate 44
destroy 162
- up *destroy* 162
tear-gas 663, 727
tearful 839
tearing passion 839
tears: draw – 830
shed – 839
- in one's eyes
excited 824
sad 837
tease *annoy* 830
spite 907
teaser *difficult* 704
teasing 830
teat 250
tea-table talk 588
technic 698
technica, memoria – 505
technical
conformable 82
workmanlike 698
- college 542
- education 537
- knowledge 698
- school 542
- term 564
technicality
special 79
cant term 563
formulary 697
technique 556, 698
technocracy 698
technology 698
techy 901
tedious 841
while away the – hours 681
tedium 841
teem
produce 161
productive 168
abound 639
- with *multitude* 102
teemful 168
teeming *crowd* 72
teemless 169
'teens 98
in one's – 127, 129
teeter 314
teeth 330, 781
armed to the – 673, 717, 722
between the – 405
cast in one's – 938
chattering of – 383
have cut one's eye – 698
in the – of 704, 708
grind one's – 900
the run of one's – 815
set one's – 604
show one's – 900
in spite of one's – 708, 744
make one's – chatter 385, 860
set the – on edge
scrape 331
saw 397
stridor 410
pain the feelings 830
tee 66
teetotalism 953, 958
teetotum 312, 840
teg 366
tegument 223
teind 99
teinoscope 445
tekel upharsin 668
telautograph 553
telegram 532
telegraph

go beyond the length of one's – 738
tethered *firm* 150
tetrachord 413
tetractic 95
tetrad 95
tetrahedral 95
tetrahedron 244
tetrarch 745
text *prototype* 22
topic 454
meaning 516
printing 591
–book 542, 596
textile 219, 329
textuary 983*a*, 985
texture *mixture* 41
roughness 256
fabric **329**
Thais 962
Thalia 599
Thalmud 985
Thames on fire
set the – 471
never set the – 501, 701
thane *nobility* 875
thank 916
no – you 764
– one's stars 838
– you for nothing 917
thankful 916
rest and be – 265, 831
thankless
painful 830
ungrateful 917
thank-offering 916, 990
thanks to 155
thanksgiving
gratitude 916
worship 990
that 79
– is 118
– is to say **79**
– being so 8
at – time 119
thatch *roof* 223
thaumatrope 445
thaumaturgist 994
thaumaturgy 992
thaw *melt* 335
heart 382
heating 384
calm the mind 826
pity 914
Thearchy
authority 737
Deity 976
theater
spectacle 441
school 542
drama 599
arena 728
amusement 840
tribunal 966
théâtre: coup de –
appearance 448
prodigy 872
display 882
jeu de – 448, 872
nom de – 565
theatrical 599
affected 855
ostentatious 882
Theban, learned – 492
theca 223
thé dansant 840
theft 775, 791
theism 984, 987
theistic *of God* 976
theme *topic* 454
dissertation 595
Themis 922
then *time* 106
therefore 476
thence
caused by 155
departure 293
therefore 476
thenceforward 121
theocracy 976, 995
theodolite 217, 244
theogony 983
theologicum, odium –
misjudgment 481
false piety 988
churchdom 995
theology **983**
theomancy 511
theopathy 987
theopneustic 985
theorbo 417
theorem
topic 454
maxim 496
supposition 514
theoretical 514
theorize 155, 514
theory
attribution 155
knowledge 490
supposition 514
theosophy 983, 984
therapeutics 655, 662
therapy 662
there 183, 186
thereabouts
almost 32
place 183
near 197
thereafter 117
thereby 631
– hangs a tale 154
therefore
attribution 155
reasoning 476
motive 615
therein 221
thereof 9
theretofore 116
thereupon 106, 117
therewith
accompanying 88
means 632
theriac 662
thermal 382
thermion 330
thermogenic 382
thermology 382
thermometer
heat **389**
thermonuclear 316
thermopile 389
thermoscope 389
Thersites 936
thesaurus
list 86
book 593
words 562
store 636
thesis *theme* 454
proposition 514
dissertation 595
Thespian 599
Thetis 341
theurgist 994
theurgy 992
thews and sinews 159
thick *crowded* 72
numerous 102
broad 202
dense 321
semiliquid 352
turbid 426
dirty 653
friends 888
come – 102
in the – of
middle 68
imbedded 228
action 680
lay it on –
cover 223
redundance 641
flattery 933
– of the action 682
– of the fray 722
through – and thin 173, 604*a*
thick-coming
many 102
repeated 104
frequent 136
– fancies 515
thicken 35
thickens, the plot – 682
thicket 367
thick-head 501
thickness **202**, 204
thick-ribbed 159
– ice 383
thickset *short* 201
broad 202
dense 321
thick-skinned 376, 823
thick-skull 499, 501
thief **792**
set a – to catch a thief 791
like a – in the night
unexpected 508
concealment 528
dishonorable 940
thievery 791
thieves' Latin 563
thimble
receptacle 191
defence 617
thimbleful 25, 32
thimblerig 545
thimblerigger 792
thin *subduct* 38
few 103
small 193
narrow 203
rare 322
scanty 640
– end of the wedge 66
– out 371
thing *substance* 3
matter 316
just the – 924
the – 926
– to do 625
– of naught 4
know a – or two 698
things
events 151
clothes 225
chattels 780
as – go 613
thingumbob 563
think 451, 484
only – 873
reason to – 472
– aloud 589, 703
– better of 607, 658
– fit 600, 602
– highly 931
– ill 932
– likely 472
– no more of
inattention 458
forgive 918
– of *intend* 620
– out 457
as one –s proper 600
– twice 605, 864
– upon
remember 505
thinker 500
thinking principle 450
thinness **203**
thin-skinned
physically sensible 375
morally sensitive 822
fastidious 868
irascible 901
third 93
trisection 94
music 413
– degree 461
– heaven 981
– part 94
– person 664
– power 92
thirdly 93
thirst 965
– for knowledge 455
thirsty soul 959
thirteen 98
thirty-nine articles 983*a*
thirty-one
cards 840
this 79
– that or the other 15
at – time of day 118
thistle *prickly* 253
thistle-down 320
thither 278
thole 821
– pin 215
Thompson submachine gun 727
thong *fastening* 45
scourge 975
Thor 979
thorn *sharp* **253**
bane 663
painful 830
plant a – 830
spiteful 907
– in the flesh 663, 830
– in the side
badness 649
bane 663
annoyance 830
thorns: sit on –
physical pain 378
moral pain 828
fear 860
on – for 868
thorny 253, 704
thorough 52
thorough-bass 413, 415
thorough-bred
intrinsic 5
horse 271
skill 698
fashionable 852
thoroughfare 260, 627
thorough-going 52
thoroughly, do – 729
thorough-paced 31
thorp 189
though
compensation 30
qualification 469
opposition 708
thought *little* 32
reflection **451**
idea 453
give a – to 457
not to be – of 610, 761
organ of – 450
quick as – 274
seat of – 450
subject of – 454
want of – 458
who could have – it? 508
– of 454
thoughtful 451, 498
thoughtless
incogitant 452
inattentive 458
careless 460
improvident 674
thoughts:
– that breathe 574
– elsewhere 458
thousand 98, 102
one in a – 648, 948
thraldom 749, 750
thrash 972
Thraso 887
Thrasonic 884, 885
thread
arrange 60
series 69
weak 160
filament 205
pass through 302
not have a dry – 339
hang by a – 665

manage 692
bargain 769
delight 827, 829
amusement 840
– of 595
– oneself to 827
– well 906
treatise 593, 595
treatment
painting 556
conduct 692
ill – 649
medical – 662
treaty 769
treble
three 93
shrill 410
childish – 581
tree *pedigree* 166
plant 367
gallows 975
top of the – 210
up a – 704
as the – falls 151
– of knowledge 493
treenail 45
trefoil 92
trek 266
trellis 219
tremble
fluctuate 149
weakness 160
shake 315
cold 383
emotion 821
fear 860
make one – 860
trembling:
– in the balance 475, 665
– to its fall 160
tremblingly alive 822
tremendous 830, 860
tremendously 31
tremolo 415
tremor
agitation 315
emotion 821
fearful 860
tremulous
agitated 315
– *voice* 583
irresolute 605
fear 860
trench *moat* 232
furrow 259
concavity 252
defence 717
– mortar 727
– on *near* 197
trespass 303
moral trespass 925
trenchant
energetic 171
assertive 535
concise style 572
vigorous language 574
important 642
emotion 821
discourteous 895
censure 932
trench-coat 225
trencher *plate* 191
layer 204
trenches, open the – 716
trend *tendency* 176
bend 278
deviate 279
trennel 45
trepan 260
snare 545
borer 262
trephine 260, 267
trepidation
agitation 315
emotion 821
excitement 825
fear 860
tres juncta in uno 92
trespass
go beyond 303
vice 945
guilt 947
tress 256
trestle 215
trevet 215
[*and see* trivet]
trews 225
trey 92
triad 92
triagonal 244
trial *inquiry* 461
experiment 463
essay 675
difficulty 704
adversity 735
suffering 828, 830
lawsuit 969
punishment 972
– of temper 824
triality 92
trialogue 588
triangle 92, 244
music 417
punishment 975
triangular duel 720
triarchy 737
tribe *race* 11
assemblage 72
class 75
clan 166
tribulation 828
tribunal 966
tribune
rostrum 542
judge 967
tributary *river* 348
giving 784
tribute
compensation 30
donation 784
money paid 809
reward 973
pay – to 928, 931
trice 113, 633
– up 43
in a – 113
trichotomy 94
trichroism 440
trick *deception* 545
trait 550
habit 613
contrivance 626
skill 698
artifice 702
– *at cards* 775
play –s
bungle 699
cunning 702
amusement 840
ridicule 856
– of fortune 509
– out 847, 851
–s of the trade 702
trickery *deceit* 545
finery 851
trickle 295, 348
trickster
deceiver 548
cunning 702
rogue 792
tricksy *cheery* 836
pretty 845
ornamented 847
tricolor
variegated 440
flag 550
tricycle 272
trident 92, 341
triennial
periodical 138
plant 367
triennium 92
trifid 94
trifle *small* 32
neglect 460
folly 499
unimportant 643
not to be –d with 744
not stick at –s 604
– time away 683
– with *neglect* 460
deceive 545
disrespect 929
trifler 460, 501
trifling 499, 643
wit 842
triforium 1000
triform 92
trifurcate 94
trigamy 903
trigger 633
draw the – 722
Trigger, Sir Lucius O' – 887
trigon 244
trigonometry 244
trihedral 93
trilateral 236, 244
trilogistic 93
trilogy 93
drama 599
trill *stream* 348
sound 407
music 416
trillion 98
trim *state* 7
adjust 27
dress 225
form 240
lie 544
waver 605
change sides 607
clean 652
beautify 845
adorn 847
scold 932
flog 972
in – order 58
trimmer *fickle* 607
apostate 941
selfish 943
trimming
border 231
ornament 847
dishonesty 940
trinal 92
trine 93
trinitrotoluene 727
trinity 92
– Sunday 998
Trinity, Holy – 976
trinket 643, 847
trinkgeld 784
trinal 93
trinomial 92
trio *three* 92
music 415
triolet 597
trip *jaunt* 266
run 274
fall 306
leap 509
mistake 495
bungle 699
fail 732
vice 945
guilt 947
– up *deceive* 545
overthrow 731
tripartition 94
triplane 273
triple 93
– crown 747, 999
triplet *three* 92
verse 597
triplex 93
triplication 93
triplicity 93
tripod 215
tripos 461
tripotage 588
tripping [*see* trip]
style 578
nimble 682
caught – 491
trippingly on the tongue 584
Triptolemus 371
trireme 273
trisection 94
triste 837
tristful 837
trisulcate
trisected 94
furrow 259
trite
known 490
conventional 613
– saying 496
tritheism 984
Triton *sea* 341
– among the minnows
superior 33
huge 192
important 642
trituration 330
trium literarum, homo – 792
triumph
success 731
trophy 733
exult 838
celebrate 883
boast 884
triumvirate 92, 737
triune 93
Triune God 976
trivet 215, 386
right as a – 650, 924
trivia 643
trivial
unmeaning 517
trifling 643
useless 645
troat 412
trocar 262
trochaic 597
trochee 597
trochilic 312
trodden: down– 749
well – 613, 677
Troglodyte 893
troika 92
troll
roll 312
fairy 980
trollop 962
trolley 272
– omnibus 272
trombone 417
tronk 752
troop 72, 726
raise –s 722
– carrier
aeroplane 726
trooper 726
lie like a – 544
swear like a – 908
troop-ship 726
trop, de – 641
trope 521
Trophonius, cave of – 837
trophy 551, 733
tropical 382
troposphere 338
trot 266, 274
– out 525, 882
troth *belief* 484
veracity 543
promise 768
by my – 535
plight one's – 902
trothless 544, 940
trotters 266
trottoir 627
troubadour 597
trouble *disorder* 59
derange 61
exertion 686
difficulty 704
adversity 735
pain 828
painful 830
bring into – 649
get into – 649, 732
in – 619, 735
take – 686
– one's head about 682
– one for 765
– oneself 686
troubled waters, fish in – 704
troublesome 686, 704, 830
troublous 59, 173
– times 713
trough *hollow* 252
trench 259
conduit 350
trounce 932, 972
troupe 72

U

illogical 477
unconquerable
strong 159
persevering 604*a*
– will 604
unconquered 719
unconscientious 940
unconscionable
excessive 31
unprincipled 945
unconscious
ignorant 491
insensible 823
unconsenting 603, 764
unconsidered 452
unconsolable 837
unconsolidated 47
unconsonant 24
unconspicuous 447
unconstitutional 925, 964
unconstrained 748, 880
unconsumed 40
uncontested 474
uncontradicted 488
uncontrite 951
uncontrollable
violent 173
necessity 601
emotion 825
uncontrolled
free 748
excitability 825
uncontroverted 488
unconventional 83, 614
unconversant 491, 699
unconverted
dissenting 489
irreligious 989
unconvinced 489
uncooked 674
uncopied 20
uncork 750
uncorrupted 939
uncounted 475
uncouple 44
uncourteous 895
uncourtly 851, 895
uncouth
- *style* 579
ugly 846
vulgar 851
uncover
denude 226
open 260
disclose 529
bow 894
uncreated 2
uncritical 931
uncropped 50
uncrown 756
unction
emotion 821, 824
divine functions 976
piety 987
extreme – 998
lay the flattering – to one's soul 834, 858
unctuous *oily* 355, 894
flattering 933
hypocritical 988
unctuousness 355
unculled
unused 678
relinquished 782
unculpable 946
uncultivated
vulgar 85
ignorant 491
unprepared 674
uncurbed 748
uncurl 246
uncustomary 83
uncut 50
undamaged (648)
undamped 340
undated
without date 115
waving 248
undaunted 861
undazzled 498
undebauched 939
undeceive 527, 529
undeceived 490
undecided
inquiring 461
uncertain 475
irresolute 605
leave – 609*a*
undecipherable 519
undecked 849
undecomposed 42
undefaced 845
undefended 725
undefiled
honest 939
innocent 946
chaste 960
undefinable
uncertain 475
unmeaning 517
unintelligible 519
undefined
invisible 447
uncertain 475
undeformed 845
undemolished 50
undemonstrable 485
undemonstrated 475
undemonstrative 826
undeniable 474, 478
undeplored 898
undepraved 939
undeprived 781
under *less* 34
below 207
subject to 749
range – 76
– advisement 454
– age 127
– agent 758
– arrest 751
– breath 405
– the conditions 8
– one's control 743
– cover
covered 223
hidden 528
safe 664
– the domination of 737
– one's eyes 446
– foot [*see below*]
– full strength 651
– the head of 9
– lock and key 664
– the mark 34
– press of 744
– protest 489, 744
– restraint 751
– the rule of 737
– seal 467
– subjection 749
– the sun 1
– way 282
underbid 794
underbreath 405
underbred 851
underclothing 225
undercurrent
cause 153
stream 348, 349
latent 526
opposing 708
underestimation 483
underfed 640
underfoot 207
tread – 739
undergo 151
– a change 144
– pain 828
undergraduate 541
underground
low 207
deep 208
latent 526
hidden 528
underhand 526, 528
– dealing 528
underhung 250
underived 20
underlessee 779
underlet 787
underlie 207, 526
underline
mark 550
emphatic 642
underling
servant 746
clown 876
undermine
weaken 158
burrow 252
damage 659
stratagem 702
hinder 706
undermost 211
underneath 207
undernourished 640
underpaid 817
underpin 215
underplot 626
underprop 215
underrate 483
underreckon 483
undersell 796
underset 215
undershot 250
undersign 467
undersized 193
understand
know 490
intelligible 518
latent 526
be informed 527
give one to – 572
– by 516, 522
– one another 709, 714
understanding
agreement 23
intellect 450
intelligence 498
come to an – 488
intelligible 518
agree 714
pacification 723
compact 769
good – 714, 888
by a mutual – 526
with the – 469
understate 489
understood
meaning 516
implied 526
customary 613
understrapper 746
understudy 134
undertake
endeavor 676
promise 768
undertaker 363
undertaking 625, 676
undertone 405
undertow 348
undervalue 483
underwood 367
underwrite
promise 768
compact 769
insurance 771
underwriter 758
undescribed 83
undeserved 925
undeserving of belief 485
undesigned 621
undesigning 703
undesirable 647, 830
undesired 830, 866
undesirous 866
undespairing 858
undestroyed
existing 1
whole 50
persisting 141
undetermined
chance 156
inquiry 461
uncertain 475
unintelligible 519
irresolute 605
undeveloped 526
undeviating
uniform 16
unchanged 150
straight 246
direct 278
persevering 604*a*
undevout 989
undigested 674
undignified 940
undiminished 31, 35, 50
undirected 279, 621
undiscernible 447, 519
undiscerning
blind 442
inattentive 458
undisciplined 608
undisclosed 526, 528
undiscoverable 519
undiscovered 526
undiscriminating 465*a*
undisguised
true 494
manifest 525
sincere 543
undismayed 861
undisposed of 678, 781
undisputed 474
undissembling 543
undissolved
entire 50
dense 321
undistinguishable 465*a*
undistinguished 465*a*
undistorted 246, 494
undistracted 457
undisturbed
quiescent 265
repose 685
unexcited 826
undivided 50, 52
undo *untie* 44
reverse 145
destroy 162
neutralize 179
not do 681
undoing *ruin* 735
undone *failure* 732
adversity 735
pained 828
hopeless 859
undoubted 474
undubitably 488
undraped 226
undreaded 861
undreamt of 452
undress *clothes* 225
nude 226
simple 849
undressed 226, 674
undried 339
undrilled 674
undrooping 604*a*
undueness 925
undulate 248, 314
unduly 32
undutiful 945
undying 112, 150
une aile, ne battre que d' – 683
unearned 925
unearth *eject* 297
disinter 363
inquire 461
discover 480*a*
unearthly
immaterial 317
Deity 976
demon 980
heavenly 981
pious 987
uneasy 828
uneatable 395
unedifying 538
uneducated 491, 674
unembarrassed 705, 852
unembodied 317
unemotional 823

unemployed 678, 681
unencumbered 705, 927*a*
unendeared 898
unending 112
unendowed 158
– with reason 450*a*
unendurable 830
unenjoyed 841
unenlightened 491, 499
unenslaved 748
unenterprising 864
unentertaining 843
unenthralled 748
unentitled 925
unenvied 929, 930
unequal 28, 139
inequitable 923
– to 640
unequalled 33
unequipped 674
unequitable 923
unequivocal
great 31
sure 474
clear 518
unerring
certain 474
tone 494
innocent 946
unessayed 678
unessential 643
unestablished 185
uneven *diverse* 16*a*
unequal 28
irregular 139
rough 256
uneventful 643
unexact 495
unexaggerated 494
unexamined 460
unexampled 83
unexceptionable
good 648
legitimate 924
innocent 946
unexcitable 826
unexcited 823, 826
unexciting 174
unexecuted 730
unexempt 177
unexercised 674, 678
unexerted 172
unexhausted 159, 639
unexpanded 195, 203
unexpected
exceptional 83
inexpectation 508
unexpensive 815
unexplained
not known 491
unintelligible 519
latent 626
unexplored
neglected 460
ignorant 491
unseen 526
unexposed 526
unexpressed 536
unexpressive 517
unextended 317
unextinguished 173, 382
unfaded 428
unfading 112
unfailing 141
unfair *false* 544
unjust 923
dishonorable 940
unfaithful 940
unfaltering 604*a*
unfamiliar 83
unfashionable 83, 851
unfashioned 241, 674
unfasten 44
unfathomable
infinite 105
deep 208
mysterious 519
unfavorable
out of season 135
hindrance 706
obstructive 708
– chance 473
unfeared 861
unfeasible 471
unfed 640, 956
unfeeling 376, 823
unfeigned 543
unfelt 823
unfeminine
manly 373
vulgar 851
unfertile 169
unfetter 750
unfettered 748
unfinished 53, 730
unfit
inappropriate 24
impotence 158
inexpedient 647
unskilful 699
wrong 923
undue 925
unfitted
not prepared 674
unfix 44
unfixed 149
unflagging 604*a*
unflammable 385
unflattering 494, 703
unfledged
young 127, 129
unprepared 674
unflinching
firm 604
persevering 604*a*
brave 861
unfold
straighten 246
evolve 313
interpret 522
manifest 525
disclose 529
– a tale 594
unforbidden 760
unforced 602, 748
unforeseen 508
unforfeited 781
unforgettable 505
unforgiving 919
unforgotten 505
unformed 241, 674
unfortified
pure 42
powerless 158
unfortunate
ill-timed 135
failure 732
adversity 735
unhappy 828
– woman 962
unfounded 546
unfrequent 137
unfrequented 893
unfriended
powerless 158
secluded 893
unfriendly
opposed 708
hostile 889
malevolent 907
unfrock 756, 972
unfrozen 382
unfruitful 169
unfulfilled 713, 925
unfurl
unfold 313
– a flag 525, 550
unfurnished 640, 674
ungainly 846, 895
ungallant 895
ungarnished 849
ungathered 678
ungenerous 819, 943
ungenial 657
ungenteel 851, 895
ungentle 173, 895
ungentlemanly
vulgar 851
rude 895
dishonorable 940
ungifted 499
unglorified 874
unglue 47
ungodly 989
ungovernable
violent 173
disobedient 742
passionate 825
ungoverned 748
ungraceful
- *language* 579
ugly 846
vulgar 851
ungracious 895, 907
ungrammatical 568
ungranted 764
ungrateful 917
ungratified 832
ungrounded
unsubstantial 4
erroneous 495
ungrudging 816
unguarded
neglected 460
spontaneous 612
unprepared 674
in an – moment
unexpectedly 508
unguem, ad – 494, 650
unguent 356
unguibus et rostro 686
unguided
ignorant 491
impulsive 612
unskilled 699
unguilty 946
unhabitable 187
unhabituated 614
unhackneyed 614
unhallowed 988, 989
unhand 750
unhandseled 123
unhandsome 940
unhandy 699
unhappy
adversity 735
pain 828
dejected 837
make – 830
unharbored 185
unhardened
tender 914
innocent 946
penitent 950
unharmonious 24, 414
unharness 750
unhatched 674
unhazarded 664
unhealthy 655, 657
unheard of
exceptional 83
improbable 473
ignorant 491
wonderful 870
unheated 383
unheed, -ed 460
unheeding 458
unhesitating
belief 484
resolved 604
unhewn 241, 674
unhindered 748
unhinge 61, 158
unhinged
impotent 158
insane 503
failure 732
unhitch 44
unholy 989
unhonored 874
unhook (44)
unhoped 508
unhorsed 732
unhostile 888
unhouse 297
unhoused 185
unhurt 670
unicorn
monster 83
carriage 272
unideal *existing* 1
no thought 452
true 494
unification 48, 87
uniform
homogeneous 16
simple 42
orderly 58
regular 80
dress 225
symmetry 242
livery 550
uniformity 16
unilluminated 421
unimaginable 471, 473
wonderful 870
unimaginative 576, 843, 868
unimagined 1, 494
unimitated 20
unimpaired 670
unimpassioned 826
unimpeachable
certain 474
true 494
due 924
approved 931
innocent 946
unimpeached 931, 946
unimpeded 705, 748
unimportance 643
unimpressed 838
unimpressible 823
unimproved 659
unincreased 36
unincumbered
easy 705
exempt 927*a*
uninduced 616
uninfected 652
uninfectious 656
uninflammable 385
uninfluenced
obstinate 606
unactuated 616
free 768
uninfluential 172, 175*a*
uninformed 491
uningenuous 544
uninhabit, -able, -ed 187, 893
uninitiated 491, 699
uninjured
perfect 650
healthy 654
preserved 670
uninjurious 656
uninquisitive 456
uninspired 823
uninstructed 491
unintellectual 452, 499
unintelligent 499
unintelligibility 519
unintelligible 519
- *style* 571
render – 538
unintentional
necessary 601
undesigned 621
uninterested 456, 841, 843
unintermitting
unbroken 69
durable 110
continuing 143
persevering 604*a*
uninterrupted
continuous 69
perpetual 112
unremitting 893
unintroduced 893
uninured 614
uninvented 526
uninvestigated 491
uninvited 893
uninviting 830
union
agreement 23
junction 43
combination 48
concurrence 178
workhouse 189
party 712
concord 714

unpurposed 621
unpursued 624
unqualified
incomplete 52
impotent 158
certain 474
unprepared 674
inexpert 699
unentitled 925
– truth 494
unquelled 173
unquenchable
strong 159
desire 865
unquenched
violence 173
heat 382
unquestionable 474
unquestionably 488
unquestioned 474, 488
unquiet
motion 264
agitation 315
excitable 825
unravel *untie* 44
arrange 60
straighten 246
evolve 313
discover 480*a*
interpret 522
disembarrass 705
unreached 304
unread 491
unready 674
unreal
not existing 2
erroneous 495
imaginary 515
unreasonable
impossible 471
illogical 477
misjudging 481
foolish 499
exorbitant 814
unjust 923
unreclaimed 951
unrecognizable 146
unreconciled 713
unrecorded 552
unrecounted 55
unreduced 31
unrefined 851
unreflecting 458
unreformed 951
unrefreshed 688
unrefuted 478, 494
unregarded
neglected 460
unrespected 929
unregenerate 988
unregistered 552
unreined 748
unrelated 10
unrelenting 914*a*, 919
unreliable
uncertain 475
irresolute 605
dangerous 665
unrelieved 835
unremarked 460
unremembered 506
unremitting
continuous 69
continuing 110
unvarying 143
persevering 604*a*
unremoved 184
unremunerated 808
unrenewed 141
unrepealed 141
unrepeated 87, 103
unrepentant 951
unrepining 831
unreplenished 640
unrepressed 173
unreproached 946
unreproved 946
unrequited 806, 917
unresented 918
unresenting 826
unreserved
manifest 525
veracious 543
artless 703
unresisted 743
unresisting 725
unresolved 605
unrespected 929
unrest 149, 264
unrestored 688
unrestrained
capricious 608
unencumbered 705
free 748
unrestricted
undiminished 31
free 748
unretracted 535
unrevenged 918
unreversed 143
unrevoked 143
unrewarded 806, 917
unrhymed 598
unriddle 480*a*, 529
unrig 645
unrighteous 945
unrip 260
unripe
young 127
sour 397
immature 674
unrivalled 33
unroll *evolve* 313
display 525
unromantic 494
unroot 301
unruffled
calm 174
quiet 265
unaffected 823
placid 826
unruly *violent* 173
obstinate 606
disobedient 742
unsaddle 756
unsafe 665
unsaid 526
unsaleable
useless 645
selling 796
cheap 815
unsaluted 929
unsanctified 988, 989
unsanctioned 925
unsated 865
unsatisfactory
inexpedient 647
bad 649
displeasing 830
discontent 832
unsatisfied 832, 865
unsavouriness 395
unsay *recant* 607
unscanned 460
unscathed 654
unschooled 491
unscientific 477
unscoured 653
unscriptural 984
unscrupulous 940
unseal 529
unsearched 460
unseasonable 24, 135
unseasoned 614, 674
unseat 756
unseemly
inexpedient 647
ugly 846
vulgar 851
undue 925
vicious 945
unseen
invisible 447
neglected 460
latent 526
unseldom 136
unselfish 942
unseparated 46
unserviceable 645
unsettle *derange* 61
unsettled
mutable 149
displaced 185
uncertain 475
– in one's mind 503
unsevered 50
unsex 146
unshaded 525
unshaken 159
– belief 484
unshapely 846
unshapen 241
unshared 777
unsheathe
– the sword 722
unsheltered 665
unshielded 665
unshifting 143
unship 185, 297
unshocked 823
unshorn 50
unshortened 200
unshrinking 604, 861
unsifted 460
unsightly 846
unsinged 670
unskilfulness 699
unslaked 865
unsleeping 604*a*, 682
unsmooth 256
unsociable 893
unsocial 893
unsoiled 652
unsold 777
unsoldierlike 862
unsolicitous 866
unsolved 526
unsophisticated
simple 42
genuine 494
artless 703
unsorted 59
unsought
avoided 623
unrequested 766
unsound
illogical 477
erroneous 495
deceptive 545
imperfect 651
– mind 503
unsown 674
unsparing
abundant 639
severe 739
liberal 816
with an – hand 818
unspeakable 31, 870
unspecified 78
unspent 678
unspied 526
unspiritual 316, 989
unspoiled 648
unspotted
clean 652
beautiful 845
innocent 946
unstable 218
changeable 149
uncertain 475
irresolute 605
precarious 665
– equilibrium 149
unstaid 149
unstained
clean 652
honorable 939
unstatesmanlike 699
unsteadfast 605
unsteady
mutable 149
irresolute 605
in danger 665
unstinted 639
unstinting 816
unstirred 823, 826
unstopped
continuing 143
open 260
unstored 640
unstrained
turbid 653
relaxed 687
– meaning 516
unstrengthened 160
unstruck 823
unstrung 160
unstudied 460
unsubject 748
unsubmissive 742
unsubservient
useless 645
inexpedient 647
unsubstantial 4
weak 160
rare 322
erroneous 495
imaginary 515
unsubstantiality 4
unsuccessful 732
unsuccessive 70
unsuitable
incongruous 24
(*inexpedient* 647)
– time 135
unsullied *clean* 652
honorable 939
(*guiltless* 946)
unsung 526
unsupplied 640
unsupported
weak 160
(*unassisted* 706)
– by evidence 468
unsuppressed 141
unsurmountable 471
unsurpassed 33
unsusceptible 823
unsuspected
belief 484
latent 526
unsuspecting
hopeful 858
unsuspicious
belief 484
artless 703
hope 858
unsustainable 495
unsweet 395
unswept 653
unswerving
straight 246
direct 278
persevering 604*a*
unsymmetric 83
unsymmetrical 59, 243
unsystematic 59
untainted *pure* 652
healthy 654
honorable 939
untalked of 526
untamed 851, 907
untarnished 939
untasted 391
untaught 491, 674
untaxed 815
unteach 538
unteachable 499, 699
untenable
powerless 158
illogical 477
undefended 725
untenanted 187, 893
unthanked 917
unthankful 917
unthawed 321, 383
unthinkable 471
unthinking
unconsidered 452
involuntary 601
unthought of 452, 460
unthreatened 664
unthrifty
unprepared 674
prodigal 818
unthrone 756
untidy 59, 653
untie 44, 750
– the knot 705
until 106
– now 118
untilled 674
untimely 135
– end 360
untinged 42
untired 689
untiring 604*a*

untitled 876
untold
countless 105
uncertain 475
latent 526
secret 528
untouched
disused 678
insensible 823
untoward
ill-timed 135
bad 649
unprosperous 735
unpleasant 830
untraced 526
untracked 526
untractable 606, 699
untrained
unaccustomed 614
unprepared 674
unskilled 699
untrammelled 705, 748
untranslatable 523
untranslated 523
untravelled 265
untreasured 640
untried *new* 123
not decided 461
untrimmed 674, 849
untrodden *new* 123
impervious 261
not used 678
untroubled 174, 721
untrue 495, 546
untrustworthy
uncertain 475
erroneous 495
danger 665
dishonorable 940
untruth 544, 546
untunable 414
unturned 916
untutored
ignorant 491
unprepared 674
artless 703
untwine 313
untwist 313
unused
new 123
unaccustomed 614
unskilful 699
unusual 83
unusually *very* 31
unutterable 31, 519, 870
unvalued
underrated 483
undesired 866
disliked 898
unvanquished 748
unvaried
continuing 143
- *style* 575, 576
unvarnished
true 494
- *style* 576
unreserved 703
simple 849
tale 494, 543
unvarying 16, 143
unveil 525, 529
unventilated 261
unveracious 544
unversed 491
unvexed 831
unviolated 939
unvisited 893
unwakened 683
unwarlike 862
unwarmed 383
unwarned 508, 665
unwarped judgment 498
unwarrantable 923
unwarranted
illogical 477
undue 925
illegal 964
unwary 460
unwashed 653
great – 876
unwatchful 460
unwavering 604*a*
unweakened 159
unwearied
persevering 604*a*
indefatigable 682
refreshed 689
unwedded 904
unweeded garden 674
unweeting 491
unweighed 460
unwelcome 830, 893
unwell 655
unwept 831
unwholesome 657
unwieldy
large 192
heavy 319
cumbersome 647
difficult 704
ugly 846
unwilling 489
unwillingness 603
unwind *evolve* 313
unwiped 652
unwise 499
unwished 866
unwithered 159
unwitting
ignorant 491
involuntary 601
unwittingly 621
unwomanly 373
unwonted 83, 614
unworldly 939
unworn 159
unworshipped 929
unworthy
shameful 874
vicious 945
– of belief 485
– of notice 643
unwrap 246
unwrinkled 255
unwritten
latent 526
obliterated 552
spoken 582
- law 697, 963
unwrought 674
unyielding
tough 323
resolute 604
obstinate 606
resisting 719
up
aloft 206
vertical 212
effervescing 353
excited 824
the game is – 735
prices looking – 814
time – 111
– in arms
prepared 673
active 682
opposition 708
attack 716
resistance 719
warfare 722
– and at them 716
– and doing 682
– and down 314
– on end 212
– in 698
– to [*see below*]
all – with
destruction 162
failure 732
adversity 735
up to
time 106
power 157
knowing 490
skilful 698
brave 861
– the brim 52
- date 123
– one's ears 641
– one's eyes 641
– the mark
equal 27
sufficient 639
good 648
due 924
– snuff 702
-- this time
time 106
past 122
Upas tree 663
upbear 215, 307
upbraid 932
upcast 307
upgrow 206
upgrowth 194, 305
upheaval 146
upheave 307
uphill
acclivity 217
ascent 305
laborious 686
difficult 704
uphoist 307
uphold
continue 143
support 215
evidence 467
aid 707
praise 931
upholder 488, 711
upholstery 633
uplands 180, 206, 344
uplift 307, 658
upon:
– my honor 535
– oath 535
– which 117, 121
upper 206
– boxes, – circle 599
– classes 875
– hand
influence 175
success 731
sway 737
– story
summit 210
intellect 450
wisdom 498
– ten thousand 875
be on one's –'s 804
uppermost 210
say what comes – 612
– in the mind
thought 451
topic 454
attention 457
– in one's thoughts
memory 505
upraise 307
uprear 307
upright
vertical 212
honest 939
uprise 305
uprising 742
uproar
disorder 59
violence 173
noise 404
uproarious 825
uproot 301
ups and downs of life 151, 735
upset *destroy* 162
invert 218
throw down 308
defeat 731
excite 824
disconcert 874
– the apple cart 732
upshot *result* 154
judgment 480
completion 729
upside down 218
upstairs 206
upstart
new 123
prosperous 734
plebeian 876
upturn 210
upwards 206
– of 33, 100
uranology 318
urban 189
urbane 894
urbis conditæ, anno – 106
urceole 998
urchin
child 129
small 193
wretch 949
imp 980
urge *violence* 173
impel 276
incite 615
hasten 684
beg 765
urgent
required 630
important 642
haste 684
request 765
urn *vase* 191
funereal 363
heater 386
cinerary – 363
usage 613, 677
usance 806
use *habit* 613
waste 638
utility 644
employ 677
property 780
make good – of 658
in – 677
be of – to *aid* 707
benevolence 906
– one's discretion 600
– one's endeavor 675
– a right 924
– up 677
used to 613
used up
deteriorated 659
disuse 678
fatigue 688
weary 841
satiated 869
useful 644
render – 677
useless 645
user, right of – 780
usher
guard 263
receive 296
teacher 540
servant 746
courtesy 894
wedding 903
– in *precedence* 62
begin 66
precession 280
announce 511
– into the world 161
usque ad nauseam 841
U.S.S. 726
ustulation 384
usual
general 78
ordinary 82
customary 613
usufruct 677
usurer
lender 787
merchant 797
credit 805
miser 819
usurious 819
usurp *assume* 739
seize 789
illegal 925
– authority 738
usurpation
insolence 885
usurper 737
usury 806
utensil 191, 633
uti possidetis
permanence 141
possession 777
retention 781
utilitarian 677, 910
utility 644
general – *actor* 599

censure 932
detract 934
vilipendency 930
villa 189
village 189
- talk 588
villager 188
villain
servant 746
serf 876
knave 941
rascal 949
villainous 649, 945
- saltpetre 727
villainy 940
villein [*see* villain]
villenage 749, 777
villi 256
villous 256
vim 171
vin: - d'honneur 292, 894
not think - ordinaire of oneself 880
vinaigrette 400
vincible 158
vincture 43
vinculo matrimonii, separatio a - 905
vinculum **45**
- matrimonii 903
vindicate 467, 937
- a right 924
vindication **937**
vindicator 919
vindictive 901, 919
vine 367
- grower 371
vinegar 397
- aspect 846
vinery 191
vineyard 371, 691
vingt et un 840
vintage 371, 636
vintner 637
viol 417
violate
disobey 742
non-observance 773
undue 925
dereliction 927
ravish 961
- a law 83
- the law 964
- a usage 614
violence **173**
arbitrary 964
do - to *bad* 649
non-observance 773
undue 925
violent 173
excitable 825
- death 360, 361
in a - degree 31
lay - hands on 789
violet 437
violin 417
violinist 416
violoncello 417
viper *snake* 366
bane 663
evil-doer 913
bad man 949
- in one's bosom 667
virago 901
virent 435
vires acquirit eundo
increase 35
energy 171
velocity 274
virescence 435
Virgilianae, sortes - 621
virgin *new* 123
girl 129
woman 374
spinster 904
good 948
pure 960
- forest **367**
- soil
ignorance 491
untilled 674
the - Mary 976
virginals 417
virginibus puerisque 960
viribus, totis - 686
viridity 435
virile
adolescent 131
strong 159
manly 373
virtu 850
article of - 847
virtual 2, 5
- image 443
virtue *power* 157
courage 861
goodness **944**
purity 960
by - of 157, 631
in - of 737
make a - of necessity *no choice* 609*a*
skill 698
submit 725
compromise 774
bear 826
virtueless 945
virtuoso 416, 850
virtuous 944, 960
virulence
energy 171
noxiousness 649
insalubrity 657
discourtesy 895
anger 900
malevolence 907
virulent 932
virum volitare per ora 531
virus 655, 663
vis:
- comica 842
- conservatrix 670
- inertia
power 157
inertness 172
insensibility 823
- medicatrix 660, 662
- mortua 157
- a tergo 284
- viva 157
visa 488
visage 234, 448
vis-à-vis *front* 234
opposite 237
carriage 272
viscera 221
viscid 352
viscount 875
viscous 352
vise 781
Vishnu 979
visibility **446**
visible 446
be - 448
become - 448
darkness - 421
- radiation 420
vision *sight* **441**
phantasm 443
dream 515
specter 980
organ of - 441
visionary
inexistence 2
unsubstantial 4
impossible 471
imaginary 515
heterodox 984
visionless 442
visit *arrival* 292
social 892
courtesy 894
- upon 972
pay a surprise - 647
visitation
disease 655
adversity 735
suffering 828
-s of Providence 976
- of the sick 998
visiting:
- card 550
on - terms 888, 892
visitor *incomer* 294
director 694
friend 890
visor 530
vista
convergence 260
sight 441
appearance 448
expectation 507
visual 441
- organ 441
vitability 359
vitæ, elixir - 662
vital *life* 359
important 642
vitality
stability 150
strength 159
life 359
vitalize 359
vitals 221
vitamin impendere vero 535, 939
vitamines 298
vitiate 659
vitiated 655
viticulture 371
vitreous 323, 425
vitrify 323
vituperate 908, 932
vituperator 936
viva! 873, 931
vivace *music* 415
vivacious
active 682
sensitive 822
cheerful 836
vivamus, dum vivimus - 840
vivandière 797
vivarium 370
vivâ voce 582
vive *glory be to* 873
on the qui - 824
vivendi
modus - 723
- causa 359
vivid *energetic* 171
sensibility 375
light 420
color 428
distinct 518
- memory 505
vivify 159, 359
vivisection 378
vixen *fox* 366
female 374
shrew 901
viz. [*see* videlicet]
vizier *director* 694
mask 530
shield 717
deputy 759
vizor 530
vobis, sic vos non - 791
vocable 562
vocabulary 562
vocal 415, 580
- training 537
vocalist 416
vocalize 580
vocation 625
voce, sotto - 581
vociferation
loud 404
cry 411
voice 580
vogue *custom* 613
fashion 852
fame 873
vogue la galère
persevere 604*a*
amusement 840
voice *sound* 402
cry 411
judgment 480
promulgate 531
affirmation 535
express 566
human - **580**
speak 580
choice 609
give one's - for 488
raise one's - 411, 582
still small -
faint sound 405
conscience 926
want of - 581
warning - 668
- against 489, 708
- of the charmer 933
make one's - heard 175
- of the tempter 615
voiced 561
voiceless 581
void *unsubstantial* 4
absence 187
emit 297
null and - 964
- of foundation 546
- of suspicion 484
voidance 297
voiturette 274
voiturier 268
volplaner 267
volant 267
volapuk 560
volatile *light* 320
gaseous 334
vaporizable 336
irresolute 605
capricious 608
volatility 111
vol-au-vent 298
volcanic
violent 173
heat 382
burnt 388
excitable 825
volcano
violence 173
heat 382
furnace 386
pitfall 667
on a - 665
volitant 267
volitare per ora, virum - 531
volitation 267
volition 600
volley
collection 72
violence 173
report 406
attack 716
volonté, à - 600
volo sic jubeo, sic - 600, 741
volt 466
voltaic electricity 157
volte face 283
voltigeur 726
volto sciolto i pensieri stretti, il - 544
voluble 584
volume *great* 31
part 51
bulk 192
book 593
speak -s
evidence 467
intelligible 518
inform 527
- of smoke 330
voluminous 573, 641
voluntary *overture* 64, 415
will 600
willing 602
donation 784
voluntas, stet pro ratione - 600
volunteer *will* 600
willing 602
endeavor 676
combatant 726
offer 763
voluptas, sua

worth – 646
– away time
inaction 681
pastime 840
– speaking of 9, 134
whilom 122
whilst 106
whim *fad* 481
fancy 515
caprice 608
wit 842
desire 865
whimper 839
whimsey 515, 865
whimsical [*see* whim] 853
whimwam 608, 643
whin 367
whine 411, 839
whinyard 727
whip *collect* 72
coachman 268
strike 276
stir up 315
urge 615
hasten 684
director 694
flog 972
scourge 975
– and spur 274
– away 293
– hand 731, 737
– in 300
– on 684
– off 293
– up 789
whipcord 205
whipper-in 694
whippersnapper 129
whipping-post 975
whipster 129
whir *rotate* 312
sound 407
whirl *rotate* 312
flurry 825
whirligig 312
whirlpool *rotate* 312
agitation 315
water 348
danger 667
whirlwind
disorder 59
agitation 315
wind 349
reap the –
product 154
fail 732
ride the –
resolution 604
authority 737
whisk *rapid* 274
circuition 311
agitation 315
– off 297
whisker 256
whisket 191
whisky
vehicle 272
drink 298
whisper
faint sound 405
tell 527
conceal 528
stammer 583
stage – 580
– about
disclose 529
publish 531
– in the ear
voice 580
whist *hush* 403
cards 840
whistle *wind* 349
hiss 409
play music 416
musical instrument 417
clean as a –
thorough 52
perfect 650
neatly 652
pay too dear for one's –
inexpedient 647
unskilful 699
dear 814
police – 669
wet one's –
drink 298
tipple 959
– at 930
– for *request* 765
desire 865
– jigs to a milestone 645
– for want of thought
inaction 681
whit *small* 32
whit-leather 327
Whit-Monday 840
white 430
– of the eye 41
– feather 862
– flag 723
– frost 383
– heat 382
– horses 348
– lie *equivocal* 520
concealment 528
untruth 546
plea 617
– liver 862
– as a sheet 860
– slave 962
stand in a – sheet 952
mark with a – stone 642, 931
whitechapel
vehicle 272
Whitefriars 996
whiteness **430**
whitewash
cover 223
whiten 430
cleanse 652
ornament 847
justify 937
acquit 970
whitewashed
get – 808
whitewasher 935
white wings 652
whitey-brown 433
whither
tendency 176
direction 278
inquiry 461
whitlow 655
whittle 44, 253
whittled
drunk 959
Whitsuntide 998
whiz 409
who 461
– goes there? 669
– would have thought? 508, 870
whoa! 265
whole *entire* **50**
healthy 654
make – 660
as a – 50
on the – 476, 480
go the – hog 729
the – time 106
– truth
truth 494
disclosure 529
veracity 543
wholesale
large scale 31
whole 50
abundant 639
trade 794
wholesome 656
wholly 50, 52
whoop 411
war – 715, 722
whop *flog* 972
whoopee 840
whopper *lie* 546
whopping *huge* 192
whore 962
whoredom 961
whoremonger 962
whorl 248
why *cause* 153
attribution 155
inquiry 461
indeed 535
motive 615
– not 868
wibble-wabble 314
wick 388, 423
wicked 945
the – *bad men* 949
impious 988
the – one 978
wicker 219
wicket 66, 260
wide 202
– apart 15
–awake *hat* 225
intelligent 498
– away 196
– berth 748
– of the mark
distance 196
deviation 279
error 495
– of *distant* 196
– open 194, 260
– of the truth 495
– world 180, 318
in the – world 180
widen 194
– the breach 713, 900
wide-spread
great 31
dispersed 73
space 180
expanded 194
widow 905
widowhood 905
width 202
wield
brandish 315
handle 379
use 677
– authority 737
– the sword 722
wieldy 705
wife 903
wig 225
wigging 932
wiggle 315
wight 373
wigwam 189
wild 851
unproductive 169
violent 173
plain 344
inattentive 458
mad 503
shy 623
unskilled 699
excited 824, 825
untamed 851
rash 863
angry 900
licentious 954
run – 825
– animals 366
– beast *fierce* 173
evil-doer 913
– goose chase
caprice 608
useless 645
unskilful 699
– imagination 515
sow one's – oats
grow up 131
improve 658
amusement 840
vice 945
intemperance 954
Wild, Jonathan –
thief 792
bad man 949
wilderness
disorder 59
unproductive 169
space 180
solitude 893
wild-fire 382
spread like –
violence 173
influence 175
expand 194
publication 531
wile 545, 702
wilful
voluntary 600
obstinate 606
will
volition **600**
resolution 604
testament 771
gift 784
at – 600
at one's own sweet – 608
have one's own – 600, 748
make one's – 360
tenant at – 779
– be 152
– for the deed 774, 937
– of Heaven 601
– he nil he 601
– power 600
– and will not 605
– you 765
Will o' the wisp
luminary 423
imp 980
willing or unwilling 601
willingness **602**
willow 839
willy-nilly 601, 744
wilted 659
wily 702
wimble 262
wimple 225
win 731, 775
– the affections 897
– golden opinions 931
– the heart 829
– laurels 873
– out 33
– over *belief* 484
induce 615
content 831
wince
bodily pain 378
emotion 821
excitement 825
mental pain 828
flinch 860
winch 307, 633
wind *convolution* [*see below*]
velocity 274
blast **349**
life 359
against the – 278, 708
before the – 278, 734
cast to the –s
repudiate 610
disuse 678
not observe 773
relinquish 782
close to the – 278
fair – 705
to the four –s 180
get – 531
get the – up 860
see how the – blows
direction 278
experiment 463
foresight 510
fickle 607
in the – 151, 152
lose – 688
sail near the –
direction 278
skill 698
sharp practice 940
outstrip the – 274
preach to the –s 645
raise the – 775
scatter to the –s 756
see where the – lies 698
short –ed 688
sport of –s and waves 315
sound of – and limb 654
take the – out of one's sails

render powerless 158
hinder 706
defeat 731
touched in the – 655
what's in the – ? 461
– ahead 708
– bag 584
in the –'s eye 278
– the horn 416
hit between – and water 659
– and weather permitting
qualification 469
possibility 470
wind *blast* [*see above*]
convolution 248
deviate 279
circuition 311
– round the heart 897
– up *strengthen* 159
prepare 673
complete 729
- *accounts* 811
windbag 884
wind instruments 417
wind-bound 706
windfall 618
wind-gauge 349
wind-gun 727
winding 248, 311
winding-sheet 363
windings and turnings 248
wind-jammer 273
windlass 307, 633
windless 688
windmill 312
tilt at –s 638
window 260
make the –s shake
loud noise 404
– dressing 544
wind-pipe 351
wind-up 67
windward, to – 236, 278
windy 349
wine 298, 959
put new – into old bottles 699
look upon the – when it is red 953
wine-bibbing 959
wine-cooler 387
wineglass 191
wing *extension* 39
part 51
side 236
fly 267
side-scene 599
instrument 633
refuge 666
army 726
clip the –s 275
lend –s to 707
on the –
motion 264
flying 267
transference 270
departure 293
take – *journey* 266
fly 267
depart 293
under the – of
safe 664
with –s *active* 682
– one's flight 293
– one's way 267
on the –s of the wind 274
wing-commander 747
winged *swift* 274
wink 443, 550
tip the – 550, 527
– at
be blind to 442
disregard 458
neglect 460
permit 760
forgive 918
– of sleep 683
winning [*see* win]
pleasing 829
courteous 894
lovable 897
winnings 775
winnow *sift* 42
exclude 55
inquire 461
pick 609
clean 652
– the chaff from the wheat 465
winsome 829, 836
winter 126, 383
– of our discontent 832
– garden 840
– sports 840
wintry 126
wipe *dry* 340
clean 652
disrespect 929
flog 972
give one a –
rebuke 932
– away 552
– the eyes
relieve 834
– off old scores 807, 952
– the tears 914
wire *ligature* 45
filament 205
telegraph 527, 534
pull the –s 693
wire-drawn
long 200
wireless 531
– telegram 532
– telegraph 534
– telephone 534
wire-puller 526, 694
wire-worm 913
wiry *strong* 159
wis 514
wisdom **498**
have cut one's – teeth 698
worldly – 864
wise
intelligent 498
sage 500
manner 627
in such – 8
word to the – 695
– in one's own conceit 880
– after the event 135
– man 500
– maxim 496
dine not –ly but too well 953
wiseacre 493, 500,
wiser, nobody the – 528
wish *will* 600
intention 620
desire 865
do what one –es 748
– at the bottom of the Red Sea 832
– the father to the thought
misjudge 481
credulous 486
hope 858
desire 865
– joy 896
– well 906
wishing-cap 993
wish-wash
unmeaning 517
wishy-washy
languid 160
insipid 391
feeble style 575
unimportant 643
wisket 191
wisp 72
wistful
thought 451
care 459
feeling 821
desire 865
wit *intellect* 450
wisdom 498
humor **842**
humorist 844
mother – 498
soul of – 572
to – 522
at one's –'s end 475, 704
witch *oracle* 513
ugly 846
sorceress 994
– doctor 994
witchcraft 992
witchery
attraction 615
pleasing 829
sorcery 992
witching time 126, 421
witenagemote 696
with *added* 37
mixed 41
ligature 45
accompanying 88
means 632
go – 178
– all its parts 52
– regard to 9
– a vengeance 31, 52
– a witness 31
withal
in addition 37
accompanying 88
enough 639
withdraw
subduct 38
absent 187
turn back 283
recede 287
depart 293
– from
recant 607
relinquish 621
dislike 867
withe 45
wither 195, 659
– one's hopes 837
withered *weak* 160
disease 655
withering
harsh 739
painful 830
contempt 930
censure 932
withers 250
– unwrung 159, 323
withhold *hide* 528
restrain 751
prohibit 761
retain 781
stint 819
– one's assent 764
within 221
derived from – 5
place – 221
keep – 221
– an ace 32
– bounds
small 32
shortcoming 304
restraint 751
– call 197
– compass
shortcoming 304
temperate 953
– the mark 304
– one's memory 505
– reach 197, 705
without *unless* 8
subduction 38
exception 83
absence 187
exterior 220
circumjacent 227
exemption 777a
derived from – 6
not be able to do – 630
– alloy 827
– ballast 605, 945
– ceasing 136
– ceremony 881
– charge 815
– fear of contradiction 535
– a dissentient voice 488
– end 105, 112
– exception 16, 79
– excuse 945
– fail 474, 604*a*
– God 989
– a leg to stand on 158
– limit 105
– measure 105
– notice 508
– number 105
– parallel 33
– a rap 804
– reason 499
– regard to 10
– reluctance 602
– reserve 525
– rhyme or reason 615*a*
– a shadow of turning 141
– stint 639
– warning 508
withstand 708, 719
withy 45
witless 491
witling 501, 844
witness [*see* 441]
spectator 444
evidence 467
voucher 550
call to – 467
witness-box 966
wits 450
live by one's –
deceive 545
skill 698
cunning 702
steal 791
dishonorable 940
set one's – to work
think 451
invent 515
plan 626
all one's – about one
care 459
intelligence 498
skill 698
one's – gone a woolgathering 458
witsnapper 844
witticism 842
wittingly 620
wittol 962
wive 903
wiveless 904
wizard *sage* 500
proficient 700
sorcerer 994
wizen *wither* 195
throat 260
woad 438
wobble 605
woe 828
– betide 908, 914
– is me 839
– to 908
woebegone 828, 837
woeful 649, 830
woefully *very* 31
wold 344
wolf *ravenous* 865
cry – *false* 544
alarm 669
fear 860
hold the – by the ears 704
keep the – from the door 359
unable to keep the – from the door 804
– at the door 667, 804
– and the lamb 923